THE CONCISE OXFORD
DICTIONARY OF
MUSIC

THE CONCISE OXFORD

DICTIONARY OF
MUSIC

BY

PERCY A. SCHOLES

SECOND EDITION

EDITED BY

JOHN OWEN WARD

LONDON   OXFORD   NEW YORK

OXFORD UNIVERSITY PRESS

Oxford University Press, Walton Street, Oxford OX2 6DP

OXFORD LONDON GLASGOW
NEW YORK TORONTO MELBOURNE WELLINGTON
IBADAN NAIROBI DAR ES SALAAM LUSAKA CAPE TOWN
KUALA LUMPUR SINGAPORE JAKARTA HONG KONG TOKYO
DELHI BOMBAY CALCUTTA MADRAS KARACHI

BOARDS EDITION ISBN O 19 311302 3
PAPERBACK EDITION ISBN O 19 311307 4

First edition 1952
Second edition 1964
Reprinted with corrections 1966, 1969 (twice),
1972 (twice), 1973, 1974, 1975, 1977 (twice),
and 1978

Printed in Great Britain
at the University Press, Oxford
by Vivian Ridler
Printer to the University

ON DICTIONARIES OF MUSIC

AND THIS ONE IN PARTICULAR

OF dictionaries of music there is no end! The present writer, looking round his shelves, sees there over fifty—British, American, French, Belgian, Swiss, German, and Italian. And those are only a fraction of what exist. Some of the fifty run into ten or twelve volumes; some are single volumes. Some are purely biographical; others offer merely alphabetically arranged strings of definitions of the musical terms in use; whilst still others, like the present one, are mixed, including biographies of composers and performers of all countries and periods, theoretical terms, terms of expression, and general articles on various historical and other phases of music.

The Beginnings of Musical Dictionary-making

The earliest of the collection is the first that ever existed. This is the work of the Flemish musician, Tinctor, who published it at Treviso about 1498—little more than forty years from the invention of printing from type.

This famous little work is in Latin (*Terminorum musicae diffinitorium*), and a good long time was to elapse before the various European countries began to produce musical dictionaries in their own vernaculars. Apparently the first in the English language was by a London musician who must surely have been of French parentage or descent, one Jacques Grassineau (or 'James Grassineau, Gent.', as he styles himself on the title-page). His book appeared in 1740. The worth of the book was attested in a short expression of approval opposite the title-page by three well-known London musicians (Pepusch, arranger of *The Beggar's Opera*; Greene, organist of St. Paul's Cathedral; and Galliard, a popular composer of the day), but they did not, and could not, declare that it was very original, for it was largely borrowed from a French dictionary of music of nearly forty years earlier—Brossard's (1703).

The Modern Musical Dictionaries

For a long time, so far as musical works of reference in the English language are concerned, this Grassineau had the whole field to himself, but gradually, from the end of the eighteenth century, other such books appeared, the slow procession culminating at last in that great standard book (on the whole the best large-scale work of its sort in any language), Grove's *Dictionary of Music and Musicians*, the first edition of which trickled out over a period of eleven years, volume one appearing in 1878 and volume four in 1889. Its editor, George Grove ('Sir George' from 1883), was a remarkably versatile man—to mention just a few of his occupations, a civil engineer in Jamaica and Bermuda, chief founder and Secretary of the Palestine Exploration Fund, first Secretary of the Crystal Palace, and, lastly, Director of the newly founded Royal College of Music. Later editions of this monumental work have been edited by J. A. Fuller-Maitland, H. L. Colles, and Eric Blom.

During the present century there have, of course, appeared a considerable number of American works of the kind. Of these perhaps the soundest to date have been Baker's *Biographical Dictionary of Musicians* (first published 1900), Oscar Thompson's *International Cyclopedia of Music and Musicians* (1938), and Apel's *Harvard Dictionary of Music* (1944).

The Purpose of the Present Dictionary

The present book is in some measure a reduction of the author's *Oxford Companion to Music*—a reduction in size and, of course, in price. It is intended to serve the purpose of those music-lovers who desire a smaller book at a smaller cost. However, the *Concise* possesses just a few features that are lacking from the *Companion* —e.g. some hundreds of short biographical entries of vocal and instrumental performers and conductors, as distinct from composers, and some hundreds of entries concerning individual compositions (operas, symphonic poems, song cycles, &c.).

Like the *Companion*, the *Concise* has very many cross-references, these last making for easy access to any information the book contains, in an attempt to justify the hopeful promise now proclaimed: '*If it's in the book you can find it.*'

Will readers collaborate?

And now an appeal must be made to readers. The great Dr. Johnson, when, two centuries ago, he issued his famous English Dictionary, admitted candidly that there must be *some* errors in it, and, as a matter of fact, any book of reference, consisting as it does of a mass of detail, cannot fail to suffer from occasional slips in writing or printing. The author has been greatly helped in improving the successive editions of the *Oxford Companion* by the kindness of readers possessing special knowledge or unusually keen powers of observation who have generously responded to his frank invitation to let him know of any defect in either accuracy or comprehensiveness that may have come to their notice, and he trusts that a similar invitation, which he hereby extends, may bring a similar generous response. A line or two on a postcard takes merely a couple of minutes to write and may result in making the book more useful to many readers of later editions. All communications of this sort will be gratefully received and promptly acknowledged.

And with that invitation the author sends his latest work into the world, hoping that his friends of the wide musical public will find it helpful.

(*From the original preface*)

PREFACE TO SECOND EDITION

LIBRARIANS should note that the appearance of the present reset edition does not mean that the previous impressions are now so much waste paper. In all reference books undergoing a continuous process of revision, new material can be incorporated only by reducing the space devoted to subjects likely to be of least interest to readers. In this edition, many new names have been included, and many names of passing or local importance have sadly been removed to make way for them. Serious students will in any case refer to Baker and the various editions of Grove.

J. O. W.

August 1963

ACKNOWLEDGEMENTS

To the following the author's gratitude is warmly expressed:

KENNETH A. WRIGHT, O.B.E., M.Eng., Hon. F.T.C.L., Chevalier of the Legion of Honour, whose unique knowledge of the composers and performers of all the European countries, acquired during his long service with the British Broadcasting Corporation, had been freely put at the author's disposal and freely drawn upon.

The late W. MCNAUGHT, B.A., Editor of the *Musical Times*, who read and checked much of the book in typescript.

NICOLAS SLONIMSKY, editor of several of the leading American books of musical reference, whose passion for exactitude in the dates of birth and death of the world's musicians has led him into researches which have enabled him to make a valuable contribution to the accuracy in this particular of the present book.

R. F. NEWTON, of London, whose researches as to the dates and places of birth and death of British musicians have also contributed to the book's accuracy.

H. K. ANDREWS, M.A., D.Mus., sometime Organist of New College, Oxford, and Lecturer in Music in the University, who has minutely checked many of the articles and made valuable suggestions.

PHILIP J. TAYLOR, sometime Organist of Magdalen College, Oxford, who has carefully gone through the whole of the proofs.

The late LL. S. LLOYD, C.B., M.A., formerly Principal Assistant Secretary to the Department of Scientific and Industrial Research, author of *Music and Sound*, &c., and E. G. RICHARDSON, B.A., Ph.D., D.Sc., Reader in Physics at King's College (Durham University), Newcastle-on-Tyne.

THOMAS B. PITFIELD, composer, poet, and draughtsman, for whose careful work on some illustrations of this book the author cannot feel too grateful.

THE JOHN COMPTON ORGAN COMPANY LTD., who took immense pains to provide the book with a really beautiful drawing of a modern organ console.

J. OWEN WARD, M.A. Oxon., long my capable assistant in the production of my recent books, who has been of great service in the preparation of this one.

ACKNOWLEDGEMENTS

Thanks are also due to the following firms for granting permission to reproduce illustrative material in this volume:

Serpent	From Walter Wood, *The Romance of Regimental Marches* (William Clowes & Son Ltd.), by permission of Messrs. Boosey & Hawkes Ltd.
The Action of a Modern Upright Piano	A section of a Schwander action. By permission of Messrs. Herrburger Brooks Ltd., the makers of this action.
Frame, Soundboard, and Strings of Grand Pianoforte	From Hutschenruyter, *Geschiednis van de Piano*. By permission of Muziekuitgeverij J. J. Lispet.
Harmonics of Trombone	From Carse, *Musical Wind Instruments*. By permission of Messrs. Macmillan & Co. Ltd.
An Artificial Larynx	From Wood, *Sound Waves and Their Uses*. By permission of Messrs. Blackie & Son Ltd.
The Vocal Cords and Associated Cavities	From Paget, *Human Speech*. By permission of Messrs. Routledge & Kegan Paul Ltd.
A Reed Pipe	From Smith, *Sound in the Organ and Orchestra*. By permission of Messrs. William Reeves, Bookseller, Ltd.
Vibrations of a Stretched String; Harmonics; Vibrations made Visible	From Jeans, *Science and Music*. By permission of the University Press, Cambridge.
Ancestor of the Gramophone	From Hamilton, *Sound and its Relation to Music*. By permission of Messrs. Theodore Presser Co.
Difference Tone Production	From Wood, *Sound Waves and Their Uses*. By permission of Messrs. Blackie & Son Ltd.

ABBREVIATIONS

THE abbreviations used in this book are believed to be either such as are in common use and therefore known to all readers, or so obvious as to be self-explanatory; nevertheless, for the sake of completeness, a list of most of them is given here.

abt.	about	G.C.V.O.	Knight Grand Cross of the Victorian Order
adj.	adjective		
adv.	adverb	Ger.	German
Amer.	American	Gr.	Greek
arr.	arranged	G.S.M.	Guildhall School of Music (London)
Assoc.	Association		
asst.	assistant	hon.	honorary
B.B.C.	British Broadcasting Corporation	Ill.	Illinois
		Ind.	Indiana
B.Mus.	Bachelor of Music	Inst.	Institute
Brit.	Britain, British	I.o.W.	Isle of Wight
c.	century	It.	Italian
C.B.E.	Commander of the Order of the British Empire	K.B.E.	Knight Commander of the Order of the British Empire
'cellist	violoncellist		
cf.	*conferatur* (Lat.), compare		
C.H.	Companion of Honour	K.C.V.O.	Knight Commander of the Victorian Order
chor.	chorus		
Coll.	College	Lambeth	Designation of degree conferred by Archbishop of Canterbury, whose Palace is at Lambeth. (See *Degrees and Diplomas* 1)
comp.	composed		
Conn.	Connecticut		
Corpn.	Corporation		
cs.	centuries		
C.V.O.	Commander of the Victorian Order	Lat.	Latin
		lit.	literally
D.B.E.	Dame Commander of the Order of the British Empire	M.A.	Master of Arts
		M.B.E.	Member of the Order of the British Empire
Dept.	Department		
D.Litt.	Doctor Literarum (Lat.), Doctor of Letters	Me.	Maine
		Mich.	Michigan
D.Mus.	Doctor of Music	Middx.	Middlesex
Ed.	Editor	Minn.	Minnesota
Edn.	Edition	M.Mus.	Master of Music
Eng.	English	Mo.	Missouri
estd.	established	MS.	Manuscript
Fest.	Festival	MSS.	Manuscripts
Fr.	French	M.V.O.	Member of the Victorian Order
F.R.S.	Fellow of the Royal Society		
F.R.S.L.	Fellow of the Royal Society of Literature	N.C.	North Carolina
		N.J.	New Jersey

nr.	near	R.C.M.	Royal College of Music, London
N.S.W.	New South Wales (Australia)	res.	resident
N.Y.	New York	R.I.	Rhode Island
N.Z.	New Zealand	Sec.	Secretary
O.B.E.	Officer of the Order of the British Empire	Soc.	Society
		Staffs	Staffordshire
OCM	*Oxford Companion to Music*	s.v.	*sub voce* = 'under that word' (referring to the place in this book where information will be found)
Orch.	Orchestra, orchestral		
Pa.	Pennsylvania		
perf.	performed, performance		
prod.	produced	T.C.L., T.C.M.	Trinity College of Music, London
Prof.	Professor	transl.	translated, translation
publ.	published	Univ.	University
q.v.	*quod vide* (Lat.), which see	Va.	Virginia
R.A.M.	Royal Academy of Music, London	Wis.	Wisconsin
		8ve	octave

ALPHABETIZATION

WHERE the title of an entry consists of more than one word the complete title governs the position in which the entry appears. Thus, for instance, the following series of five entries:

	Concert		Concert
	Concertante		Concert Halls
	Concert Halls	*not*	Concert Master
	Concertina		Concertante
	Concert Master		Concertina

That is to say, the order of entries is strictly alphabetical, taking into consideration *the whole wording of the titles*.[1] (This appears to be the convention most generally adopted; it is that of Grove's *Dictionary of Music*, the *Encyclopaedia Britannica*, the *Harvard Dictionary of Music*, &c.)

[1] Except that in names of persons the *surname* only is taken into account. Note also that, as is most usual in works of reference, surnames beginning *M'*, *Mc*, or *Mac* are all treated as though spelt *Mac*.

TABLES OF NOTATION AND NOMENCLATURE

TABLE 1
VALUES OF NOTES

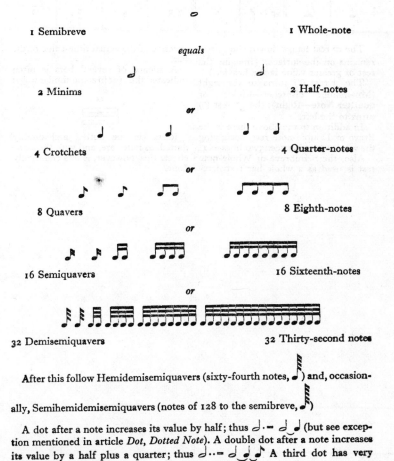

1 Semibreve	1 Whole-note

equals

2 Minims	2 Half-notes

or

4 Crotchets	4 Quarter-notes

or

8 Quavers	8 Eighth-notes

or

16 Semiquavers	16 Sixteenth-notes

or

32 Demisemiquavers	32 Thirty-second notes

After this follow Hemidemisemiquavers (sixty-fourth notes, ♪) and, occasionally, Semihemidemisemiquavers (notes of 128 to the semibreve, ♪)

A dot after a note increases its value by half; thus ♩· = ♩ ♪ (but see exception mentioned in article *Dot, Dotted Note*). A double dot after a note increases its value by a half plus a quarter; thus ♩·· = ♩ ♪ ♬ A third dot has very occasionally been used; thus ♩··· = ♩ ♪ ♬ ♬

For the rarely used Breve (the value of 2 semibreves) see Table 3.

TABLE 2
VALUES OF RESTS

(*Compare* TABLE I *above*)

𝅝	𝅗𝅥	𝅘𝅥	𝅘𝅥𝅮	𝅘𝅥𝅯	𝅘𝅥𝅰	𝅘𝅥𝅱	𝅘𝅥𝅲
▬	▬	𝄾 or 𝄼	𝄾	𝄿	𝄿	𝅀	𝅁

The 𝅝 rest hangs down; the 𝅗𝅥 rest remains on the surface. (Imagine the rest of greater value is the heavier.)

The 𝅘𝅥 rest (𝄾) turns to the right (Mnemonic: cRotchet—Right; or quaRter Note—Right); the 𝅘𝅥𝅮 rest (𝄾) turns to the left.

In addition to the above there is the Breve or Double-note rest, occupying the whole space between two lines—▬.

Also, the Semibreve or Whole-note rest is used as a whole-bar rest, irrespective of the actual time-value of the bar.

A silence of several bars is often indicated thus (or in some similar way):

Rests can be dotted and doubly dotted, as notes are, and with the same effect: this, however, is less commonly done.

TABLE 3

NAMES OF THE NOTES AND REST VALUES

ENGLISH, ITALIAN, FRENCH, GERMAN, AND AMERICAN

	ENGLISH	ITALIAN	FRENCH	GERMAN	AMERICAN
𝄺	breve	breve	carrée (square) *or* brève	Doppeltakt-note (double measure note)	double whole-note.
𝅝	semibreve	semibreve	ronde (round)	Ganze Taktnote (whole measure note)	whole-note.
𝅗𝅥	minim	minima *or* bianca (white)	blanche (white)	Halbe (half) *or* Halbenote *or* Halbe Takt-note	half-note.
𝅘𝅥	crotchet	semiminima *or* nera (black)	noire (black)	Viertel (quarter)	quarter-note.
𝅘𝅥𝅮	quaver	croma	croche (hook)	Achtel (eighth)	eighth-note.
𝅘𝅥𝅯	semi-quaver	semi-croma	double-croche (double-hook)	Sechzehntel (sixteenth)	sixteenth-note.
𝅘𝅥𝅰	demisemi-quaver	biscroma	triple-croche (triple-hook)	Zweiund-dreissigstel (thirty-second)	thirty-second note.
𝅘𝅥𝅱	hemidemi-semi-quaver	semi-biscroma	quadruple-croche (quadruple-hook)	Vierundsech-zigstel (sixty-fourth)	sixty-fourth note.

(The word 'Rest' is in Italian *Pausa*; in French *Silence* or *Pause*; in German *Pause*.)

The *English* names of the longer notes are based upon the old Latin names of the early Middle Ages.

The earlier *Italian* names are similar.

The *French* names stand alone as being purely descriptive of the appearances.

The German names are arithmetical and the American practically a translation of them. It must be admitted that the American and German names require no remembering, being logically descriptive of time-values. They are, then, undoubtedly the best, and the American names are now largely adopted in the Commonwealth.

TABLE 4

THE CLEFS

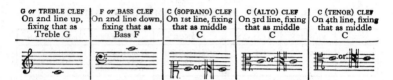

| G *or* TREBLE CLEF On 2nd line up, fixing that as Treble G | F *or* BASS CLEF On 2nd line down, fixing that as Bass F | C (SOPRANO) CLEF On 1st line, fixing that as middle C | C (ALTO) CLEF On 3rd line, fixing that as middle C | C (TENOR) CLEF On 4th line, fixing that as middle C |

The above shows the one note, middle C, represented in five different ways. The Soprano Clef is found in the older German choral music. The Alto Clef, formerly used for the Alto Voice and certain instruments, is still in use for the Viola. The Tenor Clef was formerly used for the Tenor Voice and is still in use for the higher notes of the Violoncello, for the Tenor Trombone, &c.

(See also, in the body of the book, *Great Staff*.)

TABLE 5

PITCH NAMES OF THE NOTES

IN ENGLISH, GERMAN, FRENCH, AND ITALIAN

	C	D	E	F	G	A	B
English	C	D	E	F	G	A	B
German	,,	,,	,,	,,	,,	,,	H
French	ut *or* do	ré	mi	fa	sol	la	si
Italian	do	re	,,	,,	,,	,,	,,

Note that B flat in English is B in German, and that B in English is H in German.
(See reference to this in the article *B*.)

TABLE 6

INFLECTION OF NOTES

SHARP	DOUBLE SHARP	FLAT	DOUBLE FLAT
Raising the note a half-step or semitone	Raising the note a full-step or tone	Lowering the note a half-step or semitone	Lowering the note a full-step or tone
♯	×	♭	♭♭

After a Sharp or Flat the Natural Sign ♮ restores the note to its normal pitch.

After a Double Sharp or Double Flat the Sign ♯ or ♭ (or ♮♯ or ♮♭) changes the pitch of the note to that of a single Sharp or Flat.

After a Double Sharp or Double Flat the Sign ♮ (rarely given ♮♮) restores the note to its normal pitch.

Any of these various signs is understood to affect not only the note before which it immediately occurs, but also, unless contradicted, any other notes on that same line or space of the staff throughout the measure (bar), and if the last note of the measure is thus inflected and is tied to the same note at the opening of the next measure, that latter also is understood to be included in the inflection.

TABLE 7

NAMES OF INFLECTIONS OF NOTES

Additions are made to the names of the notes as shown below:

	♯	×	♭	♭♭	♮
English	sharp	double-sharp	flat	double-flat	natural
German	Cis Dis Eis Fis Gis Ais •His (The sign is called *Kreuz*)	Cisis Disis Eisis Fisis Gisis Aisis •Hisis (The sign is called *Doppel-kreuz*)	Ces Des Es Fes Ges As •B (The sign is called *Be*)	Ceses Deses Eses Feses Geses Ases •Bes (The sign is called *Dop-pel-Be*)	The sign is called *Quad-rat* or *Auflösungs-zeichen* ('release-sign')
French	dièse	double-dièse	bémol	double-bémol	bécarre
Italian	diesis	doppio diesis	bemolle	doppio bemolle	bequadro

On account of one or two little irregularities in the German names it has been thought best to set these out in full. Notice particularly the names marked • (see Table 5).

TABLE 8

MAJOR AND MINOR KEY-SIGNATURES

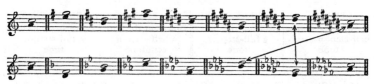

(Seldom used.)

The white note in each case represents the major key, the black note the minor key with the same signature (called 'Relative Minor').

It will be observed that, starting from C, the keynotes of the Sharp Keys rise five notes (a Perfect 5th) each remove, and that the keynotes of the Flat Keys fall five notes (a Perfect 5th) each remove.

It will also be observed that in the Sharp Major Keys the keynote is immediately above the last sharp.

And that in the Flat Major Keys the keynote is four notes below the last flat (i.e. is at the pitch of the last flat but one in the signature).

And that three notes down any Major Scale we come to the keynote of its Relative Minor or, to state it the other way, three notes up any Minor Scale we come to the keynote of its Relative Major.

Note that keys with six sharps (F♯ major and D♯ minor) are (on keyboard instruments) the equivalents of the keys with six flats (G♭ major and E♭ minor), and that keys with seven sharps (C♯ major and A♯ minor) are the equivalents of the keys with five flats (D♭ major and B♭ minor). Thus composers use either one or the other of these signatures.

The order of the sharps in the signatures is by rising fifths, and the order of the flats is by falling fifths.

Sharps → F C G D A E B ← *Flats*

That is, the one order is the other reversed.

TABLE 9

MAJOR AND MINOR IN FRENCH, GERMAN, AND ITALIAN

(in speaking of keys and scales)

ENGLISH	FRENCH	ITALIAN	GERMAN
major	majeur	maggiore	dur (i.e. 'hard')
minor	mineur	minore	moll (i.e. 'soft')

The above adjectives are used also of intervals, except for the German language, in which a major interval is called *gross* (i.e. big) and a minor one *klein* (i.e. small).

TABLE 10

TIME-SIGNATURES

Simple Duple

Compound Duple

Simple Triple

Compound Triple

Simple Quadruple

Compound Quadruple

Each Simple time has a corresponding Compound time. The beat in the Simple times is of the value of a plain note; in the Compound times of the value of a dotted note.

In other words, the beat-note value in the Simple times is divisible into halves, quarters, &c., and that in the Compound times into thirds, sixths, &c. The grouping of notes in a measure (bar) by means of the hooks of their tails (when they have such) should accord with these divisions, as shown above.

If the time-signature be regarded as a fraction it is to be understood in terms of Whole-notes, i.e. Semibreves; e.g. $\frac{3}{2}$ = three halves of $\circ$, i.e. $\frac{6}{4}$ = six quarters of $\circ$, and so on.

But note the difference between $\frac{3}{2}$ and $\frac{6}{4}$ (which are obviously of the same total time-duration per measure, yet differ in grouping and hence in rhythmic effect). And so with $\frac{3}{4}$ and $\frac{6}{8}$, and $\frac{3}{8}$ and $\frac{6}{16}$. On the other hand, between $\frac{3}{2}$ and $\frac{4}{4}$, $\frac{2}{2}$ and $\frac{4}{8}$, &c., there is little difference.

Occasional signatures other than those shown are to be met with, e.g. $\frac{3}{1}$ in one of Bach's Partitas (in effect each bar can be considered two bars of $\frac{3}{4}$).

Mixed bars of $\frac{2}{4} + \frac{3}{4}$ or $\frac{3}{4} + \frac{2}{4}$ (Quintuple Time) nowadays occur and are shown as $\frac{5}{4}$; mixed bars of $\frac{4}{4} + \frac{3}{4}$ or $\frac{3}{4} + \frac{4}{4}$, shown as $\frac{7}{4}$, and so on. There is, indeed, nothing to prevent a composer inventing any time-signature that he feels will help him to express the rhythm of any passage of his music.

TABLE 11

IRREGULAR RHYTHMIC GROUPINGS

(Duplets, Triplets, Quadruplets, &c.)

Duplet or Couplet	Two in the time of three:
Triplet (see also under 'Sextolet' below)	Three in the time of two:
Quadruplet	Four in the time of three:
Quintuplet	Five in the time of four—or of three:
Sextolet or Sextuplet (and Double Triplet)	Six in the time of four: (really a triplet it will be seen) · If a grouping of 3 + 3 is desired it should be written as below: (really a double triplet)
Septolet, or Septuplet, or Septimole	Seven in the time of four—or of six:

Various other combinations are possible, and it is hardly possible to list them or to lay down rules. When an irregular combination occurs the performer should observe the other notes of the measure, and he will quickly realize into what fraction of the measure the irregular grouping is to be fitted.

Note on Tables 12–16

These tables are concerned with the interpretation of the most usual signs for Ornaments or Graces. It must be understood, however, that such signs have carried different meanings in the usage of different periods, countries, and individual composers. Nothing less than a whole book can cover the subject, so that the information given here must be accepted as merely a useful generalization.

For the general subject see the article *Ornaments and Graces*, and for a full treatment consult Dannreuther's *Musical Ornamentation* (2 vols., Novello and H. W. Gray Co.) or some similar work.

TABLE 12

ACCIACCATURA AND MORDENT

(a) The **Acciaccatura**.

The principal note retains its accent and practically all its time-value. The auxiliary note is theoretically timeless; it is just squeezed in as quickly as possible before the principal note is heard. Some pianists of high repute even play the two notes simultaneously, immediately releasing the Acciaccatura and retaining the principal note (*Acciaccatura* is Italian for a 'crushing in'). Compare the Appoggiatura (Table 13)—a totally different thing. (For the use of the Acciaccatura sign before a shake see Table 16.)

Sometimes two or more small notes are shown before the principal notes, and then they generally amount to *Acciaccature* (being in most cases performed on the 'crushed-in', or timeless and accentless, principle), although they have no strokes through their tails, and although the name *Double Appoggiatura* or *Triple Appoggiatura* is often given them.

Note a combination of Acciaccatura with spread chord (for spread chords see Table 18):

performed as though notated—

Although, as above stated, the Acciaccatura is theoretically timeless, it nevertheless must take a tiny fragment of time from somewhere. In the cases shown above (which we may look upon as the normal ones) it takes it from the note which follows. In two other cases, however, it takes it from the note which precedes: (1) when, harmonically, and by considerations that common sense must determine, it clearly attaches to that note and not the following one; (2) when, in piano music, it appears in the bass followed by a chord in the left hand or in both hands—the composer's intention being to get the advantage of a richer harmony by sounding the bass note in a lower octave and then holding it by the pedal whilst the chord is played; in this case the chord (as a whole) is to be heard on the beat, the Acciaccatura slightly preceding it.

(b) The Upper and Lower Mordents.

Upper Mordent (in German 'Pralltriller') Upper Mordent with inflected note.

Lower Mordent (in German simply 'Mordent') Lower Mordent with inflected note

In the case of the *Upper Mordent* these 'crushed in' notes are the main note itself and the note above; if the latter is to be inflected in any way the

necessary sign (♯ ♭ ♮ × ♭♭) appears *above* the mordent sign.

In the case of the Lower Mordent the 'crushed in' notes consist of the note itself and the note below; if this latter is to be inflected in any way the necessary sign appears *below* the Lower Mordent sign (the interval is generally that of a semitone).

Mordent comes from Italian *mordere*, 'to bite'. There is a confusion in the use of names. The terms 'Mordent' and 'Inverted Mordent' are very commonly used for the two forms, but some call the first one shown above the 'Mordent' and the second one the 'Inverted Mordent', and others reverse these titles. The one way of avoiding all misunderstanding is always to use the words 'Upper' and 'Lower' (see article *Mordent*).

TABLE 13

THE APPOGGIATURA

(See note at head of TABLE 12, also entry under *Appoggiatura*)

(a) With Ordinary and Dotted Notes.

The Appoggiatura (Italian, from *appoggiare*, 'to lean') is not a timeless 'crushed in' note like the Acciaccatura (see Table 12); it is as important melodically as the note on which it 'leans', from which it takes normally half the time-value—or if the note on which it leans is dotted, two-thirds the time-value. (Note, however, that the exact interpretation of the Appoggiatura in different periods and circumstances goes far beyond the scope of this book.)

(b) With Tied Notes.

When the Appoggiatura 'leans upon' two tied notes, it normally takes the whole of the time-value of the first of these to itself (see reservation in previous column).

(c) With a Chord.

As the Appoggiatura leans only upon one note of the chord the other notes are unaffected.

TABLE 14

THE TURN

(See note at head of TABLE 12)

A turn (also called *Gruppetto*—Italian for 'grouplet') implies a figure of four notes—the note above, the note itself, the note below, and the note itself. This figure is performed *after* the note itself or *instead of it*, according as the turn sign is placed *after* the note itself or *over* it.

The inflection of the upper or lower note of the turn (in either form) is shown by the placing of a sharp, flat, natural, &c., sign above or below.

When the turn occurs after the note there is a good deal left to the taste of the performer as regards the division of the time available. The general principle seems to be that the turn is to be performed pretty quickly. To bring this about, the first example just given (if occurring in a slow tempo) might be treated thus:

whilst in a very quick tempo it might be treated as follows (indeed there might be no time to treat it in any other way):

The number of different examples given in different textbooks is very large, and no two textbooks quite agree, but the above statement gives the chief general principles accepted by all.

TABLE 15

THE INVERTED TURN

(With three alternative signs for it)

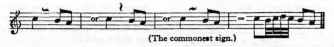

(The commonest sign.)

The principles laid down as to the Turn (Table 14) apply, of course, to the Inverted Turn, which begins with the *lower* auxiliary note, instead of the upper one.

TABLE 16

THE SHAKE OR TRILL

(See note at head of TABLE 12)

Essentially the Shake is an alternation of the note written and the note above.

But there is a diversity to be found in (a) its beginning, (b) its ending, and (c) the number of intervening alternations of the two notes.

(a) The Beginning of the Shake.

We may consider that nowadays the above beginning (i.e. on the written note itself) is the normal one.

But in the earlier music (up to and including Haydn and Mozart) it is generally intended that the shake shall begin on the upper of the two notes—

And, also, in music of any date, when the principal note is preceded by the same note the shake begins on the upper note, the principal note having already been sufficiently emphasized.

But nowadays if in any circumstances a composer wishes the shake to begin on the upper note he usually precedes it with an *Acciaccatura* sign, so as to leave no doubt.

Though the *Acciaccatura* sign is used, no real *Acciaccatura* is in-tended—the *Acciaccatura* proper (see Table 12) being a note 'crushed in' without time and without accent, whereas here the note in question gets a recognizable fraction of time and takes the accent from the note it displaces. Strictly speaking, then, the use of the *Acciaccatura* sign in this connexion is illogical and unfortunate.

It should be noted that the question whether a shake begins on the upper or the lower note is much more than that way of stating the question seems to imply. The question which of the two notes is to be accentuated is involved, and the whole colour of the shake depends on this.

Occasionally composers indicate that they intend a turn or inverted turn to precede the shake, the following being the best way of showing this intention:

(b) The Ending of the Shake.

All sorts of treatment may be demanded by the context, but one almost invariable rule is that the shake shall end on the written note itself.

Usually a turn precedes this (normally involving a triplet in order to fit the notes in).

Sometimes, to make sure of the insertion of the turn, modern writers insert in their notation the two extra notes at the end.

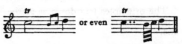

When a chain of shakes occurs, sometimes only the last one is ended with a turn.

(c) The 'Body' of the Shake.

The number of alternations of the written note and the note above is left to the taste of the performer. He will naturally insert many more when the written note is a long one in a slow tempo than when it is a short one in a quick tempo.

Sometimes, in the latter case, the shake really ceases to be such, nothing being left of it but the turn—

—or even less than that in cases where a turn is not felt to be suitable.

Inflected notes (sharps, flats, naturals, &c.) are indicated as follows:

Often a wavy line follows the sign 'tr'

Note. As with other 'ornaments' that of the shake differs in the details of performance in the music of different periods and different composers. The above gives a fairly safe generalization as to the practice of today, and in modern editions of old works where there is needed any departure from the rules here laid down it will generally be found that the editor has called attention to this.

TABLE 17

SIGNS OF RELATIVE INTENSITY

pp pianissimo or very soft	*p* piano or soft	*mf* mezzo forte or moderately loud	*f* forte or loud	*ff* fortissimo or very loud

Some composers have also used *ppp*, *pppp*, *fff*, and *ffff*, &c.—the meaning being obvious.

crescendo, i.e. increasing gradually in power.

decrescendo, or *diminuendo*, i.e. decreasing or diminishing gradually in power

See, in addition, the Signs of Accentuation, Table 24.

TABLE 18

PIANOFORTE SIGNS FOR 'SPREADING' OF CHORDS

('Arpeggioed', i.e. harp-fashion)

WRITTEN · PLAYED

Instead of attacking the notes of the chord simultaneously, play them from the bottom upwards, holding each as struck. (Occasionally in old music the notes are to be played from the top downwards and the question as to which is intended is sometimes a difficult one.)

Sometimes the wavy line is not continuous between the two staves, and then it is to be understood that the composer intends the arpeggio effect to go on in the two hands simultaneously.

It is to be noted that all spread chords should be so played as not to destroy the rhythm of the passage.

For the combination of spread chord with Acciaccatura see Table 12 (a).

TABLE 19

PIANOFORTE RIGHT-HAND AND LEFT-HAND SIGNS

LEFT			RIGHT	
L.H. Left Hand	M.S. Mano Sinistra (Italian)	M.G. Main Gauche (French)	R.H. Right Hand	M.D. Mano Destra (Italian) or Main Droite (French)

TABLE 20

REPEAT MARKS (FOR PASSAGES)

:‖ means return to ‖: or, if that does not occur, to the beginning of the piece.	D.C. or *Da Capo*, literally 'From the head', i.e. return to the beginning.	D.S. or *Dal Segno*, i.e. from the sign, meaning return to the mark :S:.	A.S. (rare) or *Al Segno*, i.e. to the sign. Usually the expression is *D.C. al Segno e poi la Coda*, i.e. 'From the beginning to the :S: and then the Coda'.	*Bis* means perform the passage twice.

To avoid needless writing or engraving (especially in orchestral music) the repetition of a short passage is often indicated as below:

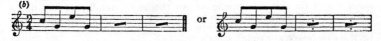

Sometimes when a section is marked to be repeated it ends in a way suitable for the return to the beginning, and, having been repeated, ends in a way suitable to proceed to the next section (or to close the whole composition if nothing more follows). The two endings are then shown thus:

Or instead of the '1', there may be used the expression '1^(ma) Volta', or 'Prima Volta', or '1st Time'.

And instead of the '2', there may be used the expression '2^(da) Volta', or 'Seconda Volta', or '2nd Time'.

When a return to the opening of the piece, or of some section of it, is indicated but only a part is to be repeated and then the piece brought to an end,

the word *Fine* ('end') shows where to stop.

For instance, a Minuet is often followed by another Minuet called 'Trio' (see *Trio*), after which the first Minuet is to be repeated and then an end to be made. In this case the word 'Fine' is placed at the end of the first Minuet to indicate that this is the place to conclude when performing the repetition.

TABLE 21

REPEAT MARKS (FOR NOTES)

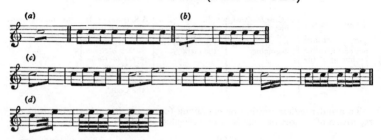

There is a 'catch' in (c) and (d), the convention not being quite logical. In (c) (three examples are given) the time-value to be filled is that of *one* of the notes shown (in this case minim or half-note); in (d) the time-value to be filled is that of *both* of the notes shown (in this case quavers or eighth notes).

Note. If *Tremolo* (or *Trem.*) is added to any of the above or similar signs the notes concerned should be repeated very rapidly and without any attention to the exact number of repetitions attained during the time-value available.

TABLE 22

THE VARIOUS USES OF THE CURVED LINE

The Tie or Bind

The two notes become one (see also article *Tie or Bind*).

The Slur, or Legato (or Bowing Mark)

All the notes affected by the curve are to be played smoothly. In string music they are to be played in one movement of the bow.

The Phrase Mark

See article *Phrasing*.

The Syllable Mark

The mark is to make clearer the fitting of the notes to the syllables.

The   sun— sinks to rest

The Portamento Mark

Instead of jumping cleanly the singer is to slide from the one note to the other, taking all intervening pitches en route. The same effect is possible on bowed instruments, but here a wavy line is sometimes the indication.

for   ev - er - more

See also *Staccato Marks*, on following page.

TABLE 23

STACCATO MARKS

This table gives a rough and generally accurate interpretation of the various marks, but is not to be taken too literally or mathematically.

MEZZO-STACCATO (shorten the note by about ¼)	STACCATO (shorten the notes by about ½)	STACCATISSIMO (shorten the notes by about ¾)
Written		

Played (approximately)

The sign (i.e. a combination of accent marks and staccato marks) indicates a combination of pressure with a slight detachment.

TABLE 24

SIGNS OF ACCENTUATION

attack	agogic accent (see *Agogic*)	fz forzato — 'forced'	sf or sfz sforzato — 'forced'	marcato 'marked', i.e. emphasized

TABLE 25

PAUSE SIGNS

Pause	*lunga pausa* long pause	*G.P.* 'General Pause'—an intimation in an orchestral score that the whole orchestra pauses.

TABLE 26

OCTAVE SIGNS

8va or 8	8va bassa or 8va sotto	toco	con 8
'Ottava', i.e. perform an 8ve higher than written.	Perform an 8ve lower than written ('sotto' = under).	'Place', i.e. (after playing an 8ve higher or lower) resume the playing as written.	Play the passage not in single notes, as marked, but in octaves.[1]

[1] The added line of 8ves will be *above* if the passage is in the treble of a pianoforte piece, and *below* if it is in the bass.

CONCISE DICTIONARY OF MUSIC

A (It.), **À** (Fr.). 'At', 'by', 'for', 'with', 'in', 'to', 'in the manner of', &c. For expressions beginning with À or À see under their principal words.

'A 2' in orch. scores and parts directs (*a*) 2 instruments that normally play separate parts (e.g. the 2 oboes or 2 flutes) to play in unison, or (*b*) 2 instruments that normally play in unison (e.g. the first violins) to divide in order to play the separate parts provided for them.

A.A.G.O. See *Degrees and Diplomas* 4.

Aallottaret (Sibelius). See *Oceanides*.

Ab (Ger.). 'Off' (in organ music applied to a stop no longer required).

A B A, A formula used by theorists meaning Simple Ternary Form (see *Form* 2).

Abaco, (1) **Evaristo Felice dall'** (b. Verona 1675; d. Munich 1742). Violinist and composer of the court of Munich; wrote music of the Corelli type.

(2) **Giuseppe Clemens Ferdinand dall'** (b. Brussels 1709; d. Verona 1805). Son of preceding; 'cellist and composer of string music.

Abailard. See *Abélard*.

Abandonné (Fr.). 'Negligent' (in such an expression as *Un rhythme un peu abandonné*—'rhythm rather free-and-easy'). **Abbandono** (It. 'abandon'). 'Free, impassioned style.' So the adverb, *abbandonatamente*, &c.

Abbassare (It.). 'To lower', e.g. to tune down a string of an instrument of the violin family, so as to obtain a note normally out of the compass.

Abbellimenti (It. 'embellishments'). See *Ornaments or Graces*; also Tables 12–16.

Abbott, Emma (b. Chicago 1850; d. Salt Lake City 1891). Operatic soprano. Studied Milan and Paris. Toured U.S.A. with own 'English Grand Opera Company'.

A.B.C.M. See *Degrees and Diplomas* 2.

Abdämpfen (Ger. 'to damp off'). To mute.

Abduction from the Seraglio. See *Entführung*.

Abegg Variations for Piano by Schumann (his op. 1, 1830). Written on a theme made out of the notes A–B–E–G–G, and dedicated to his friend Meta Abegg. (Cf. similar case s.v. *Carnaval*.)

(For the German name 'B' for B flat see *B* and *B-A-C-H*.)

Abeille, L' ('The Bee'). See *Schubert, Franz* (of Dresden).

Abel, Karl Friedrich (b. Cöthen 1723; d. London 1787). Pupil of Bach at Leipzig; orch. player under Hasse at Dresden; spent latter part of life in London as last great exponent of viola da gamba, composing chamber music and symphonies, and associated with J. C. Bach (see *Bach* 5) in concert undertakings.

Abencérages, Les. Opera by Cherubini. Libretto by V. J. E. de Jouy, based on Florian's novel, *Gonzalve de Cordove* (1st perf., Paris 1813, unsuccessful; its overture survives).

Abend (Ger.). 'Evening'; **Abendlied.** 'Evening Song.'

Aber (Ger.). 'But.'

Abert, Hermann (b. Stuttgart 1871; there d. 1927). Musical scholar of very high reputation; many valuable books, of which recasting of Jahn's (q.v.) standard life of Mozart specially important. Prof. at Univ. of Leipzig (1920) and then of Berlin (1923).

Aberystwyth (hymn tune). See *Parry, Joseph*.

Abgestossen (Ger.). See *Abstossen*.

Abilità, Aria d'. See *Aria*.

B

Abingdon, Henry. See *Abyngdon.*

Ab initio (Lat.). 'From the beginning.'

Ablösen (Ger.). 'To loosen from one another', &c. There are various applications, e.g. to separate the notes (i.e. play staccato).

Abnehmend (Ger. 'off-taking'). 'Diminuendo.'

Abraham, Gerald Ernest Heal (b. Newport, I.O.W., 1904). Active author on musical subjects; authority on Russian music; ed. of *Monthly Musical Record.* On B.B.C. staff 1935–47, again 1962–7; 1947–62 first Prof. of Music Univ. Liverpool.

Abraham Lincoln. See *Bennett, Robert Russell.*

Abrupt Cadence. See *Cadence.*

Abruzzese (It.). A song or dance in the style of the Abruzzi district, to the east of Rome.

Abschiedssymphonie (Haydn). See *Farewell Symphony.*

Absent-minded Man (Haydn). See *Distratto.*

Absetzen (Ger.). Same sense as *Ablösen* (q.v.).

Absil, Jean (b. Peruwelz, Belgium 1893). Composer of strongly modernistic tendency. Works include concertos for piano and violin, choral music, chamber music, piano music, &c.

A.B.S.M.; A.B.S.M.(T.T.D). See *Degrees and Diplomas* 2.

Absolute Music. Instrumental music which exists simply as such, i.e. not 'Programme Music' (q.v.). See *Abstract Music.*

Absolute Pitch (Sense of). That sense which some people possess of the actual pitch of any note heard, as distinct from *Relative Pitch,* which implies the recognition of a note as being a certain degree of the scale or as lying at a certain interval above or below another note heard. The sense of Relative Pitch can readily be acquired by practice, the sense of Absolute Pitch much less readily.

Absolute pitch is really an innate form of memory: the possessor of it retains in his mind (consciously or unconsciously) the pitch of some instrument to which he has been accustomed and instinctively relates to that pitch every sound heard. Many good musicians possess the faculty; as many others do not: its possession or non-possession is, then, not in itself a proof of either high or low musical capacity.

The possession of this sense is on occasion extremely useful, but may sometimes become an embarrassment, as, for instance, when a singer possessing it is called upon to read music accompanied by an instrument tuned to what is to him 'the wrong pitch', necessitating on his part a conscious transposition of the vocal line that is before him in the notation.

Abstossen (Ger.). (1) 'To detach notes from one another', i.e. to play staccato. (2) In organ playing, 'To cease to use a stop'. (*Abgestossen* is the past participle.)

Abstract Music. Same as *Absolute Music* (q.v.). As Ger. writers use the term (*Abstrakte Musik*) it has a different meaning—music lacking in sensitiveness, 'dry' music, 'academic' music.

Abt, Franz Wilhelm (b. nr. Leipzig 1819; d. Wiesbaden 1885). Opera and choral conductor; composer of many graceful songs and part-songs.

Abu Hassan. One-act operetta by Weber. (Prod. Munich 1811; London 1825; New York 1827.)

Abwechseln, Abzuwechseln (Ger., various terminations according to person, case, &c.). 'To change.' Used of one orch. instrument alternating with another in the hands of the same player, &c.

Abyngdon (Abingdon, Habyngton, &c.), **Henry** (abt. 1420–97). Singer, organist, and composer (none of whose works has been preserved). Precentor of Wells Cathedral and Master of the Children of the Chapel Royal. The first person known to have taken a music degree at Cambridge (B.Mus. 1463).

Sir Thomas More wrote two laudatory epitaphs upon him.

Academic Festival Overture (*Akademische Festouvertüre*). Brahms's op. 80, 1st perf. 1881 at a concert in celebration of the composer's receiving an honorary doctorate from the Univ. of Breslau (cf. *Tragic Overture*). A sort of fantasia on traditional Ger. students' songs, closing with *Gaudeamus igitur*—which has, on occasion, been sung as well as played (first with the composer's sanction, at Cambridge 1882).

Academy of Ancient Music. London Soc. for performance of old music; apparently founded 1726 as 'Academy of Vocal Music'. Survived until 1792. (Not to be confused with 'Concert of Ancient Music', q.v.)

Academy of Vocal Music. See *Academy of Ancient Music.*

A Cappella (It.). See *Cappella.*

Accarezzevole; accarezzevolmente (It.). 'Caressing'; 'caressingly'.

Accelerando; accelerato (It.). 'Accelerating'; 'accelerated'; i.e. getting gradually quicker (see reference under *Rubato*).

Accent. (1) See *Rhythm*; *Syncopation.* (2) The name is also applied to the simplest forms of plainsong tones (see *Plainsong*), i.e. very slightly inflected monotones.

Accento (It.). 'Accent' (see *Accent* above). So *accentato*, 'accented'.

Accentué (Fr.). 'Accented.'

Accentus. (1) The part of the Roman Catholic liturgy which is chanted only by the priest or his representative, as distinct from the *Concentus*, which is chanted by the congregation or choir. (See *Gradual*.) (2) See *Accent* 2 above.

Acciaccato (It. 'Broken down', 'crushed'—e.g. of a hat). The sounding of the notes of a chord not quite simultaneously, but from bottom to top. ('Vehement', 'violent', 'forcible', are translations given in some musical works of reference, but there does not seem to be warrant for this.)

Acciaccatura. See Table 12.

Acciaio, Istrumento d'. (It. 'Instrument of steel'.) Mozart's name for his Glockenspiel in *The Magic Flute*. (See *Percussion* 1 c.)

Accidental. The sign indicating momentary departure from the key signature by the raising or lowering of a note by means of a sharp, flat, natural, &c. It holds good throughout the measure (bar) unless contradicted, and where it occurs attached to the last note of the measure and this note is tied to a note in the next measure it holds good for that latter note also.

In some modern 'Atonal' music (see *Harmony* 3) any accidental occurring is understood to affect merely the note before which it is placed, as was often the case in earlier music (e.g. 17th c.).

A.C.C.O. See *Degrees and Diplomas* 2.

Accompagnato (It.). 'Accompanied.'

Accompanied Fugue. See *Form* 6.

Accompaniment. The term as ordinarily used today implies the presence of some principal performer (vocalist, violinist, &c.) more or less subserviently supplied with a background by some other performer or performers (pianist, orch., &c.). This is not the original use of the word, which carried no suggestion of subservience, 'Sonata for Harpsichord with Violin Accompaniment' being a common 18th-c. term.

The subservience nowadays is marked by the manner in which some vocalists treat their accompanists, demanding an undue artistic deference, a too limited body of piano tone, &c. This is the more to be regretted when songs by 19th-c. composers (Schubert, Schumann, Brahms, Wolf, &c.) or 20th-c. composers are performed, in which the piano part is elaborate and, indeed, in importance approaches the vocal part. In the performance of such songs we have an example of demands on *ensemble* (q.v.) almost like those of a piece of chamber music, in which all players are on equal terms.

For Hymn Accompaniment see *Hymns and Hymn Tunes* 6; for Additional Accompaniments see article under that head; for Plainsong Accompaniment see *Plainsong* 4; for Accompanied Cadenza see *Cadenza.*

Accoppiare (It.). 'To couple' (organ). Hence *Accoppiato*, 'Coupled'; *Accoppiamento*, 'Coupling' (the noun).

Accord (Fr.). (1) 'Chord.' (2) 'Tuning.' **Accordare** (It.). 'To tune.' **Accordato, accordati** (It. masc. sing., and plur.); **accordata, accordate** (fem. sing., and plur.). 'Tuned.' (The word is sometimes seen as a part of some expression indicating that a particular tuning is required, e.g. of the kettle-drums.) **Accordatura**. 'Tuning.'

Accordeon or **Accordion**. See *Reed-Organ Family* 3.

Accorder (Fr.). 'To tune.' Hence *Accordé*, 'Tuned'.

Accordo (It.). 'Chord.'

Accoupler (Fr.). 'To couple' (organ). So *accouplé*, 'coupled'; *accouplement*, 'coupling', 'coupler' (nouns); *accouplez*, 'couple' (imperative).

Accursed Hunter (Franck). See *Chasseur maudit*.

Accusé, Accusée (Fr. masc., fem.). 'Emphasized.'

Achron, (1) (**Akhron**, &c.), **Joseph** (b. Lozdzieje, in Russian Lithuania, 1886; d. Los Angeles 1943). Fine violinist; student of Jewish traditional music and composer of music influenced thereby. Settled in U.S.A. 1917. (2) **Isidor** (b. Warsaw 1892; d. New York 1948). Pianist, conductor, and composer. Brother of the above and also settled in U.S.A. (1922).

Acht (Ger.). (1) 'Eight.' (2) 'Care.'

Achtel or **Achtelnote** (Ger.). 'Eighth' or 'Eighth-note', i.e. Quaver (see Table 3); so *Achtelpause* for the corresponding rest. *Achtstimmig*, 'In 8 voices' (i.e. 8 parts).

Acis and Galatea. 'Serenata' or 'Pastoral Opera' by Handel. (1st perf. Cannons, abt. 1721; London 1732.)

Ackté, Aino (b. Helsingfors, Finland, 1876; there d. 1944). Operatic soprano; début Paris 1897; wide range of roles but especially famous in Strauss (*Salome*).

Acoustic Bass. Organ stop with two rows of pipes—those mentioned under *Quint* (q.v.).

Acoustics. Properly, anything pertaining to the sense of hearing, but, as commonly used, (*a*) The branch of science which concerns itself with the properties, production, and transmission of sound, or, secondarily, (*b*) The quality of a building as regards suitability for the clear hearing of speech or music. The secondary meaning (*b*) is treated under the heading *Concert Halls*.

(1) Sound is due to the vibrations of a source, such as a musical instrument, which are transmitted through the air and which set the ear-drum in vibration at the same rate.

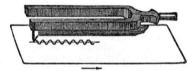

VIBRATIONS MADE VISIBLE

The trace of a vibrating fork can be obtained by drawing a piece of paper or smoked glass under it and moving it steadily forward or backward.

(2) The PITCH of a sound depends on the rapidity of those vibrations, rapid vibrations producing what we call a 'high' pitch and slow ones what we call a 'low' pitch. (See also 5 below.) The rate of vibration per second we call the 'frequency' of the note.

(3) The LOUDNESS of a sound depends on the 'amplitude' of the vibrations; for instance, a violin string violently bowed will swing backwards and forwards for a considerable distance on each side of its line of repose and so produce big vibrations in the air, and thus a loud sound, whereas one gently bowed will swing only a short distance on each side and so produce small vibrations in the air, and thus a soft sound.

(4) The initial VIBRATING AGENCIES in the case of the violin, guitar, &c., are

strings; in that of the harmonium, concertina, oboe, clarinet, bassoon, the reed pipes of organs, &c., small 'reeds' of wood or metal; in that of brass instruments the lips of the player communicating their vibrations to the column of air in the tube; in that of the flute and the 'flue' pipes of an organ a sharp edge or lip, which on receiving a jet of air sets in vibration the column of air in the tube; in that of the drum a sheet of parchment; in that of the voices of birds, animals, and human beings, the vocal cords.

(5) The smaller of these instruments produce the more rapid vibrations and the larger the slower ones: thus the oboe has a higher general pitch than its relative the bassoon, a violin than a violoncello, a stopped string than the same string left 'open', a boy's voice than a man's voice, &c. But other factors enter into the control of pitch. For instance, *mass* (the thinner strings of a violin vibrate more quickly than the thicker ones and so possess a higher general pitch) and *tension* (a violin string tightened by turning the peg rises in pitch).

HARMONICS

The Tuning Fork is perhaps the only instrument free from these. It sounds practically only its own fundamental (which accounts for its 'colourless' tone quality), whereas when a note is played on the Violin (for example) many simultaneous harmonics occur and 'colour' the tone.

(6) The varying QUALITY of the sound produced by different instruments and different voices is explained as follows. Almost all vibrations are compound, e.g. a sounding violin string may be vibrating not merely as a whole but also at one and the same time in halves, thirds, quarters, and other fractions, and these fractions are

producing notes according to their varying lengths, such as are not easily identifiable by the ear but are nevertheless present as factors in the ensemble of the tone. It is the absence or presence, or greater or lesser comparative strength,

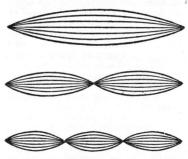

VIBRATIONS OF A STRETCHED
STRING

The string simultaneously vibrates as a whole and also in two and three equal parts, respectively (and also, of course, in other smaller parts). Its vibration as a whole produces the fundamental note; in halves the note an octave higher; and in thirds the note a twelfth higher—and so on with the smaller simultaneous divisions not here shown.

of the various secondary sounds thus produced (called harmonics, overtones, or upper partials) which conditions the quality or 'timbre' of the note. (This is the hitherto accepted theory of quality in tone: for a modern modification or elaboration of it see *OCM*, s.v. *Acoustics* 6.)

(7) We may now consider in a little detail the HARMONICS, OVERTONES, or UPPER PARTIALS just referred to. (These three words are not quite synonymous but can be treated as such here.) Taking the note G as the *Fundamental Note* (otherwise called 'First Harmonic') of a particular tube or string, the *Harmonic Series*, carried to a reasonable height, would be as follows:

Theoretically the series proceeds upwards to infinity: practically, however, it can be taken as fading gradually into silence as it ascends. It will be noted that, taking any particular note of the series (as G, D, or B), the numbers of its harmonics double with each octave as the series ascends. The numbers attached to the harmonics represent also the ratios of the frequencies of the various harmonics to the fundamental. Thus if the frequency of the low G is 96 vib./sec., that of the B in the treble stave (5th harmonic) is $5 \times 96 = 480$ vib./sec.

Whilst these harmonics are normally heard in combination some of them can, on some instruments, be separately obtained. By a particular method of blowing, a brass tube, instead of producing its no. 1 harmonic, or fundamental, can be made to produce its no. 2 or 3, or some other harmonic. By lightly touching a string, or a length of string (i.e. a stopped string), at its centre and then bowing it, it can be made to produce (in a peculiar silvery tone quality) its no. 2 harmonic; by doing the same at a third of its length it will, similarly, produce its no. 3 harmonic and so with some other harmonics. (The notational sign that a note is to be produced as a harmonic is an 'o' above it. 'Natural' Harmonics are those produced from an open string; 'Artificial' Harmonics those produced from a stopped string.)

At one period the only notes obtainable from a horn or trumpet were the harmonics that belonged to the fundamental note of its length of tube. Crooks and shanks were introduced which, inserted in the instrument, lengthened it and so altered its fundamental note and, hence, its whole harmonic series. (A crook is a curved piece of tube: a shank a straight one: their functions are identical.) Whilst any particular crook or shank was in use the player was still limited to the relevant harmonic series with all its gaps: then valves were introduced, in place of the crooks or shanks, and the length of the tube could be immediately changed and rechanged, thus making it possible to change the whole harmonic series without delays and making easily and rapidly available any

note whatever that was required by picking a harmonic series in which it conveniently occurred. On the woodwind, similar changes in effective length are secured by covering or uncovering side-holes in the tube by the fingers.

(8) Many vibrating bodies, however, produce overtones which are not members of the harmonic series. The more closely these overtones are related to members of a harmonic series, the more pleasant is the combined sound to the ear. An irregular piece of metal,

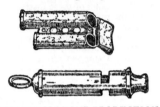

DIFFERENCE TONE PRODUCTION

Referee's whistles, showing two tubes giving strong low-pitch difference tone.

roughly struck, will give out a number of vibrations of unrelated frequencies, producing an 'unmusical' sound, or 'noise'; the same piece of metal carefully shaped and struck can give out vibrations that accord with the harmonic series of the fundamental note of the piece of metal, and will produce a 'musical' tone. (For a fuller consideration of this subject see *OCM*, s.v. *Acoustics* 8.)

(9) The normal TRANSMISSION OF SOUND, as already indicated, is through the air. The vibrations of a string, a drum-head, the vocal cords, or whatever it may be, set up similar vibrations in the nearest particles of air; those communicate them to other particles, and so on, until the initial energy is gradually exhausted.

(10) The expression SOUND WAVES is often used but it is liable to mislead, suggesting shapes of air-motion similar to those of water-motion. What happens is that one unit of air, coming under alternate pressure and release of pressure, is alternately condensed and relaxed, that it then passes on its pressures and releases of pressure to the adjacent unit and, as energy is lost,

gradually resumes quietude. There is no change of position of the unit, since each particle of air merely swings forward and backward; what occurs is a pressure and then a relaxation of the pressure which if it reaches the ear-drum of an animal or human being sets

TRANSMISSION OF SOUND

'I have five young assistants, A, B, C, D, and E, placed in a row, one behind the other, each boy's hand resting against the back of the boy in front of him. E is foremost, and A finishes the row behind. I suddenly push A; A pushes B and regains his upright position; B pushes C; C pushes D; D pushes E; each boy, after the transmission of the push, becoming himself erect. E, having nobody in front, is thrown forward. . . .' (Tyndall, *On Sound*, 1875).

up a similar series of pressures and relaxations there (= 'vibrations') and so causes the subjective effect we call 'sound'. Diagrams in textbooks of acoustics, showing 'Sound Waves' are, then, merely diagrams and not pictures, and when photographs of 'Sound Waves' are given, they are merely photographs, greatly enlarged, of marks made by some recording instrument so contrived as to represent the vibrations in wave form. (Cf. *Phonodeik*.)

(11) A somewhat difficult conception is that of the SUPERPOSITION OF VIBRATIONS. Clearly, as we are able to hear more than one note at a time, this must occur, i.e. a unit of pressure and relaxation in the air is divided simultaneously into smaller units of pressure and relaxation and, moreover, is overlapped by still other units of pressure and relaxation. The reader who finds himself unable to picture such a confused state of affairs must, in a brief treatment like the present one, be advised to take the word of the scientists for the existence of the phenomenon and to pass on to the next section of the subject

(12) We come now to the SPEED OF SOUND. Sound vibrations, travelling through the air, move very slowly as compared with light vibrations, which travel through the ether. Temperature affects the density of the air and thus affects the speed of the passage of the vibrations, but normally it may be put at about $12\frac{1}{2}$ miles per minute, the speed of light approaching a million times this speed. (Some air-flight speeds since 1948 exceed sound speed.)

(13) Pitch, as we have seen, depends upon the FREQUENCY OF THE VIBRATIONS of the sounding-agent. The vibrations in the air have obviously the same frequency as those of the agent. If the lowest C on the piano has a vibration frequency of 32 per second, the next C above has 64 per second, and so, doubling with each octave ascended, to the 8th and highest C on the larger instruments, with 4,096 per second.

(14) There is a PITCH-LIMIT OF AUDIBILITY, differing with different individuals. The low C of a large organ (an 8ve below the lowest C of the piano) is as low a note as most ears can accept as such: it has 16 vibrations per second and below that number most people feel the vibrations merely individually as such, not as combining to constitute a musical note. Upwards a few people can hear notes two 8ves above the highest note of the piano: an 8ve higher still nobody can hear anything.

(15) When two notes near to one another in vibration frequency are heard together their vibrations necessarily coincide at regular intervals and thus reinforce one another in the effect produced. This periodical reinforcement is called a BEAT. When the piano tuner is tuning one string of a certain note to another string of that note a beat can be heard diminishing in its frequency until at last, as he correctly adjusts the tension of the string, it gradually disappears and his work on that string is accomplished. When the rate of beating exceeds 20 per second, the sensation of a note low in the bass is aroused.

(16) When two loud notes are heard together they give rise to a third sound (a COMBINATION or RESULTANT TONE) corresponding to the difference between the two vibration numbers: this

(low in pitch) is called a *Difference Tone*. They also give rise to a fourth sound (another Combination Tone—high and faint) corresponding to the sum of the two vibration numbers: this is called a *Summation Tone*. For a fuller explanation of these phenomena see any textbook of acoustics, and for the practical use of Difference Tones by violinists, as a check on the tuning of double stops, and by organ builders ('Acoustic Bass', 'Resultant Bass', or 'Harmonic Bass') as a means of cheaply providing the effect of costly deep-pitched stops see *OCM*, s.v. *Acoustics* 9.

(17) There is REFLECTION OF SOUND, just as there is a reflection of light, as we experience when we hear an echo.

(18) Similarly there are SOUND SHADOWS, caused by some obstruction which impedes the passage of vibrations which reach it. However, sound vibrations tend to work or 'diffract' round an object as light vibrations do not, unless the light obstacle is very small like a pin-point, and, moreover, not every solid obstruction will create a complete 'shadow'. Most solids will transmit sound vibrations, more or less strongly, whereas only a few solids (glass, &c.) will transmit light vibrations.

(19) The term RESONANCE is applied to the response of an object to the sounding of a given note, i.e. its taking up the vibrations of that note. Thus if of 2 tuning-forks of the same pitch and placed near to one another one be sounded, the other will be set in vibration and will also give out the note. The first fork is then a *Generator* of sound and the second a *Resonator*. It is often found that a particular window in a church will vibrate when a particular organ note is sounded, and that a metal or glass object in a room will similarly respond to a particular note of the piano.

What has just been described is true resonance ('re-sounding') in the strict scientific sense of the word. There is also a less strict use of the word, which is sometimes applied to the vibration of floor, walls, and ceiling of a hall, not limited to a particular note but adapting themselves to any note played or sung. A hall may be either too resonant for the comfort of performers and hearers or too little so—too 'dead' (a hall with echo is often spoken of as 'too resonant', but there is an obvious clear distinction to be made between the mere reflection of sounds and the sympathetic reinforcements of them).

The sound board of a piano, and the back and belly of a violin, by vibrating in sympathy with the sounds emitted by the strings, amplify these enormously, so that most of the sound we hear does not come from its original source (the string) but is the effect of resonance.

For the phenomena of the reception and recognition of sound by the listener see *Ear and Hearing*.

Acta Musicologica. See *Musicology*.

Action. The mechanism of a piano, organ, or similar instrument.

Action, Ballet d', or **Pas d'.** A ballet with a dramatic basis.

Action Song. A children's song with some measure of expressive or dramatic movement by the singers.

Act Tune (or **Curtain Tune**, or **Curtain Music**). A 17th- and 18th-c. term for music between the acts of a play whilst the curtain was down.

Actus Tragicus. Bach's well-known early cantata (no. 106) *Gottes Zeit ist die allerbeste Zeit* ('God's Time is the best'). It appears to have been written for an occasion of mourning on the death of some public personage.

Adagietto (It.). (1) Slow, but less so than *Adagio*. (2) A short *adagio* composition.

Adagio (It. 'At ease'). 'Slow' (not so slow as *Largo*, however). A slow movement is often called 'an Adagio'. *Adagissimo*, 'Extremely slow'.

Adam, Adolphe Charles (b. Paris 1803; there d. 1856). Successful composer of operas, ballets, choral works, church music, &c.; music critic and prof. at Conservatory. (See *Giselle*.)

Adam de la Halle (or 'de la Hale') (b. abt. 1231, probably at Arras; d. Naples 1288). Famous trouvère (see *Minstrels* 2); his *Play of Robin and Marion* (precursor of Opéra Comique

—see *Opera* 7) still published and occasionally performed. Early composer of motets, &c.

Adam le Bossu (i.e. 'Adam the Hunchback'). Same as Adam de la Halle (q.v.).

Adams, (1) Thomas (b. London 1785; there d. 1858). London organist of high reputation as executant, extemporizer, and composer.

(2) **Suzanne** (b. Cambridge, Mass., 1872; d. London 1953). Operatic and concert soprano. Début Paris 1894; Metropolitan Opera, New York, 1899. Enjoyed Brit. popularity in oratorio.

(3) **Thomas** (d. 1918). Composer of popular anthems, &c.

(4) **Stephen.** See *Maybrick, Michael.*

Adam's Apple. See *Larynx; Voice* 5.

Adam Zero. Ballet by Bliss. (1st perf. London 1946.)

A.D.C.M. See *Degrees and Diplomas* 2.

Added Sixth, Chord of. In Key C the chord F–A–C–D and similarly in other keys, i.e. the subdominant chord plus the 6th from the bass, or, looked at in another way, the 1st inversion of the (diatonic) supertonic 7th.

Addinsell, Richard (b. Oxford 1904). Trained Oxford and R.C.M. Popular Brit. composer of music for films, of marches, &c. (See *Warsaw Concerto.*)

Addison, John (b. West Chobham 1920). Trained R.C.M. (on staff 1950–7). Comp. of successful music for film and stage, also orchestral and chamber music.

Additional Accompaniments. When there is performed today an oratorio or the like, of the 16th to 18th cs., it is often impossible to reproduce the score exactly as written, since some of the instruments no longer exist and others have changed in tone-quality, tone-quantity, or compass. Hence a degree of adaptation is unavoidable, and this sometimes takes the shape of additions to the score. A familiar example of such additions is found in the instrumental parts Mozart wrote into Handel's *Messiah* for an occasion when no organ was available to provide the figured bass (q.v.), as it was provided in

Handel's own performances: these are often nowadays used even when an organ is present, and, indeed, modern audiences are so used to hearing them that many people regard them as a part of the work and feel aggrieved if they are omitted. (Cf. *Franz, Robert.*)

Addolcendo. *(*It.*).* 'Becoming *dolce*' (q.v.).

Addolorato (It. 'grieved'). 'In a saddened style.'

Adel (Ger.). 'Nobility.'

Adelaïde. Famous soprano solo cantata by Beethoven (op. 46; abt. 1795); usually sung by a tenor. Original has piano accompaniment. Poem by Matthisson. Liszt wrote a piano 'transcription' of the song (1839).

Adeste Fideles ('O come, all ye faithful'). This Latin hymn and tune probably date from the early 18th c. The late G. E. P. Arkwright detected that the first part of the tune closely resembled a tune which appeared in a Paris Vaudeville of 1744 (where it was described as 'Air Anglais') and suggested that it was probably an adaptation of some popular tune eked out, in the hymn setting, with reminiscences of the air 'Pensa ad amare' from Handel's *Ottone* (1723). This view is supported by more recent researches. In 1947 a pamphlet by Dom John Stéphan, of Buckfast Abbey, Devon, discussed a newly discovered MS. of the *Adeste Fideles* tune in the handwriting of John Francis Wade, a Latin teacher and music copyist of Douay who died in 1786. The pamphlet advances good reasons for believing this to be 'the first and original version', dating from between 1740 and 1743, and attributes both the original (Latin) words and the compilation of the music to Wade himself.

À deux cordes (Fr.). 'On two strings.'

Adiaphonon. An early tuning-fork piano of the class of the dulcitone (see *Percussion* 1 e).

Adieu, Sweet Amaryllis. See *Wilbye.*

Adieu to the Piano. Once-popular piece wrongly attributed to Beethoven. (Origin unknown.)

Adieux, l'Absence, et le Retour, Les (Beethoven). Piano Sonata in E flat, op. 81*a*. Fr. title given by the composer himself, who also applied the description *Sonate caractéristique*.

Adirato (It.). 'Angered' (irate).

Adler, (1) **Guido** (b. Moravia 1855; d. Vienna 1941). Distinguished musicologist; editor of old music and of well-known History of Music; author of learned works; prof. Univ. of Prague and then that of Vienna.
(2) **Larry** (b. Baltimore 1914). Virtuoso on Harmonica (Mouth Organ; see *Reed Organ Family* 2). Has toured the world both as music-hall (vaudeville) and recital artist, and as soloist with symphony orchs., &c., revealing unsuspected capabilities of his instrument.

Ad libitum (Lat.), or *Ad lib.* 'At will'—as to (*a*) Rhythm, tempo, &c.; (*b*) Inclusion or omission of some voice or instrument; (*c*) Inclusion or omission of some passage; (*d*) The extemporizing of a cadenza (q.v.).

A due corde (It.). 'On two strings.'

Adventures in a Perambulator. Orchestral Suite by J. A. Carpenter (q.v.). (1st perf. Chicago 1915.)

Aehnlich or **Ähnlich** (Ger.). 'Similar', 'like.'

Aengstlich or **Ängstlich** (Ger.). 'Anxious.'

Aeolian Harp (from Aeolus, the fabled keeper of the winds). An instrument consisting of a box about 3 ft. long with, on its upper surface, catgut strings of different thicknesses but tuned in unison. It could be placed along the width of a window ledge or elsewhere where the wind could catch it and set the strings in vibration, and they, being at low tension, vibrated in such a way that their harmonics (rather than their fundamental sounds: cf. *Acoustics* 7) were evoked. The harmonics produced varied with the thickness of the strings and the velocity of the wind, so that a chordal effect was produced. The period of the Aeolian

Harp seems to have been from the end of the 16th c. or beginning of the 17th to near the end of the 19th.

Aeolian Harp (pianoforte composition). See *Gottschalk*.

Aeolian Mode. See *Modes*.

Aeolina or **Aeoline.** Soft organ stop of 8-foot length and pitch, supposed to imitate *Aeolian Harp* (q.v.). Sometimes it is tuned to 'beat' with another soft stop (cf. *Organ* 2, near end).

Aequal (Ger.). Old organ term for '8-foot'.

Aeroforo (It.). Aerophor (see below).

Aerophor. A device (patented 1912) to help wind-instrument players. A small bellows, worked by a foot, supplies wind by a tube to a corner of the mouth, leaving the player free to breathe uninterruptedly through the nose. Richard Strauss has once or twice written passages actually requiring the use of this apparatus (which in one score he calls *Aerophon*).

Aeterne Rex Altissime. See *O Salutaris Hostia*.

Aetherophone. Same as Etherophone. See *Electric Musical Instruments* 1.

Aeusserst (Ger.). Same as *Äusserst*, i.e. 'Extremely'.

Aevia. This 'word' consists of the vowels of 'Alleluia' (q.v.). It is used as an indication in somewhat the same way as *Evovae* (q.v.).

Affabile (It. 'affable'). 'In a gentle, pleasing manner.'

Affaiblissant (Fr. 'weakening'). *Diminuendo.*

Affannato (It. 'panting'). 'In a distressful manner.' **Affannoso; affannosamente** (It.). 'Distressed'; 'distressingly'.

Affekt (Ger.). 'Fervour.' So *affektvoll*, 'full of fervour'.

Affetto (It.). 'Affection.' **Affettuoso, affettuosa** (masc., fem., 'affectionate'). 'With tenderness.' *Affettuosamente*, 'affectionately'. **Affezione,** 'affection'.

Afflitto (It.). 'Afflicted.' So *afflizione*, 'affliction'.

Affrettare (It.). 'To hurry.' Hence *affrettando*, 'hurrying'; *affrettato*, *affrettoso* (or *affrettuoso*), 'hurried'; *affrettatamente*, 'in a hurrying manner'.

Afranio, Canon. See *Phagotum*.

Africaine, L'. Tragedy-opera by Meyerbeer. Libretto by Scribe. (Prod. Paris, London, and New York, 1865.)

African Music Society. Founded 1947 'to encourage research into African music and its allied arts', &c. Headquarters Johannesburg. See *Tracey, H. T.*

Afro-American Symphony. See *Still, W. G.*

Afternoon of a Faun (Debussy). See *Après-midi*.

Age of Anxiety. See *Bernstein, L.*

Age of Steel (Prokofief). See *Pas d'Acier*.

Agevole (It. 'comfortable'). 'Lightly and easily'—not laboured. So *agevolezza*, 'ease'.

Aggiustamente, aggiustatamente (It.). 'Exact' (in point of rhythm).

Aggradevole (It.). 'Agreeable.'

Agiatamente (It.). 'Comfortably', 'freely'—with suitable liberty as to speed, &c. (not to be confused with *Agitatamente*, q.v.).

Agilement (Fr.), **agilmente** (It.). 'In an agile manner', implying speed and nimble execution. **Agilité** (Fr.), **agilità** (It.). 'Agility.' For *Aria d'agilità*, see *Aria* (e).

Agincourt Song. A famous 15th-c. song commemorating the victory of 1415 : it is for 2 voices with chorus for 3.

Agitato; agitatamente (It.), **agité** (Fr.), **agitirt, agitiert** (Ger.). 'Agitated'; 'agitatedly' **Agitazione, agitamento** (It.). 'Agitation.' (Cf. remark s.v. *Agiatamente*.)

Agnew, Roy E. (b. Sydney, N.S.W., 1893; there d. 1944). Pianist; composer of piano sonatas and smaller pieces, also chamber and orch. music, songs,

&c. British career but latterly on staff State Conservatory of N.S.W., Sydney.

Agnus Dei. See *Mass*; *Requiem*; *Common Prayer*.

Agogic. (1) An adjective indicating a variety of accentuation—not that which is bound up with the regular pulsation of the music (the 2 beats in a measure, or whatever it may be), but that which is called for by the nature of any particular phrase of the music. The first note of a phrase is often felt to suggest a slight lingering which confers the effect of an accent and this is one example. Similarly a leap to a note lower or higher than those that have preceded, or a strong discord proceeding to a concord, suggests a slight effect of accentuation (by lingering, or by pressure, or both) and there are other examples.

The complementary term to 'Agogic Accent' (accent of movement) is 'Dynamic Accent' (i.e. accent of force), which implies the normal and regular rhythmic accentuation of a composition.

(2) In a wider sense 'Agogic' covers everything connected with 'expression'—*rallentando, accelerando, rubato*, the pause, accent of the kind above described, &c.

Agon. Ballet by Stravinsky. (Prod. Los Angeles 1957.)

Agrémens or **agréments** (Fr.). 'Grace notes.' (See *Ornaments or Graces*; also Tables 12–16.)

Agreste (Fr.). 'Rural.'

Agricola, (1) Alexander (b. Netherlands 1446; d. Valladolid 1506). Composer of masses, motets, &c.

(2) **Martin** (1486–1556). Cantor at Magdeburg; important theoretical writer.

(3–4) **Johann Friedrich** (1720–74) and **Benedetta Emilia** (1722–80). Husband and wife, former a pupil of Bach, organist, composer, and writer on music; latter a fine soprano singer. Both employed at court of Frederick the Great (q.v.).

A.G.S.M. See *Degrees and Diplomas* 2.

Agujari, Lucrezia—familiarly known as 'La Bastardella' (b. Ferrara 1743; d. Parma 1783). Operatic soprano of remarkable tone-quality, compass, and agility.

Ägyptische Helena, Die ('The Egyptian Helen'). Opera by Richard Strauss; libretto by Hofmannsthal (q.v.). (1st perfs. Dresden, Vienna, Berlin, New York, all 1928.)

Ähnlich or **aehnlich** (Ger.). 'Similar', 'like'.

Ai (It.). 'At the', 'to the', &c.

Aida. Tragic opera by Verdi. Libretto by Ghislanzoni. (Prod. Cairo 1871; New York 1873; London 1876.)

Aigu, aiguë (Fr. masc., fem.). 'Shrill', 'high in pitch'. In organ music *Octaves aiguës* means 'Super-octave Coupler' (see *Organ* 2).

Ainsworth, Henry. See *Hymns and Hymn Tunes* 7.

Air. (1) Melody. (2) A composition of a melodious character.

Air de caractère (Fr.). In ballet, music for 'characteristic' occasions— an entry of warriors, and the like.

Air on the G String. See *G string*.

Air with Variations. See *Form* 5.

Ais (Ger.). A sharp (see Table 7).

A.I.S.C. See *Degrees and Diplomas* 2.

Aise (Fr.). 'Ease.' So *À l'aise*, 'At ease', 'unhurried'.

Aisis (Ger.). The note A double sharp (see Table 7).

Ajouter (Fr.). 'To add.' So the imperative, *Ajoutez*.

Akademische Festouvertüre (Brahms). See *Academic Festival Overture*.

Akhron. See *Achron*.

Akimenko (Akimyenko, &c.), **Feodor** (b. Kharkof 1876; d. Paris 1945). Pupil of Balakiref and Rimsky-Korsakof; composer of piano and chamber music, and opera, &c.

Akkord (Ger.). 'Chord.'

Akkordieren. 'To tune.'

Al (It.). 'At the', 'to the', 'in the', &c., i.e. the same as *A* (q.v.), with the article added.

A.L. (Amelia Lehmann). See reference under *Lehmann, Liza*.

À la, à l' (Fr.). 'To the', 'at the', 'on the', 'with the'. Also 'in the manner of'. (See *Mesure*.)

Ala and Lolli (Prokofief). See *Scythian Suite*.

Alabiev (Alabief, Alabiew), **Alexander** (b. Tobolsk 1787; d. Moscow 1851). Precursor of national Russian school; composer of songs (especially *The Nightingale*) and an opera.

À la corde (Fr. 'at the string'). The bow kept on the string, ensuring a *legato* movement from note to note.

Alain, Jehan (b. Paris 1911; killed nr. Saumur 1940). Organist and composer for organ, piano, chamber combinations, &c.—127 opus numbers in all.

Alalà. A plainsong-like type of Spanish folk song, in 4-line verses, much decorated in its melody at the taste of the singer.

A.L.A.M. See *Degrees and Diplomas* 2.

À la pointe d'archet (Fr.). 'At the point of the bow.'

Alard, Jean (Delphin) (b. Bayonne 1815; d. Paris 1888). Fine violinist; active teacher of violin; author of a *Violin School*; editor and composer of violin works.

Albanese, Licia (b. Bari 1913). Operatic soprano. Début Parma 1935; Metropolitan 1940. Since then resident in U.S.A.

Albani, Emma (b. nr. Montreal 1847; d. London 1930). Originally Marie Louise Cécilie Emma Lajeunesse, taking professional name from Albany, N.Y., where spent early life. Soprano vocalist. Pupil of Lamperti, &c. Became very highly esteemed as opera and oratorio singer. Retired 1911, henceforward practising as teacher. D.B.E. 1925.

Albéniz, (1) **Pedro I** (b. Biscay, N. Spain, abt. 1755; d. San Sebastian 1821). Monk in charge of cathedral music at San Sebastian and composer of church music.

(2) **Pedro II** (b. Logroño, Castile, 1795; d. Madrid 1855). Like namesake above, at one time in charge of music at cathedral of San Sebastian; also court organist at Madrid. Able pianist and minor piano composer.

(3) **Isaac** (Manuel Francesco) (b. Camprodon, Catalonia, 1860; d. Cambo les Bains, France, 1909). Able pianist and composer for piano. Led a very adventurous life, playing when young in Central and South America. Conducted Zarzuelas (q.v.) in Spain; studied in Paris, and came under Debussy's influence. Lived mainly in London and Paris. His piano works are numerous and he was one of the first Spanish composers to exploit native rhythmic and melodic idioms. He wrote some operas.

See *Iberia.*

Albert (Queen Victoria's Prince Consort; b. Rosenau, Germany, 1819; d. Windsor 1861). Well trained in music; organist and minor composer, especially of church music. (See *Albert Hall; Chapel Royal; Ancient Concert.*)

Albert, Eugen d', really Eugene Francis Charles (b. Glasgow 1864; d. Riga 1932). Son of a London ballet master and composer. Won a scholarship at the National Training School of Music (now R.C.M.); early acquired high repute as pianist and at 17 won the Mendelssohn Scholarship for study abroad at Vienna and under Liszt. Added fresh reputation as composer of operas, especially *Tiefland* (q.v.), and wrote 2 piano concertos, a symphony, chamber music, &c., also editing piano classics. Had 6 successive wives, discarded Brit. nationality and railed at the country that had given him his early training.

Albert Hall, Royal (London). Built 1871 in memory of Prince Albert, consort of Queen Victoria, on part of site of 1851 Exhibition which he had promoted. Largest London hall, seating nearly 10,000. Many great musical enterprises, orchestral, choral, &c. (Cf. *Concert.*)

Albert Herring. Comic opera by Britten. Libretto by Eric Crozier, based on story by Maupassant. (Prod. Glyndebourne and Lucerne 1947.)

Alberti Bass. That simple (and often commonplace) kind of accompaniment to a melody which consists of 'broken chords', e.g.:

It takes its name from an It. composer who favoured it, Domenico Alberti (abt. 1710–40).

Albicastro, Henrico (Italianized form of real name: Heinz Weissenburg). Late 17th- and early 18th-c. Swiss mercenary soldier. Fine violinist and able composer of string sonatas and concertos.

Alboni, Marietta (b. in the Romagna 1823; d. in France 1894). Contralto. Pupil of Rossini (believed to have been his only one). From 20th year international operatic artist, with highest success.

Alborada (Sp. 'dawn'). 'Morning music' (cf. *Aubade*). This word has come to have a special application to a type of instrumental music with a good deal of rhythmic freedom and often played on bagpipe (or rustic oboe) and small drum.

Alborada del gracioso (Ravel). See *Miroirs.*

Albrechtsberger, Johann Georg (b. nr. Vienna 1736; there d. 1809). Organist of court (1772) and cathedral (1792) at Vienna; active composer, but best remembered as teacher of composition (pupils including Beethoven) and as author of many theoretical works, including once-important textbook of composition (1790; widely used in Engl. translation).

Albumblatt (Ger. 'Album Leaf'). A fancy title for any brief and slight instrumental composition.

Albumblätter ('Album-leaves'). By Schumann. 20 Piano pieces (op. 124, 1832–45, publ. 1854).

Album-leaves (Schumann). See above.

Alcestis ('Alceste'). Italian tragedy-opera by Gluck. Libretto by Calzabigi, based on Euripides. Has important preface: see *Gluck* and *Opera 2.* (Prod. Vienna 1767; London 1795; still in the international repertory.)

Other operas of this name include that by Lully (1674). See also *Alkestis.*

Alchemist, The. See *Scott, Cyril.*

A.L.C.M. See *Degrees and Diplomas* 2.

Alcock, (1) **John I** (b. London 1715; d. Lichfield 1806). Choir-boy of St. Paul's Cathedral; organist of various churches, of Lichfield Cathedral, and again of parish churches. Composer of church music, glees, and instrumental music, and author of a novel. D.Mus., Oxford.

(2) **John II** (b. Plymouth 1740; d. Walsall 1791). Son of the above. Organist and church music composer.

(3) **Walter Galpin** (b. Edenbridge, Kent, 1861; d. Salisbury 1947). Assistant organist of Westminster Abbey; organist of Chapels Royal (1902); of Salisbury Cathedral (1916); composer of church music, &c. D.Mus., Durham; M.V.O. Knighted 1933.

Alcuin (b. York abt. 735; d. Tours abt. 804). Friend and counsellor of Charlemagne at Aix-la-Chapelle; later Abbot of Tours. Author of treatise *De Musica.*

Alcuno, alcuna, alcun' (It. masc., fem.; the plurals are *alcuni, alcune,* &c.). 'Some.'

Aldrich, (1) **Henry** (b. London 1647; d. Oxford 1710). Successively undergraduate, tutor, canon, and dean of Christ Church, Oxford, and twice Vice-Chancellor of the University. Classical scholar, theologian, heraldist, architect, musical theorist, and composer of church music and catches.

(2) **Richard** (b. Providence, R.I., 1863; d. Rome 1937). Graduated Harvard. Became well known and esteemed music-critic (*N.Y. Times* 1902–24). Several useful books.

Aleko. See *Rachmaninof.*

Alembert, Jean le Rond d' (b. Paris 1717; there d. 1783). Philosopher, mathematician, acoustician, and general writer on music; contributor to the famous Encyclopédie (1751–72). Supporter of Gluck (q.v.) against the Piccinists (see *Piccini*).

Alessandro, Victor (Nicholas) (b. Waco, Texas, 1915). Trained Eastman School and St. Cecilia, Rome. Conductor (Oklahoma 1938; San Antonio 1951).

Alexander, Arthur (b. Dunedin, N.Z., 1891; d. Chinnor, Oxon., 1969). Pianist, composer. Trained R.A.M. under Matthay and Corder. On staff of R.C.M. Publ. songs, piano pieces, &c. (Married Freda Swain, q.v.)

Alexander Balus. Oratorio by Handel. (1st perf. London 1748.)

Alexander Nevsky. By Prokofief. Music for a film (1938), later developed into a Cantata (op. 78. 1st perf. Moscow 1939: broadcast New York 1943). Suite B.B.C. 1941; Proms. 1942.

Alexander's Feast. Setting by Handel of Dryden's ode, with some changes and additions. (1st perf. London 1736.)

Alexander's Ragtime Band. See *Berlin, Irving.*

Alexandra Palace (North London). Similar to Crystal Palace (q.v.). Opened 1873. Organ and other music features (cf. *Cunningham, George*). Centre of B.B.C.'s earlier television activities.

Alexandre. See *Reed-Organ Family* 5, 6.

Alexandrof (Alexandrov, Alexandrow), **Anatol** (b. Moscow 1888). Pupil of Taneief; composer of songs, piano sonatas, orch. works, &c.

Alfano, Franco (b. Naples 1876; d. San Remo 1954). Comp. of operas; orch. works; cha. music, &c. Completed Puccini's *Turandot.* Successively head of conservs. of Bologna (1919), Turin (1924), Pesaro (1947).

Alfonso and Estrella (Schubert). See *Rosamunde.*

Alfred (Arne). See under *Masque*; *Rule Britannia.*

Alfvén, Hugo (b. Stockholm 1872; d. Falun 1960). Violinist and director of music at Univ. of Uppsala (1910–39); composer of symphonies, &c.

Aliquot Scaling. See *Pianoforte.*

Alison (or Allison), **Richard** (end of 16th c. and beginning of 17th). Composer of madrigals, &c., and compiler of famous book of metrical psalm tunes (1599; see reference s.v. *Anglican Chant*).

Alkan (real name Morhange), **Charles Henry Valentin** (b. Paris 1813; there d. 1888). Remarkable pianist and composer of piano music of high difficulty, great ingenuity, and often very descriptive character.

Alkestis. Opera by Boughton. Libretto based on Gilbert Murray's translation of Euripides. (Prod. Glastonbury 1922; London 1924.)

All', alla (It.). 'To the', 'at the', 'on the', 'with the'; also 'in the manner of'.

Alla breve. See *Breve*.

Alla Breve Fugue (Bach). For organ. In D major. So nicknamed because the time-signature is *alla breve* (see *Breve*).

Allam, Walter Edward (b. London 1902). Educated King's Coll., Cambridge (M.A.), and R.C.M. Since 1929 attached Dept. of Music, Leeds Univ. Prominent in north of England, as conductor, composer, pianist, and lecturer. Compositions include symphony, Mass for 5 voices, chamber music, songs, &c. D.Mus., London.

All Among the Barley. See *Stirling*.

Allant (Fr.). (1) 'Going', i.e. 'active', 'brisk'. (2) 'Going on', in sense of continuing, e.g. Debussy's *Allant grandissant*—'Going on growing', 'continuing to grow' (i.e. to grow louder).

Allargando (It. 'Enlarging'). Getting slower and slower, and fuller in tone.

Alle (Ger.). 'All.' Thus if one violin has been playing alone all are now to enter. *Alle ersten* means all the first violins and *Alle zweiten* (sometimes *zwoten*) all the second.

Alle (It.). 'To the' (fem. plur.).

Allegramente (It.), **allègrement** (Fr.). 'Brightly', 'gaily'.

Allegretto (It.). 'Pretty lively' (but not so much so as *allegro*). **Allègrezza.** 'Mirth', 'cheerfulness'.

Allegri, Gregorio (b. Rome 1582; there d. 1652). Priest, tenor singer, and composer amongst other things of a celebrated *Miserere*, long kept as exclusive possession of Sistine Chapel, in service of which place the last part of his life was spent.

Allegro (It.). 'Merry', i.e. quick, lively, bright. Often used also as the title of a composition or movement in that style. The superlative is *Allegrissimo*.

Allein (Ger.). 'Alone', e.g. *Eine Violine allein*, 'One violin alone'.

Alleluia. This Latin form of Hebrew exclamation, meaning 'Praise Jehovah' (see *Hallelujah*), was added to certain of the responds (q.v.) of the Roman Catholic Church, suitably joyful music for it being grafted on to the traditional plainsong and, in time, itself becoming traditional; such a passage ends with the word 'Jubilate'. The Alleluia is omitted from Septuagesima to Easter Day, and in Requiem Masses, &c., a Tract (q.v.) taking its place.

Alleluia Symphony. In Breitkopf's edn. of Haydn's Symphonies, no. 30, in C (1765). Incorporates part of a plainsong alleluia.

Allemand (Fr.). 'German.'

Allemande (Fr., lit. 'German': in older days spelt 'Almand', 'Almayne', 'Almain', &c.). The name of 2 distinct types of composition, both (to judge by the name) of German origin.

(1) A dance whose music has 4 beats to the measure (sometimes treated in the time signature as 2 long beats). It has been made much use of by 17th- and earlier-18th-c. composers as the first movement of the suite (q.v.)—or the first but for a prelude. In character it is serious but not heavy and in speed moderate: it is in simple binary form (see *Form* 1) and each half opens with a short note (or several short notes) at the end of a measure (normally other phrases than the opening one begin in the same way, and especially that which opens the second half of the movement).

(2) A peasant dance still in use in parts of Germany and Switzerland. It is in triple time and suggests the waltz. Occasionally composers have called a composition of this type a *Deutscher Tanz* (plur. 'Deutsche Tänze'), or simply *Deutsch* (plur. 'Deutsche').

Allen, (1) Hugh Percy (b. Reading 1869; d. Oxford as result of street accident 1946). Organ scholar Christ's Coll., Cambridge, organist cathedrals of St. Asaph (1897) and Ely (1898); then of New Coll., Oxford (1901–18); Prof. of Music, Oxford Univ. (1918) and general inspirer of Oxford musical activities; Director of R.C.M. (1918–37). M.A., D.Mus., Oxford; hon. degrees of many universities. Knighted 1920; G.C.V.O. 1935.

(2) **E. Heron.** See *Heron-Allen.*

Allen Instruments. See *Electric Musical Instruments* 2.

Allentamento, allentando (It.). 'Slowing.'

Allgemeiner deutscher Caecilienverein. See *Cecilian Movement.*

Allin, Norman (b. Ashton-under-Lyne 1884; d. Hereford 1973). Operatic and concert bass. Trained Royal Manchester Coll. of Music. Became member of Beecham Opera Co. (see *Beecham*). High reputation as opera, oratorio, and concert artist. On staff of R.A.M. 1935–60; C.B.E. 1958.

Allison, Richard. See *Alison.*

Allison's Psalter. See reference s.v. *Anglican Chant.*

Allmählich, allmählig, allmälig (Ger.). 'Gradually.'

Allo. Short for *Allegro* (q.v.).

Allonger (Fr. 'To lengthen' the notes). To slacken in speed.

Allora (It.). 'Then.'

Allt, Wilfrid Greenhouse (b. Wolverhampton 1889; d. London 1969). Assistant organist, Norwich Cathedral, 1910; organist of St. Giles's Cathedral, Edinburgh, 1915, and choral conductor in Edinburgh; Principal, T.C.M., 1944–65. Pres. R.C.O. 1962–5.

All through the Night. The tune usually known outside Wales by this title is that of the Welsh folk song *Ar Hyd y Nos.* An English setting to which it was formerly heard was 'Here beneath a willow weepeth poor Mary Ann'—words by the novelist, Mrs. Amelia Opie (1769–1853).

Allure (Fr.). 'Gait', 'manner'.

Alma Redemptoris Mater. See *Antiphons of the Blessed Virgin Mary.*

Alphorn, Alpenhorn, or **Cor des Alpes.** A Swiss peasant instrument used for the evening calling of the cattle scattered over the summer pastures of the mountains (cf. *Ranz des Vaches*). It is made of wood and varies in length from about 7 to 12 feet. It has a mouthpiece much like that of the cornet (q.v.) and can play merely notes of the harmonic series (see *Acoustics* 7).

Alpine Symphony. By Richard Strauss (op. 64; 1915). A detailed 'programme work', continuous but in 22 sections ('Night', 'Sunrise', 'The Ascent begins', 'On the Glacier', 'Moments of Danger', and the like).

Als (Ger.). 'As', 'like', 'when', 'than'.

Alsager, Thomas Massa (b. 1779; d. 1846). Enthusiastic amateur musician, showing great activity, especially, in Beethoven propaganda. (See reference under *Criticism of Music.*)

Al segno (It.). 'To the sign', meaning 'Go to the mark 𝄋'. This may mean '*Go back* to the sign' (the same, in that sense, as *Dal Segno*, q.v.), or it may mean '*Continue* until you reach the sign' (see remarks under *Da Capo*; also Table 20).

Also (Ger.). 'Thus.'

Alsop, Ada (b. Darlington, Co. Durham, 1915). Soprano. Popular artist, particularly in oratorio, singing with all leading Brit. choral societies.

Also Sprach Zarathustra (Strauss). See *Nietzsche*, 'Thus spake Zoroaster'.

Alt. (1) 'High.' The note G above the treble stave marks the beginning of notes spoken of (in reference to the voice) as *in alt*, and the G above as *in altissimo*. This is the usual acceptance of those terms. (2, Ger.) The Alto (Contralto) voice: or, as an adj. prefixed to the name of an instrument (e.g. Althorn), it implies an alto pitch. (3, Ger., with various terminations according to gender, number, and case) 'Old.'

Alta (It. fem.; for masc. see *Alto*). 'High', e.g. *Ottava alta*, 'High octave' i.e. one 8ve higher than shown.

Altered Chord. An American synonym for Chromatic Chord (see *Chromatic Chords*).

Alternative (It.). A name applied in early 18th-c. music in dance style to a contrasting middle section (later called 'Trio', q.v.). Sometimes it is used of a whole composition, apparently implying that the 2 sections can be alternated at will.

Altflügelhorn. See *Saxhorn and Flügelhorn Families* 2.

Altgeige (Ger.) = 'Alto fiddle', i.e. properly, the viola. But see *Viola alta*.

Althorn. See *Saxhorn and Flügelhorn Families* 2.

Altissimo. See *Alt*.

Altiste (Fr.). (1) A player of the 'alto', i.e. of the viola (see *Violin Family*). (2) An alto singer (see *Alto Voice*).

Alto (It. 'high'). Applied (*a*) to the highest adult male voice (see *Alto Voice*); (*b*) to various instruments of roughly the vocal alto pitch (see several entries following this) and, especially in Fr., the viola (see *Violin Family*).

Alto Clarinet. See *Clarinet Family*.

Alto Clef. See Table 4.

Alto (Flügelhorn). See *Saxhorn and Flügelhorn Families* 1 b, 2.

Alto Moderne. See *Viole-Ténor*.

Alto Rhapsody. Brahms's op. 53 (1869), a setting for Contralto, Men's Chorus, and Orch. of part of a poem of Goethe. It was inspired by a love disappointment—the engagement to another of a daughter of the composer's old friends the Schumanns.

Alto (Saxhorn). See *Saxhorn and Flügelhorn Families* 1.

Alto Staff. See under *Great Staff*.

Alto Trombone. See *Trombone Family*.

Alto Viol. See *Viol Family* 2 b.

Alto Voice. A type of male falsetto chiefly cultivated in Britain, where church music and the glee provide for its use. In the performance of the choruses of oratorios, &c., it has been gradually superseded by the woman's contralto voice (also sometimes, after the Ger., called 'alto').

Altposaune (Ger.). Alto trombone (see *Trombone Family*).

Altra, altre. See *Altro*.

Altra volta (It.). 'Encore' (q.v.).

Altro, altri; altra, altre (It. masc. sing. and plur.; fem. sing. and plur.). 'Another', 'others'.

Altschuler, Modest (b. Mogilef, Russia, 1873; d. Los Angeles 1963). Violoncellist and conductor. Pupil Moscow Conserv. of Arensky, Taneief, and Safonof. Emigrated New York; organized Russian Symphony Orch. and toured widely, thus introducing modern Russian music. Later settled Los Angeles.

Alvarez, (1) **Albert Raymond Gourron** (b. Bordeaux 1861; d. Nice 1933). Operatic tenor. After appearances in Fr. provinces and Belgium appeared Paris Opéra 1892; became its leading tenor. Also popular London and New York.

(2) **Marguerite d'** (b. Liverpool 1886; d. Alassio 1953). Operatic and concert contralto. London début 1911. Career largely in U.S.A.

Alvary—really Achenbach, **Max** (b. Düsseldorf 1856; d. in Thuringia 1898). Operatic tenor. Trained by Stockhausen. As Wagner exponent well known on both sides of Atlantic.

Alwyn, William (b. Northampton 1905). Trained R.A.M.; later on its staff (composition). For a time orch. flautist. Composer of violin, piano, and oboe concertos, symphonies, string quartets, piano music, film music, &c.

Alzato, alzati; alzata, alzate (It. masc. sing. and plur.; fem. sing. and plur.). 'Raised', 'lifted off' (of a mute or mutes, &c.).

Am (Ger.). 'At the', 'on the', 'to the', 'by the', 'near the'. (See *Frosch*; *Griffbrett*; *Steg*.)

Amabile (It.). 'Lovable', so *amabilità*, 'lovableness'.

Amahl and the Night Visitors. 1-act television opera (the first such) by Menotti. (Prod. New York 1951.)

Amalgamated Musicians' Union. See *Musicians' Union*.

Amarevole; amarezza (It.). 'Bitterly', 'bitterness'.

Amati. See *Violin Family*.

Amazing Mandarin, The (also translated as 'The Miraculous Mandarin' or 'The Wonderful Mandarin'). Pantomime-ballet by Bartók (1919; broadcast London 1932).

Amboss (Ger.). 'Anvil' (see *Percussion Family* 2 s).

Ambros, August Wilhelm (b. nr. Prague 1816; d. Vienna 1876). High legal official in Prague and Vienna and keen musicologist, writing important History of Music (completed after his death by other hands); also other literary works and compositions.

Ambrose, Saint. See *Modes*; *Plainsong* 3.

Âme (Fr. 'soul'). The sound-post (q.v.) of the violin, &c. The fanciful French name doubtless comes from its importance to the whole tone-quality of the instrument, which depends much on its correct position. The Italians say *anima*, which likewise means 'soul'.

Amelia goes to the Ball. Opera by Menotti; libretto by himself, transl. G. Meade. (Prod. Philadelphia and New York 1937.)

Amen. 'So be it.' The (Hebrew) terminal word of prayer in Jewish, Christian, and Mohammedan worship. It has been extended by composers, innumerable times, into a long composition, as, for instance, the 'Amen Chorus' of Handel's *Messiah*. For liturgical use shorter settings have been made, as Gibbons's Threefold Amen and Stainer's Sevenfold Amen. The DRESDEN AMEN comes from the Threefold Amen of the Royal Chapel of Dresden (common also throughout Saxony); its composer was J. G. Naumann (q.v.).

Amen Cadence. See *Cadence*.

America (tune). See *God save the Queen*.

American Academy (Rome). See *Prix de Rome*.

American Federation of Musicians. A trade-union organization; founded 1895 and very prominent under the presidency (1942–62) of James C. Petrillo.

American Fingering. Same as 'English Fingering' (see *Fingering*, last par.).

American Guild of Organists. See *Degrees and Diplomas* 4.

American in Paris, An. Orchestral piece by Gershwin. (1st perf. New York 1925.)

American Institute of Musicology, Rome (with office in Cambridge, Mass.). Superseded the Inst. of Renaissance and Baroque Music founded by Armen Carapetyan (q.v.) in 1944. Possesses extensive archives, with photographic collection of source material (especially 14th and 15th cs.). Holds summer sessions with distinguished staff. Has undertaken publication (in 20 vols.) of complete works of Dufay &c.

American National Association of Organists. See *Profession of Music*.

American Organ. See *Reed-Organ Family* 6.

American Quartet. Name sometimes attached in the U.S.A. to Dvořák's String Quartet in F, op. 96 (1893); written in the U.S.A. and exhibiting some of the characteristics of Negro song; elsewhere also known as the *Nigger Quartet*.

American Society of Composers, Authors, & Publishers (known as 'ASCAP'). Founded 1914 to protect copyrights, performing rights, &c.

American Terminology of Music (compared with British). Whilst some of the American usages here listed are general, others may possibly be local or confined to certain writers or groups.

(1) The worst confusion arises from the different usage as concerns the words NOTE and TONE. Such expressions as '3 tones lower' or 'the scale of 5 tones' have quite different meanings to the Amer. and the Brit. reader. A Brit. reader, finding these expressions in an Amer. book or journal, must

be careful to understand, merely, '3 notes lower' and 'scale of 5 notes', and an Amer. reader finding such expressions in a Brit. book must be careful to translate them into Amer. as, precisely, '3 whole-steps lower' or 'a scale of 5 whole-steps'. (The Amer. contention as concerns 'Note' is that to use it for a *sound* is wrong because it 'names a *notation* element'. This is to defy more than 5 centuries of Eng. usage, including that of Chaucer, Shakespeare, Milton, &c., and also to ignore earlier Amer. usage.)

(2) Eng. BAR = Amer. MEASURE, the former term being often reserved in America for the actual bar-*line*.

(3) Eng. SEMIBREVE, MINIM, &c. = Amer. WHOLE-NOTE, HALF-NOTE, &c.

(4) Eng. NATURAL (after a sharp or flat) = Amer. CANCEL.

(5) Eng. NATURALS, in the sense of the white finger keys of a piano, &c. = (with some Amer. writers) LONG KEYS.

(6) Eng. NATURAL NOTES (of brass instruments) = (with some Amer. writers) PRIMARY TONES.

(7) Eng. TO FLATTEN and TO SHARPEN = Amer. TO FLAT and TO SHARP.

(8) Eng. ORGAN (generally) = Amer. PIPE ORGAN (to distinguish from the various reed organs).

(9) Eng. AMERICAN ORGAN = (often) Amer. CABINET ORGAN.

(10) Eng. GRAMOPHONE = Amer. PHONOGRAPH.

(11) Eng. (gramophone) RECORD = Amer. DISK sometimes used.

(12) Amer. APPLIED MUSIC means performed music: hence university courses in Applied Music are simply courses in instrumental or vocal technique and interpretation.

(13) The Eng. term FOLK SONG is often used in the U.S.A. in a loose way, covering not only the traditional peasant songs but also any songs which have become very widely known by people in general. (Cf. *Folk Lore*.)

(14) Eng. NURSERY RHYMES = (sometimes) Amer. MOTHER GOOSE SONGS.

(15) Eng. FIRST VIOLIN or *Leader* (of an orch.) = Amer. CONCERT MASTER.

(16) Eng. CONDUCTOR (of an orch.) = (often) Amer. LEADER (and Eng. *to conduct* = Amer. *to lead*).

(17) Eng. PART-WRITING = Amer. VOICE-LEADING.

America Rediscovered (Hewitt). See *Tammany*.

America, the Beautiful. Poem by Katherine Lee Bates, written in 1893 (begun on the summit of Pike's Peak, Colorado). Tunes composed for it number 60, the 2 most in use being respectively by Will C. Macfarlane and S. A. Ward.

Amfiparnaso, L'. By Orazio Vecchi. A string of pieces in madrigal style, in 3 acts with a prologue; not intended to be staged. (Prod. Modena 1594; pub. 1597; perf. London with puppets 1946.)

Amico Fritz, L' ('Friend Fritz'). Popular romantic opera by Mascagni. Libretto based on story by Erckmann-Chatrian. (Prod. Rome 1891; London and Philadelphia 1892; New York 1893.)

Amor brujo, El ('Love, the Magician'). Ballet by Falla, based on an Andalusian gipsy tale. (Prod. Madrid 1915; in concert form London 1921 and Philadelphia 1922. As ballet London 1931.)

Amore (It.). 'Love.' So *amorevole*, *amoroso*, 'loving'; *amorevolmente*, *amorosamente*, 'lovingly'. See also below.

Amore (It.), **Amour** (Fr., 'Love'). A word often found in the names of certain forms of old instruments, and generally implying a lower pitch than the ordinary and a claim to a sweeter tone. In bowed instruments it indicates, too, the possession of sympathetic strings (q.v.).

Amore dei tre re, L' ('The Love of the Three Kings'). 3-act tragedy-opera by Montemezzi. Libretto is the play by Sem Benelli. (Prod. Milan 1913; New York and London 1914.)

Amorevole; amorevolmente; amoroso; amorosamente (It.). 'Loving'; lovingly'.

Amour (Fr.). 'Love' (see also *Amore*).

Ampleur (Fr.). 'Breadth.'

Amplifiers. See *Concert Halls*. Electric amplifiers are now a part of the equipment of all radio studios, &c.

A.Mus.L.C.M. See *Degrees and Diplomas* 2.

A.Mus.T.C.L. See *Degrees and Diplomas 2.*

An (Ger.). 'On', 'by', 'to', 'at'. In organ music it signifies that the stop in question is to be drawn.

Anacreon in Heaven, Anacreontic Song. See *Star-spangled Banner.*

Anacréon, ou L'Amour fugitif. Opera by Cherubini. (Prod. Paris 1803; unsuccessful but the overture is still famous.)

Anacreontic Society. See *Clubs for Music Making*; *Star-spangled Banner.*

Anacrusis (plur. *Anacruses*). An unstressed syllable at the beginning of a line of poetry or an unstressed note or group of notes at the beginning of a phrase of music.

Analytical Notes. The descriptions of compositions which appear on Annotated Programmes (q.v.).

Anblasen (Ger.). 'To blow.'

Anche (Fr.), **ancia** (It.). 'Reed.'

Anche. (It.). 'Also.'

Ancient Concert (or 'Concert of Antient Music'). Important London subscription series (1776–1849). The royal and noble 'Directors' (e.g. George III, Prince Albert, Duke of Wellington) took turns to choose programmes. Another name was 'King's Concert', or, in Queen Victoria's time, 'Queen's Concert'. Attempts to revive it in 1868 and 1870. (Sometimes confused with Academy of Ancient Music, 1726–92, q.v.) See *Hanover Square.*

Ancient Mariner, The. See *Barnett, John Francis.*

Ancora (It.). 'Still', or 'yet' (in both senses, i.e. 'remaining' and 'even'), e.g. *Ancora forte* = 'Still loud'; *Ancora più forte* = 'Still more loud'. The word is also used for 'Again', i.e. repeat. (In all these senses, compare the Fr. word *Encore.*)

Andacht (Ger.). 'Devotion.' So *andächtig* (or *andaechtig*), 'devotional'.

Andaluz, andaluza (Sp.), **andalouse** (Fr.). Vaguely applied to several Spanish dances common in Andalusia, e.g. the Fandango (q.v.), Malagueña (q.v.), and Polo (q.v.).

Andamento (It. 'Going'—suggesting running). A fugue subject of greater length than ordinary and often of a running character (cf. *Attacco*).

Andante (It., from *andare*, 'to go'). 'Moving along', 'flowing' (slowish but not slow). The word is often used as a title for a composition. **Andantino.** A diminution of *andante.* Unfortunately, some composers use it meaning a little slower than *andante*, and others as meaning a little quicker. (If a performer, use your own judgement; if a composer, avoid the ambiguous term.)

Andauernd (Ger.). 'Lasting', i.e. 'continuing'.

Ander, andere, &c. (Ger.; various terminations according to gender, number, case). 'Other.'

Anderson, (1) Lucy—*née* Philpot (b. Bath 1790; d. 1878). Pianist—the earliest woman to play at London Philharmonic concerts (1822; see *Royal Philharmonic Society*). Teacher of Queen Victoria. (For husband see below.)

(2) **George Frederick** (b. London 1793; there d. 1876). Violinist. Master of Queen's Musick 1848–70. (For wife see above.)

(3) **William Robert** (b. Blackburn 1891). At first organist (B.Mus., Durham, &c.); then ed. of *Music Teacher* (1920–5), Extension Lecturer of London Univ., &c.; extensive contributor to musical press (sometime broadcasting critic of *Musical Times*); author of books on music.

(4) **Marian** (b. Philadelphia 1902). Contralto vocalist of Negro race. Very high international reputation as to both voice and artistic and expressive singing.

An die ferne Geliebte ('To the Distant Beloved'). Song Cycle by Beethoven, with piano accompaniment (op. 98; 1816). Poems (6) by Aloys Jeitteles. (There is also a Beethoven song, *An die Geliebte*, 1811; poem by Stoll.)

Andno. Short for *Andantino* (q.v.).

André, Franz (b. Brussels 1893). Chief conductor Belgian Radio Symphony Orch. since its earliest days. On staff Brussels Conservatory.

Andrea Chénier. Successful 4-act tragedy-opera by Giordano; libretto by Illica. (Prod. Milan and New York 1896; London 1903.)

Andreae, (1) **Volkmar** (b. Berne 1879; d. Zürich 1962). Conductor at Zürich and director of Conserv. 1914–49; compr. of operas, orch. music, &c.

(2) **Hans.** Son of above. Well-known harpsichordist.

Andrews, (1) **Hilda**—Mrs. G. M. Lees (b. Birmingham 1900). Musicologist. Ed. of Byrd's *Ladye Nevells Booke* (q.v.), North's *Musicall Gramarian* (= part of his *Memoires of Musick*), Memoir of Sir Richard Terry (q.v.), &c. Compiler of Catalogue of MS. Music in Buckingham Palace Library. Translator of French musical works. B.Mus., Birmingham, 1923.

(2) **Herbert Kennedy** (b. Comber, Co. Down, 1904; d. Oxford 1965). Organist (1938–56) and Fellow (from 1944) New College, Oxford, and Univ. Lecturer. Author *Oxford Harmony*, vol. ii, also books on Palestrina and Byrd.

Andriessen, (1) **Willem** (b. Haarlem 1887; d. Amsterdam 1964). Pianist and composer. Director of Amsterdam Conservatory. Composer of choral and orch. works, &c. Brother of (2) below.

(2) **Hendrik** (b. Haarlem 1892). Director of Utrecht Conservatory (1937–49). Composer of choral works, symphonies, sonatas, organ music, &c. Brother of the above.

Anerio, (1) **Felice** (b. abt. 1560; d. 1614). Palestrina's successor as composer for Papal Chapel. (See reference under *Plainsong* 3.) For brother see below.

(2) **Giovanni Francesco** (b. 1567; d. Graz 1630). Brother of above; a priest; musical director to King of Poland and later active in Rome.

Anfang (Ger.). 'Beginning.' *Anfangs*, 'at the beginning'. *Wie anfänglich*, 'as at the beginning'.

Angelica, angélique. Instrument of the lute type popular abut 1700.

Angelus, The. See *Naylor, Edwin.*

Angemessen (Ger.). 'Suitable to.'

Angenehm (Ger.). 'Agreeable.'

Anglais, anglaise (Fr. masc., fem.). 'English' (see also below).

Anglaise (Fr. 'English'). A term of variable meaning sometimes used by 18th-c. composers as the title of a hornpipe or country dance—or any-thing else which is thought to have an English character.

Anglebert, d', (1) **Jean Henri** (b. Paris 1628; there d. 1691). Pupil of Chambonnières and his successor as court harpsichordist; composer of effective music for harpsichord and organ.

(2) **Jean Baptiste Henri** (b. Paris 1661; there d. 1747). Son of above; his successor in court appointment and in turn succeeded by Couperin.

Anglican Chant. This is a simple type of harmonized melody used in the Anglican Church (and nowadays often in other English-speaking Protestant churches) for singing unmetrical texts, principally the Psalms and the Canticles (when these latter are not sung in a more elaborate setting). The main principle is that of the traditional Gregorian tones (q.v.), i.e. a short melody is repeated to each verse of the text (or sometimes to two or more verses; see below), the varying numbers of syllables in the different lines of the words being accommodated by the flexible device of a RECITING NOTE at the opening of each line—this being treated as timeless and so capable of serving as the vehicle for many or few syllables, whilst the succeeding notes are sung in time and (normally) take one syllable each. The 1st part of the chant has 3 measures and the 2nd part 4.

Although now considered to be, and often spoken of as, an exclusively English product, this form of chant may be said to have had very near relatives in other countries. Some early harmonized treatment of the plainsong (e.g. by Josquin des Prés abt. 1445–1521) comes extremely near it. The FALSOBORDONE of Italy was of the same general character (see *Faburden* for a description). In England very many examples of the falsobordone type were produced by all the leading composers of the early Reformation period (Tallis, Morley, Byrd, Gibbons, and their contemporaries) in their settings of the prose psalms. At a later epoch, and in another part of Europe, we find examples in which Bach sets a piece of prose to a piece of plainsong in quite the Anglican chant style (see the Sanford Terry collection of Bach's Chorales, 245–7, 332–3). Enough has now been said to show that the commonly supposed clear distinction between plainchant and Anglican chant is, in principle, non-existent—that Anglican chant is an offshoot of the harmonized plainchant which was very common throughout Christendom during the 16th and 17th centuries.

Almost immediately after the Restoration we find a few plainsong harmonizations appearing in print, set out in the way of our present single Anglican chant. It was a small step to the composition of original chants. The number of chants composed since the end of the 17th c. is very great, and the quality very variable. During the 18th c. there was a strong tendency to the provision of chants of a florid and sometimes flippant character and during the 19th that of a sentimentally chromatic type. The 20th c. has seen a strong movement towards dignity in church music and weaker specimens of the Anglican chant have increasingly tended to fall out of use.

Confident statements as to the introduction of DOUBLE CHANTS (accommodating two verses of the text instead of one) have been made, all ascribing it to the early 18th c.: the date is, however, pushed back by the appearance in Allison's Psalter of 1599 of a form of the chant now known as Flintoft's, and by a specimen of the same kind of thing (the application of the Double Anglican Chant principle to metrical verses) in Crowley's Psalter, half a century before that. The double chant form is also found in Byrd. TRIPLE CHANTS have in recent times been composed for use with two or three psalms whose verse arrangement seems to call for them: a few Quadruple Chants also exist, but in use they become very tiresome. There are also a certain number of 'Changeable Chants'—changeable in the matter of their mode, i.e. they can be sung in either the major or minor according as different sections of the

psalm or canticle call for joyful or more sober treatment. Single chants with 5 measures (2+3) have been tried, in place of those with 7, and double chants with 10 instead of 14.

Up to the Oxford Movement of the 19th c. the Anglican chant was in very little use except in cathedrals and other collegiate churches. Presumably, so long as the chanting was confined practically to trained choirs, singing together daily and going through the whole psalter 12 times a year, the method of dividing between the reciting note and the more regularly rhythmic part of the chant the varying numbers of syllables in the different verses could be picked up by experience—though the results cannot have been extremely or uniformly good. With the Oxford Movement of the early and mid-19th c., however, as the desire for a 'fully choral' service was extended and the prose psalms were now almost universally sung, some method of indicating to ordinary choirs the portion of the verse to be recited and the portion to be inflected became necessary. In 1837 had appeared the first attempt to present in printed form a method of 'pointing': its author was Robert Janes, organist of Ely Cathedral. Since then almost innumerable pointed versions of the Psalms and Canticles have appeared, with a considerable variety of methods of indicating the allocation of the syllables to the notes.

Anglican Parish Church Music. A great part of the general subject of Anglican Church Music is treated under a number of separate heads as follows: *Common Prayer, Psalm, Plainsong, Anglican Chant, Service, Anthem, Cathedral Music, Precentor, Vicar Choral, Chapel Royal, Parish Clerk, Hymns and Hymn Tunes*, and (smaller articles) *Preces, Responses, Litany, Magnificat, Nunc Dimittis, Use of Sarum*, &c. It remains to sketch briefly the conduct and development of music in the worship of the ordinary parish churches—a subject which has been a good deal neglected by historians.

At the Reformation the Roman Catholic liturgy and customs were taken over into the new Church of

England services, with the use of the vernacular but otherwise a minimum of change. There must have been up to this date a clear distinction of musical custom between the many monastery and cathedral churches and the ordinary town and village parish churches. Few parish churches, it would appear, when the Reformation came possessed anything of the nature of a choir, but, to judge from indications that remain, a surprising number (though probably very far from a majority) possessed organs. These were usually small instruments (see *Organ* 4) and, by modern standards, exceedingly clumsy in manipulation. In the parish churches, where the music was simple, they can have had little function beyond helping the priest and congregation in the performance of the plainsong. As a very considerable party in the Church of England desired thorough reform, on the Calvinistic lines, a good many parish church organs were removed or allowed to decay. The 'clerks' (lay or in minor orders) who had formerly, in the chancel, assisted the priest in the responsive parts of the service, now (perhaps in some places gradually) became reduced to one 'parish clerk' (q.v.), upon whom devolved the leading of the people's verses of the (read) prose psalms and the responses, which latter may in some places have been chanted to the new adaptation of the old plainsong and in others merely uttered in a speaking voice. A metrical psalm (see *Hymns and Hymn Tunes* 3) was often also included in the service, as what we would today call a hymn, and this was announced, read, and led by the parish clerk, sitting at his desk. The degree of ritual in churches varied very greatly, as did the degree of faithfulness in adherence to the official Prayer Book. The general standard of church life was in many parishes too poor for us to suppose that any one troubled if the musical part of the service was on a low level—or, indeed, if no musical part existed.

With Laud's appointment as Archbishop of Canterbury (1633) not merely did the High Church attitude find its expression in worship but seemliness in the conduct of services probably became more general. In 1644, whilst Laud was in prison, came the parliamentary decree that all church organs should be silenced and church music reduced to its simplest. The parish church became in some places Independent and in others Presbyterian, and no music was now heard beyond metrical psalms sung by the congregation. With the restoration of the monarchy in 1660 the Church of England became officially episcopal again, the Common Prayer was resumed, and a great body of the clergy was expelled. It does not appear that organs were quickly replaced in the parish churches in general. The music in most churches was still confined to the congregational metrical psalms led by the parish clerk (probably usually only one psalm in a service), so that the amount and character of the music during the Commonwealth and after the Restoration must in most churches have been just the same—a fact not usually realized. Very many complaints as to the character of the singing are scattered through 18th- and early 19th-c. Eng. literature. Perhaps partly as a result of the lack of organs there grew up during the later 18th c. a remarkably widespread custom of employing small orchs. in church. Such an orch., with a small choir, occupied the west gallery; together they led the metrical psalms or hymns and performed occasional simple anthems. In the towns at this period the presence of an organ was more common than in the villages, and the singing was most often led by the 'charity children' of the parish—i.e. either the children of the various free (weekday) schools for the poor or, as the term is sometimes used in the later 18th and earlier 19th c., the Sunday School children, who were once a week receiving free instruction in reading, writing, the Catechism, and the Bible, and were marched to church to join in the service. The many thousands of charity children of London, gathered once a year in St. Paul's Cathedral, formed a choir that greatly impressed Haydn in 1792 and Berlioz in 1851.

The disappearance of the church orch. is due in the first instance to the introduction of the barrel-organ and then to that of the harmonium. The barrel-organ (see *Mechanical Reproduction of Music* 10) appeared in church in the late 18th c. and quickly overspread the country; the harmonium (see *Reed-Organ Family* 5) was introduced from France in the 1840's and was followed by the Amer. organ (see *Reed-Organ Family* 6). The blow to village music-making was forceful and with enhanced decorum came diminished musical interest and variety. The Oxford Movement of the early 19th c. accentuated this desire for decorum and introduced a fashion for male choirs, surpliced and sitting no longer in the west gallery but in the chancel, and for the chanting of the responses and the psalms (see *Anglican Chant*). The old type of service lingered, however, in a good many churches until nearly the end of the 19th c. A stimulus to the development of music in the greater parish churches was given when Hook, vicar of Leeds from 1837 to 1859 (later Dean of Chichester), instituted a professional choir performing full daily (evening) cathedral services. To some extent it may be said that ambition has now over-reached itself, and there are many influential voices heard urging the smaller churches not to attempt music beyond a reasonable measure of difficulty. A discussion of the sort of music proper to various types of churches will be found in the Report of the Archbishops' Committee on Music in Worship (1922). The foundation of the Royal Coll. of Organists in 1864 (see *Profession of Music*) has done much for the improvement of music in the Anglican Church, as has also that of the Church Music Soc. (1906); that of the School of Eng. Church Music in 1927 (since 1945, Royal School of Church Music, q.v.) may be expected to do much also.

The development of musical conditions in the Anglican Church in other parts of the Commonwealth than England has, roughly speaking, followed that of the mother country, period by period, and the same may almost be said of the U.S.A.

Angore (It.). 'Pain', 'anxious wish'.

Angoscia (It.). 'Anguish.' So *angoscioso, angosciosamente,* 'with anguished feeling'.

Angreifen (Ger.). 'To seize', 'to attack'.

Angst (Ger.). 'Anguish', 'anxiety'.

Ängstlich or **aengstlich** (Ger.). 'Anxious', 'uneasy'.

Anhalten (Ger.). 'To hold on.' So *anhaltend,* 'holding on'.

Anhang (Ger.). Anything 'hanging on to' something else. A supplement, hence 'Coda'.

Aniara. 2-act 'science-fiction' opera by Blomdahl. Libretto by E. Lindgren. (Prod. Stockholm 1959.)

Anima. (It. 'soul'.) The sound-post of a violin, &c. (cf. *Âme* and *Sound-post*).

Animando (It.). 'Animating.' So *animandosi,* 'becoming animated'; *animato,* 'animated'. **Animé** (Fr.). 'Animated.'

Animo; animoso (It.). 'Spirit'; 'spirited'. So the adverb, *animosamente.*

Anmut or **anmuth** (Ger.). 'Grace.' So *anmutig,* 'graceful'.

Anna Magdalena Books (Bach). See *Klavierbüchlein.*

Ann Arbor. See *Festival.*

Années de pèlerinage ('Years of Pilgrimage'). By Liszt. Three books of Piano Pieces (1835–83) based on scenes and incidents in his travels. Book One is a recasting of the *Album d'un voyageur* (1835).

Annie Laurie. The poem is by William Douglas of Fingland (c. 1800), but has been much altered by various people, especially by Lady John Douglas Scott (1810–1900; cf. *Loch Lomond*), who also wrote the air. The date of first publication is 1838. The heroine of the song was a real person and Douglas was in love with her (she married another, however).

Annotated Programmes. The beginning of the practice of providing elucidations of music in the programme of a concert cannot be positively dated. Possibly the earliest example is the programme of a Concert of Catches and Glees, given by Arne at Drury Lane Theatre in 1768. It has a preface explaining the nature of the catch and the glee, and the various items are provided with historical and critical notes. Fifteen years later (1783)

Frederick the Great's Capellmeister, J. F. Reichardt (q.v.), founded in Potsdam a regular Tuesday performance and provided in his programmes both the words of the songs and 'historical and aesthetic explanations enabling the audience to gain a more immediate understanding'. It is of interest to note that one of the earliest annotated programmes known is of Amer. origin. It is that of the 'First Uranian Concert', given in Philadelphia on 12 April 1787. Soon after this (1790) the device is found in regular application at Biberach, in Swabia, where J. H. Knecht (q.v.), introduced it in his capacity of orch. conductor. In Covent Garden Theatre, during Lent 1801, was given the 1st Brit. perf. of Mozart's *Requiem*: the director of the performance, the well-known John Ashley, provided a book of words with more than 3 pages of biographical and historical information. John Thomson (q.v.) provided annotated programmes for the concerts of the Professional Soc. of Edinburgh, and, as Reid Prof. of Music in the Univ. of Edinburgh, similar programmes for the University concerts. John Ella, long prominent in London musical life as the director of a chamber music organization, the Musical Union (1845–80), is often spoken of in Britain as the introducer of annotated programmes: it will be seen that he had been anticipated, but it was probably the utility of his analytical notes over so long a period that formally established the practice, and thenceforward it became a common one.

The most important series of annotated programmes ever issued in Britain is that supplied for 40 years (1856–96) by Sir George Grove (with help as to the more modern works) for August Manns's famous Saturday orch. concerts at the Crystal Palace. Other famous series have been those of the Queen's Hall, London, 1908–27, by Rosa Newmarch (q.v.), assisted in later part of period by Blom (q.v.); and those of Tovey (q.v.) at Edinburgh and Philip Hale (see *Criticism*) at Boston (1901–34). The art of writing Programme Annotations is particularly well developed in U.S.A.

The same general intention as that of an annotated programme is seen in the advance articles that Weber during his opera conductorships at Prague (1813) and Dresden (1817) used to contribute to the local papers. Wagner at Dresden (1846) inserted a valuable treatise on Beethoven's 9th symphony.

See reference s.v. *Evans's Supper Rooms.*

Anreissen (Ger. 'to tear at'). 'Use a very forceful *pizzicato*' (q.v.).

Anschlag (Ger.). (1) What is sometimes called a 'Double Appoggiatura' (see Table 12), but consisting of the notes immediately below and above the principal note. (2) Touch (on, or of, a keyboard instrument). (3) 'Attack', &c.

Anschmiegend (Ger. 'bent to', 'shaped to'). 'Compliant', 'yielding'.

Anschwellend (Ger. 'swelling'). *Crescendo.*

Ansell, John (b. 1874; d. Marlow 1948). Trained G.S.M. Musical director various London theatres. B.B.C. 1925–30. Composer of popular overtures, &c.

Ansermet, Ernest (b. Vevey, Switzerland, 1883; d. Geneva 1969). Conductor. Began life as schoolmaster (mathematics) in Lausanne. In 1915, owing to illness of conductor of Kursaal, Montreux, came forward in his chosen line. Later founded *Orchestre de la Suisse Romande*, performing Geneva, Lausanne, &c.; also did much conducting in Paris, London, &c., for Diaghilef (see *Ballet*). Visiting conductor in U.S.A. and South America. Stravinsky and modernists his speciality.

Ansia (It.). 'Anxiety.'

Anson, Hugo (b. Wellington, N.Z., 1894; d. London 1958). Educ. Cambridge and R.C.M.; from 1939 Registrar of latter. Composer of chamber music, &c., and of national song, *New Zealand.*

Anstatt (Ger.). 'Instead of.'

Anstimmen (Ger.). 'To tune.'

Anstrich (Ger.). 'Stroke' of bow. (Cf. *Strich.*)

Answer in Fugue. See *Form 6.*

Antar. (1) 'Symphonic Suite' by Rimsky-Korsakof (op. 9; 1868; revised 1876, 1897, and 1903). Based on an oriental tale by Sennkovsky. (2) See *Dupont, Gabriel.*

Antecedent. See *Canon.*

Antheil, George (b. Trenton, N.J., 1900; d. New York 1959). Of Polish descent; when resident in Paris he produced much music once considered of highly revolutionary character, representative of the present machine age. Composed operas, ballets, film music, orch. works, &c., and was also an endocrinologist. (See *Transatlantic.*)

Anthem. (See first the article *Antiphon.*) The anthem may be considered as the English-speaking Protestant Churches' equivalent of the Latin motet (q.v.), from which it has sprung. It is an Anglican creation. In the liturgy of the Church of England there is a place provided for it (see *Common Prayer*), and churches other than that have given it an equivalent place somewhere after the middle or towards the end of the service. It constitutes in ordinary churches the one great occasion when the choir alone undertakes the duty of song, and when an elaboration impossible and unsuitable in other parts of the service becomes proper and effective. It is usually accompanied by organ, so different from the motet (in the strict application of the latter term): it has frequently passages for solo voices, individually or in combination.

The Eng. anthem repertory is large and varied, and includes many noble works, as well as a great deal that is trivial. The principal styles of anthem composition might be set forth in 'periods' somewhat like the following:

(1) THE PERIOD OF CONTRAPUNTAL UN-ACCOMPANIED ANTHEMS (the motet, but with Eng. words, as one might say). This lasted from the time of the Reformation until the death of the last of the great Eng. choral school, about a century beginning 1550 (i.e. the late Tudor and early Stuart period).

(2) THE EARLIER PERIOD OF THE ACCOM-PANIED ANTHEM, using solo voices and organ, and sometimes stringed and later other orch. instruments and recitative (a period on the whole of less gravity). This covered the period from the Restoration of the monarchy to the death of George I.

(3) THE PERIOD OF THE HANDELIAN AN-THEM (with a certain 18th-c. solidity and dignity)—say 1730 to 1800.

(4) THE EARLY NINETEENTH-CENTURY AN-THEM (with a more modern tinge)—say 1800 to 1875.

(5) THE LATER VICTORIAN ANTHEM (with an added grace and tunefulness but sometimes a tendency towards prettiness and sentimentality).

The word 'Anthem' is often loosely used, as, for instance, in the term 'National Anthem'. The 'Easter Anthems' of the Anglican Prayer Book are a collection of Biblical passages of relevant character, nowadays usually sung to an Anglican chant. For 'Verse Anthem' and 'Full Anthem' see *Verse.*

Anthony, Trevor (b. Ammanford, Carmarthenshire, 1913). Bass. Trained R.A.M. Lay vicar Westminster Abbey 1937–46. Recitalist, broadcaster, soloist with Brit. orchs., choral societies, and opera companies.

Anticipation. See *Harmony* 2 g.

Antico, antica; antichi, antiche (It. masc., fem., sing.; masc., fem. plur.). 'Antique', 'ancient'.

Antill, John (b. Sydney, N.S.W., 1904). Active in various capacities in opera and later Senior Music Presentation Officer of Australian Broadcasting Commission. Ballet Suite, *Corroboree* (on Australian aboriginal dances), had 1st Brit. perf. 1946; then as ballet, Sydney 1950.

Antiphon. (1) In the Roman Catholic Church it is a short extract consisting of a verse of a psalm and/or other traditional passage intoned or sung during the recitation of Divine Office (q.v.) before and after the psalm or canticle, which is itself responsively sung by the singers divided into two bodies. The antiphon may serve to enforce the meaning of the psalm, or to introduce a Christian application of the original Jewish text. It is attached very particularly also to the Canticles Benedictus and Magnificat, where it gives the keynote of the Feast, and Nunc Dimittis, where it emphasizes the intention of the service of Compline (q.v.). It is sung in complete form only at the greater feasts. The plainsong tune of the antiphon, though not the same as the 'tone' of the psalm (see *Plainsong* 2), is in keeping with it as to mode, &c.

(2) Many antiphons now exist without psalms and they are sometimes sung to settings by composers, instead

of to the original plainsong—hence the Eng. word 'anthem', derived from 'antiphona', for an independent piece of choral music not an essential part of the service.

Antiphonal, Antiphonary, or Antiphoner. Properly the Roman Catholic Church's collection of traditional plainsong antiphons (see *Antiphon*), but the word has come to be more comprehensively used as meaning the book containing all the plainsong for the Divine Office, as distinct from the Gradual (q.v.), which contains the plainsong for the Mass.

Antiphonal Singing. See *Service*.

Antiphonary, Antiphoner. Same as *Antiphonal* (q.v.).

Antiphons of the Blessed Virgin Mary. There are 4, each with its season: (*a*) during Advent and until the Purification of the Virgin Mary, *Alma redemptoris mater*; (*b*) thence until Wednesday in Holy Week, *Ave regina coelorum*; (*c*) thence until Whitsun, *Regina coeli laetare*; (*d*) from the Octave of Whitsun until Advent, *Salve regina, mater misericordiae*.

Anvil. See *Percussion Family* 2 s.

Anvil Bone. See *Ear and Hearing*.

Anwachsend (Ger. 'Growing'). 'Swelling out in tone.'

Anzublasen (Ger.). 'To be blown.'

Apaisé (Fr. 'pacified'). 'More peaceful.'

À peine (Fr.). 'Hardly', 'barely'. So *à peine entendu*, 'barely audible'.

Apel, Willi (b. Konitz 1893). Studied musicology at various German universities and in 1935 settled in U.S.A. joining staff of Harvard Univ., &c., and publishing many learned works, including *Harvard Dictionary of Music* (1944, 1969).

Aperto (It. 'open'). (1) 'Clear', 'distinct'. (2) Broad in style.

ApIvor, Denis (b. Collinstown, Eire, 1916). Trained choir schools Christ Church (Oxford) and Hereford, and under Hadley and Rawsthorne. Prolific composer of ballets, concertos, chamber music, &c.

Apocalyptic Symphony. See *Bruckner's Symphonies*.

Apollo Musagetes ('Apollon musagète', 'Apollo, Leader of the Muses'). Ballet by Stravinsky. (Prod. Paris 1927.) Music also heard in concert form.

Apollonicon. See *Mechanical Reproduction of Music* 11.

Apostles, The. Oratorio by Elgar. (1st perf. Birmingham Fest. 1903. New York and Cologne 1904.)

Appalachia. 'Variations on an Old Slave Melody' by Delius. For Orch. with some use of Baritone Solo and Chorus. (1st perf. Elberfeld 1904.)

Appalachian Spring. Ballet by Copland for Martha Graham. (Prod. Washington, D.C., 1944.) Also orch. suite 1945.

Appassionata Sonata (Beethoven). For Piano. In F minor, op. 57. So entitled by its first publisher.

Appassionato, appassionata (It. masc., fem.). 'Impassioned'; so *appassionatamente*, 'passionately'; *appassionamento*, 'passion'.

Appena (It.). 'Hardly', 'scarcely' (like the Fr. *à peine*).

Appenato (It. 'pained'). 'As if distressed.'

Applied Music. See *Degrees and Diplomas* 3.

Appoggiando; appoggiato (It. 'leaning'; 'leaned'). (1) Each note passing very smoothly to the succeeding one (i.e. *portamento*, q.v.). (2) 'Stressed.'

Appoggiatura (or 'Leaning Note'). See Table 13. (1) Properly an unprepared suspension, if such a contradictory term may be allowed (see *Harmony* 2 f), whether it be shown in full-sized type as a part of the chord in which it momentarily appears or as a small note printed just before that chord. Having a harmonic status it is not an 'ornament' in the same sense as, for instance, the Acciaccatura. (2) The same term is (unetymologically) applied to a note which is not a 'leaning' note but a note of the chord before which it appears and the treatment is the same as that indicated in Table 13.

Appreciation of Music. The words 'Musical Appreciation', taken together, have come to be accepted as the most usual time-table and textbook name for a form of educational training designed to cultivate in the pupil an ability to listen to seriously conceived music without bewilderment, and to hear with pleasure music of different periods and schools and varying degrees of complexity.

A history of musical appreciation as a subject in the educational course remains to be written. (There is a brief attempt at this in the present author's *Music—the Child and the Masterpiece*, 1935; in the Amer. ed. called *Music Appreciation—its History and Technics*.)

The fact of the existence of an *art of listening* seems to have been first prominently acknowledged by Nägeli (q.v.) of Zürich, who lectured to amateurs and in 1826 published a book for their use, and then by the great musicologist Fétis (q.v.), who in 1829 came to London to give a series of lectures on *La Musique mise à la portée de tout le monde* ('Music put within Everybody's Reach'); in 1830 he published a book with the same title, which was translated into several languages (19 eds. known to the present writer). Definite experimentation with this sort of teaching, on any large scale and in class, began only towards the very end of the 19th c., and it seems to have begun more or less simultaneously in America and Britain. The terms 'Appreciate' and 'Appreciation', in a musical application, first came into use in the U.S.A. In 1906 appeared *How to Appreciate Music*, by Gustav Kobbé, and in 1907 *The Appreciation of Music*, by T. W. Surette and D. G. Mason. In 1910 the appreciation publications of Stewart Macpherson (q.v.) began, and he became the first notable Brit. exponent of the subject.

The MUSIC MEMORY CONTEST, a device for inducing close attention to, and the memorizing of, the main themes of a great listening repertory, began in New Jersey in 1916 and was quickly taken up all over the U.S.A.; it has, up to the present, never been adopted in Britain. Special CONCERTS FOR CHILDREN became common in both countries.

The 'appreciative' idea has gained ground in many other countries than Britain and the U.S.A., largely stimulated by the facilities offered by the growing gramophone repertory.

Apprenti sorcier, L' ('The 'Prentice Sorcerer'). Symphonic Poem ('Scherzo') by Dukas. Based on a poem by Goethe which, in turn, is based on a dialogue in Lucian (2nd c. A.D.). The 'prentice, in his master's absence, tries one of his spells and, to his consternation, cannot countermand it. (1st perf. Paris 1897. London and New York 1899.)

Appuyé, appuyée (Fr. masc., fem. 'supported'). 'Emphasized.'

Aprahamian, Felix (b. London 1914). Music critic (*Sunday Times* staff from 1948) and writer especially on French music. Active in numerous musical organizations.

Après (Fr.). 'After.'

Après-midi d'un faune, Prélude à l' ('Prelude to "The Afternoon of a Faun"'). Debussy's orchestral reproduction of the languorous atmosphere of the famous eclogue of Mallarmé. On a sultry afternoon a half-awakened faun has seen a vision of nymphs fleeing down a glade—and so on. 1st performance 1894. (Explanation of the words 'Prélude à' is that it was intended that there should be a set of 3 pieces—*Prélude, Interlude*, and *Paraphrase finale*.) Has been treated as ballet (Diaghilef's Company, 1912).

Aptommas. See *Thomas* (4) and (6 b).

A punta d'arco (It.). 'With the point of the bow.'

Äqual (Ger.). Old organ term for '8 foot'.

Aquarelle (Fr.). 'Water-colour'; sometimes musically applied to a piece of delicate texture.

Aquin. See *Daquin*.

Arabella. 3-act opera by Richard Strauss. Libretto by Hofmannsthal. (Prod. Dresden 1933; London 1934.)

Arabesque (Fr., Eng.), **Arabeske** (Ger.). A florid element in Arabian architecture, hence a florid melodic figure in music, or a composition based on such. A popular example is Schumann's *Arabesque* for Piano (op. 18, 1839).

A.R.A.D. Associate of the Royal Academy of Dancing, London (founded 1927; chartered 1936).

Arada (Sp. 'ploughed land'). A type of folk song associated with ploughing.

Aragonesa (Sp.), **aragonaise** (Fr.). A Spanish dance deriving from Aragon.

A.R.A.M. See *Degrees and Diplomas* 2.

Aranyi, d'. The sisters; both eminent violinists. (1) **Adila** (b. Budapest 1888; d. Florence 1962). Trained Budapest Conservatory. Married and professional name 'Fachiri'. (2) **Jelly** or **Yelli** (b. Budapest 1895; d. Florence 1966). Trained Budapest Conservatory; pupil of Hubay and her great-uncle, Joachim. Both sisters resident in London and Brit. subjects.

Arbeau, Thoïnot—pen name (sort of anagram) of Jehan Tabourot (b. Dijon 1519; d. Langres 1595). Priest. Author of famous book on the dance, *Orchésographie* (1589).

Arbitrary Minor Scale. Same as 'Melodic' Minor Scale (see *Scale*).

Arbós, Fernandez—in full Enrique Fernandez (b. Madrid 1863; d. San Sebastian 1939). Violinist; pupil of Vieuxtemps and Joachim. After positions in Germany and Spain settled in Britain as performer, conductor, and teacher (R.C.M.), also visiting the U.S.A. (See *Iberia*.)

Arcadelt (or Arkadelt, Arcadet, Arcadente, &c.), **Jacob** (b. abt. 1510; d. 1568—both dates very variously stated). Distinguished Netherlands composer attached to St. Peter's and Sistine Chapel, Rome; then in Paris. Famous composer of madrigals, masses, &c.

Arcata (It.). Stroke of bow (violin, &c.): the words *in giù* (meaning 'down') or *in su* (meaning 'up') often follow.

Arcato (It.). 'Bowed' (after a passage of *pizzicato*).

Archadet, Jachet = Arcadelt, Jacob (q.v.).

Archangelsky (Archangelski), **Alexander** (b. in government of Penza,

Russia, 1846; d. Prague 1924). Spent life in service of Russian church as choral conductor and composer; first to introduce women's voices into choirs of Orthodox church.

Archbishop of Canterbury's Degrees. See *Degrees and Diplomas* 1.

Archbishops' Committee on Church Music. See *Anglican Parish Church Music*.

Archduke Trio (Beethoven). Piano Trio in B flat, op. 97 (1811). So nicknamed from dedication to Archduke Rudolph.

Archer, Frederick (b. Oxford 1838; d. Pittsburgh 1901). Organist (Merton Coll., Oxford; Alexandra Palace, London; Brooklyn; Pittsburgh, &c.). Also conductor, composer of organ works, author of organ tutor, &c.

Archers of Switzerland, The. Early American Ballad Opera by Benjamin Carr. (Prod. New York 1796.)

Archet (Fr.). 'Bow' (violin, &c.).

Archi (It.). 'Bows' (violin, &c.); the singular is *Arco*.

Archlute. Large double-necked theorbo (see *Lute*).

A.R.C.M. See *Degrees and Diplomas* 2.

A.R.C.O. See *Degrees and Diplomas* 2.

Arco (It.). 'Bow.' Used alone or in *coll'arco* ('with the bow'), after a passage marked *pizzicato* ('Plucked'). The plural is *archi*.

Ardemment (Fr.). 'Ardently.'

Ardente (It.). 'Ardent.'

Arditi, Luigi (b. Piedmont 1822; d. Brighton 1903). Opera conductor in Britain and America; composer of operas; best known by a vocal waltz, *Il Bacio* ('The Kiss').

Ardito (It.). 'Bold.' So *arditamente*, 'boldly'.

Ardore (It.). 'Ardour.'

Arensky (Arenski), Antony (b. Novgorod 1861; d. Finland 1906). Prof. of Composition at Conservatory of Moscow and then director of music in Imperial Chapel at St. Petersburg; composer of operas, symphonies, piano music, &c.

Arethusa, The. The poem closely describes a naval engagement that took place in the English Channel in June 1778. The tune, generally attributed to Shield (q.v.), was merely harmonized by him, being a country dance tune once popular as *The Princess Royal*.

Aretino, Guido. See *Guido d'Arezzo*.

Aretusa. See *Vitali, Filippo*.

Arezzo. See *Guido d'Arezzo*.

Ar hyd y nos. See *All through the Night*.

Aria (It. 'Air'). From the 18th c. onwards this has had the definite implication of a more or less lengthy and well-developed solo vocal piece in 3 sections, the 1st and 3rd being identical and the 2nd contrasting with them. Arias used to be rather minutely classified as (*a*) *Aria cantabile*, slow and smooth; (*b*) *Aria di portamento*, in long notes and dignified, to be sung with smooth progression from one note to the next; (*c*) *Aria di mezzo carattere*, more passionate and with orchestral accompaniment, this latter often elaborate; (*d*) *Aria parlante*, declamatory; (*e*) *Aria di bravura*, or *Aria d'agilità*, or *Aria d'abilità*, requiring great command over the voice; (*f*) *Aria all' unisono*, with the accompaniment in unison or 8ves with the vocal part; (*g*) *Aria d'imitazione*, imitative of bird song, hunting horns, and the like; (*h*) *Aria concertata*, with elaborate accompaniment; and so on.

See *Cadenza*, also cf. *Recitative*.

Ariadne auf Naxos ('Ariadne on Naxos'). 1-act opera by Richard Strauss originally intended for perf. in Molière's comedy *Le Bourgeois gentilhomme*. Libretto by Hofmannsthal. (Prod. Stuttgart 1912; London 1913; revised version dispensing with the Molière play, Vienna 1916; London 1924; New York 1934.) Also Opera by Benda (q.v.) 1775.

Ariane et Barbe-bleue ('Ariadne and Bluebeard'). Fantasy-opera by Dukas. Libretto, Maeterlinck's play. (Prod. Paris 1907; New York 1911; London 1937.)

Arietta (It.). A shorter and simpler Aria (q.v.). Usually it lacks any middle section. The term is sometimes applied to a piece of instrumental music (not always in an appropriate manner).

Ariettes oubliées (Debussy). Song settings of 6 poems by Verlaine. (1888: dedicated to Mary Garden, q.v.)

Arioso. (1) A recitative of the more melodious type. (2) A short melodious passage at the beginning or end of an aria. (3) A short air in an opera or oratorio.

Ariosti, Attilio (b. Bologna 1666; d. abt. 1740). Monk who obtained dispensation to devote himself to music and occupied various court positions in Germany and Austria; colleague in London of Handel and Bononcini as director of opera enterprise ('Royal Academy of Music') and composer of operas, &c.; performer on and composer for viola d'amore (see *Viol Family* 3 i).

Arkadelt. See *Arcadelt*.

Arkansas Traveller. See *Guion*.

Arkwright, Godfrey Edward Pellen (b. Norwich 1864; d. Highclere 1944). Distinguished musicologist; edited a comprehensive 'Old English Edition' and a valuable quarterly, *The Musical Antiquary* (1909–13). See *Adeste Fideles*.

Arlecchinesco (It.). In the spirit of a Harlequinade.

Arlecchino. 1-act opera. (Ger.) libretto and music by Busoni. (Prod. Zürich 1917.)

Arlésienne, L' ('The Maid of Arles'). Daudet's play, with choral and orch. music by Bizet (Paris 1872). The composer's 2 orch. Suites from the music have concert popularity.

A.R.M.C.M. See *Degrees and Diplomas* 2.

Armide. 5-act Fr. opera by Gluck. Libretto by Quinault, based on Tasso's *Jerusalem Delivered*. (Prod. Paris 1777; London 1906; New York 1910.)

Very many operas with the same title by other composers, including Haydn (1784). Lully's (1686) has the same libretto as Gluck's.

Armonia, armonica (It.). (1) 'Harmony.' (2) 'Wind band.'

Armonioso; armoniosamente (It.). 'Harmonious'; 'harmoniously'.

Armstrong, Thomas Henry Wait (b. Peterborough 1898). Trained Oxford (M.A., D.Mus.) and R.C.M. Organist Exeter Cathedral 1928; Christ Church Cathedral, Oxford, 1933–55. Choragus of Oxford Univ. 1938–53. Principal, R.A.M., 1955–68. Composer of choral works, church music, chamber music, &c. Knighted 1957.

Arne, (1) Thomas Augustine (b. London 1710; there d. 1778). The leading Brit. composer of his day (operas; tuneful songs still sung, including *Rule Britannia*, q.v.; oratorios; keyboard music, &c.). D.Mus. Oxford.

See *Annotated Programmes; Artaxerxes; Judith; Love in a Village; Masque.*

(2) **Michael** (b. London 1740; there d. 1786). Son of above. Lived for a time in Hamburg. Composed stage music, &c.; his song *The Lass with a delicate air* is still heard.

Arnell, Richard Anthony Sayer (b. London 1917). Composer. R.C.M. 1935–9. B.B.C. consultant in U.S.A. 1943–5, where a number of his works were written and performed. Compositions include symphonies, concertos for piano, violin, &c., chamber music and songs; also music for film *The Land*, play *Caligula*, &c. On staff T.C.M. 1948–64.

Arnold, (1) John (b. Great Warley, Essex, 1720; d. 1792). Composer of songs, catches, &c.; best known as ed. of music used in collections of metrical psalm tunes (cf. *Samuel Arnold* below).

(2) **Samuel** (b. London 1740; there d. 1802). Musician of multifarious activities—Organist of Chapel Royal and Westminster Abbey; composer to Covent Garden Theatre, proprietor of Marylebone Gardens (see *Concert*), conductor of the Academy of Ancient Music (q.v.), &c. Composer of many popular operas, of church music, &c.; ed. of Handel's works in 36 vols. and of a supplement to Boyce's *Cathedral Music* in 4 vols. (see *Boyce*); also of a book of metrical psalm tunes (not to be confused with those of his namesake above). D.Mus., Oxford.

(3) **Frank Thomas** (b. Rugby 1861; d. Bath 1940). Lecturer in German

at Cardiff Univ. Coll. and author of a very thorough historical work on figured bass (1931).

(4) **John Henry** (1887–1956). Authority on Plainsong and ed. of collections, &c., for use in Anglican Church. D.Mus., Lambeth.

(5) **Malcolm (Henry)** (b. Northampton 1921). Trained R.C.M. Orchestral trumpeter, then very prolific composer (6 symphonies, 8 concertos, &c.).

Arnould, Madeleine Sophie (b. Paris 1740; there d. 1802). Soprano singer and actress. Début at 17 and thenceforward the leading lady of the Paris lyric stage till retirement in 1778.

Arpa (It.). 'Harp.'

Arpège (Fr., from *arpe*, 'harp'). **Arpeggio** (It.; pl. *arpeggi*). A chord 'spread'—i.e. the notes heard one after the other from the bottom upwards, or sometimes from the top downwards.

Arpeggiare (It.). To play chords as arpeggios. So the present and past participles, *arpeggiando* and *arpeggiato.*

Arpeggione or Guitare d'amour. Sort of guitar-shaped six-stringed violoncello with a fretted finger-board (see *Frets*) and played with a bow. Complete existing repertory consists of one sonata by Schubert.

Arpicordo. An earlier It. name for Harpsichord.

Arraché (Fr. 'torn'). An extreme form of *pizzicato*.

Arrangement or Transcription. Adaptation of a piece of music for another medium than the one for which it was originally composed. Sometimes, too, 'Transcription' means a rewriting for the same medium but in a style easier to play. (In the U.S.A. there appears to be a tendency to use 'Arrangement' for a free treatment of the material and 'Transcription' for a more faithful treatment.)

Arrau, Claudio (b. Chile 1904). Pianist. 1st recital Santiago, age 5. Studied Santiago Conservatory and Berlin. Début Berlin 1915; U.S.A. 1924. Then world tours.

Ars antiqua. See under *Ars nova* below.

Arsin et Thesin, Per. See *Canon.*

Ars nova. The terms *Ars antiqua* and *Ars nova* ('Old Art' and the 'New Art') came into use at the beginning of the 14th c. to mark a change that then took place in music. The 'Ars nova' was characterized by a greater variety of rhythm, more shapely melodic curves, and more independently moving voice-parts. The 'Ars antiqua' is particularly associated with the school of Paris and the 'Ars nova', in its inception, with that of Florence. The It. madrigal may be looked upon as the later full flower-ing of the 'Ars nova'.

Artaxerxes. Arne's most successful Opera. Libretto an Eng. translation of Metastasio. (Prod. London 1762; Dublin 1765; New York 1828.) Many Operas on this subject, e.g. Hasse (1730), Gluck (1741).

Art de toucher le clavecin, L' ('The Art of playing the Harpsichord'). By Couperin (1716). With instructions and illustrative compositions.

Articolato (It.), **articulé** (Fr.) 'Well-articulated'; so *articolazione* (It.). 'Articulation.'

Artificial Harmonics. See *Acoustics* 7.

Artig (Ger.) (1) 'Well-behaved', 'agreeable'. So the adverb *artiglich*, and the noun *Artigkeit.* (2) Note that *-artig* often appears as a suffix in the sense of 'like'. So *marschartig*, 'march-like'.

Artikuliert (Ger.). 'Well-articulated.'

Art of Fugue (*Die Kunst der Fuge*). Posthumous and unfinished work of Bach designed to establish the possi-bilities of one simple subject in the various types of fugal and canonic writing.

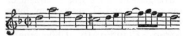

It is not clear what medium was in-tended to be employed, or, indeed, whether actual performance was in view. Modern edns. for piano and ver-sions for stringed instruments and for orch. have appeared.

Art of Playing the Harpsichord (Couperin). See *Art de toucher le clavecin.*

Artôt, AlexandreJoseph Montagney (b. Brussels 1815; d. nr. Paris 1845). Violinist, touring world. Composer for violin and for chamber combina-tions.

Arts Council of Great Britain. Body established 1946 by Royal Charter, and supported by government grant (£11,900,000 in 1971), as successor to the Council for the Encouragement of Music and the Arts ('C.E.M.A.', 1939). 20 persons selected by the Chancellor of the Exchequer in con-sultation with the Minister of Educa-tion, plus a small professional staff, in-cluding the Music Director. It has a long list of 'Associated Organiza-tions' (orchestras, opera companies, ballet companies, festivals, &c.), which it subsidizes. Address, 105 Piccadilly, London.

Arundell, Dennis Drew (b. London, 1898). Cambridge M.A., B.Mus., sometime fellow of St. John's Coll. and Univ. lecturer on music and Eng. drama. Wide variety of musical and dramatic enterprises, Cambridge, Sad-ler's Wells, radio actor, &c. Composer of incidental music. Book on Purcell, &c.

Arytenoid Cartilages. See *Larynx.*

A.S. = *Al segno* (q.v.).

As (Ger.). The note A flat (see Table 7).

Asas or Ases (Ger.). The note A double flat (see Table 7).

A.S.C.A.P. See *American Society of Composers, Authors, and Publishers.*

Ashdown Ltd., Edwin. London music publishing firm (1860), suc-cessors to Wessel firm (dating from 1825). Address, 19 Hanover Square, London, W. 1. Cf. *Enoch.*

Ashley, John. See *Annotated Pro-grammes.*

Ashton, (1) **Hugh.** See *Aston.*
(2) **Algernon Bennet Langton** (b. Durham 1859; d. London 1937). Active composer, pianist, and teacher, known to a wide public by his letters to the press (republished in 2 vols.) on every possible subject and his

exploration of London cemeteries, with frequent agitation for repair of tomb-stones of great men in all walks of life.

(3) **Frederick** (b. Ecuador 1906). Educ. in Peru and Dover. Notable choreographer (Sadler's Wells from 1936) of ballets, e.g. *Romeo and Juliet, Les Patineurs, Sylvia, La Fille mal gardée*, &c. Knighted 1962; C.H. 1970.

Aspiratamente (It.). 'Aspiringly.'

Aspirate. See *Voice* 11.

Aspro, aspra (It. masc., fem.). 'Rough', 'harsh'. So the adverb *aspramente* and the noun *asprezza*, 'asperity'.

Assai (It.). 'Very', 'extremely' (formerly this word was synonymous with the French 'Assez', but the meanings have drifted somewhat).

Assassinio nella cattedrale ('Murder in the Cathedral'). 2-act opera by Pizzetti, based on the play of T. S. Eliot. (Prod. Milan 1958.)

Assez (Fr.). 'Enough', but the usual and best translation is 'fairly', e.g. *assez vite*, 'Fairly quick'.

Assieme (It.). 'Together.'

Associated Board of the Royal Schools of Music. Founded 1889, partly to combat effect of numerous spurious examining bodies, being a combination, for the conduct of local and school examinations, of the Royal Academy and Royal Coll. of Music, and also (since 1947) the Royal Manchester Coll. of Music and the Royal Scottish Academy of Music. (See also *Degrees and Diplomas* 2.)

Association of Musical Competition Festivals. See *Competitions in Music.*

Aston, or Ashton, Aystoun, &c., **Hugh** (active in earlier 16th c.). Composer of church and virginal music, and pioneer of true instrumental style.

Astorga, Baron d' = Emanuele Gioacchino Cesare Rincón (b. Sicily 1680; d. (?) Spain abt. 1757). Amateur singer, harpsichordist, and able composer—especially of Cantate da Camera and of a famous *Stabat Mater* (abt. 1707).

Asturiano, Asturiana (Sp. masc., fem.). Pertaining to Asturias (province of Spain in Bay of Biscay, now Oviedo).

Astuzie femminile, Le ('Female Wiles'). Opera by Cimarosa. (Prod. Naples 1794; London 1804; reorchestrated by Respighi 1920, and then revived in Paris, London, &c., somewhat in ballet form.)

A suo beneplacito, A suo bene-placimento. Same as *Ad libitum* (q.v.).

As Vesta was from Latmos Hill. See *Weelkes.*

Atalanta in Calydon (Bantock). See *Choral Symphony* 3.

A.T.C.L. See *Degrees and Diplomas* 2.

Atempause (Ger. 'breath pause'). Very slight pause on a weak beat in order to give greater effect to the following strong beat.

Athaliah. Oratorio by Handel. (1st perf. Oxford 1733.)

Athalie. By Mendelssohn, being Incidental Music to Racine's drama (op. 74; 1843). Overture and *War March of the Priests* are the chief parts now heard, the latter domestically in piano arrangement.

Atkins, Ivor Algernon (b. Llandaff 1869; d. Worcester 1953). Organist of Worcester Cathedral (1897–1950). Conductor Worcester Festivals; composer. Ed. Bach Passions, &c. D.Mus., Oxford. Knighted 1921.

Atonality. See *Harmony* 3.

A.T.S.C. See *Degrees and Diplomas* 2.

Attacca (It.). The imperative, 'Attack!' Used at the end of a movement as meaning 'Start the next movement at once'.

Attacco. Very short *motif* (q.v.) used as material for imitation (see *Counterpoint*). Or as fugue subject (cf. *Andamento*).

Attack. Prompt and decisive beginning of a note or passage.

Attack on the Mill (Bruneau). See *Attaque du moulin.*

Attaque (Fr.). 'Attack.' The *Chef d'attaque* in an orch. is the leading violin (Amer. 'Concert-master').

Attaque du moulin, L' ('The Attack on the Mill'). Tragedy-opera by Bruneau. Libretto based on story by Zola. (Prod. Paris 1893; London 1894; New York 1910.)

Attendant Keys. See *Modulation.*

Atterberg, Kurt (b. Gothenburg 1887). Engineer turned composer and writer on music and as such subsidized by the Swedish Government. His 6th symphony won the £2,000 prize offered by Columbia Graphophone Co. in the year of the centenary of Schubert's death (1928)—an award which raised violent discussion in various countries. His opera, *Fanal*, is regarded as one of the few 'national' operas of Sweden. Sec. Roy. Acad. Mus., Stockholm, 1940–53.

Attey, John (active in early 17th c.). Publ. a book of lute songs (the last of such to appear—1622).

At the Boar's Head. See *Holst, G. T.*

At the Hunting-place (Haydn.) See *Auf dem Anstand.*

Attwood, Thomas (b. London 1765; there d. 1838). Boy chorister in Chapel Royal; pupil in Vienna of Mozart; host and friend in London of Mendelssohn; organist of St. Paul's Cathedral, 1796–1838; composer of theatre music and church music.

See reference under *Rule, Britannia!*

Au (Fr.). 'To the', 'at the', &c.

Aubade (Fr., from *Aube* 'dawn'). 'Early morning music' (cf. *Serenade*—'evening music').

Aubade of the Clown (Ravel). See *Miroirs.*

Auber, Daniel François Esprit (b. Caen 1782; d. Paris 1871). In youth in business in London; then prominent in Paris as composer of instrumental music and later of operas, collaborating in the latter with the dramatist, Scribe; in all wrote about 40 operas, of which amongst the best known are *Masaniello* (see *Muette de Portici*), *Fra Diavolo* (q.v.), *The Bronze Horse* (see *Cheval de bronze*), *The Crown Diamonds* (see *Diamants de la couronne*), and *The Black Domino* (see *Domino noir*). Had a fund of melody and a gift for effective orchestration. In 1842 became head of the Paris Conserv. and in 1857 musical director to Napoleon III.

Aubert, (1) **Jacques** (b. 1689; d. 1753). Famous Parisian violinist and composer of music for violin and for the stage.

(2) **Louis François Marie** (b. Paramé, Brittany, 1877; d. Paris 1968). Pupil of Fauré; at one time prominent as pianist, later as composer of songs, piano music, fairytale opera *The Blue Forest*, &c.

Auch (Ger.). 'Also', 'but'.

Audace (Fr.). 'Audacity'; (It.) 'audacious'.

Au dessous (Fr.). (1) 'Beneath'. (2) 'Less than.'

Audibility, Pitch-limit of. See *Acoustics* 15.

Audran, Edmond (b. Lyons 1840; d. nr. Paris 1901). Church organist at Marseilles and composer first of church music and later (with high success) of comic operas (see *Poupée*).

Auer, Leopold (b. Hungary 1845; d. nr. Dresden 1930). Violinist and violin teacher. Pupil of Joachim, &c. Resident from time to time in Germany and Russia; also taught in London and New York. Teacher of many of most famous violinists of period and author of books on violin playing. Publ. compositions and arrangements for his instrument.

Auf (Ger.). 'On', &c., e.g. *Auf der G*, like the Italian *Sul G*, means 'On the G' (string).

Auf dem Anstand ('At the Hunting-place') or **Mit dem Hörnersignal** ('With the Horn Call'). Nicknames for Haydn's Symphony in D, no. 31 in Breitkopf edn. of the Symphonies.

Auf einer Gondel (Mendelssohn). See *Gondola Song 2.*

Aufforderung zum Tanz ('Invitation to the Dance'). Piano piece by Weber (op. 65, 1819), representing a ballroom scene. Often heard in arrangement for orch. by Berlioz (1841), and sometimes, much changed, in one by Weingartner. Adopted by Russian Ballet as music for their *Le Spectre de la rose.*

Aufführen (Ger.). 'To perform.' So *Aufführung*, 'performance' (also 'development'); *Aufführungsrecht*, 'performing right' (often followed by the word *vorbehalten*, i.e. 'reserved').

Aufgeregt (Ger.). 'Excited.'

Aufgeweckt (Ger. 'Wakened up'). 'Lively.'

Aufhalten (Ger. 'To hold up'). 'To retard.'

Auflage (Ger.). 'Edition.'

Auflösen (Ger. 'To loosen', 'release', &c.). (1) To resolve a discord. (2, in harp playing) To lower again a string that has been raised in pitch. So the noun **Auflösung**. **Auflösungszeichen** ('release-sign'). The sign for the natural (see Table 7).

Aufschlag (Ger.). 'Up-beat' ('downbeat' being *Niederschlag*).

Aufschnitt (Ger. 'slit', &c.). A portion omitted, a 'cut'.

Aufschwung (Ger.). 'Up-soaring', 'flight', e.g. *Mit Aufschwung*, 'In a lofty (i.e. impassioned) spirit'.

Aufstrich (Ger.). 'Up-stroke' of bow ('Down-stroke' being *Niederstrich*).

Auftakt (Ger.). 'Up-beat' ('downbeat' being *Niederschlag*).

Aufzug (Ger. 'Up-pull' of curtain). 'Act.'

Augener. London Music Publishers (catalogue now owned by Galliard Ltd. (q.v.)) Estd. 1853. Proprietors of *Monthly Musical Record* (1871–1961).

Augengläser (Ger. 'Eye-glasses'). Word used by Beethoven on the title-page of his duet for violin and violoncello—'mit 2 Augengläser obbligato', being merely a jocular reference to the 2 spectacled players for whom it was composed.

Augmentation and Diminution in melodic parts are, respectively, the lengthening and shortening of the time-values of the notes of those parts. Thus (to take one instance) in a fugue the subject may (especially towards the end) appear in longer notes, the device adding dignity and impressiveness. (See also following entries.)

Augmentation, Canon by. See *Canon*.

Augmented Intervals. See *Interval*.

Augmented Sixth. The chords of the Augmented 6th are Chromatic Chords (q.v.). The three most usual, to which pointless names have been given, are as follows (taking key C as our example):

(*a*) CHORD OF THE ITALIAN 6TH, A flat–C–F sharp. (*b*) CHORD OF THE FRENCH 6TH, A flat–C–D–F sharp. (*c*) CHORD OF THE GERMAN 6TH, A flat–C–E flat–F sharp.

'Italian'　　'French'　　'German'

The above shows them all as based upon the flattened Submediant (A flat) but they can also be taken based upon the flattened Supertonic (D flat–F–B, &c.) and occasionally upon the Subdominant.

The German 6th is the commonest and serves as a convenient pivot for modulation, since not only can it be taken as based on the flattened Submediant in one key and quitted as based on the flattened Supertonic in another, or vice versa, but, by enharmonic change (see *Interval*), can be transformed into the Chord of the Dominant 7th of another key and so quitted (e.g. the A flat–C–E flat–F sharp above mentioned can be treated as A flat–C–E flat–G flat, i.e. as the Chord of the Dominant 7th of key D flat). And there are other possibilities.

Augmented Triad. See *Harmony* 2 d.

Auld Lang Syne. The poem is a recasting by Robert Burns (final form publ. 1794) of a popular song (probably in origin a folk song) then current in various versions. The tune we now have is sometimes stated to be by Shield (q.v.): something like it certainly appeared in his opera *Rosina*, as a part of the Overture (Covent Garden, 1783), where it is so treated as to imitate Scottish bagpipe music. *Sir Alexr. Don's Strathspey* (issued possibly a year later than the perf. of Shield's opera) seems to have a very good claim to be the original; it may have been already current and have become known to Shield, who was brought up at Durham, i.e. not very far from the Scottish border. The air is in the Pentatonic Scale (see *Scales*), like many Scottish tunes.

There is, of course, a strong resemblance between the tunes of *Auld Lang Syne* and *Comin' thro' the rye* (q.v.). There is also another tune, *O can ye labour lea, young man*, with a still closer resemblance to *Auld Lang Syne*. Still another, *Roger's Farewell*, seems to be a near relation.

Auld Robin Gray. The words of this song were written in 1771 by Lady Anne Barnard (*née* Lindsay). The tune to which we now sing it is not the original one, but was composed by a Somerset clergyman, the Rev. William Leeves, in 1772.

Aura (It.). Jew's harp (q.v.).

Auric, Georges (b. Lodève, Hérault, France, 1899). Pupil of d'Indy. As composer a member of 'Les Six' (see *Six*). His works include orch. and piano music, ballets, film music, &c. 1962–8 administrator of Paris Opera.

Aurora's Wedding (Tchaikovsky). See *Sleeping Princess*.

Aurresku. A sort of Basque folk dance. The *Zortziko* (q.v.) forms a part of it.

Aus (Ger.). 'Out of', 'from', &c.

Ausdruck (Ger.). 'Expression.' So *ausdrucksvoll*, 'expressively'.

Ausfüllgeiger (Ger. 'Filling-out fiddler'). A *Ripieno* (q.v.) violinist.

Ausgabe (Ger. 'out-giving'). 'Edition.'

Ausgehalten (Ger. 'held out'). 'Sustained.'

Aushalten (Ger. 'To hold out'). 'To sustain'; so *aushaltungszeichen*, 'holding-out sign', i.e. pause.

Aus Holbergs Zeit (Grieg). See *Holberg Suite*.

Aus Italien ('From Italy'). 'Symphonic Fantasia' by Richard Strauss (op. 16; 1886).

Aus meinem Leben (Smetana). See *From my Life*.

Ausschlagen (Ger. 'to beat out'). 'To beat time.'

Ausser (Ger.). 'Outer', 'out of', 'in addition to'.

Äusserst (Ger.). 'Extremely.'

Aussi (Fr.). (1) 'Also.' (2) 'As', in the sense of 'as much'. (3) 'Therefore.'

Austen = Aston (q.v.).

Austin, (1) **Frederic** (b. London 1872; d. London 1952). Baritone. opera director (especially concerned in revival of *The Beggar's Opera* and *Polly*, 1920–3), and composer orch., choral, piano music, &c. B.Mus., Durham.

(2) **Ernest** (b. London 1874; d. Wallington, Surrey, 1947). Brother of above. After the age of 30 abandoned business life for music and became known by huge 'Narrative Poem' for organ in 12 sections (*The Pilgrim's Progress*) and many smaller works.

(3) **Sumner Francis** (b. Anerley, Kent, 1888). Operatic and concert baritone (Carl Rosa Co., Old Vic., Sadler's Wells, &c.); Technical Director, Sadler's Wells. M.A., Oxford.

(4) **Richard** (b. Birkenhead 1903). Son of (1) above. Orch. conductor of repute (Bournemouth 1934–40). Trained R.C.M., later on staff.

Austral, Florence (b. nr. Melbourne, Australia, 1894; d. Newcastle, N.S.W., 1968). Operatic and concert soprano. Opera début (Brünnhilde) Covent Garden 1922. Wide tours.

Austria (hymn tune). See *Emperor's Hymn*.

Auszug (Ger.). (1) 'Extract.' (2) 'Arrangement' (q.v.).

Authentic Cadence. See *Cadence*.

Authentic Modes. See *Modes*.

Autoharp. Type of easily played zither (q.v.), played with the fingers or a plectrum. Chords are produced by depressing keys.

Automaton violinists, &c. See *Mechanical Reproduction of Music* 9.

Autre; autres (Fr.). 'Other'; 'others'.

Auxetophone. A sound-multiplier first suggested by Edison and developed by Sir Chas. A. Parsons and Horace Short. By its means the sound of an ordinary gramophone record can be made to carry for half a mile. (Cf. *Bullphone*.)

Auxiliary Note. This may be described as a variety of Passing Note (see *Harmony* 2 g), which, instead of passing *on* to another note, passes *back* to the note it has just left. Such a note may (as may a Passing Note) be either diatonic or chromatic. Shakes, Mordents, and Turns (see Tables 12–16) offer examples of the Auxiliary Note applied decoratively.

Avant (Fr.), **avanti, avante** (It.). (1) 'Before', 'preceding'. (2) 'Forward.'

Avec (Fr.). 'With.'

Ave Maria ('Hail Mary'). Prayer consisting partly of the salutations of the Archangel Gabriel and Elizabeth to the Virgin Mary and partly of matter added in the 15th c. Often set by composers (for Gounod's setting see *Meditation*).

Ave Regina Coelorum. See *Antiphons of the Blessed Virgin Mary.*

Ave Verum Corpus ('Hail, true body'). Hymn (anonymous and of unknown date) possessing its own plainsong and also frequently set by composers (Josquin des Prés, Byrd, Mozart, Cherubini, S. Wesley, Gounod, Elgar, &c.), such motet settings being frequently sung in the Roman office of Benediction. Translations sometimes begin *Jesu, Word of God Incarnate, Jesu, Blessed Word of God Incarnate,* or *Word of God Incarnate.*

Avison, Charles (b. Newcastle-on-Tyne 1709; there d. 1770). Pupil in London of Geminiani; organist of the parish church of his native town; composer of 50 concertos and author of much discussed *Essay on Musical Expression* (1752). Browning includes him in his *Parleyings with certain People of Importance in their Day.*

Avison Edition. Edition of works by Brit. composers, carried out under the auspices of Soc. of Brit. Composers (q.v.).

Avitahl, Theodore (b. Bacau, Rumania, 1933). Condr., Belgian radio. St. Louis Orch. from 1963.

Avoided Cadence. See *Cadence.*

Avshalomov, Jacob (b. Tsingtao, China, 1919). Educ. Pekin and Reed Coll., Portland, Ore. Composer and conductor. Columbia Univ. 1947; Portland Junior Symph. 1954. Works, mainly for chorus and orch., reflect his varied background.

Awake, Aeolian Lyre. See *Danby, John.*

Awakening of the Lion, The. See *Kontski.*

Ayre. See *Madrigal.*

Aystoun = Aston (q.v.).

Azione (It.). (1) 'Action.' (2) 'Drama.'

Azora, Daughter of Montezuma. Opera by Henry Hadley. (Prod. Chicago 1917; New York same year.)

B

B. In Ger. this means B *flat* (B natural being called 'H'). Thus what is called B flat in Ger. is our B double flat. (See Table 7.)

Babbitt, Milton (b. Philadelphia 1916). Studied at Princeton Univ.; mathematician and composer of increasingly abstract works, the latest of these employing electrophonic means.

Babell, William (b. abt. 1690; d. London 1723). A celebrated harpsichordist and violinist, and composer for his instruments.

Babin, Victor (b. Moscow 1908; d. Cleveland 1972). Pianist and composer. Trained at Riga Conserv. and under Schnabel. In U.S.A. from 1937; successful two-piano team with wife Vitya Vronsky (q.v.). Compositions include two-piano concerto. From 1961 director Cleveland Institute of Music.

Baby Grand. See *Pianoforte.*

Baccaloni, Salvatore (b. Rome 1900; d. New York 1969). Operatic bass (Rome 1922; La Scala 1926; Covent Gdn. 1928; Chicago 1930; Metropolitan 1940) outstanding in comic parts.

Bacchanalia. Riotous dancing or singing in honour of Bacchus, the god of wine.

Bacchetta (It. 'stick'). (1) Drumstick. (2) Baton. The plural is *bacchette*—e.g. *bacchette di legno*, 'wooden drumsticks'; *bacchette di spugna*, 'sponge-headed drumsticks'. (See *Percussion Family* 1 a.)

Bace Dance. Basse Danse (q.v.).

Bach (The Family). They were active musically for generations, records remaining of 53 who occupied positions as organists, town musicians, &c. The plan adopted here is to treat first the most important member of the family, then 4 of his sons, and after that an earlier member of the family.

(1) **Johann Sebastian** (b. Eisenach, in Thuringia, 1685; d. Leipzig 1750). He occupied successively posts as choir-boy, violinist in the orch. of a prince, organist of town churches, chief musician in a court, and cantor of a municipal school, having charge of the music in its associated churches. That last position (1723) was at Leipzig, with whose St. Thomas Church and School his name is now inseparably associated.

He played many instruments, and as clavichordist, harpsichordist, and organist was supreme in his day.

He was twice married and had 20 children, of whom several attained eminence as musicians. Towards the end of his life he became blind.

His musical production falls pretty clearly into 3 categories corresponding to the main posts he held—(1) chiefly organ works; (2) chiefly works for other instruments and for the orch. of his day; (3) chiefly church works, such as cantatas for the weekly services, passion music, and masses (for the words of the Mass, expressing no distinctively Roman Catholic doctrines, were kept in use in the Lutheran church).

Bach's work closed a phase—that of the late contrapuntal school, of which the fugue was the most definite expression, and that of North German Protestantism, which found its inspiration largely in the *chorale* (q.v.); he represents also the period of the climax of the form of the suite (q.v.), soon to be superseded by the sonata (q.v.). After his death interest trended in the new direction and his works (few of which had by then been printed) fell into obscurity: the revival of their appreciation was largely due to Mendelssohn in Germany and Samuel Wesley in England. They now enjoy the highest admiration of every music lover.

See also under *Actus Tragicus*; *Alla Breve Fugue*; *Art of Fugue*; *B-A-C-H*; *Brandenburg Concertos*; *Chaconne*; *Choral Prelude*; *Christmas Oratorio*; *Chromatic Fantasy and Fugue*; *Coffee Cantata*; *Corelli Fugue*; *Dorian Toccata and Fugue*; *English Suites*; *Expression*; *Fiddle Fugue*; *Fingering*; *Forkel*; *Frederick the Great*; *French Suites*; *Fuga alla Giga*; *German Suites*;

Giant Fugue; *Goldberg*; *History* 5; *Horn, K.F.*; *Invention*; *Italian Concerto*; *Klavier*; *Klavierbüchlein*; *Klavierübung*; *Lob und Ehre*; *Magnificat*; *Mass in B minor*; *Motet*; *Musical Offering*; *Organ Mass*; *Orgelbüchlein*; *Passion Music*; *Peasant Cantata*; *Phoebus and Pan*; *Pianoforte*; *Saint Anne's Fugue*; *Saint John Passion*; *Saint Matthew Passion*; *Saints in Glory Fugue*; *Schafe können sicher weiden*; *Schemelli Hymn Book*; *Terry, C. S.*; *Tonus Peregrinus*; *Wachet auf*; *Wedge Fugue*; *Widor*; *Wise Virgins*; *Wohl mir, dass ich Jesum habe*; *Wohltemperirte Klavier, Das*.

(2) **Friedemann**—in full Wilhelm Friedemann (b. Weimar 1710; d. Berlin 1784. J. S. Bach's 2nd child and eldest son). He was a learned and able musician, but lacked stability and died poor and embittered. Some of his keyboard works are still published.

(3) **Karl** (or **Carl**) **Philipp Emanuel** (b. Weimar 1714; d. Hamburg 1788. J. S. Bach's 5th child and 3rd son). For 28 years he held a position at the court of Frederick the Great (q.v.) at Potsdam. He was a notable composer and takes a high place in the history of music as the chief founder of the sonata-symphony style, then to be developed by Haydn, Mozart, and Beethoven. For the last 21 years of his life he was resident in Hamburg, as director of music in its 5 chief churches. His keyboard music is still published and performed. (See references under *Sonata*; *Fingering*; *Haydn*.)

(4) **Johann Christoph Friedrich** (b. Leipzig, 1732; d. Bückeburg 1795. J. S. Bach's 16th child and 9th son). He held various musical posts and composed chamber music, keyboard sonatas, concertos, symphonies, &c., some of which are still published and in use. (For another Johann Christoph see 6.)

(5) **Johann Christian** (b. Leipzig 1735; d. London 1782. J. S. Bach's 18th child and 11th son). He was for a time organist of Milan Cathedral, but came to London, where he spent a quarter of a century as an opera and concert director and music master in the family of George III; hence he became known as 'the English Bach'. He wrote operas and symphonies, and also compositions for the harpsichord which are obtainable in modern edns. (Cf. *Abel*; *Hanover Square*.)

We now pass back to an earlier generation:

(6) **Johann Christoph** (b. Arnstadt 1642; d. Eisenach 1703. Cousin of J. S. Bach's father). He wrote music which was appreciated by both J. S. Bach and C. P. E. Bach. Most of it remains in MS. but some keyboard and choral works exist in print, including the motet known in English-speaking countries as *I wrestle and pray*. (For another Johann Christoph see 4.)

B-A-C-H. As in German use both B and H exist as names of notes (H = B; B = B flat), it is possible to use the composer's name as a 4-note musical theme. Bach himself so used it, and so have many other composers—an instance generally overlooked being that of Beethoven in the slow movement of his string quartet op. 59, no. 2 (in the bass).

       B   **A**   **C**   **H**

Bachauer, Gina (b. Athens 1913). Pianist. Trained Athens Conserv. and École Normale, Paris; teachers included Cortot and Rachmaninof. Début 1935. Recitalist and soloist at orch. concerts in Athens, Middle-Eastern centres, Paris, London, &c. Wife of Alec Sherman (q.v.).

Bachaus. See *Backhaus*.

Bach Choir. Founded in London 1875–6 by Otto Goldschmidt (q.v.), his wife, Jenny Lind (who led the sopranos), and A. D. Coleridge (barrister and amateur tenor), initial object being earliest complete Brit. perf. B minor Mass. Still active (see *Jacques, Reginald*). Many choirs of similar name since formed in Britain and elsewhere (e.g. Bethlehem, Pa., 1900; 1st conductor J. Frederick Wolle).

Bache, (1) **Francis Edward** (b. Birmingham 1833; there d. 1858). Fine pianist and active composer, whose early death disappointed many who had expected to watch a notable development. (2) **Walter** (b. Birmingham 1842; d. London 1888). Brother of the above. Pupil of Liszt and popularizer of his works in Britain. (3) **Constance** (b. Birmingham 1846; d. Montreux, Switzerland, 1903). Sister of the two above. Led a useful life of literary work and lecturing, especially on Russian music.

Bachelor of Music. See *Degrees and Diplomas* 1, 3.

Bach Trumpet. See *Trumpet Family*.

Bacio, Il. See *Arditi*.

Backer-Gröndahl, (1) **Agathe Ursula** (b. Holmestrand, Norway, 1847; d. nr. Oslo 1907). Pupil of von Bülow, a fine pianist and popular composer of songs and piano music. (2) **Fridtjof** (b. Oslo 1885; there d. 1959). Son of the above. Pianist and composer.

Backfall. See *Organ* 1.

Backhaus (or Bachaus), **Wilhelm** (b. Leipzig 1884; d. Villach, Austria, 1969). Pianist. Trained Leipzig Conserv. and under d'Albert &c. Made first concert tour age 16; later toured world. On staff Royal Manchester Coll. of Music for a period from 1905.

Back Turn. Same as *Inverted Turn* (see Table 15).

Bacon, Ernst (b. Chicago 1898). Winner of Pulitzer Prize 1932, and Guggenheim Fellowship. Opera conductor, pianist, and teacher (Head of Music Dept. Univ. Syracuse). Musical journalist, and composer of symphonies, theatre music, songs, &c.

Bacon and Greens. See *Saint Patrick's Day*.

Badarczewska, Tekla (b. Warsaw 1838; there d. 1861). Known to fame as the composer (at 18) of a tasteless piano composition which has been (and perhaps still is) one of the best sellers the music trade has ever known—*The Maiden's Prayer*.

Badinage, badinerie (Fr.). 'Playfulness.'

Badings, Henk (b. Java 1907). Began as engineer, but studied music with Pijper and at 30 joined staff of Rotterdam Conserv.; director, Conserv. of The Hague, 1941. Prolific composer of orch., choral, chamber, piano, and organ works.

Badura-Skoda, Paul (b. Vienna 1927). Pianist. Trained Vienna; after prize-winning appearances at European contests he embarked on a series of world tours. Many recordings; specialist in Mozart and with wife Eva author of book on interpretation of his piano music.

Bagatelle (Fr., Ger.). 'Trifle.' So a short unpretentious instrumental composition. (Ger. plur. *Bagatellen*.)

Bagpipe Family. Forms of the bagpipe have existed for at least 3,000 years and it is today one of the most nearly ubiquitous of instruments, being known to very many races in Europe and Asia. Its essentials are that (*a*) It is a reed-pipe wind instrument (see *Reed*), and (*b*) Interposed between the medium supplying the wind and the reed-pipe is a bag serving as a reservoir and so preventing any undesired breaking of the flow of sound by the player's necessity to take breath.

Variable characteristics are: (*c*) The source of the wind-supply to the reservoir may be either the mouth of the performer or a small bellows held

ANCIENT ROMAN BAGPIPE
(Utricularium)

It still survives as the *Zampogna* of the Abruzzi peasants.

under his arm and by it contracted and expanded. (*d*) The reed-pipe (*Chanter*) from which the various notes of the tune are obtained by means of a series of holes or keys may, or may not, be accompanied by one or more other reed-pipes each confined to a single note (*Drones*), these being tuned to the Tonic or Tonic and Dominant (i.e. the *Doh* and *Soh*) of the key of the instrument (cf. 'Pedal', s.v. *Harmony* 2 i).

(*e*) The reed may be either single, like that of the clarinet family, or double like that of the oboe family; in practice the chanter reed is usually (perhaps always) double, whilst the drone reeds vary in different types of instrument.

Sackpfeiff.

OLD GERMAN BAGPIPE

(From Agricola, *Musica instrumentalis deudsch*; Wittemberg, 1528.)

The compass of nearly all bagpipes is limited to one 8ve but on some few types a second 8ve can be obtained.

Further constructional details cannot be given here but a brief account may be offered of the various Brit. forms of the instrument. (*a*) The SCOTTISH HIGHLAND BAGPIPE, or GREAT PIPE, is mouth-blown and possesses a conical-bore chanter and 3 drones (2 A's and a D, or 2 D's and an A, or 2 high A's and one low A). The tone

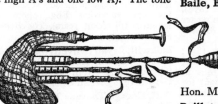

SCOTTISH HIGHLAND PIPE
(18th Century)

is penetrating and best heard in the open air; the scale is peculiar, and indeed unique—that of A major with a natural G and with the C and F pitched between sharp and natural. (*b*) The SCOTTISH LOWLAND BAGPIPE is much the same as the foregoing, but bellows-blown. (*c*) The NORTHUMBRIAN BAGPIPE is also bellows-blown but sweet and gentle in tone and normal as to scale (G major): it has

usually 4 drones: its chanter pipes are end-stopped, so that when the player closes all the finger-holes at once sound from them ceases, making possible a characteristic crisp *staccato*. (*d*) The IRISH 'UNION' BAGPIPE (the assertion that the word is a corruption of *Uillean* is unfounded). This is bellows-blown and sweet in tone; it has 3 drones. Its scale is a nearly chromatic one.

There have been other local British forms of the bagpipe but the above seem to be the sole survivors, though there may be recorded a movement which attempts to revive the IRISH WAR PIPE (mouth-blown and powerful in tone).

Cf. *Musette.*

Baguette (Fr. 'stick'). In musical use (1) Drumstick (*baguettes de bois*, wooden drumsticks; *baguettes d'éponge*, sponge-headed drumsticks). (2) Stick of bow of violin, &c. (3) Conductor's baton.

Bahr-Mildenburg (*née* Mildenburg), **Anna von** (b. Vienna 1872; there d. 1947). Wagnerian soprano. Bayreuth début 1897; Covent Garden 1906. Married poet, Hermann Bahr, and with him wrote book on Bayreuth and Wagner. On staff Munich Conservatory from 1920.

Baile, Bayle (Sp.). Ballet or dance.

Baillie, Isobel (b. Hawick, Scotland, 1895). Soprano vocalist of high artistic sensibility. Trained Milan. First London appearance 1923; then at all chief Engl. Festivals, &c.; U.S.A. 1933. Hon. M.A., Manchester. C.B.E. 1951.

Baillot, Pierre—in full Pierre Marie François de Sales (b. nr. Paris 1771; d. Paris 1842). Violin virtuoso of great reputation, composer of 9 violin concertos, &c., and prof. of the Paris Conserv.

Baines, (1) **William** (b. Horbury, Yorks. 1899; d. York 1922). Composer of piano works, &c., who unfortunately died before his development was complete.

(2) **Anthony Cuthbert** (b. London 1912). Bassoonist. Educated Christ Church, Oxford (B.A.); then at R.C.M. Bassoonist with London Philharmonic

Orch. 1935–9 and 1946–8; then orch. conductor. Founder-member of Galpin Soc. (see *Galpin, F. W.*).

Bainton, Edgar Leslie (b. London 1880; d. Sydney 1956). Trained R.C.M. and then lived as pianist, teacher, and Director of Conserv. in Newcastle-on-Tyne for many years. Director of State Conserv., Sydney, N.S.W. (1933–47). Prolific composer.

Bairstow, Edward Cuthbert (b. Huddersfield 1874; d. York 1946). Articled to Sir Frederick Bridge at Westminster Abbey; then various organist's positions, including Leeds Parish Church (1906) and York Minster (1913 to death). Successful voice trainer and choral conductor. Composer of church music, &c. Prof. of Music at Durham Univ. 1929 to death. D.Mus., Durham; Hon. D.Mus., Oxford; Hon. D.Litt., Leeds. Knighted 1932.

Baiser de la fée, Le ('The Fairy's Kiss'). Allegorical Ballet by Stravinsky, music based on themes from Tchaikovsky. (Prod. Paris 1928; London with new choreography 1935.)

Baisser (Fr.). 'To lower' (e.g. a string of the violin, &c.).

Baker, (1) Sir Henry Williams (b. London 1821; d. nr. Leominster 1877). Clergyman and baronet. Hymn writer and ed. *Hymns Ancient and Modern* (see *Hymns and Hymn Tunes* 4).

(2) **Theodore** (b. New York 1851; d. Dresden 1934). Musical writer; after business training studied mus. in Leipzig; literary ed. (1892–1926) for G. Schirmer; books include valuable biographical dictionary (1900; 5th edn., 1958, ed. N. Slonimsky).

Bakst, Leon. See *Ballet*.

Balakiref (Balakirev, Balakirew, &c.), **Mily** (b. Nijni-Novgorod 1837; d. St. Petersburg, now Leningrad, 1910). Of 'good birth' and acquainted with the music of the peasants around his home. Friend of Oulibichef, the authority on Mozart, who employed a private orch. (this afforded knowledge of the classics and experience of the principles of orchestration). Meeting with Glinka led to nationalist leanings. Started in St. Petersburg a Free School of Music;

collected and publ. folk-tunes; founded the group called 'The Five' (q.v.). Composed brilliant piano music (showing Lisztian leanings), 2 symphonies, &c.

See also *Islamey*; *King Lear*; *Russia*; *Tamara*.

Balalaika. Russian guitar, triangular in shape with (normally) 3 strings, and a fretted finger-board. It exists in various sizes. Associated with it, in Balalaika Bands, are the *Domra*, a somewhat similar instrument, and the *Gusli* (q.v.).

Balanchine, George (b. St. Petersburg 1904). Noted choreographer. With Diaghileff 1925–9; in U.S.A. from 1933.

Baldwin Company. Piano makers of Cincinnati. Date from 1862.

Balfe, Michael William (b. Dublin 1808, d. Rowney Abbey, Herts., 1870). His musical life was spent in the theatre, as orch. violinist, then as singer, later as manager, and finally as a highly popular composer. Lived for a time in Paris and Berlin and produced his operas there and in St. Petersburg. Having made a fortune bought an estate and settled down as an English country gentleman. His instinct for pleasant melody is seen in his one surviving Eng. opera (a favourite till recent years), *The Bohemian Girl* (q.v.).

Balkwill, Bryan (Havell) (b. London 1922). Trained R.A.M. Conductor (Glyndebourne from 1950; Covent Garden 1958; Welsh Opera 1963–7).

Ball, George Thomas Thalben. See *Thalben-Ball.*

Ballabile (It.). 'In a dance style.'

Ballad. Properly a song to be danced to (Lat. *Ballare*, 'to dance'; cf. 'ballet') but from the 16th c. or earlier the term has been applied to anything singable, simple, popular in style, and for solo voice. Shakespeare shows us the balladsinger, who was also ballad-seller, hawking his wares ('broadsides' or 'broadsheets'): these often described some interesting event of the day (actual or imaginary), marvellous, tragic, heroic, &c., the new poems (sung to old and known tunes) being

The vvofull Lamentation of *William Purcas*, vvho for murthering his Mother at *Thaxted* in *Essex* was executed at *Chelmsford.*

To the tune of, *The rich Merchant.*

The Swan before her death,
   most pleasantly doth sing :
But I a heavie hearted note
   with teares my hands doe wring,
With teares my hands doe wring,

Yea, once I lov'd it well,
  oh to to well indeed :
For that I did in drinke ore-gone,
  my woe-tyr'd soule doth bleed.
For this soule spotted fault,

Her words I would not heare,
  in rage I drew my knife,
To take deare life away from her,
  by whom I had my life.
The sight of which did make

A BALLAD SHEET
(This shows merely the head of the sheet)

usually in the traditional ballad metre —the 'common metre' of our hymn books. Hundreds of these broadsides

THE BALLAD SELLER
Singing his wares through the streets.

can be seen in libraries such as that of the Brit. Museum, as they have been collected and preserved by enthusiasts

of different periods. Each is generally adorned with a rude woodcut, often ostensibly picturing the event described but sometimes totally irrelevant.

The word 'ballad' was in the 19th c. also attached to the simpler type of 'drawing-room song'—sometimes called 'Shop Ballad', possibly originally to distinguish it from the hawked variety. Hence the Eng. 'Ballad Concerts' inaugurated by the music publisher, John Boosey, in 1867.

For Ballad Opera see *Opera* 5.

Ballade. A term given by Chopin to a long, dramatic type of piano piece (in his case strongly Polish in inspiration), supposedly the musical equivalent of a stirring poetical ballad (q.v.) of the heroic type. Brahms, Liszt, Grieg, and others have later used the title.

Balladenmässig (Ger.). 'In ballad style.'

Ballad Horn. Sort of Saxhorn. Different makers apply the name to different varieties. (See *OCM*, **s.v.** *Saxhorn and*

Flügelhorn Families 2 c and footnote thereon.)

Ballad of the Doom of Oleg. Cantata by Rimsky-Korsakof (op. 58). Text a Russian legend as retold by Pushkin. (1st Brit. perf. Newcastle-on-Tyne 1909.)

Ballad Opera. See *Opera* 5.

Ballerino, Ballerina (It.). Ballet dancer—male and female respectively.

Ballet. (For the general subject of dancing see *Dance*; cf. also *Masque* and *Pantomime*.)

Spectacular dancing has existed amongst many races and in many periods, but the ballet, as we today understand the word, was largely developed in the courts of France and Italy during the 16th and 17th cs. and especially in that of Louis XIV (reigned 1643–1715), where Lully (q.v.) was in charge of the music. The ballets of this period were danced by the court itself and were very formal (gavottes, minuets, chaconnes, &c.), heavy dresses being worn, with wigs, high heels, and other trappings of court life.

Even in the days of the great ballerina CAMARGO (before the public 1726–51), who was an innovator, dress was pretty ample, skirts still falling below the knees; however, she introduced a more vigorous style of motion. NOVERRE (1727–1810) succeeded in banishing the conventions hitherto ruling as to the use of mythological subjects, set order of dances, elaborate dresses, &c., and he thus made himself the founder of the Dramatic Ballet, or *ballet d'action*. He established the 5-act ballet as an entertainment in its own right: he collaborated with Gluck and Mozart in ballets for opera, and wrote an important treatise on the ballet. Other great masters of this period were DAUBERVAL (1742–1806), GAETANO VESTRIS (1729–1808), and PIERRE GARDEL (1758–1840). Vestris was the founder of a family of *maîtres de ballet*, active in 3 generations (1747–1825), and of several important ballerinas.

By the end of the 18th c. the ballet had almost discarded the last of its stately court influences and had developed gymnastic virtuosity—some conventionality, however, remaining, in that motion was confined too exclusively to the legs and feet. Dancing on the *pointe* (that is, on the tips of the toes) came in only about 1814; it calls for arduous practice, requires special shoes, and carries a danger of dislocation; MARIE TAGLIONI (career from 1822 to 1847) was its first notable exponent. The Romantic Movement (cf. *Romantic*) was now in being and this soon brought into the ballet an attempt at ethereal informality. The costume grew shorter and the skin-tight (*Maillot*, from its Parisian inventor) was daringly introduced.

From the mid-19th c. great spectacular ballets, of a realistic and topical character, became common, and much effective ballet music was written, especially by Fr. composers: the appearance of Delibes's *Coppélia* (1870) marks an epoch.

A reaction is shown in the work of the Amer. danseuse, ISADORA DUNCAN (1878–1927), who took her attitudes from Greek vases and mingled with her motions some learned from the birds, the waves, and other natural exponents of grace in action: she spent some time in Russia, and influenced the dancer FOKINE (1880–1942) and the impresario DIAGHILEF (1872–1929). St. Petersburg (now Leningrad) and Moscow had long had their great royal schools of ballet and had cultivated its technique to the highest degree of polish and the two men just mentioned introduced the new classical and naturalistic ideals, added nationalistic traits and, with their famous 'RUSSIAN BALLET', toured Europe, creating everywhere a new interest in the art. The male dancer had receded into the background and they brought him well to the front again. Their troupe included such notabilities as PAVLOVA, KARSAVINA, and LOPOKOVA (amongst the women) and NIJINSKY and MASSINE (amongst the men). Composers were commissioned to write special music (e.g. STRAVINSKY—*The Firebird, Petrouchka, The Rite of Spring*, &c.), and painters (e.g. BAKST) to design, with bold colour contrasts, scenery, costumes, &c.

Amongst 20th-c. ballet composers are Ravel (*Daphnis and Chloe*, 1910),

Roussel (*The Spider's Feast*, 1912), John Alden Carpenter (*Krazy Kat*, 1921; *Skyscrapers*, 1926), Bartók (*The Wooden Prince*, 1916), and Vaughan Williams (*Job*, 1931). Some of the scores of the ballets above mentioned have attained popularity in the concert-room, divorced from their action. On the other hand, much concert-room music has been used for ballet (e.g. Debussy's *The Afternoon of a Faun*, whole Beethoven Symphonies, and much Chopin).

Almost from the beginnings of opera ballet has been one of its frequent ingredients (Lully, Purcell, Gluck, Meyerbeer, Glinka, Borodin, and other Russian composers of their period, Wagner in the Paris version of *Tannhäuser*, Strauss in *Salome*, &c.): in some cases the dance element has been dragged into the scheme by the hair of its head, to satisfy an audience that wished for that kind of relief, but most of the composers just mentioned introduced it merely when the plot of the opera, at some point, offered a suitable opportunity, or actually demanded dancing.

The most common technical terms in connexion with ballet are, in this book, explained under their own headings. For almost all the ballets mentioned in the present article there are separate entries under their own names.

Ballet de Cour (Fr.). Court ballet of the 17th c. (Cf. *Masque*.)

Ballett. See *Madrigals*.

Ballo (It.). 'Ball', 'dance'; so *tempo di ballo*, which can mean (*a*) At a dancing speed, or (*b*) A dance-style movement.

Ballo, Di (Sullivan). See *Di Ballo*.

Ballo in Maschera, Un ('A Masked Ball'). 3-act tragedy-opera by Verdi, based on Scribe's *Gustav III*. (Prod. Rome 1859; London, Dublin, and New York 1861.)

Baltimore. See under *Schools of Music*.

Baltzar, Thomas (b. Lübeck abt. 1630; d. London 1663). Early violinist and the most accomplished up to his period heard in England (see Evelyn's Diary, &c.). Appointed leader of band of Charles II, 1661. Buried Westminster Abbey.

Bamboo Pipe. A simple instrument of the recorder type (see *Recorder Family*), which was introduced into schools in the U.S.A. in the 1920's and later into those of Great Britain, the players usually making their own instruments.

Bamboula. (1) Primitive negro tambourine (see *Percussion Family* 2 m) in use in the West Indies. (2) Dance to which this is the accompaniment.

Bampton, Rose (b. Cleveland 1909). Operatic soprano (at first mezzo). Trained Curtis Institute. Metropolitan début 1932.

Banatanka. Sort of Serbian Dance.

Banchieri, Adriano (b. Bologna 1568; there d. 1634). Renowned organist, composer, and theorist; also a poet and playwright.

Band. An orchestra—or nowadays, more generally, a body of wind-instrument players. (Formerly a company of chorus singers also.)

See *Brass Band*; *Military Band*.

Band; Bände (Ger.). 'Volume'; 'volumes'.

Bandoneon. See *Reed-Organ Family* 3.

Bandore or **Bandora.** See *Cittern*.

Bandsman's College of Music. See *Degrees and Diplomas* 2.

Bandurria. See *Cittern*.

Banister, (1) **John** (b. London 1630; d. there 1679). Violinist, leader of the band of Charles II; composer and Britain's first organizer of public concerts (see *Concert*).

(2) **Henry Charles** (b. London 1831; d. there 1897). Teacher, composer, &c. Trained R.A.M. (later on staff, as also on that of G.S.M., &c.). Several popular textbooks.

Banjo. An instrument of the same general type as the guitar (q.v.), but the resonating body is of parchment strained over a metal hoop and it has an open back. There are from 4 to 9 strings (usually 5 or 6), passing over a low bridge and 'stopped' against a fingerboard, which is often without frets (q.v.): one is a *melody string* (thumb string, or *chanterelle*), the others providing a simple accompaniment of chords. Some examples have gut strings (played with the finger-tips) and others wire strings (played with a plectrum). The ultimate origin of this instrument is supposed to be Africa, and it was in use amongst the slaves of the Southern U.S.A.; then, in the 19th c., it became the accepted instrument of 'Negro Minstrels' (q.v.) and in the 20th found a place in jazz bands. These last sometimes used a *Tenor Banjo*, with a different scheme of tuning (resembling that of the violin family). The *Zither Banjo* is of small size and has wire strings.

Banjolin. An instrument of the banjo type, but with a short, fretted neck, like that of a mandoline. It has 4 single (or pairs of) strings, played with a plectrum.

Banner of St. George. Cantata by Elgar. Text by Shapcott Wensley. (1st perf. Kensington 1897.)

Bantock, Granville (b. London 1868; there d. 1946). Trained at R.A.M., toured as conductor of a theatrical company and became musical director at New Brighton, nr. Liverpool. From 1900 Principal of the School of Music in Birmingham and from 1908 Prof. of Music in the Univ. there; in 1934 became Chairman of Corporation of T.C.M.

Prolific composer of part-songs; choral-orch. music on the large scale; songs; orch. music; &c. His composition passed through Eastern and Gaelic phases. Hon. M.A., D.Mus., Edinburgh. Knighted 1930.

See also *Atalanta in Calydon; Dante and Beatrice; Fifine at the Fair; Hebridean Symphony; Omar Khayyám; Pierrot of the Minute; Pilgrim's Progress; Sappho Songs.*

Bantock Society. Founded 1946 to produce gramophone recordings of, and generally popularize, Bantock's work. First president, Sibelius.

Bar, Bar Line. See *Notation; Rhythm; Measure.*

Barabau. Comic Ballet by Rieti. (Prod. London 1925.)

Barati, George (b. Győr, Hungary, 1913). First 'cellist, Budapest Opera (1936–8); in U.S.A. from 1939 as teacher, 'cellist, and conductor; con-ductor, Honolulu Symphony Orch. 1950–66. Composer of orch. and other works.

Barbarie, Orgue de. See *Mechanical Reproduction of Music* 5.

Barbary Bell. See *Saint Patrick's Day.*

Barber, Samuel (b. West Chester, Pa., 1910). Studied Curtis Institute 1923–32. Won Amer. Rome Prize 1935, and, two years running (1935–6) and again in 1958, Pulitzer Prize. Also Guggenheim Fellowship 1945. Prominent composer of orch. and chamber music, choral music, songs, &c., and an opera, *Vanessa* (q.v.). Brilliant technician with predominantly lyrical and expressive style. D.Mus. 1945.

Barber of Bagdad (Cornelius). See *Barbier von Bagdad.*

Barber of Seville, The (Rossini; also Paesiello). See *Barbiere.*

Barber's Shop Music. One of the regular haunts of music in the 16th and 17th cs. was the barber's shop. Here customers awaiting their turn found some simple instrument (apparently almost always the *Cittern*, q.v.), on which they could strum. The barbers themselves, in their waiting time between customers, took up the instrument and thus came to possess some repute as performers. Of the Spanish barbers Cervantes in *Don Quixote* (1604) says: 'Most or all of that faculty are players on the guitar and song makers.' In Eng. lit. of the 16th and 17th cs. the allusions to the barbers as musicians are numerous.

The musical proclivities of barbers ceased in England in the earlier part of the 18th c. It is said that they took to periwig-making (i.e. added an occupation that filled their vacant time) and forgot their music. Apparently the tradition was maintained longer in America. Steinert, the great Boston musical instrument dealer, speaks of a man with whom he lodged in Georgia about 1860, 'As once upon a time he had been a barber he knew how to play the guitar.' The expression 'Barbershop harmony' (meaning a banal style of writing) is still current in the U.S.A.

Barbiere di Siviglia, Il ("The Barber of Seville'); at early performances called *Almaviva o sia l'Inutile Pre-cauzione* ('Almaviva, or The Useless Precaution'). Comedy-opera by Rossini. Libretto based on Beaumarchais. (Prod. Rome 1816; London 1818; New York 1819.) An earlier opera of the same name, by Paesiello 1782.

Barbier von Bagdad, Der ('The Barber of Bagdad'). Comedy-opera by Cornelius. (Prod. Weimar, under Liszt, one perf. 1858; New York and Chicago 1890; London 1891. Most perfs. since 1884 have been of a revision and re-orchestration by Mottl.)

Barbirolli, John (b. London 1899; d. there 1970). Orch. and opera conductor. Studied as 'cellist at T.C.M., and R.A.M. Founded chamber orch. and joined Queen's Hall Orch. Conductor of Scottish Orch., Glasgow, 1933; New York Philharmonic (following Toscanini) 1936; Hallé Orch. Manchester, 1943 (also Houston, Texas, from 1961). Knighted 1949. Gold medal R. Phil. Soc. 1950. C.H. 1969. Married the oboist Evelyn Rothwell (q.v.).

Barcarolle. Boat song or an instrumental composition with a steady rhythm like that of oarsmen (in compound duple or compound quadruple time).

Barcarolle from *The Tales of Hoffmann* (q.v.). Retrieved by Offenbach from his much earlier Opera, *Die Rheinnixen*, 1864 (a failure). In this it figured as a *Goblin's Song*.

Bardd. See *Eisteddfod*.

Bardgett, Herbert (b. Glasgow 1894; d. Leeds 1962). Choral trainer and conductor. Nottingham Harmonic Soc.; chorus master Huddersfield Choral Soc., Hallé Choir, Leeds Festival. Conductor children's concerts of Hallé and Liverpool Philharmonic Orchs.

Bardi, Giovanni (1534–1612), Count of Vernio. In his house at Florence in 1600 were held the first operatic performances (see *Opera* 1).

Bärenhäuter, Der. See *Wagner, Siegfried*.

Bärenreiter-Verlag (Kassel). Important German publishers. Founded Augsburg 1924 by Karl Vötterle.

Emphasis on old music; many musicological publications including the monumental encyclopedia, *Musik in Geschichte und Gegenwart* (see *Blume*).

Bargiel, Woldemar (b. Berlin 1828; there d. 1897). Stepbrother of Clara Schumann, disciple of Robert Schumann, and composer of repute.

Baring-Gould, Sabine (b. Exeter 1834; d. Lew Trenchard, Devon, 1924). Country squire and rector Lew Trenchard. Collected and published folk songs. Wrote popular hymns (e.g. *Onward, Christian Soldiers*, 1865).

Bariolage (Fr.). Effect in violin playing—rapid alternation of open and stopped strings.

Baritone. See *Voice* 14.

Baritone (Saxhorn). See *Saxhorn and Flügelhorn Families* 1.

Barkarole (Ger.). 'Barcarolle' (q.v.).

Barkworth, J. E. (1858–1929). See *Romeo and Juliet*.

Barless Iron Frame. See *Pianoforte*.

Barley Shot. This 'Welsh folk-tune' is a Scottish air, *O gin I were fairly shut of her* ('shut' — 'rid'). The title became abbreviated in some collection to 'Fairly shut', and then corrupted, presumably through somebody mentioning it and being misheard, into 'Barley Shot'.

Bärmann, (1) **Heinrich Joseph** (b. Potsdam 1784; d. Munich 1847). Famous clarinettist for whom Weber's clarinet works were composed. Composer especially for combinations including his instrument. (2) **Karl I** (b. Munich 1811; there d. 1885). Son of above and also famous clarinettist. Publ. Clarinet Method. (3) **Karl II** (b. Munich 1839; d. Boston, Mass., 1913). Pianist. Pupil of Liszt and others. Settled Boston 1881. Publ. piano pieces. Son of Karl I (above).

Barnard, Mrs. See *Claribel*.

Barnard's Collection. See *Cathedral Music*.

Barnby, Joseph (b. York 1838; d. London 1896). Trained R.A.M., then organist. Mus. director Eton Coll. 1875; Principal G.S.M. 1892. Great choral conductor; composer of anthems, services, hymn-tunes, oratorios, part-songs—all at one time highly popular and some still in use. Knighted 1892.

Barn Dance. An Amer. dance of rural origin, perhaps taking its name from the festivities usual in the building of a new barn. It is in simple quadruple time.

Barnett, (1) John (b. Bedford 1802; d. Cheltenham 1890). Of Ger. descent; father's original name 'Beer'. Successful boy vocalist on opera stage and later composer of stage music, especially opera *The Mountain Sylph* (1834). Last 50 years in Cheltenham as singing teacher. (2) **John Francis** (b. London 1837; d. 1916). Nephew of above. Became prof. of R.A.M. and eminent solo pianist, also successful and varied composer (cantata, *The Ancient Mariner*, 1867).

Barocco (It.), **Barock** (Ger.), **Baroque** (Fr.). 'Bizarre.' Applied to the elaborately fanciful 17th- and 18th-c. architecture of Germany and Austria and, by association, nowadays to the German and Austrian music of the same period (e.g. that of Bach; in some countries the name *Baroque Organ* is given to the organ of the Bach period). The current musical use of the word has none of the value judgement implied by Rousseau (in 1767) and Burney (in 1773), who used the word as meaning 'coarse' or 'uncouth'.

Barraqué, Jean (b. 1928). Composer, pupil of Messiaen, and pursuing still further the paths opened by that master.

Barraud, Henry (b. Bordeaux 1900). Studied Paris Conserv. from 1926 (states he was expelled for being too 'musically daring') and worked under Dukas, Aubert, &c. Orch. and choral works, chamber music, &c. In charge organization of music Paris International Exposition 1937. Mus. Director, Paris Radio, 1945.

Barre (Fr.). See *Capotasto*.

Barrel Organ. See *Mechanical Reproduction of Music* 10.

Barrère, Georges (b. Bordeaux 1876; d. Kingston, N.Y., 1944). Flautist. Trained Paris Conserv. Then in chief Paris orchs. In New York from 1905. Founded Barrère Wind Ensemble, Barrère Little Symphony, &c. Composed flute music, &c.

Barrett, Thomas A. See *Stuart, Leslie.*

Barri, Odoardo—real name Edward Slater (b. Dublin 1844; d. London 1920). Enormously popular composer of Eng. drawing-room songs (e.g. *The Boys of the Old Brigade*, 1874).

Barrington, Rutland—really George Rutland Fleet (b. Penge 1853; d. London 1922). Operatic bass. Début 1873. Joined D'Oyly Carte Co. and from 1877 a leading Gilbert and Sullivan exponent. After 1892 appeared in long succession of musical plays, e.g. *Geisha* 1896 and 1906. Paralytic seizure ended career 1919. Wrote for *Punch* and published 2 books of reminiscences (1908, 1911).

Barrios, Angel (b. Granada 1882). Violinist; composer for orch. and the stage; also of guitar music of a high class.

Barsanti, Francesco (b. Lucca abt. 1690; d. London abt. 1760). Settled London 1714, playing oboe and flute at opera. Then in Scotland, returning London abt. 1750 and playing viola in orchs. Some orch. compositions occasionally heard today.

Bartered Bride, The (Czech *Prodaná Nevěsta*; Ger. *Die verkaufte Braut*). 3-act light opera by Smetana. (Prod. Prague 1866; London 1895; New York 1909.)

Barth, Hans (b. Leipzig 1897; d. Jacksonville, Fla., 1956). Pianist and composer. Taken to U.S.A. at age 10. Became known as recitalist, &c., and held various teaching positions. Composed works employing microtones and invented quarter-tone piano.

Barthélemon, François Hippolyte (b. Bordeaux 1741; d. London 1808). Violinist and composer. Settled London 1764 and remained there with exception of continental tours and residence in Dublin 1771–3. Wrote operas and other stage music, violin pieces, &c.; also tune to Ken's Morning Hymn still found in all hymn collections.

Bartlet or **Bartlett, John** (end of 16th c. and beginning of 17th). Eng. lutenist and composer of songs of the ayre type (see *Madrigal*).

Bartlett, Ethel (b. London 1900). Pianist. Trained at R.A.M. Married fellow-student Rae Robertson (q.v.) and with him established high international reputation in interpretation of music for 2 pianos. Latterly resident U.S.A.

Bartók, Béla. (b. in Torontal district of Hungary, now in Rumania, 1881; d. New York 1945). Student of the conserv. of Budapest; as a young composer ardent admirer successively of Brahms, Liszt, Wagner, and Strauss. Collector of Hungarian, Slovak, and Rumanian folk songs, and later of Arab music. At 26 Prof. of his old conserv. His progress as composer was at first made difficult by lack of appreciation and even definite opposition, but in time this died down and he won his way to high rank internationally.

Compositions include stage works, choral and orch. music, string quartets, violin concerto and sonatas, a viola concerto, 3 piano concertos, &c., their style being often uncompromisingly 'modern' and individual.

See also *Amazing Mandarin*; *Cantata Profana*; *Mikrokosmos*; *Wooden Prince*; *Duke Bluebeard's Castle*; *Pianoforte Playing*.

Barton, William. Early 17th-c. clergyman whose metrical version of the Psalms (1644) went through many edns.; one of the earliest writers, moreover, of original hymns as distinct from mere psalm versifications.

Barylli, Walter (b. Vienna 1921). Violinist: début 1936; leader Vienna Philharmonic Orch.; Barylli Quartet.

Baryton. See *Viol Family* 3 g.

Basilar Membrane. See *Ear*.

Baskische Tänze (Ger.). Basque dances, such as the *Pordon Danza*, *Zortziko*, and *Ezcudantza* (see under these heads).

Baskische Trommel (Ger.). 'Basque drum', i.e. the tambourine (see *Percussion Family* 2 m).

Basoche, La (i.e. the ancient Guild of Lawyers). Popular Comic Opera by Messager. (Prod. Paris 1890; London 1891; New York 1893.)

Basques. Same as *Baskische Tänze* (see above). *Pas de Basque* (Fr.) is sometimes a general term with the same meaning, but it may indicate a particular dance of the Basque peasantry—one with very varied rhythms.

Bass (usually pron. 'base'). (1) The lowest part of the harmony. (2) The lowest of the male voices (see *Voice* 14, 16). (3) The lowest of any type of instrument.

Bassa (It. fem.). 'Low' or 'Bass' (q.v.).

Bassani (or Bassano, or Bassiani), (1) **Giovanni.** Venetian instrumental composer of the late 16th and early 17th cs.

(2) **Giovanni Battista** (b. Padua abt. 1657; d. Bergamo or Ferrara 1716). Fine violinist and popular composer of works for violin, operas, masses, &c.

Bass-Bar. In a bowed instrument the strip of wood glued under the belly along the line of the lowest string and supporting one foot of the bridge.

Bass Clarinet. See *Clarinet Family* b.

Bass Clef. See *Great Staff*; Table 4.

Bass Drum. See *Percussion Family* 2 k.

Basse (Fr.). 'Bass' (q.v.).

Basse chantante (Fr.). *Basso cantante* (see *Voice* 16).

Basse chiffrée, basse continue (Fr.). Figured bass (q.v. and cf. *basso continuo*).

Basse Danse (Fr.). An early dance type which became extinct in the 16th c. but was probably the ancestor of other dances which survived it (cf. *Branle*). The first word meaning 'low', it has been supposed that the name indicated humble origin, or (more plausibly) that it arose from the fact that the feet were generally kept low, i.e. were glided, not lifted (cf. *Haute Danse*). The time is generally simple duple but sometimes triple, and occasionally a mixture of the two. Sometimes the music falls into 3 parts:

(a) *Basse Danse*, (b) *Retour de Basse Danse* ('Return of the Basse Dance'), and (c) *Tordion* (or 'Tourdion').

Basse de Flandres or Bumbass. Much the same as *Bladder and String* (q.v.).

Basse d'harmonie (Fr.). Ophicleide (see *Cornett and Key Bugle Families*).

Basset Horn. See *Clarinet Family* f.

Bassettflöte(Ger.). A 17th- and 18th-c. name for a Recorder (see *Recorder Family*) of low pitch. Sometimes it was called *Bassflöte*.

Bassflicorno. See *Tuba Group* 4.

Bassflöte. See *Bassettflöte*.

Bass Flute. (1) See *Flute Family*. (2) Organ stop in pedal department; 8-foot length and pitch.

Bass Horn. See *Cornett and Key Bugle Families*.

Bassi (It.). Plur. of *Basso*, 'low', 'bass'.

Bassiani. See *Bassani*.

Basso (It. masc.). 'Low' or 'Bass' (q.v.).

Bass Oboe. See *Oboe Family* i.

Basso cantante. See *Voice* 16.

Basso continuo (It. 'Continuous bass'). Figured bass (q.v.) from which in concerted music the 17th- and 18th-c. harpsichordist played.

Basson (Fr.). Bassoon (see *Oboe Family* c).

Basson russe (Fr.). Russian bassoon, so called (see *Cornett and Key Bugle Families*).

Bassoon. (1) See *Oboe Family* c. (2) Organ *Reed Stop* (see *Organ* 2); of 16-foot length and pitch; generally in pedal department.

Bassoon, Double. See *Oboe Family* d.

Bassoon, Russian. See *Cornett and Key Bugle Families*.

Basso ostinato (It. 'Obstinate bass'). Ground bass (q.v.).

Basso profondo. See *Voice* 16.

Bassposaune (Ger.). Bass trombone (see *Trombone Family*).

Bass-Saite (Ger. 'Bass string'). The lowest string on any (bowed or plucked) instrument.

Bass Saxhorn. See *Tuba Group* 3.

Bass Staff. See under *Great Staff*.

Bass Trombone. See *Trombone Family*.

Basstrompete (Ger.). Bass trumpet (see *Trumpet Family* f).

Bass Trumpet. See *Trumpet Family* f.

Bass Tuba. See *Tuba Group* 1 b, 2 b, c.

Bass Viol. See *Viol Family* 2 c.

Bastardella, La. See *Agujari*.

Bastien und Bastienne. One-act Operetta by the 12-year-old Mozart. Libretto a transl. of Favart's parody on Rousseau's *Le Devin du village* (see *Rousseau*). (Prod. in the garden-theatre of Mesmer, the introducer of mesmerism, Vienna, 1768: never again performed until in Berlin 1890; since then in many languages and countries, including England 1894.)

Bat, The (Strauss). See *Fledermaus*.

Bate, Stanley (Richard) (b. Plymouth 1913; d. London 1959). Trained R.A.M.; at first pianist, then composition pupil of Vaughan Williams and Nadia Boulanger. In U.S.A. 1946–50. Composer of 4 symphonies, concertos, chamber music, incidental music, &c.

Bates, Joah (b. Halifax, Yorks, 1741; d. London 1799). Fellow King's Coll., Cambridge; then civil servant. Keen and competent musician; initiator and conductor Ancient Concert (q.v.); also one of initiators and conductor Commemoration of Handel (1784). Wife was Sarah Harrop.

Bateson, Thomas (b. abt. 1570; d. Dublin 1630). Organist of Chester Cathedral and then of Christ Church Cathedral, Dublin. Composer of fine madrigals.

Bath, Hubert (b. Barnstaple 1883; d. Uxbridge 1945). Composer of stage, film, and other (chiefly light) music. Was for some years in charge of park bands in London. Wrote 1st symphony for brass band, *Freedom*.

Batiste, Antoine (Édouard) (b. Paris 1820; there d. 1876). Paris organist; teacher of Solfeggio at Conserv. and author of books on the subject. Most widely known by organ compositions of the lighter type, especially a popular *Andante* which was long a world best-seller.

Baton. See *Conducting*.

Batten, Adrian (b. 1585–90; d. London 1637). Organist of St. Paul's Cathedral, London, and active composer of church music.

Batterie (Fr.). (1) The noisier percussion instruments. (2) Any rhythmic formula for the drums such as those used in the army for signalling.

Battishill, Jonathan (b. London 1738; there d. 1801). London organist, theatre musician, and composer for church, stage, and glee clubs, some of whose music is still heard. His fine anthem, 'O Lord, look down from Heaven', is famous.

Battistini, Mattia (b. Rome 1856; d. nr. there 1928). Operatic baritone of enormous European reputation; highly esteemed as exponent of *bel canto*; great popularity in Britain (never appeared in U.S.A.); last London appearances (in Queen's Hall recitals) 1922–3.

Battle Cry of Freedom ('We'll rally round the flag, boys!'). Words and music are by Dr. George Frederick Root (1820–95). Written at the time of the American Civil War it became a marching song of the Northern troops.

Battle Hymn of the Republic. See *John Brown's Body*.

Battle of Prague, The. See *Kotzwara*.

Battle of the Huns (Liszt). See *Hunnenschlacht*.

Battle of Victoria (Beethoven). See *Wellington's Victory*.

Battle Symphony (Beethoven). See *Wellington's Victory*.

Battre (Fr.). 'To beat': hence such expressions as *battre à deux temps*, 'to beat two in a bar'.

Battuta, A (It.). 'To the beat'—same as *A tempo*, i.e. return to normal speed (after a *rallentando* or *accelerando*).

Baudrier, Yves (b. Paris 1906). At first law student, then composer; founder of group, 'La Jeune France' (q.v.).

Bauer, (1) **Harold** (b. New Malden, Surrey, 1873; d. Miami 1951). From age 9 made frequent public appearances as violinist; then, 1892, as pianist (London newspaper notices show him within 3 weeks in that year as leader of string quartet, solo violinist, and piano recitalist). After some study with Paderewski appeared as pianist throughout Europe and U.S.A., settling in New York. Published many piano arrangements, &c.

(2) **Marion (Eugenie)** (b. Walla Walla, Washington State, 1887; d. South Hadley, Mass., 1955). Musical journalist, author, and lecturer; composer of orch., choral, and chamber music, &c.

Bauerncantate (Bach). See *Peasant Cantata*.

Bauernleier (Ger.). 'Hurdy-gurdy' (q.v.).

Bavarian Highlands (Elgar). See *Scenes from the Bavarian Highlands*.

Bax, Arnold Edward Trevor (b. London 1883; d. Cork 1953). Trained at R.A.M., then became known as prolific and valued composer of chamber, piano, choral, and orch. music (7 symphonies; concertos for piano, 'cello, viola, violin, &c.)—much of it with Celtic mystic tinge, originating in Irish sympathies. Hon. D.Mus., Oxford (1934), Durham (1935), Nat. Univ. Eire 1947. Knighted 1937; Master of the King's Musick 1942. K.C.V.O.

See also *Garden of Fand*; *Tintagel*.

Baylis, Lilian (1874–1937). See *Sadler's Wells*; *Victoria Hall*.

Bay of Biscay. This bold song comes from an opera *Spanish Dollars* (Covent Garden, 1805), by John Davy (q.v.); he is said to have taken the melody from some Negro sailors whom he heard singing it in London. The words are by Andrew Cherry, an actor and playwright of Irish birth and London fame.

Bay Psalm Book. See *Hymns and Hymn Tunes* 7.

Bayreuth. See *Wagner, Richard.*

Bazzini, Antonio (b. Brescia 1818; d. Milan 1897). Highly successful solo violinist and then ardent chamber music player. Head of Milan Conserv. 1882. Composer of popular violin solo, *La Ronde des lutins* ('The Dance of the Elves'), and other things.

B.B.C. British Broadcasting Corporation (see *Broadcasting of Music*, also *Alexandra Palace*).

B.B.C.M. See *Degrees and Diplomas* 2.

B.B.C. Symphony Orchestra. Founded 1930; cond. Boult; Sargent 1950; Schwarz 1957; Dorati 1963; C. Davis 1967; Boulez 1971.

B Dur (Ger.). The key of B flat major (not B major, cf. *B*).

Be (Ger.). The sign ♭ (see Table 7).

Beach, Amy Marcy. Mrs. H. H. A. Beach, *née* Cheney (b. in New Hampshire 1867; d. New York 1944). Won an early reputation as pianist and then became more widely known as composer. Her *Gaelic Symphony* is spoken of as the first symphony of importance produced in America.

Beale, William (b. Cornwall 1784; d. London 1854). Successively choirboy of Westminster Abbey; midshipman in Brit. Navy; Gentleman of Chapel Royal; Organist of Trinity Coll., Cambridge, and then of London suburban churches. Writer of glees, &c., some of them still popular.

Bear, The (Haydn). See *Ours, L'*.

Bearbeitet (Ger. 'worked-over'). 'Arranged.' *Bearbeitung*, 'arrangement' (q.v.).

Beard, (1) **John** (b. 1716; d. Hampton 1791). Famous operatic tenor (Macheath in *Beggar's Opera*, &c.). Also Handel's tenor in many oratorios.

(2) **Paul** (b. Birmingham 1901). Violinist appearing in public since age 6. Studied R.A.M. (later on staff). Chief violin in turn of many of chief Brit. orchs. (B.B.C. Symph. Orch. 1936–62.) O.B.E. 1952.

Bearded Gamba. See *Gamba* (organ stop).

Béarnaise, La. See *Messager*.

Beat. See *Acoustics* 15; *Rhythm*.

Beating Reed. See *Reed*.

Beatitudes, The. Oratorio by Franck. (1st perf. Paris 1879. Glasgow 1900; Cardiff 1902.)

Béatrice et Bénédict. Comedy-opera by Berlioz. Libretto by the composer, based on Shakespeare's *Much Ado*. (Prod. Baden 1862; Glasgow 1936.)

Beaucoup (Fr.). 'Much.'

Beautiful Blue Danube, The. The most popular of the 400 Viennese Waltzes of Johann Strauss, jun. (op. 314).

Beautiful Maid of the Mill (Schubert). See *Schöne Müllerin, Die*.

Beauty Stone, The. Romantic Opera by Sullivan. Libretto by Comyns Carr and Pinero. (Prod. Savoy Theatre, London, 1898.)

Bebend (Ger.). 'Trembling', i.e. *Tremolo* (q.v.).

Bebung (Ger. 'trembling'). A tremolo effect obtained by rocking the finger on a string of a bowed instrument or on a key of a clavichord (cf. *Bebend*, above).

Bécarre (Fr.). The natural sign (see Table 7).

Bechstein. Piano-making firm, founded Berlin 1856 (London branch 1879).

Beck, Conrad (b. Schaffhausen, Switzerland, 1901). Swiss composer long resident in Paris; has written chamber music, symphonies, concertos, &c., contrapuntal in texture and austere in tone. Since 1949 director music programmes Basle radio.

Beck. Short for *Becken*, 'cymbals'.

Becken (Ger.). 'Cymbals' (see *Percussion Family* 2 o).

Becker, John J. (b. Henderson, Ky., 1886; d. Wilmette, Ill., 1961). Engaged in various musical activities in St. Paul, Mo.; Prof. Mus. Barat Coll., Ill., 1943. His many orchestral and choral works have bold individuality, but attained few performances.

Beckwith, John Christmas (b. Norwich on Christmas Day 1750; there d. 1809). Brilliant organist of St. Peter Mancroft's Church, Norwich, and, finally, of the Cathedral; composer of church music.

Bécourt. See *Ça ira!*

Bedächtig Ger. 'careful', 'thoughtful'). 'Steady and unhurried.'

Bedarfsfall (Ger.). Lit. 'need-case'. So *Im Bedarfsfalle*, 'in case of need'.

Bedeutend (Ger.). 'Important', i.e. 'considerably'.

Bédos de Celles, Dom Francis (b. Caux 1709; d. Saint-Denis 1779). French Benedictine, famous as organ builder and author of important book, *L'Art du facteur d'orgues* ('The Art of the Organ-builder', 1766–8).

Bee, The ('L'Abeille'). See *Schubert, Franz* (of Dresden).

Bee-Bee-Bei. See *Rubbra.*

Beecham (Father and Son). Sir **Joseph** Beecham (d. 1916) was the proprietor of certain well-known pharmaceutical products and hence enabled to become a munificent patron of music. He was given baronetcy, his son **Thomas** (b. nr. Liverpool 1879; d. London 1961), who had been knighted in 1914, inheriting this. The latter, from 1905 onwards, was prominent as orch. and opera conductor, and impresario of opera (1909–20) and ballet. Introducer to London of the Russian Ballet (1911); propagandist for music of Delius, &c. As conductor his reputation was world-wide.

Bee's Wedding, The (Mendelssohn). See *Spinning Song.*

Beethoven, Ludwig van (b. Bonn 1770; d. Vienna 1827). The Shakespeare of music, reaching the heights and plumbing the depths of the human spirit—'Tone-poet', to use the term by which he expressed his own ambition.

He came of a musical family, his grandfather and father being musicians in the service of the Elector of Bonn. At 13 he himself became useful in the court music as orch. harpsichordist; at 17 the Elector sent him to Vienna, where he remained for 3 months, receiving some teaching from Mozart; at 22 he returned to that city, profiting by further teaching from Haydn and Albrechtsberger.

In Vienna he now remained, largely supported by a body of aristocratic music-lovers who valued his skill as pianist and his already evident genius as composer. Deafness overtook him soon after the age of 30, and at last became total, but this did not interfere with his activity as composer.

As an artist he stands supreme in several departments, the world's finest symphonies (see below) and overtures being amongst the 9 of each which he wrote, its finest string quartets amongst his 17 (see below), and its noblest piano sonatas amongst his 32 (see below), whilst his great Mass in D has no rival in power and feeling but the one in B minor of Bach. In his one opera *Fidelio* (q.v.) he made a contribution to the permanent repertory of the theatre.

See also under *Adelaide; An die ferne Geliebte; B-A-C-H; Calm Sea; Choral Fantasia; Christ on the Mount of Olives; Clementi; Concerto; Consecration of the House; Coriolanus Overture; Creation' Hymn; Diabelli Variations; Egmont Overture; Emperor Concerto; Funeral Marches; Ghost Trio; Hummel; In questa tomba; Jena Symphony; King Stephen; Kreutzer; Mass in D; Namensfeier Overture; Orchestra 2; Ox Minuet; Pianoforte Playing; Prometheus; Prometheus Variations; Rage over a Lost Penny; Ruins of Athens; Rule Britannia; Scherzo; Spring Sonata.*

Beethoven's Concertos are as follows:
PIANOFORTE. No. 1, C (op. 15. Really no. 2). No. 2, B flat (op. 19, composed before 1795. Really no. 1). No. 3, C minor (op. 37, composed 1800). No. 4, G (op. 58, composed abt. 1805). No. 5, E flat (op. 73, nicknamed 'Emperor', composed 1809). There are also the following: Early Concerto in D (one movement only, abt. 1790). Rondo in B flat (incomplete; finished by Czerny). Conzertstück (either never finished or latter part lost; 2 completions, by Joseph Hellmesberger in the 1870's and by Juan Manén more recently). Violin Concerto (see below) arranged by the composer himself.
VIOLIN. Concerto in D (op. 61, composed 1806).
PIANOFORTE, VIOLIN, AND VIOLONCELLO. Triple Concerto in C (op. 56, composed abt. 1804).

Beethoven's Pianoforte Sonatas number 32, ranging from op. 2 (publ. 1796) to op. 111 (composed 1822).

See *Adieux, Appassionata, Dramatic, Grande Sonate Pathétique, Hammerklavier, Moonlight Sonata, Pastoral Sonata, Waldstein.*

Beethoven's String Quartets (17 in number) are as follows: Op. 18, nos. 1–6, in F, G, D, C minor, A, and B flat (composed abt. 1798–1800). Op. 59, nos. 1–3, in F, E minor, and C (nicknamed the *Rasoumoffsky Quartets*, because dedicated to the Count of that name, Russian Ambassador at Vienna, and a keen Quartet player; composed before 1807). Op. 74 in E flat (nicknamed the *Harp Quartet* from the pizzicato arpeggios in the 1st movement; composed 1809). Op. 95 in F minor (composed 1810). Op. 127 in E flat (composed 1824). Op. 130 in B flat (composed 1825; finale 1826 to replace the original finale, the 'Great Fugue'; see below). Op. 131 in C sharp minor (composed 1826). Op. 132 in A minor (composed 1825). Op. 133 (*Grosse Fuge*, q.v., 'Great Fugue', originally composed as finale of op. 130). Op. 135 in F (composed 1826).

Beethoven's Symphonies are as follows: No. 1, in C (op. 21, 1st perf. 1800). No. 2, in D (op. 36, 1st perf. 1803). No. 3, in E flat (the *Eroica*, q.v., op. 55, composed 1804). No. 4, in B flat (op. 60, composed 1806). No. 5, in C minor (op. 67, 1st perf. 1808; cf. *Victory Symphony*). No. 6, in F (op. 68, 1st perf. 1808; see *Pastoral Symphony*). No. 7, in A (op. 92, composed 1812). No. 8, in F (op. 93, composed 1812). No. 9, in D minor (op. 125, composed 1823; see *Choral Symphonies*).

See also *Jena Symphony* and *Wellington's Victory* (sometimes called 'Battle Symphony').

Begeistert (Ger.). 'Inspired', 'enthused'; *Begeisterung*, 'inspiration', 'exaltation'.

Beggar's Opera. The pioneer Ballad Opera (see *Opera* 5), opening with a dialogue between a beggar (professing to be its author) and a player, and consisting of a spoken play of low life interspersed with ballads set to well-known folk and other tunes. Dialogue by the poet Gay; music chosen and arranged by Pepusch. At once a parody of It. opera and a political satire. (Prod. 1728; a famous revival was that of 1920 with the music reharmonized and reorchestrated by Frederic Austin.)

Other 20th-c. re-arrangements performed have been those of E. J. Dent (1944) and Benjamin Britten (1948). There was a sequel *Polly*, performance of which was forbidden by the Lord Chamberlain, so that it did not reach the stage until 1777. It, also, had an early 20th-c. revival (London 1922).

See also *Weill, Kurt*, for 'Die Dreigroschenoper'.

Beggar Student, The ('Der Bettelstudent'). Millöcker's most famous operetta; libretto by F. Zell and R. Genée—cf. *Boccaccio* by Suppé. (Prod. Vienna and New York 1883, London 1884.) Translated into many languages.

Begleiten (Ger.). 'To accompany.' Hence *Begleitung*, 'accompaniment'; *Begleitend*, 'accompanying'.

Behaglich (Ger.). 'Agreeably.'

Behend (Ger.). 'Nimble.' So *Behendig*, 'nimbly'; *Behendigkeit*, 'nimbleness'.

Beherrscher der Geister (Weber). See *Ruler of the Spirits*.

Beherzt (Ger.). 'Courageous.'

Behnke, Emil (b. Stettin 1836; d. London 1892). Had long London career as voice specialist and wrote important works on voice training, &c.

Beide (Ger.). 'Both.'

Beinahe (Ger.). 'Almost.'

Beinum, Eduard van (b. Arnheim, Holland, 1901; d. Amsterdam 1959). Conductor, Amsterdam Concertgebouw, &c. From 1949 for a time conductor of London Philharmonic Orch.

Beispiel (Ger.). 'Example.'

Beisser (Ger., 'biter'). 'Mordent' (see Table 12).

Beklemmt, Beklommen (Ger.). 'Oppressed.'

Belaief (Belaiev, Belaiew, Byelyayeff, and other transliterations of the Russian), **Mitrofan** (b. St. Petersburg 1836; there d. 1904). He was a well-to-do timber merchant who loved and practised music and made himself a central force in the nationalist musical movement, one of his chief services to that movement being the foundation of a publishing house.

See *Vendredis*.

Bel canto (It. 'beautiful song'). A term covering the remarkable qualities of the great 18th-c. It. singers, and suggesting rather performance in the lyrical style, in which tone is made to tell, than in the declamatory style. (See *Opera* 2.)

Belebend, Belebt (Ger.). 'Animating', 'animated'. *Belebter*, 'more animated'.

Belieben (Ger.). 'Pleasure', 'will'. So *nach Belieben* = *ad libitum* (q.v.) and *beliebig* = 'optional'.

Bell. (1) This popular and ubiquitous musical instrument varies in weight from over 100 tons to a fraction of an ounce. For public bells the most usual bell metal is a bronze of 13 parts copper to 4 parts tin: the shape and proportions are the result of very intricate calculations in order to secure good tone and tuning—the latter not only of the *Strike Note* with its attendant overtones (see *Acoustics* 6, 7) but also of the deep tone which persists after these have died away, i.e. the *Hum Note*, which should be an 8ve below the Strike Note. Some bell foundries have a long period of experience to guide them: the oldest one now existing is that of Messrs. Mears & Stainbank, of Whitechapel, London, which dates from 1570.

(2) There are 2 chief ways of sounding ordinary church bells, *Chiming* (the clapper moved mechanically just sufficiently to strike the side of the bell) and *Ringing* (in which the bell is swung round full circle).

(3) A *Ring* of church bells may consist of any number from 5 to 12. With 5 bells 120 variations of order, or *Changes*, are possible; with 12 bells they number almost 480 millions. *Change Ringing*, a characteristic British practice, is a hobby with many men. Various standard Changes are described by various traditional names, as 'Grandsire Triples', 'Bob Major', or 'Oxford Treble Bob'. The oldest society of Change Ringers in England is the Soc. of Coll. Youths, founded in 1637. London churches possess 100 peals.

(4) On the continent of Europe 'rings' are unknown but the *Carillon* is there an ancient institution—especially in Belgium and Holland. This consists of a series of anything up to 70 bells played by skilful artists from a manual and pedal console somewhat similar to that of an organ but more cumbrous. Tunes and simple accompanying harmonies can be performed. At the hours and their halves and quarters the carillon is set in operation by clockwork. There are now some carillons in Britain and in the U.S.A.

(5) *Tubular Bells* are often seen in the orch. (see *Percussion Family* 1 b) and are also now used (electrically operated from a keyboard) in church towers. *Electrotonic Bells* (cf. *Electric Musical Instruments*) are now being made.

(6) Many composers have introduced bell effects into their work, from Handel (*Saul*) and Bach (*Schlage doch*) to Wagner (*Parsifal*) and Elgar (*Carillon*). Many others have imitated bell effects in keyboard composition (Byrd, Liszt, Grieg, Debussy, &c.).

(7) *Handbells* are small bells with handles: they are arranged in pitch order on a table and played by several performers, each in charge of several bells. They are used for the practice of change ringers and also as an entertainment.

For mechanically sounded bells see *Mechanical Reproduction of Music* 1.

Bell Anthem. Purcell's *Rejoice in the Lord alway*. The popular name (which dates from the composer's lifetime) alludes to the pealing scale passages of the instrumental introduction.

Belle au bois dormant (Tchaikovsky). See *Sleeping Princess*.

Belle Hélène, La. Highly popular Opera of Offenbach. (Prod. Paris 1864; London 1866; New York 1867.)

Bellezza, Vincenzo (b. Bitonto, Bari, Italy, 1888; d. Rome 1964). Conductor. Trained Naples Conserv. Career, principally as opera conductor, in Rome, New York, London, Paris, South America, &c.

Bell Gamba. Organ stop. See *Gamba*.

Bell Harp. A sort of psaltery (q.v.) invented in the early 18th c. by John

Simcock, of Bath. It resembled (roughly) a zither or dulcimer, with 8 strings stretched over a sounding-board. The player swung it in the air, holding it with the fingers and plucking the strings with plectra attached to the thumbs. (The origin of the word 'bell' as a part of the name is doubtful; possibly the swinging motion suggested it.)

Bellicoso (It.). 'Warlike.' So, too, the adverb, *bellicosamente*.

Bellini, Vincenzo (b. Catania, Sicily, 1801; d. nr. Paris 1835). Celebrated and highly popular composer of opera of the days when vocal melody and vocal agility were its most valued constituents. Friend of Chopin, who admired his melodic gift.

See *Norma*; *Puritani di Scozia*; *Sonnambula*.

Bell Lyra. A portable form of Glockenspiel (see *Percussion Family* 1 c). It is mounted on a rod held perpendicularly in the left hand whilst the right hand holds the beater.

Bellows. See *Organ* 1.

Bellows and Tongs. One of the burlesque means of music-making common in the 18th c. Presumably the sound evoked was merely that of adroit rhythmic tapping. (For instruments of similar humble standing see *Saltbox*; *Bladder and String*; *Tongs and Bones*; *Marrow Bone and Cleaver*.)

Bell Rondo (Paganini). See *Campanella*.

Bells, The. See *Rachmaninof*.

Bells of Aberdovey. This is not a Welsh folk song, as claimed in very many books of such songs, but appears to be the composition of Charles Dibdin (q.v.). He published it as his in 1785 and it appeared many times subsequently in volumes of his songs, not figuring in any of the numerous Welsh collections before 1844. The false attribution probably springs from the fact that the song was first heard in Dibdin's Drury Lane opera, *Liberty Hall*, from the mouth of a comic Welsh character.

Bells of Corneville (Planquette). See *Cloches de Corneville*.

Bells of Zlonice. See *Dvořák's Symphonies*.

Belly. The upper surface of a stringed instrument, over which the strings are stretched.

Belmont, John. See *Pianoforte*.

Belshazzar. Oratorio by Handel. (1st perf. London 1745.)

Belshazzar's Feast. (1) Oratorio by Walton. Text compiled by Osbert Sitwell. (1st perf. Leeds Fest. 1931.) (2) Suite for small orch. by Sibelius (1906: for play by Hjalmar Procope).

Belustigend (Ger.). 'Amusing', 'gay'.

Bemberg, Hermann-Emmanuel— also known as **Henri** (b. Paris 1859; d. Berne 1931). Trained under Dubois and Massenet. Composer of operas and of successful songs in the lighter Fr. style.

Bémol (F.), **bemolle** (It.). 'Flat' (see Table 7).

Ben, bene (It.). 'Well' or 'much'.

Benda, Georg (or Jiri) **Antonin** (b. Alt-Benatek, Bohemia, 1722; d. Köstritz 1795). Came of a remarkable musical family of whom 7 or 8 members can be found in larger books of reference. As a composer he is particularly important for his contribution to melodrama (q.v.).

Bene (It.). 'Well' or 'much'.

Benedicite. *The Song of the Three Holy Children* (Shadrach, Meshach, and Abednego) whilst in Nebuchadnezzar's fiery furnace. It is not in the Hebrew version of the book of Daniel, but comes from the Septuagint, or early Greek translation of the Old Testament. It is one of the canticles of the Anglican service (see *Common Prayer*) and from its form it presents something of a problem as to musical setting.

'Benedicite', by Vaughan Williams, for Soprano, Chorus, and Orch. (Prod. Leith Hill Fest. 1929); combines the text of the canticle with a poem by J. Austin (1613–69).

Benedict, Julius (b. Stuttgart 1804; d. London 1885). Son of a Jewish banker and pupil of Weber; opera conductor successively in Vienna,

Naples, and London, in which last city (1835) he settled; successful composer of operas (especially *The Lily of Killarney*, q.v.), oratorios, cantatas, &c. Knighted 1871.

Benediction. A blessing such as that with which a service ends: more specifically an informal rite in the Roman Catholic Church, closing the office (see *Tantum ergo* and *O salutaris hostia*).

Benedictus. As a single word this has two applications. (1) In the Roman Catholic Mass it means the *Benedictus qui venit*, i.e. simply the words 'Blessed is he that cometh in the name of the Lord', which complete the *Sanctus* section of the Mass (see *Mass*; also *Common Prayer*). (2) It is also applied to the song of Zacharias (Luke 1. 68 et seq.), 'Blessed be the Lord God of Israel', which is sung daily at Lauds (q.v.) in Roman Catholic churches and in the English Prayer Book occurs in the Order for Morning Prayer (see *Common Prayer*).

Beneplacito, Beneplacimento (It.). 'Good pleasure.' Preceded by the words *A suo* ('At one's') this has the same sense as *Ad libitum* (q.v.).

Benet, John. See *Bennet*.

Benevoli, Orazio (b. Rome 1605; d. there 1672). Of French extraction, he held various church music posts, chiefly in Rome, and from 1646 at the Vatican. His works include masses for multiple choirs in the Venetian manner.

Ben-Haim, Paul—originally Frankenburger (b. Munich 1897). Israeli composer (emigrated 1933). Works include symphonies, a piano concerto, chamber music, and songs.

Benjamin, Arthur L. (b. Sydney, N.S.W., 1893; d. London 1960). Pianist and composer. Studied R.C.M.; returned to native country, and then settled in London as a piano prof. at the College. Composed music in many forms, including some for films, a symphony, and 4 operas.

Benjamin Cosyn's Virginal Book. A MS. collection of music, chiefly for virginal (see *Harpsichord Family*) made (1622–43) by Benjamin Cosyn, organist of Dulwich Coll. and then of the

Charterhouse. It is now in the Brit. Museum. It was publ. in 1923.

Bennet (or Benet), John (late 16th and early 17th c.). Life circumstances obscure but remembered as the composer of fine madrigals.

Bennett, (1) William Sterndale (b. Sheffield 1816; d. London 1875). Came of a musical family. At 8 became choirboy at King's Coll., Cambridge; at 10 passed on to the R.A.M., where 7 years later Mendelssohn found him and, struck with his powers, invited him to Germany; here Schumann wrote enthusiastically of him. Later life did not fulfil this early promise, perhaps because it was loaded with the labours of pianoforte teaching, the Principalship of the R.A.M., the Professorship of Music at Cambridge, and much conducting, to all of which he conscientiously bent his full powers. He was knighted in 1871 and is buried in Westminster Abbey.

Work most performed is probably his oratorio, *The Woman of Samaria* (q.v.), but the best of him is probably to be found in the works of 30 years earlier, as, for instance, the delicate overtures, *The Naiads* (1836) and *The Wood Nymphs* (1837). (See also *May Queen*.)

(2) **Joseph** (b. Berkeley, Glos., 1831; d. Purton, Glos., 1911). Critic of *Daily Telegraph* and author of many oratorio libretti for Brit. composers and of various books.

(3) **Robert Russell** (b. Kansas City, Mo., 1894). Widely known by his symphony *Abraham Lincoln* (1931) and succeeding works. Much associated with musical comedy and film and broadcasting activities, and known as a skilful arranger and orchestrator.

(4) **Richard Rodney** (b. Broadstairs 1936). Trained at R.A.M. and under Boulez. Composer of an opera (*The Mines of Sulphur*, 1965), a symphony (1966), and other orch. and chamber music works.

Benoît, Peter (Léopold Léonard) (b. Harlebeke, Flanders, 1834; d. Antwerp 1901). Stands as one of the chief promoters of the Flemish musical movement, in the interests of which he founded a school of music at Antwerp, and wrote propagandist articles and pamphlets, and composed choral works to libretti in the Flemish language. Amongst works are a *Rubens Cantata* (1877), calling for huge resources, including the bells of Antwerp Cathedral, and a *Children's Oratorio*, in which effective use is made of a large choir of children.

Benvenuto Cellini. Romantic opera by Berlioz. (A failure on Paris production 1838; revived at Weimar by Liszt 1852; London 1853. The Overture is often heard.)

Bequadro (It.). The natural sign (see Table 7).

Bequem (Ger.). 'Comfortable' = *Commodo* (q.v.).

Bercement (Fr. substantive). 'Rocking', 'lulling', 'swaying'.

Berceuse (Fr. *Bercer*, 'to rock to sleep'). A lullaby or an instrumental composition (in compound duple time) suggesting such. The popular piano piece of this name, and in this style, by Chopin, is his op. 57 (1844).

Berceuse de Jocelyn (Godard). See *Jocelyn*.

Bereite vor (Ger.). 'Make ready', 'prepare' (such-and-such an organ stop).

Bereits (Ger.). 'Already', 'previously'.

Berezovsky (Beresowsky, &c.), (1) **Maxim** (b. in Ukraine 1745; d. St. Petersburg 1777). As he had a fine voice Catharine the Great sent him to study in Italy (cf. *Bortniansky*). On return he tried to obtain a position from which he could reform the music of the Russian Church, and, failing, killed himself in a fit of madness. He left some operas, church music, and songs.

(2) **Nicolai** (b. St. Petersburg 1900; d. New York 1953). Violinist in Moscow and then in New York Philharmonic Orch. 1922–7. Orchestral conductor, composer of symphonies, concertos for viola and for 'cello, chamber music, &c.

Berg, (1) **Alban** (b. Vienna 1885; there d. 1935). He was a disciple of Schönberg and a leading composer of his school. He wrote chamber music, orch. music, &c., but the work that attracted the greatest public attention was the opera *Wozzeck* (q.v.); he left unfinished another opera *Lulu* (q.v.).

See also *Note-row*.

(2) **Natanael** (b. Stockholm 1879; there d. 1957). By profession an army veterinary surgeon yet long President of the Soc. of Swedish Composers, being himself composer of a number of operas, ballets, choral works, &c.

Bergamasque (Fr.), **bergamasca** (It.). See *Bergomask*.

Berganza, Teresa (b. Madrid 1934). Operatic mezzo-soprano. Début Madrid 1955; Glyndebourne 1958; London 1960; New York 1962.

Berger, (1) **Francesco** (b. London 1834; there d. 1933). His life of almost a century embraced a long career of piano teaching, the composition of piano pieces and songs and literary-musical works. For nearly 30 years he served as Secretary of the Philharmonic Soc.

(2) **Erna** (b. Dresden 1900). Operatic soprano, of high reputation in such Mozart roles as the 'Queen of the Night' in the *Magic Flute*.

(3) **Arthur** (b. New York 1912). Composer and writer on music; pupil of Piston, Nadia Boulanger, and Milhaud. Some years as teacher and musical journalist in New York, then on staff of Brandeis Univ. He has written chamber music, songs, and other things; a book on Copland, and many critical pieces.

Bergerette (Fr. *berger*, 'shepherd'). A shepherd's song or simple composition supposed to be in the style of such.

Bergliot (Grieg). Recitation to orch. accompaniment: poem by Björnsen (op. 42).

Bergomask (Eng.), **bergamasque** (Fr.), or **bergamasca** (It.). Originally a peasant dance from the district around Bergamo in North Italy: it was usually in simple duple time. However, the term has sometimes been used by composers without any definite significance.

Bergonzi, Carlo (b. Cremona abt. 1683; there d. 1747). Maker of violins in Stradivarius style; succeeded by his son and grandsons.

Bergsma, William (b. Oakland, Calif., 1921). Composer. Trained Stanford Univ. and Eastman School; pupil of Hanson and B. Rogers. Many prizes. On staff Juilliard School from 1946; Prof. Washington Univ., Seattle, 1963. Compositions, mostly lyrical, contrapuntal, and unassertive, include orchestral works, chamber music, and an opera, *The Wife of Martin Guerre* (1955).

Bergsymphonie (Liszt). See *Ce qu'on entend.*

Beringer, Oscar (b. nr. Baden, Germany, 1844; d. London 1922). Enjoyed a highly successful early career as pianist, and then became a leading London piano teacher (on staff of R.A.M.). A number of his compositions were at one time known to the public.

Berio, Luciano (b. Oneglia 1925). Composer (pupil of Ghedini and Dallapiccola) whose orchestral and chamber music works, of the most advanced school, have aroused heated discussion. As an employee of the Italian radio, he has organized radio and other concerts for the propagation of contemporary music, and has special interest in electrophonic music.

Bériot, (1) Charles Auguste de (b. Louvain 1802; d. Brussels 1870). One of the most celebrated violinist virtuosi of his period, also mechanic, landscape painter, and sculptor. The great contralto, Malibran, was his first wife and he was her second husband. The last 12 years of his life were spent in inactivity through blindness and paralysis of his left arm. He left 7 violin concertos, a number of pieces for 2 violins, &c., as also a *Violin School* which enjoyed much popularity. For son see below. See also *Osborne, G. A.* (2) **Charles Wilfrid de** (b. Paris 1833; d. London 1914). Son of above, a fine pianist and, as Prof. of the Paris Conserv., teacher of Granados, Ravel, and other musicians who achieved fame. He wrote piano concertos, &c.

Berkeley, Lennox Randal Francis (b. nr. Oxford 1903). Partly of Fr. descent and musical education. Composer of piano, chamber, orch., and choral music, &c. Also operas, *Dinner*

Engagement (1952), and *Nelson* (1954). C.B.E. 1957.

See *Jonah.*

Berlin, Irving—originally Baline (b. Russia 1888). Came to U.S.A. as child. Composer of quantities of highly popular songs (e.g. *Alexander's Ragtime Band* 1911), musical comedies, film music, &c. See *God bless America.*

Berliner, Emile. See *Gramophone* 2.

Berlin Philharmonic Orchestra. Founded 1882. Conductors include Klindworth (1884), Nikisch (1897), Furtwängler (1922), and Karajan (1954).

Berlioz, Louis Hector—known merely as Hector (b. nr. Grenoble 1803; d. Paris 1869). The greatest musical figure in the Fr. romantic movement. Shakespeare was a passion with him, and so were the Brit. romantic writers, such as Scott, Moore, and Byron.

In youth he was sent by his father, a doctor, to study medicine in Paris, but there studied music instead, winning at a fifth attempt the much-coveted Rome Prize.

His compositions tended to the grandiose, employing large resources (e.g. *Te Deum, Requiem*), and sometimes to the gruesome (e.g. *Fantastic Symphony*, with its 'March to the Scaffold' and its 'Witches' Sabbath'). The value of his work is a matter of eternal dispute, some finding it commonplace and naïve and others maintaining that when it is performed with understanding very high qualities reveal themselves. He introduced the principle of the *Idée fixe* ('Fixed idea'), a recurring theme, common to all the movements of a composition but varied in shape and treatment according to the fluctuating demands of the dramatic scheme (cf. *Metamorphosis of Themes*; *Leading Motive*, s.v. *Wagner*).

In addition to the numerous compositions there remain many volumes of literary production, partly the result of a quarter of a century's work as music critic of the *Journal des Débats*; the important *Treatise on Orchestration* must also be mentioned.

Amongst his many journeys abroad in his capacity of conductor (usually of his own works) were 3 to London, in 1848, 1852, and 1855.

See also *Béatrice et Bénédict*; *Benvenuto Cellini*; *Carnaval romain*; *Childhood of Christ*; *Corsaire*; *Fantastic Symphony*; *Faust*; *Francs juges*; *Funeral Marches*; *Harold in Italy*; *King Lear*; *Lélio*; *Octo-Bass*; *Opera* 3; *Rakoczy March*; *Requiem*; *Rob Roy Overture*; *Romeo and Juliet*; *Symphonie funèbre et triomphale*; *Symphony*; *Te Deum*; *Troyens*; *Waverley*.

Bernac, Pierre (b. Paris 1899). Baritone vocalist. Sensitive and artistic concert singer; frequently associated in joint recitals with Poulenc (q.v.).

Bernard, Anthony (b. London 1891; there d. 1963). Studied under Holbrooke and Ireland. Organist, piano accompanist, and conductor. Conductor of British National Opera Co. (1926), at Shakespeare Memorial Theatre, Stratford-on-Avon (1932–42), Canterbury and Cambridge fests., of London Chamber Singers and of London Chamber Orch., which he founded in 1921, reviving much old music.

Berners, Lord Gerald Hugh Tyrwhitt-Wilson (b. Bridgnorth 1883; d. London 1950). Entered diplomatic service, composing under name of Gerald Tyrwhitt until he succeeded to the barony of Berners in 1918. Amongst compositions are the one-act opera *Le Carrosse du Saint Sacrement* (Paris 1924), a number of ballets (see *Triumph of Neptune*), and smaller things; in these there is evident a sense of irony, and some appear to be of the nature of parody. Held London exhibitions of his paintings and published literary works of an autobiographical character.

Bernstein, Leonard (b. Lawrence, Mass., 1918). Studied at Harvard and Curtis Institute. Pianist, orch. conductor of great popularity (New York Philharmonic 1958–69), and skilful composer of lively ballets (*Fancy Free*, q.v., 1944) and musical comedies (*On the Town*, 1944; *Candide*, 1957; *West Side Story*, 1958), as well as symphonies (*Jeremiah*, 1944; *The Age of Anxiety*, 1949) and other serious works.

Bersag Horn or **Bersaglieri Bugle.** Bugle (q.v.) with a single valve, lowering the pitch a 4th. Made in different sizes. Became popular with bugle bands during the 1914–18 war. Presumably of It. origin (*Bersaglieri* = a sharpshooter corps of It. army).

Berté, Heinrich (1858–1924). See *Dreimäderlhaus*.

Bertini, Henri Jérôme (b. London 1798; d. nr. Grenoble 1876). Prolific composer for the piano, and especially of piano studies which have long been much used by teachers of the instrument.

Bertrand, René. See *Electric Musical Instruments* 1.

Beruhigen (Ger.). 'To make restful.' So *beruhigt*, 'restful'; *beruhigter*, 'more restful'; *beruhigend*, 'becoming restful'; *beruhigt*, 'become restful' (past participle); *Beruhigung*, 'calming' (noun).

Berwald, Franz Adolf (b. Stockholm 1796; there d. 1868). Violinist. Composer of 6 symphonies, 2 operas, chamber music, and songs. Works much praised by some who know them.

Bes (Ger.). B double flat (see Table 7).

Beschleunigen (Ger.). To 'speed up'; hence the adj. *beschleunigt*, &c.

Beseelt (Ger.). 'Animated.'

Bessy Bell and Mary Gray. See *Vicar of Bray*.

Best, William Thomas (b. Carlisle 1826; d. Liverpool 1897). Recognized as the greatest concert organist of his period, the chief centre of his activities being the St. George's Hall, Liverpool, of which he was organist from 1855 to 1894. Arranged much orch. and other music for his instrument.

His manners were independent and his utterances caustic and many tales illustrating these traits are still current.

Bestimmt (Ger.). (1) 'Decided' in style. (2, applied to a particular line in the score) 'Prominent'.

Betend (Ger.). 'Praying.'

Bethlehem. Choral-drama by Boughton. Libretto based on medieval Coventry Play. (Prod. Glastonbury 1916.)

Bethlehem, Pa. See *Festival*; *Bach Choir*.

Betont (Ger.). 'Stressed', 'emphasized'. **Betonung,** 'accentuation'.

Betrübnis (Ger.). 'Sadness.' **Betrübt,** 'saddened'.

Bettelstudent. See *Beggar Student.*

Betti, Adolfo (b. Bagni di Lucca 1873; there d. 1950). Violinist. Trained Liège Conserv. 1st violin Flonzaley Quartet (see *Coppet*) throughout its existence (1903–29).

Bevin, Elway (end of 16th and beginning of 17th cs.). Organist of Bristol Cathedral, composer of church music still performed, and author of a noted book on musical theory.

Beweglich (Ger.). 'Agile.' So *Beweglichkeit,* 'agility'. **Bewegt.** (1) 'Moved', i.e. 'speeded'. (2) 'Moved', i.e. emotionally. **Bewegter.** 'Quicker.' **Bewegung.** (1) 'Rate of motion', 'speed'. (2) 'Emotion.' (3) 'Com-motion.'

Bianca. (It. 'White'). Minim or Half-note (see Table 3).

Bianca. Opera by Henry Hadley. (Prod. New York 1918.)

Bibelorgel, Bibelregal (Ger.). Bible Regal (see *Reed-Organ Family* 1).

Biber, Heinrich Ignaz Franz von (b. Wartenberg, Bohemia, 1644; d. Salzburg 1704). Great violinist and con-siderable composer for his instrument.

Bible Regal. See *Reed-Organ Family* 1.

Biblical Songs. By Dvořák (op. 99, 1894). Ten settings of passages from the Psalms.

Biches, Les. Ballet by Poulenc. (Prod. Monte Carlo 1926.)

Bicinium (Lat.) A two-voice song.

Bien (Fr.). (1) 'Well.' (2) 'Very.'

Biene, Auguste van (b. Holland 1850; d. England 1913). Violoncellist. Came to London as child and played in streets; discovered by Sir Michael Costa (q.v.). Composed the enorm-ously popular *The Broken Melody* and played it (in music halls, &c.) over 6,000 times.

Biggs, E. Power (b. Westcliff-on-Sea 1906). Trained R.A.M. Notable career as concert organist in U.S.A. (naturalized 1938), specializing in authentic perfs. of older works, often on reconstructions of old instruments.

Bigophone, Bigotphone. Improved mirliton (q.v.) introduced by Bigot, a Frenchman, in the 1880's. Often made up to resemble the various brass instru-ments.

Bihari, János (1764–1827). See *Rákóczy March.*

Bilitis, Chansons de (Debussy). See *Chansons.*

Billings, William. See *Hymns and Hymn Tunes* 7.

Billington, Elizabeth—*née* Weichsel (b. London abt. 1768; d. nr. Venice 1818). Soprano. Youthful prodigy as pianist and composer. Became highly popular opera prima donna. Subject of some scandalous false 'Memoirs' (1792) to which she replied with *An Answer to the Memoirs.*

Billy Budd. 4-act opera by Britten. Libretto by E. M. Forster and Eric Crozier, after Melville. (Prod. London 1951; New York television 1952.)

Billy the Kid. 'Character-ballet' by Copland (1938). Also Suite derived therefrom.

Binary Form (Simple and Com-pound). See *Form* 1 and 3.

Binchois, Gilles (b. abt. 1400; d. Soignies 1460). Soldier who turned musician, becoming a chaplain to Philip the Good and composing church music and chansons (q.v.).

Bind. See *Tie or Bind.*

Binet, Jean (b. Geneva 1893; d. Trélex-sur-Nyon 1960). Well-known Swiss composer of choral, orch., and chamber works; pupil of Jaques-Dalcroze and Bloch. Taught in U.S.A. and Belgium.

Bing, Rudolf (b. Vienna 1902). After administrative experience in German opera houses he came to England (naturalized 1946), becoming manager of Glyndebourne (q.v.) in 1935 and mus. director of the Edinburgh Festival in 1947. Gen. Manager of the Metropo-litan Opera 1949–72; knighted 1971.

Bingham, Seth (b. Bloomfield, N.J., 1882; d. New York 1972). Organist (pupil of Widor and Guilmant) and teacher of composition (Columbia

Univ.). Composer of choral, orch., and chamber works, &c.

Birchall, Robert (d. London 1819). Music publisher (est. abt. 1784) and concert manager.

Bird Organ. See *Mechanical Reproduction of Music* 6.

Bird Quartet (Haydn). See *Vogelquartett*.

Birds, The (*Gli Uccelli*). Suite for Small Orch. by Respighi. Based on 17th- and 18th-c. bird-pieces for lute and for harpsichord. Five movements —*Prelude, Dove, Hen, Nightingale, and Cuckoo.* (1st perf. São Paulo, Brazil, 1927; Cincinnati 1928.)

Birmingham Festival. See *Festival.*

Birmingham and Midland Institute School of Music. Developed originally from the penny classes of Richard Rickard in singing (1864) and violin (1882). (The Midland Inst. itself, a general educational organization, had been incorporated in 1854.) Principal 1900, Bantock; 1934, A. K. Blackall; 1945, C. M. Edmunds; 1956, Sir Steuart Wilson; 1960, Gordon Clinton.

Birmingham, City of, Orchestra. Founded 1920. First conductor Appleby Matthews (q.v.). Then Boult 1924; Heward 1930; Weldon 1943; Schwarz 1951; Panufnik 1957; Rignold 1960; Louis Fremaux 1969.

Birthday of the Infanta. Ballet by J. A. Carpenter, after Oscar Wilde. (Prod. Chicago 1919; Suite based on it 1920.) Also Dance-Pantomime composed by Schreker.

Bis (Fr. 'twice'). (1—at a concert) 'Encore!' (2—in a score) 'Repeat the passage'.

Bis (Ger.). 'Until.'

Bisbigliato (It.). 'Whispered.'

Biscroma (It.). Demisemiquaver or thirty-second note (see Table 3).

Bishop, (1) **Henry (Rowley)** (b. London 1786; there d. 1855). Famous London opera conductor and composer, and Prof. of Music successively at the Univs. of Edinburgh and Oxford. Of his very many glees some are still sung and the whole English-singing

world knows his song *Home, Sweet Home* (q.v.).

In 1842 Queen Victoria knighted him.

(2) **Thomas Brigham.** See *John Brown's Body.*

Bispham, David (Scull) (b. Philadelphia 1857; d. New York 1921). Operatic and concert baritone. Pupil of Lamperti, &c. Prominent in Wagner roles. Latterly abandoned opera for very successful recital work.

Bitonality. See *Harmony* 3.

Bittend (Ger.). 'Entreating.'

Bittner, Julius (b. Vienna 1874; there d. 1939). At first lawyer, and as such successful, but turned to music and composed, with equal success, operas, songs, chamber music, &c., as well as editing a musical journal.

Bizet, Georges—really Alexandre César Léopold (b. Paris 1838; there d. 1875). At the Paris Conserv. won the Rome Prize. On return to Paris made efforts to win recognition as opera composer, producing *The Pearl Fishers* (see *Pêcheurs de perles*), *The Fair Maid of Perth* (see *Jolie fille de Perth*), and *Djamileh* (q.v.). The real 'hit' came with *Carmen* (Paris, 1875; based on Mérimée's story), but success was not immediate and the composer died three months after the first perf. and too early to realize that he had 'done it at last'. (Productions in 1878 in London, Dublin, New York, and Philadelphia. See *Nietzsche.*)

Incidental music to Daudet's play, *L'Arlésienne* (q.v.), overture to Sardou's *Patrie*, two suites, *Rome* and *Children's Games* (see *Jeux d'enfants*), and a Symphony in C, are all tuneful and attractively scored.

Bizzarro (It.). 'Bizarre', 'whimsical'.

Björling, Jussi (b. Stora Tuna, Sweden, 1911; d. Stockholm 1960). Tenor vocalist. Earliest appearances in U.S. with family vocal quartet (including father and 2 brothers). Then studied Royal Opera School, Stockholm, making operatic début in that city 1930. From 1932 sang in Scandinavian cities, Dresden, Prague, Paris, Salzburg, Buenos Aires, &c. Also appearances in U.S. from 1937; later there resident.

Blacher, Boris (b. Newchwang, China, 1903). German composer, trained in Berlin. Active as teacher; on staff Berlin Hochschule from 1948 (director 1953). Works, in closely organized 'mathematical' style, include several operas, as well as orch. pieces and chamber music.

Black Bottom. Sort of foxtrot (q.v.) which had short ballroom career in U.S.A. and Great Britain during the 1920's.

Black Dyke Band. Brass band, founded 1855, in connexion with mills of same name in village of Queensbury, Yorkshire. Has always held high place in band world, winning many prizes and touring both sides of the Atlantic.

Black Domino, The (Auber). See *Domino Noir*.

Black-eyed Susan. Words of this song are by Gay (abt. 1720). There have been a number of different tunes to it, the one now known being by Leveridge (q.v.).

Black Key Étude. No. 5 (in G flat major) of Chopin's 12 *Grandes Études* for piano (op. 10; publ. 1833). The right hand confines itself to the black keys.

Black Knight, The. Cantata by Elgar. Setting of Longfellow's transl. of Uhland. (1st perf. Worcester Choral Soc. 1893.)

Black Pudding. The Serpent (see *Cornett and Key Bugle Families*).

Blacksmith. See *Greensleeves*.

Bladder and String. One of grotesque means of music-making common in the 18th c. Hogarth's print, *The Beggar's Opera Burlesqued*, shows it to have consisted of a 5-foot pole held in one hand, with an inflated bladder attached two-thirds of the length down, and a single string passing over this to the two ends of the pole and 'bowed' by some sort of a stick held in the other hand. (For instruments of similar humble standing see *Saltbox*; *Bellows and Tongs*; *Tongs and Bones*; *Marrow Bone and Cleaver*.)

Blagrove Family. (1) **Richard.** Nottingham violinist; published *New and Improved System of Playing the Violin* (1828). (2) **William.** Also Nottingham violinist and brother of above (d. London 1858). (3) **Henry Gamble** (b. Nottingham 1811; d. London 1872). Violinist. Son of Richard. Appeared in public at age 5. Trained R.A.M. and in Germany under Spohr. 'A recognized leader and solo player at all the highest concerts in England' (*Mus. Times* obituary). (4) **Richard Manning** (b. Nottingham 1826; d. London 1895). Trained R.A.M. (later on staff). Became a leading viola player and noted performer on (and composer for) concertina; also piano accompanist. (5) **Arthur Richard** (d. Ashtead, Surrey, 1946). 'Cello player. Pupil of Piatti. Son of (4). (6) **Stanley F.** (d. Guildford 1943). Violinist. Also son of (4). (7) **Mrs. Richard**—*née* Freeth (d. 1899). Pianist. Trained Paris. Wife of (4).

Blanc, Giuseppe. See *Giovinezza*.

Blanche (Fr. 'White'). The minim or half-note (see Table 3).

Blanik (Smetana). See *My Fatherland*.

Blasinstrumente (Ger. 'blowing instruments'). Wind instruments.

Blasis, Carlo. Great early 19th-c. ballet-master, whose academy at Milan became the most celebrated in Europe. He spent some time in England.

Blasmusik (Ger. 'blowing music'). Music of wind instruments.

Blech (Ger. 'Sheet metal'). The Brass. *Blechmusik*, 'Brass band'.

Blech, (1) **Leo** (b. Aachen 1871; d. Berlin 1958). Conductor. Trained Berlin Hochschule. Known chiefly as opera conductor in German cities. (Berlin Opera 1909–37; 1949–54). Also composer of operas, &c.
(2) **Harry** (b. London 1910). Violinist and conductor. Formed Blech String Quartet 1937; London Symphonic Players 1946; London Mozart Players 1949.

Bleiben (Ger.). 'To remain.' So *Bleibt*, 'Remains', in organ music, means that the stop in question remains in use.

Blending the Registers (in vocal practice). So gaining control of the voice that the break between one register and another (see *Voice* 4) is hardly noticeable.

Blessed Damozel, The (*La Damoiselle élue*). Setting by Debussy (1887) of Rossetti's poem. For female voices (solo and chorus) and orchestra.

Blessing and Honour. See *Lob und Ehre*.

Blest Pair of Sirens. See *Parry, C. H. H.*

Bliss, Arthur (b. London 1891). Studied at Cambridge (B.A., B.Mus.) and at R.C.M. under Stanford and Vaughan Williams.

As composer has exhibited independence, sometimes writing for unusual instrumental combinations. His fresh and vigorous works include large-scale choral and orch. compositions, film music, and ballet music. For a short time Prof. of Music in the Univ. of California, Musical Director of the B.B.C. 1942-4. Hon. D.Mus. Edinburgh, London, Cambridge; knighted 1950; Master of Queen's Music 1953; K.C.V.O. 1969; C.H. 1971.

See also *Adam Zero*; *Checkmate*; *Colour Symphony*; *Miracle in the Gorbals*; *Morning Heroes*; *Olympians*; *Pastoral*.

Blitheman, William (d. 1591). Famous organist of Queen Elizabeth's Chapel Royal; composer of church music and virginal music—the latter important for its influence on his successor in the organistship, John Bull.

Blitzstein, Marc (b. Philadelphia 1905; d. Fort-de-France, Martinique, 1964). Of Russian Jewish descent. Studied Univ. Philadelphia, Curtis Inst., and Berlin; Guggenheim Fellowship 1940. Composer of highly 'modernistic' and experimental works for stage, films, orch., &c. (see *Cradle will Rock*).

Bloch, (1) **Ernest** (b. Geneva, Switzerland, 1880; d. Portland, Ore., 1959). Trained in Switzerland, Belgium, Germany, and France. Opera *Macbeth* (perf. Paris 1910) called attention to his gifts. Some time active as conductor in Switzerland and then went to U.S.A. as conductor for the dancer, Maud Allan, and there remained (naturalized 1924), occupying various educational positions, actively composing music often based on Jewish themes and expressive of his racial sympathies, and gradually accumulating a body of warm admirers scattered through various countries, many of whom feel that the world has not yet done him full justice.

See also *Schelomo*; *Winter-Spring*.

(2) **Suzanne** (b. Geneva 1907). Daughter of (1). Studied with her father, and with Sessions and Nadia Boulanger. Lecture-recitalist on old music; res. New York.

Block Flute (Ger. *Blockflöte* = recorder). Organ stop; metal pipes; 2-foot length and pitch; a very robust piccolo type.

Blockx, Jan (b. Antwerp 1851; there d. 1912). Pupil of Benoît (q.v.) who rose to be Principal of the Royal Conservatory of Antwerp: like his master a strong propagandist for the national Flemish musical movement. Composer of operas and cantatas, often to Flemish texts.

Blodwen. Opera by Joseph Parry—the first by a Welsh composer. (Prod. Aberdare 1878.)

Blom, Eric Walter (b. Berne 1888; d. London 1959). Of Danish descent but a Brit. citizen. Active as writer of annotated programmes; music critic *Manchester Guardian* 1923-31; *Birmingham Post* 1931-46; then ed. 5th edn. of Grove's *Dictionary of Music*. Mus. critic *Observer* 1949. Translator and author of many books on musical subjects. Ed. *Music and Letters* 1937-50, and from 1954. C.B.E. 1955, Hon. D.Litt. Birm.

Blomdahl, Karl-Birger (b. Växjö 1916; d. Stockholm 1968). Swedish composer, pupil of Hilding Rosenberg. Works include symphonies, concertos, chamber music, and a successful opera, *Aniara* (1959; q.v.).

Bloss (Ger.). 'Mere', 'merely'.

Blossom Time. See *Dreimäderlhaus*.

Blow, John (b. nr. Newark 1649; d. Westminster 1708). One of first choir-boys of the Chapel Royal when its music recommenced after the Commonwealth and Protectorate; later an organist of it and of Westminster Abbey; thought to have been one of Purcell's masters. Songs, harpsichord music, and church music have high value; sometimes exhibiting great harmonic boldness.

See *Venus and Adonis*.

Bluebeard's Castle (Bartók). See under *Duke*.

Blue Bells of Scotland (properly 'Bell' and not 'Bells'). This song first appears at the very end of the 18th or the beginning of the 19th c., as one sung by the famous London actress, Mrs. Jordan (an Irishwoman), at Drury Lane Theatre. Origin of words and tune not known.

Blue Bonnets over the Border. Poem is by Sir Walter Scott; tune an old Scottish one.

Blue Danube, The. The most popular of the 400 Viennese Waltzes of Johann Strauss jr. (op. 314).

Blue Forest, The. See *Aubert, Louis F. M.*

Blues. As heard since about 1920, a sort of bitter-sweet jazz song or dance-song; written in quadruple time, generally moving at slow speed and in more or less flowing style over an unvarying 12-bar bass. Stanzas are of 3 lines, each covering 4 bars of music. The 3rd and 7th of the key are often prominent, being played somewhere between the major and minor form of the interval, and are known as 'blue notes'.

The earlier (almost entirely Negro) history of the Blues is traced by oral tradition as far back as the 1860's, the conventional harmonic foundation being largely a European contribution. Later developments for mass consumption include 'Rhythm and Blues' and 'Rock and Roll'.

Blume, Friedrich (b. Schlüchtern 1893). Musicologist. After studying medicine, philosophy, and music at Eisenach, Munich, Berlin, and Leipzig he embarked on a distinguished career as editor of old music and writer of scholarly studies on a wide variety of musical subjects. From 1943 he directed the preparation of the monu-

mental *Musik in Geschichte und Gegenwart*.

Blumenfeld, Felix (b. in district of Kherson, Russia, 1863; d. Moscow 1931). Studied at the Conservatory of St. Petersburg, became a fine pianist, and joined its staff as a teacher of his instrument; later one of the conductors of the State Opera House.

Composer of piano music, chamber music, songs, &c.

Blumenstück ('Flower-piece'). By Schumann. For Piano (op. 19, 1859).

Blumenthal, Jacob (b. Hamburg 1829; d. London 1908). Pianist to Queen Victoria; piano teacher to the ladies of London high-life, and composer of piano music and songs for the drawing-rooms of the Brit. Isles.

Blüthner. Piano-making firm, founded Leipzig 1853.

B.M. (1) Bandmaster. (2) See *Degrees and Diplomas* 3.

B.M.I. See *Broadcast Music Inc.*

B Moll (Ger.). The key of B flat minor (not B minor; see *B*).

B.Mus. See *Degrees and Diplomas* 1, 3.

B.N.O.C. Brit. National Opera Co. (q.v.).

Boar's Head Carol. See *Carol*.

Boatswain's Mate, The. One-act Comedy-opera by Ethel Smyth (q.v.). Libretto based on W. W. Jacobs' story. (Prod. London 1916.)

Bobillier, Marie. See *Brenet*.

Boccaccio. Opera by Suppé; libretto by F. Zell and R. Genée—cf. *Beggar Student* by Millöcker. (Prod. Vienna 1879, Boston and New York 1880.) Many translations.

Bocca chiusa (It. 'Closed mouth'). A wordless humming (in choral music).

Boccherini, Luigi (b. Lucca 1743; d. Madrid 1805). Fine 'cellist and composer of enormous quantities of chamber music (over 250 string trios, quartets, and quintets, as well as symphonies and vocal works). Contemporary of Haydn and resembling him in ideals, methods, and general spirit. ('The' Minuet comes from one of his 125 String Quintets—op. 13. no. 5.)

Bocedization. 16th c. system of naming notes of scale (Bo–Ce–Di, &c.), somewhat on principal of hexachordal names (see *Hexachord*) or Tonic Sol-fa (q.v.). Introduced by Waelrant (q.v.).

Boceto (Sp.). 'Sketch.'

Bochsa, Nicolas, in full Robert Nicolas Charles (b. Montmédy, Lorraine, 1787; d. Sydney, N.S.W., 1856). Official harpist to Bonaparte and to Louis XVIII; inventor or perfector of modern harp technique, author of

Boehm Flute. See *Boehm System.*

Boehm System. Takes its name from Theobald Boehm (1793–1881), a player of the flute who replaced the former clumsily placed holes of his instrument by keys enabling the cutting of the holes in their proper acoustical positions, yet leaving them in easy control of the fingers. This improvement has been universally adopted for the flute and applied also to the oboe and (more rarely) to the bassoon and clarinet.

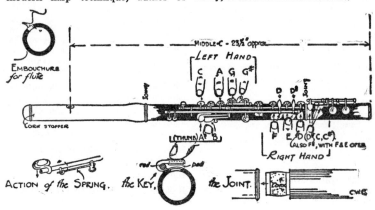

THE BOEHM FLUTE

In this instrument every detail is acoustically and mechanically perfect

famous Harp Method, and composer both of harp music and of operas; notable and successful criminal (forger, condemned in absence by the Paris court to 12 years imprisonment, bigamist, and other things; when death approached apparently recognized his danger and met it by composing a solemn Requiem, which was duly performed at funeral and may have been effective).

Bodanzky, Artur (b. Vienna 1877; d. New York 1939). Conductor. Trained Vienna Conserv. as violinist. Took various positions as theatrical and orch. conductor. Assistant to Mahler at Vienna Opera 1903. Conducted 1st Brit. perf. *Parsifal,* Covent Garden 1914. Then at Metropolitan Opera, New York, to death.

Bodda (or Bodda-Pyne). See *Pyne* 3.

Boëllmann, Léon (b. Ensisheim, Upper Alsace, 1862; d. Paris 1897). Studied organ in Paris under Gigout under whom acquired high ability. Became organist of the Paris church of St. Vincent de Paul; wrote good organ music and music for other instruments, including the well-known symphonic variations for 'Cello and Orch.

Boëly, Alexandre Pierre François (b. Versailles 1785; d. Paris 1858). Organist of church of St. Germain l'Auxerrois, Paris, and one of the first Fr. organists to appreciate and play Bach; composed chiefly for the keyboard instruments, and influenced César Franck and others who were working for a worthier development of Fr. music, especially instrumental.

Boesset (or Boësset, or Boisset), **Antoine** (b. abt. 1585; d. Paris 1643).

Director of music at Court of Louis XIII and son-in-law of Guédron (q.v.); had an outstanding melodic gift but lacked dramatic strength, so that his music was superseded by that of Lully (q.v.).

Boethius. See *Education and Music* 1.

Bog. Short for *Bogen* (see below).

Bogen (Ger.). (1) 'Bow.' So *Bogenstrich*, 'bow stroke'. (2) Short for *Krummbogen* (q.v.). (3) The Tie or Bind (see Table 22).

Bohème, La ('Bohemia'—in the figurative sense). 4-act romantic opera by Puccini. Libretto by Giacosa and Illica, after Murger. (Prod. Turin 1896; Manchester and London 1897; Los Angeles 1897; New York 1898.)
 Leoncavallo has an opera of the same name (1897).

Bohemian Girl, The. Highly popular romantic opera by Balfe. (Prod. London 1843; Dublin, New York, and Philadelphia 1844; Sydney, Vienna, and Hamburg 1846.) See reference under *I dreamt.*

Bohemia's Meadows and Forests (Smetana). See *My Fatherland.*

Bohémien, Bohémienne (Fr. masc., fem.). 'Gipsy' (based on old idea that gipsies came from Bohemia).

Bohm, Karl (b. Berlin 1844; there d. 1920). Composer of great fecundity and high saleability, his publisher, Simrock, who was also that of Brahms, declaring that profits on the compositions of the one provided capital for the publication of those of the other; these lucrative productions were largely of the nature of tuneful piano music, violin music, and songs.

Böhm, (1) **Georg** (b. Thuringia 1661; d. Lüneburg 1733). A minor J. S. Bach, composer of suites, passions, preludes and fugues, chorale preludes, &c.
 (2) **Karl** (b. Graz 1894). Operatic and orch. conductor. Has held posts at Munich, Darmstadt, Dresden, Vienna, &c. Some compositions.

Boïeldieu, François Adrien (b. Rouen 1775; d. nr. Paris 1834). At 18 had an opera performed and continued on the path thus entered, winning fame at 25 with *The Caliph of Bagdad* in Paris (see *Calife*); for some years directed the Royal Opera at St. Petersburg; then opened a second and highly successful Paris career with *La Dame blanche* (q.v.).

Bois (Fr.). 'Wood.' So (*a*) *Avec le bois d'archet = Col legno*, i.e. playing 'with the wood of the bow' instead of the hair; (*b*) *Les bois*, 'The wood-wind'; (*c*) *Baguette de bois*, 'Wooden-headed drumstick'.

Boisset. See *Boesset.*

Boîte (Fr. 'Box'). Swell box of organ.

Boîte à joujoux, La ('The Toy-box'). Children's ballet by Debussy but orchestrated for him by Caplet. (1st perf. Paris 1919.)

Boito, Arrigo (really Enrico) (b. Padua 1842; d. Milan 1918). Enjoyed double operatic fame, as librettist (Verdi's *Othello* and *Falstaff*) and composer.
 See *Mefistofele; Nerone.*

Bok, Mary Louise—née Curtis (b. Boston, Mass., 1876; d. 1970). Married (1) publisher and music patron Edward William Bok (1863–1930). (2) Efrem Zimbalist (q.v.). Founder and President of Curtis Inst. of Music, Philadelphia (1923), which provides free tuition for gifted young musicians.

Bolero. Spanish dance in simple triple time, almost same as *Cachucha* (q.v.) but danced by a couple or several couples. The accompaniment is of (or includes) the dancers' own voices and the castanets (see *Percussion Family* 2 q): the motions of the arms are an important feature.
 Ravel's ballet, *Bolero* (1928) consists practically of a single orch. *crescendo* (lasting 17 minutes), repetitive as to theme and thus without contrast except as to the instruments employed.

Bolshoi Theatre (= 'Great Theatre'), Moscow. Founded 1776; 2,000 seats. Home of Moscow opera and ballet.

Bombard. One of the bass sizes of the ancient *shawm* (see *Oboe Family*)—but in France, apparently, a shawm of any size was called a Bombard.
 Note that the Bombardon has nothing in common with it, being a brass instrument (see *Tuba Group* 2), as is

the It. *Bombarda*, which is the euphonium (see *Tuba Group* 2).

Bombarda (It.). 'Euphonium' (see *Tuba Group* 2).

Bombarde, Bombardon. Powerful organ *Reed Stop* (see *Organ* 2), often in pedal department and sometimes of 32-foot pitch. (But see also *Clavier des Bombardes*.)

Bombardon. See *Tuba Group* 2.

Bonavia, Ferruccio (b. Trieste 1877; d. London 1950). Studied violin, &c., in Milan and spent 10 years as member of Hallé Orch., Manchester; from 1920 a music critic of London *Daily Telegraph*. Wrote valuable books on Verdi, &c., and composed music for strings (quartet, octet, &c.).

Bonavia-Hunt, Rev. Noel (Aubrey) (b. London 1882). M.A. Oxon. Noted writer on organ and related matters; some compositions for the instrument.

Bonci, Alessandro (b. Cesena 1870; d. Viserba 1940). Lyric tenor. Of world popularity chiefly (but not exclusively) in opera. Début Parma 1896; London 1900; New York 1906.

Bond, (1) **Jessie** (b. Liverpool 1853; d. Worthing 1942). Contralto. Trained at R.A.M. as pianist; later in singing by Manuel Garcia. Popular member of Savoy Gilbert and Sullivan cast.

(2) **Carrie Jacobs**—*née* Jacobs (b. Janesville, Wis., 1862; d. Glendale, Calif., 1946). Composer of innumerable popular sentimental songs (*A Perfect Day*, *A Cottage in God's Garden*, &c.).

Bonduca, or **The British Heroine.** Incidental Music by Purcell to a play adapted from Beaumont and Fletcher on the story of Boadicea (1695).

Bones. Two pieces of a rib bone of an animal held between the fingers and rhythmically clacked—the 19th-c. Negro minstrels' (q.v.) equivalent of the castanets.

Bongos. Small Cuban drums, bucket-shaped vessels, cut out of the solid wood, bound with brass, and having strong vellum heads. Two of them are fixed together by a bar of metal. They are played with the thumb and fingers by dance-band practitioners.

Bonnet, Joseph (Élie Georges Marie) (b. Bordeaux 1884; d. nr. Quebec 1944). Organ pupil of Guilmant; at 22 organist of St. Eustache, Paris; toured widely in Europe and America. Organ compositions have wide popularity.

Bonnie Annie. See *John Peel*.

Bonnie Dundee. Poem by Sir Walter Scott written for his play *The Doom of Devorgoil* (1830). Tune is the old one of *The Jockey's Deliverance*. (There was a 'Bonnie Dundee' song current before Scott's, with different metre and melody; he took a part of his refrain from this.)

Bononcini or Buononcini Family (father and sons). (1) **Giovanni Maria** (b. Modena 1642; there d. 1678). Held important positions in his native place; active composer and author of treatise on music. (2) **Giovanni Battista** (b. Modena 1670; d. Vienna 1747). Court composer at Vienna for 11 years; famous as composer in various It. cities and in London, in which latter for a time an operatic rival of Handel. (3) **Marc Antonio** (really Antonio Maria; b. Modena 1677; there d. 1726). Also an opera composer famous in Italy and England.

Bonporti (or **Buonporti**), **Antonio Francesco** (b. Trent 1672; d. Padua 1749). Composer of instrumental music of good quality, apparently attached to the court of the Emperor at Vienna. Ten 'Inventions' for Violin and figured bass, *c.* 1715. (Bach's use of word apparently taken from this.)

Boosey & Hawkes, Ltd. London Music Publishers, Instrument Manufacturers, &c. (295 Regent Street, W. 1). Boosey founded 1816; Hawkes 1865. Amalgamation 1930. (See *Ballad*.)

Bord. Paris piano-making firm; established 1843.

Bordes, Charles (b. Vouvray, Indre-et-Loire, 1863; d. Toulon 1909). Pupil of César Franck who became organist of Paris church of St. Gervais, where he founded a choral body for the performance of the earlier church music under the name of 'Les Chanteurs de St. Gervais' (later an independent body); with Guilmant and d'Indy founded also the Schola Cantorum for the study of church music (1894). Collected and published old church music and Basque folk tunes, and composed music for piano, orch., &c.

Bordoni, Faustina. See under *Hasse.*

Bore of a wind instrument. Diameter of its tube ('wide bore', 'narrow bore', 'tapering bore', &c.).

Borgioli, Dino (b. Florence 1891; there d. 1960). Operatic and concert tenor of high international reputation. Début Milan 1918; Covent Garden 1925; U.S.A. 1928. (Graduate in law; also painter.)

Bori, Lucrezia—Lucrecia Borja y Gonzalez de Riancho (b. Valencia 1887; d. New York 1960). Operatic lyric soprano. Début Rome 1908; Paris 1910; Metropolitan 1912. Retired 1936.

Boris Godunof. Opera by Mussorgsky. Libretto based on poem of Pushkin. Composed 1869; rewritten 1872 and in this form, but with cuts, prod. at St. Petersburg 1874; somewhat shortened version published in vocal score 1874. Cut, revised, and re-orchestrated by Rimsky-Korsakof and thus performed St. Petersburg 1896, and widely elsewhere; new edn. of this 'retouched' 1908. Thus 5 versions in all. Original 1st and 2nd versions of the composer published 1928 and then perf. (Leningrad 1928; London and Paris 1935).

Borkh, Inge (b. Mannheim 1921). Operatic soprano. Début Lucerne 1940; Bayreuth 1950; San Francisco 1953; Covent Garden 1955.

Borodin (Borodine), Alexander (b. St. Petersburg 1833; there d. 1887). Medical man, prof. of chemistry, and founder of women's medical school. When a young man met Balakiref (q.v.) and became a member of the group of composers known as 'The Five' (q.v.), writing 2 symphonies, 2 string quartets, songs, piano music, and opera *Prince Igor* (q.v.). Not a voluminous composer, nor one of the most emphatically national, but highly competent, original in his ideas, and entirely sincere.

See also *In the Steppes of Central Asia; Polovetz Dances; Chopsticks.*

Borowski, Felix (b. Burton, Westmorland, England, 1872; d. Chicago 1956). Of mixed Polish and Brit. descent but naturalized in U.S.A. Once violinist and teacher of violin in Chicago; then music critic there. Composer of orch., chamber, vocal music, &c.

Borre, Borree, Borry. Old English spellings of *Bourrée* (q.v.).

Borren, Charles Jean Eugène van den (b. Brussels 1874; d. there 1966). Lawyer; then librarian of Brussels Conserv., Prof. of Music at Univ. of Liège, &c. Ed. of works of Filippo di Monte and author of many learned musicological works, e.g. *The Sources of Keyboard Music in England* (1914).

Bortniansky, Dimitri (b. in Ukraine 1751; d. St. Petersburg 1825). Having a fine voice was sent by Catharine the Great to Italy (cf. *Berezovsky*): on return in 1779 put in charge of the imperial choir, which he brought to a high standard of excellence. Composer of church music (publ. long after his death under the editorship of Tchaikovsky) and of some instrumental music.

Borwick, Leonard (b. Walthamstow 1868; d. Le Mans 1925). Pianist. Pupil of Clara Schumann; 1st Brit. appearance 1890, soon winning high reputation, national and international, as scholarly, vigorous player of eclectic repertory.

Bösendorfer. Viennese piano-making firm, founded 1828. *Bösendorfersaal* (concert-room) opened 1872.

Bossi, (1) **Marco Enrico** (b. nr. Lake Garda 1861; d. during an Atlantic crossing 1925). Noted organist and composer for his instrument. (2) **Renzo** (b. Como 1883; d. Milan 1965). Son of (1) A considerable composer and a teacher of composition in the Conservatory of Milan.

Boston, Mass. See *Education* 3 ; *Festival*; *Schools of Music.*

Boston Symphony Orchestra. Founded 1881 by Henry Lee Higginson and very richly endowed. Conductors include Henschel (1881), Gericke (1884), Nikisch (1889), Paur, Muck, Max Fiedler, Rabaud, Monteux

Koussevitzky, Munch (1949), Leinsdorf (1962), and Steinberg (1969).

Botstiber, Hugo (b. Vienna 1875; d. Shrewsbury 1941). Musical scholar; ed. of old Austrian music; authority on Haydn (completing Pohl's biog.)

Bote & Bock. German music publishers; founded Berlin 1838; Wiesbaden branch from 1948.

Bottesini, Giovanni (b. in Lombardy 1821; d. Parma 1889). At the age of 11 applying for admission to the Conservatory of Milan and finding there was only one vacancy and that for a student of double-bass took up that instrument, passed examination and so embarked on the career which was to establish him as greatest double-bass player ever known. Composed double-bass music and also operas, oratorios, and other works: was moreover an opera conductor successful in many centres including London.

Bouche fermée (Fr.). 'Closed mouth singing', i.e. humming.

Bouchés, Sons (Fr.). Stopped notes in horn playing (see *Horn Family*; also *Gestopft* and *Schmetternd*).

Bouffons (or *Mattachins*, or *Matassins*). Old sword dance of men wearing armour of gilded cardboard.

Bouffons, Guerre des. 'War of the Comedians' in Paris, 1752. A quarrel over an opera by Destouches led to the invitation to Paris of troupe of It. comedians, who made much stir with their perf. of Pergolese's comic opera *The Maid as Mistress* ('La Serva Padrona', q.v.). The Fr. literary and musical world split into two factions, favouring respectively It. and Fr. opera.

Boughton, (1) **Rutland** (b. Aylesbury 1878; d. London 1960). Studied at R.C.M. under Stanford and others; later on staff of Birmingham School of Music under Bantock. Devoted himself to vast project of Arthurian music drama, with Glastonbury as intended locale; here festivals were held, until at last the scheme was dropped.

The opera *The Immortal Hour* (q.v.) had remarkable success; other operatic works have been performed. In 1938 a Civil List pension was awarded.

See also *Alkestis; Bethlehem.*

(2) **Joy** (b. Bournemouth 1913; d.

1963). Daughter of the above. A leading oboist.

Bouhy, Jacques (Joseph André) (b. Pepinster, Belgium, 1848; d. Paris 1929). Baritone and famous vocal teacher. Had distinguished opera career and trained many well-known singers.

Boulanger, (1) **Nadia** (b. Paris 1887). Won the Second Rome Prize in 1908; has composed orch. music, songs, &c., and holds high international repute as teacher of composition and conductor. In U.S.A. at intervals since 1924. Director American Conservatory, Fontainebleau, 1948.

(2) **Lili** (b. Paris 1893; there d. 1918). Sister of the above and first woman to win the First Rome Prize (1914). At her death, 4 years later, left symphonic poems, choral works, &c.

Boulevard Solitude. Opera in 7 scenes by Henze. (Prod. Hanover 1952; London 1962.)

Boulez, Pierre (b. Montbrison 1925). Composer, pupil of Messiaen, and a notable member of the most advanced school. Active conductor (Cleveland Orch.; 1971 N.Y. Phil., also B.B.C. Symph. Orch.)

See *Marteau sans Maître.*

Boult, Adrian (Cedric) (b. Chester 1889). Educated Westminster School, Oxford (M.A., D.Mus.), and Leipzig Conservatory. From 1924 in charge of the Birmingham City Orch. (q.v.); 1930–42 Musical Director of B.B.C.; and 1941–9 its Conductor in chief; London Philharmonic Orch. to 1957; then Birmingham again. Knighted 1937. C.H. 1969.

Boulton, Sir Harold Edwin, Baronet (1859–1935). Ed. of several collections of songs and author of song poems. (See *Skye Boat Song*.)

Bourdon. (1) A dull-toned pedal stop found on every organ, however small; end-plugged; 8-foot length and 16-foot pitch. (2) The lowest string on the lute or violin. (3) A very large and deep-toned bell. (4) A drone string of the hurdy-gurdy (q.v.). (5) A drone pipe of the bagpipe (q.v.).

Bourgault-Ducoudray, Louis Albert (b. Nantes, 1840; d. nr. Paris 1910). Student of Paris Conservatory under Ambroise Thomas; then conductor of a Paris choral body which revived compositions of Palestrina, Bach, and others. Composer of choral works, operas, &c. Prof. of History of Music at Conservatory and collector of folk music of his native Brittany and of Greece.

Bournemouth Municipal (later **Symphony**) **Orchestra.** Founded by Dan Godfrey (q.v.) in 1893 and the first such permanent organization in Britain, with a notable record for introduction of British music. Later conductors include Richard Austin (1934), Rudolf Schwarz (1947), Charles Groves (1951), Silvestri (1961), George Hurst (1969).

Bourrée (Fr.: sometimes by older Eng. composers spelt Borry, &c.). A dance style very like the gavotte (q.v.) but with its phrases beginning at the three-quarter measure instead of at the half measure. It is sometimes found in the classical suite in a ternary arrangement: (*a*) 1st Bourrée, (*b*) 2nd Bourrée, (*c*) 1st Bourrée again.

Bout (Fr.). 'End', e.g. *Avec le bout de l'archet*, 'With the end (point) of the bow'.

Boutade (Fr. = *Jeu d'esprit*, &c.). Improvised dance or other composition.

Boutique fantasque, La. Ballet music arranged from Rossini's works by Respighi. (Prod. London 1919.)

Bow. See *Viol Family*; *Violin Family*.

Bowed Harp. Name misleadingly applied to the Crwth (q.v.).

Bowen, Edwin York (b. London 1884; d. there 1961). Trained R.A.M. (later on staff). Fine pianist and minor composer in romantic style of piano, orch., and chamber music, &c.

Bower, John Dykes (b. Gloucester 1905). Educated Cambridge (M.A., B.Mus.). Organist Truro Cathedral (1926), New Coll., Oxford (1929), Durham Cathedral (1933), St. Paul's Cathedral, London (1936–67). C.V.O. 1953; knighted 1968; Hon. Sec. R.C.O.).

Bowing (of a stringed instrument). (1) General technique of the use of the bow. (2) Grouping of the notes in one movement of the bow as an element of phrasing (q.v.).

Bowing Mark. See Table 22.

Bowles, (1) **Michael (Andrew)** (b. Riverstown, Co. Sligo, 1909). Trained Irish Army School of Music and Natl. Univ. of Ireland (B.Mus.). Mus. director, Dublin Radio, 1940–8. Cond. N.Z. Nat. Orch. 1950–3; then res. Indianapolis. Compositions for orch., &c.

(2) **Paul (Frederic)** (b. New York 1910). Widely travelled collector of folk music, composer of music for theatre, orch., chamber, and choral music, &c., and successful author.

Boyau (Fr.). 'Catgut.'

Boyce, William (b. London 1710; there d. 1779). Notable London organist and composer of church, orch., and stage music; master of orch. of George III. Overtaken by deafness and devoted rest of life to collection and publication of finest compositions of the English Cathedral composers (cf. *Greene* and *Arnold, Samuel*; also see *Cathedral music*).

See *Heart of Oak*.

Boyden, David (b. Westport, Conn., 1910). Violinist and musical scholar, trained Harvard and Hartt Coll., Conn. On staff Univ. California, Los Angeles.

Br. Short for *Bratschen* (Ger.), i.e. violas.

Brabançonne, La. Belgian national anthem. Written and composed at time of the 1830 demonstration in Brussels which led to the separation of Belgium from Holland. Author of the words was a Fr. actor then in Brussels, named Jenneval, and the composer of the music was Campenhout (q.v.). The name comes from 'Brabant'.

'Braccio' and 'Gamba'. All the viols were held downwards (cf. *Viol Family*), and to them was given the general name of *Viole da gamba*, i.e. 'leg-viols', a description afterwards restricted to the latest survivor of the family, the bass viol.

On the other hand the smaller members of the violin family were held upwards, and, by analogy, all the members of this family (including even those which from their size had to be held downwards) came to be called *Viole da braccio*, i.e. 'arm-viols'. Later this term became limited to the alto violin, i.e. the viola (still in Ger. called *Bratsche*).

This information is here given in order to correct a common misunderstanding as to the application of the terms.

Brace. Perpendicular line, with bracket, joining the 2 staves in piano music, &c.

Bradbury, (1) **Ernest** (b. Leeds 1919). Music critic and lecturer. Studied composition with Sir Edward Bairstow. Staff *Yorkshire Post* from 1947.

(2) **W. B.** See *Hymns and Hymn Tunes* 7.

Brady, Nicholas (b. Bandon, Co. Cork, 1659; d. Richmond, Surrey, 1726). Anglican divine and minor poet (see *Hymns and Hymn Tunes* 3).

Braga, Gaetano (b. in the Abruzzi 1829; d. Milan 1907). Violoncellist. Toured widely. Wrote many operas and a 'cello method. Remembered today by a highly popular Serenade for his instrument.

Braham (orig. Abraham), **John** (b. London 1774; there d. 1856). Tenor vocalist of European fame; sang in 1st perf. of Weber's *Oberon*; composed operas and widely popular songs (e.g. *The Death of Nelson*, from his opera *The Americans*, 1811). Made fortune as a musician and lost it as theatre manager.

Brahe, May. See *Morgan, Mrs. Mary Hannah.*

Brahms, Johannes (b. Hamburg 1833; d. Vienna 1897). Son of humble double-bass player in theatre orch. Locally trained by good teachers. At 20 came to notice of Joachim and Liszt, who helped him forward; then extolled by Schumann in his musical journal. For time had a position in a German court; finally settled in Vienna and there spent the last 35 years of his life.

Composer of 4 symphonies (see below), 2 piano concertos, a violin concerto, a double concerto for violin and 'cello; much fine chamber music and piano music, many songs, and choral and choral-orch. compositions (e.g. the *German Requiem*, q.v.). In all his output shows himself to be a Ger. romantic working in the Ger. classical forms, but not a romantic of the type that delights in programme music (q.v.): all this considered, he may be called Germany's outstanding classic-romantic. (See *Classical Music*; *Romantic*.)

See also *Academic Festival Overture*; *Alto Rhapsody*; *Haydn Variations*; *History* 7; *Joseffy*; *Liebeslieder-Walzer*; *Meistersinger Sonata*; *Nänie*; *Paganini Transcriptions*; *Rinaldo*; *Song of Destiny*; *Song of the Fates*; *Thuner-Sonata*; *Tragic Overture*; *Triumphlied*.

Brahms's Symphonies are as follows: No. 1, in C minor (op. 68, 1876); No. 2, in D (op. 73, 1877); No. 3, in F (op. 90, 1883); No. 4, in E minor (op. 98, 1885).

Brailowsky, Alexander (b. Kief 1896). Pianist. Trained Vienna under Leschetizky. Début Paris 1919; New York 1924. Has toured world, giving recitals—especially of complete Chopin piano works.

Brain, (1) **Aubrey (Harold)** (b. London 1893; d. London 1955). Horn player. Trained R.C.M. Then principal horn in many leading Brit. orchs. (B.B.C. 1928–46). For sons see below. (2) **Leonard** (b. London 1915). Oboe and cor anglais player. Son of (1). Trained R.A.M. Principal in various leading Brit. orchs. (Royal Philharmonic 1946). (3) **Dennis** (b. London 1921; d. Hatfield 1957). Horn player. Son of (1). Trained R.A.M. Notable orch. player and soloist, fully maintaining father's reputation.

Braithwaite, Warwick (b. Dunedin, N.Z., 1896; d. London 1971). Orch. and operatic cond. Trained R.A.M. Mus. director for B.B.C. at Cardiff and cond. National Orch. of Wales, &c., 1922–30; Sadler's Wells Opera 1933–43; Covent Garden 1949–52; Australian opera 1954; Welsh Nat. Opera 1956; Sadler's Wells 1960.

Brandenburg Concertos. Bach's set of 6 'Concerti Grossi' (see *Concerto*) for various combinations. Commissioned by Christian Ludwig, Margrave of Brandenburg (1721). They are as follows:

(1) F MAJOR. 2 Horns, 3 Oboes, and Bassoon, Strings (including 'Violino Piccolo', i.e. small violin), Harpsichord.

(2)* F MAJOR. In 2 groups, plus Continuo—(a) *Concertino*: Trumpet,

Flute, Oboe, Violin; (b) *Ripieno*: Strings; (c) Harpsichord.

(3) G MAJOR. 3 groups of Strings (each Violin, Viola, Violoncello), Double-bass and Harpsichord.

(4)* G MAJOR. In 2 groups, plus Continuo—(a) *Concertino*: Violin and 2 Flutes; (b) *Ripieno*: Strings; (c) Harpsichord.

(5)* D MAJOR. In 2 groups, plus Continuo—(a) *Concertino*: Harpsichord, Flute, Violin; (b) *Ripieno*: Strings (no 2nd Violins); (c) Harpsichord for the Continuo.

(6) B FLAT MAJOR. (No violins.) 2 Violas, 2 Viole da Gamba, Violoncello, Harpsichord.

It will be seen that the three marked * are true Concerti Grossi in the traditional style of contrasting groups (see *Concerto*).

Brandram, Rosina—Mrs. Butcher (b. 1846; d. London 1907). Contralto and actress, famous in Gilbert and Sullivan operas.

Branle (also spelt 'Bransle', &c.). Rustic round-dance of Fr. origin, at one time carried out to the singing of the dancers: name comes from *branler*, 'to sway', and refers to one of the characteristic motions of the dance. Became popular at the court of Louis XIV but had earlier than this been taken up in England (Shakespeare calls it 'Brawl'; Pepys' 'Brantle'). The music was usually in simple duple time but had a resemblance to that of the gavotte (q.v.).

Brannigan, Owen (b. nr. Newcastle-on-Tyne 1908; d. there 1973). Operatic and concert bass. Trained G.S.M. In Sadler's Wells Co. 1942, Glyndebourne (q.v.), &c.

Branscombe, Gena, otherwise Mrs. John Tenney (b. Picton, Ontario, 1881). Pupil in Germany of Humperdinck. Resident in U.S.A. Choral conductor and composer of choral music, orch. music, &c.

Bransle, Brantle. See *Branle*.

Bras (Fr.). 'Arm.'

Brass. This term, technically used, covers wind instruments formerly made of that metal, some of which, however, are now sometimes made of other metals; it does not include instruments formerly of wood but now sometimes of metal, nor does it include metal instruments with reed mouthpieces, e.g. saxophone and sarrusophone. For method of tone-production in the brass see *Acoustics* 4. It makes use of the harmonic series (see *Acoustics* 7). Each instrument possesses a mouthpiece of the nature of a cup or funnel to be pressed against the player's lips, which vibrate within it something like the double reed of the oboe family (see *Reed*): the shape of this mouthpiece

BRASS MOUTHPIECES
Horn, Cornet, and Trumpet

affects the quality of the tone, a deep funnel-shaped mouthpiece (e.g. horn) giving more smoothness, and a cup-shaped mouthpiece (e.g. trumpet) more brilliance. The shape of the bell with which the tube ends also affects the character of the tone as does the nature of the tube's bore, i.e. cylindrical or conical.

'Natural' brass instruments, playing merely the notes of the harmonic series of their 'fundamental' note, are no longer in artistic use, a system of valves having been introduced which makes it possible instantaneously to change the fundamental note of the instrument and so to have at command the notes of another whole harmonic series. (The trombones have always formed a class apart, as they possess a sliding arrangement by which the length of the tube can be changed and a fresh fundamental, with its series of harmonics, thus quickly obtained.)

In addition to its concert-room use in the orch. this family is very important in open-air use, i.e. in military band (q.v.) and brass band (q.v.).

With this article should be read the following: *Acoustics* 7; *Whole-tube and Half-tube*; *Horn Family*; *Trumpet Family*; *Trombone Family*; *Saxhorn and Flügelhorn Families*; *Tuba Group*; *Cornet*; *Duplex Instruments*.

Brass Band. This type of combination is found all over Europe and in countries settled by Europeans, but highest standard of performance is possibly reached in north of England, where its popularity is very great. The constituent instruments of such a band cannot be easily enumerated, as they differ widely. Usually they include members of the cornet and saxhorn families, plus trombones and percussion; sometimes there are added saxophones (which are not brass instruments in the usually accepted application of the word, functioning, as they do, by means of reeds).

All the wind instruments of the brass band except the bass trombone are scored for as transposing instruments (q.v.). Their keys being B flat and E flat, their notation shows, respectively, 2 flats less (or 2 sharps more) than the sounding effect, or 3 flats less (or 3 sharps more). With exception of bass trombones and percussion all are notated in treble clef: save E flat cornet, where the sound is a minor third higher than the notation, all the sounds are lower, the intervals of the discrepancy ranging from a second below (B flat cornet) to 2 octaves and a second below (B flat bombardon). Thus a brass band score is rather puzzling to an unaccustomed reader.

Cf. *Brass* above and for the individual instruments found in brass bands see under the following heads: *Cornet*; *Saxhorn and Flügelhorn Families*; *Tuba Group*; *Trombone Family*.

See also *Military Band*.

Bratsche (Ger.). 'Viola' (see *Braccio and Gamba*). So *Bratschist*, 'viola player'.

Braunfels, Walter (b. Frankfurt-on-Main 1882; d. Cologne 1954). Piano pupil of Leschetizky and a fine per-

former. For 8 years a director of the Cologne Conserv. Composer of neo-romantic music in many forms.

Brautlied (Ger.). 'Bridal song.'

Bravoure (Fr.). (1) 'Bravery', 'gallantry'. (2) Same as *Bravura* (see below).

Bravura (It.). 'Skill', e.g. *Aria di bravura*, a brilliant aria making great demands on the singer.

Brawl, Brawle. Old Eng. name for *Branle* (q.v.).

Breaking of voice. (1) Place in the voice range where the registers change (see *Voice* 4). (2) The permanent change in character (especially in the male voice) which occurs at puberty (see *Voice* 5).

Bream, Julian (b. London 1933). Guitarist and lutenist. Won R.C.M. Exhibition aged 12 and studied piano and 'cello there; later given special scholarship as student of guitar. Advised and encouraged by Segovia (q.v.).

Breathe soft, ye winds. See *Paxton, W*.

Brecht, Bert. See *Gebrauchsmusik*; *Weill*.

Breit (Ger. 'Broad'). Sometimes the equivalent of *Largo* (q.v.) and sometimes applied to bowing, e.g. *Breit gestrichen*, 'Broadly bowed'.

Breitkopf & Härtel. Very important Leipzig music publishing house. History (under various proprietors and as book printers and publishers) goes back to 1542; the first Breitkopf took over in 1719; Härtel family entered 1795; Breitkopf family dropped out 1800. Earliest musical publication 1756. Monumental complete edns. of various composers a speciality; many musical periodicals at various times.

Brema, Marie—really Minnie Fehrman (b. Liverpool 1856; d. Manchester 1925). Operatic and concert mezzo-soprano. Late début (long after marriage) 1891. Wagner roles (Bayreuth, New York, &c.). Finally on staff Royal Manchester Coll. of Music. (Name 'Brema' from Ger. father's place of birth, Bremen.)

Bremner, Robert (1720–89). Important music publisher; at first Edinburgh (1754); then London (1762).

Brenet, Michel—really Antoinette Christine Marie Bobillier (b. Lunéville 1858; d. Paris 1918). Musicologist. Author of biographies of Ockeghem, Palestrina, Handel, Grétry, &c., an historical dictionary of music (posthumous), and many other works of research.

Brenhines Dido. This 'Welsh Air' first appeared as such in a publication of 'Blind' Parry, 1781. It is an adaptation of an Eng. song, Dr. John Wilson's *Queen Dido*, which appeared in his *Cheerful Ayres* (Oxford, 1660).

Brent, John. See *Pianoforte.*

Bretón, Tomás (b. Salamanca 1850; d. Madrid 1923). Began musical life as café violinist and rose to position of conductor of Madrid opera and director of Madrid Conservatory of Music. Like Albéniz (q.v.) fought for the cause of Spanish musical nationalism, his special contribution being the artistic treatment of the operatic form of the Zarzuela (q.v.). He also wrote symphonic poems, chamber music, choral music, &c.

Bréval, Jean Baptiste (b. 1756; d. 1825). Paris 'cellist who had a reputation as composer of orch. and chamber works.

Breve (‖◻‖). Formerly the *short* note of music, but as the longer notes have fallen into disuse and shorter ones been introduced it has become the longest (twice the length of the semibreve). *Alla breve* means (it is not clear why) 'Take the minim as your beat-unit' (the same effect may be indicated by the time-signature $\frac{2}{2}$, or $\mathbb{C}$, or sometimes $\frac{4}{2}$).

Breviary. See *Liturgy.*

Brewer, (1) **Thomas** (b. 1611). Composer of catches, music for viols, &c.

(2) **Alfred Herbert** (b. Gloucester 1865; there d. 1928). Chorister Gloucester Cathedral. Organist Exeter Coll., Oxford; then at R.C.M. Organist Gloucester Cathedral and conductor Festival 1896 to death. Church, &c., composer. D.Mus., Lambeth. Knighted 1926.

Brian, Havergal (b. Dresden, Staffs., 1876; d. Shoreham 1972). Self-taught composer of 32 symphonies, 5 operas, and various choral works, all on a very large scale, and mostly unperformed.

Bridal Marches. See *Wedding Marches.*

Bride of Dionysus, The. See *Tovey.*

Bridge. (1) In stringed instruments, the piece of wood that supports the strings and communicates their vibrations to the belly (q.v.). (2) For the use of the word in composition see *Form* 3.

Bridge, (1) **(John) Frederick** (b. nr. Birmingham 1844; d. London 1924). Organist of Westminster Abbey for over 40 years; on the staff of the R.C.M. 1883–1924; many years Chairman of T.C.M.; Prof. of Music London Univ., Gresham Prof. (1890), conductor of Royal Albert Hall Choral Soc., &c. Active in musical antiquarian research; composer of church music, oratorios, &c.; author of textbooks; D.Mus., Oxford. Knighted 1897. For brother see below.

(2) **Joseph (Cox)** (b. Rochester 1853; d. St. Albans 1929). Brother of the above. Organist of Chester Cathedral (1877), Prof. of Music Durham Univ. (1908). Chairman of Board of T.C.M. (1925–9). M.A., D.Mus., Oxford.

(3) **Frank** (b. Brighton 1879; d. Eastbourne 1941; no relative of the two above). Pupil of Stanford at R.C.M. Won high repute as viola player, chamber music coach, conductor, and composer for orch., chamber combinations, and the voice.

Bridgetower, George Augustus Polgreen (b. 1780; d. Peckham 1860). Violinist (mulatto, having African father). Début Paris 1789. Thenceforward lived largely in London, but also Rome and Paris. Beethoven's 'Kreutzer' Sonata composed for him and first played by him and composer, Vienna 1803. Apparently B.Mus., Cambridge, 1811.

Bridgewater, (Ernest) Leslie (b. Halesowen, Worcs., 1893). Pianist and composer. Musical director various theatres. Light music section B.B.C.

1935–42. Composed pianoforte concerto and much incidental music for stage and films.

Brief Life (Falla). See *Vida breve*.

Brigg Fair. 'English Rhapsody' for orch. by Delius. Based on Lincolnshire folk song. (1st perf. Basle 1907; Liverpool 1908.)

Bright, Dora (Estella)—Mrs. Knatchbull (b. Sheffield 1863; d. Babington, Som., 1951). Pianist and composer. Trained R.A.M. Composed piano concertos, chamber music, &c. In later years also wrote on music.

Brighton Camp. See *Girl I left behind me*.

Brillant, brillante (Fr. masc., fem.), **brillante** (It.). 'Brilliant.'

Brindisi (It. 'Toast'). Jovial song to accompany the drinking of a health.

Brinsmead, John & Sons, Ltd. London piano-makers. Est. 1836. Edgar Brinsmead (d. 1907) wrote *History of the Pianoforte* (1868; 2nd ed. 1879).

Brio (It.). 'Vigour', 'spirit', 'fire'. So the adj. *Brioso*.

Brisé (Fr. 'Broken'). Applied (*a*) to a chord played in arpeggio fashion, or (*b*) to string music played in short, detached movements of the bow.

Bristow, G. F. See *Rip van Winkle*.

Britannia, The Pride of the Ocean. Words written in 1842 by Irish journalist, Stephen Joseph Mean (d. 1890), tune at the same period by Thomas E. Williams, of London (d. 1854)—the composer of the duet *The Larboard Watch*. An American version of the words, *Columbia, the Gem of the Ocean*, was provided by one Thomas à Becket, who in 1876 put forward a claim to be both author and composer of this song: it has been pointed out that 'gem of the ocean' is a 'very odd metaphor to apply to a continent over 3,000 miles broad, and bounded by land on two of its sides'.

British Council. Formed 1935 to spread in foreign countries interest in Britain and its cultural activities. Centres in various parts of the world, with libraries, help towards perf. of Brit. music, &c. It receives a considerable government grant. Musical Director, John Cruft (q.v.).

British Empire, Order of the (founded 1917). Five grades, as follows: (1) G.B.E., Knights Grand Cross (prefix 'Sir' before 1st name) and Dames Grand Cross (prefix 'Dame'). (2) K.B.E., Knight Commander (prefix 'Sir'), and D.B.E., Dame Commander (prefix 'Dame'). (3) C.B.E., Commanders. (4) O.B.E., Officers. (5) M.B.E., Members.

British Federation of Musical Competition Festivals. Founded 1921. First President, Sir Henry Hadow (q.v.). Address 106 Gloucester Place, London, W. 1. See *Competitions in Music*.

British Grenadiers. Original words date from the very end of the 17th c. but a later version now sung includes an allusion to Battle of Waterloo. Origin of tune unknown: earliest copy dates from *c*. 1740.

British Musicians' Pension Society. Founded 1909. Helps both members and non-members; has a Convalescent Home, &c. Address 13 Archer Street, London, W. 1.

British National Opera Company (1922–9). Founded by members of Beecham Co. (see *Beecham*) to carry on its work.

British Sound-recording Association. Formed, in 1936, by a number of engineers and amateur enthusiasts 'with the primary purpose of uniting in one organization all persons, in England and abroad, whether professionals or amateurs, engaged or interested in the art and science of sound recording'. Conducts experiments and encourages research, and arranges lectures and demonstrations, &c.

British Terminology of music (compared with American). See *American Terminology*.

Britten, (Edward) Benjamin (b. Lowestoft 1913). Displayed gifts as composer at early age and at age 12 became pupil of Frank Bridge (q.v.); later at R.C.M. studying composition under John Ireland (q.v.). Rapidly developed technical assurance and a style owing little to immediate Eng. predecessors. In Canada and U.S.A.

1939-42, at about this time composing series of vocal works *Les Illuminations*, *Seven Sonnets of Michelangelo*, &c., which culminated in the operas *Peter Grimes* (1945); *The Rape of Lucretia* (1946); *Albert Herring* (1947); *Billy Budd* (1951); *Gloriana* (1953); and *The Turn of the Screw* (1954). C.H. 1953. O.M. 1965.

See entries for all the above; also *Beggar's Opera*; *Ceremony of Carols*; *Let's Make an Opera*; *Midsummer Night's Dream*; *Noye's Fludde*; *Serenade*; *Sinfonia da Requiem*; *Spring Symphony*; *War Requiem*.

Britton, Thomas (b. Higham Ferrers, Northants., 1651; d. London 1714). See under *Concert*.

Broadcasting of Music. The history of broadcasting may be briefly traced as follows: 1830, Faraday discovered that it is unnecessary for two electric circuits to be in actual physical contact for electric energy to pass between them; 1863, Clerk Maxwell demonstrated the existence of electro-magnetic 'waves'; 1888, Hertz produced such 'waves' in the ether (some, however, give the priority to Hughes, of Kentucky); 1894, Lodge showed that signals could be transmitted without wires by means of the 'Hertzian Waves'; 1895-6, Marconi evolved a method of propagating and receiving the waves (again, however, some consider Hughes to have been the pioneer) and the Brit. Post Office gave opportunities of displaying and developing the Marconi system; 1898, Messages were communicated over a distance of 12 miles; 1901, The distance covered was now 1,800 miles; 1904, A telegraphic service to ships at sea was inaugurated and progress was by now also being made in wireless communication by telephony; 1919, Broadcasting as an entertainment was begun in the U.S.A. by amateur experimenters; 1920, The first Brit. broadcasting station was opened by the Marconi Co. at Writtle, nr. Chelmsford, and the first U.S.A. station was opened at Pittsburgh, Penn., and the latter, still operating ('KDKA'), was regarded as world's first fully organized station; 1922, Four of chief Brit. electrical manufacturers formed the Brit. Broadcasting Co.; 1923, World-first Opera

Broadcast (Mozart's *The Magic Flute*) took place from Covent Garden; 1925, Daventry high-power station opened, disseminating programmes from the London station; 1927, The (private) Brit. Broadcasting Co. became the (government controlled) Brit. Broadcasting Corporation, with 2¼ million licences; 1936, Television effectively began in Britain.

'PUNCH' AS PROPHET

(A du Maurier picture in *Punch's Almanack for 1878*)

Musical Mistress of House ('on hospitable thoughts intent'). 'Now, recollect, Robert, at a quarter to nine turn on "Voi che Sapete" from Covent Garden; at ten let in the Quartet from "Rigoletto" full on. But mind you close one tap before opening the other!'
Buttons. 'Yes, Mum!'

The organization and control of broadcasting differ in different countries. As we have seen, in Britain they are a government-authorized monopoly; in the U.S.A., however, they are in the hands of commercial companies which recoup their expenditure and make their profit by 'selling time' to advertisers who 'sponsor' programmes.

The method of broadcasting may be thus briefly outlined. A small apparatus is made to give a minute alternating current of high 'frequency' (i.e. with extremely rapid vibrations—some millions per second). This is repeatedly amplified until it amounts to several horse-power, and transmitted from wires stretched from lofty masts which send it out through the ether (at the speed of light, which travels through the same medium). A microphone is arranged to control the original minute alternating current, automatically weakening or strengthening it according to the nature of the sounds that impinge on the diaphragm: thus if the frequency of the minute alternating current were 1,000,000 per second and that of the sound 1,000 per second (= roughly C above the treble staff) it would increase and diminish the million-per-second current 1,000 times per second, and so on with sounds of other pitches. Receiving sets are so constructed as to cancel out the high-frequency vibrations, handing on only the rises and falls in the current, so that the frequency of the vibrations passed to the listener's loud-speaker corresponds to that of the original sound given to the microphone. That is the principle of radio transmission by 'amplitude modulation' ('AM').

In another common system ('FM'), it is the *frequency* of the alternating current which is varied by the frequency of the sound to be broadcast. As timbre (see *Acoustics* 6) is a matter of harmonic notes of various pitches, that also is concerned in the foregoing explanation, and as for intensity (loudness), that, of course, is a matter of the amplitude of the original vibrations (see *Acoustics* 3) communicated to the diaphragm of the transmitting set.

The speed of the transmission by 3 methods varies widely as follows: (*a*) *Sound through the air* (e.g. in a concert room), at the rate of ⅕ of a mile per second. (*b*) *By wire* (e.g. Telephone or Electrophone); a mile in a fraction of a second, the fraction depending on the electrical properties of the wire and apparatus. (*c*) *Through the ether* (Radio Broadcasting), the speed of light, i.e. 186,330 miles per second. Thus the speed of radio transmission is of the order of a million times that of concert-room transmission.

Broadcast Music Inc. ('BMI'). American performing rights society, comparable with ASCAP but owned by the broadcasting industry. Founded 1939.

Broadwood, (1) **John.** See *Pianoforte.* (2) **John & Sons, Ltd.** London piano-making firm, successors to Shudi (q.v.); firm was 'Shudi & Broadwood' 1770; 'John Broadwood & Son' 1795; 'John Broadwood & Sons' 1807. (3) The Rev. **John** (1798–1864). Brother of H. F. Broadwood of the piano firm, and one of the earliest modern folk-song collectors. (4) **Lucy** (b. London 1858; d. Camberley, Surrey 1929). Daughter of H. F. Broadwood of the piano firm, and thus niece of (3), whose interests she actively followed; helped to found Eng. Folk Song Soc. (1898) and served as its Hon. Sec. 1904–8 and 1914–18.

Brockway, Howard A. (b. Brooklyn 1870; d. New York 1951). Composer and pianist. Trained Berlin. Then various important educational positions Baltimore and New York. Composer of orch. and chamber works, &c., and collector of Kentucky mountain tunes.

Brodsky, Adolf (b. Taganrog, on Sea of Azov, Russia, 1851; d. Manchester 1929). Violinist. Trained Vienna Conservatory under Hellmesberger. Joined staff of Moscow Conservatory and then that of Leipzig. Toured internationally as solo violinist (London 1882; New York 1891). Leader of Hallé Orch., Manchester, 1895; then succeeded Hallé as Principal Royal Manchester Coll. of Music; formed Brodsky Quartet. Hon. D.Mus., Manchester (1902).

Broken Cadence. See *Cadence.*

Broken Consort or **Broken Music.** See *Consort.*

Broken Octave. See under *Short Octave.*

Bronwen (Holbrooke). See *Cauldron of Anwyn.*

Bronze Horse (Auber). See *Cheval de bronze.*

Brosa, Antonio (b. Taragona, Spain, 1896). Violinist. Settled in London 1914; founded Brosa Quartet; as soloist and chamber music player showed special interest in works of contemporary composers.

Brossard, Sébastien de (b. Dompierre, Orne, 1655; d. Meaux 1730). Church musician and composer, remembered today as author of early *Dictionnaire de musique* (1703).

Brosses, Charles de (b. Dijon 1709; d. Paris 1777). Geographer, philologist, lawyer, and President of Parliament of Burgundy, hence usually spoken of as 'President de Brosses'; important to musical historians from his letters on travel in Italy which include useful information on musical conditions of the period.

Brott, Alexander (b. Montreal 1915). Violinist, conductor, and composer. Trained McGill Conservatory (later on staff) and New York Juilliard School. Leader, McGill Quartet, Les Concerts Symphoniques, &c. Annual tours of Europe as composer-conductor. Compositions include orch. suite *From Sea to Sea* and chamber music. (Eliz. Sprague Coolidge Prize twice for latter.)

Brouwenstijn, Gré (b. Den Helder 1915). Dutch lyric-dramatic soprano. Leading singer at Amsterdam Opera, then successful appearances at Covent Garden (1951), Bayreuth (1954), &c.

Brown, Arthur Henry (b. Brentwood 1830; d. there 1926). Parish organist, authority on plainsong, and composer of 800–900 hymn tunes, many of high popularity and to be found in every collection in English-speaking world (e.g. *The day is past and over*).

Brown, J. Hullah. See *Violinda*.

Browne, Robert (abt. 1550–abt. 1633). See *Puritans and Music*.

Browning, Robert (1812–89). The poet; see *Avison*; *Galuppi*.

Brownlee, John Donald Mackenzie) (b. Geelong, Australia, 1900; d. New York City 1969). Operatic and concert baritone. Studied Paris. Introduced by Melba at her Covent Garden farewell (1926); 10 years at Paris Opéra; then Metropolitan, New York (from 1937). Dir. Manhattan School of Mus. 1957.

Bruch, Max (b. Cologne 1838; d. Friedenau 1920). Long active as conductor of various musical bodies including (1880–3) Liverpool Philharmonic Soc.; composer of choral works, works for violin and orch. (especially G minor Concerto), and 'cello and orch., &c. (see *Kol Nidrei*).

Bruckner, Anton (b. Ansfelden, Upper Austria, 1824; d. Vienna 1896). Came before public first as church musician and concert organist (giving recitals in Paris, London, &c.); then, in his forties, settled in Vienna, devoting himself increasingly to composition, and producing 9 symphonies (see below), 3 masses, a Requiem, a Te Deum, and many other works on a large scale. In form and style is, like Brahms, a classic-romantic, but, unlike him, shows some Wagner influence. Has in Germany and Austria a very high reputation not fully accepted beyond their frontiers, perhaps on account of a certain naïvety, repetitiveness, and apparent lack of faculty of self-criticism—faults which some of his ardent admirers maintain are outweighed by the musical beauty and emotional content of his work.

Bruckner's Symphonies are as follows: No. 1, in C minor (1866, revised 1891); No. 2, in C minor (1872, revised 1876 and again 1877); No. 3, in D minor (1873, revised 1877 and again 1888); No. 4, in E flat, the *Romantic* (1874, revised 1880); No. 5, in B flat (1877, revised 1878); No. 6, in A (1881); No. 7, in E (1883); No. 8, in C minor, the *Apocalyptic* (1887, revised 1890); No. 9, in D minor (1896: the finale of this remained incomplete).

For some time shortened and 'improved' versions of these works, by various hands, had currency.

There are also early Symphonies in F minor (1863) and D minor (1864, revised 1869).

Brüll, Ignaz (b. Prossnitz, Moravia, 1846; d. Vienna 1907). Toured as pianist and became known as composer of operas, orch. works, and chamber music; member of the Brahms group in Vienna.

Brume (Fr.). 'Mist.'

Brummeisen (Ger. 'Humming-iron'). Jew's Harp (q.v.).

Bruneau, Alfred—in full Louis Charles Bonaventure Alfred (b. Paris 1857; there d. 1934). At Paris Conservatory its best 'cellist and student of composition under Massenet. Made name in 1891 by opera *Le Rêve* (based on Zola's novel), then looked on as very 'advanced': one of best known of its several successors is *L'Attaque du moulin* (q.v.). Wrote also a Requiem, songs, &c.; was active as musical critic and wrote books on music. Member of the Institute.

Brunskill, Muriel (b. 1899). Operatic and concert contralto. Trained by Blanche Marchesi, &c. Début London 1920. In Brit. National Opera Co. 1922–7. Has toured many countries.

Bruscamente (It.). 'Brusquely.'

Bruscantini, Sesto (b. Porto Civitanova, Macerata, 1919). Operatic buffo bass-baritone. Début La Scala 1949; Glyndebourne 1950. Married to Sena Jurinac (q.v.).

Brushes, Wire. See *Percussion Family* 2 w.

Brustwerk (Ger.). 'Choir Organ' (see *Organ* 1).

Btb. Short for *Basstuba* (see *Tuba Group*).

Buccolico (It.). 'Bucolic', 'rustic'.

Buch der hängenden Gärten. By Schönberg. Settings for Solo Voice and Piano of 15 poems by Stefan George (op. 15; 1908).

Buck, (1) **Zechariah** (b. Norwich 1798; d. Newport, Essex, 1879). Choirmaster and then organist (1825–72) of Norwich Cathedral; famous as trainer of choir-boys; minor composer of church music. D.Mus., Canterbury.

(2) **Dudley I** (b. Hartford, Conn., 1839; d. Orange, N.J., 1909). Studied in Germany and France and then became organist of churches in various cities of U.S.A. Composer of much church music and other choral music; author of some books on musical subjects.

(3) **Dudley II** (b. Hartford, Conn., 1869; d. Fairfield, Conn., 1941). Son of above; well-known tenor, New York (1902), and singing teacher in Chicago (1939).

(4) **Percy Carter** (b. London 1871; d. there 1947). Studied R.C.M. (later on staff); then organ scholar Worcester Coll., Oxford; organist of cathedrals of Wells and Bristol; Director of Music Harrow School (1901–27); Prof. of Music Dublin Univ. (1910–20); Musi-

cal Adviser to London Education Committee (1925–37); Prof. of Music, London Univ. (1925–38); author of thoughtful books on music; composer of organ and choral works. M.A., D.Mus., Oxford. Knighted 1935.

(5) **Vera**—Mrs. B. J. Gilchrist (b. Kew, Victoria, Australia, 1903). Composer and pianist. Vice-Pres. Guild of Australian Composers. In London 1930–8, appearing in stage and radio productions of lighter kind. Composer musical comedy, songs, and piano works.

Buckwheat Notation. American adaptation of the staff notation for sight-singing purposes, on lines of system briefly described under *Lancashire Sol-fa*, but with a music type which has differently shaped heads for the notes bearing the 4 names in use, *fa, sol, la, mi*. It dates from the late 18th c., and is still in use in the 'Bible Belt' or 'Fundamentalist Region' of the southern United States.

Ye nations round the earth rejoice,

'OLD HUNDRED'

In the Buckwheat Notation. (From *The Easy Instructor; or A New Method of Teaching Sacred Harmony*, Philadelphia 1798. The tune is in the tenor, as was the British and American custom at that period)

Bucolico (It.). 'Bucolic', 'rustic'.

Buée (Fr.). 'Mist.' So Debussy's *Comme une buée irisée*, 'Like an iridescent mist'.

Buesst, Aylmer (b. Melbourne 1883; d. St. Albans 1970). Appeared as child pianist; studied violin under César Thomson and Wilhelmj; opera conductor in Germany and Britain; on staff of R.A.M., R.C.M., and G.S.M. Publ. book on Wagner's *Ring*. Asst. Director Music B.B.C. 1933–6.

Buffa (It.). 'Comic' (see *Opera* 7).

Buffet d'orgue. (Fr.). 'Organ case.'

Buffo, Buffa (It. masc., fem.). 'Comic.'

Buffonesco (It.). 'Buffoon-like', 'droll'. So the adverb *buffonescamente*.

Buffoon (Prokofief). See *Chout*.

Bugle. Brass or copper instrument of treble pitch, with wide tube of conical bore, moderate-sized bell, and cup-shaped mouthpiece. Notes are merely a few of those of the harmonic series (see *Acoustics* 7) and it is mainly a means of military signalling or (in bugle bands) simple accompaniment of marching. Cf. *Last Post*. (For Key Bugle see *Cornett and Key Bugle Families*.)

Bugle à clefs. Key Bugle (see *Cornett and Key Bugle Families*).

Bühnenfestspiel, Bühnenweihfestspiel. See *Festspiel, Festival*.

Bukofzer, Manfred F. (b. Oldenburg, Germany, 1910; d. Oakland, Cal., 1955). Trained Univs., Heidelberg, Berlin, and Basle (Ph.D.), and under Hindemith. Academic position in Basle; then Univ. California. Author of *Music in the Baroque Era*, &c. (See also *Sumer is icumen in*.)

Bull, (1) **John** (b. England abt. 1562; d. Antwerp 1628). Choir-boy in Queen Elizabeth's Chapel Royal; organist Hereford Cathedral and then Chapel Royal; D.Mus., Oxford and Cambridge, and first Gresham Prof. of Music (see *Gresham Professorship*). Then one of organists in Chapel Royal, Brussels, and finally Antwerp Cathedral.

His importance is as a highly skilled performer on and ingenious composer for the virginals, so that he ranks as one of the founders of keyboard performance and the keyboard repertory.

See *God Save the King*; *Parthenia*.

(2) **Ole Borneman** (b. Bergen, Norway, 1810; d. nr. there 1880).

Norwegian patriot violinist who toured the world playing Scandinavian melodies, earning great sums and founding in U.S.A. a Norwegian colony and in the capital of his own country a conservatory of music (both of which schemes proved abortive).

Bullock, Ernest (b. Wigan 1890). Pupil of E. C. Bairstow (q.v.) at Leeds Parish Church; sub-organist Manchester Cathedral (1912–15); organist Exeter Cathedral (1919–28); Westminster Abbey (1928–41); Prof. of Music in Univ. of Glasgow and head of Royal Scottish Academy of Music (1941); R.C.M. (1953–60). Church and organ music, part-songs, &c. D.Mus., Durham; C.V.O. (1937). Knighted 1951.

Bullphone. A 'loud-speaker' invented in the U.S.A. in the late 1930's, which glories in a range of 25 miles. (Cf. *Auxetophone*.)

Bull Roarer. See *Thunder Stick*.

Bülow, Hans Guido von (b. Dresden 1830; d. Cairo 1894). At first student of law; then abandoned this for music, becoming disciple of Liszt and Wagner (married Liszt's daughter Cosima, who left him and married Wagner). Fine pianist, able conductor (positions at Hanover, Meiningen, Hamburg, Berlin, and extensive tours; see *Conducting*). Man of forceful personality and power and of ready, significant, and tart speech.

Bumbass or **Basse de Flandres.** Much the same as *Bladder and String* (q.v.).

Bumpus, John Skelton (b. London 1861; there d. 1913). Wrote *History of English Cathedral Music* (1908), &c.

Bundfrei. See *Clavichord*.

Bunting, Edward (b. Armagh 1773; d. Dublin 1843). Famous pioneer student of Irish folk tunes, harp music, &c., publishing standard collections (1796 to 1840).

Buonamici, Giuseppe (b. Florence 1846; there d. 1914). Pianist of high distinction (pupil of Liszt and Bülow). Played in London 1887–93. Teacher of world fame, ed. of the piano classics, and composer.

Buononcini. See *Bononcini.*

Buonporti. See *Bonporti.*

Burden, or **Burthen.** A recurring line after each stanza of a ballad, &c.

Burgmüller, (1) **Norbert** (b. Düsseldorf 1810; d. Aix-la-Chapelle 1836). Composer considered to be of great promise in his day, especially by Schumann. Died before reaching maturity, leaving a quantity of symphonic and other works. (2) **Joh. Friedrich** (b. Regensburg 1806; d. Beaulieu, Seine-et-Oise, 1874). Brother of above; also a composer, chiefly of piano music for children.

Burkhard, (1) **Paul** (b. Zürich 1911). Composer and conductor of operettas and other light music (conductor Beromünster Radio Studio Orch. since 1947).
(2) **Willy** (b. nr. Bienne, Switzerland, 1900; d. Zürich 1955). Studied at Conservs. of Berne, Leipzig, and Munich, and then became teacher of composition and piano in Berne; later resident at Montana and Davos. Composer of orch., chamber, and choral music, last-named including an austere oratorio, *The Vision of Isaiah* (1936), which has received considerable recognition. Opera, *Die Schwarze Spinne* (Zürich 1949).

Burla (It.). 'Jest.' So *burlando*, 'jestingly'; *burletta*, a musical farce, &c. (Cf. *Burlesco*.)

Burleigh, (1) **Henry Thacker** (b. Erie, Penn., 1866; d. Stamford, Conn., 1949). Baritone vocalist. Composer of songs and arranger of melodies of his own (Negro) race.
(2) **Cecil** (b. Wyoming (town), N.Y., 1885). Successful violinist (pupil of Sauret, &c.), violin teacher, and composer for violin and for orch.

Burlesco, burlesca (It. masc., fem.). 'Burlesque', 'jocular' (cf. *Burla*). So the adverb, *burlescamente*.

Burletta (It.). A musical farce (cf. *Burla*).

Burmester, Willy (b. Hamburg 1869; there d. 1933). Violinist. Pupil of Joachim. Of great technical skill and sensitive artistry. Toured Britain and U.S.A. Some string compositions.

Burney, Charles (b. Shrewsbury 1726; d. London 1814). Organist (London churches, King's Lynn, finally Chelsea Hospital); minor composer; traveller in search of material for History of Music (4 vols. 1776–89); author of 2 books narrating his travel experiences in France, Italy, Germany, &c., also of a Life of Metastasio and other things. Man of wide musical and general interests, intimate with and greatly esteemed by Johnson, Garrick, Reynolds, Burke, and many other leaders of politics, science, art, literature, and social life of his period. Father of the novelists Fanny and Sarah Harriet Burney, of the writer on South Sea exploration, Admiral James Burney (one of Cook's officers in his circumnavigation), and of the celebrated Greek scholar, Charles Burney, jun.

See references under *Criticism of Music*; *Pianoforte Playing*; *Rousseau.*

Burrell, Mary (1850–98). Daughter of Sir John Banks, Regius Prof. Medicine, Trin. Coll. Dublin; wife of Hon. Willoughby Burrell (after her death Lord Gwydyr). Amassed enormous collection Wagner documents of every kind; planned complete life of Wagner so based but only immense 1st vol. published, covering merely 21 years. Other material now at Philadelphia (Catalogue published 1929).

Burthen. See *Burden.*

Busby, (1) **Thomas** (b. London 1755; there d. 1838). London organist; composer of choral works, &c.; busy author of Dictionary of Music, History of Music, and many other books. D.Mus., Cambridge.
(2) **Thomas R.** (d. 1933). Horn player. One of founders of London Symphony Orch. (q.v.) and its secretary for 1st 18 years.

Busch, (1) **Carl** (b. Bjerre, Denmark, 1862; d. Kansas City 1943). Naturalized as citizen of U.S.A. and long resident in Kansas City, Mo. Active composer of choral music, &c.; possessor of notable collection of old instruments. Knighted by King of Denmark (1912).

(2, 3, 4) The brothers **Fritz** (1890–1951), orch. and opera conductor in many important German centres, also Copenhagen, Stockholm, New York, Glyndebourne, &c.; Hon. D.Mus., Edinburgh, 1935; **Adolf** (1891–1952), violinist, leader of notable string quartet (founded 1912), prolific composer of orch. works, &c., conductor of chamber orch. Hon. D.Mus., Edinburgh, 1935; from 1940 in New York (cf. *Serkin*); and **Hermann** (b. 1897), eminent violoncellist.

All the brothers left Germany in disapproval of the Nazi régime and assumed Swiss nationality.

(5) **William** (b. London 1901; d. Woolacombe, Devon, 1945). Pianist and composer. London début as pianist 1927; then toured Holland, Germany, and U.S.A. Composer of piano concerto, 'cello concerto, chamber music, songs, &c.

Bush, (1) **Alan Dudley** (b. Dulwich 1900). Studied at R.A.M. (later on staff). Composer of chamber music, choral music, &c., and prominent in a 'leftish' musical-political movement.

(2) **Geoffrey** (b. London 1920). Studied Oxford. Composer of stage, orch., choral, and chamber music, &c.

Busk. Former Jazz term (see *Jazz*) meaning to improvise on a set of harmonies.

Busnois, Antoine (d. Bruges 1492). A pupil of Ockeghem, and a leader in the early Netherlands school of composition.

Busoni, Ferruccio Benvenuto (b. Empoli 1866; d. Berlin 1924). Of half-Italian, half-German parentage. World-famous pianist (début, aged 8) and composer of 4 operas (see *Turandot*; *Arlecchino*; *Doktor Faust*), orch. and chamber music, and piano music—in his later works to be classed amongst the anti-romantics. Piano teacher of great renown—Moscow, Berlin, Boston (New England Conservatory, 1891–3), Vienna, Bologna, Zürich, &c. Edited Liszt's piano works, Bach's '48', &c. Many transcriptions; some books. See also *Jarnach*; *Pianoforte Playing.*

Busser, Henri Paul (b. Toulouse 1872). Pupil of Gounod, Franck, and Widor at the Paris Conservatory and at 21 won the Prix de Rome. In 1902 became conductor at the Opéra. Has composed some operas and orch., choral, and organ works.

Butt, Clara (b. Southwick, Sussex, 1873; d. London 1936). Contralto. Trained R.C.M. and Paris. Enormously popular concert singer throughout Brit. Empire (often with husband R. Kennerley Rumford, q.v.). D.B.E. 1920.

Butterfly's Wings Étude for Piano. Chopin's op. 25, no. 9, in G flat. Nickname without authority.

Butterworth, George (Sainton Kaye) (b. London 1885; killed in action in France 1916). Educated at Eton, Oxford, and R.C.M. Active in revival of Eng. folk song and dance, and a delicate composer whose early end was greatly deplored.

See *Shropshire Lad.*

Button. Pin at the end of a violin, &c., which bears the pull of the strings.

Buxtehude, Dietrich (b. Oldesloe, Holstein (then under Danish rule), 1637; d. Lübeck 1707). One of fathers of organ playing and organ composition, his fame being so great that J. S. Bach when a young man walked 200 miles to hear him. Some of his church cantatas and organ works are still to be heard.

By Celia's Arbour. See *Horsley William.*

Byrd, William (b. probably at Lincoln 1542 or 1543; d. probably at Stondon, Essex, 1623). Pupil of Tallis; at about 20 organist of Lincoln Cathedral, and later (jointly with Tallis) of Queen Elizabeth's Chapel Royal. Composer of church music, string music, keyboard music, and madrigals, all of highest quality, in some anthems approaching sublimity. One of fathers of Eng. Music, and as such revered by all instructed Eng. musicians.

See *Ladye Nevells Booke; Non nobis Domine; Parthenia; Service.*

By the Waters of Minnetonka. See *Lieurance*.

Byzantine Music. By this is meant the Christian liturgical song (often highly ornamented) of the Eastern Roman Empire (capital Byzantium = Constantinople = Istanbul). It appears to derive from a far-back source common to it and to the plainsong of the Western Church. It is being increasingly studied by musicologists. See also *Greek Church*; *Tillyard; Wellesz*.

C

C.A. *Coll' arco* (q.v.).

Cabaletta or **Cabbaletta** (It.). A term with a troublesome number of meanings: (1) Short aria (q.v.) of simple and much reiterated rhythm, generally with repeats. (2) Sort of song in rondo form, sometimes with variations. (3) Recurring passage in a song, first appearing simply and then varied (some authorities make a triplet accompaniment a necessary qualification for the title). (4, a 19th-c. term) Final section of an elaborate operatic duet or aria, in which section the music often settles down to a steady rhythm.

Cabinet Organ. See *Reed-Organ Family* 6. **Cabinet Pianoforte.** See *Pianoforte.*

Caccia (It.). 'Chase', 'hunt', e.g. *alla caccia*, 'in hunting style'. (For 'Oboe da caccia' see *Oboe Family*; 'Corno da caccia = Hunting Horn—see *Horn Family*.)

Caccini, Giulio (b. Rome abt. 1546; d. Florence 1618). One of most important of early Florentine operatic experimenters (see also *Peri* and *Gagliano*). His book of songs (*Nuove musiche* = 'New Musics'; 1602) is the typical example of the early monodic style.

Cachucha. Graceful Spanish dance for a single performer. Its music is not unlike that of the bolero (q.v.).

Cadence or **Close.** Any melodic or harmonic progression which has come to possess a conventional association with the ending of a composition, a section, or a phrase.

The commonest harmonic cadences are the following:[1] (*a*) PERFECT CADENCE

[1] The definitions which follow accord with the most usual British practice. The terminology used in harmony textbooks and musical works of reference in the U.S.A. often departs somewhat from this. A large number of such books have been consulted, and they have been found to vary considerably in their application of the terms. Most (not all) of them, however, agree in one particular—the term *Perfect Cadence* being reserved for the form of *Authentic Cadence* (Dominant chord–Tonic chord) in which the last melody note is a duplication of the bass note, i.e. is the tonic and not the 3rd or 5th of the chord.

(or FULL CLOSE). Chord of the Dominant followed by that of Tonic. (*b*) INTERRUPTED CADENCE. Chord of the Dominant followed by that of Submediant. (*c*) IMPERFECT CADENCE (or HALF CLOSE). Chord of the Tonic or some other chord followed by that of Dominant. (*d*) PLAGAL CADENCE. Chord of the Subdominant followed by that of Tonic.

Perfect   Interrupted   Imperfect

Plagal   Phrygian

To any of the Dominant chords above mentioned the 7th may be added. Any of the chords may be taken in inversion (see *Harmony* 2 e), but if that is done in the case of the Perfect Cadence its effect of finality (i.e its 'perfection') is lost.

The term PHRYGIAN CADENCE is applied by various writers to (i) in major key a cadence ending on the chord of the Dominant of relative minor (e.g. in Key C major E–G sharp–B), or (ii) any sort of Imperfect Cadence (Half Close) in minor mode, or (iii) 1st inversion of Subdominant chord followed by Dominant chord (e.g. in Key C the chord A–C–F followed by the chord G–B–D). (It seems best to confine the name to the cadence (i) above, which is fairly common in Bach and for which no other name is available, whereas (ii) and (iii) are simply varieties of the Imperfect Cadence.)

For the cadences employing the *Tierce de Picardie* see under that term.

Other terms in use (too many!) are the following:

ABRUPT CADENCE = Interrupted Cadence (see above). AMEN CADENCE = Plagal Cadence (see above). AUTHENTIC CADENCE = Perfect Cadence (Full Close; see above). AVOIDED CADENCE = Interrupted Cadence (see above). BROKEN CADENCE = Interrupted Cadence (see above). CHURCH CADENCE = Plagal Cadence (see above). COMPLETE CADENCE = Perfect Cadence (Full Close; see above). DECEPTIVE CADENCE = Interrupted Cadence (see above). DEMI-CADENCE = Imperfect Cadence (Half Close; see above). DOMINANT CADENCE = Imperfect Cadence (Half Close; see above). EVADED CADENCE = Interrupted Cadence (see above). FALSE CLOSE = Interrupted Cadence (see above). GREEK CADENCE = Plagal Cadence (see above). HALF CADENCE = Half Close (see Imperfect Cadence, above). INVERTED CADENCE = A Perfect or Imperfect Cadence (Full Close or Half Close; see above) with its latter chord inverted. (Some confine the name to the Perfect Cadence thus changed; others extend it to all cadences having either chord, or both, inverted.) IRREGULAR CADENCE = Interrupted Cadence (see above). MIXED CADENCE. The term is used in 2 ways—both of them superfluous. (1) A 'mixing' of the Plagal and Imperfect Cadences, consisting of Subdominant-Dominant, this being merely the Imperfect Cadence in one of its commonest forms. (2) A mixing of the Plagal and Perfect Cadences, consisting of the Perfect Cadence preceded by the Subdominant—making 3 chords, instead of the usual 2. This is merely the Perfect Cadence led up to in one of its commonest manners and should not require any special name. RADICAL CADENCE = any cadence of which the chords are in root position, i.e. the roots of the chords in the bass. SEMI-PERFECT CADENCE = Perfect Cadence (see above) with the 3rd or 5th of the Tonic in the highest part. SURPRISE CADENCE = Interrupted Cadence (see above). SUSPENDED CADENCE = A hold-up before the final cadence of a piece, as that in a concerto (or, in former times, an aria) for the solo performer to work in a cadenza (q.v.).

Cadenza is merely Italian for 'Cadence' (q.v.) but has come to mean a flourish (properly, improvised) inserted into the final cadence of any section of a vocal aria or a solo instrumental movement. The conventional final cadence consists, harmonically, of 3 chords, the 2nd inversion of the Tonic Chord, and the Dominant and Tonic Chords in root position (i.e. $^6_4$ $^5_3$ on the Dominant bass, followed by $^5_3$ on the Tonic bass). The interpolated Cadenza begins on the first of these chords, the orchestra becoming silent and joining in again only when the soloist, after a display of vocal or instrumental virtuosity, indicates by a long trill that he is ready to be rejoined by his fellows in the final chords or in any passage elaborated out of them.

In the operatic aria conventional practice admitted 3 Cadenzas—one at the end of each of its 3 sections (see *Aria*), the most elaborate being reserved for the last, in the hope of 'bringing down the house' by its display of vocal gymnastics. The term *Melisma* has been used for the vocal cadenza.

Distrust of the inventive ability or discretion of the performer has led some composers to provide cadenzas written out in full. Mozart, for instance, provided such for some of his piano concertos and so did Beethoven. Brahms, in his violin concerto, was perhaps the last composer to leave the invention of a cadenza to the performer, but his friend Joachim at once supplied one for it and this has since almost invariably been associated with it.

From Beethoven onwards (in a part of the cadenza of his so-called 'Emperor' Concerto for piano) there have been instances of the ACCOMPANIED CADENZA: Elgar's Violin Concerto offers a fine example of this.

Cf. *Point d'orgue.*

Cadenzato (It.). 'Cadenced', i.e. rhythmic.

Cadman, Charles Wakefield (b. Johnstown, Penn., 1881; d. Los Angeles 1946). Composer of melodic gifts who made much use of American Indian themes. Wrote operas (see *Shanewis*; *Witch of Salem*), orch. suites, a symphony, chamber music, &c., and very many songs.

Caeremoniale Episcoporum. In the Roman Catholic Church the book which provides instructions completing the Rubrics of the Pontifical and Missal (see *Liturgy*). It is of special importance to the choirmaster and organist for the laws it lays down.

Cage, John (b. Los Angeles 1912). Pupil of Schönberg carrying the pioneering spirit further than his master. Composes for a 'prepared piano', i.e. one with addition of divers objects to the strings—screws, bolts, rubber bands, bamboo slats, hairpins, &c. (cf. *Marinetti*). Not only may the quality of sound thus produced bear no relationship in timbre to that of the normal piano, but the pitch of the various notes may be altered and totally unexpected. His music is described as 'disembodied beauty of sound without association, without precedented timbre or form, without aesthetic antecedent'.

Cahier (Fr.). 'Part' of a book, e.g. *Cahier I* = 'Part I', &c.

Ça ira! (Fr. for 'that will go', i.e. 'will succeed'). This expression, many times repeated, made up about half the words of a revolutionary song which is said to have originated on that October night in 1789 when the mob marched to Versailles to bring the King and royal family to Paris, and which became the musical accompaniment to almost every incident of the Terror. The words, by a popular singer of the day, Ladré (some say Poirier), give the impression of having been more or less extemporized for the occasion, and they varied from period to period with the varying phases of the Revolution. The tune adopted was that of a popular contredanse, called *Carillon national*, by a theatre violinist of the day, Bécourt. This song was regarded as the official song of the Revolution. (Cf. *Carmagnole*.)

Caisse (Fr.). 'Box', hence 'drum'.

Caisse claire (Fr. 'claire' = 'clear', distinct). Snare drum, otherwise side drum (see *Percussion Family* 2 i).

Caisse, Grosse (Fr. 'grosse' = 'large'). Bass drum (see *Percussion Family* 2 k).

Caisse roulante (Fr. 'roulante' = 'rolling'). Tenor drum (see *Percussion Family* 2 j).

Caisse sourde (Fr. 'sourde' = 'dull', as opposed to 'claire'; see *Caisse claire*, above). Tenor drum (see *Percussion Family* 2 j).

Caix d'Hervelois, Louis de (b. Paris abt. 1670; there d. 1760). Famous performer on and composer for the viola da gamba, some of whose works are now often performed by 'cellists.

Calando (It. 'lowering'). *Diminuendo*, with also *rallentando*.

Calcando (It. 'trampling'). Much the same as *accelerando*, i.e. quickening gradually.

Caldara, Antonio (b. Venice 1670; d. Vienna 1738). Occupied various musical posts in Italy, Spain, and Austria. Wrote over 70 operas and over 30 oratorios, as well as motets, masses, string sonatas, &c.

Caledonian Hunt's Delight. See *Ye Banks and Braes*.

Calife de Bagdad, Le. Opera by Boïeldieu. (Prod. Paris 1800; London 1809; New York 1827.)

Calino casturame (or *Calen o custureme*). Tune alluded to by Shakespeare in *Henry V* (Act IV, sc. iv). It is to be found in the Fitzwilliam Virginal Book (q.v.). In *A Handefull of Pleasant Delites*, 1584, the words 'Caleno Custureme' are interpolated as a refrain between every two lines of the poem. 'When as I view your comly grace'. Possibly a perversion of the Irish 'Cailín, ó cois t Suire, mé' ('I am a girl from the banks of the river Suir').

Caliph of Bagdad (Boïeldieu). See *Calife*.

Calkin, (1) **James** (b. London 1786; there d. 1862). Pianist and composer of orch., chamber, and piano music. (2) **James Joseph** (b. 1813; d. London 1868). Son of (1). A violinist. (3) **Joseph** (b. 1816; d. London 1874. Son of (1), though the duplication of the name seems unusual). Well-known tenor vocalist, singing teacher, and song composer; known as 'Tenielli Calkin' (his mother being a Tenniel). (4) **John Baptiste** (b. London 1827; there d. 1905). Also son of (1) above. Held organ posts in Ireland and then London, where he was also a prof. at G.C.M. and T.C.M. Popular composer of church music, glees and part-songs, solo songs, and piano and organ music. (5) **George** (b. London 1829; date and place of death unknown).

Also son of (1) above. Well-known 'cellist, organist, composer, arranger of organ voluntaries, and choral conductor. (6) **Joseph** (b. London 1781; there d. 1846). Probably a brother of (1) above. Orch. violinist; also bookseller (Calkin & Budd). His son (7) **Joseph George** was also a bookseller, and taught the violin.

Callas (really Calogeropoulos), **Maria** (b. New York 1923). Dramatic coloratura soprano. Trained Athens Conserv. from 1936, returning to N.Y. in 1945. Début Verona 1947; Covent Garden 1952; Chicago 1954.

Callcott, (1) **John Wall** (b. London 1766; there d. 1821). Prominent London musician; untiring provider of glees and catches, some of them still to be heard. D.Mus., Oxford. (2) **William Hutchins** (b. London 1807; there d. 1882). Son of the above and like him a glee composer; active too as an arranger for the piano of orch. and other music.

Caller Herrin'. Poem is by Lady Nairne, music by Nathaniel Gow (q.v.), who wrote it about 1798 as a harpsichord piece, incorporating the traditional fishwives' cry of Edinburgh with the bells of St. Andrew's Church—and thus, a quarter of a century later, prompting Lady Nairne's muse.

Calliope. American term for a steamblown mechanical organ (see *Mechanical Reproduction* 13).

Calmato, calmando (It.). 'Calmed'; 'calming'.

Calme (Fr.). 'Calm.'

Calm Sea and Prosperous Voyage, The (*Die Meeresstille und glückliche Fahrt*). (1) Choral-Orch. setting by BEETHOVEN (op. 112; 1815) of Goethe's poem. (2) Concert-overture by MENDELSSOHN (op. 27; 1832), based on the same poem (1st perf. London 1836).

Calore (It. 'heat'). 'Passion.' So the adj. *caloroso.*

Calthumpian Concert. See *Charivari.*

Calvary (Brit. name for *Des Heilands letzte Stunden*, 'The Last Hours of the Saviour'). Oratorio by Spohr. (1st perf. Cassel 1835. London 1837.)

Calvé, Emma—real name Rosa Cal-

vet (b. Décazeville, dept. Aveyron 1858; d. Millau, in same dept., 1942), Soprano vocalist, whose brilliant career on both sides of Atlantic was chiefly in Fr. and It. opera (*Carmen* her greatest role).

Calvin, Jean (b. Noyon, Picardy, 1509; d. Geneva 1564). Scholar, theologian, and religious reformer, making Geneva 'the Protestant Rome'. Banished instruments and choirs from churches which accepted his ideas, but had no objection (as it is commonly stated he had) to music and the other arts. The English and Scottish Puritans owed many of their ideals and principles to him, and his views on church music tended to its simplification in England and Scotland and to the development of the metrical psalm and congregational singing. (See *Puritans; Hymns and Hymn Tunes* 3.)

Calvocoressi, Michel Dimitri (b. Marseilles 1877; d. London 1944). Of Greek parentage. Had career in Paris as music critic, author, and lecturer on music; settled in London. Was an early student of Russian music and associated with Diaghilef opera enterprise; wrote books on Russian composers and other musical subjects; provided many translations of Russian libretti, contributed in various languages to many musical journals.

Camargo. See *Ballet.*

Cambert, Robert (b. Paris abt. 1628; d. London 1677). Harpsichordist and organist; colleague in Paris of Perrin (see *Lully*), who obtained a monopoly for the performance of opera in the Fr. language, Cambert's *Pomone* (1671) being the earliest Fr. opera. On Lully taking over the monopoly, Cambert went to England, where, it it said, he was murdered by his valet.

Camberwell Green (Mendelssohn). See *Spring Song.*

Cambiare (It.). 'To change.'

Cambridge University. See *Degrees.* The Professors of Music have been—1684 Nicolas Staggins; 1705 Thos. Tudway; 1730 Maurice Greene; 1755 John Randall; 1799 Chas. Hague; 1821 J. Clarke-Whitfeld; 1836 Thos. A. Walmisley; 1856 W. Sterndale Bennett; 1875 G. A. Macfarren; 1887

C. V. Stanford; 1924 Charles Wood; 1926 E. J. Dent; 1946 Patrick Hadley; 1962 Thurston Dart; 1965 Robin Orr.

Camden, Archie (b. Newark Notts., 1888). Bassoonist. Trained Royal Manchester Coll. of Music. Then in Hallé Orch.; B.B.C. Orch. 1933; Royal Philharmonic Orch. 1946. Conductor of London Stock Exchange Orch.

Camera (It.). 'Chamber'—as opposed to hall, opera-house, &c. (For 'Cantata da Camera', see *Cantata*; for 'Concerto da Camera', see *Concerto*; for 'Sonata da Camera', see *Sonata*; also *Suite*.)

Cameron, (1) **Basil** (b. Reading 1885). Conductor. Trained Berlin Hochschule. Conductor in turn of municipal orchs. of Torquay, Hastings, and Harrogate; then of chief London orchs. (B.B.C. &c.), also those of San Francisco (1930–2), Seattle (1932–8), &c. C.B.E. 1957.

(2) **Douglas** (b. Dundee 1902). Violoncellist. Trained R.A.M. (later on staff). Appears frequently as soloist with leading Brit. orchs. Also member Blech String Quartet (see *Blech, Harry*).

Camidge Family. Supplied the organists of York Minster for a century— **John** (1735–1803), in office 1756–99; his son **Matthew** (1758–1844), in office 1799–1842; *his* son **John** (1790–1859), in office 1842–8; a Cambridge and Canterbury D.Mus.

In addition there are the last-named's son **Thomas Simpson** (1828–1912) who deputized at York for his paralytic father's last 10 years and then held other posts; and *his* son **John** (1853–1939), organist of Beverley Minster 1875–1933.

Camminando (It.). 'Walking', 'proceeding', used in a sense of 'covering the ground', 'pushing on'.

Campana; campane (It.). 'Bell'; 'bells', e.g. those used in the orch. (See *Percussion Family* I b; *Bell* 5.)

Campanella (It.). 'Little bell.' (The plur., *campanelle*, is sometimes used for Glockenspiel—see *Percussion Family* I c.)

Campanella. Piano piece by Liszt, one of his 6 *Transcendent Studies of*

Execution based on Paganini, dedicated to Clara Schumann (1838; see *Paganini Transcriptions*), the work of Paganini here transcribed being *Rondo à la Clochette* ('Bell Rondo') from B minor Violin Concerto. Liszt had previously used same theme in his *Grande fantaisie de bravoure sur 'La Clochette'* for Piano and Orch. (1832).

Campanetta (It.). Glockenspiel (see *Percussion Family* I c).

Campanini, (1) **Italo** (b. Parma 1845; d. nr. there 1896). Operatic tenor. Début Odessa 1869; took part 1st perf. *Lohengrin* in Italy (Florence) 1871; London début 1872; then Russia and U.S.A. (took part in opening perf. Metropolitan Opera House 1883. For brother see below. (2) **Cleofonte** (b. Parma 1860; d. Chicago 1919). Operatic conductor and impresario. Conducted 1st U.S.A. perf. Verdi's *Othello*, Metropolitan Opera 1888. Great reputation in U.S.A. Chief conductor at Hammerstein's New Manhattan Opera House 1906–9: Chicago Opera 1910 and in general charge there 1913 to death. Wife was Eva Tetrazzini (q.v.).

Campbells are coming, The. This popular Scottish tune first appeared in print in 1745, at which time it was used as a country dance under the title *Hob and Nob*, but about the same period it is also found with its present title. There are many contradictory statements as to its origin.

Campenhout, François van (b. Brussels 1779; there d. 1848). Wellknown tenor; also opera composer; now remembered by his composition of the Belgian national anthem, *La Brabançonne* (q.v.).

Campian or **Campion, Thomas** (b. London 1567; there d. 1620). Medical man, one of most charming of Elizabethan poets, composer of delicate lute songs; author of treatises on prosody and counterpoint.

Campo, Conrado del—in full, Conrado del Campo y Zabaleta (b. Madrid 1879; d. there 1953). Composer of symphonic poems, operas, chamber music, choral music, &c.

Campoli, Alfredo (b. Rome 1906). Violinist. Came to Britain as child.

London début age 11. High reputation as exponent first of light and later of serious music.

Campra, André (b. Aix-en-Provence 1660; d. Versailles 1744). Director of the music in several provincial cathedrals and then in that of Notre Dame, Paris, to which his music attracted crowds; at about age of 40 turned to the stage and won renown especially by his opera-ballets.

Canadian Boat Song. (1) The tune is a French-Canadian folk song (*Dans mon chemin*); the poem is by Thomas Moore, who heard the tune when visiting Canada in 1804.

(2) But there is another 'Canadian Boat Song' the authorship of which is extremely obscure, the question cropping up periodically in the press. This is the song of which the very beautiful stanza is so often quoted:

From the lone shieling of the misty island
Mountains divide us, and the waste of seas—
Yet still the blood is strong, the heart is Highland,
And we in dreams behold the Hebrides.

Amongst persons to whom the lines are often attributed are the novelist John Galt, the 12th Earl of Eglinton (1739–1819), Lockhart (who possibly wrote the last 2 stanzas), John Wilson (whose claim disappears under scrutiny), and David Macbeth Moir, otherwise 'Delta', who possibly wrote the first 3 stanzas. The poem apparently first appeared in *Blackwood's Magazine* in 1829, and it is found set to music in a posthumous publication, *A Selection of Songs and Marches, &c.*, composed by Hugh, late Earl of Eglinton. Scott is accepted by some as the author.

Canadian Broadcasting Corporation. Founded 1936, superseding former Radio Commission founded 4 years earlier. Headquarters Toronto.

Canadian College of Organists. Founded 1909 (called Canadian Guild of Organists until 1920). Holds diploma exams. and maintains local centres. (See *Degrees and Diplomas* 2.)

Canadian Guild of Organists. See above.

Canaries (or *Canarie*, or *Canary*). An old dance in rhythm something like the gigue (q.v.) but with all its phrases beginning on the 1st beat of the measure with a note a beat and a half long.

Can-can (or *Chahut*). A boisterous (and latterly indecorous) Parisian dance of the quadrille pattern.

Canción (Sp.). 'Song.' There are diminutives—*Cancioncica, Cancioncilla, Cancioncita*. The *Canción Danza* is a Spanish dance-song.

Cancrizans. See *Canon*.

Candide. See *Bernstein, L.*

Caniglia, Maria (b. Naples 1906). Dramatic soprano. Début Turin 1930; London 1937; New York 1938.

Canntaireachd. Curious Scottish Highland bagpipe notation, in which syllables stand for recognized groups of notes.

Canon. The word means 'rule' and, musically, it is applied to that sort of counterpoint (q.v.) in which one melodic strand gives the rule to another, or to all the others, which must, at an interval of time, imitate it, note for note. Simple forms of choral canon are the *Catch* (q.v.) and the *Round* (q.v.).

CANON AT THE OCTAVE is one in which the voices (human or instrumental) are at that pitch-interval from one another. *Canon at the Fifth*, or at any other interval, is similarly explained.

A Canon for 2 voices is called a CANON TWO IN ONE (and similarly with *Canon Three in One*, &c.). A CANON FOUR IN TWO is a double canon, i.e. one in which 2 voices are carrying on 1 canon whilst 2 others are engaged on another.

CANON BY AUGMENTATION has the imitating voices in longer notes than the one that they are imitating. CANON BY DIMINUTION is the reverse of this.

CANON CANCRIZANS is a rather useless type in which the imitating voice gives out the melody backwards ('Cancrizans' from Lat. *Cancer* = 'crab'; but crabs move sideways; however, such writing is often crabbed): other names for it are CANON PER RECTE ET RETRO (or RECTUS ET INVERSUS) and RETROGRADE CANON.

A PERPETUAL CANON or INFINITE CANON is a Canon so arranged that each voice, having arrived at the end, can begin again, and so indefinitely. The converse is FINITE CANON.

STRICT CANON is that in which the intervals of the imitating voice are exactly the same as those of the voice imitated (i.e. as regards their quality of major, minor, &c.).

In FREE CANON the intervals remain the same numerically, but not necessarily as to quality (e.g. a major 3rd may become a minor 3rd).

That voice in a canon which first enters with the melody to be imitated is called DUX ('leader') or ANTECEDENT, and any imitating voice is called COMES ('companion') or CONSEQUENT.

There exists CANON BY INVERSION, in which an upward interval in the *Dux* becomes a downward one in the *Comes*, and vice versa. CANON PER ARSIN ET THESIN has the same meaning, but also another one, i.e. Canon in which notes that fall on strong beats in the *Dux* fall on weak beats in the *Comes*, and vice versa.

Choral Canon in which there are non-canonic instrumental parts is ACCOMPANIED CANON.

Passages of canonic writing often occur in compositions that, as wholes, are not canon, and in addition to actual canonic composition there exists a great deal of composition with a similar effect but which is too free to come under that designation, being mere CANONIC IMITATION.

Cf. *Sumer is icumen in*, and *Non nobis*.

Canonical Hours. See *Divine Office*.

Cantab. (*Cantabrigia* = Cambridge). Indicates a Cambridge degree.

Cantabile (It. 'singable' or 'singingly'). 'With the melody smoothly performed and well brought out.' (For *Aria Cantabile* see *Aria*.) **Cantando** (It.), 'singing'.

Cantata (It. 'Sung'; fem. of 'Cantato'). A word of rather different meanings, according to the period as to which it is employed. (1) In the 17th c. and often in the 18th it meant an extended vocal solo (with recitatives and arias) of the kind then popular in cultured It. society. A secular composition of this type was called a *Cantata da camera* ('Room Cantata'); a sacred one, *Cantata da chiesa* ('Church Cantata'). (2) In the 18th c., however, the term came to be also applied to a work for several solo voices, chorus, &c., much like a short oratorio or an opera without scenery or acting (e.g. Bach's *Coffee Cantata* and *Peasant Cantata* and his many church cantatas). This latter is the sense in which the word was used in 19th-c. Britain and is still used.

Cf. *Canzona*.

Cantata profana. By Bartók; 1st perf. London (1934). Narrative setting of a legend; solo voice, chorus, and orch.

Cantate (Fr., Ger.). 'Cantata.'

Cantate Domino. The 98th Psalm, 'O sing unto the Lord a new song'. See *Common Prayer*. (In the Prayer Book of the American Episcopal Church part of the *Cantate Domino* is joined to part of the *Venite*.)

Cantatrice (It.). 'Female singer.'

Cante flamenco. Type of melody popular in Andalusia and used in both song and dance. A branch of *Cante hondo* (q.v.). The significance of the word Flamenco ('Flemish') is much disputed. The term is especially applied to gipsy music, but it seems to have acquired a very comprehensive meaning nowadays and to take in almost anything.

Cante hondo or **Cante jondo** (*hondo* or *jondo* means 'deep'). Type of popular Spanish song, with a good deal of repetition of the note, much melodic decoration, and the use of some intervals that do not occur in the accepted European scales. The Phrygian cadence (see *Cadence* s.v. 'Phrygian Cadence' i) is much used. (Cf. *Cante flamenco*.)

Canterbury Degrees. See *Degrees and Diplomas* 1.

Canterbury Pilgrims, The (1) Opera by STANFORD, prod. London 1884. (2) Opera by DE KOVEN, prod. New York and Philadelphia 1917. (3) Cantata by DYSON, Winchester 1931. (4) Opera by JULIUS HARRISON.

Canti carnascialeschi (It. 'carnival songs'; singular is *canto carnascialesco*). Gay processional madrigals of an early simple sort, with several stanzas to the same music, something like the Eng. Ayre (see *Madrigal*) but with the tune in the tenor. They were a part of the social life of Florence in the 15th and 16th cs.

Canticle. A Bible hymn (other than a psalm) as used in the liturgy of a Christian church. Common Prayer (q.v.) uses the term only for the *Benedicite*, but usage applies it also to other hymns as above limited and also to the *Te Deum* (cf. *Common Prayer*). In the

Roman Catholic Church the Canticles drawn from the New Testament are called the *Evangelical Canticles* or *Major Canticles*, in distinction from those drawn from the Old Testament, which are called the *Minor Canticles*.

(*Canticles* is also the alternative name for the Old Testament book, *The Song of Solomon*.)

Cantiga. A Spanish or Portuguese folk song; also a type of religious song.

Cantilena. (1) Smooth, melodious (and not rapid) vocal writing or performance. (2, now obsolete) Short song. (3) In choral music, the part carrying the main tune. (4) Type of solfeggio (q.v.) in which appeared all the notes of the scale.

Cantilène (Fr.). Same as *Cantilena* (q.v.).

Cantillation. Chanting in free rhythm, in plainsong style. The term is most used in connexion with Jewish liturgical music.

Cantiones sacrae. See *Motet*.

Canto (It.). 'Song', 'melody'. So *Col Canto*, 'With the song', i.e. the accompanist to take his time throughout from the performer of the melody.

Canto fermo. See *Harmony* 1; *Counterpoint*; *Conductus*; *Gymel*.

Cantor. The precentor or director of the music in a Ger. Protestant church, or the leading singer in a synagogue.

Cantoris. Properly that side of the choir of a cathedral, &c., on which the Precentor sits but now normally the north side.

Cantuar. Indicates a Canterbury degree (see *Degrees and Diplomas* 1).

Cantus (Lat.). 'Song.' In the 16th and 17th cs. applied to the uppermost voice in choral music. For **Cantus firmus**, however, see references to *Canto fermo* (It.) under *Conductus*; *Gymel*; *Counterpoint*.

Cantus choralis. See *Chorale*. For **Cantus figuratus, Cantus mensuratus,** and **Cantus planus,** see *Plainsong*.

Canu penillion (Welsh). 'Penillion singing' (see *Penillion*).

Canzona or **canzone** (It., plur. *canzoni*). (1) Type of poem of period of the troubadours (see *Minstrels*, &c.); hence musical setting of such a poem, solo or choral. (2) Short instrumental composition somewhat resembling choral music of more or less the fugal type, and sometimes in several movements.

The *Canzona cantata* and *Canzona sonata* were respectively the 'sung' and 'played' canzona (later abbreviated to 'Cantata' and 'Sonata', i.e. the adjectives used as nouns).

Canzonet, or **canzonetta.** Diminutive of *Canzona* (see above). Applied to certain madrigals and later to a light, flowing kind of simple solo song.

Caoine. Irish funeral song, with wailing (the Eng. spelling is 'Keen').

Capell, Richard (b. Northampton 1885; d. London 1954). Music critic of London *Daily Mail* (1911–31) and then of *Daily Telegraph*, interrupting his work during 1914–18 as member of the Brit. force in France (Military Medal) and during 1939–45 as War Correspondent of his journal in France, North Africa, Greece, &c. Wrote valuable books on *Schubert's Songs*, &c., and also on the war and on post-war position in Greece.

Capella. See *Cappella*.

Capelle (Fr.). Same as Ger. *Kapelle* (q.v.).

Capellmeister. See *Kapellmeister*.

Capet, Lucien (b. Paris 1873; there d. 1928). Violinist. Trained Paris Conserv. Founded Capet Quartet. Famous teacher. Some compositions and books.

Capitán, El. Very successful operetta by Sousa. Libretto by C. Klein; lyrics by T. Frost. (Prod. Boston 1896; New York the same year; London 1899.)

Caplet, André (b. Havre 1878; d. nr. Paris 1925). Studied at Paris Conservatory and won Prix de Rome (1901); early became known as capable conductor (Boston Opera Co. 1910–14); close friend of Debussy and first conductor of some of his works. Composed songs, choral and orch. music, chamber music, &c.

Capocci, (1) Gaetano (b. Rome 1811; there d. 1898). Organist and director of choir St. John Lateran. Composer of church music. For son see below. **(2) Filippo** (b. Rome 1840; there d. 1911). Like father became organist St. John Lateran (1875); succeeded him as director of choir 1898. Famous performer and composer for his instrument.

Caponsacchi. See *Hagemann*.

Capotasto, capo d'astro, capodastro (It.); **capodastère** (Fr.), **capodaster** (Ger.). Lit. 'head' of the 'touch' or 'feel', i.e. the 'nut', or raised portion of the top of the finger board of a stringed instrument, which 'touches' the strings and defines their length at that end. Another name is *Barre* (Fr.). A movable capotasto has sometimes been used, which can be placed at any point in the length of the strings (in 'cello playing the thumb acts as such and in the 18th c. was sometimes so called). In U.S.A. the name *capotasto* is reserved for this type.

Cappella, Capella (It., the former being the correct spelling). 'Chapel.' *A cappella* or *alla cappella* (applied to choral music) meaning 'in the church style' and, by this, 'unaccompanied' (like the 16th-c. church music). A rarer sense of these expressions makes them synonymous with *alla breve* (see *Breve*).

Capriccio (It.); **caprice** (Eng. and Fr.). (1) Term applied to some of the 16th-c. It. madrigals and, later, to a kind of free fugue for keyboard instruments, and later to any light quick composition. (2) In the early 18th c. the word was sometimes used for 'Cadenza'. (3) *A capriccio* means 'According to the fancy (caprice) of the performer'.

Capriccio. Opera by Richard Strauss. Libretto by Clemens Krauss. (Prod. Munich 1942.)

Capriccio espagnol. Symphonic Suite by Rimsky-Korsakof, op. 34 (1887).

Capriccio italien. Symphonic Poem by Tchaikovsky, op. 45 (1880).

Capriccioso (It.), **capricieux** (Fr.). 'Capricious', hence in a lively, infor-mal, whimsical style. So the adverb *capricciosamente*.

Caprice. See *Capriccio*.

Caractacus. Cantata by Elgar. Text by H. A. Acworth. (1st perf. Leeds Fest. 1898.)

Carapetyan, Armen (b. Persia, of Armenian parents, 1908). Musicologist. Educated Teheran, then Sorbonne and Harvard Univ. (M.A., Ph.D.). Also studied violin under Capet and composition under Malipiero. In 1944 founded Inst. of Renaissance and Baroque Music, Rome, which was superseded by the 'American Inst. of Musicology' of which he is Director.

Carcelera (Sp.) from *carcel*, 'jail'. Sort of *Saeta* (q.v.)—supposedly a prisoner's song.

Cardillac. Opera by Hindemith (op. 39, 1926). Libretto based on story by E. T. A. Hoffmann. (Prod. Dresden 1926; London, concert form 1936.)

Card Party (Stravinsky). See *Jeu de cartes*.

Cardus, Neville (b. Manchester 1889). Joined staff of *Manchester Guardian* 1917 and became its music critic on death of Samuel Langford in 1927. Also cricket-critic of this paper, and author of books on his subjects and an autobiography (1947, &c.). Position on *Sydney Morning Herald* 1941–7. C.B.E. 1964. Knighted 1967.

Caressant (Fr.). 'Caressing.'

Carey, (1) Henry (b. abt. 1690; d. London 1743). Wrote much music for theatre, &c. (Not the composer of *God save the Queen* as often stated.)
(2) **(Francis) Clive (Savill)** (b. Sible Hedingham, Essex, 1883; d. London 1968). Baritone. Trained R.C.M. (on staff 1946–53), &c. Toured with Eng. Singers (q.v.), sang in opera, served as producer at Sadler's Wells, and composed incidental music for plays. On staff of conservs. of Adelaide (1939) and then Melbourne (1942–5). Active in Eng. folk song movement, &c. C.B.E. 1955.

Carezzando; carezzevole (It.). 'Caressing'; 'caressingly'.

Carillo. See *Carrillo*.

Carillon. Recitation with Orch. Poem by Cammaerts, music by Elgar—largely based on a bell motif and composed as a tribute to Belgium 1914 (op. 75). Later arranged for alternative perf. without declamation.

Carillon. (1) See *Bell* 4. (2) Organ stop; a *Mixture* (q.v.) of 3 ranks (12th, 17th, 22nd): chiefly in U.S.A.

Carillon national. See *Ça ira!*

Carissimi, Giacomo (b. Marino, nr. Rome, 1605; d. Rome 1674). Brought to perfection the recitative style and introduced more instrumental variety into the cantata and oratorio. Some of his sacred music is still heard.

Carl Rosa Opera. See *Rosa*.

Carlton, Richard (b. abt. 1558; d. abt. 1638). A Norfolk vicar and notable madrigal composer.

Carmagnole. Originally the name of sort of short coat, worn in north Italian district of Carmagnola, and brought into France by workmen from that district. The insurgents of Marseilles in 1792 (cf. *Rouget de Lisle*) introduced it to Paris, where it became identified with the Revolution. A round dance of the time was given the name and a song with the refrain, 'Dansons la Carmagnole, vive le son du canon', to a very catchy air, became identified with revolutionary festivities such as executions. The authorship of both words and music is unknown. (Cf. *Ça ira!*)

Carman's Whistle. This is a tune to be found, with variations by Byrd, in the Fitzwilliam Virginal Book (q.v.). It is that of a ballad which was published in 1592.

Carmen (Lat.). (1) 'Tune', 'song', 'strain', 'poem'. (2, in 14th- and 15th-c. parlance) Voice part of a composition (as distinguished from the instrumental parts), or the uppermost part of a choral composition.

Carmen. See *Bizet*.

Carmina Burana. 'Scenic cantata' by Orff, on Latin text. (Prod. Frankfurt 1937.)

Carnaval: Scènes mignonnes ('Dainty Scenes'). Set of 21 Piano pieces by Schumann (op. 9, 1834–5), 'built for the most part on the notes

A–S–C–H, the name of a small Bohemian town where I had a lady friend, but which, strange to say, are also the only musical letters in my name'. (AS is Ger. for A flat, and H for B; S is sometimes treated by Schumann as ES, i.e. E flat. Where the 4 notes appear alone they are not meant to be played.) Cf. *Abegg*.

Carnaval. Ballet by Fokine, set to the above music. (Prod. St. Petersburg 1910.)

Carnaval romain, Le. Most popular of the Concert-overtures of Berlioz. (op. 9, 1843.) The themes come from his unsuccessful opera, *Benvenuto Cellini*, in which it has sometimes (as he suggested) been used as an introduction to the 2nd Act.

Carnegie, Andrew (b. Dunfermline 1835; d. Lenox, Mass., 1919). Scot who made fortune in Pittsburgh steel industry, establishing funds which have endowed many musical activities, making grants for organs, providing sets of gramophone records for U.S.A. educational institutions, financing publication of contemporary and old music (e.g. great edn. of Engl. church music of Tudor period), building New York's largest concert hall (Carnegie Hall, 1891), founding in Pittsburgh Carnegie Inst. with organ, and Carnegie Inst. of Technology (with music department), &c. Chief media for these benefactions have been Carnegie Corporation of New York and Carnegie United Kingdom Trust (headquarters Dunfermline).

Carnegie Hall, New York. Chief concert hall of city. Opened 1891, Andrew Carnegie (q.v.) providing most of funds. Until 1898 called 'Music Hall'.

Carner, Mosco (b. Vienna 1904). Took doctorate at Univ. of Vienna and then developed as orch. and operatic conductor. Settled in London 1933, conducting, writing upon music, &c. Important book on Puccini (1959).

Carnival. (1) By DVOŘÁK: See *Triple Overture*. (2) By GLAZUNOF: Concert-overture (op. 45).

Carnival at Paris. Orch. piece by Svendsen (op. 9, abt. 1874).

Carnival of Animals. Amusing 'Grand Zoological Fantasy' by Saint-

Saëns for Orch., with Piano, Xylophone, and Harmonica (metal plates struck with hammer). Fourteen brief movements—(1) *Introduction and Royal Lions' March*; (2) *Hens and Cocks*; (3) *Hémiones—Swift Animals*; (4) *Tortoises*; (5) *The Elephant*; (6) *Kangaroos*; (7) *Aquarium*; (8) *Long-eared Personages*; (9) *The Cuckoo in the Depths of the Wood*; (10) *The Aviary*; (11) *Pianists*; (12) *Fossils*; (13) *The Swan*; (14) *Finale*.

Carnival of Venice. Name given to a number of popular instrumental compositions, more or less of the nature of variations on the air of a certain popular Venetian tune. (See under *Paganini*.)

Carol. A religious seasonal song, usually joyful, in the vernacular and sung by the common people. All Christian nations, Western and Eastern, have carols, some of them evidently of pagan origin but taken over and adapted in the early days of Christianity. The nature of the carol varies: it may be dramatic, narrative, or lyrical.

The Christmas carols of France are called Noëls (Noël = Christmas) and, through the Norman, the word has survived in Britain as 'Nowell', sometimes found as the refrain of a carol. Those of Germany are called 'Weihnachtslieder', i.e. Christmas Eve Songs.

One of the oldest printed Eng. Christmas carols is the *Boar's Head Carol*, long sung as the traditional dish is carried in on Christmas Day at Queen's Coll., Oxford; it was printed in 1521. This is but one of a large group of carols associated with good cheer as an element in Christmas joy.

As the Eng. and Scottish Puritans of the 17th c. disapproved of keeping religious feasts they, of course, discouraged Christmas celebrations of every kind, including carols.

From the later 19th c. the singing of carols in England, which had long become a matter of door-to-door visitation, often of a very pleasant and picturesque nature, tended to be degraded into petty beggary: in every district little children in groups paraded from door-to-door to door-step, from the end of November onwards, building up a Christmas fund by the extortion of what may very fairly be called 'hush money'. At the same period what may be described as the 'Ancient and Modern' movement (see *Hymns and Hymn Tunes* 4) brought into popularity a poorish type of newly composed music of very Victorian idiom, and also somewhat weakly harmonized versions of the old carol tunes; these were the musical counterpart of the imitative Gothic church architecture of the period. However, towards the beginning of the 20th c. a movement for better Christmas music made itself felt, and especially one for the revival of the genuine traditional carols.

Carolan. See *O'Carolan*.

Caro mio ben. See *Giordani, Giuseppe*.

Carpenter, John Alden (b. Park Ridge, Ill., 1876; d. Chicago 1951). Studied Harvard. Wealthy business man who attained popularity as composer of orch. works, piano pieces, songs, &c. (see *Adventures in a Perambulator*; *Birthday of the Infanta*; *Krazy Kat*; *Sea Drift*; *Skyscrapers*).

Carr, (1) Frank Osmond (b. nr. Bradford 1858; d. Uxbridge 1916). Composer of highly popular light comedy operas, &c. (e.g. *His Excellency* 1894; libretto by W. S. Gilbert). M.A., Cambridge; D.Mus., Oxford.

(2) **Howard** (b. Manchester 1880; d. London 1960). London theatre conductor; composer of light operas and orch. music, songs, &c. In Australia 1928–38 on staff of Sydney Conservatory, &c.

(3) **Benjamin.** See *Opera* 6.

Carrée (Fr. 'square'). The double whole-note or breve (q.v.).

Carreño, Teresa—in full María Teresa (b. Carácas, Venezuela, 1853; d. New York 1917). Pianist. When she was 9 family settled in New York where she appeared with highest success. Later studied under Gottschalk (q.v.) and Rubinstein (q.v.), and became equally well known in Old and New Worlds. Had a period as operatic soprano and another (short) as operatic conductor. Carried varied musical tastes into matrimony—(1) the violinist Sauret 1872; (2) the baritone vocalist G. Tagliapietra 1875; (3) the pianist-composer d'Albert 1892–5; (4) Tagliapietra (brother of 2nd husband) 1902 to death. Not, as often stated, composer of Venezuelan National Anthem.

Carrillo, Julián (b. San Luis Potosí, Mexico, 1875; d. Mexico 1965). Studied Leipzig and became violinist in the Gewandhaus Orch. under Nikisch; held important positions in native country and then settled New York. Developed a system of microtonal composition (see *Microtones*); works include symphonies, operas, masses, chamber music, &c.; also theoretical treatises.

Carrodus Family (orig. Carruthers). (1) **John Tiplady** (b. nr. Keighley, Yorks., 1836; d. London 1895). Violinist. Début at 9. Then pupil of Molique. Became leading violinist of chief London orchs. and provincial fest. orchs., &c.; recitalist and composer for his instrument. For his sons see below.

Sons of above. (2) **Bernhard Molique** (d. Ross, Hereford, 1936), violinist. (3) **Ernest Alexander** (d. 1938), Britain's leading double-bass player. (4) **John**, violoncellist and organist. (5) **Robert**, violinist. (6) **William O.** (d. Greenford, Middlesex, 1942), flautist.

On one occasion father and the 5 sons appeared together in orch. of Three Choirs Fest. (Hereford 1894). In 1895, when Keighley conferred town's freedom to celebrate jubilee of public appearance of founder of this musical family, all above plus his wife and sister appeared as performers—i.e. 8 of the same name.

(7) **Constance** (b. Preston). Mezzo-contralto. Trained Roy. Manchester Coll. of Music. Specialist in European folk song. Numerous broadcasts, also tours in Britain and Europe.

Carroll, Walter (b. Manchester 1869; there d. 1955). Manchester church musician and teacher (prof. at Royal Manchester Coll. of Music and lecturer at Univ.); Musical Adviser to Education Committee (1918–34). Composer of highly successful piano (and latterly violin) music for children. Author of works on musical education. D.Mus., Manchester.

Carrosse du Saint-Sacrement, Le. See *Berners*.

Carse, Adam—formerly A. von Ahn Carse (b. Newcastle-on-Tyne 1878; d. Great Missenden, Bucks., 1958). Trained at R.A.M. (later on staff); a music master at Winchester Coll. for 13 years. Composer of many orch. works, chamber music, and educational music, and high authority on history of orch.; ed. of neglected classics.

Carte, Richard D'Oyly (b. London 1844; there d. 1901). Concert agent and producer of light operas, who became impresario of Gilbert and Sullivan; built Savoy Theatre, 1881 (hence term for G. and S. works, 'Savoy Opera'). Widow (d. 1913) and then son **Rupert** (1876–1948) and granddaughter **Bridget** in turn succeeded in proprietorship and management of 'D'Oyly Carte Opera Co.'

Carter, (1) Ernest Trow (b. Orange, N.J., 1866; d. Stamford, Conn., 1953). Piano pupil of William Mason (q.v.); and studied composition in Germany; member of the Bar (1891) but continued to devote himself to music, holding various academic musical positions and organistships. Composed operas, ballets, orch. works, &c. B.A., Hon. Mus.Doc., Princeton; M.A., Columbia.

(2) **Elliott Cook** (b. New York 1908). Studied Harvard and in Paris under Nadia Boulanger. On staff Peabody Conserv. 1947; Columbia Univ. 1948; Yale Univ. 1960. Composer of operas, ballets, orch., choral, and chamber music. Pulitzer Prize 1960.

Caruso, Enrico (b. Naples 1873; there d. 1921). Tenor vocalist of highest popularity in It. and Fr. opera, winning fabulous financial rewards for both appearances in person and gramophone records.

Carvalho, (1) Léon. See under *Miolan-Carvalho*.

(2) (*née* Miolan), **Caroline Marie Félix** (b. Marseilles 1827; d. nr. Dieppe 1895). Operatic soprano of international popularity; created several of soprano parts in Gounod's operas.

Caryll, Ivan (really Felix Tilkin; b. Liège 1861; d. New York 1921). Active in England and America; composed many popular musical comedies (*The Earl and the Girl, Our Miss Gibbs*, &c.).

Casadesus. The following members of this large (originally Spanish) family, all born in Paris, are the best known: (1) **Francis Louis** (1870–1954). Opera condr.; founder and Dir. (1918–22), Amer. Conserv., Fontainebleau; comp. operas, orch. music, &c. (2) **Robert Guillaume** (1878–1940). Brother of (1). Pianist and composer. (3) **Henri Gustav** (1879–1947). Brother of (1). Viola-player. Member of Capet (q.v.) Quartet. Founded New Soc. of Ancient Instruments (toured with it Europe and U.S.A.); made collection of old instruments (now in Boston Orch.'s museum). Composer of light operas and ballets, &c. (4) **Marcel Louis Lucien** (1882–1914). Brother of (1). Violoncellist. Killed in World War I. (5) **Marius Robert Max** (b. 1892). Son of (1). Violinist. Composer of operas, chamber music, &c. (6) **Robert Marcel** (1899–1972). Son of (2). Pianist, touring Europe and U.S.A., &c. Composer of concertos for piano, violin, &c., and other orch. and piano works. Dir. Piano Dept., Amer. Conserv., Fontainebleau, till 1949.

Casals, Pau—formerly Pablo, but later changed to the Catalan form (b. Vendrell, Catalonia, 1876; d. Rio Piedras, P.R., 1973). World's greatest 'cellist, also a conductor (founded Barcelona orch.) and composer. Became an exile from his native country in 1939, with victory of Franco and re-incorporation of Catalonia in Spain. (See *Suggia*.)

Casella, Alfredo (b. Turin 1883; d. Rome 1947). Studied under Fauré at Paris Conserv. and then enjoyed international success as pianist and orch. conductor. As composer ranks as an anti-romantic and a supporter of the national It. movement for a style of composition less based on a 'predominance of vocal melodramatic melody'.

Cassa (It. 'box'). Any drum of a large size, generally the bass drum (see *Percussion Family* 2 k).

Cassa grande, or **Gran cassa** (It. 'big box'). Bass drum (see *Percussion Family* 2 k).

Cassadó, Gaspar (b. Barcelona 1897; d. Madrid 1966). Violoncellist. Pupil of Casals. Many compositions and arrangements for 'cello.

Cassandra. See *Gnecchi*.

Cassa rullante (It. 'rolling box'). Tenor drum (see *Percussion Family* 2 j).

Cassation, Cassazione. See *Suite*.

Casse-noisette (Tchaikovsky). See *Nutcracker*.

Casson, Thomas. See *Positive Organ*.

Castagnette (It.), **castagnettes** (Fr.). 'Castanets' (see *Percussion Family* 2 q).

Castanets. See *Percussion Family* 2 q.

Castelnuovo-Tedesco, Mario (b. Florence 1895; d. Hollywood, Cal., 1968). Pupil of Pizzetti. Composer of songs, choral music, piano pieces, and operas, showing a sense of delicate refinement. In California from 1948.

Castillane (Sp.). Dance of the Province of Castile.

Castle Hyde. See *Last Rose of Summer*.

Castor and Pollux. See *Rameau*.

Castrato Singer or **Evirato Singer**. See *Voice* 5.

Catalán (Sp.), **Catalane** (Fr.). Spanish dance type deriving from Catalonia.

Catalani, (1) **Alfredo** (b. Lucca 1854; d. Milan 1893). Composer of very popular operas, especially *La Wally* (1892). (2) **Angelica** (b. Sinigaglia 1780; d. Paris 1849). Operatic soprano of highest possible fame. Great range and flexibility. In London and elsewhere received enormous fees (spent largely on charitable schemes). Heard at some Engl. festivals.

Catch. A round (q.v.); but the term is now often used in a less general sense which confines its application to such rounds as, in the singing, afford a laugh by the way the words are heard, as for instance in the one *Ah, how Sophia*, which in the singing suggests 'Our house afire', the later line 'Go fetch the Indian's borrowed plume' similarly suggesting 'Go fetch the engines!'

Catch Club = Noblemen and Gentlemen's Catch Club (q.v.).

Cathedral Music and Musicians in Britain. The present article is concerned with cathedral music in Britain from the date when this became a distinctively Brit. thing, i.e. from the Reformation.

What are known as the cathedrals of the *Old Foundation* are Bangor, Chichester, Exeter, Hereford, Lichfield, Lincoln, Llandaff, St. Asaph, St. David's, St. Paul's (London), Salisbury, Wells, and York—13 in all: these were already cathedrals, and cathedrals only, at the suppression of the monasteries under Henry VIII in 1536–9. What are known as the *New Foundation* cathedrals are (a) Canterbury, Carlisle, Christ Church at Dublin (the position of St. Patrick's Cathedral in the same city is peculiar and cannot be gone into here), Durham, Ely, Norwich, Rochester, Winchester, and Worcester, and (b) Bristol, Chester, Gloucester, Oxford, and Peterborough —14 in all. Of these, those marked (a) had previously been both monasteries and cathedrals and now became merely the latter, whilst those marked (b) became cathedrals for the first time, new sees being set up. In the Old Foundation cathedrals the Precentor (q.v.) is a 'dignitary' generally ranking next to the Dean: in cathedrals of the New Foundation the Precentor is usually merely a minor canon. The Old Foundation cathedrals (whose statutes all dated from a time when organs were primitive and organists had little importance) barely recognized the organist as a special official, but in drafting the statutes of the New Foundation cathedrals he was generally taken into account (the exceptions are Winchester and Ely). In the Old Foundation cathedrals the office of Master of the Choristers was often a separate one; in those of the New Foundation this was rare. In addition to the cathedrals certain other churches, similarly equipped, functioned as centres of musical activity, such as Westminster

Abbey, St. George's Chapel in Windsor Castle, and the larger colleges of Oxford and Cambridge Univs. It can be taken that what follows applies to them, as to the cathedrals. (The Chapel Royal, London, is discussed, under its own name, elsewhere in this volume.)

A large number of new cathedrals have come into existence as the result of the 19th- and 20th-c. desire for more efficient organization; they are usually old parish churches converted to diocesan use, but one or two are new buildings (Truro, Liverpool). They have none of them been sufficiently lavishly financed to undertake the traditional full daily cathedral programme. There are also a certain number of cathedrals of the Anglican communion in Ireland, in addition to the two mentioned above, and in Scotland, in which latter, however, the original buildings (e.g. Glasgow Cathedral) were deprived of cathedral status on the completion of the Reformation under Knox, and, where still in existence, are in use as Presbyterian churches.

At the time of the Reformation, and for a century afterwards, there were two currents of religious thought contending for the control of the service of the Church. One school would much reduce or even abolish choirs and organs and the other would fully retain them. From Cranmer's time composers were urged to write syllabically (that is a note to a syllable) and with plain chordal progressions rather than counterpoint: these limitations (prompted by the good motive of enabling the congregation to hear the words) tended somewhat to restrict the interest of the music, and have led to the rather marked differentiation of what we call the 'Anglican style' from the style of church music in Britain in pre-Reformation days and in other countries.

Under the musical Tudors cathedral music was fostered: under the early Stuarts it somewhat declined. Nevertheless, up to the beginning of the Civil War cathedral music flourished considerably and produced a body of composition of which any country might be proud (though admittedly the Chapel Royal must have the credit for much of this). A very important collection of cathedral music was printed in

1641, that of Barnard, a minor canon of St. Paul's. In that same year a House of Lords Committee advised 'That the Music used in cathedral and collegiate churches be framed with less curiosity', i.e. with less elaboration. The following year civil war broke out and the Puritan soldiery, as yet undisciplined, destroyed some cathedral organs and music books. In 1644 an Act was passed for the removal of 'superstitious monuments', and this included organs. The statement that orders were given for the destruction of music books is incorrect; however, church music during this period was, in England, Wales, and Ireland, reduced to the unaccompanied congregational singing of metrical psalms. (For a general treatment of the musical condition of the period see the article *Puritans and Music*.)

When King and Church came to power again in 1660 a great era of organ building began. There was a dearth of singers, especially boys, whose line of music was for a little time, in some cathedrals, supplied by men singing falsetto or by wind instruments. In order to re-establish the tradition Edward Lowe (formerly organist of Christ Church Cathedral, Oxford) brought out his *Short Direction for the Performance of Cathedral Service* (1661; reprinted with additions 1664). Rev. James Clifford's collection of anthem words as used at St. Paul's and other cathedrals (1663) shows about 400 anthems as in use—a considerable repertory to have reinstated in such a short time. It also gives the earliest Anglican chants ever printed: the use of such chants was long confined to the cathedrals (see *Anglican Chant*).

Thence onward there has been no break in the continuity of cathedral services, but there have been periods of the grossest neglect on the part of those charged with their conduct. S. S. Wesley's agitation all through his varied cathedral life is well known. Partly, perhaps, as a result of his heroic battlings and those of some others, and partly, certainly, as a result of the Oxford Movement, the conditions of cathedral music began greatly to improve after the middle of the 19th c. Genuine difficulties came in the years following the First World War, when the funds available would in some places no longer suffice; in some cathedrals, instead of two choral services daily only one was given, and other severe economies were undertaken.

An innovation that must receive comment is the increasing and now great use of the cathedrals for performance of the finest large-scale music by amateur choirs forming a sort of auxiliary to the smaller professional bodies. It may, then, be fairly claimed that the Eng. cathedral is once again an influential centre of national musical activity.

A further word may be added as to collections of cathedral music. Barnard's 17th-c. collection has already been referred to. Two valuable publications of the later 18th c. should be mentioned: Boyce's *Cathedral Music* came out 1760–78: it was the first collection of anthems and services to be printed in score instead of in separate part books, and its contents covered nearly 300 years of Eng. cathedral composition. Arnold's collection followed, as a supplement to Boyce, in 1790. The era of cheap music, of services and anthems printed in score, in handy size, and sold for a few pence, dates from the middle of the 19th c. and is much associated with the name 'Novello'.

See *Vicar Choral*.

Catoire (Katuar, and other transliterations), **George** (b. Moscow 1861; there d. 1926). Of partly Fr. descent. Pupil of Liadof and protégé of Tchaikovsky. His compositions (which show relatively little national Russian influence) include orch. music, piano music, and songs.

Cat's Fugue. Harpsichord Fugue of D. Scarlatti, being one of his so-called Sonatas. Nickname alludes to a story

that the fugue's subject originated in the sounds made by a cat walking over the keys.

Catterall, Arthur (b. Preston 1883; d. London 1943). Violinist. Pupil of Brodsky at Royal Manchester Coll. of Music. Leader of Hallé Orch., B.B.C. Orch., &c., and of own string quartet (1910–25).

Cat Valse for Piano. By Chopin (op. 34, no. 3 in F). Nickname recalls a legend concerning the composer's cat running over the keyboard, and so suggesting a certain appoggiatura passage. Cf. *Dog Valse*.

Caucasian Sketches. By Ippolitof-Ivanof. 4 pieces (op. 10)—*In the Mountain Pass*; *In the Village*; *In the Mosque*; *March of the Sirdar*.

Cauldron of Annwyn, The. Opera-trilogy by Holbrooke. Libretto by 'T. E. Ellis' (Lord Howard de Walden). It consists of the following: (1) *The Children of Don* (London 1912; Vienna 1923); (2) *Dylan, Son of the Wave* (London 1914); (3) *Bronwen* (Huddersfield 1929).

Caurroy, François Eustace du (b. nr. Beauvais 1549; d. Paris 1609). Canon of the Sainte Chapelle in Paris, prior of a monastery, and Superintendent of Music to Henri IV. Famous in his day as a composer of church and instrumental music, some of which has been republished in recent times.

Caustun (or Causton or Cawston), **Thomas** (d. London 1569). Gentleman of the Chapel Royal under Mary and Elizabeth; composer of church music still sung.

Cavaillé-Col, Aristide (b. Montpellier 1811; d. Paris 1899). Greatest member of a Fr. family of organ builders which was prominent from the 18th c.

Cavalieri, Emilio di (b. abt. 1550; d. Rome in 1602). In the service of the Medici court at Florence, and a member of the little group that brought into existence opera (see *Opera*); composer of the first oratorio (see *Oratorio*), and one of the earliest composers to use figured bass (q.v.).

Cavalier of the Rose (Strauss). See *Rosenkavalier*.

Cavalleria Rusticana ('Rustic Chivalry'). Dramatic opera by Mas-cagni. Libretto based on a story by Giovanni Verga. (Prod. Rome 1890; Philadelphia, New York, and London 1891.) See *Intermezzo* 3.

Cavalli, Pietro Francesco (b. Crema, Lombardy, 1602; d. Venice 1676). Important composer of operas, church music, &c., belonging to the second phase of the 'New Music' or 'monodic style' (see *History of Music* 4).

Cavatina. (1) Practically the same as arietta (q.v.), i.e. a sort of aria with only one section instead of the normal aria's three. (2) A term for an instrumental piece, generally rather short and rather slow.

Cave, Alfred (b. London 1902). Violinist. Trained R.A.M. and under Auer and Flesch. Solo player; leader Birmingham City Orch., Æolian Quartet, &c.

Cavendish, Michael (b. abt. 1565; d. 1628). Composer of lute songs and madrigals.

Cawston. See *Caustun*.

CB. Short for *Contrabassi*, i.e. string double-basses.

C.B.E. See *British Empire, Order of the*.

C Clef. See *Great Staff*; Table 4.

Cebell. An old Eng. type of gavotte rather quicker than the ordinary. Contrasting high and low passages seem to have been a feature.

Cecilia, Saint (martyred in Sicily abt. A.D. 176). The association of music's patron saint with music is very obscure, apparently dating merely from the 15th c. (There is a theory that it arose from the misreading of an antiphon for her day.) The first recorded musical fest. in her honour was in abt. 1570 at Evreux in Normandy; the earliest recorded date of a Brit. musical celebration is 1683. Such celebrations on her day (22 Nov.) were long widespread over Europe. Innumerable paintings and stained glass windows depict the Saint playing the organ—always one of many centuries later than A.D. 176.

Cecilian Movement. A movement for the reform of Roman Catholic church music, inspired, in the first instance, by the labours of Dr. Karl

Proske (1794–1861), canon and choir-master of Ratisbon Cathedral, and of the brothers Mettenleiter, his col-laborators. These stimulated the priest, Dr. Franz Xaver Witt (1834–88), a pupil of Proske and of one of the Mettenleiters, to the foundation of the Allgemeiner Deutscher Caecilienverein (General Ger. Soc. of St. Cecilia), which received the formal sanction of the Holy See. The principles of the society may be briefly laid down as follows: (1) The Gregorian Chant is basically the true music of the Church. (2) The It. music of the late 16th c. is the best of all harmonized church music that has appeared. (3) The Viennese school of church music (the Masses of Haydn, Mozart, &c.) is quite unecclesiastical and should be disused. (4) Modern music may and should be composed for church use, but it should respect the tradition and spirit of 'the ages of faith'. Unfortunately, after the death of Witt, when the society came under the direction of Dr. Franz Xaver Haberl (1840–1910), a great deal of dull amateurish music was published, and, moreover, commercial motives entered into the work of the publishing or-ganization. Inaccurate eds. of the poly-phonic music were issued and an edn. of plainsong based on the spurious 16th-c. 'Medicean' text (see *Plainsong*).

Cédez (Fr. 'give way'). 'Diminish the speed.' The present and past parti-ciples are *cédant*, *cédé*.

Celere (It.). 'Quick', 'speedy'. Hence *celerità*, 'speed'; *celeramente*, 'with speed'.

Celesta. See *Percussion Family* 1 d.

Céleste (Fr.). (1) Sort of soft pedal on old-fashioned pianos, interposing a strip of cloth between hammers and strings. (2) The *Voix Céleste* stop on the organ (see *Organ* 2).

Celibidache, Sergiu (b. Rumania 1912). Studied philosophy, mathe-matics, and music in Berlin. Principal conductor Berlin Philharm. Orch. 1945; many successful tours in Europe, England, N. and S. America.

Cellier, Alfred (b. London 1844; there d. 1891). Successful composer of light opera, *Dorothy* (prod. London 1886, New York 1887) being the best-known example of his work, and active as opera conductor. Composed also orch. and choral works, &c.

'Cello. Short for 'Violoncello' (see *Violin Family*).

Celtic Harp. See *Clàrsach*.

C.E.M.A. See *Arts Council*.

Cembalist. Harpsichord player (see *Cembalo*).

Cembalo (It.). (1) 'Dulcimer.' Hence the term *clavicembalo* ('keyed dulci-mer'), used for harpsichord. This shortened back to 'cembalo' came to mean (*a*) the harpsichord, or (*b*) the figured bass (q.v.) from which a harpsi-chord accompanist was required to construct his part. (In old organ music it sometimes means the manual part, as distinct from the pedal part.) Beet-hoven in one of his 4 'Hammerklavier' (piano) sonatas has used the expression *Tutto il cembalo* (i.e. 'the whole harpsi-chord') for *Tutte le corde* (q.v.).
(2) Cembalo in old It. often means 'cymbal'.

Cendrillon ('Cinderella'). Opera by Massenet. (Prod. Paris 1899; New Orleans 1902; Philadelphia 1911; New York 1912; London, but with puppets, 1928; Swindon 1939.)

Cenerentola, La ('Cinderella'). Opera by Rossini. (Prod. Rome 1817; London 1820; New York 1826.)

Centennial Overture. See *Pratt, Silas G.*

Cento, Centon, Centone. See *Pas-ticcio*.

Central Music Library, London (116 Buckingham Palace Road, S.W. 1.) Established 1948 on initiative of Mrs. Winifred Christie Moór (gift of £10,000). First director, Miss Dorothy Lawton—long in charge New York Pub-lic Music Library (d. Bournemouth 1960.) (Musical people not resident in London may borrow books and music by application through their local Pub-lic Library.)

Ceòl beag (Gaelic, 'little music'). That part of Scottish Highland bag-pipe repertory comprising marches, strathspeys (q.v.), and reels (q.v.). (Cf. *Ceòl mor* and *Ceòl meadhonach*.)

Ceòl meadhonach (Gaelic, 'middle music'). That part of Scottish Highland bagpipe repertory comprising folk songs, lullabies, croons, and slow marches. (Cf. *Ceòl beag* and *Ceòl mor*.)

Ceòl mor (Gaelic, 'big music'). That part of Scottish Highland bagpipe repertory comprising salutes, gatherings, and laments, as also tunes composed in memory of some historical event. (Cf. *Ceòl beag* and *Ceòl meadhonach*.)

Ce qu'on entend sur la montagne ('What one hears on the Mountain'. Ger. title *Bergsymphonie*, 'Mountain Symphony'). Symphonic poem for piano by Liszt (scored by Raff 1849; by composer himself 1854). Based on Victor Hugo's *Feuilles d'automne*, no. 5.

Ceremony of Carols. By Britten (1942). 9 medieval carols set for treble voices and harp.

Cernikoff, Vladimir (b. Paris 1882; d. London 1948). Pianist. London début 1908; then lived London.

Certon, Pierre (d. 1572). Pupil of Josquin des Prés and master of boys of Sainte Chapelle, Paris; composed many masses, motets, and chansons (see *Chanson*).

Ces (Ger.). C flat (see Table 7).

Ceses (Ger.). C double flat (see Table 7).

Cesti, Marc Antonio (b. Arezzo, Tuscany, 1623; d. Florence 1669). Franciscan monk who studied under Carissimi and served in turn as musical director of the Medici court at Florence, as a member of the papal choir in Rome, and as assistant musical director of the Imperial Court in Vienna. Composer of operas, solo cantatas, &c., belonging (like the works of Cavalli) to the second phase of the new 'monodic' style (see *History of Music* 4).

Chabrier, Emmanuel—in full Alexis Emmanuel (b. Ambert, Puy-de-Dôme, 1841; d. Paris 1894). Civil servant in Paris who associated with the symbolist poets, the impressionist painters, and the Franck group of musicians: a brilliant pianist who made a hit as an opera composer and resigned his official position, becoming assistant to the great conductor Lamoureux, and helping in the preparation of his early performances of Wagner in Paris. His orch. rhapsody, *España* (1st perf. Paris 1883), had a great success; the opera *Le Roi malgré lui* (Paris 1887) still keeps the boards. Melodically he is sometimes vulgar but his harmonic and orch. experiments entitle him to be looked upon as a forerunner of Debussy and Ravel.

Chaconne (or *Ciacona*, &c.) and Passacaglia (or *Passecaille*). These two forms early became practically indistinguishable. Both were originally slow dances of 3-in-a-measure rhythm, and the music of both was erected on a ground bass (q.v.). In some specimens this bass theme passes into an upper part. In others whilst there is no actual ground bass the music falls into a number of quite short sections similar to those which are written over a ground bass. Lully, Rameau, and other composers of their period and a little later, often ended an opera with a movement of this type. Bach, in his instrumental music, has left magnificent examples of the Chaconne or Passacaglia, and Beethoven and Brahms have done the same, though not using either of those names. A universally known Chaconne of Bach is that which closes the 2nd Partita (D minor) for unaccompanied violin—often played by recitalists without its companion movements.

Chacony. Old Eng. for 'Chaconne' (q.v.).

Chadwick, George Whitefield (b. Lowell, Mass., 1854; d. Boston 1931). Studied in Germany and then became organist and teacher in Boston, serving for half a century on the staff of the New England Conserv., most of the time as Director. He left 3 symphonies, symphonic suites and tone-poems, 5 string quartets, a piano quintet, and much other music. No man did more to lay the foundations of an Amer. school of composition and for many years before his death he was honoured as the doyen of his country's composers.

See *Tam O'Shanter*

Chahut. See *Can-Can.*

Chains, Iron. See *Percussion Family* 2 y.

Chaleur (Fr.). 'Warmth.' So *chaleureux, chaleureusement*, 'with warmth'.

Chaliapine (Shaliapin), **Feodor Ivanovich** (b. Kazan, Russia, 1873; d. Paris 1938). Bass vocalist, especially celebrated, as both singer and actor, as exponent of leading roles in Russian opera (Mussorgsky, Rimsky-Korsakof, &c.), but also greatly admired in certain It. and Fr. works. Song recitals latterly a feature of his activities. (Cf. *Song of the Volga Boatmen.*)

Challen, Charles H., & Son, Ltd. (Hermitage Road, London, N. 4.) Pianoforte makers; established 1804.

Chalumeau. See under *Clarinet Family.*

Chamberlain, Houston Stewart (b. Portsmouth 1855; d. Bayreuth 1927). Writer on aesthetics, philosophy, &c. (*Foundations of the 19th Century*, 1891, prepared way for Nazi doctrines). Settled Bayreuth 1908; wrote many books on Wagner and married his daughter Eva. Naturalized German during First World War.

Chamber Music. A term which was originally meant (as Burney puts it abt. 1805) to cover such music as was not intended 'for the church, the theatre, or a public concert room'. As now used it has lost any implication as to place of performance and excludes, on the one side, solo vocal music and music for a single instrument (or for a solo instrument with mere accompaniment), and, on the other, orch. and choral music, &c., including merely all seriously intended instrumental music for 2, 3, 4, or more instruments, played with a single instrument to a 'part', all the parts being on equal terms. Thus it comprises such things as duet sonatas for violin and piano or 'cello and piano, sonatas for some wind instrument and piano, trios for strings or for 2 stringed instruments and piano, quartets for strings or for 3 stringed instruments and piano, instrumental quartets, sextets, septets, and octets, &c. Of all these types the most important is the string quartet:

the instruments employed in it are 2 violins, viola, and 'cello, the double-bass having very rarely a place in chamber music.

The modern conception of chamber music may be said to date from Haydn. For a century and more before his time nearly all music was supplied with a figured-bass (q.v.), guided by which a harpsichordist extemporized a background: going behind this figured-bass period (i.e. the 17th c. and a large part of the 18th) we find something more like our idea of chamber music in the 16th-c. music for viols: this, however, was usually little differentiated in idiom and style from choral music (such as the madrigal) and was thus hardly truly instrumental.

All the greatest composers have contributed to the now abundant repertory of chamber music, and so far have we departed from the early 19th-c. idea of the meaning of the term that 'Chamber Concerts' are common. Such concerts date effectively from the 1830's when the Müller Brothers String Quartet began touring Europe with a fine classical repertory. Since that period there have been many world-famous string quartets. Despite much concert-room performance, however, chamber music still retains some right to its name, since it is often treated as 'the music of friends' and is much practised privately.

Chambonnières, Jacques Champion de (b. 1602; d. Paris abt. 1672). His father was harpsichordist to Louis XIII as he himself became to Louis XIV, who ennobled him. Compositions for his instrument important and still published.

Chaminade, Cécile (b. Paris 1857; d. Monte Carlo 1944). Skilful pianist; her own playing helped to popularize her music for her instrument, much of which is of the lighter, graceful kind; she also wrote orch. music, ballets, and songs.

Champêtre (Fr.). 'Rustic.' Hence *Danse champêtre*, a peasant dance in the open air.

Chandos Te Deums (2); **Jubilate; and Anthems** (12). By Handel, for Duke of Chandos and perf. at his palace at Cannons, nr. Edgware, Middlesex (1718-20).

Changeable Chants. See *Anglican Chant*.

Change Ringing. See *Bell* 3.

Changez (Fr.). 'Change' (imperative).

Changing Note or **Nota Cambiata** (It.). An idiomatic melodic formula whose salient characteristic is the leap of a third away from an unessential note. The earliest form (in the polyphonic age) was a 3-note figure, (*a*). This was soon joined and eventually superseded by a 4-note idiom, (*b*). In the harmonic age of counterpoint (from Bach and Handel onwards) a variety of other changing note figures appear, (*c*) (*d*) (*e*).

In U.S.A. the term *Cambiata* is in common use for 'changing note'. Also when the leap of a third is in the direction opposite to that of the step-wise movement the term *Échappé*, or *Escape Tone*, is sometimes used, and, where the movement is back to the original note, the term *Returning Tone*.

Chanson (Fr. 'song'). A vague word with many applications, especially: (1) Any sort of simple verse-repeating song. (2) A type of song, for several voices or for one voice with accompaniment, that grew up in France and north Italy in the 14th c. and flourished until the end of the 16th—really a kind of early madrigal of the 'ayre' type (cf. *Madrigal*).

Chanson sans paroles. See *Song without Words*.

Chansons de Bilitis. By Debussy. Three solo settings (1897) of prose poems of Pierre Louÿs.

Chant. See *Anglican Chant*. For Gregorian Chant see *Plainsong*.

Chantant (Fr. 'singing'). In a singing style. Sometimes the past participle is used, *chanté* ('sung').

Chanter. See *Bagpipe Family*.

Chanterelle (Fr.). The highest string of the violin, &c. (See under *Banjo*.)

Chanteurs de St. Gervais. See *Bordes*.

Chanty. See *Shanty*.

Chapeau tricorne (Falla). See *Three-cornered Hat*.

Chapelle (Fr.). See *Kapelle*.

Chapel Royal. No one institution has been more useful in fostering Eng. musicianship and promoting the development of Eng. music than the Chapel Royal—by which must be properly understood not a building but a body of clergy and musicians (like German 'Kapelle', q.v.).

Existing records of the Chapel go back to 1135. During the reign of Edward IV (1461-83) the Chapel consisted of 26 chaplains and clerks, 13 minstrels (a very wide term), 8 choirboys and their master, and a 'Wayte', or musical watchman, sounding three times nightly. Under Richard III (1483-5) a press-gang system was authorized (though the practice of pressing seems to have existed earlier); this remained in operation for about a couple of centuries: representatives of the Chapel were now definitely entitled to travel about the country listening to all the best cathedral choirs, and robbing them of any boys whose voices marked them out as fit to sing before the King. Under Henry VIII (q.v.), a practical musician, the musical staff of the Chapel rose to 79. Edward VI had a chapel of 114, and Mary the same. Under Elizabeth (1557-1603) and James I (1603-25), the Chapel's personnel was of the highest distinction. Such servants as Tye, Tallis, Byrd, Gibbons, Morley, Tomkins, and Bull would do honour to any monarch in any age. These brought church music to a level not exceeded even by the musicians of the Sistine Chapel at Rome; they developed the Eng. madrigal, and they laid the very foundations of artistic keyboard music. With the death of Charles I in 1649 the Chapel ceased. Cromwell was a great lover of music and kept up a small body of domestic musicians, but he did not maintain a princely state, and, of course, he did not approve of choirs as an instrument of public worship (see *Puritans*). In 1660 came back a King, and the Chapel was recalled to help him in his devotions. Charles II, after lively music from Lully at the court of Louis XIV, wanted such music at the Eng. court. A talented choir-boy, Pelham Humfrey, was sent abroad to learn foreign styles; a younger boy, Purcell, without going abroad, was very apt to learn, and these youths and others, as they matured, largely trained by Captain Henry Cooke (q.v.), were quickly able to put to good use the new resources (such as the band of 24 fiddlers in church) with which the King had provided himself. Purcell, from 1677 to his death in 1695, was 'Composer in Ordinary' to the Chapel.

Under William and Mary, Anne, and the Georges, we hear less of the Chapel. George III was a keen music lover, but, like these other monarchs, he had musicians in his employ beyond those of his Chapel; he spent little time in London, and when at Windsor had no need of his 'Chapel Royal', in the technical sense, since the Chapel of St. George, in Windsor Castle, had its own distinct staff, as it still has. The great days, then, were over, but a line of organists continued, the name of almost every one of whom is well known to the student of Eng. musical history. Some clever boys still got their training in the Chapel. Sullivan was one.

Today the 'Chapel Royal' consists of a body of clergy, choirmen, and boys ('Priests in Ordinary', 'Gentlemen', and 'Children'), and the organist charged with the conduct of the Sunday services. Their place of duty is chiefly the chapel of St. James's Palace, but they have other places of duty at Buckingham Palace and Marlborough House.

Distinct from the Chapel Royal is the private band of the monarch, presided over since the days of Charles II by an official called 'Master of the King's Musick'; the band used to play to the monarch at meals and at state ceremonies and to combine with the gentlemen and children of the Chapel Royal for the performance of King's Birthday Odes and New Year's Day Odes, and its string section used to take part in the services of the Chapel Royal. It accompanied the monarch wherever he went. At Queen Victoria's accession the band had come to be merely a small body of wind-instrument players, but the music-loving Prince Consort reorganized it (in 1840) as an orch. Edward VII abandoned the custom of giving State Concerts and the band at present exists in little more than name; it consists of 30 eminent orch. players, but is rarely called upon to perform. Elgar was Master at the time of his death, being succeeded by Walford Davies (1934), Bax (1941), and Bliss (1953). (See also *Boyce*; *Eccles, John*; *Stanley*.)

Chaplin, the sisters **Nellie** (pianist and harpsichordist; d. 1930), **Kate** (violinist and treble violist; d. 1948), **Mabel** (cellist and bass violist). During the first 3 decades of the 20th c. they contributed notably to the revival of the old domestic instruments, the old music, and the old dances.

Chappell, William (b. London 1809; there d. 1888). Founded Musical Antiquarian Soc. (1840). Ed. *Popular Music of the Olden Time* (2 vols. 1855–9; new edn. by H. E. Wooldridge 1893). Cf. *Chappell & Co.*

Chappell & Co. Ltd. London Music Publishers, Piano Makers, &c. (50 New Bond St., W. 1). Founded 1812. Wm. Chappell (see above) was member of firm.

Chapple, Stanley (b. London 1900). Pianist, conductor, and teacher. Principal London Academy of Music 1934–5; then on staff G.S.M. Settled U.S.A., head of Music School of Univ. of Washington, Seattle 1948–63.

Chapuis, Auguste Paul Jean-Baptiste (b. Dampierre-sur-Salon 1868; d. Paris 1933). Pupil at Paris Conserv. of Massenet, Franck, and Dubois; became Paris organist, music inspector of Paris schools; composer of operas, &c.

Chaque (Fr.). 'Each', 'every'.

Characteristic Piece, or Charakterstück (Ger.). Vague term occasionally applied by composers to a shorter instrumental composition (especially for piano); apparently much the equivalent of *Stimmungsbild* (Ger.), 'Mood-picture'.

Character Notation. Same as *Buckwheat Notation* (q.v.)

Charakterstück. See *Characteristic Piece*.

Charger, Se (Fr.). 'To take upon oneself.' (*Ils*) *se chargent*, '(They) take upon themselves', i.e. they undertake.

Charity Children as Choirs. See *Anglican Parish Church Music*.

Charivari (Fr.). Extemporized music of a violent kind made with any household utensils, &c., that lie to hand, generally before the house of a person who has incurred communal disapprobation. Equivalents are *Rough Music* (Eng.); *Chiasso* (It. 'uproar'); or *Scampanata* (It. 'bell ringing'); *Katzenmusik* (Ger. 'cat music'); *Shivaree, Calthumpian Concert* (Amer.).

Charleston. A sort of fox-trot long popular among the Negroes of the Southern States. Its rhythmic characteristic is that its bars, of 4 crotchets value, are divided into unequal halves of respectively 3 and 5 quavers' value. From about 1925 it had a short popularity in Amer. and European ballrooms, and about 1950 came briefly into vogue again.

Charlie is my darling. The poem is by Lady Nairne, though there seems to have been an earlier Jacobite song of the same name. The tune is an old Scottish traditional one.

Charpentier, (1) Marc Antoine (b. Paris 1634; there d. 1704). Pupil of Carissimi in Rome. Returning to Paris associated himself with Molière in the performance of his plays. Had a high reputation as a composer of light music and also left operas, oratorios, and masses.

(2) **Gustave** (b. Dieuze, Lorraine, 1860; d. Paris 1956). Pupil of Massenet at Paris Conservatoire and winner of Prix de Rome. Two compositions often heard are the early orch. piece, *Impressions of Italy*, and the opera *Louise* (q.v.), in which latter he manifests his sympathy with the Parisian working girls, for whom he founded a recreative and educational institution.

Chasins, Abram (b. New York 1903). Of Russian parentage. Accomplished pianist and as such has toured Europe; has served on teaching staff of the Curtis Inst., Philadelphia, and as music adviser (1943) and director (1947) of the *New York Times* radio station. Compositions include piano concertos and solos, orch. music, &c.

Chasse, Cor de (Fr.). 'Hunting horn' (see *Horn Family*).

Chasse, La ('The Hunt'). Nickname for (1) Haydn's Symphony in D, no. 73 in Breitkopf edn. of the Symphonies; reference is to the final movement. (2) Mozart's String Quartet in B flat, K. 458; the reference is to the opening subject.

Chassé (Fr.). In ballet, the 'chasing' away of one foot by a touch from the other.

Chasseur maudit, Le ('The Accursed Hunter'). Symphonic Poem by Franck (1882), based on a ballad by Bürger.

Chatterton, Julia (b. 1886; d. London 1936). Founder of International Folk-Song and Folk-Lore Soc. Collected 1,000 songs in Greece, Balkan countries, Spain, &c. Also collector of and performer on out-of-the-way instruments.

Chausson, Ernest (b. Paris 1855; d. nr. Mantes-sur-Seine 1899). Man of wealth; trained for law; became pupil of Massenet at Paris Conserv. and then transferred himself to Franck circle (see *Franck*). For a time secretary of French National Musical Soc. Compositions (orch., operatic, &c.) show influence of Franck, Wagner, and Brahms, and latterly of Debussy; songs are notable. Killed by bicycle accident on own estate.

See *Tempest, The*.

Chávez, Carlos (b. nr. Mexico City 1899). Considered to be leading Mexican composer. Founder and conductor of Mexican Symphony Orch. 1928 (retired 1949) and has been the head of both National Conserv. and Government Dept. of Fine Arts. Has had success in his own country and elsewhere.

Che (It.). 'Who', 'which'.

Checkmate. Ballet by Bliss. (1st perf. by Sadler's Wells company, Paris 1937; then over 100 perfs. in Britain; as Suite, New York 1939.)

Cheer, Boys, Cheer. See Russell, H.

Chef d'attaque (Fr. 'chief of the attack'). Orch. leading violin (Eng.), or concert-master (Amer.).

Cherniavsky, Mischel (b. Uman, S. Russia, 1893). Violoncellist. Played before Czar age 7; toured world from age 9. Resident London and naturalized British.

Cherry Ripe. Poem by Herrick (1648); music by C. E. Horn (q.v.).

Cherubini, Maria Luigi Carlo Zenobio Salvatore (b. Florence 1760; d. Paris 1842). Life mainly spent in Paris, where he became director of the national Conserv. Learned contrapuntist and writer on counterpoint (in this said to have been assisted by Halévy) and voluminous and successful composer of music for stage and church, &c., of which both Beethoven and Mendelssohn thought highly. (See *Abencérages*; *Anacréon*; *Deux journées*; *Lodoïska*; *Medea*.)

Chester, J. & W., Ltd. Music Publishers; firm founded Brighton 1860; London 1915 (Eagle Court, E.C. 1). Issues a journal called *The Chesterian*.

Chester Waits. See *Wait*.

Chesterian. See *Chester, J. & W., Ltd.*

Chest of Viols. Any complete set of viols of different sizes (so called from the fact that such a set was often kept in a specially contrived chest).

Chest Register. See *Voice* 4.

Cheval de bronze, Le ('The Bronze Horse'). 'Fairy-opera' by Auber; libretto by Scribe. (Prod. Paris and London 1835; New York 1837.)

Chevalet (Fr. 'trestle'). Bridge of bowed instruments, &c.

Chevé, Emile J. M. See *Galin-Paris-Chevé*.

Chevillard, Camille Paul Alexandre (b. Paris 1859; d. nr. there 1923). Son-in-law, assistant (1886), and then (1897) successor of La-

moureux in the conducting of his concerts; also (1913) conductor at Opéra. Composer of orch. and chamber music, &c.

Cheville (Fr.). Peg, e.g. of a stringed instrument.

Chiaro, chiara (It. masc., fem.). 'Clear', 'unconfused'. Hence *Chiaramente*, 'clearly', 'distinctly; *chiarezza*, 'clarity', 'distinctness'.

Chiasso. See *Charivari*.

Chiave (It.). 'Clef'. (See Table 4.)

Chica (Sp.). Early form of Fandango (q.v.).

Chicago Musical College. See *Schools of Music*.

Chicago Symphony Orchestra. Founded 1891 by Theodore Thomas (q.v.); later conductors include Frederick A. Stock (1905), Defauw (1942), Rodzinski (1947), Reiner (1953), Martinon (1963), Solti (1969).

Chieftain, The (Sullivan). See *Contrabandista*.

Chiesa (It.). 'Church.' Hence 'Aria da Chiesa' (an aria for church use); 'Cantata da Chiesa' (see *Cantata*); 'Concerto da Chiesa' (see *Concerto*); 'Sonata da Chiesa' (see *Sonata*).

Chifonie (Fr.). Early name for hurdy-gurdy (q.v.).

Child, William (b. Bristol 1606; d. Windsor 1697). One of organists of Charles I and, after Commonwealth and Protectorate, of Charles II. Left much church music, including some still heard.

Childhood of Christ, The (*L'Enfance du Christ*). Oratorio by Berlioz. (1st complete perf. Paris 1854; Manchester 1880; a selection New York 1884. Sometimes staged as opera.)

Child of Our Time, A. Choral-Orch. work by Tippett, with a sociological text and some use of Negro Spirituals. (1st perf. London 1944.)

Children of Bethlehem. See *Pierné*.

Children of Don (Holbrooke). See *Cauldron of Anwyn*.

Children's Corner. Piano pieces by Debussy (1906-8) dedicated to his little daughter. With Eng. titles (explained by influence of Eng. governess)—*Doctor Gradus ad Parnassum* (cf. *Gradus ad Parnassum*); *Jimbo's Lullaby* ('Jimbo' is composer's mistake for 'Jumbo'); *Serenade for the Doll*; *Snow is dancing*; *The Little Shepherd*; *Golliwogg's Cakewalk*.

Children's Crusade, The (*La Croisade des enfants*). Oratorio by Pierné. (1st perf. 1904; New York 1906.)

Children's Death Songs (Mahler). See *Kindertotenlieder*.

Children's Games (Bizet). See *Jeux d'enfants*.

Children's Oratorio. See *Benoît*.

Children's Overture. See *Quilter*.

Chimes of Normandy, The (Planquette). See *Cloches de Corneville*.

Chiming of Bells. See *Bell* 2.

Chinese Crash Cymbal. This differs in shape from the normal cymbal (see *Percussion Family* 2 o). The cup is much shallower and its edge turns up. It is made of a special alloy peculiar to the Chinese, and when struck with a drum stick gives a brilliant crash; its home is the dance band.

Chinese Crescent. Same as *Turkish Crescent* (q.v.).

Chinese Temple Block. See *Korean Temple Block*.

Chinese Wood Block. Oblong block of wood, 7 or 8 inches long, with slots cut in it. Struck with stick of a snare drum gives a hard, hollow tone. Other names are *Clog Box* and *Tap Box*. Jazz movement seems to have brought it into use.

Ching, James (b. Thornton Heath, Surrey, 1900; d. 1962). Pianist. Studied Oxford (M.A., B.Mus.), R.A.M. and R.C.M., Berlin, and Leipzig. Founded own Pianoforte School. Several books on pianoforte technique.

Chiroplast. Hand-rest for piano practice, once a part of the Logier system's equipment (see *Logier*).

Chisholm, Erik (b. nr. Glasgow, 1904; d. Rondebosch, nr. Cape Town, 1965). Trained Scottish National Academy of Music and Univ. of Edinburgh (D.Mus.). Held posts in Nova Scotia and Singapore. Conductor various opera and ballet companies in Britain. Musical critic of Scottish journals. Active promoter of contemporary music activities in Glasgow. From 1946 in Cape Town as director of S. African Coll. of Music and Dean of Faculty of Music at Univ. Compositions include symphonies, piano concertos, ballets, &c.

Chissell, Joan Olive (b. Cromer, Norfolk, 1919). Trained R.C.M. (ed. of its Magazine). Extra-mural Music Lecturer of Univs. Oxford and London. Contributor to various musical periodicals (assistant music critic of *The Times* 1947). Author of book on Schumann.

Chitarrone. See *Lute Family*.

Chiuso, chiusa (It. masc., fem.). 'Closed', 'stopped' (see *Horn Family*).

Chladni. See *Clavicylinder*.

CHM. See *Degrees and Diplomas* 2, 4.

Chocolate Soldier, The. Operetta by Oscar Straus. Libretto based on Bernard Shaw's *Arms and the Man*. (Prod. Vienna 1908; New York 1909; London 1910.) (Ger. title *Der tapfere Soldat*—'The Brave Soldier'.)

Choeur (Fr.). 'Chorus', 'choir'. But *Grand Choeur*, besides meaning 'Big Chorus' and 'Full Choir', means 'Full Organ' (or a composition for such).

Choir or **Chorus.** (1) A *Mixed Voice* Choir (or Chorus) is one of both women and men. (2) A *Male Voice Choir* is (usually) of men only, but may be of boys and men. (3) A *Double Choir* is one arranged in 2 equal and complete bodies, with a view not merely to singing in 8 parts but also to responsive effects, &c. (4) Architecturally, the choir is that part of a cathedral which, in a church other than a cathedral, is called the chancel.

Choir Organ. See *Organ* 1.

Choke Cymbals. Two ordinary cymbals (see *Percussion Family* 2 o), fixed face to face on a rod, with a device by which their pressure one on the other can be adjusted, according to the tone-quality desired. They are played with a drumstick, giving a short, sharp crash. The Jazz movement seems to be responsible for their coming into use.

Chopin, Frédéric François (b. Zelazowa Wola, Poland, 1810; d. Paris 1849). Of half Polish, half Fr. parentage and spent about half life in Warsaw and half in Paris. As pianist showed qualities of both delicacy and fire, and so, too, in his many compositions for his instrument: the nocturne style he took from the Irishman Field (q.v.), and there is in such music of his also to be seen the influence of the It. Bellini: the Polish side of him comes out in his Polonaises and Mazurkas. With Schumann and Mendelssohn he stands as one of the great leaders of one branch of the Romantic Movement in music.

Consumption brought to an early end a brief career which had already endowed pianists with a new repertory, including 27 Études, 25 Preludes, 19 Nocturnes, 52 Mazurkas, 13 Polonaises, 15 Valses, 4 Impromptus, a Barcarolle, a Berceuse, 3 Sonatas, and 2 Concertos—nearly all being of so definitely personal a stamp as to be unmistakably the work of no one but him.

See also under *Ballade*; *Berceuse*; *Black Key Étude*; *Butterfly's Wings Étude*; *Cat Valse*; *Dog Valse*; *Funeral Marches*; *Hexameron*; *Mazurka*; *Minute Valse*; *Nocturne*; *Pianoforte Playing*; *Raindrop Prelude*; *Revolutionary Étude*; *Rubato*; *Scherzo*; *Shepherd Boy Étude*; *Sylphides*; *Winter Wind Étude*.

Chopsticks. A certain quick waltz tune for piano 4 hands, transmitted from generation to generation of schoolgirls. It is performed with the flat hands held perpendicularly, the notes being struck by their sides (i.e. with the outsides of the little fingers), with a tonic-dominant vamping (q.v.) bass part and an occasional touch of glissando (q.v.). In Fr. *Côtelettes* ('Cutlets') and in Ger. *Koteletten Walzer*. There is a famous collection of compositions based on the tune—*Paraphrases*, by Borodin, Cui, Liadof, Rimsky-Korsakof, and Liszt.

Choragus. (1) In the life of Ancient Greece the leader of a chorus. (2) An official peculiar to the Univ. of Oxford. When the Lectureship or Professorship in Music was founded and endowed by William Heyther in 1626, he laid it down that a subordinate official, called Choragus, was to conduct practices of music twice a week. The office still exists (but not with that duty). For a time, during the late 19th c., there was also an assistant official called Coryphaeus.

Choral or Chorale (first spelling is the Ger. form, second the Eng.). See *Hymns and Hymn Tunes* 2 for a brief discussion of the subject. The following remarks may be added here.

Whilst, in general speech today, when we mention 'Chorales' we refer to the hymn tunes, Protestant in origin, treated of in the article alluded to above, this is not the strict meaning of the Ger. word 'Choral'. Originally it is a word belonging to the unreformed Church and means the ecclesiastical *Plainsong* (q.v.), the *Cantus choralis*. Properly, the 'Choral' in the Ger. Roman Catholic Church is that part of the plainsong sung by more than 1 voice (the 'Concentus' as distinguished from the 'Accentus'), but this distinction of terminology is not always observed. A good deal of metrical Latin hymnody had come to have a place in the service, and Luther drew largely upon this in translation; the plainsong melodies, in some cases, were taken into the Protestant service, a number of what we now call 'chorales' being, indeed, such melodies adapted and harmonized for 4 voices. The congregation had no recognized part in the music of the pre-Reformation Church, and one of Luther's most striking innovations was in the provision of hymns and tunes for their singing: these largely took the place of the plainsong of the choir in the unreformed Church, and it was natural that the same name 'choral' should be employed.

The first Lutheran chorales had not the regular rhythms that they later took on. They had often a mixture of 2-in-a-measure and 3-in-a-measure, and, indeed, a good deal of the free rhythm of plainsong. With the Lutheran chorales, as with the Genevan and Eng. and Scottish hymn tunes, the melody was at first in the tenor. During the 17th c. it gradually became usual to place it in the treble, as today.

The repertory of the Ger. chorale

may be said to have been completed in Bach's day. He himself composed only about 30—making, however, 400 reharmonizations of existing chorale melodies. Since then few have been composed, and whilst in England the manufacture of hymn tunes is still a fairly flourishing musical industry, in Germany it may be said to have stopped; there every hymn has its traditional tune (though sometimes several have the same tune) and nobody thinks of disjoining the two.

It has always been the custom that the congregational singing of chorales should be in unison. It was long usual to precede the singing of a chorale by the playing of an organ prelude (see *Choral Prelude*) and to interpolate short interludes between every 2 lines (see Mendelssohn's arrangements of chorales in *St. Paul*). Chorale singing has often been surprisingly slow.

Chorale Partita. See *Choral Prelude*.

Choral Fantasia. By Beethoven, for Piano, Choir, and Orch. (Op. 80; 1st perf., with the composer at the piano, Vienna 1808.) The words are those of a poem by Christoph Kuffner.

Choral Prelude or **Chorale Prelude** (Ger. *Choral Vorspiel*). Out of the custom of playing organ preludes and interludes to the chorale grew up the technique of 2 special forms of composition, one based upon a treatment of the chorale melody, often taken line by line and surrounded by other melodic parts woven together into elaborate counterpoint, and the other not reproducing the chorale intact but suggesting it to the minds of the hearers by taking its first few notes as the theme to be elaborated. For a north German congregation, to whom the melodies were all known from childhood, such a piece of organ music had great interest and significance.

Amongst the composers who helped to develop this form were Sweelinck (1562–1621), Scheidt (1587–1654), Pachelbel (1653–1706), Buxtehude (1637–1707), Reinken (1623–1722), and Böhm (1661–1733). Such of Bach's forebears as were organists also naturally took their part in the working out of the form, and he himself crowned the labours of all his predecessors and contemporaries by presenting the form in perfection.

In addition to the Chorale Preludes of Bach there are certain early works which he called CHORALE PARTITAS, the word Partita here, as with certain other composers, having not the usual sense of a suite (q.v.) but that of an air with variations. The number of variations corresponds to the number of the verses of the hymns, and each variation seems to be designed to re-express the thought of the corresponding verse. Since Bach many other Ger. composers have written chorale preludes.

To some extent the same form has been cultivated in England. Purcell has a Voluntary on the *Old Hundredth* that, in its primitive way, is quite on the lines of the Bach Chorale Prelude. In the late 19th c. and early 20th there was a revival of interest in this form amongst Brit. composers.

Choral Symphony. A symphony making more or less use of a chorus, or a symphony entirely for voices used in groups, on orch. lines as to contrasts of tone-colours. (There are also other varieties.)

Some examples are: (1) By BEET-HOVEN (his 9th and last symphony, in D minor (op. 125), with solo vocalists and chorus in final movement). Commissioned by the London Philharmonic Soc. (1st perf. Vienna 1824; London 1825; New York 1846.) (2) By HOLST. Setting for Solo Soprano, Chorus, and Orch. of poems of Keats. (1st perf. Leeds Fest. 1925.) (3) BANTOCK styled his *Atalanta in Calydon* a 'Choral Symphony'. It is a setting of Swinburne for voices only. (1st perf. Manchester 1912.) (4) See *Morning Heroes*.

Two other works that are in effect Choral Symphonies are Mahler's 8th Symphony (see *Symphony of a Thousand*) and the *Sea Symphony* of Vaughan Williams.

Choral Vorspiel. See *Choral Prelude*.

Chord. See *Harmony*; also *Augmented Sixth, Chromatic Chords, Diminished Seventh, Dominant Seventh, Leading Seventh, Neapolitan Sixth.*

Chording. (1) A choir-trainer's term for bad and good intonation of the notes sounded together in chords.

(2) In U.S.A. the term means the improvised strumming of accompanimental chords on a banjo, &c.

Choreographic Poem. A *symphonic poem* (q.v.) developing dance rhythms and expressing the dance spirit.

Choreography, Choregraphy. The art of dance composition in ballet.

Chorley, H. F. See *Criticism of Music.*

Chorus. (1) See *Choir or Chorus.*
(2) Old name for Bagpipe (see *Bagpipe Family*). (3) Old stringed instrument—generally the crwth (q.v.).

Chorus Reed. Any organ reed stop (see *Organ* 2) which is not intended for solo use.

Chotzinoff, Samuel (b. Vitebsk, Russia, 1889; d. New York 1964). Pianist and critic. Graduated Columbia Univ. 1912. Had career as accompanist. Became critic of various New York journals and served on staff of Curtis Inst., Philadelphia. Mus. Director, Natl. Broadcasting Corpn., New York.

Chout ('Buffoon'). Ballet by Prokofief. (Op. 21; prod. Paris and London 1921.) Also as Orch. Suite.

Christ and his Soldiers. Oratorio (intended for child listeners) by John Farmer. (1st perf. Harrow School 1878.)

Christe Eleison. See *Mass.*

Christians, Awake. See *Wainwright, John.*

Christie, (1) **John** (b. 1882; d. Glyndebourne 1962). Educated Eton (where later a master) and Cambridge (M.A.). Founded Glyndebourne Opera Fest. (see *Glyndebourne* and *Mildmay, Audrey*). C.H. 1954.

(2) **Winifred** (b. Scotland 1882; d. London 1965). Pianist. Trained R.C.M. and under Harold Bauer, &c. In U.S.A. 1915–20. Married Emanuel Moór (q.v.) and demonstrated his double-keyboard piano (see *Central Music Library*; *Keyboard*).

Christmas Concerto (*Fatto per la notte di Natale*—'Made for Christmas Night'). By Corelli, being his Concerto

Grosso in G minor. op. 6, no. 8, in G minor.

Christmas Eve. Opera by Rimsky-Korsakof. Based on a fairy-tale by Gogol. (Prod. St. Petersburg 1895.) An Orch. Suite made from its music is sometimes heard.

Christmas Oratorio (*Weihnachts Oratorium*). Bach. Text by Picander and the composer. Really 6 cantatas for perf. in Leipzig on 6 days from Christmas to Epiphany. (1734; 1st Brit. perf. London 1861; 1st Amer. perf., in part, Boston 1877.)

Christmas Pieces (Ger. title *Kinderstücke*, 'Children's Pieces'). For Pianoforte by Mendelssohn (op. 72; 1842). Composed at Denmark Hill for the children of the house (his relatives, the Beneckes).

Christmas Symphony (Haydn). See *Weihnachtssymphonie.*

Christmas Tree, The. See *Rebikof.*

Christoff, Boris (b. Bulgaria 1919). Bass. Trained Rome. Appeared in concerts 1946; Covent Garden and New York Metropolitan 3 years later.

Christ on the Mount of Olives (*Christus am Ölberge*). Oratorio by Beethoven. (1st perf. Vienna 1803. London 1814; various Eng. versions of words, including one, *Engedi*, changing subject to story of David.)

Christopher Columbus. Early overture by Wagner. Intended for a play by Theodore Apel. (1st perf. Leipzig 1835. London 1905.) Also opera by Milhaud. (1st perf. Berlin 1930.)

Christus. (1) Oratorio by LISZT. (1st perf. Budapest 1873; Boston, Mass. 1880. As opera, Budapest 1938.) (2) Unfinished oratorio by MENDELSSOHN. (1st perf. Birmingham Fest. 1852.)

Christus am Ölberge (Beethoven). See *Christ on the Mount of Olives.*

Christy Minstrels. See *Negro Minstrels.*

Chromatic. See *Diatonic and Chromatic.*

Chromatic Chords. Chords which include one or more notes not in the diatonic scale of the prevailing key of the passage in which they occur. The Chord of the *Augmented 6th* (q.v.) is an example.

Chromatic Fantasy and Fugue. By Bach for harpsichord (probably about 1720). The Fantasy largely in *bravura* passages, the fugue (in 3 voices) one of Bach's longest for the domestic keyboard instruments.

Chromatic Harp. See *Harp.*

Chromatique (Fr.). 'Chromatic.'

Chrotta. Another name for Crwth (q.v.).

Chrysander, Karl Franz Friedrich (b. Mecklenburg 1826; d. Bergedorf 1901). Authority on Handel, editing complete works for Ger. Handel Soc. and writing a great biography (1858–67; never completed). Worked also on other musicological subjects, publishing works of Palestrina, Schütz, Corelli, Couperin, and Bach, and discovering autograph of Bach's B minor mass. Friend of Brahms.

Church, John (b. 1675; d. 1741). Gentleman of Chapel Royal and Chorister of Westminster Abbey. Author of *Introduction to Psalmody*; composer of church music and fine songs in Purcell vein.

Church Cadence. See *Cadence.*

Church Company, John. Philadelphia music publishing firm, est. 1859; operated since 1930 by Presser Co. (q.v.).

Church Modes. See *Modes.*

Church Music. The public exercises of the Jewish religion gave a large place to music. In the temple of Solomon, at the outset, 'four thousand praised the Lord with instruments' and 'the number of them that were instructed in the songs of the Lord was two hundred, fourscore and eight'. Before the last of the Temples of Jerusalem was destroyed, after 1,200 years of musical service, the system of synagogues had spread, and with it a liturgical service making large use of song, but no longer with instruments. When Christianity came there was at first no break with the Jewish Church; Christians still attended the Temple at Jerusalem and the synagogues (as Christ himself did), and in their separate Christian meetings they carried on the musical tradition. We find Paul exhorting the Ephesians and Colossians to use psalms, hymns, and spiritual songs. Hebrew and Greek elements probably mingled in the worship music that grew into a traditional corpus during the first 3 centuries of Christianity and was further codified from time to time. It appears that the use of instruments was not favoured. It is said that the introduction of the organ into Christian worship was due to Pope Vitalian in the 7th c. The process of systematization and development of the Church's song may be traced in other articles in this volume (especially *Liturgy, Plainsong, Mass, Schola Cantorum, Harmony*).

Throughout the ages there have been alternating processes of the accumulation of undesirable musical practices and of reform. Thus Pope John XXII, in the early 14th c., forbade the use of secular melodies as a basis for the polyphonic settings of the Mass (cf. *Missa sine Nomine*). The Council of Trent (1545–63) recommended bishops to 'exclude music in which anything impious or lascivious finds a part' and there seems to have been a danger a little later of polyphonic music being altogether prohibited, largely on the ground of the inaudibility of the words involved in the interweaving of the voices (the edicts of 2 recent Popes are mentioned under *Motu Proprio*). The Reformed Churches, also, have had their complaints and struggles. See *Common Prayer*, and *Puritans and Music.*

The Orthodox (or Greek) Church today, like the Calvinistic Churches of the 16th and 17th cs., forbids the use in worship of any instrument.

Church Music Society (British). Founded 1906. Its objects are the encouragement of a high standard in the choice and perf. of music in worship. It is predominantly Anglican in membership. Cf. *Royal School of Church Music.*

Church of England. See *Anglican Parish Church Music.*

Church Windows (*Vetrate di chiesa*). Four 'Impressions for Orchestra' by Respighi. (1st perf. Boston 1927; London 1928.)

Ciacona. See *Chaconne*.

Cid. Le. Opera by Massenet. Libretto based on Corneille. (Prod. Paris 1885; New York 1897.) Also opera by Cornelius (his last, prod. Weimar 1865).

Cifra, Antonio (b. probably nr. Terracina abt. 1584; d. Loreto 1629). Held many important church music positions in Italy and had high reputation as composer of church music, madrigals, chamber music, and organ music.

Cigány (Hungarian). 'Gipsy.' What are called *Cigány Bands* seem to consist normally of strings, clarinet, and dulcimer.

Cimarosa, Domenico (b. nr. Naples 1749; d. Venice 1801). Had triumphant international career as composer of operas—the *Secret Marriage* (see *Matrimonio Segreto*), *Astuzie Femminile* (q.v.), and over 60 others; possessed a special gift for gay comedy; as to musical style might be called 'the Italian Mozart'. Of revolutionary views; helped to welcome the Fr. republican army in Naples in 1799 and on the return of the Bourbon monarchy was arrested and for a short time imprisoned. He died soon after.

Cimbal, cimbalom, Cimbelom, &c. Dulcimer (q.v.).

Cincinnati. See *Festival*; *Schools of Music*.

Cincinnati Symphony Orchestra. Founded 1895. 1st regular conductor Franz van der Stucken (1896–1907).

Cinderella (Massenet). See *Cendrillon*.

Cinderella (Rossini). See *Cenerentola*.

Cinelli (It.). 'Cymbals' (see *Percussion Family* 2 o).

Cinq (Fr.). 'Five.'

Cinq, Les. See *Five*.

Cinque (It.). 'Five.'

Cinque Pace, Cinque Passi. See *Pavan and Galliard*.

Cinquième (Fr.). 'Fifth.'

Cioè (It.). 'That is.'

Cipher, Ciphering. Continuous sounding of a note on the organ, due to some mechanical defect.

Cis (Ger.). C sharp (see Table 7).

Cisis (Ger.). C double sharp (see Table 7).

Cither. Cittern (not 'Zither').

Cittern (also Cithern and other spellings). Wire-stringed instrument of great antiquity, played with a plectrum until end of 16th c. and thereafter often with the fingers. In shape it somewhat resembled a lute (see *Lute Family*) but it had a flat back. In England during the 18th c. it was miscalled the *English Guitar*. Of the same general type were the *Orpharion* (or *Orphareon*), or *Pandore* (or *Bandore* or *Bandora*), a bass instrument. The Spanish *Bandurria* and *Laud* are also forms of cittern.

(Note that the Gittern, q.v., was a different instrument.)

City Center, New York. Founded 1944 in abandoned theatre. Home of enterprising opera and ballet at popular prices; moved to Lincoln Center 1966.

Civettería (It.). 'Coquetry', 'flirtatiousness'. So *civettando*, 'coquetting'; *civettescamente*, 'coquettishly'.

Cl. = 'Clarinet'.

Claflin, Avery (b. Keene, N.H., 1898). Educated Harvard. Business man but also composer (operas, orch. and choral music, chamber music, &c.).

Clagget, Charles (1740–abt. 1795). Irish violinist, who settled in London and became a very ingenious inventor (improved violins, keyboard instruments, and wind instruments; cf. *Inventionshorn*).

Clair de lune. The third movement of Debussy's *Suite bergamasque*.

Claire, Caisse (Fr.). Side drum (see *Percussion Family* 2 i).

Clairon (Fr.). Bugle (q.v.); also a 4-foot stop on some Fr. organs.

Claque. Body of concert-goers hired by concert-giver to ensure his receiving applause adequate to his own opinion of his merits ('His' here being understood as a common gender pronoun).

Claquebois (Fr. 'clack-wood'). Xylophone (see *Percussion Family* 1 f).

Clarabel, Clarabella, or **Claribel Flute.** Much the same as *Hohlflöte* (q.v.).

Clari, or **The Maid of Milan.** Opera by Bishop, his most celebrated work, in which first appears the song *Home, sweet Home*. (Prod. London and New York 1823.)

'Claribel'—really Mrs. Barnard (b. 1830; d. Dover 1869). Wrote quantities of gentle, tuneful songs which greatly touched the hearts of her contemporaries (*Come back to Erin* now possibly the only survivor).

Claricembalo and **Clarichord.** Misspellings (apparently) of *Clavicembalo* ('Harpsichord') and *Clavichord*.

Clarina. See *Clarinet Family*.

Clarinet Family. All members of this family possess cylindrical tube and single reed, this of the 'beating' variety

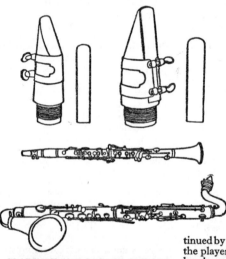

CLARINET AND BASS CLARINET
and their mouthpieces and reeds

(cf. *Reed*)—differing from Oboe Family in these particulars. As the reed blocks one end of the tube, the pipe acts as a 'stopped' one (cf. *Organ* 2), sounding 8ve lower than it would have done if left open. Like other cylindrical tubes the clarinet overblows at the interval not of its 1st upper partial, the interval of an 8ve (as the flute and oboe do), but at its 2nd (the interval of a 12th). The notes of the instrument's 1st 8ve are obtained in the normal way and the gap of a 5th before the overblowing begins has to be filled by additional side-holes which leave the tone weaker at this point and the fingering somewhat more awkward. All members of the family have great powers of *pianissimo* and of *crescendo* and *diminuendo*—greater than those of any other wind instrument. Double, triple, and flutter tonguing are possible (see *Tonguing*).

The family is of relatively recent introduction (very end of 17th c.), but derives from a family on somewhat similar lines, that of the CHALUMEAU (apparently merely in popular use): the word 'Chalumeau' is still in use to define the lowest part of the compass of the clarinet.

Chief members of the family are: (*a*) CLARINET IN C, B FLAT, OR A—the normal treble instrument. The existence of these 3 pitches was to enable the composer to use any key without creating undue difficulty for the player (cf. *Transposing instruments*). The C instrument is now not much used, on account of inferior tone, but figures in the scores of classical composers. (*b*) BASS CLARINET. Its range lies an 8ve below that of one of the above (usually of that of the B flat instrument). It differs somewhat in shape, its lower end being curved upwards and ending in a bell, and its upper one continued by a tube bent downwards to reach the player's mouth. Except in military band music it is treated as a transposing instrument, its music being notated either in the treble clef and a 9th higher than the sound (Fr. method), or in the bass clef a 2nd above the sound (Ger. method).

Other members of the family which must be mentioned are (*c*) HIGH E FLAT CLARINET, a 4th above the B flat instrument. It is found in all military bands and occasionally figures in orch.

scores. It is a transposing instrument, its music being notated a minor 3rd lower than the sound. (d) HIGH D CLARINET. This serves the same purpose as the E flat Clarinet, but is much rarer. It is a transposing instrument, being written for a tone lower than the sound. (e) ALTO CLARINET—IN E flat and F. The E flat instrument is practically a military band instrument and, even so, now rare. The F instrument is practically a modernized Basset Horn (see below). Both are written for in the treble clef and are transposing instruments. (f) BASSET HORN. A tenor instrument in appearance like the Bass Clarinet, with a pitch a 5th below that of the little-used C Clarinet. It also is a transposing instrument. (g) PEDAL CLARINET, or CONTRABASS CLARINET, or DOUBLE-BASS CLARINET. This is related to the Bass Clarinet much as the Double Bassoon is related to the ordinary Bassoon, or the stringed Double-Bass to the 'Cello. It is almost entirely a military band instrument. Its part is written a 9th higher than the sound. (The word 'pedal' has no reference to any part of the construction and the origin of its use is not very clear.) (h–j) Three rather obscure modern instruments related to the clarinet family by possessing a single reed are the CLARINA, the HECKELCLARINA or HECKELCLARINETTE, and the HOLZTROMPETE (all these were invented with the object of supplying Wagner's *Tristan* shepherd boy with a suitable instrument for his rural pleasures, but are not much used by him, the Cor Anglais being preferred).

Clarinet Flute. Organ flue stop, end-plugged; 4-foot length and 8-foot pitch; slightly reedy in quality.

Clarinet Quintet. See *Quintet*.

Clarinet Stop. Reed stop (see *Organ* 2) smoother than Oboe; 8-foot pitch or occasionally 16.

Clarion. Organ stop like *Trumpet* (q.v.) but of 4-foot pitch.

Clark, (1) **Richard** (b. Buckingham 1780; d. 1856). Singer in the choirs of Westminster Abbey, St. Paul's Cathedral, and the Chapel Royal. Zealous but unintelligent or unscrupulous musi-

cal antiquarian whose statements should never be depended upon.

(2) **Frederick Scotson** (b. London 1840; there d. 1883). Clergyman, schoolmaster, admired organist, founder of a London school of organ playing, and popular composer for his instrument.

(3) **Edward** (b. Newcastle-on-Tyne 1888; d. London 1962). Conductor. For some time connected with Diaghilef (see *Ballet*). With B.B.C. in various capacities 1923–36. Especially interested in contemporary developments in composition. (President Internat. Soc. Contemp. Music from 1945.) Married Elisabeth Lutyens (q.v.).

Clarke, (1) **Jeremiah** (b. abt. 1670; d. 1707). Organist of St. Paul's Cathedral and active composer of songs, harpsichord music, theatre music, and church music—some of the last-named still being in use. Came to a sad end; being disappointed in love shot himself.

See also *Trumpet Voluntary.*

(2) **Stephen** (b. Durham; d. Edinburgh 1797). Musical ed. of Johnson's *Scots Musical Museum* (6 vols. 1787–1803)—the great repository of Scottish national song.

(3) **Rebecca** (b. Harrow 1886). Viola player and composer. Trained R.C.M.; won 2nd Coolidge Prize for Sonata for Viola and Piano 1919. Has appeared as quartet player and soloist in many countries and has composed songs, &c. Resident in New York. Married James Friskin (q.v.).

(4) **Douglas** (b. 1893; d. Warwick 1962). Educated Cambridge (M.A., B.Mus.). Went to Winnipeg 1927; Dean of Faculty of Music McGill Univ., Montreal, 1930–55; cond. Montreal Symphony Orch. 1930–41. Returned to England 1958. Composer of orch. and other works.

Clarke-Whitfeld, John (b. Gloucester 1770; d. Hereford 1836). Organist at different times of 4 Irish and Eng. cathedrals and 2 Cambridge colleges. D.Mus. of 3 univs. and Prof. of music at Cambridge. As a composer of church music enjoyed great popularity; some of it still in use.

Clàrsach. The ancient small Celtic harp, revived in Scotland during the 20th century.

IRISH CLÀRSACH

Reputed to be that of King Brian Boru (926–1014) but probably of a somewhat later period. Now in the Library of Trinity College, Dublin

Clashpans. Old name for cymbals (see *Percussion Family* 2 o).

Classical Music. (1) Music of a more or less formal nature, with emphasis on beauty and proportion rather than on emotional expression (thus in antithesis to 'Romantic', q.v.). (2) Music of permanent value, not ephemeral. (3, amongst less educated people) Music with no 'tune' in it.

Claudin. See *Jeune, Claude le.*

Clausula. Cadence. Some medieval terms are *Clausula vera*, Perfect cadence; *Clausula falsa*, Interrupted cadence; *Clausula plagalis*, Plagal cadence; and so on.

Clavecin (Fr.). Harpsichord (*not* Clavichord).

Claves. Round sticks of hard wood 7 or 8 inches long. The player (in dance bands and the like) holds one over the upturned finger-nails of his left fist and beats it with the other held lightly in the right hand. A Cuban instrument.

Clavicembalo. See *Cembalo.*

Clavichord. In appearance this, when opened, resembles a small rectangular piano—often in form of a box to be placed on a table but sometimes possessing its own legs: a long side of the rectangle faces the player and the strings run horizontally parallel with that side. Method of tone-production is not, as with harpsichord and spinet by plucking, or, as with piano, by hammering, but by a sort of pressure stroke from below, by small pieces of metal, called *Tangents*. A peculiarity of these is that they are not only agents setting the strings in vibration but also agents in 'stopping' the strings (acting in this capacity as a violinist's finger does). The point where a tangent impinges on the string is the point at which the string should be stopped in order to produce the required note: the string is thus divided into two portions by the tangent but only the longer of these portions can vibrate, the other end of

CLAVICHORD

the string being permanently 'damped' by a piece of felt. In earlier examples (up to, say, 1730) there was an economy of string, since the tangents operated by 2 or more adjacent finger-keys might share a string on which to operate, each meeting it at the exact point called for by the note associated with one of the finger-keys in operation. (It will be realized, then, that the notes represented by such associated finger-keys could not be obtained simultaneously.) This type of clavichord was termed *Fretted*—presumably by analogy with the same word as applied to viols and lutes, &c. (see *Frets*); or, in Ger., *gebunden* (= 'bound together'). In later examples every finger-key possessed its monopoly of 1 string, and the term now used was *Unfretted* or (Ger.) *bundfrei* (= free of binding).

The tone of the clavichord is soft and ethereal: its power can be modified by the touch, as with the piano: a sort of prolongation of a note, called *bebung* (Ger. for 'tremolo'), is a characteristic effect.

The original period of popularity of the clavichord was an extended one—from the 14th c. to the end of the 18th or a little later. It and the harpsichord, less sensitive, but more varied in tone quality and more powerful, existed side by side from the beginning of the

16th c. onwards. During the 20th c. it has come again into some use.

Clavicylinder. Keyboard instrument invented by the acoustician, Chladni (1756–1827), having a glass cylinder, worked by a pedal and revolving against strips of wood, glass, or metal brought into action by the keys.

Clavicymbal. Eng. form of It. 'Clavicembalo', i.e. harpsichord (q.v.).

Clavicytherium. An upright spinet or harpsichord (q.v.).

Clavier. See *Klavier*.

Clavier à lumières, 'Keyboard of Lights'. See *Prometheus* (Scriabin).

Clavier des bombardes (Fr.). That organ manual having *Trumpet* and *Tuba*.

Clavier de récit (Fr.). *Swell Organ*; see *Organ 1*.

Clavierübung. See *Klavierübung*.

Clay, Frederick (Emes) (b. Paris 1838; d. Great Marlow, Bucks., 1889). Composer of theatre music and of highly popular songs (*I'll sing thee Songs of Araby, The Sands of Dee, She wandered down the mountain side*, &c.). See *Lalla Rookh*.

Clear Flute. Organ stop much like *Waldflöte* (q.v.).

Clef. See *Notation*; *Great Staff*; Table 4.

Clemens non Papa—name applied to Jacob (or Jacques) Clement (b. abt. 1510; d. abt. 1556). Important composer of Flemish school; many masses, motets, &c. (Conjectural explanations of sobriquet—(*a*) to distinguish from Pope Clement VII, and (*b*, more credible) to distinguish from Flemish poet Jacobus Papa.)

Clementi, Muzio (b. Rome 1752; d. Evesham, Worcs., 1832). At 14 a prodigy pianist; adopted and educated by an Eng. gentleman. Won European reputation as composer, pianist, and piano teacher (among his pupils being Field, Kalkbrenner, and J. B. Cramer). His collection of piano studies, *Gradus ad Parnassum*, is famous. He may be regarded as the first genuine composer for the piano (i.e. uninfluenced by the old harpsichord style) and as a com-

poser of piano sonatas was admired (and imitated) by Beethoven. Past middle life he successfully took to piano manufacturing in London (Clementi & Co., later Collard & Collard).

See *Pianoforte playing*; *Fingering*.

Clemenza di Tito, La ('The Mercy of Titus'). It. Opera by Mozart; libretto based on Metastasio. (Prod. Prague 1791; London 1806.) Also Opera by Gluck (1752).

Clérambault, Louis Nicholas (b. Paris 1676; there d. 1749). Noted Paris organist and composer for keyboard instruments and voice. His 4 books of Fr. cantatas are the best of their period.

Cleva, Fausto (Angelo) (b. Trieste 1902; d. Athens 1971). Operatic cond., mainly U.S.A.: Cincinnati 1934; San Francisco 1942; Metropolitan 1950, &c.

Cleveland Symphony Orchestra. Founded 1918; conductors include Nikolai Sokoloff, Rodzinski (1933), Szell (1946), Maazel (1973).

Cliburn, Van (= Harvey Lavan Jnr.; b. Shreveport, La., 1934). Pianist, studied with his mother and at the Juilliard School under Rosina Lhévinne. Début age 13; in 1958 became widely known as first American to win Tchaikovsky Prize in Moscow.

Clifford, (1) **James.** See *Cathedral Music*.

(2) **Julian I** (b. London 1877; d. 1921). Trained Leipzig, &c. At first pianist; then conductor Birmingham Symphony Orch., Harrogate Municipal Orch. Composed orch. and piano music, songs, &c.

(3) **Julian II** (b. London 1903). Son of above and also conductor. Trained R.C.M. and in Brussels. Has conducted leading Brit. orchs. At one time Musical Director of Municipal Orchs. of Hastings, Harrogate, Bexhill.

(4) **Hubert John** (b. Bairnsdale, Victoria, 1904; d. visiting Singapore 1959). Trained Melbourne Conserv. and R.C.M. Empire Music Supervisor B.B.C. 1941–4. On staff R.A.M. from 1944. Musical Director of Korda-British Lion Group of Film Producers 1946–50. Compositions include a symphony (1940), also light music under pseudonyms.

Clinton Family. Wind-instrument-playing family of whom the following seem to be the most important. (1) **Arthur** (b. abt. 1827). Clarinettist of repute. Father of the two following. (2) **James** (b. Newcastle 1853; d. London 1897). Leading London clarinettist of his day. (3) **George A. Arthur** (b. Newcastle-on-Tyne 1850; d. London 1913). Clarinettist. Began age 10 in volunteer band. At 17 in Queen Victoria's Private Band, then 24 years in Crystal Palace Orch. (also Covent Garden). On staff R.A.M., T.C.M., and Kneller Hall (q.v.). Brilliant performer; ed. of clarinet studies.

Clinton, (Francis) Gordon (b. Broadway, Worcs., 1912). Baritone. Trained R.C.M.; on staff from 1949. Principal Birmingham School of Mus. 1960.

Cloak, The (Puccini). See under *Trittico*.

Cloches (Fr.). 'Bells', e.g. those used in the orch. (see *Bell*; *Percussion Family* 1 b).

Cloches de Corneville, Les ('The Bells of Corneville'). Very popular operetta by Planquette. (Prod. Paris and New York 1877; London and Edinburgh, as *The Chimes of Normandy*, 1878.)

Clochette. Small bell.

Clochette, La (Paganini–Liszt). See *Campanella*.

Clocks, Musical. See *Mechanical Reproduction of Music* 4.

Clock Symphony (Ger. *Die Uhr*, 'The Clock'). Nickname of the 11th of Haydn's 'London Symphonies' (q.v.)—no. 101 in Breitkopf edn. (Key D). The slow movement suggests 'tick-tock'.

Clog Box. See *Chinese Wood Block*.

Close. The same as *Cadence* (q.v.).

Close Harmony. See *Harmony* 2 b.

Closson, Ernest (b. nr. Brussels 1870; d. there 1950). On staff of Conserv. of Brussels and then that of Mons. Active music critic and musicologist; author of books on Beethoven, Grieg, History of the Piano, &c.; collector and ed. of Belgian folk songs.

Cloud-capt Towers, The. See *Stevens, Richard*.

Club Anthem. See *Turner, W*.

Clubs for Music Making. Clubs meeting weekly for chamber-music practice, &c., were in 17th c. common in London, the university cities, &c. Catch Clubs were also common then and later (the NOBLEMEN AND GENTLEMEN'S CATCH CLUB, founded 1761, still meets once a month, as do several other Catch and Glee Clubs of rather later origin).

The London Club, CONCENTORES SODALES, was founded in 1798 and was still alive in 1864 or later. The ANACREONTIC SOCIETY lasted from 1766 to 1794. The OXFORD UNIVERSITY MUSICAL CLUB was founded in 1872 and the OXFORD MUSICAL UNION in 1884; these two combined in 1916. Cambridge has had similar activities. The OXFORD AND CAMBRIDGE MUSICAL CLUB, in London, long maintained a good club house and held weekly meetings for the performance of chamber music. (Revived 1952.)

Clutsam, George H. (b. Sydney, N.S.W., 1866; d. London 1951). Pianist; then critic and composer. Acted as accompanist to Melba, &c.; settled in London 1889, as accompanist, &c.; music critic of *Observer* 1908–18. Composed symphony, songs, and (esp.) operettas, &c. (see *Dreimäderlhaus*).

Clutsam Keyboard. See *Keyboard*.

Cluytens, André (b. Antwerp 1905; d. Paris 1967). Operatic conductor: Antwerp 1927; other posts; then Paris Opera 1944; Opéra Comique 1949.

Coach-horn. See *Post-horn*.

Coates, (1) Albert (Henry) (b. St. Petersburg 1882; d. nr. Cape Town 1953). Of half English, half Russian parentage. Studied in Leipzig and travelled widely as conductor, at last settling in S. Africa in 1946. Compositions include operas *Samuel Pepys* (1929), *Pickwick* (London 1936), and *Tafelberg se Kleed* ('Table Mountain in Cloud', 1952).

(2) **John** (b. nr. Bradford 1865; d. nr. London 1941). Tenor vocalist (originally baritone) of high artistic aims and achievements; successful equally in opera (including Wagner),

oratorio, and (especially latterly) recitals of Eng. songs, old and contemporary.

(3) **Henry** (b. London 1881; d. 1963). London music critic, then on staff of London Univ., T.C.M., and G.S.M. Book on Palestrina; some compositions; M.A., Cambridge; Ph.D., London.

(4) **Eric** (b. Hucknall, Notts., 1886; d. Chichester 1957). Trained R.A.M. At first viola player, then composer of songs, orch. music, &c., usually of the lighter type, and conductor of own works in many countries.

(5) **Edith Mary** (b. Lincoln 1908). Operatic contralto. Trained T.C.M. Active and successful career at Old Vic. and Sadler's Wells, Covent Garden, &c.

Cobb, (1) Gerard Francis (b. Nettlestead 1838; d. Cambridge 1904). Fellow of Trinity Coll., Cambridge. President of Univ. Board of Musical Studies (1877–92) and Univ. Musical Soc. (1874–84). Prolific composer—church music, songs, and part-songs, chamber music, piano music, &c.

(2) **Richard Barker.** See *Temple, Richard.*

Cobbett, Walter Willson (b. Blackheath, London, 1847; d. London 1937). Amateur violinist and especially chamber-music enthusiast, who spent money freely on prizes for compositions and on the production of a great *Cyclopedic Survey of Chamber Music* (1929; revised 1963).

Cochlea. See *Ear and Hearing.*

Cockaigne (legendary name of an imaginary country, later humorously applied to the home of the Cockneys). Concert-overture by Elgar, evocative of memories of the busy life of London. (Op. 40; 1901.)

Cockram. See *Passing By.*

Cocteau, Jean (b. Maisons-Lafitte, France, 1891; d. Paris 1963). Copious poet and prose writer, draughtsman, choreographer, writer and director of surrealist films, and playwright; at one time acrobatic airman, at another opium addict, &c.; all his phases exemplar and expositor of the Parisian *avant-garde* and in music propagandist, successively, for Debussy, Ravel, Satie,

'**Les Six**' (q.v.), Stravinsky, Markevitch, and Messiaen. Associated with Diaghilef in various ballet innovations.

Coda (It. 'Tail'). Passage added to any composition, or section of such, to give a stronger sense of finality (cf. *Codetta,* below).

Codetta (It. 'Little tail'). (1) Short or less important Coda (see above), e.g. the one at the end of the exposition in sonata form (see *Form* 3). (2) In fugue (see *Form* 6) an episodical passage occurring in the exposition.

Codiad yr ehedydd. See *Rising of the Lark.*

Coerne, Louis Adolphe (b. Newark, N.J., 1870; d. Boston, Mass., 1922). Active composer in various forms, including the earliest Amer. opera to be produced in Europe (*Zenobia,* Bremen 1905). Ph.D. of Harvard, the book *The Evolution of Modern Orchestration* and the opera score being accepted as his thesis.

Coffee Cantata (Ger. *Kaffeecantate*). Humorous cantata by Bach (1732). Libretto, by Picander, turns on the growing fondness for coffee at the time it was composed. Has been staged as an opera (e.g. Glasgow 1925).

Coffey, Charles. See *Devil to Pay.*

Coffin, Hayden—in full Charles Hayden (b. Manchester 1862 of Amer. parents; d. 1935). Baritone vocalist and actor, famous in operetta and musical comedy. Made his name by singing of *Queen of my Heart* in *Dorothy* (see *Cellier*).

Cogli, Coi (It.). 'With the' (plur.).

Cohen, Harriet (b. London 1895; d. there 1967). Pianist. Trained R.A.M.; pupil of Matthay; successful in both Britain and U.S.A.; wide repertory but specialized in music of Bax. Published piano arrangements of Bach. C.B.E. 1938.

Col, coll', colla, colle (It.). 'With the', e.g. *col basso,* 'with the bass'; *colla voce,* 'with the voice' (indication to accompanist to be subservient, i.e. as to time details).

Colascione. A kind of lute (q.v.) with a small circular body, a very long neck, and (usually) only 3 strings.

Cold and Raw. Song of D'Urfey (1653–1723) set to an old tune *Stingo*, or *Oil of Barley*.

Coleman, Charles. See *Siege of Rhodes.*

Coleridge, Arthur Duke (1830–1913). See *Bach Choir.*

Coleridge-Taylor, Samuel (b. London 1875; d. Croydon 1912).

Son of an Englishwoman and a West-African Negro medical man at that time practising in London. Appeared in public as boy violinist; studied under Stanford at R.C.M. Recommended by Elgar to the committee of the Gloucester Fest.; produced at it (1898) orch. Ballad in A minor and thus came prominently before the public. A few weeks later came the choral-orch. *Hiawatha's Wedding Feast* followed by *The Death of Minnehaha* (1899) and *Hiawatha's Departure* (1900), as well as choral-orch., orch., and chamber works, &c., and incidental music for plays, &c.

His daughter **Avril** (b. London 1903) is a conductor of standing who has toured extensively in S. Africa, &c. She is also a composer.

See also *Faust*; *Sea Drift.*

Colinda. A type of Rumanian Christmas song.

Coll', colla, colle (It.). See *Col.*

Coll' arco. 'With the bow'; i.e. after a passage marked *pizzicato*. (Sometimes shortened to *c.a.*)

Colla parte (It. 'with the part'), **colla voce** (It. 'with the voice'). An indication to an accompanist carefully to take his tempo and rhythm from the soloist.

Colla punta dell' arco (It.). 'With the point of the bow.'

Collard and Collard. See *Clementi.*

College of Saint Nicolas. See *Royal School of Church Music.*

Col legno (It. 'with the wood'). Striking the strings with the stick of the bow, instead of playing on them with the hair.

Colles, Henry Cope (b. Bridgenorth 1879; d. London 1943). Educated at the R.C.M. and Oxford (M.A., B.Mus.; later Hon. D.Mus.). Music critic of *The Times* (1905–43), ed. of 3rd and 4th edns. of Grove's *Dictionary of Music,* and author of several books on music.

Collingwood, Lawrance Arthur (b. London 1887). Conductor; studied Oxford, G.S.M., and St. Petersburg. Has conducted much opera in London (Old Vic and Sadler's Wells; Mus. Director latter 1940–7). Compositions include opera *Macbeth* (Sadler's Wells 1934), and orch. and chamber music, &c. C.B.E. (1948).

Collins, (1) **H. B.** (=Henry Bird) (b. Ipswich 1870; d. Birmingham 1941). Trained R.C.M. Became organist Birmingham Oratory 1915. High authority on early polyphonic music.

(2) **Anthony** (b. Hastings 1893). Viola player and then conductor and composer of film music, orch. and chamber music, &c.

Colmonell Use. See *Use of Sarum,* &c.

Colofonia (It.). 'Colophony', or bow resin.

Colomba. Opera by Mackenzie. (Prod. London 1883; Hamburg and Darmstadt 1884.)

Colonne, Édouard—but originally Judas (b. Bordeaux 1838; d. Paris 1910). Trained at Paris Conserv. Became leading violin of Paris Opera and then founder and conductor of famous orch. bearing his name. Paid conducting visits to Britain, Russia, the U.S.A., &c.

Colophony (Fr. *colophane*; It. *colofonia*; Ger. *Kolophon*). Resin for bow of stringed instruments.

Colorato, colorata (It. masc. and fem.) or **figurato, figurata** (It. masc. and fem). Treated in the manner of *Coloratura* (q.v.). (Cf. *Musica figurata.*)

Coloratura (It.), **Koloratur** (Ger.). The extempory or written decoration of a vocal melody in the shape of runs, roulades, and cadenzas of all kinds.

Coloratura soprano. One with a light flexible voice equal to the demands of passages of *Coloratura.*

Colour and Music. There is a natural tendency to find analogies between sound and colour, and even to develop definite theories as to a scientific relationship between them based on the fact that both are the result of vibrations (those of sound, however, relatively slow vibrations in the air; those of light and colour extremely rapid vibrations in the ether); such theories, however plausible at first sight, are on consideration seen to be erroneous, for the 8ve of notes has no definite relationship to the scale of colours and any comparison of the two is arbitrary. Many persons experience a mental association between keys and colours but this association is purely subjective and personal, differing widely with different individuals (for instance to Rimsky-Korsakof the key of C major was white whilst to Scriabin it was red).

There have, from the 17th c. onwards, been many suggestions that musical effects and colour effects should be combined and experiments in this direction ('Colour Organs', &c.) continue to be made. Interesting and beautiful results may be thus obtained, of which composers have sometimes tried to take advantage—e.g. Scriabin (q.v.) in his *Prometheus* and Schönberg (q.v.) in his *Die glückliche Hand* ('The Lucky Hand'), the scores of both of which include a line of notation for a play of colours on a screen during the musical performance.

For a fuller and more systematic discussion of the whole subject the reader may be referred to the 14-column treatment of it in the *Oxford Companion to Music*.

Cf. *Colour Symphony*.

Colour Symphony. By Arthur Bliss (1922). When composing this work he experienced sensations of colour, and hence headed his 4 movements 'Purple', 'Red', 'Blue', and 'Green'. These titles have obvious symbolical associations.

Colpo (It.). 'Stroke', e.g. *Colpo d'arco*, a stroke of the bow.

Columbia, The Gem of the Ocean. See *Britannia, the Pride of the Ocean*.

Combination Pedals. See *Organ* 2.

Combined Counterpoint. See *Counterpoint*.

Comb Instruments. See *Mechanical Reproduction of Music* 7.

Come (It.). 'As', 'like', 'as if'; *come prima*, 'as at first'; *come stà*, 'as it stands'; *come sopra*, 'as above'.

Come back to Erin. Eng. song (not Irish) by 'Claribel' (q.v.).

Comes. See *Canon*.

Comic Opera. See *Opera* 7.

Comin' thro' the Rye. Scottish or imitation-Scottish song (not certain which), with tune resembling one in a London pantomime of 1795 and also resembling tunes of *Auld Lang Syne* (q.v.) and other songs. Poem partly same as one by Burns.

Comique (Fr.). 'Comic' (but see *Opera* 7).

Comma. A minute interval such as that resulting when a rising succession of untempered 5ths (cf. *Temperament*) and a similar succession of 8ves arrive at what is ostensibly the same note, but is not really quite such.

Comme (Fr.). 'As', 'as if', 'like', &c.

Committee for the Promotion of New Music (15 Half Moon Street, Piccadilly, London, W. 1). Founded 1943 by the Arrangers', Composers', and Copyists' Section of the Musicians' Union (q.v.). First President Dr. Ralph Vaughan Williams. Holds Recitals, 'Experimental Rehearsals', &c., and after a hearing of works so tried out selects the best for inclusion in a *List of Recommended Works*. Up to 1948 there had been so presented works of 160 composers. Some works presented gramophonically recorded by Decca Record Co. Later called 'Society for the Promotion of New Music'.

Commodo or **comodo** (It.). 'Convenient', i.e. without any suspicion of strain, e.g. *tempo comodo*, at a comfortable, moderate speed. So the adverb, *comodamente*.

Common, in liturgical parlance, means that the part of service to which it is applied is regular and invariable (as distinguished from variable parts, called 'Proper' of such and such a day of the church's year). See *Mass*.

Common Chord. See *Harmony* 2 d.

Common Metre. See *Hymns and Hymn Tunes* 8.

Common Prayer, Book of. The complete service book of the Anglican Church, containing everything authorized for use except the Lessons, Anthems, and Hymns. It thus fulfils the same purposes as the Roman Catholic Church's Missal, Breviary, Manual, and Pontifical (see *Liturgy*). From the musician's point of view, the main difference between the Roman Breviary and Missal and the Prayer Book's order of Morning and Evening Prayer and Communion lies in the greater simplicity of the latter, in both the part for the minister and that for the people. The choir has, properly, no standing, save that in both Morning and Evening Prayer there is a place where occurs the indication 'In Quires and Places where they sing, here followeth the Anthem'. In practice, however, a good deal (or even the whole) of the people's part is in larger churches and cathedrals reserved for the choir, as the people's representative: one or two metrical hymns (not mentioned in the Prayer Book though allowed by the Injunctions of 1559) constitute there the only opportunity of the people's joining vocally in the service.

Provision is made for the reading or singing of the whole of the Psalms in rotation in each month of daily morning and evening services (see *Psalm*). At Morning Prayer the *Venite* (Ps. 95) is normally sung before the Psalms for the day.

The Canticles (q.v.) are as follows: At Morning Prayer, the *Te Deum* (or, at certain seasons, the *Benedicite*) and the *Benedictus* (or, on one or two occasions, the *Jubilate*); at Evening Prayer, the *Magnificat* (or, rarely, the 98th Psalm, *Cantate Domino*) and *Nunc Dimittis* (or, again rarely, the 67th Psalm, *Deus Misereatur*).

In the order of Holy Communion occur 4 of the 5 great passages from the Ordinary of the Mass (see *Mass*)—*Kyrie, Gloria in Excelsis, Credo*, and *Sanctus*, this last without its *Benedictus qui venit* section. (The custom has grown up, however, of setting both the *Benedictus qui venit* and the *Agnus Dei* in composed 'services' and the practice

was declared lawful by the Lincoln judgement of 1892; thus translated adaptations of settings of the Roman Mass have become available.)

The remainder of the order for the 3 services consists of prayers spoken or chanted by the minister, Preces and Versicles (see *Preces*) spoken, monotoned, or chanted by him, with Responses by the people, similarly treated (see *Responses*), and Lessons read. It has become a common practice to accompany the monotoned Creed by varied harmonies on the organ, so enabling choir and congregation to maintain the pitch. The Psalms (including the *Venite*) are either said or sung to Anglican Chants (see *Anglican Chant*) or Gregorian Tones (q.v.), and when the Canticles are not sung to some composed setting they are treated in the same way. The Litany (q.v.), to be sung or said after Morning Prayer on Sundays, Wednesdays, and Fridays, is, if sung, generally set to plainsong, either in unison or with descant.

Merbecke in 1550 published 'The Book of Common Prayer noted'. This consisted of monophonic setting, in mensurable music, mainly original, of the Communion office, Mattins and Evensong, the Office for the Burial of the dead and 'the Communion when there is no burial'. Terry (Proceedings Mus. Assoc., Session 45) points out that 'there is no authentic plainsong throughout the book excepting the Versicles and Responses at the opening of Mattins and Evensong and those which occur later on in those services'. Merbecke's noting of the versicles and responses was used as the basis for most of the later Tudor settings (e.g. Tallis's two settings).

Common Time. Another name for ₄ time (see Table 10). The C sometimes used instead of the figures ₄ does not stand for 'common': it dates from the period when triple time (called 'perfect') was indicated by a full circle and quadruple time (called 'imperfect') by a broken circle.

Community Singing (or **Community Music**). A rough definition of 'Community Singing' would be 'the audience as its own vocal performer'. This, looked on by many as a recent activity, is in reality a very ancient one. Obviously any sort of hymn sung by a congregation is an example of community singing, and as an early instance of Eng. community singing on a large scale may be mentioned the singing of metrical psalms outside St. Paul's Cathedral, London, in the first flush of enthusiasm after the Reformation. Stow (1559) says: 'You may now see at Paul's Cross, after the service, 6000 people, young and old, of both sexes, singing together.'

Addison in the *Spectator* (1711) tells us that community singing was common in the French opera of his day:

'I have sometimes known a performer on the stage do no more in a celebrated song than the clerk of a parish church, who serves only to raise the Psalm, and is afterwards drown'd in the musick of the congregation.'

It has, however, been claimed that this practice was Italian in its origin. A somewhat similar practice shortly sprang up in England and Ireland. Thus Colley Cibber's ballad-opera, *Love in a riddle* (Drury Lane, London, 1729), included an invitation to the audience issued by the mouth of the chief comedian:

Then, freeborn boys, all make a noise,
  As France has done before us;
With English hearts all bear your parts,
  And join the jolly chorus.

The present-day expression 'Community Singing' apparently originated in the U.S.A., where the practice was definitely organized in camps during the First World War, official 'Song Leaders' being appointed. A similar practice already obtained in the Brit. Army. After the war Gibson Young developed a community-singing movement in Australia, and later came to England, where he did the same. In 1925 a London newspaper (Lord Beaverbrook's *Daily Express*) took up the movement as a journalistic 'stunt' and organized meetings for community singing in the Royal Albert Hall (seating 10,000) and elsewhere. But the actual pioneer of the modern Brit. community singing movement appears to be R. E. Jeffrey of the B.B.C., who carried out successful experiments in Aberdeen in March 1924, so slightly anticipating the Beaverbrook scheme.

Special song books for community singing have been published in Britain and the U.S.A.

In certain manufacturing districts of the north of England ordinary audiences can pretty effectively join a choir in the singing of the 4 voice-parts of Handel's 'Hallelujah Chorus', and that is, perhaps, community singing at the point of greatest cultivation attainable.

Comodo (It.). See *Commodo*.

Compass of Voices. See *Voice* 14.

Compère, Loyset (b. abt. 1440; d. St. Quentin 1518). Possibly a pupil of Okeghem; later Canon and Chancellor of the Cathedral of St. Quentin and an important composer of church music.

Competitions in Music.[1] The musical competition is a venerable institution. Putting aside the celebrated contest between Phoebus and Pan, there were the Pythian Games of the 6th c. B.C. (which were especially musical contests), the Eisteddfod of Wales, traditionally dating back to the 7th c., the Song Contest of the Minnesingers at the Wartburg in the 13th c., the 'Puys' (meetings of minstrels) of the Middle Ages, and so on.

In England in the late 18th c. choral competitions were sometimes held at country taverns. In the 19th c. a very great extension of competition activity took place. In 1853 the Brass Band Contests of the Belle Vue Gardens, Manchester, began, followed in 1855 by 'Prize Glee Singing'. In 1860 at the Crystal Palace there took place its first Tonic Sol-fa Competition, with choirs from England and Scotland; Bradford held a competition in solo and choral singing in 1864; in 1872 and some following years there were important choral competitions at the Crystal Palace; in 1874 there were such competitions in Manchester and Liverpool. In 1876 a Pianoforte-playing competition took place at Portsmouth; it was called by the Amer. term of 'Bee' and was followed by a swarm that for a few years flew vigorously about the country. In 1881 Sheffield held a general musical competition; and (surprisingly)

---

[1] In the U.S.A. the usual term is not 'Competition' but 'Contest'.

Fr. male-voice and mixed-voice choral societies, wind-bands, and orchs., came over to Brighton and held there a great competition. In 1882 a Temperance Choral Competition was held at the 'Royal Victoria Coffee Hall' (the 'Old Vic'), London, and in 1883, on the east side of London, the Stratford Musical Fest. began its useful activities of many years. The above list does not claim to be exhaustive but is sufficient to discredit the frequent statements such as, 'In 1885 Miss Mary Wakefield, at Kendal, sowed the first seeds of the competition festival movement', or 'begun by J. S. Curwen'.

During the closing years of the 19th c. musical competition activities developed into a regular 'movement'. In 1904 an Assoc. of Musical Competition Fests. (now 'British Federation of Music Festivals') was formed: and in 1905 it was estimated that 50,000 competitors were engaged every year (this does not include the Welsh organizations, for which see *Eisteddfod*). The movement spread to Canada, Australia, and other parts of the Brit. Empire. A Canadian Fest. that has been held annually from 1908 is that of the Alberta Musical Fest. Assoc., held in turn at Calgary, Edmonton, and Lethbridge, Alberta.

The Irish national competition, the Feis Ceoil, was founded in 1897; it has usually been held in Dublin.

In the U.S.A. the earliest musical competition recorded appears to be that of Dorchester, Mass., in 1790, at which two rival choirs competed. It was in the 1920's that a general competition movement grew up, and it was largely connected with the high schools. From 1914 intercollegiate singing contests became frequent.

Musical competitions have been fairly common in Germany from the 1880's or earlier. They have also taken place in many other European countries.

In several countries there have been many competitions for composition held under very varied auspices. They have embraced all types of music.

For 'Music Memory Contests' see under *Appreciation of Music*.

Compiacevole (It.). 'Pleasing. So *compiacevolmente*, 'pleasingly'; *compiacimento*, 'pleasure'.

Complete Cadence. See *Cadence*.

Compline (meaning 'completion'). The 8th and last of the *Canonical Hours* (see *Divine Office*) of the Roman Catholic Church.

Componiert (Ger.). 'Composed.'

Composé (Fr.). (1) 'Composed.' (2) 'Compound.'

Composer's Counterpoint. See *Counterpoint*.

Composers' Guild of Great Britain (84 Drayton Gardens, London, S.W. 10). Affiliated to the Soc. of Authors (same address). Exists to protect the interests of composers. First President: Dr. R. Vaughan Williams.

Composition, etymologically, is the 'putting together'—of words to make a poem or piece of prose, of notes to make a waltz or symphony, of details to make a picture. In music the 'putting together' consists chiefly in (*a*) combining successive notes to make *Melody*; (*b*) combining simultaneous notes to make *Harmony*; (*c*) combining melodies to make *Counterpoint*; (*d*) combining *Phrases* to make *Sentences* and sentences to make long passages; (*e*) combining *Themes* and their treatment to make pieces or *Movements* of pieces; (*f*) combining movements to make the *Cyclic Forms* (sonata, symphony, &c.). The combining of timbres in *Orchestration* may also be held to constitute a part of composition. (See separate entries under these various heads.) The object of the composer is dual: he desires to express his emotions and to satisfy his sense of craftsmanship and design.

There are, in a sense, no 'RULES' of composition. What have been formulated as such by theorists in textbooks are an attempt at a codification of the processes of successful composers of the past and may be disregarded by any composer of the present who feels that he can gain the effect he desires without accepting such control.

Composers who have been asked to define their mental processes of composition all claim the initial impulse of something called INSPIRATION but admit that whilst this element is essential it has to be followed by labour and the application of a craftsmanship previously acquired in the student stage and then increasingly developed by continual practice. The inspiration thus referred to is in some cases merely a mood which clamours for expression or a musical idea (or 'theme') which 'comes into the head' and demands development: there have, however, been composers whose inspiration has on occasion been of the nature of a scheme of modulations (e.g. Franck on occasion), or the form of a piece (e.g. Ravel in his second violin sonata), without, as yet, any musical material to be used in carrying out the modulations or form. And so on—the nature of inspiration being apparently surprisingly various. Some composers have courted inspiration by extemporizing at the piano. Others have been stimulated by a non-musical 'programme' (see *Programme Music*) which they were impelled to express in tones. Some (e.g. Schubert) have felt an impulse to compose a song, and on reading a poem which strongly impressed them have been inspired with the musical style and material they ultimately adopted in it.

It is observable that composition in the late 19th and 20th cs. had become a much more laborious and serious undertaking than it had been in the 16th, 17th, and 18th. PRODUCTIVITY in that earlier period was very much higher. Philippe de Monte (in the 16th c.) composed over 1,000 madrigals and 300 motets. In the 18th c. composers normally threw off sonatas, string quartets, symphonies, &c., in sets of 6 or more. Handel wrote *Israel in Egypt* in 29 days and *Messiah* in 22; Bach wrote 5 complete sets of Church Cantatas for each Sunday of the year and his contemporary Telemann 12 such sets (i.e. over 600 in all). Mozart's greatest 3 symphonies were composed in the brief period of 2 months. Operas also in the 18th c. were often 'mass produced'. Even in the early 19th c. we find Schubert, who died at the age of 30, composing over 600 songs and, later, Hugo Wolf, who died at the age of 42, composing 500. Wholesale com-

position, however, had in general ceased with the end of the 18th c.

ORIGINALITY in Composition is exceedingly difficult to define. There seem to be two qualities passing under that name: (*a*) Actual novelty in melody, harmony, form, orchestration; and (*b*) The strong expression of personality. There have been composers who could take a theme (e.g. a fugue subject; cf. *Form* 6) that seemed to possess, in itself, little originality, or even to be rather trite, and yet out of it produce a moving and 'original' composition.

The above is a mere summary of some of the main thoughts which come to one as one considers the nature of Composition and its practice in different periods and by different composers, the whole subject being very much more fully developed in *OCM*.

Cf. *Expression*; *Interpretation*.

Composition Pedals. See *Organ* 2.

Compound Binary. See *Form* 3.

Compound Interval. See *Interval*.

Compound Time (Duple, Triple, Quadruple). See Table 10.

Compter (Fr.). 'To count.' *Comptent*, 'count' (plur.), as an indication in an orch. score that the instruments in question have fallen out for the moment and are merely 'counting their bars'—'marking time'.

Comte Ory, Le ('Count Ory'). 2-act comedy-opera by Rossini. French libretto by Scribe and Delestre-Poirson. (Prod. Paris 1828.)

Comus. See *Lawes, Henry*.

Con (It.). 'With.'

Concentores sodales. See *Clubs for music making*.

Concentus. See under *Accentus*.

Concert. The word means, properly, a *performing together* (vocal or instrumental or both), and is so used in older literature, but has come to be applied to almost any sort of public musical performance.

World's earliest concerts in modern sense seem to have been those of JOHN BANISTER in his London house 1672–8. THOMAS BRITTON, a charcoal hawker but a learned and cultured man, followed at once with his series 1678–1714. (Note, however, that before the time of Banister programmes of music preliminary to plays were common in London theatres, earliest of which record has been found being in 1602.)

Earliest records of any concert in American Colonies are those of Boston and Charleston, both 1731.

PROMENADE CONCERTS, with audience on its feet, go back to the London pleasure places called 'Gardens' (e.g. Vauxhall, 1660–1859; Marylebone, abt. 1650–1776; Ranelagh, 1742–1803). In 1830's the conductor MUSARD, in Paris, carried on concerts on similar lines and in 1838 'Promenade Concerts à la Musard' were advertised in London. Thereafter many enterprises of this kind (Jullien, q.v.; Balfe, q.v.; Rivière, &c.), of which Queen's Hall Promenade Concerts, conducted by Henry Wood (q.v.) from 1895 to last illness, still continue—transferred to Royal Albert Hall on enemy destruction of Queen's Hall 1941.

Concertante (It.). (1) 'Of the nature of a concerto.' (2) The concertante instruments in the old Concerto Grosso (see *Concerto*) were those to which were confided the solo sections, as distinct from the Ripieno (q.v.) instruments, which played in the full sections. Cf. *Concertino*.

Concertata, Aria. See *Aria*.

Concertato. See *Concerto*.

Concert Flute. (1) Organ stop, sometimes on principle of *Harmonic Flute* (q.v.): usually on Solo Manual; generally 4-foot pitch. (2) See *Flute Family*.

Concertgebouw Orchestra. Headquarters the Concertgebouw ('Concert-building'), Amsterdam, constructed 1888. Conductor 1945–59, Eduard van Beinum, 1961, Bernard Haitink.

Concert Grand. See *Pianoforte*.

Concert Halls should be not so large that (a) Some members of the audience lose the softer passages of the music or feel the effect of the whole to be muffled, or that (b) Any echoes which occur are heard so long after the notes evoking them as to become confused with following notes (a high ceiling is likely to produce this distressing effect unless broken up by panels, i.e. 'coffered'). The materials of walls and ceiling should be neither too reverberatory nor too absorbent ('dead'). Curved surfaces, such as an apse at the back of the platform, are undesirable, as the various parts of the curve reflect sound in such a way that, by the principle of focus, they produce intensification of sound at various points in the auditorium. Columns, alcoves, and other interruptions in the route of the sound should be avoided and the floor should be raked, so that the front rows of the auditors do not impede the passage of the sound to the ears of the back rows. Ventilation should be so contrived as not to admit outside noises. Amplifiers and loud speakers can be used (as they nowadays often are) to get over difficulties due to original faulty designing of the hall.

For Resonance see *Acoustics* 19.

Concertina. See *Reed-Organ Family* 4.

Concertino. (1, in older usage) The solo instrumental group in the Concerto Grosso (cf. *Concertante*; *Concerto*). (2, in more modern usage) A shorter and lighter variety of the Concerto.

Concert Master. See *Leader*.

Concerto (It. and Eng.). As the word's original significance is merely that of a performance 'together' of several instrumentalists or vocalists it has necessarily had many applications at different periods. By the end of the 17th c. it had come to be used by the It. violinist-composer school (Corelli, &c.) as implying a type of composition in which a small body of solo strings was heard in alternation and combination with a larger body of orch. strings. The larger body was called *Ripieno* (i.e. 'full') and the smaller *Soli*, *Concertino*, *Concertato*, or *Concertante*. The Concerto of this period resembled the Sonata of the same period in that it consisted of 3 or more contrasted movements. As there were 2 types of Sonata, the *Sonata da Chiesa* ('Church Sonata', with abstract movements) and the *Sonata da Camera* ('Chamber Sonata', with dance-style movements), so there were 2 types of Concerto, the CONCERTO DA CHIESA and the CONCERTO DA CAMERA. Concerti of these types were very definitely established in favour when Corelli wrote his *Concerti Grossi* (1712). A *Concerto Grosso* ('Great Concerto') is really nothing more than what has just been described—a work in which the antiphonal idea is developed, i.e. the alternation and combination of *Ripieno* and *Concertino* groups of instruments. The most famous Concerti Grossi are three of the *Brandenburg Concertos* of Bach, each with a different combination of instruments (see *Brandenburg Concertos*).

Concertos with a solo part in place of the Concertino also existed in the Concerto Grosso period, and these may be considered to be the ancestors of the present-day type of Concerto, which we may call the VIRTUOSO CONCERTO, in whose scores we see the words *Solo* and *Tutti* ('all') in place of *Concertante* and *Ripieno*. To this type Mozart contributed between 40 and 50 examples with solo parts for various instruments, and Beethoven 5 for piano, 1 for violin, &c. The general plan is that of the later Sonata (q.v.) and Symphony but (for some rather obscure reason) with only 3 movements instead of 4.

In this more modern kind of Concerto the CADENZA (q.v.) became a feature.

Among less common uses of the word 'Concerto' we have an example in the *Italian Concerto* (q.v.) of Bach, which is written for a single performer.

Cf. *Concertino*; *Concertstück*.

Concerto Accademico. Original title of the Concerto for Violin and Strings by Vaughan Williams (1925).

Concert of Ancient Music, also known as 'Ancient Concert', or 'King's Concert'. London series under royal and aristocratic management, 1776–1849, with passing attempts at revival in 1867 and 1870. No music less than 20 years old in programmes. (Not to be confused with 'Academy of Ancient Music', q.v.)

Concerto Russe. For Violin. By Lalo (1883).

Concert Overture. See *Overture*.

Concert Pitch. See *Pitch*.

Concertstück (Ger.) means literally 'Concert-piece' but generally with the first word understood in the sense of 'concerted', i.e. with some solo instrument operating in combination with orch. Briefer concertos of the less formal kind and without breaks between sections (i.e. in what is called 'one movement') are often so designated.

Conchita. Opera by Zandonai. (Prod. Milan 1911; London 1912; New York 1913.)

Concitato (It.). 'Roused up', 'stirred'. So *concitamento, concitazione*, 'agitation'.

Concone, Giuseppe (b. Turin 1810; there d. 1861). Celebrated singing teacher and composer of vocal studies.

Concord. See *Harmony* 2 f.

Concrete Music. See *Musique Concrète*.

Concordant Intervals. See *Interval*.

Conducting. The method of holding together an instrumental or choral force, and securing from it the most musical effect possible, has varied in different periods. From an early time it was usual in choral performance to mark the beat, and probably to indicate entries of the various voices, with a roll of paper or a short stick (at one period called a *Sol-fa*). During the 17th c. and the earlier 18th, in France (and possibly elsewhere), it was common for the director of the forces loudly to thump out the beat on the floor with a long stick, or on a table with a shorter one. Then came in the practice of conducting from a harpsichord, the player of which, presumably with the score before him, would, by his performance, control the tempo and prevent the players scattering, and probably to some extent suggest the interpretation.

During the earlier 19th c. the keyboard instrument tended to go out of use, the control being left to the leading 1st violinist, who by vigorous sawing or by waving his bow would give the tempo to his fellows, to some extent, doubtless, suggest expression, and ward off dangers of various natures. Something like the modern practice of baton conducting came in earlier in Germany than in Britain. Beethoven seems to have conducted (very badly) with a baton. No baton seems to have been seen in the London concert room until later in the 19th c. Spohr is sometimes said to have introduced it in 1820, but this is doubtful.

It will be realized that conductorship must, throughout the long period above covered, have been of a very elementary character, and that, hence, orch. and choral performances must often have been of a merely rough-and-ready

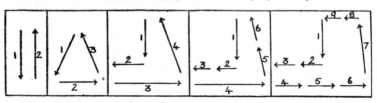

SCHEME OF BATON MOTIONS
(2, 3, 4, 6, and 9 beats in a bar)

character. Real refinement in orch. performance was introduced by Johann Stamitz (q.v.), at Mannheim, in the mid-18th c., but the example seems to have been very slowly followed. The initiation of the modern standard (what we may call 'Virtuoso Conductorship') may probably be attributed to von Bülow who was employed at various Ger. centres from 1864 to 1885 and, of course, achieved a high reputation as a conductor of the works of Beethoven and of Wagner.

Conductus. A type of church composition of the 12th and 13th cs. In that period the process of composition consisted in adding voice-parts to an existing melody ('Canto fermo'). If this melody were not plainsong but secular or original the term 'conductus' was used. (This seems to be the word's general significance.)

Confiteor. See *Mass.*

Confutatis. See *Requiem.*

Conjunct Motion. See *Motion.*

Cons, Emma. See *Victoria Hall.*

Consecration of Sound (Spohr). See *Weihe der Töne.*

Consecration of the House, The (*Die Weihe des Hauses*). Concert-overture composed by Beethoven (op. 124)

for the opening of the Josephstadt Theatre in Vienna, 1822.

Consecutive Fifths or Octaves. See *Harmony* 2 j.

Consequent. See *Canon.*

Conservatoire National (Paris). See *Schools of Music.*

Conservatorio. See *Schools of Music.*

Conserver (Fr.). 'To preserve.' So *conservant le rhythme*, 'preserving rhythm'.

Console. See *Organ* 3.

Console Piano. See *Pianoforte.*

Consonance. See *Harmony* 2 f.

Consonants. See *Voice* 10.

Con sordino (It.). 'With mute' (see *Mute*).

Consort. An old spelling of 'concert'; its sense is any body of performers performing together.

For *Consort of Viols* see *Viol Family* 2. A *Whole Consort* was one in which all the instruments were of strings, or all of wind; a *Broken Consort* one in which there was an admixture of the 2 types (cf. Shakespeare, 'broken music').

Consort Viol. See *Viol Family* 3 d.

Consul, The. 3-act tragedy-opera, libretto and music by Menotti. (Prod. New York 1950; London 1951.)

Conte (Fr.). 'Tale.' Sometimes used as a 'fancy title' for a piece of instrumental music.

Contes d'Hoffmann (Offenbach). See *Tales of Hoffmann.*

Contest. See *Competitions in Music.*

'Continental' Fingering. See *Fingering*.

Continuo. See *Figured Bass*.

Contrabandista. Two-act comic opera by Sullivan. Libretto by Burnand. (Prod. by German Reed, St. George's Hall, London, 1867; another version, *The Chieftain*, at Savoy Theatre 1894.)

Contrabass. (1) Double-bass (see *Violin Family*). (2) Organ stop. Much same as *Violone* (q.v.).

Contrabass Clarinet. See *Clarinet Family*.

Contrabass Trombone. See *Trombone Family*.

Contrabass Tuba. See *Tuba Group* 1 c.

Contradanza. See *Country Dance*.

Contraltist. A Castrato Singer (see *Voice* 5) with a voice of contralto range.

Contralto. See *Voice* 14.

Contrapuntal. The adj. of 'Counterpoint' (q.v.).

Contrary Motion. See *Motion*.

Contra-violin. Slightly bigger than the normal violin and with somewhat thicker strings, which gives it an individual 'colour'. It was intended by its inventor (Charles Newbold of Jersey, Channel Islands, 1917) for the player of Second Violin parts.

Contredanse. See *Country Dance*.

Conus, George (b. Moscow 1862; there d. 1933). Pupil of Serge Taneief at Moscow Conserv. and later prof. there. Composed orch. music, piano music, songs, &c., and was much esteemed as a theorist.

Converse, Frederick Shepherd (b. Newton, Mass., 1871; d. nr. Boston 1940). Pupil at Boston of Chadwick and Paine, whose ideals he adopted, and of Rheinberger at Munich. Composed well-wrought orch. music, chamber music, operas, choral music, piano music, and songs, and was very much esteemed for his lofty idealism.

Cook, (1) **Thomas Aynsley** (b. London 1836; d. Liverpool 1894). Operatic bass. Trained by Staudigl (q.v.). Début Manchester 1856. Joined Carl Rosa Co. 1874. Had repertory of about 100 operas. Appeared up to a fortnight before death. (Daughter was wife of Eugène Goossens II, and hence he was grandfather of Eugène III, Leon, Adolphe, Sidonie, and Marie.)

(2) **(Alfred) Melville** (b. Gloucester 1912). Organist. Pupil of Sumsion; D.Mus., F.R.C.O.; asst. org. Gloucester Cath. 1932; Leeds 1937; org. Hereford Cath. 1956.

Cooke, (1) **Henry** (b. probably abt. 1616; d. Hampton Court 1672). Choir-boy in Chapel Royal; later joined the royalist forces and became captain; at Restoration returned to Chapel Royal as Master of the Children, amongst which children were Pelham Humfrey, John Blow, and Henry Purcell. Was favourably known not only as their teacher but as composer of music for stage and church, as actor and as singer. Both Pepys and Evelyn praise him.

See *Siege of Rhodes*.

(2) **Benjamin** (b. London 1734; there d. 1793). Organist of Westminster Abbey; his church music and glees are still sung.

(3) **Thomas Simpson** (b. Dublin 1782; d. London 1848). Music-seller and leader of a theatre orch. in Dublin; successful as tenor singer and long attached in this capacity to Drury Lane Theatre in London. Famous singing teacher, and popular composer of theatre music and glees (e.g. *Strike the Lyre*).

(4) **William Waddington** (b. West Keel, Lincs., 1868; d. 1940). Pianist and composer. Trained R.C.M. and under Leschetizky. Début Crystal Palace 1900. On staff G.S.M. for 40 years.

(5) **James Francis** (b. Bay City, Mich., 1875; d. Philadelphia, Pa., 1960). Author and composer. Studied Würzburg Conserv., &c. Editor *Étude* 1908–49; President Theo. Presser Co. (q.v.) 1925–36. Also President Presser Foundation (q.v.) from 1918. Chev. de la Légion d'honneur; 15 hon. doctorates.

(6) **Arnold Atkinson** (b. Gomersall, Yorks., 1906). Studied at Cambridge (D.Mus. 1948) and under Hindemith at Berlin; became musical director of Festival Theatre, Cambridge, and then

some years on staff of Royal Manchester Coll. of Music, later on that of T.C.M. Composer of chamber music, orch. music (*Daily Telegraph* Prize for overture 1934), &c.

(7) **Deryck (Victor)** (b. Leicester 1919). Musicologist. Educ. Cambridge (M.A.). B.B.C. 1947–59; book *The Language of Music*. See *Mahler's Symphonies*.

Coolidge, Mrs. Elizabeth Sprague (b. Chicago 1864; d. Cambridge, Mass., 1953). Pianist, composer, and patron of music. Founder of chamber music festivals (Pitsfield, Mass.; then Washington, D.C.). Coolidge Foundation at Library of Congress (with Auditorium given by her) for concerts and festivals; awards of prizes and medals to contemporary composers of all countries. Many universities recognized value of her work by conferring honorary degrees.

Cooper, (1) **George** (d. London 1843). London organist of repute (assistant organist St. Paul's Cathedral and organist St. Sepulchre's).

(2) **George** (b. London 1820; there d. 1876). Organist. Played occasionally at St. Paul's Cathedral from age 11, assistant organist there at 18 (succeeding his father, resigned—see above). Organist St. Sepulchre's, Chapel Royal, &c. Publ. many organ arrangements.

(3) **Gerald Melbourne** (b. 1892; d. London 1947). Well-to-do and enthusiastic and public-spirited music-lover, who promoted annual series of London chamber concerts, at which old music was revived and contemporary music brought before public. Produced popular edn. Purcell, &c. Hon. Sec. Royal Philharmonic Soc. (1929–32) and other positions.

(4) **Martin Du Pré** (b. Winchester 1910). Studied under Wellesz (q.v.). Music critic *London Mercury* (1935), *Daily Herald* and *Spectator* (1946), *Daily Telegraph* (1954). Editor *Musical Times* (1953). Author of books on Bizet, Gluck, &c. B.A. (Oxon.).

Coperario. See *Coprario*.

Coperto (It. 'covered'). A term used of drums muted by being covered with a cloth.

Copla. (1) A Spanish popular poem

and song in short stanzas (see *Seguidilla*), sometimes extemporized. (2) A solo movement in a *Villancico* (q.v.).

Copland, Aaron—original name Kaplan (b. Brooklyn 1900). Studied in America and under N. Boulanger in Europe (Guggenheim Fellowship 1925–6), and settled in New York. Highly successful composer of popular ballets, film music, &c., as well as works (3 symphonies, piano music, &c.) in a less accessible idiom. Books on appreciation, aesthetics, &c. Active 'committeeman', and altogether one of the most influential figures in his profession. Hon. D.Mus., Princeton, 1955. (See *Appalachian Spring*; *Billy the Kid*; *El Salón México*; *Lincoln Portrait*; *Quiet City*; *Rodeo*; *Tender Land*.)

Coppel (Ger.). 'Coupler' (organ).

Coppélia. See *Delibes*.

Coppet, Edward J. de (b. New York 1855; there d. 1916). Of Swiss origin. Wealthy musical patron. Founded Flonzaley Quartet (named from his Swiss estate, where they practised before each winter season); first appearance in public 1904, thereafter touring U.S.A. and Europe as well as performing in patron's New York home. Disbanded 1927. See *Betti*; *Pochon*.

Coprario (or **Coperario**), **John**—really John Cooper (b. abt. 1570; d. 1627). Played lute and viola da gamba and composed pieces for those instruments and for the organ, as also songs, music for masques, &c. Changed name during a visit to Italy and then retained the improvement.

Coprifuoco, coprifoco (It. 'curfew'). Occasional title for an instrumental composition, sometimes with bell effect.

Coq d'Or, Le. See *Golden Cockerel*.

Cor (Fr.). Properly horn (see *Horn Family*) but the term forms a part of the name of several instruments which are not horns (see below).

Cor anglais. (1) See *Oboe Family*. (2) Organ reed stop like *Oboe* (q.v.), generally 8-foot pitch but sometimes 16.

Corant, coranto. See *Courante*.

Corbett, William (abt. 1669–1748). London violinist and composer. Lived a good deal in Italy and there made large collection of violins, &c., and of music. Works for various string and wind combinations; also songs and some theatre music.

Corda, corde (It. sing., plur.). 'String', 'strings'. (1, Piano music) *Una corda*, 'one string', i.e. use the 'soft' pedal which causes the hammers (on a grand piano) to strike only one string for each note. (2, Violin music, &c.) *Corda vuota*, 'empty string', i.e. 'open string'.

Corde (Fr.). 'String'. (In Italian the same spelling means 'strings'—see *Corda*.)

Corde à jour, corde à vide (Fr.). 'Open string' (q.v.).

Cor de chasse. Hunting horn (see *Horn Family*).

Cor de nuit (Fr. 'night-horn', i.e. 'watchman's horn'). Organ flue stop; end-plugged; of 4-foot length and 8-foot pitch; of very characteristic tone quality.

Corder, Frederick (b. London 1852; there d. 1932). Composer of operas, &c., who settled down as composition prof. of the R.A.M. (where he had himself been trained) and there became responsible for the training of a long line of composers. (See *Society of British Composers*.)

Cor des Alpes. See *Alphorn*.

Cor d'harmonie (Fr.). Horn, with or without valves (see *Horn Family*).

Corea (Sp.). A dance accompanied by song. Hence the adjective *Coreado*.

Corelli, (1) Arcangelo (b. nr. Milan 1653; d. Rome 1713). In his day the violin was superseding the viol and he became the new instrument's first great player, teacher, and composer, so winning universal fame and leaving behind him an imperishable memory.

See *Christmas Concerto*.

(2) **Franco** (b. Ancona 1923). Dramatic tenor. Début Spoleto 1951; London 1957; New York 1961.

Corelli Fugue (Bach). For Organ. In B minor. So nicknamed because on subjects from Corelli.

Coriolanus Overture. Composed by Beethoven (op. 62; 1807) for a revival

in Vienna of the tragedy by the Austrian dramatist H. J. von Collin.

Cor mixte. See *Corno Alto and Corno Basso*.

Cornelius, (1) Peter (b. Mainz 1824; there d. 1874). Friend of Wagner and colleague of his at Munich; favourably remembered by cultured solo singers and intelligent choralists for his poetical songs and part-songs. His opera *The Barber of Bagdad* had only one performance (see *Barbier von Bagdad*) until its composer had been many years in the grave.

(2) **Peter** (b. nr. Fredensborg, Denmark, 1865; d. Copenhagen 1934). Operatic tenor renowned in Wagner roles. Début Copenhagen 1892, and thereafter in Bayreuth, London, &c.

Cornelius March. By Mendelssohn (op. 108; 1841). Composed for a Dresden fest. in honour of the painter Cornelius (1783–1867).

Cornet or cornet à pistons. An instrument of brass (or other metal), of bore partly cylindrical (cf. *Trumpet*) and partly conical (cf. *Horn*), with a cup-shaped mouthpiece. Like both

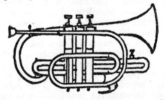

trumpet and horn it operates on the harmonic series (cf. *Acoustics* 7), filling in the gaps by the use of valves which, singly or in combination, lengthen the tube so giving new fundamentals of 1 semitone to 6 lower, and consequently as many new harmonic series. Its tone is of a quality between that of the horn and that of the trumpet. Owing to the width of its bore it has great flexibility. Double and triple tonguing are possible (see *Tonguing*). Like the trumpet as found in most Brit. orchs. it is constructed so that its primary key can be either B flat or A, as desired: this removes some of the difficulties of playing in the extreme flat and sharp keys, as in the one case the player is eased of 2 flats and in the other of 3 sharps. There exists also a cornet in E flat, almost exclusively for wind-band use. In all these 3 keys the cornet is a transposing instrument (q.v.), its music being written a tone or minor 3rd higher, or a minor 3rd lower, according as the instrument is in one or other of those keys.

The cornet's first orch. appearance seems to have been in Rossini's opera, *William Tell*, in 1829. By the 1890's it had almost driven the trumpet out of the orch., but it has had to relinquish that position of advantage and is now chiefly found in brass and military bands.

Cornet Stop. Organ stop of Mixture type (see *Mixture*): usually of 4 or 5 ranks. *Mounted Cornet* is one placed high on its own sound-board so as to be well heard. (See *Voluntary 5*.)

Cornett and Key Bugle Families. (This family is not to be confused with that of the modern cornet, and the very ancient spelling with the double 't' has been adopted by the present writer, as it has by some of his predecessors, to mark an essential distinction.)

The Cornett and Key Bugle families, both now obsolete, have affinities (*a*) with the wood-wind instruments, in the method of varying the notes by the use of holes in the tube; and (*b*) with the brass instruments in the fact that the vibrating agent is the lips of the player (see *Brass*) applied to a cup-shaped mouthpiece. The difference between the two families is that (*a*) in the Cornett family the first 8ve of notes is obtained by successively uncovering the holes in the tube, and the second 8ve by doing the same and overblowing, whereas (*b*) in the Key Bugle Family *each note* obtained by uncovering a hole gives rise to a series of notes, i.e. a section of the harmonic series (see *Acoustics* 6 and 7).

The CORNETT FAMILY for centuries consisted of merely a wooden tube, usually leather-covered (occasionally an ivory tube), either straight or curved (in the arc of a circle or in 2 such arcs like a flattened 'S', or, in the case of one member of the family, in a zigzag shape) or turned back on itself like a bassoon. Its members have been as follows: (*a*) SMALL CORNETT, straight or arc-

shaped, and with a compass of a 4th below that of the cornett proper; (*b*) CORNETT proper (the one intended when the noun is used without any adjective), like the preceding but for pitch; (*c*) GREAT CORNETT, S-shaped and tenor in pitch; (*d*) SERPENT, a later (16th-c.) form, of bass pitch, 8 feet long

SERPENT
Bombardier Browning, the last serpent player of the Royal Artillery (1847)

and hence zigzag shaped as its name suggests, to bring its whole tube within reach of the player's fingers; (*e*) BASS HORN or KEYED HORN, no horn at all but an improved form of the serpent—that reptile without its wriggles and merely bent back on itself; (*f*) RUSSIAN BASSOON, a variety of the preceding.

The members of the KEY BUGLE FAMILY were: (*a*) KEY BUGLE (or 'Keyed Bugle'), a treble instrument of the ophicleide type; (*b*) OPHICLEIDE, of Brass and shaped like its colleague of the other family, the Bass Horn (3 sizes existed, alto, bass, and double bass, but only the bass was ever much used and it is now completely superseded by the bass tuba; see *Tuba Group*).

The *Cornett* is mentioned in Eng. writings as early as the 10th c. In the directions for Shakespeare's plays it is often called for, and it had some church use in both France and England. Bach prescribes its use in 11 of his church cantatas, almost always to support the treble voices in a chorale melody. The

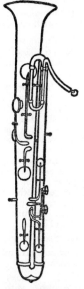

OPHICLEIDE

Serpent enjoyed, perhaps, its greatest popularity in France, where in the 18th c. it was much in use as a church instrument: some Eng. players of it were famous, and it was much heard in wind-bands and also in the orch. (Handel, Mendelssohn, and Wagner have included it in some of their scores.) The *Bass Horn* and *Russian Bassoon* had short careers at the end of the 18th c. and beginning of the 19th.

The *Ophicleide* had a part in orch. scores of Mendelssohn, Berlioz, Wagner, and other notable composers, and was much heard in wind-bands. The *Key Bugle* was introduced about 1810 and enjoyed about a quarter of a century of popularity, losing this when

the modern cornet came on the scene.

Cornetta (It.). Cornet (q.v.). *Cornetta signale* ('signal cornet'), means 'bugle', i.e. the simple military one; *cornetta a chiavi*, 'key bugle'.

Cornetto (It.). Cornet (q.v.).

Cornet Voluntary. See *Voluntary*.

Corney Grain. See *Grain*.

Cornish, William. See *Cornyshe*.

Corno (It.). Properly horn (see *Horn Family*), but the term forms a part of the name of several instruments that are not horns (e.g. *corno inglese* = cor anglais; see *Oboe Family*).

Corno alto and **corno basso** (It. 'high horn' and 'low horn'). (1) Old names for horn players who specialized in the high and low registers respectively. (In early 19th-c. France there was a middle category, *cor mixte*.) (2) In modern scores the terms are used to distinguish, e.g. the horn in B flat which transposes down one note, and that which transposes down an 8ve plus one note.

Corno a macchina (It.). Valve horn (see *Horn Family*).

Corno a mano (It. 'hand horn'). The natural French Horn (see *Horn Family*).

Corno a pistoni (It.). Valve horn (see *Horn Family*).

Corno basso. See *Corno alto*.

Corno cromatico (It. 'chromatic horn'). Valve horn (see *Horn Family*).

Corno da caccia. Hunting horn (see *Horn Family*).

Corno di bassetto. (1) Basset horn (see *Clarinet Family* f). (2) Organ stop much like *Clarinet* (q.v.), but of broader tone.

Corno dolce. A soft organ stop generally of flute (*not* horn) type; 8-foot length and pitch (occasionally 16).

Corno inglese (It.). Cor anglais (see *Oboe Family*).

Cornone (It.). Great Cornett (see *Cornett and Key Bugle Families*).

Cornopean. Organ stop like *Trumpet* (q.v.) but softer.

Corno torto (It. 'twisted horn'). Great cornett (see *Cornett and Key Bugle Families*).

Corno ventile (It.). Valve horn (see *Horn Family*).

Cornyshe (or **Cornish**), **William** (b. abt. 1465; d. 1523). Composer, actor, playwright, and pageant master about the court of Henry VIII, whom he accompanied, with 10 choir-boys, to the Field of the Cloth of Gold. Some of his church music and also jovial secular songs survive.

Coro (It.). 'Choir', 'chorus'. *Gran coro*, in organ music, means 'full organ'.

Cor-oboe. Organ flue stop of 8-foot length and pitch, and somewhat reedy quality.

Coronach. See *Corranach*.

Coronation Concerto. Nickname of Mozart's Piano Concerto in D, K.537, perf. at Frankfort, 1790, on occasion of coronation of Leopold II.

Coronation Mass. Mozart's in C, K. 317. So nicknamed, apparently, from some association with the annual crowning of a reputedly miracle-working image of the Virgin, nr. Salzburg.

Coronation of Poppea, The (Monteverdi). See *Incoronazione di Poppea*.

Corps de Ballet (Fr.). The whole ballet troupe of any particular theatre.

Corps de réchange (Fr.). Crook of a brass instrument (see *Trumpet Family*; *Horn Family*).

Corranach (also Coronach). (1) Highland Scottish and Irish funeral dirge. (2) Person performing such a dirge.

Corregidor, Der ('The Mayor'). The only opera of Hugo Wolf. (Prod. Mannheim 1896; London 1934.) The plot, based on novel by Alarcón, is the same as that of Falla's ballet, *The Three-cornered Hat* (q.v.).

Corrente. See *Courante*.

Corri, Domenico (b. Rome 1746; d. London 1825). Prominent singing-master in Edinburgh and impresario, author of music textbooks, and music publisher (in London from abt. 1790).

Corroboree. See *Antill, John*.

Corsaire, Le. Concert-overture by Berlioz, an early work (1831; revised 1855). Based on Byron's poem.

Cor simple (Fr.). Natural Horn (see *Horn Family*).

Corta. See *Corto*.

Corte. See *Corto*.

Cortège (Fr.). 'Procession.'

Cortèges ('Processions'). 'Fantasy Overture' by Rawsthorne (1945).

Corti. See *Corto*.

Corto, corta (It. sing. masc. and fem.), **corti, corte** (It. plur. masc. and fem.). 'Short.'

Cortot, Alfred (b. Nyon, Switzerland, 1877; d. Lausanne 1962). Pianist and conductor. Trained Paris Conserv. (1907–17 on staff). Début as pianist, Paris 1896. Then (1898–1901) an assistant at Bayreuth. Conducted 1st perf. in France of *Dusk of the Gods*, Paris 1902; carried on active Wagner propaganda; also introduced many contemporary Fr. orch. works. From 1905 toured widely with Thibaud and Casals as trio; also as piano recitalist. Edited Chopin, Schumann, Liszt. Publ. articles and books.

Coryphaeus. See under *Choragus*.

Cosacco, cosacca (It. masc., fem.). 'In the Cossack style.'

Cosaque (Fr.). Cossack dance in simple duple time with continual *accelerando*.

Così fan tutte, ossia La Scuola degli amanti ('Thus do all [women], or the School for Men in Love'). 2-act It. comedy-opera by Mozart. Libretto by da Ponte. (Prod. Vienna 1790; London 1811; New York 1922.)

Costa, Michael Andrew Agnus (b. Naples 1806; d. Brighton 1884). Came to England at age 21 and then remained, climbing to a dominating position as conductor of opera, oratorio, and orch. works, in which last capacity he established a new standard. As a composer won approval by the oratorios *Naaman* and *Eli* (q.v.). Knighted 1869.

Cosyn, Benjamin. See *Benjamin Cosyn's Virginal Book*.

Côtelettes. See *Chopsticks*.

Cotillon. An elaborate ballroom dance popular in the 19th c. as the final dance of the evening. It was a sort of country dance (q.v.), performed by any number, all imitating the leading couple, who chose their figures out of a large number available. In the course of the dance almost every gentleman would have as partner almost every lady. The music was simply that of various waltzes, mazurkas, &c.

Cottage Pianoforte. See *Pianoforte.*

Cotton, John (late 12th or early 13th c.). Writer of an important treatise on music; thought to have been an Englishman.

Coulisse (Fr. 'Groove', 'Sliding-piece', &c.). (1) Slide of trombone and slide trumpet (see *Trombone Family*; *Trumpet Family*). (2, followed by the words *à accorder*) Tuning slide of a wind instrument.

Council for the Encouragement of Music and the Arts. See under *Arts Council.*

Council of Trent. See *Church Music*; *Lauda Sion*; *Veni Sancte*; *Victimae Paschali.*

Counter-exposition. See *Form* 7.

Counterpoint. The term derives from the expression *punctus contra punctum*, i.e. 'point against point' or 'note against note'. A single 'part' or 'voice' added to another is called 'a counterpoint' to that other, but the more common use of the word is that of the combination of simultaneous 'parts' or 'voices', each of significance in itself and the whole resulting in a coherent texture. In this sense Counterpoint is the same as *Polyphony.*

The art of counterpoint developed gradually from the 9th c. onwards and reached its highest point at the end of the 16th c. and beginning of the 17th (Palestrina, Lassus, Victoria, Byrd, &c.; cf. *History of Music* 2), and when, at a later date, attempts were made to formulate rules for students of the art they were based on the practice of that period of culmination. The chief theorist responsible for the formulation of those rules was Fux (q.v.) who published, in 1725, a book which still shows its influence in modern text-books of STRICT COUNTERPOINT (or 'Student's Counterpoint'), a form of training intended to be preparatory to the practice of FREE COUNTERPOINT (or 'Composer's Counterpoint').

In Strict Counterpoint the processes are studied under 5 heads, the result of an analysis which dissects the practice of the art into 5 SPECIES. Following the practice of early composers a CANTO FERMO ('fixed song') is employed, i.e. a short melody, set by the master, against which another melody is to be written by the student—or, it may be, several such melodies. It is usually set out with one note to a measure (bar).

The Species are as follows:

I. The added voice proceeds at the same pace as the *Canto Fermo*, i.e. with 1 note to a measure.

II. The added voice proceeds at twice (or 3 times) the pace of the *Canto Fermo*, i.e. with 2 notes or 3 to a measure.

III. The added voice proceeds at 4 (or 6) times the pace of the *Canto Fermo*, i.e. with 4 notes to a measure.

IV. The added voice proceeds (as in Species II) at the rate of 2 notes to 1, i.e. 2 to a measure; but the second note is tied over to the first note of the following measure, i.e. Syncopation (q.v.) is introduced.

V. (Sometimes called FLORID COUNTERPOINT.) The added voice employs a mixture of the processes of the other 4 species and also introduces shorter notes (quavers).

The use of Strict Counterpoint as a method of study has latterly tended to decline, its 'rules' being felt by many teachers to be too rigid.

COMBINED COUNTERPOINT ('strict' or 'free') is that in which the added voices are in different species. INVERTIBLE COUNTERPOINT is such as permits of voices changing places (the higher becoming the lower, and vice versa), the effect still remaining happy. DOUBLE COUNTERPOINT is Invertible Counterpoint as concerns 2 voices. TRIPLE COUNTERPOINT is that in which 3 voices are concerned, which are capable of changing places with one another, so making 6 positions of the voice parts possible. QUADRUPLE AND QUINTUPLE COUNTERPOINT are similarly explained, the first allowing of 24 positions and the second of 120.

IMITATION is common in contrapuntal composition—one voice entering with a phrase which is then more or less exactly copied by another voice. When the Imitation is strict it becomes *Canon* (q.v.). See *Linear Counterpoint*.

Countersubject. See *Form 7*.

Countertenor. Male alto. See *Voice 5* and cf. *Alto Voice*.

Count of Luxemburg, The (*Der Graf von Luxembourg*). Opera by Lehár (1909).

Country Dance (Eng.), **contredanse** (Fr.), **contradanza** (It.). This type of dance is of Brit. origin and its various foreign names have come ¦about from a plausible false etymology ('counter-dance', one in which the performers stand opposite to one another—as distinguished from a round dance). The term is generic and covers a whole series of figure dances deriving from the amusements of the Eng. village green. Such dances became popular at the court of Queen Elizabeth, and during the Commonwealth were systematically described by Playford (q.v.) in his *English Dancing Master*. In the early years of the 19th c. the waltz and quadrille drove the country dance out of the English ballroom (with the exception of the popular example known as *Sir Roger de Coverley*); the folk-dance movement of the 20th c., however, brought it into considerable use again. Scotland has throughout retained a number of its country dances.

Country Gardens. See *Vicar of Bray*.

Coup d'archet (Fr.). 'Bow-stroke' or 'bowing'.

Coup de glotte. See *Voice 4*.

Coupé (Fr.). In ballet, like the Chassé (q.v.) but the displaced foot goes into the air.

Couperin, François (b. Paris 1668; there d. 1733). One of the 9 (at least) of his name and family who were prominent in Paris music, the earliest born 1626 and the latest dying about 1850. This one, as distinguishing mark (and mark of distinction), is often known as 'Couperin the Great' ('Couperin le Grand'). At 25 was organist of the chapel of Louis XIV at Versailles and at 28 also of St. Gervais, Paris. His fame today rests on his abundant, well-conceived, delicate, and effective harpsichord music—much of it bearing fanciful titles and of the nature of what is now called 'programme music'.

See also *Art de toucher le clavecin*; *Suite*.

Couperin's Tomb (Ravel). See *Tombeau de Couperin*.

Coupler. See *Organ 2*.

Couplet. (1) Episode in the early Fr. rondo (e.g. Couperin; see *Form 4*). (2) Same as *Duplet* (see Table 11).

(3) The 2-note slur (♪♪)—the 2nd note of which should be slightly curtailed (♪♪).

Coupleux. See *Electric Musical Instruments 4*.

Couppey. See *Le Couppey*.

Coupure (Fr. 'Cut'). Portion omitted.

Courante, or **corrente**, or **coranto**, or **corant** (lit. a 'running'). As met with by performers and students today the music based on this old dance-type falls into 2 classes:
(*a*) The It. variety, in a rapid tempo and in simple triple time. (*b*) The Fr. variety, similar to the above, but with a mixture of rhythms, simple triple and compound duple (3-in-a-measure and 6-in-a-measure, the end of each of the 2 sections into which the music falls, especially, being in the latter rhythm). Occasionally in Bach's keyboard examples the conflicting rhythms are found together, one in each hand.

In the classical suite the courante followed the allemande (cf. *Pavan and Galliard*). Occasionally it was, in turn, followed by 'Doubles', i.e. variations on itself.

Courroie (Fr.). 'Strap.'

Courtauld, (Mrs.) Elizabeth Theresa Frances (d. London 1932). Generous patron of London music, organizing Covent Garden seasons 1925–7 and then a 'Concert Club' (orch. concerts at Queen's Hall at low prices).

Couvert, couverte (Fr. masc., fem.). 'Covered.'

Covent Garden Theatre, London. Built 1732; rebuilt after fires 1809,

1858; opera performed there sporadically until in 1847 it became definitely an opera house. Government ownership from end 1949.

Coward, (1) **Henry** (b. Liverpool 1849; d. Sheffield 1944). Successively apprentice in cutlery works, school teacher, school principal, and professional musician (B.Mus., Oxford, 1889; D.Mus. 1894). Through whole career ardent exponent of Tonic Sol-fa, which had laid the foundation of his own musical culture. At end of 19th c. initiated, by the example of his Sheffield Fest. Choir, a new standard in choral singing and for nearly 50 years held supreme position as trainer of choral bodies, touring with them both hemispheres (cf. *Harriss, Charles*). Knighted 1926.

(2) **Noel** (b. Teddington 1899). Playwright. Author and composer of popular musical plays, &c.

Cow-bell. The ordinary cow-bell of the mountain districts of central Europe, with the clapper removed. It is fixed to a drum and struck with the stick of a snare drum.

Cowell, Henry (b. Menlo Park, Calif., 1897; d. Shady, N.Y., 1965). Pianist; also composer who went his own way, experimenting with instrumental effects and trying to find a common basis for Eastern and Western musical art (Guggenheim Fellowship 1931); composed lavishly for orch. and chamber combinations and for piano, conducted a musical journal, and published expositions of his revolutionary musical theories.

Cowen, Frederick Hymen (b. Jamaica 1852; d. London 1935). Came to England in infancy; at 6 published a waltz and at 8 an operetta. Early made a name as pianist; studied in Germany, and on return quickly became known as composer and conductor; for a time conducted the Hallé Orch. at Manchester. His compositions range from mass-produced Victorian 'shop ballads' to songs of considerable artistic merit; they also include operas and oratorios (see *Ruth*), and attractive works for orch. Knighted 1911.

Cox and Box. Musical Farce by Sulli-

van. Libretto by Burnand after Maddison Morton. (1st public perf. Adelphi Theatre, London, 1867; New York 1875.)

Cracovienne (Fr.), **Krakowiak** (Polish). A Polish dance from the district of Krakow. It is in a lively $\frac{2}{4}$, with a characteristic syncopation:

Cradle will rock, The. One-act light opera by Blitzstein. (Prod. New York 1937.)

Craft, Robert (Lawson) (b. Kingston, N.Y., 1923). Conductor. Trained Juilliard Sch., Columbia Univ., and under Monteux. Pupil of Stravinsky and notable interpreter of his music and personality, also of Webern, &c.

Cramer, (1) **Wilhelm** (b. Mannheim 1745; d. London 1799). Came to London at age 27 and attained a high position as solo violinist and as leader of all the chief orchs. His compositions are unimportant. (2) **Franz,** or **François** (b. Schwetzingen 1772; d. London 1848). Son of Wilhelm, above; his career resembled that of his father. (3) **Johann Baptist** (b. Mannheim 1771; d. London 1858). Another son of Wilhelm; lived in London all his life except its first year. Piano pupil of Clementi and attained a high reputation as pianist, touring Europe widely. Wrote quantities of piano studies (still in use), also 100 sonatas and many concertos (both these now superseded); founded (1824) the music publishing firm of Cramer & Co. (still active).

Cramer & Co. London Music Publishers and Piano Makers, &c. (139 New Bond St., W. 1). See *Cramer* (3).

Crash Cymbal. See *Chinese Crash Cymbal.*

Crawford, (1) **Ruth Porter** (b. East Liverpool, Ohio, 1901; d. Chevy Chase, Md., 1953). Composer of chamber music, &c.

(2) **Hector William** (b. Melbourne 1913). Trained Melbourne Conserv. and founded its orch. 1938. Latterly engaged in radio enterprises.

Craxton, Harold (b. London 1885; d. there 1971). Pianist, with special reputation as accompanist. Trained at R.A.M. (later on staff); pupil of Matthay. Specialist in and ed. of the Eng. music of the 16th to 18th cs., Composer of music for his instrument.

Creation, The (*Die Schöpfung*). Oratorio by Haydn. Words from *Genesis* and *Paradise Lost* transl. into Ger. and re-transl. into Eng. (1st perf. Vienna 1798; London 1800; in part, Bethlehem, Pa., 1811; in full, Boston 1819.)

Creation Mass (Haydn). See *Schöpfungsmesse.*

Creation's Hymn (*Die Ehre Gottes aus der Natur*, 'Nature's Praise of God'). Song by Beethoven, with Piano accompaniment. One of a set of 6 settings of poems by Gellert (op. 48; 1803).

Creatures of Prometheus, The (Beethoven). See *Prometheus.*

Crécelle (Fr.). 'Rattle' (see *Percussion Family* 2 r).

Credo. See *Mass; Common Prayer.*

Credo Mass. Mozart's Mass in C, K. 257 (1776). It has acquired the name from the prominent way in which the word 'Credo' is always given out in unison.

Creed. Three creeds are in use in the Roman Catholic and Anglican Churches—the *Apostles' Creed* (probably the earliest); the *Nicene Creed* (framed by the Council at Nicaea in Bithynia, A.D. 325); and the *Athanasian Creed* (really much later than Athanasius, and dating from the 5th or 6th c.). The Roman Catholic Church has also the *Creed of Pope Pius* (1564). For some particulars of the place of the creed in the service of the church, and of its music, see *Mass* ('Credo') and *Common Prayer.*

Creighton, Robert. See *Creyghton.*

Cremona (1) (corruption of 'Cromorne'; see *Krumhorn*). Organ stop much like *Clarinet* (q.v.). (2) The Italian town. See *Violin Family.*

Creole Music. The indigenous music of Latin America. It has distinctive rhythms, and melodies often accompanied by a short bass phrase much repeated with slight changes. The castanets (see *Percussion Family* 2 q) are used.

Crescendo (It.). 'Increasing' (in tone, i.e. getting gradually louder). See Table 17.

Crescendo Pedal. An organ device which gradually brings into action all the stops.

Crespin, Régine (b. Marseilles 1927). Dramatic soprano. Début Paris 1951; Bayreuth 1958; London 1960; New York 1962.

Creston, Paul—original name Joseph Guttoveggio (b. New York 1906). Resident in New York as organist and teacher. Winner of Guggenheim Fellowship 1938 and grant from Amer. Academy of Arts and Letters 1943. Largely self-taught composer of 5 symphonies, 12 concertos, &c., chamber music, choral works, &c.

Creyghton (or Creighton), Robert (b. abt. 1639; d. Wells 1734). Canon and precentor of Wells Cathedral; composed church music which is still in use.

Creyghtonian Seventh. Mannerism of Creyghton (see above), being preceding of final Perfect Cadence (see *Cadence*) by subdominant chord with 7th added (e.g. in key C, F–A–C–E).

Cricoid Cartilege. See *Larynx.*

Crispino e la comare. See *Ricci, F.*

Crist, Bainbridge (b. Lawrenceburg, Ind., 1883; d. 1969). Lawyer (LL.B.) who, after some years of practice, took up study of music in Europe and established himself as singing teacher (Boston, &c.) and as composer. Long list of orch. and choral works and songs.

Cristofori. See *Pianoforte.*

Critic, The, or An Opera Rehearsed. Comedy-opera by Stanford. Libretto based on Sheridan's play. (Prod. London 1916.)

Criticism of Music. It is perhaps fair to say that the serious criticism of current musical activities began in Germany with the issue of actual musical journals. Such publications have, since the initial attempts, played an important role in Ger. musical life.

In the strategic centre of Vienna the greatest name has been that of Hanslick (q.v.), who was critic of various papers there from 1848 to 1895. He is famous for his support of Schumann and

Brahms and notorious for his opposition to Liszt and Wagner.

Active musical criticism in France (which for this purpose means Paris) may be said to have begun with the pamphlet-fisticuffs of the 'Guerre des Bouffons', 1752–4 (see *Bouffons*), and to have received a fresh stimulus from the similar struggles between the Gluckists and Piccinists, 1776–9 (see *Piccini*). The first Fr. periodical definitely devoted to music was the *Journal de musique française et italienne* (1764–8).

The great names of the Fr. Encyclopedia (1751–72) are great names also in the history of Fr. musical discussion at the period—Diderot, d'Alembert, Rousseau, Grimm; there has never been another period or another country where the best intellects devoted themselves to the discussion of music as those in Paris did at this period. Later names of high importance are those of Fétis, who in 1826 founded his *Revue musicale* and who served as critic of the *Temps* and the *National*, and Berlioz, whose critical writing in the *Journal des Débats* from 1835 to 1863 was very vigorous.

In the very thoughtful introductory chapter of the last volume of Burney's *History of Music* (1789) he says: 'Musical criticism has been so little cultivated in this country that its first elements are hardly known.' Burney's *History* itself, in its later chapters, abounds in candid expressions as to the composers and executants of his day (especially opera singers), and as these are brought down to the very musical season preceding the issue of the volume it may be said to approach the condition of criticism of current activities.

The *Morning Post* (founded 1772, amalgamated with the *Daily Telegraph* 1937) was the first amongst Brit. newspapers to give systematic reports of plays and concerts, but the earliest to employ a professionally trained musician as critic is said to have been *The Times*, the step being taken through the influence of one of the managers of the paper, T. M. Alsager (q.v.), who was a keen enthusiast for music. The great tradition of Eng. musical criticism may be said to have been established by two men in particular, J. W. Davison (1813–85), who was music critic of *The Times* from 1846 to 1879, and H. F. Chorley (1808–72), who was music critic of the (weekly) *Athenaeum* from 1833 to 1868.

The publication of British musical periodicals seems to have begun with that of the *New Musical and Universal Magazine* (1774–5). More important was the *Musical Quarterly Magazine* (1818–28), and other early and important journals were the *Harmonicon* (1823–33) and the *Musical World* (1836–91). The still-existing *Musical Times* in its earliest form dates from 1841 and in more or less its present form from 1844.

The statement is sometimes seen that Brit. critics are, by the law of libel, unfairly restricted in the expression of opinion. This is not so. They are quite free to state their opinions of performances or compositions, however severe these may be—or even however unjust (see any book upon the law as it concerns journalists).

In the U.S.A. *Dwight's Journal of Music* (1852–81) fought the battle of Chopin, Mendelssohn, and Schumann, but only lukewarmly supported the more radical innovators, Berlioz, Wagner, and Liszt. Amer. critics of the daily press who did a great deal to inform and lead public opinion were Horace Howland and Frederick Schwab on the *New York Times*, and William Fry (q.v.) and John Rose Green Hassard (1866–88) on the *New York Tribune*. The last-named held a position of outstanding influence; he was one of the most discerning champions of Wagner and other contemporary composers. From the closing years of the 19th c., musical criticism in the U.S.A. became very important, such names as those of Finck (1854–1939), Krehbiel (1854–1923), Hale (1854–1934), Henderson (1855–1937), Huneker (1860–1921), and Aldrich (1863–1937) being almost as familiar to, and respected in, the European musical world as in the American. A younger band of writers (not confined to the East) seems likely to maintain the tradition.

Croce, Giovanni Dalla (b. nr. Venice abt. 1558; d. Venice 1609). Priest and composer of motets, madrigals, &c.

Croche (Fr. 'Hook'). The quaver or eighth-note (*not* the crotchet; see Table 3).

Croft, William (b. Warwickshire 1678; d. Bath 1727). Organist of the Chapel Royal, and of Westminster Abbey. Composer of distinguished church music that remains in use (including the setting of the Burial Service); also of accomplished harpsichord music (available in a modern edn.).

Croisade des enfants (Pierné). See *Children's Crusade*.

Croiser (Fr.). 'To cross' (*croiser les mains*, 'to cross hands'). So *croisant*; *croisé*, 'crossing'; 'crossed'.

Croix sonore. See *Electric Musical Instruments* 1.

Croma (It.). Quaver or Eighth-note (see Table 3).

Cromatico, cromatica (It. sing. masc., fem.); **cromatici, cromatice** (It. plur. masc., fem.). 'Chromatic.' The *Corno cromatico* is the Valve Horn (see *Horn Family*).

Cromorne. On Fr. organs a delicate type of clarinet stop (but cf. *Krumhorn*).

Cromwell. See *Deering*.

Crooks (and **Shanks**). See *Acoustics* 7; *Horn Family*; *Trumpet Family*.

Crooks, Richard (b. Trenton, N.J., 1900). Operatic and concert tenor. Début U.S.A. 1922. Long member of Metropolitan Opera Co.

Crooning. An excessively sentimental type of singing, introduced by radio entertainers, called 'Crooners', at first in U.S.A. (about 1929 or 1930) and afterwards elsewhere. They sing very softly and the tone is built up by electrical amplification.

Crosby Hall. 15th-c. London hall (in 'City') used for musical activities 1842 to early years of 20th c.: then removed and rebuilt Chelsea and used for other purposes.

Cross, Joan (b. London 1900). Operatic soprano. Trained T.C.M. as violinist and then as vocalist. Appeared Old Vic (see *Victoria Hall*), Sadler's Wells (q.v.), Covent Garden, &c. C.B.E. 1951.

Crossley, Ada (b. Australia 1874; d. 1929). Contralto. Pupil in London of Santley (q.v.); in Paris of Mathilde Marchesi (q.v.). Melbourne début 1892; London 1895. Gained high oratorio reputation in English-speaking countries.

Crossley-Holland, Peter (Charles) (b. London 1916). M.A. (Oxon.). Composer and writer on music. On Arts Council 1943; B.B.C. 1948. Numerous compositions; books on folk music, oriental music, &c.

Crot. Crwth (q.v.).

Crotch, William (b. Norwich 1775; d. Taunton 1847). At 4 years old was giving daily organ recitals in London; at 11 pupil-assistant to the organist of King's and Trinity Colleges, Cambridge; at 14 composer of an oratorio performed in that city; at 15 organist of Christ Church Cathedral, Oxford; at 19 B.Mus.; at 22 Prof. of Music in Oxford Univ., and at 24 D.Mus. Later Principal of the R.A.M.

Became a man of high musical learning, but not the great composer he had been expected to become; his oratorio *Palestine* (1812) had, however, great popularity and one item from it, *Lo, Star-led Chiefs*, is still widely sung at Epiphany-tide. Was an able water-colour painter.

Crotchet (♩). The 'Quarter-Note', i.e. a quarter the time-value of the whole-note or semibreve. (Avoid confusion with the Fr. *Croche*, i.e. 'hook', which means quaver or 8th-note, *Noire*, i.e. 'black', being crotchet.) See Table 1.

Crouch, Frederick Nicholls (b. London 1808; d. Portland, Maine, 1896). At 9 was playing in the orch. of a London theatre; then became a sailor and returned to theatre as 'cellist; sang in the choirs of Westminster Abbey and St. Paul's Cathedral; studied at the R.A.M.; emigrated to U.S.A., practising his profession in various cities and fighting in the Civil War on the Confederate side. Prod. many popular compositions of which one is still in use—the song *Kathleen Mavourneen* (q.v.).

Crowd. Crwth (q.v.). Hence *crowder*, old Eng. for 'fiddler'.

Crowe, Alfred Gwyllym (b. Bermuda 1835; d. 1894). Military bandmaster, orch. conductor, and composer. Trained Kneller Hall (q.v.). Turned to popular orch. conducting with great success (Covent Garden Promenade Concerts 1881; Llandudno 1893). Composed waltzes, &c. (especially the very popular *See-Saw Waltz*).

Crowley's Psalter. See *Anglican Chant*.

Crown Diamonds (Auber). See *Diamants de la couronne*.

Crown Imperial. Orch. March by Walton (1937). Coronation March for George VI commissioned by the B.B.C. Title comes from a line of the poet Dunbar (abt. 1460–1525).

Crucible, The. Opera by Robert Ward. Libretto by B. Stambler after the play by Arthur Miller. (Prod. New York 1961.)

Crucifixion. See *Stainer, John*.

Crucifixus. See *Mass*.

Cruft, (1) **John I** (b. 1857; d. 1937). Viola player. Carl Rosa Co., &c. (2) **Eugene** (b. London 1887). Doublebass player. Son of (1). Trained R.C.M. (later on staff). Beecham Orch. 1909; London Symphony Orch.; B.B.C., &c. M.V.O. 1953. (3) **John II** (b. London 1914). Oboist and cor anglais player. Son of (2). Trained R.C.M. (later on staff). London Symphony Orch., &c. Musical Dircetor British Council 1959.

Cruiskin (or **Cruiskeen) Lawn** (= 'Little Jug Filled'). Famous Irish drinking song of unknown origin.

Cruit. Crwth (q.v.).

Crusaders, The. See *Gade*.

Crwth or **Crowd** (or *Rote* or *Rotte*). An ancient bowed instrument. It had a more or less rectangular frame of which the lower part was filled in to form a sound box, the upper half being left with openings on each side of the strings: through one of these openings the left hand passed to stop the strings whilst the right manipulated the bow. In the 6th c. it seems to have been looked on as a distinctively Brit. instrument and it lingered (in fast-dwindling use) in the ancient Brit.

fastness of Wales even so late as the early 19th c. (A modern name, *Bowed Harp*, is misleading.)

 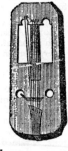

THE CRWTH

The first is as depicted in a 13th-century manuscript: it shows only 3 strings: the second is a more modern Breton instrument with 6 strings

Crystal Palace. Immense glass building built originally as the home of the 1851 Exhibition and then transferred from Hyde Park to Sydenham (nr. South London) where, under Manns daily orch. programmes (with a series of important Saturday Concerts to 1901) were feature. Gigantic Handel Fests. from 1857. Fire destroyed building in 1936. See *Annotated Programmes*.

Csárdás. See *Czardas*.

Ctesibius. See *Hydraulus*.

Cuckoo. Simple 2-note wind instrument, imitating call of the bird, used in Toy Symphonies (q.v.).

Cuckoo, The (harpsichord composition). See *Daquin*.

Cuénod, Hugues (b. Vevey, Switzerland, 1902). Tenor. Trained Lausanne, Basle, and Vienna. Lives in Paris and thence tours in many countries.

Cui, César (b. Vilna 1835; d. Petrograd, now Leningrad, 1918). Of Fr. origin. In Russian army attained rank of general. Was a member of the nationalist group of 'The Five' (q.v.), but his own music not very distinctively Russian. Compositions include operas, songs, piano pieces, &c. (See *Chopsticks*.)

Cuivre (Fr.). 'Copper', 'brass'. Hence *Les Cuivres* are the brass instruments of the orchestra.

Cuivré (Fr.). 'Brassy', i.e. (in music for the horn, &c.) the tones are to be forced, with a harsh, ringing timbre.

Culp, Julia (b. Groningen, Holland, 1880; d. Amsterdam 1970). Contralto with great international reputation for interpretation of *Lieder*.

Cummings, (1) William Hayman (b. Sidbury, Devon, 1831; d. London 1915). Tenor singer of high repute, then a prof. of singing at R.A.M., and Principal of G.S.M. (1896–1910). Active musical antiquary.

(2) **Henry** (b. Dublin 1906). Baritone. Trained R.A.M. and under John Coates (q.v.). Popular oratorio and stage singer.

Cum sancto Spiritu. See *Mass*.

Cundell, Edric (b. London 1893; d. there 1961). Began professional life as horn player at Covent Garden theatre; studied piano at T.C.M. (on staff 1920–37). Principal G.S.M., 1938–59. Orch. conductor; composer of chamber music, orch. music, songs, &c. C.B.E. 1949.

Cunningham, George Dorrington (b. London 1878; d. Birmingham 1948). Recital organist. Trained R.A.M. Organist of Alexandra Palace, London (1901), Birmingham Town Hall (1924); conductor City of Birmingham Choir; M.A., D.Mus.; also held church positions.

Cunning-Man, The. See under *Rousseau*.

Cupo (It.). 'Dark', 'sombre'.

Curtain Music or **Curtain Tune.** See *Act Tune*.

Curtall. See *Oboe Family*.

Curtin, Phyllis (b. Clarksburg, W. Va., 1930). Operatic soprano. Début New York 1953; Vienna 1960.

Curtis Institute, Philadelphia. See *Schools of Music*; *Bok*.

Curtis, Natalie—Mrs. Paul Burlin (b. New York 1875; d. Paris 1921). Pianist (pupil of Busoni, &c.) but best known for patient research in music of Amer. Indians and later of Negroes. Many valuable publications.

Curwen, (1) John (b. Heckmondwike 1816; d. Manchester 1880). Congregational minister and founder of the Tonic Sol-fa method of sight-singing, as also (1863) of the publishing firm bearing his name. (See *Sight-Singing*; *Tonic Sol-fa*; *Hullah*; *Education 1*.) (2) **John Spencer** (b. Plaistow 1847; d. London 1916). Continued his father's activities; wrote useful *Studies in Worship Music* and ed. *The Musical Herald*. (3) **Annie Jessy** (*née* Gregg; b. Dublin 1845; d. 1932). Wife of John Spencer, above; applied the sound educational principles of her father-in-law to piano teaching in a series called *The Child Pianist*; also wrote on *The Psychology of Music Teaching*. (4) **J. Curwen & Sons, Ltd.** London Music Publishers (29 Maiden Lane, W.C. 2). Founded by John Curwen in 1863 to publish material for his movement and later extended its range.

Curwen Memorial College. See *Degrees and Diplomas 2*.

Curzon, Clifford (b. London 1907). Pianist of international reputation. Trained R.A.M. and also under Schnabel, Landowska, and Nadia Boulanger. Married (1931) Lucille Wallace. C.B.E. 1958.

Cushion Dance (or, in Ger., *Kissentanz*, or *Polstertanz*). An old dance in which a participant chose a partner by dropping a cushion before him or her. (Cf. *Trescone*.)

Cusins, William George (b. London 1833; d. in the Ardennes 1893). Pianist of high standing; organist of Queen Victoria's private chapel and 'Master of the Queen's Musick'; 16 years conductor of Philharmonic Soc.'s orch. (1867–83); composer of oratorios, orch. works, &c. Knighted 1892.

Custard, (1) Walter Henry Goss (b. 1871). Held many important organists' positions. 1917–55, organist, Liverpool Cathedral. B. Mus., Oxford.

(2) **Reginald Goss** (b. 1877; d. Dorking 1956). Organist. St. Margaret's, Westminster, 1902–13; Bishopsgate Inst. 1914–39. Composed organ music and publ. many organ arrangements; book on Pedalling, &c.

Cutner, Solomon. See *Solomon*.

Cuvelier, Marcel (b. Brussels 1899; d. Venice 1959). Combined legal training at Free Univ., Brussels, with musical training at the Conserv., later holding administrative posts in musical world—Sec. to International Federation of Concerts, Administrator of Brussels Symphony Orch.; sec.-general of music section of U.N.E.S.C.O.

Cyclic Form. (1) A term applied to those types of composition (Suite, Sonata, Symphony, Concerto, &c.) which consist of several 'movements' (see *Movement*) akin to a cycle of Poems, in which each item is complete, yet the series, by suitability of subject-matter, mood, &c., forms a whole.

(2) In a more particularly musical sense the term is by some writers restricted to a composition consisting of several movements bound together by the use of some musical subject-matter common to all.

Amongst Eng. writers the former and more general sense (1) is usually intended.

Cyklus (Ger.). 'Cycle'. So *Liedercyklus*, 'Song-cycle' (q.v.).

Cylinder or **rotary valve.** A special type of valve in brass instruments, in much use in some European countries but in Britain and U.S.A. applied to the Fr. horn only. Occasionally the term is used for any kind of valve, e.g.

in the It. 'Trombone a Cilindri' (valve trombone; see *Trombone Family*).

Cymbalon. 'Dulcimer' (in Hungary, &c.).

Cymbals. See *Percussion Family 2 o*.

Cymbalum orale (medieval Lat.). 'Jew's Harp' (q.v.).

Cymbel. Organ stop; a brilliant type of *Mixture* (q.v.).

Czaar und Zimmermann ('Czar and Carpenter'). Opera by Lortzing. Libretto on story of Peter the Great. (Prod. Leipzig 1837; New York 1857; London 1871.)

Czardas, or **Csárdás,** or **Tchardache.** One of the national dances of Hungary. It is in two parts which alternate—a slow *Lassu* and a rapid *Friss*.

Czar Saltan. See under *Legend*.

Czar's Bride, The. Opera by Rimsky-Korsakof. (Prod. Moscow 1899; New York 1922; London 1931.)

Czerny, Carl (b. Vienna 1791; there d. 1857). Pupil of Beethoven, teacher of Liszt, and a notable piano pedagogue, publishing popular piano studies, &c., and reaching his op. 1000. (See *Pianoforte Playing*; *Hexameron*.)

Czibulka, Alphons (b. Szepes-Váralla, Hungary, 1842; d. Vienna 1894). Bandmaster in Austrian army and composer of popular operettas and dance music, as also light piano music (e.g. popular *Stéphanie Gavotte*).

Czimbal, Czimbalom, Czimbalon. Same as *Zimbalon*, i.e. a sort of developed dulcimer (Hungary, &c.).

D

D' (Fr., abbrev. of *De*). 'Of.'

Da (It.). 'Of', 'from'.

Da capo (It. 'from the head'). A term meaning 'Go back to the beginning, start again, and continue until you come to the word *Fine* ("End")', or the pause mark (⌢).' Sometimes the expression used is *da capo al segno* ('From the beginning to the sign') or *da capo al fine* ('From the beginning to the word *Fine*', i.e. 'End'). Occasionally there follow the words *poi segue la coda*, meaning that, arrived at the point indicated by the above expressions, a jump is to be made to the final passage of the piece (which is generally marked 'Coda').

D.C. is an abbreviation for *Da Capo*.

Dafne. See *Schütz*; also *Peri*.

Dafydd y Garreg Wen, i.e. David of the White Rock, otherwise David Owen (1720–49; cf. *Rising of the Lark*). The tune called by his name is supposed to have been composed by him on his death-bed, on awakening from a trance in which he believed himself to have heard it in heaven. Sir Walter Scott wrote words to it, *The Dying Bard*.

Dalayrac, Nicolas (b. in the Haute Garonne 1753; d. Paris 1809). Composer of about 60 popular operas.

d'Albert. See *Albert*.

Dalcroze. See *Jaques-Dalcroze*.

Dale, Benjamin James (b. London 1885; there d. 1943). Brilliant student of R.A.M., of which later became a prof. and (1937) warden. Piano sonata in D minor (1905) on an original plan attracted much attention: amongst other works many for viola.

Dalibor. Very successful opera by Smetana. (Prod. Prague 1868 and then in many countries.)

Dallam. A family of organ builders active in England during the late 16th c. and 17th c.

Dallapiccola, Luigi (b. Pisino, Istria, 1904). Pianist and composer; trained at Conservatory of Florence and later on staff there; extensive and varied list of works, showing distinct 'modern' tendencies—use of Note-row (q.v.), &c.

See *Prigioniero*; *Scale*.

Dalley-Scarlett, Robert (b. Sydney 1887; d. Brisbane 1959). Educated in Australia where active as organist, conductor, and organizer of various musical societies (Sydney, Brisbane, Adelaide); broadcasting and literary work. A few compositions. D.Mus., Adelaide.

Dal segno (It. 'from the sign'). 'Return to the sign 𝄋: and repeat thence to the word *Fine* (= "End"), or to a double bar with a pause sign (⌢) above it.'

D'Alvarez, Marguerite. See *Alvarez*.

Daman. See *Damon*.

Dame blanche, La. ('The White Lady'). The chief opera of Boïeldieu. Libretto by Scribe, based on Scott's *The Monastery* and *Guy Mannering*. (Prod. Paris 1825; London 1826; New York 1827.)

Damnation de Faust, La (Berlioz). See *Faust*.

Damoiselle élue, La (Debussy). See *Blessed Damozel*.

Damon (or **Daman**), **William** (d. before 1593). Foreign musician employed in England at Queen Elizabeth's court; composed anthems, lute music, &c., and publ. notable collection of metrical psalm tunes.

Damp. To check the vibrations of an instrument (e.g. kettledrum) by touching it in some way. For damping on the pianoforte see that instrument (cf. *Gedämpft*).

Dampers. See *Pianoforte*.

Dämpfer (Ger.). 'Mute' (q.v.). *Mit Dämpfern*, 'with mutes'.

Dämpfung, 'Muting', or (pianoforte) 'Soft-pedalling'.

Damrosch, (1) **Leopold** (b. Posen 1832; d. New York 1885). Doctor of medicine and violinist; settled U.S.A. 1871; there prominent as conductor and composer. D.Mus., Columbia Univ., New York. Father of (2) and (3) below. (Cf. *Mannes, David.*) (2) **Walter Johannes** (b. Breslau 1862; d. New York 1950). Went to U.S. with father (above) and succeeded him as conductor of opera and oratorio, &c., becoming particularly prominent as

Dance. In every age and amongst every race dancing has existed either as recreation or as a religious manifestation or as both.

In Europe all countries have their traditional ('folk') dances. To take an example, those of England are numerous, falling into three classes—for men alone the Sword Dance and the Morris Dances and for men and women together the Country Dances.

There has always been a tendency

THE DANCING LESSON
(By Cruikshank, 1822)

sponsor of Wagner's works there. Conductor New York Symphony Soc. 1885–1927. Active and useful general musical career (latterly in connexion with radio). Composer of operas &c. Autobiography 1923. (3) **Frank** (b. Breslau 1859; d. New York 1937). Valuably active in New York as supervisor of music in public schools (1897–1905); choral and orch. conductor; founder of Inst. of Musical Art (later merged in Juilliard School), &c. D.Mus., Yale.

Danby, John (b. London 1757; there d. 1798). Organist of chapel of Spanish Embassy, London; successful composer of fine glees (e.g. *Awake, Aeolian Lyre*).

for some of the peasant dances of the different countries to pass into polite use, their steps and music then becoming sophisticated. For some earlier typical examples see under *Allemande, Bergomask, Bourrée, Branle, Canaries, Chaconne and Passacaglia, Courante, Dump, Gavotte, Hay, Jig, Minuet, Passamezzo, Passepied, Pavan and Galliard, Rigaudon, Sarabande, Volta.* The rhythms and styles of some of the above, from the 16th c. onwards, supplied conventional models for instrumental compositions (see *Suite*). The Dances later popular in polite circles (some of them of rustic origin) were the *Minuet* and the Eng. *Country Dance* (17th c.); *Cotillon* and *Écossaise* (18th c.); *Waltz, Quadrille, Polka,*

Schottische, Mazurka, Barn Dance (19th c.), and some of these also were taken as models by instrumental composers. (For the characteristic developments of the dance and its music in the 20th c. see under *Ragtime*; *Jazz*. For dancing as a spectacle see under *Masque* and *Ballet*; for the religious and moral objections which sometimes restricted or opposed dancing see under *Puritans and Music*. For all the dances mentioned in the present article and about 100 more see entries under their own names.)

Dance goes on (Delius). See *Life's Dance*.

Dance of Death. See *Danse macabre*.

Dance of the Elves, The. See *Bazzini, Antonio*.

Dance Rhapsody. Two Orch. Pieces of this name by Delius. (No. 1, 1st perf. Hereford Fest. 1909. No. 2, 1916, 1st perf. London 1919.)

Dancla, Jean Baptiste Charles (b. Fr. Pyrenees, 1817; d. Tunis 1907). Prominent violinist and prolific violin composer.

Danco, Suzanne (b. Brussels 1911). Soprano. Début Genoa 1941; London 1951.

Dandrieu, Jean François (b. Paris 1682; there d. 1738). Paris priest who composed ably for organ and harpsichord, much of his music for latter being still in use.

Danican. See *Philidor*.

Daniel. See *Danyell*.

Daniel Jazz. By Gruenberg. For tenor vocalist and 8 instruments.

Daniels, Mabel (Wheeler) (b. Swampscott, Mass., 1878). Composer and teacher. Trained Boston and Munich. Many choral and orch. works.

Dannreuther, Edward George (b. Strasbourg 1844; d. Hastings 1905). Settled in London as prominent pianist and teacher. Ardent supporter of Wagner; founded Wagner Soc. (1872); transl. some of Wagner's prose works; organized Wagner concerts; had much to do with the London Wagner Fest. of 1877, serving as Wagner's host on that occasion.

Danse (Fr.). 'Dance.'

Danse champêtre. See *Champêtre*.

Danse macabre ('Dance of Death'). (1) Symphonic poem by Saint-Saëns (op. 40; 1874). In waltz style. Inspired by poem of Henri Cazalis which same composer had earlier set as a song and

DANSE MACABRE

(One of Holbein's series of woodcuts of the 'Totentanz')

which was, in turn, obviously inspired by some of the many early series of pictures such as that of Holbein (1538). There is a quotation of the *Dies Irae* in the music. (2) Liszt has provided both a piano transcription of the above (1876) and an independent piece of his own for piano and orch., *Todtentanz* ('Death Dance'). Cf. *Todtentanz*.

Danses polovtsiennes (Borodin). See *Polovetz Dances*.

Dans mon chemin. See *Canadian Boat Song*.

Dante and Beatrice. 'Poem for Orchestra.' By Bantock. (1st perf. 1901 as *Dante*; revised 1911.)

Dante's Divina Commedia, Symphony to. By Liszt (1856). In U.S.A. known as *Dante Symphony*. It has a choral ending.

Danton. See *Lopatnikof*.

Danton's Tod. Opera by Einem, after Büchner's play. (Prod. Salzburg 1947; then Vienna, Hamburg, &c.)

Danyell or **Daniel, John** (b. in 1560's; d. 1630). Lutenist and member of Queen Elizabeth's Chapel Royal. B.Mus., Oxford, 1604. On evidence of a book of his music for voices and lute of which one copy remains (Brit. Museum) ranks high as a composer. (For his period very chromatic.)

Danza (It.). 'Dance.'

Danza española (Sp.). 'Spanish dance' (in some parts of South America applied to a particular type, generally in simple duple rhythm).

Daphne. See *Gagliano*.

Daphnis and Chloë. Ballet ('Choreographic Symphony') by Ravel (1910). Prod. by Diaghilef's Russian Ballet (Paris 1912; London 1914), with Nijinsky and Karsavina in the title roles. Two Concert Suites reproduce its music, 'No. 2' being the better known. Wordless choir a feature.

Daquin or **d'Aquin, Louis Claude** (b. Paris 1694; there d. 1772). Child prodigy harpsichordist and organist (latterly of Fr. Chapel Royal); amongst his harpsichord pieces heard today is the popular *The Cuckoo*.

D'Aranyi. See *Aranyi*.

Dargason. An English folk tune, used from the 16th c. onwards for a country dance. It is also used for the folk song *It was a maid of my country*.

d'Argo. See *Argo*.

Dargomijsky (Dargomyszki, &c.), **Alexander** (b. govt. of Toula 1813; d. St. Petersburg 1869). Early showed musical talent. Became civil servant but meeting Glinka was led to adopt musical life. Had views on opera resembling those of Wagner (then unknown in Russia): his opera *The Stone Guest* (q.v.), finished after his death by Cui and Rimsky-Korsakof, became the Bible of the contemporary Russian School. Copious writer of songs, &c.

See *Russalka*.

Darke, Harold Edwin (b. London 1888). Trained at R.C.M. (later on staff); organist St. Michael's, Cornhill, 1916–66; notable organ recitalist and choral trainer and composer for organ, choir, &c. Hon. M.A., Cambridge, and Fellow King's College; D.Mus., Oxford. Wife Dora Garland (q.v.).

Dart, Robert Thurston (b. London 1921; d. there 1971). Organist and harpsichordist. Studied R.C.M. and Univ. Coll., Exeter. Professor Cambridge (1962) and London (1964); writer on musical subjects. Special interest, music 15th–17th cs. Artistic Dir. Boyd Neel Orch. 1955.

Darunter (Ger.). 'There-under' 'there-amongst', &c.

Das (Ger.). 'The' (neuter sing.).

Dasselbe (Ger.). 'The same.'

Dauberval. See *Ballet*.

Dauer (Ger.). 'Duration.' **Dauernd.** 'Enduring', in the sense of lasting, continuing.

Daughter of Jairus, The. Popular Oratorio by Stainer. (1st perf. Worcester Fest. 1878.) The duet *Love divine, all loves excelling* has been much sung.

Daughter of Madame Angot, The (Lecocq). See *Fille de Madame Angot*.

Daughter of the Regiment (Donizetti). See *Fille du Régiment*.

Dauvergne, Antoine (b. Moulins 1713; d. Lyons 1797). Violinist and composer of music for violin and for orch., also for stage and church; Superintendent of King's Music.

Davey, Henry (b. Brighton 1853; there d. 1929). Researcher in and writer on music; author of a valuable *History of English Music* (1895 and 1921).

David, (1) **Félicien César** (b. Cadenet, in south of France, 1810; d. St. Germain-en-Laye 1876). Studied at Paris Conserv. Accepted Christian-Socialist ideas of Saint-Simonians; travelled in Holy Land and publ. collection of Oriental Melodies for piano; composed chamber and orch. music; especially known by symphonic ode *The Desert* (1844).

(2) **Ferdinand** (b. Hamburg 1810; d. nr. Klosters, Switzerland, 1873). Violinist and leader of Mendelssohn's Leipzig Gewandhaus Orch.; wrote 5 violin concertos and ed. many of the

violin classics. Pupil of Spohr and teacher of Joachim and Wilhelmj.

(3) **Paul**—in full Julius Peter Paul (b. Leipzig 1840; d. Oxford 1932). Son of Ferdinand above and like him a violinist. Settled in England as music master of Uppingham School, whence he exerted influence on the development of Eng. public school music.

Davidsbündler-Tänze.   Eighteen 'Characteristic Pieces for Piano' by Schumann (op. 6; 1837; revised 1850). The 'Davidsbund' ('League of David') was an imaginary society whose members, the 'Davidsbündler', were pledged to slay all 'Philistines'. Some members represented real persons (Mendelssohn, Stephen Heller, Clara Schumann, under fanciful names); others were borrowed from the writings of Jean Paul Richter, and still others were specially invented: they figured in fanciful articles in Schumann's musical journal, the *Neue Zeitschrift für Musik*.

Davie, Cedric Thorpe (b. London 1913). Of Scottish descent. Studied at R.C.M. and in Germany; on staff of Royal Scottish Academy of Music and organist in Glasgow. Composer of choral and orch. music, &c., often with a Scottish subject. Prof. of Music St. Andrews Univ. 1948. O.B.E.; F.R.A.M.

Davies, (1) Mary (b. London 1855; d. 1930). Mezzo-soprano. Trained R.A.M. Won great popularity Brit. festivals, &c. Retired 1900. President Welsh Folk-music Soc.; Hon. D.Mus., Wales.

(2) **Ben**—in full Benjamin Grey Davies (b. nr. Swansea 1858; d. Bath 1943). Tenor vocalist. Trained R.A.M. Successful in opera; then long a popular favourite in oratorio, concerts, and recitals, in Britain and U.S.A.

(3) **Fanny** (b. Guernsey 1861; d. London 1934). Pianist. Pupil of Mme Schumann and a player of similar artistic aims, tastes, and style. Popular in Britain and elsewhere in recitals and chamber music.

(4) **Edward Harold** (b. Oswestry 1867; d. Adelaide 1947). Went to Australia 1887 and trained Univ. Adelaide (D.Mus.—earliest in Commonwealth); later on Univ. staff and

Director of Conserv. (1919–47). Active as organist and conductor. Expeditions into central Australia to study and record music of Aborigines. Brother of (5) below.

(5) **Henry Walford** (b. Oswestry 1869; d. nr. Bristol 1941). Choir-boy at St. George's Chapel, Windsor Castle; scholar of R.C.M.; organist of various London churches, especially that of the Temple (1898). Prof. of Counterpoint at R.C.M.; conductor of Bach Choir, London; Prof. of Music at University Coll., Aberystwyth, and Director of National Council of Wales; organist of St. George's Chapel, Windsor, and Master of the King's Musick; highly popular as broadcasting lecturer on music. Knighted 1922.

As composer first widely recognized on performance of oratorio *Everyman* (q.v.); style tended to mysticism and delicacy, but not without flashes of humour.

(6) **Evan Thomas** (b. Dowlais 1879; d. Aberdare 1969). Dir. of Music Univ. Coll., Bangor (1920–43); comp. songs, part-songs, and chamber music.

(7) **Tudor** (b. nr. Porth, Wales, 1892; d. London 1958). Operatic and concert tenor. Trained R.C.M. Sang Brit. National Opera Co.; Old Vic. and Sadler's Wells; Covent Garden; Paris Opéra; U.S.A., &c.

(8) **Ffrangcon.** See *Ffrangcon-Davies*.

(9) **Frances Joan** (b. London 1912). Pianist. Studied R.A.M. Soloist in Britain and on Continent; regular broadcaster.

(10) **(Albert) Meredith** (b. Birkenhead 1922). R.C.M. and Oxford. Organist and conductor St. Albans 1947; Hereford 1949; Asst. Condr. Birmingham Orch. 1957; B.B.C. Welsh Orch. 1960. Guest conductor Covent Garden, Sadler's Wells, English Opera Group.

(11) **Peter Maxwell** (b. Manchester 1934). Studied R.M.C.M., later under Petrassi and Sessions. Compositions reflect his interest in music of the earlier periods, esp. 16th c.

Davis, Colin (b. Weybridge 1927). Trained R.C.M. At first clarinettist; came to notice as Mozart opera conductor. B.B.C. Scottish Orch. to 1959;

Sadler's Wells 1961; B.B.C. Orch. 1967; Covent Garden 1971. C.B.E. 1965.

Davison, (1) **Archibald Thompson** (b. Boston, Mass., 1883; d. Brant Rock, Mass., 1961). Studied Harvard (M.A. 1907; Ph.D. 1908) and, as organist, under Widor at Paris. On staff of Harvard 1909–54 (prof. from 1940). Active as choral conductor (Harvard Glee Club 1912–33), author, composer. Hon. D. Mus., Oxford, &c.

(2) **James William.** See *Criticism of Music*; *Goddard, Arabella.*

Davy, (1) **Richard** (end of 15th c. and beginning of 16th). Organist of Magdalen Coll., Oxford; later a priest. Composer of church music.

(2) **John** (b. nr. Exeter 1763; d. London 1824). Articled to William Jackson, organist of Exeter Cathedral; then went to London and became prominent composer of lighter kinds of theatre music. Some of his songs (e.g. *The Bay of Biscay*, q.v.) have passed into the permanent popular repertory.

Dawson, (1) **Frederick** (b. Leeds 1868; d. Lymm, Ches., 1940). Pianist; could play Bach's '48' from memory at age 10; pupil of Hallé and Rubinstein. Of high Brit. and continental reputation but latterly dropped out of sight through ill health.

(2) **Peter** (b. Adelaide 1882; d. Sydney 1961). Bass. Studied in London (1902) under Santley, Covent Garden début 1909. Became popular with large public in Britain, Australia, New Zealand, &c. Gramophone artist from 1904 (13 million records sold). Then in family business in Sydney, but continuing appearances in Britain. Publ. songs under name J. P. McCall.

(3) **William Levi** (b. Anniston, Alabama, 1898). Trombonist and composer. Of Negro race; Director of Music at Tuskegee (1931). Has composed *Negro Folk Symphony*, &c.

Day, Alfred (b. London 1810; there d. 1849). Doctor of medicine who wrote a *Treatise of Harmony* (1845), tracing origin of chords then in use to natural harmonic series; his views were adopted by Macfarren in his very widely used *Rudiments of Harmony* (1860), &c., and also by Prout in first 15 edns. (1889–1901) of his *Harmony, its Theory and Practice.*

Dazu (Ger.). 'Thereto', i.e. (in organ playing) the stops mentioned are now to be added to the others.

D.B.E. See *British Empire, Order of the.*

D.C. = Da Capo (q.v.).

De, D' (Fr.). 'Of', 'from'.

Deacon, Harry Collins (b. London 1822; there d. 1890). Eminent singing teacher; master of Sims Reeves and a great number of the most popular Brit. vocalists of his day. Pianist (especially active as accompanist).

Deaconing. See *Hymns and Hymn Tunes* 5.

Dead City, The ('Die tote Stadt'). The chief opera of Erich Korngold. Libretto by P. Schotte, based on Rodenbach's novel, *Bruges la morte.* (Prod. Hamburg and Cologne 1920; New York 1921.) Many translations.

Dead Marches. See *Funeral Marches.*

Dean, Winton (Basil) (b. Birkenhead 1916). Educated Cambridge. Musical scholar and author of articles and books esp. on Bizet and Handel.

Dean Paul, Lady. See *Poldowski.*

Deas, James Stewart (b. Edinburgh 1903). Educated Edinburgh Univ. (M.A., B.Mus.); musical training under Weingartner. Conductor of Edinburgh Opera Co. 1931–3; also various orchs. Mus. critic, *The Scotsman* (1939–48). Prof. of Music Sheffield Univ. 1948.

Death and the Maiden Quartet. Nickname of Schubert's String Quartet, No. 14, in D minor (1826), of which the 2nd movement consists of variations on the composer's song, *Death and the Maiden.*

Death and Transfiguration (*Tod und Verklärung*). Symphonic Poem by Richard Strauss (op. 24; 1889). The score is prefaced by a poem written by Alexander Ritter in order to detail the music's imaginative basis, point by point (A sick man on his mattress in a 'squalid garret', &c., and on to 'Sounds of Triumph, Deliverance, Transfiguration!').

Death of Jesus (Graun). See *Tod Jesu.*

Death of Minnehaha (Coleridge-Taylor). See *Hiawatha.*

Death of Nelson. By Braham (q.v.).

Debain, A. F. See *Reed-Organ Family* 5.

De Bériot. See *Bériot.*

Debile (It.), **débile** (Fr.). 'Weak.'

De Boeck. See *Boeck.*

Debole (It.). 'Weak.'

Debora e Jaèle. Opera by Pizzetti. (Prod. Milan 1922.)

Deborah. Oratorio by Handel. (1st perf. London 1733.)

De Bréville. See *Bréville.*

De Brosses. See *Brosses.*

Debussy, Claude Achille (b. St. Germain-en-Laye. 1862; d. Paris 1918). From age of 12 student at Paris Conserv.; 10 years later won Rome Prize and so was able to work quietly for 3 years in Rome. At 32 (1894) produced his tone-poem *Prelude to 'The Afternoon of a Faun'* (see *Après-midi*), based on a poem of the symbolist poet Mallarmé: this won high admiration yet provoked much discussion as did the composer's one string quartet about the same time. At 40 (1902) roused still more active argument by the opera *Pelléas and Mélisande* (q.v.), which struck many people as being one long recitative. In 1911 provided incidental music to d'Annunzio's *Martyrdom of St. Sebastian* (see *Martyre*). During his fifties was seized by a painful malady of which he at last expired.

That characteristic of his music which made it appear so novel in style is a delicate suggestiveness in harmonic and orch. expression rather than plain and blunt statement: this allies him to the Fr. Impressionist painters and Symbolist poets, by whom he was much influenced. His numerous piano compositions have gradually made his style familiar to a wide circle and the novelty of his idiom has ceased to be an impediment to appreciation. On careful analysis it was realized that there are present in all his work the classic qualities of precision, balance, and the skilful treatment of melodic themes, much of the special and personal flavour coming from the use of a melodic scale of whole-tones (see *Scales*) and also from the use of harmonies based on a minute study of the

effect of overtones (see *Acoustics* 6 and 7). There is a strong programmatic element in his music (see *Programme Music*), not, however, crudely presented but of the nature of delicate suggestion. (See *Impressionism.*)

See also under *Ariettes oubliées*; *Blessed Damozel*; *Boîte à joujoux*; *Chansons de Bilitis*; *Children's Corner*; *Clair de lune*; *Enfant prodigue*; *Estampes*; *Fêtes galantes*; *Île joyeuse*; *Images*; *Jeux*; *Khamma*; *Marche écossaise sur un thème populaire*; *Mer*; *Negro Minstrels*; *Nocturnes*; *Préludes*; *Printemps*; *Proses lyriques*; *Six épigraphes antiques.*

Début (Fr. 'beginning'). First public appearance.

Decani. Properly that side of the choir of a cathedral, &c., on which the Dean sits, but now normally the south side.

Deceptive Cadence. See *Cadence.*

Déchant (Fr.). 'Descant' (q.v.).

Décidé (Fr.), **deciso** (It.). 'Decided.' 'With decision' (i.e. firmly, not flabbily). So the It. superlative, *decisissimo.*

Decimette. A composition for 10 performers.

Declamando; declamato (It.). 'Declaiming'; 'declaimed', i.e. in a declamatory style.

Découpler (Fr.). 'To uncouple.'

Decrescendo; decresciuto (It.). 'Decreasing'; 'decreased', i.e. getting gradually softer. See Table 17.

Deering, or Dering, Richard (d. 1630). Born in England but some time in Italy; settled in London as a professional musician but later became organist to the convent of Eng. nuns at Brussels; still later returned and became one of the musicians of the court of Charles I. Like some other composers of the period he wrote amusing choral pieces based on the cries of London street vendors; also composed music for viols, Eng. anthems, and Latin motets—the last the favourite music of Oliver Cromwell.

Défaut (Fr.). 'Fault' or 'lack'. So *à défaut de*, 'In the absence of'.

Defauw, Désiré (b. Ghent 1885; d. Gary, Ind., 1960). Violinist and conductor. London début 1910; own string quartet from 1913; conducted

Brussels Conserv. orch. from 1920; established the *Orchestre nationale de Belgique* 1937; in U.S.A. from 1939; cond. Chicago Symphony 1943-9.

Degeyter. See *Internationale*.

Degrees and Diplomas in Music. (1) BRITISH UNIVERSITY DEGREES. The degrees in music given by Brit. and Irish universities are Bachelor ('B.Mus.' or 'Mus.B.') and Doctor ('D.Mus.' or 'Mus.D.'), music being like medicine in proceeding straight from 'Bachelor' to 'Doctor' without the intermediate 'Master' (exceptions—Cambridge, since 1893, has all 3 degrees; Wales and Birmingham have also the 3 degrees).

The universities conferring musical degrees, with the dates from which they have been conferred, are as follows: Cambridge (1463), Oxford (abt. 1499), Dublin (1615), London (1879), Durham (1892), Edinburgh (1893), Manchester (1894), Univ. of Wales (1905), Birmingham (1905), National Univ. of Ireland (1908), Sheffield (1931), Glasgow (1933), Leeds (1946), Nottingham (1948), Bristol (1951), Belfast (1953), Hull (1955). It will be seen that some universities do not yet confer such degrees.

For 350 years after Oxford and Cambridge began to grant degrees in music the conditions were very vague. Apparently the degrees were sued for and refused or granted, the composition and performance before the Univ. of an 'exercise' (at what was called an 'Act') being expected. Definite examinations were instituted during the professorship of Sterndale Bennett at Cambridge (in 1857) and that of Ouseley at Oxford (in 1862).

In several universities it is possible to obtain by research in musical subjects the degree of Litt.B., Litt.D., and Ph.D. (or B.Litt., D.Litt., and D.Phil.)—Bachelor and Doctor of Letters, and Doctor of Philosophy.

By an old custom dating from the 13th c., the Archbishop of Canterbury (by virtue of his former office of Legate of the Pope) has the power to grant degrees, and he sometimes exercises this power by conferring the doctorate of music. These degrees are known as 'Canterbury Degrees' (D.Mus. Cantuar.) or (from the Archbishop's London palace, from which they are issued) 'Lambeth Degrees'.

Various universities in the Dominions and Colonies confer musical degrees, their requirements being not so much standardized as those of the universities of the old country. As some of these universities possess conservatories of music and teach performance this receives more recognition as a degree qualification.

At some Brit. universities music can now be taken as one of the subjects for a degree in Arts.

(2) BRITISH DIPLOMAS. The issue of degrees in music in Britain is well controlled. On the other hand, there is so large a number of genuine diplomas that the public is bewildered by them, and added to these a certain (happily diminishing) number of bogus diplomas given by private groups of individuals posing as public bodies.

The diploma-conferring bodies in the list now to be given are commonly recognized as genuine public bodies. Their diplomas are usually graded as follows: (*a*) Associateship, (*b*) Licentiateship (not always present), (*c*) Fellowship. This is not quite invariable, however; for instance, the Royal Academy of Music confers Licentiateship upon external or internal candidates and Associateship (of at least equal grade) upon internal candidates. Fellowship is reserved by some institutions as a purely honorary distinction.

ROYAL ACADEMY OF MUSIC (founded 1822). F.R.A.M. (limited to 150 distinguished past students); Hon. R.A.M. (honorary members); A.R.A.M.; L.R.A.M. (open to non-students and with the differentiation, 'teacher' or 'performer'); SPECIAL DIPLOMA of the Teachers' Training Course.

ROYAL COLLEGE OF MUSIC (founded 1883, succeeding the National Training Coll. of Music, founded 1873). F.R.C.M. (honorary, limited to 50); Hon. R.C.M. (distinguished non-students); Hon. A.R.C.M. (distinguished past students); A.R.C.M. (by examination, open to non-students and with the differentiation, 'teacher' or 'performer'); M.Mus. R.C.M. ('Master of Music'—severe and varied tests; open to non-students); Teachers' Training Course certificate awarded to selected students from certain colleges for a 1-year course.

ASSOCIATED BOARD. The R.A.M. and R.C.M. combine, under the title 'Royal Schools of Music, London' (from 1947 with also Royal Manchester Coll. and Royal Scottish Academy), to confer in the Dominions and Colonies the diploma, formerly known as 'L.A.B.' (Licentiate of the Associated Board), now entitled 'L.R.S.M., London'. This is the Overseas equivalent of the L.R.A.M. and the A.R.C.M.

The teacher's diploma, G.R.S.M. (Graduate of the Royal Schools of Music), is open only to internal students at the R.A.M. and R.C.M. after 3 years' work, including Teaching Course.

ROYAL COLLEGE OF ORGANISTS (founded 1864). A.R.C.O.; F.R.C.O., with an additional (optional) diploma entitling the candidate to add the letters Ch.M. (i.e. 'Choirmaster'). In 1936 the Archbishop of Canterbury instituted a Diploma in Church Music to the examination for which he admits only F.R.C.O.s holding the Ch.M. diploma, who on passing his examination become A.D.C.M.s.

TRINITY COLLEGE OF MUSIC (founded 1872). A.T.C.L.; L.T.C.L.; F.T.C.L. (these in executive subjects—as Teacher or Performer); A.Mus.T.C.L.; L.Mus. T.C.L. (these in theoretical subjects). G.T.C.L.; Hon. F.T.C.L.; Hon. T.C.L. (F.T.C.L. awarded also for orig. composition.)

GUILDHALL SCHOOL OF MUSIC AND DRAMA (founded in 1880). A.G.S.M. (internal students); L.G.S.M. (internal and external students); F.G.S.M. (honorary—limited to 100); G.G.S.M. (internal students); Hon. G.S.M. (honorary—limited to 100).

ROYAL MANCHESTER COLLEGE OF MUSIC (founded 1893). A.R.M.C.M. (after a 3 years' course and examination) and F.R.M.C.M. (honorary only).

BIRMINGHAM AND MIDLAND INSTITUTE SCHOOL OF MUSIC (founded 1887). A.B.S.M.; A.B.S.M. (T.T.D.), Teacher's Training Diploma; L.B.S.M.; G.B.S.M. (after Graduate Course); F.B.S.M. (honorary).

ROYAL SCOTTISH ACADEMY OF MUSIC (founded 1929, succeeding the Glasgow Athenaeum School of Music). Dip. R.S.A.M. and (in musical education) Dip.Mus.Ed. R.S.A.M. (both after a full course in the Academy and examination).

LONDON COLLEGE OF MUSIC. Founded in 1887 as a proprietory examining body working for profit, the validity of its diplomas was not usually admitted in official musical circles. In 1941, however, it changed its constitution, becoming an incorporated body not working for profit. Diplomas include A.L.C.M., L.L.C.M., F.L.C.M., A.Mus.L.C.M., L.Mus.L.C.M.

TONIC SOL-FA COLLEGE, or CURWEN MEMORIAL COLLEGE (founded 1863). A.T.S.C.; L.T.S.C.; F.T.S.C.

INCORPORATED STAFF SIGHT-SINGING COLLEGE (founded 1896; now ceased). A.I.S.C.; F.I.S.C.

INCORPORATED SOCIETY OF MUSICIANS (founded 1882) at one time gave the diploma L.I.S.M., and this is, presumably, still valid.

ROYAL SOCIETY OF TEACHERS (founded, as 'Teachers' Registration Council', 1912). Musicians were accepted for membership of the society, having, like teachers of other subjects so admitted, the right to use the description M.R.S.T. By 1944 Education Act no new members accepted, functions being taken over by new National Advisory Council.

ROYAL MILITARY SCHOOL OF MUSIC (Kneller Hall). Graduation is indicated by the letters p.s.m., meaning 'passed school of music'.

BANDSMAN'S COLLEGE OF MUSIC. This is a young examining body (1931), not for profit and with unpaid officials and described as 'The National Institution of the Brass Band Movement'. It awards, after examination, 3 diplomas, B.B.C.M. ('Bandmaster'), A.B.C.M., and L.B.C.M.

OVERSEAS SCHOOLS OF MUSIC. Some of the universities in different parts of the Commonwealth, having schools of music attached, grant a diploma.

The Canadian College of Organists grants diplomas of A.C.C.O. and F.C.C.O.

(3) AMERICAN DEGREES. The number of universities, colleges, schools of music, &c., conferring Mus.B. is now very great, and owing to the varying laws of different states the standing of these institutions and the value of their degrees vary widely. Mus.B. (or B.Mus. or B.M.) generally signifies the successful carrying out of a 4 years' course of study, which may be largely execution (or, as it is called in the U.S.A., 'Applied Music'). More than in Britain, the study of music is allowed to count towards a degree in Arts, Science, and Philosophy, so that many musicians take the B.A., M.A., B.Sc., and Ph.D. The degree of M.Mus. (or Mus.M., or M.M.) exists also. Some institutions confer a masters' degree in Sacred Music—M.S.M. The degree of Mus.D. is practically exclusively reserved as an honorary distinction.

(4) AMERICAN DIPLOMAS. The U.S.A., fortunately, does not possess the bewildering variety of diploma-conferring institutions of Britain, nor any alphabetical distinctions of any kind so much valued. The Amer. Guild of Organists (1896) confers diplomas of Associateship and Fellowship— A.A.G.O. and F.A.G.O.: when the

examination as choirmaster is passed the letters Ch.M. may be added.

(5) DEGREES AND DIPLOMAS OTHER THAN BRITISH AND AMERICAN. It is, of course, quite impossible to give particulars here of the degrees and diplomas in music of all countries, but in general it may be said that outside the English-speaking world specifically musical degrees are not given. For the Ger. doctorate in Philosophy (Ph.D.) and the Fr. doctorate in Letters (Dr.ès Lettres) a thesis upon a musicological subject may be presented.

Degrigny. See *Grigny*.

Dehors (Fr.). (1) 'Outside.' (2) 'Prominent.' Sometimes the expression is *En dehors*.

De la (Fr.). 'Of the', 'from the'.

Delamarter, or **De Lamarter, Eric** (b. Lansing, Mich., 1880; d. Orlando, Fla., 1953). Prominent Chicago organist and teacher, and conductor (assistant conductor of Chicago Symphony Orch. 1917–36, &c.); music critic of several Chicago papers. Composer of numerous orch. and chamber works, songs, and piano and organ pieces.

Delannoy, Marcel (b. Ferté Alais 1898; d. Paris 1962). Composer of operas, ballets, songs, piano music, &c.

de Lara. See *Lara*.

Delattre, Roland. See *Lassus*.

Delibes, (Clément Philibert) Léo (b. St. Germain-du-Val, Sarthe, 1836; d. Nantes 1891). Studied at the Paris Conservatory and quickly took a place in the musical life of the capital as the composer of successful ballets (*Coppélia* 1870, *Sylvia* 1876), operettas, and operas (see *Lakmé*; *Roi l'a dit*). Light-handed, he provided graceful melody, pleasant harmony, and piquant orchestration.

Delicato (It.). 'Delicate.' So *delicatamente* 'delicately'; *delicatissimo*, 'as delicately as possible'; *delicatezza*, 'delicacy'.

Délié (Fr. 'Untied'). (1) The notes separated from each other, i.e. staccato. (2) Unconstrained in style. (3) Supple (fingers).

Delirio (It.). 'Frenzy.' So *delirante*, 'frenzied'.

Delius, Frederick, or **Fritz** (b. Bradford, Yorks., 1862; d. Grez-sur-Loing, France, 1934). His father and mother were German, the former, however, being of Dutch descent. Early in life settled in Florida as an orange grower; then became a piano teacher in Virginia, and later studied at Leipzig, where (1888) he made his first public appearance as composer with a suite, *Florida*, soon afterwards giving in London a programme of his own works, which puzzled the public and the critics and led to little advance in reputation: his definite acceptance came later largely through the efforts of the conductor Beecham. His operas had their first performance in German (see *Koanga*; *Village Romeo and Juliet*; *Fennimore and Gerda*). His output includes orch. variations and rhapsodies, &c., concertos for piano, 'cello, violin, and violin and 'cello, choral-orch. pieces, a *Mass of Life* and a *Requiem* (both settings of Nietzsche), chamber music, and songs.

From his middle thirties he spent most of his time on a small property he had acquired near Fontainebleau, and there he ended his life, crippled and blind (see *Fenby, Eric*).

He may be classed, roughly, as a Romantic of the Impressionist School; his harmonic idiom, which tends to chromaticism, is very individual.

See also under *Appalachia*; *Brigg Fair*; *Dance Rhapsody*; *Eventyr*; *Hassan*; *In a Summer Garden*; *Life's Dance*; *Mass of Life*; *North Country Sketches*; *On hearing the first Cuckoo in Spring*; *Paris*; *Requiem*; *Sea Drift*; *Song before Sunrise*; *Song of Summer*; *Song of the High Hills*; *Songs of Farewell*; *Summer Night on the River*.

Delizioso (It.). 'Delicious', 'sweet'. So the adverb, *Deliziosamente*.

Della Casa, Lisa (b. nr. Berne 1919). Operatic lyric soprano. Début 1941; Zürich 1943–50; Glyndebourne 1951; Metropolitan 1947.

Deller, Alfred (b. Margate 1912). Counter-tenor singer. Trained in local parish choir, then self-taught. Lay Clerk, Canterbury Cathedral, 1940–7; St. Paul's Cathedral Choir 1947. Frequent soloist in broadcast and other concerts of music of 16th–18th cs.

Dello Joio, Norman (b. New York 1913). Composer, pianist, and teacher. Trained Juilliard. Many awards. On staff Sarah Lawrence Coll. 1945; Mannes Sch. 1957. Prolific composer of operas, ballets, orch., and chamber music.

Del Mar, Norman Réné (b. London 1919). Conductor. Trained R.C.M. Conductor English Opera Group (q.v.) 1948–56; Yorkshire Symph. Orch. 1954–5; B.B.C. Scottish Orch. 1960. On staff G.S.M. 1952.

Del Monaco, Mario (b. Florence 1915). Dramatic tenor. Trained Pesaro. Début Milan 1941; Metropolitan 1950. World career; many recordings.

De los Angeles, Victoria (b. Barcelona 1923). Lyric soprano. Trained Barcelona Conserv. Début Madrid 1944; Covent Garden and Metropolitan 1950. Highest world-wide reputation.

del Riego. See *Riego*.

Delvincourt, Claude (b. Paris 1888; killed in road crash 1954). Studied under Widor and others at the Paris Conserv. and in 1913 won the Rome Prize. Amongst his compositions is the dance poem *L'Offrande à Siva*. Director of Paris Conserv. from 1941.

Démancher (Fr., from *manche*, 'neck'). (1) To shift the left hand along the neck of a violin, &c. (2) To shift the left hand close to the bridge.

Demessieux, Jeanne Marie-Madeleine (b. Montpellier 1921; d. Paris 1968). Organist. Trained Montpellier and Paris Conservatories. Then 5 years under Marcel Dupré. First recital Paris 1946, later London and Edinburgh (1948), &c. Won enthusiastic praise as interpreter and composer, and particularly for remarkable powers of improvisation. Organist of church of Saint-Esprit, Paris, from age 12.

Demi (Fr.). 'Half.'

Demi-cadence. See *Cadence*.

Demi-jeu (Fr. 'Half-play'). In organ and harmonium music, &c., 'At half power of the instrument'.

DeMille, Agnes (b. New York 1909). Well-known choreographer, esp. of musical plays, &c.

Demi-pause (Fr.). Half-rest, minim rest.

Demisemiquaver (𝅘𝅥𝅯). The Thirty-second note, i.e. $\frac{1}{32}$ the time-value of the whole-note or semibreve (see Table 1).

Demi-ton (Fr.). Semitone.

Demi-voix (Fr.). 'Half voice', i.e. Half the vocal power (= It. *mezza voce*).

Demuth, Norman (b. South Croydon 1898; d. Chichester 1968). A choir-boy at St. George's Chapel, Windsor Castle, and then at R.C.M. From 1930 on the staff of the R.A.M. Wrote symphonies, concertos, ballets, chamber music, choral music, books, &c.

Demütig, demüthig (Ger.). 'Meek.' So, too, *demutsvoll, demuthsvoll*. And the noun *Demütigung, Demüthigung*.

Denison, John Law (b. Reigate, Surrey, 1911). Trained R.C.M. Horn player in B.B.C. Orch., &c. Asst. mus. director British Council 1946; Arts Council (q.v.) director 1948. Mgr. Festival Hall 1965. C.B.E. 1960.

Dennoch (Ger.). 'Nevertheless.'

Densmore, Frances (b. Red Wing, Minn., 1867; d. there 1957). Authority on music of Amer. Indians; innumerable valuable publications.

Dent, Edward Joseph (b. Ribston Hall, Yorks., 1876; d. London 1957). Educated at Eton and King's Coll., Cambridge; M.A., B.Mus. Prof. of Music in that univ. 1926–41; also Hon. D.Mus., Oxford. Had wide influence as President of the International Soc. for Contemporary Music (1923–37; q.v.) and of the International Musicological Soc. Active as a practical translator of opera libretti and as a sound author on many musical subjects; some compositions. (Cf. *Beggar's Opera*.)

Denza, Luigi (b. nr. Naples 1846; d. London 1922). Composer of hundreds of popular songs (e.g. *Funiculì, Funiculà*, 1880, which Strauss, thinking it to be a Neapolitan folk song, introduced into his early suite, *Aus Italien*). For the last quarter-century of his life was a prof. of singing in the R.A.M., London.

Deppe, Ludwig (b. nr. Lippe, Germany, 1828; d. Bad Pyrmont 1890). Conductor, composer, and famous piano teacher.

De profundis ('Out of the deep'). Psalm 129 in the Vulgate (following the Septuagint) and 130 in the Eng. Authorized and Revised versions (following the Hebrew). It is one of the 7 Penitential Psalms (see *Psalm*) and has a place in the Office of the Dead of the Roman Catholic Church, where, of course, its traditional plainsong is attached to it. It has been set by composers many times.

Der (Ger.). 'The' (masc. sing.).

Derb (Ger. Various terminations according to gender, case). 'Firm', 'solid', 'rough'.

De Reszke, Jean, Édouard, and **Josephine.** See *Reszke.*

Dering. See *Deering.*

Derselbe (Ger.). 'The same.'

Des (Fr.). 'Of the' (plur.).

Des (Ger.). 'Of the' (masc. and neut. sing.); also the note D flat (see Table 7).

Descant. Like 'Faburden' (q.v.) a puzzling term because at different periods used with different significances, chief of which are as follows: (1) A melody sung above the Plainsong (which latter normally in the tenor). (2) a part extemporized by a singer to a non-extemporized part sung by another singer. (3) The art of composing or singing part-music. (4) The soprano part in choral music. (5) In modern hymn singing, a freely written soprano part added to a hymn tune whilst the tune itself is sung by the choir's tenors or by the congregation (cf. 1 above).

Descant Viol. See *Viol Family* 2 a.

Desert, The. See *David, Félicien.*

Deses (Ger.). D double flat (see Table 7).

Desiderio (It.). 'Desire.' Hence *con desiderio*, 'longingly'.

Desinvolto, desinvoltura (It.). 'Ease.'

Desmond, Astra—Mrs. Neame (b. 1898). Operatic and concert mezzo-soprano. Educated Westfield Coll., London (B.A., London): singing under Blanche Marchesi (q.v.), &c. Became notable exponent of Elgar's works. Tours in many countries and sings in 12 languages. Has written on songs of Grieg, Dvořák, and Sibelius. C.B.E.

Dessous (Fr.). 'Below', or (as a noun) 'lower part'.

Dessus (Fr.). 'Above', or (as a noun) 'upper part'.

Destinn or **Destinnova** (really Kittl), **Emmy** (b. Prague 1878; d. Budejovice 1930). Operatic soprano of highest fame as vocalist and actress.

Desto (It.). 'Wide-awake', i.e. in a buoyant, sprightly manner.

Destouches, André Cardinal (b. Paris 1672; there d. 1749). Studied under Campra (q.v.) and rose to be Superintendent of the King's Music and director of the Opera under Louis XV. Wrote ballets, operas, and some church music. (See *Bouffons, Guerre des.*)

Destro, destra (It. masc., fem.). 'Right', e.g. *mano destra*, 'right hand'. *Destro* also means 'dexterous'.

De suite (Fr.). (1) 'One following the other.' (2) 'Immediately.'

Détaché (Fr. 'Detached'). 'Staccato.' (1) *Grand détaché*, Staccato with a full bow for each note. (2) *Petit détaché*, Staccato with the point of the bow for each note. (3) *Détaché sec*, same as *Martelé* (q.v.).

Detached Console. See *Organ* 3.

Determinato (It.). 'Determined.'

Detroit Symphony Orchestra. Founded 1872 on a small scale: enlarged 1914. Conductor, 1952 Paul Paray; 1964 Sixten Ehrling.

Dett, Robert Nathaniel (b. Drummondville, Quebec, 1882; d. Battle Creek, Mich., 1943). Negro composer whose fluent and agreeable style sometimes displayed a measure of racial feeling. Trained at Oberlin Conservatory, Harvard Univ., Columbia Univ., and elsewhere. Head of the vocal dept. of Hampton Inst., Va. Hon. D.Mus., Oberlin and Harvard.

Dettingen Te Deum and Anthem. By Handel, to celebrate defeat of French at Dettingen, nr. Frankfort, 1743. (1st perf. Chapel Royal, London, that year.)

Deus misereatur. The 67th Psalm, 'God be merciful unto us and bless us'. In the Anglican Prayer Book (see *Common Prayer*) it is found as an optional part of the marriage service in the place of Ps. 128, and in the evening service as an alternative to *Nunc Dimittis*.

Deuteromelia. See *Ravenscroft, Thomas.*

Deutlich (Ger.). 'Distinct.'

Deutsch (Ger.). 'German.' (But see also *Allemande* 2.)

Deutsch, Otto Erich (b. Vienna 1883; d. there 1967). Writer of many important books and articles on Mozart, Handel, and, especially, Schubert. Settled in Cambridge, England; there active in musical research. Returned Vienna 1952.

Deutscher Tanz, Deutsche Tänze. See *Allemande* 2.

Deutsches Requiem, Ein (Brahms). See *German Requiem.*

Deutschland über Alles. ('Germany beyond everything' or 'Germany before everything'), known also as the *Deutschlandlied* ('Germany Song'). A poem of aspiration for the unity of the Ger. peoples written in the period which preceded the 1848 revolutionary disturbances, by August Heinrich Hoffmann (generally called Hoffmann von Fallersleben; 1798–1874). There is in it nothing whatever of the ideal of world-conquest; it is innocent love of country that is expressed. The tune is that which Haydn wrote as the Austrian national anthem, the *Emperor's Hymn* (q.v.).

Deux (Fr.). 'Two.' *À deux*. For 2 voices or instruments, or (occasionally) short

for '**À deux temps**' (see *Deux temps*). In orch. music, however, this expression has two (opposite) meanings, (*a*) Two separate instrumental parts are now merged in one line of music, (*b*) One instrumental part is now divided, the players becoming 2 bodies.

Deuxième (Fr.). 'Second.'

Deux journées, Les. Cherubini's chief opera. Generally known in Britain as *The Water Carrier*. (Prod. Paris 1800; London 1801; New Orleans 1811.)

Deux temps (Fr. 'Two beats'). (1) In $\frac{2}{2}$ time. (2) But *Valse à deux temps* has the following varied meanings; (*a*) In normal Waltz ($\frac{3}{4}$) time with 2 dance steps to a measure, on the 1st and 3rd beats; (*b*) In $\frac{6}{4}$ or $\frac{6}{8}$ time, with steps on the 1st and 4th beats; (*c*) Having 2 values of beat, as in Gounod's *Faust* where 2 waltzes are combined, one of them in $\frac{3}{4}$ time and the other in $\frac{3}{2}$, 2 measures of the $\frac{3}{4}$ being heard against 1 measure of the $\frac{3}{2}$ and thus rhythmically conflicting.

Development (also called *Free Fantasia*, or *Working-out*. Fr. *Développement*; Ger. *Durchführung*, i.e. 'Through-leading'; It. *Svolgimento*, i.e. 'Unfolding'). The treatment of the detailed phrases and motifs of a previously heard theme ('subject') in such a way as to make new passages, often of a modulatory nature. (See *Form* 3 for the employment of this process in Compound Binary Form and 6 for its employment in Fugue.)

Devil and Daniel Webster, The. 1-act opera by Douglas Moore. Libretto by Benét. (Prod. New York 1939.)

Devil's Trill Sonata (*Trillo del Diavolo*, or *Sonata del Diavolo*). By Tartini. The legend explaining this name has been told as follows:

'Tartini dreamt one night that he had enter'd into a compact with the Devil, who promis'd to be at his service on all occasions. After making several Trials of his Obedience, he gave the Devil his Violin, in order to discover what sort of a Musician he was, when to his great astonishment he heard a Solo so exquisitely beautiful that he awoke with surprise and delight, and instantly seizing his Instrument, he endeavoured, but in vain, to express what he had just heard. He, however, composed the following Solo, which he named *Il Sonata del Diavolo*, which has always been esteemed his Masterpiece.' (Inscription on the 1st Brit. edn., abt. 1810.)

There is a song by Panseron based on the story (with violin obbligato) and a ballet (also with a solo violin part) has also been based on it (London 1893).

Devil to Pay, The. Ballad Opera by C. Coffey. (Prod. London 1731; Charleston 1736; New York 1751.) Much performed in Britain and the North American colonies, also in Germany where it initiated the movement for 'Singspiel' (q.v.). It was also imitated in France and Italy.

Devin du village, Le. See *Rousseau*.

Devoto (It.). 'Devout', 'with devotion'.

Devozione (It.). 'Devotion.'

D'Hardelot. See *Hardelot*.

Di (It.). 'By', 'from', 'of'.

Diabelli, Antonio (b. nr. Salzburg 1781; d. Vienna 1858). Pupil of Michael Haydn and friend of Joseph Haydn. Popular composer and teacher (providing, amongst other things, useful piano-fodder for young pianists), and, finally, music publisher.

Diabelli Variations. By Beethoven, for Piano (op. 120; 1823). On a Waltz by Antonio Diabelli (see above). Fifty other composers wrote one each, as commissioned, but Beethoven did not stop till he had provided this set of 33.

Diabolus in musica (Lat. 'The devil in music'). The Tritone (q.v.).

Diaghilef. See *Ballet*.

Dialogues des Carmélites, Les. 3-act tragedy-opera by Poulenc, libretto by Bernanos. (Prod. Milan 1957.)

Diamants de la couronne, Les ('The Crown Diamonds'). Opera by Auber. (Prod. Paris 1841; New York 1843; London 1844.)

Diamond, David (Leo) (b. Rochester, N.Y., 1915). Studied at Eastman School, &c., and in Paris; won Juilliard Award and Guggenheim Fellowship (1938 and 41). Composer of symphonies and other orch. music (includ-

ing concertos for violin, and for harpsichord), chamber music, choral music, &c.

Diapason. The Greek derivation of this word defines its sense as 'through all'. (1) Its chief musical use today is as the name of certain organ stops (see *Organ* 2), probably originally referring to the fact that these extended through the whole compass as some other stops did not. (2) In French the word has come to mean a pitch-fixing instrument (pitch pipe or tuning-fork), perhaps because from its note is decided the standard of pitch of the whole series of notes. (3) In French the term *Diapason normal* has also a pitch connotation, implying the generally accepted pitch in which the A (2nd space of treble staff) has 435 vibrations per second.

Diapason Phonon. Organ stop of Open Diapason type (see *Organ* 2); lips of pipes are leathered, so refining tone. Invention of Hope-Jones; 1855–1914 (cf. *Diaphone*).

Diapason Voluntary. See *Voluntary*.

Diapente (Greek). The interval of the perfect 5th.

Diaphone. Loud type of organ Open Diapason stop (see *Organ* 2) with vibratory apparatus. (Invention of Hope-Jones; 1855–1914.)

Diaphony. The same as Organum (see *History of Music* 2), but some define it as a freer form of this, admitting other intervals than the perfect ones (see *Interval*), and others speak of it as a later form, admitting of contrary motion, crossing of parts, &c.

Diaphragm. See *Voice* 3.

Diarmid. Opera by MacCunn. Libretto by the Marquis of Lorne. (Prod. Edinburgh 1897.)

Diatonic and Chromatic. The *Diatonic Scales* (see *Scale*) are those of the major and minor keys, and diatonic passages, intervals, chords, and harmonies are such as are made up of the notes of the key prevailing at the moment. The Modes (q.v.) must also be considered diatonic. The *Chromatic Scales* (see *Scales*), as also chromatic passages, intervals, chords, and harmonies, are such as introduce notes not forming a part of the prevailing key.

Di Ballo, Overture. Concert-overture by Sullivan (1870).

Dibdin, Charles (b. Southampton 1745; d. London 1814). Choir-boy of Winchester Cathedral, music-shop assistant in London; actor-singer, stage composer, and public entertainer, singing his own songs; author of novels, musical textbooks, and other things. Remembered today as a writer of bold or tender sea songs (e.g. *Tom Bowling*). (See *Bells of Aberdovey*.)

Dichterliebe ('Poet's Love'). Cycle of 16 songs by Schumann, op. 48 (1840), being settings of Heine.

Dichtung (Ger.). 'Poem' (see *Symphonic Poem*).

Dick (Ger.). 'Thick.'

Dickie, Murray (b. nr. Glasgow 1924). Tenor. Trained Vienna Conservatory and under Borgioli (q.v.). With New London Opera Co. 1946–8; then Covent Garden Co., &c.

Dickinson, (1) **Edward** (b. West Springfield, Mass., 1853; d. Oberlin, Ohio, 1946). Organist and authority on church music; for long period Prof. of Music History at Oberlin College.

(2) **Clarence** (b. La Fayette, Ind., 1873; d. New York 1969). Prominent as organist and choral conductor in Chicago and New York; composer and ed. of music, and author on many musical subjects; from 1912 to 1945 in charge of music at Union Theological Seminary, New York.

Diction. Properly, verbal phrasing, or style in the choice of words, but singing teachers use the term in the sense of 'enunciation'.

Diddling. A Lowland Scottish practice similar to the Highland practice of *Port à Beul* (q.v.). Dance tunes are sung to nonsense syllables such as 'dee-diddle-di-de'. In rural districts competitions are held.

Dido and Aeneas. Only actual opera by Purcell. Libretto by Nahum Tate. (Prod. at London boarding-school for girls, probably 1689; reached public stage 1700: again 1895, and since then revived in many cities of different countries.)

Die (Ger.). 'The' (fem. sing.; masc., fem., neuter plur.).

Dieci (It.). 'Ten.'

Diepenbrock, Alphonse (b. Amsterdam 1862; there d. 1921). Schoolmaster, self-taught as musician; composed music for church and stage, songs, &c., and wrote on musical subjects.

Dieren, Bernard van (b. Rotterdam 1884; d. London 1936). Father Dutch, mother Irish; spent most of life in London as a journalist, composing a variety of works in an original idiom and collecting around him a small but ardent band of admirers. Wrote a book on the sculptor Epstein and musical essays publ. as *Down among the Dead Men* (1935).

Dièse (Fr.). 'Sharp' (see Table 7).

Dieselbe (Ger.). 'The same.'

Dies Irae. See *Requiem*. The poem is by Thomas of Celano (d. abt. 1250). The plainsong tune has occasionally been introduced into instrumental music, as in Berlioz's 'Fantastic' Symphony and Saint-Saëns's *Danse Macabre*.

Diesis (It.). (1) 'Sharp' (see Table 7). (2) In acoustical theory the minute interval between the sum of three major 3rds (in perfect tuning) and an 8ve.

Dies Natalis. By Finzi. A setting of words by Traherne, for Soprano or Tenor and Strings (1940).

Dietro. (It.). 'Behind.'

Difference Tone. See *Acoustics* 9.

Digital. Any one of the keys making up the keyboard of a piano or similar instrument.

Digitorium. A small portable apparatus for the use of keyboard players wishing to strengthen their fingers. It usually had no more than 5 keys and these had strong springs so that considerable force was required to depress them (cf. *Virgil Practice Clavier*). Its inventor was Myer Marks and date of its introduction probably about the middle of the 19th c.

Diluendo (It. 'dissolving'). 'Dying away.'

Dilungando (It.). 'Lengthening.'

Diminished Intervals. See *Interval.*

Diminished Seventh. As an interval (q.v.) this chiefly occurs with the Leading Note as the lower note (e.g. in Key C the two notes would be B–A flat). It forms a part of the CHORD OF

Key C   Key A

Key F♯   Key E♭

(Obviously the modulation might in each case equally well have been to the minor key instead of the major.)

THE DIMINISHED 7TH (in key C consisting of the notes B–D–F–A flat). The theoretical explanation of the chord is that it is the chord of the Minor 9th (G–B–D–F–A flat) with the root omitted. This cord is particularly serviceable as a pivot for neat and easy modulation on account of its protean versatility (e.g. the B–D–F–A flat above mentioned may be enharmonically changed into B–D–F–G sharp, or B–D–E sharp–G sharp, &c., thus turning it into an inversion of the Chord of the Diminished 7th in some other key, in which it may be quitted).

Diminished Triad. See *Harmony* 2 d.

Diminuendo (It. 'diminishing'). 'Gradually getting softer.' See Table 17.

Diminution. See *Augmentation.*

Diminution, Canon By. See *Canon.*

Di molto (It. 'of much'). 'Very.'

d'Indy. See *Indy.*

Dinorah. Pastoral Opera by Meyerbeer. Libretto founded on a Breton legend. (Prod., as *Le Pardon de Ploërmel*, Paris and London 1859; New Orleans 1861; New York 1862.)

Di nuovo (It.). 'Anew.'

Dioclesian (in full *The Prophetess or the History of Dioclesian*). So-called 'Opera' of Purcell (1690). Dialogue by Betterton, adapted from Beaumont and Fletcher.

Diphthongs. See *Voice* 9.

Diplomas in Music. See *Degrees and Diplomas.*

Dip. Mus. Ed. R.S.A.M. See *Degrees and Diplomas* 2.

Dip. R.S.A.M. See *Degrees and Diplomas* 2.

Direct. The sign ∾ at the end of a page or line (in older music) to give warning of the next note.

Directorium Chori. In the Roman Catholic Church the book containing all the tones to be used in the Mass (see *Gregorian Tones*).

Dis (Ger.). D sharp (see Table 7).

Discant. Same as 'Descant' (q.v.).

Discord. See *Harmony* 2 f.

Discordant Intervals. See *Interval.*

Discreto (It.). 'Discreet', 'reserved'.

Discrezione, discretezza. 'Discretion', 'reserve'.

Disinvolto (It.). 'Self-possessed', hence easy-going in manner.

Disis (Ger.). D double sharp (see Table 7).

Disjunct Motion. See *Motion.*

Disk. Gramophone Record.

Disperato (It.). 'Desperate.' So, too, *disperabile, disperante*, whilst *disperazione* means 'despair'.

Dissoluto punito, Il. See *Don Giovanni*.

Dissonance. See *Harmony* 2 f.

Dissonanzen Quartett or **Les Dissonances.** Ger. and Fr. nicknames for Mozart's String Quartet in C, K. 465, on account of the nature of the much-discussed introduction.

Distanza (It.). 'Distance.'

Di Stefano, Giuseppe (b. nr. Catania 1921). Lyric tenor. Début 1946; Metropolitan 1948; Covent Garden 1961.

Distin Family. Prominent in Britain during mid-19th c., especially as a saxhorn ensemble. The following list does not seem to be quite complete. (1) **John** (1793–1863). Player of trumpet. (2) **George** (d. 1848). Horn player. (3) **Henry.** Instrument maker. (4) **Theodore** (1824–93). Baritone vocalist and composer of songs, part-songs, and church music.

Distinto (It.). 'Distinct', 'clear'.

Distratto, Il ('The Absent-minded Man'). Nickname for Haydn's Symphony in C, no. 60 in Breitkopf edn. of the Symphonies. The material is derived from incidental music previously composed for a play of the same name.

Dital Harp. An instrument invented in 1798 by Edward Light, a teacher of guitar: it was at first called *Harp Guitar*. By 'dital' is meant a finger-key (actually played by the thumb), as opposed to 'pedal' (cf. *Harp*): each dital raised the pitch of a string by a semitone. Another name was *Harp Lute*, the appearance of the instrument suggesting the body of a lute continued upwards by that of a small harp.

Dithyramb (Eng.), **dithyrambe** (Fr.), **ditirambo** (It.). A wild choral hymn in ancient Greece and thus a fancy name occasionally adopted for some composition of passionate character.

Ditson, Oliver & Co. Boston (Mass.) music publishing firm. Estd. 1835. Operated since 1931 by Presser Co. (see *Presser*).

Dittersdorf, Karl Ditters von (b. Vienna 1739; d. nr. Neuhaus, Bohemia, 1799). Lesser contemporary of Haydn

and Mozart, his activities, like theirs, centring within some of the princely courts of mid-Europe. Had high repute as violinist, and as composer provided an ever-flowing stream of string quartets, symphonies, &c. Original name 'Ditters', the addition to it resulting from his ennoblement by the Emperor.

Div. See *Divisés*.

Diver, The. See *Loder* 1.

Diversions. Occasional synonym for variations (see *Form* 5).

Divertimento (It. 'amusement'). (1) See *Suite*. (2) An easy-going fantasia on airs from some opera, &c.

Divertissement (Fr.). (1) Entr'acte (q.v.). (2) Series of dances, songs, &c., inserted in an 18th-c. Fr. opera. (3) Fantasia (q.v.) in popular style.

Divina Commedia, Symphony to. By Liszt, based on Dante (1856). In U.S.A. known as *Dante Symphony*.

Divine Office. The Canonical Hours of the Roman Catholic Church (see *Matins, Lauds, Prime, Terce, Sext, None, Vespers*, and *Compline*: these are daily said by all the clergy and in cathedral and monastic churches are daily said or sung). Also *Matins* and *Evensong* in the Church of England.

Divine Poem. By Scriabin, being his 3rd Symphony (op. 43; 1903) inspired by some of his theosophical ideas and expressive of his mystical feelings. (1st perf. Paris 1905; New York 1907; London 1913.)

Divisés (Fr.), **divisi** (It.). 'Divided' (used, for instance, where the 1st violin part shows double notes and the players, instead of attempting to play both, by double stopping, are to divide themselves into 2 groups to perform them). The abbrev. 'Div.' is often seen.

Divisions. (1; 17th and 18th cs.) The splitting up of the notes of a tune into shorter notes, i.e. a form of variation; this was especially common in viol playing and was done extempore. (2) Long vocal runs, as in Bach, Handel, and other 18th-c. composers.

Division Viol. See *Viol Family* 3 e.

Divoto; divotamente (It.). 'Devout'; 'devoutly'. So too, *divozione*, 'devoutness'.

Dix (Fr.). 'Ten.' Hence *Dixième*, 'Tenth'.

Dixie. The song *Dixie* is by Daniel Decatur Emmett (q.v.), one of the 'negro minstrels' (q.v.) so popular during a great part of the 19th c. He wrote it in 1859 as a 'walk around' song. The Southern sentiment he expresses in it was purely histrionic, and when war broke out it was a blow to him, as a Northerner, to find his song adopted as a marching song by the Southern troops and a rallying song for the Southern cause.

Dixon, (Charles) Dean (b. New York 1915). Eminent Negro conductor. Trained Juilliard. French radio 1949; Gothenburg 1952; Frankfurt radio 1960.

Djamileh. Opera by Bizet. Libretto based on de Musset's poem *Namouna*. (Prod. Paris 1872; Dublin and Manchester 1892; London 1893.)

Djinns, Les ('The Jinns'). Symphonic Poem for Piano and Orch. by Franck (1884), based on verses by Victor Hugo which describe a night flight of the Jinns over an oriental city.

D.Litt., D.Mus. See *Degrees and Diplomas* 1.

Do, Doh. See *Ut*; *Tonic sol-fa*.

Dobbs, Mattiwilda (b. Atlanta, Ga., 1925). Coloratura soprano. Début Holland Fest. 1952; Covent Garden 1954; Metropolitan 1957.

Dobrowen, Issay (Alexandrovich) (b. Nijni Novgorod 1894; d. Oslo 1953). Conductor and composer. Trained Moscow Conserv. and under Godowsky. Had conducting experience Russia and Germany and frequently (1932–5) in U.S.A., with chief orchs. Composer of theatre music, piano and violin concertos, piano pieces, &c.

Doch (Ger.). 'Yet', 'still', 'nevertheless'.

Doctor of Music. See *Degrees and Diplomas* 1, 3.

Doctor Syntax. 'Pedagogic Overture' by Walton (1921).

Dodecaphonic Scale. See *Scale*.

Dodecaphonist Technique. The

technique of *Note-row* (q.v.) composition.

Doglia (It.). 'Sorrow.' So *doglioso*, 'sorrowful'; *dogliosamente*, 'sorrowfully'.

Dog Valse for Piano. Chopin's op. 64, no. 1, in D flat (cf. *Minute Valse*), or op. 34, no. 3 in F (cf. *Cat Valse*). Confusion occurs in the application of the nickname; the composer is supposed to have improvised a valse after seeing a dog running round after its own tail.

Doh, Do. See *Ut*; *Tonic Sol-fa*.

Döhler, Théodor von (b. Naples 1814; d. Florence 1856). Popular pianist and composer of music for piano—largely of the brilliant kind.

Dohnányi, Ernö (formerly Ernst) **von** (b. Pozsony—Pressburg, or Bratislava —1877; d. New York 1960). Studied at the Conservatory of Budapest; as a remarkable pianist welcomed throughout Europe and U.S.A. Taught piano at Conservatory of Berlin, then (1916–39) settled in Budapest, where for two periods was Director of the Conservatory; then Musical Director Hungarian Broadcasting Corporation. From 1947 in U.S.A.

Composer of 2 piano concertos, 2 symphonies, 2 operas, church music, &c.; romantic and eclectic in style—not nationalistic like that of Bartók and Kodály.

Doigt (Fr.). 'Finger'; hence *doigté*, 'fingering'.

Doit, doivent (Fr.). 'Must' (3rd person sing. and plur. respectively).

Doktor Faust. Last opera of Busoni; libretto by himself. Completed by P. Jarnach. (Prod. Dresden 1925; in concert form London 1937.)

Dolcan (Organ stop). Same as *Dolce* (q.v.).

Dolce (It.). 'Sweet' (with the implication of 'soft' also). Hence *dolcissimo*, 'very sweet'; *dolcemente*, 'sweetly'; *dolcezza*, 'sweetness'.

Dolce (organ stop). Soft open metal diapason (see *Organ* 2); pipes are of inverted conical shape; 8-foot length and pitch.

Dolente (It.). 'Doleful', 'sorrowful'. So the adverb *dolentemente* and the superlative *dolentissimo*.

G

Doles, Johann Friedrich (b. Steinbach, Saxe-Meiningen, 1715; d. Leipzig 1797). One of Bach's pupils and one of his successors at Leipzig; voluminous composer of church music, songs, &c.—light in style and not at all Bachian.

Doll, The (Audran). See *Poupée*.

Dollar Princess, The (Ger. *Die Dollarprinzessin*). Very popular operetta by Leo Fall. (Prod. Vienna 1907; London, Atlantic City, and New York 1909.)

Dolmetsch, Arnold (b. Le Mans 1858; d. Haslemere 1940). Became a high authority on almost every type of ancient European instrument, making and playing clavichords, harpsichords, viols, lutes, recorders, &c., teaching his family to do so, and reviving and editing the music. Hon. D.Mus., Durham; Civil List Pension; Chevalier of Legion of Honour. His eldest son **Rudolf**, a finished harpsichordist, disappeared at sea during the Second World War; other members of the family continue the varied activities with the family name, **Carl Frederick** (b. France 1911) being a distinguished recorder player (C.B.E. 1954).

Dolore (It.). 'Dolour', 'pain'. Hence *doloroso*, 'dolorous', 'painful', and the adverb, *dolorosamente*.

Dolores, Antonia. See *Trebelli*.

Dolukhanova, Zara (b. Moscow 1918). Soprano. Trained Gneissen Mus. Sch.; Member of Bolshoi Opera; many world tours.

Dolzflöte (Ger.). Same as It. *Flauto dolce*, i.e. a soft-toned organ stop of flute tone.

Domestic Symphony (*Symphonia Domestica*). By Richard Strauss (op. 53; 1903; 1st perf. New York 1904), dedicated to 'My Dear Wife and our Boy'. A piece of detailed 'Programme Music' with headings explaining the events represented. Strauss also wrote for left-hand pianist (Paul Wittgenstein) and orch. a *Parergon to the Symphonia Domestica* ('Parergon' = ornamental accessory, or secondary work), to some extent based on the same material.

Dominant. (1) 5th degree of major or minor scale. (2) *Modes.*

Dominant Cadence. See *Cadence*.

Dominant Seventh. A chord consisting of the common chord of the Dominant with the 7th from its root added, e.g. in key C it is G–B–D–F (cf. *Harmony* 2 f, s.v. 'Discord', &c.). It normally resolves on the Tonic or Submediant chord, the note constituting the 7th falling a semitone. The three inversions of the Dominant Seventh chord are, of course, in common use.

Domine Deus. See *Mass*.

Domine Jesu Christe. See *Requiem*.

Dominicus Mass, or **Pater Dominicus Mass.** Mozart's Mass in C, K. 66 (1769). Written for the first celebration of mass by a young priest who had taken that name.

Domino noir, Le ('The Black Domino'). Very popular comedy-opera by Auber. (Prod. Paris 1837; 4 London theatres 1838; New Orleans 1839; New York 1843.)

Domra. See *Balalaika*.

Dona nobis pacem. (1) See *Mass*. (2) Cantata by Vaughan Williams. (1st perf. Huddersfield 1936.) Text from the Bible, Walt Whitman, and John Bright ('Angel of Death' speech of 1855).

Don Carlos. 4-act opera by Verdi. Libretto (in Fr.) on the play of Schiller. (Prod. Paris 1867; London, in It., same year; New York 1877; 1st Eng. perf. London 1938.)

Don Giovanni (full title, *Il Dissoluto punito, o sia Don Giovanni*, i.e. 'The Rake Punished, or Don Juan'). It. comedy-opera by Mozart. Libretto by da Ponte. (Prod. Prague 1787; London 1817; New York 1826.)

Doniach, Shula (b. Samara, now Kuibishev, Russia, 1905). Woman composer, pianist, conductor, writer, &c. In England from infancy. Trained R.A.M., then Berlin, Vienna, &c.; also influenced by 2 years in Palestine.

Donington, Robert (b. Leeds 1907). Musicologist and player of viola da gamba and treble viol. Scholar Queen's Coll., Oxford (B.A., B.Litt.); then with Dolmetsch at Haslemere. Hon. Sec. and Editor, Dolmetsch Foundation 1933-8. Specialist early English instruments and music. Author of *Musical Instruments* (1949), &c.

Donizetti, Gaetano (b. Bergamo 1797; there d. 1848). Composed 60 operas, many of which enjoyed performances all over the civilized world; had a gift of tune and knew how to write for singers in the days when opera was, above all, a display of vocal tone and technique.

See also *Don Pasquale*; *Elisir d'amore*; *Favorita*; *Fille du régiment*; *Linda di Chamounix*; *Lucia di Lammermoor*; *Lucrezia Borgia*; *Home, Sweet Home*.

Don Juan (Mozart). See *Don Giovanni*.

Don Juan. Symphonic Poem by Richard Strauss (op. 20; 1888) based on a dramatic poem by Lenau. Also Ballet by Gluck (Vienna 1861).

Don Juan de Mañara. See *Goossens, Eugene III*.

Donne curiose, Le ('The Inquisitive Women'). Opera by Wolf-Ferrari. (Prod., in Ger., Munich 1903; New York 1912.)

Donovan, Richard (Frank) (b. New Haven, Conn., 1891; d. there 1970). Organist (pupil of Widor), choral cond., member of Mus. Faculty at Yale; Prof. of Mus. 1947-60. Composer of symphonic works, chamber music, &c.

Don Pasquale. Popular comedy-opera; libretto and music by Donizetti. (Prod. Paris and London 1843; Dublin 1844; New York 1846.)

Don Quixote, The Comical History of. Incidental music by Purcell to play by D'Urfey. 1694-5.

Don Quixote. 'Fantastic Variations on a Theme of Knightly Character'. Symphonic Poem by Richard Strauss (op. 35; 1897) with solo viola and 'cello. Based on Cervantes.

Dont, Jacob (b. Vienna 1815; there d. 1888). Violinist. Trained Vienna Conserv. and became well-known performer. Wrote violin concertos, studies, &c.

Dopo (It.). 'After.'

Doppel (Ger.). 'Double.'

Doppel B or **Doppel-be.** The Double Flat (see Table 7).

Doppelchor (Ger.). 'Double chorus.'

Doppelfagott (Ger.). 'Double Bassoon' (see *Oboe Family*).

Doppelflöte. (Ger., lit. 'double flute'). Wooden organ stop; sometimes end-plugged pipes: generally 8-foot pitch (name comes from pipes having 2 mouths, one on each side).

Doppelfuge (Ger.). 'Double fugue' (see *Form* 6).

Doppelkreuz (Ger.). 'Double sharp' (see Table 7).

Doppeln (Ger.). 'To double.'

Doppelschlag (Ger. 'double stroke'). The turn.

Doppeltaktnote (Ger. 'double-measure-note' or 'two-bar note'). The Breve, or Double Whole-note.

Doppelt so schnell (Ger.). 'Double as fast.'

Doppio (It.). 'Double.' So *Doppio diesis*, *Doppio bemolle*, 'double sharp', 'double flat' (see Table 7); *Doppio movimento*, 'double speed' (i.e. twice the preceding speed).

Doppler Family. (1) **Albert Franz** (b. Lemberg 1821; d. nr. Vienna 1883). Flautist in Budapest and then Vienna. Composer of operas, orch. works, flute concertos, &c. Brother of (2). (2) **Karl** (b. Lemberg 1825; d. Stuttgart 1900). Flautist, like his brother above. Opera conductor and composer. (3) **Arpad** (b. Budapest 1857; d. Stuttgart 1927). Pianist and composer. For a few years in New York. Son of (2) above.

Dorati, Antal (b. Budapest 1906). Conductor. Studied Budapest Academy and Univ. of Vienna. Early career mainly as operatic conductor (Budapest, Dresden, Münster, &c.); then specialized in ballet. Has also conducted leading orchs. in Europe, N. and S. America, and Australia. Some compositions and arrangements of ballet suites; settled U.S. (naturalized 1947); condr. Dallas 1945; Minneapolis 1949-60; B.B.C. 1963; Washington, D.C. 1970; also Stockholm.

Dorfmusikanten Sextett (Mozart). See *Musikalische Spass*.

Dorian Mode. See *Modes*.

Dorian (or Doric) Toccata and Fugue (Bach). For Organ. In D minor. So nicknamed because original copy omitted signature and thus suggested Dorian Mode.

(As originally notated.)

Dorothy. See *Cellier*.

Dot, Dotted Note. A dot placed after a note lengthens it by half. Observe, however, that in music up to and including Bach and Handel the addition intended was merely *approximately* half, something being left to the decision of the performer, e.g. a dotted quaver and a semiquaver in one part, played against a triplet of quavers in another part, might accommodate itself

to that latter rhythm,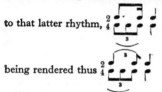

being rendered thus

Also in a very slow movement ♩. ♪ might be rendered ♩.. ♫ It was, indeed, to meet this latter case that the DOUBLE DOT (the second dot adding half the value of the first one) was in 1769 introduced by Mozart's father, Leopold Mozart, and it is still in use.

Double (Fr.). An old term for 'Variation', e.g. *Air avec doubles* = 'Air and Variations'.

Double Action. See *Harp*.

Double Appoggiatura. See Table 12.

Double Bar. The double perpendicular line marking the end of a composition or of some section thereof. (It may or may not coincide with a single bar line and if it does not do so has no rhythmic function.)

Double-Bass. See *Violin Family*.

Double-Bass Clarinet. See *Clarinet Family*.

Double Bassoon. See *Oboe Family*.

Double-Bass Saxhorn. See *Tuba Group* 3.

Double-Bass Trombone. See *Trombone Family*.

Double-Bass Tuba. See *Tuba Group* 1 c.

Double-Bass Viol. See *Viol Family* 3 d.

Double-bémol (Fr.). 'Double flat' (see Table 7).

Double C, &c. Sometimes used to indicate the note C, &c., two lines below the bass stave.

Double Chant. See *Anglican Chant*.

Double Choir (or Chorus). One arranged in 2 equal and complete bodies with a view not merely to singing in 8 parts but also to responsive effects, &c.

Double Chorus or Choir. See *Choir or Chorus*.

Double Concerto. A concerto with 2 principal instruments.

Double Counterpoint. See *Counterpoint*.

Double-croche (Fr. 'double-hook'). Semiquaver or Sixteenth-note (see Table 3).

Double-Curtall. See *Oboe Family*.

Double-dièse (Fr.). 'Double sharp' (see Table 7).

Double Dot. See *Dot*.

Double English Horn. Organ stop of Hope-Jones invention: 16-foot *chorus reed* (q.v.).

Double Flat. The sign ♭♭, which placed before a note lowers its pitch by a whole-step, or tone (see Table 6).

Double Fugue. A fugue with 2 subjects (see *Form* 6).

Double-handed. Said of the players of a band that is convertible from wind to strings or to full orch.

Double Harp. See *Harp*.

Double Horn. See *Horn Family*.

Double Keyboard. See *Pianoforte*.

Double Open Diapason. Stop of 16-foot pitch. (For 'Diapason' see *Organ* 2.)

Double Organ. (1, old term.) Either one with a full keyboard, descending to 8-foot C or 12-foot G, or one with 2 manuals. (2, modern term occasionally used in U.S.A.) One with a separate 'sanctuary' division.

Double Pedal. See *Harmony* 2 i.

Double Quartet. See *Quartet*.

Double Reed. See *Reed*.

Double-sharp. The sign ✕ which, placed before a note, raises it by a whole-step or tone.

Double Stopping (of a stringed instrument). Stopping and playing on 2 strings at a time (used, loosely, also when one of the strings is 'open', or even both of them).

Double Suspension. See *Harmony* 2 f.

Double Tonguing. See *Tonguing.*

Double Triplet. See Table 11.

Doublette 2 (Fr.). The organ stop in Eng. called the *Fifteenth.*

Double Virginal. One of which the keyboard descended to C below bass stave.

Double Whole-note. 'Breve' (see Table 3).

Douce, doux (Fr. fem., masc.). 'Sweet.' Hence *doucement*, 'sweetly'.

Douglas, (1) **Clive Martin** (b. Rushworth, Victoria, 1903). Conductor and composer. Educated Univ. of Melbourne. For some time conductor Australian Broadcasting Commission orchs. (Tasmania 1936; Queensland 1941–7; Victoria 1953). Melbourne Conserv. from 1959. Compositions include operas and orch. and chamber works.

(2) **Keith**—in full, George Keith (b. 1903; d. St. Leonards on Sea 1950). Conductor; also initiator and director of many musical enterprises. Educated Oxford. Founded Bradford Philharmonic Concerts, &c., and conducted orch. 1925–31; conducted Carl Rosa Opera Co. (q.v.) 3 years. Hon. Sec. Royal Philharmonic Soc. (from 1932), &c.

(3) **(Richard) Roy** (b. Tunbridge Wells 1907). Has composed for unusual chamber music combinations; orch. composer and arranger, especially of music for ballet and films; orch. pianist, organist, celesta player, &c.

Douleur (Fr.). 'Sadness.' So *douloureux, douloureus* (masc., fem.), 'sad'; *douloureusement,* 'sadly'.

Douthitt, Wilfrid. See *Graveure.*

Doux, douce, doucement. See *Douce*, above.

Dowland, (1) **John** (b. nr. Dublin 1562; d. London 1626). The greatest lute player of his age, holding, at different periods, positions as such at the court of the King of Denmark and at that of Charles I in London. His songs with lute accompaniment have been republished and testify to his skill and taste as composer. He was able to boast that music of his had been published in 8 continental capitals. Many of the poets and dramatists of his day mention him with admiration.

(2) **Robert** (b. abt. 1586; d. 1641). Son of the above and his successor in his Eng. royal office. He published a collection of lute music by various composers.

Down Among the Dead Men. This bold drinking song (the 'dead men' being the empty bottles under the table) has been in print, words and music, since 1715, but is probably earlier. Its authorship is unknown. The words have existed in many forms, adapted to the political circumstances of different periods.

Downes, (1) **Olin**—in full, Edwin Olin (b. Evanston, Ill., 1886; d. New York 1955). Music critic *Boston Post* (1906) and then *New York Times* (1924). Author of some popular books on music.

(2) **Ralph** (b. Derby 1904). Organist. Trained R.C.M. (on staff 1954) and Oxford (M.A., B.Mus.). On staff Princeton Univ., U.S.A. (1928). Then organist London Oratory (1936). Composer of organ music.

Down in a Flowery Vale. See *Festa.*

Down in the Valley. 1-act folk opera by Kurt Weill. (Prod. Indiana Univ. 1948.)

Doxologia, Doxology (from the Greek *Doxa*, 'Glory', and *Logos* 'Discourse'). Any liturgical formula of praise, as the *Gloria patri* ('Glory be to the Father', &c., i.e. the 'Lesser Doxology', or 'Doxologia parva', used at the end of the Psalms), or the *Gloria in excelsis Deo* ('Glory to God in the highest'—the 'Greater Doxology', or 'Doxologia magna').

The 'Greater Doxology' is a part of the Roman Mass (sung to differing plainsong according to the feast); properly it should be left to the priest until the words 'Et in terra pax', when the choir should enter, but composers such as Bach, Mozart, and Beethoven have ignored this. In its Eng. wording the 'Greater Doxology' is a part of the Anglican Communion Service.

In the non-liturgical Protestant churches 'The Doxology' usually means a metrical form of the Lesser Doxology, generally that sung to the tune *Old Hundredth*—'Praise God from whom all blessings flow', &c., from Bishop Ken's (1637–1711) Morning and Evening Hymns, 'Awake, my soul' and 'Glory to Thee'.

D'Oyly Carte. See *Carte*.

Drabant. An aristocratic Polish dance ceremony popular during the 18th and early 19th cs. It began with a solemn march and then changed to an *Obertass* (q.v.).

Dragonetti, Domenico (b. Venice 1763; d. London 1846). Double-bass virtuoso. In London from 1794 to death and for over half a century occupied at concerts all over kingdom same desk as his friend the 'cellist Lindley (q.v.). Composer for his instrument. In manners a notorious eccentric.

Dragons de Villars, Les. See *Maillart*.

Dramatic Sonata. A nickname for Beethoven's Piano Sonata in D minor, op. 31, no. 2.

Dramatic Soprano. See *Voice* 16.

Drame Lyrique. One of the Fr. names for opera (e.g. Debussy uses the term for his *Pelléas et Mélisande*).

Dramma Lirico (It.). Same as Fr. *Drame lyrique* (q.v.).

Dramma per musica (It. 'Drama by Music 'or 'Drama through Music'). A term a good deal used by It. composers of opera from its earliest days to the 18th c. (cf. *Opera* 3).

Drammatico (It.). 'Dramatic.'

Drängend (Ger.). 'Urging forward', 'hurrying'.

Draper, Charles (b. Odcombe, Som., 1869; d. London 1952). Clarinettist of high standing in Britain. Trained R.C.M. On its staff as also G.S.M., T.C.L.

Drawstop. See *Organ* 1.

Drdla, Franz (b. Saar, Moravia 1868; d. 1944). Composer of operas, &c., but best known by violin compositions (especially his *Souvenir*).

Dream, The. Nickname of the Adagio of Haydn's String Quartet no. 48 in F, often described as op. 50, no. 5.

Dreaming (Schumann). See *Träumerei*.

Dream of Gerontius, The. Oratorio by Elgar. Setting of Newman's poem. (1st perf. Birmingham Fest. 1900; Düsseldorf 1902; Chicago 1903.)

Drehleyer or Drehleier (Ger.). Hurdy-gurdy (q.v.).

Drei (Ger.). 'Three.' **Dreifach.** 'Threefold' (see *Fach*).

Dreigroschenoper, Die. See *Weill, Kurt.*

Dreimäderlhaus, Das. Operetta ostensibly reproducing scenes from Schubert's life. The music is some of Schubert's, irresponsibly treated by the Hungarian-Ger. musician Heinrich Berté (1916). An American version, arr. by Sigmund Romberg, appeared as *Blossom Time* (1921) and an English version, arr. by G. H. Clutsam, as *Lilac Time* (1923).

Dreinfahren (Ger.). 'To talk roughly', &c.

Dresden, Sem (b. Amsterdam 1881; d. The Hague 1957). Principal of the Conserv. at The Hague; composer of orch. and chamber music, songs, &c.

Dresden Amen. See *Amen*.

Drigo, Riccardo (b. Padua 1846; there d. 1930). Pianist and for many years director of the Imperial Theatre at St. Petersburg. Had a vein of melody and his ballets had great success, especially *Harlequin's Millions*, of which the Serenade is everywhere known.

Dringend (Ger.). 'Urgent', 'pressing on'. So the comparative *dringender*.

Drink to me only with thine eyes. The poem is by Ben Jonson (1616), but is closely based on expressions in certain of the Letters of Philostratus (3rd c.). The tune cannot be traced back beyond about 1770. The usual attribution to a Colonel Mellish seems to be unwarranted, as he is understood to have been born in 1777.

Dritte (Ger., various grammatical terminations). 'Third.'

Driving Note. An old-fashioned term for a suspended or retarded note (see *Harmony* 2 f), or any note causing syncopation by anticipating the succeeding accent.

Drohend (Ger.). 'Threatening.'

Droit, droite (Fr. masc., fem.). 'Right', e.g. *main droite*, 'right hand'. But *droit* as a noun means 'right' in another sense, e.g. *Droits d'execution*, 'Performing Rights'.

Drone. See *Bagpipe Family*.

Drouet, Philip. See *Partant pour la Syrie*.

Droz, H. U. J. See *Mechanical Reproduction of Music* 9.

Drum. See *Percussion Family*.

Drum and Fife Bands. See under *Fife*. The drums in such bands are of the side drum (snare drum) type (see *Percussion Family* 2 i).

Drum-roll Symphony (Ger. *Paukenwirbel*). Nickname for the 11th of Haydn's 'London Symphonies' (q.v.), no. 103 in Breitkopf edn. of the Symphonies (in E flat). The opening of the introduction accounts for the name. (Not to be confused with *Paukenschlag*; see *Surprise Symphony*.)

Drumslade. Old Eng. word for drummer (especially in army).

Drury Lane Theatre (London). Built 1696, rebuilt 1791–4, burned 1809, re-opened 1812. From the time of Arne onwards the scene from time to time of notable operatic enterprises. (See reference under *Annotated Programmes*.)

D.S. = *Dal segno* (q.v.).

Du (Fr.) 'Of the' (masc. sing.).

Dub. Old Eng. for 'tabor'. See *Recorder Family* 2.

Dubensky, Arcady (b. Viatka, Russia, 1890; d. Tenafly, N.J., 1966). Violinist; served as member of New York orchs. Compositions, whilst adopting traditional rather than experimental style, often break new ground in the media employed (e.g. Fugue for 18 violins, another for 4 bassoons, a suite for 9 flutes, and an overture for 18 toy trumpets and 2 bass drums); also works for normal orch., operatic works. &c.

Dubinushka. Rimsky-Korsakof's Orch. Variations on a Russian people's song. When 1st perf. (St. Petersburg 1905) it led to the Composer's ejection from his post as Principal of the St. Petersburg Conservatory and a consequent strike of the students.

Dublin. See under *Schools of Music*.

Dubois, (1) **Théodore**—in full François Clément Théodore (b. Rosnay, Marne, 1837; d. Paris 1924). Had a brilliant career at the Paris Conserv. ending with the winning of the Rome Prize; returning from Rome became organist, and at age 40 succeeded Saint-Saëns at the Madeleine. For 9 years was head of the Conserv. (see allusion to resignation s.v. *Ravel*). Wrote for concert and church; and classroom (theoretical treatises).

(2) **Léon** (b. Brussels 1859; d. there 1935). Studied at Brussels Conserv. and won its Rome Prize (1885): became head of the Conserv. (1912–25). Wrote operas, &c.

Ducasse. See *Roger-Ducasse*.

Du Caurroy. See *Caurroy*.

Ducoudray. See *Bourgault-Ducoudray*.

Due (It.). 'Two.' So (1) *A due*, either (a) Divided between 2 instruments or voices, or (b) 2 instruments or voices to be joined in playing the same line of notes. (2) *Due corde*, 'Two strings' (*a*, Violin music, &c.) Divide the passage over 2 strings; (*b*, Piano music) No longer play *Una corda* (see *Corda*).

Duet (Fr. *duo*; Ger. *Duett*; It. *duo* or *duetto*). Any combination of 2 performers (with or without accompaniment), or a composition for such.

Duets for Pianoforte. See *Pianoforte Playing*.

Dufay, Guillermus or **Gulielmus** (b. in Low Countries, possibly Hainault, before 1400; d. Cambrai 1474). Chorister at Cambrai Cathedral; went to Rome and to other cities with the then wandering Pope, singing in the Papal Choir; took degree of Master of Arts at Sorbonne; became canon of Cambrai and Bruges and later of Mons; then lived in Savoy and also at Court of Burgundy, but spent last 30 years at Cambrai. The greatest Netherlands composer of that great period of Netherlands composers; wrote both church music and lively secular pieces. (See *American Inst. Musicology*.)

Duftig. (Ger.). 'Misty.'

Dukas, Paul (b. Paris 1865; there d. 1935). Studied at Paris Conservatory and later became a prof. of composition there. As a composer influenced by Lalo. Symphonic scherzo *The 'Prentice Sorcerer* (see *Apprenti Sorcier*) highly successful, but opera *Ariadne and Bluebeard* (see *Ariane et Barbe-Bleue*) considered his masterpiece; in his forties burnt all unpublished compositions and publ. no more. Was a conscientious editor of Scarlatti and Rameau and wrote much musical criticism.

Duke, (1) John Woods (b. Cumberland, Maryland, 1899). Pianist and composer. Member of Music Faculty at Smith Coll., Northampton, Mass., 1923. Works include chamber music and some orch. music.

(2) **Vernon.** See *Dukelsky*.

Duke Bluebeard's Castle. One-act opera by Bartók. (Op. 11; 1911. Prod. Budapest 1918.)

Dukelsky, Vladimir (b. Pskov, Russia, 1903; d. Santa Monica, Cal., 1969). Studied at Kiev Conserv.: eventually settled in Hollywood. Prolific composer of ballets, operas, &c., and orch. and chamber music (lighter works under name of 'Vernon Duke').

Dulce domum. This is a Winchester Coll. Song. The composer is John Reading (q.v.). The original poem, by an unknown author, is in Latin. There have been various Eng. translations; that generally used is one of several proposed by readers of the *Gentleman's Magazine*, in which correspondence on the subject appeared in March 1796.

Dulcet. Organ stop: a Dulciana (q.v.) of 4-foot length and pitch.

Dulcian (Ger. organ term). Soft reed stop of 8 or 16 feet (not same as Eng. *Dulciana*, q.v.).

Dulciana. Soft organ stop usually in Britain of diapason class (see *Organ* 2), and in U.S.A. of string-toned class.

Dulciana Mixture. Organ Mixture stop (see *Mixture*) of soft tone, generally on Swell or Echo manual.

DULCIMER (OR 'HACKBRETT')

(From Virdung's *Musica getutscht*, Basle, 1511 —the earliest printed book on musical instruments)

Dulcimer. A shallow closed box over which are strung wires to be struck with 2 wooden hammers held in the player's 2 hands. It is in Hungary, Rumania, and Bohemia that it is in most use. (In Kentucky an instrument called by this name is really a form of psaltery or zither, the strings being plucked.)

See also *Pantaleon*; for Glass Dulcimer see *Harmonica* 2.

Dulcitone. See *Percussion Family* 1 e.

Dumbarton Oaks. Concerto for 15 instruments by Stravinsky (1938). Name taken from that of residence (in Washington, D.C.) of American patron of music, Robert Woods Bliss.

Dumb Girl of Portici (Auber). See *Muette*.

Dumka (plur. *Dumky*). A type of Slavonic folk ballad, alternately elegiac and madly gay, and often in the minor.

Dumky Trio. By Dvořák (op. 90; 1891), for piano, violin, and 'cello. In style of *Dumka* (see above).

Dump, Dumpe. Title of some Eng. pieces of the 16th–early 17th cs., often in variation form, and possibly elegiac in intention.

Dumpf (Ger.). 'Dull', 'muted'.

Duncan, Isadora. See *Ballet*.

Dunelm. Indicates a degree of Durham Univ.

Dunhill, Thomas Frederick (b. London 1877; d. Scunthorpe, Lincs. 1946). Wrote orch. and piano music, songs (especially for children), and chamber music, a successful light opera *Tantivy Towers*, &c., also a book, *Chamber Music*.

Duni. See *Duny*.

Dunkel (Ger.). 'Dark.' So *Dunkler*, 'darker'.

Dunn, (1) **Geoffrey Thomas** (b. London 1903). Operatic and concert tenor. Trained R.A.M. (later on staff). Also active as producer, translator of many libretti, and librettist.

(2) **John** (b. Hull 1866; d. Harrogate 1940). Violinist. Trained Leipzig Conserv. Of high Brit. reputation.

(3) **Edward** (b. Manchester 1899). Conductor, lecturer, &c. Trained Royal Manchester Coll. Mus. Musical director, Bath and Buxton; from 1935 conductor Durban Civic Orch. Books on aesthetics, &c.

Dunstable, John (b. ? Dunstable, probably between 1380 and 1390; d. ? London 1453). Applied his delicate perception to the principles of counterpoint and achieved a great advance in choral composition; thus acquired an enormous reputation all over Europe.

Duny, or Duni, Egidio Romoaldo (b. nr. Naples 1709; d. Paris 1775). Had great success as opera composer all over Italy, also in London and Paris, settling in the latter city and there attaining great popularity; one of the important members of the 18th-c. group of Fr. comic-opera composers.

Duo (It. and Fr.). 'Duet' (q.v.).

Duodecuple Scale. See *Scales*.

Duodrama. Same as Melodrama (q.v.), but restricted to 2 speakers.

Duolo (It.). 'Grief.'

Duparc, Henri—in full Marie Eugène Henri Fouques (b. Paris 1848; d. Mont de Marsan 1933). A favourite pupil of Franck; influenced a good deal by Wagner; one of the founders of the National Musical Soc. His songs, which are few, are of high importance; ill health silenced almost the last 50 years of his life.

Duplet. See Table 11.

Duple Time. See Table 10.

Duplex Instruments (Brass). These exist in 2 types: (a) Those planned to produce 2 qualities of tone by the provision of 2 bells of different bore, and (b) Those planned to play in either of 2 different keys (i.e. from either of 2 different fundamental notes; see *Acoustics* 7) without change of quality of tone (e.g. the double-horn in F and B flat) by the provision of double lengths of valve tubing.

Duplex Scaling. See *Pianoforte*.

Dupont, (1) **Auguste** (b. nr. Liège 1827; d. Brussels 1890). A prof. of piano at Brussels Conserv. and composer of much romantic piano music.

(2) **Gabriel** (b. Caen 1878; d. nr. Paris 1914). Pupil of Widor. Composed piano and orch. music, operas, &c.; put his whole heart into an opera, *Antar*, which was in rehearsal in 1914 when on one and the same day war was declared and he died: when it reached performance 7 years later it was highly spoken of by some of the best critics.

Duport, (1) **Jean Pierre** (b. Paris 1741; d. Berlin 1818). Famous 'cellist for whom Beethoven composed 2 sonatas; he himself also composed for his instrument. (2) **Jean Louis** (b. Paris 1749; there d. 1819). Brother of above and an even greater 'cellist; the present system of fingering the instrument is largely his; also composed for it.

Dupré, Marcel (b. Rouen 1886; d. nr. Paris 1970). Pupil of Guilmant and Widor; succeeded latter as organist of St. Sulpice; some years acting-organist of Notre-Dame; toured widely as recitalist. Composer of choral works and noted improviser. Dir. Paris Conserv. 1954–6.

Duprez, Louis Gilbert (b. Paris 1806; d. nr. there 1896). Operatic tenor of high fame in France, Italy, and other countries. Created many parts in works of Meyerbeer, &c. Some compositions; also books on singing and reminiscences.

Dupuis, Thomas Sanders (b. London 1733; there d. 1796). London organist, latterly (1779) at Chapel Royal; Haydn meeting him as he was leaving the Chapel kissed him in recognition of his able extemporization. D.Mus., Oxford, 1790. Composed piano and organ music, glees and church music, &c.; some of church music still in use.

Dur. (1, Ger.) 'Major' in the sense of major *key*, e.g. *Dur Ton* or *Dur Tonart*, 'Major key', *A dur*, 'A major'. (2, Fr.) 'Hard.'

Duramente (It.). 'With hardness', 'harshness', 'sternness'.

Durante, Francesco (b. nr. Naples 1684; d. in that city 1755). Enjoyed high celebrity as teacher of composition, pupils including very many of most notable It. composers of his period. Composed mainly for church.

Durch (Ger.). 'Through.' **Durchaus.** 'Throughout.' **Durchkomponiert** or **durchcomponiert** ('through-composed'). Applied to songs of which the music is different for each stanza of the poem. **Durchdringend** ('through-forcing'). 'Penetrating', 'shrill'. **Durchführung** ('through-leading'). 'Development' (q.v.). **Durchweg.** (1) 'Throughout', 'altogether'. (2) 'Generally', 'nearly always'.

Dureté (Fr.). 'Hardness', 'severity'.

Durey, Louis (b. Paris 1888). As composer influenced by Satie (q.v.) and Stravinsky. One of the group 'Les Six' (see *Six*) but abandoned it in 1921.

Durezza (It.). 'Hardness', 'severity'.

Duro (It.). 'Hard', 'firm'.

Dur Ton, Dur Tonart (Ger.). 'Major key.'

Duruflé, Maurice (b. Louviers 1902). Studied as organist and composer at Paris Conserv. and came to hold international position as organ executant and improviser and composer for his instrument.

Dushkin, Samuel (b. Suwalki, Poland, 1891). Violinist. Trained New York and Paris. Successful tours in U.S.A. and elsewhere.

Dusk of the Gods (Wagner). See *Ring des Nibelungen*.

Dussek (Dušík), Jan Ladislav (b. Caslav, Bohemia, 1760; d. nr. Paris 1812). Enjoyed European fame as pianist and composer for piano; praised by Haydn; now remembered by 2 or 3 sonatas out of over 50 he left.

Düster (Ger.). 'Sombre.'

Dux. See *Canon*.

Dvořák, Antonin (b. nr. Prague 1841; d. in that city 1904). Began life as a butcher boy; studied music, in poverty, in Prague; at 21 gained admission to the orch. of the National Theatre in Prague as a viola player; later gained a good post as organist, and began to be known as orch. composer: an opera *King and Collier* (1871) established his position and the Austrian Government gave him a small pension; Brahms greatly encouraged him and helped him to get a publisher. The *Stabat Mater* (q.v.) made him widely known in Britain. From 1892 to 1895 was in New York as head of the National Conserv.; then returned to Prague as head of its Conserv.

Compositions include 9 operas and 9 symphonies (see below), overtures, concertos for violin, for piano, and for 'cello, chamber music, piano solos and duets, a *Requiem* (q.v.), a *Te Deum* (q.v.), the popular, though gruesome, cantata *The Spectre's Bride* (q.v.), songs, part-songs, &c. Characteristic features are personal harmonic idiom, fresh and vital orchestration, and the influence of folk tune, chiefly Bohemian, but in a few works Negro.

See also *American Quartet*; *Biblical Songs*; *Dumky Trio*; *Humoresque*; *Russalka*;

Saint Ludmila; *Slavonic Dances*; *Slavonic Rhapsodies*; *Songs my mother taught me*; *Suk*; *Te Deum*; *Triple Overture*.

Dvořák's Symphonies. These are frequently wrongly numbered. The correct order is as follows: 1, C minor (no op. no.; 1865), called *Bells of Zlonice*. 2, B flat (no op. no.; 1865). 3, E flat (no op. no. but originally called 'op. 10'; 1873). 4, D minor (no op. no. but originally 'op. 13'; 1874). 5, F (op. 76, originally 'op. 24', and generally called 3rd; 1875). 6, D (op. 60, 1880; generally called 1st). 7, D minor (op. 70, 1885; generally called 2nd). 8, G (op. 88, 1889; generally called 4th). 9, E minor, *From the New World* (op. 95, 1893; generally called 5th).

Dvorsky, Michel. See *Hofmann, Josef.*

Dwight's Journal of Music. See *Criticism.*

Dyer, Louise B. M. (Mrs. Hanson; b. Melbourne 1890; d. Monaco 1962). See *Lyrebird Press.*

Dying Poet, The. See *Gottschalk.*

Dyke, (Edward) Spencer (b. St. Austell 1880; d. London 1946). Violinist. Trained R.A.M. (later on staff). Formed well-known quartet and edited violin classics and studies.

Dykes, John Bacchus (b. Hull 1823; d. Ticehurst, Sussex, 1876). Precentor of Durham Cathedral and later vicar of a parish in that city; became a highly popular composer of church music, especially hymn tunes (in quantities).

Dylan (Holbrooke). See *Cauldron of Anwyn.*

Dynamic Accent. See under *Agogic.*

Dynaphone. See *Electric Musical Instruments* 1.

Dyson, George (b. Halifax, Yorks., 1883; d. Winchester 1964). Trained R.C.M., won Mendelssohn scholarship and spent some years in Italy and Germany; became music director of several 'public' schools, including Winchester; 1937–52 was head of R.C.M. As composer has prod. large-scale orch. works and choral works, chamber music, &c. M.A., D.Mus., Oxford; Hon. LL.D., Aberdeen and Leeds. Knighted 1941; K.C.V.O. 1953.

See also *Canterbury Pilgrims*; *In Honour of the City*; *Quo Vadis.*

Dzerzhinsky, Ivan (b. Tambov 1909). He studied in Moscow and Leningrad. He has composed piano music (including concertos); operas (including *Quiet flows the Don* (Moscow 1936) and *Virgin Soil Upturned*, based on Sholokhov's novels (1937); also *Volochaevko Days*); incidental music for plays and films, &c.

E

E (It.). 'And.'

Eadie, Noël (b. Paisley 1901; d. London 1950). Operatic soprano. Covent Garden(1931), Chicago(1932), Glyndebourne, &c.

Eames, Emma (b. Shanghai 1867, of U.S.A. parents; d. New York 1952). Operatic soprano. Début Paris Opera 1889. Popular New York and London.

Ear and Hearing. The human ear consists of 3 portions, the outer one, which collects the vibrations of the air (see *Acoustics*), the middle one, which conveys them onward, and the inner one, which receives them and passes on its sensations to the brain, where what we call the sensation of 'sound' thus originates.

The OUTER EAR consists of (*a*) The visible exterior auricle, commonly called 'the ear', and (*b*) A short tube ending with a membrane which we call the 'ear-drum'.

The MIDDLE EAR has a chain of 3 small bones called, from their shapes, the *Hammer*, *Anvil*, and *Stirrup*: these bones are joined together by elastic cartilage. The Hammer is attached to the inner side of the ear-drum and the Stirrup to a membrane which covers an aperture in the wall of the inner ear: the Anvil connects the two. The Middle Ear is in communication with the outer air by means of the *Eustachian Tube*, which connects it with the upper part of the throat: one purpose this serves is to assimilate the pressure of the air on the inner side of the ear-drum to that on the outer side, thus avoiding undue strain.

The structure of the INNER EAR is too intricate for description here. The essential part, from the musician's point of view, is the *Basilar Membrane*, about an inch and one-third long, which runs along the middle of a canal filled with liquid. The canal is in spiral form, reminding one of a snail shell, hence its name *Cochlea*. According to the current theory, the sensation of pitch is believed to be localized in various 'levels' (localities) of the basilar membrane, which is in contact with a series of about 20,000 very fine fibres. These fibres are connected, by means of the auditory nerve, with the brain and it is by them that the sensation we call sound arises. It may be noted that everyone has a pitch beyond which his sense of hearing *suddenly* ceases to exist. It is not uncommon for the hearing to suffer as regards high pitches whilst remaining normal for middle and lower pitches.

Two dangers concerning the ear should be known to all: (*a*) The pinching of the nostrils when blowing the nose, which results in the forcing of air violently through the Eustachian Tube into the middle ear, and (*b*) The removal of foreign bodies from the ears of children or adults by other than a medical man, which may result in injury to the ear-drum.

Earl of Ross's March. See under *Marche écossaise*.

Easdale, Brian (b. Manchester 1909). Trained R.C.M. (A.R.C.M. as solo pianist). Composed operas and orch., chamber, and film music.

East or Easte. See *Este*.

Easter Anthems. See *Anthem* (end).

Eastern Church. See *Greek Church*.

Eastman, George (b. Waterville, N.Y., 1854; d. Rochester 1932). Wealthy manufacturer (inventor of Kodak, &c.) and munificent patron of music. Founder at Rochester, N.Y., of Symphony orch. and school of music.

Eastman School of Music. See *Schools of Music*.

Easton, (1) **Florence** (b. Middlesbrough 1884; d. New York 1955). Operatic and *Lieder* soprano. Spent early life Canada. Then trained R.A.M. and Paris. Operatic début Moody-Manners Co. 1903. Then in U.S.A. and Berlin (Royal Opera 1907–13). Metropolitan Opera, New York, 1917 and later.

(2) **Robert** (b. Sunderland 1898). Operatic and concert bass. Covent Garden, &c., and chief Brit. festivals.

Ebdon, Thomas (b. Durham 1738; there d. 1811). Organist of Durham Cathedral and composer of church music still in use.

Ebenfalls (Ger.). 'Likewise', 'in the same way'.

Ebenso. 'Just as' (followed by adj.).

Eccard, Johannes (b. Mühlhausen, Thuringia, 1553; d. Berlin 1611). Pupil at Munich of Orlandus Lassus; voluminous and able composer of sacred and secular choral music.

Eccles, or **Eagles,** (1) **Solomon I** (b. London 1618; there d. 1683). Composer and teacher of virginals and viol; turned Quaker and publicly burned his instruments and music; behaved eccentrically, mending shoes in pulpit of church and having to be removed by the constable, and during the Plague (1666) running about London with a brazier on his head calling on men to repent: accompanied the founder of Quakerism, George Fox, to West Indies and went also to New England. (2) **Solomon II.** Apparently distinct from Solomon I though formerly confused with him; possibly his son and possibly the musician of that name who was one of the King's musicians. (3) **Henry I.** Probably brother of Solomon I; violinist and as such member of King's band (1689). (4) **John** (b. London abt. 1650; d. Kingston-on-Thames 1735). Eldest son of Solomon I; eminent composer of stage music; became member of King's band (1700); left songs, choral music, and keyboard music that is still sometimes heard. (5) **Henry II** (abt. 1652–1742). Second son of Solomon I; went to Paris and became member of band of Louis XIV; composer of violin music still in use. (6) **Thomas** (abt. 1680–1740). Youngest son of Solomon I; a mere tavern fiddler.

Ecclesiastical Modes. See *Modes.*

Échappé. See under *Changing Note.*

Écharpe (Fr.). 'Scarf.' So *Pas d'écharpes,* 'Scarf dance'.

Échelle (Fr. 'ladder'). 'Scale' (but *Gamme* is the more usual word for the musical scale). **Échelette** (Fr. 'little ladder'). 'Xylophone' (see *Percussion Family* 1 f).

Echo. See *Acoustics* 17; *Concert Halls.*

Echo Cornet. Organ stop of gentle tone (see *Cornet Stop*).

Echo Gamba. A soft type of organ stop (see *Gamba*).

Echoklavier (Ger., lit. 'Echo-keyboard'). Choir Organ—not Echo Organ (see *Organ* 1).

Echo Organ. See *Organ* 1.

Eckerberg, Sixten (b. Hjälterad, Sweden, 1909). Conductor, pianist, composer. Trained Stockholm Conserv. and under Weingartner, &c. Conductor in Scandinavian and other European centres. Compositions include symphonies, piano concerto, songs, &c.

Éclatant (Fr.). (1) 'Brilliant', 'gorgeous'. (2) 'Piercing'.

Eclogue. Short pastoral poem (sometimes used as title of a piece of music).

Eco (It.). 'Echo.'

École (Fr.). 'School.'

Écossaise. A sort of contredanse (see under *Country Dance*) in 2-in-a-measure rhythm. The origin of the name is a mystery, since there seems to be nothing Scottish about the character of the music. (It is *not* the same as the Schottische, q.v.)

Ed (It.). 'And'—form of *E* (see above) as used before a vowel.

Edel (Ger.). 'Noble.'

Eden. Oratorio by Stanford. (1st perf. Birmingham Fest. 1891.)

Edinburgh. See *Annotated Programmes; Festival.*

Edinburgh, Duke of. See *Royal Amateur Orchestral Society.*

Edison, Thomas Alva. See *Gramophone; Megaphone; Auxetophone.*

Edmunds, Christopher Montague (b. Birmingham 1899). Trained Birmingham School of Music (on staff 1927; Principal 1945–56) and Manchester Univ. (D.Mus.). Composer of operas, symphonies, &c.

Education and Music. (1) GENERAL HISTORY OF MUSIC IN EDUCATION IN EUROPE. In the great days of ANCIENT GREECE all education was divided into

2 categories, 'Music' and 'Gymnastic'. These terms indicated a dichotomy between the culture of the mind and that of the body, and by 'Music' was meant every form of literary and artistic culture, including what we today call by that name. The important place which Plato gives to music (in our sense) in the scheme of education outlined in his *Republic* is well known.

Less attention appears to have been given to education in the ROMAN civilization, and music seems not to have enjoyed any special prominence.

In EARLY CHRISTIAN EUROPE education came into the hands of the Church, and as a subject of education music was considered chiefly from the point of view of the church service. It was important that the traditional plainsong (q.v.) should be passed on intact, and its singing doubtless formed a part of the curriculum in many schools. The University Curriculum was modelled on a division of the Seven Liberal Arts into 'Trivium' and 'Quadrivium', the 'Trivium' consisting of Grammar, Dialectic, and Rhetoric, and the 'Quadrivium', of Geometry, Arithmetic, Music, and Astronomy. 'Music' included both the knowledge of plainsong and that of the acoustical theories of Boethius (A.D. 470–524), whose 5 books recorded the theory of the Greeks. Candidates for degrees were expected to be thoroughly grounded in these arts (the 'Trivium' for the bachelor's degree and the 'Quadrivium' for the master's), and consequently every man of higher learning possessed a theoretical knowledge of music.

FEUDALISM provided for the secular musical education of the knightly classes, since the arts of chivalry taught to the young included the making and singing of verses, the playing of the lute, and so forth.

The RENAISSANCE, with its cultivation of Humanism and its new emphasis on the joy of life, brought a renewed and discriminating study of all forms of art; the movement looked back to Greek civilization for its models, and so music necessarily received attention.

The religious REFORMATION which followed, especially on its Lutheran but also on its Calvinistic side, encour-

aged the use of music in education. Thus was established a tradition which lasted on in Germany, so that 2 centuries later we find Frederick the Great (reigned 1740–86) laying it down that the schools of his dominion should provide a singing lesson thrice weekly.

The SONG SCHOOLS of Europe played an important part in musical education for about 1,000 years (see *Schola Cantorum*). There were at one time hundreds of such schools scattered up and down the Brit. Isles, and they functioned actively until the dissolution of the monasteries (1523–39), under Henry VIII, and of the chantries (1547), under Edward VI, brought most of them to an end. Some of the Scottish song schools survived the Reformation and had the duty allotted to them of leading the metrical psalms in Presbyterian worship.

Some allusion must be made to the 18th- and 19th-c. Fr., Swiss, Ger., and It. educational reformers. JEAN-JACQUES ROUSSEAU gives a well-thought-out scheme of musical training in his *Émile, ou de l'éducation* (1762). He demands that the songs used shall be simple and undramatic. The reading of music should come later, when the love of music has been awakened; in his exposition of this principle there is some anticipation of the Curwen (q.v.) doctrine of 'the thing first and then the sign.' Rousseau shows himself very modern in advising that every child should be exercised in the composition of melodies, and he argues forcibly and rationally in favour of what we call the 'movable doh' rather than the 'fixed doh' (and of the 'lah' minor also: cf. *Tonic Sol-fa*).

The Swiss PESTALOZZI (1746–1827) laid great stress on the value of the school use of national songs and fully recognized the cultivation of song as having a harmonizing influence on character. His one-time associate, the Ger. FROEBEL (1782–1852), the initiator of the Kindergarten movement, strongly advocated the cultivation of singing 'not with the aim of making some sort of an artist out of every pupil ... but with the simple and explicit intention of securing for each pupil complete development of his nature, that he may be conscious of its wealth of interest and energy, and, in particular, may be able to appreciate true art'.

The treatment of music in the educational method of MARIA MONTESSORI, which method began to make a stir with the publication of her first book in 1912, was a disappointment to musicians. She knew too little of the art of music to realize the best way of incorporating it in her system.

(2) MUSIC IN BRITISH EDUCATION SINCE THE 16TH CENTURY. Eng. writers on education during the 16th and 17th cs. commonly considered music as a valuable part of the curriculum. Amongst these are SIR THOMAS ELYOT (in his *The Governour* in 1531), MULCASTER (headmaster of Merchant Taylors' School, 1561–86, and of St. Paul's School, 1596–1608), and MILTON (*Tractate of Education*, 1644). There seems to have been in the 18th c. a considerable decline in the attention given and the importance attached to music as a part of the educational curriculum. It dropped out altogether in boys' schools and in the girls' schools took the status of a mere decorative 'accomplishment'.

With the growth of POPULAR EDUCATION IN ENGLAND music received a new recognition, and instruction in singing at sight became common (see *Mainzer*; *Hullah*; *Tonic Sol-fa*). The elementary schools, indeed, for some time gave music more systematic attention than did the 'PUBLIC SCHOOLS' (in England this term means the big boarding-schools, some of them very ancient, for the boys of the upper classes), and hence the poorer had a privilege denied the richer. However, Thring, headmaster of Uppingham School from 1853 to 1887, set an example by his recognition of the value of the arts including music, and since that period the musical resources of all the 'public schools' have been enormously enlarged and they are now doing a great work for the musical culture of the country.

Following this movement has come a corresponding one for the fuller recognition of music in the UNIVERSITIES, at which opportunities are now increasingly provided for the gaining of a taste for music as a refined recreation and also for serious training of a professional character—generally only so far as 'paper work' of every kind is concerned (see *Degrees and Diplomas*).

A feature of musical education throughout the Brit. Empire from the late 1870's onward has been a system of LOCAL EXAMINATIONS in piano, violin, theory, &c., conducted by the musical colleges at many hundreds of centres. This system does not obtain in any European country except Britain, nor does it obtain in the U.S.A.; it is common, however, throughout the Brit. Commonwealth, examiners being sent from the London institutions.

From about 1920 onwards a wonderful widening of musical activity came about in Brit. schools—percussion bands (for the youngest children), pipe-making and playing, class teaching of piano and of stringed instruments, school orchs., melody composition by children, Dalcroze Eurhythmics (see *Jacques-Dalcroze*), the addition of instrumental and theoretical music (as an optional subject) to the syllabuses for the various School-leaving Certificates, the general use of the gramophone in schools, the giving of lessons by radio, and special concerts for children.

A great extension of the practice of holding Holiday Courses for music teachers took place from about the same time, and the great schools of music now added to their curriculum schemes of study in musical educational method.

(3) MUSIC IN EDUCATION IN THE UNITED STATES OF AMERICA. Although the Brit. colonies in America were founded at a period when musical culture in England was at one of the highest levels it has ever attained, there seems to be no record that the art took any place in the curriculum of the schools. That curriculum was probably in general rather severely utilitarian (as was natural in a new country), religious, and (in the best schools) classical. The work of LOWELL MASON (q.v.), from about 1830 onwards, led to a great advance. He conducted musical conventions, founded the Boston Academy of Music (1832), published educational textbooks and collections of music, and (1838) succeeded in introducing music into the public

schools of Boston (public schools in the wide Amer. sense). By 1933 the U.S.A. had gone ahead of all nations in the world in the provision of school orchs. and was rapidly developing a very high standard in *a cappella* choral singing (for a reference to 'Musical Appreciation' see the article devoted to that subject). The foundation of the National Supervisors' Conference in 1907, with its growth during the next 50 years to an attending membership of over 30,000, was a great encouragement to progress. (Name later changed to 'Music Educators' National Conference'.) There has been a readiness in the U.S.A. to adopt experimental methods in school music, and it has been a leader in many new activities.

Music takes, on the whole, a larger place in the Amer. university than in the Brit. Many universities have schools of music attached to them, in which all branches of the art are taught. The first chair in music in any university in the U.S.A. was occupied at Harvard by J. K. Paine (q.v.) from 1875 to 1905—a period that was very fruitful.

Articles upon cognate subjects in this volume are: *Appreciation of Music*; *Sight-Singing*; *Tonic Sol-fa*; *Pianoforte Playing and Teaching*; *Degrees and Diplomas*; *Broadcasting*; *Memory*; *Society for the Advancement of Musical Education*.

Edward. See *Loewe*.

Edwards, Richard (b. Somerset abt. 1523; d. London 1566). Master of the Children of the Chapel Royal; wrote poems, of which one is quoted by Shakespeare in *Romeo and Juliet* ('When griping grief'); acted a play before Queen Elizabeth who was highly pleased with it; wrote a book of 'comic short stories' (unfortunately lost); composed the early madrigal, *In going to my naked bed*.

E.F.D.S.S. English Folk Dance and Song Soc. (q.v.).

Effects. A very comprehensive dance-band term applied to imitative instruments, such as baby-cry, cock-crow, horse-trot, locomotive, sleigh-bells, &c.—and even nose-blow!

Effleurer (Fr.). 'To touch very lightly.'

Égal, égale (Fr. masc., fem.). 'Equal.' So *également*, 'equally'.

Egdon Heath. Symphonic Poem by Holst (op. 47). Inspired by Thomas Hardy's description, in *The Return of the Native*, of a lonely mysterious Dorset plain. Its sub-title is 'Homage to Thomas Hardy'. (1st perf. New York, Cheltenham, and London 1928.)

Egk, Werner (b. Bavaria 1901). Composer and conductor (some years Berlin State Opera). Director of Berlin Hochschule 1950–3. President German Composers' Soc. See *Peer Gynt*.

Églogue (Fr.). 'Eclogue' (q.v.).

Egmont Overture. From Beethoven's Incidental Music (op. 84; 1810) for a performance of Goethe's historical drama of *Egmont*—the Flemish noble who withstood Philip of Spain and was beheaded by the Duke of Alva (1567).

Eguale (It.). 'Equal.' So *egualità*, *egualezza*, 'equality'; and *egualmente*, 'equally'. *Voci eguali*, 'equal voices' (q.v.).

Egyptian Ballet. See *Luigini*.

Egyptian Helen (Strauss). See *Ägyptische Helena*.

Ehlers, Alice (b. Vienna 1890). Pianist (pupil of Leschetizky) and harpsichordist (pupil of Landowska). Many tours in Europe and U.S.A.: now resident California.

E.H. Short for *Englisches Horn* (Ger.), i.e. Cor anglais (see *Oboe Family*).

Ehre Gottes, Die (Beethoven). See *Creation's Hymn*.

Ehrling, Sixten (b. Malmö 1918). Pianist and conductor. Trained Stockholm Conserv.; Stockholm Opera 1944; Detroit Orch. 1964.

Eichheim, Henry (b. Chicago 1870; d. nr. Santa Barbara, Calif., 1942). Violinist in Boston Symphony Orch. 1890–1912; composer of chamber music, piano pieces, songs, &c., influenced by his numerous visits to the Far East.

Eifer (Ger.). 'Zeal', 'ardour'. **Eifrig.** 'Zealous', i.e. ardent in style.

Eighteen-twelve (1812) Overture. Concert-overture by Tchaikovsky (op. 49; 1880), vividly and noisily recalling the repulse of Napoleon's invasion of

Russia in 1812. Original idea was performance in a public square in Moscow, with an enormous orch., a brass band, the cathedral bells, and cannon.

Eighth Note. 'Quaver' (see Table 3).

Eile (Ger.). 'Haste.'

Eileen Aroon. See *Robin Adair*. Thomas Moore (q.v.), in his Irish Melodies, set to the original *Eileen Aroon* tune the lyric 'Erin, the tear and the smile'.

Eilen (Ger.). 'To hurry'; hence *eilend*, 'hurrying' (i.e. *accelerando*). *Eilig*, 'speedy'.

Ein, Eine (Ger. masc., fem.; various terminations according to grammatical case—*em, en, er, es*). 'One', 'A'.

Eine kleine Nachtmusik (Mozart). See under *Kleine*.

Einem, Gottfried von (b. Berne 1918). Trained Berlin, resident Salzburg. Composer of opera *Dantons Tod* (q.v.), also orch. and chamber music.

Einfach (Ger.). 'Simple', 'single'.

Ein' feste Burg (in Eng. 'A Safe Stronghold'). Hymn of Luther; tune adapted by him from a plainsong melody. Much used by composers, e.g. in Meyerbeer's *The Huguenots*, Mendelssohn's *Reformation Symphony*, and Wagner's *Kaisermarsch*.

Einige (Ger., various terminations according to gender, number, case). 'Some.'

Einlenken (Ger., verb or noun). 'To turn back', or 'a turning back'.

Einmal (Ger.). 'Once.'

Einstein, Alfred (b. Munich 1880; d. El Cerrito, Calif., 1952). Eminent musicologist; Ph.D., Munich (thesis on Ger. repertory for viola da gamba). Ed. of 9th to 11th edns. Riemann's *Musiklexikon* 1919–29; music critic in Berlin and ed. of *Zeitschrift für Musikwissenschaft* 1918–33. In London and Italy 1933–8; U.S.A. 1939. Some years Prof. of Music Smith Coll., Northampton, Mass. Many valuable books (*The Italian Madrigal*, 1949) and reviser of Köchel's catalogue of Mozart's works. See *Köchel*.

Einstimmig (Ger.). 'One-voiced', i.e. for one part.

Eintritt (Ger.). 'Entrance', 'beginning'.

Einzeln (Ger.). 'Single.'

Eis (Ger.). E sharp (see Table 7).

Eisenberg, Maurice (b. Königsberg 1900). Violoncellist. Trained Peabody Conserv., then pupil of Becker, Klengel, Casals, &c. Début with Philadelphia Orch. 1916: then member of that orch. European tours. On staff Paris École Normale 1929. Returned U.S.A. 1937.

Eisis (Ger.). E double sharp—if that note exists anywhere (see Table 7).

Eisler, Hanns (b. Leipzig 1898; d. Berlin 1962). Pupil of Schönberg; first came into notice as composer of work for voices and piano called *Newspaper Cuttings* and then wrote other 'musical cartoons' based on current events; when Nazis took power all his published compositions were destroyed; from 1937 resident in New York and Hollywood, producing compositions of various types, including film music. In 1948 he was deported and returned to Europe.

Eisteddfod (plur. *Eisteddfodau*). The word means a session (from *eistedd*, 'to sit'). The national Welsh gathering of this name is one of bards, and dates in its present form from 1817, though it is said to date back, in one form or another, as far as the 7th c. with a break during the complete 18th c. and a few years before and after it. It now takes place annually in one Welsh town or another. Degrees of *Ofydd* (Ovate), *Bardd* (Bard), and *Pencerdd* (Chief Musician) are conferred on candidates who pass various tests and there is also a strong choral and competitive side to the gathering. Many local Eisteddfodau also exist, and these are purely of the nature of Competition Festivals. 'International Eisteddfodau' have been held annually from 1947.

Eitner, Robert (b. Breslau 1832; d. nr. Berlin 1905). Distinguished musicologist. Works include standard Biographical-bibliographical Dictionary (10 vols. 1900–4), &c.

Élan (Fr.). 'Dash', in the sense of impetuosity.

Élargir (Fr.). 'To broaden', i.e. to take more slowly. So *élargi*, 'broadened'; *élargissant*, 'broadening'; *élargissez*, 'broaden' (imperative).

El Capitán. See *Sousa*.

Electric Action. See *Organ* 1.

Electric Musical Instruments. Electricity is used in one type of Pianola as a motive power (see *Mechanical Reproduction of Music* 13) and in many pipe organs as a communicating power (see *Organ*); it is also used in a more subtle way, in Gramophone (Phonograph) recording and reproducing (see *Gramophone or Phonograph*). The present consideration of the subject does not concern such applications of electricity as these, but (*a*) instruments which use electrical vibrations transmitted through the ether, and (*b*) instruments which use such vibrations in materials in the instrument itself (which latter might be called 'semi-electric').

(1) ETHER WAVE INSTRUMENTS. The general principle of all these instruments is the employment of electronic valve oscillators, sometimes employed singly, more often 'heterodyning' or 'beating' together, i.e. the combining of 2 electric currents of which the vibrations differ in frequency. The rapidity of the vibration of the component currents is, in itself, far too great to produce the phenomenon we call 'sound' (cf. *Acoustics* 15), but the conflict (or 'interference') of the 2 produces 'beats' of a lower rapidity (cf. the production of 'differential tones', under *Acoustics* 14) and when these are passed to a loud-speaker sound is created. Apparently all instruments embodying this principle include also a means of amplifying the vibrations on the lines of the loud-speaker of a broadcasting set or an electric gramophone. Amongst instruments in some way applying the principle have been the following: *c.* 1924, Mager's *Spherophone*; 1927, Thérémin's *Etherophone*, *Thérémin*, or *Théréminovox*; *c.* 1930, Langer and Halmagyi's *Emicon*; Trautwein's *Trautonium*; *c.* 1932, Martenot's *Ondium Martenot*, or *Ondes Musicales*; Obouhof's *Croix Sonore*; 1933, The *Mellertion*; Bertrand's *Dynaphone*; Taubmann's *Electronde*; 1936, Helberger

and Lertes's *Hellertion*; 1938, Mager's *Partiturophone*; The Wurlitzer *Electronic Piano*. Some of these are purely melodic, others not so limited. Some are designed to produce microtones (q.v.); one, the *Mellertion*, is built to a 10-division 8ve instead of the normal 12-division one.

(2) SEMI-ELECTRIC BOWED AND PLUCKED INSTRUMENTS. The *Vierling Violin and Violoncello* are played in the usual way but the tone amplification is effected not by a sound-board but by being picked up by electro-magnets or electric condensers and conveyed to an amplifier (similar to that of a radio set) and issued through a loud-speaker. The *Allen Instruments* (U.S.A.) are on much the same lines; they comprise complete sets of stringed instruments, both bowed and plucked. The 5-string violoncello of Karapetoff and the *Electrofonic Violin* of Moss and Bartley apply similar principles. The Fr. *Radiotone* (about 1931) has a keyboard by means of the mechanism attached to which a single metal string is 'stopped' at various points. The string is vibrated by revolving circular 'bows', and is thus made to affect electro-magnets, which, in turn, affect amplifiers and a loud-speaker: this instrument can, if desired, be built into an organ. *Electric Guitars, Mandolines*, &c., have been on the market since 1936 or a little earlier.

(3) SEMI-ELECTRIC PIANOS. The pioneer in this field was Nernst, of Berlin, whose principles are applied in various ways in the instruments now to be mentioned.

In the *Neo-Bechstein Piano* (1931) the strings are set in vibration by hammers (but with less force than in the normal instrument): there is no sound-board, the vibrations being picked up and amplified (on the lines of a radio set), and then, turned into sound vibrations again, given out from a loud-speaker cabinet. The volume or tone is controlled by a pedal acting on the amplifier and, even on a single note or chord, can be swelled or diminished at will. The quality of tone can be adjusted to the taste of the purchaser by changes of the relative strength of the harmonics (see *Acoustics* 6, 7). These are the main principles; details cannot be gone into here. The *Vierling Piano* appears to be constructed on somewhat the same principles and so, too, the *Electrochord*, which applies patents of Vierling. The *Miessner Piano* is similar but has a system of buttons and dials for the amplification of particular sets of harmonics (see *Acoustics* 6, 7), thus producing changes of timbre. Several of the above instruments admit of a broadcasting set and a gramophone being built in.

(4) ELECTRIC ORGANS, &c. Electrophonic organs of various makes are now in use. These produce their tone not from pipes but by means of rotating disks with pick-ups. The latter may work on the electro-magnetic, or electro-static, principle. The pioneers in this type of instrument seem to have been Coupleux and Givelet. The Amer. Ranger exhibited such an organ, the *Rangertone*, in 1931, and in 1935 the Hammond Co. of Chicago put on the market the *Hammond Organ*, which has been widely taken up. Comptons, of London, have also pipeless organs on sale. The *Orgatron* of the Everette Piano Co., New Haven, Mich., is also a pipeless instrument. The *Novachord* is a domestic instrument which claims to reproduce the tone of the organ or almost any other instrument: it employs a series of Thermionic valves.

(5) INSTRUMENTS USING THE PHOTO-ELECTRIC CELL. These are operated from a keyboard. The *Rhythmicon*, or *Poly-rhythmophone* is the joint invention of Thérémin (see 1) and the Amer. composer Cowell: it is really a new variety of percussion instrument. The *Photona* is a 2-manual keyboard instrument in which the tones are produced by rotating disks inserted between a light-source and a photo-electric cell. Other instruments employing the photo-electric cell are Spielman's *Super-Piano* and the *Welte Photophone*. The *Sound-film* is briefly alluded to under *Gramophone* 4. Cf. *Musique Concrète*.

Electrochord. See *Electric Musical Instruments* 3.

Electrofonic violin. See *Electric Musical Instruments* 2.

Electronde. See *Electric Musical Instruments* 1.

Electrone. One name for the *Electrophonic Organ* (see *Electric Musical Instruments* 4).

Electronic. See *Electrophonic*.

Electrophone. (1) Form of telephone from theatres and music halls to the home (in use from the 1880's to the advent of radio broadcasting). (2) Instrument using electric bells, invented and written for by the Dutch composer, Daniel Ruyneman (b. 1886).

Electrophonic, Electrotonic (sometimes mangled into *Electronic*, which properly would have a more general signification). Applied to methods of producing tone electrically, i.e. without strings, pipes, &c. See *Electric Musical Instruments*.

Electrophonic Organ (or 'Electronic' Organ). See *Electric Musical Instruments* 4.

Elegantemente (It.). 'Elegantly.'

Elegia, elegiaco (It.). 'Elegy' 'elegiac' (see below).

Élégie (Fr.), **Elegy.** A song of lament or an instrumental composition with that suggestion.

Elegy for Young Lovers. Opera by Henze. Libretto by Auden and Kallman. (Prod. Schwetzingen 1961.)

Elektra. 1-act opera by Richard Strauss. Libretto, by Hofmannsthal, based on Sophocles. (Prod. Dresden 1909; New York and London 1910.)

Element, Ernest (b. Wolverhampton 1909). Violinist. Studied with Paul Beard (q.v.), Henry Holst (q.v.), and Flesch (q.v.), afterwards holding positions in Brit. orchs. (chief violin many years City of Birmingham Orch.). Also prominent in chamber music.

Elevatio (Lat.), **Elevation** (Eng.). Music (choral or organ) performed during the Elevation of the Host in the Roman Catholic Church is known by this name.

Elevato (It.). 'Elevated' in spirit.

Elevazione (It.). 'Elevation' (of spirit).

Élève (Fr.). 'Pupil.'

Elfenreigen. See *Reigen*.

Elgar, Edward (William) (b. Broadheath, nr. Worcester, 1857; d. Worcester 1934). Son of a Worcester organist and music-seller. Long a violinist and violin teacher, but gradually came forward as composer, the Eng. fest. system giving him his chance to do so; at 42 his *Enigma Variations* placed him in the first rank; next year the oratorio *The Dream of Gerontius* revealed him (a Roman Catholic) as a composer of a distinctively mystical turn of mind. *The Apostles* and *The Kingdom* emphasized this. His many orch. works include symphony in A flat (1908), violin concerto (1910), symphony in E flat (1911), 'symphonic study' *Falstaff* (1913), 'cello concerto (1919), songs, part-songs, chamber music, &c. A distinctively Brit. composer, temporarily welcomed in other countries, only to fall into the background of public consciousness there at a later date. His music has both tenderness and nobility and is masterly in orchestration.

Prof. of Music in Birmingham Univ. 1905–8. Many hon. degrees; knighthood 1904; Order of Merit 1911; K.C.V.O. 1928; baronetcy 1931, &c.

See also *Apostles*; *Banner of St. George*; *Black Knight*; *Caractacus*; *Carillon*; *Cockaigne*; *Dream of Gerontius*; *Enigma Variations*; *Falstaff*; *Froissart*; *Go, song of mine*; *Grania and Diarmid*; *Greek Anthology*; *In the South*; *Kingdom*; *King Olaf*; *Light of Life*; *Music Makers*; *Nursery Suite*; *Polonia*; *Pomp and Circumstance*; *Scenes from the Bavarian Highlands*; *Sea Pictures*; *Severn Suite*; *Spirit of England*; *Starlight Express*; *Wand of Youth*.

Eli. Oratorio by Costa. (1st perf. Birmingham Fest. 1855.) *The March of the Israelites* from this work was long popular with amateur pianists.

Elias ('Elijah'). See *Mendelssohn*.

Elijah. See *Mendelssohn*.

Elinson, Iso (b. Moghileff, Russia, 1907; d. London 1964). Pianist. Studied Petrograd Conserv.; became Brit. subject. Gave numerous recitals espec. of Beethoven complete sonatas, Bach '48', &c. On staff Royal Manchester Coll. Mus.

Elisir d'amore, L' ('The Lovepotion'). 2-act comedy-opera by Donizetti. Libretto by Romani, after Scribe. (Prod. Milan 1832; London 1836; Dublin and New York 1838.)

Elkin & Co. Ltd. London music publishing firm (20 Kingly St., W. 1).

Ella, John. See *Annotated Programmes*.

Ellerton, John Lodge (b. Cheshire 1801; d. London 1873). Prolific and once popular composer (7 It. operas, 2 Ger., 2 Eng.; 6 masses; 6 symphonies; over 60 songs; over 60 glees; over 40 string quartets, &c., all now entirely forgotten except by the compilers of works of reference).

Ellington, 'Duke' (Edward Kennedy Ellington, b. 1899). Famous Amer. Negro jazz composer and pianist.

Ellis, Alexander John—original name Sharpe (b. London 1814; there d. 1890). Author of important books on phonetics and acoustics, especially pitch (yet stated to be tone-deaf, working entirely by calculation). Translator of *Sensations of Tone* by Helmholtz (q.v.). Sixth Wrangler and D.Sc., Cambridge; F.R.S., &c.

Elman, Mischa (b. Russia 1891; d. New York 1967). Violinist. Pupil of Auer. Began world fame at age 13. Publ. some compositions.

Éloigner (Fr.). 'To put farther away.' So *s'éloignant* 'getting farther away'.

El Salón México. Orch. piece by Copland. Based on popular Mexican melodies. (Prod. by Mexico Symphony Orch. 1937.)

Elvey, (1) **George Job** (b. Canterbury 1816; d. Windlesham, Surrey, 1893). Organist of St. George's Chapel, Windsor Castle, 1835–82, and composer of services and anthems. D.Mus., Oxford. Knighted 1871. (2) **Stephen** (b. Canterbury 1805; d. Oxford 1860). Brother of George, above. D.Mus., Oxford, organist of New Coll., St. John's Coll., and the Univ. Church. His pointed psalter attained wide use. Some church music still performed.

Elwell, Herbert (b. Minneapolis 1898). Pupil of Bloch (q.v.) and Nadia Boulanger (q.v.). U.S.A. Rome Prize 1926. Then on staff Cleveland Inst. and Music Critic *Cleveland Plain Dealer*. Many and varied compositions.

Elwes, Gervase Cary (b. nr. Northampton, England, 1866; killed by train in station of Boston, Mass., 1921). Tenor vocalist; pupil of Bouhy, Victor Beigel, &c. Of high artistic aims and reputation in oratorio and recitals. (Gervase Elwes Fund, to perpetuate memory, became present Musicians' Benevolent Fund, q.v.)

Elyot, Sir Thomas. See *Education* 2.

Embouchure. In the playing of brass instruments and the flute, the mode of application of the lips, or their relation to the mouthpiece. (But in the original Fr. use the word means also the mouthpiece itself.)

Emerald Isle, The. Posthumous Comic Opera by Sullivan, completed by Edward German. Libretto by Basil Hood. (Prod. Savoy Theatre 1901.)

Emer's Farewell. See *Londonderry Air.*

Emicon. See *Electric Musical Instruments* 1.

Emmanuel, Maurice—in full Marie François Maurice (b. Bar-sur-Aube 1862; d. Paris 1938). Learned musicologist and active composer of operas, symphonies, chamber music, &c.

Emmett, Daniel Decatur (b. Mount Vernon, Ohio, 1815; there d. 1904). Printer's devil, soldier, member of a circus troupe, and founder of the first group of comedians with blackened faces ('Negro Minstrels', q.v.); composer of *Dixie* (q.v.), *Old Dan Tucker*, and similar songs.

Emozione (It.). 'Emotion.'

Emperor Concerto (Beethoven). Piano Concerto in E flat, op. 73 (1809). Origin of the Eng. nickname uncertain; it is unknown in Germany.

Emperor Jones, The. See *Gruenberg.*

Emperor Quartet (Haydn). See *Emperor's Hymn* and *Kaiserquartett.*

Emperor's Hymn ('Gott erhalte Franz den Kaiser', i.e. 'God preserve the Emperor Francis'—the tune being found in many hymn-books under the name *Austria*. This was the national hymn of Austria from the time of the composition of the tune by Haydn (1797) to the setting up of the Republic in 1918, and after that the tune was officially retained, but other words adopted—those of Ottokar Kernstock, *Sei gesegnet ohne Ende* ('Thine be never-ending blessings'). The original

words were by Lorenz Leopold Haschka (1749–1827). Haydn, whose instructions were to compose something approaching in merit the Eng. *God save the King*, took one of the Croatian folk melodies of his childhood, which probably suggested itself to him as fitting metrically and rhythmically the opening lines, and altered and extended its later part. He used this tune as the basis of a set of variations in his string quartet in C usually numbered as op. 76 no. 3 (hence called 'Kaiser' Quartet or 'Emperor' Quartet). For the application of the tune in Germany see *Deutschland über Alles.*

Empfindung (Ger.). 'Feeling', 'sentiment'; hence *Empfindungsvoll*, 'feelingly'.

Emphase (Fr., Ger.). 'Emphasis.'

Emporté (Fr. 'Carried away'). 'Excitedly.'

Empressé (Fr.). 'Eager.'

Ému (Fr.). 'Moved', 'affected' (in the sense of 'touched').

En (Fr.). 'In', 'whilst', &c. Used in such expressions as, *en accélérant*, 'accelerating'; *en rondeau*, 'in rondo style', &c.

Enchaînez (Fr., lit. 'Chain together'). 'Join up' (i.e. next movement to be played without break).

Enchanted Grove (Ballet). See *Tombeau de Couperin.*

Enclume (Fr.). 'Anvil' (see *Percussion Family* 2 s).

Encore in Fr. means 'again', and in Eng. has been adopted as the word of demand for the repetition of a performance (properly, perhaps, of the same piece, but it is often used of a mere return to the platform to give additional performance, whether of the same or another piece). The verb 'to encore' has also come into use.

Although, as above stated, the word 'encore' is Fr., its entry into the Eng. language was by corruption of the It. *ancora* (with the same meaning), which word, from the early 18th-c. onwards, was in use amongst the audience of the It. Opera in London (indifferently with the words *altra volta*, 'another time'). The word the Fr. themselves use is *bis* (Lat. 'twice'), with the verb *bisser*. An inhuman demand is sometimes made upon the generosity and physical endurance of a soloist who has concluded a heavy concerto and is then expected to sit down again and play one or more solo pieces.

End-plugged. See *Organ* 2.

Energia (It.). 'Energy.' So *energico*, 'energetic'.

Enesco, Georges (orig. George Enescu; b. Dorohoiû, Rumania 1881; d. Paris 1955). Music student and orch. violinist in Vienna; then studied at Paris Conserv. under Marsick, Fauré, and Massenet, and developed into a brilliant virtuoso and able teacher (one of the teachers of Menuhin) as well as a successful composer, with a personal style, to some extent influenced by the folk music of his native country.

Enfance du Christ (Berlioz). See *Childhood*.

Enfant et les sortilèges, L'. 1-act 'Fantaisie lyrique' by Ravel. Libretto by Colette. (Prod. Monte Carlo 1925; Paris 1926.)

Enfant prodigue, L' ('The Prodigal Son'). (1) DEBUSSY's Prix de Rome Cantata, 1884. (Prod. as 1-act opera London and Boston 1910 and subsequently in many countries.) (2) Wordless Play with Music by WORMSER. (Prod. Paris 1890; London 1891.) (3) There have been one or two operas with this name, e.g. AUBER's (Paris 1850). (4) Ballet by PROKOFIEF (Paris 1929).

Enfasi (It.). 'Emphasis.'

Enfatico; Enfaticamente (It.). 'Emphatic'; 'Emphatically'.

Engedi (Beethoven). See *Christ on the Mount of Olives*.

Engel, Carl I (b. nr. Hanover 1818; d. London 1882). Pianist and teacher who settled in London and wrote books on piano playing, &c. Became great authority on ancient musical instruments.

Carl II (unrelated to I: b. Paris 1883; d. New York 1944). Studied at universities of Strasbourg and Munich,

migrated to U.S.A. and engaged in music publishing (especially with Schirmer, of New York); ed. *Musical Quarterly* (q.v.) and served as chief of Music Division of Library of Congress, Washington (1921–35). Active in promoting musicological research.

Engelstimme (Ger. 'Angel-voice'). The *Vox Angelica* stop on the organ.

Enger (Ger. 'Narrower'). 'Drawn together', i.e. 'quicker'.

Englisches Horn (Ger.). 'English horn', i.e. *Cor anglais* (see *Oboe Family*).

English Concertina. See *Reed-Organ Family* 4.

English Fingering. See *Fingering*.

English Folk Dance and Song Society. A combination, dating from 1932, of the Eng. Folk Song Soc. (founded 1898) and the Eng. Folk Dance Soc. (founded 1911). Headquarters are at Cecil Sharp House, North London. There are many local branches in different parts of the country. English Folk Festivals, on a large scale, are held annually in the Royal Albert Hall, and a journal and magazine are published.

See also *Folk Song*; *Broadwood, Lucy*; *Kidson, Frank*; *Sharp, Cecil*; *Howes, Frank*.

English Guitar. See *Cittern*.

English Horn. See *Oboe Family*.

English Hymnal. See *Hymns and Hymn Tunes* 4.

English Opera. See *Opera* 5.

English Opera Group. Non-profit-making company founded 1947 by Benjamin Britten, Eric Crozier (writer), and John Piper (painter). One aim is 'To encourage composers to write for the operatic stage and poets and playwrights to tackle the problem of writing libretti in collaboration with composers'. Has carried out performances (operas, festivals, and concerts) in various parts of Britain and also abroad. Managed by Covent Garden from 1961.

English Schools Music Association. This now carries on the work of the Tonic Sol-fa Assoc. (founded by John Curwen in 1853). The annual festivals are continued, at which some thousands of children are assembled (long at the Crystal Palace; then at the Alexandra Palace).

English Singers, The. Group of 6 able vocalists founded (1920) for public perf. of Eng. madrigals. Travelled widely on both sides Atlantic. Later re-formed as 'New English Singers' and then 'English Singers Quartet'.

English Suites. Set of 6 Keyboard Suites by Bach, posthumously published. Title seems to have arisen from the existence in the possession of Bach's youngest son, John Christian, of a MS. copy of which the 1st movement of the 1st suite bore the unexplained words *fait pour les Anglais* ('made for the English'). Cf. *French Suites* and *German Suites*.

English Terminology of Music (compared with American). See *American Terminology*.

Enharmonic Interval. See *Interval*.

Enigma. Orch. 'Variations on an Original Theme', by Elgar (op. 36; 1899), sketching the idiosyncrasies of 13 friends, and of the composer himself. His explanation of the title is: 'Through and over the whole set, another and larger theme "goes", but is not played.' Many ingenious guesses have been made at the identity of this mysterious, unheard theme.

Enlevez (Fr. 'Take up'). 'Remove' (e.g. pedal or mute).

Enoch & Sons. London music publishing firm (19 Hanover Sq., W. 1). Estd. 1869. Now merged in Ashdown (q.v.).

En Saga ('A Saga'). Symphonic Poem of Sibelius (op. 9; 1892, revised 1901). No clue is offered as to the poetic details represented.

Ensalada (Sp. 'salad'). Kind of comic choral *quodlibet* (q.v.) in the 16th c. and later.

Ensemble (Fr. 'together'). (1) Any combination of performers, but especially one-to-a-part combinations. (2) The quality in perf. implying the greater or lesser exhibition of the co-operative spirit, with unanimity of attack, 'give and take', and balance of tone; so such expressions as 'Good ensemble' and 'Poor ensemble'.

A *Morceau d'ensemble* (e.g. in an opera) is a piece in which several performers combine.

Entendre (Fr.). 'To hear.' So *entendu*, *entendue* (masc., fem.), 'heard'.

Entfernt (Ger.). 'Distant' (in reality or effect). So *Entfernung*, 'distance'.

Entführung aus dem Serail, Die ('The Escape from the Seraglio'). Ger. Opera by Mozart. (Prod. Vienna 1782; London 1827 as *The Seraglio*; Brooklyn 1860.) See *Singspiel*.

Entr'acte (Fr.). Interval between the acts, or music then performed.

Entrada (Sp.). Same as *Entrée* (q.v.).

Entrain (Fr.). 'Vigour', 'dash', 'go'.

Entrata (It.). 'Entrance', or 'beginning'.

Entrechat (Fr.). In ballet, a vertical jump into the air, during which the feet are repeatedly crossed.

Entrée (Fr.). (1) A 17th- and 18th-c. term for an instrumental piece before a ballet. (2) An act in an opera-ballet of which every act is self-contained (in this use a corruption of *entremets*, 'side-dish', an old title for a sort of masque). (3) The moment of opening of any part of a work.

Entremes (Sp.). (1) A comic musical intermezzo in a play. (2, later use) A type of brief humorous independent play.

Entrückung (Ger. the state of absence, hence of being rapt away). 'Rapture.'

Entschieden (Ger.). (1) 'Decided', 'resolute'. (2) 'Decidedly', i.e. considerably.

Entschlossen (Ger.). 'Determined' in style. So *Entschlossenheit*, 'determination'.

Entusiasmo (It.). 'Enthusiasm.' So *entusiastico*, 'enthusiastic'.

Enunciation. See *Form* 3.

Éolides, Les. Symphonic Poem by Franck (1876), based on the poem by

Leconte de Lisle, an evocation of the flight of the breezes over Southern lands.

Epidiapente (Ger.). A term used in connexion with canon (q.v.)—'At the fifth'.

Epiglottis. The cartilage at the root of the tongue, which during swallowing covers and protects the vocal cords.

Episode. See *Form* 4, 7.

Episodical Form. Another name for rondo form (see *Form* 4).

Epithalamium. Marriage song.

Éponge, Baguette d' (Fr.). Sponge-headed drum-stick.

Equabile (It.). 'Equable.'

Equale (It., plur. *equali*, but in modern It. these words would be *eguale, eguali*). (1) Equal. (2) 18th-c. term for a funeral quartet of trombones or music for such (e.g. Beethoven's).

Equal Temperament. See *Temperament*.

Equal Voices (It. *Voci eguali*; Lat. *Voces aequales*; Ger. *Gleiche Stimmen*). A choral composition is said to be for 'equal voices' when it is for voices of the same kind, generally for 2 sopranos, or 3 sopranos (school music and music for ladies' choirs). In such music, in fairness to the voices of the performers, the parts are usually so arranged that sometimes one voice and sometimes another is at the top. Occasionally the term is less correctly used as implying 'for children's voices' (unmixed with adults), or 'for women's voices' (unmixed with men's), or 'for men's voices' (unmixed with women's).

Équivaut (Fr.). 'Is equivalent to.'

Érard. Paris piano-making and harp-making firm; estd. abt. 1780 (London branch 1786). See *Harp*.

Erede, Alberto (b. Genoa 1908). Conductor. Trained Univ. of Genoa and Basle Conserv., where pupil of Weingartner (q.v.). Associate conductor (with Fritz Busch) Glyndebourne 1934–9; musical director Salzburg Opera Guild 1935–8; It. Radio Orch. 1945–6; musical director and conductor New London Opera Co.

1946–8; on staff Metropolitan, New York, 1950–6; then in Germany.

Ergriffen (Ger.). 'Gripped', or emotionally moved. So *Ergriffenheit*, 'emotion'.

Erhaben (Ger.). 'Sublime'; hence *Erhabenheit*, 'sublimity'.

Erlanger, (Baron) Frédéric d' (b. Paris 1868; d. London 1943). Son of Ger. father and Amer. mother; himself naturalized Brit. subject. Composed operas, &c. (at first under name Frédéric Regnal).

Erleichterung (Ger.). An 'easing', i.e. a simplified version.

Erl King, The (*Der Erlkönig*). Poem by Goethe, set by a number of composers, including —(1) SCHUBERT, 1815; the famous setting with the vigorous piano accompaniment. (2) LOEWE, 1818. (3) J. F. REICHARDT, praised by Mendelssohn as the finest setting. (4) CORONA SCHRÖTER; a very simple and unimportant setting, 1782 (apparently the earliest setting of all).

Erlkönig. See *Erl King*.

Erlöschend (Ger.). 'Becoming weaker.'

Ermangelung (Ger.). 'Default', i.e. lack.

Ermattend, ermattet (Ger.). [As if] 'Becoming tired out', 'tired out'.

Ernani. Tragic opera by Verdi, after V. Hugo. (Prod. Venice 1844; London 1845; New York and Boston 1847.)

Erniedrigen (Ger.). 'To lower' (pitch).

Ernst, ernsthaft (Ger.). 'Earnest', 'serious'.

Ernst, Wilhelm—in full Heinrich Wilhelm (b. Brünn, otherwise Brno, Moravia, 1814; d. Nice 1865). As young violinist followed Paganini from town to town studying his methods, and later himself won high fame as a virtuoso of his instrument, for which he composed many works, some of them still in use.

Ero e Leandro ('Hero and Leander'). Opera by Mancinelli. Libretto by Boito. (Prod. in concert form at Norwich Fest. 1896; as opera in

Madrid 1897; London 1898; New York 1899.) Also an Opera by Bottesini (1879).

Eroica Symphony, or Sinfonia Eroica (Beethoven). The 3rd (in E flat, op. 55; 1804). The title is authentic. It was in the first MS. called *Bonaparte*, the title-page being indignantly torn off when the composer received the news that the 'hero' had become Emperor.

Eroica Variations (Beethoven). Another name for *Prometheus Variations* (q.v.).

Eroico, eroica (It. masc., fem.). 'Heroic.'

Erotikon (Gr.). 'Love-song.'

Ersatz (Ger.). 'Substitute' (noun).

Erschüttert (Ger.). 'Shaken', i.e. agitated.

Erst, erste (Ger. masc., fem.; various terminations according to grammatical case—*em, en, er, es*). 'First.'

Ersterbend (Ger.). 'Dying away.'

Erste Walpurgisnacht (Mendelssohn). See *First Walpurgis Night*.

Erstickt (Ger.). 'Suffocated', 'stifled'.

Erwartung ('Suspense'). Schönberg's orch. accomp. Monodrama (1909) for solo Sop.; text by Marie Pappenheim. 1st perf. I.S.C.M. (Prague) 1924.

Erweitert (Ger.). 'Widened', 'broadened' (i.e. slower and with steadiness).

Erzähler (Ger. 'Narrator'). Soft organ stop of 8-foot length and pitch: a variety of *Gemshorn* (q.v.). The 2nd harmonic (see *Acoustics* 7) should be almost as strong as the fundamental.

Erzürnt (Ger.). 'Irritated.'

Es (Ger.). E flat (see Table 7). Also the pronoun 'it'.

Esaltato (It.). 'Excited', 'exalted'.

Esatto, esatta (It. masc., fem.). 'Exact.' So *esattezza*, 'exactness'.

Escape from the Seraglio (Mozart). See *Entführung*.

Escape Tone. See under *Changing Note*.

Esecuzione (It.). 'Execution.'

Esercizio, esercizi (It.). 'Exercise', 'exercises'.

Eses (Ger.). E double flat (see Table 7).

Eskdale, George (b. Tynemouth 1897; d. London 1960). Internationally known trumpet virtuoso. Trained Kneller Hall (q.v.). Then in chief London orchs. (L.S.O. from 1932) and on staff R.A.M.

Esmeralda. Opera by Goring Thomas (q.v.). Other operas of this name by Dargomijsky (1847), &c.

Esotica, esotica (It. masc., fem.). 'Exotic.'

Espagne (Fr.). 'Spain.' **Espagnol, Espagnole** (Fr. masc., fem.), **Espagnolo** or **Espagnuolo, Espagnola** or **Espagnuola** (It. masc., fem.). 'Spanish.'

España. See *Chabrier*.

Espirando (It.). 'Expiring', 'dying away'.

Esplá, Oscar (b. Alicante 1886). Has been principal of the Conservatory of Madrid, and composed orch. works, ballets, operas, &c., influenced by his study of the folk music of eastern Spain, and using as tonal basis a scale of his own devising. Books on musical subjects.

Esposito, Michele (b. nr. Naples 1855, d. Florence 1929). After training at conserv. of his native city went to Paris; then to Dublin (1882), where became chief piano prof. at the Royal Irish Academy of Music, later founding the Dublin Orch. Composer of chamber and orch. music, &c. Hon. D.Mus., Dublin.

Espressione (It.). 'Expression.' **Espressivo.** 'Expressively.'

Esquisse (Fr.). 'Sketch' (q.v.).

Essential Note. An actual note of a chord, as distinct from a Passing Note, Suspension, Appoggiatura, &c. These latter are 'Unessential Notes'.

Essipoff, Annette (b. St. Petersburg 1851; there d. 1914). Pianist. Pupil of Leschetizky (q.v.) and for a period (1880–92) his wife. High international reputation.

Est. See *Este*.

Estampes ('Prints' or 'Engravings'). By Debussy (1903). Set of 3 Piano pieces: (1) *Pagodas*; (2) *Evening in Granada*; (3) *Gardens under Rain*. (The last makes use of 2 traditional Fr. song-tunes, heard through the splash.)

Estampie (Fr.), **Estampida** (Provençal). Type of Troubadour tune for dancing, sometimes with words, in form of a rondeau (q.v.).

Este, or **Easte**, or **East**, or **Est**, (1) **Thomas** (b. abt. 1535; d. abt. 1608). Great music publisher, issuing works of nearly all the Elizabethan madrigalists, books of metrical psalm tunes, &c. (2) **Michael** (b. abt. 1580; d. abt. 1648). Thought to be son of the above. Organist of Lichfield Cathedral and composer of madrigals, anthems, and fancies for viols.

Estey Organ. See *Reed-Organ Family* 7.

Esther. Oratorio by Handel. (1st perf. as Masque, *Haman and Mordecai*, Cannons 1720.)

Estinguendo (It.). 'Extinguishing', i.e. dying away.

Estinto (It. 'extinct'). As soft as possible.

Estompé (Fr.). 'Toned down.'

Estravaganza (It. 'extravagance'). A composition of an erratic type (cf. *Extravaganza*).

Estremamente (It.). 'Extremely.'

Estribillo (Sp.). A choral movement at the beginning or end of a *Villancico* (q.v.).

Estudiantino, estudiantina (Sp. masc., fem.). 'In the spirit or style of a party of students.'

Esultazione (It.). 'Exultation.'

Et (Fr., Lat.). 'And.'

Éteindre (Fr.). 'To extinguish.' So *éteint*, 'extinguished'.

Étendue (Fr. 'extent'). 'Compass', 'range'.

Eterne rex altissime. See *O Salutaris Hostia* ('Eterne' is a medieval spelling of 'Aeterne').

Etherophone. See *Electric Musical Instruments* 1.

Ether Wave Instruments. See *Electric Musical Instruments* 1.

Et incarnatus est. See *Mass*.

Et in Spiritum Sanctum. See *Mass*.

Et in unum Dominum. See *Mass*.

Étoile du nord, L' ('The North Star'). Romantic opera by Meyerbeer. Libretto by Scribe. (Prod. Paris 1854; London 1855; New York 1856.)

Eton College Manuscript. Famous book of choral music at Eton Coll., of date between 1490 and 1504.

Étouffer (Fr. 'To stifle'). 'Damp'—with violin-mute, piano-pedal, &c. The imperative is *étouffez*, the past participle *étouffé*. So *étouffoir*, 'Damper' (piano pedal).

Et resurrexit. See *Mass*.

Étude (Fr. 'study'). Any composition intended as a basis for the improvement of the performer may be so entitled. In piano music the term is especially applied to a short piece restricted to the exploitation of one kind of passage. This type was carried by Chopin into the realm of poetry and so Études suitable for public perf. came into existence.

Études d'exécution transcendante (Liszt). See *Paganini Transcriptions*.

Études en forme de variations (Schumann). See *Études symphoniques*.

Études symphoniques. By Schumann (op. 13, publ. 1837; revised edn. 1852). Full original title (in Fr.) was *Études en forme de Variations (XII Études symphoniques) pour le Pianoforte. Dédiées à son ami William Sterndale Bennett*.

Etwas (Ger.). 'Some', 'something', 'somewhat'.

Euchorics. Brit. name (abt. 1930 onwards) for art of verse-speaking in chorus.

Eugen Onegin. Opera by Tchaikovsky. Libretto based on poem of Pushkin. (Prod. Moscow 1879; London 1892; New York 1920.)

Eulenburg. See *Payne, Albert*.

Eulenstein, Charles (b. Heilbronn, Würtemburg, 1802; d. Styria 1890).

Remarkable virtuoso of the Jew's Harp, touring widely; lived many years in Scotland and England.

Euouae. See *Evovae.*

Euphonium. See *Tuba Group* 2 a.

Eurhythmy (*Eu* = Gr. 'good', 'well'). An activity of followers of the Ger. apostle of 'Anthroposophy', Rudolf Steiner (1861–1925), representing 'the inner movement' of the spoken word or of music 'through the medium of the whole body'. There have been many similar activities with similar names (cf. *Jaques-Dalcroze*).

Euryanthe. Weber's only 'Grand' Opera. (Prod. Vienna 1823; London 1833; New York 1887.)

Eustachian Tubes. Those communicating between the Pharynx (q.v.) and the ear (see *Ear and Hearing*).

Evaded Cadence. See *Cadence.*

Evangelical Canticles. See *Canticles.*

Evangelimann, Der ('The Evangelist'). Extremely successful tragedy-opera by Kienzl. (Prod. Berlin 1895; London 1897; Chicago 1923; New York 1924.)

Evangelist, The (Kienzl). See *Evangelimann.*

Evans, (1) **David Emlyn** (b. Newcastle Emlyn, Wales, 1843; d. London 1913). Composer of church and choral music, &c., and ardent worker for music in Wales; collected Welsh folk tunes and compiled biographical dictionary of Welsh musicians.

(2) **David** (b. Resolven, Glam., 1874; d. Rhos. Denbigh, 1948). Prof. of Music at Univ. Coll., Cardiff, 1908–39, ed. of journal *Y Cerddor* ('The Musician'), and of books of hymn tunes; composer of Welsh choral works, &c. D.Mus., Oxford.

(3) **Edwin I** (b. London 1844; there d. 1923). Organist and author of a large number of books on varied musical subjects.

(4) **Edwin II** (b. London 1874; there d. 1945). Son of the above. Prominent London music critic, with a special interest in all contemporary composition. President of International Soc. for Contemporary Music.

(5) **(Charles) Warwick** (b. London). Violoncellist. Trained R.C.M. Chamber player who has devoted talents to London String Quartet (q.v.), which he founded in 1908.

(6) **Nancy** (b. Liverpool 1915). Operatic mezzo-sop. Covent Garden, Glyndebourne, &c.

(7) **Geraint** (b. Pontypridd 1922). Lyric baritone. Début London 1948; San Francisco 1959; Scala 1960, &c. Notable Figaro, Falstaff, &c. C.B.E. 1959; knighted 1969.

Evans's Supper Rooms. Famous London combination of restaurant and concert hall built 1855; had permanent choir performing nightly; annotated programmes a feature.

Éveillé (Fr.). 'Awakened.'

Evensong. Formerly a synonym for Vespers (q.v.). Also the service of Evening Prayer in the Anglican Church, which is based on the ancient offices of Vespers and Compline (q.v.).

Eventyr—Once upon a Time. Orch. Ballad by Delius, based on Scandinavian fairy-tales. (1st perf. London 1919.)

Everyman. (1) By WALFORD DAVIES. (1st perf. Leeds Fest. 1904.) Oratorio based on medieval Mystery-play. (2) By SIBELIUS (op. 83; 1916). Incidental Music to Hofmannsthal's version of the play. (3) See *Scott, Charles Kennedy.*

Evirato (It. 'Unmanned'). 18th-c. type of male singer whose boy-soprano voice had been preserved by castration; (see *Voice* 5).

Evocación (Sp.). 'Evocation', 'invocation'.

Evovae or **Euouae.** This 'word' consists of the vowels of 'seculorum, Amen', being the last words of the Gloria Patri (see *Doxologia*), and is used as a name for the cadential endings of the Gregorian Psalm tones. These letters are, indeed, often placed under the notes of the plainsong as an abbreviation of the words they represent. Cf. *Aevia.*

Exactement (Fr.). 'Exactly.'

Exalté (Fr.). 'Exalted', 'very excited'.

Exercise. (1) An instrumental passage purely for technical practice and with little or no artistic interest. (2) In the 18th c. a keyboard suite. (3) For the word in its university sense see *Degrees and Diplomas* 1.

Exeter Hall. In Strand, London, 1830–1907. Chief choral centre to 1880 (see *Sacred Harmonic Society*).

Expert, Henry (b. Bordeaux 1863; d. Tourettes-sur-Loup (Alpes Maritimes) 1952). Eminent musicologist, specializing in the Fr. 16th-c. composers.

Exposition. See *Form* 3, 6.

Expressif (Fr.). 'Expressive.'

Expression, we may almost say, is that part of a composer's music which he has no full means of committing to paper and must therefore leave largely to the artistic perception of the performer. Such guidance as he can offer is in the shape of terms roughly indicating the speed to be adopted and the spirit to be expressed, and further, in that of conventional signs such as those shown in Tables 17 and 18 and 22–25. The general convention as to the verbal terms in use is to take them from the It. language, but Fr., Ger., and Brit. composers have at times drawn also on their own languages. Some modern music (and older music as edited by modern musicians) is over-marked, both as to terms and signs—so much so as to become confusing and to defeat its aim.

For a means of indicating speed more precisely than the conventional terms can do, see under *Metronome*: it may, however, be frankly stated that this means has sometimes been carelessly used by composers and indiscreetly used by editors, so that 'metronome marks' at the head of compositions or movements cannot be accepted as sacred. Indeed as regards the observance of any indications of expression some latitude must be allowed to the 'interpreter'; there have been cases where a composer, having heard a performer's rendering of his work, has admitted that though it transgressed in some way his original intention the result was as good as, or even better than, the effect he himself had in mind.

Rubato (q.v.) is a powerful element in 'Expression'—and one which the composer has no means whatever of indicating.

It is exceedingly doubtful whether before the later 18th c. really expressive playing was expected of any combination of choralists or instrumentalists. Bach's very inferior forces at Leipzig and the fact that they were constantly called upon to produce music just written (e.g. the Church Cantatas) must have precluded refinement in perf.; Mozart (as we know from his letters) would sometimes perform a concerto or other elaborate composition completely unrehearsed (e.g. the overture to *Don Giovanni*). The long-common system of leaving the direction of the orch. jointly to the leading violinist and a harpsichordist, with no baton conductor (see *Conducting*), must have made attention to detail impossible. We owe the rise of standard in orch. perf., in the first instance, to Johann Stamitz, at Mannheim, in the 18th c., and in the 19th to the teaching of Berlioz and the example of Wagner and Von Bülow. On the other hand, we cannot but believe that the solo instrumental perf. of such sensitive, accomplished, and inspired musicians as Bach and Mozart was always highly expressive. It would appear, then, that a dual standard existed—one for solo perf. and another for concerted perf.

Expressionism. A term borrowed from the vocabulary of a group of painters who began to come into notice about 1912. These professed to record in paint not impressions of the outer world but their 'inner experiences'. In music the idea of Expressionism seems to be the casting off of rules of every kind, so leaving untrammelled the recording of the 'inner experiences'. Schönberg is regarded as the leading exponent of this theory—which seems a little strange in view of the very formal character of some of his music (his use of the Note-row, q.v., &c.).

Expression Stop. See *Reed-Organ Family* 5.

Expressive Intonation. See *Temperament*.

Extemporization. See *Improvisation*.

Extension Organ. See *Organ* 3.

Extravaganza. Term sometimes applied to musical works of a grotesque or caricatural character (e.g. Gilbert and Sullivan's *Trial by Jury*).

Extrêmement (Fr.). 'Extremely.'

Ezcudantza. Basque fest. dancet for 2 performers with accompaniment of pipe and tabor, and sometimes of voice.

F

Fa. The 4th degree of the major scale, according to the system of vocal syllables derived from Guido d'Arezzo (see *Hexachord*), and so used (spelt *Fah*) in Tonic Sol-fa (also in that system the 6th degree of the minor scale; see *Tonic Sol-fa*). In many countries, however, the name has become attached (on 'fixed-doh' principles; see *Sight-Singing*) to the note F, in whatever key this may occur. (See Table 5; also *Lancashire Sol-fa*.)

Faber, Heinrich. See *Vulpius*.

Faburden (Eng.), **fauxbourdon** (Fr.), **falsobordone** (It.). This term has had a surprisingly large number of different applications at different periods.

(1) In very early use it meant the accompanying of a Plainsong melody with *parallel added parts—in 3rds and 6ths*.

(2) In the 15th c. it meant any added part to such a plainsong melody, the *two moving at the same rate*. It was apparently used especially of such passages interpolated amongst unison singing of the plainsong, e.g. in the psalms.

(3) About the same period it was also used of the same kind of liturgical singing as that mentioned under (2), but without plainsong in any of the voices. (This is sometimes spoken of as *free* Faburden as distinct from the previous type, spoken of as *strict*.)

(4) The name came also to be given to a sort of chanting in which the whole of a phrase was declaimed on one chord, except that the cadence was harmonized as such. (The same music was used for every verse of a psalm, &c., as is done today with the Anglican Chant, q.v.)

(5) The name was also sometimes applied to a sort of monotoning.

(6) And to a drone bass, such as that of a bagpipe.

(7) In 16th- and 17th-c. Eng. usage it was sometimes applied to the tenor part of a metrical psalm tune, &c., which part then usually carried the melody.

(8) It was also applied to a refrain to the verses of a song.

(9) Nowadays (cf. *Descant*) the word is used in Britain for a freely-written soprano part added to a hymn tune whilst the tune itself is sung by the choir's tenors or by the congregation, or (more commonly of recent years) for a 4-part harmonization with the tune in the tenor—this last a revival of the old English practice.

When this word is used in old musical treatises or in modern musical historical works any of the above senses may be intended and the reader should use his discretion.

Cf. *Descant*; *Gymel*.

Façade. By Walton. 'An entertainment for reciting voice and instruments'—21 poems of Edith Sitwell, originally (1923) read through a megaphone to the accompaniment of flute, clarinet, trumpet, saxophone, 'cello, and percussion. Two Orch. Suites later made from the music (1926 and 1938). A selection of the pieces is the music of a very successful ballet.

Fach (Ger.). 'Fold', as *Zweifach* or *2-fach*, 'twofold'; *Dreifach* or *3-fach*, 'threefold'; *Vierfach* or *4-fach*, 'fourfold'. The commonest use of these words is in indicating a division of (say) the first violins of an orch., but there is an organ application indicating the number of ranks in a mixture stop (q.v.).

Fachiri, Adila. See *Aranyi*.

Facile (Fr.). 'Easy.' **Facilement** (Fr.), **facilmente** (It.). 'Easily', i.e. fluently and without an effect of striving.

Facilità (It. 'facility'). (1) 'Ease', 'fluency'. (2) 'Simplification.'

Fackeltanz (Ger.). Properly 'Torch dance', but more often a torchlight procession to music.

Fading or **Fadding.** An Irish dance of the 16th and 17th cs.

Fadinho. Much the same as Fado (q.v.).

Fado. A type of popular Portuguese song and dance with guitar accompaniment, apparently dating from about 1850.

Fa fictum. A term used in connexion with the Hexachords (q.v.)—the note B flattened (in the Soft Hexachord).

Fagan, Gideon (b. Somerset West, S. Africa, 1904). Conductor. Trained South African Coll. of Music and R.C.M. Conductor B.B.C. Northern Orch. 1939–42; Johannesburg Orch. 1949–52. Guest conductor to South African and Brit. orchs. and Musical Director to various London theatrical productions. Some compositions show South African influences.

F.A.G.O. See *Degrees and Diplomas* 4.

Fagott (Ger.), **fagotto** (It.). Bassoon (see *Oboe Family*).

Fagotto. Organ stop, same as *Bassoon* (q.v.).

Fah. See *Fa.*

Fahren (Ger.). 'To go.' So *Fahren sogleich fort*, 'Go on at once'.

Faible (Fr.). 'Feeble', weak in tone.

Fair at Sorochintzy, The. Posthumous Opera by Mussorgsky (various versions completed by other composers). Libretto by composer, based on Gogol. (After a few early incomplete perfs. prod. Petrograd 1917; New York 1930; London 1934.)

Faire (Fr.). 'To do', 'to make'.

Fairies, The (Wagner). See under *Feen.*

Fair Maid of Perth (Bizet). See *Jolie fille.*

Fairy Queen, The (Purcell). Incidental music to an adaptation of *A Midsummer Night's Dream*, not properly an 'Opera'. (Prod. 1692; score then lost; found 1901 in library of R.A.M.; since then various perfs. in Eng., Fr., and Ger.)

Fairy's Kiss (Stravinsky). See *Baiser de la fée.*

Faites (Fr.). 'Do', 'make' (imperative).

Fa-la. Same as ballett (see *Madrigal*), the refrain being a setting of these syllables.

Falkner, (Donald) Keith (b. Sawston, Cambs., 1900). Oratorio and concert bass vocalist. At first in Navy; then trained R.C.M. (later on staff) and Berlin, Vienna, and Paris. Won high place in esteem of publics of Commonwealth and U.S.A. Music Officer for Italy of Brit. Council (q.v.) 1946–50. On staff Cornell Univ. 1950. Dir. R.C.M. 1960–74. Knighted 1967.

Fall (Old Eng.). 'Cadence.'

Fall, Falle, &c. (Ger.). 'Case', e.g. in the expression *Im Falle*, 'In case'.

Fall, Leo (b. Olmütz 1873; d. Vienna 1925). Light opera composer of great international popularity. See *Dollar Princess.*

Falla, Manuel de (b. Cadiz 1876; d. Argentina 1946). Pupil of Pedrell (q.v.). When nearly 30 won prize for best national opera with *La Vida breve* (q.v.) which then waited 8 years before reaching performance. Lived for some time in Paris, and associated with Debussy, Ravel, and Dukas. Ballet *The Three-Cornered Hat* (q.v.) performed by Diaghilef troupe, 1919; *Love the Magician* (see *Amor brujo*) is another successful ballet. *Master Pedro's Puppet Show* (see *Retablo de Maese Pedro*) is a marionette-opera, *Nights in the Gardens of Spain* (q.v.) a composition for piano and orch. Keen student of native folk music, whose idiom enters into all his compositions.

(Spanish usage requires when using surname alone to write 'Falla', not 'de Falla' as is often done.)

Fall of Babylon, The (*Der Fall Babylons*). Oratorio by Spohr. (1st perf. Norwich Fest. 1842.)

False Close. See *Cadence.*

False Relation. See *Harmony* 2 h.

Falsettist. A singer who uses the method of voice production called falsetto (see *Voice* 5; also cf. *Alto Voice*).

False Vocal Cords. See *Voice* 4.

Falsobordone (It.). Same as Eng. *Faburden* (q.v.).

Falstaff. (1) Symphonic Study by Elgar (op. 68; Leeds Fest. 1913). Highly detailed piece of programme music based on passages in Shakespeare's *King Henry IV* and *Henry V.* (2) The only humorous opera of Verdi and his last. Libretto by Boito, after Shakespeare's *Merry Wives.* (Prod. Milan 1893—see *Mascheroni*; London 1894; New York 1895.) (3–4) Also operas by Salieri (1799) and Balfe (1838).

Fanciulla del West, La (Puccini). See *Girl of the Golden West*.

Fancy. An old Eng. word corresponding to the It. 'fantasia' and used for a type of composition for a group of viols (cf. *Viol Family*), as also, occasionally, for compositions for other instruments. (Cf. *In Nomine*; also *Phantasy*.)

Fancy Free. 1-act ballet by Leonard Bernstein. (Prod. New York 1944.)

Fandango. A lively Spanish dance believed to be of South American origin. It is in simple triple or compound duple time, and of ever-increasing speed—with sudden stops during which the performers (a single couple) remain motionless, and with intervals during which the performers sing. The castanets are used (see *Percussion Family* 2 q).

Fandanguillo. A sort of fandango.

Fanfare. (1, Eng.) Flourish of trumpets. (2, Fr.) Either flourish of trumpets or Brass Band (as distinct from *Harmonie*, a band of brass and woodwind).

Fantaisie (Fr.), **Fantasia** (It. and Eng.). Lit. 'fancy', hence any kind of composition in which form is of secondary importance, as (*a*) One suggestive of extemporization; (*b*) Strings of tunes out of an opera, &c.; (*c*) In 16th c. and earlier, an instrumental composition of a very contrapuntal character.

Free Fantasia is another name for the development section in Sonata Form (see *Form* 3).

Fantaisie norvégienne (Lalo). See *Rapsodie norvégienne*.

Fantasiestücke ('Fantasy Pieces'). By Schumann, 2 books of Piano pieces (op. 12; 1838). Also 3 pieces (op. 111; 1851).

Fantastico (It.), **fantasque** (Fr.), **fantastisch** (Ger.). 'Fantastic', 'whimsical', 'capricious'.

Fantastic Symphony (*Symphonie fantastique*). By Berlioz (op. 14; 1830); inspired by his passion for the Irish Shakespearian actress, Henrietta Smithson, whom he afterwards married. An advanced example of romantic 'Programme Music'. The movements are entitled (1) *Dreams, Passions*; (2) *A Ball*; (3) *Scene in the Fields*; (4) *March to the Scaffold*; (5) *Witches' Sabbath*.

Faraday, (1) **Michael.** See *Broadcasting of Music*.

(2) **Philip Michael** (b. London 1875; there d. 1944). Composer of comic operas, songs, &c.

Farandole. A lively dance in compound duple time in use in southern France and northern Spain. To the accompaniment of the galoubet and tambourin (see *Recorder Family* 2) the participants dance through the streets of the town.

Farcing or **Farsing.** The practice of inserting tropes (q.v.) into the plainsong of the Roman Catholic Liturgy, or into polyphonic settings of it. So we speak of a 'farced Kyrie', &c. (The word comes from the Lat. *Farcire*, 'To stuff'. 'Farce', in theatrical parlance, derives from the same word, from the practice of introducing comic interludes into the primitive miracle plays and the like.)

Farewell, Manchester. The tune is the favourite *Felton's Gavotte*, a harpsichord piece by Rev. William Felton (q.v.), of Hereford, composed about 1740. It has been stated that it was played in front of the army of the Young Pretender when they left Manchester.

Farewell Symphony (*Abschiedssymphonie*). Nickname of a Haydn Symphony—in F sharp minor (no. 45 in Breitkopf edn. of his Symphonies). In the last movement the players one by one blow out their candles and depart.

Farina, Carlo (b. Mantua abt. 1600; d. abt. 1640). One of earliest writers of virtuoso music for violin (publ. 1626–8).

Farinelli, (1) **Michel** (b. 1649). Fr. violinist and singing master (real name 'Farinel'; in Eng. literature of this period sometimes 'Fardinel' or 'Faronell').

(2) **Jean Baptiste,** or **Giovanni Baptista.** Brother of the above; in the

service of George I of England; composer of flute concertos, &c.

(3) Real name **Carlo Broschi,** 'Farinelli' being stage name (b. Andria 1705; d. Bologna 1782). The most celebrated *castrato* singer of his time.

Farjeon, Harry (b. New Jersey 1878; d. London 1948). His father was the well-known Eng. novelist. Trained at the R.A.M., of which he later became a prof. Composer and writer on music.

Farmer, (1) **John I** (end of 16th c. and beginning of 17th). Organist of Christ Church Cathedral, Dublin; then lived in London. Wrote charming madrigals.

(2) **John II** (b. Nottingham 1836; d. Oxford 1901). Directed the music at Harrow School (1862–85), providing it with numerous tuneful songs, settings of the words of his colleague, Edward Bowen; then became organizer of musical activities at Balliol Coll., Oxford. Composed oratorio (intended for young audiences (*Christ and his Soldiers* (q.v.), &c.

(3) **Henry George** (b. Birr, Ireland, 1882; d. Law, Lanarkshire, 1966). Educated at Glasgow Univ. (M.A., Ph.D., D.Litt.). Mus. director of various theatres 1910–47, at same time establishing reputation by many books and papers on military, Scottish, and (esp.) Arabic music.

Farnaby, (1) **Giles** (about 1560–1640). Composer of charming short pieces for virginals and of madrigals. (2) **Richard** (dates unknown). Son of the above; left a little keyboard music.

Farnam, W. Lynnwood (b. Sutton, Quebec, 1885; d. New York 1930). Organist. Trained R.C.M. Held posts in Montreal 1904–13; then Boston and New York. Virtuoso recitalist, touring widely. Head of organ dept. Curtis Institute.

Farnon, Robert (Joseph) (b. Toronto 1917). Trumpeter (C.B.C. Orch. 1936–42); conductor (Canadian army orch. 1943–6); then res. Britain. Much lighter mus. for films, radio, &c., also serious works.

Farrant, (1) **Richard** (b. abt. 1530; d. Windsor 1581). Organist to Queen Elizabeth in St. George's Chapel, Windsor; nowadays remembered by a little church music. (*Lord for Thy Tender Mercies' Sake* now said not to be by him but by John Hilton, senior or junior, or possibly Tye; the service 'Farrant in D minor' is by John Farrant; see below).

(2) **John.** Organist of Ely Cathedral 1567–72. See reference above.

Farrar, (1) **Geraldine** (b. Melrose, Mass., 1882; d. Ridgefield, Conn., 1967). Operatic and concert soprano. Studied Paris and Berlin. Début with Royal Opera Co., Berlin, 1901, becoming member of that Co. With Metropolitan Opera, New York, 1906–22. Brilliant international career in opera; also highly successful in films.

(2) **Ernest Bristow** (b. Blackheath, nr. London, 1885; killed in action in France 1918). Trained at the R.C.M. and became an organist. Left a few compositions—delicate and pointing to the existence of real talent.

Farrell, Eileen (b. Willimantic, Conn., 1920). Concert and opera soprano (Metropolitan 1960) of great range and power. Indiana U. 1971.

Farrington, Joseph (b. Preston 1881; d. Orpington, Kent, 1960). Operatic and concert bass. In choir King's Coll., Cambridge, 3 years; then St. Paul's Cathedral 16 years. Active in B.N.O.C. and Sadler's Wells, &c. Reputation as oratorio singer.

Farruca. An Andalusian dance of gipsy origin.

Farsing. See *Farcing.*

Farwell, Arthur (b. St. Paul, Minn., 1872; d. New York 1952). Composer. At first studied engineering, then musical composition under Humperdinck (q.v.) in Germany, and Guilmant (q.v.) in Paris. Made study of music of Amer. Indians, his compositions showing its influence.

Fasch, (1) **Johann Friedrich** (b. nr. Weimar 1688; d. Zerbst, Anhalt, 1758). Pupil of Kuhnau at Leipzig Thomas-School; afterwards active in establishment of a 'Collegium Musicum', which later developed into the celebrated Gewandhaus concert organization. Became Court Capellmeister at Zerbst; his compositions admired by Bach. (2) **Carl Friedrich Christian** (b. Zerbst 1736; d. Berlin 1800). Son of the above, and colleague of C. P. E.

Bach in the service of Frederick the Great. Later founded a Berlin organization which developed into the Singakademie. Skilful composer, valued by Beethoven.

Faschingsschwank aus Wien ('Viennese Carnival Pranks'). A set of 5 Piano Pieces by Schumann (op. 26; 1839).

Fasola. See *Lancashire Sol-fa.*

Fassung (Ger.). 'Drafting', &c. Hence *neue Fassung*, 'new version'.

Fast (Ger.). 'Almost.'

Fastoso (It.). 'Pompous.' So *fastosamente*, 'pompously'.

Father O'Flynn. The words are by A. P. Graves; the music is an Irish folk song collected by him in County Kerry.

Fatto per la notte di Natale (Corelli). See *Christmas Concerto.*

Fauré, Gabriel Urbain (b. Pamiers 1845; d. Paris 1924). Organist in Paris (including the Madeleine); also prof. of composition at the Conservatory and its Director 1905–20. Prolific composer, highly thought of, especially by his countrymen, for his operas, orch. works, chamber music, songs, &c. Revered by his juniors, many of whom were his pupils (e.g. Ravel, Florent Schmitt, Roger-Ducasse).

See also *Pelléas et Mélisande*; *Pénélope*; *Requiem.*

Faure, Jean Baptiste (b. Moulins 1830; d. Paris 1914). Operatic baritone of great repute. Trained Paris Conserv. (of which later on staff). Début Opéra Comique 1852; Covent Garden 1860. Chief baritone Paris Opéra 1861–76. Composer of songs (e.g. *Les Rameaux*), author of book on singing.

Fausset (Fr.). 'Falsetto' (see *Voice* 5).

Faust. (1) GOUNOD's highly popular opera. (Prod. Paris 1859; London, Dublin, and New York 1863.) Libretto by Barbier and Carré based on Goethe. (2) SPOHR and many other composers have written operas on the same subject. (3) BERLIOZ's 'Dramatic Legend' *La Damnation de Faust* (1846) has since 1893 occasionally been staged as an opera. (4) BOITO. See *Mefistofele*. (5) SCHUMANN's *Scenes from Goethe's Faust*

(1844–53) is a setting in cantata form. (6) COLERIDGE-TAYLOR wrote incidental music to Stephen Phillips's *Faust* (op. 70; 1908). (7) FAUST OVERTURE (Wagner). Composed in Paris in 1840 and recast in 1855. Intended to be the 1st movement of a *Faust Symphony*. (8) FAUST SYMPHONY. By LISZT (1854). 'In Three Character Pictures—after Goethe.' *Faust*; *Gretchen*; *Mephistopheles* (with, in the finale, Solo Tenor and Male Chorus).

Cf. *Doktor Faustus.*

Fauxbourdon (Fr.). Same as Eng. *Faburden* (q.v.).

Favart, Charles Simon (b. Paris 1710; there d. 1792). Playwright and theatre manager in Paris, influential in development of opéra comique; wrote 150 opera libretti (including some for Grétry and Gluck). His wife, an actress, vocalist, and dancer, collaborated. See *Bastien und Bastienne.*

Favola d'Orfeo (Monteverdi). See *Orfeo.*

Favorita, La ('The Favourite'). Romantic opera by Donizetti. (Prod. Paris 1840; London 1843; New Orleans 1843; New York 1845.)

Fayrfax, Robert (b. Deeping Gate, Lincs., 1464; d. St. Albans 1521). Organist of Abbey of St. Albans and there interred. Composer of church music and in his day accounted the leading composer of the country.

F.B.S.M. See *Degrees and Diplomas* 2.

F.C.C.O. See *Degrees and Diplomas* 2.

F. Clef. See *Great Staff*; Table 4.

Fedora. Tragedy-opera by Giordano. (Prod. Milan 1898; London and New York 1906.)

Feen, Die ('The Fairies'). 1st opera of Wagner. Libretto based on Gozzi. (Composed 1833; posthumously produced Munich 1888.)

Feierlich (Ger.). This has a double meaning—in the mood of 'Holy Day' (solemn) or in that of 'Holiday' (rejoicing), a 'Feier' being a public celebration of the one kind or the other.

Feinberg, Samuel (b. Odessa 1890). Pianist and composer. Trained Moscow Conserv. (later on staff). As composer influenced by Scriabin.

Feis Ceoil. See *Competitions*.

Feldpartita (Ger.). A composition for wind band, of the type of *partita* (q.v.) or of *divertimento*.

Felice (It.). 'Happy.'

Fellowes, Edmund Horace (b. London 1870; d. Windsor 1951). Minor canon of St. George's Chapel, Windsor Castle. Widely admired for his great work in editing the complete works of all the Eng. composers of madrigals (36 vols.), lute songs (23 vols.), complete works of Byrd (20 vols.), as also books on (and much church music of) the same period. Autobiography (1946) and many miscellaneous works. M.A., B.Mus., Oxford, Hon. D.Mus., Dublin (1917) and Oxford (1939), M.V.O. (1931), C.H. (1944). Hon. Librarian St. Michael's Coll., Tenbury, 1918–48.

Feltkamp, Johannes Hendricus (b. Leyden, Holland, 1896). Flautist. Trained Royal Conserv., The Hague, then various orch. appointments, including France and Italy. Finally specialized in solo and chamber music work; frequent foreign tours with own trio. Seven years conductor Amsterdam Chamber Orchestra.

Felton, William (b. Drayton 1715; d. Hereford 1769). Anglican clergyman, a vicar-choral of Hereford Cathedral, an organist, harpischordist, and composer of keyboard concertos, &c. (See *Farewell, Manchester*.)

Female Wiles (Cimarosa). See *Astuzie femminile*.

Fenby, Eric William (b. Scarborough 1906). After local training and the occupancy of organ positions went to France to serve as amanuensis to the blind and paralysed Delius, as to his experiences with whom he has written a book. Own compositions mostly in smaller forms but include a symphony.

Fennimore and Gerda. Last opera of Delius. (Prod. Frankfort 1919.)

Ferguson, Howard (b. Belfast 1908). Studied with Harold Samuel and at R.C.M., where he held a scholarship for composition. Has written chamber music, songs, some orch. music, &c. On staff R.A.M.

Ferial. The word comes from the Lat. *feria*, 'feast day', but has by etymological perversity come to mean an ordinary day, as distinguished from a feast. Hence the application of 'Ferial Use' to liturgy and music. (For the Ferial and Festal Responses see *Responses*.)

Fermamente (It.). 'Firmly.'

Fermata (It.), **Fermate** (Ger.). A pause ⌢. (Sometimes the use is a special one—the pause mark in a concerto which indicates the point where the cadenza begins; see *Cadenza*.)

Fermer (Fr. 'to close'), **fermé** ('closed'). A word used in organ music. (1) Close the swell box. (2) Put a particular stop out of action.

Fermezza (It.). 'Firmness.'

Fermo (It.). 'Firm', in style of performance. (For *canto fermo* see *Counterpoint*.)

Ferne (Ger.). 'Distance', e.g. *Wie aus der Ferne*, 'As if out of the distance'.

Fernflöte (Ger., lit. 'Far Flute', i.e. 'Distant Flute'). Soft organ stop of metal; 8-foot length and pitch.

Fernwerk (Ger.; cf. *Ferne*, above). Echo Manual of organ.

Feroce (It.). 'Ferocious.' So *ferocità*, 'ferocity'.

Ferrabosco, (1) **Alfonso I** (b. Bologna 1543; there d. 1588). Composer of madrigals and motets and music for viols; from about 1560 to 1578 in the service of Queen Elizabeth of England. Father of (2) **Alfonso II** (b. Greenwich abt. 1575; there d. 1628). Spent whole life in England, being in service of James I and Charles I. (3, 4, 5) **Alfonso III, Henry,** and **John.** Apparently sons of Alfonso II, and like their father and grandfather in royal service in England. John became organist of Ely Cathedral and left church compositions.

Ferrero, Willy (b. Portland, Maine, 1906; parents Italian; d. Rome 1954). Orch. conductor. Appeared as such at age 6 in Rome and then with great success in Britain and elsewhere. Studied Vienna, taking diploma as composer at age 18. Then active in Italy.

Ferrier, Kathleen (b. nr. Preston 1912; d. London 1953). Contralto vocalist. Pupil of Roy Henderson (q.v.). Concert and oratorio artist; operatic début in title role of Britten's *Rape of Lucretia*, 1946. Highest possible international reputation. C.B.E. 1953.

Ferroud, Pierre Octave (b. nr. Lyons 1900; killed in motoring accident in Hungary 1936). Pupil of Florent Schmitt; music critic and composer with notable talent for orchestration.

Fertig (Ger.). 'Ready', dexterous, finished in style. So *Fingerfertigkeit*, Fluent finger technique.

Fervaal. Opera by d'Indy. Libretto by composer. (Prod. Brussels 1897; Paris 1898.)

Fervente (It.). 'Fervent.' **Fervido, fervidamente.** 'Fervid'; 'fervidly'.

Fervore. 'Fervour.'

Fes (Ger.). F flat. **Feses** (Ger.). F double flat (see Table 7).

Fest (Ger.). 'Festival.'

Festa (It.). 'Festival.' So *festevole*, 'merry', *festevolmente*, 'merrily'.

Festa, Costanzo (b. nr. Turin abt. 1490; d. 1545). Musical director at the Vatican; church music still in use in Rome; composed madrigals (one well known in its Eng. version, *Down in a Flowery Vale*).

Festal. Applied in the distinction of ecclesiastical feast days from ordinary, or Ferial days (see *Ferial* and *Responses*).

Feste Burg, Ein' (Luther). See *Ein' feste Burg.*

Festevole (It.). 'Merry.' Hence *festevolmente*, 'merrily'.

Festgesang ('Festival Song'). By Mendelssohn, for Male Chorus and Orch. Composed for the Gutenberg Centenary at Leipzig 1840. (The English hymn-tune, *Hark, the Herald Angels Sing*, is an adaptation of one of its numbers.)

Festin de l'araignée (Roussel). See *Spider's Feast.*

Festing, Michael Christian (d. London 1752). Violinist, opera director, and composer of violin music, choral works, songs, &c.

Festival. This word, as applied to musical performances, apparently first came into use at the end of the 17th c. with the *Festival of the Sons of the Clergy*, when what had been a mere annual charity sermon in aid of distressed families of the clergy, dating from 1655, blossomed out with the Restoration into something artistically important: from 1698 an orch. was employed. This celebration continues annually but is merely a musical service on grand lines. The *Three Choirs Festival*, alternating between the cathedral cities of Gloucester, Hereford, and Worcester, and combining their choral forces, began in a similar primitive way (1715) and was similarly expanded in scope (1724); it occupies several days. The *Birmingham Festival* began in 1768 and lasted until 1912, being held for a period triennially but in general at irregular intervals. Other important Festivals are those of *Norwich* (1770 onwards) and *Leeds* (1858, 1874, and then triennially). At the *Handel Commemoration* of 1784 (in Westminster Abbey and the Pantheon) was assembled the biggest body of choral and orch. performers ever seen in the world up to that date: it was followed by further events of the same sort in 1785-6-7 and 1791. The *Crystal Palace Handel Festivals* began in 1857 and after a time became triennial. There have been very many other Eng. festivals. SCOTLAND has had a few early festivals (*Edinburgh* 1815-19-24-43 and also the Reid Concert Festivals, 1874, &c.; *Glasgow* 1860 and 1873). In 1947 an important annual series of Edinburgh 'International Festivals' was inaugurated. In WALES the *Harlech Festival* has been held in the castle annually since 1867 and there have been many other Welsh festivals (see *Eisteddfod*).

In the U.S.A. there is greater festival activity than in any other country in the world. What were in effect festivals on a limited scale were at first often called 'Conventions'. The *Handel and Haydn Society, of Boston, Mass.* (founded 1815), held a gathering in 1857 as did *Worcester, Mass.*, in 1858, and *Cincinnati* in 1871. Several universities have organized regular festivals (beginning with the *Univ. of Michigan*, Ann Arbor, in 1893). There are chamber music festivals, opera festivals, Bach festivals (especially Bethlehem, Pa., since 1900), summer open-air festivals, &c.

FRANCE is hardly a festival country. Nor is ITALY, though important festivals are held annually at Florence ('Maggio musicale') and Venice. In GERMANY the *Lower Rhine Festival* (dating from 1817) has been held annually at Cologne, Düsseldorf, and Aachen, &c., in turn. After the First World War festivals in Germany and Austria (e.g. Salzburg) were organized as attractions for tourists. Many Ger. festivals have been of the nature of celebrations of particular composers, held in the place of their birth. The Wagner performances at Bayreuth have always been called by the name of 'Bühnenfestspiel', i.e. 'stage-festival-performance'.

The *International Society for Contemporary Music* has held annual festivals from 1922, visiting a number of different countries.

What are often called 'Competition Festivals' are treated under the heading *Competition*.

Festival Song (Mendelssohn). See *Festgesang*.

Festivo (It.). 'Festive'; so *festivamente*, 'festively'.

Festklänge. Symphonic Poem by Liszt (1853), written in celebration of his intended marriage with Princess Sayn-Wittgenstein.

Festlich (Ger.), **festoso** (It.). 'Festive' (so the It. superlative *festosissimo*).

Festspiel (Ger. 'Festival-play'). A term applied to certain musical stage works, or works in which music has

some part. Wagner extended the term in the title to his *Ring* tetralogy, which he called a *Bühnenfestspiel* ('Stage-festival-play') and still further in the title of his *Parsifal*, described as a *Bühnenweihfestspiel* ('Stage-consecration festival-play').

Fête galante. 1-act opera by Ethel Smyth. Libretto based on story by Maurice Baring. (Prod. Birmingham and London 1923.)

Fêtes galantes. By Debussy. Two series, each of 3 song settings of Verlaine (1892 and 1904).

Fétis, François Joseph (b. Mons 1784; d. Brussels 1871). Active and learned musicologist and general musical researcher, especially famous for his indispensable *Biographie universelle des musiciens* (8 vols., 1835–44; 2nd edn. 1860–5; supplement by A. Pougin, 2 vols., 1878–80). Also author of many theoretical works and prolific composer of symphonies, operas, masses, &c. Director of Brussels Conserv. (1833 to death).

See *Appreciation of Music*; *Criticism of Music*.

Feuer (Ger.). 'Fire.' So *feurig*, 'fiery'.

Feuermann, Emanuel (b. Galicia 1902; d. New York 1942). Violoncellist. Played in public from age 11; chief teacher of his instrument Cologne Conserv. age 17–21; at Berlin Hochschule 1929–33; then settled in New York to escape Nazis.

Feuersnot ('Fire-famine'). 1-act opera by Richard Strauss. (Prod. Dresden 1901; London 1910; Philadelphia 1927.)

Feuersymphonie (Haydn). See *Fire Symphony*.

Feuille d'album (Fr.). 'Album leaf' (see *Albumblatt*).

Feux d'artifice (Debussy). See *Fireworks*.

Ff. = *Fortissimo*, i.e. very loud.

Ffrangcon-Davies, (1) **David Thomas** (b. Bethesda, Wales, 1855; d. London 1918).Concert and oratorio baritone (at first tenor). Studied Oxford and became clergyman. Then trained G.S.M. and first appeared as vocalist aged 35, at once winning high reputation as sensitive and conscientious artist. Publ. (1906) *The Singing of the Future*; nervous breakdown and cessation of public appearances the following year. (Surname originally 'Davis', not 'Davies', and 'Ffrangcon' added as name of hills near his birthplace.) (2) **Gwen** (b. London 1896). Daughter of above. Soprano vocalist (specially prominent in Boughton's *Immortal Hour*, q.v., 1919 and later); then popular as actress in spoken drama.

Fg. Short for *Fagott*, i.e. bassoon (see *Oboe Family*).

F.G.S.M. See *Degrees and Diplomas* 2.

F holes. The sound-holes in the belly of a violin, &c.—roughly in the shape of an *f*.

Fiacco (It.). 'Weak', as though tired out. So the adverb *fiaccamente* and the noun *fiacchezza*.

Fiata, Fiate (It.). 'Time', 'times', in the sense of 'once' (*una fiata*), 'twice' (*due fiate*), &c.

Fiato (It.). 'Breath.' Hence wind instruments are *stromenti a fiato*.

Fibich, Zdeněk (b. Všeborice, or Šebořice, Bohemia, 1850; d. Prague 1900). Studied in Leipzig, Paris, and elsewhere, spent some years in Vilna, Poland, and then settled in native place, devoting himself to composition, and producing numerous works—orch., chamber, stage, &c.

Fickenscher, Arthur (b. Aurora, Ill., 1871; d. San Francisco 1954). Pianist and organist, trained Munich. Prof. of Music, Univ. of Virginia. Invented 'Polytone' instrument which provides for 60 notes in 8ve. Composer of orch. and chamber music, &c.

Fiddle. Colloquial name for any kind of bowed instrument, especially the violin.

Fiddle Fugue (Bach). For Organ. In D minor. So nicknamed because existing in earlier form for Violin solo.

Fidelio, oder Die eheliche Liebe ('Fidelio, or Married Love'). Beethoven's only opera. (Prod. Vienna 1805, with changes 1806, in present form 1814; London 1832; New York

and Philadelphia 1839.) The heroine is called Leonora and 3 of the 4 attempts at an overture for the work bear her name. Their correct chronological order is as follows—'Leonora No. 2' (1805); 'Leonora No. 3' (1806); 'Leonora No. 1' (for a perf. that did not take place, 1807); *Fidelio* (1814). The last is the one now used with the opera, the others (especially 'No. 3') being heard in concert performance, and frequently between the scenes of a performance of the opera. (See *Singspiel*.)

Fiedler, (1) Max—in full August Max (b. Zittau 1859; d. Stockholm 1939). Pianist and then conductor. Trained Leipzig Conserv. (later on staff). Conducted London Symphony Orch. 1907; Boston Symphony Orch. 1908–12. Then Berlin, &c. Composed orch. music, &c.

(2) **Arthur** (b. Boston, Mass., 1894). Conductor. Trained Berlin; member Boston Symph. Orch. (viola) 1915. From 1930 cond. 'Boston Pops' Orch. in very successful annual summer series with repertory ranging from standard classical to popular. Many recordings and guest engagements.

Field, John (b. Dublin 1782; d. Moscow 1837). Pupil in Dublin of Giordani and at 9 appeared in public as a pianist. Two years later his father settled in London and he there became a pupil of Clementi, playing before Haydn, who predicted a great future for him. Clementi used him to display the instruments in his piano warehouse and then took him abroad on a business tour; arrived at St. Petersburg (Leningrad) he parted from his employer and there settled as a fashionable piano teacher, often making European tours as virtuoso. Enjoyed high fame as composer for piano—his concertos being much played (later greatly praised by Schumann): the style and name of the 'Nocturne' are of his devising and were later taken over by Chopin; Liszt published an edition of his Nocturnes, preceded by a panegyric.

Field-Hyde, (1) **F. C.** (b. Baldock 1866; d. Bath 1958). Studied singing under Manuel Garcia and held lectureships at colleges connected with Cambridge Univ. and London Univ.; also

R.A.M., &c. Competition adjudicator and author of books on class-singing, ear-training, and voice-training. (See *Tremolo*.) (2) **Margaret** (b. Cambridge 1905). Lyric soprano. Studied under father (see above) and at Frankfort and Paris. Début 1928. Has toured under Brit. Council auspices.

Field-Marshal Death (Mussorgsky). See *Songs and Dances of Death*.

Fier, fière (Fr. masc., fem.). 'Proud.' So *fierté*, 'pride'. (But in painting this word is sometimes used for 'boldness of touch', and it may be that it should sometimes be so interpreted in music.)

Fierezza (It.). 'Fierceness.' (In painting used in same sense as Fr. *fierté*, so that remark above may apply.)

Fifths Quartet (Haydn). See *Quintenquartett*.

Figaro (Mozart). See *Nozze di Figaro*.

Figlia del reggimento (Donizetti). See *Fille du régiment*.

Figural, figured (Eng.); **figuré** (Fr.); **figurato** (It.); **figural, figuriert** (Ger.). 'Florid.' (1) A 'figured chorale' is one in which the melody is accompanied by quicker notes in the other voice-parts. (2) In solo vocal music the word implies *Coloratura* (q.v.).

Figuralmusik. See *Musica figurata*.

Figurato, figurata (It. masc. and fem.). Same as *colorato, colorata*, i.e. treated in the manner of *Coloratura* (q.v.).

FIGURED BASS

The tune *Ephraim* in Horsley's *Collection of Psalm Tunes*, 1828

Fiero (It.). (*a*) 'Fierce', 'fiery'. (*b*) 'Haughty.' So the adverb *fieramente*, with the same implications, and *fierezza* above.

Fife (in Ger. *Trommelflöte*, 'drum-flute'). A small high-pitched side-blown flute (in a Drum and Fife Band the piccolo; see *Flute Family*. But such bands now include also flutes of larger sizes). Cf. *Whiffle*.

Fifine at the Fair. 'Orch. Drama' (i.e. Symphonic Poem) by Bantock. Based on Browning's poem of same name but with added sub-title, *A Defence of Inconstancy*. (1st perf. Birmingham 1912.)

Fifteenth. On organ a high-pitched Diapason stop (for 'Diapason' see *Organ* 2); 2-foot length and pitch on manuals, 4-foot on pedal.

Fifth. See *Interval*. (For 'Consecutive' and 'Hidden' Fifths see *Harmony* 2 j.)

Figure. (1) In MUSICAL CONSTRUCTION this word usually carries the same meaning as *Motif* (q.v.). We also speak of a *Figure of Accompaniment*, meaning the germ out of which, by repetition at different pitch-levels, a certain sort of song accompaniment, &c., is evolved.

(2) In DANCING the word implies a set of evolutions by the dancers as a body, such as makes a distinct division of the dance as a whole. A *Figure Dance* is one in which this element is prominent, as distinguished from a *Step Dance*, in which it is largely or entirely absent.

Figured Bass (or *Thorough Bass*, or *Continuo*). The shorthand of harmony, a mere bass line with figures under or over it which enabled a keyboard accompanist (in the 17th and 18th cs.) to know from what series of chords he should extemporize his part (for in that period accompaniment to a vocal or violin solo, or to church music, &c., was rarely written in full).

Long after composers had abandoned the practice of writing figured basses, harmony teachers used them as exercises and examiners as tests, the bass and its figures being provided and the student being expected to write out from that indication the full harmonies, observing the code of rules conventionally accepted (avoidance of consecutives, &c.), and producing as artistic a result as he could compass. As an educational device, however, the figured bass now tends rapidly to disappear.

Figuriert. See *Figural*.

Filer la voce, filar il tuono (It.), **filer la voix, filer le son** (Fr.). Lit. 'to draw out the voice' or 'draw out the tone', i.e. the *messa di voce* (q.v.), but sometimes understood as merely holding out a long note without the *crescendo* and *diminuendo*.

Fille de Madame Angot, La ('The Daughter of Madame Angot'). Highly popular operetta by Lecocq. (Prod. Brussels 1872, run of 500 nights; Paris with similar run; London and New York 1873.) A ballet suite, *Mam'zelle Angot*, by Gordon Jacob, is based on the operetta.

Fille du régiment, La ('The Daughter of the Regiment'; in It. version *La Figlia del reggimento*). Popular Romantic opera by Donizetti. (Prod. Paris 1840; New Orleans and New York 1843; London 1847.)

Filtz, Anton (b., possibly in Bohemia, abt. 1730; d. Mannheim 1760). Pupil and leading 'cellist in the orch. of J. Stamitz at Mannheim. Composed during his short life over 40 symphonies, as also 'cello and flute concertos, chamber music, &c.

Fin (Fr.). 'End.'

Fin (It.). Same as *Fino* (q.v.).

Final. See *Modes*.

Finale. The last movement of a cyclic work (sonata, &c.), the closing portion of an opera, and so on.

Finck, Henry Theophilus (b. Bethel, Missouri, 1854; d. Rumford Falls, Maine, 1926). Graduated Harvard, then studied Ger. universities. On staff

New York Evening Post 1881. Its music ed. 1888–1924. Wrote innumerable books on music. See under *Criticism*.

Fine (It.). 'End.'

Fingal's Cave. See *Mendelssohn*.

Finger Board. In a stringed instrument, the long strip of hard wood over which the strings are stretched.

Finger Organ. See s.v. *Hand Organ*.

Fingering of Keyboard Instruments. The methods of applying the fingers to a keyboard have varied greatly at different periods and with different players, but have since the end of the 18th c. come to be standardized on something like our modern principles. Before this period there was a good deal of passing of the 3 middle fingers over one another and comparatively little use of the thumb and little finger: this was partly due to the fall of the keys being much shallower than with our modern instruments, which allowed of the fingers being used almost flat on the keys, and also to the modest requirements of the gentler music of the day, calling for less dashing about the keyboard than that to which we have now become accustomed. Bach told his son Emanuel that in his young days the great players used the thumb merely in big stretches: he himself used it freely and abandoned the old flat position of the fingers for a curved one; nevertheless he to some extent continued the practice of passing one finger over another. He disregarded the old principle of 'good' fingers, to be used on the 'good' (i.e. accented) notes and 'bad' ones to be used on the 'bad' (i.e. unaccented) ones, insisting that all the fingers must be brought to an equal condition of 'goodness'. Emanuel Bach worked out his father's principles to something nearer a logical conclusion and thus ranks as one of the founders of modern fingering practice. The only finger-crossing he retained was that of the longest finger over the index finger —the longer one over the shorter, and so not quite unreasonable. It must be remembered that the favourite instrument of these 2 great players was the clavichord, with its singing quality. The pianoforte killed finger-crossing, since it demanded an actual blow (properly a blow by pressure—one sufficient to *throw* the hammer at the strings, yet so exactly controlled as to throw it with either the greater force required by a fortissimo or the lesser required by a pianissimo).

It was Clementi (the founder of a real pianoforte style in composition— cf. *Pianoforte Playing*) who firmly established the modern principles of fingering: his use of the thumb was the same as ours, except that he did not use it on the black keys, as is sometimes done today. These modern principles include the division of a scale into 2 groups of 3 and 4 notes respectively, with the thumb as the pivot between them, the playing of arpeggio passages on the basis of the 8ve, some adaptation of fingering to the hand of the individual player, the planning of the fingering of a passage by working backwards from the point at which it is ultimately to arrive, and the division of such a passage into 'physical groups' as units, each of these being considered as a chord.

Organ fingering follows much the same principles as piano fingering but, as the nature of the instrument generally calls for a very perfect legato, more substitution of finger is required, a key often being depressed by one finger and then held by another, so freeing the first one for use on another key.

There have been various methods of marking the printed copies of music with the composer's or editor's suggested fingering. What was called the 'English' system employed a cross for the thumb and then numbered the fingers up to '4' for the little one (as they are numbered in violin music). What was long called the 'Continental' system used '1' for the thumb, and the other figures for the fingers up to '5' for the little one. The latter system is now almost universal (cf. *Zimmermann*).

Fingersatz (Ger.). 'Fingering.'

Finite Canon. See *Canon*.

Finlandia. Symphonic Poem by Sibelius (op. 26; 1899). An expression of patriotic sentiment based on original themes of national character.

Finn, William J. (b. Boston, Mass., 1881; d. New York 1961). Roman Catholic priest. Distinguished conductor and trainer of church choirs ('Paulist Choristers' of Chicago and New York; notable foreign tours). Composer and author in his field.

Fino (It.). 'As far as', e.g. *Fino al segno*, 'As far as the sign (𝄋)'.

Finzi, Gerald (b. London 1901; died Oxford 1956). Studied under Bairstow in York and R. O. Morris in London; lived quietly, writing esp. songs and other vocal pieces (see *Dies Natalis*), choral works, and a 'cello concerto.

Fiocco, (1) Pietro Antonio (b. Venice 1650; d. Brussels 1714). Director of the royal orch. at Brussels, holder of other posts there, and composer of church music, &c.

(2) **Joseph-Hector** (b. Brussels 1703; d. there 1741). Choirmaster successively of the Cathedrals of Antwerp and Brussels, harpsichordist, and composer.

Fiorillo, (1) Federigo (b. Brunswick 1755; d. 1823 or later). Violinist. Roved widely; 6 years in London. Composed the much-used *Six Caprices or Études*, also violin concertos and chamber music.

(2) **Dante** (b. New York 1905). Self-taught composer, but winner of Guggenheim Fellowship and of Pulitzer Prize (1939). Composer of many symphonies, concertos, chamber music, &c.

Fioritura (It. 'flowering'; plur. *fioriture*). That agile decoration of a melody common in the 18th-c. operatic aria, &c., or in its perf., for it was often extemporized by the singer. Violinists and pianists also, at one period, indulged themselves in a similar way. (Cf. *Ornaments*.)

Fipple flutes. See *Recorder Family*.

Firebird, The ('L'Oiseau de feu'). Russian Fairy-tale Ballet by Stravinsky; also heard in the form of 2 orch. Suites. (Prod. Paris 1910.)

Fire-Famine (Strauss). See *Feuersnot*.

Fire Symphony (*Feuersymphonie*). Nickname for Haydn's Symphony in A, no. 59 in Breitkopf edn. of the Symphonies.

Fireworks. By Stravinsky. Orch. piece (1908). Also (*Feux d'artifice*) final piece in Debussy's 2nd book of Preludes for Piano (1910).

Fireworks music. Instrumental Suite by Handel, composed for and perf. at pyrotechnic display in Green Park, London, to celebrate Peace of Aix-la-Chapelle, 1749.

Firkušný, Rudolf (b. Napajedla, Czechoslovakia, 1912). Pianist. Trained Prague Conserv., &c. European tours and broadcasts from 1939; from 1941 resident U.S.A. Composed piano concerto, songs, &c.

First of August. This tune, claimed as a Welsh folk tune, first came into notice in Britain at the opening of the 18th c. when a party of Swedish dancers used it: it was then called *The New Swedish Dance*. Later it was attached to a song in praise of the Hanoverian succession, called *The Glorious First of August* (George I came to the throne on 1 Aug. 1714).

First of May. By Shostakovich; his 3rd Symphony (op. 20; 1929). Inspired by both the emotions evoked by Nature in spring-time and those evoked by the efforts of Man in time of Revolution. It has an *ad lib.* choral ending.

First Post. See *Last Post*; *Tattoo*.

First Violin. See *Violin Family*.

First Walpurgis Night (*Die erste Walpurgisnacht*). Mendelssohn's setting, for Solo Vocalists, Chorus, and Orch., of Goethe's ballad. Walpurgis Night is the spring fest. when witches ride to the Brocken in the Harz Mountains. (Op. 60, 1831; revised 1843.)

Fis (Ger.). F sharp (see Table 7).

F.I.S.C. See *Degrees and Diplomas 2*.

Fischer, (1) Carl, Inc. New York music publishers. Estd. 1872.

(2) **J. & Brother.** New York music publishers. Estd. (at Dayton, Ohio) 1864.

(3) **Edwin** (b. Basle 1886; d. Zürich 1960). Pianist. Trained at Stern Conserv. Berlin. Conductor of societies at Lübeck, Munich, and Berlin. European tours as pianist (specializing in Bach and Mozart); ed. old piano

music; some books and compositions. From 1942 res. Lucerne.

Fischer-Dieskau, Dietrich (b. Berlin 1925). Opera and concert baritone. Trained Berlin Hochschule; then soldier and prisoner of war; Berlin Opera 1948; then world career; outstanding reputation as interpreter of Lieder.

Fisher, (1) William Arms (b. San Francisco 1861; d. Brookline, Mass., 1948). Pupil of H. W. Parker and Dvořák, vocal composer, ed. of musical publications, author of a book on music, &c.

(2) **Sylvia** (b. Melbourne 1910). Dramatic soprano. Début Melbourne 1932; Covent Garden from 1949; Chicago 1959.

Fisis (Ger.). F double sharp (see Table 7).

Fistoulari, Anatole (b. Kiev 1907). Conductor (child prodigy as such). After continental and U.S.A. appearances settled London, conducting chief orchs. there.

Fitelberg, (1) Gregor or Gregorz (b. Livonia 1879; d. Katowice 1953). Trained at Warsaw Conserv. and became leader and then conductor of Warsaw Orch.; travelled for a time as conductor of Diaghilef's Russian Ballet. Works include symphonic poems, chamber music, &c. (2) **Jerzy** (b. Warsaw 1903; d. New York 1951). Son of above. Studied largely in Berlin. Composer of orch. works and a good deal of music for stringed instruments—including violin and 'cello concertos. Resident U.S.A. One of his several string quartets won Coolidge Award (1936).

Fitzwilliam Virginal Book. A MS. collection of music for virginals (see *Harpsichord Family*) made by Francis Tregian in the early 17th c. (see *Music and Letters*, July 1951 and Jan. 1952), and constituting our largest treasury of such music. It has been published (1894–9; see *Fuller-Maitland*). It was formerly erroneously called 'Queen Elizabeth's Virginal Book'; its present name comes from its having been the property of Viscount Fitzwilliam (d. 1916) and being now preserved in the Fitzwilliam Library of Cambridge University.

Five, The. Name given to a group of 19th-c. Russian composers who (following up the work of Glinka and Dargomijsky) definitely established a Russian School of composition. The members were Balakiref, Cui, Borodin, Mussorgsky, and Rimsky-Korsakof.

Five Tudor Portraits. 'Choral Suite' with Solo Vocalists and Orch., by Vaughan Williams; settings of poems by John Skelton, 1460–1529. (1st perf. Norwich Fest. 1936, London 1937.)

Fixed-doh. See explanation under *Movable-doh.*

Fjelstad, Øivin (b. Oslo 1903). Début 1921 as violinist; 1931 as conductor; chief conductor, Norwegian Radio from 1935. Some compositions.

Fl. Short for 'Flute'.

Flageolet. (1) See *Recorder Family* 2. (2) Soft Organ stop; 2-foot length and pitch.

Flageolet Notes, Flageolet Tones. The harmonics of the violin, this being the Fr. and Ger. description of them.

Flageolett, Flageolettöne (Ger.). Flageolet (see *Recorder Family* 2), 'Flageolet Notes' (see above).

Flagstad, Kirsten Marie (b. nr. Oslo 1895; d. Oslo 1962). Dramatic soprano. Début Oslo 1913. Long known only in Scandinavian countries; then Bayreuth 1933; New York 1934; London 1936; also Australia. Famous in Wagnerian roles. Retired 1953.

Flamenco. See *Cante flamenco.*

Flat (♭). (1, Noun). The sign which, placed before a note, lowers its pitch by a semitone. See Table 6. (There is a slight difference of usage in the language of Britain and the U.S.A.—in the former 'to flatten' and 'flattened'; in the latter 'to flat' and 'flatted'.) (2, Adj.) Flat singing or playing is such as departs from correct intonation on the downward side.

Flatter (Fr.). 'To caress', e.g. *flatter la corde*, 'To caress the string', to bow delicately.

Flatterzunge. See *Tonguing.*

Flat Twenty-first (Organ). Rank in a Mixture stop, sounding 2 octaves and a minor 7th above normal (i.e. interval of minor 21st = compound minor 7th).

Flautando, flautato (It.). Lit., 'fluting' and 'fluted'—referring to the producing of flute-like tones from the violin, &c., either by (*a*) bowing near the finger-board with the point of the bow or (*b*) using harmonics (cf. *Flageolet Notes*).

Flautendo. A Debussy term, apparently a misspelling of *flautando* (q.v.)

Flauti (It., sing. *flauto*). 'Flutes.'

Flautina. Organ stop; a *Gemshorn* (q.v.) of 2-foot length and pitch.

Flauto (It., plur. *flauti*). 'Flute' (see *Flute Family*; *Recorder Family*).

Flauto dolce. Organ stop; much the same as *dolce* (q.v.), but rather more flute-like.

Flauto magico (Mozart). See *Magic Flute.*

Flauto traverso. Organ stop of 4-foot length and pitch.

Flebile; flebilmente (It.). 'Mournful'; 'mournfully'.

Flecha, Mateo (b. Catalonia abt. 1530; there d. 1604). Churchman and composer of church music and secular choral music; attached for some time to Imperial Court at Prague.

Fledermaus, Die ('The Bat'). Operetta by Johann Strauss jr. (Prod. Vienna and New York 1874; London 1876.)

Flehend (Ger.). 'Entreating.'

Flem, Paul Le. See *Le Flem.*

Flesch, Carl (b. Hungary 1873; d. Lucerne 1944). Violinist and teacher of violin. Pupil of Marsick and others. Early high reputation Germany and Austria. Chief violin prof. Curtis Inst., Philadelphia, 1924–8; taught also in London; wrote an autobiography, books on violin playing, and publ. edns. of classical concertos, &c.

Flessibile; flessibilità (It.). 'Flexible'; 'flexibility'.

Fleta, Miguel (b. Albalate, Spain, 1893; d. Burgos 1938). Operatic tenor. Début Trieste and Madrid 1919–20; Metropolitan, New York, 1923.

Flicorno. See *Tuba Group* 4.

Fliegende Holländer, Der ('The Flying Dutchman'). Opera by Wagner. (Prod. Dresden 1843; London 1870; Philadelphia 1876; Dublin, New York, and New Orleans 1877.)

Fliessend (Ger.). 'Flowing.' So *fliessender*, 'more flowing'.

Flight and Robson. See *Mechanical Reproduction of Music* 11.

Flight of the Bumble Bee (Rimsky-Korsakof). See *Legend of Tsar Saltan*.

Fling. A particularly vigorous type of Scottish Highland reel.

Flintoft, Luke (b. probably Worcester, date unknown; d. London 1727). Gentleman of Chapel Royal and (being in orders) minor canon of Westminster Abbey. It is claimed that he originated the Double Anglican Chant of which a specimen by him (in G minor) is today in all chant books (but see *Anglican Chant*).

Flonzaley Quartet. See *Coppet*.

Flood, William Henry Grattan (b. Lismore, Ireland, 1859; d. Enniscorthy 1928). Organist of several Irish (Roman Catholic) cathedrals; composer of church music, and untiring musical antiquarian, making large claims for Irish descent of Eng. composers, also Irish origin of Eng. tunes.

Flora. See *Furry Dance*.

Flora gave me fairest flowers. See *Wilbye*.

Floral Dance. See *Furry Dance*.

Florida Suite. Early orch. work of Delius. (1887; 1st perf. Leipzig 1888; London 1937.)

Florid Counterpoint. See *Counterpoint*.

Florodora. See *Stuart, Leslie*.

Flos Campi. Suite by Vaughan Williams (1926) for Viola solo, Small Orch., and wordless voices. Based on *Song of Solomon*.

Flötenuhr. See *Mechanical Reproduction of Music* 4.

Flotow, Friedrich von (b. Mecklenburg 1812; d. Darmstadt 1883). Born into nobility and educated for diplomatic service; discovered rich vein of flowing melody and gave life to theatre; of nearly 20 operas, *Martha* (q.v.) now best remembered.

Flotter (Fr.). 'To float' (referring to an undulating movement of the bow in violin playing, &c.). **Flottant.** 'Floating.'

Flourish. (1) A trumpet call of the fanfare type. (2) In a more general sense any florid instrumental passage.

Flower, (1) **Eliza** (b. Harlow, Essex, 1803; d. Hurstpierpoint 1846). London organist; composer of anthems and hymns and the once-familiar chorus, *Now pray we for our country*. (The poet of *Nearer my God to Thee*, Mrs. Sarah Flower Adams, was sister of Eliza, who wrote its original tune—not now sung.)

(2) **Newman**—in full Walter Newman, 1879–1964. Chairman of book-publishing firm of Cassell & Co., Ltd. Author of books on Sullivan, Schubert, and (especially) Handel. Knighted 1938.

Flowers of the Forest. The melody is an old Scottish one. The original words are lost—all but a few lines which were incorporated by Jane Elliott in her version in the middle of the 18th c. The words now usually sung are by Mrs. Cockburn and were written a little later (about 1765). Mrs. Cockburn's version properly has its own tune but is now generally sung to the same one as Jane Elliott's. (The Forest is a district of Selkirk and Peebles; the 'Flowers' are its young men.)

Flow gently, Deva. See *Parry, John Orlando*.

Floyd, Carlisle (b. Latta, S. Carolina, 1926). Composer and pianist. Educated univs. of Spartanburg (S.C.) and Syracuse (N.Y.). On staff Florida State Univ. from 1947. Composer of operas, esp. the successful *Susannah* (q.v.).

Flüchtig (Ger.). 'Fleet', 'agile'. The comparative is *flüchtiger* and the noun *Flüchtigkeit*.

Flue Pipe and **Flue Stop.** See *Organ* 2.

Flügel (Ger. 'wing'). The grand piano, or, formerly, the harpsichord. (Cf. *Kielflügel*; *Pedalflügel*.)

Flügelhorn. See *Saxhorn and Flügelhorn Families.*

Fluido (It.). 'Fluid.' So *fluidità, fluidezza,* 'fluidity'.

Flüssig (Ger.). 'Fluid', 'flowing'. So *flüssiger,* 'more flowing'.

Flute. See *Flute Family.*

Flûte (Fr.). 'Flute' (see *Flute Family; Recorder Family; Organ* 2).

Flûté (Fr.). Same as *flautando* (q.v.).

Flûte à cheminée (Fr., 'Chimney flute'). Same as *Rohrflöte* (q.v.).

Flute amabile. Organ stop, same as *Flûte d'amour* (q.v.).

Flûte à pavillon (Fr., lit. 'tented flute'). Organ stop of 8- or 4-foot length and pitch; each pipe ends in a sort of bell-tent structure.

Flûte d'amour (Fr., lit. 'love flute'). (1) See *Flute Family.* (2) Soft Organ stop, in Britain, of 8- or 4-foot length and pitch, and in U.S.A. of 2-foot length and 4-foot pitch (being end-plugged).

Flute Family. This very ancient family has 2 branches, which are separately treated in the present book, the end-blown branch receiving attention under the heading *Recorder Family* and the present article concerning only the side-blown branch ('Transverse Flute').

The transverse flute is a cylindrical tube with a more or less conical (parabolic) head: the tube is stopped at one end. The player blows across a side hole in the head and his breath sets in vibration the column of air inside the tube. Acoustically the tube acts as an open one; the mouth-hole serves to prevent its acting as stopped and thus sounding an 8ve lower (cf. *Organ* 2).

There is a range of three 8ves. The lowest 8ve is produced by altering the effective length of the tube by the action of keys closing finger-holes; the next 8ve similarly but with increased wind-pressure; the 8ve above that by a system of 'cross-fingering' too complicated for brief description. The quality of the lowest 8ve is rather thick and somewhat like that of the clarinet; that of the middle 8ve smooth and clear; that of the highest 8ve bright

and penetrating. Agility is a characteristic of the instrument, shakes and some tremolos being easy and also rapid reiterations of notes (by processes described under *Tonguing*).

Flutes were originally made of wood, but silver and other metals are now common. The present structure and mechanism are due to Theobald Boehm (see *Boehm System,* and for a further attempt at improvement see *Giorgi Flute*).

AN 18TH-CENTURY FLUTE PLAYER
(From *The Compleat Tutor for the German Flute* 1780)

The members of the family in use in the orch. today are (1) The CONCERT FLUTE; (2) The PICCOLO (or *Octave Flute*), whose pitch is an 8ve higher than that of the Concert Flute; and (3) The so-called BASS FLUTE, with a pitch a 4th (or 5th) lower than that of the Concert Flute (really, then, an Alto Flute and so named in some languages). The old FLÛTE D'AMOUR (with a pitch a 3rd below that of the Concert Flute) is now obsolete. The Concert Flute is sometimes called 'Flute in D' (from its natural scale), and sometimes 'Flute in C' (from its present usual lowest note). It is not treated as a 'transposing instrument' (see *Transposing Instruments*), being written for as it sounds. The Bass Flute is a transposing instrument, being written for as a 4th higher than it sounds.

The first to introduce the side-blown flute into orch. music was perhaps

Lully; in the mid-18th c. Bach and Handel sometimes indicate that they want the side-blown instrument and sometimes that they want the end-blown one. From Haydn onwards it can be taken that the side-blown one is intended.

Flûte harmonique (Fr.). (1) Mouth organ (see *Reed Organ Family* 2). (2) A certain organ stop.

Flute Quartet. See *Quartet*.

Flute Stop (on organ). See *Doppelflöte, Fernflöte, Flauto traverso, Flûte d'amour, Grossflöte, Harmonic Flute, Hohlflöte, Rohrflöte, Spitzflöte, Suabe Flöte, Waldflöte, Zauberflöte,* &c.

Flutter Tonguing. See *Tonguing*.

Flying Dutchman, The (Wagner). See *Fliegende Holländer*.

Focoso (It.). Fiery.

Foerster, (1) **Josef Bohuslav** (b. Prague 1859; d. Stara Boleslav 1951). Son of another Josef, also a musician. Worked in Hamburg, then in Vienna; then settled in Prague, holding position of importance. Composed symphonies, operas, &c.

(2) **Adolph Martin** (b. Pittsburgh 1854; there d. 1927). Composer of symphonies and chamber music, piano and organ music, and songs; Pittsburgh teacher and conductor.

Fogg, Eric—in full Charles William Eric (b. Manchester 1903; d. London 1939). Son of a well-known Manchester musicians; choir-boy of Manchester Cathedral; from early age fluent composer; from 1924 on staff of B.B.C.

Foggin, Myers (b. Newcastle-on-Tyne 1908). Pianist and conductor. Trained R.A.M.; 1936–49 conducted People's Palace Choral and Orch. Society. Musical director, Toynbee Hall, 1946; then Director of Opera, R.A.M., and later Warden. Principal, T.C.L., 1965.

Foire des enfants. See *Toy Symphony*.

Fois (Fr.). 'Time', e.g. *première fois*, 'First time'; *deux fois*, 'Twice'.

Fokine. See *Ballet*.

Foldes, Andor (b. Budapest 1913). Pianist. Pupil of Dohnányi. World-wide concert career; in U.S.A. from

1939; some piano compositions, and a book on piano technique.

Folge (Ger.). 'Succession', 'series', 'continuation'.

Folgen (Ger.). 'To follow'; so the various parts of the verb, as *folgt,* 'follows'.

Foli (real name Foley), **Allan James** (b. Tipperary 1835; d. Southport 1899). Bass vocalist. After training in Naples appeared with high success in opera in various It., Fr., Br., Russ., and Amer. centres. In Britain enjoyed fame as an oratorio singer.

Folía or Follía (accent on the 'i'). Originally a type of wild Portuguese dance. One of the various extant melodies used (a very simple one) has enjoyed remarkable popularity during 3½ centuries, being used by very many composers as the basis of instrumental music (of the air-with-variations type) or of vocal music. The best-known example is Corelli's 12th Sonata for violin and harpsichord. The ground bass there associated with it is found in many other examples.

Folk Dance. See *English Folk Dance and Song Society*.

Folk Lore. Properly, the whole body of peasant knowledge and art of any country, and quite wrongly applied by continental (and some Amer.) writers to folk music in particular.

Folk Mass. See *Mass*.

Folk Song. Song which has grown up amongst the peasantry of any race, being transmitted orally from generation to generation and sung without accompaniment. Its idiom commonly expresses racial characteristics, so that its source can be identified or guessed at when it is heard (compare the difference of flavour between Eng. and Irish folk song). Folk songs are always verse-repeating (q.v.) and are often not in the modern scales but the old modes.

Societies exist for the collection and publication of the folk songs of England, Wales, and Ireland and, in view of the danger of the disappearance of peasant art of every kind under the conditions of modern life (advance of education, easy transport, migration to the towns, broadcasting, &c.), their labours have come none too soon. Many composers have in their works made use of the melodies or idioms of folk song (the Eng. Elizabethan keyboard composers, also Haydn, Grieg, Dvořák, Albéniz, Stanford, Vaughan Williams, &c.).

(An occasional use of the term Folk Song as a mere synonym for 'Popular Song' is regrettable as tending to confuse categories.)

See *Sharp, Cecil*; *English Folk Dance and Song Society*.

Follía. See *Folía*.

Fonds d'orgue. 'Foundation Tone' and also 'Foundation Stops' (cf. *Foundation*). *Jeux de Fonds* definitely means the Foundation Stops (i.e. all the stops except the Mutation and Mixture stops). See *Organ* 2.

Fontane di Roma (Respighi). See *Fountains of Rome*.

Foot ('8-foot', '4-foot', '2-foot', '16-foot', &c.). See *Organ* 2.

Foote, Arthur William (b. Salem, Mass., 1853; d. Boston 1937). Studied at New England Conserv., Boston, and under J. K. Paine at Harvard; pursued long and fruitful career as Boston teacher and as composer of orch. and chamber works, piano pieces, songs, &c. Also wrote or collaborated in musical textbooks.

Forbes, (1) **Robert Jaffrey** (b. Stalybridge 1878; d. Manchester 1958). Trained Royal Manchester Coll. of Music, of which later Principal (1929-53). Accomplished pianist and orch. and operatic conductor. Lecturer Manchester Univ. C.B.E. (1948).

(2) **Watson** (b. St. Andrews 1909). Viola player. Trained R.A.M. and under Sevčik. Prominent chamber-music and orch. player. Has publ. arrangements for viola.

Ford, Thomas (b. abt. 1580; d. London 1648). Lutenist and composer of lute songs, &c.

Forest, The ('Der Wald'). Opera by Ethel Smyth. Libretto (Ger.) by composer. (Prod. Berlin and London 1902; New York 1903.)

For he's a jolly good fellow. See *Malbrouck s'en va-t-en guerre*.

Forkel, Johann Nikolaus (b. nr. Coburg 1749; d. Göttingen 1818). Organist and director of music at Univ. of Göttingen; wrote many useful books on music, including one of the earliest histories and the first biography of Bach.

Forlana, or **Furlano** (It.), or **Forlane** (Fr.). A popular old It. dance in compound duple time—a sort of gigue.

Form. It is obvious that (*a*) a piece of music which passed throughout from one musical idea to another, with always something new, would exact a degree of attention on the part of the listener which would become too mentally fatiguing to allow of any pleasurable sensation, whilst (*b*) a piece which consisted entirely of the repetition of one musical idea would equally (to sophisticated audiences at all events, as distinct from the members of primitive races) become extremely tiresome. A skilful arrangement of musical material in such a way as to avoid both these extremes thus becomes necessary, and as the art of composition has developed, means of avoiding these extremes have been increasingly devised; the result of this has been that whereas in (say) the 16th and 17th cs. instrumental compositions were practically all very brief (e.g. a movement in a keyboard suite of Byrd or Purcell), by the 19th c. they were frequently long (e.g. a sonata or symphony movement of the later Beethoven). This implies an enormous growth in the understanding of the principles of Form and in mastery of the application of those principles. Despite, however, all experiment on the part of innumerable composers, the forms so far devised can be classified into no more than 6 categories, all of them exploiting the idea of contrast plus variety both in the domain of Thematic Material and in that of Key (combinations of these are, of course, possible, e.g. in Simple Ternary Form each section can be in Binary Form, and so on).[1]

(1) SIMPLE BINARY FORM (e.g. in the movements of Bach's keyboard suites) has no

[1] All the following descriptions must be taken as useful generalizations. The details given are the normal, from which, of course, individual works may vary.

strong contrast of material. The 1st section opens, of course, in the Tonic key and then (subject to an exception shortly to be mentioned) modulates, as it ends, into the key of the Dominant. The 2nd section then opens in that 2nd key and, before it ends, modulates back to the 1st. There are, then, 2 distinct main cadences, or points of rest, the 1st in the Dominant and the 2nd in the Tonic. The exception just referred to is this: If the piece is in a minor key the 1st section sometimes ends in the relative major. This form, although it sometimes attained fairly considerable dimensions in the 18th c., is unsuitable for very long pieces, since the variety offered to the listener is almost entirely confined to details of treatment and the element of key, the thematic material employed throughout being the same. Since the period that ended with the death of Bach and Handel, this form has been little used.

(2) TERNARY FORM. This is one of the most commonly used forms for short compositions. It consists of a 1st section (more or less complete and self-contained), a 2nd section, contrasting as to musical material and key (normally in the Dominant or the Tonic Minor or Relative Major), and then the 1st one repeated. See *ABA*.

(3) COMPOUND BINARY FORM (also known as SONATA FORM, because often employed in the first or some other movement or movements of a Sonata; and as FIRST MOVEMENT FORM for the same reason). This derives historically from the Simple Binary Form but has developed into something more resembling Ternary Form. Like the Simple Binary it falls into 2 sections, of which the 1st modulates to the Dominant and the 2nd takes us back to the Tonic. But the sections have become elaborated as follows:

1st Section. Strain I (called *First Subject*) in Tonic key; followed by Strain II (called *Second Subject*) in Dominant key. Those 2 strains (or 'Subjects') are generally contrasted in character. This section is called the *Enunciation* or *Exposition*.

2nd Section. Some *Development* (also called 'Working-out' or 'Free Fantasia': see *Development*) of the material in the previous section, followed by a repetition (*Recapitulation*) of that section, but this time with both subjects in the Tonic key so that the piece may end in the key with which it opened.

Details are the following: (*a*) There is a *Bridge Passage*, leading (in both sections) from the First Subject to the Second; (*b*) At the end of each section there is some sort of a closing passage (*Coda*).

A tendency towards the evolution of Simple Binary Form into Compound Binary Form may be observed in some of J. S. Bach's movements, but its first real exploita-

tion is connected with the name and fame of his son, C. P. E. Bach, and its further exploitation and elaboration with the names of Haydn, Mozart, Beethoven, and their contemporaries. This form is still in frequent use, but there has latterly been a growing tendency to modify it in detail.

(4) RONDO FORM. This may be considered an extension of Ternary Form. Let the 3 sections of that form be indicated by the formula A, B, A; then the Rondo Form must be indicated by A, B, A, C, A, D, A, or some variant of this. (The sections B, C, D are often spoken of as *Episodes*.)

SONATA-RONDO FORM, as its name implies, offers a combination of the Compound Binary and Rondo Forms. The general plan is as follows: 1st Section. Subject I, Subject II in another key, Subject I repeated. 2nd Section. Development of the previous Subject-material. 3rd Section. Subject I and Subject II again, but the latter this time in the same key as Subject I.

Sometimes the Development above mentioned is replaced by new material. And there are other variants.

(5) AIR WITH VARIATIONS. This form, which from the 16th c. to the present day has been popular with composers of every class from the most trivial to the most serious, consists, as the name implies, of one theme (or 'Subject'), first played in its simplicity and then many times repeated with elaborations, each variation thus taking on its own individuality.

(6) FUGUE FORM.[1] In all the forms above mentioned there may be much or little interweaving of melodic strands (i.e. counterpoint), but such interweaving is of the very essence of the Fugue. The texture of a Fugue is made up of a certain fixed number of such strands. If the idea is strictly carried out we find the composition spoken of as a 'Fugue in Four Parts', or in 'Four Voices' (or whatever the number of strands may be). Not all of the parts are necessarily present together, but in any case their fixed number is never exceeded. Thus, for whatever medium the Fugue is composed (it may be, for instance, for keyboard), it is thus, in a sense, laid out as though for a choral body, and that is why, as we have seen, the word 'voices' is often used for the melodic strands of which the texture is woven.

These 'voices' enter at the outset one after the other, with a scrap of melody, or *Subject* (different from the 'Subject' of, say, a Sonata movement, in that it is merely melodic and short). When all have entered we have come to the end of what we call the *Exposition*. Then (normally) there comes an *Episode* or passage of connective tissue (usually a development of something that has appeared in the exposition) leading to another entry or series of entries of the

[1] See footnote on p. 207.

Subject—and so on until the end of the piece, entries and episodes alternating.

Contrasts of key constitute an important element in fugal construction. In the Exposition the Subject first appears, naturally, in the Tonic key; the 2nd voice to enter with it does so a 5th higher (or lower), i.e. in the Dominant key, the name *Answer* now being attached to it; the 3rd one is a repetition of the Subject (in a higher or lower 8ve), and so on, Subject and Answer thus appearing alternately, according to the number of 'voices' engaged, and Tonic and Dominant keys thus also alternately. One function of the Episodes is to effect modulation to various related keys, so that the later entries may have the advantage of this variety, but once the Exposition is over it is not considered necessary that further series of entries shall always alternate as to keys in the Subject–Answer manner.

In addition to the Subject there is often a *Countersubject* appearing in the Exposition and probably later in the Fugue. It is of the nature of a melodic accompaniment to the Answer and Subject (generally in double counterpoint—see *Counterpoint*). The voice which has just given out the Subject or Answer then goes on to the Countersubject whilst the next voice is giving out the Answer or Subject and so on.

Sometimes in later entries we have an overlapping of the Subject, each voice, as it gives out, not waiting for the previous voice to finish it but breaking in, as it were, prematurely. This device, which is called *Stretto*, tends to increase the emotional tension of the entry in which it occurs.

Occasionally, after the Exposition (and possibly before the 1st Episode) we find a *Counter-Exposition*, much like the 1st Exposition in that the same 2 keys are employed. Appearances of the Subject (in the Exposition or elsewhere) are sometimes separated by something of the Episode nature but shorter, called a *Codetta*.

There exist 2 types of FUGUE WITH TWO SUBJECTS (or DOUBLE FUGUE), one in which the 2 Subjects appear from the outset (in double-harness, so to speak) and another in which the 1st Subject is treated for a certain time, the other then appearing and being likewise treated, after which we find the 2 combined. In choral fugues (e.g. in an oratorio movement) there is sometimes a free instrumental part, and then we have an ACCOMPANIED FUGUE. The device of PEDAL (see *Harmony* 2 i) is often employed in fugue, especially near its close.

An explanation must now be given of a detail sometimes present in the Answer. There are cases in which, instead of its being an exact replica of the Subject (a *Real Answer*), it is, for reasons not easily explained in so short a treatment as the present, slightly changed in 1 or 2 of its intervals

(*Tonal Answer*). So we speak of a *Real Fugue* and a *Tonal Fugue* (an absurdity since the tonal treatment may not extend beyond the exposition).

A shortened type of fugue is sometimes called a FUGHETTA. A passage in fugal style, not in itself an actual fugue, is called FUGATO.

Combinations of several movements in different forms (Suite, Sonata, Symphony, Concerto, &c.) are called CYCLIC FORMS.

There are very many types of composition to which distinctive names are given, each representing not a 'Form' but rather a style in which one of the above forms is presented; such, for instance, are the Nocturne, the Gavotte, the Barcarolle, the Concertstück, and so on (over 150 of these styles will be found separately treated under their own names in the present book).

Format de poche (Fr.). 'Pocket-size' (score, &c.).

Formes, (1) **Karl Johann** (b. Mülheim 1815; d. San Francisco 1889). Operatic bass. Début Cologne 1841. Then at Mannheim 1843–8. London début 1849; U.S.A. 1857. (2) **Theodor** (b. Mülheim 1826; d. nr. Bonn 1874). Operatic tenor. Brother of the above and toured with him in U.S.A. Died insane.

Fornsete. See *John of Fornsete.*

Forrester, Maureen (b. Canada 1931). Contralto; trained Berlin. Début Montreal 1953; New York 1957. Successful concert appearances esp. in works of Mahler, &c.

Forster, Will. See *Will Forster's Virginal Book.*

Forsyth Bros., Ltd. Music firm, including publishing (Hallé's Pianoforte series, &c.) in its business since 1872. (Manchester and 34 Berners St., London, W. 1.)

Forsyth, Cecil (b. Greenwich 1870; d. New York 1941). Trained R.C.M. Orch. viola player; then light opera conductor in London. Settled New York 1914. Composed comic operas, orch. and choral music, &c., and wrote standard book on orchestration (1914), &c.

Fort (Ger.). (1) 'Forwards', 'continually'. (2) 'Away'—in organ music this means that the stop in question is now to be silenced.

Forte (It.). 'Strong', i.e. loud (abbrev. *f*). So *fortissimo*, 'very strong' (abbrev. *ff*, or *fff*); *fortemente*, 'strongly'.

Fortfahren (Ger.). 'To go forward.'

For the fallen (Elgar.) See *Spirit of England.*

Fortissimo (It.). See *Forte.*

Fortner, Wolfgang (b. Leipzig 1907). Composer. Trained Leipzig Conserv. and Univ. On staff of Heidelberg Church Music Institute. Compositions include symphonies, a violin concerto, ballet music, &c., also piano and chamber music.

Fortsetzung (Ger.). 'Continuation.'

Fortunatus. See *Pange, lingua.*

Fortune my foe. Old song, alluded to by Shakespeare (*Merry Wives*), Ben Jonson, and many other Elizabethan playwrights. Became the most popular 'hanging tune', i.e. vehicle for the words put into the mouths of criminals at public executions and hawked around the gallows. Appears in the Fitzwilliam Virginal Book (q.v.).

'Forty-eight, The' (Bach). See *Wohltemperirte Klavier, Das.*

Forty-part Motet. See *Tallis.*

Forza (It.). 'Force', 'vigour'. So *forzando*, 'forcing'; *forzato*, 'forced'.

Forza del destino, La ('The Force of Destiny'). Opera by Verdi. Libretto by F. M. Piave, based on a Spanish drama of 1835. (Prod. St. Petersburg 1862; Rome 1863; London 1867.) Many translations.

Foss, (1) (orig. Fuchs) **Lukas** (b. Berlin 1922). Came as boy to U.S.A.; studied in Paris, at Curtis Inst., Philadelphia, and under Hindemith at Yale. Pianist Boston Symph. Orch. 1944–50. On staff Univ. Calif. 1953. Cond. Buffalo Symphony Orch. 1963–9. Has composed ballets and other orch. music, songs, choral music, &c., with experiments in 'ensemble improvisation'.

See *Jumping Frog.*

(2) **Hubert James** (b. Croydon 1899; d. London 1953). First manager and

musical ed. (1924) of music dept. of Oxford Univ. Press, author of books on music, ed. of journal, *Music Lover*; authority on printing.

Foster, (1) **Stephen Collins** (b. Pittsburgh 1826; d. New York 1864). Southerner by descent and depicted in 175 songs, humorous or sentimental, the life of the southern white and Negro population (e.g. *My Old Kentucky Home, Swanee River = Old Folks at Home*). See *Negro Minstrels*. Commemorated by a memorial museum on the campus of Univ. of Pittsburgh.

(2) **Ivor Llewellyn** (b. Pontypridd, Glam., 1870; d. Bridgend, Glam., 1959). Operatic and concert baritone. Trained R.C.M. Popular 'ballad' singer and fest. artist. See (6) below.

(3) **Muriel** (b. Sunderland 1877; d. London 1937). Mezzo-soprano. Trained R.C.M. and won international repute, with special fame in Britain as sensitive and expressive oratorio singer.

(4) **Roland** (b. Dundalk, Ireland, 1879). Vocal teacher. Trained G.S.M. (later on staff). Since 1915 on staff N.S.W. State Conserv., Sydney. Author books on singing.

(5) **Arnold (Wilfred Allen)** (b. Sheffield 1898; d. London 1963). Trained R.C.M.; pupil of Vaughan Williams. Succeeded Holst (q.v.) as director Morley Coll., London (1928–40); conducted Eng. Madrigal Choir same period. Music-master Westminster School (1926–61). Arranged Eng. folk dances for orch. and for piano and composed choral, orch., and chamber music, &c.

(6) **Megan** (b. Tonypandy, S. Wales, 1898). Soprano. Pupil of father (see 2 above). Popular concert artist.

Fouetté (Fr. 'Whipped'). In ballet, a spectacular step introduced from Italy; the dancer is propelled into a turn (pirouette) by a whipping circular movement of one leg, while standing on the point of the other.

Fougueux, fougueuse (Fr. masc., fem.). 'Impetuous.'

Foulds, John Herbert (b. Manchester 1880; d. Calcutta 1939). Began professional life as 'cellist in Hallé Orch.; composed much and varied music, including *World Requiem* (1923; calls for enormous forces); experimented in use of microtones. Maud MacCarthy (1881–1967) was his wife.

Foundation. In organ parlance this word is used in 2 different senses. (1) *Foundation Tone* is that of all the more dignified stops (Diapason, the more solid of the Flute stops, &c.). (2) *Foundation Stops* are all the stops except the Mutation and Mixture stops (see *Organ* 2 and cf. *Fonds d'orgue*).

Fountains of Rome ('Fontane di Roma'). Symphonic Poem by Respighi (1916), in 4 sections, each with the name of a famous fountain. 1st perf. Rome 1917; New York 1919; London 1921.)

Four-hand Pianoforte Music. See *Pianoforte Playing*.

Fournier, Pierre (b. Paris 1906). Violoncellist. Entered Paris Conserv. aged 12 (later on staff). As chamber player frequently associated with Schnabel and Szigeti, attaining high international reputation. Also soloist with leading European and Amer. orchestras.

Four Rustics, The (Wolf-Ferrari). See *I Quattro rusteghi*.

Four Saints in Three Acts. Opera by Virgil Thomson. Libretto by Gertrude Stein. (Prod. Hartford, Conn., 1934; then New York and Chicago.)

Fourth. See *Interval*.

Fourth of August (Elgar). See *Spirit of England*.

Fox-Strangways, Arthur Henry (b. Norwich 1859; d. nr. Salisbury 1948). Educated Oxford (M.A. 1882) and Hochschule, Berlin. Then master at Dulwich Coll. and Wellington Coll. (music-master of latter 1893–1901). London music critic from 1911 (*Observer* 1925–39); founder and 1st ed. (1920–37) *Music and Letters*; author of *Music of Hindustan* (1914); part-author of life of Cecil Sharp; active translator of German Lieder.

Fox-trot. An Amer. ballroom dance to music of a sort of march-like ragtime, slow or quick. From about 1913 it spread to all the world's ballrooms. The *Charleston* and *Black Bottom* are varieties of it.

F.R.A.D. Fellow of the Royal Academy of Dancing (founded 1927; chartered 1936).

Fra Diavolo. Light Opera by Auber. (Prod. Paris 1830; London and New York 1831.)

Frais, fraîche (Fr. masc., fem.) 'Fresh.' So *fraîcheur*, 'freshness'.

F.R.A.M. See *Degrees and Diplomas* 2.

Franc (or Le Franc), **Guillaume** (b. Rouen abt. 1505; d. Lausanne 1570). Huguenot composer, precentor successively at the cathedrals of Geneva and Lausanne, under the Calvinistic dispensation, and ed. of a book of metrical psalms (1565).

Franc, franche (Fr. masc., fem.). 'Frank', 'open-hearted', 'bluff'.

Français, française (Fr. masc., fem.). 'French.'

Française. Old round dance in triple or compound duple time. Very popular in the 1830's.

Françaix, Jean (b. Le Mans 1912). Pupil in composition of Nadia Boulanger and in piano of I. Philipp. First symphony in Paris 1932 provoked loud protest. Prolific composer of orch. works, ballets, &c.

Francesca da Rimini. Opera by ZANDONAI. Libretto after d'Annunzio. (Prod. Turin and London 1914; New York 1916.)

There are also operas with the same title by GOETZ (1877), RACHMANINOF (1906), &c., a Symphonic Fantasia by TCHAIKOVSKY (op. 32, 1876; based on picture by Gustave Doré), and a Symphonic Poem by HENRY HADLEY (1st perf. Boston 1905).

All the above are based on the story in Dante's *Inferno*, Canto V.

Francescatti, (Réné) Zino (b. Marseilles 1905). Violinist. Appeared as prodigy from age 5. Settled Paris 1927, then U.S.A. First-rank international career. Officer of the Legion of Honour.

Franchetti (Baron), Alberto (b. Turin 1860; d. Viareggio 1942). Wealthy Italian trained in Germany; composer of operas and orch. and chamber works.

Franchezza (It.), **franchise** (Fr.). 'Freedom of spirit', 'boldness'.

Franchomme, Auguste Joseph (b. Lille 1808; d. Paris 1884). Fine 'cellist; wrote chamber music, a 'cello concerto, &c. Intimate friend of Chopin.

Franciscus. See *Tinel, E.*

Franck, (1) César (Auguste Jean Guillaume) (b. Liège 1822; d. Paris 1890). Trained at Paris Conserv., and in later life (aged 50) became an organ prof. there. Compositions long attracted little notice, but he was surrounded by a group of pupils who revered him (cf. *d'Indy*): first real public success as composer came when he was 68, with performance of his String Quartet; following month was knocked down by omnibus and so badly injured that he did not long survive.

His life was that of a saint but (despite experiences that would have soured most men) a cheerful one: some of his early works are trivial but the Symphony, the Prelude, Choral, and Fugue (piano), the Prelude, Aria, and Finale (piano), the Symphonic Variations (piano and orch.), some bigger organ works, &c., display undoubted mastery. Style is very personal (and somewhat limited) in its idiom; he shows influence of Bach, Beethoven, and Liszt both in the general feeling behind his work and in some of the forms adopted.

See also *Béatitudes*; *Chasseur maudit*; *Djinns*; *Éolides*; *Redemption*.

(2) **Joseph** (b. Liège 1820; d. Paris 1891). Brother of César; minor composer, chiefly of church music; author of textbooks.

(3) **Eduard** (b. Breslau 1817; d. Berlin 1893—Unrelated to César and Joseph). Prof. of piano in various conservatories; composer of sound chamber music, piano sonatas, &c.

Francs juges, Les ('The Judges of the Secret Court'). Overture by Berlioz (op. 3; abt. 1827), written for an intended opera.

Frank, Alan (Clifford) (b. London 1910). Writer and broadcaster on music. Editorial staff Oxford Univ. Press 1927; head of music dept. from 1948. His wife is Phyllis Tate.

Frankel, Benjamin (b. London 1906; d. there 1973). A watchmaker's apprentice. Then trained in Germany and at G.S.M. (later on staff). At one time earned his living as a jazz-band violinist, &c. Composer of 7 symphonies and other orchestral and chamber music, film music, &c.

Frankenstein, Alfred (Victor) (b. Chicago 1906). Educ. Univs. of Chicago (on staff 1932–4) and Yale. Mus. (also painting) critic *San Francisco Chronicle* from 1934.

Franklin, David (b. London 1908). Operatic bass. Appeared Glyndebourne 1936–9; Covent Garden, 1946–50, &c. Frequent broadcasts.

Fransella, Albert (b. Amsterdam 1865; d. 1935). Flautist. Pupil of his father and de Jong (q.v.): joined latter's orch. at Manchester. Then Scottish, Crystal Palace, and Queen's Hall Orchs. Formed London Wind Sextet, and a Wind Trio. On staff G.S.M.

Franz, Robert (b. Halle 1815; there d. 1892). First came into prominence when near 30, as a song composer; as such praised by Schumann and also by Mendelssohn and Liszt. Then a nervous malady and deafness overtook him, and his admirers had to raise money to support him. Songs number about 350—nearly all for mezzo-soprano, and lyrical rather than dramatic; also did much work as ed. of Bach and Handel, to whose music he supplied additional accompaniments (now put aside as insufficiently in consonance with the composers' styles).

Frapper (Fr.). 'To strike.' So *frappant*; *frappé*, 'striking'; 'struck'.

Fraser, M. Kennedy-. See *Kennedy-Fraser*.

Fraser-Simson, Harold (b. London 1878: d. Croy, Inverness, 1944). Popular composer of songs, operettas, ballets, &c.

Frauenchor (Ger.). 'Women's Choir.'

Frauenliebe und Leben ('Women's Love and Life'). Cycle of 8 songs by Schumann (op. 42; 1840), settings of poems by the Ger. romantic poet Chamisso.

Frau ohne Schatten, Die ('The Woman without a Shadow'). Opera by Richard Strauss. Libretto by Hofmannsthal. (Prod. Vienna 1919.)

F.R.C.M. See *Degrees and Diplomas* 2.

F.R.C.O. See *Degrees and Diplomas* 2.

Freddo (It.). 'Cold.' So *freddamente*, 'coldly'; *freddezza*, 'coolness', 'indifference'.

Frederick the Great (b. Berlin 1712; d. Potsdam 1786). Maintained, according to the court custom of the day, a domestic body of musicians, including, at different times, several of importance as composers (e.g. Quantz, C. P. E. Bach); was himself an ardent flautist and composed lavishly for his instrument (works still publ.). J. S. Bach visited his court at Potsdam in 1747, and the *Musical Offering* (q.v.) is the result.

See references under *Education and Music* 1; *Agricola* 3, 4.

Fredonner (Fr.). 'To hum.'

Freebooter Songs. See *Wallace, William.*

Free Canon. See *Canon.*

Free Counterpoint. See *Counterpoint.*

Free Faburden. See *Faburden.*

Free Fantasia. Same as 'Development' in Compound Binary Form, &c. (see under *Development* and also *Form* 3).

Freed, Isadore (b. Brest Litovsk 1900). Pianist and composer, pupil of Bloch, d'Indy, Joseph Hofmann, &c. On staff Curtis Inst. 1924; Temple Univ. 1935; Hartt Coll. of Mus. 1944. Composer of orch. and chamber music, &c.

Freer, Dawson (b. Croydon 1886). Vocal teacher. For some years on staff of T.C.M. and R.C.M.; then taught privately in London. Author of practical books on vocal technique, &c.

Free Reed. See *Reed.*

Frei, freie, &c. (Ger., various terminations according to case, &c.). 'Free.'

Freie Kombination (Ger.). 'Free Combination'—one of the facilities provided on an organ for preparing registration.

Freischütz, Der ('The Marksman'). Opera by Weber—one of the most popular of all Ger. operas. (Prod. Berlin 1821; at 4 London theatres, Edinburgh, and Philadelphia 1824; Dublin and New York 1825.)

Fremstad, Olive (b. Stockholm 1871; d. Irvington-on-Hudson 1951). Operatic mezzo-soprano. As a child a prodigy pianist; then taken U.S.A.; became piano teacher but developed as singer (trained under Lilli Lehmann in Berlin, &c.). After Ger. opera successes appeared Metropolitan Opera 1903. Special reputation as Wagner interpreter.

French Harp. Mouth organ.

French Horn. See *Horn Family.*

French Overture. See *Overture.*

French Sixth. See *Augmented Sixth.*

French Suites. Name (possibly unauthorized) given to a set of 6 Keyboard Suites by Bach. Its origin lies perhaps in their grace and delicacy of treatment. Cf. *English Suites, German Suites.*

Frenetico, frenetica (It. masc., fem.). 'Frenzied.'

Frequency of Sound Vibration. See *Acoustics* 2, 8, 13; *Broadcasting of Music.*

Frere, Walter Howard (b. nr. Cambridge 1863; d. Mirfield, Yorks., 1938). Authority on liturgical music, publishing results of much valuable research. Author of important introduction to Historical Edn. of *Hymns Ancient and Modern* (1909). Superior (Anglican) Community of Resurrection, Mirfield, 1902–13 and 1916–22. Bishop of Truro 1923–34.

Fresco (It.). 'Fresh', 'cool'. So the adverb *frescamente.*

Frescobaldi, Girolamo (b. Ferrara 1583; d. Rome 1643). Organist of St. Peter's, Rome, and in high repute as a player; composer of organ music (some still played today); also wrote madrigals and motets. Through his pupils (Froberger, &c.) had much influence on course of Ger. music. (See *Germani.*)

Frets in a stringed instrument are raised lines across the finger-board (originally cords tied round it) marking the positions the fingers should assume in order to produce the particular notes. (Cf. *Viol Family* 1 e; *Lute*; *Mandoline*; *Guitar*; *Banjo*; *Balalaika*.)

Fretta (It.). 'Haste.' Hence *frettevole, frettoso, frettoloso, frettolosamente,* 'hurried'.

Fretted. See *Frets*; *Clavichord*.

Frettevole, Frettoso, &c. See *Fretta*.

Freude (Ger.). 'Joy.' So *freudig,* 'joyful'.

Freund, John Christian (b. London 1848; d. Mt. Vernon, N.Y., 1924). Educated Oxford Univ. Settled New York 1871, engaging in musical journalism (founded *Musical America* 1898).

Fricker, Peter Racine (b. London 1920). Studied R.C.M.; then under Mátyás Seiber. Varied compositions— chamber music, orch., &c. 4th symph. 1966. Mus. director Morley Coll., London, 1953. Res. Santa Barbara 1965.

Frid, Geza (b. Hungary 1904). Pupil of Kodály and Bartók; composer of chamber music, &c. Res. Holland.

Fried, Oskar (b. Berlin 1871; d. Moscow 1941). Horn player; then conductor of important Berlin organizations, choral and orch. Made European tours. Conductor Tiflis opera from 1934. Many compositions.

Friedemann Bach (Opera). See *Graener*.

Friedheim, Arthur (b. St. Petersburg 1859; d. New York 1932). Pianist. Pupil of Anton Rubinstein and Liszt (for some years his secretary and companion). Resident at various periods London, Chicago, Munich, Toronto, New York, &c. Compositions for piano, operas, &c. Edited Chopin's works, &c.

Friedman, Ignaz (b. nr. Cracow 1882; d. Sydney 1948). Pianist. Pupil of Leschetizky. Toured world. Lived latterly Australia. Composed piano and chamber music, &c. Edited Chopin (complete piano works), also Schumann, Liszt, and Neupert.

Frisch (Ger.). 'Fresh', i.e. brisk and lively.

Friskin, James (b. Glasgow 1886; d. New York 1967). Trained at R.C.M. as pianist and composer; settled in New York 1914; produced chamber music, &c. Married Rebecca Clarke.

Friss or Friszka. See *Czardas*.

F.R.M.C.M. See *Degrees*, &c. 2.

Froberger, Johann Jacob (b. Stuttgart 1616; d. Héricourt 1667). Court organist at Vienna and composer of important keyboard works.

Froebel. See *Education and Music* 1.

Frog Quartet (Haydn). See *Froschquartett*.

Fröhlich (Ger.). 'Happy.'

Froid (Fr.). 'Cold.' So *froidement,* 'coldly'.

Froissart. Concert-overture by Elgar, inspired by a passage in Scott's *Old Mortality* in which Claverhouse speaks of his enthusiasm for the Froissart Chronicles. (Op. 19; Worcester Fest. 1890.)

From Bohemia's meadows and forests (Smetana). See *My Fatherland*.

From Italy (Strauss). See *Aus Italien*.

From my life (*Aus meinem Leben*). By Smetana, being 2 String Quartets, in E minor (1876) and C minor (1882). Some, however, attach the name merely to the first of these. See also under *Smetana*.

From the Bavarian Highlands (Elgar). See *Scenes from the Bavarian Highlands*.

From the New World. See *Dvořák's Symphonies*.

Frosch (Ger. 'frog'). The nut of the bow of the violin, &c. So *am Frosch,* 'at the nut'.

Froschquartett('Frog Quartet'). Nickname of Haydn's String Quartet no. 49, in D, sometimes described as op. 50, no. 6. The reference is to the character of the chief theme of the finale.

Frottola (It., plur. *frottole*). A late 15th- and early 16th-c. popular unaccompanied choral form, a sort of simple madrigal. The same music was sung to the various verses and the tune was in the highest part. Thus it resembled the Eng. ayre (see *Madrigal*).

Früher (Ger.). 'Earlier', 'previously'.

Frühlingslied (Mendelssohn). See *Spring Song*.

Frühlingsrauschen (Sinding). See *Rustle of Spring*.

Frühlingssonate (Beethoven). See *Spring Sonata*.

Fry, William Henry (b. Philadelphia 1813; d. Santa Cruz 1864). Composer of 1st notable Amer. opera (*Leonora*, Philadelphia 1845; New York 1858; on It. model of early 19th c.); *Notre Dame de Paris* followed some years later (1864). One of the pioneers of music criticism in U.S.A.

Fryer, Herbert—in full George Herbert (b. London 1877; d. there 1957). Pianist. Trained R.A.M. and R.C.M.; then under Busoni, &c. Prominent recitalist from 1898, touring extensively in Europe and throughout English-speaking world. On staff Inst. Musical Art, New York, 1914–16; on that of R.C.M. 1916–47.

F.T.C.L. See *Degrees and Diplomas* 2.

F.T.S.C. See *Degrees and Diplomas* 2.

Fuchsova, Liza (b. Brno, Czechoslovakia, 1913). Pianist, trained Prague Conserv. (then on staff). European concerts and broadcasts particularly of modern (espec. Brit.) music. Brit. resident from 1939.

Fuga alla giga, i.e. 'Fugue in Jig-style' (Bach). For Organ. In G. So nicknamed from the nature of its rhythm.

Fugara. Organ stop; a rather rougher toned variety of *Gamba* (q.v.).

Fugato. A passage in fugal style (see *Form* 6).

Fughetta. A short Fugue (see *Form* 6).

Fugue. See *Form* 6.

Fuguing Tunes. See *Hymns and Hymn Tunes* 4.

Führend (Ger.). 'Leading.'

Fuleihan, Anis (b. Cyprus 1900; d. Stanford, Calif., 1970). Went to U.S.A. at 15; composer, pianist, and conductor. Indiana U. 1947; dir. Nat. Conserv. Beirut 1953; cond. Tunis 1963–5.

Full, as applied to Anthems and other music in the church service. See *Verse*.

Full Close. See *Cadence*.

Fuller, Frederick (b. Kirkham, Lancs., 1909). High baritone. Studied univs. Liverpool, Paris, Munich, Harvard (M.A.). Trained singing New York, France, Germany, &c. Recitalist of wide repertory, espec. Iberian and Latin-American music.

Fuller Maitland, John Alexander (b. London 1856; d. nr. Carnforth 1936). Music critic of *The Times*, 1889–1911; good pianist and harpsichordist; publ. books, ed. 2nd edn. of Grove's *Dictionary of Music*; ed. (in collaboration with W. Barclay Squire) Fitzwilliam Virginal Book; one of pioneers of Eng. folk-song movement by publication (in collaboration with Lucy Broadwood) of *English County Songs* (1893). Hon. D.Litt., Durham.

Füllflöte (Ger.). A 'full-toned' (i.e. loud) flute stop on the organ.

Fülligstimmen (Ger. 'full-toned voices'). Organ stops of loud tone.

Full mixture. Organ Mixture stop (see *Mixture Stop*) of which pipes are of Diapason scale.

Full Organ. As an indication in organ music, directs the player to use Great coupled to Swell, with all the louder stops on both manuals.

Full Score. See *Score*.

Füllstimme (Ger., lit. 'Filling-voice'). (1) A middle strand in the texture of a composition (choral or instrumental) which may be looked upon as merely accessory. (2) An additional orch. part (cf. *Ripieno*), &c. (3) The mixture stop of an organ.

Full to Mixtures. Organ composers' term meaning use all loud stops except Reeds (see *Mixture Stop* and *Organ* 2).

Full Trichord. See *Pianoforte*.

Fumagalli, Adolfo (b. nr. Milan 1828; d. Florence 1856). Pianist and composer of pieces of the lighter kind—some still popular.

Fundamental Bass. See *Harmony* 2 e.

Fundamental Discord. See *Harmony* 2 g.

Fundamental Note. See *Acoustics* 7.

Funèbre (Fr.), **funebre** (It.). 'Funeral', &c. So *marche funèbre*, 'funeral march'.

Funeral Marches. Amongst the best known of these (all of them in some public use on occasions of mourning) are the following: (1) HANDEL's *Dead March in Saul* (from the oratorio of that name); (2) The 2nd movement of BEETHOVEN's 3rd Symphony (*Eroica*); (3) The 3rd movement of CHOPIN's 2nd Piano Sonata (in B flat minor, op. 35); (4) CHOPIN's *Marche funèbre*, op. 72 b in C minor.
There are also (5) BEETHOVEN's March 'sulla morte d'un eroe' ('on the death of a hero'), which is a movement in his Piano Sonata in A flat, op. 26; (6) MENDELSSOHN's *Song without Words* no. 28, in E minor (the title 'Funeral March' not, however, authentic); (7) The Funeral March for Siegfried from WAGNER's *Dusk of the Gods*; (8) GRIEG's Funeral March for Nordraak (Military Band, but scored also by Halvorsen for Orch.); (9) BERLIOZ's *Funeral March for the Last Scene of 'Hamlet'* (op. 18, no. 3; 1848). And there are others.

Funeral March of a Marionette. Orch. witticism by Gounod, originally intended to become one movement of a Burlesque Suite.

Funeral Heroid (Liszt). See *Héroïde funèbre*.

Fünf (Ger.). 'Five.' So **fünfstimmig,** 'five-voiced', i.e. in 5 'parts' or 'strands'.

Funiculì, funiculà. See *Denza*.

Fuoco (It.). 'Fire', i.e. a combination of force and speed. (But *focoso*, 'fiery'.)

Für (Ger.). 'For.'

Furia (It.). 'Fury.' So *furioso, furibondo,* 'furious'; *furiosamente,* 'furiously'.

Furiant. A Bohemian dance type, rapid and of decided yet often-changing rhythm.

Furieux; furieusement (Fr.), **furioso, furibondo; furiosamente** (It.). 'Furious'; 'furiously'.

Furmedge, Edith (b. London 1898; there d. 1956). Operatic and concert contralto. Pupil and then wife of Dinh Gilly. Appeared Covent Garden, &c.

Furniture or **fourniture** (in organ terminology). A powerful *Mixture Stop* (q.v.).

Furore (It.). (1) 'Fury'. (2) 'Enthusiasm'.

Furry Dance. An ancient processional dance at Helston, Cornwall, sometimes called 'Floral Dance' or 'Flora'. It resembles the Farandole (q.v.).

Furtwängler, Wilhelm (b. Berlin 1886; d. nr. Baden-Baden 1954). Orch. and opera conductor. Pupil of Rheinberger, Mottl, &c. Held important posts as conductor in Berlin, Leipzig, Vienna, &c., and conducted in Britain and U.S.A. Potsdam Mus. Academy 1947. Then permanent conductor Vienna Philharmonic Orch.

Fury over a Lost Groschen. See *Rage over a Lost Penny*.

Futurism. See *Marinetti*.

Fux, Johann Joseph (b. Hirtenfeld, Upper Styria, 1660; d. Vienna 1741). Voluminous composer and learned theorist, especially notable as codifier of rules of 'Strict Counterpoint' (see *Counterpoint*; *Gradus ad Parnassum*).

Fuyant (Fr.). 'Fleeing.'

G

G (in Fr. organ music) = *grand orgue*, i.e. 'Great Organ'.

Gabrieli, or **Gabrielli**, (1) **Andrea** (b. Venice abt. 1510; there d. 1586). Pupil of Willaert (q.v.) and served under him at St. Mark's, Venice, later becoming one of its organists: famous throughout Europe as choral and organ composer. The great Dutch master Sweelinck one of his pupils. (2) **Giovanni** (b. Venice 1557; there d. 1612). Nephew of the above; also became one of organists of St. Mark's; like uncle enoyed international fame. Schütz one of his pupils.

Gabrilowitsch, Ossip (Solomonovich) (b. St. Petersburg 1878; d. Detroit 1936). Pianist and orch. conductor. Pupil of Rubinstein, Leschetizky, &c. Won high international reputation as pianist; became conductor of Detroit Orch. 1918, later conducting also Philadelphia Orch. in partnership with Stokowski. Married Mark Twain's daughter.

Gade, Niels Vilhelm (b. Copenhagen 1817; there d. 1890). Began composing in nationalistic vein, but Leipzig training prevailed and influence of Mendelssohn and Schumann swamped his racial and individual traits. Assistant some time to Mendelssohn as conductor and succeeded him for short period; then returned to Copenhagen as organist and conductor. Visited England to conduct cantata *The Crusaders* (Birmingham Fest. 1876), which long enjoyed Brit. popularity; composed also 8 symphonies, violin concerto, graceful piano works, songs, &c.

Gadsby, Henry Robert (b. London 1842; d. Putney 1907). Boy chorister of St. Paul's Cathedral who as composer was self-taught. On staff G.S.M. &c. Prolific and popular provider of orch. and chamber music, cantatas, church music, &c.

Gadski, Johanna (Emilia Agnes) (b. Pomerania 1872; d. Berlin 1932).

Operatic and *Lieder* soprano. Especially famous in London and New York as Wagner interpreter.

Gaelic Symphony. See *Beach, Amy Marcy.*

Gafori, Gaforio, Gafuri, &c., **Franchino** (b. Lodi 1451; d. Milan 1522). Famous theoretical writer (*Practica musicae*, 1496).

Gagliano, Marco da (b. Gagliano, nr. Florence, 1575; d. Florence 1642). Canon and musical director of St. Lorenzo, Florence; founder there of famous musical society (Accademia degl' Elevati); leading musician of that city and one of the early group of opera composers (see also *Peri* and *Caccini*): his *Daphne* perf. at Mantua 1608; wrote also madrigals and church music.

Gagliarda (It.). Galliard (see *Pavan and Galliard*).

Gagnebin, Henri (b. Liège 1886). Swiss by parentage, and head of Conservatory of Geneva (1925); composer of orch. and chamber music; as also an oratorio of original type and 'modern' harmony (*St. Francis of Assisi*, 1935).

Gai; gaiement (Fr.). 'Gay'; 'gaily'. So *gaîté*, 'gaiety'.

Gaillard. Galliard (see *Pavan and Galliard*).

Gaio, gaia (It. masc., fem.). 'Gay.' So *gaiamente*, 'gaily'.

Gajo (It.). Older spelling of *Gaio* (q.v.).

Gál, Hans (b. Brunn-am-Gebirge, Austria, 1890). Distinguished musicologist and well-known composer; from 1938 in Edinburgh.

Galant, galamment (Fr.); **galan.** (Ger.); **galante, galantemente** (It.). 'Gallant', 'gallantly'.
Cf. *Style galant.*

Galanterien (Ger.), **galanteries** (Fr.). In the classical Suite (q.v.) movements which were not looked upon as essential to the scheme but rather as interpolations of light relief. They usually comprised any of the following: Minuet, Gavotte, Bourrée, Passepied, Loure, Polonaise, Air.

Cf. *Style galant.*

Galanter Stil (Ger.). See *Style galant.*

Galilei, Vincenzo or **Vincentino** (b. Florence abt. 1520; there d. 1591). One of famous group of Florentine musicians who originated opera; singer, violinist, lutenist, composer, and theorist; father of the great astronomer, Galileo Galilei.

Galin-Paris Chevé. A Fr. sight-singing system on movable-doh lines and with a practical device for acquiring the sense of time-values of notes (Pierre Galin, 1786–1821; Aimé Paris, 1798–1866, and Nanine Paris, d. 1868; Emile J. M. Chevé 1804–64). Cf. *Tonic Sol-fa.*

Gallegada. See *Muiñeira.*

Galliard. See *Pavan and Galliard*; *God save the King.*

Galliard Ltd. London Music Publishers (148 Charing Cross Road, W.C. 2).

Galli-Curci, Amelita—Mrs. Homer Samuels (b. Milan 1882; d. La Jolla, Calif., 1963). Coloratura soprano. Trained Milan Conserv. as pianist; self-trained as singer, by making gramophone records of her singing and studying defects. Début Rome 1909; Chicago 1916; Metropolitan 1921. Retired 1937.

Galliera, Alceo (b. Milan 1910). Conductor. Trained Milan Conserv. (later on staff, as also of Siena Conserv.). Became conductor of orch. of La Scala, &c. Has also appeared in many other European cities.

Galli-Marié, Marie Célestine Laurence—formerly Marié de l'Isle (b. Paris 1840; d. nr. Nice 1905). Operatic mezzo-soprano. Début Strasbourg 1859. The earliest Carmen (Paris 1875). High international fame—especially for vivid acting.

Gallop, Rodney Alexander (b. Folkestone 1901; d. 1948). Brit. Foreign Office official, student of folk music (Basque country, Portugal, Mexico, &c.). C.M.G. 1946.

Gallus. See *Handl.*

Galop or **Galopade.** A lively round dance in simple duple time, with a change of step, or hop, at the end of every phrase of the music.

Galoubet and Tambourin. See *Recorder Family* 2.

Galpin, Francis William (b. Dorchester 1858; d. Richmond 1945). Anglican clergyman (Canon Emeritus of Chelmsford Cathedral); erudite antiquarian, of especial authority in history of musical instruments. Hon. D.Litt., Cambridge. (A Galpin Society carries on his work.)

Galuppi, Baldassare (b. Island of Burano, nr. Venice, 1706; d. Venice 1785). Studied under Lotti and became eminent as opera composer, visiting London and St. Petersburg and composing operas for their theatres; placed in charge of music in St. Mark's, Venice; was an able harpsichordist and composed for his instrument (but Browning's poem, *A Toccata of Galuppi's*, describes an imaginary composition).

Gamba (or **Viola da Gamba**). (1) See *Braccio and Gamba*; *Viol Family* 2. (2) String-toned organ stop: 8-foot length and pitch (sometimes 4 or 16-foot). Metal pipes often tapering towards top and sometimes widening again into an inverted bell—hence *Bell Gamba.* A variety with a small roller before mouth of each pipe is *Bearded Gamba.*

Gamelan. A type of orch. common in the East Indies, with bowed and woodwind instruments, gongs, drums, rattles, marimbas, &c.

Game of Cards (Stravinsky). See *Jeu de Cartes.*

Gamme (Fr.). 'Scale.'

Gamut. (1) Properly, the note G at the pitch now indicated by the lowest line of the bass staff. Greek G or 'gamma' was used for its designation, and as the note just mentioned was the 'Ut' (or as we should now say, 'Doh') of the lowest Hexachord (q.v.) this portmanteau word came into use as a name for it. (2) By extension the word came to be used as a comprehensive name for the whole series of Hexachords as displayed in writing. Shakespeare (*Taming of the Shrew*) shows knowledge of the Gamut in that sense and Pepys writes of 'conning his Gamut'. (3) By a further extension it came to mean 'scale' in general (cf. Fr. 'gamme'). (4) And it came also to mean the whole range of musical sounds from the lowest to the highest.

Gangar. A 'walking' dance of Norway.

Ganz (Ger.). 'Quite', 'whole', e.g. *ganzer Bogen*, 'whole bow'; *gänzlich*, 'Completely'.

Ganz, (1) **Wilhelm** (b. Mainz 1833; d. London 1914). Pianist and conductor. Settled in London 1850; accompanist to Jenny Lind and many leading violinists; also orch. violinist. Founded 'Mr. Ganz's Orchestral Concerts' 1880–2; prof. of singing G.S.M. Composed piano music and songs.

(2) **Rudolph** (b. Zürich 1877). Pianist (pupil of Busoni, &c.) and then conductor. Became U.S.A. citizen; on piano staff Chicago Musical Coll. (1901), principal 1934–54. Conductor St. Louis Orch. 1921–7. Composer orch., choral, and piano works. Hon. D.Mus. several U.S.A. institutions.

Ganze, Ganze Note. Same as *Ganzetaktnote* (see below).

Ganze Pause. Semibreve rest.

Ganzetaktnote (Ger. 'whole-measure note', or 'whole-bar note'). The whole-note or semibreve.

Garaguly, Carl (b. Budapest 1900). Conductor and violinist. Trained Budapest Conserv. under Hubay and later in Berlin. Appearances in Hungary as violinist from age 7, later in Germany, Austria, Sweden, &c. Leader of Stockholm Symphony Orch. and in 1941 appointed its conductor.

Garbo (It.). 'Manners' (in a good sense), 'bearing', 'grace'. So *garbato*, *garbatamente*, 'elegantly', 'gracefully'; *garbatissimo*, 'very graceful'; *garbatino*, 'rather graceful'; *garbatezza*, 'gracefulness'.

Garcia, (1) **Manuel del Popolo Vicente** (b. Seville 1775; d. Paris 1832). Great operatic tenor, opera

composer, and highly successful singing-master (Paris, London, New York, &c.). (2) **Manuel Patricio Rodriguez** (b. Madrid 1805; d. London 1906, aged 101). Son of the above; singing-master of overwhelming reputation and inventor of the Laryngoscope (q.v.): on staff of R.A.M. 1848–95. (3) **Maria Felicia**—known by her first married name of **Malibran** (b. Paris 1808; d. Manchester 1836). Daughter and pupil of the first Manuel; an operatic contralto of unbounded reputation. Her second husband was de Bériot (q.v.). (4) **Pauline** —in full Michelle Pauline, known by her married name of **Viardot**, or **Viardot-Garcia** (b. Paris 1821; there d. 1910). Another daughter and pupil of the first Manuel and a celebrated operatic mezzo-soprano (of unusually extended compass): a piano pupil of Liszt and wrote operas and songs. (5) **Gustave** (b. Milan 1837; d. London 1925). Son of the second Manuel; a successful operatic baritone; on staff of R.A.M. and R.C.M. as teacher of singing. (6) **Albert** (b. London 1875; there d. 1946). Son of Gustave and like him a baritone; on staff of R.C.M., G.S.M., and T.C.M.

Gardel, Pierre. See *Ballet*.

Garden of Fand, The. Symphonic Poem by Bax (1913). Inspired by Irish legend. Lady Fand's 'garden' was the ocean, of which her father was the Lord. (1st perf. Chicago and London 1920; Paris 1923.)

Garden, Mary (b. Aberdeen 1874; d. there 1967). Operatic soprano. Taken U.S.A. as child. Trained Paris; début there in *Louise* 1900: created part heroine *Pelléas and Mélisande* 1902. U.S.A. début New York 1907. Manager Chicago Opera 1921–3.

'Gardens' (London). See reference under *Concert*.

Garder (Fr.). 'To keep', 'to hold', with the imperative *gardez*.

Gardiner, Henry Balfour (b. London 1877; d. Salisbury 1950). Educated at Charterhouse and Oxford and in Germany; for a time a music-master at Winchester Coll.; composed attractive orch. and other music and before war of 1914–18 was active in promoting interest in works of contemporary countrymen by series of London concerts. See *Shepherd Fennel's Dance*.

Gardner, (1) **Samuel** (b. Elizabethgrad, Russia, 1891). Taken as child to U.S.A. Became violinist (pupil of Loeffler, q.v.). In Kneisel Quartet, &c. Conductor. On staff Inst. of Musical Art, New York. Compositions largely for violin.

(2) **John (Linton)** (b. Manchester 1917). Composer. Educ. Oxford (B.Mus.). On staff Repton Sch. 1939–40; Air Force 1941; Covent Garden coach 1946; Morley Coll. 1952; R.A.M. 1956. Composer of opera *The Moon and Sixpence*, a symphony, and choral music, also music for plays and films.

Garland, (1) **John** = Johannes de Garlandia (early 13th c.). Learned Eng. theologian and grammarian, composer and theoretician, resident in Oxford and Paris (identity, however, somewhat uncertain).

(2) **Dora** (b. 1893). Violinist. Trained R.C.M. Became leader of Queen's Hall Orch. 1918, later appearing with same as soloist. Married Harold Darke (q.v.).

Garreta, Juli (b. San Feliu 1875; there d. 1925). Catalan watchmakercomposer, who wrote effective sardanas, orch. music, chamber music, &c.

Garrett, George Mursell (b. Winchester 1834; d. Cambridge 1897). Organist of St. John's Coll., Cambridge, and composer of sound church music.

Gaspard de la nuit. Set of piano pieces by Ravel (1908)—(1) *Ondine*; (2) *Le Gibet* ('The Gibbet'); (3) *Scarbo*. Based on Aloysius Bertrand's romantic prose-ballads of the same title, which bear the sub-title, 'Fantaisies à la manière de Rembrandt et de Callot' (1842).

Gassmann, Florian Leopold (b. Brüx, Bohemia, 1723; d. Vienna 1774). Pupil of Padre Martini. After a short career in Italy he became court ballet composer at Vienna and then Kapellmeister there. His operas had great success in their time.

Gastein Symphony. See *Schubert's Symphonies*.

Gastoldi, Giovanni Giacomo (b. Caravaggio abt. 1555; d. Mantua 1622). Choirmaster of ducal chapel at Mantua abt. 1581 to death; accomplished composer of church music and madrigals.

Gastoué, Amédée (b. Paris 1873; d. Clamart 1943). Eminent church musician and plainsong expert (on staff of Schola Cantorum, q.v.); authority on early Fr. music, and bibliographer; author of a long list of books on his subjects and also a composer of masses and motets.

Gate of Life. See *Leoni*.

Gathering Note. This term, which has to do with hymn tunes, is applied in two slightly different ways:

(a) To the single treble note (or sometimes pedal note) with which old organists used to precede the first or every verse of a hymn, as a signal, presumably, to the congregation to open their mouths and be ready. (At some time if the treble note was used, it was often given an ictus by the use of the semitone below it as an acciaccatura.)

(b) To the note, longer than the succeeding notes, with which each line of some hymn tunes begins, probably put there by the composer with a similar purpose. This latter kind of gathering note was very usual in the 4-lined common-metre English tunes (see *Hymns and Hymn Tunes* 8) from the last quarter of the 16th c. to the last quarter of the 17th, and is sometimes found in tunes of the 18th c. Steggall, Hullah, and one or two others in the 1860's tried to reinstate these gathering notes, but without success. The *English Hymnal* of 1906 (see *Hymns and Hymn Tunes* 4), on grounds of rhythmic variety, repeated this attempt.

Gathering Psalm. The first psalm in old Scottish Presbyterian worship. So called from the fact that at one time it was sung as the congregation was assembling—like the organ's opening voluntary today.

Gatti, (1) **Guido Maria** (b. Chieti 1892; d. 1973). Editor of several It.

musical journals, author of books on various phases of It. music, &c.; joint-author of dictionary of music; frequent contributor to musical press of various countries; organizer of concerts, &c.

(2) **Gabriella** (b. Rome 1912). Operatic and concert soprano. Trained Acad. St. Cecilia, Rome; winner of high awards. Successful tours abroad in England and elsewhere.

Gatti-Casazza, Giulio (b. Udine 1869; d. Ferrara 1940). Operatic impresario. Scala, Milan, 1898; then Metropolitan, New York, 1908–35. (Cf. *Alda.*)

Gaubert, Philippe (b. Cahors 1879; d. Paris 1941). At Paris Conserv. student of flute and then its prof., as also conductor of orch. of its concert society (1919–38); conductor, too, of the Grand Opéra. Composer of orch. and chamber music, operas, and songs.

Gauche (Fr.). 'Left.' *Main gauche,* 'left hand'.

Gaudeamus igitur. See under *Academic Festival Overture.*

Gaul, Alfred Robert (b. Norwich 1837; d. King's Norton 1913). Birmingham organist who attained high popularity as composer of cantatas (see *Ruth*; *Holy City, The*).

Gauntlett, (1) Henry John (b. Wellington, Shropshire, 1805; d. London 1876). Church musician (lawyer by profession). Organ reformer; designed 56 organs for Hill (q.v.); student of plainsong; published over 25 collections of church music of various kinds and said he believed he had composed 10,000 hymn tunes. (2) **Ambrose**—grandson of above (b. London 1890). Violoncellist. Trained G.S.M. and R.A.M. (later on staff). Principal 'cellist Covent Garden Opera Orch.; B.B.C. Symphony Orch. 1935–47. Also player of viola da gamba (see *Viol Family* 2 c, 4).

Gavotte. A dance form deriving from the Pays de Gap in France, whose inhabitants are known as 'Gavots'. Its music is in simple quadruple time and in steady rhythm; each phrase opens on the 3rd beat of a measure. Often it is found followed by a *musette* after which the Gavotte is repeated.

Gay, Maria (b. Barcelona 1879; d. New York 1943). Operatic soprano. Début Brussels 1902, Covent Garden 1906, Metropolitan Opera 1908—all these as Carmen. Retired 1927. Married G. Zenatello.

Gayarre, Julian (b. nr. Pamplona 1843; d. Madrid 1890). Operatic tenor. Trained Madrid Conserv. Then appeared Milan, Vienna, St. Petersburg, South American centres, &c.; Covent Garden 1877. Founded at Madrid vocal school for poor Spanish boys.

Gazza ladra, La ('The Thieving Magpie'). Opera by Rossini. (Prod. Milan 1817; London 1821; Philadelphia 1827.)

G.B.E. See *British Empire, Order of the.*

G.B.S.M. See *Degrees and Diplomas* 2.

G Clef. See *Great Staff*: Table 4.

Gd.Ch. = 'Grand Chœur' (Fr.), i.e. 'Full Choir', or 'Full Organ'.

Gebet (Ger.). 'Prayer.'

Gebrauch (Ger). 'Use', e.g. *Pedalgebrauch*, 'Use of the pedal' (in piano playing).

Gebrauchsmusik (Ger. 'utility music'). A type of music of some 20th-c. pre-Nazi German and Austrian composers (e.g. Hindemith, Křenek, Kurt Weill) who, under the teaching of the revolutionary poet Bert Brecht, opposed the idea of 'Art for art's sake' and maintained the necessity of preserving contact with the masses by finding inspiration in subjects of actuality and using musical idioms in everyday use.

Gebunden (Ger.). 'Bound.' (1) In the sense of 'tied' or 'slurred'. (2) See *Clavichord.*

Gedact or **Gedeckt** (Ger. 'covered'). Soft organ stop approaching flute quality: name comes from end-plugged pipes; 8-foot pitch, or 16, or 4 (occasionally 2).

Gedämpft (Ger.). 'Damped', i.e. (stringed and brass instruments) muted; (drums) muffled; (piano) soft-pedalled.

Gedda, Nicolai (b. Sweden 1925). Operatic tenor. Trained Stockholm Conserv. Début Stockholm 1952;

Covent Garden 1954; Metropolitan 1957.

Gedeckt. See *Gedact*.

Gedehnt (Ger.). 'Stretched out', i.e. sustained. So *gedehnter*, 'more sustained' or 'prolonged'.

Gedicht (Ger.). 'Poem.'

Gedichte von Mörike (Wolf). See under *Mörike*.

Gedike. See *Goedicke*.

Gefallen (Ger.). 'Pleasure', in the phrase *nach Gefallen*, 'At one's own pleasure' (= *Ad libitum*; q.v.).

Gefällig (Ger.). 'Agreeable', in a pleasant sort of way, effortless and cheery.

Gefühl (Ger.). 'Feeling'; hence *gefühlvoll*, 'full of feeling'.

Gegen (Ger.). 'Towards', 'near', 'about', 'against', 'counter'.

Gehalten (Ger.). 'Held out', i.e. sustained; so *gut gehalten*, 'well sustained'.

Gehaucht (Ger.). 'Whispered.'

Geheimnisvoll (Ger. 'full of secrecy'). 'Mysterious.'

Gehend (Ger.). 'Going', i.e. *andante* (q.v.).

Gehörig (Ger.). 'Proper', 'suitable'.

Geige (Ger.; plur. *Geigen*). Originally any bowed instrument, now the violin.

Geigen Principal or **Geigen** (Ger. '*Geige*', 'fiddle'). Organ stop; a slightly string-toned diapason of 8-foot length and pitch, or sometimes 4-foot.

Geiringer, Karl (b. Vienna 1899). Distinguished musical scholar; 1923–38 in charge of library and instrument collection of historic 'Friends of Music' society at Vienna. Author of many books and articles, especially on Brahms and Haydn. Prof. Boston Univ. 1941–62; then Univ. California (Santa Barbara).

Geisha, The. Popular Operetta by Sidney Jones. (Prod. London and New York 1896; thereafter in many countries and languages.)

Geist (Ger.; cf. Eng. 'ghost'). 'Spirit', 'soul'.

Geister Trio, Das (Beethoven). See *Spirit Trio*.

Geistlich (Ger., cf. *Geist* above). 'Spiritual.' So *geistliches Lied*; *geistliche Lieder*, 'spiritual song'; 'spiritual songs'.

Gekneipt (Ger.). 'Plucked' (i.e. *pizzicato*).

Gekoppelt (Ger.). 'Coupled' (organ).

Gelassen (Ger.). 'Quiet', 'calm'.

Geläufig (Ger., from *laufen*, 'to run'). 'Fluent', 'nimble'. So *Geläufigkeit*, 'fluency'.

Gemächlich (Ger.). 'Comfortable', i.e. unhurried. So *gemächlicher*, 'more leisurely'.

Gemässigt (Ger.). 'Moderate' (i.e. with regard to speed).

Gemendo, gemebondo (It.). 'Moaning.'

Gemessen (Ger.). 'Measured.' (1) Precise (in time values). (2) At a moderate speed. (3) Grave, heavy in style.

Geminiani, Francesco (b. Lucca abt. 1680; d. Dublin 1762). Highly admired violinist and composer for stringed instruments (pupil of Corelli); wrote early violin method; lived a good deal in London, Dublin, and Paris.

Gemshorn (Ger., lit.'Chamois Horn'). Light-toned organ stop with conical pipes, generally of 4-foot length and pitch but sometimes 8 or 2.

Gemüt(h) (Ger.). 'Feeling.' So *gemütvoll*, 'feelingly'. (But *gemütlich* = 'easy-going', 'comfortable'.)

Genannt (Ger.). 'Called', 'known as'.

Genau (Ger.). 'Exact'; hence *Genauigkeit*, 'Exactitude'.

Gendron, Maurice (b. Nice 1920). 'Cellist. Trained Paris Conserv. Tours in Britain and elsewhere. Many transcriptions for 'cello.

Generalbass (Ger.). 'Figured Bass' (q.v.).

General Crescendo Pedal. See *Crescendo Pedal*.

General Pause. Rest or pause for all the executants.

Generator of Sound. See *Acoustics* 19.

Generoso (It.). 'Generous', lofty in style.

Gentil, gentille (Fr.). 'Gentle', 'pleasant', 'pretty'; hence the adverb *gentiment*.

Gentile (It.). 'Gentle', 'delicate'; so the adverb *gentilmente* and the noun *gentilezza*.

Gentlemen's Concerts, Manchester. Began 1744; ceased 1920. Owned own hall from 1777.

Gérardy, Jean (b. Spa 1877; there d. 1929). Violoncellist. First public appearance at 11, in trio with Paderewski and Ysaÿe, performing in Belgium and then in England. As adult attained preeminent position on both sides of Atlantic.

Gerhard, Roberto (b. Valls, Tarragona, Catalonia, 1896; d. Cambridge 1970). Last pupil of Pedrell (q.v.) and then pupil of Schönberg; composed orch. music, chamber music, piano music, opera, ballets, songs, &c. C.B.E. 1967.

Gerhardt, Elena (b. Leipzig 1883; d. London 1961). Soprano vocalist. Studied Leipzig Conserv. and under Nikisch, who often appeared as her accompanist. Début 1903; after early appearances in opera turned to oratorio and (especially) Lieder singing, in which last branch won extremely high international reputation. Settled in London 1934 as teacher.

Gericke, Wilhelm (b. nr. Graz 1845; d. Vienna 1925). Conductor Linz, Vienna, &c. Boston Symphony Orch. 1884–9 and 1898–1906.

German. A sort of *Cotillon* (q.v).

German, Edward—really Edward German Jones (b. Whitchurch, Shropshire, 1862; d. London 1936). Studied at R.A.M. and then played in orchs., soon becoming a theatre conductor. As composer showed gift for charming melody and light orchestration and soon became leading provider of incidental music to plays (3 dances written for *Henry VIII*, 1892, became universally known). Light operas (e.g. *Merrie England*, q.v.) had great success; also wrote symphonies, suites, and rhapsodies. Knighted 1928.

See also *Princess of Kensington*; *Richard the Third*; *Theme and Six Diversions*; *Tom Jones*; *Welsh Rhapsody*.

German Concertina. See *Reed-Organ Family* 4.

Germani, Fernando (b. Rome 1906). Organist. Trained Conserv. Rome and Papal Inst. Sacred Music. Has toured widely as recitalist both sides Atlantic, in several cities performing Bach's whole organ output; also various organ concertos with leading orchs. For 2 years directed advanced organ course at Curtis Institute (q.v.). From 1948 chief organist St. Peter's, Rome. Editor Frescobaldi's complete organ works, composer organ music, and author articles on organ subjects.

German Polka. See *Schottische*.

German Reed Entertainments. See *Reed, T. G.*

German Requiem, A (*Ein deutsches Requiem*). Oratorio (not a Requiem Mass) by Brahms, op. 45. (1st perf., in part, Vienna 1867; almost complete Bremen 1868; complete Leipzig 1869; London, in a private house, 1871—see *Loder, Kate*—publicly 1873.)

German Sixth. See *Augmented Sixth*.

German Suites. Unauthorized title for the set of 6 keyboard Partitas by Bach. (Cf. *French Suites*; *English Suites*; *Klavierübung*.)

Gerontius. See *Dream of Gerontius*.

Gershwin, George (b. Brooklyn 1898; d. Hollywood 1937). Jazz pianist and popular composer who came forward prominently in 1924 with *Rhapsody in Blue* (q.v.); also composed piano concerto, orch. music (see *American in Paris*), musical comedy *Of thee I sing* (1931), Negro folk-opera *Porgy and Bess* (prod. Boston and New York 1935), &c.

Gerster, Etelka (b. Hungary 1855; d. nr. Bologna 1920). High coloratura operatic soprano of great fame. For over 20 of last years of life conducted a vocal school in Berlin.

Gertler, André (b. Budapest 1907). Violinist. On staff Brussels Conserv. Repertory of classical and modern works. Many tours with Bartók.

Gerührt (Ger.). 'Moved' (in the emotional sense).

Ges (Ger.). G flat (see Table 7).

Gesang der Parzen (Brahms). See *Song of the Fates*.

Gesangvoll (Ger.). 'Song-like.'

Geschlagen (Ger.). 'Struck.'

Geschleift (Ger.). 'Slurred', i.e. *legato*.

Geschlossen (Ger.). 'Closed.'

Geschmack (Ger.). 'Taste'; hence *geschmackvoll*, 'tastefully'.

Geschöpfe des Prometheus, Die (Beethoven). See *Prometheus*.

Geschwind (Ger.). 'Quick.'

Geses (Ger.). G double flat (see Table 7).

Gesprochen (Ger.). 'Spoken.'

Gesteigert (Ger.). 'Increased', i.e. *crescendo*, or, it may be, *sforzando*.

Gestopft (Ger.). 'Stopped.' (1) Applied to horn notes produced with the bell of the instrument more or less closed by the hand. (2) An equivalent for *Gedämpft* (q.v.).

Gestossen (Ger.). 'Detached', i.e. *staccato*.

Gesualdo, Carlo, Prince of Venosa (b. Naples 1560; there d. 1613). Modernist madrigalist, harmonies passing far beyond most advanced then in use; stands quite alone, belonging to no 'school'. In 1590 murdered his first wife and her lover.

Geteilt, getheilt (Ger.). 'Divided', e.g. of violins—corresponding to *divisi* (q.v.). Sometimes abbreviated, *get.*

Getragen (Ger.). 'Carried', i.e. sustained.

Gevaert, François (Auguste) (b. nr. Oudenarde 1828; d. Brussels 1908). Succeeded Fétis as director of Brussels Conserv. and like him was author of many valuable musicological and theoretical works. Composed choral music, opera, &c.

Gewandhaus ('Cloth Hall'). In Leipzig; setting for celebrated concert series since 1781.

Gewichtig (Ger.). 'Weightily' (either in a more literal or more figurative sense, the latter amounting to 'With dignity').

Gewidmet (Ger.). 'Dedicated.'

Gewöhnlich (Ger.). 'Usual'—employed to countermand previous indication that the instrument concerned was to play in some unusual way, e.g. the violin after it has been playing *am Griffbrett* (near the fingerboard).

Gezogen (Ger.). 'Drawn.' (1) Drawn out, sustained. (2) Same as *portamento* (q.v.).

G.G.S.M. See *Degrees and Diplomas* 2.

Ghedini, Giorgio Federico (b. Piedmont 1892; d. Nervi 1965). Trained Turin Conserv. (on staff to 1937) and Bologna. On staff Parma Conserv. 1938; Milan Conserv. 1942. Composer of operas, orch., chamber, and church music, &c. Ed. of old It. music.

Ghiribizzo (It.). 'Caprice.' So *ghiribizzoso*, 'capricious'.

Ghost Trio. Nickname of Beethoven's Pfte. Trio, op. 70, no. 1. It alludes to the mysterious opening of the 2nd movement.

Giannini, (1) **Vittorio** (b. Philadelphia 1903; d. New York 1966). Trained Conserv. Milan; then Juilliard School of Music. Won Rome Prize (q.v.) and spent 4 years in Rome. On staff Juilliard School, &c. Composed operas, orch. works, a requiem (Vienna 1937), chamber music, songs, &c., also music for educational films. (2) **Dusolina** (b. Philadelphia 1902). Soprano. Opera and concert tours in U.S.A., Australia, and Europe. Sister of (1).

Gianni Schicchi (Puccini). See under *Trittico*.

Giant Fugue (Bach). For Organ. In D minor. So nicknamed from the stalking figure in the pedal.

Giardini, Felice de (b. Turin 1716; d. Moscow 1796). Brilliant violinist highly successful in London, where he was resident for long periods, and active as opera manager and composer, &c.

Gibbons, (1) **Edward** (b. abt. 1568; d. abt. 1650). Member of choir of King's Coll., Cambridge, and then Exeter Cathedral; a little church music by him survives. (2) **Ellis** (b. Cambridge 1573; d. 1603). Brother of the above and now known by 2 madrigals. (3) **Orlando** (b. Oxford 1583; d. Canterbury 1625). Brother of the two above. Choir-boy at King's Coll., Cambridge, and (at 21) organist of Chapel Royal, as later of Westminster Abbey. Considered to be the country's finest keyboard executant; composer of dignified church music, madrigals, and music for viols and for virginals; one of greatest names in the national roll of musicians of his period. (See *Parthenia*.) (4) **Christopher** (b. London 1615; there d. 1676). Son of Orlando and like him organist of Westminster Abbey; composed anthems, string fantasias, &c.

Gibbs, (1) **Richard.** Organist of Norwich Cathedral in early part of 17th c.; left a little church music.

(2) **John.** A shadowy personage to whom some of the work generally credited to Richard is by some assigned.

(3) **Joseph** (1699–1788). Ipswich organist; composer of excellent string sonatas.

(4) **(Cecil) Armstrong** (b. nr. Chelmsford 1889; d. there 1960). Studied at Cambridge (B.A., D.Mus.) and R.C.M. (later on staff). Composed comic operas, songs, chamber music, &c.

Gibet (Ravel). See *Gaspard de la nuit.*

Gibson, Alexander (b. Motherwell, Scotland, 1926). Conductor. Trained Glasgow Univ., R.C.M., Salzburg, &c. On staff Sadler's Wells 1951; B.B.C. Scottish Orch. 1952; Cond. Sadler's Wells 1954 (mus. director from 1957); mus. director Scottish Nat. Orch. from 1959. C.B.E. 1967.

Gieseking, Walter (Wilhelm) (b. Lyons 1895 of Ger. parents; d. London 1956). Pianist of high international reputation (appeared in Britain from 1923; later in U.S.A.); composer of chamber music, &c.

Giga. See *Gigue.*

Gigg, Gigge. Old Eng. spellings of *Jig* or *Gigue* (q.v.).

Gigli, Beniamino (b. Recanati 1890; d. Rome 1957). Operatic, concert, and film tenor. Trained Liceo S. Cecilia, Rome. Soon became internationally famous (New York 1920; London 1930)—especially in Puccini and Verdi.

Gigout, Eugène (b. Nancy 1844; d. Paris 1925). Noted Paris organist and well-known organ composer; pupil and son-in-law of Niedermeyer and member of staff of his church music school.

Gigue or Giga. A rustic Eng., Scottish, and Irish dance type (cf. *Jig*), of which the music runs along quickly in a rhythm of groups of 3 beats ($\frac{3}{8}$, $\frac{6}{8}$, $\frac{9}{8}$, $\frac{12}{8}$, &c.): often there is a long-short effect, a sort of merry limp (e.g. ♩ ♪♩ ♪). Pieces in gigue style came to be the customary closing movements of the suite: the form was binary, and, with Bach, the 2 halves often opened in something like fugal style (cf. *Form* 6), the subject of the 1st half being often inverted as that of the 2nd half. (Just occasionally Bach applied the term 'gigue' to a piece that was not such, being in plain 2-in-a-measure or 4-in-a-measure time.)

Gigues (Debussy). See under *Images.*

Gilbert, (1) **William Schwenk** (b. London 1836; drowned when bathing in lake in his own grounds at Harrow Weald 1911). Sullivan's most famous and most successful librettist in his comic operas; wrote also the *Bab Ballads*, &c. Knighted 1907.

(2) **Henry Franklin Belknap** (b. Somerville, Mass., 1868; d. Cambridge, Mass., 1928). Edward MacDowell's earliest composition pupil and the first serious Amer. composer to recognize the possibilities of Negro musical idioms.

Gilchrist, Anne Geddes (b. Manchester 1863; d. nr. Lancaster 1954). Well-known authority on Brit. folk song, also on history of hymn tunes. O.B.E.; F.S.A.

Gilels, Emil (b. Odessa 1916). Pianist, trained Odessa and Moscow Conservs. Appeared Vienna 1933, then worldwide career. U.S.A. 1955. On staff Moscow Conserv.

Giles, or Gyles, Nathaniel (b. Worcester abt. 1560; d. Windsor 1633). Organist of Worcester Cathedral and then of St. George's Chapel, Windsor Castle; learned musician who left much church music.

Gilly, Dinh (b. Algiers 1877; d. London 1940). Operatic baritone. Covent Garden début 1911; very popular England; joined Beecham Co. Taught in London. Cf. *Furmedge, Edith*.

Gilman, Lawrence (b. Flushing, N.Y., 1878; d. Sugar Hill, N.H., 1939). Distinguished and popular music critic (on *New York Herald-Tribune* 1923–39); author of books on Strauss, Debussy, MacDowell, &c.

Gilmore, Patrick Sarsfield (b. nr. Dublin 1829; d. St. Louis 1892). Bandmaster ('Gilmore's Band', Boston). Organized monster Festivals in Boston ('Peace Jubilees') 1869 and 1872, with respectively 11,000 and 22,000 performers, choral and orchestral. Claimed to be composer of *When Johnny comes marching home*.

Gimel. See *Gymel*.

Gioco (It.). 'Play', 'game'. So *con gioco, giochevole, giochevolmente,* 'Playfully'.

Gioconda, La. 4-act opera by Ponchielli. Libretto by Boito, based on Victor Hugo's play, *Angelo, Tyrant of Padua*. (Prod. Milan 1876; London and New York 1883.)

Giocondo, giocondoso (It.). 'Jocund.' So the adverbs *giocondevole, giocondamente,* and the nouns *giocondità, giocondezza*.

Giocoso (It.). 'Jocose.' So the adverb *Giocosamente*.

Gioia, Gioja (It.). 'Joy.' So *gioiante, gioioso, gioioso, gioiosamente,* 'joyfully'.

Gioielli della Madonna, I ('The Jewels of the Madonna'). Opera by Wolf-Ferrari. (Prod. Berlin 1911; Chicago, New York, and London 1912.)

Giordanello. See *Giordani Family*.

Giordani Family—father (Carmine), 2 daughters, and 3 sons, all of whom settled in Britain where they were active in operatic enterprises, &c. Two of the sons are of importance. (1) **Tommaso** (b. Naples abt. 1740; d. Dublin 1806). Opera singer in London; then settled in Dublin; active as opera

organizer, teacher, and composer. (2) **Giuseppe,** popularly called 'Giordanello' (b. Naples abt. 1753; d. Termo 1798). Associated with his brother's opera enterprises in Dublin but returned to Italy in 1782. Composed operas, church music, and instrumental music. The favourite song, *Caro mio ben*, is probably by him.

Giordano, Umberto (b. Foggia 1867; d. Milan 1948). Opera composer of the Mascagni stamp, most popular work being *Andrea Chénier* (q.v.; see also *Fedora*; *Madame Sans-Gêne*).

Giorgi Flute. A form of end-blown concert flute (see *Flute Family*), introduced in 1896 by T. C. Giorgi. It is built on strictly correct acoustical principles but does not appear to have established itself.

Gioviale; giovialità (It.). 'Jovial'; 'joviality'.

Giovinezza (It.). The official Fascist party song. Words by Salvatore Gotta; tune by Giuseppe Blanc.

Gipps, Ruth (b. Bexhill 1921). Studied at R.C.M. as pianist &c.; became for a time oboist in Birmingham Orch. Has composed symphonic poems, concertos, and chamber music for woodwind instruments, piano music, &c. D.Mus., Durham.

Gipsy Baron (Strauss). See *Zigeunerbaron*.

Giraffe. See *Pianoforte*.

Girl I left behind me, The. The words can be traced back to the end of the 18th c.: so can the tune, sometimes known as *Brighton Camp*. It is played in the Brit. Army on occasions of departure.

Girl of the Golden West, The (*La Fanciulla del West*). Opera by Puccini. Libretto based on Amer. play of David Belasco. (Prod. New York 1910; London, Liverpool, Rome, &c., 1911.)

Girl with the Flaxen Hair (Debussy). See *Préludes*.

Gis (Ger.). G sharp (see Table 7).

Giselle. Highly popular Ballet; music by Adolphe Adam (q.v.). On a story by

Théophile Gautier, based on a legend recorded by Heine, in his *Germany*. (Prod. Paris 1841.)

Gisis (Ger.). G double sharp (see Table 7).

Gitano, gitana (Sp. masc., fem.). 'Gipsy.' For *Seguidillas gitanas* see *Playeza*.

Gitlis, Ivry (b. Haifa 1922). Violinist; pupil of Flesch, Enesco, and Thibaud. International career; noted as interpreter of modern works.

Gittern. A sort of early guitar (q.v.) with gut strings—not to be confused with the Cittern (q.v.).

Giù (It.). 'Down', e.g. *arcata in giù*, 'down-bowed'.

Giubilo, giubilio (It.). 'Joy.' So *giubiloso*, 'joyous'; *giubilante*, 'jubilant'.

Giucante, giuchevole (It.). 'Playful.'

Giulio Cesare ('Julius Caesar') 3-act opera by Handel. Libretto by Haym (Prod. London 1724.)

Giulivo (It.). 'Joyous.' So the superlative *giulivissimo* and the adverb *giulivamente*.

Giuoco (It.). Same as *gioco* (q.v.)—and so with derivatives.

Giustamente (It.). 'With exactitude' (i.e. unvarying speed and rhythm).

Giustezza. 'Exactitude.' **Giusto, giusta** (It. masc., fem.). 'Just.' This word is used in the two senses (*a*) exact, (*b*) appropriate (e.g. *tempo giusto* puzzlingly means either 'strict time' or 'suitable time').

Givelet. See *Electric Musical Instruments* 4.

Glanville-Hicks, Peggy (b. Melbourne, Australia, 1912). Trained Melbourne Conserv. and R.C.M. London. Then under Nadia Boulanger, Wellesz, &c. Has composed much orch., chamber, stage, and film music, &c. Long res. U.S.A.; then in Greece.

Glänzend (Ger.). 'Brilliant.'

Glareanus. See *Modes*.

Glasgow. See *Festival*; *Schools of Music*.

Glasharmonika (Ger.). Musical Glasses (see *Harmonica* 1).

Glass Dulcimer. See *Harmonica* 2.

Glasses, Musical. See *Harmonica* 1.

Glatt (Ger.). 'Smooth.' So *Glätte*, 'Smoothness'.

Glazunof (Glazounow, &c.), Alexander (b. St. Petersburg 1865; d. Paris 1936). As a youth attached to the group of nationalist Russian composers; later showed more cosmopolitan sympathies in his style; composed 8 symphonies (first at age 16 performed by Balakiref), piano and violin concertos, ballets, chamber music, &c. (no operas); on staff of St. Petersburg (Leningrad) Conserv. and later its director. The Soviet govt. conferred on him the title of 'People's Artist of the Republic', but he soon after left for France, and there remained.

See also *Carnival*; *Stenka Razin*.

Glee. A choral composition in a number of short self-contained sections, each expressing the mood of some particular passage of the poem set, the music predominantly harmonic (i.e. in blocks of chords), rather than contrapuntal. Properly it is for male solo voices and unaccompanied. Its great period, during which a remarkable series of able composers made lavish contributions to the repertory, was from about 1750 to about 1830, after which latter date it gradually gave way to the part song (q.v.). It is a purely Eng. form, and was much fostered by the popularity of glee clubs. (Note that in U.S.A. this name has been applied to university musical clubs with much more general aims.)

Gleemen. See *Minstrels* 1.

Gleich (Ger.). 'Like' (in the sense of similar), 'equal'. So *gleichsam*, 'as it were', 'as if', &c.; *gleichmässig*, 'equal'; *gleichstark*, 'of equal strength'; *gleiche Stimmen*, 'Equal Voices' (q.v.).

Gleitend (Ger.). Gliding' (= *glissando*, q.v.).

Gli, glie (It. masc., fem.). 'The' (plur.).

Glière, Reinhold (b. Kief 1875; d. Moscow 1956). Pupil of Taneief and Ippolitof-Ivanof at Moscow Conserv.;

later a prof. there. Composed symphonies and symphonic poems (showing fine grasp of orch. effect), chamber music, operas, ballets, &c.

Glinka, Michael (b. in govt. of Smolensk 1804; d. Berlin 1857). Brought up on father's country estate, where he heard much folk music, as also performances of his uncle's private orch.; in St. Petersburg had a few lessons from Field (q.v.); went to Italy, where he studied It. opera (Bellini, Donizetti, &c.). Nearing 30 decided to write a Russian opera and went to Berlin to acquire technique by study under great teacher, Dehn; then returned and wrote *A Life for the Czar* (1836); *Russlan and Ludmilla* followed (1842). Spent 2 years in Spain and wrote orch. music based on Spanish folk tunes.

The Father of the Russian National School of composition and one of the founders of the Romantic School.

See also *Kamarinskaya*; *Life for the Czar*; *Russlan and Ludmilla.*

Gli Scherzi (Haydn). See *Russischen Quartette.*

Glissando (bastard It., from the Fr. *Glisser*, 'To slide'). (1, piano) A drawing of a finger down or up a series of adjacent notes. (2, bowed instruments) Passing from one note to another on the same string (or part of the way to this other), in much the same manner as above and with much the same effect—with the difference that the pitches passed through, instead of representing the fixed tones and semitones of a scale, are infinite in number.

Glisser; glissant (Fr.). 'To slide'; 'sliding'. See above for explanation.

Gli Ucelli (Respighi). See *Birds.*

Glock, William (b. London 1908). Studied music in Cambridge and Berlin; active as music critic (London *Observer* 1940–5), general writer on music, lecturer, and pianist. Dir. Dartington Hall 1948; Controller of Music, B.B.C. 1959–72. Editor, *The Score.*

Glöckchen. Small bell.

Glocke; Glocken (Ger.). Bell; Bells (see *Bell*; *Percussion Family* 1 b).

Glockenspiel. See *Percussion Family* 1 c.

Gloria in Excelsis Deo ('Glory to God in the highest'). The 'Doxologia Magna' (see *Doxologia*), an amplification of the song of the angels announcing the birth of Christ. It occurs in the Roman Mass (q.v.) and in the Communion Service of the Anglican Church (see *Common Prayer*).

Gloriana. Opera by Britten. Libretto by William Plomer. (Prod. Covent Garden 1953.)

Gloria Patri. See *Doxologia.*

Glorious Apollo. See *Webbe, Samuel I.*

Glorious First of August. See *First of August.*

Glory to thee, my God, this night. See *Tallis's Canon.*

Glory to the Soviet Pilots. See *Goedicke.*

Glotte, Coup de. See *Voice* 4.

Glottis. See *Voice* 4.

Glover, Sarah Ann. See *Tonic Sol-fa.*

Gluck, (1) Christoph Willibald von (b. nr. Neumarkt, Bavaria, 1714; d. Vienna 1787). In his twenties was composing operas in Italy and in his thirties in London, in which latter place he also appeared as a performer on some sort of musical glasses—claimed to be his own invention. He then travelled much, producing new operas in many European cities. His life henceforth fell into 3 periods spent mainly in Vienna (1749–73), Paris (1773–9), and Vienna again (1779 to death).

In the first Vienna period his most important operas where *Orpheus and Eurydice* (1762), which reached a new level of musical value and dramatic fitness, and *Alcestis* (1767), of which the preface set out a statement of Gluck's now definitely dramatic principles.

Of the Paris period (a period of strife between his supporters and those of the more conventional Italian Piccini) the chief productions were *Iphigenia in Aulis* (1774) and *Iphigenia in Tauris* (1779). The principles to which he was now committed make him the first greatly effective reformer of the opera before Wagner, a century later. Apart from the valuable innovations they present his operas have the advantage of containing much purely beautiful music. He is, then, one of the art's heroic figures.

See also *Alembert*; *Armide*; *Calzabigi*; *Iphigénie en Aulide*; *Iphigénie en Tauride*; *Piccini*; *Opera 2*.

(2) **Alma**—original name Reba Fiersohn (b. Bucharest 1884; d. New York 1938). Soprano vocalist. Brought to New York as child. Made début at Metropolitan Opera House 1909; studied in Berlin with Sembrich and attained high position in public esteem; 1st husband's name (1906) was Gluck; married (1914) Zimbalist.

Glückliche Hand, Die ('The Lucky Hand'). Short dramatic work by Schönberg (op. 18; 1913), employing orchestra, voices, pantomime and dramatic action, and play of colour (cf. *Colour and Music*). Text by composer. (1st perf. Vienna 1924. Philadelphia 1930.)

Glühend (Ger.). 'Glowing.'

Glyndebourne Festival Theatre. Opened in 1934 on the private estate of Mr. John Christie, Glyndebourne, nr. Lewes, Sussex (cf. *Mildmay, Audrey*). Opera performances of a high standard have been given and were made accessible to London residents by the provision of a special train service. In 1954 Mr. Christie created the Glyndebourne Arts Trust Ltd., handing the property to it.

Glynne, (1) **Walter** (b. Gowerton, Glamorganshire, 1890). Tenor vocalist. Trained R.C.M. Varied career as recitalist, broadcaster, and soloist at leading Brit. festivals and concerts.

(2) **Howell** (b. Swansea 1906; d. Toronto 1969). Bass vocalist. Studied with Ben Davies and von Warlich, &c. Principal bass (buffo, &c., roles) Carl Rosa 1931, Sadler's Wells 1951, Covent Garden. Concert appearances, oratorio, radio, &c.

Gnecchi, Vittorio (b. Milan 1876; d. there 1954). Wrote a number of operas in a pioneering spirit, including *Cassandra* (1905) about which dispute arose some years later on account of the resemblance between its musical themes and those of Strauss's *Elektra* (1909), and *La Rosiera* (1910), 1st perf. 1927), said to be the 1st opera employing quarter-tones (see *Microtones*).

Gniessin (Gniessine, Gnessin, Gnyesin, &c.), **Michael** (b. Rostov 1883; d. Moscow 1957). Studied under Rimsky-Korsakof; son of a Rabbi and a zealous partisan of Jewish racialism in music, established himself as one of leading composers of Jewish school. Operas, *The Maccabeans*, *The Youth of Abraham*, &c.; many orch. and chamber works, songs, &c.

Gnomenreigen. See *Reigen*.

Gnyesin. See *Gniessin*.

G.O. (in Fr. organ music) = *Grand Orgue*, i.e. 'Great Organ'.

Gobbi, Tito (b. Bassano del Grappa, Italy, 1915). Operatic baritone. Studied law at Padua; singing in Milan. Début Rome 1938; international career from 1947; Covent Garden 1950; Metropolitan 1956.

Godard, Benjamin (Louis Paul) (b. Paris 1849; d. Cannes 1895). Violinist who had much success as composer of violin concertos, symphonies, chamber music, operas, and songs. Name kept alive by a trifle, the Berceuse from the opera *Jocelyn* (q.v.).

God bless America. By Irving Berlin. Composed 1918 but first attained popularity 1938 and much sung during Second World War.

God bless the Prince of Wales. The words of this song were written in Welsh by Ceiriog Hughes and the music at the same time by Brinley Richards. They were published together in 1862. The tune has become the official one of the Brit. Royal Air Force.

Goddard, (1) **Arabella** (b. nr. Saint-Malo 1836; d. Boulogne 1922). Pianist (of Brit. origin). Famous child prodigy; then pupil of Kalkbrenner and Thalberg. Achieved great international reputation. Married her Eng. musicmaster, J. W. Davison (see *Criticism*), music critic of London *Times*.

(2) **Scott** (b. Ore, Sussex, 1895; d. 1965). Trained R.C.M. Schoolmaster 1913–28, then music critic (*Morning Post* 1928; *News Chronicle* 1938–55).

Godfrey Family. Remarkable musical family, prominent from opening of 19th c., 9 or 10 (mostly military bandmasters) being found in larger reference books. Best remembered is **Daniel Eyers Godfrey** (1868–1939), i.e. Sir Dan Godfrey, knighted 1922, who conducted Bournemouth Municipal Orch. 1893–1934, making the town a centre, especially, for the introduction of works of Brit. composers.

God in nature (Beethoven). Same as *Creation's Hymn* (q.v.).

God is a spirit. See *Woman of Samaria.*

Godowsky, Leopold (b. nr. Vilna, Poland, 1870; d. New York 1938). World-famous pianist, piano teacher, and composer of piano music. Long resident in U.S.A.

God save America. See *God save the Queen.*

God save George Washington. See *God save the Queen.*

God save the Queen. The tune of the Brit. 'National Anthem' must long have been the best-known tune in the world, having at one time or another been borrowed by about 20 countries as that of their official national song. The popularity of the words and tune in Britain seems to date from the time of the landing of the Young Pretender, in 1745, when they were introduced in London theatres and widely taken up by the people at large. But there is some evidence that they had been previously used—in 1688, 'when the Prince of Orange was hovering over the coast'. The authorship of both words and tune is obscure. The common attribution to Henry Carey is quite untenable.

The tune is in rhythm and style a galliard. There is a Geneva tune of this type with some phrases resembling some in *God save the Queen*; it was introduced in 1603 at a banquet celebrating the 1st anniversary of the unsuccessful attempt of the Duke of Savoy to seize the city (the 'Escalade'). An Eng. Christmas carol printed in 1611, *Remember, O thou man*, shows similar resemblances. Much stronger resemblances are seen in a keyboard piece of John Bull (abt. 1562–1628),

though this is in the minor, and his name is sometimes attached to the tune. There are also other tunes with similarities of metre and rhythm and with melodic phrases that are common to them and *God save the Queen.*

As for the words, the cry 'God save the King!' is found in passages in the authorized Eng. version of the Old Testament in connexion with 3 personages, Saul, Absalom, and Jehoash, and it goes behind this version to the Coverdale version of 1535. The prayer appointed to be read in churches on the anniversary of the Gunpowder Plot (5 Nov. 1605) contains passages which might be the origin of part of the 2nd verse of the 'Anthem'. And there are other loyal phrases in Eng. literature which suggest themselves as the origin of portions of the poem.

In the Amer. colonies and the U.S.A. the tune has at different times been sung to many different sets of words— *God save America, God save George Washington, God save the Thirteen States*, and the like. The present words *My country, 'tis of thee*, date from 1831 and are the work of the Rev. Samuel Francis Smith. The name usually given to the tune is *America.*

Very many composers have introduced the tune into their compositions or based compositions upon it—Beethoven, Weber, Brahms, &c.

God save the Thirteen States. See *God save the Queen.*

Gods go a-begging, The. Suite of orch. pieces arranged by Beecham from Handel. It has been used for ballet purposes.

God's time is the best (Bach). See *Actus Tragicus.*

Goedicke (Gedike, &c.), Alexander Fedorvich (b. Moscow 1877). Composer and pianist; a prof. at Moscow Conserv.; has written operas, cantatas (e.g. *Glory to the Soviet Pilots*), 3 symphonies, &c.

Goehr, (1) **Walter** (b. Berlin 1903; d. Sheffield 1960). Trained Berlin and under Schönberg. Mus. Dir. various Ger. theatres. Attached Ger. Radio 1925–31; attached Gramophone Co. 1933–9. Conductor B.B.C. Theatre

Orch. (1946–9), then free-lance. On staff Morley Coll., London. Composer of radio, theatre, and film music. Ed. Monteverdi, &c.

(2) **Alexander** (b. Berlin 1932). Son of (1). Trained R.M.C.M. and Paris Conserv.; composer of orch., vocal, and chamber works in polyphonic style, using note-row methods.

Goethe songs by Hugo Wolf (1889). 51 poems (1888 and later). Piano accompaniment, but some later orchestrated by the composer.

Goetschius, Percy (b. Paterson, N.J., 1853; d. Manchester, N.H., 1943). Considerable composer but reputation rested rather on activities as teacher of composition and writer of textbooks.

Goetz, Hermann (b. Königsberg 1840; d. nr. Zürich 1876). Spent life as organist, &c., in Switzerland. Fame rests chiefly on opera *The Taming of the Shrew* (see *Widerspenstigen Zähmung*), but he wrote many other things, including important symphony in F.

See *Francesca da Rimini*.

Goldberg, (1) **Johann Gottlieb** (b. Danzig 1727; d. Dresden 1756). One of best keyboard pupils of Bach, who wrote for him the famous and difficult *Goldberg Variations* at the request of a count who required music nightly to solace his sleeplessness. There are 30 variations, for double-keyboard harpsichord, and they are elaborate and difficult. (Cf. *Klavierübung*.)

(2) **Reuben** (b. London 1894; d. Johannesburg 1948). Violoncellist. Studied R.A.M.; then pupil of Casals. Settled South Africa. At one time in New York with Metropolitan Opera Orch., &c.

(3) **Simon**—or Szymon (b. Poland 1909). Violinist. Studied Berlin. Début age 12. At age 17 leader Dresden Philharm. Orch.; then Berlin Philharm. Orch.; U.S.A. 1942; founded Netherlands Chamber Orch. 1955. Numerous tours, solo and chamber music. (See *Kraus, L.*)

Golden Cockerel, The ('Le Coq d'Or'). Fantasy-Opera by Rimsky-Korsakof. Libretto based on a poem by Pushkin. (Prod. Moscow 1909; London 1914; New York 1918). The *Hymn*

to the Sun is sometimes separately performed. Ballet treatments of the Opera have been seen and an Orch. Suite has been made from its music.

Golden Legend, The. Cantata by Sullivan; setting of Longfellow. (1st perf. Leeds Fest. 1886.)

Golden Sonata. Nickname of the 9th of Purcell's 'Sonatas of Four Parts'.

Goldmark, (1) **Carl** (b. Keszthely, Hungary, 1830; d. Vienna 1915). Violinist, pianist, and composer of operas (especially *Queen of Sheba*, Vienna 1875; see *Königin*), orch. and choral works, chamber music, &c. Also an autobiography. (2) **Rubin** (b. New York 1872; there d. 1936). Nephew of Carl above. Studied in New York (under Dvořák and others) and in Vienna, and then occupied various positions in U.S.A.

Goldovsky, Boris (b. Moscow 1908). Pianist and conductor. Trained conservs. of Moscow, Berlin, Budapest. In U.S.A. from 1930. Opera director, New England Conserv., Boston, from 1942. Noted opera coach and broadcaster.

Goldschmidt, Otto (b. Hamburg 1829; d. London 1907). Pupil in composition of Mendelssohn at Leipzig Conserv.; appeared as pianist in London; conducted at Jenny Lind's concerts in U.S.A. and married her there (1852); lived with her at Dresden and then London (1858 to death); on staff of R.A.M. (vice-principal); founded Bach Choir (q.v.). Composed choral works, &c. (Not to be confused with another Otto Goldschmidt—a Paris pianist, b. 1846.)

Golestan, Stan (b. Vaslui, Rumania, 1875; d. Paris 1956). Studied in Paris with d'Indy and Roussel and remained there as music critic of *Figaro* and composer (*Rumanian Rhapsody*, &c.).

Golliwogg's Cakewalk (Debussy). See *Children's Corner*.

Golschmann, Vladimir (b. Paris 1893—of Russian parents). Ballet conductor in Paris (Diaghilef, &c. See *Ballet*). Conductor of St. Louis Orch. 1931–58; Denver 1964. Amer. citizen 1947.

Goltermann, Georg Eduard (b. Hanover 1824; d. Frankfort-on-Main 1898). Eminent 'cellist and composer for his instrument.

Gombert, Nicolas (b. South Flanders abt. 1500; d. probably after 1556). Distinguished pupil of Josquin des Prés; held church positions in Brussels and Madrid (1537), in which latter city seems to have become chief musician to Charles V.

Gompertz, Richard (b. Cologne 1859; d. Dresden 1921). Violinist. Pupil of Joachim. Lived in Cambridge, England (1880); then on staff of R.C.M. (1883). In Dresden from 1899.

Gondola Song. (1) A barcarolle (q.v.) type of composition, supposed to recall the singing of Venetian gondoliers at their work. It is generally in 6-in-a-measure time, or some similar compound time.

(2) Name given by Mendelssohn to 3 of his *Songs without Words*—nos. 6, 12, and 29 (in G min., F sharp min., and A min.), and also to another Piano piece: *Auf einer Gondel*, 'On a Gondola' (in A maj. 1837).

Gondoliera. See *Siciliano.*

Gondoliers, The, or The King of Barataria. Comic Opera by Gilbert and Sullivan. (Prod. Savoy Theatre, London, 1889; New York and Cape Town 1890.)

Gong. See *Percussion Family* 2 p.

Go no more a-rushing. See *Under the spreading Chestnut Tree.*

Good, Margaret (b. London). Pianist. Trained R.A.M. Recitalist in Britain specializing in 'cello sonatas with husband William Pleeth.

Goodall, Reginald (b. Lincoln 1905). Conductor. Trained R.C.M., &c. Attached Sadler's Wells, Glyndebourne, Covent Garden, &c.

Good-bye. Highly popular 'Drawing-room Song' by Tosti. In the theatrical profession deemed unlucky. 'You try whistling Tosti's *Good-bye* or *I dreamt that I dwelt in marble halls*, and see what happens. You'll get thrown out on the pavement' (J. and C. Gordon, *The London Roundabout*).

Good-humoured Ladies, The. Ballet by Massine, based on play by Goldoni, set to music of D. Scarlatti arranged by V. Tommasini.

Goodson, Katharine (b. Watford 1872; d. London 1958). Pianist. Trained R.A.M. and Vienna under Leschetizky. Début London 1897. Distinguished international career. Married Arthur Hinton.

Goofus. An instrument introduced in the 1920's, or thereabouts. It looks like a saxophone, but has 25 finger-holes, each with its own reed, and is thus capable of producing chords.

Goose of Cairo, The (Mozart). See *Oca del Cairo, L'.*

Goossens, (1) **Eugene I** (b. Bruges 1845; d. Liverpool 1906). Trained Brussels Conserv.; became successful opera conductor in Belgium and other countries; settled in England, directing the Carl Rosa Opera Co. in its heyday; then resident Liverpool as organist of a Roman Catholic church. Wife was the dancer Madame Sidonie. (2) **Eugene II** (b. Bordeaux 1867; d. London 1958). Son of Eugene I. Trained Brussels Conserv. and R.A.M., London; like his father conducted Carl Rosa Opera Co. Married daughter of the operatic bass, T. Aynsley Cook, q.v. (She died in 1946.) (3) **Eugene III** (b. London 1893; d. Hillingdon, Mdx., 1962). Conductor and composer. Son of Eugene II. Trained Bruges Conserv. and R.C.M. (1907–12). Began career as violinist with Queen's Hall Orch. 1911, but soon became conductor. Like father and grandfather did some service with Carl Rosa Opera Co.; then Beecham Co., Brit. Nat. Opera Co., and Russian Opera and Ballet, &c. From 1923 in U.S.A.; Rochester Philharmonic Orch. and (from 1931) Cincinnati Orch. Australia 1947–56 as director of Conservatory of New South Wales and conductor of Sydney Symphony Orch. Compositions include operas *Judith* (London 1929) and *Don Juan de Mañara* (London 1937); Oratorio, *Apocalypse* (1951). Kt. 1955. (4) **Leon** (b. London 1896). Also son of Eugene II. First oboist of Queen's Hall Orch. at 17 and soon recognized as leading player. (5–7) Other children of Eugene II are **Adolphe,** fine horn player, killed in war of 1914-18; and **Sidonie** and **Marie,** gifted harpists.

Goossens-Viceroy, Alice Leontine Melanie (b. Brussels). Singer and teacher. Trained Brussels Conserv., then sang at Monnaie, Brussels, till First World-War. Toured Australia and joined staff Sydney Conserv.

Gopak (also transliterated **Hopak**). A lively dance of Little Russia: it is in 2-in-a-measure time.

Gordian Knot Untied, The. Incidental Music by Purcell to a play by an unknown author (1691).

Gordon, (1) **Jacques** (b. Odessa 1899; d. Hartford, Conn., 1948). Violinist. Trained Imperial Conserv., Odessa. Went to U.S.A. 1914 and continued study Inst. Musical Art, New York. In 1921 joined staff Chicago Conserv., and became leader Chicago Symphony Orch. Also formed own string quartet. From 1942 on staff Eastman School of Music.

(2) **Gavin (Muspratt)** (b. Ayr 1901; d. London 1970). Trained at R.C.M. under Vaughan Williams and others. As composer known esp. for ballet music (e.g. *The Rake's Progress* 1935). Sadler's Wells staff 1951-8; also bass singer and film actor.

Gorgheggio. This term (from the It. *gorgheggiare,* 'to trill', or 'warble') is applied to any long, rapid passage in which one vowel takes many notes.

Gorr, Rita—orig. Geimert (b. Ghent 1926). Mezzo-soprano. Début Antwerp 1949; Covent Garden 1959; Metropolitan 1962.

Go, song of mine. By Elgar. 6-part unaccompanied setting of poem by Cavalcanti, transl. Rossetti (1st perf. Hereford Fest. 1909).

Goss, (1) **John I** (b. Hampshire 1800; d. London 1880). Pupil of Attwood and succeeded him as organist of St. Paul's Cathedral; wrote dignified church music (anthem, *The Wilderness,* &c.). Knighted 1872; D.Mus., Cambridge, 1876.

(2) **John II** (b. London 1894; d. Birmingham 1953). Baritone. Began life as errand boy, &c.; got engagement with touring concert party; became

pupil of Beigel, &c. Developed into sensitive artist; toured many parts of world. Edited song books, &c.; also wrote novel. In Vancouver 1940-50.

Gossec, François Joseph (b. Vergnies, in what is now Belgium, 1734; d. Paris 1829). When 17 went to Paris and was taken up by Rameau; composed symphonies (the first in France), string quartets, &c., showing originality, and by his operas won high fame; greatly admired as an orchestrator. For 80 years a leading musician of Paris, composing music for public occasions.

Götterdämmerung (Wagner). See *Ring des Nibelungen.*

Gott erhalte Franz den Kaiser. See *Emperor's Hymn.*

Gottes Zeit (Bach). See *Actus Tragicus.*

Gottschalk, Louis Moreau (b. New Orleans 1829; d. Rio de Janeiro 1869). Son of an Eng. Jew and a Fr. Creole. Clever pianist; at 15 played in Paris and was praised by Chopin. Toured as virtuoso pianist and spectacular conductor. His piano compositions now faded (*The Aeolian Harp, The Dying Poet,* &c.).

Goudimel, Claude (b. Besançon abt. 1514; d. Lyons 1572). Great church musician, writing masses, motets, and tunes for the metrical psalms of Marot and Béza (sung by both Protestants and Roman Catholics until forbidden to latter by authority); definitely associated with Huguenots and perished in massacre of St. Bartholomew.

Gould, (1) **Morton** (b. Richmond Hill, N.Y., 1913). Trained Juilliard and N.Y. Univ. Infant prodigy, then career as successful composer of brilliant theatre and film music, also some symphonic pieces.

(2) **Glenn (Herbert)** (b. Toronto 1932). Pianist. Trained Toronto Conserv. Début age 14; New York 1955; then international career.

Gounod, Charles François (b. Paris 1818; d. nr. there 1893). At Paris Conserv. won Rome Prize and in Rome studied with interest the older church music, especially that of 16th c.; on return became church organist and studied for priesthood but abandoned the idea. Solemn Mass (1st perf. London 1851) brought him into prominence, and was followed almost immediately by opera *Sapho*, and 8 years later by *Faust*: other operas include *Romeo and Juliet*. During Franco-German War (1870) settled in London, there remaining 5 years: his sacred works popular in Britain and elsewhere, especially *The Redemption*. Had a lyric gift, a dramatic gift, and a gift of colourful orchestration, all of which made for popular appeal, but is today felt to have inclined too much to the sentimental and even effeminate.

See also *Faust*; *Funeral March of a Marionette*; *Meditation*; *Mireille*; *Mors et Vita*; *Philémon et Baucis*; *Redemption*; *Romeo and Juliet*; *Sapho*; *Seven Last Words*; *Weldon* 2.

Gow, (1) **Niel I** (b. nr. Dunkeld, Perthshire, 1727; there d. 1807). Famous fiddler at balls, &c.; collector and player of traditional reels and strathspeys. (2) **Donald**. Brother of Niel I; notable 'cellist. (3) **William** (b. 1751; d. 1791). Son of Niel I and equally famous in same capacities. (4) **Nathaniel** (b. Inver, nr. Dunkeld, 1763; d. Edinburgh 1831). Son of Niel I, brother of William, and almost as famous as they in same capacities; active publisher of Scots dance music. (See *Caller Herrin'*.) (5) **Niel II** (b. Edinburgh abt. 1795; there d. 1823). Son of Nathaniel, associated with him in publishing business; composer of songs still current.

Goyescas. See *Granados*.

G.P. (1) 'General Pause' (q.v.). (2) 'Grand et Positif' (Fr.), i.e. 'Great and Choir Organs to be coupled'.

G.P.R., in Fr. organ music = 'Grand-Positif-Récit', i.e. 'Great, Choir, and Swell coupled'.

G.R. = 'Grand Récit' (Fr.), i.e. 'Great and Swell Organs coupled'.

Grace, Harvey (b. Romsey 1874; d. Bromley, Kent, 1944). Organist (Chichester Cathedral 1931–8), composer and ed. of organ works, writer on organ and church music; ed. of *Musical Times* (1918 to death); adjudicator at competitions, and man of wide general musical interests deeply con-

cerned for widening of public appreciation of good music.

Grace Notes. See *Ornaments*.

Gracieux, Gracieuse (Fr. masc., fem.). 'Graceful.'

Gradatamente (It.). 'Gradually.'

Gradevole (It.). 'Pleasing'; so the adverb *gradevolmente*. **Gradito**. 'Pleasant'; so the adverb *graditamente*.

Gradual. (1) The Respond (q.v.) sung in the service of the Mass between the Epistle and Gospel. (2) The book containing the Concentus of the traditional plainsong of the Mass, i.e. it is the choir's (or congregation's) musical companion to the Missal—in which last the only music is the Accentus (q.v.) or priest's parts.

Cf. *Antiphonal*.

Graduellement (Fr.). 'Gradually.'

Gradus ad Parnassum ('Steps to Parnassus'—the abode of the muses). A fancy title given to dictionaries of Latin, Greek, &c., and borrowed by Fux for his treatise on counterpoint and by Clementi for his great collection of piano studies.

Graener, Paul (b. Berlin 1872; there d. 1944). Theatre conductor, encouraged by Brahms as composer; wrote orch. music, many operas (*Friedemann Bach* 1931), chamber music, &c. Resident in London 1896–1908, conducting at Haymarket Theatre and on staff of R.A.M.

Graf von Luxemburg, Der. See *Count of Luxemburg*.

Graham, (1) **John** (b. 1859; d. London 1932). Writer on music; on staff *Musical Herald* (latterly ed.) 1887–1921, and leading tonic sol-faist. Early collector of Eng. folk songs.

(2) **Martha** (b. Pennsylvania 1893). Dancer and choreographer of great influence in the development of modern dance.

Grail. (1, liturgically and musically) the same as 'Gradual' (q.v.), i.e. the Respond sung in the Mass between the Epistle and the Gospel. (2, 'Holy Grail') the vessel which according to tradition was used by Christ at the Last Supper and then by Joseph of

Arimathea to receive the blood at the Crucifixion (as such figuring in Wagner's *Parsifal*).

Grain, Richard Corney (b. Teversham, Cambs., 1845; d. London 1895). Highly popular vocal entertainer 'at the piano'.

Grainger, Percy Aldridge (b. Melbourne, Australia, 1882; d. White Plains, N.Y., 1961). From age of 10 educated at Frankfurt; later studied with Busoni; at 18 appeared in London as pianist; influence of his friend Grieg led to interest in folk music and making English folk tunes basis of some compositions. Style very personal; general character of his temperament and production might be characterized as 'breezy'. From 1915 in U.S.A., where naturalized.

Gramophone (or **Phonograph**). (1) THE EDISON INVENTION. The idea of recording sound by attaching a needle to a membrane vibrating in sympathy and by allowing its point to mark a plate travelling at a fixed speed dates from as early as the beginning of the 19th c., the object being to add to acoustical knowledge as to the differences in the vibrations evoked by sounds of various pitches and timbres. Edison, in the U.S.A., in 1877 constructed such an apparatus, with the intention that it should be used in a 'dictating machine': this he called *The Phonograph—the Ideal Amanuensis*, and the records, on wax cylinders, he called *Phonograms*. Here was the origin of the 'Dictaphone' now in use in business offices, but about 20 years later (1897 or 1898) the device is found to be in considerable musical use.

(2) THE BERLINER IMPROVEMENTS. Emile Berliner, a German-born citizen of the U.S.A., had, however, by 1888 obtained patents for important improvements—a circular plate of a shellac mixture instead of a waxed cylinder, and a horizontal motion of the needle instead of a perpendicular one (i.e. a motion making lateral impressions on the sides of a spiral track instead of the previous 'hill and dale' impressions), and his principles were in time developed and universally adopted.

(3) THE APPLICATION OF ELECTRICITY. So far the processes used had been purely 'Acoustic', the result of the direct action of sound vibrations. In 1925 appeared the earliest electrically made records, in which the vibrations had been received by means of a microphone (cf. *Broadcasting*) and converted into electrical vibrations, causing, in turn, mechanical vibrations in a needle travelling over the recording disk. It

ANCESTOR OF THE GRAMOPHONE

Edison's first Phonograph (1877)
Since the waxed cylinder was turned by hand there was, in both recording and reproducing, a difficulty in maintaining perfect regularity of speed, and hence of pitch

was found that by the use of electric-made records, very much more faithful reproductions could be secured, and the acoustic-made record in time disappeared from the market. The motive power of the Edison and early Berliner instruments had been supplied by a handle turned by the operator. This had been superseded by a clock-spring device, which in the more expensive instruments was, in turn, superseded by electric power obtained by plugging to the domestic electric circuit: such instruments also reproduced the sounds by electric means, reversing the process of electrical recording as above described. The new apparatus was very commonly combined with one for the reception of radio broadcasting. The bugbear of short-playing records (cutting up an extended composition into record sides of under 5 minutes) was early recognized; but it was only in 1948 that (at first in the U.S.A.) all the problems inherent in trying to combine a narrower groove and slower speed without loss of 'high fidelity' throughout the greater part of the range of audible frequencies was satisfactorily solved.

(4) WIRE AND TAPE RECORDERS, in which sound is recorded and reproduced by means of variations in the magnetic patterns of a long strip of magnetizable substance such as wire, steel tape, or (later) metallic oxide on a plastic ribbon base, were much developed in Germany during the Second World War, and soon afterwards were being marketed commercially in great quantities. The same system was by 1958 in use for the recording of television programmes. Sound is recorded on film by means of the Photo-electric cell (see *Electric Musical Instruments* 5), which has also been used for recording on paper.

See *British Sound-Recording Association.*

Gramophone, The. British monthly journal. Founded (1923) and ed. Compton Mackenzie.

Gran (It.). 'Great', 'big'.

Granadina. A kind of fandango (q.v.) of Granada, in southern Spain: it has the same harmonic and vocal peculiarities as the malagueña (q.v.).

Granados, or **Granados y Campina,** (1) **Enrique** (b. Lérida, Catalonia, 1867; d. 1916). Pupil of Pedrell (q.v.) and, as pianist, of de Bériot (son of violinist) in Paris; founded a school of music in Barcelona and directed it up to his death. Enjoyed high reputation as pianist and wrote effectively for his instrument, employing distinctively national idioms (cf. *Albéniz*); set of piano pieces *Goyescas* based on pictures of great Spanish painter Goya (1746–1828); made an opera out of these (1st perf. New York 1916; composer and wife present and on returning lost their lives when liner *Sussex* sunk by German submarine; prod. Paris 1919, &c.). (2) **Edward** (b. Barcelona 1894; d. Madrid 1928). Son of Enrique; conductor and composer known by several stage compositions, especially in form of Zarzuela (q.v.).

Gran cassa. 'Big box', i.e. bass drum (see *Percussion Family* 2 k).

Gran coro. 'Full Organ.'

Grand, grande (Fr. masc., fem.). 'Great', 'big'.

Grand Canyon Suite. See *Grofé.*

Grand chœur (Fr., sometimes abbrev. *Gd. chœur* or *Gd. Ch.*). 'Large Choir', or 'Full Organ' (q.v.).

Grand détaché (Fr.). See *Détaché.*

Grand Duke, The, or The Statutory Duel. Comic Opera by Gilbert and Sullivan. (Prod. Savoy Theatre, London, also Berlin, 1896; New York 1937.)

Grand duo (Schubert). See *Schubert's Symphonies.*

Grande Duchesse de Gérolstein, La. One of Offenbach's most popular operas. Libretto by Meilhac and L. Halévy. (Prod. Paris, New York, and London 1867.)

Grandes études de Paganini (Liszt). See *Paganini Transcriptions.*

Grande sonate pathétique (Beethoven). For Piano, in C minor, op. 13. So entitled (in Fr.) by the composer.

Grandezza (It.). 'Grandeur', 'dignity'. **Grandioso** (It.). 'With grandiloquence.'

Grandisonante (It.). 'Sonorous.'

Grandjany, Marcel (b. Paris 1891). Harpist. Trained Paris Conserv. Début Paris 1909; tours of Europe and U.S.A. On staff Amer. Conserv., Fontainebleau, 1921–35, then settled U.S.A.; on staff Juilliard School 1938. Compositions for harp.

Grand jeu (Fr.). 'Full Organ' (or Harmonium, of which a combination stop is so named).

Grand Opera. See *Opera* 7.

Grand orchestre (Fr.). (1) 'Full orchestra.' (2) 'Large orchestra.'

Grand orgue (Fr.). (1) 'Full Organ', or 'Great Organ' (see *Organ* 1). (2) 'Pipe Organ'—as distinct from 'Reed Organ', i.e. from 'American Organ' or 'Cabinet Organ'.

Grand Pianoforte. See *Pianoforte.*

Grand pirouette. See under *Pirouette.*

Grand prix de Rome. See *Prix de Rome.*

Grand Staff, or **Grand Stave.** See *Great Staff.*

Gran gusto (It.). 'Great taste.'

Grania and Diarmid. Drama by W. B. Yeats with incidental music by Elgar (op. 42; 1902).

Gran tamburo. Big drum, i.e. the Bass drum (see *Percussion Family* 2 k).

Gratias agimus. See *Mass*.

Grau, Maurice (b. Brünn 1849; d. Paris 1907). Impresario. Managed Anton Rubinstein's 1st U.S.A. tour, 1872, and tours of many other instrumental and vocal celebrities. Then opera New York, &c., 1890–1903.

Graun, Carl Heinrich (b. Wahrenbrück, Saxony, 1704; d. Berlin 1759). For 20 years musical director at Potsdam to Frederick the Great; able singer and composer for voice, and successful opera composer; latterly wrote much church music (see *Tod Jesu*).

Grave (It., Fr.). (1, as a term of expression) 'With slow speed and solemnity'. (2, as a term of pitch) 'Low'. In Fr. organ music *octaves graves* means 'Sub-octave Coupler'.

Gravement (Fr.), **gravemente** (It.). 'Gravely.'

Grave Mixture. Organ *Mixture Stop* (q.v.) of 2 ranks (12th and 15th).

Graves, (1) **Alfred Perceval** (b. Dublin 1846; d. Harlech 1931). Inspector of schools, poet, leader in revival of Irish letters; collaborated with Stanford and Charles Wood in publication of Irish folk songs, &c. (see *Londonderry Air*; *Father O'Flynn*). (2) **Charles Larcom** (b. Dublin 1856; d. Carlisle 1944). Journalist (on *Punch* staff, &c.). Miscellaneous author. Life of Grove (1903); also of Sir Hubert Parry (2 vols. 1926). Brother of above.

Graves, Octaves (in Fr. organ music). 'Sub-octave Coupler.'

Graveure, Louis; real name Wilfrid Douthitt (b. London 1888; d. Los Angeles 1965). Concert and opera vocalist. Pupil of Clara Novello Davies. He made himself the mystery man of the vocal world by appearing in New York in 1914 as a baritone, clean-shaven and calling himself 'Douthitt', and then the following year bearded, calling himself 'Graveure', and steadily denying identity with 'Douthitt'. In 1928 and later he appeared still as 'Graveure', but beardless and a tenor.

Gravicembalo. An It. name for the harpsichord. The word is supposed to be a corruption of 'Clavicembalo'.

Gravità (It.). 'Gravity', 'seriousness'.

Gray, (1) **Alan** (b. York 1855; d. Cambridge 1935). Took law degrees (LL.B. and LL.M.) at Cambridge and then turned to music, taking D.Mus. and becoming director of music, Wellington Coll., and then organist of Trinity Coll., Cambridge (1892–1930). Composed festival cantatas, &c., and (especially) church and organ music. (2) **Cecil** (b. Edinburgh 1895; d. Worthing 1951). Author of books on Gesualdo, Sibelius, 'Peter Warlock' (i.e. his friend Philip Heseltine, q.v.), &c.; also books of essays, and a somewhat speculative history of music. Composer of operas (*Women of Troy*, &c.).

Gray, H. W. New York music publishing company, founded 1906, taking over American branch of Novello & Co.

Grazia; grazioso; graziosamente (It.). 'Grace'; 'graceful'; 'gracefully'.

Graziös (Ger.). 'Gracious', 'graceful'.

Great Cornett. See *Cornett and Key Bugle Families*.

Greater Doxology. See *Doxologia*.

Great Fugue (Beethoven). See *Grosse Fuge.*

Great Organ. See *Organ* 1.

Great Pipe. See *Bagpipe Family.*

Great Service. See *Service.*

Great Staff or **Great Stave** (or **Grand Staff** or **Stave**). This is a fictional notational device rather unnecessarily introduced by musical pedagogues for the purpose of explaining the clefs—

$$\flat, \; \text{©} \; \text{and} \; \parallel \; \text{or} \; \parallel.$$

The two staves in common use are brought near together. It suffices then to place between them one extra line for Middle C ('middle' in a double sense: in the middle of this diagram, as it is in the middle of the piano keyboard). The C Clef is placed on this line. The Treble (or G) Clef now comes 2 lines above and the Bass (or F Clef) 2 lines below.

The TREBLE STAFF, BASS STAFF, SOPRANO STAFF (in some choral use in Germany still), the ALTO STAFF (in use in older choral music, in music for the Viola, &c.) and the TENOR STAFF (in use in the older choral music, for the Trombone, &c.)—all these are seen as but sections of the one 'Great Staff', with Middle C as the connexion.

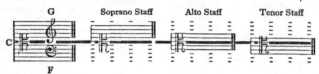

Greaves, Thomas (end of 16th c. and beginning of 17th). Lutenist who wrote ayres and madrigals.

Greef, Arthur de (b. Louvain 1862; d. Brussels 1940). Prof. of piano at Conserv. of Brussels; virtuoso of his instrument and composer for it and for orch., &c.

Greek Anthology, Songs from the. By Elgar. Set of 5 male-voice part-songs (op. 45; 1903).

Greek Cadence. See *Cadence*.

Greek Church and Music. The 'Greek' or 'Orthodox' or 'Eastern' Church (in full, the 'Holy Oriental Orthodox Catholic Apostolic Church') includes all those Eastern Christian bodies which own their allegiance to or retain communion with the four ancient patriarchates of Jerusalem, Alexandria, Antioch, and Constantinople (now Istanbul). It includes the Hellenic Church, the Russian Church, the national churches of Serbia, Rumania, Bulgaria, &c. A branch of the Gr. Church has existed in London since the middle of the 17th c.; there are others in Liverpool and Manchester. The U.S.A. has cities with a large Eastern population and a good many Gr. churches exist there.

The Gr. Church possessed anciently many liturgies, but now uses that of the patriarchate of Jerusalem (or of St James in the East), which exists in a longer form called that of St. Basil (used only on certain days of the year), and a shorter form, called that of St. Chrysostom. This liturgy was originally in Greek, but the service is now conducted either in Greek or in Old Slavonic, or, in certain countries, in other languages. When the liturgy is sung in Greek the modern pronunciation is used.

The treatment of music in the Gr. Church is conditioned (*a*) by the decision of the Council of Laodicea (A.D.367) that, in order to avoid corruption of the ancient Byzantine plainsong, the congregations should be deprived of all vocal part in the service, only trained choirs acquainted with the tradition being allowed to sing; and (*b*) by adherence to the early Christian prohibition of the use of instruments in worship.

A characteristic that at once strikes the Western visitor to a Gr. Church where the plainsong is in use is the fact that throughout an entire piece of plainsong the tonic of the mode is hummed (preferably by a boy); the intention is to keep the singer of the plainsong in the key. A nasal quality in the voice-production and the force employed (legacies of Turkish times) fall strangely on Western ears. The singing is properly entirely in unison.

In Russia, from the 15th c., attempts have been made to create a purely Russian church music, and the ancient plainsong was, in some measure, departed from in favour of harmonized song. In the 18th c. Russian church music received a strongly It. cast from the influence of the It. composers attached to the Russian court, especially Sarti and Galuppi. Bortniansky (1751–1825) and Berezovsky (1745–77), both trained in Italy, are examples of Russian church-music composers thus, in some measure, influenced. Amongst later composers who have provided music for the Russian church have been Turchaninof, Lvof, Archangelsky, Glinka, Balakiref, Rimsky-Korsakof, Gretchaninof, Tchaikovsky, Rachmaninof, Kalinnikof, and Kastalsky (all these appearing in this volume under their own names).

Greenbaum (1) Hyam (b. Brighton 1901; d. Bedford 1942). At first violinist; Queen's Hall Orch., Brosa Quartet &c. Conductor of B.B.C. Television Orch. 1936-9, and Revue Orch. 1939-42. Friend and interpreter of Schönberg, Van Dieren, Lambert, &c. Wife was Sidonie Goossens (q.v.). (2) **Kyla** (b. Brighton 1922). Pianist. Sister of (1). Specialist in modern music.

Greenberg, Noah (b. New York 1919; d. there 1966). Choral conductor. Founded New York Pro Musica 1952; largely responsible for revival of interest in medieval and renaissance music, through international tours and recordings.

Greene, (1) Maurice (b. London 1695; there d. 1755). Organist of St. Paul's Cathedral and Chapel Royal, Master of the King's Musick (1735), Prof. of Music at Cambridge (1730) and D.Mus.; composer of songs, theatre music, a service and anthems that are still performed. Began a great collection of Eng. cathedral music, bequeathed to his friend Boyce (q.v.), who carried it further and published it.

(2) **Harry Plunket** (b. co. Wicklow 1865; d. London 1936). Baritone vocalist. Studied in Germany and Italy and in London; made early reputation in opera and then turned to oratorio and song recitals—in which latter drew on a very large and varied repertory including songs specially written for him by Parry, Stanford, and others. His book *Interpretation in Song* has high value.

(3) **Eric Gordon** (b. London 1901; d. there 1966). Tenor vocalist. Educ. Winchester Cathedral Choir School and studied organ there. Entered Westminster Bank; became organizer of musical activities of its staff; resigned to pursue career as vocalist 1936. Studied R.A.M. from 1922 and built reputation as singer. Joined New English singers (see *English Singers*) 1934. Specialized in oratorio, especially Bach.

Green Mansions. Opera for broadcasting by Gruenberg (New York 1937).

Greensleeves. This is the tune twice mentioned by Shakespeare in *The Merry Wives of Windsor*: it is also mentioned by other writers of this period and later. It is first referred to in 1580, when it is called 'a new Northern Dittye', but there is evidence that it is of somewhat earlier date. There seem to be many ballads to the tune, as also some examples of its being converted to pious uses, as, for instance (again in 1580), 'Green Sleeves moralized to the Scripture'. During the Civil War of the 17th c. *Greensleeves* was a party tune, the Cavaliers setting many political ballads to it. From this period the tune is sometimes known as *The Blacksmith*, and under that name Pepys alludes to it (23 April 1660). Vaughan Williams has composed an orch. fantasia on the tune (adapted from his opera, *Sir John in Love*).

Gregorian Association. Brit. body founded 1870 to promote and improve use of Plainsong (q.v.). Publications are issued and an Annual Fest. is held in St. Paul's Cathedral.

Gregorian Chant. Same as *Plainsong* (q.v.).

Gregorian Modes. See *Modes*.

Gregorian Tones. The 8 plainsong melodies prescribed for the psalms in the Roman Catholic Church, one in each of the 8 Modes (see *Plainsong 3; Modes; Anglican Chant*). They have alternative endings (or 'inflexions') so as to connect properly with the varying antiphons which follow them (see *Antiphon*). The *Tonus Peregrinus* (q.v., = 'Alien Tone') is additional to the 8. See also *Parisian Tones*.

Grelots (Fr.). Little bells (e.g. sleigh bells, sometimes used in the orch.).

Gresham Professorship of Music. Sir Thomas Gresham (abt. 1519-1579), founder of the Royal Exchange, London, bequeathed his house to the Corporation of the City of London and the Mercers' Co. for the founding of a college with 7 resident professors and gratuitous instruction in astronomy, geometry, music, law, medicine, and rhetoric. John Bull (q.v.) was 1st Prof. of Music (in office 1596-1607). The provision made is now merely a series of popular lectures by the Prof. (at present Peter M. S. Latham, q.v.).

Gresnick (or Gresnich), Antoine Frédéric (b. Liège 1755; d. Paris 1799). Educated in Rome and Naples and lived for some years in London as chief musician to Prince of Wales and composer of operas: also wrote Fr. operas for Lyons and Paris, generally with high success, yet died in discouragement through failure of one or two of them.

Gretchaninof (Gretchaninow, &c.), Alexander (b. Moscow 1864; d. New York 1956). Pupil of Rimsky-Korsakof: his long list of works includes songs, operas, church music, and music for children (including children's operas). In New York from 1941.

Grétry, André Ernest Modeste (b. Liège 1741; d. Montmorency, nr. Paris, 1813). As a choir-boy was dismissed as lacking in ability; inspired by visit of an It. opera company, and encouraged by a sympathetic teacher, began to compose; tramped to Rome and studied there; on way to Paris spent year at Geneva, meeting Voltaire and receiving encouragement from him; gradually won favour as composer, producing 50 operas in Paris (e.g. *Richard Coeur-de-Lion*, q.v.). His operas are melodious and true settings of the words, but somewhat thin in texture and not very ably orchestrated. He left some sacred music and theoretical and critical treatises: publication of his complete works (musical and literary) undertaken by Belgian govt. in 1883.

Gr. Fl. Short for *Grosse Flöte*, i.e. the normal flute.

Grieg, Edvard Hagerup (b. Bergen 1843; there d. 1907). His mother was a fine pianist and became his first teacher; on advice of Ole Bull he was sent to Leipzig (cf. *Gade*); then he settled for a time in Copenhagen, but returned to Norway, founding a musical society at Christiania (now Oslo) and conducting it for 13 years; married his cousin Nina Hagerup, a fine singer who helped to popularize his songs. Liszt much encouraged him, especially praising his piano concerto (which remains

one of the most popular ever written). Wrote no symphony and no opera, but 3 violin sonatas, one string quartet, incidental music to Ibsen's *Peer Gynt* (q.v.), and a quantity of piano pieces in smaller forms and some of it easy to perform and simple in style, thus appealing to a wide public. A large portion of his output is distinctively Norwegian, based on peasant musical idioms, melodic, harmonic, and rhythmic. Frequently visited Britain and was Hon. D.Mus., Cambridge (1894), and Oxford (1906).

See also under *Funeral Marches*; *Holberg Suite*; *Huldigungsmarsch*; *Sigurd Jorsalfar*; *Halvorsen*.

Grier, (Hugh) Christopher (b. Derby 1922). Educ. King's College, Cambridge (B.A., B.Mus.). Brit. Council music officer for Scandinavia 1947; music critic, *The Scotsman*, 1949.

Griff (Ger. 'grip' or anything 'gripped' or 'grasped'). The knob on the handle of a drumstick. **Griffbrett** (Ger. 'grip-board'). Fingerboard of the violin, &c. Thus *am Griffbrett = sul tasto* (It.), i.e. bow on or near the fingerboard (see *gewöhnlich*).

Griffes, Charles Tomlinson (b. Elmira, N.Y., 1884; d. New York 1920). Studied in Berlin and worked there professionally for a time; then returned to U.S.A. as music teacher in a school in Tarrytown. His compositions attracted wide notice only after his early death; they include orch. music (e.g. *The Pleasure Dome of Kubla Khan*, q.v.), pieces for string quartet, a dance drama, piano music, and songs.

Grigny, Nicolas de; also spelt **Degrigny** (b. nr. Rheims 1672; there d. 1703). Famous organist of Rheims Cathedral and composer of organ music (this valued by Bach).

Griller, Sidney (b. London 1911). Violinist; trained R.A.M.; founded 1928 (with 3 fellow students) Griller String Quartet which soon won international reputation. On staff Univ. Calif. from 1949.

Grimmig (Ger.). 'Grim', 'furious'.

Grimson Family. (1) **Samuel Dean.** Violinist and viola player, prominent in London orch. and chamber music in 1870's and onwards. The individuals who follow are his children. (2) **Annie** (b. London). Pianist. Trained R.C.M. and under Matthay. London début 1899. Took high place as soloist. Composer of symphony, &c. (3) **Amy** (b. London 1872). Pianist and violoncellist. Trained R.C.M. and under Matthay. Soloist and teacher. (4) **Jessie**. Violinist. Trained R.C.M. and under Wilhelmj. Début Crystal Palace. Founded Grimson Quartet. First woman violinist-member Queen's Hall Orch. (5) **Robert**. Violoncellist. Trained R.C.M. and Berlin. On staff of Basle Conserv.; then in England. (6) **Harold Bonarius** (b. London). Violinist. Pupil of Sauret and Wilhelmj. Leading violinist Torquay Orch., &c.

Grinke, Frederick (b. Winnipeg 1911). Violinist. Trained R.A.M. and then under Adolf Busch and Carl Flesch. Became a member of Kutcher Quartet (see *Kutcher*) and then leader of Boyd Neel Orch. (see *Neel*).

Grisi, (1) **Giuditta** (b. Milan 1805; d. nr. Cremona 1840). Operatic mezzo-soprano of high quality. Before public 1823 to marriage 1834. (2) **Giulia** (b. Milan 1811; d. Berlin 1869). Operatic soprano of international celebrity. Sister of above. Before public from age 17 to near end of life (latterly only in concerts). Second husband was Mario. (3) **Carlotta** (b. in Istria 1819; d. Geneva 1899). Most famous ballerina of her period. Cousin of 2 vocalists above.

Groaning Stick. Thunder stick (q.v.).

Grob (Ger.). 'Coarse', 'rough'.

Grofé, Ferde (Ferdinand Rudolf von Grofe) (b. New York|1892). Conductor, composer, and arranger, esp. of popular *Grand Canyon Suite* (1931).

Gros, grosse (Fr. masc., fem.). 'Great', 'big'. (In the case of an organ stop this means of low pitch, e.g. 16 feet instead of 8 feet.)

Gross, grosse, &c. (Ger., various terminations according to case, gender, and number). 'Great', 'large'. So *grösser*, 'greater'.

Grosse caisse (Fr.). 'Big box', i.e. 'Bass Drum' (see *Percussion Family* 2 k).

Grosse Fuge ('Great Fugue'). 'The most gigantic fugue in existence.' Composed by Beethoven as the last movement of his String Quartet in B flat (op. 130), but then detached and printed as a separate work. Sometimes played by the whole string section of an orch.—a practice said to have been initiated by von Bülow.

Grosse Orgelmesse ('Great Mass with Organ'). Popular name for Haydn's Mass No. 4, in E flat, in which the organ has an important part. (Cf. *Kleine Orgelmesse.*)

Grosse Quartette (Haydn). See *Sonnenquartette.*

Grosses Orchester (Ger.). 'Full orchestra.'

Grosse Trommel (Ger.). 'Great drum', i.e. 'Bass Drum' (see *Percussion Family* 2 k).

Grossflöte (Ger.) 'Large Flute'. (1) The normal flute. (2) Metal organ stop of 8-foot length and pitch.

Grossmith, George (b. London 1847; there d. 1919). Entertainer and vocalist. Before public since 1870. Appeared in Gilbert and Sullivan from 1877 (*Sorcerer*) to 1888 (*Yeomen of the Guard*); thenceforward chiefly occupied with his personal entertainments. Composed incidental music to some plays. (The actor Weedon Grossmith, 1854–1919, was his brother.)

Gros tambour (Fr.). 'Great drum'. Same as *grosse caisse* (q.v.).

Grosz, Wilhelm (b. Vienna 1894; d. New York 1939). Took doctorate at Univ. of Vienna and studied music at conservatory. Held position as opera conductor Mannheim. In London 5 years, removing to New York shortly before death. Composer of operas and other theatre music, orch. and chamber music, film music, songs, &c.

Grotesk (Ger.). 'Grotesque.'

Grotrian-Steinweg. Brunswick piano-making firm, succeeding Theodor Steinweg 1865.

Grottesco (It.). 'Grotesque.'

Ground or Ground bass. Perhaps the earliest type of variation. It consists of a short bass phrase repeated many times with varied upper parts, and was much cultivated during the Purcell and Handel–Bach periods.

See *Sumer is icumen in*; *Folia*; *Chaconne and Passacaglia*.

Grove, George (b. Clapham 1820; d. Sydenham 1900). Man of great versatility and varied occupations (all useful to society). Civil engineer, building lighthouses in West Indies, secretary to Soc. of Arts (1850) and Crystal Palace on its opening (1852); founder of Palestine Exploration Fund and ed. of Smith's *Dictionary of the Bible*, author of a *Primer of Geography*, ed. of *Macmillan's Magazine* (1868–83), 1st Director of R.C.M. (1883 to death), ed. of famous *Dictionary of Music and Musicians* (4 vols. 1879–89; later edns. by other hands). D.C.L., Durham, LL.D., Glasgow. Knighted 1883.

See *Annotated Programmes*.

Groven, Eivind (b. Telemark, 1901). Composer, musicologist, and folk music collector. Studied Norway and Germany. Works include principally orchestral and vocal-orchestral compositions.

Groves of Blarney. See *Last Rose of Summer*.

Groves, Charles (b. London 1915). Trained R.C.M. B.B.C. chorus master 1938; asst. cond. B.B.C. Theatre Orch. 1942; Northern Orch. 1946; Bournemouth 1951; dir. Welsh National Opera 1961; Liverpool Philharmonic 1963. O.B.E. 1958.

Grovlez, Gabriel (b. Lille 1879; d. Paris 1944). Studied as pianist at Paris Conserv.; taught piano for many years at Schola Cantorum; then became successful operatic conductor. Composer of piano music, symphonic poems, ballets, comic operas, &c., and ed. of old Fr. music.

G.R.S.M. See *Degrees and Diplomas 2*.

Gr. Tr. Short for *Grosse Trommel* (q.v.).

Gruenberg, (1) **Louis** (b. nr. Brest-Litovsk 1884; d. Los Angeles 1964). Taken to U.S.A. in childhood but studied Vienna Conserv. and under Busoni in Berlin. Early career as pianist (début Berlin 1912). Then settled permanently in U.S.A., becoming known as composer of operas (e.g.

Emperor Jones, prod. New York 1933), orch. music, chamber music, and piano works, &c., in some showing leanings towards jazz idioms.

See also *Daniel Jazz*; *Green Mansions*; *Hill of Dreams*.

(2) **Erich** (b. Vienna 1924). Début age 7, then trained Jerusalem Conserv. In London from 1946. Leader Boyd Neel Orch.; Stockholm Philharmonic 1956; L.S.O. 1962; R.P.O. 1971.

Grumiaux, Arthur (b. Villers-Perwin, Belgium, 1921). Violinist. Trained Charleroi, Brussels, Paris. Début Britain 1945; then tours Europe, &c.

Grundstimmen (Ger. 'ground voices'). Foundation-stops of an organ.

Grüner-Hegge, Odd (b. Oslo 1899). Conductor and composer. Studied under Weingartner: début as pianist 1918. Cond. Oslo Philharm. Society from 1931. Dir. Norwegian Opera 1960. Works include piano and chamber music.

Gruppetto. It. name for 'Turn' (see Table 14).

G.S.M. Guildhall School of Music (q.v.).

Gsp. Short for *Glockenspiel*.

G string (violin). The lowest string, with a rich tone, so that composers occasionally direct that a passage shall be played on it alone (Bach's 'Air on the G string' is really the 2nd movement from that composer's 3rd orch. suite in D, rearranged by Wilhelmj (in 1871) as a violin solo in key C, the melody a 9th lower and with pianoforte accompaniment).

Guajira. A type of Cuban folk dance.

Guaracha, Guarracha. A type of Mexican folk dance in two sections, respectively in 3-in-a-measure and 2-in-a-measure time.

Guarneri. See *Violin Family*.

Guarracha. See *Guaracha*.

Gucht, Jan van der (b. Ongar, Essex, 1906). Tenor vocalist. Trained under Henschel (q.v.), &c. Varied career as recitalist, broadcaster, soloist with Brit. orchs. and choral societies, &c.

Gueden, Hilde (b. Vienna 1917). Operatic lyric soprano. Trained Vienna Conserv. Début Vienna 1940; Munich 1941; Rome 1942; London 1947; Edinburgh 1948; Metropolitan 1951. 'Kammersängerin' 1950.

Guédron (or **Guesdron**), **Pierre** (b. Beauce, Normandy, 1565; d. Paris 1621). Singer in chapel of Henry IV, later composer to it, &c., and still later musical director to Mary of Medici; composed ballets, &c. (in sense of drama anticipating Lully): work in general tended in same direction as that of the Florentine group of the same period (see *Opera* 1).

Guerre des bouffons. See *Bouffons*.

Guerrero, (1) **Pedro.** 16th-c. Spanish composer of lute music, church music, &c. For his brother see below. (2) **Francisco** (b. Seville 1528; there d. 1599). Brother and pupil of the above. He held important church positions and composed both church and secular music which was published in several countries.

Guerriero, Guerriera (It. masc., fem.). 'Warlike.'

Guesdron. See *Guédron*.

Guggenheim Fellowship (U.S.A. and Latin America). Benefaction of Mr. and Mrs. J. S. Guggenheim. As regards awards to musicians these are for composition and research—generally to cover study in Europe.

Gui, Vittorio (b. Rome 1885). Orch. and operatic conductor, composer of operas, symphonic poems, songs, &c.; also writer of critical articles.

Guido d'Arezzo, or **Guido Aretino,** &c. (b. Paris abt. 995; d. Avellano 1050). (Takes his name from It. town where he long resided—not born there.) Learned Benedictine of great fame as musical theoretician. (See *Hexachord; Sight-singing; Tonic Sol-fa*.)

Guidonian Hand. See *Hexachord*.

Guilbert, Yvette (b. Paris 1865; d. Aix-en-Provence 1944). Actress, diseuse, and singer; highly popular both sides Atlantic for over half a century (1885–1940).

Guildhall School of Music (London). Founded 1880; present building 1887. Under control of Corporation of City of London. Principals Weist-Hill (1880), Barnby (1892), Cummings (1896), Ronald (1910), Cundell (1938), Thorne (1959), Percival (1965).

Guillaume Tell ('William Tell'). Fr. Opera by Rossini; libretto based on Schiller's play. (Prod. Paris 1829; London 1830; New York 1831.) This opera has been given under many different names and with many different libretti (often changed for political reasons). Another opera of the name by Grétry (1791).

Guillemain, Gabriel (b. Paris 1705; suicide nr. there 1770). Notable composer of music for strings, chamber music combinations, and harpsichord.

Guilmant, Félix Alexandre (b. Boulogne 1837; d. Paris 1911). Studied organ with Lemmens, and soon won high position as recitalist; at 34 became organist of church of Trinity, Paris, where he remained for 30 years; on staff of Paris Conserv. and with Bordes and d'Indy founded the Schola Cantorum. Many effective organ compositions; also ed. early organ music.

Guimbarde (Fr.). Jew's harp (q.v.).

Guion (Guyon), David Wendel Fentress (b. Ballinger, Texas, 1895). Studied piano with Godowsky in Vienna; in composition self-taught; has occupied many academic positions. As composer especially popular for felicitous transcriptions of popular and traditional Amer. melodies (*Turkey in the Straw, Arkansas Traveller*, &c.); many songs.

See *Shingandi*.

Guiraud, Ernest (b. New Orleans 1837; d. Paris 1892). At Conserv. of Paris won Rome Prize; on return to Paris chiefly occupied as opera composer; also wrote orch. music, &c., and a *Treatise of Instrumentation*. On staff of Conserv. where Debussy was one of his pupils.

Guitar. An ancient and widely distributed instrument somewhat of the lute type (cf. *Mandolin*) but with a flat or only slightly rounded back, played, like the lute, with the fingers, not with a plectrum. Its sides have inward curves something like those of the violin family. The normal modern guitar has 6 strings. Its culture is today highest in Italy and (especially) Spain: one form of Spanish guitar is the *Vihuela*. In Britain there is an active Philharmonic Soc. of Guitarists, with branches in various provincial centres (also branches Australia and Ceylon), and there are similar societies in Austria, France, and North and South America.

GUITAR

Scaramouche (1608–94), famous Italian comedian, popular in France at the courts of Louis XIII and Louis XIV

Guitare d'amour. See *Arpeggione*.

Gulbranson, Ellen—*née* Norgren (b. Stockholm 1863; d. Oslo 1947). Operatic soprano, repeatedly engaged at Bayreuth (as Brünnhilde 1896 onwards); also Berlin, London, Paris, &c.

Gundry, Inglis (b. London 1905). Studied at Oxford and R.C.M. During the war of 1939–45 served in the Navy (latterly musical adviser to Admiralty education department). Has composed operas, ballets, orch. music, &c.

Gung'l, Joseph (b. Zsàmbèk, Hungary, 1810; d. Weimar 1889). A schoolmaster who turned military bandmaster and composed quantities of popular dances and marches.

Guntram. First Opera of Richard Strauss. (Prod. Weimar 1894.)

Guridi, Jesus (b. Vitoria, Spain, 1886; d. Madrid 1961). Of Basque birth, he collected Basque folk songs and used them in his compositions (chiefly operas, musical comedies, and choral pieces). Director of Madrid Conserv.

Gurlitt, Cornelius (b. Altona 1820; there d. 1901). Became chief organist of native town and one of later 19th c.'s most liberal, artistic, and successful providers of piano fodder for the young; also composed operas, chamber music, &c.

Gurney, Ivor (b. Gloucester 1890; d. Dartford 1937). Choir-boy and then assistant organist at Gloucester Cathedral; won scholarship to R.C.M., served in 1914–18 war and was wounded and gassed; returned to College and appeared before public as composer of delicate songs, piano music, and chamber and orch. music. Effect of war injuries compelled cessation of work and seclusion in mental hospital for many years, and in it he died.

Gurrelieder ('Songs of Gurra'). Setting by Schönberg of Danish poems by Jens Peter Jacobsen transl. into Ger. (No op. number; composed 1900–11). Employs 5 Vocal Soloists, a Speaker (in *Sprechgesang*, q.v.), 3 four-part Male Choruses, an eight-part Mixed Chorus, and very large Orch. (See *Percussion* 2 y.)

Gusla, or **Gusle**, or **Guzla**. An ancient one-stringed bowed instrument still popular in some Slavonic regions (not to be confused with 'Gusli', below).

Guslar. A player on the *Gusli* (q.v.).

Gusle. See *Gusla*.

Guslee. See *Gusli*.

Gusli, or **Guslee**. Russian instrument of the zither class (not to be confused with 'Gusla', above). Of great antiquity.

Gusto (It.). 'Taste' (i.e. Sense of fitness as to speed, force, phrasing, &c.). So *gustoso*, 'Tastefully'.

Gut (Ger.). 'Good', 'well'.

Guyon. See *Guion*.

Guzla. See *Gusla*.

Gwineth, Gwynedd, &c. (16th c.). Clergyman and controversial writer on religion; composer whose music is almost all lost. D.Mus., Oxford, 1531.

Gyles, Nathaniel. See *Giles*.

Gymel or **Gimel.** The word comes from the Lat. *gemellus* and has been used in music in 3 senses, all with the idea of twinship.

(1) It describes a style of singing alleged to have been common in parts of Britain as early as the 10th or 11th c. Whilst one body of singers took the tune of a song another body would extemporaneously add a part in 3rds beneath it (cf. *Faburden* 1).

(2) It is applied to a type of composition found in the 14th and early 15th cs. in which, whilst the main tune, or canto fermo, was sung in a lower voice, 2 upper voices sang an accompaniment in which they moved independently of the other voice but in 3rds with one another.

(3) We find the term used in 16th-c. choral music. In the parts for any particular voice we may find the word 'gymel' meaning that the singers of that part are here divided—our *divisi*, in fact. The restoration of the *status quo* is then indicated by the word *Semel*.

Gyrowetz, Adalbert (b. Budweis, Bohemia, 1763; d. Vienna 1850). Highly successful composer of 60 symphonies, chamber music, operas, ballets, and masses—in the Haydn style, not very original (thus he fell at last into neglect and died in poverty).

H

H. Ger. for B (B flat being in that language called B).

Haas, Karl (Wilhelm Jacob) (b. Karlsruhe 1900; d. 1970). Conductor and editor. Educ. Heidelberg and Munich. At first music adviser, Karlsruhe and Stuttgart radio, &c. In England from 1939. Founded London Baroque Ensemble 1941, specializing in perfs. of wind music of that period. Many recordings, arrangements, &c.

Hába, (1) **Alois** (b. Vyzovice, Moravia, 1893; d. Prague 1972). Studied in Prague, Vienna, and Berlin; then settled in Prague as a member of the staff of its Conserv. Has applied in his composition and teaching a system of microtones (q.v.); in 1931 produced microtonal opera, *The Mother*; professes to use a 'non-thematic' process, i.e. one eschewing elements of repetition and symmetry. (2) **Karel** (b. Vyzovice, Moravia, 1898). Brother and pupil of the above, and on occasion adopts his microtonal system.

Habanera. A slow Cuban dance (Habana = Havana), which became very popular in Spain. It is in simple duple time and dotted rhythm.

Habanera, La. See *Laparra*.

Habeneck, François Antoine (b. Mézières, Ardennes, 1781; d. Paris 1849). Paris violinist and violin teacher of high repute, also composer for his instrument. Notable as founder of Société des Concerts du Conservatoire and as conductor, being first to introduce Beethoven's symphonies into France.

Haberl, Franz Xaver. See *Cecilian Movement*.

Habyngton, Henry. See *Abyngdon*.

Hackbrett (Ger. 'chopping board'). 'Dulcimer' (q.v.).

Haddon Hall. Romantic opera by Sullivan. Libretto by S. Grundy. (Prod. Savoy Theatre, London, 1892.)

Hadley, (1) **Henry Kimball** (b. Somerville, Mass., 1871; d. New York 1937). Well known as conductor in Europe (1904–9) and in U.S.A. (1909 Seattle Symphony Orch.; 1911–15 New York Philharmonic Orch., &c.); also conducted in Japan. As composer left 4 symphonies, many overtures, 7 operas, chamber music, over 100 songs, &c.; a sure technician somewhat after the model of Wagner. D.Mus., Tufts Coll., French Order of Merit, &c.

See also *Bianca*; *Francesca da Rimini*; *Lucifer*; *Ocean*; *Salome*.

(2) **Patrick (Arthur Sheldon)** (b. Cambridge 1899; d. London 1973). Studied at Univ. of Cambridge and R.C.M. (on staff 1925); lecturer Cambridge 1939; Prof. of Mus. 1946–63. Has composed much orch. and chamber music, choral music, &c.

Hadow, William Henry (Sir Henry Hadow) (b. Ebrington, Glos., 1859; d. London 1937). Successively scholar, lecturer, and fellow and tutor of Worcester Coll., Oxford; Principal of Armstrong Coll., Newcastle-on-Tyne (1909–19), then Vice-Chancellor of Univ. of Sheffield (to 1930); in numberless ways served Brit. general and musical education. Wrote 2 series of *Studies in Modern Music* (1894–5) and other books on musical subjects, and ed. *The Oxford History of Music* (1901 onwards). M.A., B.Mus., Hon. D.Mus., Oxford; Hon. LL.D., D.Litt., &c., of several other univs.; knighted 1918; C.B.E. 1920. Married in later life daughter of Rev. John Troutbeck.

Haendel. See *Handel*.

Haendel, Ida (b. nr. Warsaw 1923). Violinist. Trained Warsaw Conserv. and under Flesch. Resident England since age 16. Has toured widely.

Haffner Serenade and Symphony. Nicknames of Mozart's Suite in D, K. 250 (1776), and Symphony in D, K. 385 (1782), composed for the Haffner family of Salzburg.

Hageman, Richard (b. Leeuwarden, Holland, 1882; d. Beverly Hills, Calif., 1966). Emigrated to U.S.A.

1907. Operatic and orch. conductor. Composed opera, *Caponsacchi* (New York 1931) and many songs.

Hagerup, Nina (b. nr. Bergen 1845; d. Copenhagen 1935). Vocalist. Wife of Grieg and singer of his songs.

Hahn, Reynaldo (b. Carácas, Venezuela, 1875; d. Paris 1947). Went to Paris in infancy and there remained; at 11 entered Conserv., becoming pupil of Massenet. Composer of many operas, songs, &c.; efficient conductor with special interest in Mozart's operas.

Hahnebüchen (Ger.). 'Coarse', 'heavy'.

Haieff, Alexei (b. Siberia 1914). Composer; trained Juilliard and under Nadia Boulanger. In U.S.A. from 1932. Works include orch. and esp. chamber music in spare, contrapuntal, 'neoclassic' style.

Hail Columbia. The words are by Joseph Hopkinson (son of Francis Hopkinson, q.v.), and were written in 1798 when war between Great Britain and France was in progress and there seemed to be a danger of the U.S.A. being drawn into the struggle. They were written to fit the tune known as *The President's March*—probably composed by Philip Phile or Phylo, leading violin of a Philadelphia orch.

Hail, smiling morn. See *Spofforth*.

Hailstone Chorus. Realistic movement in Handel's oratorio *Israel in Egypt* (1738).

Hail, true Body. See *Ave verum corpus*.

Halb, Halbe (Ger., various grammatical terminations). 'Half.' **Halbe** or **Halbenote.** Half-note or minim (see Table 3). **Halbe-pause.** 'Half-rest', i.e. minim rest (see Table 3). **Halbe Taktnote.** See Table 3.

Halbprinzipal (Ger.). 'Half Diapason', i.e. 4-foot Principal (organ stop).

Halbsopran (Ger.). 'Mezzo-soprano.'

Halbtenor (Ger.). 'Baritone.'

Hale, Adam de la. See *Adam de la Halle*.

Hale, Philip (b. Norwich, Vt., 1854; d. Boston, Mass., 1934). Graduated Yale; practised law; then studied music under Rheinberger in Munich, Guilmant in Paris, &c. Became music critic Boston journals (*Herald* last 30 years of life). Noted as writer of excellent programme notes for Boston Symphony Orch. See under *Criticism*; *Annotated Programmes*.

Halévy (originally Lévy), **Jacques François Fromental Élie** (b. Paris 1799; d. Nice 1862). Pupil of Cherubini at Paris Conserv.; at 21 won Rome Prize, and on return made his way as opera composer, in which activity he was very productive (*La Juive*, q.v., considered his masterpiece); like Meyerbeer loved stage pageantry and grandeur. Held many official positions including a professorship at the Conserv., where Bizet was his pupil (later his son-in-law).

Half Cadence. See *Cadence*.

Half Close. See *Cadence*.

Halffter, (1) **Escriche Ernesto** (b. Madrid 1905). Orch. conductor and composer of operas, orch. music, chamber music, songs, &c. (2) **Rodolfo** (b. Madrid 1900). Brother of the above; composer of piano and chamber music, &c. Res. Mexico.

Half-note. 'Minim' (see Table 3).

Hälfte (Ger.). 'Half.'

Half-tube. See *Whole-tube and Half-tube*.

Halir, Karl (b. Hohenelbe, Bohemia, 1859; d. Berlin 1909). Violinist. Trained Prague Conserv. and under Joachim (q.v.), of whose quartet he was later a member (1893–1907). Toured U.S.A., &c.

Halka. Opera by Moniuszko. (Prod. Vilna 1848; New York 1903.)

Hall, (1) **Ernest** (b. Liverpool 1890). Trumpet player. Trained R.C.M., later on staff. Principal Covent Garden, Boston Symphony Orchs.; B.B.C. Symphony Orch. from 1930.

(2) **Marie (Paulina)** (b. Newcastle-on-Tyne 1884; d. Cheltenham 1956). Violinist. Daughter of harpist; pupil of Hildegard Werner of Newcastle, Sauret, Max Mossel, Elgar, Kruse, Ševčik, and others. On appearing in

public at 18 had immediate wide-spread success.

(3) **G. W. L. Marshall-.** See *Mar-shall-Hall.*

Halle, Adam de la. See *Adam de la Halle.*

Hallé (originally Halle), **Charles** (b. Hagen, Westphalia, 1819; d. Manchester 1895). Distinguished pianist and conductor; made his home in Manchester (1848), establishing famous orch. that still bears his name (1857), and also Royal Manchester Coll. of Music (1893). Knighted 1888. Second wife (formerly Mme Norman-Neruda) was celebrated violinist.

Hallé Orchestra (Manchester). Founded by Sir Charles Hallé (q.v.) in 1857; later conductors include Richter (1895), Beecham (1914), Harty (1920), Barbirolli (1943), Loughran (1971).

Hallelujah. It means 'Praise Jehovah' (from Hebrew *Hallel,* 'praise', and *Jah,* Jehovah). 'Alleluia' (q.v.) is the Latin form. Hallelujah Choruses (perhaps usually prompted by Rev. xix. 1) are common in music (see below).

Hallelujah Chorus. By this is usually meant one particular such chorus out of very many which exist—the chorus which so triumphantly closes Part II of Handel's *Messiah.* At the 1st London perf., in Covent Garden Theatre (23 March 1743), the whole assembly, with George II at its head, rose to its feet as this chorus opened, and remained standing to the end, thus establishing a tradition which is still maintained everywhere in Britain.

Hallelujah Organ Concerto. Handel's No. 9 in B flat (Set 2, no. 3)—so nicknamed from the appearance in the last movement of a phrase from the 'Hallelujah Chorus'.

Hallen (Ger.). 'To clang.'

Halleux, Laurent (b. Brussels 1897). Violinist. Pupil of César Thomson at Brussels Conserv. In 1915 one of founders of Pro Arte Quartet; later joined London String Quartet (q.v.).

Halling. A popular solo dance of Norway, presumed to have originated in the Hallingdal. Its music is in simple duple time and its motions are remarkably vigorous.

Halmagyi. See *Electric Musical Instruments* 1.

Halt (Ger.). 'Pause' (⌒).

Halten (Ger.). 'To hold', 'sustain'.

Halvorsen, Johan (b. Drammen, Norway, 1864; d. Oslo 1935). Studied in Stockholm, Leipzig, Berlin, and Liège; skilful violinist and obtained position as such at Aberdeen; then conductor of orch. at Bergen. Compositions reflected influence of Grieg (whose niece he married).

Hambourg Family. Father and 3 sons (all naturalized Brit. subjects) as follows: (1) **Michael** (b. Yaroslav, Russia, 1856; d. Toronto 1916). A pupil and then on staff of Moscow Conserv. (1880). Settled London 1890; Toronto 1910. The sons are as follows: (2) **Mark** (b. Bogutchar, S. Russia, 1879; d. Cambridge 1960). Pianist. Début Moscow age 10; London following year. Then pupil of Leschetizky. Toured world. Piano compositions and books. (3) **Jan** (b. Voronesz 1882; d. Tours, France, 1947). Violinist. Pupil of Sauret, Wilhelmj, Ševčik, and Ysaÿe. Toured Britain, U.S.A., &c. (4) **Boris** (b. Voronesz 1885; d. Toronto 1954). Violoncellist. In London from age 5. Pupil of Becker at Frankfurt. Toured world.

Hamerik (originally Hammerich), (1) **Asger** (b. Copenhagen 1843; d. Frederiksborg 1923). Piano pupil of von Bülow, who valued his talent as conductor and employed him in that capacity. Composed operas, &c. Director of Conserv. Peabody Inst., Baltimore, 1871–98; founded a good orch. there; then returned to Copenhagen. Knighted by King of Denmark. (2) **Angul** (b. 1848; d. 1931). Brother of Asger. Musicologist and historian of high standing. (3) **Ebbe** (b. Copenhagen 1898; d. there 1951). Son of Asger. Orch. conductor; composer of operas, symphonic works, &c.

Hamilton, Iain (Ellis) (b. Glasgow 1922). Composer. Trained R.A.M. and London Univ. (B.Mus.). Lecturer Morley Coll. 1952; Duke Univ., U.S.A., 1962. Composer of numerous original orch., choral, and chamber works, independently dissonant in idiom, some with jazz tinge. Active in professional organizations (chairman Composers' Guild 1958, &c.).

Hamlet. (1) Symphonic Poem by Liszt. (1859; 1st perf. 1876.) Intended as a Prelude to Shakespeare's play. (2) See *Thomas, C. L. Ambroise.* (3) Concert Ov. op. 67 (1888) and incid. music by Tchaikovsky.

Hammer Bone. See *Ear and Hearing.*

Hammerich. See *Hamerik.*

Hammerklavier Sonatas (Beethoven). Title-page description by the composer himself, of the piano sonatas ops. 101 (in A), 106 (in B flat), 109 (in E), 110 (in A flat). Now usually applied only to op. 106. ('Hammerklavier' is old Ger. name for Piano, as distinct from Harpsichord.)

Hammerstein, Oscar (b. Stettin 1848; d. New York 1919). Business man who became opera manager, building Manhattan Opera Houses (1898 and 1906) and producing amazing list of important novelties; thus threatened existence of Metropolitan Opera House, which eventually bought him out. Built London Opera House, Kingsway (1911), but unsuccessful and soon abandoned (became a cinema).

Hammond & Co. London music publishers (11 Lancashire Court, W. 1).

Hammond, Joan (Hood) (b. Christchurch, N.Z., 1912). Soprano. Golf champion and journalist who left Sydney 1936 to study singing in Vienna (operatic début there), France, Germany, Italy. London career from 1938. O.B.E. 1953. Retired 1965.

Hammond Organ. See *Electric Musical Instruments* 4.

Hampson. See *Hempson.*

Hampstead Heath Bank Holiday. See *Klenau.*

Hampsy. See *Hempson.*

Hanacca or **Hanakisch** (Ger.) or **Hanaise** (Fr.). A Moravian dance in simple triple time; a sort of quick polonaise.

Hand, Hände (Ger.). 'Hand', 'hands'.

Handbells. See *Bell* 7.

Handel (originally Händel or Haendel), **George Frideric** (b. Halle 1685; d. London 1759). Worked at music initially against his father's wishes; became a violinist in orch. of Hamburg opera. At 21 went to Italy, where he acquired great reputation as keyboard performer and, also, that flowing Italianate style which is seen in his composition. Then Kapellmeister to Elector of Hanover, but soon left for London, where his Elector later followed him as George I of Britain.

The early part of the London career was chiefly occupied in (Italian) opera composition and management, with fluctuations between high prosperity and deep adversity, the latter finally predominating and leading to activity in Eng. oratorio, by the products o. which his memory and reputation were to be kept alive in a period when opera of the 18th-c. It. variety had passed completely out of vogue. The most important oratorios are *Saul* (composed 1738), *Israel in Egypt* (1739; famous for its double choruses), *Messiah* (1741), *Samson* (1741), *Judas Maccabaeus* (1746), *Occasional Oratorio* (1746), *Joshua* (1747), *Solomon* (1748), *Theodora* (1749); these had their greatest popularity in a period ending about 1880, and some of them are now known to few music-lovers except by detached vocal solos and choruses. There were, also, concerti grossi, organ concertos, and harpsichord works o. permanent interest.

It will be observed that Handel and Bach were born in the same year and died within a few years of one another; both, too, ended their lives in the distress of loss of sight; the general circumstances of their lives and the style of their works are, however, in strong contrast, the one remaining in his own north German environment all his days, and also in his original middle-class station, and the other travelling abroad and moving on intimate terms in an exalted social circle; the one providing for small local audiences, apparently cultivated in their tastes and prepared to enjoy music of complex texture and deep personal feeling, and the other composing for the largest audiences music of an immediately attractive though inherently solid character ('a magnificent opportunist').

See *Acis and Galatea*; *Additional Accompaniments*; *Adeste fideles*; *Alexander Balus*; *Alexander's Feast*; *Amen*; *Athaliah*; *Chandos*; *Deborah*; *Dettingen Te Deum and Anthem*; *Esther*; *Festival*; *Fireworks Music*; *Funeral Marches*; *Giulio Cesare*; *Gods of a-begging*; *Hallelujah Chorus*; *Hallelujah Organ Concerto*; *Harmonious Blacksmith*; *Hornpipe Concerto*; *Israel in Egypt*; *Jephtha*; *Joseph*; *Joshua*; *Judas Maccabaeus*; *Kerll*; *Largo*; *Messiah*; *Occasional Oratorio*; *Pastoral Symphony*; *Rinaldo*; *Samson*; *Saul*; *Semele*; *Solomon*; *Susanna*; *Theodora*; *Water Music*.

Handel and Haydn Society. See *Festival*.

Händel Gesellschaft. The German Handel Society; see *Chrysander*.

Handel Society. (1) Founded in London in 1843 for the publication of the composer's works; after a few volumes were published, however, it was dissolved. (2) Founded in London in 1882 for the performance of the composer's (and other) music, chiefly large choral works.

Hand Horn. The 'Natural' French Horn, when designed for playing with the hand in the bell (see *Horn Family*).

Handl, Jacob—otherwise Händl, Gallus, &c. (b. Reifnitz, Carniola, 1550; d. Prague 1591). Held important church positions in Vienna, Olmütz, and Prague, and wrote masses, motets, &c., which entitle him to high rank amongst the composers of his day.

Handlo, Robert de (early 14th c.). Eng. writer on musical notation.

Hand Organ. The Barrel Organ (see *Mechanical Reproduction* 10). The word 'Hand' distinguishes it from the 'Finger Organ', i.e. the one played from a keyboard.

Handregistrierung (Ger.). Manual piston (on organ).

Handschin, Jacques (b. Moscow 1886; d. Basle 1955). Trained Paris. Various organist positions. On staff St. Petersburg (Leningrad) Conserv. Prof. Univ. Basle from 1930. Innumerable publications embodying results of musicological research.

Handtrommel (Ger.). 'Tambourine' (see *Percussion Family* 2 m).

Hanging Tunes. See under *Fortune my Foe*.

Hanover Square Rooms. Long the leading *locale* for London concertgiving; opened 1775; closed 1874. Amongst those who performed there were J. C. Bach, Haydn, Liszt, Rubinstein, Mendelssohn, Wagner (as conductor 1855), Clara Schumann, and Joachim. Ancient Concerts (q.v.) held there 1804 to cessation 1848; Philharmonic Soc. (see *Royal Philharmonic Soc.*) 1833–69.

Hänsel and Gretel. Fairy-tale opera by Humperdinck. (Prod. Weimar 1893; London 1894; New York 1895.)

Hans Heiling. See *Marschner*.

Hanslick, Eduard (b. Prague 1825; d. Vienna 1904). Great Viennese music critic; central figure of many a hot fight; Wagner's bitterest opponent and Brahms's most ardent supporter. Author of important book *On Musical Beauty* (1854; 11 German edns., also transl. into 5 other languages).

Hanson, Howard Harold (b. Wahoo, Nebraska, 1896). Won Amer. Rome Prize and spent 1921–4 at Amer. Academy in Rome, then director (until 1964) of Eastman School, Rochester, N.Y. Pulitzer Prize for Symphony No. 4 in 1944. Chamber music, piano music, songs, &c. Active conductor.

See also *Lux Aeterna*; *Merry Mount*; *Nordic Symphony*; *Pan and the Priest*; *Romantic Symphony*.

Harcadelt, Jachet—Arcadelt, Jacob (q.v.).

Hardelot, Guy d'—Mrs. Helen Rhodes, *née* Guy (b. Hardelot, nr. Boulogne, 1858; d. London 1936). Highly popular composer of Eng. songs. Trained Paris Conserv.; protégée of Gounod and Massenet, &c. Songs sung by Melba, Calvé, Maurel, &c., as also by every Brit. amateur vocalist.

Hardi; Hardiment (Fr.). 'Bold'; 'Boldly'.

Hard Palate. See *Palate*.

Harewood, George Henry Hubert Lascelles, 7th Earl of (b. 1923). Active force in music; associated with English Opera Group since inception; on Board, Covent Garden; edited own magazine *Opera* (1950–3). Director Edinburgh Festival 1961–4.

Harfe (Ger.). 'Harp.'

Hark, the Herald Angels sing. See *Festgesang.*

Harlequin's Millions. See *Drigo.*

Harmonic. See under *Harmonics.*

Harmonica. This word has been variously applied as follows:

(1) MUSICAL GLASSES. In these the tone is evoked by rubbing with the wetted finger the rims of glasses, either (*a*) Drinking glasses, these being filled with water to different heights in order to leave a larger or smaller area of glass free to vibrate, and so to produce the different notes), or (*b*) Glass basins, graduated in size, fixed to a spindle revolved by a pedal mechanism, the bottoms of the basins running in a trough of water, so as to be kept permanently damp.

Gluck, in his earlier career, performed in London on form (*a*), Mozart, as a youth, on form (*b*), for which form Beethoven and other serious composers have provided some music.

(2) GLASS DULCIMER (see *Dulcimer*)— strips of glass struck with hammers. Occasionally this has been provided with a mechanism and keyboard.

(3) The MOUTH ORGAN. See *Reed Organ Family* 2.

(4) NAIL HARMONICA. See *Nail Fiddle.*

And in other languages than English this word has still wider applications.

Harmonic Bass. Organ stop; same as *Acoustic Bass* (q.v.).

Harmonic Flute. Organ stop usually of 8-foot length but 4-foot pitch, pipes being pierced at half-length: tone silvery.

Harmonic Minor Scale. See *Scale.*

Harmonicon, The. See *Criticism.*

Harmonic Piccolo. Organ stop of 4-foot length and 2-foot pitch—on principle of *Harmonic Flute* (q.v.).

Harmonics. (1) See *Acoustics* 6, 7. (2) Organ *Mixture Stop* (q.v.), usually of 4 ranks (e.g. 17th, q.v.; 19th, q.v.; flat 21st, q.v.; and 22nd).

Harmonic Sequence. See *Sequence* 1.

Harmonic Series. See *Acoustics* 7.

Harmonic Trumpet. Organ stop (see *Trumpet*) embodying (in upper pipes, at any rate) constructional principle of *Harmonic Flute* (q.v.); 8-foot pitch.

Harmonie. The French for 'harmony' but it has also a special application, *Harmonie* (or *Musique d'Harmonie*) meaning a band of wood, brass, and percussion (as distinct from *Fanfare*, a band of merely brass and percussion), or sometimes the wind instruments of an orch.

Harmonie, Basse d'. Ophicleide (see *Cornett and Key Bugle Families*).

Harmonie, Cor d' (Fr.). French Horn—when without valves (see *Horn Family*).

Harmonie, Trompette d' (Fr.). The ordinary trumpet of today (see *Trumpet Family*).

Harmoniemesse (Ger. 'Wind-band Mass'). Popular name for Haydn's 14th Mass, in B flat, which makes a fuller use of wind instruments than is common in Haydn's Masses.

Harmoniemusik (Ger.). A band of wood, brass, and percussion.

Harmonika (Ger.). Same as *Harmonica* (q.v.).

Harmonious Blacksmith, The. Unauthorized and uncontemporary name given to an Air and Variations in Handel's 5th Harpsichord Suite of 1st Set (1720).

Harmonique (Fr.). 'Harmonic.'

Harmonische Töne (Ger.). 'Harmonics.'

Harmonium. See *Reed-Organ Family* 5.

Harmony. (1) Harmony may be described as the clothing of melody— which was left unclothed in Europe until the 9th c. and is still so left over a great part of the rest of the world as also in the peasant tunes of Europe itself. At the period mentioned (cf.

History of Music 2) the traditional plain-song of the Church, formerly sung in unison, began to be given to singers of a middle voice (hence 'tenors'—lit. 'holders' of the *canto fermo*, or 'fixed song'), whilst any higher and lower voices enwrapped it with other melodic strands, and even today composers, in much the greater proportion of their music, maintain in their minds some melody which ranks as the principal one, and which they intend the listener to recognize as such, whilst other melodies which are combined with it, or chords with which it is accompanied, rank as subsidiary.

The word CHORD, just used, may be defined as any combination of notes simultaneously performed, and even when the main process in the composer's mind is a weaving together of melodic strands he has to keep before him this combinational element, both as regards the notes thus sounded together and the suitability of one combination to follow and precede the adjacent combination.

At different periods composers have given more attention to one or the other of the two aspects of their work, (*a*) The weaving together of melodic strands and (*b*) The chords thus brought into existence from point to point.

The former aspect of the result is the *Contrapuntal* element (see *Counterpoint*) and the latter the *Harmonic* element. In less elaborate music (as, for instance, a simple song with piano accompaniment) the contrapuntal element may be unimportant or even non-existent. Counterpoint, it will be realized, necessarily implies also harmony, whilst harmony does not necessarily imply counterpoint.

The harmonic combinations (or chords) which the human ear (or rather, we may almost say, the European ear) has enjoyed, tolerated, or abhorred, at different periods, have varied greatly. Looking at the history of Harmony over a long period the resources may be said to have widened: new combinations introduced by composers of pioneering spirit have been condemned by unaccustomed ears as ugly, have then gradually come to be accepted as commonplace, and have been succeeded in their turn by other experimental combinations. The whole process is outlined, with examples, in *OCM*, and cannot be detailed here.

(2) The harmonies which 'the man in the street' accepts today without objection, and even with pleasure, may be defined as those of the Haydn or, perhaps, Haydn–Beethoven period, or of a period a little more extended. Those are, for instance, the harmonies we find in examining any popular collection of hymn tunes. The following definitions concern such harmonies as those just mentioned:

(*a*) DIATONIC HARMONY: Harmony which confines itself to the major or minor key that is in force at the moment. CHROMATIC HARMONY: Harmony which employs notes extraneous to the major or minor key in force at the moment.

(*b*) OPEN HARMONY: Harmony in which the notes of the chords are more or less widely spread. CLOSE HARMONY: Harmony in which the notes of the chords lie near together.

(*c*) PROGRESSION: The motion of one note to another note or one chord to another chord.

(*d*) TRIAD: A note with its 3rd and 5th (e.g. C–E–G). COMMON CHORD: A Triad of which the 5th is perfect. MAJOR COMMON CHORD: A Common Chord of which the 3rd is major. MINOR COMMON CHORD: A Common Chord of which the 3rd is minor. AUGMENTED TRIAD: A Triad of which the 5th is augmented. DIMINISHED TRIAD: A Triad of which the 5th is diminished.

(*e*) ROOT of a chord. That note from which it originates. (For instance, in the common chord C–E–G we have C as the root, to which are added the 3rd and 5th.) INVERSION of a chord: The removal of the root from the bass to an upper part. FIRST INVERSION: That in which the 3rd becomes the bass (e.g. E–G–C or E–C–G). SECOND INVERSION: That in which the 5th becomes the bass (e.g. G–E–C or G–C–E). THIRD INVERSION: In a 4-note chord that inversion in which the fourth note becomes the bass. (For instance, in the chord G–B–D–F the form of it that consists of F–G–B–D or F–B–G–D, &c.) FUNDAMENTAL BASS: An imaginary bass of a passage, consisting not of its actual bass notes but of the roots of its chords, i.e. the bass of its chords when uninverted.

(*f*) CONCORD. A chord satisfactory in itself (or an interval that can be so described; or a note which forms a part of such an interval or chord). CONSONANCE: The same as *Concord*. DISCORD: A chord which is restless, requiring to be followed in a particular way if its presence is to be justified by the ear (or the note or interval responsible for producing this effect). See, for instance, the examples given under *Dominant Seventh* and *Diminished Seventh*. DISSONANCE: The same as *Discord*. RESOLUTION: The satisfactory following of a discordant chord (or the satisfactory following

Fundamental Bass

of the discordant note in such a chord). SUSPENSION: A form of discord arising from the holding over of a note in one chord as a momentary (discordant) part of the combination which follows, it being then resolved by falling a degree to a note which forms a real part of the second chord. DOUBLE SUSPENSION: The same as the last with 2 notes held over.

Suspension   Anticipation   Retardation

(*g*) ANTICIPATION: The sounding of a note of a chord before the rest of the chord is sounded. RETARDATION: The same as a Suspension but resolved by *rising* a degree.

PREPARATION: The sounding in one chord of a concordant note which is to remain (in the same 'part') in the next chord as a discordant note. (This applies both to Fundamental Discords and Suspensions; see example, s.v. *Suspension* above.) UNPREPARED SUSPENSION: A contradiction in terms meaning an effect similar to that of Suspension but without 'Preparation'.

FUNDAMENTAL DISCORD: A discordant chord of which the discordant note forms a real part of the chord, i.e. not a mere Suspension, Anticipation, or Retardation. Or the said discordant note itself (e.g. *Dominant Seventh*, *Diminished Seventh*, &c.).

PASSING NOTE: A connecting note in one of the melodic parts (not forming a part of the chord which it follows or precedes).

(*h*) FALSE RELATION: The appearance of a note with the same letter-name in different parts (or 'voices') of contiguous chords,

in one case inflected (sharp or flat) and in the other uninflected.

(*i*) PEDAL (or 'Point d'Orgue'): The device of holding on a bass note (usually Tonic or Dominant) through a passage including some chords of which it does not form a part. INVERTED PEDAL: The same as the above but with the held note in an upper part. DOUBLE PEDAL: A pedal in which two notes are held (generally Tonic and Dominant).

Ped.

First line of hymn-tune *Edina* by Sir H. S. Oakeley. Here the harmonic pedal is actually a note on the organ pedal-board. It will be seen that it forms no part of the chords marked *.

(*j*) CONSECUTIVE 5ths (or 8ves): The interval of the perfect 5th occurring between 2 'parts' and followed by another perfect 5th between the same 2 parts (e.g. G–D between tenor and soprano in one chord followed by A–E in the same parts in the next chord), and similarly with the interval of the 8ve. HIDDEN 5ths (or 8ves): The progression in similar motion (see *Motion*) of 2 parts to a perfect 5th (or an 8ve) from such an interval in the same 2 parts in the previous chord that the imaginative eye of a captious examiner might see a 5th (or 8ve) in intermediate hiding (e.g. G–C in tenor and soprano proceeding to A–E in the next chord). Those who object to this progression usually do so only when the outermost parts are those involved in the crime.

Consecutive 5ths   Consecutive 8ves

Hidden 5ths   Hidden 8ves

(3) From Wagner onwards the resources of Harmony have been enormously extended, and those used by composers of the present day often submit to no rules whatever, being purely empirical, or justified by rules of the particular composer's own devising. Amongst contemporary practices are the following:

BITONALITY—in which two contrapuntal strands or 'parts' proceed in different keys. POLYTONALITY—in which the different contrapuntal strands, or 'parts', proceed in more than one key. ATONALITY—in which no principle of key is observed. MICROTONALITY—in which scales are used having smaller intervals than the semitone (see *Microtones*).

From the point of view of any 19th-c. musician Harmony is now in a state of anarchy but it is kinder (and perhaps wiser) to speak of it as passing through a stage of bold experimentation (cf. *Note row*).

In amplification of this article see *Added Sixth*, *Augmented Sixth*, and *Chromatic Chords*.

Harms Inc. See *Music Publishers Holding Corporation*.

Harold in Italy. The 2nd of the 4 Symphonies of Berlioz (op. 16; 1834). It has a solo Viola part, and was written to the commission of Paganini—who, however, never played it. Programmatic basis to be found in Byron's *Childe Harold*, the movements being entitled (1) *Harold in the Mountains*; (2) *March and Evening Prayer of Pilgrims*; (3) *Serenade*; *the Mountaineer of the Abruzzi to his Beloved*; (4) *Orgy of Brigands*.

Harp. This instrument, of very ancient lineage, can be simply defined as an open frame over which is stretched a graduated series of strings, set in vibration by plucking with the fingers. In the modern orch. harp the series is not (normally) chromatic, as it is in the piano, having merely 7 different notes with the 8ve, these being in the major scale of B—treated for convenience as that of C flat. There are 7 pedals, each affecting one note of this foundational scale; each pedal works to 2 notches, and by depressing it to its 1st or 2nd notch, respectively, the vibrating lengths of all the relevant strings are simultaneously shortened by fractions representing a semitone and a tone: thus all keys become possible, and by depressing all the pedals together the pitch of the complete instrument can be raised from C flat (the normal key) to C natural or C sharp. The usual compass is five and a half 8ves from the C flat three 8ves below middle C.

DOUBLE-ACTION HARP

Chords are normally played in more or less rapid succession of their notes, in the form understood by the word *arpeggio* (It. *arpa*, 'Harp'). The typical 'sweeping' (*glissando*) action of the hand may be used in many kinds of scale (but evidently not in the chromatic scale, however, nor in any other scale passage employing more than 8 notes to the 8ve). In addition, of course, single strings can be plucked individually or in small groups.

The instrument above described is the DOUBLE-ACTION harp, introduced by Erard (abt. 1810), the word 'double' marking its differences from its predecessors on which the pitches could be raised only a semitone. A CHROMATIC HARP (Pleyel, 1897) exists, with a string for every semitone, so requiring no pedals: on this the 'sweeping' action for chords, or diatonic scales is, of course, impossible.

Some earlier forms of the harp are (*a*) the WELSH HARP or TELYN, with 3 rows of strings, the 2 outer rows (tuned in unison or 8ves) giving the diatonic scale and the inner row the intermediate semitones: a simple modulation was effected by touching one of the inner strings. (*b*) The DOUBLE HARP (not to be confused with the Double-Action harp above described) had only 2 rows of strings, diatonically tuned: intermediate semitones could be obtained only by shortening the length of a string with the thumb, whilst plucking it with a finger.

The harp has had much solo use in Wales from time immemorial and in England domestically during the Victorian period. It was a frequent member of the early 17th-c. orch. but in later times was rarely found again in orch. use until the 19th c. (See also *Clarsach, Bell Harp, Dital Harp, Aeolian Harp*.)

Harper Family, (1) Thomas (b. Worcester 1786; d. London 1853). The leading Brit. trumpet player of his period. **(2) Thomas John** (b. London 1816; d. 1898). Successor to his father (above) as leading trumpet player of the country. **(3) and (4) Charles Abraham** (1819–93) and **Edmund** (abt. 1821–69). Also sons of (1) and both horn players.

Harp Guitar. See *Dital Harp.*

Harp Lute. See *Dital Harp.*

Harp Quartet. See *Beethoven's String Quartets.*

Harpsical. Same as harpsichord (q.v.)—an 18th-c. corruption of this word, possibly to parallel 'virginal'.

Harpsichord Family (Virginals, Spinet, Harpsichord). This type of domestic keyboard instrument was the most favoured from the beginning of the 16th c. to the end of the 18th. Moreover, from about 1600 onwards it was, in its fully developed form (that of the harpsichord proper), an indispensable supporting basis to almost every instrumental combination, 'chamber' and orch. It is now manufactured again, especially for domestic use in the performance of old keyboard music and orch. music. Its principle

of tone-production, in all its forms, is that of a plucking of the strings. These lie horizontally (an exception will be mentioned later), and when a finger-key is depressed there rises a small piece of wood, called a *Jack*, provided with a plectrum in the shape of a quill (or sometimes a leathern point): the

HARPSICHORD JACK
In contact with the string

jack, after catching the string and thus setting it in vibration, falls back, and, by means of an escapement, repasses the string without touching it. The amount of tone produced can be very little modified by the degree of pressure applied to the finger-key or the speed with which the key is depressed and in this respect the instrument differs from the clavichord and piano: slight accentuation is, however, possible.

The VIRGINAL or VIRGINALS is the oldest and simplest member of the family. It is oblong in shape, often a

THE VIRGINALS (1678)

mere box to be placed on a table, but sometimes supplied with its own legs. The strings (only one to each note) run parallel to the keyboard. The term *Pair of Virginals* was often used (cf. the old term 'pair of stairs' for 'flight of stairs', i.e. a multiple set, with perhaps the idea of gradation). The period of the virginal was roughly that of the 16th c. and the earlier part of the 17th. The Eng. virginal music of this period is of high importance: for some contemporary collections of this see *Fitz-william Virginal Book, Ladye Nevells Booke, Benjamin Cosyn's Virginal Book,* and *Will Forster's Virginal Book.* For the earliest published collection (1611) see *Parthenia.*

The SPINET. This resembles the virginals in having one string to a note, but differs from it in being not rectangular but wing-shaped, its form being roughly dictated, much as in the modern grand piano, by the graduated length of the strings, from the low notes to the high ones. The strings do not run parallel to the keyboard as with the virginals; or at right angles, as with the grand piano, but at an angle of about 45 degrees. (In the *Clavicytherium,* however, a rarer form than that above described, the strings ran perpendicularly, like those of an upright piano.) The spinet was in use

HANDEL'S SPINET

from the later 17th c. to the end of the 18th. (Note that the instruments second-hand furniture dealers in Britain sometimes offer today under the name of spinet are almost invariably square pianos: see *Pianoforte.*)

The HARPSICHORD (proper). This represents the highest development reached by the family. It is, like the spinet, wing shaped, but the strings run out at right angles to the keyboard, as they do in the modern grand piano, which, especially in specimens which attain similar size, it resembles in general appearance. There are 2 or more strings to a note and the number in use at any moment can be varied by

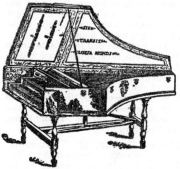

HANDEL'S HARPSICHORD
Made by Andreas Ruckers, of Antwerp, in 1651. Now in the South Kensington Museum

the use of stops like those of an organ or by pedals like those of a piano. An additional set of strings tuned an 8ve above normal, or occasionally an 8ve below it, may thus be added (cf. the organist's use of 16-foot and 4-foot stops; see *Organ* 2): later instruments possess also a swell device in which slats like those of a Venetian blind are opened and closed by means of a pedal. Often there are 2 keyboards and sometimes 3. Whilst all these combinations give considerable power of varying the degree and character of the tone, the player's power of expression is not direct, as it is on the piano, variation in finger touch having little influence.

Harris, (1) **Renatus** (b. France c. 1652; d. Salisbury 1724). One of great Eng. organ builders of Restoration period. His grandfather and father (Thomas) were also organ builders: so were his sons (Renatus and John).

(2) **Augustus** (b. Paris 1852; d. Folkestone 1896). London theatrical potentate controlling Drury Lane from 1879 and Covent Garden from 1888.

Influential in development of taste for opera, setting high standard. Introduced to Britain many famous singers and great works. Knighted 1891.

(3) **William Henry** (b. London 1883; d. there 1973). Studied at R.C.M.; organist successively of New Coll., Oxford (1919), Christ Church Cathedral, Oxford (1928), and then St. George's Chapel, Windsor Castle (1933–61). Composer of choral-orchestral setting of Francis Thompson's *The Hound of Heaven* (1919), church music, and organ music. M.A., D.Mus. Knighted 1954.

(4) **Roy (Ellsworth)** (b. Oklahoma 1898). Composer. Educated Univ. California. Early musical studies under his mother and Arthur Farwell (q.v.). Went to Paris 1926 to study under Nadia Boulanger (q.v.); Guggenheim Fellowship 1928–9. Long list of compositions includes 7 symphonies, choral, and chamber works, &c. Has taught for short periods in many places of learning.

Harrison, (1) **Julius Allen Greenway** (b. Stourport 1885; d. London 1963). Pupil of Bantock. Conductor of opera (Beecham Co., &c.); Scottish Orch.; Hastings Orch. 1930–40; B.B.C. Northern Orch.; on staff R.A.M. Many orch. and other compositions (Mass in C 1948) and several books (on Brahms, &c.).

(2) **Sidney** (b. London 1903). Pianist, adjudicator, lecturer, and author. Trained Guildhall School (later on staff). Adjudicating tours across Canada. First in Britain to give piano lessons by television.

(3) **Lou** (b. Portland, Ore., 1917). Composer and teacher, pupil of Cowell and Schönberg. On staff Mills Coll., Univ. of Calif. Composer of operas, symphonic and chamber works, ballets, &c., in many styles; critical articles on music.

Harrison sisters, (1) **Beatrice** (b. India 1893; d. nr. Oxted, Surrey, 1965). 'Cellist. Studied R.C.M. and Berlin Hochschule; appeared Queen's Hall, London, at 14½; notable player of Elgar Concerto, &c. (2) **May** (1891–1959). Violinist. 1st London appearance St. James's Hall, with Mendelssohn Concerto, Bach Chaconne, &c.,

age 13. Studied R.C.M. and then St. Petersburg under Auer. Later toured Europe with great success. (3) **Margaret.** Violinist and pianist. Début in 1918.

Harriss, Charles Albert Edwin (b. London 1862; d. Ottawa 1929). Eng. organist and composer; settled in Canada 1883; married wealthy woman, was enabled to organize choral festivals Brit. music in different cities Canada 1903; 'Musical Festival of British Empire' 1911 (with Coward, q.v., and Sheffield Choir: 6 months' Empire tour); London Festival of Empire (also 1911); performances of 10,000 singers and 500 players, London 1924; many similar large-scale enterprises. D.Mus., Lambeth, 1905.

Harrop, Sarah (b. Lancashire abt. 1756; d. London 1811). Soprano. Pupil of Sacchini. See *Bates, Joah.*

Harsanyi, Tibor (b. Hungary 1898; d. Paris 1954). Trained at Budapest Conserv.; later settled in Paris. Composer of ballets, orch. works, violin concerto, chamber music, &c.

Hart, Harte (Ger.; various terminations according to case, &c.). 'Hard'; also 'major'.

Hart, Fritz Bennicke (b. Brockley, Kent, 1874; d. Honolulu 1949). Conductor and composer. Trained R.C.M. From 1912 in Australia; conductor Melbourne Symphony Orch. and director conserv. there. Conductor Honolulu Symphony Orch. from 1931; on staff Honolulu Univ. 1937–46. Some compositions.

Hartley, Fred (b. Dundee 1905). Light music conductor, composer, and arranger. Trained R.A.M. Joined B.B.C. 1924; Light Music supervisor 1940–4; from 1945 also concerned with Australian Broadcasting Commission.

Hartmann, Karl Amadeus (b. Munich 1905; d. Munich 1963). Composer, trained Munich Academy and later under Webern. Leading representative of more modern German school and its active promoter (President of Ger. div. of I.S.C.M. 1953). Works include 6 symphonies, an opera, chamber music, &c.

Hart's Psalter. See *Stilt.*

Harty, Hamilton—in full Herbert Hamilton (b. Hillsborough, Co. Down, Ireland, 1879; d. Brighton 1941). Church organist at 12; at 21 in London and becoming known as admirable piano accompanist; later high reputation as orch. conductor (Hallé Orch. 1920–33). Composer of choral and orch. works, &c. Hon. D.Mus., Dublin and Manchester; LL.D., Belfast. Knighted 1925. Wife was Agnes Nicholls.

Harvey, Trevor (Barry) (b. Freshwater, I.O.W., 1911). Conductor. Studied Oxford (B.A., B.Mus.). B.B.C. 1935–42. Director of Music Brit. Forces Network in Germany 1945–6, also conducting Ger. orchs. Then freelance conducting.

Harwood, (1) **Edward** (b. nr. Blackburn 1707; d. 1787). Composed hymn tunes, Anglican chants, and anthems, and especially simple setting of Pope's *Vital Spark* that enjoyed immense vogue for long period.
(2) **Basil** (b. Woodhouse, Glos., 1859; d. London 1949). Organist of Ely Cathedral (1887–92), Christ Church Cathedral, Oxford (1892–1909). Composed church and organ music, also choral works for English festivals, &c. D.Mus. Oxon.

Háry János. Folk-opera by Kodály. Based on a humorous Hungarian legend of a swashbuckling hero. (1st perf. Budapest 1926.) An Orch. Suite was made from the musical material (1st perf. New York 1927).

Haskil, Clara (b. Bucharest 1895; d. Brussels 1960). Pianist. Début Vienna age 7; studied Paris Conserv. under Cortot and Fauré; then under Busoni. Distinguished international career despite lifelong physical handicaps.

Hasler. See *Hassler.*

Haslinger. Austrian music-publishing family (1) **Tobias** (1787–1842). Friend of Beethoven and from 1826 proprietor of eponymous firm. (2) **Carl** (1816–68). Son of (1) and his successor, also a pianist (pupil of Czerny) and prolific composer.

Hassan. Drama by Flecker with incidental music by Delius. (Prod. London 1923.)

Hassard, J. R. G. See *Criticism.*

Hasse, Johann Adolph (b. nr. Hamburg 1699; d. Venice 1783). Highly celebrated composer of Italianate style, resident in Dresden, Vienna, Venice, &c.; amazingly prolific (over 100 operas, masses, oratorios, symphonies, sonatas, &c.). The famous operatic soprano, Faustina Bordoni (b. Venice 1700; there d. 1781), for whom he composed certain operas, became his wife.

Hassler (or Hasler), Hans Leo (b. Nuremberg 1564; d. Frankfurt-on-Main 1612). Came of family of musicians of distinction. After early career as organist sent to Venice to study under Andrea Gabrieli; returning held positions in Augsburg, Nuremberg, &c. Wrote masses, motets, settings of chorales, madrigals, organ music, &c. Looked upon today, from the excellence of his work, as one of the fathers of Ger. music.

Hässler, Johann Wilhelm (b. Erfurt 1747; d. Moscow 1822). Able organist and pianist; composer of much music for his instruments; also vocal music. Held high position at Moscow from 1794.

Hastig (Ger.). 'Hasty', 'impetuous'.

Hastings, Thomas. See *Hymns and Hymn Tunes* 7.

Hatton, John Liptrot (b. Liverpool 1809; d. Margate 1886). Active theatre conductor and composer in London; toured widely as vocalist-entertainer, with mixed programmes that included comic songs, and sometimes Bach fugues, or *The Sleigh Ride* with bells tied to his legs. Composed 300 solo songs, some still sung (*Simon the Cellarer*, the fine *To Anthea*, &c.; also part-songs).

Hauer, Josef Matthias (b. Wiener-Neustadt 1883; d. Vienna 1959). Atonal composer, anticipating Schönberg (see *Harmony* 3). Composed piano, chamber, and orchestral music, songs, an oratorio, &c.; also wrote theoretical books.
See also *Note-row.*

Hauk (or Hauck), Minnie—Countess Hesse-Wartegg (b. New York 1851; d. Lucerne 1929). Operatic soprano of international reputation. First London and New York Carmen (both 1878). In last years blind and in poverty.

Haunted Tower, The. See *Storace*.

Haupt (Ger.). (1, noun) 'Head.' (2, adj.) 'Principal, chief.'

Hauptmann, Moritz (b. Dresden 1792; d. Leipzig 1868). Violinist, composer, and (especially) theorist. Pupil and friend of Spohr. Cantor of Leipzig Thomas School and composition teacher of Conserv. Many distinguished pupils (Joachim, Bülow, Sullivan, &c.). Important books.

Hauptsatz. See under *Satz*.

Hauptstimme (Ger.). 'Principal voice' (or part).

Hauptthema. Principal subject of a composition.

Hauptwerk (Ger. 'chief work'). Great Organ (see *Organ* 1).

Hausegger, (1) Friedrich von (b. St. Andrae, Carinthia, 1837; d. Graz 1899). Musicologist; taught history of music at Univ. of Graz and wrote valuable books on musical aesthetics, Wagner, &c. (2) **Siegmund von** (b. Graz 1872; d. Munich 1948). Son of (1). Orch. conductor and composer of operas, symphonic poems, choral works, &c.; Director of Academy of Music in Munich (1922–6). Publ. some books on musical subjects.

Hausmann, Robert (b. Rottleberode, Harz district, 1852; d. Vienna 1909). 'Cellist. Pupil of Piatti, &c., and member of Joachim Quartet.

Haut, haute (Fr. masc., fem.). 'High.'

Hautboy. (1) See *Oboe Family*. (2) Organ stop, same as *Oboe* (q.v.).

Haute (Fr.). 'High.'

Haute Danse (Fr. 'High Dance'). An old general term covering any dance in which the feet were lifted, as distinguished from the *Basse Danse* (q.v.), in which they were kept close to the floor.

Havanaise (Fr.). 'Habanera' (q.v.)—the Cuban capital being 'Habana', or in Fr. 'Havane'.

Hawaiian Guitar. See *Ukelele*.

Haweis, Hugh Reginald (b. Egham, Surrey, 1838; d. London 1901). Anglican clergyman in West End of London. Violinist and writer and lecturer (in Britain and U.S.A.) on violins, church bells, &c.; also wrote the very widely sold *Music and Morals* (1871) and *My Musical Life* (1884).

Hawes, William (b. London 1785; there d. 1846). Master of the Choristers at St. Paul's Cathedral (1812) and Chapel Royal (1817); music publisher; opera director at Lyceum Theatre; conductor of Madrigal Soc.; organist of Lutheran Church, Savoy, London. Composer of stage music, glees, &c.

Hawkins, (1) John (b. London 1719; there d. 1789). Son of a carpenter; became attorney; married money and gave up business; appointed Justice of the Peace (Chairman Middlesex Quarter Sessions). Knighted 1772. Considerable miscellaneous writer; biographer of Samuel Johnson; known to musicians by his *History of Music* (5 vols. 1776).
(2) **Isaac.** See *Pianoforte*.

Hawley, H. Stanley (b. Ilkeston, Derbyshire, 1867; there d. 1916). London pianist, editor of piano music on novel and practical lines, and general organizer of useful musical activities.

Hay, Haye, or Hey. There seem to have been several dances called by this name; they were usually round dances. The music was similar to that of the dance called *Canaries* (q.v.).

Haydn, (1) Joseph—in full Franz Joseph (b. Rohrau 1732; d. Vienna 1809). Son of a musical village wheelwright married to a musical cook; became choir-boy in Cathedral of Vienna; on voice breaking took pupils and lived sparely. Gradually won position of more importance and comfort; from 1760 to 1790 Kapellmeister to Esterházy family, with control of orch., choir, solo singers, and also opera performances; became recognized as greatest composer of period. Spent 18 months in London 1791–2 (becoming D.Mus., Oxford) and similarly 1794–5, both visits being highly successful and remunerative; received honours from many countries; at his death memorial services held in all principal European cities.

Style of composition initially based on that of C. P. Emanuel Bach, i.e. the new style of the sonata and symphony: this line of development pursued in his over 100 symphonies, about 80 string quartets, over 50 sonatas, &c.: finest of the symphonies are those composed for London (known as the 'Salomon Symphonies' from the impresario who arranged the visit and commissioned them; see *Salomon*): this line led to further development by younger contemporaries Mozart (born 24 years later) and Beethoven (born 38 years later). His very numerous works include oratorios (especially *The Creation* 1798 and *The Seasons* 1801); some operas (now disused), songs, and every form of music of the period.

See also separate entries: SYMPHONIES: *Chasse*; *Distratto*; *Drum-Roll*; *Farewell*; *Fire*; *Impériale*; *Laudon*; *London symphonies*; *Maria Theresia*; *Matin-Midi-Soir*; *Mercury*; *Mourning*; *Ours*; *Oxford*; *Paris symphonies*; *Passione*; *Philosoph*; *Poule*; *Reine*; *Roxolane*; *Schoolmaster*; *Surprise*; *Toy symphony*; *Weihnachtssymphonie*. STRING QUARTETS: *Dream*; *Froschquartett*; *Kaiserquartett*; *Lerchenquartett*; *Quintenquartett*; *Rasiermesserquartett*; *Rittquartett*; *Russischen Quartette*; *Sonnenquartette*; *Sunrise Quartet*; *Tostquartette*; *Vogelquartett*. ORATORIOS, MASSES, &c.; *Creation*; *Grosse Orgelmesse*; *Harmoniemesse*; *Heiligermesse*; *Mariazellermesse*; *Nelsonmesse*; *Paukenmesse*; *Schöpfungsmesse*; *Sechsviertelmesse*; *Seven Last Words*; *Stabat Mater*; *Theresienmesse*. OTHER WORKS: *Emperor's Hymn*; *Isola Disabitata*; *Hurdy-Gurdy*. BIOGRAPHY: *Pohl*.

(2) **Michael**—in full Johann Michael (b. Rohrau 1737; d. Salzburg 1806). Brother of Joseph. For over 40 years Kapellmeister to Archbishop of Salzburg (at the time when the Mozart family were also active in that city). Composed masses, oratorios, cantatas, &c. (over 350 church works in all), operas, 30 symphonies, organ music, &c.

Haydn Variations. By Brahms (1873), for orchestra (op. 56a) or two pianos (op. 56b). Theme is 'St. Anthony's Chorale', used by Haydn in a wind divertimento.

Haydon, Glen (b. Inman, Kansas, 1896; d. Chapel Hill, N.C., 1966). Studied Univ. of California (later on its staff) and at Paris and Vienna. Then head of music dept. of Univ. of N. Carolina (1934). Various theoretical works and compositions.

Haye. See *Hay*.

Hayes, (1) **William** (b. Gloucester 1705; d. Oxford 1777). Organist of Worcester Cathedral (1731–4) and of Magdalen Coll., Oxford (1734–7), Prof. of Music at Oxford (1741–death). D.Mus., Oxford 1749. Conducted various festivals; composed glees, canons, catches, church music; wrote one or two books on musical subjects. (2) **Philip** (b. Oxford 1738; d. London 1797). Son of William. Organist of New Coll., Oxford (1776), Magdalen Coll. (1777), and St. John's Coll. (1790). Succeeded father as Prof. of Music in Univ. D.Mus. 1777. Composer of church music, &c.

(3) **Catharine**—Mrs. Bushnell (b. Limerick 1825; d. Sydenham 1861). Operatic soprano. Trained Paris under Manuel Garcia. Great success in It. début, La Scala, Milan, 1845; London 1849. Toured world and amassed fortune.

(4) **Roland** (b. Curryville, Ga., 1887). Tenor vocalist. Pupil of Beigel, Henschel, and Lierhammer. Valued recital artist in U.S.A. and Europe, &c.; fine interpreter (being a Negro) of 'spirituals'. Hon. D.Mus., Boston, Howard, Fisk, &c., Univs.

Haynes, Walter Battison (b. nr. Worcester 1859; d. London 1900). Had a brilliant career at Leipzig Conserv.; then led life of London organist and prof. of R.A.M. Considerable composer now remembered by only a few smaller things (e.g. song *Off to Philadelphia in the Morning*).

Hayward, (1) **Henry** (b. Broseley, Shropshire, 1814; d. Wolverhampton 1884). Distinguished violinist ('The English Paganini'); pupil of Spagnoletti. Wolverhampton from about 1840. (2) **Marjorie** (b. Greenwich 1885; d. London 1953). Violinist. Trained R.A.M. under Sauret and then Prague under Ševčik. Later on staff R.A.M. (F.R.A.M.). Leader of Virtuoso String Quartet and then own Quartet and Kamaran Trio.

Hb. Short for *Hoboe*, i.e. Oboe.

Head, Michael (b. Eastbourne 1900). Trained at R.A.M., where later became a prof. of piano. Has written deft songs and sung them publicly.

Head Register. See *Voice* 4.

Hear my Prayer. By Mendelssohn (1844). For Soprano solo, Choir, and Organ (afterwards orchestrated). Composed for William Bartholomew's concerts in Crosby Hall, London (1st perf. 1845).

Heart of Oak (*not* 'Hearts of Oak'). This bold patriotic song comes from a pantomime, *Harlequin's Invasion*, written by Garrick in 1759, the music being supplied by Boyce. It is a topical song, alluding as it does to 'this wonderful year' (the victories of Minden, Quiberon Bay, and Quebec).

In 1768 an Americanized version was composed, which, as *The Liberty Song*, had enormous popularity.

Hebenstreit. See *Pantaleon*.

Hebridean Symphony. By Bantock. (1st perf. Glasgow 1916.)

Hebrides, The, or **Fingal's Cave.** See *Mendelssohn*.

Heckelclarina. See *Clarinet Family*.

Heckelclarinette. See *Clarinet Family*.

Heckelphone. See *Oboe Family*.

Heel. That end of the bow of a stringed instrument at which it is held, as distinguished from the other end, which is called 'point'.

Heftig (Ger.). 'Violent', 'impetuous'.

Heger, Robert (b. Strasbourg 1886). Operatic and orch. conductor in many Ger. cities and in Vienna (State Opera 1925–33); then Berlin (1933–45) and Munich; Covent Garden (1926–36). Composer of operas and orch. works.

Heifetz, Jascha (b. Vilna 1901). Violinist. Son of a violinist; became recognized as infant prodigy; trained conservs. of Vilna and St. Petersburg under Auer. Attained international fame; settled in U.S.A., and there naturalized 1925. Has publ. many violin arrangements.

Heilands letzte Stunden, Des (Spohr). See *Calvary*.

Heiligermesse ('Holy Mass'). Popular name for Haydn's 9th Mass, in B flat. The name comes from a special treatment of the words 'Holy, Holy' in the Sanctus.

Heimkehr aus der Fremde (Mendelssohn). See *Son and Stranger*.

Heink. See *Schumann-Heink*.

Heinze, Bernard Thomas (b. Shepparton, Victoria, 1894). Studied Univ. Melbourne and R.C.M., later in Paris under d'Indy (q.v.) and Berlin under Willy Hess (q.v.). Conducted in European centres; returned Australia 1923. On staff Univ. of Melbourne; conductor of its orch. 1924–32; Melbourne Symphony Orch. 1933–49. Knighted 1949.

Heise, Peter Arnold (b. Copenhagen 1830; d. Stockkerup 1879). Trained Leipzig Conserv. and under Gade (q.v.), &c. Composer of songs, &c. Opera *King and Marshal* still performed in Denmark.

Heiss (Ger.). 'Hot', 'ardent'.

Heiter (Ger.). (1) 'Cheerful.' (2) 'Clear.'

Helberger. See *Electric Musical Instruments* 1.

Heldenleben (Strauss). See *Hero's Life*.

Heldentenor (Ger. 'hero-tenor'). A big-voiced tenor suitable for heavy operatic parts (*Tenore robusto*).

Helicon. See *Tuba Group* 2.

Hell (Ger.). 'Clear', 'bright'.

Heller, Stephen (b. Budapest 1813; d. Paris 1888). After training in Vienna settled in Paris as member of the circle of the Romantic group, Chopin, Liszt, Berlioz, and others. An able and refined pianist and composer of quantities of graceful and accomplished piano music—mostly short pieces: these had great popularity which is not yet entirely exhausted.

Hellertion. See *Electric Musical Instruments* 1.

Hellflöte. 'Clear flute' (an organ stop).

Hellmesberger Family. All violinists of very high repute in Vienna.

(1) **Georg I** (b. Vienna 1800; d. nr. there 1873). Touring virtuoso and holder of important Vienna positions. Composer of violin concertos, &c. Teacher of Joachim, Auer, &c. (2) **Joseph I** (b. Vienna 1828; there d. 1893). Founded famous Hellmesberger String Quartet. Son of (1). (3) **Georg II** (b. Vienna 1830; d. Hanover 1852). Composed operas, &c. Son of (1). (4) **Joseph II** (b. Vienna 1855; there d. 1907). Son of (2); member of his quartet and successor as its leader. Composer of light operas, &c.

Helmholtz, Hermann Ludwig Ferdinand (b. Potsdam 1820; d. Charlottenburg 1894). Great authority on acoustics (also medical man and Prof. of Physiology various univs.). Most famous work is *Sensations of Tone* (1863 and many later edns.). Cf. *Ellis.*

Helmore, Thomas (b. Kidderminster 1811; d. London 1890). Anglican clergyman. Became master of choristers, &c., Chapel Royal, London (1846). Active worker in field of plainsong; many publications.

Helmrich, Dorothy Jane (b. New South Wales). Singer and teacher. Trained Sydney Conserv., and R.C.M. (1923); oratorio and concert work in Britain, also Lieder recitals, &c., on Continent and U.S.A. Return to Australia under broadcasting contract 1940; founder and vice-pres. of Australian C.E.M.A. (cf. *Arts Council*).

Hely-Hutchinson, Victor—in full Christian Victor (b. Cape Town 1901; d. London 1947). At 9 appeared before public with volume of compositions *A Child's Thoughts*; educated Eton, Oxford and R.C.M.; on staff of B.B.C. 1926–34; Prof. of Music, Birmingham Univ., 1934–44; then B.B.C. Music Director.

Hemidemisemiquaver (). The sixty-fourth note, i.e. of the value of a 64th of a semibreve (see Table 1).

Heming, Percy (b. Bristol 1885; d. London 1956). Baritone. Trained R.A.M., Dresden, &c. Prominent in *Beggar's Opera* revival of 1920, also Covent Garden, &c., and Empire tours.

Hemiola or **Hemiolia**. This rhythmic device consists of superimposing two notes in the time of three, or three in the time of two, e.g.:

cf. *Deux Temps.*

Hempel, Frieda (b. Leipzig 1885; d. Berlin 1955). Coloratura soprano. Trained Stern Conserv., Berlin; début in that city at Royal Opera House, becoming its leading coloratura soprano. Later toured European opera houses; also Metropolitan Opera, New York, 1912–19. From 1920 gave 'Jenny Lind' concerts U.S.A. and Britain (impersonations in mid-19th c. costume and singing Lind repertory).

Hempson, or **Hampson** or **Hampsy, Dennis,** or **Denis** or **Denys** (b. Craigmore, co. Londonderry, 1695; d. Magilligan 1807). Enjoyed high fame as player of Irish Harp and played it to the day before his death at age 112; composed some tunes still remembered.

Hen, The (Haydn). See *Poule.*

Henderson, (1) **William James** (b. Newark, N.J., 1855; d. New York 1937). Graduated Princeton. Became music critic *New York Times* (later *Sun*). Wrote solid and useful books on music; also poems, books on navigation, &c. Died by own hand. See under *Criticism.*

(2) **Roy** (b. Edinburgh 1899). Concert, oratorio, and opera baritone. Studied R.A.M. and then took high place in esteem of Brit. musical public. Has also been active as choral conductor (Nottingham, Bournemouth).

Hendl, Walter (b. West New York, N.J., 1917). Conductor, trained under Fritz Reiner at Curtis Inst. Cond. Dallas S.O. 1949; Dir. Eastman School 1964–72).

Henry VIII of England (b. Greenwich 1491; came to throne 1509; d. 1547). Played various instruments and composed masses (now lost): anthem, *O Lord, the Maker of all Thing,* long attributed to him, is now supposed to be by W. Mundy; other existing compositions (for voices and viols) probably his.

Henry the Eighth. (1) Opera by Saint-Saëns (1883). (2) Incidental Music to Shakespeare's play by Sullivan (1878); also by German (1892).

Henry of Glarus. See *Modes*.

Henry Watson Music Library. See *Watson, Henry*.

Henschel, (1) **George,** originally Isidore Georg (b. Breslau 1850; d. Aviemore, Inverness-shire, 1934). On father's side of Polish descent. At 12 appeared as pianist, at 16 as basso-profundo; studied at Leipzig Conserv.; from 1877 resident in Britain (naturalized 1890); was conductor of Boston Symphony Orch. 1881-4; then in Britain again, conducting important series of Symphony Concerts. Throughout life admired as artistic singer with fine repertory (oratorio, Leider self-accompanied, &c.); began broadcasting when near 80 and held London exhibition of paintings at 84. Knighted 1914. Long list of compositions, solo vocal, choral, piano, and orch. (2) **Helen** (b. Boston, Mass., 1882). Daughter of above and of his first wife. Studied violin at R.C.M. For many years gave vocal recitals self-accompanied: then regular broadcasts.

Henselt, Adolf von (b. Schwabach, Bavaria, 1814; d. Warmbrünn, Silesia, 1889). Brilliant piano virtuoso (pupil of Hummel) exploiting its possibilities in large number of effective compositions (especially 24 studies).

Hen Wlad fy Nhadau. See *Land of my Fathers*.

Henze, Hans Werner (b. Gütersloh, Westphalia, 1926). Composer; pupil of Fortner and Leibowitz. Outstanding non-doctrinaire member of the younger German school. Works include symphonies, concertos, and operas. Res. Italy.

See also *Boulevard Solitude*; *Elegy for Young Lovers*; *Prinz von Homburg*.

Herabstrich (Ger., lit. 'here-down-stroke'). Down-bow of violin and viola (cf. *Heraufstrich*).

Heraufstrich (Ger., lit. 'here-up-stroke'). Up-bow of violin and viola (cf. *Herabstrich*).

Herbage, Julian Livingston (b. Woking 1904). Educ. Cambridge.

On music staff of B.B.C. 1927-46. Has arranged and conducted much theatre music and done much musicological research (especially concerning 18th c.). Book on Handel's *Messiah*, &c.

Herbert, (1) **Victor** (b. Dublin 1859; d. New York 1924). Began professional life as 'cellist and composer for 'cello; then very successful conductor of military bands and of orchs.; finally as composer of almost innumerable operas and operettas (see *Natoma*) won a large and adoring public.

(2) **William Scott** (b. Melbourne 1920). Tenor. Cathedral chorister and lay clerk, St. Paul's, Melbourne. Recitalist, &c., in Australia. Since 1947 engaged in many Brit. festivals.

Herbstlied (Ger.). 'Autumn song.'

Hereford Use. See *Use of Sarum*, &c.

Here in cool grot. See *Mornington*.

Here's a health unto his Majesty. See *Savile*.

Her (His) Majesty's Theatre (London). Built 1705 (Queen Anne's reign). Many of Handel's operas had 1st performance there as had other operas later. Burnt down and rebuilt 1789 and 1867; rebuilt smaller size 1897.

Hernach (Ger.). 'Hereafter.'

Hero and Leander (Mancinelli). See *Ero e Leandro*.

Hérodiade ('Herodias'). Opera by Massenet. (Prod. Brussels 1881; London 1904; New York 1909.)

Héroïde funèbre ('Funereal Heroid'). Symphonic Poem by Liszt (1850), intended as part of a projected *Revolutionary Symphony*. (Heroid = a hero's epistolary poem, as in Ovid.)

Héroïque (Fr.), **heroisch** (Ger.). 'Heroic.'

Hérold, Louis Joseph Ferdinand (b. Paris 1791; there d. 1833). Studied under Méhul at Paris Conserv. and at 20 gained Rome Prize. On return devoted himself to opera with very great success (see *Zampa*; *Pré aux clercs*), also to ballet and piano compositions.

Heron-Allen, Edward (b. London 1861; d. Selsey 1943). Lawyer who made himself high authority on violin (*Violin-making*, 1884; *De Fidiculis Bibliographia*, 1890–4, &c.). Also on Persian poetry, marine biology, and other widely varied subjects.

Hero's Life, A (*Ein Heldenleben*). Symphonic Poem by Richard Strauss (op. 40; 1898). It has 6 connected sections—(1) *The Hero*; (2) *The Hero's Adversaries*; (3) *The Hero's Courtship*; (4) *The Hero's Battlefield*; (5) *The Hero's Works of Peace*; (6) *The Hero's Release from the World*.

Herrmann, Bernard (b. New York 1911). Conductor and composer. Studied Univ. of New York and Juilliard Graduate School. Began as radio conductor; then in Hollywood as successful composer for radio drama and films (e.g. *Citizen Kane* 1941); also dramatic cantata *Moby Dick* (New York 1940), orch. music, ballet suites, opera, &c.

Herschel, (1) **William**—originally Friedrich Wilhelm (b. Hanover 1738; d. Slough, Bucks. 1822). Hautboy player in Hanoverian guard; came to England and held Yorkshire posts as bandmaster of militia, organist, &c.; went to Bath as organist, and there composed much church music, also studying astronomy, making discoveries and on that of planet Uranus being appointed Court Astronomer to George III, about whose court the rest of his life was spent. Publ. compositions included symphony, some military music, &c. (2) **Jacob** (b. abt. 1734; d. in England 1792). Brother of William. Likewise settled in England. Publ. sonatas for 2 violins and bass. (3) **Caroline Lucretia** (b. 1748; d. Hanover 1848). Sister of William and Jacob; trained by William as singer and had success in Handel's oratorios; assisted William in his astronomical work, discovering 8 minor planets; retired to Hanover and lived to be almost a centenarian.

Herstrich (Ger., lit. 'hither-stroke'). A bow movement towards the player, i.e. the down stroke on 'cello and double-bass (cf. *Hinstrich*).

Hertz, (1) **Alfred** (b. Frankfurt 1872; d. San Francisco 1942). Had early Ger. career as opera conductor. At Metropolitan opera, New York, 1902–15. Conducted (1903) 1st perf. *Parsifal* other than at Bayreuth. San Francisco Orch. 1915–30. First conductor at Hollywood Bowl (1922).
    (2) **Heinrich Rudolph.** See *Broadcasting of Music*.

Herunterstimmen (Ger.). 'To tune down' a string to (*nach*) a specified note.

Herunterstrich (Ger. 'here-under-stroke'). Down-bow on violin and viola.

Hervorgehoben (Ger.). 'Forth-lifted'—referring to a melody which is to be made to stand out.

Hervorragend (Ger. 'forth-project-ing'). 'Prominent' (e.g. of a melody to be 'brought out'). So too, *hervortretend* (lit. 'forth-stepping').

Herz, Heinrich or **Henri** (b. Vienna 1803; d. Paris 1888). Pianist and composer. See *Pianoforte Playing*; *Hexameron*.

Herzgewächse (lit. 'heart-growths'). Setting by Schönberg (op. 20; 1911) of Maeterlinck. For high coloratura soprano, celesta, harmonium, and harp.

Herzhaft (Ger.). 'Bold'.

Herzig (Ger.). (1) 'Hearty.' (2) 'Tender', 'charming'.

Herzogenberg, Heinrich von (b. Graz 1843; d. Wiesbaden 1900). Director Bach Soc., Leipzig (1875–85); then in Berlin as prof. of composition at the Hochschule. A minor composer. His correspondence exists in an Eng. translation and he and his wife figure in Ethel Smyth's books of reminiscences.

Hes (Ger.). B flat. (Usually, however, the Germans call this note B; see *H* above.)

Heseltine, (1) **James** (b. 1692; d. Durham 1763). Organist of Durham Cathedral (1711 to death). Composed anthems which are still in use and others destroyed by him when he quarrelled with the Dean and Chapter.
    (2) **Philip** (b. London 1894; there d. 1930). Pen name 'Peter Warlock', under which name composed delicate

songs, chamber music, &c. Under real name publ. books (*Delius*; *The English Ayre*, &c.) and ed. Elizabethan lute songs. United highest ideals of art with low view of human life and died despairing—apparently by his own hand. (See *Gray, Cecil*.)

Hess, (1) **Willy** (b. Mannheim 1859; d. Berlin 1939). Violinist. Family settled in U.S.A. when he was 6; at 11 toured with the Thomas Orch.; further training under Joachim; then various continental positions and (1888–95) chief violinist of Hallé Orch., Manchester, and on staff of Royal Manchester Coll. of Music (cf. *Holst, Henry*); on that of R.A.M. (1903–4); then chief violin Boston Symphony Orchestra. Berlin Hochschule (1910).

(2) **Myra** (b. London 1890; d. there 1965). Pianist. Studied R.A.M. under Matthay and attained high reputation in Britain, U.S.A., and elsewhere. During Second World War instituted and directed daily lunch-hour concerts at National Gallery, London. Hon. LL.D., Manchester 1945, St. Andrews 1946; Hon. D.Mus. Durham and London 1946, Cambridge 1949. C.B.E. 1936, D.B.E. 1941. Philharmonic Soc. Gold Medal.

Hesse, Adolf Friedrich (b. Breslau 1809; there d. 1863). A great organist (played in England 1852); his compositions for his instrument are still in use.

Heterodyning. See *Electric Musical Instruments* 1.

Heure espagnole, L'. 1-act Opera by Ravel. (Prod. Paris 1911; London 1919; Chicago and New York 1920.)

Heward, Leslie Hays (b. Liversedge, Yorks., 1897; d. Birmingham 1943). Chorister of Manchester Cathedral and later its assistant organist. Studied R.C.M.; a music master at Eton and then at Westminster School; conductor of Cape Town Orch. 1924; Birmingham City Orch. (q.v.) 1930 to death.

Hewitt, James. See *Tammany*.

Hewson, George Henry Phillips (b. Dublin 1881). Organist of St. Patrick's Cathedral and Chapel Royal, Dublin. M.A., D.Mus. and (1935) Prof. of Music in Univ. of Dublin. Composer of church music, &c.

Hexachord. A group of 6 consecutive notes regarded as a unit for purposes of singing at sight—somewhat as the 8ve is in 'movable-doh' systems today. It was introduced (or perfected) by Guido d'Arezzo in the 11th c. and was still widely current up to the 17th.

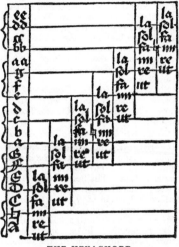

THE HEXACHORD
(From Virdung's *Musica getutscht*, Basle, 1511)

There were 3 different Hexachords, the *Hard* one beginning on G, the *Natural* one beginning on C, and the *Soft* one beginning on F. It will be realized that these overlapped in their range, and that a singer reading a piece of music might have to pass from one to another if its compass extended beyond one of those sets of 6 notes.

The names of the notes were taken from the opening syllables of 6 lines of a Lat. hymn, which syllables happened to ascend a degree with each succeeding line. These names were *Ut, Re, Mi, Fa, Sol,* and *La*. Letter names were also then in use for the notes, but these were *absolute* names, as they are still, whereas the hexachordal names were *relative* to the group in use at the moment, as their successors the modern Tonic sol-fa names are relative to the key in use at the moment (see *Tonic*

Sol-fa): the Sol-fa system (on its pitch side) may, indeed, be looked upon as a modernization of the hexachordal system, which served well in the period of simple modal music (see *Modes*) but was incapable of application to the increasing complexities of a key system.

To the Hexachords Guido added the device of what is called THE GUIDONIAN HAND. This is a plotting out of the choral singer's hand as a sort of 'modulator' (as a modern Tonic solfaist would call it); the tips and joints of the finger had notes allotted to them, so that a conscientious chorister, having once learnt their positions, carried with him a convenient means of exercising himself.

Shakespeare in *The Taming of the Shrew* (Music Lesson scene; III. i) shows a knowledge of the hexachordal system.

Cf. *Gamut*; *Bocedization*; *Tonic Sol-fa.*

Hexameron. One of the curiosities of music—Piano Variations on the march from Bellini's *I Puritani*, by 6 famous pianists (Liszt, Thalberg, Pixis, Herz, Czerny, and Chopin) who, at a charity concert in Paris in 1837, sat at 6 pianos, each in turn playing his own variation—Liszt contributing an Introduction, connecting links, and finale. Later Liszt often played the whole series in his recitals, with an orch. accompaniment that he had added.

Hexenmenuett (Haydn). See under *Quintenquartett.*

Hexentanz (Ger.). 'Witches' Dance.'

Hey. See *Hay.*

Heyner, Herbert (b. London 1881; d. Saxmundham, Suffolk, 1954). Baritone. Pupil of Fredk. King (q.v.) and Maurel (q.v.). London début 1907. Well-known oratorio singer, &c.; also Lieder. Toured Continent and U.S.A.

Heyther, William. See *Choragus.*

Hey, Tutti Tatti. See *Land o' the Leal*; *Scots wha hae.*

Heyworth, Peter (Lawrence Frederick) (b. New York 1921). Educ. Oxford. Mus. Critic *Times Lit. Supp.* 1952; *Observer* 1955.

Hiawatha. Cantata Trilogy by Coleridge-Taylor (q.v.).

Hicks. See *Glanville-Hicks.*

Hidden Fifths or Octaves. See *Harmony* 2 j.

Hier (Ger.). 'Here.'

Higgs, James (b. London 1829; there d. 1902). London organist. Editor, with J. F. Bridge (q.v.), of Bach's organ music. On staff R.C.M. Author of books on fugue and modulation. B.Mus. Oxford; D.Mus. Lambeth.

Highland Bagpipe. See *Bagpipe Family.*

High Mass. See *Mass.*

Hiles, (1) **John** (b. Shrewsbury 1810; d. London 1882). Well-known organist and arranger and composer for organ; also writer of many popular musical catechisms and textbooks. (2) **Henry** (b. Shrewsbury 1826; d. Worthing 1904). Brother of above and also organist—chiefly in Manchester, where also lecturer in composition, &c., Owens Coll. and Coll. of Music. One of founders of Incorporated Soc. of Musicians (see *Profession*). Wrote textbooks showing sturdy independence of thought (then almost alone in opposition to 'strict counterpoint'); composed many oratorios, part songs, &c.

Hill & Sons, W. E. London violinmakers founded 1717 but tracing connexion with maker of same name mentioned in Pepys's Diary.

Hill & Son, W. London Organ builders, tracing origin to Snetzler. See *Gauntlett* 1.

Hill, (1) **Thomas Henry Weist** (b. London 1828; there d. 1891). Violinist. Trained R.A.M. First to play Mendelssohn Concerto in U.S.A. Active choral conductor and 1st principal Guildhall School of Music (1880 to death).

(2) and (3) **Ferdinand Weist** and **Thomas C.** were sons of above and respectively violinist and 'cellist.

(4) (*née* Fortescue-Harrison), **Annie F.**—Lady Arthur Hill (b. 1849; d. Wokingham 1944). Composer of highly popular songs (e.g. *In the Gloaming*) and operettas.

(5) **Edward Burlingame** (b. Cambridge, Mass., 1872; d. Francestown, N.H., 1960). Instructor in music at

Harvard 1908, asst. prof. 1918, prof. 1928–37: composer of symphonies and other orch. music, piano music, choral music, &c. Author of book *Modern French Music*.

(6) **Alfred** (b. Melbourne 1870; d. Sydney 1960). Composer and conductor. Trained Leipzig Conserv., then returned Sydney (on staff Conserv.). Composer Maori cantata, operas, symphony, &c. O.B.E. 1953.

(7) **Richard S.** (b. Chicago 1901; d. Florida 1961). Studied Cornell and Oxford Univs. and under Kinkeldey. From 1939 on staff of music div., Liby. of Congress (head of Reference Section); from 1943 also ed. of *Notes*.

Hillbilly Songs. The traditional songs (largely of European origin) of the primitive peoples of the mountain regions of the south-eastern parts of the U.S.A.

Hiller, (1) **Ferdinand von** (b. Frankfurt-on-Main 1811; d. Cologne 1885). Pianist (appearing frequently in Britain) and prominent conductor; friend of all leading members of Romantic School, German and French, and left many books throwing light on their activities. Composed operas, &c.

(2) **Johann Adam.** See *Singspiel*.

Hill of Dreams. Symphonic Poem by Gruenberg. (Won Flagler Prize of $10,000 and perf. New York 1919.)

Hilsberg (properly 'Hillersberg'), **Alexander** (b. Warsaw 1900; d. Camden, Me., 1961). Violinist and conductor. Trained St. Petersburg Conserv. under Auer, &c. Joined Philadelphia Orch. 1926 and Curtis Inst. 1938. Chief Violin, Philadelphia Orch. Later known as conductor (New Orleans 1953).

Hilton, (1) **John I** (b. abt. 1560; d. 1608). Organist of Trinity Coll., Cambridge; composed anthems but sometimes difficult to say whether a particular one is by him or John II. (2) **John II** (b. 1599; d. 1657). Probably son of John I; organist of St. Margaret's, Westminster; composed church music, madrigals, catches, viol music, &c. B.Mus., Cambridge, 1626.

See *Farrant*.

Himmel, Friedrich Heinrich (b. Brandenburg 1765; d. Berlin 1814). Once of European fame as composer of operas, songs, &c.; now remembered chiefly by a small item of church music (in Eng. *Incline Thine Ear*).

Hindemith, Paul (b. Hanau, nr. Frankfurt-on-Main, 1895; there d. 1963). First known as violinist; for a time viola of Amar String Quartet; 1927–35 teacher of composition at Berlin State Conserv. Composed much for violin and for viola, also for orch., &c. Opera *Mathis der Maler* (q.v.) also supplied material for symphony of same name. Output very large and strikingly varied in resources employed, with sense of adventure and humour (cf. *Gebrauchsmusik*). *Ludus Tonalis* (12 fugues, &c., for piano) 1943. Performance of works forbidden during Nazi régime. Head of Music, Yale Univ., 1942–53; then at Zürich Univ. Books on harmony, &c. Hon. D.Mus., Oxon., 1954.

See also *Cardillac*; *Ludus Tonalis*; *Marienleben*; *Neues vom Tage*; *Nusch-Nuschi*; *Saint Francis*; *Unaufhörliche*.

Hine, William (b. Brightwell, Oxon., 1687; d. Gloucester 1730). Organist of Gloucester Cathedral (1710 to death). Left church music.

Hines, Jerome (b. Hollywood 1921). Operatic bass. Début San Francisco 1941; Metropolitan 1947; Bayreuth 1958.

Hinsterbend (Ger.). Lit. 'Away-dying'.

Hinstrich (Ger.). 'Away-stroke' (the one away from the player), i.e. the up-bow on 'cello and double-bass (cf. *Herstrich*).

Hinton, Arthur (b. Beckenham, Kent, 1869; d. London 1941). Studied at R.A.M. (and later became a prof. of composition there); also Munich under Rheinberger: wrote orch., chamber, piano, and vocal music. The pianist Katharine Goodson (q.v.) was his wife.

Hipkins, Alfred James (b. London 1826; there d. 1903). Specialist in the domestic keyboard instruments: attached firm of Broadwood from 14th year: became good pianist, clavichordist, and harpsichordist. Wrote largely on construction and history of instruments, also acoustics.

Hippolyte et Aricie. See *Rameau*.

Hirsch, (1) Paul Adolf (b. Frankfurt-on-Main 1881; d. Cambridge 1951). Business man at Frankfurt who formed remarkable music library, throwing it open to public; removed it to Cambridge 1936; sold to Brit. Museum 1947; its published catalogue, in four vols., valuable source of bibliographical reference.

(2) **Leonard** (b. Dublin 1902). Violinist. Trained Royal Manchester Coll. of Music. Left Manchester 1936 to be chief violin B.B.C. Empire Orch. Later same position in Philharmonia Orch. Much occupied with chamber music (founded Hirsch Quartet).

Hirt (Ger.). 'Herd', Herdsman'. So *Hirtenlied* ('Herdsman's Song') and similar expressions.

His (Ger.). B sharp. **Hisis,** B double sharp (if this note is anywhere to be found). See Table 7.

Hislop, Joseph (b. Edinburgh 1884). Operatic tenor. Trained Stockholm and Milan. Début Stockholm Opera 1914. Has since toured world. On staff of Stockholm Academy of Music and School of Opera.

His Majesty's Theatre. See *Her Majesty's Theatre*.

Histoire du soldat (Stravinsky). See *Soldier's Tale*.

Historical Scenes (Sibelius). See *Scènes historiques*.

History of Music. (1) Early music was entirely, or almost entirely, melodic. In that it resembles non-European music of the present time, for to this day almost all music but that of European origin (or music plainly influenced by such) is melodic.

(2) THE POLYPHONIC PHASE. When in the 10th c. the earliest glimmer of the idea of combination of voices entered people's minds it did so in the shape of a mere doubling of the traditional church melodies at the interval of a 4th or a 5th (*Organum*). Later it assumed the aspect of the addition of more or less free-moving parts to a fixed one. Towards the end of the 15th c. skill

was attained in the use of such devices as (*a*) The preparation of the ear for the coming of a discordant interval, the actual impingement of that interval and the passing of it into smooth concord, i.e. its 'resolution'; (*b*) The increase of the interest of singers and listeners by the occasional dropping into silence of a voice, so that it might re-enter with effect; (*c*) The taking up by one voice of some wisp of melody just uttered by another, i.e. the device we call 'imitation'; (*d*) The close and even exact melodic following of one voice after another—a more complete form of imitation, called 'canon'. Up to this period, and, indeed, for more than a century later (say to nearly the year 1600), the attention of composers was largely concentrated upon choral writing; not much effective composition remains for a single voice with instrumental accompaniment, for chorus with independent instrument accompaniment or for instruments without voices. (But see *Minstrels*, &c., for the Troubadours and Trouvères; also *Harpsichord*.) As the 16th c. came towards its close the phase of pure choral writing rose to its climax and the first group of composers in whose works real interest is felt today by lovers of church music or by concert audiences is that whose work was done during the 30 years or so on each side of the date 1600. This was the great period of the *a cappella* Mass and motet, of the Anglican 'service' and anthem, and of the madrigal.

It is aside from the purpose of this article to give any great number of dates and names, but a few are indispensable; and for this period of nearly 700 years the following will be sufficient:

The Earlier Group of Polyphonic Composers. ENGLAND, Dunstable (d. 1453). FLANDERS, Dufay (d. 1474); Josquin des Prés (d. 1521).

The Later Group of Polyphonic Composers. FLANDERS, Lassus (1532–94). ITALY, Palestrina (abt. 1525–94). SPAIN, Victoria (abt. 1549–1611). ENGLAND, Byrd (1543–1623).

It may be said that in the works of the latest of the composers just mentioned the modal system (see *Modes*) is seen in gradual decay, whilst the major and minor scales are seen to be rising into prominence, so that shortly after the death of the last of these composers the modal period definitely closed.

(3) THE BEGINNINGS OF ARTISTIC INSTRUMENTAL COMPOSITION. An effort was simultaneously taking place in the devising of effective techniques for instrumental perf. and instrumental composition. In the later 16th and earlier 17th cs. the viol and lute families were in their glory, as was the family of recorders (end-blown flutes); reed and brass instruments were somewhat rudimentary, as was the organ; the domestic keyboard instruments of the clavichord and harpsichord classes had attained considerable development, and the simple, early form of the harpsichord then known, the virginals, was in much use. (For all these instruments see the articles devoted to them.)

The tendency had been to write for instruments much as for voices; indeed, a group of viol players would often take up a book of madrigals and, according to the respective size and compass of their instruments, divide amongst themselves the various vocal parts. But a differentiation was then rapidly taking place. A distinction between the passages suitable for instruments, as compared with those suitable for voices, was being increasingly admitted. The development of a true keyboard style was a particular feature of the period, and the Eng. composers especially distinguished themselves in this, as also in the bringing into existence of suitable forms of keyboard music. Amongst such forms two were of outstanding importance. The first of these is the Variation. The other form was derived from dance styles of the day, consisting of a contrasted pair of dance-like movements (generally a slow pavan and quick galliard), sometimes preceded by a prelude. This is one of the sources of the later cyclic forms, the Suite (q.v.), Sonata (q.v.), Symphony (q.v.), and classical String Quartet (see *Chamber Music*), &c.

The art of combining instruments was as yet but little understood. Heterogeneous collections of instruments of all types might be brought together for a perf., but there was no standardized collection like our present-day orch.

Of composers who produced notable and permanently valuable instrumental work in this experimental period it will be sufficient here to mention the following:

SPAIN, Cabezón (1510–66), one of the earliest composers of keyboard music. ENGLAND, Byrd (1543–1623); Bull (abt. 1562–1628); Giles Farnaby (latter half of 16th c.); Orlando Gibbons (1582–1625). HOLLAND, Sweelinck (1562–1621), a famous organist and organ composer. ITALY, Frescobaldi (1583–1643), the greatest It. organist and organ composer of his day.

(4) THE DRAMATIC APPLICATION OF MUSIC. The next phase in the development of music (the 'New Music') results from the application of music to the purpose of drama. This phase is sufficiently described under the headings *Opera* and *Oratorio*, to which the reader should turn. The new style of solo-vocal writing (see *Recitative*), with its simple accompaniment of mere supporting chords, gave an immediate impetus to the monodic way of looking at music, i.e. it laid stress upon the consideration of music as a succession of simultaneously sounding groups of notes, as distinct from its consideration as a number of superposed layers of melody. The exigencies of the stage drama led to a study of instrumental resources and began to tend somewhat towards a standardization of them on the lines of the modern orch. As the basis of the combination there was always a harpsichord, at which a performer, playing from the figured bass provided by the composer, supplied an unceasing background of plucked-wire tone. It was in Italy that this new movement began and that country, which during the previous period had become especially a place of high culture of the *a cappella* choral style, now became the leading place of culture of the solo voice (maintaining pre-eminence in this department of musical activity down to the middle of the 19th c.). The It. vocal *Aria* (q.v.) became extremely important. Flanders and England, which had been to the fore during the previous period, now fell into the rear.

The names which it seems most essential to mention in connexion with the early dramatic development of music are the following:

ITALY, Caccini (abt. 1546–1618); Peri (1561–abt. 1633); Monteverdi (1567–1643); Cavalli (1602–76). FRANCE, Lully

(1632–87; Italian born). GERMANY, Schütz (1585–1672).

(5) THE NEW BALANCE OF THE HARMONIC AND THE POLYPHONIC. It is impossible to expel polyphony from music, and it quickly crept back—especially into oratorio, with its well-developed chorus-work. Comparing any choral page of Bach or Handel with many a one of Palestrina or Byrd, we find that from the point of view of the singer of any individual part they are not unlike; the differences which are more apparent to the listener spring chiefly from the following factors: (a) In the Palestrina composition the influence of the old modes may always be felt, whereas in every moment of the Bach music every phrase can be clearly assigned to either the major or the minor system—with well-defined modulations from one key to another. (b) In the Palestrina composition there is often a freer rhythm, the voice-parts largely moving each in its own rhythmic way, in accordance with the stresses of the words as uttered and with the requirements of effective expressional emphasis upon those words. Such music was written and originally printed without bar-lines. (c) If we try to reduce the Palestrina composition to a scheme of mere chords we may possibly, in some places, find ourselves in hesitation, because it has hardly been conceived as such; if we try to do the same with the Bach composition we shall find little trouble. Up to and including the Palestrina period, then, harmony was a by-product of the counterpoint, whereas in the period now under consideration harmony and counterpoint were conceived of as on equal terms.

The instrumental music was on the same lines as the choral music, and there was a great development of it. The viol family was in decline and the new violin family was ever rising into popularity. The orch. (see *Orchestra*) was still comparatively unstandardized, yet it was coming to be realized that the new violin family constituted its most effective basis. The ubiquity of the harpsichord has already been mentioned. The position of Germany in musical production was now a very strong one.

The chief instrumental form of the period was binary (see *Form*): dance rhythms formed the usual basis, and it is amazing to see what a variety of interesting allemandes, courantes, sarabandes, minuets, gigues, and the like Handel and Bach and their contemporaries constructed on these simple formal lines (see *Form* 1). The chief solo vocal form of the period was ternary (see *Form* 2): hundreds of arias (see *Aria*) were laid out in this form. In addition to these the fugue form was very common in instrumental and choral music, and, indeed, in the hands of Bach now reached perfection.

The chief names and dates of the phase are as follows:

ITALY, Corelli (1653–1713), especially a composer for the violin and its family; A. Scarlatti (1660–1725), especially a composer of operas and hence of the aria; D. Scarlatti (1685–1757), son of the foregoing and especially a harpsichord player and composer. ENGLAND, Purcell (1658–95). FRANCE, Couperin (1668–1733), especially a harpsichord composer. GERMANY, Bach (1685–1750); Handel (1685–1759).

(6) THE SONATA AND SYMPHONY, THE PIANO, AND THE GERMAN 'LIED'. The next period was that of the perfecting of the classical sonata (for 1 instrument or 2), the string trio and quartet, and the symphony (all these being merely sonatas in varying media). The articles *Form*, *Sonata*, *Symphony*, and *Chamber Music* should be referred to for an explanation of this general type of composition and of its historical development. Towards the end of the period a very forceful and dramatic quality was imported into such music by Beethoven. The orch. was now fully standardized and its harpsichord background was gradually abandoned: there was a continual kaleidoscopic play of colour, wind instruments being greatly improved and the technique of composition for all instruments becoming much more subtly developed.

The Pianoforte (invented during the previous period but only slowly perfected) now superseded the clavichord and harpsichord and lent itself readily to the strongly subjective expression of Beethoven (especially in his piano sonatas) and of Schubert (especially in a number of shorter poetical compositions—'impromptus' and the like): it also made it possible for Schubert and other composers of the period to give an adequate musical treatment to the romantic Ger. lyrical poetry of the period in that very important and abundant type of solo song called the 'Lied' (q.v.).

The principal names and dates of this period are:

GERMANY, C. P. E. Bach (1714–88), one of the principal founders of the Sonata and Symphony; Haydn (1732–1809); Mozart (1756–91); Beethoven (1770–1827); Schubert (1797–1828).

(7) THE ROMANTIC PERIOD. From Beethoven onwards music expressed emotion in that direct, detailed, and powerful manner that marks all the painting and literature of the Romantic period (see *Romantic*). Later developments of the Romantic Movement were the Nationalistic Movement (see *Nationalism in Music*), and Musical Impressionism, associated with the names of certain Fr. composers (see *Impressionism*).

The work of Wagner in the strengthening and (in a sense) rationalizing of the musical drama is discussed under his own name. His very free polyphony and his introduction of new chromatic resources brought into existence a harmony so distinctive that if a few consecutive measures are played we can infallibly ascribe them to their author. He added to both the variety of instruments in the orch. and the number of players of each individual instrument, with the result that from his middle-period works onward to our own day orch. music of every type is much more highly coloured than before. In all these matters Strauss is merely the follower and continuator of Wagner. Brahms, however, though in the nature of his thought a typical Ger. Romantic, inclined in processes to the classical side, having 'taken off' directly from Beethoven, and deviated relatively little from his methods. The application of the general Wagnerian system to orch. music led to the introduction of the *Symphonic Poem* (q.v.), a mid-19th-c. application of that type of composition that has always in some measure existed, called *Programme Music* (q.v.).

Perhaps the principal figures in the Romantic period are the following:

GERMANY, Weber (1786–1826); Wagner (1813–83); Mendelssohn (1809–47); Schumann (1810–56); Brahms (1833–97); Strauss (1864–1949). FRANCE, Berlioz (1803–69); Franck (1822–90, Belgian by birth); Debussy (1862–1918); Ravel (1875–1937). POLAND, Chopin (1810–49). HUNGARY, Liszt (1811–86). BOHEMIA, Smetana (1824–84); Dvořák (1841–1904). RUSSIA, Glinka (1804–57); Balakiref (1837–1910); Mussorgsky (1839–81); Rimsky-Korsakof (1844–1908); Tchaikovsky (1840–93); Scriabin (1872–1915). ITALY, Verdi (1813–1901); Puccini (1858–1924); Malipiero (1882–1973); Casella (1883–1947). SPAIN, Albéniz (1860–1909); Granados (1867–1916); Falla (1876–1946); Turina (1882–1949). BRITAIN, Elgar (1857–1934); Vaughan Williams (1872–1958); Holst (1874–1934); Bax (1883–1953); Walton (born 1902); Britten (born 1913).

(8) THE NEO-ROMANTICS AND THE REVOLT AGAINST ROMANCE. The musical texture of the latest of the Neo-Romantics, as we may call them, is, in places, almost totally different from anything that any composer had imagined possible 30 years before they began their work. The old distinction between concord and discord seems to be abandoned, the old key system has gone, the old forms are perceptible only as underlying the composition in the most general sort of way, and, in an orch. piece, the instruments are used in a manner that to the older Romantics would have seemed intolerably harsh: yet one can sense in their works the old romantic ideals and, indeed, some of them seem to be even overcharged with emotional content. We may take Schönberg (Austrian born: 1874–1951) as typical of this school (see *Note-row*).

Contemporary with them is another school that not only deliberately attempts to eschew romanticism but to some extent succeeds in doing so. The members of this school decry the 'subjective', which seems to mean that their music is intended to be not an expression of human feeling but merely a pattern in sounds.

A host of younger experimentalists attach themselves to this anti-romantic or neo-classical ideal, but for the purposes of the present article it will be sufficient to name 3 whose position is admitted:

RUSSIA, Stravinsky (born 1882) in his

later phases. HUNGARY, Bartók (1881–1945). GERMANY, Hindemith (born 1895).

There is some attempt going on to make use in composition of intervals smaller than have hitherto been used (see *Microtones*).

Hlzbl (Ger.). Short for *Holzbläser*, 'wood-blowers', i.e. the wood-wind department.

H.M.S. Pinafore, or The Lass that loved a Sailor. Comic Opera by Gilbert and Sullivan. (Prod. Opéra Comique, London, and also Boston and San Francisco 1878; New York and Philadelphia 1879.)

Hob and Nob. See *Campbells are Coming*.

Hobbs, John William (b. Henley 1799; d. Croydon 1877). Tenor. Boy chorister of Canterbury Cathedral; as man in 3 Cambridge coll. choirs; also St. George's Chapel, Windsor; Chapel Royal (1827); and Westminster Abbey. Popular concert singer. Composer of songs (e.g. *Phyllis is my only joy*) and glees. W. H. Cummings was his son-in-law.

Hobday, (1) Alfred Charles (b. Faversham 1870; d. Tankerton 1942). Viola player. Trained R.C.M. Leading orch. and chamber music player of high repute.

(2) **Claude** (b. Faversham 1872; d. London 1954). Double-bass player. Trained R.C.M. (afterwards on staff). Well-known orch. player.

Hobertus. See *Obrecht*.

Hoboe (plur. *Hoboen*). 'Oboe' (see *Oboe Family*).

Hoboy. See *Oboe Family*.

Hobrecht. See *Obrecht*.

Hochdruckstimmen (Ger.). 'High-pressure stops' (organ tubas).

Höchst (Ger.). 'Highest', i.e. in the highest degree (followed by some adj. or adverb).

Hochzeit des Camacho (Mendelssohn). See under *Wedding*.

Hochzeitsmarsch (Ger.). 'Wedding March.'

Hochzeitszug (Ger.). 'Wedding procession.'

Hocket (lit. 'Hiccough'). An early elementary contrapuntal device by which, in 2 vocal parts, rests were introduced in one, coinciding with notes in the other (without consideration of the effect on the words).

Hoddinott, Alun (b. Bargoed, Glam., 1929). Composer. Trained Univ. Coll. S. Wales (D.Mus. 1960; on staff 1959) and under Arthur Benjamin. Works include concertos for viola, for piano, oboe, and harp; style though not tonal is romantic in feeling, with individual approach to rhythmic problems.

Hoffmann, 'E.T.A.', i.e. Ernst Theodor Amadeus (b. Königsberg 1776; d. Berlin 1822). Govt. official, novelist and essayist, his imaginative literary works inspiring Weber, Schumann (see *Kreisleriana*), and Brahms. Also composer of operas, chamber music, piano sonatas, choral works, &c.

'Hoffman'. Alleged original name of Reményi (q.v.).

Hofmann, Josef Casimir (b. Cracow 1876; d. Los Angeles 1957). Pianist. Father an opera conductor; mother opera singer. Became pupil of Rubinstein and won high international reputation as child prodigy, renewing this when, after retirement for study, reappeared at age 18. Settled in U.S.A. 1924; head of Curtis Inst., Philadelphia (to 1938). As 'Michael Dvorsky' composer of piano music, &c.

Hofmannsthal, Hugo von (b. Vienna 1874; there d. 1929). Poet of high distinction and author of libretti of several of operas of Richard Strauss (see *Elektra, Rosenkavalier, Ariadne auf Naxos, Frau ohne Schatten, Aegyptische Helena, Arabella*).

Hogarth, George (b. nr. Oxton, Berwick, 1783; d. London 1870). London music critic and author of books on music. Son-in-law of George Thomson (q.v.) and father-in-law of Charles Dickens.

Hohlflöte (Ger. 'hollow flute', i.e. hollow-sounding flute). Organ stop of 8-foot length and pitch; metal or wood.

Hol, Richard (b. Amsterdam 1825; d. Utrecht 1904). Piano teacher, organist, choral and orch. conductor, &c. Composed symphonies, chamber music, operas, masses, &c.; wrote books on Sweelinck and ed. a journal devoted to the interests of organ playing and organ music.

Holberg Suite (*Holbergiana*; or, in Ger. title, *Aus Holbergs Zeit*, 'From Holberg's Time'). Composed by Grieg (1884) for celebration of 2nd Centenary of founder of modern Danish literature. (1st version for Piano; 2nd for String Orch.; both op. 40.)

Holborne, (1) **Anthony** (d. 1602). Englishman who publ. (1597) book of music for cittern (q.v.). (2) **William.** Brother of Anthony; contributed Ayre in 3 voices to book above mentioned.

Holbrooke, Joseph Charles (b. Croydon, London, 1878; d. London 1958). Music Hall pianist from age 12. Then trained R.A.M. Composed much and in every branch, including opera; trilogy of Wagnerian type (*The Cauldron of Annwyn*, q.v.); some books. Was long a vigorous controversialist, attacking unsympathetic critics.

Hollander, Benno (b. Amsterdam 1853; d. London 1942). Trained Paris Conserv. After touring as violin virtuoso settled London 1876. Leading violin Covent Garden, &c. Conducted own orch. at Kensington. Composer of violin concertos, chamber music, &c.

Holländer, the brothers, (1) **Gustav** (b. Leobschütz, Upper Silesia, 1855; d. Berlin 1915). Violinist and composer of violin music. Pupil of Joachim. (2) **Viktor** (b. Leobschütz, Upper Silesia, 1866; d. Hollywood 1940). Conductor, opera and operetta composer.

Hollingsworth, John (b. Enfield 1916; d. London 1963). Conductor Trained G.S.M. Appeared with London Symphony Orch. and London Philharmonic Orch. Associate Conductor Royal Air Force Symphony Orch. 1940–5. Toured U.S.A., &c. Director of Symphony Concerts, Tunbridge Wells; Musical Director Government Films Division 1947; also Associate Director Rank film organization. Then Covent Garden.

Hollins, Alfred (b. Hull 1865; d. Edinburgh 1942). Born blind yet early established high reputation as pianist

(playing concertos with the best orchs. of Britain and U.S.A., and appearing in European continental centres); later known as organist (touring Commonwealth and U.S.A.). Organist of Free (now West) St. George's Church, Edinburgh (1897 to death). Organ compositions much played. Hon. D.Mus., Edinburgh.

Hollmann, Joseph (b. Maestricht 1852; d. Paris 1927). Violoncellist. Pupil of Servais, &c., and at Paris Conserv. Composed 'cello solos and concertos, &c.

Hollywood Bowl. A natural amphitheatre near Los Angeles in California, where, since the 1920's, concerts, &c., have been given. The seating capacity is 25,000.

Holmes, (1) **John** (later 16th c.). Organist of Cathedrals of Winchester (to 1602), Salisbury (1602–10); composer of church music, madrigals, catches, &c. (2) **Thomas** (d. Salisbury 1638). Son of John; composer of catches.

(3) **Edward** (b. nr. London 1797; d. there 1859). Pianist and writer of standard life of Mozart, 1845 and later editions; *Ramble amongst the Musicians of Germany* 1828.

(4) **Alfred** (b. London 1837; d. Paris 1876). Violinist, touring widely. Settled in Paris 1864. For brother see below.

(5) **Henry** (b. London 1839; d. San Francisco 1905). Brother of above and also violinist. On staff of R.C.M. but involved in scandal (1894); then settled San Francisco. Composer of symphonies, &c.

Holmès (really 'Holmes'), **Augusta (Mary Anne)** (b. Paris 1847 of Irish parents; there d. 1903). Pupil of Franck, composer of symphonies, operas, choral works, songs, &c.

Holst (originally von Holst), (1) **Gustav Theodore** (b. Cheltenham 1874; d. nr. London 1934). Son, grandson, and greatgrandson of musicians. (Descent six-sevenths or seven-eighths British and the rest Swedish.) Began professional life as village organist, &c.; at 19 went to R.C.M., where for 5 years studied under Stanford. To earn a living became trombonist in theatre orchs. and then in Scottish Orch. Became director of music at St. Paul's Girls' School, London, 1906; also in similar capacity at Morley Coll., a working-class institution in South London. During 1914–18 war, at request of writer of this book, went to Salonica and then to Constantinople to organize musical activities amongst troops, the 'von' being dropped at this time. (From items in the above his practical bent and strong social idealism may be deduced.)

Compositions (of an original and personal character) include orch. suite, *The Planets* (perf. 1918); *The Hymn of Jesus* (1917); one-act operas, *Savitri* (prod. 1916), *The Perfect Fool* (prod. 1923), *At the Boar's Head* (prod. 1925); many choral works and smaller compositions for various instrumental combinations, &c.

See also under *Choral Symphony*; *Egdon Heath*; *Hymn of Jesus*; *Hymns from the Rig Veda*; *Ode to Death*; *Planets*; *Saint Paul's Suite*; *Savitri*.

(2) **Imogen** (b. Richmond, Surrey, 1907). Daughter of Gustav. Won scholarship in composition at R.C.M. 1927; and then a travelling scholarship; has been engaged in various useful musical enterprises and produced some compositions, a biography of her father, and a study of his music.

(3) **Henry** (b. Copenhagen 1899). Violinist. Trained Copenhagen Conserv. and then Berlin under Willy Hess (q.v.); chief violinist Berlin Philharmonic 1923; followed Hess at Royal Manchester College of Music (1931–45); R.C.M. (1945–54); then Denmark. Eminent soloist and chamber music player.

Holy City, The. Oratorio by Alfred Gaul. (1st perf. Birmingham Fest. 1882.)

'Holy Mass' (Haydn). See *Heiligermesse*.

Holz (Ger.). 'Wood'; and so 'wood-wind'.

Holzbläser (Ger., lit. 'wood-blowers'). Wood-wind players.

Holzblasinstrumente (Ger., lit. 'wood-blow instruments'). The wood-wind.

Holzflöte (Ger.). 'Wooden flute' (organ stop).

Holzharmonika (Ger., lit. 'wood-harmonica'). 'Xylophone' (see *Percussion Family* 1 f).

Holzschlägel (Ger.). Wooden drumstick.

Holztrompete. See *Clarinet Family*.

Homage March. See *Huldigungsmarsch*.

Homer, (1) **Sidney** (b. Boston, Mass., 1864; d. Florida 1953). Pupil of Chadwick (q.v.) and Munich Conserv., and for some time teacher of composition in Boston. Composer of long list of songs (some highly popular), organ works, chamber music, &c. For wife (his pupil) see below. (2) **Louise Dilworth**—*née* Beatty (b. Pittsburgh 1871; d. Florida 1947). Operatic contralto. Début Vichy 1898; Covent Garden 1899; San Francisco 1900. Attached Metropolitan Opera House 1900 onwards. For husband see above.

Home, Sweet Home. This tune is by Bishop (q.v.), who composed it for an album of national melodies (1821) and unblushingly described it as 'Sicilian Air'. Later (1823) he used it in the opera *Clari*, whose libretto was by the Amer. actor and dramatist John Howard Payne (1791–1852) and thus the present words became attached to it. Donizetti uses a version of the song in his opera *Anne Boleyn* (1830).

Hommage à Rameau (Debussy). See under *Images*.

Homme armé (Fr. 'armed man'). A 15th c. Provençal folk-tune much used as a *canto fermo* in the composition of masses in the 15th, 16th, and early 17th cs. Its original words are unknown.

Homophone. Two strings (harp) tuned to produce the same note.

Homophony is the term applied to music in which the parts or voices move 'in step' with one another, instead of exhibiting individual rhythmic independence and interest, as they do in *Polyphony* (q.v.). Thus many modern hymn tunes are *homophonic*, whereas Bach's settings of the German chorales and many of Handel's choruses are *polyphonic*.

Hon. A.R.C.M. See *Degrees and Diplomas* 2.

Hondo. See *Cante Hondo*.

Honegger, Arthur (b. Havre 1892; d. Paris 1955). Of Swiss parentage. Trained Conserv. of Zürich and Paris; member of the temporary Paris group of 'Les Six' (see *Six*). Composed orch. music, chamber music, operas, ballets, dramatic oratorios (see *King David*) and a long list of other things (see *Joan of Arc*; *Judith*; *Pacific 231*; *Rugby*).

Höngen, Elisabeth (b. Gevelsberg, Westphalia, 1906). Dramatic contralto and mezzo-soprano. Trained Berlin Univ. (musicology) and Hochschule (singing). From 1933 many appearances in opera houses of Germany and other countries; also as Lieder singer.

Hon. G.S.M. See *Degrees and Diplomas* 2.

Hon. R.A.M. See *Degrees and Diplomas* 2.

Hon. R.C.M. See *Degrees and Diplomas* 2.

Hood, Basil (1864–1917). Librettist of light operas, &c.—*Rose of Persia* (Sullivan), *Merrie England* (E. German), &c. Adapter of foreign works—*The Merry Widow*, *The Dollar Princess*, &c.

Hoogstraten, Willem van (b. Utrecht 1884; d. Tutzing 1965). Conductor. Trained Cologne Conserv. and engaged Hamburg (1911), New York (1923), and Portland, Oregon (1927–37). Then Salzburg and Stuttgart.

Hook, James (b. Norwich 1746; d. Boulogne 1827). For half a century organist at Marylebone and Vauxhall Gardens, nightly performing concertos; composed over 2,000 tuneful songs (see *Within a Mile of Edinbro' Town* and *Lass of Richmond Hill*).

Hook, Dean of Chichester. See *Anglican Parish Church Music*.

Hooton, Florence (b. Scarborough 1912). Violoncellist. Trained R.A.M. and under Feuermann. Soloist with B.B.C. from early Savoy Hill days.

As recitalist and concerto player has introduced many contemporary Brit. works.

Hopak. See *Gopak*.

Hope-Jones, Robert (b. Hooton Grange, Cheshire, 1859; d. Rochester, N.Y., 1914). A highly inventive organ builder, who introduced many electrical devices and tonal novelties (see *Diapason Phonon*; *Diaphone*; *Double English Horn*).

Hopkins, (1) **Edward John** (b. London 1818; there d. 1901). Member of family musical in several generations of which 7 or 8 members are listed in larger books of reference. For 55 years the admired organist of Temple Church, London; authority on organ construction (author with Rimbault of standard book on organ; edns. in 1855, 1870, 1877); composer of organ music, anthems, and services. D.Mus., Lambeth, 1882.

(2) **Edward Jerome** (b. Burlington, Vermont, 1836; d. Athenia, N.J., 1898). Active as organist, musical lecturer, and journalist; also as composer of great quantity and variety of music.

(3) (original name Reynolds) **Antony** (b. London 1921). Pianist and composer. Trained R.C.M. Joined staff Morley Coll., London. Composer of piano sonatas, chamber music, choral works, songs, &c. Also radio, film, and stage music, ballets, and one-act opera, *Lady Rohesia* (prod. Sadler's Wells 1948), &c.

(4) **Gerard Manley.** See *Sprung Rhythm*.

Hopkinson, (1) **Francis** (b. Philadelphia 1737; there d. 1791). Lawyer, poet, and prose writer; one of signatories of Declaration of Independence; harpsichordist, inventor of a metronome, composer of earliest piece of music by an American (the song, *My days have been so wondrous free* 1759) and other songs, cantatas, &c.; organizer of subscription concerts. (2) **Joseph** (1770–1842). Son of the above. See *Hail, Columbia*.

Hoquet. Same as *Hocket* (q.v.).

Hora Novissima. See *Parker, Horatio*.

Horenstein, Jascha (b. Kiev 1898). Conductor, pupil of Busch and

Schreker. Vienna Symph. Orch. 1923; Berlin 1925. Düsseldorf Opera 1929. Then mainly free-lance career, including U.S.A. and South America.

Horn, (1) **Karl Friedrich** (b. Nordhausen, Saxony, 1762; d. Windsor 1830). At 20 settled in London and became well-known music teacher (in 1811 to Queen Charlotte and Princesses); organist of St. George's Chapel, Windsor Castle, 1823. Collaborator with Samuel Wesley in Eng. edn. of Bach's '48'; composer of piano sonatas, &c., and author of book on thorough-bass. (2) **Charles Edward** (b. London 1786; d. Boston, Mass., 1849). Son of the above; singer and composer for London stage; emigrated to U.S.A. 1833; composed oratorios, operettas, glees, &c., and still popular songs (*Cherry Ripe*; *I've been roaming*, &c.).

Horn. (1) See *Horn Family*. (2) Organ stop like *Trumpet* (q.v.), but fuller and smoother in tone.

Horn diapason. Organ stop of string-like tone (word 'Horn' being a misnomer); 8-foot length and pitch.

Hörner (Ger.). 'Horns'.

Horn Family. The modern horn is an intricately coiled tube of over 11 ft.; it is of ¼ in. bore at one end but widens gradually until it terminates in a large bell of 11–14 in. diameter: the mouthpiece is funnel-shaped. All these details differentiate it from the trumpet (q.v.), but, like it, it is a 'half-tube' instrument (see *Whole-tube and Half-tube*). The principle on which the notes are obtained is that of all brass instruments (see *Brass*).

There are 2 main forms of the horn: the *Natural Horn* and the *Valve Horn*. The Natural Horn is restricted, at any given moment, to one pitch of the harmonic series (see *Acoustics* 7): the Valve Horn can at will be switched from the harmonic series at one pitch to that at another, so making any note of the chromatic scale instantaneously available. The Valve Horn is valuable for solo purposes or, if several such horns are present, for the performance of chords. Its technique is more difficult to acquire than that of any other instrument in the orch. and even

famous players can sometimes be heard to 'crack' on a note.

Members of the family are the following:

(*a*) HUNTING HORN: the simplest form of the Natural Horn.

(*b*) FRENCH HORN—NATURAL BUT WITH CROOKS. This is the instrument for which the older classical composers

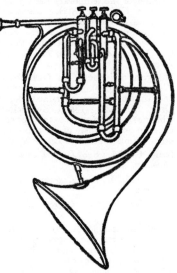

THE HORN
('French Horn' with Valves)

wrote. The *crooks* were additional lengths of tube, lowering the fundamental note and hence changing the harmonic series available: they could be inserted as needed, the composer, in his score, leaving the player a little time to effect the change. The crooks in the player's outfit were 10 in number (or sometimes 12). In addition to the treatment of the instrument as a transposing one (see *Transposing Instruments*) a point in the notation was that, by a convention, when there occurred notes low enough to demand the use of the bass clef they were written an 8ve lower than their pitch demanded. As with the trumpet all parts were written as if in Key C, with sharps and flats inserted as accidentals. Certain notes were not in tune with the modern tempered scale (see *Temperament*): they were modified by inserting a hand in the bell of the instrument ('Stopped notes'): smaller gaps in the harmonic series were filled in by a similar means of modification.

(c) FRENCH HORN WITH VALVES. This is the horn of our modern orchestras. Traditionally it is pitched in F, but other pitches exist The 'Double Horn', which is pitched in both F and B flat alto, is normally used to-day. The valves act much as the old crooks did but without the loss of time inseparable from the insertion, removal or changing of these (cf. *Trumpet*). The notation is normally the same as that of the Natural Horn with its F crook, i.e. the music is written without key signature (see (b) above), a perfect 5th higher than it is intended to sound. There is, however, a modern tendency to use a key signature, which when it appears has necessarily (from the use of the F pitch) a flat less or sharp more than the actual key (see *Transposing Instruments*).

Double and Triple Tonguing (see *Tonguing*) is very effective on the horn.

The horn is not merely an important member of the orch.: it has some place in the chamber music repertory.

For Bass Horn or Keyed Horn see *Cornett and Key Bugle Families*.

Hornpipe. The word has 2 meanings: (1) An obsolete instrument, consisting of a wooden pipe with a reed mouthpiece (a single 'beating' reed; see *Reed*), and, at the other end, a horn as 'bell' (cf. *Stockhorn*). It was common in all the Celtic parts of Britain. (2) A dance once popular in the Brit. Isles (and apparently nowhere else), to which that instrument was originally the usual accompaniment. Properly it was a solo dance; earlier examples of the music are in simple triple time, but by the end of the 18th c. this had changed to simple duple. This dance was later chiefly kept up amongst sailors.

Hornpipe Concerto. A nickname for Handel's Concerto Grosso No. 12 in B minor.

Hornpipe Quartet (Haydn). See under *Lerchenquartett*.

Horowitz, Vladimir (b. Kiev 1904). Pianist. Trained at Kiev Conserv. In early manhood attained high international artistic reputation. Retired 1936–9 through illness; then reappeared with success as before. Married daughter of Toscanini.

Horseman Quartet (Haydn). See *Rittquartett*.

Horsley, (1) **William** (b. London 1774; there d. 1858). London organist, friend of Mendelssohn; one of founders of Philharmonic Soc.; writer of textbooks; composer of favourite glees (e.g. *By Celia's Arbour*), &c. B.Mus., Oxford. (2) **Charles Edward** (b. London 1822; d. New York 1876). Son and pupil of William; pupil also of Moscheles (piano) and at Leipzig of Mendelssohn (composition); London organist; emigrated to Australia (1862), then U.S.A. Composed oratorios, &c., and wrote textbook of harmony.

Horoscope. Ballet by Constant Lambert. (Prod. Sadler's Wells 1938.)

Horst Wessel Song. This was the great song of the Ger. National Socialist or 'Nazi' party. The words are by a student, Horst Wessel, who was born in 1907 and was killed in 1930 in a Communist quarter of Berlin in which he lived as commander of a Storm Troop section of the Nazi forces. The tune is that of a music-hall song popular amongst the Ger. troops in 1914.

Hortense, Queen. See *Partant pour la Syrie.*

Hosanna. A Hebrew exclamation of praise to God, adopted also into the Gr. and Lat. languages. It was the cry of the multitudes on Christ's entry into Jerusalem (Matt. xxi. 9), and has been taken into many liturgies, as into the Roman Catholic Mass (see *Mass*).

Hoteterre Family (17th and 18th cs.). Famous Paris family of makers and players of the various wood-wind instruments; compilers of tutors and composers of music for these.

Hothby, John (b. England; there d. 1487). Carmelite monk who travelled and lived in Italy, enjoying fame as theorist and leaving behind him famous theoretical treatises and a little music.

Hotter, Hans (b. Offenbach 1909). Began as organist; then baritone vocalist. Opera contracts Prague, Hamburg (1934), Munich (1940), Vienna (1945). Guest artist Europe and S. America; notable Wotan, Kurwenal &c. Covent Garden from 1948.

Hound of Heaven, The. See *Harris, W. H.*

Hovhaness, Alan (b. Somerville, Mass., 1911). Composer. Of Armenian descent. Trained New England Conserv. A close student of Asiatic and Middle-Eastern music, many of his long list of works showing this preoccupation.

Howell, Dorothy (b. Birmingham 1898). Pianist and composer. Trained R.A.M. (later on staff). Has composed symphonic poem *Lamia* (1919; 5 London perfs. that season), pf. concerto, &c.

Howells, Herbert (Norman) (b. Lydney, Glos., 1892). Articled to Herbert Brewer (q.v.); won scholarship at R.C.M. 1920 (later on staff); succeeded Holst at St. Paul's Girls' School 1934. Has composed piano concerto, orch. music, chamber music, choral works (esp. *Hymnus Paradisi* 1950), organ music, &c. Prof. of Mus., London Univ. 1955. Active adjudicator, &c. Some critical writings. D.Mus., Oxon. C.B.E. 1954.

Howes, Frank (b. Oxford 1891). Educated Oxford Univ. (M.A.); on staff of R.C.M.; also music critic of *The Times* (assistant to Colles, q.v., 1925; succeeded him 1943–60). Author of books on Byrd, Vaughan Williams, Walton, the orchestra, and other subjects; for many years chairman of Eng. Folk Dance and Song Soc. (q.v.) and editor of its *Journal*; chairman of Musicians' Benevolent Fund. C.B.E. 1954.

Howland, Horace. See *Criticism.*

Hoyte, William Stevenson (b. Sidmouth 1844; d. London 1917). London organist. On staff R.A.M., R.C.M., and G.S.M. Composer of church and organ music, &c. D.Mus., Lambeth (1905).

Hptw. (in Ger. organ music) = *Hauptwerk* ('chief work'), i.e. 'Great Organ'.

Hr. Short for horn.

Hrf. Short for *Harfe* (Ger.), i.e. Harp.

Hrotta. Sometimes used for 'Crwth' (q.v.).

Hubay, Jenö, or **Huber, Eugen**—being Magyar and Ger. forms of same name (b. Budapest 1858; there d. 1937). Eminent violinist and famous teacher of his instrument; director of Budapest Conserv. 1919–31. Composer of symphonies, 4 violin concertos, operas, songs, &c.

Huber, Hans (b. nr. Olten, Switzerland, 1852; d. Locarno 1921). Head of the Basle Conserv. and a vigorous and varied composer—operas, oratorios, masses, a new '48' (preludes and fugues for piano 4 hands), &c.

Huberman, Bronislaw (b. Poland 1882; d. Vevey, Switzerland, 1947). Violinist. Trained Berlin under Joachim. Appeared in public, Vienna, at age 10; Brahms Concerto, with composer present, age 14; founded Palestine Symphony Orch. 1936. Two autobiographical books.

Hübsch (Ger.). 'Pretty', 'dainty'.

Hucbald (abt. 840–930). Monk of St. Amand, nr. Tournai (Belgium); wrote famous treatise *De harmonica institutione*; other treatises formerly, but not now, attributed to him.

Hudson, (1) **Eli** (b. Manchester 1877; d. London 1919). Flautist. Trained R.C.M. Took high place as soloist and London orch. player. Also as member of music hall trio, 'Olga, Elgar, and Eli Hudson'.

(2) **George.** See *Siege of Rhodes.*

Huë, Georges Adolphe (b. Versailles 1858; d. Paris 1948). At Paris Conserv. won Rome Prize; on return wrote stage music, orch. music, many songs, &c.

Hueffer, Francis (b. Münster 1843; d. London 1889). Influential music critic of London *Times*, author, and librettist. Ph.D., Göttingen.

Hughes, (1) **Herbert** (b. Belfast 1882; d. Brighton 1937). Trained at R.C.M.; publ. quantities of effective settings of Irish folk songs (a founder of Irish Folk Song Soc.) as well as original songs (sometimes humorous); also served as London music critic (*Daily Telegraph*, &c.).

(2) **Patrick Cairns** ('Spike Hughes'; b. 1908). Writer on music; light music composer; expert in jazz and in broadcasting activities, &c., and conductor.

(3) **Rev. Dom Anselm, O.S.B.** (b. London 1889). Studied Oxford (M.A.) and became Benedictine (Nashdom Abbey, Bucks.). Engaged in research in, and editorship of, publications of early polyphonic music. Sec. of Plainsong and Mediaeval Music Soc. 1926–36. Ed. of early part of *New Oxford History of Music*. Lecture tours in America.

(4) **David Edmund.** See *Broadcasting of Music.*

Hugh the Drover, or Love in the Stocks. Opera by Vaughan Williams. Libretto by Harold Child. (Prod. London 1924; Toronto 1931.)

Huguenots, Les. Meyerbeer's most popular opera. (Prod. Paris 1836; New Orleans 1839; London 1842; New York 1845.)

Huit (Fr.). 'Eight'; hence *huitième*, 'Eighth'.

Huldigungsmarsch (Ger. 'Homage March'). (1) By WAGNER (1864). Originally for Military Band. In honour of Composer's patron, King Ludwig of Bavaria. (Orch. version, partly scored by Raff, 1st perf. at foundation-stone laying of Bayreuth Opera House, 1872). (2) By LISZT. For Piano (1853; scored by Raff 1853; revised and re-scored by Composer 1857). In honour of Grand Duke of Saxe-Weimar. (3) By GRIEG (op. 56, no. 3; in the *Sigurd Jorsalfar* music); also known as 'Triumphal March'.

Hull, Percy Clarke (b. Hereford 1878; d. 1968). Chorister and then Asst. Organist Hereford Cathedral: Organist 1918–50 and Conductor of Fest. 1918–49. Knighted 1947.

Hullah, John (Pyke) (b. Worcester 1812; d. London 1884). Took up fixed-doh sight-singing method of Wilhem (q.v.) of Paris, and had enormous initial success in teaching it in London and elsewhere (ultimately superseded by Tonic Sol-fa of his lifelong rival,

Curwen); prof. of singing at King's, Queen's, and Bedford Colls., London; organist of Charterhouse; government inspector of music in Training Colls. 1872; composed successful opera (1836), many songs (e.g. *The Three Fishers*; *O that we two were maying*; *The Storm*); wrote many textbooks. (See *Sight-singing.*)

Humfrey (or **Humphrey** or **Humphrys**), **Pelham** (b. 1647; d. Windsor 1674). One of first group of Children of the Chapel Royal when its music began again at Restoration: sent by Charles II to France and Italy to perfect himself in composition; became Master of Children of the Chapel Royal and one of Composers to King. A little of his church music is still heard (especially the very simple 'Grand Chant').

Hummel, Johann Nepomuk (b. Pressburg, otherwise Pozsony, now Bratislava, 1778; d. Weimar 1837). Pupil of Mozart; at 9 toured Europe as prodigy pianist; in London for a year, having piano lessons from Clementi; studied composition in Vienna with Salieri, Albrechtsberger, and Haydn; became friend of Beethoven; remarkable virtuoso, extemporizer, and teacher; lavish composer for his instrument and author of famous instruction book; also composed masses, operas, &c.

See *Pianoforte Playing and Teaching.*

Hum note. See *Bell* 1.

Humoresque (Fr.), **Humoreske** (Ger.). A word used by some composers as a title for a lively instrumental composition. Two such pieces frequently heard are that of *Dvořák*, being No. 7 of his 8 Humoresques for Piano, op. 101 (1894), and that of *Schumann* for Piano (op. 20, 1839).

Humperdinck, Engelbert (b. nr. Bonn 1854; d. Neustrelitz 1921). Friend and helper of Wagner; as composer became famous 1893 with delightful opera *Hänsel and Gretel* (q.v.): other operas were lesser successes (see *Königskinder*).

Humphrey or **Humphrys.** See *Humfrey.*

Humphries, John (b. 1707; d. 1730). Violinist and composer for his instrument, some of whose music has been republished (not to be confused with a shadowy J. S. Humphries of about same period, also violin composer).

Humstrum. Properly a crude fiddle of the rebec type. But the word has been used both as a synonym for *hurdy-gurdy* (q.v.) and also, sometimes, for any instrument of a roughly made, simple kind.

Huneker, James (Gibbons) (b. Philadelphia 1860; d. Brooklyn 1921). Prominent N.Y. music critic and author many books—all written in a very personal forthright style. See under *Criticism*.

Hungaria. Symphonic Poem by Liszt (1854).

Hungarian Rhapsodies. See *Liszt's Hungarian Rhapsodies.*

Hunnenschlacht ('Battle of the Huns'). Symphonic Poem by Liszt (1857). Inspired by a fresco of Kaulbach.

Hunt, The (Haydn). See *Chasse.*

Hunt Quartet (Mozart). See *Chasse.*

Hunt, (1) **Thomas** (early 16th c.). Composer of church music; a madrigal of his still sung.

(2) **Henry George Bonavia** (b. Malta 1847; d. 1917). Anglican clergyman in London. Warden of T.C.M. 1872–92. Author of highly popular *Concise History of Music* (1878 and many later edns.). Ed. of popular general magazines. Composer of church music, &c. B.Mus., Oxford, 1876; D.Mus., Dublin, 1887.

(3) **John** (b. Eltham, Kent, 1905). Pianist. Trained R.A.M. and under Artur Schnabel. Before public from 1930, since touring in many countries.

Hunting Horn. See *Horn Family.*

Hüpfend (Ger., various terminations according to case, &c.). 'Hopping', i.e. 'with springing bow' (same as *spiccato*; q.v.).

Hurdy-Gurdy. A stringed instrument played by turning with the right hand a rosined wheel which serves as a bow, whilst the left operates a small keyboard with a few finger-keys like those of a piano. Two of the strings (one or the other of which is allowed to vibrate at any given moment according to the key of the music) produce the low keynote, so resembling the drone of a bag-pipe (q.v.; and see *Bourdon* and

HURDY-GURDY
(In French, *Vielle*)

Harmony 2 i). Some instruments have sympathetic strings (q.v.).

Music has been provided for this instrument by serious composers (including Haydn). It is still in some use in France.

(The vulgar application of the name to the street piano is, presumably, by mere analogy, both instruments being played by a handle.)

Huré, Jean (b. Gien, Loiret 1877; d. Paris 1930). Fine pianist, founder of music school, ed. of journal for organists, and author of books on piano and organ playing. Composed masses, symphonies, piano sonatas, &c.

Hurlstone, William Yeates (b. London 1876; there d. 1906). Brilliant student of R.C.M. and then member of its staff; showed great talent for composition and then prematurely died.

Hurtig (Ger.). 'Nimble', 'agile'.

Hüsch, Gerhard (b. Hanover 1901). Lyric baritone. Trained Hanover Conserv. Opera début Osnabrück 1923; Berlin, London 1930. High reputation as Lieder singer. On staff Munich Hochschule since 1938.

Huss, (1) **Henry Holden** (b. Newark, N.J., 1862; d. New York 1953). Pianist, teacher, and composer of orch. and chamber music, &c.

(2) **John.** See *Hymns* 2.

Hussey, Dyneley (b. India 1893). Music critic, &c. Educated Oxford (B.A.). On London *Times* (1924–47), *Saturday Review, Spectator* (1923–46), *Listener* (1946–59), &c. Books on Mozart, Verdi, &c.

Hutcheson, Ernest (b. Melbourne, Australia, 1871; d. New York 1951). Child pianist; then trained Leipzig Conserv. On staff Peabody Conserv. 1900; Juilliard 1924 (President from 1937). Composer of piano and orch. works, &c.; author of book on piano technique, &c.

Hutchings, Arthur (James Bramwell) (b. Sunbury-on-Thames 1906). Largely self-taught. First career as schoolmaster, writing meanwhile on music and conducting string orch., &c.; in 1947 appointed Prof. of Music Durham Univ. Books include *Schubert, Delius, Mozart's Concertos,* &c.; some compositions. B.A., B.Mus., Ph.D., London.

Hutschenruyter, (1) **Wouter I** (b. Rotterdam 1796; there d. 1878). Violinist, horn-player, composer, conductor, musicologist, and man of general capacity and usefulness. For his grandson see below. (2) **Wouter II** (b. Amsterdam 1859; d. The Hague 1943). Grandson of the above. Conductor of Utrecht orch.; director of

Rotterdam Municipal School of Music, &c. Composer and author of useful books on musical subjects.

H.W. (in Ger. organ music) = *Hauptwerk*, i.e. 'Great Organ'.

Hyde, (1) **Walter** (b. Birmingham 1875; d. Hampstead 1951). Tenor. Trained R.C.M. Started career in light opera; then concert singing and Wagner opera (Covent Garden; Metropolitan Opera House, New York, &c.). On staff G.S.M.

(2) **F. C. Field-.** See under *Field-Hyde.*

Hydraulus (Lat.), **Hydraulikon** (Gr.), or **Water organ.** The most ancient form of organ known, being attributed to Ctesibius the Egyptian, *c.* 250 B.C. It seems to have been in wide use over a long period. Representations of it occur on coins, ancient treatises describe it, a terra-cotta model has been dug up at Carthage, and some remains of an actual specimen of date A.D. 228 have been found in the ruins of a Roman station near Budapest. In general appearance it resembled a small organ of today and it had a keyboard with wide keys each operating on a slider under the relevant pipe. Wind was supplied to the reservoir by hydraulic means. Authorities at present differ as to the application of these means.

Hymn. See *Hymns and Hymn Tunes.*

Hymn of Jesus. Choral-orch. work by Holst. Text from the apocryphal *Acts of St. John.* (1st perf. London 1920.)

Hymn of Praise (*Lobgesang*). See *Mendelssohn.*

Hymn of Triumph (Brahms). See *Triumphlied.*

Hymns, Ancient and Modern. See *Hymns and Hymn Tunes* 4.

Hymns and Hymn Tunes (including Metrical Psalms). (1) There are many ancient LATIN HYMNS in use today and in translation they find a place in hymn-books in the Eng. language (cf. *Sequence* 2). They date from a period before the use of harmony. They quickly acquired their own plainsong melodies, and, most of them being metrical, brought into existence a type of plainsong tune that, in greater or lesser measure, still has a place in almost every hymn-book—though nowadays either harmonized or, at least, provided with an organ accompaniment.

(2) THE REFORMATION AND THE CHORALE. The Reformation in Bohemia in the 14th and early 15th cs., and in Germany, France, and England in the 16th, gave a very marked impetus to hymn writing and hymn-tune composition. Huss wrote many hymns, and the first hymn-books published in any vernacular are the collections of his followers. In Germany LUTHER made great use of hymns. The 1st Lutheran hymn-book appeared at Wittenberg in 1524. It would be difficult to overestimate the importance of the place which the Lutheran hymn tune, or 'Choral' (in Eng. usually spelt 'chorale'), has taken in Ger. life—especially, of course, in the Protestant north. For some further remarks on the subject see *Choral or Chorale*.

(3) THE METRICAL PSALM. The Calvinistic reformers in France, Switzerland, and elsewhere also greatly used hymns, or rather, in their case, metrical versions of the psalms (cf. *Calvin*). To Geneva, the headquarters of Calvinism, many Eng. and Scottish divines fled to escape persecution and so from Geneva came a number of the metrical psalm tunes now most endeared to the hearts of Eng. and Scottish congregations.

The metrical psalter of STERNHOLD AND HOPKINS (London: completed 1562) was the great treasury of sacred song of Englishmen in the 16th and 17th cs. John Day published it with melodies taken from Fr. and Ger. sources, and the following year brought out a harmonized ed. of the tunes. Other tune books that followed as companions for this psalter were Este's (1592), Ravenscroft's (1621), and Playford's (1677). Playford's was the 1st popular book to put the melody in the treble instead of the tenor. Sternhold and Hopkins was the chief book authorized in the Church of England for a third, i.e. up to 1696, when the TATE AND BRADY version appeared and was used by a number of churches in preference, though many continued to use Sternhold and Hop-

kins for over a century longer. It passed through 600 editions. Sternhold and Hopkins was after 1696 spoken of as the 'Old Version' and Tate and Brady as the 'New Version', and this 'New Version' held the field right up to the introduction of the modern hymn-book.

(It should be noted that in all the above discussion of psalm singing and psalm tunes the liturgical use of the psalms in the Church of England is not in question. The psalms for the day were in ordinary churches read in prose, in alternation of minister and parish clerk, or, in cathedrals, sung to the Anglican chants (see *Anglican Chant*): a metrical psalm would be sung in a service as a sort of religious relaxation.)

(4) THE ENGLISH HYMN. Many beautiful religious lyrics (i.e. hymns in the modern sense of the word) were meanwhile written, some of which are to be found in present-day hymn-books, but they were not at that time much used in public worship. Dr. Watts published his 1st book in 1707 and John Wesley's 1st such publication appeared in 1737 in Georgia. The Methodist movement made enormous use of hymn singing and the many later publications of the Wesleys kept it abundantly supplied. The hymn-tune books of this period are rather disappointing. Some of the fine old Genevan and other psalm tunes are there (often much disfigured), but there are many florid tunes of a very secular character, and some of secular origin. 'Fuguing Tunes', i.e. tunes in which a voice or two fell momentarily silent and then came in with an imitation of some preceding voice, were introduced amongst the hymn-singing denominations. These tunes were popular in the Amer. colonies, which produced many of their own.

From this point onwards hymn writers and hymn-tune composers became so numerous that it is difficult to summarize their activities. Just as the Evangelical movement of the 18th c. had inaugurated the popularity of the Eng. hymn, so the High Church (or Oxford) Movement of the early and middle 19th c. gave it renewed vigour, for the Anglican Church had at last accorded hymns, as distinct from metrical psalms, general acceptance—long after the nonconforming bodies had all done so. In 1861 appeared *Hymns Ancient and Modern*, which (with many additions and revisions) is still a very popular book in the Anglican communion. (Cf. *Neale, John Mason*.) With it are associated the names of such composers as W. H. Monk (q.v.), Dykes (q.v.), and Stainer (q.v.); the best of their tunes are worthy, but the second-best fall into the class rather of part song than of hymn. An attempt at a genuinely congregational selection of tunes for the Anglican Church, with less frequent tendency to the sentimental, was made in the publication of the *English Hymnal* in 1906 (new edn. 1933); both plainsong and folk song melodies were freely introduced.

(5) 'LINING-OUT' (or in America 'Deaconing'). The practice of having each line read (by minister, parish clerk, or precentor) before it was sung by the congregation probably dates from the earliest days of the introduction of metrical psalms into public worship. The practice was regarded as a temporary concession to an ignorance of reading that was expected to disappear, but, once established, it came to possess that sanctity that attaches to all ecclesiastical custom and it was exceedingly difficult to get rid of it. It lingered in a few Anglican churches of England up to the 1860's or 1870's.

(6) ORGAN ACCOMPANIMENT was for long very crude. The better-equipped organists, where lining-out did not prevail, nevertheless broke the hymn and tune into fragments by the practice of a long shake at the end of every line, or a few measures of trivial interlude, and played quite long interludes between all the verses, or, at any rate, before the last one.

(7) PSALMS AND HYMNS IN AMERICA. Nothing seems to be known of the singing of the earliest settlers—those of Virginia from 1607 onwards. Almost immediately, in the north appeared the Pilgrim Fathers, bringing with them the metrical Psalter to which they had become accustomed in Holland, that of AINSWORTH, their minister at Amsterdam. Then, in 1640, a better version was desired and a clerical committee compiled it, and printed it in the house of the President of Harvard Coll., at Cambridge, Mass., on a press given by Puritan friends in Holland but sent from England (1638). This 'BAY PSALM BOOK' had immense popularity, which did not die out for a century and a third, the last ed. (of about 70) appearing in 1773. England and Scotland adopted it to some extent.

About 1720 arose in New England a great clamour on the subject of 'SINGING BY NOTE', also called 'Regular Singing' (i.e. singing by rule), which simply meant singing the tunes as printed. Several ministers wrote vigorously on the subject. Their points are always the same. The tunes, being learnt only by ear, have diminished in number down to 8 or 10 in some congregations or half this in others; so many graces have been introduced that the tunes have become unrecognizable; the graces differ so much that no two congregations sing a tune in the same way; for want of knowledge of the notes the various members of a congregation do not keep together, and so on. The protests and attempts at reform met with the most violent opposition, but in the end good sense prevailed and the new ideas spread over all the settled parts of the North American continent.

The wrenching away from the idea of an officially limited body of sacred song tune and the development of ability in singing opened the field for the 1st American composers. WILLIAM BILLINGS was one of these. Billings (1746–1800) was self-taught but he flew high, even into what he called 'fuges' (cf. 4 above). Later came such enthusiasts as THOMAS HASTINGS (1787–1872), who wrote many hymns and tunes and did enormous work in developing choral activities in New York State, and LOWELL MASON (1792–1872), who exercised great influence.

A special phase of Amer. hymnology has been the 'GOSPEL HYMN'. It came at last into world prominence with the work of the evangelist Moody and his musical colleague Ira D. Sankey, which was actively pursued in the U.S.A. and Britain during the 1870's, 1880's, and 1890's. Moody did not himself write the words of any hymns. Moreover, in the widely circulated *Sacred Songs and Solos*, Sankey is as much compiler as composer, drawing largely on a type of tune that had already become popular in the U.S.A., the type with a lively rhythm and a harmonization consisting of little more than alternations of the 3 chief chords of the key (tonic, dominant, and sub-dominant). To this type the Amer. W. B. BRADBURY (1816–68) had been a considerable contributor, publishing many collections. The Salvation Army, founded by William Booth in 1878, has made this type of hymn and tune familiar to the members of almost every race in the world.

(8) HYMN METRES. In many hymn-tune books figures to indicate the metre are attached to hymns and tunes, either in the body of the book or in the index; these show the number of syllables in the lines and the number of lines in the stanza and facilitate the fitting of tunes to hymns. Thus the metre known as 'six-eight', or 'six-lines-eight', appears as 8 8 8. 8 8 8 or 8 8. 8 8. 8 8. according as the poet has arranged his lines (as to rhymes) in the one way or the other.

The following metres have distinct names: 8 6. 8 6, 'Common Metre' (also called Ballad Metre from its being that of the old Eng. ballads); 6 6. 8 6, 'Short Metre'; 8 8. 8 8, 'Long Metre'. The variety of metres is now astonishing, as many as 100 to 120 being found in some hymn-books.

See *Gathering Note.*

Hymns from the Rig Veda. By Holst. Some for Solo Voice and Piano; others for Female Voices, Male Voices, or Mixed Voices. (1st perf. 1911–13.)

Hymn Society of Great Britain and Ireland. A Society founded in 1936 for the study of hymnology and the en-couragement of the use of hymns and tunes of a high standard. Its officers and members are drawn from the ministry and laity of all the Protestant churches.

Hymn to the Sun (Rimsky-Korsakof). See *Golden Cockerel.*

Hymnus Eucharisticus. See *Rogers, Benjamin.*

Hypoaeolian; Hypodorian; Hypo-ionian; Hypolydian; Hypomixo-lydian; Hypophrygian. See *Modes.*

I

I (It.). 'The' (masc. plur.).

Ibach & Sons. Piano-making firm at Barmen; founded 1794 (Brit. branch 1880).

Ibéria (Debussy). See *Images* 2 b.

Iberia (Albéniz). 4 books of piano pieces (some transcribed for orchestra by Arbós).

Ibérien, Ibérienne (Fr. masc., fem.). As often loosely used this means 'Spanish', but properly it means this plus 'Portuguese'—the ancient Iberia comprising the whole peninsula.

Ibert, Jacques (b. Paris 1890; d. there 1962). Pupil of Fauré at Paris Conserv.; in 1919 won Rome Prize; 1937–55 Director of the Fr. Academy in Rome (see *Prix de Rome*). His compositions lean to the Ravel type of *Impressionism* (q.v.).

Ideale, Die ('The Ideals'). Symphonic Poem by Liszt (1857). Based on Schiller's poem.

Idée Fixe. 'Fixed Idea' (see under *Berlioz*).

Idomeneo re di Creta, ossia Ilia ed Adamante ('Idomeneus, King of Crete, or Ilia and Idamante'). It. opera by Mozart. (Prod. Munich 1781; Glasgow 1934; London 1938.)

I dreamt that I dwelt in marble halls. Song in Balfe's *The Bohemian Girl* (q.v.). See reference under *Goodbye*.

Idyll. In literature a description (prose or verse) of happy rural life, and so sometimes applied to a musical composition of peaceful pastoral character (e.g. Wagner's *Siegfried Idyll*).

Iernin. See *Lloyd, George*.

I heard a brooklet gushing. See *Loder*.

Il (It.). 'The' (masc. sing.).

Île joyeuse, L' ('The Island of Joy'). Piano piece by Debussy suggested by one or other of Watteau's two pictures, *L'Embarquement pour Cythère* (deli-cately depicted early 18th-c. scene of party about to embark for the island sacred to Venus.)

Iles, John Henry (b. Bristol 1871; d. Birchington 1951). Founder of National Band Fest., Crystal Palace (1900) and of weekly, *British Bandsman*. Organizer of world tours of leading Brit. bands. O.B.E.

Il faut (Fr.). (1) 'There is (or are) needed' (such-and-such a player or players, &c.). (2) 'It is necessary to' (followed by a verb), or 'One must'.

I'll sing thee songs of Araby (Clay). See *Lalla Rookh*.

Illuminations, Les. By Britten. Ten song-settings of poems of Rimbaud, with string accompaniment (1940).

Images ('Pictures'). (1) Two sets of piano pieces by Debussy (1905 and 1907). 1st set: (a) *Reflets dans l'eau* ('Reflections in the water'), (b) *Hommage à Rameau* ('Homage to Rameau'), (c) *Mouvement* (in Perpetual Motion). 2nd set: (a) *Cloches à travers les feuilles* ('Bells heard through the foliage'), (b) *Et la lune descend sur le temple qui fut* ('And the moon goes down over the ruined temple'), (c) *Poissons d'or* ('Goldfish').
  (2) Three pieces for Orch. by Debussy (1912): (a) *Gigues* (originally called 'Gigues Tristes'), scored by Caplet under the Composer's direction; (b) Ibéria ('Spain'), 3 continuous sections—*Par les rues et par les chemins* ('In the streets and by-ways'), *Les parfums de la nuit* ('The fragrance of the night'), and *Le matin d'un jour de fête* ('The festal morning'); (c) *Rondes de printemps* ('Spring roundelays'), making some use of the tune of the old Fr. dance-song, 'Nous n'irons plus au bois'.

Im Bedarfsfalle (Ger.). 'In case of need.'

Imbrie, Andrew (Welsh) (b. New York 1921). Composer. Educated Princeton (B.A. 1943), Univ. of

California (later on staff), and under Sessions and Nadia Boulanger. Works include a violin concerto, choral music, and chamber music, mostly in a clear, polyphonic style.

Im Falle (Ger.). 'In case.'

Imitation. See *Canon; Counterpoint.*

Imitazione, Aria d'. See *Aria.*

Immer (Ger.). 'Ever', 'always', 'still'. *Immer belebter,* 'ever more lively', or 'getting livelier and livelier'; *Immer schnell,* 'always quick', 'still quick'.

Immortal Hour, The. Very successful music-drama by Boughton. Libretto based on work by 'Fiona Macleod' (William Sharp). (Prod. Glastonbury 1914; London 1920; New York 1926.)

Impair (Fr.). 'Odd' (numbers)—as opposed to *Pair,* 'even'.

Impaziente, impazientemente (It.). 'Impatient', 'impatiently'.

Imperfect Cadence. See *Cadence.*

'Imperfect' Time. See *Common Time.*

Impériale, L' ('The Imperial'). Nickname for Haydn's Symphony in D, No. 53 in Breitkopf edn. of the Symphonies.

Imperial Mass (Haydn). See *Nelsonmesse.*

Imperioso (It.). 'Imperious'.

Impeto (It.). 'Impetus', 'impetuosity'.

Impétueux (Fr.). 'Impetuous.' **Impetuoso; impetuosamente; impetuosità** (It.). 'Impetuous'; impetuously'; 'impetuosity'.

Imponente (It.). **Imponierend** (Ger.). 'Imposing in style'. So *imponenza* (It.). 'An imposing style'.

Impresario, The (Mozart). See *Schauspieldirektor.*

Impressionism. A word originally introduced (1874) in connexion with the painters of a Fr. school of the 19th c. (Monet, Manet, &c.) in which the picture, instead of recording a mass of details, rather records what a quick glance can take in. In practice this results in the representation of the play of light upon objects rather than the objects themselves—tints and tinges

rather than shapes. By analogy the term has been applied to the type o. music with which we associate, especially, the name of Debussy, whose harmonic system conduced to an effect of dreamy vagueness. (Debussy was a great admirer of the work of the impressionist painter Whistler, and his own description of his 3 orch. 'Nocturnes' reads almost like the description of the impressionist pictures.)

Impressions of Italy. See *Charpentier, Gustave.*

Impromptu. An instrumental composition of a character (nominally, at least) suggesting improvisation (q.v.). Schubert, Chopin, and Schumann have left examples.

Improperia. The Reproaches of the Roman Catholic Liturgy, sung on Good Friday morning. They consist of passages from the prophets, responded to by the Trisagion (q.v.). The music properly is plainsong, but there are some 'fauxbourdons' (see *Faburden* 2), very simple 4-part settings of Palestrina used in the Sistine Chapel (and long kept for that place alone; cf. *Allegri*).

Improvisation, or Extemporization, has been an important element in musical activity through the centuries. Some instances are the following: (1, 12th–17th c.) The art of vocal descant (see *Descant* 2). (2, 17th and 18th cs.) The 'Divisions' (q.v.) of string players. (3, 17th and 18th cs.) The keyboard interpretation of 'Figured Bass' (q.v.). (4, 18th c.) The filling in of the Preludes to keyboard suites, which Handel and others of his period often left as mere series of chords out of which the performer was expected to develop his passages. (5, 18th c. onwards). The Cadenza in concertos. (6, especially 18th and early 19th cs.) The keyboard performances, without notes, in which Bach, Mozart, Beethoven, and others were so fertile in ideas and skilful in their exploitation.

In a Monastery Garden. See *Ketèlbey.*

In a Persian Garden. See *Lehmann.*

In a Summer Garden. Fantasy for Orch. by Delius. (1st perf. London 1909; revised version Edinburgh 1913.)

Incalcando (It. 'warming-up'). 'Getting faster and louder.'

Incalzando (It.). 'Pressing forward', 'hastening'.

Incidental Music. Music occurring incidentally in the spoken play. It dates back as far as the earliest days of the drama (Greek, Roman, Medieval). Shakespeare calls for a good deal of it. Purcell wrote much such music. So did Beethoven (Goethe's *Egmont*, &c.), Mendelssohn (*Midsummer Night's Dream*), Bizet (Daudet's *L'Arlésienne*), and Grieg (Ibsen's *Peer Gynt*), whilst many present-day plays and films offer opportunities for the provision of such music by our contemporary composers.

Inciso (It.). 'Incisive.'

Incline thine ear. See *Himmel*.

Incominciando (It.). 'Commencing.'

Incoronazione di Poppea, L' ('The Coronation of Poppea'). Last opera of Monteverdi. (Prod. Venice 1642.)

Incorporated Association of Organists. The formation of societies of Brit. organists, without distinction as to whether professional or amateur, seems to have begun at Wakefield, Yorks., in 1889. In 1913 the then existing societies federated as the 'National Union of Organists' Associations' and in 1929 this became a legal corporation under its present title. It holds annual conferences, carries on a journal, &c.

Incorporated Society of Musicians. Leading association for professionals in sphere of serious music (48 Gloucester Place, London, W. 1). See *Profession*; *Degrees and Diplomas* 2.

Incorporated Staff Sight-singing College. See *Degrees and Diplomas* 2.

Indebolendo (It.). 'Becoming weak.' So *Indebolito*, 'having become weak'.

Indeciso (It.). 'Undecided', 'capricious'.

In der Natur (Dvořák). See *Triple Overture*.

Indian Queen. So-called 'Opera' by Purcell (1695). Story adapted from tragedy by Sir Robert Howard and Dryden.

Indicato (It.). 'Indicated', i.e. prominent.

In dulci jubilo. See *Pearsall*.

Indy, Vincent d'—in full Paul Marie Théodore Vincent (b. Paris 1851; there d. 1931). Pupil, friend, and helper of César Franck (q.v.), his whole life-work being an expression of ideals he shared with him. In 1876 attended first performance of *The Ring* at Bayreuth and, enthusiastic, became one of Lamoureux's right-hand men in the introduction of Wagner to Paris audiences. Also revived older music (Monteverdi, Bach, Rameau, &c.); defended Debussy when he was assailed and as conductor insisted on performing his music. With Bordes and Guilmant founded the Schola Cantorum, a complete school of music largely with a religious aim; served as its Principal and wrote a 3-volume *Treatise of Composition* based on his teaching there. As a composer wrote operas, symphonies, tone poems, chamber music, &c., all of the most careful workmanship.

Altogether a man remarkable for width of interests, unceasing activity, and the highest aims.

See also *Fervaal*; *Legend of St. Christopher*; *Symphonie sur un chant montagnard*.

In exitu Israel (Lat.). Psalm 114 (in the Vulgate 113), 'When Israel came out of Egypt'. It is traditionally sung in the *tonus peregrinus* (q.v.). A magnificent 8-part motet setting by Samuel Wesley is well known.

Infinite Canon. See *Canon*.

Inflexion. In plainsong, the general name given to such parts as are not in monotone, i.e. including the intonation, mediation, and ending, and excluding the recitation.

Infra (It.). 'Below.'

Ingegneri, Marco Antonio (b. Verona abt. 1547; d. Cremona 1592). Choirmaster of cathedral of Cremona; teacher of Monteverdi. Publ. books of church music and madrigals which brought him into high repute as original and sensitive composer.

Ingemisco. See *Requiem*.

Inghelbrecht, Désiré (Émile) (b. Paris 1880; d. there 1965). Studied at Paris Conserv. Able conductor. Composed ballets, orch. and chamber music, songs, &c. Book, *Conductor's World*, 1954.

Inglese (It.). 'English.'

In Honour of the City. Cantatas; settings of Dunbar's poem of abt. 1500. (1) By DYSON (1st perf. Lincoln 1928). (2) By WALTON (1st perf. Leeds Fest. 1937).

In Memoriam Overture. By Sullivan, written within a week of his father's death. (1st perf. Norwich Fest. 1866.)

In modo di (It.). 'In the manner of.'

Innig (Ger.). 'Inmost', i.e. heartfelt. So the noun *Innigkeit*.

Inno (It.). 'Hymn.'

Innocenza (It.). 'Innocence.'

In Nomine. A type of Eng. contrapuntal composition (generally for a consort of viols: see *Viol Family* 2; but sometimes for keyboard or lute); it may be considered a kind of *Fancy* (q.v.), and is the earliest known instrumental music independent of either dance music or church music. The basis of all such works is almost always a version of a particular piece of plainsong (*Gloria Tibi Trinitas Aequalis*). The origin of the name *In Nomine* was long a puzzle. It is now pointed out that the prototype of the *In Nomine* form was an example by Taverner. This set the fashion for the composition of such pieces, and is identical with the setting of the words *In Nomine Domini* in the Benedictus of that composer's Mass, *Gloria Tibi Trinitas*. Thus the pioneer instrumental composition of the kind was called *In Nomine*, and other composers in adopting the form adopted also the name.

In questa tomba oscura ('In this dark tomb'). Song by Beethoven; with Piano accompaniment. The result of a competition to set a poem by Carpani, the 62 efforts by other composers being now forgotten.

Inquiet (Fr.), **inquieto** (It. 'unquiet'). 'Restless.'

Inquisitive women. The (Wolf-Ferrari). See *Donne curiose*.

Insensibile (It.). 'Imperceptible.'

Insieme (It.). 'Together', 'ensemble' (q.v.).

Inspiration. See *Composition*.

Inständig (Ger.). 'Urgent.'

Instante (It.). 'Urgent.' So *instantemente*, 'urgently'.

Institute of Renaissance and Baroque Music. See *American Inst. of Musicology*.

Instrumentation. The study of the characteristics of the various instruments. Sometimes the word is used as meaning 'Scoring for an orchestra', but it is best to apply to this the term 'Orchestration'.

Instruments are devices for provoking vibrations in the air, which vibrations, impinging on the drum of the ear, create a nervous disturbance which we call sound. They fall into 4 classes as follows: (1) STRINGED INSTRUMENTS, with a sub-classification as to whether the string is set in motion by (*a*) plucking; (*b*) the friction of a bow. (2) WIND INSTRUMENTS, with a sub-classification as to whether the air in the instrument is set in motion by (*a*) simple blowing into a tube—with or without a mouthpiece; (*b*) blowing through a reed (q.v.); (*c*) blowing through the lips, which then serve as a reed, e.g. in brass instruments. (3) PERCUSSION INSTRUMENTS, with a sub-classification as to whether the pitch is (*a*) determinate, or (*b*) indeterminate. (4) ELECTRICAL INSTRUMENTS. See *Electric Musical Instruments*.

(There are just one or two oddities which do not fall into any one of these classifications and sub-classifications, but they are not of great importance.)

Intavolatura. 'Scoring.' Used in Elizabethan times of the 'arrangement' of madrigals, &c., for keyboard performance—the choral originals having circulated merely in parts, not in score.

Interlude. Anything inserted in an entertainment, &c., especially (*a*) Short play of 16th c. interpolated during banquet or between acts of a Mystery, Morality, &c., (*b*) Organ passage of late 17th and 18th cs. played between verses of a metrical psalm or hymn.

Intermède (Fr.). See *Intermezzo*.

Intermezzo (It., plur. *intermezzi*), **intermède** (Fr.). Lit. 'in the middle' and hence a word logically of wide application—and, as will be seen, this has been further widened.

(1) It was used in 16th-c. Italy of lighter entertainment interpolated between the sections of heavier, e.g. songs or madrigals, or humorous acting between the acts of plays. (2) From this grew up the comic opera, examples of which, therefore, often bore the description 'Intermezzo' on their title-pages. (3) Nowadays, in a theatrical application, usually an instrumental passage interposed in an opera (e.g. the well-known Intermezzo in Mascagni's *Cavalleria Rusticana*). (4) Ger. musicians have sometimes applied the term to the optional movements of the classical suite (q.v.), i.e. those that are sometimes interposed after the traditional allemande, courante, and sarabande, and before the final gigue. (5) Composers have occasionally given the name to some movement in a sonata or symphony. (6) Schumann, in several works, seems to use the word as a mere synonym for 'trio'—in the old 'minuet and trio' sort of sense. (7) Schumann, Brahms, and others have loosely applied the same term to shorter independent pieces.

Intermezzo. Opera by Richard Strauss. Libretto by the composer. (Prod. Dresden 1924.)

Internationale. Official Communist song (*Arise ye cursèd from your slumbers! Arise ye criminals of want!*), words by Eugène Pottier, a woodworker of Lille; music by Degeyter (1849–1932). Russia discarded it on 1 Jan. 1944.

International Folk Music Council. Founded London 1940 at conference representing 28 countries. First president R. Vaughan Williams. Office 26 Warwick Road, London, S.W. 5.

International Musical Society. Soc. of persons devoted to musicological research having about 20 national sections, these combining for purposes of publication and conferences. Founded 1899 and brought to an end 1914 by First World War. See *International Musicological Society*.

International Musicological Society (sometimes known as International Soc. for Musical Research). Founded 1927 to resume and carry on the work of the International Musical Soc. (see above). Headquarters at Basle. Journal, *Acta Musicologica*.

International Society for Contemporary Music. Founded 1922, under the 1st presidency of E. J. Dent (q.v.), with a large number of national sections. Object pursued is holding of annual festival, varying the place year by year, at which the works of contemporary composers of all countries are given a hearing. See *Evans* (4); *Clark* (3).

International Society for Musical Research. Another name for International Musicological Soc. (q.v.).

Interpretation in music is merely the act of performance, with the implication that in it the performer's judgement and personality have a share. Just as there is no means by which a dramatist can so write his play as to indicate to the actors precisely how they shall speak his lines, so there is no means by which a composer can indicate to a performer the precise way in which his music is to be sung or played—so that no two performers will adopt the same slackenings and hastenings of speed (including *Rubato*, q.v.), the same degree of emphasis on an accented note, and so forth.

The fact that latitude thus necessarily exists for the exercise of judgement and the expression of personality often leads a certain type of performer (including, decidedly, the conductor) to seek the unusual and extreme in manner of interpretation.

Interrupted Cadence. See *Cadence*.

Interval is the term used to express the idea of difference in pitch between any 2 notes. The 'size' of any interval is expressed numerically, e.g. C to G is a 5th, because if we proceed up the scale of C the 5th note in it is G—and so on.

The somewhat hollow-sounding 4th, 5th, and 8ve of the scale are all called *Perfect*. They possess what we may perhaps call a 'purity' distinguishing them from other intervals. The other

L

intervals, as they are found in ascending the major scale from its key-note, are all called *Major* ('Major 2nd', 'Major 3rd', 'Major 6th', 'Major 7th').

If any Major interval be chromatically reduced by a semitone it becomes *Minor*; if any Perfect or Minor interval

take C to G sharp (an Augmented 5th) and C to A flat (a Minor 6th).

COMPOUND INTERVALS are those greater than an 8ve, e.g. C to the D an 8ve and a note higher, which may be spoken of either as a Major 9th or as a Compound Major 2nd.

N.B. The intervals marked * have little beyond a theoretical existence

be so reduced it becomes *Diminished*; if any Perfect or Major interval be increased by a semitone it becomes *Augmented*.

ENHARMONIC INTERVALS are those which differ from each other in name but not in any other way (so far as modern keyboard instruments are concerned, at all events). As an example

INVERSION OF INTERVALS is the reversing of the relative position of the 2 notes defining them, e.g. C to G inverted becomes G to C. It will be found that a 5th when inverted becomes a 4th, a 3rd becomes a 6th, and so on (i.e. the number-name of the new interval = 9 minus the number of the old interval). It will also be found that

Perfect intervals remain Perfect (C to G a Perfect 5th; G to C a Perfect 4th, &c.), Major ones become Minor, Minor becomes Major, Augmented become Diminished, and Diminished become Augmented.

Every interval is either CONCORDANT or DISCORDANT (cf. *Harmony* 2 f). The Concordant ones comprise all Perfect intervals and all Major and Minor 3rds and 6ths; the Discordant ones comprise all Augmented and Diminished intervals and all 2nds and 7ths. It follows from what has been said in this and the previous paragraphs that all Concordant intervals when inverted remain Concordant and all Discordant intervals remain Discordant.

In the Mosque (Ippolitof-Ivanof). See *Caucasian Sketches.*

In the Mountain Pass (Ippolitof-Ivanof). See *Caucasian Sketches.*

In the South. Concert-Overture by Elgar (op. 50; 1904). Composed at Alassio.

In the Steppes of Central Asia. 'Orchestral Sketch' or Symphonic Poem, by Borodin. A vivid piece of Programme Music of Oriental flavour, representing the approach and passing of a caravan. Composed (1880) for an exhibition of historical *tableaux vivants* to celebrate the 25th year of the reign of Czar Alexander II.

In the Village (Ippolitof-Ivanof). See *Caucasian Sketches.*

In this Dark Tomb (Beethoven). See *In questa tomba oscura.*

Intime (Fr.), **intimo** (It.). 'Intimate.' So the (It.) superlative *intimissimo.*

Intonation. (1) The opening phrase of a plainsong melody (see *Plainsong* 2), perhaps so called because it was often sung by the precentor alone and gave the pitch and (in the Psalms) the 'tone' (see *Gregorian Tones*) of what was to follow. (2) The act of singing or playing in tune. Thus we speak of a singer or violinist's 'intonation' as being good or bad. (Cf. *Intoning*, below.)

Intoning (i.e. 'Monotoning'). The singing upon 1 tone or note, as is done by the clergy in parts of the Roman,

Anglican, and other liturgies. (Cf. *Intonation*, above.)

Intrada. The It. equivalent of *Entrée* (q.v.).

Intrepido; intrepidezza (It.). 'Bold', 'boldness'. So also *intrepidamente*, 'boldly'.

Introduzione (It.). 'Introduction.'

Introit. In the Roman Catholic Church it is a passage normally consisting of an antiphon (q.v.) with one verse of a psalm and the Gloria Patri, sung at High Mass while the Celebrant recites the preparatory prayers at the foot of the altar steps, or said at a Low Mass by the Priest after these prayers. It varies according to the Mass celebrated: there is no Introit on Good Friday. In the Anglican Church the word is used in the same sense, and in certain other Protestant churches it is used for a short piece of choral music opening a service.

Invention. This is the name given by Bach to 15 of his shorter keyboard compositions in 2 parts or 'voices': they are of a highly contrapuntal type, being largely of the nature of imitation (see *Counterpoint*—end). Each of them works out some short melodic motif. Bach also left another 15 compositions in the same style, known today as his 'Three-part Inventions', but to these he himself gave the title 'Symphonies'. Cf. *Bonporti.*

Inventionshorn, Inventionstrompete. The prefix 'Inventions' has been used to characterize several novelties. The 'Inventionshorn' was the work of Charles Clagget (q.v.) who united 2 instruments, one in D and the other in E flat, in such a way that the player had both at command and could thus gain the advantage of the full chromatic scale. As for the term 'Inventionstrompete', it seems to have been applied not only to the trumpet equivalent of the Inventionshorn but also to 2 earlier novelties, one a short horn in F with crooks for every key down to B flat, and the other the 'Italian Trumpet' (coiled into horn shape).

Inversion, Canon by. See *Canon.*

Inversion of Chords. See *Harmony* 2 e.

Inversion of Intervals. See *Interval.*

Inverted Cadence. See *Cadence.*

Inverted Mordent. See Table 12.

Inverted Pedal. See *Harmony* 2 i.

Inverted Turn. See Table 15.

Invertible Counterpoint. See *Counterpoint.*

Invitation to the Dance (Weber). See *Aufforderung.*

Invitatory. In the Roman Catholic Church a short passage of Scripture or versicle sung before, between the verses of, and after the Venite (q.v.) and intended to indicate the special character of the service according to the season (omitted from the Church of England Prayer Book but nevertheless nowadays sometimes introduced). The term Invitatory Psalm, or Invitatorium, is also applied to the Venite itself (Ps. 94 in Roman usage, 95 in the Eng. Bible and Prayer Book; see *Venite*).

In Windsor Forest. Cantata by Vaughan Williams, adapted from part of his *Sir John in Love* (1931).

Iolanthe, or The Peer and the Peri. Comic opera by Gilbert and Sullivan. (Prod. Savoy Theatre, London, and New York 1882.) There is also a one-act opera *Iolanthe* by Tchaikovsky (op. 69, his last opera; prod. Petersburg 1892, and a comparative failure).

Ionian Mode. See *Modes.*

Iphigénie en Aulide. Fr. Opera by Gluck. Libretto based on Racine. (Prod. with great success Paris 1774; as revised by Wagner, Dresden 1847; Oxford 1933; Philadelphia 1935.)

Iphigénie en Tauride. Very successful Fr. Opera by GLUCK. (Prod. Paris 1779; London 1796; New York 1916.) Other operas of this name include that by PICCINNI (1781).

Ippolitof-Ivanof (Ippolitow-Iwanow, &c.**), Michail Michailovich** (b. Gatchina 1859; d. Moscow 1935). Pupil of Rimsky-Korsakof at Conserv. of St. Petersburg; later prof. and then director of that of Moscow. Made study of Caucasian music. Composed operas, orch. music (see *Caucasian Sketches*), chamber music, and songs.

I quatro [*sic*] **rusteghi** ('The Four Rustics'). Comedy-opera by Wolf-Ferrari; libretto based on Goldoni. (Prod. Munich 1906; London 1946.) Adapted by E. J. Dent as *School for Fathers.*

Ireland, John Nicholson (b. Bowdon, Cheshire, 1879; d. Washington (Eng.) 1962). Son of the authors Alexander and Anne Elizabeth Ireland. Studied composition under Stanford at R.C.M. (on staff 1923–39), and became known by chamber music; wrote delicate and effective music for piano, a popular piano concerto, orch. music, choral works, organ pieces, many fine songs, &c. Hon. D.Mus., Durham.

See also *Satyricon.*

Iris. Romantic Opera on Japanese subject by Mascagni. Libretto by Luigi Illica. (Prod. Rome 1898; Philadelphia and New York 1902; London 1919.)

Irish 'Union' Bagpipe. See *Bagpipe Family.*

Irish War Pipe. See *Bagpipe Family.*

Iron Chains. See *Percussion Family* 2 y.

Iron Frame. See *Pianoforte.*

Ironico; ironicamente (It.). 'Ironic'; 'ironically'.

Irregular Cadence. See *Cadence.*

Irresoluto (It.). 'Irresolute', 'undecided in style'.

Irving, Ernest—in full Kelville Ernest (b. Godalming 1878; d. Ealing 1953). Theatrical conductor—attached in turn to most London theatres; musical director of film company, &c.

Irwin, Robert (b. Dublin 1905). Baritone. Trained at St. Patrick's Cathedral, Dublin. Recitalist and broadcaster.

Isaac (Isaak, &c.**), Heinrich** (b. before 1450; d. Florence 1517). Spent life (mostly in service of various ruling princes) at Ferrara, Florence, Innsbruck, Vienna, Augsburg, and Constance, finally returning to Florence. Left very numerous and valuable works, sacred and secular, vocal and instrumental. One of most important composers of his period.

Isaacs, (1) **Edward** (b. Manchester 1881; d. Manchester 1953). Pianist. Trained Royal Manchester Coll. of Music, Berlin, Vienna, &c. Berlin and Manchester débuts 1904; London 'Proms' 1906. Lost sight completely 1925. Author *The Blind Piano Teacher* (1948), &c. Many compositions. M.A., B.Mus., Manchester.

(2) **Harry** (b. London 1902). Pianist. Trained R.A.M. (later on staff). Formed Harry Isaacs Trio (with Leonard Hirsch and Jas. Whitehead) 1946. Frequent broadcaster.

(3) **Leonard** (b. Manchester 1909). Pianist, &c. Son of (1) above. Trained R.C.M. and École Normale, Paris. After varied career joined B.B.C. 1936; music supervisor, European service 1941–2 and 1945–8; music programme organizer 1948–50; then in charge of music, Third Programme. Prof. Mus., Univ. Manitoba, 1963. B.Mus., London.

I.S.C.M. International Soc. for Contemporary Music (q.v.).

Islamey. Vivid 'Oriental Fantasia' for Piano by Balakiref (1869). An orch. transcription by Casella in use (1908).

Islancio (It.). 'Impetuosity.'

Island God, The. Opera by Menotti (q.v.); libretto by himself, transl. McLeish. (Prod. New York 1942.)

Island of Joy (Debussy). See *Île Joyeuse.*

Island of the Dead, The. Symphonic Poem by Rachmaninof (op. 29; 1907), based on well-known picture by the Basle painter, Böcklin (1872–1901)—a ruined temple on a water-lapped rock, with a boat approaching in which stands a figure shrouded in white.

I.S.M. Incorporated Soc. of Musicians (Britain). See *Profession.*

Isola disabitata, L'. Opera by Haydn, setting of Metastasio's libretto. (Prod. Esterházy 1779; Washington, D.C., 1936.) Another setting of the same libretto exists by Traetta (1768), and one of a libretto by Goldoni (1757) by Domenico Scarlatti.

Isometric. (Gr. *Isos* = 'equal'). Having the same rhythm in every voice or part (i.e. proceeding in chords rather than in freely moving counter-point).

Isorhythmic. (Gr. *Isos* = 'equal'). Repeating the same rhythm although the notes are different—a musical term for a principle applied in the melodic themes of some early motets.

Israel in Egypt. Oratorio by Handel famous for its double choruses. (1st perf. London 1739.) (See reference under *Kerll.*)

Israel Restored. See *Bexfield.*

Isserlis, Julius (b. Kischinev, Russia, 1889; d. London 1968). Pianist and composer. Trained Moscow Conserv. Recitalist in America and Europe. Resident London from 1938. Numerous piano compositions.

Istesso (It.). 'Same.' Used in such connexions as *L'istesso tempo*, 'The same speed'—usually meaning that, though the nominal value of the beat has changed, its actual time duration is to remain the same: for instance, the former beat may have been ♩ (say in 4 time) and the new one ♩. (say in 6 time) and these are to have the same time value.

Istrumento d'acciaio (It. 'instrument of steel'). Mozart's name for his Glockenspiel in *The Magic Flute*. (See *Percussion* 1 c.)

Italiana in Algeri, L' ('The Italian Girl in Algiers'). Opera by Rossini. (Prod. Venice 1813; London 1819; New York 1832.)

Italian Concerto. By Bach for double-keyboard Harpsichord (alone). He seems to have used the term to call attention to the facts that there are (a) passages of alternation and contrast, and (b) 3 movements, so resembling the Italian 'Concerto Grosso' (see *Concerto*).

Italian Girl in Algeria, The (Rossini). See *Italiana in Algeri.*

Italian Overture. See *Overture*; *Symphony.*

Italian Serenade. By Hugo Wolf. For String Quartet (1887). Arrangement for Small Orch. (1892), later ed. by Reger.

Italian Sixth. See *Augmented Sixth*.

Italian Song-book (Wolf). See *Italienisches Liederbuch*.

Italian Symphony by Mendelssohn (op. 90). Inspired by a visit to Italy in 1831, finished in 1833, but publ. after the composer's death 14 years later. The slow movement has come to be called the 'Pilgrims' March'. The last movement is a Saltarello.

Italian Trumpet. See *Inventionshorn, Inventionstrompete*.

Italienisches Liederbuch ('Italian Song-book'). 46 Solo Song settings, by Hugo Wolf (2 books, 1890, 1896), of poems in It. style by Heyse. Piano accompaniment, but later many were orchestrated by Wolf and others by Reger.

Iturbi, José (b. Valencia 1895). Pianist and conductor. Trained at conservs. of native place and Paris. Of great international repute in his two capacities; has conducted especially in U.S.A., and appeared in several films. Some compositions.

It was a maid of my country. See *Dargason*.

Ivanhoe. The only 'Grand' Opera of Sullivan. Libretto, based on Scott's novel, by J. Sturgis. (Prod. Royal English Opera House, London, 1891, 160 perfs.; Berlin 1895; revived London 1910.)

Ivan Susanin (Glinka). See *Life for the Czar*.

Ivan the Terrible (in the original *Pskovitianka*—'The Maid of Pskov'; the Eng. name being the invention of Diaghilef, Paris 1909). Opera by Rimsky-Korsakof. Libretto by the composer, based on a play by L. A. Mei. (Prod. St. Petersburg 1873; London 1913.)

I've been roaming. See *Horn, C. E.*

Ives, (1) **Simon** (b. Ware 1600; d. London 1662). Organist, singing teacher, and composer of songs, catches, and instrumental music.

(2) **Charles** (b. Danbury, Conn., 1874; d. New York 1954). Combined business career with music; as composer walked alone, writing in many forms and using 'advanced' ideas (microtones, combined rhythms, &c.).

Ivogün, Maria—stage name derived from real name, Inge von Günther (b. Budapest 1891). Coloratura soprano, highly popular in Germany, Britain, and U.S.A.

I wrestle and pray. See *Bach* (6), *Johann Christoph*.

J

Jabo (Sp., in old Sp. *Xabo*). A solo dance in a slow 3-in-a-measure rhythm.

Jácara (Sp., in old Sp. *Xacara*). An old Sp. song-dance.

Jack. See *Harpsichord Family*.

Jackson, (1) **William** (b. Exeter 1730; there d. 1803). Known as 'Jackson of Exeter'. Became organist of cathedral there (1777), composed large quantities of church music (including simple but highly popular Te Deum in F), and operas for London theatres. Wrote books of essays; was also painter.

(2) **William** (b. Masham, Yorks., 1815; d. Ripon 1866). Known as 'Jackson of Masham'. Self-taught musician, organist, player of many instruments; tallow chandler by trade, but later settled in Bradford as music-seller, organist, choir trainer of high repute, &c. Composed a choral symphony, oratorios, glees, church music, &c.

Jacob, (1) **Benjamin** (b. London 1778; there d. 1829). Famous organist associated with Samuel Wesley in introduction of Bach's works.

(2) **Gordon** (b. Norwood, nr. London, 1895). After service in 1914–18 war entered R.C.M.; now a prof. there. Has composed concertos for various instruments, orch. works, chamber music, part-songs, &c., and written a manual of technique of orchestration. D.Mus., London. C.B.E. 1968.

(See reference under *Fille de Madame Angot*.)

Jacobi, (1) **George** (b. Berlin 1840; d. London 1906). Had career in Paris; then came to London as conductor of Alhambra Theatre, for which composed over 100 ballets.

(2) **Frederick** (b. San Francisco 1891; d. New York 1952). Studied in New York under Rubin Goldmark and in Berlin; then assistant conductor Metropolitan Opera House, New York; taught composition at Juilliard School; lived amongst Amer. Indians of New Mexico and Arizona, and composed works based on their melodies; also composed music for Jewish service, orch., chamber, and choral music, &c.

Jacobs, Arthur (David) (b. Manchester 1922). Educ. Oxford (M.A.). Mus. critic *Daily Express* 1947–52, *Evening Standard* 1956–8; libretto translator; books on opera, &c.

Jacobs-Bond, Carrie. See *Bond*.

Jacobson, Maurice (b. London 1896). Held composition scholarship at R.C.M., studying with Stanford and Holst. Has written incidental music for theatre, ballets, &c. Managing director of Curwen music publishing firm.

Jacopone da Todi. See *Stabat mater dolorosa*.

Jacques, Reginald (b. Ashby-de-la-Zouche 1894; d. London 1969). Educated Queen's Coll., Oxford, and became its organist and a Fellow (1933); conductor Oxford Harmonic Soc. (1923–30); Oxford Orchestral Soc. (1930–6); Bach Choir, London; on staff of R.C.M.; Musical Adviser to London County Council 1936–42; Director of Music to Council for Encouragement of Music and Arts 1940–5. Founded Jacques String Orch. in 1936. Books on school music; collections of songs, &c. Lecturer. C.B.E. 1954.

Jadassohn, Salomon (b. Breslau 1831; d. Leipzig 1902). Composer and theorist. On staff of Leipzig Conserv. (D.Ph., Leipzig Univ.). Many theoretical textbooks.

Jaell, (1) **Alfred** (b. Trieste 1832; d. Paris 1882). Fine pianist and popular piano composer. (Pupil of Moscheles, q.v.). (2) **Marie,** *née* **Trautmann** (b. Steinselz 1862; d. Paris 1925). Wife of Alfred above; also clever pianist; author of works on piano playing, &c.

Jagdhorn (Ger.). 'Hunting horn' (see *Horn Family*).

Jagdquartett (Mozart). See *Chasse*.

Jäger (Ger.). 'Hunter.'

Jahn, Otto (b. Kiel 1813; d. Göttingen 1869). Distinguished archaeologist and philological scholar; author of articles and books on various composers and especially of a standard life of Mozart (1856–9 and later edns. by various hands; English transl. 1883; cf. *Abert*).

Jahreszeiten (Haydn). See *Seasons*.

Jaleadas. The 'Seguidillas Jaleadas' (see *Seguidilla*) is a vigorous type, showing the influence of the cachucha (q.v.).

Jaleo (in old Sp., *Xaleo*). Spanish solo dance in a slow 3-in-a-measure time.

Jalousieschweller (Ger. 'Venetian-blind swell'). The organ Swell Pedal.

James, (1) Ivor (b. London 1882; d. 1963). Violoncellist. Trained at the R.C.M. (later on staff). Active in chamber music (Eng. String Quartet 1909; Menges Quartet 1931). C.B.E. 1953.

(2) **Philip** (b. Jersey City, N.J., 1890). Organist, bandmaster, theatrical conductor, orch. conductor; on music staff at Columbia Univ., then a prof. at New York Univ., &c. Has composed orch., chamber, choral, and organ works, &c.; much radio work.

(3) **William Garnet** (b. Ballarat 1895). Pianist. Trained Melbourne Conserv. and under de Greef. Appeared in London 1915 onwards. Composer of songs, &c. Federal Controller of Music, Australian Broadcasting Commission.

(4) **Philip Brutton** (b. 1901). Author of *Early Keyboard Instruments* (1930). On staff of Victoria and Albert Museum; then Director of Art to Arts Council (q.v.).

Jammernd; jämmerlich (Ger.). 'Lamenting'; 'lamentable'.

Jam Session. Informal performance of jazz musicians improvising collectively on well-known tunes.

Janáček, Leoš (b. Hukvaldy, or Hochwald, now in Czechoslovakia, 1854; d. Ostrau, or Ostrava, 1928). Choir-boy at Brno; at 16 became choir-master of monastery; then studied in Prague and Leipzig, and settled in Brno for rest of life, as conductor, teacher, student of folk-music, and composer of many operas of national character (see *Jenufa*), orchestral, chamber, and choral music, a folk-mass, &c.

Janes, Robert. See *Anglican Chant*.

Janiewicz (or Yaniewicz), Felix (b. Vilna 1762; d. Edinburgh 1848). Fine violinist, living in Italy, Paris, London, Liverpool, and Edinburgh. Composed concertos, trios for 2 violins and 'cello, &c. One of original founders of Philharmonic Soc., London.

Janissary Music, Janitscharenmusik (Ger.). The Turkish type o. military music at one time popular in the European armies. The Janissaries were the Sultan's bodyguard, disbanded, after revolt, in 1826.

Janko Keyboard. See *Keyboard*.

Jannequin, Clément (b. abt. 1475, possibly in Chatellerault; d. abt. 1560 in Paris). Pupil of Josquin des Prés. Early Fr. composer of choral music, remarkable for expression of 'programmatic' ideas (battle pieces, bird song pieces, &c.; cf. *Programme Music*); also composed church music and songs, &c.

Jansen, Jacques (b. Paris 1913). Baritone. Trained Paris Conserv. Has sung Paris Opéra and Opéra-Comique, also Covent Garden, Metropolitan, and Buenos Aires, &c. Notable Pelléas: recitalist (Ravel, &c.).

Janssen, (1) Herbert (b. Cologne, 1895; d. New York 1965). Operatic baritone of unusual gifts. German début 1924; also Vienna, Paris, Barcelona, Bayreuth (1930), Buenos Aires, and London (Covent Garden 14 seasons), &c. 1939–51 with Metropolitan Opera, New York.

(2) **Werner** (b. New York 1899). Conductor. Fellow Amer. Academy in Rome 1930. Guest conductor major European orchs. Début in U.S.A. with New York Philharmonic Orch. 1934; conductor Baltimore Orch. 1938–9; Utah Symphony Orch. 1946; Portland, Oreg., 1947–9; San Diego 1952–4. Some compositions.

Japanese Fiddle. A one-stringed instrument sometimes seen in the hands of Eng. street performers and the like. (See also *Stroh Violin*.)

Jaques-Dalcroze, Émile (b. Vienna 1865; d. Geneva 1950). Swiss by parentage. Trained at Conservs. of Vienna and Paris, then on staff of Conserv. of Geneva. Developed system of musical training through rhythmic movement ('Eurhythmics'); first centre for this Hellerau, nr. Dresden; then headquarters at Geneva with branches in many parts of world; author of books on the system; also popular composer of songs, stage works, &c.

Jarnach, Philipp (b. Noisy, France, 1892). Son of the Catalan sculptor and a Ger. mother. Trained chiefly in Paris; then on staff of Conserv. of Zürich (1914–21); after that in Berlin and Cologne. Has composed orch. and chamber music, songs, &c., often elaborately contrapuntal and influenced by music of his friend Busoni (whose posthumous opera *Doktor Faust*, q.v., was entrusted to him for completion). Books on modern music, &c.

Järnefelt (Edvard) Armas (b. Viipuri, or Viborg, Finland, 1869; d. Stockholm 1958). Student of Busoni and then of Massenet; held posts in Ger. opera houses, and then returned to native country, to which, as conductor, he introduced Wagner's works; afterwards conductor in Stockholm and Helsinki. Composed orch. and choral music, piano music, &c., often with a national tinge. (A 'Praeludium' for orch. very popular with wide public; 1st Brit. perf. London 1909.)

Jarred, Mary (b. Brotton, Yorkshire, 1899). Operatic contralto. Trained R.A.M. and R.C.M. Three years member of Hamburg Opera, then (1933) Covent Garden. Of repute as oratorio artist.

Jarvis, Charles. See *Pianoforte*.

Jazz. A type of music of Amer. Negro origin. Historians hesitatingly trace the roots of jazz to Colonial days, the ultimate source, via the Caribbean, being the native music of the African Negro slaves, blended with the simpler kind of mission hymns and the spontaneous work songs of the field hands and convict chain gangs. The usual starting-point for the modern history of jazz is in the licensed brothel district of late 19th-century New Orleans, where Negro musicians entertained the customers. These 'jazzmen' were largely musically illiterate improvisers, with a background of playing in street marching bands (the instruments often a relic of the Civil War). Thus there is no surviving evidence of their work. The earliest gramophone records of jazz seem to have been made about 1916: by the early 1920's the jazz craze replaced the era of Ragtime (q.v.). For some time records were made primarily for the Negro market; but their popularity spread, and eventually jazz was adopted into the world of mass entertainment. The subsequent history of jazz is one of successive waves of new styles, seized on by an inner circle of initiates and discarded on reaching wider popularity. Of late years, younger Negroes have rejected the more popular side of jazz as contributing to the 'Negro as entertainer' stereotype: hence a school of aloof, solemn players, many of them with a conservatory background.

From the earlier 1920's serious composers have adopted some of the superficial characteristics of jazz; in the later 1950's experimenters, often followers of the school of Webern, made serious attempts to write in a style compounded of jazz and Western European music, with results widely discussed but for the most part of limited appeal for the general audience.

See *Ragtime*; *Blues*.

Jazz stick. See *Percussion Family* 2 t.

Je (Ger.). 'Always', 'ever', 'each', &c. (a difficult word to translate exactly).

Jeanne d'Arc au bûcher. See *Joan of Arc at the Stake*.

Jeannie Deans. See *MacCunn*.

Jeans, Susi (b. Vienna 1911). Organist, harpsichordist, &c. Studied Vienna and Leipzig; specialist in early keyboard music. Widow of astrophysicist Sir James Jeans.

Jebb, John (b. Dublin 1805; d. Peterstow 1886). Anglican clergyman (D.D., Canon of Hereford). Author of important books on Cathedral Service (1841), Choral Responses, and Litanies (2 vols. 1847–57), &c.

Jedoch (Ger.). 'However', 'nevertheless', 'yet'.

Jeffrey, R. E. See *Community Singing*.

Jeffries, George (d. 1685). Gentleman of Chapel Royal of Charles I. Little is known of him except that he left quantities of church music, secular songs, string music, &c.

Její Pastorkyňa (Janáček). See *Jenufa*.

Jemnitz, Alexander (b. Budapest 1890; d. Balaton-füred 1963). Studied under Reger at Leipzig. After activities as theatre conductor in Germany settled in native city. Composer of piano and organ works, chamber music, songs, &c.—latterly in a somewhat Schönbergian idiom.

Jena Symphony. Name attached to a symphony discovered at Jena in 1910, and taken by some to be an early work of Beethoven.

Jenkins, (1) **John** (b. Maidstone 1592; d. Kimberley, Norfolk 1678). Voluminous and valued composer of fancies (q.v.) for viols, as also sonatas for 2 violins, string bass, and keyboard instrument; also virtuoso on lyra viol, &c.; one of royal musicians both before and after Commonwealth, but spent most of life in private service of noble families in Norfolk.

(2) **David** (b. Trecastle, Brecon, Wales, 1848; d. Aberystwyth 1915). Pupil of Joseph Parry (q.v.). B.Mus., Cambridge; Prof. of Music in Univ. Coll., Aberystwyth. Engaged in Eisteddfod activities and co-editor of journal *Y Cerddor* ('The Musician'). Composed operas, oratorios, church music, &c.

Jensen, (1) **Adolf** (b. Königsberg 1837; d. Baden-Baden 1879). Pupil of Liszt, Gade, &c.; notable song composer in Schumann vein; also effective piano composer. Lived in Russia and Denmark, and then in various Ger. cities.

(2) **Gustav** (b. Königsberg 1843; d. Cologne 1895). Brother of above and pupil of Joachim. Active composer of chamber music; well known as ed. of old string music.

(3) **Ludvig Irgens** (b. Norway 1894). Has composed songs often to own texts (sometimes amusing), opera, oratorio, orch. and chamber music, &c.

Jenufa (original, Czech. title, *Její Pastorkyňa*, 'Her Foster-daughter'). Famous Opera by Janáček. (Prod. Brno 1904; New York 1924.)

Jephtha. (1) Last Oratorio of HANDEL. Text by Morell. (1st perf. London 1752.) (2) Oratorio by CARISSIMI.

Jeppesen, Knud (b. Copenhagen 1892). Head of Conservatory of Copenhagen and Prof. of music in Univ. there. Important musicologist, specializing particularly in Palestrina and his period in It. music (*The Style of Palestrina and the Dissonance*, 1923; Eng. edn. 1927). Long ed. of *Acta Musicologica* of International Musicological Soc.

Jepson, Helen Possell (b. Titusville, Pa., 1906). Operatic soprano. Trained Curtis Inst. Operatic début Philadelphia 1928; New York (Metropolitan Opera) 1935.

Jeremiah. See *Owen, John*.

Jeremiah (Symphony). See *Bernstein, Leonard*.

Jeritza, Maria (b. Brno 1887). Operatic soprano. Trained Prague Conserv. Début Olmütz 1910; Vienna 1913; Metropolitan, New York, 1921; Covent Garden 1925. Famous in Wagner, Strauss, and Puccini roles, &c. Autobiography, *Sunlight and Song*, 1924.

Jerusalem. (1) The boldly idealistic song known by this name, which from the 1920's assumed almost the position of a secondary Brit. National Anthem, is a setting by Hubert Parry (q.v.) of words by the poet-painter William Blake (1757–1827). The setting, first performed in 1916, was made on the suggestion of Robert Bridges, the then poet-laureate. The words are not to be confused with Blake's longer poem 'Jerusalem'. (2) See *Pierson*.

Jessie, the Flower of Dunblane. The poem is by Robert Tannahill, of Paisley (1774–1810); the air is a Scottish folk tune.

Jessonda. Spohr's most popular Opera. (Prod. Cassel 1823; London 1840; Philadelphia 1864.)

Jesu, Joy of Man's Desiring. See *Wohl mir, dass ich Jesum habe*.

Jeu (Fr.; plur. *Jeux*). (1) 'Game', 'play', &c. (2) 'Stop' (organ), e.g. *Jeux d'anche*, 'Reed Stops'; *Jeux de fonds*, 'Foundation Stops' (see *Fonds d'Orgue*); *Grand jeu* or *Plein jeu*, 'Full Organ'.

Jeu de Cartes, Le ('The Game of Cards'). Ballet by Stravinsky. Also heard as Suite. (Prod. New York 1937.)

Jeu de Clochettes (Fr.). Glockenspiel (see *Percussion Family* 1 c).

Jeu de Timbres (Fr.). Same as *Jeu de Clochettes* (q.v.).

Jeune, Claude le, or **Claudin Lejeune** (b. Valenciennes, Spanish Flanders, 1528; d. Paris 1600). Famous composer of secular choral music—chansons (sometimes descriptive, cf. *Jannequin*); also, being Huguenot, set metrical psalms (cf. *Goudimel*).

Jeune France, La. Paris group of composers banded for mutual support and propaganda, formed 1936; members being Messiaen, Jolivet, Baudrier, and Lesur (see these names).

Jeunehomme Concerto. Mozart's Piano Concerto in E flat, K. 271. The name has become attached from the fact that it was composed for the pianist, Mlle Jeunehomme.

Jeunesse d'Hercule, La ('The Youth of Hercules'). Symphonic Poem of Saint-Saëns (op. 50; 1877). The youth chooses the way of struggle instead of the way of pleasure and is rewarded by the vision of immortality.

Jeu ordinaire (Fr.). Ordinary way of playing—countermanding some behest to play in an unusual way, such as (violin, &c.) *Sur la touche*, 'Near the fingerboard'.

Jeux. See *Jeu*.

Jeux. Ballet by Debussy—on a romance of the tennis court. (1st perf. Paris 1913.)

Jeux d'enfants ('Children's Games'). By Bizet. Suite of 12 pieces for piano duet, of which 5 were scored for orch. by the composer (*Petite suite*, 1873), and later used for a popular ballet.

Jewels of the Madonna (Wolf-Ferrari). See *Gioielli*.

Jewess, The (Halévy). See *Juive*.

Jewish Church. See *Church Music*.

Jew's Harp. One of the simplest and most widely distributed instruments, being found throughout Europe and Asia. It consists of a tiny iron frame, open at one end, in which end a single strip of metal vibrates. The frame is held between the teeth and the strip then twanged by the finger. The strip, in itself, is obviously capable of producing only one note, but the harmonics of this note become available by resonance, through various shapings of the cavity of the mouth. (Cf. *Acoustics* 19 and *Voice* 6 and 7.) Thus tunes can be played.

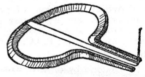

JEW'S HARP

The origin of the name 'Jew's Harp' (or 'Jew's Trump') is untraced. There seems to be no association with Jewry. The suggestion that it derives from 'Jaw's Harp' is a mere guess.

Jig. (1) A dance once popular in England, Scotland, and Ireland, in the last of which its popularity was of longest duration. For its general character and music see *Gigue*. (2) In the late 16th c. and the 17th, the term was applied to a lively song and dance item, of comic character, used to terminate theatrical performances.

Jig Fugue (Bach). See *Fuga alla giga*.

Jingles. See *Percussion Family* 2 m, *Sizzle Cymbal*.

Jingling Johnny. See *Turkish Crescent*.

Jinns (Franck). See *Djinns*.

Jirák, Karel Boleslav (b. Prague 1891). Studied with Novák and Foerster. Choral, orch., and opera conductor; prof. of composition at Prague Conserv.; then Roosevelt Coll., Chicago. Composer of opera, symphonies, chamber music, &c.

Joachim, Josef (b. Kitsee, nr. Pressburg, otherwise Pozsony, also Bratislava, 1831; d. Berlin 1907). He was of

Jewish descent. Studied Leipzig Conserv.—then under Mendelssohn's direction; at 13 visited Britain (where all his life he was to remain the greatest public favourite of all violinists). At 18 was leading violinist under Liszt at Weimar and for a time an adherent of the Liszt–Wagner 'Music of the Future' school; then (1860) reverted to Mendelssohn–Schumann–Brahms school. Taught in Berlin and there founded famous Joachim Quartet (1869). Compositions (now neglected) include 3 violin concertos and 5 overtures.

His wife was the celebrated contralto, Amelia Weiss.

Joan of Arc at the Stake. Musical mystery-play by Honegger; text by Claudel. (1935; 1st perf. Basle 1938; 40 stage perfs. in 1941; B.B.C. 1947.)

Joash. See *Silas.*

Job. (1) Oratorio by C. H. H. PARRY. (1st perf. Gloucester Fest. 1892.) (2) 'Masque for Dancing' by VAUGHAN WILLIAMS, based on Blake. (1st perf., concert form, Norwich 1930; staged London 1931.)

Jocelyn. Opera by Godard. (Prod. Brussels and Paris 1888.) Now remembered by a long-popular *Berceuse* which was added as an afterthought to please the tenor.

Jockey's Deliverance. See *Bonnie Dundee.*

Joculator. See *Minstrels* 1.

Jodelling. A type of joyous vocal expression common in Switzerland and the Tyrol, which employs an alternation of normal voice production with falsetto (see *Voice* 5).

John XXII, Pope. See *Church Music.*

John Anderson, My Jo. The poem of this song is by Burns, superseding several old poems, of various dates, which begin with the same words. The origin of the tune is disputable, there being several tunes that resemble it. ('Jo' means 'sweetheart'.)

John Brown's Body. The attribution of this song to Thomas Brigham Bishop, of Portland, Maine, is now considered to be without foundation. The tune appears to date from the late 1850's,

when it was composed for a convivial excursion at Charleston, S.C., and promptly taken up as a revivalist hymn. The words grew spontaneously amongst the men of a force occupying Fort Warren, Boston, in 1861, and refer chaffingly to a Sergeant John Brown of the regiment, the butt of many jokes connecting him with the then recently executed anti-slavery warrior of the same name. The song spread to other regiments and became universally popular, being published by Ditson in the same year.

The 'Battle Hymn of the Republic' was written by Julia Ward Howe to the same tune; the fine verse 'He is coming like the glory', not in the original, is of unknown authorship.

Johnny strikes up. See *Křenek.*

John of Fornsete (13th c.). Credited with composition of *Sumer is icumen in* (q.v.), on grounds of its being in his handwriting as keeper of records of Reading Abbey.

John Peel. Poem written by John Woodcock Graves (abt. 1820) to the old folk tune of *Bonnie Annie.* The hero of the song was a friend of the poet.

Johnson, (1) **Edward** (end of 16th c. and beginning of 17th). Composer of madrigals and virginal music.

(2) **Robert** (b. London abt. 1583; d. 1633). One of 'Musicians of the Lute' to James I and Charles I and of high reputation in his day.

(3) **Edward** (b. Guelph, Ontario, 1878; d. Toronto 1959). Operatic tenor and opera manager. Successful vocal career in Milan and other European centres and in Chicago and New York. General manager Metropolitan Opera, New York, 1935–50. C.B.E. 1935.

(4) **Horace** (b. Waltham, Mass., 1893; d. Tucson, Ariz., 1964). Musical journalist, &c., and composer of songs and orch. music of a picturesque character.

Jolie Fille de Perth, La ('The Fair Maid of Perth'). Opera by Bizet. Libretto based on Scott's novel. (Prod. Paris 1867; Manchester and London 1917.)

Jolivet, André (b. Paris 1905). Pupil of Varèse (q.v.) and Le Flem (q.v.).

His music is often for unusual combinations—3 baritones and orch., with Ondium Martenot (see *Electric Musical Instruments* 1), &c.

Jolly Roger. See *Leigh, W.*

Jommelli, Niccolò (b. nr. Naples 1714; d. in that city 1774). Famous opera composer of palmy days of It. opera; during 15 years residence in Germany adopted subtler Ger. style and on return to Italy was hissed, retired from profession, had an apoplectic stroke, and died.

Jonah. Oratorio by Berkeley. (1st perf. London 1936.)

Jonás, Alberto (b. Madrid 1868; d. Philadelphia 1943). Pianist. Trained conservs. of Madrid, Brussels, and St. Petersburg. Début Brussels 1880. Toured widely 1894–1904; director in turn of piano department Michigan Univ. School of Music and Michigan Conserv. After 10 years in Berlin settled U.S.A. again (New York, Philadelphia). Composer of piano music, &c., and author of didactic works on piano playing.

Jones, (1) Robert (end of 16th c. and beginning of 17th). Directed 'Children of the Revels of the Queen within Whytefryers', i.e. was authorized theatrical entrepreneur in days when choir-boy actors were appreciated. Composed madrigals and ayres with lute accompaniment.

(2) **Richard** (beginning of 18th c.). Leader of Drury Lane Theatre Orch. and composer of sonatas, suites, &c., for violin and harpsichord.

(3) **Edward** (b. Llanderfel, Merionethshire, 1752; d. London 1824). Famous performer on Welsh harp; publ. collection of Welsh airs, &c.

(4) **Sidney** (1861–1946). See *Geisha*.

(5) **Evlyn Howard** (b. London 1877; d. 1951). Pianist. Trained R.C.M. and in Germany under d'Albert; for a time an orch. conductor; well-known London recitalist and teacher of piano.

(6) **Parry** (b. Blaina, Monmouthshire, 1891; d. London 1963). Operatic and concert tenor. Had distinguished Covent Garden career, and appeared also at Metropolitan Opera House, New York, and in many parts of the continent of Europe, and elsewhere. O.B.E. 1962.

(7) **Trefor** (b. Cymmer, S. Wales, 1901; d. Montrose 1965). Tenor. Trained R.C.M. Successful career in oratorio and opera.

(8) **Hope.** See *Hope-Jones*.

(9) **Daniel** (b. Pembroke 1912). Composer. Educ. Univ. Coll., Swansea, (M.A.) and R.A.M. (Mendelssohn Scholarship, &c.). Symphonies, many tone-poems and numerous other orch. and chamber works, including sonata for 3 kettledrums unaccompanied.

(10) **Rev. Dr. Percy** (b. Geelong, Victoria, 1914). Trained Pontifical Inst. of Sacred Music, Rome, &c. School music inspector, Melbourne archdiocese, from 1940; choirmaster, St. Patrick's Cathedral, from 1942; Music Faculty, Melbourne Univ., &c. Books and articles on liturgy, education, &c. Ph.D., D.Mus.

(11) **Roderick** (b. Rhondda, Wales). Baritone vocalist. Trained R.A.M. Sometime vicar choral St. Paul's Cathedral. Sadler's Wells Opera Company 1945.

Jongen, (1) Joseph (b. Liège 1873; there d. 1953). Studied at Liège Conserv. and won Belgian Rome Prize; head of Brussels Conserv. 1920–39. Composed chamber, organ, orch., and piano music, songs, &c. (2) **Léon** (b. Liège 1884). Brother of above, and like him studied at Liège Conserv. and won Belgian Rome Prize. Has composed chiefly for stage, but also chamber music, piano pieces, songs, &c. Succeeded brother at Brussels Conserv. 1939.

Jongleur. See *Minstrels* 1.

Jongleur de Notre-Dame, Le. Called a Miracle Play. Opera of Massenet. (Prod. Monte Carlo 1902; Paris 1904; London 1906; New York 1908.)

Jonny spielt auf. See *Křenek*.

Jordá, Enrique (b. San Sebastian, Spain, 1911). Conductor. Studied Madrid and Paris Univs.; musical studies with le Flem (q.v.), and Dupré (q.v.). Conductor Basque Ballet and Madrid Symphony Orch.; 1948, Cape Town Orch.; 1954–63, San Francisco Orch.

Jordan, (1) **Jules** (b. Willimantic, Conn., 1850; d. Providence, R.I., 1927). Well-known vocalist and famous choral conductor (Arion Club, Providence, for 40 years). Composer of 300 songs, also an opera, church music, &c.

(2) **Arthur** (b. Dudley 1886). Tenor. Leading Wagner and other parts in Brit. National Opera Co.

(3) **Mrs.** (Actress; 1762–1816). See *Blue Bells of Scotland.*

Joseffy, Rafael (b. Hungary 1852; d. New York 1915). Pianist. Pupil of Tausig and Liszt. Soon won international reputation. Settled in New York 1879; playing of Brahms's works valuable in bringing them into popularity. Edited Chopin's works and published piano 'School', as also compositions and arrangements.

Joseph. (1) Oratorio by HANDEL. (Full title *Joseph and his Brethren.* 1st perf. London 1744.) (2) Chief opera of MÉHUL. (Prod. Paris 1807; occasionally perf. in Britain as oratorio, as an opera not before 1914; New York 1857.) (3) Oratorio by MACFARREN. (1st perf. Leeds Fest. 1877.)

Josephslegende. Ballet by Richard Strauss. (Prod. Paris and London, 1914.)

Joshua. Oratorio by Handel. Text by Morell. (1st perf. London 1748.)

Josquin des Prés (b. probably Condé, Hainault, abt. 1440; d. there 1521). Pupil of Ockeghem and one of most able contrapuntists of 15th c. Was in Rome, in service of Pope, 1486–94. Took orders and became Canon of Condé. Left many masses, motets, and secular songs (cf. *Chanson*). His work, long forgotten, was rediscovered by Burney.

Josten, Werner (b. Elberfeld 1885; d. New York 1963). In his early thirties settled in U.S.A.; joined staff of Smith Coll., Northampton (1923); there revived 17th- and 18th-c. operas, &c. Composer of orch. and chamber music, ballets, &c.

Jota, La. A dance of northern Spain, performed by one couple or more, accompanied by a guitar player, who also sings. The castanets are used (see *Percussion Family* 2 q). The time is a rapid 3-in-a-measure.

Joubert, John (b. Cape Town 1927). Composer. Trained R.A.M. On staff Univ. Coll., Hull (1951). Works include operas, concertos for piano and for violin, chamber music, &c.

Jouer (Fr.). 'To play.'

Joule, Benjamin St. John Baptist (b. Salford 1817; d. Rothsay 1895). Manchester organist and music critic. Authority on church music. (*Directorium Chori Anglicanum,* 1849 and many later edns., and other publications.)

Journals, Musical. See under *Criticism.*

Journet, Marcel (b. Grasse 1870; d. Vittel 1933). Operatic bass. Trained Paris Conserv. Début Brussels 1891. Became popular in opera houses of Europe and U.S.A. (Covent Garden début 1897; thenceforward many visits. Metropolitan Opera House, New York, 1901–8. Member of Chicago Opera Co. from 1914.)

Joyce, (1) **Patrick Weston** (b. Ballyorgan, co. Limerick, 1827; d. Dublin 1914). Great collector and ed. of Irish folk music; author also of books on Irish Social History, Irish Grammar, Irish Place Names, &c., and translator of Irish classic tales. Prof. in teachers' training college, and LL.D.

(2) **Eileen** (b. in a tent in Tasmania). Pianist, 'discovered' by Grainger (q.v.) and sent to Germany, where studied under Teichmüller; later in London with Matthay and Schnabel. Has played much in Britain and elsewhere and appeared in or recorded for many films.

Joyeux, joyeuse (Fr. masc., fem.). 'Joyous.'

Jubelnd (Ger.). 'Jubilant.'

Jubilate. The 100th Psalm, 'O be joyful in the Lord, all ye lands' (see *Common Prayer*).

Jubili. See *Pneuma.*

Judas Maccabaeus. Oratorio by Handel. Text by Morell. (1st perf. London 1747.)

Judder. See *Tremolo.*

Judenharfe (Ger.). 'Jew's Harp' (q.v.).

Judge, Jack. See *Tipperary.*

Judges of the Secret Court (Berlioz). See *Francs Juges*.

Judith. (1) Oratorio by C. H. H. PARRY. (1st perf. Birmingham Fest. 1888.) (2) Oratorios by ARNE (1761) and others. (3–5) Operas by SEROV (1st perf. St. Petersburg 1863); HONEGGER (Mézières, Switzerland, 1925); and GOOSSENS (London 1929).

Judson, Arthur (b. Dayton, Ohio, 1881). Held position Denison Univ., Ohio (Hon. D.Mus.). Then successively on staff of *Musical America*, Manager of Philadelphia Orch., and in charge of own concert agency, &c.

Juggler. See *Minstrels* 1.

Juhan, James. See *Pianoforte*.

Juilliard School of Music. See *Schools of Music*.

Juive, La ('The Jewess'). Famous Opera by Halévy. Libretto by Scribe. (Prod. Paris 1835; New Orleans 1844; New York 1845; London 1846.)

Juke boxes. Automatic coin machines for playing gramophone records, orig. installed in Amer. inns, &c. In 1945 there were said to be a quarter of a million of them. ('Juke' = 'jouke', local inns in Southern states being called 'jouke joints'; cf. Chaucerian Eng. *Jowken*, 'to rest or sleep'.)

Julia. See *Quilter*.

Julian, John (b. St. Agnes, Cornwall, 1839; d. Thirsk 1913). Vicar of Topcliffe, Yorks.; canon of York Minster; D.D. Author of the very comprehensive and reliable *Dictionary of Hym-*nology (1st edn. 1892) and some smaller works.

Julius Caesar. See *Giulio Cesare*.

Jullien, or Julien, Louis Antoine[1] (b. Sisteron 1812; d. Paris 1860). Composer and conductor of dance music and highly popular conductor of orch. music and opera. In London 1838–59; there founded Promenade Concerts (see *Concert*), at which exhibited supreme showmanship; returned to Paris, was imprisoned for debt and finally placed in asylum for the insane where soon died.

Jumping Frog of Calaveras County, The. 1-act opera by Lukas Foss, after Mark Twain. (Prod. Bloomington 1950.)

Jungfernquartette (Haydn). See *Russischen Quartette*.

Jupiter Symphony. Mozart's Symphony in C, K. 551 (1788). The nickname seems to have been first attached in a London Philharmonic Soc.'s programme in 1821.

Jürg Jenatsch. See *Kaminski*.

Jurinac, (Srebenka) Sena (b. Travnik, Yugoslavia, 1921). Soprano. Trained Zagreb. Has appeared Vienna State Opera, Salzburg, Glyndebourne, Edinburgh, &c. Also Lieder recitals. Married Sesto Bruscantini.

Jusqu'à (Fr.). 'Until.'

Juste (Fr.). 'Just', in sense of exact (e.g. in time or tune). So *justesse*, 'exactitude'.

Just intonation. See *Temperament*.

---

[1] The author of this book finds himself tempted by a blank space remaining on this page to set out Jullien's full name in all its grandeur:

Louis George Maurice Adolph Roch Albert Abel Antonio Alexandre Noé Jean Lucien Daniel Eugène Joseph-le-brun Joseph-Barème Thomas Thomas Thomas-Thomas Pierre Cerbon Pierre-Maurel Barthelemi Artus Alphonse Bertrand Dieudonné Emanuel Josué Vincent Luc Michel Jules-de-la-plane Jules-Bazin Julio César Jullien.

The sponsers at his baptism were the 36 members of the local Philharmonic Society, each of whom contributed a name to the above imposing array.

K

K. (followed by a numeral). See under *Köchel*.

Kabalevsky, Dmitri (b. St. Petersburg 1904). Pupil of Miaskovsky and hence member of Moscow group. Has written operas and symphonies (the 3rd one, *Requiem*, employing chorus).

Kaffeecantate (Bach). See *Coffee Cantata*.

Kaffir Piano. See *Marimba*.

Kahn, Otto H. (b. Mannheim, 1867; d. New York 1934). Ger. patron of Amer. musical enterprises (e.g. Metropolitan Opera, New York).

Kaisermarsch. By Wagner. (1st perf. Berlin 1871.) Flamboyant musical celebration of the victory over the French in 1870 and the election of William of Prussia as Ger. Emperor. The chorale *Ein' feste Burg* (q.v.) piously supplies some of the material.

Kaiserquartett. See *Emperor's Hymn*.

Kajanus, Robert (b. Helsingfors, Finland, 1856; there d. 1933). Orch. conductor. Pupil of Svendsen and others. Founded orch. and choir in native city. Friend of Sibelius and specialized in conducting and recording his music; composed symphonic poems, &c.

Kalevala. See *Sibelius*.

Kalinnikof (Kalinikov, &c.**), Vassily Sergeievich** (b. govt. of Orel, Russia, 1866; d. Yalta 1901). For a time opera conductor; youth of poverty had sown seeds of consumption so retired, devoting himself to composition; 1st symphony made name well known, 2nd one later; also symphonic poems, chamber music, songs, &c.

Kalisch, Alfred (b. London 1863; there d. 1933). Prominent and much respected London music critic; early supporter of Strauss and translator of his libretti.

Kalkbrenner, Friedrich Wilhelm (b. somewhere on a journey from Cassel to Berlin 1785—not 1788, as generally stated; d. Deuil, Seine-et-Oise, 1849). Highly renowned pianist and piano teacher. Composed piano concertos, études, &c., also chamber music, &c. Wrote famous piano 'Method'.

Kalliwoda, Johannes Wenceslaus (b. Prague 1801; d. Carlsruhe 1866). Violin virtuoso; over 30 years Kapellmeister at court of Donaueschingen. Composed 7 symphonies, &c., once much played.

Kamaran Trio. See *Hayward, M.*

Kamarinskaya. Orch. Fantasia by Glinka (1848). Composed in Warsaw; the name is that of a Russian dance. As now performed the music embodies revision by Rimsky-Korsakof and Glazounof.

Kaminski, Heinrich (b. nr. Waldshut, Black Forest, 1886; d. nr. Munich 1946). Conductor and composer—latter in a very polyphonic style. Wrote opera *Jürg Jenatsch*, orch., chamber, and choral works.

Kammer (Ger.). 'Chamber.' So *Kammercantate*, 'Chamber Cantata' (see *Cantata*); *Kammerduett, Kammertrio*, 'Chamber Duet', 'Chamber Trio' (i.e. one for a room rather than a concert hall); *Kammerconcert, Kammerkonzert*, either 'Chamber Concert', or 'Chamber Concerto'; *Kammermusik*, 'Chamber Music'; *Kammersymphonie*, 'Chamber Symphony' (i.e. one for a small orch.).

Kanon (Ger.). 'Canon.' For *Kanon in der Umkehrung* see *Umkehrung*.

Kantele. Finnish variety of the Gusli (q.v.), plucked with the fingers.

Kapelle (Ger.). Lit. 'chapel': a term at one period applied to the whole staff of clergy, musicians, &c., attached to a royal chapel or the like. In time it came to be used for any organized body of musicians employed at court, &c., and from this it, in time, became (what it is today) a designation for any orch. body, from symphony orch. to dance band.

Kapellmeister, or **Capellmeister** (Ger.). The director or conductor of a *Kapelle* (q.v.). So **Kapellmeistermusik** is a derogatory term applied to music of the mere composed-to-order quality.

Karajan, Herbert von (b. Salzburg 1908). Conductor. Pursued studies as engineer and musician simultaneously in Vienna. Early career as conductor at Ulm (1928) and Aix-la-Chapelle (1934). Reputation founded before 1939 in Germany, Scandinavia, and Low Countries, after the war becoming international. (Berlin Opera 1941, Berlin Philharmonic 1954; Vienna Opera 1956–64.)

Karelia. Orch. Overture and Suite by Sibelius (opp. 10 and 11; 1893). In Karelia, in the south of Finland, are best preserved the national legendary song-poems (runes), and there the composer spent his honeymoon the year before composing this work.

Karg-Elert, Sigfrid (b. Oberndorf-am-Neckar 1877; d. Leipzig 1933). Pianist, organist, harmoniumist, and composer of music for his instruments, for string instruments, and for voices. Organ music especially valued by his admirers.

Karsavina. See *Ballet.*

Kaschey the Immortal. Opera by Rimsky-Korsakof. (Prod. Moscow 1902; London, concert-form, 1933.)

Kash, Eugene, otherwise Jack (b. Toronto 1912). Violinist and conductor. Studied Curtis Institute, Philadelphia; then Prague and Vienna. Tours of Europe as violinist. Music director, Canadian Natl. Film Board 1942–50; founded children's concerts, Ottawa 1946; conductor, Ottawa Philharmonic Orch. 1950. Special interests, modern and folk music.

Kastagnetten (Ger.). 'Castanets' (see *Percussion Family* 2 q).

Kastalsky (Kastalski, &c.), **Alexander** (b. Moscow 1856; there d. 1926). Pupil at Moscow Conserv. of Tchaikovsky and Taneief. Became authority on and composer of music for Russian Church, some of works being monumental and grandiose. Compositions include 80 sacred choruses, an oratorio, an opera, &c.

Kastner, Alfred (b. Vienna 1870; d Hollywood, Calif., 1948). Harpist Trained Vienna Conserv. Held positions in Dresden, Warsaw, Budapest, Leipzig, London (Queen's Hall Orch. 1904–19; on staff R.A.M. and G.S.M.), and Los Angeles. Compositions and studies for harp.

Kate o' Gowrie. See *Lass o' Gowrie.*

Kate, the Cabin boy. See *Williams, J. Gerrard.*

Kathleen Mavourneen. The words are by an Irishwoman, Mrs. Julia Crawford, the tune by the Englishman, F. N. Crouch (q.v.), who used to sing it himself with great success.

Katims, Milton (b. New York 1909). Violist and conductor. Studied Columbia Univ. Active with radio orchs. in New York; from 1954 conductor of Seattle Symphony Orch.

Katuar. See *Catoire.*

Katzenmusik. See *Charivari.*

Kaum (Ger.). 'Barely.'

Kay, Ulysses (Simpson) (b. Tucson, Ariz., 1917). Educ. univs. of Arizona, Rochester, Yale, Columbia. Numerous grants and awards. Composer of orchestral and chamber works, music for films, &c. Music adviser to Broadcast Music Inc. (q.v.).

Kazoo. See *Mirliton.*

Kb. Short for *Kontrabass,* i.e. 'double-bass'.

K.B.E. See *British Empire, Order of the.*

Keck (Ger.). 'Audacious.' So *Keckheit,* 'audacity'.

Keel Row (*Keel* means 'Boat'). This song is closely associated with the district of Newcastle and Tyneside generally, though its 1st appearance in print seems to be in an Edinburgh publication (*A Collection of favourite Scots Tunes;* about 1770). There is thus a contention as to its origin. The tune resembles several Eng. country dances, including one printed in a *Choice Collection* of 1748.

Keen. See *Caoine.*

Keep the home fires burning. This song, popular with Brit. and Amer. soldiers and civilians during the First

World War, is, as to the music, the work of the actor-playwright-film-wright-composer Ivor Novello (1893–1951). The verses are, in the main, the work of an Amer. lady in London, Mrs. Lena Guilbert Ford, to whom the composer supplied the tune with the first line of the words, leaving her to do the rest.

Keineswegs (Ger.). 'In no way.'

Keiser, Reinhard (b. nr. Leipzig 1674; d. Hamburg 1739). For 45 years associated with the Hamburg opera, composing nearly 120 operas, and establishing a Ger. style and tradition; also composed oratorios; remarkable settings of Passion, &c.

Keith Prowse & Co. Ltd. London music publishers, &c.; founded before 1835 (159 New Bond St., W. 1).

Kéler-Béla, originally Albert von Keller (b. Bartfeld, or Bardiov, then in Hungary, 1820; d. Wiesbaden 1882). Famous waltz conductor, successor of Gung'l in Berlin (1854) and Lanner in Vienna (1855); finally settled in Wiesbaden (1870) as military bandmaster and orch. conductor. Composed brilliant music of lighter order.

Kell, Reginald (b. York 1906). Clarinettist. Trained R.C.M. Principal clarinettist in many leading orchs. On staff of R.A.M. (1936). Later resident U.S.A.

Keller, Hans (b. Vienna 1919). Writer on music. Penetrating and often controversial contributor to many journals. On staff B.B.C. from 1959.

Kelley, Edgar Stillman (b. Sparta, Wis., 1857; d. New York 1944). Teacher and author; composer of symphonies, chamber music, &c.

Kellogg, Clara Louise (b. Sumterville, S. Carolina, 1842; d. New Hartford, Conn., 1916). Operatic and concert soprano. Highly popular in London and New York. Married Moritz Strakosch.

Kelly, Michael (b. Dublin 1762; d. Margate 1826). Tenor vocalist and as such took part in 1st perf. of the *Figaro* of his friend Mozart. Composed theatre music and wrote book of *Reminiscences*.

Kelway, (1) **Thomas** (b. probably Chichester; there d. 1749). Chorister and then organist of Chichester Cathedral. Composed church music, some being still in use. (2) **Joseph** (d. probably 1782). Brother of above. Noted organist, whose extemporizations were admired by Handel; also of high repute as harpsichordist. Composed harpsichord sonatas, &c.

Kemble, Adelaide—Mrs. Sartoris (b. London 1814; d. 1879). Operatic and concert soprano. Daughter of the actor Charles Kemble. Début London 1835. Then in Italy; pupil of Pasta (q.v.), &c. Made many brilliant appearances there; then won fame in England (Covent Garden début 1841) and Germany. Retired 1842, on marriage. Several literary works.

Kempe, Rudolf (b. nr. Dresden 1910). Conductor; trained Dresden; in Leipzig 1929–49; Mus. Dir., State Opera, Dresden, 1949; many international appearances; Royal Philharmonic Orch. 1960.

Kempff, Wilhelm (b. Berlin 1895). Pianist. Trained Potsdam and Berlin. Virtuoso career; dir. Hochschule für Musik, Stuttgart, 1924–32.

Kenilworth. (1) Cantata by Sullivan. Text by Chorley. (1st perf. Birmingham Fest. 1864.) (2) See *Klein*.

Kennedy, (1) **David** (b. Perth 1825; d. Stratford, Ontario, 1886). Tenor. For some time precentor in Edinburgh Presbyterian church. Developed as singer of Scots songs and lived life of travel wherever in world Scotsmen are to be found, winning enormous popularity. Most of children became musicians (see *Kennedy-Fraser*).
(2) **Douglas Neil** (b. Edinburgh 1893. Grandson of (1) above, and nephew of Marjory Kennedy-Fraser, q.v.). For some years botanist on staff Imperial Coll. of Science. Then succeeded Cecil Sharp as Organizing Director Eng. Folk Dance Soc. O.B.E.
(3) **Lauri** (b. Sydney, 1898). 'Cellist. Début New York 1920, London 1921. Solo principal, B.B.C., London Phil. and Covent Garden Orchs., &c., 1929–37. Many world tours; resident Australia.

Kennedy-Fraser, Marjory (b. Perth 1857; d. Edinburgh 1930). Daughter of David Kennedy; in youth travelled with him and his family all over Brit. Empire and U.S.A. Made collection, arrangement, and publication of songs of Hebrides her life-work.

Kent, James (b. Winchester 1700; there d. 1776). Organist of Trinity Coll., Cambridge, and then of Winchester Cathedral and Coll. Composed church music still performed (sometimes incorporating, without acknowledgement, long passages from It. composers).

Kentner, Louis (b. Silesia 1905). Hungarian concert pianist. Studied at Budapest Conserv. As youth began recital travels and won high reputation; settled in England 1935. Some piano compositions.

Keraulophon (Gr., 'horn-pipe-voice'). Organ stop, sort of *Salicional* (q.v.), now rarely found.

Kerll (or Kerl), Johann Kaspar (b. Adorf, Saxony, 1627; d. Munich 1693). Studied in Italy, probably under Frescobaldi, and became noted organist and composer of organ works, masses, operas, &c.; Kapellmeister at Munich (1656–74); then organist of Cathedral of Vienna (1677–84); and finally returned to Munich. Influenced Handel, who 'borrowed' one of his canzonas, using it as chorus 'Israel was glad' in *Israel in Egypt*.

Kern, Jerome David (b. New York 1885; there d. 1945). Composer of many highly popular musical comedies (e.g. *Showboat* 1928) and of film music.

Kes, Willem (b. Dordrecht 1856; d. Munich 1934). Violinist and conductor. Trained Leipzig Conserv. and under Wieniawski and Joachim. Chief violin several leading Dutch orchs.; then conductor (including Amsterdam Concertgebouw 1888). Glasgow (1896), Moscow, &c. Composed orch. music, &c.

Ketèlbey, Albert W. (b. Birmingham 1875; d. I.O.W. 1959). Trained T.C.L. Theatre conductor and then composer of much highly popular orch. music (*In a Monastery Garden*, &c.).

Kettledrum. See *Percussion Family* 1 a.

Kettledrum Mass (Haydn). See *Paukenmesse*.

Keussler, Gerhard von (b. Schwanenberg 1874; d. nr. Dresden 1949). Trained under Julius Klengel as violoncellist. Then took Ph.D. Leipzig Univ. Conductor at Prague (1906); then Hamburg, &c. In Melbourne, 1931–7. Composed operas, oratorios, symphonies, &c., and publ. musicological monographs.

Key, as a principle in musical composition, implies adherence, in any passage, to the note-material of one of the major or minor scales (see *Scale*)—not necessarily a rigid adherence (since other notes may incidentally appear), but a general adherence, with a recognition of the Tonic (or 'key-note') of the scale in question as a principal and governing factor in its effect. Thus we speak of a passage as being 'in the key of' (say) C major or F minor, and also use the same terms to describe a composition (or movement) as a whole—in this latter case implying merely that the key mentioned is the one in which the piece begins and ends and is its governing one (cf. *Modulation*). If a piece of several movements is so spoken of it does not necessarily mean more than that the 1st movement (usually also the last one) is in that key.

It will be realized that all major keys are exactly alike, as are all minor keys, so that the particular key chosen for a composition is more a matter of the pitch-level desired than of anything more important (cf. *Transposition*).

The element of key crept into European music in the early 17th c., as the Modes (q.v.) gradually fell out of use: it remained of supreme importance to the end of the 19th c., but since then has shown clear signs of weakening influence. (See 'Polytonality' and 'Atonality'; s.v. *Harmony* 3.)

See also *Diatonic*; *Colour and Music*; *Form*; *Tonic Sol-fa*; *Suite*; Table 8.

Keyboard. The purpose of keyboards is to enable the 2 hands (e.g. on pianoforte or harmonium) or the 2 hands and 2 feet (organ) readily to control the sounds from a much larger number of strings, reeds, or pipes than could otherwise be controlled. One standardized apparatus of this sort, which has been gradually developed over a long period, has come to be universally adopted: it is by no means the most convenient imaginable, but the conservatism of musicians will probably prevent its supersession unless some drastic change in the scales used in music (e.g. by the general adoption of Microtones, q.v.) makes such a change imperative.

The earliest keyboard was, apparently, that of the organ, in the days when merely the melodic plainsong of the Church was played on that instrument, at first thumped out on keys as broad as the fists that operated them. In those days, and for long after the keys had been adapted for pressure by the fingers, music was still modal (see *Modes*), and at first the longer finger-keys, as we still have them, were all that were needed. With the coming into use of the practice of *musica ficta* (q.v.) a B flat was found to be desirable and space for it was made by placing a short finger-key between the A and the B natural. (It appears that a few keyboards like this still existed as late as the beginning of the 17th c.) Other finger-keys were similarly added, and our present-day keyboard of 7 different long and broad keys and 5 short and narrow ones so came into existence. This still leaves out many notes (e.g. B sharp, if required, has to be played as C, F flat as E, and so on). The restricted number of keys which the individual can manipulate, and the necessity of avoiding the high cost of providing a large number of extra organ pipes, strings, &c., precluded the provision of further finger-keys, and the difficulty was overcome by methods of tuning at first, partially, with Meantone tuning and then, fully, with Equal Temperament tuning (see *Temperament*). There have been a good many attempts at the invention of a keyboard which would be free (or largely free) from this principle of compromise, but whilst some of them have been interesting scientifically they have none of them proved of value practically in the making of music.

Ingenious invention has also taken other roads:

The B. J. MANGEOT dual-keyboard instrument (1878) had one of its manuals designed for the right hand and the other for the left, the one ascending the scale and the other descending it, so redressing the inconvenience arising from Nature's mistake in symmetrically placing the thumb at the left of the right hand and the right of the left hand.

The JANKO KEYBOARD (1882) had 6 manuals, each of them giving a whole-tone series of notes: the finger-keys of each keyboard, though coloured white and black, were all on one level and the keyboards were so arranged that the hands could wander easily over the whole 6 of them, as they do today over the rows of keys on a typewriter. The span of the 8ve was much reduced and large chords were easy. Transposition was so simple that any composition could be equally readily played in any key. Praised by Liszt, Rubinstein, &c.

The CLUTSAM KEYBOARD was the normal one except that it was curved in 2 planes, so taking account of the fact that the arms move in arcs, both horizontally and perpendicularly considered.

The EMANUEL MOÓR Duplex-coupler piano (1921) has 2 manuals, the upper one tuned an 8ve higher than the lower; these are so placed that the hand can easily pass from one to the other, or even play on both together; thus scales in 10ths are played as scales in 3rds are on the normal instrument; moreover, the 2 manuals can be instantly coupled, so that scales in 8ves can be played as scales in single notes.

These are but a few of the attempts that have been made at improvement of the keyboard, and the world has certainly not seen the end of experiment in this field.

See also *Fingering*; *Short Octave and Broken Octave*.

Keyboard of Light. See *Prometheus— the Poem of Fire*.

Key Bugle or **Keyed Bugle.** See *Cornett and Key Bugle Families*.

Keyed Horn. See *Cornett and Key Bugle Families*.

Key-note. The principal (and lowest) note of the scale out of which a passage is constructed. Same as *Tonic*.

Keys, Ivor (Christopher Benfield) (b. Littlehampton 1919). Educ. Oxford and R.C.M. Organist, composer, and teacher. Taught at Queen's Univ., Belfast, from 1947; professor of music Nottingham Univ. 1954; Birmingham 1968. Composer of choral music, &c.; critical writings.

Key Signature. See *Signature*; also Table 8.

Khamma. Egyptian Ballet by Debussy, but orchestrated by Koechlin. Commissioned by Maud Allen. (1st perf., concert form, Paris 1924.)

Khatchaturian, Aram (b. Tiflis, Armenia, 1903). Studied at Moscow Conserv. and began to compose, using Caucasian folk music idioms and pouring out works in many forms. In 1939 received Order of Lenin; in 1943 name inscribed on marble tablet in hall of Conserv.; in 1948 officially and publicly reproved (with Prokofief and Shostakovich) for 'vicious, anti-popular, and formalist trends and bourgeois ideology'.

Khovantschina ('The Khovanskys'— a 17th-c. princely family). Posthumous opera by Mussorgsky. Libretto by composer. Completed by Rimsky-Korsakof. (Prod. St. Petersburg 1886; London 1913; Philadelphia 1928; New York 1931.)

Kidson, Frank (b. Leeds 1855; there d. 1926). Authority on old Leeds Pottery and known throughout the country as the owner of an unrivalled collection of scarce old music, song books, ballads, ballad operas, &c., and as one of the little group of pioneers in the scientific collection of Eng. folk song and its publication; one of the founders of the Eng. Folk Song Soc. (cf. *Broadwood, Lucy*). His *British Music Publishers . . . from Queen Elizabeth's Reign to George the Fourth's* remains indispensable to the student of Brit. musical history wishing to trace the date of any publication of that period.

Kielflügel (Ger.). Harpsichord (*Kiel* = 'quill'; *Flügel* = 'wing'. Alluding to the plucking medium and the general shape of the instrument).

Kienzl, Wilhelm (b. Waizenkirchen, Austria, 1857; d. Vienna 1941). Studied at Conserv. of Prague and then under Rheinberger at Munich; encouraged by Liszt and associated with Wagner. Composed very popular operas *Der Evangelimann* (see *Evangelimann*) and *Der Kuhreigen* (see *Kuhreigen*).

Kiepura, Jan (b. Sosnowiec, Poland, 1902; d. Harrison, N.Y., 1966). Operatic and concert tenor. Début Warsaw 1925; also films.

Kierkegaard, Søren Aabye (1813–55). Danish Christian philosopher. His book *Either/Or* includes whimsical but psychologically profound essay with theme that since music's function is to express (rather than describe or portray) it can, best of all arts, express amatory emotion. Mozart's operas (especially *Don Giovanni*) considered to be supreme example of this.

Kikimora. By Liadof. 'Legend for Orchestra' (op. 63, publ. 1910). The title means 'Beguiling Witch'.

Kilpinen, Yrjö (b. Helsinki, otherwise Helsingfors, 1892; d. there 1959). Studied Berlin and Vienna and then taught in Conserv. of native city; pensioned by Finnish Government so that he might devote himself to composition; became notable composer of over 800 songs, also piano sonatas, &c.

Kind; Kinder (Ger. sing. and plur.). 'Child'; 'children'.

Kinderscenen ('Scenes of Childhood'). By Schumann. Thirteen short piano pieces (op. 15; 1838).

Kinderstücke (Mendelssohn). See *Christmas Pieces*.

Kindersymphonie. See *Toy Symphony*.

Kindertotenlieder ('Children's Death Songs'). By Mahler. Five song settings (1902), with orch. or piano, of poems by Rückert; posthumously published.

Kindler, Hans (b. Rotterdam 1892; d. Rhode Island 1949). Violoncellist and conductor. Internationally prominent in 1st capacity from 1912; settled U.S.A. 1914. In 2nd capacity from 1927; founded National Symph. Orch., Washington, D.C., 1931; resigned 1948.

Kindlich (Ger.). 'Childlike.'

King, (1) William (b. Winchester 1624; d. Oxford 1680). Graduate and then chaplain (1652) of Magdalen Coll., Oxford, Fellow of All Souls (1654), and finally organist of New Coll. (1664). Composed church music and songs.

(2) **Robert** (late 17th c. and early 18th). Composer, concert organizer, member of royal band. B.Mus., Cambridge, 1696. Composed many songs and some choral music.

(3) **Charles** (b. Bury St. Edmunds 1687; d. London 1748). Master of Choristers of St. Paul's Cathedral; dull composer of church music, some still in use. B.Mus., Oxford.

(4) **Frederick** (b. Lichfield 1853; d. London 1933). Baritone. Studied National Training School of Music (cf. R.C.M.). London début 1878. High reputation in oratorio. Over 40 years on staff of R.A.M. training very many leading Brit. singers.

(5) **Alexander Hyatt** (b. Beckenham 1911). Educ. Cambridge. On staff Brit. Museum 1934; in charge of its Printed Music Collection 1945. Sec. (1948) Council Union Catalogue of Old Music. Books and articles on bibliographical and musicological subjects. Contributor to *Neues Mozart Jahrbuch*, &c.

King and Collier. See *Dvořák.*

King Arthur or **The British Worthy** (Purcell). Incidental music to Dryden's play (1691)—not properly an 'Opera'.

King David ('Le Roi David'). Oratorio by Honegger. (1st perf., as a play, Mézières, Switzerland, 1921; as Oratorio, New York 1925 and London 1927.)

Kingdom, The. Oratorio by Elgar. (1st perf. Birmingham Fest. 1906. New York 1907.)

King Enzio. Early overture by Wagner (1832) for drama by Raupach.

King James's March to Ireland. See *Lochaber no more.*

King Lear (1). Early Concert-overture by BERLIOZ (op. 4; 1832). (2) Overture and Incidental Music to Shakespeare's play by BALAKIREF (1859–61). (3) Incidental Music (2 movements) by DEBUSSY (1904).

King Olaf. Cantata by Elgar. (1st perf. N. Staffs. Fest. 1896.)

King Pest. Rondo from Lambert's *Summer's Last Will* (q.v.).

King Priam. Opera by Tippett; text by composer. (Prod. Covent Garden 1962.)

King Saul. Oratorio by C. H. H. Parry. (1st perf. Birmingham Fest. 1894.)

King's Children (Humperdinck). See *Königskinder.*

King's Concert. See *Ancient Concert.*

King's Henchman, The. Opera by Deems Taylor. (Prod. New York 1927.)

King's Musick. See *Chapel Royal.*

King Stephen Overture. Composed by Beethoven (op. 117) for the production of a Prologue by Kotzebue, on the subject of King Stephen, 'Hungary's First Benefactor', written for the opening evening of the Ger. Theatre in Budapest in 1812. (Cf. *Ruins of Athens.*)

Kingston, Morgan (b. Wednesbury, Staffs., 1881; d. 1936). Operatic and concert tenor, successful Covent Garden and Metropolitan Opera 1917 onwards.

Kinkeldey, Otto (b. New York 1878). Trained in music at Columbia Univ. under MacDowell, at Univ. of Berlin (Ph.D.), &c.; held professorial post Univ. of Breslau (1910–14); then chief music librarian New York Public Library (1915–23 and 1927–30); Prof. of Music Cornell Univ. (1923–7; of Musicology 1930–46) and Librarian there 1930–46. Visiting lecturer, Harvard. D.Litt., Princeton, 1947. Author of many important papers on musicological subjects and a leader in the work of the Amer. Musicological Soc.

Kipnis, Alexander (b. Ukraine 1896). Opera and concert bass of high international reputation: fine Lieder interpreter. U.S.A. citizen (1934).

Kirby, Percival Robson (b. Aberdeen 1887). Prof. of Music in Univ. of Witwatersrand, Johannesburg, 1921–49 (M.A., D.Litt.). Author of *The Musical Instruments of the Natives of South Africa* (1934) and *The Kettledrums* (1930).

Kirbye, George (d. Bury St. Edmunds 1634). Seems to have been domestic musician in a family of his native place. Composed madrigals, &c.

Kirche (Ger.). 'Church'.

Kirchencantate (Ger.). 'Church Cantata.'

Kirchner, (1) **Theodor** (b. Neukirchen, Saxony, 1823; d. Hamburg 1903). Protégé and friend of Mendelssohn and Schumann, and composer of songs, piano pieces, chamber music, &c.

(2) **Leon** (b. Brooklyn, N.Y., 1919). Composer, pupil of Schönberg and Sessions. On staff Univ. California 1946; Univ. S. Calif. 1954; Univ. Buffalo 1959; Harvard 1961. Works include a piano concerto, songs, and chamber music.

Kirkby Lunn. See *Lunn.*

Kirkpatrick, Ralph (b. Leominster, Mass., 1911). Harpsichord and clavichord player, lecturer, and author. Studied Harvard Univ. (B.A.), now on staff of Yale University. Publ. edn. of Bach's Goldberg Variations; biography Domenico Scarlatti, &c.

Kirnberger, Johann Philipp (b. Saalfeld, Thuringia, 1721; d. Berlin 1783). Pupil of Bach; violinist and minor composer; author of many important theoretical works.

Kiss, The. See *Arditi.*

Kissentanz (Ger.). 'Cushion Dance' (q.v.).

Kit. Pocket fiddle used by dancing masters in the 18th and early 19th cs.

Kitej, The Tale of the Invisible City of, and the Maiden Fevronia. Opera by Rimsky-Korsakof. (Prod. St. Petersburg 1907; London, concert form, 1926; Ann Arbor, Mich., concert form, 1932; Philadelphia and New York, staged, 1936.)

Kitson, Charles Herbert (b. Leyburn, Yorks., 1874; d. London 1944). Organ scholar of Selwyn Coll., Cambridge, and then organist at Leicester; organist, Christ Church Cathedral, Dublin (1913–20), and Prof. of Music in Univ. of Dublin. Wrote many valuable textbooks (especially on counterpoint) and composed some church music.

Kjerulf, Halfdan Charles (b. Oslo, then Christiania, 1815; d. nr. there 1868). Successful composer of songs and also of men's voice choral music

and piano music—all of Norwegian flavour. Recognized as a national figure and as such greatly mourned when he died.

Kl. Short for *Klarinette* (Ger.), i.e. 'Clarinet' (see *Clarinet Family*).

Klagend, kläglich (Ger.). 'Lamenting.'

Klappenhorn (Ger. *Klappen* = 'keys'). 'Key Bugle': see *Cornett and Key Bugle Families.*

Klar (Ger., various grammatical endings, as *klare, klaren*). 'Clear', 'distinct'.

Klarinette; Klarinetten (Ger.). 'Clarinet'; 'Clarinets'.

Klaviatur (Ger.). 'Keyboard.'

Klavier or **Clavier** ('Keyboard' or 'Keyboard Instrument'). The word has been used familiarly in Germany for whatever domestic keyboard instrument was in fashion—harpsichord or clavichord at one period, pianoforte later.

Bach's *Das wohltemperirte Klavier* (the title of his 48 Preludes and Fugues) has been thought by most authorities to imply the use of the clavichord, but by others (partly on internal evidence) to imply that of the harpsichord. The 2 instruments were, in Bach's day, both in use and probably neither was exclusively intended.

In Eng. the word *Clavier* is used chiefly in connexion with the organ—as a synonym for 'manual' (or 'pedalboard').

Klavierauszug (Ger.). 'Piano arrangement.'

Klavierbüchlein ('Little Clavier-Book'). Three collections of keyboard music by Bach bear this title—(*a*) One put together for the instruction of his eldest son, Wilhelm Friedemann, 1720. (*b*) Similar but small collection for his young second wife, Anna Magdalena, 1722. (*c*) Larger collection for his wife, 1725; this includes some vocal pieces and theoretical material.

Klavierstück (Ger.). 'Piano piece.'

Klavierübung ('Keyboard exercise'). Bach's general title for 4 publications—(*a*) The 6 keyboard Partitas—or 'German Suites'. (*b*) Two pieces for double-

manual Harpsichord, the It. Concerto (q.v.) and the Fr. Overture or Partita in B minor. (c) Some Organ works, including the 'St. Anne' Fugue. (d) The Goldberg Variations (see *Goldberg* 1).
The name had previously (1689) been used by Kuhnau (q.v.).

Klecki. See *Kletzki*.

Kleiber, Erich (b. Vienna 1890; d. Zürich 1956). Operatic and orch. conductor of wide international reputation. Attached to many Ger. opera houses (Berlin State Opera 1923–35); New York Philharmonic 1930–2; Czech National Theatre, Prague, 1930. London concerts 1938; Covent Garden 1950–3. Argentine citizen (1938).

Klein (Ger.). (1) 'Small.' (2, of intervals) 'Minor'.

Klein, Bruno Oscar (b. Osnabrück 1858; d. New York 1911). Pupil of Rheinberger at Munich; went to U.S.A. as concert pianist (1878); also taught composition in National Conserv. (1887–92); also church organist. Composed opera (*Kenilworth*, produced Hamburg 1895), masses, orch. and chamber music, &c.

Kleine Nachtmusik, Eine ('A Little Serenade'). By Mozart (K. 525; 1787). Four movements for String Quartet or String Orch.

Kleine Orgelmesse ('Little Mass with Organ'). Popular name for Haydn's Mass No. 5, in B flat. (Cf. *Grosse Orgelmesse*.)

Kleine Trommel (Ger. 'small drum'). The side drum; otherwise 'Snare Drum' (see *Percussion Family* 2 i).

Kleinflöte (Ger. 'small flute'). Organ stop; same as *Piccolo* (see *Flute Family*).

Klemperer, Otto (b. Breslau 1885; d. Zürich 1973). Conductor of high reputation. Connected in turn with many of chief Ger. opera houses. Settled U.S.A. 1932 (Los Angeles and Pittsburgh Symphony Orchs., &c.); Budapest Opera since 1947. Some compositions (a Mass, &c.).

Klengel, (1) **August Alexander** (b. Dresden 1783; there d. 1852). Pupil of Clementi; accompanied him to St.

Petersburg and remained 1805–11; became court organist at Dresden. As composer remarkable for contrapuntal facility, writing many canons for piano (hence nicknamed 'Kanon-Klengel'), and (following example of Bach) 48 Preludes and Fugues in all keys.

(2) **Paul** (b. Leipzig 1854; there d. 1935). Pianist, violinist, conductor, composer of songs, &c. Brother of Julius, below.

(3) **Julius** (b. Leipzig 1859; there d. 1933). Brother of Paul, above. Very notable 'cellist; outstanding teacher, and composer of concertos, &c., for 'cello and music for strings generally.

Klenovsky, (1) **Nikolai Semenovich** (b. Odessa 1857; d. St. Petersburg 1915). Violinist and composer (pupil of Tchaikovsky at Moscow Conserv.). Works include ballets, incidental music to plays, orch. music, &c.

(2) **Paul.** Pen name of Sir Henry Wood as orch. arranger of Bach's organ toccata and fugue in D minor.

Kletzki (Klecki), Paul (b. Łódź, Poland, 1900; d. Liverpool 1973). Studied at State Conserv. of Warsaw and then Hochschule, Berlin. Well-known conductor. Dallas Symphony Orch. 1958. Suisse Romande 1969. Compositions include symphonies, concertos, chamber music, &c.

Kl. Fl. Short for *kleine Flöte* (Ger.), i.e. Piccolo (see *Flute Family*).

Klindworth, Karl (b. Hanover 1830; d. Stolpe, nr. Potsdam, 1916). Violinist and opera conductor; also pianist and as pupil of Liszt developed on this side and won renown as such and as piano teacher, and arranger for piano of scores of his friend Wagner, &c., and ed. of Chopin. In London 1854–68, active in Wagner propaganda there; then in Moscow (to 1881) as piano prof. at Conserv. and in Berlin as conductor and head of piano school, &c. Composed for piano. See *Wagner*.

Klingen (Ger.). 'To sound.' So *klingend*, 'resonant'.

Klose, Friedrich (b. Karlsruhe 1862; d. Locarno 1942). Teacher of composition at Basle and Munich Conservatories; composer of opera, oratorio, symphonic poems, chamber music, &c.

Klosé, Hyacinth Eléanore (b. Corfu 1808; d. Paris 1880). Famous clarinettist, prof. of his instrument at Paris Conservatory, and writer of methods for it and for saxophone.

Knappertsbusch, Hans (b. Elberfeld 1888; d. Munich 1965). Opera conductor. Trained Cologne Conserv.; then at Elberfeld (1913), Leipzig (1918), Dessau (1919), Munich State Opera (1922), Vienna State Opera (1938).

Knarre (Ger.). 'Rattle.'

Knecht, Justin Heinrich (b. Biberach, Württemberg, 1752; d. there 1817). Able organist; also conductor, and opera and concert manager (a pioneer of annotated programme, q.v.), and author of many theoretical textbooks. As composer anticipated Beethoven's *Pastoral Symphony* with work of similar intention.

Kneifend (Ger.). 'Plucking' (same as *pizzicato*).

Kneisel, Franz (b. Bucharest, 1865; d. New York 1926; German by parentage). Violinist. Orch. player Vienna and Berlin, and leading violinist Boston Symphony Orch. (1885–1903). Successful soloist; founded celebrated Kneisel Quartet (1886–1917); also active as conductor. Hon. D.Mus., Yale and Princeton.

Kneller Hall. Twickenham. Originally home of famous portrait painter, Sir Godfrey Kneller (1646–1723), now of Royal Military School of Music (founded 1857). See *Schools of Music*; *Degrees and Diplomas* 2.

Knight, Gerald Hocken (b. Par, Cornwall, 1908). Educ. Cambridge (M.A., B.Mus.) and R.C.M. Organist Canterbury Cathedral 1937–52. Director Royal School of Church Music (q.v.). C.B.E. 1971.

Knipper, Lev (b. Tiflis 1898). Composer of orch. works, operas, &c. Pupil of Jarnach and composer in a Russian manner and on broad diatonic lines.

Knorr, Iwan (b. Mewe, W. Prussia, 1853; d. Frankfurt-on-Main 1916). Brought up in Russia and after studies at Leipzig Conserv. returned there; then (1883) appointed on Brahms's recommendation prof. of composition at Conserv. of Frankfurt-on-Main, there becoming teacher of a number of Brit. students (e.g. N. O'Neill, Cyril Scott, Roger Quilter, Balfour Gardiner). Composed operas, orch., chamber, and piano music, &c., and wrote textbooks and life of Tchaikovsky.

Koanga. Opera by Delius. (Prod. Elberfeld 1904; London 1935.)

Köchel, Ludwig von (b. nr. Krems 1800; d. Vienna 1877). Botanist and mineralogist and as such accustomed to orderly classification; as admirer of Mozart undertook that of his works (thus the present-day identification as 'K. 91', &c.). Various revisions—esp. Alfred Einstein (1937). 6th ed. 1964.

Koczwara. See *Kotzwara*.

Kodály, Zoltán (b. Kecskemét, Hungary, 1882; d. Budapest 1967). Studied at Conserv. of Budapest and became a teacher of composition there. Like his friend Bartók (q.v.) collected Hungarian folk tunes. His compositions, national in spirit and modern in harmony, &c., include opera (*Háry János*, q.v.), tone poems, choral works (*Psalmus Hungaricus* 1923), chamber music. Also publ. books on music.

Koechlin, Charles (b. Paris 1867; d. Var 1950). Pupil of Massenet and Fauré at Paris Conserv. He composed much orch., chamber, and piano music, songs, &c., which make strong appeal to his disciples and relatively weak one to world in general. Also wrote theoretical treatises.

Kogan, Leonid (b. Dniepropetrovsk 1924). Violinist, trained Moscow Conserv., then on staff. Many world tours; also trio with Gilels and Rostropovitch.

Köhler, Irene (b. London 1912). Pianist. Trained T.C.M. and R.C.M. and Vienna. Début Proms. 1934. Tours Europe, India, &c. Work for films. B.Mus., London.

Köhler, Louis, in full Christian Louis Heinrich (b. Brunswick 1820; d. Königsberg 1886). Pianist, piano teacher, composer of much music for educational use (as also operas, orch. works, &c.), and writer of numerous textbooks and the like.

Kokett (Ger.). 'Coquettish.'

Kol Nidrei. For 'Cello and Orch. By Max Bruch. Hebrew melody (sung in synagogues on eve of Day of Atonement), developed for 'cello, harp, and orch. (Also arranged for 'cello and piano.)

Kolomyika. A quick Polish dance in 2-in-a-measure time, popular amongst the mountain peasants of Poland.

Kolophon (Ger.). 'Colophony', i.e. Bow Resin.

Koloratur. See *Coloratura*.

Kombination (Ger.). 'Combination.' In organ music applied to any mechanical device for preparing registration.

Komisch (Ger.). 'Comic.'

Komponiert (Ger.). 'Composed.'

Kondrashin, Kyril (b. 1914). Conductor; trained Moscow Conserv.; Leningrad Orch., &c., 1936; Bolshoi Th. 1943–56, then international tours. On staff Moscow Conserv. 1952–6.

Königin von Saba, Die ('The Queen of Sheba'). Tragedy-opera by Goldmark. (Prod. Vienna 1875; New York 1885; Manchester and London 1910.)

Königskinder ('King's Children'). By Humperdinck. Play declaimed through music (Munich and London 1897; New York 1898). Then recast as a true Opera (prod. New York 1910; Berlin, London, Milan, &c., 1911).

Kontrabass (Ger.). Double-bass—generally the stringed one.

Kontrabassposaune (Ger.). Double-bass Trombone (see *Trombone Family*).

Kontrafagott (Ger.). Double Bassoon. See *Oboe Family*.

Kontski, Antoine de (b. Cracow 1817; d. Ivanitchy 1899). Piano pupil of Field (q.v.); travelled widely as pianist and left highly popular drawing-room compositions for piano (especially *The Awakening of the Lion*—a tame one apparently); also piano concertos, opera, oratorio, symphonies, &c.

Konzert (Ger.). (1) Concert. (2) Concerto.

Konzertstück (Ger.). Same as *Concertstück* (q.v.).

Koppel (Ger.). 'Coupler' (organ).

Korbay, Francis Alexander (b. Budapest 1846; d. London 1913). Opera singer in Budapest; then temporarily losing voice toured and taught as pianist; settled in London as singer and teacher of singing (at R.A.M. 1894–1903). Arranged Hungarian songs set to Eng. words.

Korean Temple Block. An oriental addition to the 20th-c. dance-band drummer's equipment. A skull-shaped hollow block of wood is struck with the drum-stick. The *Chinese Temple Block* is similar.

Kornett (Ger.). The modern Cornet or the ancient Cornett—either.

Korngold, Erich Wolfgang (b. Brno 1897; d. Hollywood, Calif., 1957). Son of well-known Vienna music critic. Became youthful prodigy composer, causing discussion by modernity of harmonies. Varied compositions including opera *The Dead City* (q.v.). In California from 1935, composing for films, with Max Reinhardt, &c.

Kosakisch, Kosatcheck, or Kosachok. A Cossack dance, the music of which is in quick simple duple time and of ever-increasing speed, and is often in the minor.

Kostelanetz, André. Conductor; b. St. Petersburg 1901; trained at Conserv. there. Settled U.S.A. 1922 (naturalized). Conducted many orchs. in U.S.A., Britain, and other countries; attached Columbia Broadcasting System since 1930. Has characteristic style of orchestrating and arranging popular music.

Kostenka. A Serbian dance type.

Koteletten Walzer. See *Chopsticks*.

Kotzwara (Koczwara, &c.), Franz (b. Prague 1730; hanged self, London, 1791). Theatre violinist and double-bass player in various countries, settling in London (abt. 1790). Now remembered only by one simple and commonplace composition for piano, *The Battle of Prague*, of which hundreds of thousands of copies have been sold.

Kouiaviak. A French spelling of *Kujawiak* (q.v.).

Koussevitzky, Sergei Alexandrovich (b. Vishny Volotchok, Russia, 1876; d. Boston, Mass., 1951). Trained Moscow Conserv. (later on staff) and in 1903 appeared as double-bass virtuoso (recitals in England 1907–8); composed concerto, &c., for his instrument. Founded Symphony Orch. (1910) and toured Russia as its conductor; also founded publishing business for Russian music (1909–18). Later appeared in France, England, Italy, Germany, Spain, &c. Finally settled U.S.A. as conductor of Boston Symphony Orch. (1924–49), enthusiastically encouraging development of young Amer. composers.

See following entry; also *Violin Family*.

Koussevitzky Music Foundation (Boston, Mass.). Brought into existence 1943 by the conductor in memory of his wife. Aids young composers by commissioning new works, &c. Work energetically continued after his death, by his 2nd wife.

Koven, Henry Louis Reginald de (b. Middletown, Conn., 1859; d. Chicago 1920). Educated Oxford Univ., England. Composer of 19 comic operas (see *Robin Hood*) and 2 grand operas (see *Canterbury Pilgrims* and *Rip van Winkle*).

Kraft (Ger.). 'Strength', 'vigour'. So *Kräftig*, 'strong', 'vigorous'.

Kraft, (1) Anton (b. nr. Pilsen 1752; d. Vienna 1820). 'Cellist in Haydn's orch. at Esterházy; then in other princely orchs. Publ. sonatas for 'cello, &c. At one time thought to be composer of Haydn's 'cello concerto in D. (2) **Nicolaus** (b. Esterházy 1778; d. Stuttgart 1853). Son of above and also 'cellist. Like father member successively of various princely orchs. and composer for his instrument.

Krakoviak, Krakowiak. See *Cracovienne*.

Kramer, A. Walter (b. New York 1890; d. there 1969). Composer of very varied works; writer on music, ed. of *Musical America*, 1929–36.

Kraus, (1) Lili (b. Budapest 1908). Pianist. Entered Budapest Conserv.

1916; then Vienna Conserv. (later on staff)—teachers included Kodály, Bartók, and Schnabel. International reputation as recitalist (frequently associated with violinist Simon Goldberg) and soloist at orch. concerts. During World War II captured in Java by Japanese and imprisoned 3 years. Naturalized New Zealand.

(2) **Otakar** (b. Prague 1909). Operatic and concert baritone, first appearing in Czechoslovakian opera houses. In Britain from 1939—Carl Rosa Co. Glyndebourne, Covent Garden, &c.

Krauss, Clemens Heinrich (b. Vienna 1893; d. Mexico City 1954). Trained Vienna Conserv. Held conducting posts many cities, including Vienna and Munich operas. New York début 1929. Many first perfs. works of his friend Richard Strauss.

Krazy Kat. Ballet by J. A. Carpenter. (1st perf. Chicago 1921.)

Krebs, (1) Johann Ludwig (b. Buttelstädt, Thuringia, 1713; d. Altenburg 1780). One of Bach's favourite pupils; some of his organ music still heard; also wrote music for clavichord, flute, &c. (2) **Marie** (b. Dresden 1857; there d. 1900). Pianist, touring Europe. London début age 14. Highly popular in Britain; toured U.S.A.

Krehbiel, Henry Edward (b. Ann Arbor, Mich., 1854; d. New York 1923). Music critic *N.Y. Tribune* 1880 to death. Publ. both scholarly and popular books on music and ed. Eng. version Thayer's *Life of Beethoven*. See under *Criticism*.

Krein, (1) Alexander Abramovich (b. Nijni-Novgorod 1883; d. Moscow 1951). Came of a Jewish family of well-known musicians. Studied 'cello at Moscow Conserv.; then became composer, especially using ancient synagogue tunes in a modern harmonic style; recognized as a leader of Jewish-Russian musical movement. (2) **Grigory Abramovich** (b. Nijni-Novgorod 1879; d. nr. Leningrad 1955). Brother of Alexander, above. Studied composition in Germany under Reger and violin at Moscow Conserv. Compositions sometimes less racial than his brother's but equally modern in idiom. (3) **Julian Grigorovich** (b. Moscow 1913). Son of Grigory. Studied in Paris under Dukas; when 12 publ. a piano sonata; has since composed much orch. music, &c., some of it performed in U.S.A., France, Spain, &c.

Kreis (Ger.). 'Circle', 'cycle'. So *Liederkreis*, 'song cycle'.

Kreisler, Fritz (b. Vienna 1875; d. New York 1962). Studied violin under Hellmesberger at Vienna Conserv. and Massart at Paris Conserv.; then became greatest touring virtuoso of his period, though with restricted repertory—the greater classics plus trifles of his own composing or arranging; some of so-called 'arrangements' to which were attached names of more or less obscure 17th- and 18th-c. composers later revealed (1935) as being of own composition. Composed also string quartet and operettas. Hon. LL.D. Glasgow.

Kreisleriana. 'Phantasies for Pianoforte' by Schumann (op. 16, 1838; revised 1850; dedicated to Chopin). Kreisler, 'an eccentric, wild Kapellmeister', was the creation of the Ger. romantic author, E. T. A. Hoffmann.

Křenek, Ernst (b. Vienna 1900). Of partly Czech, partly Ger. origin. Studied under Schreker in Vienna and Berlin and married Mahler's daughter; in Switzerland 1923; Kassel 1925; style successively neo-romantic, atonal, jazz-influenced, e.g. in opera *Jonny spielt auf* ('Johnny strikes up', 1927; translated into 18 languages and widely performed). List of compositions extremely varied and very long. Emigrated to U.S.A. 1938 and on music staff of Vassar Coll.; then Hamline Univ., St. Paul, Minn.; Hollywood since 1947. European recital tours. Books on composition, on Ockeghem, &c.

See *Gebrauchsmusik* and *Note-row*.

Kreutzer, Rodolphe (b. Versailles 1766; d. Geneva 1831). Fine violinist to whom Beethoven dedicated violin and piano sonata which is known by his name (op. 47, in A: cf. *Bridgetower*). Composed 43 operas and 19 violin concertos, 15 string quartets, &c., and left valuable violin studies still much used.

Kreuz (Ger. 'cross'). The sign of the sharp (see Table 7).

Krieg (Ger.). 'War.' So *kriegerisch*, 'martial'.

Krips, Josef (b. Vienna 1902). Studied Vienna under Weingartner, &c. Began career aged 15 as violinist. At 22 conductor in Aussig, then Dortmund. Vienna State Opera from 1933, and on staff Vienna Conserv. In Belgrade 1938 when activities suspended by Nazis. Returned Vienna 1945; European tours, London Symphony Orch. 1950; Buffalo 1952; San Francisco 1963–70.

Krommer, Franz (b. Kamenitz, Moravia, 1759; d. 1831). Wholesale composer of music for both wind band and chamber combinations of various kinds (including quartets and quintets of flutes), also of symphonies, masses, &c.

Krumhorn, Krummhorn (sometimes corrupted into *Cromorne* or *Cremona*). Popular medieval instrument with double reed (like oboe) and cylindrical tube (like clarinet).

Krummbogen, Krummbügel (Ger. 'bent-arch'), or **Stimmbogen** ('tuning-arch'). 'Crook' (of a brass instrument—see *Horn Family*; *Trumpet Family*).

Krummhorn. See *Krumhorn*.

Kruse, Johann Secundus (b. Melbourne 1859; d. London 1927). Violinist. Pupil of Joachim. Chief violin Berlin Philharmonic 1892; member Joachim Quartet, &c. Settled in London 1897, giving chamber concerts, &c.

Kryzhanovsky, Ivan Ivanovich (b. Kief 1867; d. Leningrad 1924). Medical man who had studied composition with Rimsky-Korsakof and composed symphonic poems, chamber music, songs, piano pieces, &c.

Kubelik, (1) **Jan** (b. nr. Prague 1880; there d. 1940). Violinist. Pupil of Ševčik. Of high international reputation. Composed violin concertos, &c. Naturalized Hungarian.

(2) **Rafael**—in full Jeronym Rafael (b. Bychor, Czechoslovakia, 1914). Son of above. Conductor of Prague Philharmonic Orch. and National Opera; toured abroad, with or without his

orch.; Dir. Chicago Symphony Orch. 1950–2; Covent Gdn. 1955–8; Bavarian Radio Orch. 1961; Metropolitan Opera 1973. Comp. opera, symphonies, &c.

Kücken, Friedrich Wilhelm (b. Hanover 1810; d. Schwerin 1882). Highly popular as composer of tuneful songs.

Kuhe, William (b. Prague 1823; d. London 1912). Enjoyed European reputation as pianist. Lived in London and Brighton 1847 to death; a prof. of piano at R.A.M. 1886–1904; organized annual musical festivals in Brighton (1870–82). Composed much drawing-room music for his instrument.

Kuhlau, Friedrich (b. Ülzen, Hanover, 1786; d. nr. Copenhagen 1832). Lived in Copenhagen 1810 to death; became Court Composer, &c.; accomplished flautist; composed flute quartets, trios, duets, &c., also works for violin and for piano (especially easy sonatas and sonatinas, some still used by teachers), songs, and a number of successful operas.

Kuhnau, Johann (b. Geising, Saxony, 1660; d. Leipzig 1722). Bach's immediate predecessor at Leipzig Thomas School (1684–death) and his ablest forerunner as composer for clavichord and harpsichord; one of early writers of sonatas (as distinct from suites), and also one of early writers of 'programme music' (q.v.). See *Klavierübung*; *Sonata*.

Kuhreigen, Der ('The Ranz des Vaches'). Tragedy-opera by Kienzl. (Prod. Vienna 1911; Philadelphia and New York 1913; Liverpool and London 1914.)

Kujawiak. A quick Polish dance in 3-in-a-measure time.

Kullak, Theodor (b. Krotoschin 1818; d. Berlin 1882). Came of distinguished musical family. A leading piano teacher in Berlin, especially remembered to-

day by his several series of compositions for study of piano playing in its various branches and grades. (See *Pianoforte Playing and Teaching*.)

Kullervo. Early Symphonic Poem by Sibelius for Vocal Soloists, Chorus, and Orch. (op. 7; 1892). Kullervo is one of the leading personalities in the national Finnish epic, the *Kalevala*.

Kullmann, Charles (b. New Haven, Conn., 1903). Operatic tenor. Trained Juilliard School and Amer. Conserv., Fontainebleau. Successful appearances New York (Metropolitan Opera from 1935), Berlin, Vienna, London, &c. 1956, Indiana Univ.

Kunst (Ger.). 'Art.' So *Künstler*, 'artist'; *Kunstkenner* ('art-knower'), 'connoisseur'.

Kunst der Fuge, Die (Bach). See *Art of Fugue*.

Kunstlied (Ger.). 'Art-song' (in distinction from *Volkslied*, 'folk-song').

Kunz, Erich (b. Vienna 1909). Baritone vocalist: studied Vienna Conserv. Breslau Opera 1937–41, Vienna State Opera from 1941. Many appearances opera houses of Europe, S. America, &c.

Kurz, kurze, &c. (Ger., various grammatical terminations). 'Short.'

Kurz, Selma (b. Bietlitz 1874; d. Vienna 1933). Operatic coloratura soprano. At Vienna Opera for over a quarter of a century (1899–1926). Made great impression at Covent Garden 1904–5.

Kurzer Vorschlag. See *Vorschlag*.

Kussevitzky. See *Koussevitzky*.

Kutcher, Samuel (b. London 1899). Violinist. Appeared Queen's Hall aged 10. Trained T.C.M., G.S.M., and R.C.M. Kutcher String Quartet founded 1928.

Kyrie. See *Mass*; *Requiem*; *Common Prayer*.

L

L—*Longo*. See *Scarlatti* (2).

L' (Fr., It.). 'The' (masc. or fem. sing.).

La (It., Fr.). 'The' (fem. sing.).

La. The 6th degree of the major scale, according to the system of vocal syllables derived from Guido d'Arezzo (see *Hexachord*), and so used (spelt *Lah*) in Tonic Sol-fa, in which it is also the 1st degree of the minor scale (see *Tonic Sol-fa*). In many countries, however, the name has become attached (on 'fixed-doh' principles; see *Sight-Singing*) to the note A, in whatever key this may occur. (See Table 5; also *Lancashire Sol-fa*.)

L.A.B. See *Degrees and Diplomas* 2.

L'Abeille. See *Schubert, Franz* (of Dresden).

Labialstimme (Ger., plur. *Labialstimmen*). Flue Stop.

Lablache, Luigi (b. Naples 1794; there d. 1858). Operatic bass. Large voice, extended compass, great flexibility, fine presence, and high powers of dramatic characterization in both comic and tragic parts—which combination of qualities won him unique position. Taught Queen Victoria singing.

Labroca, Mario (b. Rome 1896). Pupil of Respighi and Malipiero; has composed operas, orch., chamber, and piano works, &c. Mus. Head, Ital. Radio.

Lac des Cygnes (Tchaikovsky). See *Swan Lake*.

Lächelnd (Ger.). 'Laughing.'

Lâcher (Fr.). 'To loosen' (e.g. snare of drum).

Lachner, (1) **Franz** (b. Rain 1803; d. Munich 1890). Spent early life in Vienna (1822–34) and there friend of Schubert and Beethoven; later at Mannheim and Munich (1836 to death). Composer of operas, masses, oratorios, 8 symphonies, chamber music, &c. (Brother of Ignaz and Vincenz, below.) (2) **Ignaz** (b. Rain 1807; d. Hanover 1895). Brother of Franz, above, and Vincenz, below; held various positions as organist and as Kapellmeister. Composer of operas, symphonies, masses, chamber music, &c. (3) **Vincenz** (b. Rain 1811; d. Karlsruhe 1893). Brother of Franz and Ignaz, above, and had career much like theirs and produced series of compositions much of same type as they, with, also, much valued men's voice partsongs. (4–6) **Theodor** (b. 1798; d. Munich 1877), **Thekla**, and **Christiane** (b. 1805). Half-brother and 2 sisters of all the above; all 3 organists and otherwise musically skilled and active. Altogether a remarkable family.

Lacombe, (1) **Louis Trouillon** (b. Bourges, France, 1818; d. St. Vaast la Hougue, nr. Cherbourg, 1884). Prominent touring pianist; teacher in Paris. Composed operas, orch., and chamber music, &c.
(2) **Paul** (b. Carcassonne 1837; d. there 1927). Friend and disciple of Bizet. Composed orch., chamber, and piano music, &c. Not related to Louis above.)

Lacrimosa. See *Requiem*.

Lacrimoso, lagrimoso (It.). 'Lachrymose', 'tearful'.

Ladye Nevells Booke, My (or 'My Lady Nevill's Book'). A manuscript collection of Byrd's music for virginal (see *Harpsichord Family*), dated 1591. It is in private possession but was published in 1926 (see *Andrews, Hilda*).

Lady Macbeth of Mtsensk. Opera by Shostakovich. (Prod. Moscow 1934; Cleveland and New York 1935; London concert perf. 1936.)

Lage (Ger.). 'Position' (e.g. in string playing).

Lagnoso, lagnevole (It.). 'Doleful.' So the adverb *lagnosamente*.

Lagrimando, lagrimoso (It.). 'Lachrymose', 'tearful'.

Lah. See *La*.

Lai, or Lay. A 14th-c. French song-form, usually 12 unequal stanzas sung to different tunes. Later examples are in several voices.

Laird o' Cockpen. Poem by Lady Nairne; tune traditional Scottish.

Laisser (Fr.). 'To allow', 'to leave'. *Laissant*, 'allowing', 'leaving'. *Laissez* is the imperative.

Lakmé. 3-act tragedy-opera by Delibes. Libretto by Goudinet and Gille. (Prod. Paris 1883; London 1885; New York 1886.)

Lalande, Michel Richard de (b. Paris 1657; d. Versailles 1726). Contemporary of Lully at court of Louis XIV; some time Superintendent of Court Music. Composed ballets and much church music.

Lalla Rookh. Cantata by Frederick Clay (Brighton Fest. 1877); it includes his most popular song, *I'll sing thee songs of Araby*.

Lalo, Édouard—in full Victor Antoine Édouard (b. Lille 1823; d. Paris 1892). Studied at Paris Conserv. As composer long failed to arouse any public interest; in 1872 luck turned with perf. by Sarasate of his 1st violin concerto; other works greatly increased his fame (see *Symphonie espagnole*; *Roi d'Ys*; *Rapsodie norvégienne*; *Concerto russe*); masterpiece is considered to be ballet *Namouna* (also is form of orch. suite), which influenced Debussy, d'Indy, and others. Deft orchestration one of his qualities. Left some good songs.

Lamarter, De. See *Delamarter*.

Lambert, (1) **Michel** (b. Vivonne, Poitou, abt. 1610; d. Paris 1696). Skilful singer, song composer, and choir trainer at court of Louis XIV. Lully married his daughter.

(2) **Alexander** (b. Warsaw 1862; d. New York 1929). Pianist. Trained Vienna Conserv. and under Bruckner and Liszt. Début New York 1881. Toured widely and settled New York 1888. Composer of piano music and study material.

(3) **Constant** (b. London 1905; d. there 1951). Pupil of Vaughan Williams at R.C.M. Opera and ballet conductor (some years Sadler's Wells, q.v.; from 1948 Mus. Adviser there). Composer of

ballets (see *Horoscope*), orch. works, choral works (see *Summer's Last Will and Testament* and *Rio Grande*), &c. Music critic and author (*Music Ho!* 1934).

Lambeth Degrees. See *Degrees and Diplomas* 1.

Lambeth Walk. The name of a London street on the south side of the Thames. A song and dance of the same name attained immense popularity from the spring of 1938 onwards. Gestures, speech, and action were incorporated in it; and it was supposed to embody suggestions of the manners of the inhabitants of the district to which its words allude.

Lament. Traditional elegiac music, e.g. amongst Scottish clans and the Irish.

Lamentando, lamentabile, lamentevole, lamentoso (It.). 'Lamenting.'

Lamentations. In the Roman Catholic Church sung as part of the service of Tenebrae (q.v.)—based on words of the prophet Jeremiah.

Lamentations (Haydn Symphony). See under *Weihnachtssymphonie*.

Lamentazione, lamento (It.). 'Lamentation', 'lament'.

Lamia. See *Howell, Dorothy*.

Lamond, Frederic A. (b. Glasgow 1868; d. Stirling 1948). Pianist. Began musical life as church organist; studied at Frankfurt and then under von Bülow and Liszt. Appeared in public at age 17; quickly attained international fame especially as Beethoven interpreter. Lived Berlin 1904–19; then in native city on staff of Royal Scottish Academy of Music.

Lamoureux, Charles (b. Bordeaux 1834; d. Paris 1899). Conductor. Trained as violinist at Paris Conserv. and played in orch. of Opéra, &c. Won great repute as conductor of Opéra and, especially, of Lamoureux Concerts (from 1881); greatly helped to popularize Wagner in France. Visits to London (with or without own orch.) did much to make Fr. composers known. (Cf. *Chevillard*.)

Lampe, (1) John Frederick (b. Saxony 1703; d. Edinburgh 1751). Settled in Britain abt. 1725; bassoon player in London opera; composer of successful stage music, &c.; composed tunes for some hymns of his friend Charles Wesley. (2) **Charles John Frederick**. Son of John Frederick, above, and like him a composer.

Lamperti, Francesco (b. Savona 1813; d. Como 1892). Celebrated singing teacher, composer of vocal studies and author of treatise on singing.

Lancashire Sol-fa. A modern name for a system of sight-singing more properly called 'Old English Sol-fa', since it was universally used in England from at least the early 17th c. and its latest textbook appeared in 1879. It is a method of solmization applied to the normal staff notation; the first 3 notes of every major scale are called *fa-sol-la*, and so are the second 3 notes, the remaining note being called *mi*; the minor scale is read as if its notes were those of the relative major. In the Amer. Colonies (and later the U.S.A.) it was called *Fasola* or, sometimes (from the special notation there used), *Patent Notes* (cf. *Buckwheat Notation*).

Lancers. See *Quadrille*.

Lancio (It.). 'Gusto.'

Landino (or **Landini**), **Francesco** (b. Florence abt. 1325; there d. 1397). Lost sight as a child, yet became clever player of organ, lute, flute, and other instruments, and as composer of madrigals, &c., one of the representative composers of his period.

Ländler. The popular Ger. dance which is probably the original of the waltz—though not so quick as this. Other names were *Schleifer* (referring to the sliding of the feet) and *Tyrolienne*.

Ländlich (Ger.). 'Country-like', 'rustic'.

Land of Hope and Glory. See under *Pomp and Circumstance*.

Land of my Fathers (*Hen Wlad fy Nhadau*). The poem of this song (which is the National Anthem of Wales) is by Evan James, of Pontypridd, the tune by James James. Both poem and tune

first appeared in print in 1860 in John Owen's *Gems of Welsh Melody*.

Land of the Mountain and Flood. See *MacCunn*.

Land o' the Leal. The poem is by Lady Nairne, and the tune is the traditional Scottish one of *Hey, tutti tatti*—also sung to Burns's *Scots wha hae* (q.v.). The song was written about 1798 and 1st publ. soon after 1800.

Landowska, Wanda (b. Warsaw 1877; d. Lakeville, Conn., 1959). Harpsichord virtuoso and authority. Long resident in France and then in U.S.A. (1941).

Lane, (1) George William Brand (b. Brighton 1854; d. Manchester 1927). Settled in Manchester, as business man, 1875; developed singing class and choral soc. work; then became concert manager, engaging eminent performers and carrying on long-famous series of concerts.

(2) **Eastwood** (b. Brewerton, N.Y., 1879). Self-taught composer. Has written piano pieces, music for light orch., &c.

Lang (Ger.). 'Long.'

Lang, Paul Henry (b. Budapest 1901). Settled in U.S.A. and became Prof. of Musicology at Columbia Univ., New York, and a leader in musicological activity. Ed. of the *Musical Quarterly* (1945) and author of *Music in Western Civilization* (1941). Mus. critic, *New York Herald Tribune* (1954–63).

Lange, Hans (b. Constantinople 1884; d. Albuquerque, N.M., 1960). Violinist and conductor. Trained Prague Conserv. under Ševčik, &c. Appeared as solo violinist. From 1923 in New York; assoc. cond. Philharmonic 1933; Chicago Orch. 1936–46; Albuquerque Civic Symphony 1950–8.

Lang-Müller, Peter Erasmus (b. Copenhagen 1850; there d. 1926). Composer of nationalist leanings; wrote orch. and choral music, operas, songs, &c.

Langer. See *Electric Musical Instruments* 1.

Langer Vorschlag. See *Vorschlag*.

Langford, Samuel (b. Manchester 1863; there d. 1927). Succeeded his father in the business of nursery gardening, and, having enjoyed in his 30's the advantage of 4 years under Reinecke at the Leipzig Conserv., combined with it remarkable activity as the much-honoured music critic (1905 to death) of *Manchester Guardian*. Cf. *Cardus*.

Langoureux; langoureusement (Fr.). 'Languorous'; 'languorously'.

Langrish, Vivian (b. Bristol 1894). Pianist. Trained R.A.M. under Matthay, &c.; later on its staff. Successful career as recitalist.

Langsam (Ger.). 'Slow.' So *langsamer*, 'slower'.

Languendo, languente, languemente (It.). 'Languishing.' **Langueur** (Fr.). 'Languor.' **Languido; languidamente** (It.). 'Languid'; 'languidly'. **Languissant** (Fr.). 'Languishing.' **Languore** (It.). 'Languor.'

Lanier (Laniere, &c.) (1) **Family.** Of Fr. origin but active in Eng. musical life (especially about the Court) for well over a century. **Nicolas** (b. London 1588; there d. 1666) was Master of King's Musick to Charles I and after Commonwealth Charles II; also Marshal of Corporation of Music. Left songs, &c. He is credited with the introduction of recitative into England. (There were 2 other Laniers with same Christian name.)

(2) **Sidney** (b. Macon, Georgia, 1842; d. Lynn, N.C. 1881). Descendant of a member of the above family who emigrated at beginning of 18th c. Delicate and accomplished poet and original thinker on principles of prosody, studying it from musical point of view; for some years earned living as flautist in Baltimore Symphony Orch.; in 1879 became Lecturer in Eng. Literature at Johns Hopkins Univ.

Lanner, Joseph Franz Karl (b. nr. Vienna 1801; there d. 1843). As conductor of dance orch. in Vienna and composer helped to generate the 19th-c. waltz fever (cf. *Strauss, Johann* 1). In addition to over 100 waltzes wrote quadrilles, galops, &c., galore.

Lanzentanz (Ger.). Same as *Pordon Danza* (q.v.).

Laparra, Raoul (b. Bordeaux 1876; killed in air-raid, Paris 1943). At Paris Conserv. pupil of Fauré and Massenet; won Rome Prize 1903; leapt into fame 1908 with perf. of his opera *La Habanera*. Wrote orch. and other music; active also as musical journalist.

Lara (real name 'Cohen'), **Isidore de** (b. London 1858; d. Paris 1935). Trained Milan Conserv. Publ. songs and wrote many operas (Covent Garden; Opéra Comique, Paris; Metropolitan Opera House, New York, &c.). During First World War organized in London hundreds of concerts to provide work for musical profession.

Larboard Watch (Williams). See *Britannia, the Pride of the Ocean*.

Larchet, John Francis (b. Dublin 1885). Prof. of Music in Dublin coll. of National Univ. of Ireland (D.Mus.). Composer of songs, &c.

Largamente (It.). 'Broadly', i.e. slowish and dignified (cf. *Largo*, below).

Large (Fr.). 'Broad', i.e. slow and dignified (cf. *Largo*, below). **Largement** (Fr.). 'Broadly' (same as It. *Largamente*; see above). **Largeur** (Fr.). 'Breadth.'

Larghetto (It.). The diminutive of *Largo* (see below). Slow and dignified, but less so than *Largo*. **Larghezza** (It.). 'Breadth' (cf. *Largo*, below).

Largo (It.). 'Broad', dignified in style; so *Largo di molto*, 'Very slow and dignified' (and similar expressions of which the separate words will be found in their alphabetical positions).

Largo (Handel. Often called by publishers 'Handel's Celebrated Largo'). An instrumental arrangement, by some person unknown, of the song *Ombra mai fu* from the opera *Serse*.

Larigot (old name for Flageolet). Organ stop; same as *Nineteenth* (q.v.).

Lark Ascending, The. 'Romance' for Solo Violin and Orch. by Vaughan Williams (1914). Inspired by a poem of Meredith.

M

Lark Quartet (Haydn). See *Lerchen-quartett*.

Larsson, Lars Erik (b. nr. Lund, Sweden, 1908). Studied at Conserv. of Stockholm and then in Vienna with Alban Berg (q.v.). Known in Sweden as conductor, critic, and composer of opera, chamber music, &c.

Laryngoscope. Apparatus for studying the interior of the larynx (q.v.) by means of mirrors. Invented by Manuel Garcia, 1854.

Larynx. The 'voice box' containing the vocal cords (see *Voice* 4). Its framework consists of 9 cartilages, including the *Thyroid* (or 'shield-shaped'), of which the point makes the protuberance in the throat called the 'Adam's Apple'; the *Cricoid* (or 'signet-ring-shaped'), and 2 *Arytenoid* (or 'ladle-shaped'). The vocal cords are attached to the Thyroid cartilage at the front and the Arytenoid cartilages at the back.

Lasalle, Jean Louis (b. Lyons 1847; d. Paris 1909). Operatic bass. Début Liège 1868; Paris Opéra 1872; Metropolitan Opera House, New York, 1892. Great international reputation. From 1901 a teacher of singing.

Lasciare (It.). 'To allow to . . . .' So the imperative *Lasciate*.

Lassen, Eduard (b. Copenhagen 1830; d. Weimar 1904). Succeeded Liszt as musical director at Weimar (1858–91). Was 2nd conductor in world to perform Wagner's *Tristan*. Composed operas and orch. music, &c.

Lassimone, Denise (b., of Fr. parents, Camberley, 1904). Pianist. Trained under Matthay at R.A.M. High reputation especially in Bach and Mozart.

Lasso. See *Lassus*.

Lass of Richmond Hill. The poem of this popular song is by a barrister, Leonard McNally, and the lass commemorated (of Richmond, Yorkshire; not Richmond, Surrey) became his wife in 1787. The music is by James Hook.

Lass o' Gowrie. Poem by Lady Nairne, founded on William Reid's *Kate o' Gowrie*; tune Scottish traditional.

Lass o' Patie's Mill. Poem by Allen Ramsay (1686–1758); tune Scottish traditional.

Lassu. See *Czardas*.

Lassus, Orlandus, or Orlando di Lasso—not 'Roland de Lattre', &c. (b. Mons abt. 1532; d. Munich 1594). The greatest representative of the Flemish school of the high polyphonic period, as his contemporaries Palestrina, Byrd, and Victoria are of the It., Eng., and Spanish schools. In early part of life travelled widely, everywhere welcomed; in Rome 1553–4 as maestro of the Lateran; from 1556 to death in Munich, together with other musicians of his race, in the service of the Court. Famous equally as composer of an enormous quantity of the finest choral music and as a trainer of choirs. Towards the end of his life suffered from attacks of severe mental depression. His 4 sons were all musicians.

Lass with a delicate air, The. See *Arne, Michael*.

Last Hours of the Saviour (Spohr). See *Calvary*.

Last Judgement, The (*Die letzten Dinge*, 'The Last Things'). Oratorio by Spohr. (1st perf. Cassel 1826. Norwich Fest. 1830; Boston 1842.)

Last Night at Bethany, The. Oratorio by C. Lee Williams. (1st perf. Gloucester Fest. 1889.)

Last Post. A British Army bugle call. The *First Post* at 9.30 p.m. calls all men back to barracks and the *Last Post* at 10 p.m. ends the day. By a natural and poetical association of ideas it has become the custom to sound the same call after every military funeral. (See also *Tattoo*.)

Last Rose of Summer. The poem is by Thomas Moore and first appeared in his *Irish Melodies* (1813). The air is that of a previous Irish song, *The Groves of Blarney*, by R. A. Millikin (about 1790), which in its turn was that of a song called *Castle Hyde*; but Moore altered it. Beethoven made a setting of the air, Mendelssohn wrote a piano fantasia on it, and Flotow used it in his opera *Martha*.

Lates, (1) **John James** (d. Oxford 1777). Oxford violinist and composer. (2) **Charles** (d. abt. 1810). Son of above. Oxford organist and composer.

Latham, Peter Morton Sturges (b. London 1894; d. there 1970). Educated at Rugby and Balliol. Gresham Professor of Music (see *Gresham Professorship*), and on staff R.A.M., Extension Lecturer 1946–64; Author of books on Brahms and Beethoven.

Laube Sonata (Beethoven). See *Moonlight Sonata*.

Laud. See *Cittern*.

Laud, William (1575–1645). See *Anglican Parish Church Music*.

Laudamus Te. See *Mass*.

Lauda Sion. One of the Sequences (q.v.) allowed to remain in the liturgy of the Roman Catholic Church when the Council of Trent (1545–63) abolished the rest. It has its traditional plainsong, but has also been set by composers. The words are by St. Thomas Aquinas (abt. 1264); they were written for the feast of Corpus Christi (on which they are still sung).

Lauda Sion. Cantata by Mendelssohn (op. 73; 1846). Composed for Corpus Christi Day for a church at Liège: a fragment of the plainsong (see above) appears in one chorus.

Laudi Spirituali (It., more correctly 'Laude Spirituali'). Popular devotional songs of the 13th c. and later, composed for the *Laudisti*, or singing confraternities of Florence and other It. cities.

Laudisti. See *Laudi Spirituali*.

Laudon Symphony. Nickname for Haydn's Symphony in C, No. 69 in Breitkopf edn. of the Symphonies. The name honours the famous Austrian field-marshal.

Lauds. The 2nd of the Canonical Hours (see *Divine Office*) of the Roman Catholic Church, formerly sung at sunrise.

Lauri-Volpi, Giacomo (b. nr. Rome 1892). Operatic tenor, trained St. Cecilia, Rome. Début Rome 1920; Metropolitan 1923; Covent Garden 1925; retired 1965.

Laut (Ger.). 'Loud.'

Laute (Ger.). 'Lute.'

Lautenmacher (Ger.). Same as *Luthier* (q.v.).

Lavallée, Calixa. See *O Canada!*

Lavolta. See *Volta*.

Lawes, (1) **Henry** (b. Dinton, Wiltshire, 1596; d. London 1662). Gentleman of Chapel Royal of Charles I; wrote music for Milton's masque of *Comus* (Ludlow Castle 1633), the Christmas songs in Herrick's *Hesperides*, &c., and greatly valued by these and other poets of the day. Brother of William below.

See *Siege of Rhodes*.

(2) **William** (b. Salisbury 1602; killed at siege of Chester 1645). Brother of Henry, above, and like him Gentleman of Chapel Royal; fought in Civil War on Royalist side. Composed vocal and instrumental music, including music for viols.

Lawrence, (1) **Thomas Bertie** (b. Liverpool 1880; d. London 1953). Choral trainer. Trained as violinist Liverpool School of Music; then some years in business. Formed famous Fleet Street Choir 1929, specializing in Eng. Tudor music.

(2) **Marjorie Florence** (b. Dean's Marsh, Victoria, 1908). Operatic and concert mezzo-soprano. Pupil of Dinh Gilly in Paris. Operatic début Monte Carlo 1932, Paris 1933, Metropolitan Opera, New York, 1935, &c. Stricken with infantile paralysis 1941. Though unable to walk, successfully reappeared in opera and concert hall 1942.

Lawton, Dorothy. See *Central Music Library*.

Lay. See *Lai*.

Lay Clerk, Lay Vicar. See *Vicar Choral*.

Lay of the Bell, The. See *Romberg, A. J.*

Lazareno, Manuel (b. Madrid 1909). Composer. Studied Madrid Conserv. Resident England since 1939; much work Latin-Amer. Service, B.B.C. Compositions include chamber and orch. music and incidental music for many radio plays, &c.

Lazarus, Henry (b. London 1815; there d. 1895). Famous clarinettist; chief Brit. player of his period and on staff of R.A.M. and Kneller Hall.

L.B.C.M. See *Degrees and Diplomas* 2.

L.B.S.M. See *Degrees and Diplomas* 2.

Le (1, Fr.) 'The' (masc. sing.). (2, It.) 'The' (fem. plur.).

Leader (1, Eng.) Principal 1st violin of the orch.—in U.S.A. called *Concert Master*. (2, U.S.A.) Conductor of the orch. (3) 1st violin of string quartet, &c.

Leading Motive or **Leitmotiv** (Ger.). See under *Wagner*, with whose Music Dramas the term first came into use. (The device it represents had, however, previously had some exemplification in the works of other composers, there being instances of something very like it in Mendelssohn, Mozart, and even older composers.) Compare also *Idée fixe* (s.v. *Berlioz*), *Motto Theme*, and *Metamorphosis of Themes*.

Leading Note. 7th degree of major scale (and of minor scale in the form in which that note lies a semitone below the tonic).

Leading Seventh. Chord of minor 7th on Leading Note of major scale (e.g. in C Major, B–D–F–A).

Lebendig (Ger.). 'Lively.' So *lebendiger*, 'livelier'.

Lebhaft (Ger.). 'Lively.' So *lebhafter*, 'livelier'; *Lebhaftigkeit*, 'liveliness'.

Lechner, Leonhard—known also as Athesinus (b. in Tyrol abt. 1550; d. Stuttgart 1606). Choir-boy in Court Chapel, Munich, under Lassus. Held various posts as schoolmaster, singer, and Kapellmeister. Composed motets, &c., and publ. collection of works of Lassus and others.

Leckie, Alexander Joseph (b. Geelong, 1881; d. Perth 1966). Trained R.C.M. B.Mus., Adelaide. Organist Cathedral, Perth, W. Australia, 1908–17; conductor various choral societies, &c.; examiner, Univ. W. Australia.

Leclair, Jean Marie (b. Lyons 1697; murdered Paris 1764). Famous violinist, also for a time ballet master at Turin; from age of 40 gave himself entirely to composition and by the demands he made on players forwarded the development of the technique of perf. of bowed instruments.

Lecocq, Charles—really Alexander Charles (b. Paris 1832; there d. 1918). Trained at Paris Conserv.; gradually won fame as melodious composer of comic operas—more than 40 in all (see *Fille de Madame Angot*).

Le Couppey, Felix (b. Paris 1811; there d. 1887). Trained at Paris Conserv. and later on its staff; famous as teacher of piano and composer of educational material for its students.

Ledger Lines. See *Leger Lines*.

Leeb, Hermann (b. Linz, Austria, 1906; later naturalized Swiss). Lutanist, guitarist, &c. Member and one of founders of Basle Schola Cantorum. On staff Conserv. Zürich and head of music department of Zürich Radio. Many tours as executant.

Leeds. See *Festival*.

Leer (Ger.). 'Empty'; applied to open strings of violin, &c.

Leeves, William. See *Auld Robin Gray*.

Lefébure, Yvonne (b. Ermont, Seine-et-Oise, 1904). Pianist. Pupil Cortot, Widor, and others. Career in Europe and U.S.A. as recitalist and soloist with leading orchs. Lecturer, contributor to musical journals, &c.

Lefébure-Wély (originally Lefébvre), **Louis James Alfred** (b. Paris 1817; there d. 1869). Infant prodigy, publicly playing organ at age 8; organist St. Roch at age 14; then trained at Paris Conserv.; organist Madeleine (1847–58); St. Sulpice (1863–death). Composed much organ music of very brilliant type, harmonium music, popular piano pieces, symphonies, chamber music, &c.

Lefebvre, Charles Édouard (b. Paris 1843; d. Aix-les-Bains 1917). Studied Paris Conserv. and won Rome Prize (1870). Composer of operas, orch., chamber, and church music.

Le Flem, Paul (b. Lézardrieux, Côtes du Nord, 1881). Trained Paris Conserv. and Schola Cantorum (q.v.). Conductor famous choral body

'Chanteurs de St. Gervais'. Composer orch., choral, chamber, and piano music, &c. Also musical journalism.

Left-hand Pianoforte Music. See *Pianoforte Playing.*

Legato, legando, legabile (It.). 'Bound', 'binding', 'in a binding fashion', i.e. performed with a smooth connexion between the notes (opposite of *Staccato*). *Legatissimo* is the superlative. (See Table 22.)

Legatura (It.). (1) 'Tie.' (2) 'Slur.' (3) 'Syncopation.'

Legende von der heiligen Elizabeth, Die (Liszt). See *Saint Elizabeth.*

Legend of Joseph (*Josephs Legende*). Ballet by Richard Strauss. (Prod. Paris and London 1914.)

Legend of St. Christopher, The. (1) Oratorio by HORATIO PARKER. (1st perf. New York 1898. In England, in part, Worcester Fest. 1902; complete Bristol Fest. 1902.) (2) Oratorio by D'INDY. (1st perf. Paris 1920.)

Legend of the Invisible City of Kitej and the Maiden Fevronia. See *Kitej.*

Legend of Tsar Saltan. Opera by Rimsky-Korsakof. Libretto based on Pushkin. (Prod. Moscow 1900; London 1933.) An interlude, *The Flight of the Bumble Bee*, is sometimes included in orch. programmes.

Legends for Orchestra, Four (Sibelius). See *Lemminkäinen.*

Léger, légère (Fr. masc., fem.). 'Light.' So *légereté,* 'lightness', *légèrement,* 'lightly'.

Leger Lines (sometimes spelt 'Ledger Lines'). Those short lines added below or above the staff when notes occur that are too high or too low to be accommodated within the staff itself.

Legge, Walter (b. London 1906). Joined His Master's Voice Co. in 1927, becoming Recording Manager; similar post Columbia Co. since 1938; as such responsible for introduction of many famous artists to the gramophone. London Music critic *Manchester Guardian* 1934–8. Asst. Artistic Director

Covent Garden 1938–9. Director of Music E.N.S.A. 1942–5. Wife is Elisabeth Schwarzkopf.

Leggero, leggere (It. masc., fem.). 'Light.' So *leggeramente* or *leggermente,* 'lightly'; *leggerezza, leggeranza,* 'lightness'; *leggerissimo,* 'as light as possible'.

Leggiadro, leggiadretto (It.). 'Graceful.' So *leggiadramente,* 'gracefully'.

Leggiero, leggiere (It. masc., fem.). 'Light.' So *leggieramente* or *leggiermente,* 'lightly'; *leggierezza, leggieranza,* 'lightness'; *leggierissimo,* 'as light as possible'.

Leggio (It., from *leggere,* 'to read'). 'Music desk.'

Legno (It.). 'Wood.' Used in the expression *col legno,* 'With the wood', i.e. tapping the strings with the stick of the bow instead of playing on them with the hair of it. So *bacchetta di legno,* Wooden-headed drum-stick (see *Percussion Family* 1 a); *strumenti di legno, stromenti di legno,* 'Wood [wind] instruments'.

Lehár, Franz (b. Komarno, or Komorn or Komaron, then in Hungary, 1870; d. Ischl, Austria, 1948). Son of military bandmaster; trained as violinist at Conserv. of Prague; then bandmaster like his father. Composed serious operas, but won great success with *The Merry Widow* (q.v.) and followed this with similar works, as also dances, marches, piano music for young, a violin concerto, &c. (Cf. *Count of Luxemburg.*)

Lehmann, (1) **Lilli** (b. Würzburg 1848; d. Berlin 1929). Coloratura, dramatic, and Lieder soprano. Daughter and pupil of well-known soprano (who was also harpist). Appeared in public age 17–55; one of Wagner's Bayreuth leading singers, creating some parts in *Ring* (1876); famous in Wagner roles on both sides of Atlantic but versatile (170 roles in operas of varying types). Great singing teacher; author of valuable books (on singing and autobiographical).

(2) **Liza**—in full Elizabeth Nina Mary Frederika (b. London 1862; d. Pinner 1918). Granddaughter of Robert

Chambers, the Edinburgh publisher, daughter of Rudolph Lehmann, the painter, and Amelia Lehmann (one-time popular song composer under her initials 'A. L.'). Had a successful career as soprano vocalist; then composed songs, especially song cycles (*In a Persian Garden*, &c.) and also light operas, and some instrumental and choral music.

(3) **Lotte** (b. Perleberg 1888.) Operatic and concert soprano vocalist. Of high reputation in Europe, Brit. Empire, U.S.A., and S. America, especially in Wagner and Strauss roles. Author of a novel and autobiographical works. Naturalized in U.S.A.

Leibowitz, René (b. Warsaw 1913; d. Paris 1972). Composer and conductor. Pupil of Webern and Schönberg, leader of their disciples in France, and author of explanatory articles and treatises. Compositions, all in strict conformity with doctrines of this school, include orchestral and chamber music, songs, &c.

Leicht (Ger.). (1) 'Light in style.' (2) 'Easy.' **Leichtigkeit.** (1) 'Lightness.' (2) 'Easiness.'

Leichtentritt, Hugo (b. Posen 1874; d. Cambridge, Mass., 1951). At age 15 went to U.S.A.; studied at Harvard and then at Berlin (D.Phil. 1901); practised in Berlin as teacher and critic; fought on Ger. side during latter part of First World War; returned to U.S.A. in 1933. On staff at Harvard. Author of many musicological works, ed. of old music, and composer of operas, orch. music, &c.

Leichtfertig (Ger.). 'Giddy', 'frivolous'.

Leid (Ger.). 'Sorrow.'

Leidenschaft (Ger.). 'Passion'; *leidenschaftlich*, 'passionately'.

Leider, Frida (b. Berlin 1888). Operatic soprano, attached especially to Berlin opera. High repute in Wagner; work continued as stage director.

Leigh, Walter (b. London 1905; killed in action in Libya 1942). Studied at Cambridge and under Hindemith in Berlin. Composed piano music, songs,

orch. and choral music, &c.; also comic operas *Jolly Roger* (1933), &c.

Leinsdorf, Erich (b. Vienna 1912). Conductor. Trained Vienna; conductor various European festivals. Metropolitan, New York, 1938; Cleveland Orch. 1943; Rochester 1947; Metropolitan 1957; Boston 1962–9.

Leise (Ger.). 'Soft', 'gentle'. So *Leiser*, 'Softer'.

Leisten (Ger.). 'To perform.' So *Leistung*, 'performance'.

Leitmotiv (Ger.). 'Leading motive' (q.v.).

Lejeune. See *Jeune, Claude Le*.

Lekeu, Guillaume (Henri) (b. nr. Verviers, Belgium, 1870; d. Angers, France, 1894). Pupil in Paris of Franck and d'Indy; composed chamber music, &c. (especially sonatas for violin and piano) that showed high promise, so that premature death was probably a great loss.

Lélio ou le retour à la vie ('Lelio, or the Return to Life'). 'Monodrama' by Berlioz (his 'Op. 14 bis', 1832). Intended as a sequel to the *Fantastic Symphony* (q.v.). It calls for Orch., Choir, 2 Tenors, a Baritone, and a Speaker.

Lemare, Edwin Henry (b. Ventnor, Isle of Wight, 1865; d. Los Angeles 1934). Trained at R.A.M.; held important organ posts and then took to recital career; in Pittsburgh (1902–5) as organist of Carnegie Inst.; municipal organist San Francisco 1921–3; similarly at Portland, Maine, 1924–9; then at Chattanooga, Tennessee. Composed and arranged much music for organ.

Lemmens, Nicolas Jacques (b. Westerloo, Belgium, 1823; d. nr. Malines 1881). Studied organ at Brussels Conserv.; then sent by Belgian govt. to study under Hesse at Breslau; appointed prof. at Brussels Conserv. (1849), and there exercised great influence. Married (1857) the leading Brit. soprano (see *Lemmens-Sherrington*, below) and lived much in England; finally opened school of church music at Malines (1879).

Composed much organ music (including *The Storm*), and compiled organ method.

Lemmens-Sherrington, Hellen—so spelt (b. Preston, Lancs., 1834; d. Brussels 1906). Soprano vocalist of highest eminence in Britain (opera and oratorio). Trained at Brussels Conserv. Married N. J. Lemmens (q.v.).

Lemminkäinen. Suite of 4 'Legends for Orchestra' by Sibelius. (Op. 22, 1893–5; 1st perf. Helsinki 1896.) Based on the Finnish national epic, the *Kalevala*. (1) *Lemminkäinen and the Maidens*; (2) *Lemminkäinen in Tuonela*; (3) *The Swan of Tuonela* (originally written as *Prelude* to a projected Opera); (4) *The Return of Lemminkäinen*.

Lene or **leno** (It.). 'Gentle.' So *lenezza*, 'gentleness'.

Lengnick & Co. London music publishing firm (160 Wardour St., W.1).

Leningrad Symphony. Name that has become attached to Shostakovich's 7th Symphony (op. 60). Composed in Leningrad in 1941, when the city, besieged, was for a long period under heavy fire. (1st Brit. perf. London 1942.)

Leno. See *Lene*.

Lent (Fr.), **lento** (It.). 'Slow.' So *lentando*; *lentato* (It.). 'slowing', 'slowed' (same as 'rallentando'); *lentement* (Fr.), *lentamente* (It.), 'slowly'; *lenteur* (Fr.), *lentezza* (It.), 'slowness'; *lentissimo*, 'very slow'.

Leo, Leonardo (b. nr. Brindisi 1694; d. Naples 1744). Wrote 60 comic and serious operas, fine church music, and music for harpsichord and for organ.

Leoncavallo, Ruggiero (b. Naples 1858; d. nr. Florence 1919). Trained at Naples Conserv.; for many years earned living as player in cafés, composing operas, &c., which did not succeed; in 1892 had enormous success with *I Pagliacci* (see *Pagliacci*); many other operas, none a real success and some complete failures. (See *Zaza*; *Bohème*.)

Leonora. Opera by William H. Fry. Also operas by Paer (1804) and Mercadante (1844). And see *Fidelio*.

Leonora Overtures (Beethoven). See *Fidelio*.

Lerchenquartett ('Lark Quartet'). Nickname of Haydn's String Quartet 'No. 66' or 'No. 67', in D, being No. 11 of the *Tostquartette* (q.v.); it is sometimes described as Op. 64, No. 5. The opening accounts for the name. It is also sometimes, by reason of the rhythm of the last movement, called the *Hornpipe Quartet*.

Lertes. See *Electric Musical Instruments* 1.

Les (Fr.). 'The' (plur.).

Les Adieux, &c. (Beethoven). See *Adieux*.

Leschetizky, Theodor (Leszetycki, Teodor) (b. Lancut 1830; d. Dresden 1915). Of Polish parentage. Virtuoso pianist and composer of piano music; teacher at St. Petersburg Conserv., 1852–78; then in Vienna, where pupils from all over world flocked to him (Paderewski, Gabrilowitch, &c.); married 3 pupils as his 2nd to 4th wives. Close analysis of movements and intense concentration on detail the characteristics of his teaching.

Leslie, Henry (David) (b. London 1822; d. nr. Oswestry 1896). Began life as 'cellist and ended it as most famous Brit. choral conductor of his day ('Henry Leslie's Choir'—a London organization of high importance). As composer remembered merely by part-songs, his oratorio, opera, and symphonies being long forgotten.

Les P'tites Michu. See *P'tites*.

Lesquercade (Fr.). Languedoc patois for 'a maiden in love'. It is used as the title of pieces by several 19th-c. Fr. musicians.

Lesser Doxology. See *Doxologia*.

Lesson. See *Suite*.

Lesto (It.). 'Quick.' So *lestamente*, 'quickly'; *lestissimo*, 'very quickly'.

Lesueur (Le Sueur), Jean François (b. nr. Abbeville 1760; d. Paris 1837). Ran through the gamut of church music from position of choir-boy at Abbeville and Amiens to the musical direction o. Notre Dame, Paris (1786); in latter developed grandiose effects, with use of orch., &c., leading to objections by purists and war of pamphlets; hence retired 1788. Now opened new career as opera composer, as music director of Napoleon (1804), and as prof. of Paris Conserv., where 12 of his students won Rome Prize (amongst them his warm admirer Berlioz, Ambroise Thomas, and Gounod). Compositions include oratorios, masses, Te Deums, &c.

Lesur, Daniel (b. Paris 1908). Organist, pianist, and composer. One of group of 'La Jeune France' (q.v.).

Leszetycki. See *Leschetizky*.

Let's Make an Opera. 'Entertainment for young people' by Benjamin Britten, illustrating the preparation of an opera. Libretto by Eric Crozier. (Prod. Aldeburgh 1949.)

Letzt (Ger., various terminations according to gender, number, case). 'Last.'

Letzten Dinge, Die (Spohr). See *Last Judgement*.

Levare (It.). 'To lift' or 'take off'. So *si levano i sordini*, 'the mutes are taken off'. The past participle *levato* (plur. *levati*) occurs. Also the imperative *levate*, 'lift off'.

Leveridge, Richard (b. London abt. 1670; there d. 1758). Bass singer of great popularity, and composer of many songs that became national favourites (e.g. *Black-eyed Susan*, q.v.; *The Roast Beef of Old England*); in old age fell into poverty and maintained by annual subscription list of admirers.

Levet. Old Eng. term for piece of music played beneath bedroom window, &c., in morning at time of rising.

Levezza (It.). 'Lightness.'

Levi, Hermann (b. Giessen 1839; d. Munich 1900). Noted operatic conductor. Held important posts Rotterdam, Munich, &c. Conducted 1st perf. *Parsifal* (Bayreuth 1882) and music at Wagner's funeral. Some compositions, revised edns. of classic operas, and book on Goethe.

Levien, John Mewburn (b. 1863; d. London 1953). Baritone and singing teacher. Trained Manuel Garcia, &c. Long on staff G.S.M. and T.C.M. and Hon. Sec., &c., Royal Philharmonic Soc. Books on Braham, Santley, &c.

Lewis, (1) **Joseph** (b. Brierley Hill, Staffs., 1878; d. nr. Dorking 1954). Choral conductor, &c. Trained Birmingham School of Music. On B.B.C. staff 1923–38; on G.S.M. staff 1946. Books on singing and conducting.

(2) **Bertha** (b. London 1887; d. Cambridge 1931). Operatic contralto. Trained R.A.M. Appeared on concert platform and in serious opera. Joined D'Oyly Carte Gilbert and Sullivan Co. 1919 and displayed remarkable histrionic gifts. Died as result of overturn of motor-car driven by her colleague Sir Henry Lytton (q.v.).

(3) **John**—in full Leslie John (b. Hereford 1910). Tenor vocalist. Trained R.A.M. Regular broadcaster since 1935. Operatic début Sadler's Wells 1936; Covent Garden same year. Also appearances in London musical productions of the lighter kind.

(4) **Anthony Carey** (b. Bermuda 1915). Studied at Cambridge (M.A., B.Mus.), and in Paris with Nadia Boulanger. On staff of B.B.C. 1935; then War service; Prof. of Music in Birmingham Univ. 1947–68; then Princ. R.A.M. Conductor; writer; composer of orch. works, &c.

(5) **Richard** (b. Manchester 1914). Tenor vocalist (after early career as boy soprano). Trained Royal Manchester Coll. Music. Covent Garden, Glyndebourne, &c., also many Continental and U.S.A. engagements, espec. in modern Brit. works. C.B.E. 1963.

Ley, Henry George (b. Chagford, Devon, 1887; d. 1962). Chorister at St. George's Chapel, Windsor Castle; held scholarship at R.C.M. (later on staff); organ scholar Keble Coll., Oxford (M.A., D.Mus.); whilst still undergraduate (1909) appointed organist of Christ Church Cathedral, Oxford; 'Precentor' (i.e. Musical Director) Eton Coll. 1926–45. Pres. R.C.O. 1933. Composed songs, part-songs, church music, &c.

Leygraf, Hans (b. Stockholm 1920). Pianist. Studied Stockholm Conserv., Munich, and Switzerland. Début aged 9 with Stockholm Symphony

Orch. First recital aged 12. Specialist as Mozart interpreter; also numerous appearances as conductor. Composer piano, orch., and chamber works.

Lezginka (Russian). A dance of the Mohammedan tribe, the Lezghins (on the Persian border).

L.G.S.M. See *Degrees and Diplomas* 2.

L.H. = Left Hand.

Lhevinne, (1) **Joseph** (b. Orel, Russia, 1874; d. New York 1944). Pianist. Trained Moscow Conservatory (later on staff). Début Moscow 1889; New York 1906. World tours. Settled U.S.A. 1919. On staff Juilliard Graduate School. For wife see below. (2) **Rosina** (b. Kief 1880). Pianist. Trained Kief Conserv. Début Moscow 1895. Settled U.S.A. with husband (above) and like him on staff Juilliard Graduate School.

Liadof (**Liadov**, &c.), **Anatol** (b. St. Petersburg 1855; d. nr. Novgorod 1914). Pupil of Rimsky-Korsakof at Conserv. of St. Petersburg; later a prof. there. Composed piano pieces (see *Chopsticks*) and some orch. tone-poems (see *Kikimora*); ed. Russian folk music.

Liaison (Fr. 'Binding'). (1) Smooth performance. (2) Slur indicating such performance. (3) Tie or bind (see Table 22).

Liapunof (**Liapunov**, &c.), **Serge** (b. Yaroslavl 1859; d. Paris 1924). Friend of Balakiref and adherent of Russian national school. Composed orch. music and piano virtuoso music, piano concertos, &c.; ed. Russian folk music.

Libel. See under *Criticism*.

Libera me. See *Requiem*.

Liberamente (It.). 'Freely' (i.e. as to tempo, rhythm, &c.).

Liber scriptus. See *Requiem*.

Libertà (It.). 'Liberty', 'freedom'.

Liberty Song. See *Heart of Oak*.

Libitum. See *Ad libitum*.

Libre; **librement** (Fr.). 'Free'; 'freely'.

Libretto (It. 'Little Book'). The literary text of an opera or oratorio.

Licenza (It.). 'Licence', 'freedom' (in such expressions as *Con alcuna licenza*, 'With some licence', i.e. freedom as to tempo and rhythm).

Lichfild, Henry (end of 16th c. and beginning of 17th). Obscure musician; possibly an amateur. Composed madrigals.

Lie, Sigurd (b. Drammen, Norway, 1871; there d. 1904). Studied in Leipzig and Berlin and practised as violinist and choral conductor in Bergen and Christiania (= Oslo). Composed orch., choral, and solo vocal works, &c.; early death deplored.

Lié (Fr.). 'Bound', i.e. (1) Slurred, or (2) Tied.

Liebe (Ger.). 'Love.'

Liebesgeige (Ger. 'Love-fiddle'). Viola d'amore (see *Viol Family* 3).

Liebeslieder-Walzer ('Love-song Waltzes'). By Brahms (op. 52, 1869, and op. 65, 1875—the latter being called *Neue Liebeslieder*, 'New Love-songs'). For Piano 4-hands, with ad lib. Vocal Quartet.

Liebesmahl der Apostel, Das (Wagner). See *Love Feast*.

Liebesoboe (Ger. 'Love-oboe'). Oboe d'amore (see *Oboe Family*).

Liebesträume ('Love Dreams'). By Liszt. Nocturnes for Piano (publ. 1850), being transcriptions of songs by the composer.

Lieblich Gedact (Ger. *Lieblich* = 'lovely'). Same as *Gedact* (q.v.).

Liebling, (1) **Georg Lothar** (b. Berlin 1865; d. New York 1946). Pianist. Pupil of Kullak (q.v.) and Liszt, &c. Début Berlin 1884. On staff G.S.M., London, 1898–1908. Then Munich and California. Hon. D.Mus. Univ. South California. Composed operas, violin and piano concertos, &c. (2) **Emil** (b. Silesia 1851; d. Chicago 1914). Pianist. Pupil of Kullak (q.v.) and Liszt. In U.S.A. from 1867 (Chicago from 1872). Many piano compositions; also musical-literary work. Brother of (1) and uncle of (3). (3) **Leonard** (b. New York 1880; there d. 1945). Pianist and journalist. Pupil of Godowsky (q.v.); then at

Berlin Hochschule. Toured both sides Atlantic. Joined staff *Musical Courier* 1902; ed. 1911 to death. Some compositions. Nephew of (1) and (2).

Lied; Lieder (Ger. 'Song'; 'Songs'). The word is applied to a distinctive type of solo vocal composition that came into being as an outcome of the Romantic movement (see *Romantic*) of the late 18th and earlier 19th cs. In this type the poem chosen is of high importance, and not a mere passenger for the vehicle, tune. The treatment of the poem may be either 'verse-repeating' or 'through-composed' (i.e. either the same for every stanza or different for each), according to the lyrical or dramatic demands of the poem. The piano part (simple or highly elaborate) is more than a mere accompaniment and, as much as the vocal part, demands an artistic interpretation. Some great names in the history of the *Lied* are Schubert (1797–1828; over 600 examples exhibiting great variety of treatment), Loewe (1796–1869), Schumann, Franz, Brahms, and Wolf.

Liedercyklus (Ger.). 'Song Cycle' (q.v.).

Lieder eines fahrenden Gesellen ('Songs of a Wayfaring Man'). By Mahler. Four song settings (1897) of poems by the composer, inspired by, or at any rate akin to, the Ger. folk collection, *Des Knaben Wunderhorn.*

Liederkranz. 'Song-wreath', i.e. same as Song-cycle (q.v.).

Liederkreis ('Song-circle'). Name applied by Schumann to his op. 24 (1840), 9 Songs by Heine, and also to his op. 39 (1842), 12 Songs by Eichendorff.

Liedersammlung. 'Song Collection.'

Liedertafel (Ger. 'Song Table'). A common name for a Ger. male-voice singing soc. Originally a more or less convivial body of which the members sat round a table with refreshments, but the aims later became more artistic.

Lied ohne Worte. See *Song without Words.*

Lied von der Erde, Das ('The Song of the Earth'). By Mahler. Cycle of 6 songs for Tenor and Contralto (or Baritone), with Orch. The composer called it a Symphony (not numbered as such, however). One of his last works and often considered his greatest. Text a transln. of six 8th-c. Chinese poems. (1st perf. Munich 1911; London 1913; Philadelphia 1916.)

Lie strewn the white flocks (Bliss). See *Pastoral.*

Lieto (It.). 'Joyous.' So *lietissimo,* 'very joyous'; *lietezza,* 'joy'.

Lieutenant Kije. Russian film with music by Prokofief (op. 60; 1933); a 5-movt. orch. suite from this.

Lieve (It.) (1) 'Light'; so *lievezza,* 'lightness'; *lievemente,* 'lightly'. (2) 'Easy'.

Life for the Czar. Opera by Glinka—the earliest important one in Russian by a Russian composer. (Prod. St. Petersburg 1836 and highly popular in Russia until Soviet Revolution; after that perf. under original title—*Ivan Susanin*—with slight libretto revisions; London 1887; Manchester 1888.)

Life on the Ocean Wave, A. See *Russell, H.*

Life's Dance. Symphonic Poem by Delius. Revision, 1911, of the earlier *The Dance goes on.* (1st perf. Düsseldorf 1904.)

Ligature. (1) The mark which in plainsong notation binds several notes into one group. (2) The slur which in modern notation of vocal music shows that the two or more notes it affects are to be fitted to one and the same syllable. (3) The tie or bind (see *Tie*)—a use of the word better avoided as unnecessary and confusing. (4) The adjustable metal band which in instruments of the clarinet family secures the reed to the mouthpiece.

Light of Life, The. Oratorio by Elgar. (1st perf. Worcester Fest. 1896.)

Light of the World, The. Oratorio by Sullivan. (1st perf. Birmingham Fest. 1873.)

Light Opera. Opera of which the subject-matter is cheerful and the musical treatment such as calls for little mental effort on the part of the listener.

Lilac Time. See *Dreimäderlhaus.*

Lilburn, Douglas Gordon (b. Wanganni, N.Z., 1915). Trained N.Z. and R.C.M. (Cobbett Prize 1939). On music staff Victoria Univ. Coll., Wellington. Compositions for films, &c.

Lilliburlero. This tune first appeared in print in 1686 in a book of 'lessons' for the recorder or flute, where it is styled merely a Quickstep. Next year it became popular set to some grotesque and satirical verses (with the mock Irish word 'Lilliburlero' as a refrain) referring to the appointment to the Lord-Lieutenancy of Ireland of General Talbot, just created Earl of Tyrconnel, whose name they several times mention. It played a part in the events leading to the discomfiture of James II and the landing of William in Northern Ireland and has remained a song of the Orange party to this day, set to another song, 'Protestant Boys'. It is thought that Purcell may be the composer, as in 1689, in his *Musick's Handmaid*, it appears, under the title 'A New Irish Tune', as a tiny piece for the harpsichord: he also used it as a ground bass (q.v.) in music for a play, *The Gordian Knot unty'd*, in 1691. The probability, however, seems to be that Purcell was simply using a popular air of the day. A tune somewhat like it appears in a Dutch metrical psalter in 1540.

Some English children now know the tune as that of the nursery rhyme 'There was an old woman tossed up in a blanket'.

Lily of Killarney, The. The most successful opera of Benedict. Libretto based on D. Boucicault's play, *Colleen Bawn.* (Prod. London and Dublin 1862; New York 1868.)

Lincoln Center. A cultural centre opened in New York in 1962, and including a concert hall, opera house, theatre, music school, &c. First President, William Schuman.

Lincoln Portrait. Orch. piece by Copland. With a part for a Speaker. (1st perf. Cincinnati 1942.)

Lind, Jenny—orig. Johanna Maria (b. Stockholm 1820; d. Malvern Wells, England, 1887). Soprano vocalist. Pupil of Manuel Garcia. Early made great international operatic reputation; Brit. début 1847; U.S.A. début 1852. At 29 abandoned opera stage for oratorio and concerts, attracting enormous audiences in Britain and U.S.A. Adored in Britain, partly on grounds of high moral character, charitable gifts, &c. One of earliest professors of R.C.M. (1883–6). Married composer-conductor Otto Goldschmidt and helped him to found Bach Choir (q.v.).

Linda di Chamounix. Romantic Opera by Donizetti. (Prod. Vienna 1842; London 1843; New York and Dublin 1847.)

Lindley Family. (1) **Robert** (b. Rotherham, Yorks., 1777; d. London 1855). Violoncellist—the chief Brit. one of the period (cf. *Dragonetti*). Composed for his instrument. Sons (2) **William** (b. 1802; d. Manchester 1869), Violinist, and (3) **Charles** (d. 1842) Violoncellist.

Linear Counterpoint. Counterpoint with emphasis on the individual strands of the fabric rather than on their harmonic implications.

Lining-out. See *Hymns and Hymn Tunes* 5.

Linke Hand (Ger.). 'Left hand.' *Links* means the same.

Linley, (1) **Thomas I** (b. Badminton 1732; d. London 1795). At first carpenter; secured some musical training (finally under Paradies in Naples) and became singing master and concertgiver in Bath; then (1774) Stanley's partner in management of oratorios at Drury Lane Theatre, London, and after Stanley's death had Samuel Arnold as partner; from 1776 partproprietor and manager of theatre; with son Thomas (see below) composed music for Sheridan's very successful *The Duenna* (1773), and following year took Sheridan (his son-in-law) as partner. Composed much other stage music, also songs, &c. (2) **Thomas II** (b. Bath 1756; drowned Grimsthorpe, Lincs., 1778). Son of Thomas I, above. Studied violin with Nardini in Florence, where the young Mozart became his close friend. Active and able young composer whose early death was greatly regretted.

NOTE. In some larger books of reference 5 other children of Thomas Linley I are included.

(3) **George** (b. Leeds 1798; d. London 1865). No relation of the above family. Settled in London and pursued literary and musical life; ed. and arranged collections of Scottish songs, &c., and composed operas and (words and music) drawing-room songs of high popularity (e.g. *Ever of thee I'm fondly dreaming*); also publ. 2 satirical books attacking London music critics.

Linz Symphony. Nickname of Mozart's Symphony in C, K. 425, composed at Linz for and first performed by the orch. of Count Thun in 1783.

Lipatti, Dinu (b. Rumania 1917; d. Geneva 1950). Pianist and composer. Trained Bucharest Conserv. and, after début and many appearances in Bucharest, and in sonata recitals with Enesco (q.v.), in Paris under Nadia Boulanger (q.v.), Paul Dukas (q.v.), and Cortot (q.v.). On staff Geneva Conserv. Works include orch. and chamber music, a concertante symphony for 2 pianos and strings, &c.

Lira. See *Lyra*.

Lirico (It.). 'Lyric.'

Liscio, liscia (It. masc., fem.). 'Smooth.'

Lisle. See *Rouget de Lisle*.

Lisley, John. Composer of a madrigal in *Triumphs of Oriana* (q.v.).

L.I.S.M. See *Degrees and Diplomas* 2.

L'Isola disabitata (Haydn, &c.). See *Isola*.

L'Istesso (It.). See *Istesso*.

Liszt, Ferencz, or **Franz** (b. Dobr'jan, otherwise Raiding, Hungary, 1811; d. Bayreuth 1886). Studied in Vienna—piano under Czerny and composition under Salieri; became acquainted with Schubert and was kissed by the admiring Beethoven; went to Paris, where much fêted; at 13 (1824) had brilliant reception in London. As young man came much into touch with Fr. romantic literary school (e.g. Hugo, Lamartine George Sand, Saint-Beuve) and also romantic painters (e.g. Delacroix) and greatly influenced by them. At end of his thirties (1849) settled in Weimar as musical director to the Prince; remained for 10 years, reviving cultural fame which that capital had enjoyed under Goethe (d. 1832); organized and conducted 1st perf. of Wagner's *Lohengrin* and brought forward works of Berlioz, &c.; relation to Wagner was close, being that of his warmest champion. From about fiftieth year made Rome chief centre; took minor orders, became known as Abbé Liszt, and now composed much church music.

Female companionship took a large place in his life, especially that of the Countess of Agoult (later known as 'Daniel Stern' the novelist) by whom he had the daughter, Cosima, who later married von Bülow and then Wagner, and Princess Sayn-Wittgenstein, whom he would have married if the Pope would have consented to divorce her from her husband.

As pianist he held a supreme position and young pianists (whom he advised or taught gratuitously) flocked to Weimar from every country. As composer, he represents (with Wagner) the mid-19th-c. school of 'The Music of the Future' (that term being coined in his house); he introduced new processes in composition, e.g. the 'Metamorphosis of Themes' (q.v.); the 'Symphonic Poem' (as name and thing) was of his introduction (see *Symphonic Poem*; *Programme Music*). The list of his productions comprises 400 original compositions and 900 'transcriptions' (for he was the world's greatest 'transcriber' or 'arranger' for piano). The influence of his compositions is seen in the work of many composers—German, Russian, French, &c., but his compositions in themselves have never come to occupy the pedestal their contemporary and later admirers prepared for them and the tradition of Liszt as executive artist overshadows the reputation of Liszt as creative artist.

See also *Adelaïde*; *Années de Pèlerinage*; *Campanella*; *Ce qu'on entend*; *Christus*; *Danse Macabre*; *Divina Commedia*; *Faust Symphony*; *Festklange*; *Hamlet*; *Héroïde Funèbre*; *Hexameron*; *Huldigungsmarsch*;

Hunnenschlacht; *Ideale*; *Liebesträume*; *Mazeppa*; *Mephisto Waltzes*; *Orpheus*; *Paganini Transcriptions*; *Préludes*; *Prometheus*; *Recital*; *Saint Elizabeth*; *Tasso*; *Todtentanz*.

Liszt's Hungarian Rhapsodies. Twenty piano compositions of which 19 were published. Of these 15 were later issued in authorized orch. versions (with modifications and sometimes changes of key) by Franz Doppler. Confusion exists as to the numbering, which differs in the two versions. For a full discussion of this see *Musical Times*, July to October 1932, and compare the lists in the 5th ed. of Grove's *Dictionary*.

Litaniae Lauretanae ('Litany of Loretto'). A 13th-c. litany (q.v.) in honour of the Virgin Mary, much sung in Italy. Palestrina composed many settings of it.

Litany. A supplication. The Roman Catholic and Anglican Churches each possess a long litany consisting of very brief expressions by the priest, each followed by some such response from the people as 'Deliver us, O Lord' or 'We beseech Thee to hear us'. The Anglican litany is a very free translation and adaptation of the chief Roman one.

Litolff, Henry Charles (b. London 1818; d. nr. Paris 1891). Of Alsatian descent. Became widely known as virtuoso pianist, and then as enlightened and enterprising publisher (one of pioneers of cheap edns. of classics), and finally as composer (operas, concertos, overtures, chamber and piano music, &c.). Piano *Spinning Song* and orch. overture *Robespierre* can still be heard.

Little Clavier-book (Bach). See *Klavierbüchlein.*

Little Organ-book (Bach.). See *Orgelbüchlein.*

Little Russian Symphony. See *Tchaikovsky's Symphonies.*

Liturgy. This, properly, means the service of the Christian Eucharist, but in ordinary usage is now applied to any written and officially authorized form of service. The evolution of liturgies

has had a great influence on the development of music, especially because, for many centuries, almost the only literate and trained musicians were those of the Church and the only fully organized music that of its services.

During the 1st few centuries of Christianity liturgies were innumerable, being largely local or territorial. The 1st Christian churches at Rome were Greek-speaking and had a Gr. liturgy; the origin of the Lat. liturgy of Rome is unknown. It overspread Europe from the 11th c.: it is comprised, for the main part, in 2 volumes, the *Missal* (compiled about 900; many revisions since), which gives the service of the Mass, or Eucharist, and the *Breviary* (11th c.), which gives the Divine Office for each day: the *Rituale*, giving the special services (baptisms, marriages, funerals, &c.), and the *Pontifical*, giving services to be performed only by bishops (e.g. ordination), complete the series. The Roman liturgy is unique in the general conformity of its language throughout the world (exceptions are certain ancient churches in Slav. countries and the Near East).

The Lutheran liturgy, as its author left it, was largely a translation, with omissions, of the Lat. liturgy—with an increased congregational element.

For related subjects see *Divine Office*; *Mass*; *Greek Church*; *Common*; *Common Prayer*; *Use of Sarum*; *Litany*; *Psalm*; *Canticle*; *Hymns*; *Respond*; *Accentus*; *Antiphon*; *Antiphonal*; *Tract*; *Creed*; *Improperia*; *Requiem*; *Te Deum*; *Trope*; *Alleluia*; *Sequence*; &c.

Liuto (It.). 'Lute.'

Liverpool Philharmonic Orchestra. Founded 1840. Resident conductors include Max Bruch, Julius Benedict, and F. Cowen; then, after a period of guest conductors: Sargent (1940), Rignold (1949), Pritchard (1957), Groves (1963). 'Royal' from 1957.

Livre (Fr.). 'Book.'

L.L.C.M. See *Degrees and Diplomas.*

Llewellyn, (1) (Thomas) Redvers (b. Briton Ferry, S. Wales, 1903). Operatic and concert baritone. Trained Cardiff Univ., then London and Italy. Operatic career Sadler's Wells; soloist at Brit. orch. concerts and choral festivals, &c. Tours of S. Africa.

(2) **Ernest Victor** (b. Kurri Kurri, N.S.W., 1915). One of Australia's foremost violinists. Leader Sydney Symphony Orchestra.

Lloyd, (1) **John Ambrose** (b. Mold, Flintshire, Wales, 1815; d. Liverpool 1874). Commercial traveller and popular composer of hymn-tunes, anthems, part-songs, &c.; also cantata *The Prayer of Habakkuk*, said to be first such work produced in Wales. Ed. collections of hymn-tunes.

(2) **Edward** (b. London 1845; d. Worthing 1927). Tenor vocalist. Westminster Abbey choir-boy; then singer in Cambridge coll. chapels, Chapel Royal, London, &c. Came prominently forward as oratorio and concert singer, &c., about 1870. Retired 1900 after career of highest popularity.

(3) **Charles Harford** (b. Thornbury, Glos., 1849; d. Slough 1919). Educated at Oxford (M.A., D.Mus.); succeeded S. S. Wesley as organist of Gloucester Cathedral (1876); then organist of Christ Church Cathedral, Oxford (1882); Precentor (i.e. Musical Director) of Eton Coll. (1892); organist of Chapel Royal, St. James's Palace (1914). Composed much choral-orch. music for provincial festivals, also church music, part-songs, &c.

(4) **Llewelyn Southworth** (b. Cheshire 1876; d. Birmingham 1956). Ninth Wrangler, Cambridge, 1898; Principal Asst. Sec. of govt. Dept. of Scientific and Industrial Research; important researcher and writer on acoustical problems; some compositions. C.B. 1921.

(5) **John Morgan** (b. Ystrady Fodwg, Wales, 1880; d. Barry 1960). Student, and then Lecturer and, finally (1933), Prof. of Music at Univ. Coll., Cardiff. D.Mus., Dublin. Compositions mainly choral.

(6) **David George** (b. Trelogan, Flintshire, 1912; d. nr. Holywell 1969). Tenor vocalist. Trained G.S.M. Soloist with choral and orch. societies. Opera at Glyndebourne (début there 1938), London, Brussels, &c.

(7) **George** (b. St. Ives, Cornwall, 1913). Violinist and composer of symphonies and operas (*Iernin*, Penzance

1934, Lyceum, London, 1935; *The Serf*, Covent Garden, London, 1938; *John Socman*, Bristol 1951.)

L.Mus.L.C.M. See *Degrees and Diplomas 2.*

L.Mus.T.C.L. See *Degrees and Diplomas 2.*

Lobgesang. See *Mendelssohn.*

Lob und Ehre ('Blessing and Honour'). A Motet long attributed to Bach, but really by G. G. Wagner (1698–1756).

Local Examinations. See *Associated Board; Education 2.*

Locatelli, Pietro Antonio (b. Bergamo 1695; d. Amsterdam 1764). Violin pupil of Corelli and himself a great violinist, introducing novel effects and advancing technique. Composed sonatas, concerti grossi, &c., for violin, also flute sonatas.

Lochaber no more. The words are by Allan Ramsay. The tune is a variant of an old Irish one, *King James's March to Ireland*, said to have been composed by the harper Miles O'Reilly (b. 1635). Scottish regiments use this tune as a lament.

Loch Lomond. The poem is attributed to Lady John Douglas Scott (cf. *Annie Laurie*). The tune may also be by her.

Locke (or **Lock**), **Matthew** (b. Exeter abt. 1630; d. London 1677). Chorister of Exeter Cathedral; during Commonwealth took part in early London opera performances, being part-composer of the first opera ever heard in England, Davenant's *Siege of Rhodes* (q.v.); on Restoration became 'Composer in Ordinary' to Charles II. Composed anthems, songs, viol music, stage music, &c. The '*Macbeth* Music' (q.v.) long attributed to him is not his.

Lockey, Charles (b. nr. Newbury, Berks., 1820; d. Hastings 1901). Tenor. In choir St. George's, Windsor; then St. Paul's Cathedral (1843). Début in oratorio 1842; sang in 1st perf. *Elijah*, Birmingham Fest. 1846. Retired, through throat trouble, 1859.

Lockspeiser, Edward (b. London 1905). Studied at R.C.M. and in Paris and Berlin. Author of many articles and books on musical subjects (e.g. *Debussy, Berlioz*, &c.). On staff B.B.C. 1942–52.

Loco (It.). 'Place'; used after some sign indicating performance an 8ve higher or lower than written and reminding the performer that the effect of that sign now terminates. Often the expression used is *al loco*, 'At the place'.

Loder, (1) Edward James (b. Bath 1813; d. London 1865). Member of distinguished musical family, of the other members of which particulars will be found in larger books of reference. His operas were successful, especially *The Night Dancers* (1846). Remembered today by songs, e.g. *I heard a brooklet gushing* (which has been praised as equal to Schubert's setting of the same poem—his *Wohin*, in *Die schöne Müllerin*), and the popular *The Diver*. (2) **Kate**—Lady Thompson (b. Bath 1825; d. Headley, Surrey, 1904). Cousin of the above. Pianist. Trained R.A.M. (later on staff). High reputation as artistic performer. After marriage to eminent surgeon retired from platform but made her London house a centre of musical activity (Brahms's *German Requiem*, q.v., had 1st Brit. perf. there, 1871). For last 30 years of life paralysed.

Lodge, Oliver Joseph. See *Broadcasting of Music*.

Lodoiska. Important opera of Cherubini. (Prod. Paris 1791; New York 1826.)

Loeffler, Charles Martin Tornow (b. Mulhouse 1861; d. Medfield, Mass., 1935). Studied violin with Massart and Joachim; played in many orchs. in Europe and U.S.A.; joined Boston Symphony Orch. on its first organization in 1882 and remained till 1903. Voluminous composer of symphonic poems, chamber music, choral music, &c.

Loeillet, (1) Jean-Baptiste—also **John** (b. Ghent 1680; d. London 1730). He became known in France as a performer on the flute, oboe, and harpsichord, then settled in London, where he

carried on concerts and introduced the side-blown flute. He wrote music for the flute, clavichord, &c. The misspelling 'Lully', adopted by one publisher of his period, still causes confusion on concert programmes. The 'John Loeillet' who appears in works of reference as a separate individual is now considered to be Jean-Baptiste. (2) **Jacques** (b. Ghent 1685; d. Versailles 1746). Brother of (1) and likewise a player of various woodwind instruments; also of the violin. He was oboist to the Elector of Bavaria in Munich; from 1727 he was maître de chapelle under Louis XV. He wrote several flute sonatas, also pieces for violin.

Loeschhorn, (Carl) Albert (b. Berlin 1819; there d. 1905). Pianist, teacher, and composer; active in various capacities in Berlin; now remembered by his piano studies, other works being forgotten.

Loewe, Carl—in full Johann Carl Gottfried (b. nr. Halle 1796; d. Kiel 1869). Singer, travelling widely as such, and composer of songs, creating a new art-form, the vividly descriptive or dramatic ballad (e.g. *Edward*); also wrote oratorios, operas, and musical textbooks. When nearing 70 fell into six-weeks' trance and some years later into another from which he never awakened. Of high importance in history of song.

See *Erl King*.

Loewenberg, Alfred (b. Berlin 1902; d. London 1950). At 23 graduated D.Phil. at Univ. of Jena. Settled in London 1934 and occupied himself in useful musicological research. In 1943 publ. the now standard *Annals of Opera*, with minutely detailed particulars of performances (1597–1940) of nearly 4,000 works.

Logan, Sinclair (b. Liscard, Cheshire, 1897). Bass-baritone (also pianist and organist with various diplomas as such). Director Worcester Coll. for Blind, Chairman Music Sub-Committee of Nat. Inst. for Blind, &c. (himself almost sightless). Extension Lecturer Univ. Birmingham. B.Mus., Durham.

Logier, Johann Bernard (b. Kaiserslautern, Palatinate, 1777; d. Dublin 1846). Came to Britain at age 10; became military bandmaster, pianist, organist, and music seller in Dublin. Promoted a system of teaching piano to many pupils simultaneously and invented Chiroplast (q.v.). Composed piano sonatas, &c., and wrote famous textbook of composition (the first one Wagner studied).

Lohengrin. Romantic opera by Wagner. (Prod. by Liszt at Weimar 1850; New York 1871; London 1875.)

See reference under *Wedding March*.

Löhr, Hermann Frederic (b. Plymouth 1872; d. 1944). Trained R.A.M. Became composer of highly popular songs (*Where my Caravan has Rested*; *Little Grey Home in the West*, &c.).

Loin, Lointain (Fr.). 'Distant', i.e. faint.

London College of Music (Great Marlborough St., London). Founded (privately) 1887. Incorporated 1939.

Londonderry Air. This most beautiful Irish melody is first found in print in the Petrie collection of 1855 (see *Petrie*), where it appears with the indication that the name of the composer is unknown. It is understood to be a genuine folk tune and bears all the marks of this. The first words known to have been set to it were 'Would I were Erin's apple blossom o'er you', by Alfred Perceval Graves; the second setting was 'Emer's Farewell', by the same poet. The words now generally sung to it ('Danny Boy') are by F. E. Weatherly.

London, George—orig. Burnstein (b. Montreal 1920). Bass baritone. Studied in Los Angeles; début there 1941, then extensive U.S. tours. Vienna 1949; Metropolitan 1951.

London Philharmonic Orchestra. Founded 1932 by Beecham (q.v.) but now self-governing. It publishes a journal, *Philharmonic Post*, and has issued a number of books on orch. questions (e.g. *Philharmonic*, 1942). Conductor 1950–7 Boult; 1958 Steinberg; 1961 Pritchard; 1967 Haitink.

London String Quartet. Founded 1908 by 'cellist Charles Warwick Evans

(q.v.). Other original members, Sammons, Petre, and H. Waldo Warner. Travelled widely and won high esteem in all parts of world. Then resident California. See also *Pennington, Primrose, Halleux*.

London Symphonies or Salomon Symphonies. Haydn's last 12, written for the London impresario, Salomon (Nos. 93–104 in Breitkopf edn. of the symphonies. No. 12, in D, is often called 'The London Symphony', but there is no justification for such special distinction). No. 1, in D (1791?). No. 2, in G, called in Germany *Paukenschlag* ('Drum-stroke'), and in England *Surprise*, q.v. (1791). No. 3, in C minor (1791). No. 4, in D (1791). No. 5, in C (1792). No. 6, in B flat (1792). No. 7, in E flat (1793). No. 8, in G, called *Militär*, 'Military', q.v. (1794). No. 9, in D, called *Die Uhr*, 'The Clock' (1794). No. 10, in B flat, called 'The Miracle' (1794–5). No. 11, in E flat, called *Paukenwirbel*, 'The Drum Roll', q.v. (1795). No. 12, in D, 'The London' (1795).

London Symphony. See *Vaughan Williams*.

London Symphony Orchestra. Founded 1904 by a secession of members of the Queen's Hall Orch., based on what was held to be their right to employ deputies. Cond. 1961 Monteux; 1965 Kertesz; 1968 Previn.

London Waits. See *Wait*.

Long, (1) **Marguérite Marie Charlotte** (b. Nîmes 1874; d. Paris 1966). Pianist. Trained Paris Conserv., of which later joined staff. Very artistic interpreter both of older and modern works.

(2) **Kathleen** (b. Brentwood 1896; d. Cambridge 1968). Pianist. Trained R.C.M., then on staff. Of international repute as recitalist. C.B.E. 1957.

Long drum. Tenor drum—but sometimes the name is applied to the Bass drum (see *Percussion Family* 2 k).

Longing Waltz (Schubert). See *Mourning Waltz*.

Long keys. See *American Terminology* 5.

Long metre. See *Hymns and Hymn Tunes* 8.

Longo, (1) **Alessandro** (b. Amantea 1864; d. Naples 1945). Pianist and Professor of Piano at Naples Conserv. Also composer. See reference s.v. *Scarlatti, Domenico*. (2) **Achille** (b. Naples 1900; there d. 1954). Son of above. Composer of orch. and chamber music, &c.

Lontano (It.). 'Distant', e.g. *come da lontano*, 'as if from a distance', i.e. faintly. So *lontananza*, 'distance'.

Lopatnikof (**Lopatnikov**, &c.), **Nicolai** (b. Reval, later Tallinn, 1903). Russian trained both as engineer and musician, living some time in Germany; since 1939 in U.S.A. Composer of orch. and chamber music, opera (*Danton*), &c.

Lopokova. See *Ballet.*

Lord, for Thy Tender Mercies' Sake. See under *Farrant.*

Loreley. Opera of Mendelssohn (op. 98, 1847), of which only part was composed when he died. Libretto by Geibel on the familiar Rhine legend. Fragments are sometimes performed concert-fashion.

Lorenz, Max (b. Düsseldorf 1902). Tenor. Studied Berlin. Dresden Opera, then 10 years Bayreuth, also Vienna Opera; visits to Covent Garden, Scala, New York Metropolitan, Rome, &c.

Loritus. Same as 'Glareanus' (see *Modes*).

Lortzing, Gustav Albert (b. Berlin 1801; there d. 1851). Both parents actors; himself lived theatre life, marrying an actress; composed many comic operas still highly popular (see *Czaar und Zimmermann*).

Los (Ger.). 'Loose', 'free in style'.

Lo, Star-led Chiefs. See *Crotch.*

Lost Chord, The. Once highly popular song by Sullivan. Setting of poem by Adelaide Anne Procter. Composed 1877, 'in sorrow at my brother Fred's death'.

Lotti, Antonio (b. probably Venice abt. 1667; there d. 1740). For a time organist of St. Mark's, Venice; composed important church music, over 20 operas, &c.

Louise. Opera of working-class life by G. Charpentier. Libretto by composer. (Prod. Paris 1900; New York 1908; London 1909.)

Loulié, (1) **Étienne** (latter part of 17th c.). Noted Paris music-master and writer of theoretical treatises; earliest inventor of a metronome.

(2) **L. A.** (names unknown) (b. Paris abt. 1775; d. probably 1830-40). Paris violinist; wrote string works still heard today. Programmes sometimes confound him with Lully or Loeillet.

Lourd, lourde (Fr. masc., fem.). 'Heavy.' So *lourdement*, 'heavily'; *lourdeur*, 'heaviness', 'weight'.

Loure. (1) An old Normandy bagpipe. (2) A rustic dance, supposedly once accompanied by the above instrument. Its music was like that of the gigue (q.v.) but slower. A feature of the rhythm was the frequent use of a figure consisting of a short note followed by a longer one—e.g.

Louré. Kind of stringed-instrument bowing—several notes in one bow movement but slightly detached from one another and with a little pressure on each. The verb *Lourer* means to play thus.

Lourié, Arthur (b. St. Petersburg 1892). For a few years after the Revolution held an official position of control in musical education; then (1921) settled in France, as composer now devoting himself largely to mystic religious music, somewhat influenced as to technique by Stravinsky (*Sonata liturgique for piano and chorus*; *Concerto spirituel for piano, chorus, and double-bass*, &c.); since 1941 in U.S.A.

Loveday, Alan Raymond (b. Palmerston North, N.Z., 1928). Violinist. Talent noted by Budapest Quartet during tour of New Zealand; benefit concert given to finance training abroad. Hence in Britain from age 11, studying under Sammons (q.v.) and at R.C.M. Solo work with Brit. orchs., &c.

Love Divine (Stainer). See *Daughter of Jairus.*

Love Feast of the Apostles, The (*Das Liebesmahl der Apostel*). 'Biblical Scene for Men's Choir and Full Orchestra' by Wagner. (1st perf. Dresden 1843.)

Love in a Village. An 'English Opera' (i.e. with spoken dialogue). Libretto by Bickerstaffe: music by Arne and 16 others. (Prod. London 1762; Dublin 1764; Philadelphia and New York soon after. Still revived occasionally.) See *Miller of the Dee.*

Love of the Three Kings (Montemezzi). See *Amore dei tre re.*

Love of Three Oranges, The. Opera by Prokofief (op. 33). Libretto by composer, based on Gozzi's play. (Prod., in Fr., Chicago, 1921; New York 1922.) Also Suite for Orch. (1923.)

Love-potion, The (Donizetti). See *Elisir d'amore.*

Lover, Samuel. See *Rory O'More.*

Loveridge, Iris (Gwendoline May) (b. London 1917). Pianist. Trained R.A.M., and with Cyril Smith and Kentner. Frequent recitalist and broadcaster.

Love-song Waltzes (Brahms). See *Liebeslieder.*

Love, the Magician (Falla). See *Amor brujo.*

Lowe, (1) **Claude Egerton** (b. London 1860; there d. 1947). Trained as pianist and violinist Leipzig Conserv. Successfully taught both his instruments in London and then repeatedly toured world as examiner for T.C.M.
(2) **Edward.** See *Cathedral Music.*

Lower Mordent. See Table 12.

Lower Rhine Festival. See *Festival.*

Lowland Bagpipe. See *Bagpipe Family.*

Lowlands (d'Albert). See *Tiefland.*

Low Mass. See *Mass.*

L.R.A.M. See *Degrees and Diplomas* 2.

L.R.S.M. See *Degrees and Diplomas* 2.

L.T.C.L. See *Degrees and Diplomas* 2.

L.T.S.C. See *Degrees and Diplomas* 2.

Luboshutz, (1) **Lea** (b. Odessa 1885; d. Philadelphia 1965). Violinist. Trained Moscow Conserv. and under Ysaÿe. Toured Europe and U.S.A. and settled in latter. On staff Curtis Inst. (see *Bok* 2). (2) **Pierre** (b. Odessa 1891; d. Rockport Me., 1971). Brother of (1). Trained Moscow Conserv. and Paris. Toured Europe and U.S.A. Specialist in 2-piano performances with wife (cf. *Nemenoff*).

Luca, Giuseppe da (b. Rome 1876; d. New York 1950). Baritone; trained St. Cecilia. Début Piacenza 1897; Milan 1904; outstanding Metropolitan artist from 1915 until 1940.

Lucas, Leighton (b. London 1903). Began life as boy in Diaghilef Ballet (see *Ballet*). Then conductor of ballet, &c. Own orch. Composer and arranger.

Lucca, Pauline (b. Vienna 1841; there d. 1908). Famous operatic soprano. Popular in London and throughout Europe.

Lucia di Lammermoor. Famous Opera by Donizetti. Libretto by Cammarano, based on Scott's novel. (Prod. Naples 1835; London 1838; New Orleans 1841; New York 1843.)

Lucifer. Symphonic Poem by Henry Hadley. (1st perf. Norfolk, Conn., Fest. 1914.)

Lucky Hand (Schönberg). See *Glückliche Hand.*

Lucrezia Borgia. Tragedy-opera by Donizetti, based on play of Victor Hugo. (Prod. Milan 1833; London 1839; New York 1844.)

Ludus Tonalis ('Play of Tone'). By Hindemith (1943). 12 three-part fugues for piano (some employing recondite devices), with Prelude, Interludes, and Postlude. Sub-title is *Studies in Counterpoint, Tonal Organization, and Piano-playing.*

Ludwig, (1) (really Ledwidge), **William** (b. Dublin 1847; d. London 1924). Operatic and concert baritone. Active in Great Britain (especially with Carl Rosa Co.) and in U.S.A. Notable in Wagner and in Irish folk songs. Retired 1911.
(2) **Emil** (b. 1881; d. Ascona Switzerland, 1948). German novelist,

playwright, and then biographer of Napoleon, Bismarck, Lincoln, Beethoven, &c.—unfortunately not entirely ceasing to be novelist when he became biographer.

Luening, Otto (b. Milwaukee 1900). Flautist, opera conductor, &c. Holder of a Guggenheim Fellowship, 1930–2, and then on coll. musical staffs (Columbia Univ.; Barnard Coll. 1944). Orch. and chamber music and opera composer, with special interest in development of electrophonic music.

Luftig (Ger.). 'Airy.'

Lugubre (It. and Fr.). 'Lugubrious.'

Luigini, Alexandre Clément Léon Joseph (b. Lyons 1850; d. Paris 1906). Trained at Paris Conserv. under Massart (violin), Massenet (composition), &c.; became fine violinist and effective opera conductor. Composed amongst other things much ballet music (e.g. well-known *Egyptian Ballet*).

Lully, Jean Baptiste (b. Florence 1632; d. Paris 1687). Taken to Paris at early age; by violin playing and talent for dance became known; at age 20 taken into service of Louis XIV, and later appointed director of special body of string players and dance composer to court.

Married daughter of Lambert (q.v.) and became associated with Molière in preparation of the mythological ballets then in favour; also composed music for some of Molière's plays. Bought from poet Perrin the monopoly for opera performances in Fr. tongue; became wealthy and was ennobled. Life said to be stained by some of worst vices; lost it through abscess caused by striking his foot with the customary long baton when conducting a Te Deum.

Works are very numerous (chiefly operas but also church compositions, &c.); notable for intelligent use of accompanied recitative with correct accentuation, &c.; established form of Fr. Overture (see *Overture*). His style influenced that of Purcell and others. See *Phaëton*.

Programmes sometimes confound Lully with John Loeillet or L. A. Loulié.

Lulu. Unfinished Opera by Alban Berg. Libretto by the composer. (Prod., in its incomplete state, Zürich 1937.) Some of the music exists also as an Orch. Suite.

Lumineux (Fr.). 'Luminous.'

Lungo, lunga (It. masc., fem.). 'Long.' So *lunga pausa* = (1) 'long pause' and (2) 'long rest'.

Lunn, (1) **Charles** (b. Birmingham 1838; d. London 1906). Author of *The Philosophy of Voice* (1874, and 7 or more further edns.) and many similar works.

(2) **Louisa Kirkby** (b. Manchester 1873; d. London 1930). Operatic and concert mezzo-soprano vocalist. Trained R.C.M. Popular on both sides of Atlantic in opera, oratorio, songs, &c.

Luogo (It.). Same as *loco* (q.v.).

Lur. (1) A prehistoric bronze trumpet. (2) A wooden trumpet-like instrument used today by herdsmen in Scandinavia, as the Alphorn (q.v.), which it somewhat resembles, is in Switzerland.

Lurline. See *Wallace, W. V.*

Lush, Ernest (b. Bournemouth 1908). Pianist. Pupil of Matthay, &c. B.B.C. staff pianist and accompanist since 1927. Also recitalist, soloist in concertos, &c.

Lusigando. A term that appears sometimes in Debussy's music. Apparently a mistake for *lusingando* (q.v.).

Lusingando (It.). 'Flattering', i.e. play in a coaxing, intimate manner. So, too, *lusinghevole, lusinghevolmente, lusinghiero, lusingante.*

Lussan, Zélie de (b. Brooklyn 1863, of Fr. parents; d. London 1949). Operatic mezzo-soprano. Opera début Boston 1885, London 1888; highly popular. Carmen at Covent Garden, &c.; also many parts in Carl Rosa and Metropolitan Opera House. Retired 1907 and settled London.

Lustig (Ger.). 'Cheerful.' So *Lustigkeit,* 'cheerfulness'; *Lustspiel,* 'comedy'.

Lustigen Weiber von Windsor, Die ('The Merry Wives of Windsor'). The most successful Opera of Nicolai.

Libretto based on Shakespeare. (Prod. Berlin 1849; New York 1863; London 1864.)

Lustige Witwe, Die (Lehár). See *Merry Widow*.

Lute Family. An ancient and widely distributed family of stringed instruments played by plucking with the fingers (not with a plectrum). In shape they are something like a half-pear, with its stalk, sliced in half, the stalk representing the finger-board (which is fretted: see *Frets*). There is no bridge and each string is duplicated in unison: the number of strings has varied at different periods and in different countries. The head, containing the peg-box, is usually bent back from the neck at an angle. Members of the family have included individuals of various sizes from the large *Chitarrone* or *Archlute* to the small *Mandora* or *Mandore*. The *Chitarrone* and *Theorbo* had a double peg-box, the set of strings attached to one box passing over a finger-board (q.v.), and those attached to the other being left free and being plucked as 'open' strings. The Chittarone was a very large theorbo corresponding to the stringed double-bass of our orchs.; it had wire strings, whilst the other had strings of gut or, in some countries, twisted silk.

Lute music was played not from a notation but from a TABLATURE (q.v.) which in the 16th and 17th cs. took the form of a staff with a space for every string and small letters (a, b, c, &c.) placed within the space to indicate the fret to be used: small marks above the staff, resembling the tails of our notes, gave the duration of the sounds.

This instrument is still in use amongst the Arabian races and has during the 20th c. seen some slight revival in Britain, where at one time it had both been the most serious solo instrument, and had very commonly provided the accompaniment for songs. In the arly days of the orch. the family was much drawn upon, its latest appearance there being probably in one or two works of Bach and Handel. Bach also wrote solo music for it and Haydn a little chamber music calling for it.

Cf. *Colascione*, and see reference under *Song*.

Luth (Fr.). Lute.

Luther, Martin (b. Eisleben, Saxony, 1483; there d. 1546). As religious leader made much use of music; himself played lute and flute; approved of professional choirs but loved also congregational singing; his hymn book of 1524 one of the first such (see *Hymns* 2): some words are his and possibly a few tunes. The tendency of his use of music in worship was to establish the chorale in the place of honour it has since occupied, thus making it a stimulus to composers (cf. *Choral* and *Choral Prelude*).

See also *Ein' feste Burg*; *Pope and Turk Tune*.

Luthier (Fr., from *luth*, 'lute'). A maker of stringed instruments, more especially those of the violin family.

Lutkin, Peter Christian (b. Thompsonville, Wis., 1858; d. Evanston, Ill., 1931). Trained Berlin, Paris, and Vienna. Became Chicago organist, and then held academic positions.

Lutoslawski, Witold (b. Warsaw 1913). A leader of the post World War II 'modernist' school, his compositions include choral, orch., and chamber music works.

Lutto (It.). 'Mourning.' So *luttoso* or *luttuoso*, 'mournful'; *luttosamente*, 'mournfully'.

Lutyens, Elisabeth (b. London 1906). R.C.M. student and then composer of orch. and chamber music, &c. Daughter of the well-known architect; married the conductor, Edward Clark.

Lux aeterna. (1) See *Requiem*. (2) By Hanson. Symphonic Poem with Viola obbligato. (Op. 24; 1st perf. Rome 1923.)

Lvof (Lvov, Lwoff, &c.), Alexis Feodorovich (b. Reval 1798; d. nr. Kovno 1870). Son of director of music in Imperial Court Chapel at St. Petersburg; entered army and rose to high rank, then turned to music and succeeded to father's position; good violinist and leader of famous string quartet; composed much unaccompanied choral music for Russian Church, also the official national anthem of Russia in use 1833 to Revolution (in Britain and America used as a hymn tune).

Lwoff. See *Lvof*.

Lyadof, &c. See *Liadof*.

Lyceum Theatre (London). Place of entertainment from 1798; known as 'English Opera House' for period from 1809. Rebuilt 1815; burnt 1830 and rebuilt.

Lydian Mode. See *Modes*.

Lympany, Moura (b. Saltash, Cornwall, 1916). Pianist. Trained R.A.M. and Vienna and under Matthay. Numerous international tours. Res. U.S.A.

LYRE PLAYERS
(From a Greek vase in the Munich Museum)

Lyra or Lira. Properly the Lyre (q.v.) but (1) in Germany an early name for the hurdy-gurdy (q.v.), whilst (2) in Italy the *lira*, *lira da braccio*, or *lira moderna* was an early bowed instrument, and (3) the *lira da gamba* (in Fr. simply *lyre*) was a bass form of the It. 'Lira', but with more strings.

Lyra Viol. See *Viol Family* 3 f.

Lyre. An instrument of the ancient Greeks, Assyrians, Hebrews, &c.; it was essentially a small harp. In later use the word has been loosely applied to certain bowed instruments (see *Lyra*).

(Eng. and other poets sometimes confuse this instrument with the lute, for which there is no warrant whatever.)

Lyrebird Press (122 R. de Grenelle, Paris). Founded (1933) by Mrs. Louise Dyer (Australian; later Mrs. Hanson-Dyer) for uncommercial publication of Byzantine Music, early Polyphonic Music, complete works of Couperin, Lully, &c. Also gramophone records of early music, &c.

Lyric. (1) A poem (not narrative) of a simple straightforward type, in stanzas. (2) Trade term for a song in a 'musical play'. (3) *Lyric Drama*, opera of all kinds. (4) *Lyric Opera*, one in which the singing outweighs the drama. (5) *Lyric Piece*, term (probably introduced by Grieg) sometimes used as title for short piano piece, &c. (6) *Lyric Soprano* (or Tenor), one of lighter quality of voice and pleasant cantabile style.

Lyric Suite. 6 movements for string quartet by Alban Berg (op. 18, 1926).

Lyrique (Fr.), **Lyrisch** (Ger.). 'Lyrical.'

Lyrisches Stück (Ger.). 'Lyric Piece' (see *Lyric* 5).

Lytton, Henry (b. London 1865; d. there 1936). Début at 17 in travelling Gilbert and Sullivan company; after 3 years succeeded G. Grossmith (q.v.) in chief comedian parts. Abandoned Gilbert and Sullivan opera 1898–1907; then resumed it with enormous success. Knighted 1930; retired 1934. (Cf. *Lewis, Bertha*.)

M

M. As is most usual in works of reference surnames beginning *M'*, *Mc*, or *Mac*. are all treated as though spelt *Mac*. This is the convention adopted in most books of reference—the *Encyclopaedia Britannica*, the British *Who's Who*, &c. (but not the American *Who's Who*).

Ma. (It.). 'But.'

Maazel, Lorin (b. Neuilly 1930). Amer. parentage. From 1939 exhibited as remarkably gifted conductor prodigy; travel scholarship to Italy 1952, continuing his touring career in Europe and S. America. Berlin Opera and radio orch. 1965; London 1971.

Macbeth. (1) Symphonic Poem by RICHARD STRAUSS (op. 23, 1887). It is, of course, based on Shakespeare's tragedy. (2) Early Opera by VERDI. (Prod. Florence 1847; Dublin 1859; later revised; 1st Eng. perf. Glyndebourne 1938). (3) Other operas of same name and on same subject include those by BLOCH (Paris 1910) and COLLINGWOOD (London 1934).

Macbeth Music. Attributed to Locke, but probably not by him. It seems to be an elaboration of music by one Robert Johnson (not the musician mentioned under that name in the present book), which he composed for Middleton's play, *The Witch* (mid-17th c.). Possibly this elaboration (1672) was the work of Purcell when a boy.

McBride, Robert Guyn (b. Tucson, Arizona, 1911). Composer, teacher, instrumentalist. Played wind instruments in jazz combinations, also with orchs. and as chamber player. Numerous compositions, some in popular jazz forms, and others more serious orch. and chamber works.

Maccabeans, The. See *Gniessin.*

McCall, J. P. See *Dawson, Peter.*

McCallum, David (b. Kilsyth, Stirlingshire, 1897). Violinist. Trained R.C.M. and Germany. Leader of Scottish Orch. 1932–6; London Philharmonic Orch. 1936–9; National Symphony Orch.; then Royal Philharmonic Orch.

MacCarthy, Maud (b. Clonmel, Ireland, 1882; d. 1967). Violinist. Pupil of Arbós. Notable recitalist and concerto player. Studied Indian music and lectured on it (e.g. Musical Assoc. 1912), performing Indian instruments. For time known (from 1st husband's name) as 'MacCarthy-Mann'; married 2nd, John Foulds (q.v.).

Macchina (It.). 'Machine, mechanism.' So *macchina a venti*, 'Wind Machine' (q.v.); *corno a macchina*, Valve Horn (see *Horn Family*); *tromba a macchina*, Valve Trumpet (see *Trumpet Family*).

McCormack, John (b. Athlone, Ireland, 1884; d. Dublin 1945). Tenor vocalist. Studied in Milan and in 1907 appeared in London with high success; in 1909 in New York similarly (became U.S.A. citizen). At first chiefly engaged in opera; later almost abandoned this for concerts and recitals. Farewell appearances 1938. Papal Count.

MacCunn, Hamish (b. Greenock 1868; d. London 1916). One of first batch of pupils at opening of R.C.M.; sprang into prominence at 19 with romantic overture *Land of the Mountain and the Flood*; later active as opera conductor and composer (*Jeannie Deans*, 1894, very successful; see also *Diarmid*); cantatas, orch. pieces, &c., chiefly on Scottish subjects.

McDonald, Harl (b. nr. Boulder, Colorado, 1899; d. Princeton, N.J., 1955). Studied in California and at Leipzig; various educational positions; also engaged in acoustical research. Compositions in various media (3rd symphony includes solo voice in 'Sprechstimme', q.v.).

MacDowell, Edward Alexander (b. New York 1861; there d. 1908). Studied piano under Teresa Carreño; then at Conservs. of Paris and Frankfurt, at latter a composition pupil of Raff; then taught at Conserv. of

Darmstadt, and from age 21, when Liszt praised his 1st piano concerto, began to gain recognition in Germany. In 1884 married former pupil, Marion Nevins (1857–1956). Returned to U.S.A. in 1888, settling in Boston; called to New York in 1896 as 1st Prof. of Music at Columbia Univ.; health failed and he resigned in 1904; brain trouble followed and then death at age 46. Admirers raised large sum to endow 'MacDowell Colony' at Peterborough, New Hampshire, on estate he had bought; here composers may spend periods of quiet work.

Compositions include, for piano, 2 concertos, 4 sonatas, and many short pieces which have attained high popularity; symphonic poems; songs, &c. All are of romantic cast, poetical, and often reflecting love of nature.

Mace, Thomas (b. prob. York abt. 1620; d. abt. 1710). Lay clerk of Trinity Coll., Cambridge; wrote quaint and useful book, *Musick's Monument* (1676), on church music, lute and viol and their music, &c.

McEwen, John Blackwood (b. Hawick 1868; d. London 1948). Graduated at Univ. of Glasgow (M.A. 1888); then studied at R.A.M. (1893), of which he later became a prof. and principal (1924–36). Composed *Solway Symphony*, overture *Grey Galloway*, piano music, much chamber music, &c. Also wrote books on theory and musical aesthetics. Hon. D.Mus., Oxford, and LL.D., Glasgow. Knighted 1932.

MacFarlane, William Charles (1870–1945). See *America the Beautiful*.

Macfarren, (1) George Alexander (b. London 1813; there d. 1887). Trained at R.A.M. and later became a prof. there (1834) and finally principal (1876 to death). Suffered from poor eyesight and at last completely blind, for some years dictating compositions to an amanuensis; works (including operas, festival oratorios, and cantatas, orch. and other instrumental music) enjoyed high popularity but are now completely forgotten; textbooks on harmony and counterpoint, at one time greatly used, likewise put aside. Prof. of Music at Cambridge 1875 and D.Mus. 1876.

Knighted 1883. (For wife and brother see below.)

See also *Joseph*; *Day, A*.

(2) **Natalia** (b. Lübeck 1828; d. Bakewell 1916). Ger. contralto vocalist; translator of Ger. operas and Lieder. From age 17 wife of George Alexander, above.

(3) **Walter Cecil** (b. London 1826; there d. 1905). Brother of George Alexander, above. Nearly 60 years a prof. of R.A.M., good pianist, composer of piano music, and ed. of piano classics.

Machaut (Machault), Guillaume de (b. Machaut, in Ardennes, abt. 1300; d. Rheims 1377). Learned priest and graceful poet; latterly a canon of Rheims; composer of earliest existing polyphonic setting of mass and many other works, sacred and secular.

Machicotage. (1) Extemporary ornamentation of plainsong by the priest. (2) Addition of an improvised 2nd part to a plainsong.

See *Plainsong* 3.

Machine à vent (Fr.). 'Wind Machine' (q.v.).

Machine drums. See *Percussion Family* 1 a.

Mächtig (Ger.). 'Mighty', 'powerful'.

Mackenzie, (1) Alexander Campbell (b. Edinburgh 1847; d. London 1935). Came of musical family; from 10 to 15 in Germany, where learnt violin (and played in orch.) and composition; then won scholarship at R.A.M.; settled for a time in Scotland; spent period in Italy composing; Principal of R.A.M. (1888–1924); in much request as choral and orch. conductor. Sevenfold Doctor (Hon. D.Mus. of 4 univs., D.LL. of 2; and LL.D.); knighted 1895. Composed operas (several produced in Germany), fest. oratorios and cantatas, orch. music, &c.—many in their day highly successful.

See also *Colomba*; *Rose of Sharon*; *Rule Britannia!*; *Tam O'Shanter*.

(2) **Compton** (b. West Hartlepool 1883). Educated Oxford. Novelist, playwright, and miscellaneous writer. Founder (1923) and ed. of the monthly

journal, *The Gramophone* (cf. *Stone, Christopher*). Rector of Glasgow Univ. 1931–4. Hon. LL.D., Glasgow; F.R.S.L., O.B.E. Knighted 1952.

Mackenzie-Rogan, John (b. 1855; d. nr. London 1932). Military bandmaster. Trained Kneller Hall. Then Queen's Royal Regiment, Coldstream Guards (1896), and Senior Director of Music, Brigade of Guards. (Retired as Lt.-Col.; C.V.O.)

Mackerras, (Alan) Charles (b. Schenectady, N.Y., 1925). Oboist and conductor; Australian parentage. Trained Sydney Conserv., then came to England 1946, establishing reputation as opera and ballet conductor (Sadler's Wells 1948); B.B.C. 1954–6; then free-lance. Lecturer and skilful arranger.

McKie, William Neil (b. Melbourne 1901). Organist. Trained R.C.M. and Oxford (M.A., B.Mus., Hon. D.Mus.). Music master Eng. public schools; then city organist, Melbourne (1931–8); Magdalen Coll., Oxford, 1938–41; Westminster Abbey 1946-63. Knighted 1953. Hon. Sec. R.C.O. 1963–8.

Mackinlay. See *Sterling*.

Maclean, (1) Charles Donald (b. Cambridge 1843; d. London 1916). Oxford M.A. and D.Mus.; Precentor (i.e. musical director) Eton Coll. (1871–5); then nearly quarter-century in Indian Civil Service; on return devoted self to musical organizing work, especially with International Musical Soc. (For son and grandson see below.) (2) **Alick**, really **Alexander Morvaren** (b. Eton 1872; d. London 1936). Son of Charles Donald, above; had career as theatre and light orch. conductor (at Scarborough 1911–death). Composed operas, choral and orch. works, &c. (3) **Quentin Morvaren** (b. London 1896; d. Toronto 1962). Son of Alick, above. Cinema organist; composer of lighter type of music.

Macleod, Annie. See *Skye Boat Song*.

MacMillan, Ernest Campbell (b. nr. Toronto 1893; d. there 1973). Came to Britain, took A.R.C.O. at age 13, F.R.C.O. and B.Mus., Oxford, at 17.

Studied at Edinburgh with Hollins and Niecks and then took Arts course at Univ. of Toronto (Honours in Modern History). Trapped at Bayreuth 1914, interned at Ruhleben and there wrote and had accepted his Oxford D.Mus. exercise and took the degree. Has since composed choral and chamber music, &c., and publ. books of Canadian folk songs. Principal of Toronto Conserv. of Music 1926–42, conductor of Toronto Symphony Orch. since 1931, Dean of Faculty of Music, Univ. of Toronto, 1926–52. Knighted 1935.

McNaught, (1) William Gray (b. London 1849; there d. 1918). Choral conductor; competition adjudicator; authority on Tonic Sol-fa; assistant Inspector of Music, government Education Dept., &c. Ed. of *Musical Times* (1909 to death) and *School Music Review*; author of books on school singing. Trained R.A.M. D.Mus., Lambeth. (2) **William** (b. London 1883; d. there 1953). Son of above. Educ. Oxford (B.A.). Leading music critic; ed. *Musical Times* (1944–53), succeeding Harvey Grace.

Maconchy, Elizabeth (b. Broxbourne, Herts., 1907). Studied at R.C.M. and then Prague, where won recognition as composer by piano concerto performed 1930. Composer of orch. and chamber music, &c.

McPhee, Colin (b. Montreal 1901). Composer of modernist tendencies settled in U.S.A. Spent years 1931–7 in Bali, Dutch East Indies, engaged in anthropological-musical research: has publ. papers on the subject and a collection of Balinese ceremonial music for piano. Compositions include theatre music, orch. and chamber music, &c. In several works makes use of Balinese idioms.

Macpherson, (1) (Charles) Stewart (b. Liverpool 1865; d. London 1941). Distinguished pupil of R.A.M.; later a prof. there, as also prof. of composition at Royal Normal Coll. for Blind. After early career as organist, conductor, and composer, devoted himself to educational treatment of music, writing valuable textbooks, producing practical edns. of piano classics, and founding Music Teachers'

Assoc.; pioneer in Britain of Musical Appreciation movement in schools (see *Appreciation of Music*).

(2) **Charles** (b. Edinburgh 1870; d. London 1927). Chorister at St. Paul's Cathedral; trained R.A.M.; later a prof. there; asst. organist St. Paul's Cathedral 1895, organist 1916 to death. Composed some church, orch., and chamber music. Hon. D.Mus., Durham.

Madame Butterfly. Tragedy-opera on Japanese subject by Puccini. Libretto based on story by John Luther Long and the play thereon by David Belasco. (Prod. Milan 1904; London 1905; New York 1906.)

Madame Sans-Gêne. Opera by Giordano. Libretto based on the play by Sardou and Moreau. (Prod. New York 1915.)

Madeira, Jean (Browning) (b. Centralia, Ill., 1924). Operatic mezzo-soprano. Trained Juilliard. Metropolitan début 1948; European career from 1954, later appearing chiefly in Vienna and New York.

Madelon, La. Favourite song of Fr. soldiers during latter part of war of 1914–18. Composed by Camille Robert.

Maderna, Bruno (b. Venice 1920; d. Darmstadt 1973). Conductor and composer (pupil of Scherchen and Malipiero), sympathetic to modern trends. Compositions include a piano concerto and other works, some including electrophonic means. Leader, with Berio, of the Italian group of advanced experimental followers of Webern.

Madetoja, Leevi (b. Uleåborg 1887; d. Helsinki 1947). Finnish composer, conductor, teacher, &c. Pupil of Järnefelt, Sibelius, d'Indy, &c. Symphonies (3), operas (2), &c.

Madriale. See *Madrigal*.

Madrigal. The word, as the name for a type of composition, is found in Italy from the late 13th c. It was applied to secular unaccompanied vocal compositions for 2 or 3 voices, with ingenious points of imitation (see *Counterpoint*—end). The form of the word used was *madriale* or *mandriale*, and at a somewhat later period this was given to a type of lyrical poem. In the 16th c. the word came again into musical use as the It. composers devoted themselves to work of the type indicated, now availing themselves of the full resources of the greatest age of contrapuntal choral composition. The corpus of It. madrigals of the 16th and early 17th cs. is very large.

At the end of the 16th c. It. madrigals were imported into England (see *Yonge*) and for a few years (up to about 1630) quantities of works in this style were provided by Eng. composers. They can be divided into 3 classes; (*a*) The *Madrigal proper*, very contrapuntal in style and publ. in part-books for the separate voices (intended to be one voice to a part); (*b*) The *Ayre*, less contrapuntal, being more like a verse-repeating soprano song, with choral or instrumental accompaniment (the latter often for lute), and publ. not in part-books but in a large book around which the performers could sit or stand; and (*c*) The *Ballett*, like the ayre, but with a dance lilt and a 'fa-la' refrain, and publ. in part-books like the madrigal proper; it was probably often danced to by the singers.

See *Triumphs of Oriana*.

Madrigal Society. Founded in London in 1741 and still existing. The members meet for supper, after which the books are handed round the table, choir-boys enter to sing the treble parts, and the singing begins. No audience. Offering of prizes for madrigal composition has been a feature of the society's activity.

Madrileña (Sp.), **Madrilène** (Fr.). A Spanish dance type deriving from the province of Madrid.

Maelzel. See *Metronome*; *Mechanica Reproduction of Music* 8, 9; *Wellington's Victory*.

Maestà, maestade (It.). 'Majesty', 'dignity'. So *maestevole*, *maestevolmente*, 'majestically'. **Maestoso**, 'majestic'. So *maestosamente*, 'majestically'.

Maestro (It.). 'Master', 'teacher', &c. *Maestro di cappella* (see *Kapellmeister*) means 'Chief Musician' or 'Musical Director' and nowadays (usually abbreviated to merely 'Maestro') 'Conductor'.

Mager. See *Electric Musical Instruments* 1.

Maggini, Giovanni Paolo (b. Brescia 1581; there d. 1630). Great violin maker.

Maggiolata (It.). 'May Song', or 'Spring Song'—either traditional or composed.

Maggiore (It.). 'Major.'

Maggot. Old Eng. for 'fanciful idea', &c.; hence applied as part of title of a pleasant piece of instrumental music (generally a country dance)—'My Lady Winwood's Maggot', and the like.

Magic Flute, The (Ger. *Die Zauberflöte*, or, in It. version, *Il Flauto magico*). Fantastic opera by Mozart. Libretto by Schikaneder. (Prod. Vienna 1791; London 1811; New York 1833.)

Magna (It.). Fem. of *magno*, 'great'.

Magnard, Albéric—in full Lucien Denis Gabriel Albéric (b. Paris 1865; d. defying Germans in his own house 1914). Educated partly at Ramsgate, England; then trained at Paris Conserv. under Dubois and Massenet; later studied with d'Indy and as composer belongs to Franck-d'Indy school. Opera *Yolande* (Brussels 1892); chamber music, symphonies, &c.

Magnificat. The hymn of the Virgin Mary ('My soul doth magnify the Lord'), as given in the gospel of St. Luke. It forms a part of the service of Vespers (q.v.) in the Roman Catholic Church and of that of Evensong in the Anglican Church (see *Common Prayer*). It has, of course, its traditional plainsong in the former, and is often sung to an Anglican chant in the latter. It is also sung both in churches and in concert performances to composed settings of which many exist—Palestrina, Lassus, Bach (see below), the Eng. church composers, Vaughan Williams, &c.

Magnificat. (1) By BACH. The text is punctuated with Chorales. (Probably 1st perf. Leipzig 1723. London, in a private house, 1852.) (2) By VAUGHAN WILLIAMS. For contralto solo, female chorus, and orch. (in which a solo flute is important). Dedicated to Astra Desmond, the solo vocalist in the 1st perf. at Worcester Fest. 1932.

Magno, Magna (It. masc., fem.). 'Great.'

Magyar. The Magyars are a Mongol race now chiefly found in Hungary. So 'Magyar' is sometimes used for 'Hungarian'. When the term is used in connexion with music, however, it usually refers to that of the very musical Hungarian gipsies.

Mahillon, Victor Charles (b. Brussels 1841; d. St. Jean, Cap Ferrat, 1924.) Curator of great collection of instruments at Brussels Conserv. and authority on instrumental construction and history.

Mahler, Gustav (b. Kalischt, Bohemia, 1860; d. Vienna 1911). Studied at Vienna Univ. and Conserv. (composition with Bruckner); then held various opera conductorships, including Vienna (1897–1907); also conducted opera in London and New York. Composed 9 symphonies, some with voices (see below); 42 songs, &c. Like Brahms a classical romantic, influenced also by Wagner. In Germany and Holland his works have been given very high rank; elsewhere they have made their way, though more slowly.

See also *Kindertotenlieder*; *Lieder eines fahrenden Gesellen*; *Symphony of a Thousand*.

Mahler's Symphonies are as follows: No. 1, in D (1888). No. 2, in C minor, 'Resurrection Symphony' (1894); with solo soprano and contralto and chorus. No. 3, in D minor (1895); with solo contralto, and boys' and female choruses. No. 4, in G (1900); with solo soprano. No. 5, in C sharp minor (1902). No. 6, in A minor (1904). No. 7, in E minor (1905). No. 8, in E flat (1907); with 8 solo vocalists, 2 mixed choruses and boys' chorus, and organ (see *Symphony of a Thousand*). No. 9, in D (1909). No. 10 (unfinished: the sketches were entrusted to Křenek, and a movement was perf. 1924; version by Deryck Cooke perf. 1964). There is also his *Lied von der Erde* (q.v.), a Symphony with solo voices.

Maid as Mistress (Pergolese). See *Serva Padrona*.

Maiden's Prayer, The. See *Badarzewska*.

Maid of Arles (Bizet). See *Arlésienne*.

Maid of Pskov, The (Rimsky-Korsakof). See *Ivan the Terrible.*

Maid of the Mill (Schubert). See *Schöne Müllerin.*

Maillart, Aimé—really Louis (b. Montepellier 1817; d. Moulins, Allier, 1871). At Paris Conserv. won Rome Prize; on return from Rome gradually became known as composer of operas (e.g. *Les Dragons de Villars*, 'Villars Dragoons', 1856).

Mailloche (Fr.). Stick of bass drum (see *Percussion Family* 2 k).

Maillot. See *Ballet.*

Main, mains (Fr.). 'Hand', 'hands', e.g. *main droite* (or *M.D.*), 'right hand'; *main gauche* (or *M.G.*), 'left hand'; *deux mains*, 'two hands'; *quatre mains*, 'four hands' (in piano music).

Maine, Basil Stephen (b. Norwich 1894). After study at Cambridge (M.A.), schoolmastering, organ-playing, and acting, became a London music critic, lecturer, author (e.g. *Elgar*, 2 vols., 1933), and composer, and finally (1939) Anglican clergyman. Admirable 'orator' in musical works calling for such (Honegger, Bliss, Walton, &c.).

Mainzer, Joseph (b. Trier, otherwise Trèves, 1801; d. Salford 1851). In turn mining engineer, priest, opera composer in Brussels and Paris, music critic, and teacher of sight-singing classes in Paris and throughout Britain (lived in Edinburgh 1847, later in Manchester). Some of his books had very large sale (especially *Singing for the Million*, 1841) and his *Musical Times and Singing-Class Circular* (1842–4) became our present *Musical Times* (1844 and still running). His methods look today very unmethodical but were widely taken up, those of Hullah (q.v.), however, competing with them, both ultimately succumbing before the system of Curwen (see *Sight-Singing*; *Tonic Sol-fa*).

Mais (Fr.). 'But.'

Maitland. See *Fuller Maitland.*

Maître (Fr.). 'Master.'

Maître de Chapelle (Fr.). Same as Ger. *Kapellmeister* (q.v.).

Maîtrise. A Fr. choir school.

Majestätisch (Ger.). 'Majestic', 'majestically'.

Majestueux, majestueuse (Fr. masc., fem.). 'Majestic'; so *majestueusement*, 'majestically'.

Majeur (Fr.). 'Major.'

Major Bass. Organ stop of 16-foot pitch, generally an *Open Diapason* (for which see *Organ* 2).

Major Canticles. See *Canticles.*

Major Common Chord. See *Harmony* 2 d.

Major Flute. Loud Organ stop of 8- or 16-foot length and pitch.

Major Intervals. See *Interval.*

Major Scale. See *Scale.*

Mal (Ger.). 'Time', in such connexions as *Erstes Mal*, 'First Time'; 2 *Mal* (or *Zweimal*), twice, &c.

Malagueña. A kind of fandango (q.v.) of Malaga, in southern Spain. A feature is some more or less improvised singing. Its peculiar harmony (particularly at the cadence) is another characteristic.

Malbrouck s'en va-t-en guerre. This is an 18th-c. Fr. nursery ditty. The tune is in Britain sung to both 'For he's a jolly good fellow' and 'We won't go home till morning'. It has had a great popularity all over Europe, to many different sets of words. It is usually stated that 'Malbrouck' is the great Duke of Marlborough, but the name 'Malbrouck' is found in literature of the Middle Ages.

Malcolm, George John (b. London 1917). Choir trainer, pianist, harpsichordist, &c. Trained R.C.M. and Balliol Coll., Oxford (M.A., B.Mus.). Master of the Music, Westminster R.C. Cathedral (1947–59); then on staff R.A.M. C.B.E. 1965.

Malcuzynski, Witold (b. Warsaw 1914). Pianist; studied Warsaw Univ., then turned to music. Grand Prix, Warsaw Chopin contest 1937. During war in America. Successful tours of Europe since 1942.

Maleingreau, Paul de (b. Trélon, N. France, 1887; d. Brussels 1956). Trained at Brussels Conserv. (under

Tinel) where later became a prof. of harmony and organ (notable as Bach performer). Composer of organ, piano, and chamber music, &c.

Male Voice Choir (or Chorus). One (usually) of men only but it may be of boys and men.

Male Voice Quartet. See *Quartet.*

Malibran. See *Garcia* 3.

Malimba. See *Marimba.*

Malinconia, malinconico (It.). 'Melancholy.' So *malinconoso, malinconioso, malinconicamente,* 'in melancholy fashion'.

Malipiero, Francesco—in full Gian Francesco (b. Venice 1882; d. Treviso 1973). Has written orch. and chamber music, &c., some of which has been widely performed; has edited works of Monteverdi and himself experimented in problems of combination of music and drama, producing many stage works. Active in providing collections of works of It. composers of 17th and 18th cs.; has written books and many articles on musical subjects. Director Conserv., Venice; Prof. of Music, Univ. Padua.

Malizia (It.). 'Malice.'

Malko, Nicolai Andreievich (b. Brailov, Russia, 1883; d. Sydney 1961). Trained St. Petersburg Conserv. under Rimsky-Korsakof, &c., and Munich under Mottl. Conducted State Opera and Ballet, St. Petersburg, 1908–18; then academic positions in Moscow, Kiev, &c., Copenhagen, Prague. Toured Europe as conductor; frequently in London. Chicago 1940; Yorkshire Symphony Orch. 1954; Sydney Symphony 1956.

Malling, (1) **Jörgen** (b. Copenhagen 1836; there d. 1905). Composer of operas, piano music, songs, &c., and well known as Danish champion of Chevé method of sight-singing (see *Galin-Paris-Chevé*).

(2) **Otto (Valdemar)** (b. Copenhagen 1848; there d. 1915). Pupil of Gade. Well-known organist, choral conductor, and member of staff of Conserv. of Copenhagen, and then its director. Composed orch., chamber,

choral, and piano music, songs, &c.; best known by organ works.

Mallinson, James Albert (b. Leeds 1870; d. Elsinore, Denmark, 1946). Lived in Australia 1898–1903. Married a Danish Lieder singer, Anne Steinhauer, in Copenhagen; then toured the world with her, giving programmes of some of the 400 songs he composed (300 pub.). In later years overseas examiner for T.C.M.

Malten (real name Müller), **Thérèse** (b. Insterburg, E. Prussia, 1855; d. Dresden 1930). Operatic soprano internationally prominent in Wagner roles.

Maltman. See *Sir Roger de Coverley.*

Ma Mère l'Oye ('Mother Goose'). Piano Duets for children's enjoyment by Ravel (1908); also orchestrated by him and, further, treated as a Ballet. Based on some of Perrault's 17th-c. fairy-stories: (1) *Sleeping Beauty*; (2) *Tom Thumb*; (3) *Empress of the Pagodas*; (4) *Beauty and the Beast*; (5) *Fairy Garden.*

Man. (1, It.) Short for *mano,* 'hand'. (2, Ger.) Short for *Manuale,* 'manual' (of organ); Man. I = 'Great'; II, 'Swell'; III, 'Choir'; IV, 'Solo' (but occasionally another numeration is used, based on position, i.e. I, 'Choir'; II, 'Great'; III, 'Swell'; IV, 'Solo').

Mana-Zucca—rearrangement of (Augusta) Zuckermann (b. New York 1887). Successively piano prodigy, operetta singer, and composer of many hundreds of works, from drawing-room ballads and piano teaching material to concertos and operas.

Mancando, mancante (It.). 'Dying away.'

Mancanza (It.). 'Lack.'

Manchega. An especially lively type of seguidilla (q.v.) that is danced in the La Mancha province of Spain.

Manchester Music Library. See *Watson, Henry.*

Mancinelli, Luigi (b. Orvieto 1848; d. Rome 1921). Opera conductor. Early career as 'cellist; principal of Bologna Conserv. (1881); for many years conducted opera seasons at Covent Garden,

London, &c. Great Wagner exponent. Composer of operas, oratorios, &c. (See *Ero e Leandro*.)

Mandoline or Mandolin. An instrument of the type of the lute (see *Lute Family*) but much less musically valuable. It has 4 (or 5) pairs of strings (each pair tuned to the same note); they are plucked with a plectrum (q.v.), generally in tremolo fashion. Some of the great composers have, on occasion, written for mandoline, including Beethoven, who left 5 solos for it with piano accompaniment.

See also *Electric Musical Instruments* 2.

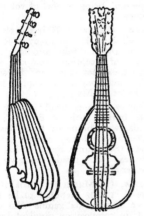

NEAPOLITAN MANDOLINE
(With 4 pairs of strings)

Mandora or **Mandore.** See *Lute Family*.

Mandriale. See *Madrigal*.

Mandyczewski, Eusebius (b. Czernowitz 1857; d. Vienna 1929). Musical scholar, pupil of Nottebohm. Taught at Vienna Conserv.; noted as editor of many works of Haydn, Beethoven, and Schubert, also those of his friend Brahms.

Manén, Joan de (b. Barcelona 1883). Violinist and composer of operas, orch. and chamber music, &c.

Manfred. 'Dramatic Poem' by Schumann (op. 115; 1849). A setting (for concert or stage use) of Byron's poem, adapted. (1st stage perf. at Weimar, by Liszt, 1852.)

Manfred Symphony. See *Tchaikovsky's Symphonies*.

Mangeot, E. J. See *Keyboard*.

Manhattan School of Music. Founded 1917 by Mrs. Janet D. Schenk for benefit of the (largely foreign-born) population of the 'Upper East Side' of New York City. Grants degrees of Bachelor and Master of Music. Address: Claremont Ave., New York.

See *Brownlee, John*.

Mani (It.). 'Hands.'

Manica (It.). 'Shift' (on violin, &c.; see *Position*).

Manichord. See *Monochord*.

Manico (It.). 'Fingerboard' (violin, &c.).

Manieren (Ger.). Ornaments or 'graces' (see *Ornaments*).

Man in Cage. See *Murrill*.

Mann, (1) **Arthur Henry** (b. Norwich 1850; d. Cambridge 1929). Choir-boy and then asst. organist at Norwich Cathedral, under Zechariah Buck (q.v.); organist of various churches and then (1876) of King's Coll., Cambridge. Had high reputation as choir trainer, Handelian, and musical antiquary.

(2) **Johann Christoph** or **Giovanni Matteo.** See *Monn*.

Männer (Ger.). 'Men.' So *Männerchor*, 'Men's Choir'; *Männerstimmen* 'Men's Voices'.

Männergesangverein (Ger. 'Men's Singing Society'). Much the same as *Liedertafel* (q.v.).

Manners, Charles—really Southcote Mansergh (b. London 1857; d. Dublin 1935). Bass vocalist and opera manager. Trained at R.A.M. and in Florence. Made début in D'Oyly Carte's Gilbert and Sullivan Co., soon winning high reputation. Married soprano Fanny Moody (q.v.) and founded (1897) well-known Moody-Manners Opera Co. for perf. of opera in English. Retired 1913.

Mannes, (1) **David** (b. New York 1866; d. there 1959). Violinist. Pupil of Ysaÿe (q.v.), &c. Leading violinist New York Symphony Orch. 1898–1912.

Founded Music School Settlement for Coloured People, New York, 1912; then his own music school 1916. Sonata Recitals with wife (see below). (2) **Clara Damrosch** (b. Breslau 1869; d. New York 1948). Pianist. Daughter of Leopold Damrosch (q.v.) and wife of above. (3) **Leopold Damrosch** (b. New York 1899; d. Martha's Vineyard, Mass., 1964). Pianist and composer; son of the two above. Pupil of Cortot, &c. Pulitzer Prize and Guggenheim Fellowship. (Also physicist and co-inventor of the 'Kodachrome' colour photography process.)

Mannheim School. Name given to the group of composers (notably Stamitz, q.v.) working in that Ger. town in the post-Bach, pre-Haydn period and active in developing the early stages of the symphony (q.v.).

Manns, August Friedrich (b. nr. Stettin 1825; d. Norwood, nr. London, 1907). Became military bandsman, player in Berlin dance orch. of Gung'l, and composer of dance music, &c. Conductor at Crystal Palace 1855–1901 and made it the country's greatest centre of enterprising orch. activity. Knighted 1903 and Hon. D.Mus., Oxford, same year.

Mano, mani (It.). 'Hand', 'hands'.

Manon. Very successful opera by Massenet. (Prod. Paris 1884; London and New York 1885.)

Manon Lescaut. Dramatic opera by Puccini. (Prod. Turin 1893; London and Philadelphia 1894; New York 1898.) Also Opera by Auber (1856).

Mansergh. See *Manners.*

Manual. See *Organ* 1.

Manuale (Ger.). Manual (of organ). See under *Man.*

Manualkoppel (Ger.). 'Manual coupler', i.e. (usually) 'Swell to Great'.

Manuel, Roland Alexis—or Roland-Manuel, or Manuel-Levy (b. Paris 1891). Pupil of Roussel and Ravel; composer of light operas, ballets, orch. music, &c., and prolific author (especially on Ravel and Falla) and musical journalist.

Manzoni Requiem (Verdi). See *Requiem.*

Maometto II (Rossini). See *Siege of Corinth.*

Maple Leaf for Ever! This Canadian national song was written and composed in 1867 by a schoolmaster, Alexander Muir (born in Scotland 1830, died 1906); since 1887 it has been officially used in Ontario schools. in Quebec *O Canada!* is preferred.

Mapleson, James Henry (b. London 1830; there d. 1901). Studied R.A.M. Operatic vocalist and orch. viola player. Became very active as London opera impresario and travelled U.S.A. with his company. (Known as 'Colonel Mapleson', being colonel of volunteer regiment.)

Mara, Gertrud Elisabeth—b. Schmeling (b. Kassel 1749; d. Reval, Russia, 1833). Violin prodigy, then soprano of exceptional compass, with internat. career esp. in Dresden, Berlin, and London. Unhappily married to 'cellist Mara.

Maracas. Dance-band instruments made from a pair of dried Cuban gourds, with beans or beads inside. Shaken by handle to produce a rattling effect. (Sometimes made of bakelite with lead shot inside, so giving a stronger effect.)

Marais, (1) **Marin** (b. Paris 1656; there d. 1728). Reputed to be best player of viola da gamba who ever lived; in composition pupil of Lully. Wrote operas and much instrumental music, latter still heard; had 19 children, almost all musicians (see below). (2) **Roland** (abt. 1680–1750). The musically most important of children of Marin Marais (above); his father's successor as performer on viola da gamba; publ. music for his instrument and a *New Method of Music* (1711).

Marbeck. See *Merbecke.*

Marble Guest (Dargomijsky). See *Stone Guest.*

Marcando; marcato (It.). 'Marking'; 'marked', i.e. each note emphasized. *Marcatissimo* is the superlative.

Marcello, Benedetto (b. Venice 1686; d. Brescia 1739). Venetian lawyer, official, poet, violinist, vocalist, and composer of celebrated settings of first 50 Psalms (6 vols., 1724–7) for 1 to 4 voices with figured-bass accompaniment; also concerti, canzoni, &c., and satire on opera composition of the day, *The Fashionable Theatre* ('Il Teatro alla Moda').

Marchal, André (b. Paris 1894). Being blind from birth, trained Inst. Nat. des Jeunes Aveugles, then Paris Conserv. Organist Saint-Germain-des-Prés, 1915–45, then Saint-Eustache. Extensive recital tours, Europe and America; wide reputation as improviser and Bach player.

Marchand, Louis (b. Lyons 1669; d. Paris 1732). Organist of Paris Chapel Royal (1708–14); some compositions. He is remembered for failing to appear for a projected 'competition' with Bach in Dresden, 1717.

Marchant, Stanley (b. London 1883; d. there 1949). Had early career as boy soprano known throughout Britain. Then trained R.A.M. Sub-organist St. Paul's Cathedral (1916), organist (1927–36). Principal R.A.M. (1936); Prof. of Music London Univ. (1937). Composed church music, &c. M.A., D.Mus., Oxford. C.V.O. 1935. Knighted 1943.

Marche (Fr.). 'March.'

Marche aux flambeaux (Fr.). 'Torchlight Procession.'

Marche écossaise sur un thème populaire. By Debussy (1891). Written for Piano Duet and later orchestrated. Commissioned by General Meredith Reed and based on a tune associated with one of his ancestors—the *Earl of Ross's March*.

Marche funèbre. See *Funeral Marches*.

Marche hongroise (Berlioz). The *Rákóczy march* (q.v.).

Märchen (Ger.). 'Tale' or 'tales'—often with some suggestion of the traditional or legendary.

Marchesi, (1) Salvatore Cavaliere de Castrone, Marchese della Rajata (b. Palermo 1822; d. Paris 1908). Baritone vocalist. Pupil of M. Garcia and himself of high fame as vocal trainer. Lived some time in London;

later in Paris. Publ. Vocal Method, &c. (2) **Mathilde** (b. Frankfurt 1821; d. London 1913). Soprano vocalist; wife of above (*née* Graumann) and like him pupil of Garcia and herself famous vocal trainer; publ. Vocal Method. Lived in London 1849–54; then in Paris. (3) **Blanche** (b. Paris 1863; d. London 1940). Soprano vocalist (at first violinist). Daughter of the two above. Had successful career in opera and concerts and settled in London as vocal trainer.

Marching through Georgia. This song commemorates General Sherman's famous march of 1864. Both the stirring, rhythmic verses, with their mixture of enthusiasm and humour, and the fine swinging tune are by Henry Clay Work (1832–84).

March of the Israelites. See *Eli*.

March of the Sirdar (Ippolitof-Ivanof). See *Caucasian Sketches*.

Marcia (It.). 'March.' So *alla marcia*, 'in march style'.

Marconi. See *Broadcasting of Music*.

Marcoux, Vanni (Jean Émile Diogène; b. Turin 1877; d. Paris 1962). Operatic baritone. Trained Paris. Début Turin 1894; Covent Garden 1905; Paris 1908; Boston 1912. Associated some years with Chicago Opera Co.

Maréchal, Maurice (b. Dijon 1892; d. Paris 1964). 'Cellist. Studied Paris Conserv. Appeared as soloist with Lamoureux Orch.; then international reputation. 1st perfs. of works by Honegger, Caplet, Ravel, &c.; Chev. Légion d'Honneur 1931.

Marenzio, Luca (b. nr. Brescia 1553; d. Rome 1599). Held important positions in Rome and Warsaw; greatly admired as composer of madrigals (tending to a harmonic scheme then advanced); these publ. at the time in many continental centres and in England.

Mareppe. See *Mechanical Reproduction of Music* 9.

Maria Egiziaca (Respighi). See *Mary of Egypt*.

Maria Theresia ('Maria Theresa'). Nickname for Haydn's Symphony in C, No. 48 in Breitkopf edn. of his

Symphonies. The Empress Maria Theresa expressed great pleasure on hearing the work.

Mariazellermesse. Popular name for Haydn's Mass No. 8, in C, possibly commissioned for the Benedictine Monastery at Mariazell, 60 miles from Vienna.

Marienleben, Das ('The Life of Mary'). Song-cycle by Hindemith to poems by Rilke (op. 27, 1922–3; revised 1936–8).

Marimba. A Latin-American instrument of African origin. It consists of strips of wood of different length with

SOUTH AFRICAN MARIMBA
(The portable variety)

(tuned) resonators underneath, the whole fixed in a frame and struck with drumsticks—in fact, a super-xylophone large enough for 4 players (or *Marimberos*), standing or sitting side by side, to perform on together. A feature of this instrument is a piece of bladder attached to each resonator, which by its vibration intensifies the sound and also contributes a buzzing effect to the lower notes.

The South African original, known to Europeans as the *Kaffir Piano*, is by natives called the Malimba.

Cf. *Vibraphone*. For adaptations of the marimba to orch. use see *Percussion* 1 g, h. See also *Creston*.

Marimba Gongs. See *Percussion Family* 1 h.

Marimberos. See *Marimba*.

Marinetti, Filippo Tommaso (b. Alexandria 1876; d. 1944). It. pioneer of completely new methods in all the arts ('The Father of Futurism'). In music advocated and practised the employment of 'noise-makers' of all kinds, and from 1909 onwards gave in Rome, Paris, London, &c., performances sometimes interrupted by the violent opposition of audiences which had laid in a lavish provision of vegetable and other missiles. Created Senator by Mussolini and put in charge of cultural side of Fascism (active to 1939 or later). Publ. *Futurismo e Fascismo* (dedicated to Mussolini) and *I manifesti del futurismo*, &c. (cf. *Cage, John*).

Marinuzzi, Gino—really Giuseppe (b. Palermo 1882; d. Milan 1945). Successful opera conductor in old and new worlds; Rome Opera 1928; La Scala 1934 until death by assassination; composer of operas, orch. works, &c.

Mario, Giovanni—really the Marchese Giovanni de Candia (b. Sardinia 1810; d. Rome 1883). Operatic tenor of highest international celebrity. Before public 1838–71. Sang much with Giulia Grisi and became her 2nd husband. After retirement held post as a museum curator in Rome.

Mariotte, Antoine (b. Avignon 1875; d. Iseux, Loire, 1944). Pupil of d'Indy (q.v.); opera conductor; principal of Orleans Conserv. (1920); composer of orch. music and many operas.

See *Salome* (2).

Maritana. Very popular opera by Wallace. (Prod. London 1845; Dublin and Philadelphia 1846; New York and Vienna 1848; Sydney and Hamburg 1849; Prague 1851.)

Markevich, Igor (b. Kief 1912). Composer and conductor. Has lived most of life in Switzerland; pupil of Nadia Boulanger in Paris, where many of his works have had their 1st performances, and where they have been greatly praised by some critics. Oratorio *Paradise Lost* (London 1932), orch. works, &c. Active amongst anti-fascists in Italy during Second World War. Book *Made in Italy* 1949.

Markiert (Ger.). 'Marked', i.e. (1) 'clearly accented', or (2) 'brought out', e.g. a melody to be emphasized, as compared with the accompaniment.

Markig (Ger.). 'Vigorous.'

Marks, Myer. See *Digitorium*.

Marksman, The (Weber). See *Freischütz*.

Marot, Clément (b. Cahors, France, abt. 1496; d. Turin 1544). Poet and courtier of time of Francis I; provided Fr. metrical versions of the Psalms.

Mârouf, Savetier du Caire ('Mârouf, Cobbler of Cairo'). Arabian Nights Opera by Rabaud. (Prod. Paris 1914; New York 1917.)

Marqué (Fr.). 'Marked', i.e. 'Emphasized' (cf. *Markiert*).

Marriage of Figaro (Mozart). See *Nozze di Figaro*.

Marrow Bone and Cleaver. The traditional music of the Brit. butchers. It is occasionally still (or was until recently) to be heard at London weddings of members of the blood-stained fraternity. (For instruments of similar humble standing see *Tongs and Bones*; *Bellows and Tongs*; *Bladder and String*; *Saltbox*.)

Marsch (Ger.). 'March.'

Marschner, Heinrich August (b. Saxony 1795; d. Hanover 1861). Encouraged in composition by Beethoven; colleague of Weber in conductorship of Dresden opera and belongs to Weber school of national Ger. romantic opera (*Hans Heiling*, Berlin 1833, an enormous success).

Marseillaise. See *Rouget de Lisle*.

Marshall, William (b. Fochabers, Moray = Elginshire, 1748; d. Craigellachie, Banffshire, 1833). Butler to Duke of Gordon, surveyor and architect, astronomer, clockmaker, farmer and factor, justice of the peace, and highly popular violinist and composer of over 100 strathspeys, as also reels, jigs, &c.

Marshall-Hall, G. W. L. (b. London 1862; d. Melbourne, Victoria, 1915). Trained R.C.M. and Germany. Ormond Prof. Music, Univ. Melbourne 1890–1900 and again 1914 (gap in university career due to unwise publication of certain poems). Founded Melbourne Orch. (1892) and Conserv.

Marsick, (1) **Martin Pierre Joseph** (b. nr. Liège 1848; d. Paris 1924). Violinist, composer, and teacher. Trained Paris Conserv. under Massart (q.v.); then Berlin under Joachim. Début Paris 1873. Thereafter toured both sides Atlantic. As teacher had many famous pupils. Composed violin concertos, &c. For son see (2) below.
(2) **Armand** (b. Liège 1877; d. Brussels 1959). Pupil of d'Indy and others; conductor of orch. and prof. at conserv. at Athens (1908–22); Bilbao (1922–7); Liège (1927–39). Composed operas, symphonic poems, &c.

Marteau (Fr.). 'Hammer' (cf. *Martelé, Martellando*).

Marteau sans maître, Le. 9 movements for alto voice and nine instruments by Boulez (1955).

Martelé (Fr.). 'Hammered'—referring to the manner of playing bowed instruments by a series of short, sharp blows with the bow upon the strings. The point of the bow is to be used for this process unless the heel is indicated by the expression *Martelé du talon* (see also *Détaché*). **Martellando; martellato** (It.). Same as *Martelé*, though the words are sometimes applied to pianoforte playing and even singing.

Martenot. See *Electric Musical Instruments* 1.

Martha. Romantic Opera by Flotow. (Prod. Vienna 1847; London 1849; New York 1852.)

Martin, (1) **George Clement** (b. Lambourn, Berks., 1844; d. London 1916). Pupil of Stainer; his deputy (1876–88) as organist of St. Paul's Cathedral and successor (1888–death). Composed church music. D.Mus., Lambeth (1883) and Oxford (1912).
(2) **Frank** (b. Geneva 1890). Swiss composer of orch., choral, and chamber works, &c., personal in style and untrammelled by conventions. For a time resident in Holland.
(3) **Easthope** (1885–1925). Composer of popular drawing-room songs (e.g. *Come to the Fair*).

Martinelli, Giovanni (b. nr. Padua 1885; d. New York 1969). Operatic tenor. At first player in army band;

début as singer Milan 1910. Covent Garden from 1912; Metropolitan Opera House, New York, from 1913.

Martini, (1) Giambattista, or **Giovanni Battista,** called 'Padre Martini' (b. Bologna 1706; there d. 1784). Franciscan friar, learned musician and musical historian, composer and famous teacher of composers.

(2) **'Martini il Tedesco'**—real name Johann Paul Aegidius Schwarzendorf (b. Freistadt, Palatinate, 1741; d. Paris 1816). Settled in France, Italianizing his name; first in Nancy (1760) and then in Paris (1764). Composed music for military band, symphonies, operas, church music, &c. On restoration of Bourbons in 1814 became director of court music.

Martinon, Jean (b. Lyons 1910). Conductor and composer. Studied at Conservs. of Lyons and Paris, pupil of Roussel and Münch. Cond. Paris Conserv. Orch. (1944); Bordeaux Symphony Orch. (1946); Chicago Orch. (1963); Paris Nat. Orch. (1968). Compositions include orchestral pieces, an opera, and chamber music.

Martinu, Bohuslav (b. Polička, Bohemia, 1890; d. nr. Basle 1959). Trained as violinist and became orch. player. Composer (largely self-taught) of chamber and orch. music, operas, ballet, &c. Paris 17 years; settled in U.S.A. 1941.

Martucci, (1) Giuseppe (b. Capua 1856; d. Naples 1909). Pianist and orch. conductor (first in Italy to produce Wagner's *Tristan*; Bologna 1888); director of Conservs. of Bologna (1886–1902) and Naples (1902–death). As composer belongs to 'New Music School' of Liszt and Wagner—symphonies, concertos, chamber and piano music, &c. For his son see below. (2) **Paolo** (b. Naples 1883). Son of Giuseppe, above; pianist and teacher, living in U.S.A.

Marty, Eugène Georges (b. Paris 1860; there d. 1908). Studied under Massenet at the Paris Conserv. and won Rome Prize (1882); on return to Paris became active as choral trainer and orch. and operatic conductor. Composed operas and orch. works.

Martyrdom of St. Sebastian (Debussy). See *Martyre de Saint-Sébastien.*

Martyre de Saint-Sébastien, Le ('The Martyrdom of St. Sebastian'). 'Symphonic Fragments' by Debussy, being parts of the incidental music he wrote for d'Annunzio's Mystery Play (Paris 1911). The sections are (1) *The Court of the Lilies*; (2) *Ecstatic Dance and Finale to Act I*; (3) *The Passion*; (4) *The Good Shepherd.*

Martyr of Antioch, The. Oratorio by Sullivan. Text by Dean Milman. (1st perf. Leeds Fest. 1880.)

Marx, (1) Adolph Bernard (b. Halle 1795; d. Berlin 1866). Lawyer who became musicologist, started a musical journal; founded (with Kullak and Stern) what is now called the Stern Conserv. Composer, but more important as writer of books on music. (2) **Joseph** (b. Graz 1882; d. there 1964). Ph.D. of Graz Univ. with thesis on 'The Functions of Intervals in Harmony and Melody for the Comprehension of Time-complexes'; prof. of theory at Vienna Academy of Music; director of it (1922) and then of the Hochschule. Admired as composer of songs and chamber music of romantic type.

Maryland, My Maryland. Words by James Ryder Randall (1861). Tune the Ger. *Der Tannenbaum* (cf. *Red Flag*).

Marylebone Gardens. See *Concert.*

Marziale (It.). 'Martial.'

Masaniello (Auber). See *Muette de Portici.*

Mascagni, Pietro (b. Leghorn 1863; d. Rome 1945). Studied at Milan Conserv.—but only for short time, not appreciating systematic academic teaching; became minor operatic conductor and then small-town piano teacher; nearing 30 leapt into fame with opera *Cavalleria Rusticana* (q.v.); though 15 or more operas followed none had lasting success (see *Amico Fritz*; *Iris*).

Mascarade (Fr.). In earlier use this means 'Masque' (q.v.) and in later use 'Masquerade', i.e. 'Masked Ball'.

Mascheroni, Edoardo (b. Milan 1852; d. Ghirla, Como, 1941). Composer and conductor of operas (chosen by Verdi to conduct 1st perf. *Falstaff*, q.v.). Works included a requiem, &c., and very popular songs.

Maschinenpauken (Ger.). Mechanically-tuned kettledrums (see *Percussion Family* 1 a).

Mask or **Maske**. Old spellings of *Masque* (q.v.), but sometimes found attached to (say) a virginals piece, and then generally implying, probably, a dance of a character fitting it for use in a masque.

Masked Ball (Verdi). See *Ballo in Maschera*.

Mason, (1) **Lowell** (b. Medfield, Mass., 1792; d. Orange, N.J., 1872). Great pioneer of school music (see *Education* 3) and promoter of choral singing; composed simple church music (see *Hymns and Hymn Tunes* 7). For his son and grandson see below. (2) **William** (b. Boston 1829; d. New York 1908). Son of Lowell, above. Studied piano and composition under best teachers in Germany and became pianist and teacher of high repute and author of books on piano playing, &c. Composed piano music, &c. (3) **Daniel Gregory** (b. Brookline, Mass., 1873; d. Greenwich, Conn., 1953). Grandson of Lowell and nephew of William, above. Asst. Prof. of Music (1910) and then Prof. (1929), Columbia Univ., New York. Many orch. and chamber music works of value and many books. (Cf. *Appreciation*.)

(4) **Colin** (b. Northampton 1924; d. London 1971). Music critic (*Manchester Guardian* 1950; *Daily Telegraph* 1964) and sympathetic writer on modern music.

Mason and Hamlin. See *Reed-Organ Family* 6.

Masonic Funeral Music (Mozart). See *Mauerische*.

Masque (or **Mask** or **Maske**). A ceremonial entertainment of the aristocracy, consisting of a combination of poetry, vocal and instrumental music, dancing, acting, costume, pageantry, and scenic decoration, applied to the representation of allegorical and mythological subjects. It was much cultivated in Italy, from which country England seems to have learnt it, then carrying it to a very high pitch of artistic elaboration. In Elizabethan times amongst the authors employed was Ben Jonson, who counts as a supreme master of the Eng. masque; he sometimes enjoyed the collaboration of the celebrated Inigo Jones as designer of the decorations and machinery. Amongst composers of masque music were Campian or Campion (q.v.), Coprario (q.v.), N. Lanier (q.v.), and A. Ferrabosco, Jun. (q.v.). From a literary point of view the most famous masque ever written is Milton's *Comus* (1634); of this the music was supplied by Henry Lawes (q.v.). Masques continued under the Puritan régime of the Commonwealth and Protectorate, some being arranged, by authority, for entertainment of distinguished foreign visitors. A late example of the masque is Arne's *Alfred* (1740), written for perf. in the garden of the Prince of Wales: from it comes the song *Rule, Britannia!* (q.v.).

The Fr. *Ballet de Cour* was practically the masque and there is a masque element in modern ballet, though this, of course, lacks the literary and lyrical elements.

Masquerade. Masked Ball.

Mass. Owing to the importance the Roman Catholic Mass holds in the minds of worshippers and the opportunities it offers for musical participation it has exercised a large influence upon the development of music. The *Proper of the Mass* (i.e. the parts which vary from season to season and day to day) has naturally usually been left to its traditional plainsong treatment. The 5 passages that are frequently set for chorus, or for chorus and soloists, are as follows: (*a*) *Kyrie* ('Lord have mercy . . .'), (*b*) *Gloria in excelsis Deo* ('Glory be to God on high . . .'), (*c*) *Credo* (' I believe . . .'), (*d*) *Sanctus*, with *Benedictus* properly a part of it, but in practice often separated ('Holy, Holy . . . Blessed . . .'), (*e*) *Agnus Dei* ('O Lamb of God . . .'). These are, properly, the congregational element in the *Ordinary of the Mass*, or *Common of the Mass*, i.e. the invariable part. From the beginning of Harmony (q.v.), innumerable musical settings for them have been provided by hundreds of composers of all European nations. A high point was reached at the end of the 16th c., when the unaccompanied choral contrapuntal style of composition reached its apogee (Palestrina in Italy, Byrd in England, Victoria in Spain, &c.). In the 17th and 18th cs. the high development of solo singing and the gradually increasing understanding of the principles of effective orch. accompaniment led to great changes in the style of musical treatment of the Mass, and the settings of the late 18th-c. and early 19th-c. composers (Haydn, Mozart, Weber, Schubert, &c.), however musically effective, have not the devotional quality of the settings of the late 16th and early 17th cs. The practice had grown up of treating the 5 passages above mentioned as the opportunity of providing an extended work in oratorio style, two outstanding examples of this being the Mass in B minor of J. S. Bach (composed 1731–8) and the Mass in D of Beethoven (composed 1818–23). These are two landmarks in the history of music.

In such large-scale works as those just mentioned the 5 passages alluded to tended to become subdivided. The great setting of Bach is as follows: (a) *Kyrie eleison* ('Lord, have mercy'), *Christe eleison* ('Christ, have mercy'), *Kyrie eleison* ('Lord, have mercy'); (b) *Gloria in excelsis Deo* ('Glory be to God on high'), *Laudamus te* ('We praise Thee'), *Gratias agimus tibi* ('We give Thee thanks'), *Domine Deus* ('Lord God'), *Qui tollis peccata mundi* ('Who takest away the sins of the world'), *Qui sedes ad dexteram Patris* ('Who sittest at the right hand of the Father'), *Quoniam tu solus sanctus* ('For Thou only art holy'), *Cum Sancto Spiritu* ('With the Holy Spirit'); (c) *Credo in unum Deum* ('I believe in one God'), *Patrem omnipotentem* ('Father almighty'), *Et in unum Dominum* ('And in one Lord'), *Et incarnatus est* ('And was incarnate'), *Crucifixus* ('Crucified'), *Et resurrexit* ('And rose again'), *Et in Spiritum Sanctum* ('And [I believe] in the Holy Spirit'), *Confiteor unum baptisma* ('I confess one baptism');

(d) *Sanctus* ('Holy'), *Hosanna in excelsis* ('Hosanna in the highest'), *Benedictus qui venit* ('Blessed is he that cometh'); (e) *Agnus Dei* ('O Lamb of God'), *Dona nobis pacem* ('Give us peace').

HIGH MASS is a Mass celebrated by a priest with deacon, sub-deacon, and other ministers, and sung throughout, either to the traditional plainsong or with the 5 passages mentioned near the beginning of this article set by some composer. SUNG MASS is practically the same as 'High Mass'; LOW MASS is performed by a priest and one clerk without choir; a VOTIVE MASS is one offered with a particular 'intention' or in honour of a saint on some day other than his feast; a NUPTIAL MASS is, of course, one offered as a part of the ceremony of marriage; the MASS OF THE PRESANCTIFIED is that of Good Friday, in which the priest does not consecrate afresh but uses the Host reserved from the Mass of the previous day; a FOLK MASS is, properly, 'Low Mass' (see above) proceeding whilst the congregation sing hymns in the vernacular, but the term has also been applied to a type of setting so simple that the congregation can sing their part. For other terms see under *Missa*.

See also *Introit*; *Gradual*; *Grail*; *Alleluia*; *Sequence 2*; *Offertory*; *Roman Catholic Church Music in Britain*; *Preface*.

Massart, Joseph Lambert (b. Liège 1811; d. Paris 1892). Violinist and teacher. On staff of Paris Conserv. Pupils included Wieniawski, Sarasate, and many other famous players.

Massé, Victor—really Félix Marie Massé (b. Lorient 1822; d. Paris 1884). Student of Paris Conserv. who won Rome Prize 1844 and on return made name as composer of songs, also operas, usually of lighter type (*Les Noces de Jeannette*, 'Jeannette's Marriage', 1853), &c.

Massenet, Jules Émile Frédéric (b. St. Étienne, Loire, 1842; d. Paris 1912). Studied at Paris Conserv., winning Rome Prize (1863), a prof. of composition at Conserv. (1878–96). Made self known in all countries by long list of melodious operas (see *Manon*; *Thaïs*; *Sapho*), also by orch. works, incidental music to plays, and 200 songs.

See also *Cendrillon*; *Cid*; *Hérodiade*; *Jongleur de Notre Dame*; *Werther*.

Mässig (Ger.). (1) 'Moderate', 'moderately', *mässiger*, 'more moderate' and *mässigen*, 'to moderate'. (2) 'In the style of' (e.g. *marschmässig*, 'in march style').

Massimo, massima (It. masc., fem.). 'The greatest.'

Mass in B Minor of Bach. Composed 1733. (1st Brit. perf., in part, Bach Soc., 1860; complete, Bach Choir, 1875.) See particulars of this work s.v. *Mass*.

Mass in D (*Missa Solemnis*) of Beethoven, op. 123; 1818–23. (1st partial perf., to Ger. words, Vienna 1824; complete but in a private house, London 1832; in public, but probably incomplete, London 1839; 1st complete public perf. St. Petersburg and Cologne 1844 and London 1846.)

Massine. See *Ballet*.

Mass in G minor of Vaughan Williams. For Vocal Quartet and Double Choir, unaccompanied. (1st perf. Westminster Cathedral 1922.)

Mass of Life. By Delius. A setting of parts of Nietzsche's *Also sprach Zarathustra*. (1st perf. London 1909.)

Mass of Pope Marcellus (Palestrina). See *Missa Papae Marcelli*.

Master of Music. See *Degrees and Diplomas* 1, 3.

Master of the King's (Queen's) Musick. See *Chapel Royal*.

Master Peter's Puppet Show (Falla). See *Retablo de Maese Pedro*.

Masters, Robert Henderson (b. London 1917). Violinist. Studied R.A.M. (later on staff). Founded Robert Masters (Piano) Quartet (1939–63); tours of Britain and Continent, also Dominions.

Mastersingers. See *Minstrels* 4.

Mastersingers (Wagner). See *Meistersinger*.

Mastersingers Sonata (Brahms). See *Meistersinger Sonata*.

Matassins or **Mattachins.** The dance also called *Bouffons* (q.v.).

Matelotte (Fr., from *matelot*, 'sailor'). A sailors' hornpipe (see *Hornpipe*).

Materna, Amalie (b. Styria 1844; d. Vienna 1918). Operatic soprano, famous in Wagner roles. Brünnhilde at 1st Bayreuth perf. (1876); earliest Kundry in *Parsifal*, &c.

Mathieson, Muir (b. Stirling 1911). Conductor. Trained R.C.M. Has appeared in concert hall, and as opera conductor at Sadler's Wells, but most prominent as conductor of film music (Music Director 1934–9 of Alexander Korda; then of J. A. Rank Organization). Also organizer and conductor of children's concerts for schools. O.B.E. 1957.

Mathis der Maler ('Matthias the Painter'—the famous artist Grünewald, abt. 1460–1530). Opera by Hindemith. Libretto by the composer. (Prod. Zürich 1938; London, concert form, 1939.) The composer also made a symphony out of some of the music.

Matin, Le Midi, Le Soir, Le ('Morning', 'Afternoon', 'Evening'). Nicknames for 3 Haydn symphonies, Nos. 6–8 in Breitkopf edn. of the Symphonies (respectively in D, C, and G). The last is also known as *La Tempesta* ('The Storm').

Matins. The 1st of the Canonical Hours in the Roman Catholic Church (see *Divine Office*) and Morning Prayer in the Anglican Church (see *Common Prayer*). In the former Church the morning observance is sometimes forestalled on the previous evening or afternoon.

Matrimonio segreto, Il ('The Secret Marriage'). Cimarosa's most important opera. Libretto based on an Eng. play by Colman and Garrick. (Prod. Vienna 1792; London 1794; New York and Philadelphia 1834. Still in the international repertory.)

Mattachins. See *Bouffons*.

Matteis, (1) **Nicolà.** It. violinist who came to London abt. 1672 and astonished by his technique (see Evelyn's *Diary*, &c.); publ. violin compositions in London, also songs, and treatise on guitar playing. For son see below. (2) **Nicholas** (d. Shrewsbury abt. 1749). Son of above. For nearly 40 years member of court orch. at Vienna and composer of ballet music there;

then (curiously) in Shrewsbury, as teacher of languages and violin (see Burney's *History of Music*).

Matthay, Tobias (Augustus) (b. London 1858; d. Haslemere, Surrey, 1945). Student and then prof. of piano at R.A.M.; gradually developed, by close observation of working of physical and psychological sides of piano playing, scientific and artistic system of piano teaching, and embodied this in books. Many of leading Brit. pianists his pupils.

Mattheson, Johann (b. Hamburg 1681; there d. 1764). Many-sided man. In younger days Hamburg opera singer and composer, and colleague and friend of Handel. For some years musical director of Hamburg cathedral and at same time Secretary of Brit. Legation. Publ. many compositions and innumerable books on various aspects of music.

Matthews, (1) **Denis** (b. Coventry 1919). Pianist. Trained R.A.M. under Craxton, winning Musicians' Co. Medal as most distinguished student. On leaving quickly established himself in public esteem. Composer of some music for his instrument.

(2) **Thomas** (b. Cheshire 1907). Violinist. Studied London, Germany, Belgium. Hallé Orch. 1925–34; London début as soloist 1936; leader, London Philharm. Orch., 1939–41, then tours of Commonwealth and Europe. Leader, Covent Garden Opera Orch. and Accademico Quartet 1950; London Symph. Orch. 1952; Scottish Orch. 1954; on staff R.A.M. Husband of Eileen Ralf (q.v.).

Mattinata (It.). A 'Morning Song', or a piece with that suggestion, i.e. the same as *aubade* (Fr.), *alborada* (Sp.), and *Morgenlied* (Ger.).

Matzenauer, Margarete (b. Temesvar, Hungary, 1881; d. Van Nuys, Calif., 1963). Eminent opera singer (both soprano and contralto parts); début Strasbourg 1901. Munich 1904; Metropolitan 1911–30. Retired 1938.

Maud. See *Somervell*.

Mauerische Trauermusik ('Masonic Funeral Music'). By Mozart. For strings and wood-wind (K. 477, 1785).

Maultrommel (Ger.). Jew's harp (q.v.).

Maurel, Victor (b. Marseilles 1848; d. New York 1923). Operatic baritone. Trained Paris Conserv. Won high international position as interpreter of Verdi (created part of Iago in *Othello*). For last 14 years of life vocal teacher in New York. Author of several books on singing, opera, &c.

Mauresco (Sp.), **Mauresque** (Fr.). 'Moorish' (see also *Moresca*).

Má Vlast (Smetana). See *My Fatherland*.

Mavra. 1-act comedy-opera by Stravinsky. Libretto based on Pushkin. (Prod. Paris 1922; London, broadcast, and Philadelphia 1934.)

Maxixe. A rather strenuous Brazilian dance in simple duple time. It enjoyed European popularity in the early years of the 19th c. and then, about 1911–13, reappeared in somewhat changed form as the tango (q.v.): both these dances were chiefly popular as exhibition dances rather than ball-room dances.

Maxwell, James Clerk. See *Broadcasting of Music*.

May, Florence (b. London 1845; d. there 1923). Pianist and author. Daughter of a well-known London musician; pupil of Brahms, of whose piano works she was an able interpreter and the standard life of whom she wrote (1905; new edn. 1948).

Maybrick, Michael (b. Liverpool 1844; d. Buxton 1913). Popular baritone. Trained Leipzig. As 'Stephen Adams' provided immense public with highly acceptable vocal fodder—*Nancy Lee*, *Star of Bethlehem*, *Holy City*, &c.

Mayer, Robert (b. 1879). London business man; founder of children's concerts in London and many other cities (1923 onwards), and of various chamber music organizations, &c. Sociological worker and author. Knighted 1939. Wife, Dorothy Moulton (q.v.).

Maynard, John (early 17th c.). Composed songs, *The XII Wonders of the World*.

May Night (Rimsky-Korsakof). See *Night in May*.

Maynor, Dorothy (b. Norfolk, Va., 1910). Eminent Negro soprano. Trained Hampton Institute and Westminster (N.J.) Choir Coll., Début 1939.

Mayor, The (Wolf). See *Corregidor*.

May Queen, The. Cantata by Sterndale Bennett. (Op. 30; composed for opening of Leeds Town Hall 1858; highly popular for many years.)

Mayr, (1) **(Johann) Simon** (b. Mendorf, Bavaria, 1763; d. Bergamo 1845). Notable opera composer, filling Italian needs around the turn of the century, until the arrival of Rossini.

(2) **Richard** (b. nr. Salzburg 1877; d. Vienna 1935). Operatic and *Lieder* bass-baritone. Début Bayreuth 1902. Then Vienna under Mahler. Covent Garden 1924; Metropolitan Opera, New York, 1927.

Mayseder, Josef (b. Vienna 1789; there d. 1863). Virtuoso violinist and violin teacher; composer especially for his instrument.

Mazas, Jacques Féréol (b. Béziers 1782; d. Bordeaux 1849). Violinist. Trained Paris Conserv. under Baillot. Enjoyed great celebrity as touring virtuoso. Composer of violin music, &c.

Mazeppa. Symphonic Poem by Liszt (1856). Based on Victor Hugo's (not Byron's) treatment of the legend of the Polish noble bound naked on an untamed horse. Also exists for 2 pianos (1855) and for piano solo (1874).

Liszt has 2 (earlier) piano pieces of the same name, (a) *Mazeppa* (publ. 1847) and (b) No. 4 of the *Études d'exécution transcendante* (1852).

Mazurka. A traditional dance of Poland (originally sung as well as danced). It spread in the mid-18th c. to Germany and then to Paris, and early in the 19th to Britain and the U.S.A. It is in triple time with a certain accentuation of the 2nd beat of each measure and an ending of the phrases on that beat: dotted notes are a feature. The speed is not great and a certain aristocratic pride of bearing, sometimes combined with a touch of wildness, helps to differentiate it from the waltz. It has entered into instrumental composition, especially with Chopin, who

left over 50 examples for piano, in which the style is greatly refined and the tempo and rhythm sometimes changed from those that are traditional.

The POLKA-MAZURKA differs from the Polka in being in triple time and from the Mazurka in having an accent on the 3rd beat of the measure.

Mazzinghi, Joseph (b. London 1765; d. Bath 1844). Pupil of J. C. Bach (q.v.), and popular composer of operas and piano music (nearly 70 sonatas); 2 simple vocal items probably keep his name still alive—duet *When a little farm we keep* (from an opera), and glee *The Wreath* ('Ye shepherds tell me').

Mazzocchi, (1) **Domenico** (b. nr. Cività Castellana 1592; d. Rome 1665). Lawyer in Rome who publ. madrigals and wrote oratorios, especially the famous *Querimonia di S. Maria Maddalena* ('Plaint of St. Mary Magdalen', 1631). Said to have been first to use < > signs for crescendo and diminuendo. For his brother see below. (2) **Virgilio** (b. nr. Cività Castellana 1597; there d. 1646). Brother of Domenico, above. Chorus master of St. Peter's, Rome; composer of earliest comic opera (1639) and of church music.

Mazzoleni, Ettore (b. Brusio, Switzerland, 1905; d. Toronto 1968). Studied Oxford Univ. and R.C.M. (later on staff there). Settled Toronto 1929, joining staff of Conserv. of which became Principal 1948.

M.B.E. See *British Empire, Order of the*.

M.D. = *Main Droite* (Fr.) or *Mano Destra* (It.), i.e. 'Right Hand'. Sometimes, also, used as an abbreviation of 'Musical Director'.

Me. See *Mi*.

Meadows White, Mrs. See *Smith* 6.

Mean-tone Temperament. See *Temperament*.

Mears and Stainbank. See *Bell* 1.

Measure. (1) An old Eng. term, normal in the U.S.A. and in the mid-19th c. reintroduced into Britain by John Curwen (q.v.), indicating the time-content of the notational space which lies between one bar-line and the next. (Cf. *Rhythm*.) (2) In older

Eng. literature, and often in Eng. poetry, any dance or dance tune; e.g. 'to tread a measure'.

Mechanical Reproduction of Music.

Innumerable instruments have been invented for this purpose, including the following:

(1) TOWER CHIMES, &c. Bells mechanically sounded came into use at least as early as the 14th c., the principle being that of a revolving barrel with pins in it which released the striking mechanism. (For the Carillon see *Bell* 4.)

(2) MECHANICAL VIRGINALS. These date, in England, from at least as early as the reign of Henry VIII. Again the barrel-and-pin principle was applied.

(3) MECHANICAL ORGANS. These date, in England, from at least as early as the reign of Elizabeth, and again the barrel-and-pin mechanism was employed.

(4) DOMESTIC MUSICAL CLOCKS, &c. These were popular in the 18th c. Handel, Haydn, Mozart, and many other prominent composers wrote music for them. The principle was again that of the barrel-and-pin. Mostly they were wind instruments—i.e. tiny organs, for which the Ger. name was *Flötenuhr* (flute-clock).

(5) The 'ORGUE DE BARBARIE'. This also was a small organ, but played by turning a handle instead of by clockwork. Such instruments were at one time common in the Eng. streets.

(6) The 'SERINETTE' or 'BIRD ORGAN'. This was a simple form of the last, intended by reiteration of a short tune to teach captive birds to sing. (*Serin*, Fr. = the domestic canary.)

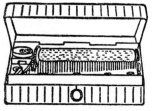

FRENCH MUSICAL BOX
(Tabatière à musique)

(7) METALLIC COMB INSTRUMENTS. These employed an application of the barrel-and-pin principle to a comb the teeth of which, being graduated in length, provided a scale of notes from which tunes could be produced. Such instruments have been very common as *Musical Boxes*, *Musical Watches*, &c., and they are still manufactured. The Fr. name for a Musical Box

on this principle is *Tabatière à musique* ('Musical Snuff-box').

(8) MAELZEL'S INSTRUMENTS. Maelzel (1772–1838) was a very ingenious inventor (cf. *Metronome*). For a time he enjoyed the friendship of Beethoven, who composed for his Panharmonicon (a mechanical orch.) *The Battle of Victoria* (1813). This, however, was but one of his many elaborate musical inventions.

(9) AUTOMATON VIOLINISTS, FLAUTISTS, TRUMPETERS, HARPSICHORDISTS, &c. Inventors of such instruments as these were Vaucanson (1709–82), H. U. J. Droz (end of 18th c.), Maelzel (mentioned above), and Mareppe (first half of 19th c.). But there were very many others.

(10) The BARREL ORGAN. This was a true organ of normal size, with a barrel-and-pin mechanism operated by turning a handle. It was exceedingly common in Eng. churches from the 1770's or earlier and many such instruments still exist in churches, but very few are still in use, one such being in Shelland, Suffolk. A domestic size of the Barrel Organ was also common and its repertory included dance music, &c. (See *Hand Organ*.)

(11) The APOLLONICON. This was the most elaborate barrel organ ever constructed: its builders were Flight and Robson, and it was publicly exhibited in London from 1817 to about 1840.

(12) The STREET PIANO (often erroneously spoken of as 'Barrel Organ'). It is in principle simply a barrel-and-pin-operated piano of a crude kind.

(13) PERFORATED ROLL INSTRUMENTS. These are operated pneumatically by paper rolls in which holes, of varying lengths and in due position, represent the notes. They date from 1842 and range from small organs, with the roll operated by a handle, to the Pianola (patented 1897) and similar instruments of which the motive-power is supplied by means of pedals by the operator or by electricity. In one form of the Pianola a master roll is mechanically punched by the playing of some pianist of high repute and the rolls made from it reproduce very exactly his interpretation of the music: this form is generally described as a *Reproducing Piano*. (The same principle has been applied to organs of large size.)

Medea. 3-act opera by Cherubini. Libretto after Euripides. (Prod. Paris 1797.)

Medesimo (It.). 'Same', e.g. *Medesimo movimento*, 'The same speed'.

Mediant. The 3rd degree of the major or minor scale. So called as being midway between the tonic and the dominant.

Mediation. See *Plainsong* 2.

Medicean Edition. See *Plainsong* 3; *Cecilian Movement.*

Meditation—Ave Maria ('Bach-Gounod'). To Bach's 1st Prelude of the '48', which consists of a delicate series of arpeggios, Gounod added a luscious 19th-c. sentimental melody.

Medium, The. 2-act chamber opera by Menotti. Libretto by composer. (Prod. Columbia Univ., New York, 1946.)

Medtner, Nicholas (b. Moscow 1880; d. London 1951). Parents were German. Trained at Moscow Conserv.—as pianist under Safonof; later prof. there (1902–3 and 1918–21); toured extensively as virtuoso pianist; settled in France and then in England (1940). Composer of much piano music including 3 concertos.
See *Mysore, Maharaja of.*

Meeresstille und glückliche Fahrt. See *Calm Sea and Prosperous Voyage.*

Mefistofele ('Mephistopheles'). Opera by Boito. Libretto by the composer, based on Goethe's *Faust.* (Prod. Milan 1868; London, New York, and Philadelphia 1880.)

Megaphone. A large speaking-trumpet. Also a device introduced by Edison for listening at a distance of some miles without the use of wires or electricity—practically an improved ear-trumpet on a large scale.

Mehr (Ger.). 'More.' Also 'many', in compounds such as *mehrstimmig* 'many-voiced', i.e. 'Polyphonic' (q.v.).

Mehrere (Ger.). 'Several.'

Mehta, Zubin (b. Bombay 1936). Studied in Vienna; won internat. competition for conductors at Liverpool in 1958; world tours; mus. director Los Angeles Philharmonic 1961.

Méhul, Étienne Nicolas, or **Étienne Henri** (b. Givet, Ardennes, 1763; d. Paris 1817). Went to Paris at 15; there met Gluck and heard his operas, which much impressed him; himself became composer of operas and before 30 famous as such, eventually producing a long list of them, as also songs, sym-

phonies, piano sonatas, &c.; his opera *Joseph* (q.v.) has kept his name alive.

Meili, Max (b. Winterthur, Switzerland, 1899). Tenor. Trained Munich. Widely travelled as recitalist, especially with programmes of earlier composers (from troubadours to Schütz, Bach, &c.). One of founders of Schola Cantorum, Basle.

Meistersinger. See *Minstrels* 4.

Meistersinger Sonata. Nickname of Brahms's 2nd Violin and Piano Sonata (in A, op. 100), of which the 1st theme slightly resembles Wagner's 'Preislied' in his *Die Meistersinger.*

Meistersinger von Nürnberg, Die ('The Mastersingers of Nuremberg'). Comedy-opera by Wagner. (Prod. Munich 1868; London 1882; New York 1886.)
See *Minstrels* 4.

Melartin, Erkki Gustav (b. Kökisalmi, otherwise Kexholm, Finland, 1875; d. Helsinki 1937). Studied in Vienna and became a prof. at Conserv. of Helsinki, and later (1911) its director. A leading Finnish composer of symphonies, symphonic poems, chamber and piano music, an opera, songs, &c.; also publ. collections of Finnish folk songs.

Melba, Nellie (b. Melbourne 1861; d. Sydney 1931). Coloratura soprano vocalist. Really Mrs. Armstrong, *née* Mitchell, taking professional name from place of birth. Began musical life as organist and pianist, studying singing after marriage; made 1st public vocal appearance in 1885 and gave concert in London 1886. Studied with Mathilde Marchesi (q.v.) and appeared in opera at Brussels 1887 and Covent Garden 1888—both with great success. Henceforth enjoyed high international reputation. Retired 1926, returning to native country. D.B.E. 1918; G.B.E. 1929.

Melchior, Lauritz (b. Copenhagen 1890). Operatic tenor (at first baritone). Studied with Victor Beigel and others. Début Copenhagen 1913. Great Wagnerian singer (Bayreuth, London, New York, &c.). Resident California. (Naturalized 1947.)

Melisma (Gr. 'song'; plur. *melismata*). A term used of passages in plainsong, or other song, in which one syllable flowers out into a passage of several notes; also sometimes applied to a vocal cadenza.

Melismata. See above, and *Ravenscroft, Thomas*.

Mellers, Wilfrid Howard (b. Leamington 1914). Writer on music and composer of orch. and chamber music, songs, &c. On staff Birmingham University.

Mellertion. See *Electric Musical Instruments* 1.

Mellish, Colonel. See *Drink to me only with thine eyes*.

Mellon, Alfred (b. London 1820; d. there 1867). Violinist and conductor. Pupil of Molique. Leading violin Birmingham theatre orch. age 16; then Covent Garden (1844). Conductor London theatres, Pyne-Harrison Opera Co. (see *Pyne* 3), Covent Garden Proms., Liverpool Philharmonic Soc., &c. Composed opera *Victorine*, &c.

Mellophone. A synonym (U.S.A.) for the Tenor Horn (see *Saxhorn and Flügelhorn Families* 1 c).

Melodia. Organ stop popular in U.S.A.; of type of *Hohlflöte* (q.v.); 8-foot length and pitch.

Melodic Minor Scale. See *Scale*.

Melodic Sequence. See *Sequence* 1.

Melodies for the Pianoforte. See *Song without Words*.

Melodrama. (1) A play (or passage in such) in which the spoken voice is used against a musical background (Gr. *melos*, 'music'). The *Ariadne* and *Medea* of Benda, in 1775, are looked upon as the virtual foundation of this type of stage activity, but they had predecessors. From time to time examples are still appearing (Strauss, Fibich, Honegger, Milhaud, Bliss, &c.). (2) The word has somehow come to have another sense—that of a highly sensational stage work, and it is in such a sense that we use the adjective 'melodramatic'.

Melody. During the thousands of years that passed from the appearance on the earth of something that may be recognized as 'man' to the date of approximately A.D. 900 all music was melodic, i.e. consisted of merely one 'line' of notes, so that if a hundred people were singing together they did so in unison (or 8ves if there were present both men and women or children). The music of many primitive races still remains purely melodic, as does European folk song and also plainsong. Many apparently simple folk melodies will be found, on examination, however, to be highly organized, e.g. as regards the use at different pitch levels of some simple, brief *motif* (q.v.), the adroit use of a high note as a point of climax, &c.; many such melodies will be found to be cast in some definite form, as, for instance, Simple Ternary form (see *Form* 2).

Rhythm (q.v.) is an important element in melody, whether it be the prose rhythm of primitive music, plainsong, and the compositions of some modern composers, or the metrical rhythm of most other music. Indeed this element is so much a governing factor in the effect of a melody that if, whilst the notes of a popular melody are left intact, the rhythm is drastically altered it becomes difficult to recognize the melody. The rhythm of many melodies is extraordinarily subtle and repays close study.

Once Harmony (q.v.) had become an element in music it began to influence Melody in this way—that melodic passages are often found to be based on the notes of a chord (with or without added decorative or intermediate notes).

The quality of originality in melody is rather intangible. Apparently it lies mainly in mere detail, since, looked at critically, what we accept as an original melody is often found closely to resemble some previous and quite well-known melody. It is often difficult to see what has led to the popularity of a particular melody, or what it is that gives some melodies something like eternal life, whilst others prove to be merely ephemeral: as regards this latter question of durability, however, it will generally be found that the long-lived melodies possess a logical organization—a quality the value of which, apparently, the popular mind subconsciously recognizes.

Racial and national feeling expresses itself strongly in melody, particular scales, intervals, and rhythms being typical of the music of particular races or nations.

Melody in F of Rubinstein. Early and highly popular composition for piano; one of *Two Melodies*, op. 3.

Mélopée (Fr.). 'Melopoeia' (the art of composing songs; the musical side of dramatic art); the term covers declamatory song, recitative, &c.

Melophone. See *Regondi*.

Melusina (in full, *Overture to the Story of the Lovely Melusina*; Ger. title, *Die schöne Melusine*). Concert-overture by Mendelssohn (1833). Prompted by the opera, *Melusine*, by Conradin Kreutzer. (1st perf. London Philharmonic Soc. 1834.)

Même (Fr.). 'Same', e.g. *même mouvement*, 'same speed'.

Memory in Music. The whole of musical composition, performance, and enjoyment depends upon memory. The Composer could not write with effect the simplest passages if he did not remember at least their melodic and harmonic units as he has heard them before, and which he is combining in new relationships. The Performer, likewise, is guided by his memory of music previously performed or heard, which that before him resembles, or from which it differs in some way which he can recognize. The enjoyment of the Listener, in even the simplest composition, is conditioned by his ear's familiarity with more or less similar melodic and harmonic passages, similar key relationships, and the like. The indispensable tool of memory, then, is 'ASSOCIATION': nothing (in music or otherwise) can be remembered unless there be something already known with which the mind can (consciously or otherwise) connect it. This is the principle upon which all systems of 'Memory Training' (general or musical) are founded.

In piano performance, as an example, three main forms of association are employed: (*a*) those connected with the manual processes involved—the 'feel' of a passage, the length of a leap, &c.; (*b*) those connected with the notational appearance of a passage; and (*c*) those connected with a mental analysis of the form of a composition, the underlying harmonic scheme of its passages, their build-up by the use of such familiar devices as scales, arpeggios, broken chords, and so on. These may be called respectively *Tactile Memory*, *Visual Memory*, and *Analytical Memory*, and performers who are good memorizers probably use all of them in varying degrees.

There are some curious anomalies in current practice in the use of memory in public performance. Pianists are now expected to play from memory (many of them doubtless unduly limiting their repertory by the necessity of conforming to the custom), whilst organists rarely do so: solo vocalists, of course, depend on memory in opera, but not in oratorio; string players do so in solo performance but not in the playing of trios, quartets, &c., and so on. There is an increasing tendency amongst orch. conductors to do their work from memory.

Astounding feats of musical memory are recorded of many well-known musicians: for some of these the reader must be referred to *OCM*.

For Music Memory Contests see under *Appreciation of Music*.

Men (It.). Same as *meno*, 'less'.

Mendel, (1) **Hermann** (b. Halle 1834; d. Berlin 1876). Eminent writer; author of great musical *Conversations-Lexikon* in 12 vols.

(2) **Arthur** (b. Boston 1905). Musical scholar. Studied Harvard and Paris, then worked as teacher, journalist, choral condr., and editor (G. Schirmer 1930–8; Associated Music Publrs. 1941–7). Chairman of mus. dept., Princeton Univ., 1952. Authority on Bach and his period.

Mendelssohn (really **Mendelssohn-Bartholdy**), **Felix**, in full Jacob Ludwig Felix (b. Hamburg 1809; d. Leipzig 1847). Grandson of the famous philosopher, Moses Mendelssohn, and son of a banker; trained by sound

Berlin teacher, Zelter, and became young friend of Goethe; before 15 had written many symphonies, an opera and other things, and at 17 the beautiful overture to *A Midsummer Night's Dream*; early became active propagandist for music of Bach, long neglected. From 20 to 24 travelled extensively, spending much time in Britain, where always warmly welcomed—as accomplished pianist, organist, and composer; as result of visit to Scotland wrote (1830; op. 26) *Fingal's Cave* ('Hebrides') overture (1st perf. London Philharmonic Soc. 1832). Town director of music in Düsseldorf 1833–5; then conductor of famous Gewandhaus Concerts, Leipzig; also head of new Leipzig Conserv. (1843), which he organized.

Two oratorios greatly added to popularity in Britain and elsewhere, *St. Paul* (Düsseldorf, May 1836; Liverpool, Oct. 1836; New York 1838), and *Elijah* (Birmingham Fest. 1846, the composer conducting; Hamburg 1847; New York 1851); between these came the *Lobgesang* ('Hymn of Praise', a Symphony-Cantata, Leipzig, June 1840; Birmingham Fest., Sept. 1840; Boston 1842). The 6 Organ Sonatas were written for and 1st publ. in England (1845); the very popular *Songs without Words* for piano were also composed for England (1830 onwards). Several of his grandchildren settled or were born in England and became British subjects.

See also *Athalie*; *Calm Sea and Prosperous Voyage*; *Christmas Pieces*; *Christus*; *Cornelius March*; *Festgesang*; *First Walpurgis Night*; *Funeral Marches*; *Gondola Song*; *Hear my Prayer*; *Italian Symphony*; *Lauda Sion*; *Loreley*; *Melusina*; *Midsummer Night's Dream Music*; *Reformation Symphony*; *Scotch Symphony*; *Son and Stranger*; *Song without Words*; *Spinning Song*; *Spring Song*; *Trumpet Overture*; *Wedding March*; *Wedding of Camacho*.

Mendelssohn Scholarship. This Brit. benefaction was founded shortly after Mendelssohn's death in 1847, the 1st holder (Arthur Sullivan) being appointed in 1856. It was originally awarded either to a young performer or composer, but is now reserved to the latter. The beneficiary may pursue his education either at home or abroad.

Ménestrandie. See *Minstrels* 1.

Ménestrel, Ménestrier. See *Minstrels* 1.

Mengelberg, (1) **Willem**—in full Josef Willem (b. Utrecht 1871; d. Chur, Switzerland, 1951). Orch. conductor. Trained Cologne Conserv., &c. Conductor of Amsterdam Orch. 1895–1945; appeared in U.S.A. from 1905; Britain 1911–14. Worked to popularize Mahler in Holland. After Second World War charged with Nazi collaboration, 'forbidden to exercise his profession in public in any manner whatever for a period of six years 1945–51', and died in exile. (2) **Rudolf**—in full Kurt Rudolf (b. Crefeld 1892; d. Monte Carlo 1959. Cousin of above. A director of Concertgebouw Orch., Amsterdam; composer of choral, solo vocal, orch. works, &c.; author of books on Mahler, &c.

Menges, (1) **Isolde** (b. Hove 1893). Violinist. Pupil of Sauret and Auer. Appeared successfully in Britain, U.S.A., &c. On staff of R.C.M. (1931); leader of Menges String Quartet (also 1931). (2) **Herbert** (b. Hove 1902). Brother of above. Appeared in public as violinist age 4. Trained as pianist by Mathilde Verne and de Greef; composition at R.C.M. Musical director Old Vic. 1931 and again 1944; conductor Sadler's Wells 1941–4; Brighton Philharmonic Orch. 1945; also several London orchs.

Mennin, Peter (orig. Mennini) (b. Erie, Pa., 1923). Trained Oberlin Conserv. and Eastman School (Ph.D. 1947); then taught at Juilliard School (1947–58); dir. Peabody Conserv. 1958; pres. Juilliard 1962. Compositions have won many awards; they are mainly orchestral, and include concertos, 7 symphonies, and choral and chamber music.

Meno (It.). 'Less.'

Men of Prometheus (Beethoven). See *Prometheus*.

Menotti, Gian-Carlo (b. Cadigliano, Italy, 1911). Studied at Milan Conserv.; then went to U.S.A. (1928) and studied at Curtis Inst. Compositions include many vivid operas performed at Metropolitan Opera House,

New York, in London, and elsewhere; orch. works, &c. (Cf. *Amahl*; *Amelia goes to the Ball*; *Consul*; *Island God*; *Medium*; *Telephone*.)

Menter, Sophie (b. Munich 1846; d. nr. there 1918). Pianist. Daughter of well-known 'cellist. Pupil of Tausig and protégée of Liszt. On staff of St. Petersburg Conserv. 1883–7. For some years wife of Popper (q.v.). Composed some piano music.

Menuet (Fr.), **Menuett** (Ger.), **Menuetto** (this last common spelling being incorrect). *See Minuet.*

Menuhin, (1) **Yehudi** (b. New York 1916). Violinist with outstanding reputation from early age. First appearance San Francisco aged 7, followed by prodigious list of successes in all parts of the world (New York, aged 9, Berlin 11, London 13, &c.). Pupil of Enesco and Adolf Busch. Retired after world tour in 1935, reappearing 1937. Worked indefatigably for entertainment of military forces in Second World War. Hon. D.Mus., Oxford, 1962; Hon. K.B.E. 1965. (2) **Hephzibah** (b. San Francisco 1920). Pianist. First appeared San Francisco aged 8, then recitals with brother (above) in Europe and America. Married and settled in Australia (1938), continuing career there.

Mephistopheles (Boito). See *Mefistofele.*

Mephisto Waltzes. By Liszt. Expressive of the wildly diabolic and originating in the Faust legend. There are 4 numbered as follows: (1) For Orchestra, being the 2nd movement (*Der Tanz in der Dorfschenke*, 'The Dance in the Village Tavern') of the *Two Episodes from Lenau's 'Faust'* (1858–9); dedicated to Tausig; arranged also for Piano, 2 and 4 hands. (2) For Orchestra (1881); dedicated to Saint-Saëns; arranged also for Piano, 2 and 4 hands. (3) For Piano (1883); dedicated to Marie Jaell. (4) For Piano (1885); unpublished.

There is also a *Mephisto Polka* for Piano (1883; same date as the 3rd of the Waltzes).

Mer, La. Three 'Symphonic Sketches' by Debussy (1905). (1) *De l'aube à midi sur la mer* ('From dawn to noon on the sea'); (2) *Jeux de vagues* ('The play of the waves'); (3) *Dialogue du vent et de la mer* ('Dialogue of wind and sea').

Merbecke (or **Merbeck**, or **Marbeck**), **John** (b. Windsor abt. 1510; d. there abt. 1585). Organist of St. George's Chapel, Windsor Castle; during reign of Henry VIII condemned to be burnt as heretic, but pardoned and returned to his duties; publ. earliest Concordance of whole Eng. Bible and theological and controversial books; for *The Booke of Common Prayer Noted* (1550) see *Common Prayer* (end); also *Responses.* Composed 5-part mass, Latin motets, &c. B.Mus., Oxford, 1549.

Mercadante, (Giuseppe) Saverio (Raffaele) (b. Altamura, S. Italy, 1795; d. Naples 1870). Opera composer of European reputation (nearly 60 operas), also composed church music, instrumental music, and songs. Lived in turn in most of chief cities of Italy, in Madrid, Lisbon, Paris, and Vienna. Became blind 1862 but continued composition by means of an amanuensis.

Mercury Symphony (Merkur). By Haydn. Nickname for Haydn's Symphony in E flat, No. 43 in Breitkopf edn. of his symphonies.

Merikanto, (1) **Oskar** (b. Helsinki, Finland, 1868; there d. 1924). Studied in Germany and then settled in native city as organist and later opera conductor. Composed operas, &c.; publ. collection of Finnish folk songs. For his son see below. (2) **Aarre** (b. Helsinki 1893; d. there 1958). Son of (1). Composer of orch., chamber, and piano works.

Merkel, Gustav (b. nr. Bautzen, Saxony, 1827; d. Dresden 1885). Fine organist and composer of effective organ works.

Merkur (Haydn). See *Mercury Symphony.*

Merrick, Frank (b. Bristol 1886). Pianist. Son of sound musician, Dr. Frank Merrick (1854–1941), and his pupil; studied also with Leschetizky. On staff Royal Manchester Coll. of Music (1911) and then R.C.M. (1929).

Has composed orch. works (including completion of 'Unfinished Symphony' 1928), piano concertos, &c.

Merrie England. Highly popular Operetta by Edward German. Libretto by Basil Hood. (Prod. London 1902.)

Merrill, Robert—orig. **Miller** (b. Brooklyn 1917). Operatic baritone. First successes as popular singer, then operatic career after Metropolitan début 1945.

Merriman, Nan (b. Pittsburgh 1920). Operatic mezzo-soprano. Début Cincinnati 1942; numerous broadcasts and recordings. Retired 1965.

Merry Mount. Opera by Hanson. Libretto based on Hawthorne. (Prod. New York 1934.)

Merry Widow, The (Ger., *Die lustige Witwe*). Highly popular Operetta by Lehár. (Prod. Vienna 1905; London and New York 1907.)

Merry Wives of Windsor, The (Nicolai). See *Lustigen Weiber von Windsor*.

Mersenne (or Mersennus), Marin (b. Oizé, Maine, France, 1588; d. Paris 1648). Theologian, philosopher, mathematician, and musician; wrote books of musical theory, especially *Harmonie Universelle* (1636–7). Valued today for information on contemporary instruments.

Merulo, Claudio (b. Coreggio 1533; d. Parma 1604). Famous organist of St. Mark's, Venice (later at Mantua and Parma); composer of organ music, motets, and madrigals.

Messa di Voce (It. 'placing of the voice'). A *crescendo* and the *diminuendo* on one long held note (cf. *Filar la voce*).

Messager, André (Charles Prosper) (b. Montluçon 1853; d. Paris 1929). Pupil of Saint-Saëns; organist St. Sulpice, Paris, 1874, and then at other Paris churches. Became active as opera conductor from 1898, for various periods attached to Opéra Comique, Grand Opera, and Covent Garden, London; also orch. conductor, taking Paris orch. to U.S.A. and Canada. As opera composer made his mark with *La Béarnaise* (Paris and London, 1885), following this with many other successes (see *Basoche*; *P'tites Michu*;

Véronique; *Monsieur Beaucaire*). Married an Englishwoman, Hope Temple, the song composer, but they separated. Debussy's *Pelléas and Mélisande* was dedicated to him, its 1st conductor.

Messa per i defunti (It.). Requiem Mass (see *Requiem*.)

Messe des morts (Fr. 'Mass of the Dead'). Requiem Mass (see *Requiem*).

Messiaen, Olivier Eugène Prosper Charles (b. Avignon 1908). Parisian organist. Composer of organ, orch., and choral music, original in form and daring in harmony, and strongly expressive of religious mysticism. Has explained his highly personal theories in 2 vols. entitled *Technique de mon langage musical* (1944).

Messiah. Oratorio by Handel. Libretto selected from Scripture by Charles Jennens. Composed 22 Aug.–14 Sept. 1741, i.e. 3½ weeks. (1st perf. Dublin 13 April 1742; London 23 March 1743. New York in part 1770; Boston complete 1801. Publ. posthumously 1767.)

See also under *Additional Accompaniments*; *Pastoral Symphony*.

Messing (Ger.). 'Brass.' So *Messinginstrumente*, 'brass instruments'.

Mesto (It.). 'Mournful', 'sad'. So *mestizia*, 'sadness'.

Mesure (Fr.). (1) Measure, bar. (2) Time; e.g. *à la mesure* = *a tempo*.

Metà (It.). 'Half.'

Metallic Comb Instruments. See *Mechanical Reproduction of Music* 7.

Metamorphosis of Themes. A process associated especially with the practice of Liszt in his compositions. A piece of Programme Music (q.v.) would be based upon some musical passage representative of some person or idea, and as the music progressed, and the circumstances imagined altered in accordance with the underlying literary or dramatic scheme of the composition, the theme would change in character.

Cf. *Idée fixe* (s.v. *Berlioz*), *Leading Motive* (s.v. *Wagner*), and *Motto Theme*.

Metastasio, The Abbé—really Pietro Trapassi (b. Rome 1698; d. Vienna 1782). Grocer's son who, heard at 11 publicly improvising verses in streets of Rome, was adopted and educated by a wealthy man. Devoted himself to providing opera composers with libretti; became the most celebrated in this line in Europe; amongst the multitude of composers who set his libretti were Gluck, Handel, and Haydn. His general poetical works appeared in innumerable edns. and were translated into many languages. He lived in Vienna as court poet for the last half-century of his life.

Metre. The rhythmic element in poetry, covering (*a*) Number of lines in each stanza; (*b*) Number of syllables in a line; (*c*) Arrangement of syllables as to accentuation—or in ancient languages as to 'quantity'. (For metres of hymns see *Hymns and Hymn Tunes* 8.)

Metrical Psalm. See *Hymns and Hymn Tunes* 3.

MAELZEL'S METRONOME

Metronome. An apparatus for fixing the Tempo (q.v.) of a composition. The commonest form now in use is the clockwork one of Maelzel (1772–1838); hence such indications at the head of a piece of music as M.M. ♩ = 100 (i.e. the ♩ beat to be taken at the speed of Maelzel's Metronome set at 100 beats to a minute). In the late 1940's a Swiss firm put on the market a metronome the size and shape of a watch; there are also electrically operated metronomes.

Cf. *Expression.*

Metropolitan Opera House (New York). Built 1883. Seats 3,500; also 600 standing places. Chief opera house in U.S.A. until replaced by new building in Lincoln Center (q.v.) in 1966.

Mettenleiter. See *Cecilian Movement.*

Mettere (It.), **mettre** (Fr.). 'To put'; hence (It. imperative) *mettete il sordino*, 'put on the mute'. *Mettez* (Fr. imperative) often means 'put into action' an organ stop.

Metzler & Co. London music publishers, &c. (139 New Bond St., W. 1). Estd. 1812. Early speciality was instruments of reed-organ type.

Meyerbeer, Giacomo—real name Jacob Liebmann Beer (b. Berlin 1791; d. Paris 1864). Won early reputation as pianist but turned to opera, at first Italian; works performed in Italy; but from 1831, after performance of *Robert the Devil* (see *Robert le Diable*), in Paris; made that capital his headquarters; in this and following works cultivated the grandiose in stage effect and in music (see *Africaine*; *Dinorah*; *Étoile du Nord*; *Huguenots*; *Prophète*); also active in Berlin, where he was appointed Royal Director of Opera. Had high ability and, if vulgar, the courage of his vulgarity; hence effective.

Meyerowitz, Jan (b. Breslau 1913). Studied composition under Zemlinsky in Berlin and under Casella, Respighi, and Molinari in Rome. Came to U.S.A. in 1946 (naturalized 1951). Taught at Tanglewood and Brooklyn College. Many compositions, including 5 operas.

Mezza (It. fem.), **Mezzo** (It. masc.). 'Half', e.g. *Mezza voce*, 'Half-voice', i.e. half the vocal (or instrumental) power possible. (Not to be confused with *Messa di Voce*, q.v.). *Mezzo forte*, 'Half-loud', i.e. neither loud nor soft.

Mezzo carattere, Aria di. See *Aria.*

Mezzo-Soprano. See *Voice* 14.

Mezzo-Staccato. See Table 23.

MF. = *Mezzo forte*, 'Half-loud.'

M.G. = *Main gauche* (Fr.), i.e. 'Left hand.'

Mi. The 3rd degree of the major scale, according to the system of vocal syllables derived from Guido d'Arezzo (see *Hexachord*), and so used (spelt *Me*) in Tonic Sol-fa (q.v.), in which it is also the 5th degree of the minor scale. In many countries, however, the name has become attached (on 'fixed-doh' principles; see *Sight-Singing*) to the note E, in whatever key this occurs. (See Table 5; also *Lancashire Sol-fa*.)

Miaskovsky (Myaskovski, &c.), Nicolas (b. Novo-Georgievsk 1881; d. Moscow 1950). Studied under Rimsky-Korsakof at the Conserv. of St. Petersburg, fought in the war of 1914–18; then became a prof. at Conserv. of Moscow. Composed 27 symphonies and some piano sonatas, songs, &c. In style shows influences of Glazunof and Tchaikovsky, his idiom, however, being necessarily more modern.

Michelangeli, Arturo Benedetto (b. Brescia 1920). Pianist. Trained Milan Conserv., then on staff Conserv. of Bologna 1938–42. First prize International Musical Competition of Geneva 1939, after which attained world-wide reputation.

Michelangelo Sonnets (Britten). See *Seven Sonnets*.

Mi contra fa. The tritone (q.v.).

Microtones are any intervals smaller than a semitone. They occur in certain exotic scales and have also been exploited by some late 19th- and 20th-c. composers. Quarter-tone pianos have been constructed, but the readiest means of producing microtonal music is offered by the bowed instruments (on which, as in vocal music, microtones are even sometimes produced unintentionally).

See *Hába; Carrillo*; *Stein*.

Middelschulte, Wilhelm (b. Werne, Germany, 1863; there d. 1943). Organist. Settled Chicago 1891. Composed organ music.

Middleton, Hubert Stanley (b. Windsor 1890; d. Cambridge 1959). Studied R.A.M. and Cambridge (M.A., D.Mus., also D.Mus., Oxford). Organist Truro Cathedral 1920. Ely 1926; Trinity Coll., Cambridge, 1931; Univ. Lecturer in Music.

Midi, Le (Haydn). See under *Matin*.

Midsummer Night's Dream. (1) Opera by Britten; libretto by the composer and Peter Pears, after Shakespeare. (Prod. Aldeburgh 1960; London and Hamburg 1961; New York 1963.) (2) See *Thomas, C. L. Ambroise*.

Midsummer Night's Dream Music. By Mendelssohn. Overture (op. 21) composed at age 17 (1st perf. Stettin 1827; London 1829). Incidental Music to play (op. 61, 1843; 1st perf. Potsdam 1844; see reference under *Wedding March*).

Miessner Piano. See *Electric Musical Instruments* 3.

Mignon. Very popular opera by Ambroise Thomas. Libretto based on Goethe's *Wilhelm Meister*. (Prod. Paris 1866; London 1870; New York 1871.)

Migot, Georges (b. Paris 1891). Pupil of Widor, d'Indy, and Guilmant; wounded in war of 1914–18, recovering but slowly and partially. Composer of orch., choral, chamber, theatre, and piano music; has written books on music and is a competent painter. In all activities shows strong nationalistic leanings.

Mihalovici, Marcel (b. Bucharest 1898). Studied under d'Indy in Paris, then attached to younger Fr. and Russian group there. Has composed operas, ballets, orch. and chamber music, &c.

Mikado, The, or The Town of Titipu. The most widely popular of the Gilbert and Sullivan Comic Operas; versions in about a dozen languages. (Prod. Savoy Theatre, London, and also Chicago, New York, and Sydney 1885.)

Mikrokosmos. By Bartók. Six Albums containing 153 'Progressive Piano Pieces', from the utmost simplicity to extreme difficulty (1926–37).

Milán, Don Luis. Spanish lutenist (see *Song*).

Milanollo Sisters. Violinists giving joint performances. **Domenica Maria Teresa** (b. Savigliani 1827; d. Paris 1904) and **Maria** (b. Savigliani 1832; d. Paris 1848). So long as younger sister lived they played together both in duet and solo (in latter case sharing the movements of a concerto between them); great success in Paris and London. Elder sister continued public appearances to 1857.

Milanov, Zinka (b. Zagreb 1906). Operatic soprano. Pupil of Ternina; début 1927, then Yugoslav career until

1936. From 1937 regularly heard at Metropolitan and other Amer. opera houses.

Milanuzzi (or **Milanuz**), **Carlo** (early 17th c.). Augustinian who held many positions as organist and composed much church music.

Mildenburg. See *Bahr-Mildenburg*.

Mildmay, Audrey (b. Hurstmonceaux 1900; d. Glyndebourne 1953). Operatic soprano. Carl Rosa Co., Sadler's Wells, Glyndebourne (q.v.—founded by her husband John Christie, q.v.). Special reputation in Mozart.

Miles, (1) **Philip Napier** (b. nr. Shirehampton, Glos., 1865; d. nr. Bristol 1935). Wealthy landowner who studied music in Germany and also under Parry; conductor of choral soc. on his estate and bore expense of opera festivals at Bristol. Composed several operas. Hon. LL.D., Bristol.

(2) **Maurice** (b. Surrey 1908). Conductor. Trained R.A.M. and Salzburg. Then in B.B.C., and successively conductor of the orchs. of Buxton and Bath (1936) and of the Yorkshire Symphony Orch. (1947).

Milford, Robin (b. Oxford 1903; d. Lyme Regis 1959). Son of Humphrey Milford, Publisher to the Oxford University Press. Studied at R.C.M. under Vaughan Williams, Holst, and R. O. Morris; then became school music-master. Composer of oratorio *A Prophet in the Land* (1931); violin concerto (1937), piano music, various choral works, songs, &c.

Milhaud, Darius (b. Aix-en-Provence 1892). Trained Paris Conserv. (1910–15) and under d'Indy and others. Member of the temporary modernist group of 'Les Six' (see *Six*); has worked on polytonal lines (see *Harmony* 3), producing orch. and chamber music, ballets, operas, &c. Escaped to U.S.A. in 1940, joining staff of Mills Coll., Oakland, Calif. Later travelled between America and France.

See also *Printemps*; *Saudades*.

Milieu (Fr.). 'Middle'; hence *milieu de l'archet*, 'middle of bow'—and so forth.

Militaire (Fr.), **militare** (It.), **militär** (Ger.). 'Military.'

Militärtrommel (Ger.). Side drum; (see *Percussion Family* 2 i).

Military Band. This term is used in Britain either for an actual army (or naval or air-force) band or for one on the same model, i.e. one comprising both brass and wood-wind instruments. The composition of such bands varies widely in different countries, and even in different regimental or other units of the same country. One common Brit. combination is as follows:

(*a*) 1 piccolo (or flute, or both); 1 oboe; 1 small clarinet; 12–14 ordinary clarinets, 2 bass clarinets; 1 alto and 1 tenor saxophone; 2 bassoons. (*b*) 4 horns, 2 baritones, 2 euphoniums, 4 bombardons. (*c*) 4 cornets; 2 trumpets; 3 trombones. (*d*) 2 drummers with a variety of percussion instruments. Sometimes, when conditions of performance allow, a stringed double-bass, or two, may appear, as an alternative to the same number of bass wind instruments. Bands in U.S.A. vary from the above scheme merely in detail: there has been a great development of such bands in the High Schools in that country.

The score and parts of the military band, unlike those of the brass band (q.v.), employ the ordinary orch. system of notation.

Military Symphony. Nickname of the 8th of Haydn's 'London Symphonies' (q.v.). Uses certain military instruments in·some movements.

Milkina, Nina (b. Moscow 1919; now British). Pianist; trained London under Matthay and Craxton, then Paris Conserv. Recitals and broadcasts, especially Mozart.

Miller, (1) **Edward** (b. Norwich in 1730's; d. Doncaster 1807). From 1756 organist of Doncaster Parish Church; composed harpsichord music, &c. Southey in *The Doctor* has much about him.

(2) **Dayton Clarence** (b. Strongsville, Ohio, 1866; d. Cleveland 1941). Acoustician and authority on flute family (owning large collection now in Library of Congress, Washington). Many books on his subjects. See *Phonodeik*.

(3) **Philip (Lieson)** (b. Woodland, N.Y., 1906). Studied Manhattan and Juilliard Schools; Music Div., N.Y.

Public Library from 1927; chief 1959–66. Many articles, esp. on singers and their recordings.

Miller of the Dee, The. The words were first printed in 1762, when they appeared in Arne's opera *Love in a Village*; but it is almost certain that the song was then an old one. The tune exists in many versions as an Eng. folk song, set to various words: it is found in several of the early 18th-c. ballad operas from 1728 onwards.

Millikin, R. A. See *Last Rose of Summer*.

Millöcker, Karl (b. Vienna 1842; d. nr. there 1899). Prolific and popular composer of tuneful Viennese operettas and for some years issued monthly album of piano compositions. (Cf. *Beggar Student*.)

Mills, (1) **Richard** (b. Llanidloes 1809; d. 1844). One of earliest Welsh theorists; composed and edited collections of hymn tunes and anthems.

(2) **Sebastian Bach** (b. Cirencester 1838; d. Wiesbaden 1898). Pianist. Pupil of Cipriani Potter (q.v.) and Sterndale Bennett (q.v.); then Leipzig Conserv. Début Gewandhaus 1858; New York 1859. Settled New York but toured Europe widely. High reputation as performer and teacher.

Milner, (1) **Arthur** (b. Manchester 1894). Organist, teacher, and composer of a number of works for his instrument.

(2) **Anthony** (b. Bristol 1925). Trained R.C.M. under R. O. Morris and took lessons from Seiber. Lecturer, writer, pianist, and composer of a number of works, chiefly choral.

Milophone. Mouth organ (see *Reed Organ Family* 2).

Milstein, Nathan (b. Odessa 1904). Violinist. Pupil of Auer, Ysaÿe, &c. Appeared in public at 19 and quickly gained high international reputation. Has publ. many arrangements for violin.

Milton, (1) **John I** (b. abt. 1563; d. London 1647). Able composer of church music, a few madrigals, viol music. For his son see below. (2) **John II** (b. London 1608; there d. 1674). Son of John I. The great poet; an amateur organist and a keen lover of music, as his poems testify.

See reference under *Education* 2; *Masque*.

Mime. A play in dumb show or an actor in such (cf. *Pantomime*). Obviously a great deal of ballet (q.v.) includes miming as an ingredient.

Mimodrama. Any play (musical or other) of which the action is carried on in dumb show (cf. *Pantomime*).

Minaccevole; minaccevolmente (It.). 'Menacing'; 'menacingly'. So also *minacciando, minaccioso, minacciosamente*.

Minder (Ger.). 'Less.'

Mineur (Fr.). 'Minor.'

Minim ($\textrm{d}$), The 'Half-Note'—i.e. half the time-value of the semibreve or 'whole-note' (see Table 1). **Minima** (It.). Minim (see Table 3).

Minne (Ger.). 'Love'; so *Minnelied*, 'love song'.

Minnesingers. See *Minstrels* 3.

Minor Canon. In English cathedrals of the 'New Foundation' (see *Cathedral Music and Musicians in Britain*) a member of the clerical staff (but not of the chapter) engaged in intoning the priest's part of the service.

Minor Canticles. See *Canticles*.

Minor Common Chord. See *Harmony* 2 d.

Minore (It.). 'Minor.'

Minor Intervals. See *Interval*.

Minor Scale. See *Scale*.

Minstrels, Troubadours, Trouvères, Minnesingers, Mastersingers.

(1) JONGLEURS AND MINSTRELS. In every age and country there has been some class of men professionally devoted to musical amusement. The Roman name for such a person was JOCULATOR, which points to some exercise of the art on its lighter side. From this came the Fr. Joglar, later JONGLEUR, and the Eng. JUGGLER. The words 'Jongleur' and 'Juggler' descended in dignity and came to refer merely to the lighter side of the professional work of the public entertainers in question.

A difference of social grade was marked in the 14th c. by the introduction of a new term for the higher-class public entertainers, the musician class—that of MÉNESTRIER, which was really at this time pretty well the equivalent of 'professional musician'. The profession itself was known as that of *ménestrandie*. Soon the word MÉNESTREL grew out of the former word. England had always had musical entertainers of the various grades, as, for instance, the Saxon 'gleemen', and the close political connexion with France brought to it the name used in that country, which in England changed slightly into 'minstrel'. Control of the profession of minstrel (the formation of a fraternity, or guild) seems to have begun in London and in other cities at least as early as 1350, and various ordinances and Royal Charters are in existence (1500, 1518, 1574, &c.) which detail the objects sought and the conditions imposed.

(2) TROUBADOURS AND TROUVÈRES. The activity of the Jongleur or Minstrel class, as has just been seen, can be traced from almost the beginnings of history down to comparatively modern times. That of the troubadours was of much briefer duration, being only about 200 years—from the end of the 11th c. to the latter part of the 13th. The art of the jongleurs and minstrels was exercised in all parts of Europe; it had no one country as its headquarters. That of the troubadours and trouvères was confined to the south of France, with overflows into northern Spain and northern Italy and central and northern France—so confined, that is to say, except so far as those who exercised it travelled at times to other countries, and to some extent inspired these with the desire of imitation (see *Minnesingers* below). The activities of the Troubadour and Trouvère class often transcended those of a profession, becoming rather the occupation of certain gifted members of the nobility, and they even numbered kings amongst their practitioners (e.g. Richard Lion Heart of England, who was partly Provençal by origin). The distinction between troubadour and trouvère is one of locality and language. The troubadours lived in southern France, in Provence, and used the Provençal

tongue. The trouvères were in central and northern France and spoke the Fr. tongue. Roughly it may be said that the activity of the trouvères began and ended half a century later than that of the troubadours.

The art of the troubadours and trouvères represents one of the greatest refinements in the processes of poetry that the world has ever seen. A fair body of troubadour music remains.

(3) MINNESINGERS (from *Minne* = Love). These were the Ger. counterpart of the troubadours and trouvères, with whom they were contemporary (though they began a little later) and from whom their art derived (though it assimilated also native folk influences). Like the troubadours and trouvères, they were largely of knightly rank. The art of the Minnesingers declined about the same time as that of the troubadours and trouvères.

(4) MASTERSINGERS (in Ger. *Meistersinger*). After the decline of the aristocratic Minnesingers the trader and craftsman classes of Germany took up their dual art and practised it, with added complexities and under very academic regulations. Almost every city had its guild. Throughout the 14th, 15th, and 16th cs., and into the 17th c., these guilds were active, and that of Ulm was dissolved only in 1839, its last member (the last of the Mastersingers) dying in 1876. The conduct of a Mastersingers' Guild was very much what Wagner has shown us in *The Mastersingers of Nuremberg*, and the very names of the characters of that opera are for the most part those of actual personages. Certain of the themes in Wagner's music-drama are actual Mastersinger tunes. Hans Sachs, the dignified and genial elder hero of Wagner's music-drama, lived from 1494 to 1576, i.e. he came near the end of the Mastersinger period. He was a prolific poet, playwright, and composer.

Minstrels (Debussy). See *Préludes*.

Minuet (Eng.), **Menuet** (Fr.), **Minuetto** (It.), **Menuett** (Ger.).[1] Of the innumerable dance styles of Europe

[1] The spelling 'Menuetto' does not exist in any language, though Beethoven and others have used it.

this is the one which has left the greatest mark upon music. It began as a rustic dance in France, was admitted to Court in the mid-17th c. and became refined, was soon ubiquitous in the ballrooms of Europe, and then declined in favour after about 1790. As an instrumental dance type it was early taken up by composers, becoming one of the optional movements of the Suite (see

posers the force employed was here, for contrast, reduced to 3 performers. (In the Minuet-Trio movement of some of the piano sonatas of Beethoven and others the Trio is in 3-part harmony, so maintaining the tradition.) After the Trio the original Minuet reappears, so that not only are the 2 parts in Ternary Form but so is also the piece as a whole.

LEARNING THE MINUET
(By Cruikshank, 1835)

Suite and *Galanterien*): it also figured in overtures—even in those to some of Handel's oratorios. In the period following Bach and Handel it became a frequent movement in the Sonatas, String Quartets, and Symphonies, &c., of Haydn, Mozart, and their contemporaries. It was supplanted, however, in some works of Haydn and many of Beethoven by the Scherzo (q.v.) which had gradually developed out of it.

The Minuet is in 3-in-a-measure time and its tempo is unhurried. Normally (after the earliest days) it has been in Ternary Form (see *Form* 2). With it is usually associated another Minuet—called 'Trio', from the fact that in the orch. minuets of some of the Fr. com-

Minute Valse for Piano. Chopin's Op. 64, No. 1, in D flat—supposed to take merely 1 minute to play, hence the nickname. (But cf. *Dog Valse*.)

Miolan-Carvalho, Caroline Marie Felix (b. Marseilles 1827; d. nr. Dieppe 1895). Operatic soprano. Trained Paris Conserv. (from age 14) under Duprez. Paris début 1849; Covent Garden 1854. Held in highest esteem (especially in Paris) as exponent of Gounod roles. Husband was Léon Carvalho (1825–97), the famous Paris opera impresario.

Miracle in the Gorbals. Ballet by Bliss (1st perf. London 1944).

Miracle Plays, Mysteries, and **Moralities.** The custom of teaching Bible stories by means of sacred dramas (often in church) is venerable. These dramas were known as *Miracle Plays* (or, simply, *Miracles*), another name, given by writers on the subject (apparently first in the 18th c.), being *Mystery*. Of similar character were the plays which personifying virtues and vices taught moral lessons—such as *Moralities*. Religious plays of such types as these are recorded as early as the 4th c. In England there are records of them from the 11th c. to the 16th and even today there are relics of them in the rural performances of mummers in the north of England (e.g. the play of St. George and the Dragon).

Corpus Christi was in some cities a great occasion for plays in the streets (at Chester 24 such played in the 1 day, moving to different locations, with the whole 24 at each of these). As a good deal of singing entered into the scheme of some of the plays we may see in them the germ of the coming oratorio and opera.

Miraculous Mandarin (Bartók). See under *Amazing*.

Mireille. Opera by Gounod, based on poem of Mistral. (Prod. Paris, London, Dublin, and Philadelphia 1864.)

Mirliton (Fr.). The instrument known in Britain as the 'Tommy Talker' or 'Kazoo'—a short tube with a membrane at each end into a side hole of which tube one sings or hums. The result is a kind of caricature of oboe tone (cf. *Bigophone*).

Miroirs ('Mirrors'). Set of Piano pieces by Ravel (1905), of which he scored one (1912) for Orch., *L'Alborada del gracioso* ('The Aubade of the Clown').

Mirror Canon, Mirror Fugue. (1) One which can be played forwards or backwards, the effect in both cases being the same. (2, less common) One in which all the voices and all their intervals can be inverted, the lowest voice becoming the highest, and, in each voice, melodic progression by an upward interval of a 5th becoming melodic progression by a downward interval of a 5th, and so on.

The mirror is visualized placed (1) at the end of the melody, at right angles to the stave lines; (2) above, and parallel to, the stave.

Mirrors (Ravel). See *Miroirs*.

Mise (Fr.). 'Putting' (noun). *Mise de voix = Messa di voce* (q.v.).

Miserere. Ps. 51 (50 in Roman Catholic numeration). In the Roman Catholic Church it is sung in the service of Lauds (q.v.). It has frequently been set by composers. (See *Allegri*.)

Misón, Luís (d. 1766). See *Tonadilla*.

Missa ad Fugam, or **Missa ad Canones.** A mass in a fugal or canonic style.

Missa Brevis ('Short Mass') is a mere setting of the Kyrie and Gloria, as was customary in the Lutheran Church.

Missa Cantata ('Sung Mass'). Practically the same as 'High Mass' (see *Mass*).

Missa de Angelis. A particular plainsong Mass, very popular both in the Roman and some Anglican churches: it seems to date from the 14th and 15th cs. but to have been modified in the 17th c. and possibly the 18th, so that it does not altogether reproduce the true spirit of plainsong.

Missa in tempore belli (Haydn). See *Paukenmesse*.

Missal. See *Gradual; Liturgy*.

Missa lecta ('Read Mass'). Same as 'Low Mass' (see *Mass*—end of article).

Missa Papae Marcelli ('Mass of Pope Marcelli'). By Palestrina. The Pope Marcellus II, who resigned after only a few weeks, showed a desire to promote a reform in church music and this Mass is traditionally associated with the circumstance. But the romantic legend that has grown around the occurrence has no historical basis.

Missa privata or **Missa lecta** ('Private Mass' or 'Read Mass'). Same as 'Low Mass' (see *Mass*—end of article).

Missa pro defunctis. The *Requiem* (q.v.).

Missa quarti toni ('Fourth Mode Mass') and similar titles were attempts (in periods up to the late 16th c.) to find a somewhat distinctive description by mentioning the Mode (see *Modes*) in which the music was written.

Missa sine nomine ('Mass without Name'). In the early days of contrapuntal music it was common to use an existing melody (plainsong or secular song) as the *canto fermo* (see *Counterpoint*) and the mass then took its name from this melody. A mass composed on an original *canto fermo* was, then, called a 'Missa sine nomine'. (For the 14th-c. prohibition of the use of secular *canti fermi* see a remark under *Church Music*.)

Missa solemnis (Beethoven). See *Mass in D.*

Missa supra voces musicales ('Mass on the musical notes') means a mass written on a *canto fermo* (see *Counterpoint*) consisting of merely a fragment of scale—the Hexachord (q.v.).

Mistero, misterio (It.). 'Mystery.' So the adj. *misterioso* and the adverb *misteriosamente.*

Mistico (It.). 'Mystic.'

Misura (It.). 'Measure.' (1) In the Eng. sense of 'bar'. (2) In the general sense of regularity. So *alla misura*, 'in strict time'; *senza misura*, 'without strict time'. And so, too, *misurato*, 'measured', i.e. strictly in time.

Mit (Ger.). 'With.' Very many terms of expression begin with this word. (The adjectives and nouns which follow it in such terms of expression will be found in their alphabetical positions.)

Mitchell, (1) **William John** (b. New York 1906; d. Binghampton, N.Y., 1971). Musical scholar. Studied Columbia Univ.; on staff from 1932, prof. 1952–68.

(2) **Howard** (b. Lyons, Nebraska, 1911). Studied 'cello at Peabody Conserv. and Curtis Inst.; leading 'cellist, Nat. Symphony Orch. in Washington, then assistant (1944) and finally permanent (1949–70) conductor. Assiduous supporter of contemporary music.

(3) **Donald** (b. London 1925). Critic, specializing in modern music; founder and ed. of *Music Survey* (q.v.). Ed. books on Britten and Mozart. Large scale biog. of Mahler.

Mit dem Hörnersignal (Haydn). See *Auf dem Anstand.*

Mitleidig (Ger.). 'Pitiful.'

Mitropoulos, Dimitri (b. Athens 1896; d. Milan 1960). Conductor, pianist, composer. Studied Athens Conserv. and in Germany under Busoni, &c. Appeared as conductor in all parts of Europe, then with Minneapolis Symphony Orch. (from 1937), and New York Philharmonic Orch. (1950–8). Composer of an opera, and orch., chamber, and piano works, &c.

Mitte (Ger.). 'Middle', e.g. *Auf der Mitte des Bogens*, 'In the middle of the bow'.

Mixed Cadence. See *Cadence*. **Mixed Sequence.** See *Sequence* 1.

Mixed Voice Choir (or **Chorus** or **Quartet**). One of both women and men.

Mixed Voices. A term used in choral music meaning men's and women's voices, together, as, for instance, in the normal soprano, alto, tenor, and bass ('S.A.T.B.') combination.

Mixolydian Mode. See *Modes.*

Mixture stop. Organ stop in which each finger-key (or pedal-key) played operates on a group of pipes corresponding to some of the higher harmonics of the note of that key. The group may be of from 2 to 7 pipes and the stop is then spoken of as having that number of *Ranks*. It cannot be used alone, but adds brightness when combined with stops of normal pitch in 'Full Organ', &c. Cf. *Sesquialtera.*

M.K. = *Manualkoppel* (Ger.), i.e. 'Manual Coupler' (in organ music—followed by an indication of the particular manuals to be coupled).

Mlada. Opera by Rimsky-Korsakof. Libretto by composer. (Prod. St. Petersburg 1892.)

Mlynarski, Emil (Simon) (b. Lithuania 1870; d. Warsaw 1935). Pupil of Auer, Rubinstein, and Liadof. International career as violinist, conductor (Scottish Orch. 1910–16; then Warsaw Opera and Conserv.); on staff of Curtis Inst., Philadelphia 1929–31. Composer of orch. works, operas, &c. (See *Polonia* 3.)

M.M. (1) See *Metronome*. (2) See *Degrees and Diplomas* 3.

M.Mus. See *Degrees and Diplomas* 1, 2, 3.

Moab (hymn tune). See *Roberts, John.*

Moby Dick. See *Herrmann.*

Modal. Pertaining to the modes (q.v.).

Moderato (It.), **modéré** (Fr.). 'Moderate' (i.e. in point of speed). So the adverbs *moderatamente, modérément.*

Modes. That form of scale called 'the Modes' (or, with too limited a suggestion, the *Church Modes* or the *Ecclesiastical Modes*) dominated European music for 1,100 years (say A.D. 400 to A.D. 1500), strongly influenced composers for another hundred years (say to A.D. 1600), and has since reappeared from time to time in the work of some composers, especially in the present century. Throughout that total period of 1,500 years the plainsong of the Church, which is entirely 'modal', has continued to accustom the ears of fresh generations to the melodic effect of the Modes.

The available material of music at the period when the Modes became accepted was that which we could nowadays conveniently describe as represented by the white keys of the piano or organ, whose notes constitute (with slight differences of tuning) the scale which in the 4th c. B.C. Pythagoras and the Gr. thinkers of his period had worked out scientifically. In the 2nd c. A.D. the Greeks were using this scale in 7 different ways; Gr. influence was strong in the early Christian Church and when the famous Bishop of Milan, St. Ambrose (abt. 340–97), undertook to set in order the music of the Church he accepted the Gr. scale but laid it out in 4 Modes (i.e. manners) of using its notes. It has been usually accepted that Pope Gregory (St. Gregory the Great, abt. 540–604) elaborated the Ambrosian system, adding 4 more modes.[1] To these 8 modes 4 more were later added, making 12.

[1] The statement here given as to the parts played by Saints Ambrose and Gregory is the traditional one which has appeared over and over again in all authorities for several centuries. It is conveniently clear-cut but is now questioned, a present tendency being to regard the modal system as one which in large measure grew up amongst the singers, being adopted by them as a practical measure.

What the Ambrosian modes were like may be found by playing on the piano 8ve scales of white notes beginning respectively on the notes D, E, F, and G. These are not like our 12 major scales (which are all alike as to intervals), or our 12 minor scales (which are similarly all alike), inasmuch as a melody played in one of the major scales or one of the minor scales and then in another is merely altered in pitch, whereas a melody played in one of the Modes and then in another is altered in some of its intervals and hence in its general effect. The 5th and 1st notes of an Ambrosian mode were of special importance. The 5th, the DOMINANT, was much used as a Reciting Note in plainsong, and the 1st, the FINAL, as a cadence note, closing a passage.

In Gregory's day the 4 Ambrosian modes were described as the AUTHENTIC MODES and the set of 4 which he added as the PLAGAL MODES. These Plagal modes were merely new forms of the others, being the same 4 taken in a compass lying not between Final and Final of the corresponding authentic modes but between their Dominant and Dominant, the Final, on which the cadences fell, thus coming in the middle. In order to avoid having the Reciting Note at the very top or bottom of the series of notes a new one was chosen, lying 3 notes below the original one, and this was now regarded as the Dominant. The whole series was now as follows (A = Authentic and P = Plagal):

Mode I (A)	Range	D-D	with Dominant		A
II (P)	,,	A-A	,,	,,	F
III (A)	,,	E-E	,,	,,	C[1]
IV (P)	,,	B-B	,,	,,	A
V (A)	,,	F-F	,,	,,	C
VI (P)	,,	C-C	,,	,,	A
VII (A)	,,	G-G	,,	,,	D
VIII (P)	,,	D-D	,,	,,	C[1]

[1] The Dominants of the two modes so marked (one of them Authentic and the other Plagal) would normally be B, but this being found an unsuitable note C was adopted instead.

It will be noted that the odd-numbered Modes are the Authentic ones and the even-numbered the Plagal.

Nearly a thousand years after Gregory a Swiss monk, Henry of Glarus, or Henricus Glareanus, brought forth, in a book called

Dodecachordon (1547), a theory that there should, historically, be 12 modes instead of 8. He added modes on A and C (none on the unsuitable B), with their Plagal forms, so that the table above was added to as follows:

IX (A) Compass A-A with Dominant E
X (P)   ,,   E-E ,,   ,,   C
XI (A)   ,,   C-C ,,   ,,   G
XII (P)   ,,   G-G ,,   ,,   E

Glareanus gave his 12 modes what he thought to be their original Gr. names and these (though incorrect) have become accepted:

I. Dorian   VIII. HypoMixoly-
II. HypoDorian   dian
III. Phrygian   IX. Æolian
IV. HypoPhrygian   X. HypoÆolian
V. Lydian   XI. Ionian
VI. HypoLydian   XII. HypoIonian
VII. Mixolydian

It should be clearly understood that the difference between the various modes is not one of *pitch* but of the order in which fall the tones and semitones. Any mode could be taken at another than its original pitch (i.e. transposed), but in that case its intervals remained as before. Thus we could set out the whole series as beginning on C, when the Dorian and Lydian (to take two examples) would appear as follows:

The Authentic Modes shown uniformly with C as final (with the semitones marked)

I. Dorian.

V. Lydian.

With the development of harmonized music the modal system in time tended to disintegrate: the two Authentic Modes added by Glareanus (the Ionian and Æolian) were felt to be the most suited to harmony and have remained as our 'major' and 'minor'. The other modes, however, are in use in plainsong, some folk song, and occasionally in the work of certain composers.

There is much more to be said on the Modes but at least a general conspectus has been given and for details the reader must be referred to *OCM*.

Modinha. Type of song (not folk song) popular in Portugal.

Mödl, Martha (b. Nuremberg 1912). Operatic soprano (at first mezzo). Début 1944; Düsseldorf 1945-9; Bayreuth 1951; Covent Garden 1949.

Modo (It.). (1) 'Manner', e.g. *in modo di*, 'in the manner of'. (2) 'Mode' (see *Modes*).

Modulation means change of key (q.v.) in the course of a passage. The simplest and most natural modulations are those to what are called the *Related Keys* (or *Attendant Keys*), i.e. to the Relative Minor (or Major as the case may be), to the Dominant and its Relative Minor (or Major), and to the Subdominant and its Relative Minor (or Major).

(The Tonic Minor or Major is really a Related Key, modulation to it being simple and common, but is not usually so described.)

Modulator. See *Tonic Sol-fa*.

Modus Lascivus. The Ionian mode, the same as our major scale of C.

Moeran, Ernest John (b. Heston, Middx., 1894; d. Kenmare, Ireland, 1950). Of Irish descent but largely Norfolk residence; studied under John Ireland and at the R.C.M. Compositions include orch., chamber, choral, piano, and other works (Symphony in G minor 1937; violin concerto 1942).

Moffat, Alfred Edward (b. Edinburgh 1866; d. London 1950). Composer and editor. After 6 years' music study in Germany devoted himself especially to discovery, editing, and republication of old and neglected compositions, vocal and instrumental, particularly those of the 18th c.

Möglich (Ger.). 'Possible.' Thus *so rasch wie möglich*, 'as quick as possible'. The superlative is *Möglichst*.

Moins (Fr.). 'Less.'

Moiseiwitsch, Benno (b. Odessa 1890; d. London 1963). Pianist. Pupil of Leschetizky. Settled in Britain 1908; naturalized 1937. Of high reputation in all parts of world.

Moitié (Fr.). 'Half.'

Molinari, Bernardino (b. Rome 1880; d. Rome 1952). Conductor. Trained Conserv., Rome. From 1912 for many years attached to Augusteo, Rome. Wide and frequent conducting tours of Europe and America.

Molique, Wilhelm Bernhard (b. Nuremberg 1802; d. Stuttgart 1869). Remarkable violinist, pupil of Spohr; settled in London 1849–66. Compositions include 6 violin concertos, chamber music, &c.

Moll (Ger.). 'Minor', in the sense of key, e.g. *A moll*, 'A minor'; *Moll Ton*, or *Moll Tonart*, 'minor key' (see Table 9).

Molle; mollemente (It.). 'Gentle'; 'gently'.

Molloy, James Lymon (b. Cornolore, Ireland, 1837; d. Hambledon 1909). London barrister by profession but known in all Brit. homes by his songs (*Darby and Joan*; *Love's Old Sweet Song*, &c.).

Molto (It.). 'Much', 'very', e.g. *molto allegro*, 'very quickly'.

Moment Musical (Fr.). One of the many terms introduced in the early 19th c., when pianoforte composition was being developed on the romantic side, to designate a type of piece of brief length. Apparently Schubert was the first to use it. (The older spelling *Momen* is sometimes found.)

Mompou, Federico (b. Barcelona 1893). Composer of piano music, often of an advanced character as to harmony, &c.

Monckton, Lionel (b. London 1862; there d. 1924). Educ. Oxford. Highly successful composer of songs for musical comedies (*The Arcadians*, *A Country Girl*, *Our Miss Gibbs*, &c.). At one time a music critic of *Daily Telegraph*.

'Monday Pops'. See *St. James's Hall*.

Mondonville, Jean Joseph Cassanea de (b. Narbonne 1711; d. nr. Paris 1772). Noted Paris violinist; Superintendent of Music to Louis XV;

one of the protagonists on the Fr. side in the 'Guerre des Bouffons', 1752–4 (see *Bouffons*). Composed operas, oratorios, motets, and instrumental music.

Moniuszko, Stanislaw (b. Ubiel, prov. of Minsk, 1819; d. Warsaw 1872). Musical director Warsaw opera house and noted in Poland as composer; 16 operas (see *Halka*); 7 masses; orch. and chamber works; over 270 songs.

Monk, (1) **Edwin George** (b. Frome, Somerset, 1819; d. Radley, nr. Oxford, 1900). Organist and music-master at Radley Coll. (1848); organist York Minster (1859–83). Composed church music, and edited books of hymn tunes and Anglican chants, &c. D.Mus., Oxford (1856).

(2) **William Henry** (b. London 1823; there d. 1889). Connected with King's Coll., London, as organist, &c. (1847); prof. of vocal music there (1874). Like his namesake (unrelated) above edited books of hymn tunes, &c. (e.g. *Hymns Ancient and Modern* 1861); many of his own hymn tunes remain favourites today. Hon. D.Mus., Durham.

(3) **Cyril** (b. Sydney, 1882). Violinist. Appeared first as pianist, then studied violin in London. Recital tours, New Zealand, &c.; founded Australian String Quartet. On staff, Sydney Conserv.

Monks' March, or **The Monks of Bangor's March.** The tune is first found in Playford's Dancing Master (1665), where it is given as the march of General Monk. (The association with the monks of Bangor in their march to Chester 1,000 years before General Monk's time is thus seen to be an error.)

Monn, (1) **Georg Matthias** (b. Lower Austria 1717; d. Vienna 1750). Organist of a Vienna church; composer of symphonies, a 'cello concerto, chamber music, &c. Some confusion appears to exist with a certain Johann Christoph Monn (also described as Giovanni Matteo Monn or Mann). A symphony in E flat, sometimes heard, cannot be securely ascribed to one or the other.

(2) **Johann Christoph** or **Giovanni Matteo.** See *Georg Matthias*, above.

Monochord. Rather a scientific instrument than a musical one. It was in use in Ancient Egypt and Ancient Greece and is still in use by physicists of today.

It consists of a soundbox over which is stretched a single string which can be divided at any point by a movable bridge, the position of which can be exactly determined by a scale of measurements on the surface over which it moves. The ratios of intervals, and similar acoustical facts, were discovered by its means. It is said that it was also used for teaching intervals to singers, and for giving the pitch to a choir. (In the early days of the clavichord the fact that this had only one string to each note caused it sometimes to be spoken of as a Monochord—sometimes changed to *Manichord*.)

Cf. *Tromba Marina.*

Monodic. Sometimes used as synonymous with monophonic (q.v.), but more properly denotes a particular type of accompanied solo song which developed around 1600, characterized by recitativo-like design of the voice part and by figured-bass accompaniment.

Monodrama. Same as melodrama (q.v.), with the restriction that it is for a single speaker.

Monophonic. Having one 'line' of notes—as distinct from (a) *Homophonic* (several lines of notes but moving together as chords, and without rhythmic individuality in the lines) and (b) *Polyphonic* (several lines of notes, each with individuality and moving with some independence).

Monsieur Beaucaire. Opera by Messager. Libretto based on a story by N. Booth Tarkington. (Prod. Birmingham, London, and New York 1919; Montreal 1920; Paris 1925.)

Monsigny, Pierre Alexandre (b. nr. St. Omer 1729; d. Paris 1817). Of noble family; held various official positions (Inspector-General of Canals, &c.); good violinist and famous composer of comic operas; had gift of graceful melody and counts as one of best opera composers of his country and period.

Montagu-Nathan, Montagu—orig. Montagu Nathan (b. Banbury 1877; d. London 1958). Violinist, then mus. journalist; books on Russian music.

Monte, Filippo di, or Philippe de Mons (b. Mechlin, Malines, abt. 1521; d. Prague 1603). One of greatest composers of later part of great Flemish period; even considered a rival of Palestrina; musical director at court of Holy Roman Empire (1568–death; Vienna and then Prague). Publ. over 1,000 madrigals, also many masses and motets.

Montéclair, Michel Pignolet de (b. Andelot, N.E. France, 1667; d. St. Denis, nr. Paris, 1737). One of earliest performers on modern double-bass; also famous teacher of violin. Composed operas, instrumental music (including for flute), &c.; wrote also violin method (1720), and theoretical works.

Montemezzi, Italo (b. nr. Verona 1875; there d. 1952). Student of engineering; took up music late and studied at Milan Conserv. and achieved fame with opera *L'Amore dei tre re* (see *Amore*). Composed other operas, orch. works, &c.

Monter (Fr.). 'To raise.' So the imperative *montez.*

Montessori. See *Education and Music* 1.

Monteux, Pierre (b. Paris 1875; d. Hancock, Me., 1964). Trained at Paris Conserv. (violinist); then became orch. viola player. Conducted Diaghilev Russian ballet 1911–14 and later; toured U.S.A. with it. Paris Opéra (1913–14); Covent Garden; Metropolitan, New York (1917–18); Boston Symphony Orch. (1919–24); Orchestre Symphonique de Paris (1928); San Francisco (1935–52); London Symphony Orch. (1961).

Monteverdi (or **Monteverde**), **Claudio** (b. Cremona 1567; d. Venice 1643). Early opera composer; applied the ideas of 'The New Music' (see *History of Music* 4; *Caccini*); used great harmonic freedom, varied orch. accompaniment, and sensitive and dramatic recitative; travelled extensively and held many important It. positions; many books of madrigals; some masses.

See *Orfeo*; *Incoronazione di Poppea*; *Vespers*.

Monthly Musical Record. See *Augener*; *Westrup*; *Abraham*.

Moody, (1) **Fanny** (b. Redruth 1866; d. Dundrum, Co. Dublin, 1945). Operatic soprano. Début with Carl Rosa Co. 1887, thereafter Drury Lane and Covent Garden seasons, &c. Married Southcote Mansergh ('Charles Manners', q.v.) 1890.

(2) **Charles Harry** (b. Stourbridge, Worcs., 1874; d. 1965). Organist Wigan Parish Church 1896; Coventry 1899; Ripon Cathedral 1902–52. Condr. of important Yorkshire choirs. Various church music compositions and literary works. C.B.E. 1920; D.Mus., Lambeth, 1923.

Moody and Sankey. See *Hymns and Hymn Tunes* 7.

Moody-Manners Opera Co. See *Manners, Charles*.

Moon and Sixpence. See *Gardner*.

Moonlight Sonata (Beethoven). Nickname of the Piano Sonata in C sharp minor, op. 27, no. 2 (1801), from the poet Rellstab's remark that the 1st movement reminded him of moonlight on Lake Lucerne. Also called *Laube Sonate* ('Arbour Sonata'), from a tradition as to the place of its composition.

Moór, Emanuel (b. Hungary 1863; d. nr. Vevey, Switzerland, 1931). Had early pianist career, both sides Atlantic. Composed operas, symphonies, &c. Invented new form of instruments of violin family and Duplex-coupler Piano (cf. *Keyboard* and *Christie, Winifred*).

Moore, (1) **Thomas** (b. Dublin 1779; d. Bromham, Wilts., 1852). As Scott made his native Scotland romantic so he did his native Ireland; publ. collections of traditional Irish Melodies with poems written for them (1807 onwards); London society favourite, singing and playing these (e.g. *The Harp that once*, *The Last Rose of Summer*, *The Minstrel Boy*).

See *Canadian Boat Song*; *Eileen Aroon*; *Last Rose of Summer*; *Saint Patrick's Day*.

(2) **Mary Carr** (b. Memphis, Tenn. 1873; d. Ingleside, Calif., 1957). Composer of several operas which have enjoyed perf. on various stages of the Western U.S.A. Also of orch. and chamber music, &c.

(3) **Douglas (Stuart)** (b. Long Island 1893; d. Greenport, L.I., 1969). Studied at Yale, in Paris with d'Indy and Nadia Boulanger, and with Bloch; won Pulitzer Prize for further European study (1926), Associate Prof. of Music (1926), and then Prof. (1940–63), Columbia University, New York. Composer of operas, symphonic poems, chamber and piano music, songs, &c. (Cf. *Devil and Daniel Webster*.)

(4) **Gerald** (b. Watford 1899). Spent boyhood in Canada touring as pianist. Associated as accompanist with many of world's greatest singers and violinists. Author of book *The Unashamed Accompanist* (1943). C.B.E. 1954.

(5) **Grace** (b. Jellico, Tenn., 1901; killed in air accident nr. Copenhagen 1947). Soprano. At first in café music and musical comedy. Opera début Metropolitan Opera 1928; Covent Garden 1935. Also appeared in films.

Moqueur (Fr.). 'Mocking', 'waggish'.

Morales, Cristóbal (b. Seville abt. 1500; d. Málaga 1553). Priest, singer in Sistine Chapel, Rome; then held various positions in his native Spain. Held high place as composer of church music, much of his music being printed in different cities of Europe; still very highly esteemed.

Moralities. See *Miracle Plays*.

Morasco. Same as *Moresca* (q.v.).

Morbido; morbidezza (It.). 'Soft', 'gentle'; 'softness', 'gentleness'. (Not 'morbid', and 'morbidity' as stated in some books.)

Morceau (Fr.). 'Piece.' So *Morceau symphonique*, 'Symphonic piece'. (For *Morceau d'ensemble* see *Ensemble*.)

Mordent. See Table 12. (In addition to the 2 forms of this ornament there shown there are others used by the older composers: these, however, are in modern edns. set out in full and so need not be given here.)

Moreau, Jean Baptiste (b. Angers 1656; d. Paris 1733). Organist of cathedral of Langres and then at Dijon; went to Paris and taken into royal service; composed music for dramatic divertissements and especially music for Racine's *Esther* (1689). Renowned singing master and song composer.

Morel, Jean (b. Abbeville 1903). Trained in Paris; taught at Amer. Conserv. at Fontainebleau (1921–36) and Brooklyn Coll. (1940–3). Conducting career in France and the Americas. Juilliard School from 1949.

Morendo (It.). 'Dying.'

Moreno, Stephen (b. Navarre, Spain, 1890). Benedictine monk (now at New Norcia, W. Australia). Composer of innumerable religious and some secular works.

Moresca, Moresco, Morisca, or Morisco. A Moorish dance. Apparently the name (which was common from the 15th c. to the 17th) did not carry any settled implications as to rhythm and style. Often it was applied to any rough-and-ready grotesque dance employing costumes representing animals, &c. (cf. *Morris*).

Moresque (Fr.). Same as *Moresca* (q.v.).

Morgan, Mrs. Mary Hannah (b. Melbourne; d. Sydney 1956). Song-composer ('May Brahe'). Went to England 1912; published over 300 songs (*I passed by your window*, &c.).

Morgenblätter (Ger.). This can mean either 'Morning leaves' (i.e. the foliage) or 'Morning newspapers'. It occurs in musical use by the waltz composer Johann Strauss II, who, it is clear from the picture on the cover of the original edn., intended the second meaning. The waltz was, indeed, composed for a ball of the journalists of Vienna.

Morgenlied (Ger.). 'Morning song.'

Mori, (1) **Nicholas I** (b. London 1796; there d. 1839). Violinist and music publisher. Pupil of Viotti. A leading violinist in all orchs. of his day. For sons see below. (2) **Frank** (b. London 1820; d. Chaumont, France, 1873). Son of (1). Composer of cantatas, songs, vocal exercises, &c. Also

music publisher (firm of Lavenu). (3) **Nicholas II** (b. 1822). Also son of (1). Composer of choral works, &c.

Mörike Songs (*Gedichte von Mörike*). Fifty-three solo song settings by Hugo Wolf (1888). Piano accompaniment.

Morini, Erica (b. Vienna 1905). Violinist. Pupil of Ševčik. As child appeared Leipzig Gewandhaus under Nikisch (q.v.). New York début 1921; London 1924. Naturalized U.S.A.

Morisca, Morisco. See *Moresca*.

Morison, Elsie Jean (b. Victoria, Australia, 1924). Lyric soprano. Trained Melbourne Conserv. and R.C.M. Sadler's Wells 1948; Covent Garden 1953.

Morley, Thomas (1557–1602). Organist of St. Paul's Cathedral, and Gentleman of Chapel Royal; composed songs for some of Shakespeare's plays; given monopoly of music printing by Queen Elizabeth. Composed church music, very fine madrigals, fine songs, and instrumental music, and wrote *A Plaine and Easie Introduction to Practicall Musick* (1597).

See *Triumphs of Oriana, The.*

Morley College. Founded 1889 as adult non-vocational education centre. Directors of music dept. include Holst (1907), Arnold Goldsbrough (1924), Arnold Foster (1928), Michael Tippett (1940), Fricker (1953), John Gardner (1965), Michael Graubart (1969).

Mormorando, mormorante, mormorevole, mormoroso (It.). 'Murmuring.'

Morning Heroes. By Bliss. 'Symphony for Orator, Chorus, and Orchestra', with text from various sources. (1st perf. Norwich Fest. 1930.)

Mornington, Earl of—Garrett Colley Wellesley (b. Co. Meath 1735; d. London 1781). Father of the Duke of Wellington. Was remarkable child musician, as performer on violin, harpsichord, and organ; Prof. of Music, Dublin Univ., 1764–74. Composed fine glees (e.g. *Here in cool grot*) and some church music.

Morris or Morrice. A type of Eng. folk dance for men. The dancers wear bells on their ankles, &c.: sometimes they are accompanied by persons dressed to represent characters (the Queen of the May, the Fool, &c.). The music is usually in duple or quadruple time. Some Eng. villages possess morris troops whose origin goes back to an unknown antiquity.

MORRIS DANCE
From a picture by Vinckenboom
(temp. James I)

Morris, (1) **Reginald Owen** (b. York 1886; d. London 1948). Educated at Oxford (M.A., D.Mus.) and R.C.M. (later on staff). Publ. a number of theoretical works, especially an important one on 16th-c. contrapuntal technique (1922). Composer of orch. and chamber music, &c.

(2) **Harold Cecil** (b. San Antonio, Texas, 1890; d. New York 1964). Pianist. On staff Inst. of Musical Art, New York (1921); Juilliard School (1922–39). Composer of many orch. and chamber works, &c.

Morrison, Angus—in full Stuart Angus (b. Maidenhead 1902). Pianist. Trained R.C.M. (on staff since 1926). Recitalist in Britain and abroad.

Morrow, Walter (1850–1937). Trumpet player. Trained R.A.M. Début 1873. Leading player in London orchs. and famous soloist. Introduced special instrument for playing Bach's highlying trumpet parts (cf. *Trumpet Family*).

Mors et Vita. Oratorio by Gounod. (1st perf. Norwich Fest. 1884.)

Mortari, Virgilio (b. nr. Milan 1902). Pupil in Milan Conserv. of Bossi and Pizzetti; pianist and composer of operas, chamber music, songs, &c.

Moscheles, Ignaz (b. Prague 1794; d. Leipzig 1870). Neat and brilliant pianist; resident in London 1826–46; then appointed director piano dept.

Leipzig Conserv. by its 1st head, Mendelssohn. Composed 8 piano concertos, piano solos, chamber music, &c.

See *Pianoforte Playing.*

Mosè in Egitto ('Moses in Egypt'). Opera by Rossini. (Prod. Naples 1818; London 1822; New York 1835.) Early Brit. and Amer. performances often had changed libretti and sometimes garbled music also. The famous 'Prayer' from the original version of the opera long had much currency in choral circles.

Moser, (1) **Andreas** (b. Hungary 1859; d. Berlin 1925). Violinist (pupil, friend, and biographer of Joachim and with him ed. of Beethoven's quartets and many violin works). (2) **Hans Joachim** (1889–1967). Son of (1). Musicologist and lexicographer (*Das Musik Lexikon*, 1931, &c.) and author of many books on mus. history.

Moses and Aaron. 2-act opera (3rd act incomplete) by Schönberg. Libretto by composer. (Prod. Zürich 1957.)

Mosso (It.). 'Moved', e.g. *più mosso*, 'More moved' = quicker.

Mossolof, Alexander Vassilievich (b. Kief 1900). Trained at Moscow Conserv.; accomplished pianist. Composer of operas, ballets, orch. works, piano music, songs, &c., sometimes of very original character.

Moszkowski, Moritz (b. Breslau 1854; d. Paris 1925). Solo pianist and composer of attractive piano music of lighter (but still sound) type, also orch. music, an opera, &c. Lived in Paris from 1897; often visited Britain.

Motet. The church choral form of the motet superseded that of the conductus (q.v.). From the 13th c. and into the 15th or early 16th both were in use: then the conductus gradually died out and the motet continued and, in a greatly developed form, may be said to be alive today.

The motet from the first had more contrapuntal freedom than the conductus. Its parts moved in different lengths of notes according to the rhythmic schemes of the day, which cannot be gone into here. When we come to the period of Palestrina and Byrd we find the motet grown into a great medium of the most able expression of the finest musical thought. Palestrina wrote about 180 motets. An alternative for 'motets' frequently used at this period is 'Cantiones Sacrae'. Bach wrote 6 magnificent motets, all in German, and 4 of them are for 8 voices: the great *Singet dem Herrn* ('Sing ye to the Lord') is one of them. These are for voices unaccompanied (i.e. with no written accompaniment, though some think that an instrumental support doubling the voice parts was used), but by this time choral works with independent accompaniment were taking on the name, and indeed the word is henceforth very loosely applied—even to pieces for solo voice with accompaniment. The true motet continued to be written, however.

The moments when motets may be introduced into the Roman Catholic service are at the Offertory, during the Elevation of the Host, and during processions and other ceremonies for which the liturgy does not prescribe any particular text to be sung.

Cf. *Anthem.*

Mother, The. See *Hába.*

Mother Goose (Ravel). See *Ma mère l'oye.*

Mother Goose Songs (Amer.) = *Nursery Rhymes* (Eng.).

Motif (Fr.), **Motiv** (Ger.), **motivo** (It.), **motive** (Eng.). The briefest intelligible and self-existent melodic or rhythmic unit, consisting of 2 notes or more: almost any passage of music will be found, on examination, to consist of a development of some motif. (The principle of the Motif finds a great extension in Wagner, where it is not necessarily so atomic as the above definition suggests, being sometimes an extended phrase. Cf. *Leading Motive; Wagner.*)

Motion. (1) In the combination of any 2 'voices' or 'parts' of a composition, if they proceed in the same direction (notationally considered) they are said to be in *Similar Motion*, if in opposite directions in *Contrary Motion*. If one part holds (or repeats) a note and the other part moves up or down from it there is *Oblique Motion*. Similar Motion in which the parts proceed by the same

intervals (numerically considered) is *Parallel Motion*. (2) In the shaping of a single part progress by step is called *Conjunct Motion* and progress by leap *Disjunct Motion.*

Moto (It.). 'Motion', e.g. *con moto*, 'with motion' = quickly.

Moto perpetuo. See *Perpetuum mobile.*

Moto precedente (It.). 'Preceding motion' (i.e. same speed as what has just gone before).

Motteggiando (It.). 'Bantering.'

Mottl, Felix (b. nr. Vienna 1856; d. Munich 1911). Studied at Vienna Conserv.; then became assistant to Wagner in preparing first Bayreuth Festival (1876); held many important official positions as conductor; many London visits 1894 onwards, especially as Wagner conductor; also composer, but not prolific or important as such.

Motto Theme. A device akin to that of the *Leading Motive* of Wagner, the *Idée fixe* of Berlioz, and *Metamorphosis of Themes* of Liszt. It arises from the attaching of some symbolical significance to a musical theme which reappears at intervals during the course of a piece of Programme Music, and is intended to bring that significance to the mind of the listener whenever it is heard.

Motu Proprio. Lit. 'Of his own motion'. A sort of Bull issued by the Pope, reserved for the internal administrative affairs of the Church. The word is often heard in connexion with church music on account of the Motu Proprio of Pius X, issued in the year of his becoming Pope (1903). It was of the nature of an Instruction upon Sacred Music; it laid down general principles recognized everywhere by cultured, intelligent, and devout musicians as being sound, and placed emphasis especially upon the importance of the traditional plainsong and of the 'classical polyphony' of the time of Palestrina which ultimately derived from it. Modern compositions were not prohibited, but they were to be such as 'by their merit and gravity are not unworthy of the liturgical functions'. Theological students were to receive instruction in the music of the Church. The ancient 'Scholae Cantorum' were to be revived and attached to the principal churches everywhere (see *Schola Cantorum*). About the same time as this Motu Proprio was issued the papal support was definitely given to the monks of Solesmes in their long-continued labours for the purity of plainsong and the official Vatican edition was the result.

In 1928 Pope Pius XI issued a constitution commanding the restoration to the congregation of their part of the Common of the Mass (see *Mass*; *Common*).

Moule-Evans, David (b. Ashford, Kent, 1905). Won Mendelssohn Scholarship and studied R.C.M. (later on staff). Has composed orch. works (Symphony and *Spirit of London* overture), &c. D.Mus., Oxford.

Moulton, Dorothy—Lady Mayer (b. London 1888). Soprano. Trained under Wm. Shakespeare and von zur Mühlen. Opera appearances with Carl Rosa Co.; then specialized Lieder and modern songs. Co-founder with husband Sir Robert Mayer of Children's Concert organization.

Mountain Sylph, The. See *Barnett, John.*

Mountain Symphony (Liszt). See *Ce qu'on entend.*

Mounted Cornet. Organ stop. See *Cornet Stop.*

Mount of Olives (Beethoven). See *Christ on the Mount of Olives.*

Mouret, Jean Joseph (b. Avignon 1682; d. Charenton 1738). Held various official musical posts in Paris. Composed operas, ballets, motets, and effective music for string and wind instruments.

Mourning Symphony (*Trauersymphonie*). By Haydn. Nickname of Haydn's Symphony in E minor, No. 44 (abt. 1772), in Breitkopf edn. of his Symphonies.

Mourning Waltz (Ger. *Trauerwalzer*), or **Sad Waltz** (Fr. *Valse Triste*, but cf. entry under this name), or **Longing Waltz** (*Sehnsuchtswalzer*). Unauthorized publishers' titles for Schubert's op. 9, no. 2, for Piano.

Moussorgski. See *Mussorgsky.*

Mouth Organ. See *Reed Organ Family* 2.

Mouton, Jean (b. nr. Boulogne abt. 1470; d. St. Quentin 1522). Pupil of Josquin des Prés and master of Willaert and thus in the full succession of the Netherland contrapuntists who in the early 16th c. had such importance; in earlier part of career employed at court of Louis XII and his successor Francis I; latterly a canon of St. Quentin. Left fine masses, motets, &c.

Mouvement (Fr.). 'Movement' (either in the sense of motion or in the derived sense of section of long composition). *Mouvement perpétuel* is the same as *perpetuum mobile* (q.v.).

Mouvt. is an abbreviation of *Mouvement*; sometimes (as in Debussy) the meaning is 'Return to the proper speed' (e.g. after 'Rit.').

Mouvementé (Fr.). 'Bustling', 'animated'.

Mouvement Perpétuel. See *Perpetuum Mobile.*

Movable-doh. A term applied to that system of sight-singing in which *Doh* is the name applied to the keynote of every major scale, *ray* to the 2nd note, *me* to the 3rd, and so on—as distinct from the *Fixed-doh* system in which C is, in every key in which it occurs, called *doh*, D called *ray*, and so on. (See *Sight-Singing, Tonic Sol-fa.*)

Movement. A composition cast in any 'Cyclic Form' (q.v.) consists of several shorter compositions, each, as a rule, complete in itself, and all so designed (as to fitness for one another, contrast, &c.) as to combine effectively into a larger composition (see *Suite, Sonata, Symphony, Concerto,* &c.). These shorter compositions are necessarily, for purposes of variety, different in speed (i.e. quicker and slower) and hence are called 'Movements'.

Movente (It.). 'Moving.' **Movimento.** 'Motion.'

Moyse, Marcel (b. St. Amour, Jura, France, 1889). Flautist. Trained Paris Conserv. (later on staff, as also of conservatories of Geneva, Zürich, and Lucerne). Has toured widely with Trio of members of his family. Chevalier of Legion of Honour.

Mozart, (1) (Johann Georg) Leopold (b. Augsburg 1719; d. Salzburg 1787). Violinist of high reputation in service of Prince Archbishop of Salzburg; composer of many symphonies and other orch. works, piano and organ works, and chamber music; author of famous *Violin School* (1756 and later edns.; translated into various languages—Eng. 1948). Father of Anna and Wolfgang Amadeus, below.

See reference under *Dot.*

(2) (Maria) Anna, or **Marianne** (b. Salzburg 1751; there d. 1829). Daughter and pupil of Leopold, above. Child prodigy harpsichordist; became music teacher in Salzburg; married; spent last decade of life in widowhood, blindness, and relative poverty.

(3) Wolfgang Amadeus—according to baptismal register Joannes Chrysostomus Wolfgangus Theophilus (b. Salzburg 1756; d. Vienna 1791). Son and pupil of Leopold, above. At 6 clever harpsichordist; spent 6th to 10th years chiefly in touring with sister and father the courts and capitals of Europe (in London for 15 months, 1764–5); appointed to musical staff of Salzburg; further extended tours in Italy and elsewhere followed, up to 1781 (age 25) when settled in Vienna; married and lived sparely; was intimate with Haydn (a quarter-century older), who fully recognized his genius; instrumental compositions at first based on those of Haydn, but Haydn's later influenced by his; at 35 died of uraemia.

Compositions include the following: OPERAS: especially *Figaro, Don Giovanni*, and *The Magic Flute.* ORCHESTRAL WORKS: nearly 50 symphonies, especially 3 in 1788 (E flat, G minor, and C, now called *Jupiter*, q.v.), concertos, serenades, &c. CHAMBER MUSIC: string quartets and quintets, piano trios and quartets, &c., sonatas for piano and violin, &c. PIANO WORKS: sonatas, variations, miscellaneous pieces. CHURCH MUSIC: masses, &c. VOCAL MUSIC: arias and Lieder, duets, trios, and quartets.

See also *Additional Accompaniments; Bastien und Bastienne; Chasse; Clemenza di Tito; Coronation Concerto; Coronation Mass; Così fan tutte; Credo Mass; Dissonanzen Quartett; Dominicus Mass; Don Giovanni; Entführung aus dem Serail;*

Expression; Haffner; Harmonica 1; *Idomeneo; Istrumento d'acciaio; Jeunehomme Concerto; Jupiter Symphony; Kierkegaard; Kleine Nachtmusik; Köchel; Linz Symphony; Magic Flute; Mauerische Trauermusik; Musikalischer Spass; Nozze di Figaro; Oca del Cairo; Orchestra* 2; *Organ Solo Mass; Paris Symphony; Pianoforte Playing; Prague Symphony; Prussian Quartets; Requiem; Schauspieldirektor; Stadler Quintet; 'Twelfth Mass'.*

Mozart and Salieri. Opera by Rimsky-Korsakof. A setting of Pushkin's dramatic poem. (Prod. Moscow 1898; London 1927; Forest Park, Pa., 1933.)

MP. = *Mezzo piano*, 'half-soft'.

Mr. Pepys. See *Shaw, Martin.*

M.R.S.T. Member of the Royal Soc. of Teachers (see *Degrees and Diplomas* 2).

M.S. = *Mano sinistra* (It.), i.e. 'left hand'.

M.S.M. See *Degrees and Diplomas* 3.

M.T.N.A. Music Teachers' National Assoc. (see *Profession of Music*).

Much Ado About Nothing. Opera by Stanford, based on Shakespeare. (Prod. London 1901; Leipzig 1902.)

Muck, Karl (b. Darmstadt 1859; d. 1940). Orch. and operatic conductor. Prominent in Wagner. Boston Symphony Orch. 1906–8; 1912–18; interned in U.S.A. 1918 as enemy alien.

Müde (Ger.). 'Tired', 'languid in style'.

Mudge, Rev. Richard (b. Bideford, Devon, 1718; d. nr. Birmingham 1763). His 6 Concerti (Walsh, 1749) have been exhumed and found to be effective compositions of the pre-Haydn period.

Mudie, Michael Winfield (b. Manchester 1914; d. Brussels 1962). Conductor. Trained R.C.M. Chiefly engaged with opera (Royal Carl Rosa 1935; Covent Garden; Director Sadler's Wells 1948–52). Retired through ill-health 1952.

Muette de Portici, La ('The Dumb Girl of Portici', but known in Britain as *Masaniello*). Opera by Auber. (Prod. Paris 1828; London and Edinburgh 1829; New York 1831.)

Muffat, (1) Georg (b. Megève, Savoy, 1653; d. Passau 1704). Organist of Strasbourg Cathedral, &c., then in Salzburg and Passau. Composed concerti grossi, organ music, &c. For son see below. (2) **Gottlieb** (b. Passau 1690; d. Vienna 1770). Son of Georg, above. Organist in royal service in Vienna. Composed organ and harpsichord music.

Muffling (of drums). See *Mute*; *Percussion Family* 1 a.

Mühelos (Ger.). 'Effortless.'

Mühlen. See *Zur Mühlen*.

Mühlfeld, Richard (b. Salzungen 1856; d. Meiningen 1907). Celebrated clarinettist, Meiningen and Bayreuth orchs., whose playing prompted Brahms's late group of clarinet works.

Muiñeira, or **Muñeira.** A type of Spanish dance and song in compound duple time. It is popular in Galicia, and another name for it is *Gallegada*.

Muir, Alexander. See *Maple Leaf for ever!*

Mukle, May (b. London 1880; there d. 1963). Violoncellist. Trained R.A.M. Toured extensively on 5 continents until end of her life. Many compositions specially written for her by Vaughan Williams, Holst, &c. Chamber music player. Founded (1933) M.M. ('Mainly Musicians') Club, London.

Mulcaster. See *Education* 2.

Mulet, Henri (b. Paris 1878). Paris organist and composer for organ.

Mullinar, Michael (b. Bangor 1895). Pianist and composer. Trained R.C.M. Accompanist to City of Birmingham Orch. 1922–38; then in London. Dedicatee of Vaughan Williams's 6th symphony.

Mullings, Frank Coningsby (b. Walsall 1881; d. Manchester 1953). Opera and concert tenor. Trained Birmingham and Midland Institute (later on staff). Début Coventry 1907; London 1911. Later Beecham and British National Opera Companies. On staff Royal Manchester College of Music.

Münch, Charles (b. Strasbourg 1891; d. Richmond, Va., 1968). Conductor.

At first violinist (pupil Carl Flesch, q.v.). On staff Leipzig Conservatory and leader Gewandhaus Orchestra. Début as cond. Paris 1933; London 1938. Boston Symph. Orch. 1948–62.

Münchinger, Karl (b. Stuttgart 1915). Trained Leipzig; formed (1945) and cond. Stuttgart Chamber Orch. (many tours and recordings).

Munck, (1) François de (b. Brussels 1815; there d. 1854). Violoncellist. Pupil and then on staff of Brussels Conserv. In London 1848–53. (2) **Ernest de** (b. Brussels 1840; d. 1915). Violoncellist. Settled London. On staff R.A.M. 1893.

Mundharmonika (Ger.).'Mouth harmonica', i.e. mouth organ (see *Reed Organ Family* 2).

Mundy, (1) William (abt. 1529–abt. 1591). Vicar-choral of St. Paul's and Gentleman of Queen Elizabeth's Chapel Royal; left good church music, still sung. For son see below. (2) **John** (d. 1630). Like father (above) Gentleman of Chapel Royal; organist Eton Coll. and then St. George's Chapel, Windsor Castle. D.Mus., Oxford, 1624. Composed madrigals and keyboard music.

Muñeira. See *Muiñeira*.

Munsel, Patrice (Beverly) (b. Spokane, Wash., 1925). Operatic coloratura soprano. Début Metropolitan 1943 (youngest ever at that theatre); successful international career.

Munter (Ger.). 'Lively.'

Murciana. A kind of fandango (q.v.) of Murcia, in southern Spain, with the same peculiarities as the malagueña (q.v.).

Murder in the Cathedral. See *Assassinio nella cattedrale*.

Murdoch, William David (b. Bendigo, Victoria, Australia, 1888; d. Holmbury St. Mary, Surrey, 1942). Pianist. Trained Melbourne and R.C.M. Attained prominence as solo and chamber music player. On staff of R.A.M. Composed piano and vocal music; wrote books on Chopin and Brahms.

Muris, Jean de (end 13th c. and 1st half 14th). Mathematician and writer of treatises on musical theory.

Murmelnd (Ger.), **murmurando** (It.). 'Murmuring.'

Murrill, Herbert Henry John (b. London 1909; d. there 1952). Studied at R.A.M. (later a prof. there) and at Oxford. London organist, school music-master, and then B.B.C. (Head of Music 1950); composer of orch. music, stage music (including opera *Man in Cage* 1929), chamber and piano music, songs, &c.

Murska, Ilma (b. Zagreb 1836; d. Munich 1889). Operatic soprano with wide vocal range and great dramatic powers. Début Florence 1862; London 1865. Then world fame.

Musard, Philippe (1793–1859). Fr. violinist who developed into popular orch. conductor. Cf. *Concert.*

Mus.B. See *Degrees and Diplomas* 1, 3.

Muscadin. A term occasionally found in Engl. virginal music; apparently it is a kind of hornpipe (q.v.).

Mus.D. See *Degrees and Diplomas* 1, 3.

Musette. (1) A type of Fr. bagpipe (q.v.) very popular in aristocratic circles of the late 17th c. and the early 18th. It was not mouth-blown but bellows-blown, and had 4 or 5 drones, all enclosed in 1 cylinder. (2) A kind of gavotte in which a persistent bass note imitates the drone of the above instrument.

Musgrave, Thea (b. Edinburgh 1928). Studied at Edinburgh Univ. and under Boulanger. Recital pianist and composer of works (esp. operas and chamber music) using note-row methods but also influenced by folk-song style.

Musica falsa (It. 'false music'). Same as *Musica ficta* (q.v.).

Musica ficta (Lat. 'feigned music'). A sharpening or flattening of certain notes, conventionally prescribed or permitted in modal music (see *Modes*) in order to avoid certain awkward intervals or for other purposes. Its one-time prevalence necessitates a good deal of knowledge of early custom on the part of modern editors of music up to and including that of the 16th c.

Cf. *Fa fictum.*

Musica figurata (It.), or **Figuralmusik** (Ger.). The term has 2 meanings: (1, the commoner meaning) Contrapuntal music in which the various melodic strands move more or less independently, shorter notes in one voice against longer in others—as distinct, that is, from mere 'note against note' counterpoint. (2, the less common meaning) Decorated melody in plainsong, &c., as distinct from the more sober type (such decorated plainsong is also known as *musica colorata*— 'coloured music').

Musical America. American monthly magazine, with wide coverage of musical events. Founded 1898; merged with *High Fidelity* 1965. (See *Kramer.*)

Musical Antiquary. See *Arkwright.*

Musical Appreciation. See *Appreciation of Music.*

Musical Association. See *Royal Musical Association.*

Musical Box. See *Mechanical Reproduction of Music* 7.

Musical Comedy. The term used to be applied to any sentimental-humorous play with plenty of light music in it.

Musical Competition Festivals. See *Competitions in Music.*

Musical Examiner, The. Eng. weekly musical journal (1842–4). Ed. J. W. Davison (see *Criticism*).

Musical Glasses. See *Harmonica* 1.

Musical Joke (Mozart). See *Musikalischer Spass, Ein.*

Musical Offering, The (*Das musikalische Opfer*). Collection of contrapuntal treatments of a single subject, composed by Bach 3 years before his death, and dedicated to Frederick the Great, who, during Bach's visit to Potsdam in 1747, had given him that subject upon which to extemporize.

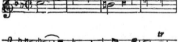

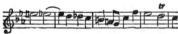

Some of the pieces are for keyboard, others for no particular medium. There are 2 for flute (Frederick's own instrument) with violin and figured bass. Modern performing arrangements exist for various combinations. (Cf. *Art of Fugue*.)

Musical Opinion and Music Trade Review. Brit. monthly journal (26-27 Hatton Garden, London, E.C.1). Founded 1877.

Musical Quarterly. Founded 1915 (G. Schirmer Inc., 609 Fifth Avenue, New York). Editors O. G. Sonneck (to 1928); Carl Engel (to 1944); Gustave Reese (1945); Paul H. Lang. See also under *Criticism*.

Musical Saw. Same as *Singing Saw* (q.v.).

Musical Switch. A popular type of composition constructed out of snatches of popular tunes dovetailed into each other so that the attention is no sooner running on one line than it is 'switched' to another.

Musical Times. See under *Criticism*.

Musical Union. See *Annotated Programmes*.

Musical World, The. Important Brit. weekly musical journal (1836-91). Ed. first by Cowden Clarke; then (1844-85) J. W. Davison (see *Criticism*).

Music and Letters. Brit. musical quarterly. Founded 1920 by A. H. Fox-Strangways; 1937 ed. Eric Blom; 1950 Richard Capell; 1954 Blom; 1959 Westrup.

Musica parlante (It. 'talking music'). A term used by the early Florentine opera composers to describe their invention, *Recitative* (q.v.).

Musica reservata. A term (first appearing in middle of 16th c.) of which meaning is in some doubt. One view applies it to an extreme form of *Musica ficta* (q.v.), another to music employing an unusual reserve in the use of figuration and ornaments, and still another merely to what would nowadays be spoken of as music for extreme 'highbrows'.

Music drama. See *Wagner*.

Music Educators' National Conference. See *Education* 3.

Musicians' Benevolent Fund. A Brit. organization dating from 1921, originally founded in memory of the singer Gervase Elwes (1866-1921). Address: St. Cecilia's House, 7 Carlos Place, London, W. 1.

Musicians' Company. Ancient London Guild, which long claimed to be operating on royal charter of 1604, granted to it as successor of ancient London Soc. of Minstrels, which charter, however, was revoked 1636. New Charter granted in 1950. The Company dines regularly, offers prizes for composition, &c., and occupies a definite and useful position in Brit. musical life.

Musicians' Union. This trade union was established in 1921 by a combination of the earlier Amalgamated Musicians' Union and National Orchestral Union. It fixes minimum rates of payment, &c., and maintains a 'Political Fund'. Address: 29 Catherine Place, London S.W. 1. (Cf. *Committee for Promotion*.)

Music in Education. Brit. bi-monthly journal (Novello & Co. Ltd.). First publ. as *Music in Schools* 1937; changed title 1944.

Music Makers, The. By Elgar. Ode for Contralto, Chorus and Orchestra; setting of a poem by A. O'Shaughnessy. (1st perf. Birmingham Fest. 1912.)

Musico. Another name for Castrato Singer (see *Voice* 5).

Music of the Future. See *Liszt*.

Musicology. This is a word of comparatively recent adoption into the Eng. language (from the Fr. *Musicologie*). It may be said to cover all study of music other than that directed to proficiency in performance or composition.

Amongst the divisions of musicology are acoustics; the physiology of voice, ear, and hand; the psychology of aesthetics and, more directly, of musical appreciation and of musical education; ethnology so far as it bears on music (including folk songs, folk dances, &c.); rhythm and metrics; modes and scales; the principles and development of instruments; orchestration; form; theories of harmony; the history of music; the bibliography of music; terminology—and so forth.

The International Musical Soc. (1900–14) had as its purpose the promotion of musicological study, and its post-war successor made its purpose clear in its name—'Société Internationale de Musicologie' (founded 1928, organ *Acta Musicologica*). There are also national musicological societies in many countries. A Brit. musicological soc. (The Royal Musical Assoc.) has existed since 1874. An Amer. Musicological Soc. was founded in 1934.

In Germany many universities have chairs of musicology (Musikwissenschaft—lit. 'Musical Knowledge'); in France one or two; in Holland two (Amsterdam and Utrecht). The first Amer. univ. to establish such a chair was Cornell (1930).

Music Publishers Holding Corporation. New York firm, combining (1929) a number of previously independent firms (Harms, Remick, Witmark, New World).

Music Review, The. Brit. quarterly (3 Petty Cury, Cambridge). Founded 1940. Ed. Geoffrey Sharp.

Music Survey. Brit. quarterly. Founded 1948; discontinued 1953.

Music Teacher, The. Brit. monthly. Transformation of *The Music Student* (founded 1908).

Music Teachers' Association. Active and useful Brit. body founded 1908 by Stewart Macpherson. Its centre is London, but it possesses a number of local sections. Object is to improve the standard of music teaching.

Music Teachers' National Association of America. Founded 1876 and still usefully active. Annual Conference is important event. See *Profession of Music*.

Musikalische Opfer, Das (Bach). See *Musical Offering*.

Musikalischer Spass, Ein ('Musical Joke'). By Mozart. Also known as *Dorfmusikanten-Sextett* ('Village Musicians' Sextet'). For String Quartet and 2 Horns (K. 522, 1787); satirizing amateur composing and performing.

Musikalisches Gesangbuch. See *Schemelli Hymn Book*.

Musikwissenschaft. See *Musicology*.

Musin, Ovide (b. nr. Liège 1854; d. Brooklyn 1929). Violinist. Trained Liège Conserv. (later on staff) and Paris Conserv. Toured world. In London 1877–82. Settled New York 1908. Publ. Violin Method, &c.

Musique concrète ('Concrete Music'). Term coined by Paris group experimenting with electrically combined series of previously recorded sounds, usually natural noises rather than those produced by electronic means. (See *Electric Musical Instruments*.)

Musique d'harmonie. See *Harmonie*.

Mus.M. See *Degrees and Diplomas* 1, 3.

Mussorgsky (Musorgsky, Moussorgski, &c.), Modeste Petrovich (b. Karevo, Pskov, 1839; d. St. Petersburg, 1881). An official in a Russian guards regiment and then (1863) a civil servant, who whilst retaining this latter position devoted himself to composition; was greatly influenced by Dargomijsky and a pupil of Balakiref, and a prominent member of the Russian nationalistic group of composers known as 'The Five' (q.v.). The musical expression of realism was a characteristic of his songs, operas, orch., choral, and piano works.

See also *Boris Godounof*; *Fair at Sorochintzy*; *Khovantschina*; *Night on the Bare Mountain*; *Pictures at an Exhibition*; *Song of the Flea*; *Songs and Dances of Death*.

Mustel Organ. See *Reed-Organ Family* 7.

Muta (It.). 'Change', e.g. of kettledrum tuning. *Muta D in C* means 'Change tuning from D to C' (thus no connexion with the word 'mute'). So also for change of crook in brass instruments. (Cf. *Mutano*.)

Mutano (It.). 'Change' 3rd person plur. '[they] change'. (Cf. *Muta*.)

Mutation Stop. Organ stop sounding not at normal pitch, 8ve pitch, &c., but at pitch of one of the non-8ve harmonics. See *Quint, Twelfth, Seventeenth, Nineteenth, Flat Twenty-first*.

Mute. A silencer, partial or complete. (1) In BOWED INSTRUMENTS a small clamp to be placed on the bridge, producing a silvery tone. (2) In BRASS INSTRUMENTS a pear-shaped stopper to be pushed into the bell (a similar contrivance is occasionally used with wood-wind instruments). (3) With the KETTLEDRUMS muting was formerly effected by placing a cloth over the parchment but it is usual now to employ sponge-headed drumsticks instead.

Muth, Mut (Ger.). 'Courage', so *muthig, mutig,* 'bold'.

Muzio, Claudia (b. Pavia 1889; d. Rome 1936). Dramatic operatic soprano. Début Messina 1910; Covent Garden 1914; Metropolitan 1916; with Rome Opera 1928–35.

Myaskovski. See *Miaskovsky.*

My Aunt Margery. See *Sir Roger de Coverley.*

My Country, 'tis of Thee. See *God save the Queen.*

Myers, Rollo Hugh (b. Chislehurst 1892). Educ. Oxford (M.A.). Paris Music Correspondent London *Times* and then *Telegraph,* 1920–34. Attached B.B.C. 1935–44. Brit. Council officer Paris 1945–6. From 1948 Ed. *Chesterian* and *Music To-day* (organ of International Soc. Contemporary Music, q.v.). Author books on contemporary music. Officier d'Académie (Palmes académiques).

My Fatherland (*Má Vlast*). Cycle of 6 Symphonic Poems by Smetana (1874–9), as follows: (1) *Vyšehrad* ("The High Castle"—a rock in the Vltava river, once the seat of the royal house). (2) *Vltava* (The river Moldau). (3) *Sàrka* (Leader of the Bohemian Amazons). (4) *From Bohemia's Meadows and Forests.* (5) *Tabor* (Stronghold of the blind leader of the Hussites). (6) *Blanik* (Mountain in southern Bohemia where sleep the Hussites who will arise to help their country in its worst need).

My Old Kentucky Home. See *Foster, Stephen Collins.*

Mysliviczek, Joseph (b. nr. Prague 1737; d. Rome 1781). Successful composer of over 30 Italian operas, as well as instrumental works; much admired by Mozart.

Mysore, Maharaja of, H.H. Sir Sri Jaya Chamarajendra Wadiyar Bahadur (b. 1919). Large-scale patron of music. Early plans to become concert pianist destroyed by 2nd World War. His Musical Foundation (1947) has sponsored recordings (by H.M.V.) of works of Medtner, &c. He has also promoted London concerts. (B.A. Univ. Mysore 1938; now its Chancellor.)

Mysteries. See *Miracle Plays.*

Mysteriös (Ger.). 'Mysterious.'

Mystery. See *Miracle Plays.*

N

Naaman. See *Costa.*

Nabokof, Nicolai (b. Lubcha, near Minsk, 1903). Pupil of Busoni; settled in U.S.A. Has composed ballets, orch., choral (oratorio *Job* 1931), chamber, and piano works, &c.

Nabucodonosor (Nabucco; 'Nebuchadnezzar'). 4-act opera by Verdi. Libretto by Solera. (Prod. Milan 1842.)

Nach (Ger.). 'After', 'in the manner of', 'according to', 'towards', 'to'. *Nach und nach*, 'bit by bit'; *nach Es* '[Tune now] to E flat'; &c.

Nach Belieben. *Ad libitum* (q.v.).

Nachdruck (Ger.). 'Emphasis.' So *nachdrücklich*, 'emphatic'.

Nachez, Tivadar (b. Budapest 1859; d. Lausanne 1930). Violinist. Pupil of Joachim. Attained high international repute; lived London from 1889; then (1916) California and elsewhere. Composed chamber music, violin concerto, &c.

Nachgehend (Ger.). 'Following.'

Nachlassend (Ger. 'leaving behind'). 'Slackening in speed.'

Nachschlag (Ger. 'after-stroke'). (1) The 2 notes that end the turn closing a shake (see Table 16). (2) Any ornamental note or notes indicated as to be added after another note (for the varieties see a specialist book on ornaments): such notes decorate the note that follows them but their time-value is subtracted from the one they follow, and it is in this sense that they are an 'after-stroke'.

Nachspiel (Ger. lit. 'afterplay'). The equivalent of Postlude (q.v.).

Nachtanz (Ger. 'after-dance'). A term applied to the second of the 2 contrasted dance tunes which were common as pairs from the 15th c. to the 17th, i.e. Pavan and Galliard, Passamezzo and Saltarello, Allemande and Courante, Sarabande and Gigue. (The saltarello, especially, is known by this name.)

Nachthorn (Ger.). Organ stop, same as *Cor de nuit* (q.v.).

Nachtmusik (Ger. 'night-music'). A serenade—and especially a suite intended to be used as such.

Nachtstück (Ger. 'night-piece'). (1) The Ger. equivalent of Nocturne, q.v. (2) A piece of solemn character, such as suggests the feelings of night.

Nach und nach (Ger.). 'Bit by bit.'

Nach wie vor. 'After as before', i.e. 'As on the previous appearance'.

Nadeshda. See *Thomas, A. Goring.*

Naenia (Lat.). 'Dirge.' Cf. *Nänie.*

Nagel, Wilibald (b. Mülheim a.d. Ruhr 1863; d. Stuttgart 1929). Musicologist and pianist; author of many valuable books; lived in London 1893–6, collecting material for his *History of Music in England* (down to end of 17th c.; 2 vols., 1894–7).

Nägeli, Hans Georg (b. Wetzikon, nr. Zürich, 1773; d. Zürich 1836). From age 19 music publisher in Zürich; as such in touch with all composers of the day, including Beethoven, some of whose works he was first to publish; revived many old works and publ. earliest correct edn. of Bach's '48'. Promoter of school music; author of educational books and collections of material; also of critical works. (See *Appreciation of Music.*)

Nahe (Ger.). 'Near.'

Naiads, The. See *Bennett, William Sterndale.*

Naïf, naïve (Fr.), **Naiv** (Ger.). 'Artless.' So *naïvement* (Fr.), 'artlessly'.

Nail Fiddle or **Nail Violin** or **Nail Harmonica.** An 18th-c. instrument consisting of a semicircular board with nails, graduated in size, fastened round the curve: it was held in the left hand and bowed by the right hand.

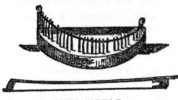

NAIL FIDDLE

Nairne, Baroness (1766–1845). Composed poems (frequently of great merit) for the old Scottish tunes.

Name-day Overture (Beethoven). See *Namensfeier*.

Namensfeier Overture. Composed by Beethoven (op. 115) for the Name-Day festivities of the Emperor Francis II, 1814; not perf. until 1815.

Nämlich (Ger.). (1) 'The same.' (2) 'Namely.'

Namouna. See *Lalo*.

Nänie (*Naenia*—Roman dirges). Choral Ode by Brahms (op. 82; 1881), a setting of Schiller ('Even the beautiful die', &c.).

Napoleon, Ode to (Schönberg). See under *Ode*.

Napolitana (It.), **Napolitaine** (Fr.). A light and simple type of madrigal, presumably of Neapolitan origin, and much like the Villanella (q.v.). But during the 20th c. a certain type of music-hall song took the name 'Napolitana': it had usually verses in the minor and choruses in the major.

Napravnik (Naprawnik, &c.), **Edward Frantsovich** (b. Bohemia 1839; d. St. Petersburg 1916). Studied music in Prague; accepted positions in St. Petersburg from 1861, including conductorship of Royal opera (1869) and symphony concerts. Composed 4 operas, 4 symphonies, chamber and choral music, &c. From character of his music counts as a Russian composer.

Nardini, Pietro (b. Leghorn 1722; d. Florence 1793). Tartini's best pupil and violinist of very high reputation.

Composed violin concertos, sonatas, &c., string quartets, flute music.

Nares, James (b. Stanwell, Middx., 1715; d. London 1783). Organist of York Minster and then of Chapel Royal; composed church music (still in use), catches and glees, harpsichord music, &c.

Narrante (It.). 'Narrating', i.e. in a declamatory manner.

Nasal tone. Vocal tone of that quality which is associated with what is called 'speaking through the nose'. The precise method of its production is not yet clear.

Nash, Heddle (b. London 1896; there d. 1961). Tenor vocalist. Choirboy Westminster Abbey. Then trained in Milan. Appeared in opera in Italy and on return became popular in opera and oratorio in Britain. Mozart roles a speciality.

Naso; nasetto (It. 'nose'; 'little nose'). The point of the bow of the violin, &c.

National Federation of Music Societies. A Brit. organization founded in 1935 by the Incorporated Soc. of Musicians, with help from the Carnegie Trust. It aims at encouraging choral societies, &c. (Address: 4 St. James's Square, S.W. 1.)

Nationalism in Music. The folk music of different races varies in melodic style and idiom in ways that express distinctions of racial feeling, and the work of composers of those races, unless purely conventional in style, commonly varies in a corresponding way. This latter phenomenon became strongly marked in the middle of the 19th c., when composers of northern races who had for some time been trained in Germany, or had accepted Ger. conventions, began consciously to throw off the Ger. influence and to allow their native idioms free play. This was a branch of the larger 'Romantic' Movement (see *Romantic*), the promoters of which sought vivid emotional expression rather than classic beauty. Thus Chopin, of mixed Polish and Fr. origin, often adopted Polish dance rhythms and forms, yet exhibited the Fr. grace; Liszt attempted to express the Hungarian spirit; Smetana and

Dvořák showed Bohemian traits; Grieg, Norwegian; Glinka, Balakiref, Borodin, Mussorgsky, and Rimsky-Korsakof, Russian; Albéniz, Granados, Falla, and Turina, Spanish; Sibelius, Finnish. In Britain Parry was distinctively English, Mackenzie to some extent Scottish, and Stanford Irish. In U.S.A. there were some attempts at the achievement of a national style by the employment of Amer. Indian or Negro idioms, but this device, in the hands of composers of European descent, was a rather too self-conscious effort and obviously artificial.

National Music Supervisors' Conference. See *Education* 3; also *Profession.*

National Orchestral Union. See *Musicians' Union.*

National Training School of Music (London). Founded 1873; succeeded by Royal Coll. of Music (q.v.) in 1882. Principals, Sullivan (1873), Stainer (1881).

National Union of Organists' Associations. See *Incorporated Association of Organists.*

National Youth Orchestra of Great Britain, consisting of talented boys and girls aged 13 to 19. First meeting in Bath, summer of 1947; second in Cambridge. Such orchs. had been in existence many years earlier in the U.S.A.

Natoma. Opera by Victor Herbert. (Prod. Philadelphia, New York, Baltimore, and Chicago 1911.)

Natural (1) A note that is neither raised ('sharpened' or 'sharped') nor lowered ('flattened' or 'flatted'). (2) The sign ♮, which, after a note has been raised by a sharp or double-sharp or lowered by a flat or double-flat, restores it to its original pitch. After a double-sharp or double-flat the change to a single one is indicated by either the single one, or sometimes ♮♯ or ♮♭. (See Table 6.)

Naturale (It.). 'Natural' (one sense being 'in the natural or usual manner'—so rescinding some direction to perform in an unusual manner).

Natural Harmonics. See *Acoustics* 7.

Natural Horn. See *Horn Family.*

Natural Trumpet. See *Trumpet Family.*

Nature's Praise of God. Same as *Creation's Hymn* (q.v.).

Natürlich (Ger.). 'Natural' (in same sense as given under *Naturale*).

Naumann, Johann Gottlieb (b. nr. Dresden 1741; d. Dresden 1801). Prolific composer of operas (successful in many countries) and of church music (the 'Dresden Amen'), symphonies, &c.

Nava, Gaetano (b. Milan 1802; there d. 1875). Famous singing teacher; composer of vocal studies, &c.

Navarraise. A Spanish dance deriving from the province of Navarre.

Naylor, (1) **John** (b. Stanningley, nr. Leeds, 1838; d. on voyage to Australia 1897). Organist York Minster from 1883. Composer of oratorios, church music, &c. D.Mus., Oxford. (2) **Edward Woodall** (b. Scarborough 1867; d. Cambridge 1934). Son of above. Studied Cambridge (M.A., D.Mus.) and R.C.M. Organist and lecturer Emmanuel Coll., Cambridge. Composer of church music, &c., and gained Ricordi Prize for opera *The Angelus* (Covent Garden 1909; revived 1921). Author of valuable musicological papers; also books on *Shakespeare and Music* (1896) and *Fitzwilliam Virginal Book* (1905).
(3) **Ruth Winifred** (b. Adelaide 1908). Soprano. Trained Adelaide, at R.C.M., Salzburg, and Paris. Opera career in Britain; Covent Garden, Sadler's Wells; Eng. Opera Group, &c.

Ne (Fr.). (1) If the word *pas* or *point* also occurs this is a simple negative. (2) If *jamais* follows the meaning is 'never'. (3) If *que* follows immediately, or almost so, the meaning is 'only'.

Neal, Mary (b. 1860; d. Gomshall, Surrey, 1944). Pioneer (before Cecil Sharp) in work of preserving and bringing into wider use the Eng. folk dances. Introduced them through Espérance Club (for working girls),

London, and sent out teachers under an 'Association for the Revival and Practice of Folk Music'. C.B.E.

Neale, John Mason (b. London 1818; d. East Grinstead 1866). High-church Anglican clergyman. Translator of ancient Lat. and Gr. hymns and himself a hymn writer (in *Hymns Ancient and Modern*, 1861, one-eighth of the hymns his—original or translations). Many hymnological publications.

Neapolitan Sixth. One of the chromatic chords. It is the major common chord on the flattened supertonic, in its 1st inversion (thus in key C it consists of F–A♭–D♭).

Neben (Ger.). 'Near', 'at the side of', &c. But in a number of compound words the meaning is 'additional', 'accessory', &c. So *Nebenthema*, 'subsidiary theme'; *Nebenstimmen* or *Nebenregister*, the mutation stops of an organ.

Nebensatz. See under *Satz*.

Nebst (Ger.). 'Together with', 'including'.

Nebuchadnezzar. See *Nabucadonosor*.

Neck. The projecting portion of a violin, &c., that carries the fingerboard and terminates in the peg-box.

Neel, (Louis) Boyd (b. London 1905). Conductor. At first naval cadet; then qualified as medical man. Founded Boyd Neel String Orch. 1933 and with it travelled widely in Old and New Worlds. Dean of Toronto Conserv. 1953; orch. directed by Thurston Dart from 1955. C.B.E. 1953.

Negli (It. masc. plur.). 'In the', 'at the', &c.

Negligente, negligentemente (It.). 'Negligently', i.e. with insouciance.

Negro Folk Symphony. See *Dawson, William Levi*.

Negro Ministrels. The Negro Minstrel type of entertainment had about 60 years of popularity. Its origin is said to have been in the singing of the song 'Jim Crow' by Thomas Rice, at Pittsburgh, in 1830. From 1843 there became popular in the U.S.A. a troupe called the Virginian Minstrels—with which was connected Dan Emmett,

who for it composed 'Dixie' (q.v.). Their type of programme became an accepted public entertainment. The performers were white men with blacked faces, singing what purported to be Negro songs, imitating the Negro speech, cracking Negro jokes, playing the banjo and the bones (q.v.), dancing, &c. Many composers catered for them, writing simple melodies to sentimental or humorous verses: the most famous of such composers is Stephen Foster (q.v.), and with his name is associated that of Christy, who introduced his songs by means of his famous 'Christy Minstrels' troupe. Towards the end of the 19th c. Negro Minstrels were a feature of every considerable Brit. coast resort, performing many times daily on the sands. They were later almost everywhere superseded by the 'Pierrots'.

Debussy's piano pieces *Minstrels* and *Golliwogg's Cake Walk* record his interest in this type of popular musical activity.

Negro Spirituals. See *Spirituals*.

Nehmen (Ger.). 'To take.'

Nei (It.). 'In the' (see *Nel*).

Nel (It.). 'In the.' Other forms (according to gender, number, &c.) are *nello, nella, nell', nelle, nei, negli*.

Nelsonmesse ('Nelson Mass'). Popular name for Haydn's 11th Mass, in D minor. It is said that a trumpet passage at the beginning of the Benedictus was connected in his mind with news received of the battle of Aboukir (1798): another story says that it was performed during Nelson's visit to Eisenstadt (1800). In Britain it is usually called the *Imperial Mass* and spoken of as No. 3.

Nemenoff, Genia (b. Paris 1905—of Russian parents). Pianist. Trained Paris Conserv. under Philipp, &c. Toured Europe. Settled in New York. See *Luboschutz, Pierre*.

Nenia (It.). 'Dirge.'

Neo-Bechstein Piano. See *Electric Musical Instruments* 3.

Neo-Classical, Neo-Romantic. See *Romantic*.

Ne pas (Fr.). 'Not' (the 2 words are usually separated by a verb).

Nera (It. 'black'). Crotchet or Quarter-note (see Table 3).

Neri, St. Philip. See *Oratorio*.

Nernst, W. See *Electric Musical Instruments 3*.

Nerone ('Nero'). Posthumous opera by Boito, scenically and musically elaborate; libretto by composer. Completed by Tommasini and Toscanini. (Prod. Milan 1924.)

Other operas of this name by Mascagni (1935), &c.

Nerveux (Fr.). 'Nervous', 'sinewy'.

Net, nette (Fr. masc., fem.), **netto, netta** (It. masc., fem.). 'Clear'; so *nettement* (Fr.), *nettamente* (It.), 'clearly'.

Neue Liebeslieder (Brahms). See *Liebeslieder*.

Neues vom Tage (*News of the Day*). Satirical comedy-opera by Hindemith (1929).

Neuf (Fr.). 'Nine'; hence *neuvième*, 'ninth'.

Neukomm, (Chevalier) Sigismund von (b. Salzburg 1778; d. Paris 1858). Favourite pupil of Haydn; spent last part of life in France (ennobled by Louis XVI) and Britain; very highly prized in latter as composer of 1,000 works, little and big, including songs, &c., once of the highest popularity, now utterly forgotten.

Neuma, Neumae (medieval Lat.). 'Neum', 'Neums' (see *Notation*).

Neums, Neumes. See *Notation*.

Neun (Ger.). 'Nine.'

Neupert, Edmund (b. Christiania 1842; d. New York 1888). Pianist of high repute. Settled New York 1882. Composed light and elegant piano music; also studies, &c. (Cf. *Friedman, Ignaz*.)

Neuvième (Fr.). 'Ninth.'

Nevada—original surname Wixom; Mrs. R. S. Palmer, (1) **Emma** (b. nr. Nevada City, Calif., 1859; d. Liverpool 1940). Operatic and concert soprano of high standing in Italy, England, France, and U.S.A. (For daughter see below.) (2) **Mignon** (b. Paris 1886). Soprano; daughter of the above and, like her, of international repute (named

'Mignon' from the opera of that name of Ambroise Thomas, q.v., who was witness at her mother's marriage to her father, an Eng. medical man). Début Rome; Covent Garden 1910.

Neveu, Ginette (b. Paris 1919; killed in air crash 1949). Violinist. Trained Paris Conserv. and under Flesch (q.v.). First appeared aged 7 at Concerts Colonne. Won Wieniawski Prize, Warsaw, aged 15; then brilliant international career.

Nevin, (1) **Ethelbert Woodbridge** (b. Edgeworth, Penn., 1862; d. New Haven, Conn., 1901). Studied and lived much in various European centres; composed highly popular piano music and songs (see *The Rosary*). For his brother see below. (2) **Arthur Finley** (b. Edgeworth, Penn., 1871; d. Sewickley, Penn., 1943). Brother of Ethelbert, above. Studied in Berlin; became Prof. of Music at Univ. of Kansas, &c.; carried out research in Amer. Indian Music; composed operas, orch. suites, piano music, songs, &c.

New England Conservatory, Boston. See *Schools of Music*.

New English Music Society. See *Bernard*.

New English Singers. See *English Singers*.

New Foundation. See *Cathedral Music*.

Newman, (1) **Robert** (b. 1859; d. London 1926). Bass. Trained R.A.M. On opening of Queen's Hall (1893) became manager; started Promenade Concerts (see *Concert*, and *Wood, Henry J.*) 2 years later. Showed enormous enterprise and great acumen during over 30 years' tenure of this post.

(2) **Ernest** (b. Liverpool 1868; d. Tadworth, Surrey, 1959). Up to 1903 (under original name, William Roberts) engaged in Liverpool bank, writing on economics and banking, and also (under assumed name) on philosophy, literature, and music (*Gluck and his Operas* 1895; *Study of Wagner* 1899). Then 2 years teacher of solo singing, &c., at Birmingham. Music critic *Manchester Guardian* 1905, *Birmingham Post* 1906, *Observer* 1919, *Sunday Times* 1920–58. Numerous and valuable books, especially on Wagner

(great *Life* in 4 vols., 1933-47); performing translations of Wagner libretti, &c.

(3) **Sidney Thomas Mayow** (b. London 1906). Educated Christ Church, Oxford (M.A.) and R.C.M. Hon. D.Mus. (Durham). Lecturer in music Durham Univ. 1936-41, then Reid Prof. of Music, Edinburgh. Has broadcast as pianist and as conductor.

Newmarch, Rosa Harriet ('Mrs. Newmarch', *née* Jeaffreson; b. Leamington 1857; d. Worthing 1940). Her name was long associated in England with the writing of the programme notes for the Queen's Hall Orch.'s concerts and of books on Russian music and musicians, the Russian arts, and Russian thought, also Czech music.

New Music. A term which, in one shape or another, crops up from time to time in the history of the art: (1) About 1300 in Italy and France in the 'Ars Nova' (q.v.). (2) About 1600 in Italy, in the *nuove musiche* (see *Opera* 1 and *Caccini*). (3) After 1850, in Germany, when the productions of Liszt and Wagner were often spoken of as the 'New Music'.

News of the Day (Hindemith). See *Neues vom Tage.*

Newspaper Cuttings. See *Eisler.*

New Swedish Dance. See *First of August.*

Newton, Ivor (b. London 1892). Associated as pf. accompanist with very many international artists. Has toured extensively Europe, America, Australia.

New World Music Corporation. See *Music Publishers Holding Corporation.*

New World Symphony. See *Dvořák's Symphonies.*

New York Philharmonic Orchestra. Formed 1928 by union of Philharmonic Soc. of N.Y. (1842) and the N.Y. Symphony Soc. (1878). Conductors include Toscanini (1928); Barbirolli (1936); Rodzinski (1943); Mitropoulos (1950); Bernstein (1958); Boulez (1971).

Nibelungen March. A vulgar concoction attributed to military band programmes to Wagner—apparently on the strength of 2 brief themes from *Siegfried* in the middle.

Nicholl, Horace Wadham b. Tipton, nr. Birmingham, 1848; d. New York 1922). Organist; emigrated to U.S.A. 1871, occupying organ and editorial posts there. Composed organ and orch. music, oratorios, songs, &c.

Nicholls, (1) **Frederick** (b. Birmingham 1871). Music teacher in Liverpool and composer of many popular songs and piano pieces. Several books.

(2) **Agnes** (b. Cheltenham 1877; d. London 1959). Dramatic soprano. Trained R.C.M. Highly esteemed opera, oratorio, and concert artist. Married Hamilton Harty (q.v.) 1904. C.B.E.

(3) **John Whitburn** (b. Bendigo, Victoria, 1916). Trained R.C.M. City organist, Hobart, from 1940, also Cathedral organist and choirmaster.

Nicholson, (1) (or **Nicolson**) **Richard** (b. abt. 1570; d. Oxford 1639). Master of choristers, Magdalen Coll., Oxford, and earliest Prof. of Music in the Univ. Composed church music, madrigals, and 1st known song cycle (*The Wooing of Joan and John*).

(2) **Sydney Hugo** (b. London 1875; d. Ashford, Kent, 1947). Educated at New Coll., Oxford (M.A., B.Mus.; D.Mus., Lambeth, 1928), and R.C.M.; organist Cathedrals of Carlisle (1904) and Manchester (1908); Westminster Abbey (1918-28). Founded School of Eng. Church Music (from 1945 Royal School of Church Music, q.v.) and directed it. Knighted 1938.

Nicht (Ger.). 'Not', e.g. *nicht gedämpft*, 'not muted'—contradicting an earlier direction.

Nicodé, Jean Louis (b. nr. Poznán 1853; d. Dresden 1919). As a child left Poland for Germany; finally settled in Dresden as teacher and conductor and toured as pianist. Composed chiefly orch. and piano works.

Nicolai, Karl Otto Ehrenfried (b. Königsberg 1810; d. Berlin 1849). Very successful in Italy and Germany as opera conductor and composer (see *Lustigen Weiber von Windsor*).

Nicolini (1)—really Nicolino Grimaldi (b. Naples abt. 1673). Highly celebrated castrato contralto. In London 1708-11 and 1714-17. Principal part in many of Handel's operas. Addison praises him in *Spectator*.

(2)—really Ernest Nicolas (b. St. Malo 1834; d. Pau 1898). Operatic tenor. Trained Paris Conserv. Successful in France and Italy. London début 1866; U.S.A. 1881. Stage colleague of Patti and then the 2nd of her 3 husbands.

Nicolson. See *Nicholson* 1.

Niecks, Frederick (b. Düsseldorf 1845; d. Edinburgh 1924). Settled in Scotland as violinist and organist 1868; man of learning and writer of valuable articles and books on music; Prof. of Music, Univ. of Edinburgh 1891–1914. Hon. D.Mus., Dublin, 1898.

Nieder (Ger.). 'Down.' So *niederdrücken*, 'to press down'.

Niedermeyer, Abraham Louis (b. Nyon, Switzerland, 1802; d. Paris 1861). Settled in Paris as young man and attempted career as opera composer; then turned to another branch of activity, founding Niedermeyer School of Church Music (many wellknown musicians there trained; still flourishing) and composing masses, motets, &c. (still in use).

Niederschlag (Ger.). (1) 'Downbeat'—'up-beat' being *Aufschlag*. (2) 'Down-stroke' of the bow—another term being **Niederstrich.**

Nielsen, Carl August (b. Island of Funen, Denmark, 1865; d. Copenhagen 1931). Protégé of Gade (q.v.); became opera conductor, &c., in Copenhagen. Composed operas, symphonies, violin concerto, chamber and piano music, &c. (See *Telmányi*.)

Niente (It.). 'Nothing', e.g. *quasi niente*, 'almost nothing' (in point of tone).

Nietzsche, Friedrich (b. Röcken, Saxony, 1844; d. Weimar 1900). As Prof. of Classical Philology at Univ. of Basle (1869–70) came into touch with Wagner, then resident at Lucerne (see *Wagner*); in his *The Birth of Tragedy from the Spirit of Music* (1872) hailed Wagnerian Music Drama as the successor of Gr. tragedy; later (1876) publ. *Richard Wagner in Bayreuth*; these 2 books aroused great discussion in Ger. philosophical and musical

circles. At a later period he abandoned his support of the Wagnerian principles and publ. *The Case of Wagner* (1888) and *Nietzsche versus Wagner* (1889), setting up Bizet's *Carmen* as his new ideal, and crying 'We must Mediterraneanize music'. His remaining years were a miserable period of insomnia, drug-taking, egotistic hysteria, and mental collapse.

He had in friendly circles enjoyed a reputation as an extemporizer on the piano and he left a mass of amateurish compositions, a complete edn. of which was begun in 1924 but probably did not proceed far beyond the 1st volume; a few songs, however, had been publ. in 1864 and a work for choir and orch. (*An das Leben*, 'To Life') in 1887.

His doctrine of the 'Superman', in the allegorical prose-poem, *Thus spake Zoroaster* (1883–5), was one of the incitements to Germany's crimes of 1914–18 and thus to those of 1939–45. Strauss based a tone-poem on it (with the same title, op. 30, 1896) and Delius drew from it the text of his *A Mass of Life* (1905).

Nigger Quartet. See *American Quartet.*

Night Dancers, The. See *Loder.*

Nightingale. An imitative instrument used in an oratorio of Alessandro Scarlatti (q.v.), in the 'Toy Symphonies' of Haydn and Romberg, &c.

Nightingale, The ('Le Rossignol'). (1) 'Lyrical Tale' by Stravinsky, based on fairy-story of Hans Andersen, with Chinese subject. At first treated as Opera (Paris and London 1914; New York 1926) but transformed into Symphonic Poem (1917) and then into Ballet. (2) See *Alabiev.*

Night in May. Opera by Rimsky-Korsakof. Libretto by composer, based on Gogol. (Prod. St. Petersburg 1880; London 1914.)

Night on the Bare Mountain. Composition freely arranged and orchestrated by Rimsky-Korsakof from a passage in Mussorgsky's *Sorochintsy Fair*. This is the form of the work familiar in concert programmes, and is not to be confused with Mussorgsky's virtually unknown *St. John's Night on the Bare Mountain* (1867).

Nights in the Gardens of Spain ('Noches en los jardines de España'). 'Symphonic Impressions' for Piano and Orch., by Falla. (1st perf. Madrid 1916.) 3 sections: (*a*) *At the Generalife*—a garden near Granada; (*b*) *Dance in the Distance*; passing without break to (*c*) *In the Gardens of the Sierra of Cordova*.

Nijinsky. See *Ballet*.

Nikisch, (1) **Artur** (b. Hungary 1855; d. Leipzig 1922). Violinist, pianist, and conductor. Child prodigy pianist, appearing publicly at age 8. Trained Vienna Conserv. At 17 one of 1st violins at laying of foundation-stone of Bayreuth theatre; then member of Vienna Court Orch. At 24 conductor of Leipzig Opera; from 34 to 38 of Boston Orch.; then Budapest Opera, Leipzig Gewandhaus, and Berlin Philharmonic. Many London visits and toured U.S.A. with London Symphony Orch. Notable accompanist of pupil Elena Gerhardt (q.v.). Some compositions. (2) **Mitja** (b. Leipzig 1899; d. Venice 1936). Pianist. Son of above. Pupil of Teichmüller. U.S.A. début 1923.

Nilsson, (1) **Christine** (b. nr. Wexiö, Sweden, 1843; d. Stockholm 1921). Operatic and oratorio soprano of high popularity on both sides of Atlantic. Before public 1864–91. (2) **Birgit (Marta)** (b. Karup, Sweden, 1918). Dramatic soprano, pupil of Joseph Hislop in Stockholm. Début Stockholm 1946; Glyndebourne 1951; San Francisco 1956; Covent Garden 1958; Metropolitan 1959; notable Brünnhilde, Isolde, &c.

Nin, Joaquín—Nin y Castellanos (b. Havana, Cuba, 1879; d. there 1949). Of Spanish parentage; pupil in Paris of Moszkowski and d'Indy; student and then teacher at Schola Cantorum. As pianist in high repute for interpretation of old keyboard music; edited old Spanish keyboard, violin, and vocal music. Composer of piano music, &c., and writer of books on music. For son see below.

Nin-Culmell, Joaquín (b. Berlin 1908). Son of the above, but Cuban citizen, now resident in U.S.A. Pupil of Dukas and Falla. Composer of piano music, &c.

Nineteenth. Organ mutation stop (see *Organ* 2). Length and pitch 1⅓ foot, pitch being thus a 19th (2 octaves and a fifth) above normal.

Ninety-fourth Psalm (Organ piece). See *Reubke*.

Ninna-Nanna, Ninnarella (It.). 'Cradle song.'

Ninth. See *Interval*. A 'Chord of the Ninth' is a Common Chord (see *Harmony* 2 d) plus the 7th and 9th.

Nobel, Felix de (b. Haarlem 1907). Conductor and pianist. Trained Amsterdam Conserv., later on staff Conserv. of The Hague. Since 1937 conductor of Netherlands Chamber Choir. As pianist was accompanist for Dutch Radio; now member Concertgebouw Quintet and Amsterdam Chamber Music Soc.

Nobile (It.). 'Noble.' So *nobilmente*, 'nobly'; *nobiltà*, 'nobility'.

Nobilissima visione (Hindemith). See *Saint Francis*.

Noble, (1) **Thomas Tertius** (b. Bath 1867; d. Rockport, Mass., 1953). Trained R.C.M. Asst. to Stanford as organist of Trinity Coll., Cambridge, 1890; organist Ely¦ Cathedral 1892, York Minster 1898–1912, St. Thomas's Church, 5th Avenue, New York, 1912–47. Comp. church music, &c. Hon. M.A.; D.Mus., Lambeth. (2) **Dennis** (b. Bristol 1899; d. Spain 1966). Operatic baritone. Began career in choir of Westminster Abbey; then transferred to stage, studied in Italy, and appeared successfully in Britain, on the Continent, and in U.S.A.

Noblemen's and Gentlemen's Catch Club (for brevity merely 'Catch Club'). Founded in London 1761 and still functioning. The prizes it has offered for catches, canons, and glees have led to much composing activity. See *Clubs for Music Making*.

Noblezza (It.). 'Nobility.'

Noces, Les (Stravinsky). See *Wedding*.

Noces de Jeannette, Les. See *Massé*.

Noch (Ger.). 'Still', 'yet', in the sense either of continuance or of 'even', e.g. *noch leise*, 'still softly', *noch leiser*, 'still more softly'.

Noche (Sp.). 'Night.'

Nocturne (Fr. and now Eng.), **Notturno** (It.). (1) Any composition which suggests the calm beauty of night may be so described (Haydn has a Notturno for flute, oboe, 2 horns, and strings, and several for hurdy-gurdy, q.v.). (2) The Irish composer, John Field (1782–1837), gave the name to a type of short, slow piano piece in which a melody in the right hand (often much embellished) is accompanied by some form of broken chords in the left: Chopin then took up this style and infused it with intenser romantic feeling. In general such a piece is in Simple Ternary Form (see *Form* 2).

Nocturnes by Debussy. Three orch. pieces (1899). (1) *Nuages* ('Clouds'); (2) *Fêtes*; (3) *Sirènes* ('Sirens'—with use of women's voices, wordless).

Node (of a vibrating string). Point of rest between two vibrating portions.

Noël (Fr.) or **Nowell** (Eng.). The word means 'Christmas', and is also used as meaning a Christmas carol (see *Carol*).

Nohl, Carl Friedrich Ludwig (b. Westphalia 1831; d. Heidelberg 1885). Author of books on Beethoven, Mozart, &c.

Noire (Fr.). The Eng. 'crotchet' or Amer. 'quarter-note' (see Table 3).

Nomenclature. See *Notation*.

Non (Fr., It.). 'Not.'

None. The 6th of the Canonical Hours (see *Divine Office*) of the Roman Catholic Church. Properly it takes place at 3 p.m. (i.e. the 'ninth hour').

Nonet (Eng.); **Nonette** (Fr.); **Nonetto** (It.); **Nonett** (Ger.). Any combination of 9 instruments or any piece of music intended for them. Such compositions are comparatively rare.

Nonnengeige (Ger. 'nun-fiddle'). The Tromba Marina (q.v.).

Non Nobis Domine. Famous vocal canon commonly attributed to Byrd. The most usual version is for 3 voices.

Nono, Luigi (b. Venice 1924). Composer, pupil of Maderna and Scherchen. One of the most radical and commercially successful of the advanced Italian followers of Webern.

Norcome (or **Norcombe**), **Daniel** (b. Windsor 1576; d. before 1626). Member of choir of St. George's Chapel, Windsor Castle; became Roman Catholic and went (as instrumentalist) to vice-regent's chapel, Brussels; then at Danish court and in Venice. Now remembered by a madrigal and some music for viol.

Nordica (really Norton), **Lillian** (b. Farmington, Maine, 1857; d. Java 1914). Operatic and concert soprano. Had early concert successes in U.S.A. Studied Milan and came out in opera under new name. Covent Garden début 1887; Bayreuth 1894; thereafter specially prominent in Wagner works.

Nordic Symphony. By Hanson. (Op. 21; 1st perf. Rome 1922.)

Nordquist, Conrad—in full Johan Conrad (b. Vänersborg, Sweden, 1840; d. there 1920). Trained Stockholm Conserv. (later on staff). Prominent conductor, composer, and teacher.

Nordraak, Richard (b. Christiania, now Oslo, 1842; d. Berlin 1866). Despite brief life important as one of founders of Norwegian school of composition and as having influenced Grieg. Composed incidental music to plays, songs, and choral and piano music.

Norfolk Rhapsodies. Three Orch. pieces by Vaughan Williams (1906–7). Based on folk tunes collected by composer in Norfolk. (The first idea was that the 3 should constitute the movements of a Symphony.)

Norma. Bellini's most successful opera. Libretto by Romani. (Prod. Milan 1832; London 1833; Dublin, Philadelphia, and New York 1841.)

Norman-Neruda. See *Hallé*.

North, Hon. Roger (1653–1734). Wrote *Memoires of Musick* (1728), of which the book mentioned under *Andrews, Hilda* forms part.

Northcote, Sydney (b. Glamorganshire, Wales, 1897; d. London 1968). Ed. R.C.M., then Oxford. On staff Guildhall School of Music, 1928–41;

then Natl. Music Adviser, Carnegie U.K. Trust. Writer on music and musical education.

North Country Sketches. For Orch., by Delius. (1913–14; 1st perf. London 1915.) 4 movements—(a) *Autumn*; (b) *Winter Landscape*; (c) *Dance*; (d) *The March of Spring*.

North Star, The (Meyerbeer). See *Étoile du Nord*.

Northumbrian Bagpipes. See *Bagpipe Family*.

Norwich. See *Festival*.

Norwich Sol-fa. See *Tonic Sol-fa*.

Noskowski, Zygmunt (b. Warsaw 1846; d. Wiesbaden 1909). Active in various musical activities in native city; invented a notation for blind. Operas, symphonies, chamber music, piano works, songs, &c. Noted teacher.

No Song, No Supper. See *Storace*.

No Surrender! This is a tune used by the Protestants of Northern Ireland (cf. *Lilliburlero*), having a traditional connexion with the siege of Londonderry. The present words date only from 1826, being by Mrs. Charlotte Elizabeth Tonna, who wrote other Orange party songs.

Nota cambiata. See *Changing Note*.

Notation and Nomenclature in music are devices for which the human being long felt no need and although every race has its music they are still unknown to the larger part of the world's population. They are apparently purely European in origin and even in Europe thousands of tunes exist which have been transmitted by one generation to another without achieving the dignity of being recorded on paper until there arose the modern movement for collecting the music of the peasantry (cf. *Folk Song*). The plainsong of the Church, also, must, in the earlier centuries of the Christian era, have been communicated orally.

The naming of notes by letters of the alphabet goes back as far as the Ancient Greeks; the Romans also possessed an alphabetical system. In both cases, however, this nomenclature served rather the purposes of scientific discussion than those of performance.

An early (7th-c.) system of notation was that of NEUMS or NEUMES, i.e. signs of which the original generating forms were merely the grave and acute accents plus a horizontal line, but which developed into the elaborate system still in use in the plainsong manuals of the Church. They are now precise (at all events as to pitch), so that an instructed singer can 'read' from them, but for long they were merely approximate in their indications, serving to inform the singer as to which of the plainsong melodies in his repertory he was expected to sing and to remind him of its general melodic curves and rhythms. Our conventional signs for the Turn and the Trill are derived from details of the Neum notation. The present exactitude in the indication of pitch has been effected by adding to the one line of the early Neum notation. Plainsong now uses a STAFF of 4 lines and other music one of 5. The CLEF derives from the Neum notation: attached to the Staff it fixes the pitch of one of its lines as middle C or some other note (see Table 4) and, one note being thus precisely indicated, all others are likewise decided.

PROPORTIONAL NOTATION of an exact character (i.e. as to the time values) began in the 10th c. when the primitive developments of polyphonic music (as distinct from the previous purely melodic music) brought about its necessity. Definite notes, of different shapes according to their intended proportionate length, were now devised and from them is derived our present series of semibreve, minim, &c. BAR LINES became common only during the 16th and 17th cs. (earliest use 1448): they were at first casually drawn as mere aids to the eye—the idea of making them of equal time-value coming later. Their first use was in choral scoring, the object being to exhibit the coincidence of the different voices; the separate voice-parts for the use of the singers did not, therefore, possess them.

The Staff Notation has gradually become very elaborate but is still (rationally considered) incomplete and in many ways imperfect. It would appear, however, that if music continues to grow in complexity (cf. *Microtones* for an example) the present staff notation must some day break down. Certain simple but practical reforms, however, could be pretty easily effected, one example being the adoption of (say) the crotchet (quarter-note) as the invariable beat-value. The only reformed notation that has so far widely established itself is that called TONIC SOL-FA (q.v.) which, in practice, is almost confined to choral music, and is widely current only in the English-speaking countries of the world.

See Notation Tables on pp. xiii–xxx; also *Great Staff*.

Note. (1) A written sign representing the pitch and duration of a single musical sound. (2) A single sound of musical pitch. (3) A finger-key of the pianoforte. (4) For Amer. use of the word see *American Terminology* 1.

Note-row (*Tonreihe*, Amer. 'Tone-row'). A highly artificial composing procedure used by Schönberg and other composers of his set. It employs the Dodecaphonic Scale (see *Scales*). The following is a description of it by Schönberg's pupil and friend, Wellesz, in his pamphlet *Arnold Schönberg* (1945).

'A melodic skeleton has to be thought out, consisting of the twelve tones [i.e. "notes"] of the chromatic [more correctly "dodecuple"] scale, to provide a suitable pattern for the intended composition. No tone should be repeated before the row comes to an end. The pattern appears (1) in its original form, (2) in its inversion, (3) in the crab ["cancrizans"; cf. the reference to this word s.v. *Canon*], and (4) in the crab inversion. . . . The twelve-tone [i.e. "dodecuple"] system is applied both horizontally and vertically: all the harmonies are built upon chords consisting of tones of the row [arranged in the order in which they appear in the series]. Discordant chords therefore prevail. Consonances are rare, or—as Schönberg once put it—they are not excluded but have to be introduced carefully.'

To this may be added that though the order of the notes of the pattern is not to be varied the rhythm in which they are presented may be. Moreover any note in the melodic group may appear an 8ve higher or lower than it did originally (the interval of a 2nd becoming that of a 9th, for example) and the whole group can be used at any

higher or lower level (resembling transposition in diatonic music).

Amongst composers who have adopted the Note-row system (either as above or in some variant) are Berg, Webern, Hauer, and Křenek, together with very many of their juniors.

Notes. Organ of (Amer.) Music Libraries Association; founded 1934. See *Hill, R. S.*

Notre Dame de Paris. See *Fry, W. H.*

Nottebohm, Martin Gustav (b. Lüdenscheid, Westphalia, 1817; d. Graz 1882). Pupil of Schumann and Mendelssohn; noted piano teacher, minor composer, musicologist of repute, and author of valuable books on Beethoven.

Notturnino (It.). A miniature nocturne.

Notturno. See *Nocturne.*

Nourri, bien (Fr. 'well-nourished'). 'With full, rich tone' (cf. *Nutrendo*; *Nutrito*).

Nourrit, Adolphe (b. Paris 1802; d. Naples 1839). Operatic tenor. Pupil of Manuel Garcia I. Début Paris Opéra 1821. High success followed. Later studied Italy under Donizetti. Not satisfied with Italy's reception of his singing committed suicide by jumping from window.

Nováček, Ottokar Eugen (b. Fehertemplon, otherwise Weisskirchen, Hungary, 1866; d. New York 1900). Brilliant violinist. Composed violin music, string quartets, piano concerto, &c.

Novachord. See *Electric Musical Instruments* 4.

Novaes, Guiomar (b. Brazil 1895). Pianist. Trained Paris Conserv. age 14–16 under Philipp, &c. Toured both sides Atlantic (New York début 1915).

Novák, Vitězslav (b. Kamenice-on-Lipa, otherwise Kamenitz, Bohemia, 1870; d. near Prague 1949). Pupil of Dvořák at Conserv. of Prague, of which he later became a prof. and afterwards Rector (1919–22). As composer at first accepted ideals of Ger. romantics (Schumann, &c.); later studied Bohemian folk music and used its idiom as basis (operas, symphonic poems, piano music, songs, &c.).

Nove (It.). 'Nine.'

Novelette (Eng.), **Novellette** (Ger.). A term introduced by Schumann as the title for 8 pieces of his for piano. They have no individual titles but each, says the composer, is to be taken as the musical equivalent of a romantic story. A few other composers have used the term: it carries with it no special connotation as to form.

Novello & Co. Ltd. London Music Publishers (27/28 Soho Square, London). See *Novello Family* (1) and (2); *Gray, H. W.*

Novello Family; a gifted musical family of which the most important members were: (1) **Vincent** (b. London 1781; d. Nice 1861). London Roman Catholic organist; composed church music and revived more: publ. Purcell's in 5 vols.; masses of Mozart, Haydn, Beethoven, &c.; vols. of Eng. anthems by Croft, Greene, Boyce, &c.; also organ music. Out of one of his publications (1811) grew the firm of Novello & Co. See (2). (2) **(Joseph) Alfred** (b. London 1810; d. Geneva 1896). Son of above. Bass vocalist of repute who definitely founded Novello firm (1829) on basis of collections of his father. Retired to Nice 1856; then to Geneva. (3) **Clara Anastasia** (b. London 1818; d. Rome 1908). Daughter of Vincent. Brilliant soprano vocalist (opera and oratorio), well known 1833–60. (4) **Mary Sabilla** (d. Geneva 1904). Also daughter of Vincent, and also soprano vocalist, but through throat weakness ceased appearance; translated theoretical books into English.

Novello, Ivor. See *Keep the home fires burning.*

Noverre. See *Ballet.*

Nowell (Eng.) or **Noël** (Fr.). A Christmas carol (see *Carol*). The word means 'Christmas'.

Now pray we for our country. See *Flower, Eliza.*

Noye's Fludde ('Noah's Flood'). 1-act opera by Britten. Libretto is a 16th-cent. Chester miracle play. (Prod. Aldeburgh 1958.)

Nozze di Figaro, Le ('The Marriage of Figaro'). It. comedy-opera by Mozart. Libretto by da Ponte based on Beaumarchais. (Prod. Vienna 1786; London 1812; New York 1824.)

Nuance. Musically used the word implies those delicate differences of intensity and speed which, largely, make up the 'life' of a performance.

N.U.I. National University of Ireland.

Nuit sur le mont chauve, Une. See *Night on the Bare Mountain.*

Nunc Dimittis. The Song of Simeon in St. Luke's Gospel ('Lord, now lettest Thou thy servant depart in peace'). It is a part of the service of Compline (q.v.) in the Roman Catholic Church and of that of Evensong in the Anglican Church (see *Common Prayer*). It has its traditional plainsong in the former and is often sung to an Anglican Chant in the latter. It has also been set innumerable times by church composers (see *Service*).

Nun's Fiddle. The Tromba Marina (q.v.).

Nuove Musiche. See *Caccini, Opera* 1.

Nuovo, nuova (It. masc., fem.). 'New.' Hence *di nuovo*, 'anew'.

Nuptial Mass. See *Mass.*

Nur (Ger.). 'Only.'

Nursery Rhymes (Eng.) = *Mother Goose Songs* (Amer.).

Nursery Suite. By Elgar. For Orch. (op. 86, 1931). Composed for the then Duchess of York and her children, the Princesses Elizabeth and Margaret Rose. It has been used for a Ballet.

Nusch-Nuschi. Burmese Marionette-play with music by Hindemith (op. 20, 1921). The dances sometimes appear in concert programmes.

Nut (stringed instrument term). (1) The slight ridge over which the strings pass on leaving the pegs. (2) That contrivance at one end of the bow by which is adjusted the tension of the hairs.

Nutcracker and the Mouse King, The. Ballet by Tchaikovsky (op. 71, prod. St. Petersburg 1892). Based on the *Histoire d'un Casse-noisette* of A. Dumas, a version of E. T. A. Hoffmann's story. The NUT-CRACKER SUITE for Orch. (op. 71*a*) was compiled from the ballet's music.

Nutrendo; nutrito (It. 'nourishing'; 'nourished'). Metaphors carrying one of the following two suggestions: (1) Full, rich tone. (2) Well-sustained tone. (Cf. *Nourri*.)

O

O, Od (It.). 'Or.'

Oakeley, Herbert Stanley (b. Ealing 1830; d. Eastbourne 1903). Studied at Oxford and Leipzig; good organist; Prof. of Music at Univ. of Edinburgh 1865–91; M.A., Hon. D.Mus., Oxford, Cambridge, Dublin; LL.D., Aberdeen; D.C.L., Toronto; Knighted 1876. Composed chiefly choral music.

Obbligato (It.—sometimes, incorrectly, *obligato*), **obligé** (Fr.), **obligat** (Ger.). (1) Attached to the 'part' of any instrument in a score the implication often is (and always should be) that the part in question is essential to the effect. (2) But, unfortunately, ambiguity has been imported by the use of the word in the very opposite sense, i.e. as a part that may be omitted if desired.

O.B.E. See *British Empire, Order of the*.

Oben (Ger.). 'Over', 'above'.

Ober (Ger.). 'Over', 'upper'.

Oberek. A type of Polish dance.

Oberlin College Conservatory of Music. See *Schools of Music*.

Libretto by Planché. (Prod. London 1826; Dublin 1827; New York 1828.)

Obertas, Obertass. A national Polish round dance of rather wild character in a quick simple-triple time (see *Drabant*).

Obertus. See *Obrecht*.

Oberwerk (Ger. 'upper-work'). 'Swell Organ.' (Abbrev.—'Obw' or 'O.W.')

Obligat, obligato, obligé. See *Obbligato*.

Oblique motion. See *Motion*.

Oblique stringing. See *Pianoforte*.

Oboe. (1) See *Oboe Family*. (2) Organ Reed stop (see *Organ* 2) of 8-foot pitch; imitative of instrument whose name it bears.

Oboe da Caccia. See *Oboe Family*.

Oboe d'amore. See *Oboe Family*.

Oboe Family. All members of this family possess a double reed (see *Reed*) and a conical tube. In essentials the family is very ancient, going back to the beginning of the Christian era.

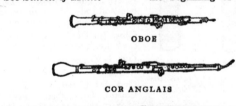

OBOE

COR ANGLAIS

BASSOON

Oberlin, Russell (b. Akron, Ohio, 1928). Counter-tenor. Trained Juilliard Sch., &c. With New York Pro Musica 1953–9, then solo career. Covent Garden 1960.

Oberon, or the Elf-King's Oath. Eng. Fairy-tale Opera by Weber.

The medieval SHAWMS or SCHALMEYS (high-pitched instruments) and POMMERS and BOMBARDS (low-pitched ones), and the CURTALL and DOUBLE CURTALL were members of this family. The HAUTBOY (or HOBOY; see reference under *Wait*) was a coarser form of our present Oboe, which latter may be said, roughly, to date from the time of Haydn and Mozart.

The chief existing members of the family are: (*a*) OBOE, with a peculiarly penetrating pleasant tone. (*b*) COR ANGLAIS (or 'English Horn'—but neither English in origin nor a horn), being an alto oboe with a pitch a 5th below that of the oboe; to avoid its being a little too long for the player's convenience the reed is inserted in a metal tube which is bent back. (*c*) BASSOON, the bass member of the family, of which the whole tube is bent back on itself and the reed brought within reach of the player's mouth by a curved tube. (*d*) DOUBLE BASSOON, resembling the bassoon but longer and in pitch an 8ve lower. The *Cor Anglais* is a transposing instrument, its music being written a 5th higher than it is to sound (see *Transposing Instruments*); the others are non-transposing.

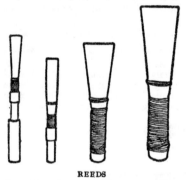

REEDS

From left to right—Oboe, Cor Anglais, Bassoon, and Double Bassoon

The following must also be mentioned: (*e*) OBOE DA CACCIA (obsolete), a predecessor of the cor anglais, which nowadays, in old music, takes its place. (*f*) OBOE D'AMORE (obsolete except for revival in a few modern scores); it is intermediate in size between the oboe and the cor anglais, has a pear-shaped bell, which gives it an individual tone-colour, and is a transposing instrument, its music being written a minor 3rd higher than the effect desired. (*g*) B FLAT OBOE, a high-pitched instrument used in some military bands; it is a

transposing instrument written for a minor 3rd lower than it sounds. (*h*) TENOROON (obsolete), a small bassoon, a 5th higher in pitch than the normal bassoon. (*i*) HECKELPHONE, a sort of baritone oboe, used by Strauss and Delius. It is generally written for in the treble clef an 8ve higher than it sounds. (Possibly when some composers specify 'bass oboe' they mean this instrument.) (*j*) SARRUSOPHONE, a wind-band instrument, made of brass. It exists in 6 sizes (in Keys E flat and B flat) from that of the oboe to that of the double bassoon; it is a transposing instrument.

Cf. *Boehm System.*

Obouhof. See *Electric Musical Instruments 1.*

Oboussier, Robert (b. Antwerp 1900; d. Zürich 1957). Swiss composer who studied in Germany and lived for some years as a music critic in Paris; then similarly employed in Berlin, but lacking sympathy with Nazi ideals left it in 1938 and settled in Zürich. Composer of orch., chamber, and piano music, &c., and author of books on musical subjects.

Obrecht (or **Hobrecht**, or **Obertus**, or **Hobertus**), **Jacob** (b. Bergen-op-Zoom abt. 1453; d. Ferrara 1505). Active in church music in Low Countries and Italy. Many compositions survive and have high importance.

Obw. (in Ger. organ music) = *Oberwerk*, i.e. 'Swell Organ'.

O.C. = *Organo corale* (It.), i.e. Choir Organ.

Oca del Cairo, L' ('The Goose of Cairo'). Unfinished comedy-opera by Mozart (K. 422, 1783). Libretto by G. Varesco. (Patched-up Fr. version, *L'Oie du Caire* prod. Paris 1867; London, in It., 1870; new version by H. F. Redlich, London, in It., 1940; other versions have been heard, e.g. Salzburg 1936.)

O Canada! One of the national songs of that country, popular especially amongst the Fr.-Canadian population. The music, by Calixa Lavallée, composed in 1880, was originally a hymn in honour of St. John the Baptist. The tune is officially adopted for regimental bands in Canada. In the non-Fr. part of Canada the alternative national song *The Maple Leaf for Ever!* remains very popular (see *Maple Leaf*).

O can ye labour lea, young man. See *Auld Lang Syne*.

Ocarina. A small, more or less egg-shaped wind instrument, of metal or earthenware, in the closed chamber of which the air is set in vibration from without (the only instrument on this principle). Its prototype exists amongst certain primitive races.

OCARINA
(A late and improved model)

O'Carolan, Turlough (1670–1738). Famous Irish harper and composer for the harp.

Occasional Oratorio, by Handel. Some of the music comes from previous works by the same composer. (1st perf. London 1746.)
See reference under *Rule, Britannia!*

Ocean, The. (1) Rubinstein's 2nd Symphony (op. 42); 1857 in its original form but later extended to 7 movements (1st perf. Königsberg 1857; New York 1871; Crystal Palace, London, 1877). (2) Symphonic Poem by Henry Hadley (1st perf. New York 1921).

Oceanides. Symphonic Poem by Sibelius (op. 73, 1914). The name recalls the sea nymphs of Gr. mythology, who have their Finnish counterpart, the *Aallottaret*—which was at first the title used.

Ockeghem (Okeghem, Ockenheim, &c.**), Jean de** (b. Dender, E. Flanders, abt. 1425; d. Tours abt. 1495). Became chaplain and composer to Charles VII in Paris; then treasurer of Abbey at Tours. Left masses, motets, chansons, &c., showing great progress of polyphonic composition at his period.

O come, all ye faithful. See *Adeste Fideles*.

Octandre. Same as *Octet* (q.v.). Properly it means an 8-stamened plant.

Octave. (1) See *Interval*. (For 'Consecutive' and 'Hidden' Octaves see *Harmony* 2 j; for 'Octave Signs' see Table 26.) (2) Organ stop, same as *Principal* (q.v.) in Brit. and Amer. organs.

Octave Flute. Piccolo (see *Flute Family*).

Octave quint. Organ stop same as *Twelfth* (q.v.).

Octaves graves, Octaves aiguës in Fr. organ music mean respectively the sub- and super-octave couplers.

Octavin (Fr.). The 'Fifteenth' stop of the organ. So *Octavin harmonique,* 'Harmonic Piccolo'.

Octet (Fr. *Octuor* and *Octette*; It. *Ottetto*; Ger. *Oktett*). Any combination of 8 performers or any piece of music composed for such. The normal String Octet is for 4 violins, 2 violas, and 2 'cellos. Various octet combinations of wind and strings exist.

Octo-bass. A string double-bass 10 feet high introduced by the great Paris *luthier*, J. B. Vuillaume, in the 1840's, and recommended by Berlioz. The stopping was done by levers actuated by the left hand and the feet, the bowing in the normal way.

October Symphony. The 2nd by Shostakovich (1927). Its actual title is *A Dedication to October* (the month in which the Bolshevik Revolution of 1917 took place).

Octuor. See *Octet*.

Od (It.). 'Or.'

Ode. Properly a chorus in a Gr. play. Any exalted poem in the style of an address, generally of moderate length.

Oder (Ger.). 'Or.'

Ode to Death. By Holst. Choral-Orch. setting of Whitman. (Leeds Fest. 1922.)

Ode to Napoleon. By Schönberg. For Speaker (in *Sprechgesang*, q.v.),

Piano, and String Quartet (Op. 41) or String Orch. (Op. 41 B). A setting of Byron's vituperative poem. (1st perf. New York 1945.)

O Deutschland, hoch in Ehren ('O Germany, high in honours'). The poem is by Ludwig Bauer (1832–1910), a schoolmaster of Augsburg, and was written in 1859. The tune, by the Englishman Henry Hugo Pierson, was written as a sea-song and Bauer adopted it.

Odington, Walter de (end of 13th c. and beginning of 14th). Monk of Evesham who left important treatises on mathematics and astronomy and one on music.

O.E. = *Organo espressivo* (It.), i.e. Swell Organ.

Oedipus Rex. 'Opera-Oratorio' by Stravinsky. Original Fr. text by Cocteau but translated into Latin by J. Danielou, and so performed. (Prod. Paris 1927; Boston and New York, concert form, 1928; New York, staged, 1931; London, concert form, 1936.)

Œuvre (Fr.). 'Work.'

Offen (Ger.). 'Open.'

Offenbach, Jacques—real name Jakob Wiener (b. Cologne (father from Offenbach) 1819; d. Paris 1880). Son of a Jewish cantor. Settled in Paris as a boy and there lived ever after. Early career was as violoncellist; later as a highly successful composer of light operettas (see *Orphée aux Enfers*; *Belle Hélène*; *Grande Duchesse de Gérolstein*; *Tales of Hoffmann*). A strange association of bad luck attached to his name, so that theatrical people, &c., crossed themselves when it was mentioned.

Offertory, Offertoire, or Offertorium. The Offertory of the Mass consists of an Antiphon (q.v.), a part of the Proper (cf. *Common*) of the Mass, sung just after the Credo, whilst the Priest is preparing the bread and wine and offering them upon the altar. The plainsong setting of the Antiphon is generally insufficient to occupy the time, so there may be interpolated a motet (sometimes one which repeats the words of the antiphon just heard), or an organ voluntary. In the Anglican

service the place of the Offertory is now usually taken by a hymn.

Office. The 'Hour Services' of the Roman Catholic Church ('The Divine Office', q.v.). Also used for Anglican Matins and Evensong, and (though loosely) in the phrase 'The Office of the Holy Communion'.

Office Hymn. A liturgical hymn appointed for the Office, or Service of the day (see above).

Öffnen (Ger.). 'To open.'

Offrande à Siva, L'. See *Delvincourt*.

Off to Philadelphia in the Morning. See *Haynes*.

Oficleide (It.). 'Ophicleide' (see *Cornett and Key Bugle Families*).

Of thee I sing. See *Gershwin*.

Ofydd. See *Eisteddfod*.

Ogdon, John (b. Mansfield, Notts., 1937). Pianist, trained R.M.C.M. and with Denis Matthews, Petri, &c. London Prom début 1959; Spoleto 1960; Tchaikovsky prize 1962; New York 1963. Some compositions.

O gin I were fairly shut of her. See *Barley Shot*.

O gladsome light (Sullivan). See *Golden Legend*.

Ogni (It.). 'All', 'every'.

Ohne (Ger.). 'Without', e.g. *ohne Dämpfer*, 'without mute'.

Oil of barley. See *Cold and Raw*.

Oiseau de feu (Stravinsky). See *Firebird*.

Oiseau-Lyre. See *Lyrebird*.

Oistrakh, (1) David (b. Odessa 1908). Violinist; studied Odessa Mus. Sch.; début at age 19, then international career as foremost Russian player. (2) Igor (b. Odessa 1931). Son of (1) and also a notable violinist.

Okeghem. See *Ockeghem*.

Oktave (Ger.). 'Octave'. So *Oktav-flöte*, 'octave flute', i.e. piccolo; *Oktavkoppel*, 'octave coupler'.

Oktet. See *Octet*.

Olczewska, Maria (real name Marie Berchtenbreiter) (b. Bavaria 1892). Operatic contralto. Attached Vienna Opera. Covent Garden début 1924;

Metropolitan 1933; active as teacher (Vienna Conserv.) from 1947. Special reputation in Wagner roles.

Old Dances and Airs for the Lute. Three Orch. Suites by Respighi (1918-24-31). The 3rd is for Strings alone.

Old Dan Tucker. See *Emmett.*

Old English Sol-fa. See *Lancashire sol-fa.*

Old Folks at home. See *Foster, Stephen Collins.*

Old Foundation. See *Cathedral Music.*

Old Hall Manuscript. Early 15th-c. collection of church music found in the library of St. Edmund's Coll., Old Hall, Hertfordshire, first described in 1903 and publ. 1933-5. It offers a valuable opportunity of studying the choral style of a period abt. 1415. (Cf. *Ramsbotham, Alexander.*)

Old Hundredth (Eng. name) or **Old Hundred** (Amer. name). A metrical psalm tune that holds pre-eminence on account of its age, traditions, and dignity. Its origin is uncertain. Its name indicates that it was set to the hundredth psalm in the 'old' version of the metrical psalms, i.e. Sternhold and Hopkins as distinct from Tate and Brady (see *Hymns and Hymn Tunes* 3); the edn. of this version in which it first appeared was Day's of 1563. But the history of the tune goes back rather further to Marot and Béza's Genevan Psalter of 1551, in which it is attached to the 134th psalm. A form of the tune appears even earlier, in the Antwerp collection, *Souter Liedekens* (1540). In some Ger. and other settings it appears in 3-in-a-measure rhythm.

See *Doxologia.*

Old King Cole. Ballet by Vaughan Williams. (Prod. Cambridge 1923.)

Oldman, Cecil Bernard (b. London 1894; d. there 1969). After study at Oxford joined staff of Brit. Museum (1926), becoming at length (1947-59) Keeper of the Printed Books. Learned musicologist and writer, esp. on Mozart. C.B. 1952. Hon. D.Mus. Edinburgh 1956.

'Old Vic.' See *Victoria Hall.*

Ole (Sp.) A gipsy type of Seguidilla (q.v.), also known as *Polo* or *Romalis.*

Oliphant (Old Eng. 'elephant'). An ivory hunting-horn in use from A.D. 800 or perhaps earlier.

Oliver Ditson Co. See *Ditson.*

O Lord, the maker of all thing. See *Henry VIII.*

Olsen, Ole (b. Hammerfest, Norway, 1850; d. Oslo 1927). Studied in Leipzig and became piano teacher, conductor, &c., in Oslo. Compositions show nationalistic leanings—operas, symphonic poems, songs, &c.

Olympians, The. Opera by Bliss; libretto by J. B. Priestley. (Prod. London 1949.)

O'Mara, Joseph (b. Limerick 1865; d. Dublin 1927). Operatic tenor. Trained Italy. London début in production Sullivan's *Ivanhoe* 1891; Covent Garden 1893. Principal tenor Moody-Manners Co. 1902-10; formed own touring company 1912.

Omar Khayyám. By Bantock. For Solo Voices, Chorus, and Orch. (in 3 parts, respectively 1st perf. Birmingham Fest. 1906; Cardiff Fest. 1907; Birmingham Fest. 1909. Then as a whole in London and in 1912 Vienna).

Ombra mai fù. See *Largo* (Handel).

Omphale's Spinning-wheel (Saint-Saëns). See *Rouet d'Omphale.*

On a Gondola (Mendelssohn). See *Gondola Song.*

Ondeggiando, ondeggiante, ondeggiamento (It.). 'Undulating', i.e. tremolo or vibrato, or (also) any swaying effect.

Ondes musicales, Ondium martenot. See *Electric Musical Instruments* 1.

Ondine (Ravel). See *Gaspard de la nuit.*

Ondříček, Franz (b. Prague 1857; d. Milan 1922). Violinist. Pupil of Massart at Paris Conserv. Toured world with high success. Part author of *New Method of Learning Higher Technique of Violin.* Composer of concerto, &c.

Ondulé (Fr.). 'Undulating', i.e. tremolo or vibrato, or (also) any swaying effect.

O'Neill, Norman (b. London 1875; there d. as result of street accident 1934). Grandson of W. H. Callcott, grand-nephew of William Horsley. Made special name as composer and conductor of stage incidental music. Wife (Adine Rückert, d. 1947) was well-known pianist.

One-step. An Amer. dance of the jazz period, in simple duple time and rather more vigorous than the fox-trot (q.v.).

Ongarese (It.). 'Hungarian.'

On hearing the first cuckoo in Spring. Orch. piece by Delius. (1911; 1st Brit. perf. London 1914.)

Onslow, George (b. Clermont-Ferrand 1784; there d. 1853). Grandson of 1st Lord Onslow; mother French; man of means. Good pianist and 'cellist, who attained high (but now faded) fame as composer of operas, symphonies, and quantities of chamber works (over 30 each string quartets and quintets), &c.; elected to Inst. of France in succession to Cherubini.

On the Steppes (Borodin). See *In the Steppes.*

On Wenlock Edge. Song Cycle by Vaughan Williams; settings of poems from Housman's *A Shropshire Lad* (1909). Cf. *Shropshire Lad.*

Op. Short for *Opus* (q.v.). For the plur. *Opp.* is often used.

Open diapason. See *Organ* 2.

Open harmony. See *Harmony* 2 b.

Open notes. The notes on the unstopped strings of any bowed or plucked instrument.

Open pipes (Diapason, &c.). See *Organ* 2.

Open string. A string of a bowed or plucked instrument when not 'stopped' by the fingers.

Oper (Ger.). 'Opera.'

Opera may be defined as drama set to music—entirely or partially, but in either case in such a degree that the musical part of the entertainment ranks as an essential, and not an incidental, element (i.e. mere 'musical plays' and the like are not covered by the term).

(1) The date of the 1st operas is usually given as the turn of the 16th–17th cs., but there had been many precursors (see *Miracle Plays, Sacre Rappresentazioni, Masque, Pastoral* 1). It may be looked upon as a late product of the Renaissance, being an attempt to reproduce what its Florentine founders believed to have been the ancient Gr. presentation of drama, with what now came to be called recitative (q.v.) as, at this period, its most essential element. The earliest examples were PERI'S *Dafne* (1597), which is now lost, and his *Eurydice* (1600): the latter was in part composed by CACCINI, who in the same year reset the whole text (see *Peri* and *Caccini*). Early landmarks in the history of the new form (*Le Nuove Musiche*, 'The New Musics') are MONTEVERDI's *Orpheus* (Mantua 1607) and *Coronation of Poppea* (Venice 1642): with him we find a considerable development of the *Aria* (see *Monteverdi* and *Aria*). Towards the end of the century (from 1679 onwards) came the unresting activity of ALESSANDRO SCARLATTI, who wrote 115 operas, and is regarded as the founder of the Neapolitan School. As the century advanced some operatic activity developed in countries other than Italy especially in France, where, from 1672, LULLY, in setting libretti in the Fr. language, developed a style of his own.

(2) In the 18th c. It. opera became a highly conventionalized form, with the display of vocal tone and agility (Bel Canto, q.v.) as an outstanding characteristic. A class of highly skilled and generously paid It. singers (including 'castrati'; see *Voice* 5) had come into existence and their performance in tuneful works by It. composers, sung in the original language, were a feature of musical life. In London during the 1st half of the century HANDEL was active in the production of operas in the It. language and convention. In Paris RAMEAU, from 1733, was putting on the boards operas in the Fr. language and in a style different from that of the It. composers, with much expressive declamation and original harmonies and orchestration: he may be regarded as the true founder of definitely Fr. opera. The 2nd half of the century is notable in the history of opera for the reforms of GLUCK, his

Orpheus (Vienna 1762) and, still more, his *Alcestis* (Vienna 1767) marking a return to the original principle of the 1st It. opera composers, i.e. emphasis upon dramatic fitness and effect. *Orpheus* is the earliest full-length opera that still maintains a place in the regular repertory. Vienna at this period had become an important centre of opera production. Not only was Gluck there but also his prolific rival Hasse, and, moreover, the world's most wholesale supplier of operatic libretti, Metastasio (q.v.). MOZART wrote two of his greatest operas in Vienna (*Figaro*, in Italian, 1786; *The Magic Flute*, in German, 1791): these are works of the highest class and their place in the repertory (with also *Don Giovanni*, Prague, 1787) is permanently assured.

(3) Despite the example of Gluck, It. opera maintained its tradition of vocal display and tuneful attractiveness. In the 19TH CENTURY such names come to mind as those of DONIZETTI (1797–1848), BELLINI (1801–35), and ROSSINI (1792–1868) with later, VERDI (1813–1901), the last of whom, however, in his later works developed a more genuinely dramatic style (*Aida*, 1871; *Othello*, 1887; *Falstaff*, 1893). Meantime, in Germany, BEETHOVEN'S *Fidelio* (1805; present form 1814) and the operas of WEBER (especially *Der Freischütz*, 'The Marksman', 1821) had carried further the principles of the use of the Ger. language and the expression of the Ger. romantic spirit. Thus we are led on to WAGNER (q.v.), who, like Gluck, ranks as one of the greatest reformers of opera in his determination not to sacrifice dramatic truth of expression to mere musical attractiveness; indeed he discarded the term opera in favour of 'music drama', so returning to the idea of the earliest opera composers, who had sometimes used the term 'Dramma per Musica'. The formidable list of Wagner's works shows an increasing grasp of the means of applying his principles, with, at the same time, a continual development of his outstanding accomplishment as a musician (*The Flying Dutchman*, 1843; *Tannhäuser*, 1845; *Lohengrin*, 1850; *Tristan and Isolde*, 1865; *The Mastersingers*, 1868; *Rhinegold*, 1869; *The Valkyrie*, 1870; *Siegfried*, 1876; *The*

Dusk of the Gods, 1876. All these dates are those of 1st perf.). During the middle part of the century the Ger. MEYERBEER was producing in Paris, in French, his flamboyant romantic works (*Robert the Devil*, 1831; *The Huguenots*, 1836; &c.). BERLIOZ, in France, at the same period, was demonstrating his bold originality (*Benvenuto Cellini*, 1838; *Beatrice and Benedict*, 1862; *The Trojans*, 1864), whilst the tuneful GOUNOD, in a succession of works (especially *Faust*, 1859, and *Romeo and Juliet*, 1867), was at the same period winning the suffrages of a wide public. BIZET's many operas must be mentioned (especially *Carmen*, 1875), as also the very many melodious works of MASSENET, MESSAGER, and SAINT-SAËNS (*Samson and Delilah*, 1877). Indeed it must be recognized that during the late 19th c. Fr. Opera reached a notable season of efflorescence. Spanish opera composers of the latter part of the century included PEDRELL (1841–1922) and ISAAC ALBÉNIZ (1860–1909). (For a light traditional Spanish operatic form see *Zarzuela*.) A notable addition to the operatic repertory was made during this century by Russian composers, especially GLINKA (*A Life for the Czar*, 1836), DARGOMIJSKY (*Russalka*, 1856; *The Stone Guest*, 1872); RIMSKY-KORSAKOF (*Ivan the Terrible*, 1873); MUSSORGSKY (*Boris Godounof*, 1874); BORODIN (*Prince Igor*, 1890); and TCHAIKOVSKY (*Eugen Onegin*, 1879). Czech composers were SMETANA (from 1866 to 1882) and DVOŘAK (from 1874 to 1904). The century saw the coming into existence of many national schools of composition, and, as will have been realized, this has left its mark on the world's operatic repertory.

(4) In 20TH-CENTURY Germany, following Wagner, we see STRAUSS emerge (*Salome*, 1905; *Elektra*, 1909; *The Rose Cavalier*, 1911; &c.). In Italy, following Verdi, we see PUCCINI (attaining fame rather before the actual opening of the century with *La Bohème*, 1896, and *Tosca*, 1900, which were followed by *Madame Butterfly*, 1904; &c.): his works are characterized by easy-flowing It. melody, pointed dramatic (or even melodramatic) effect, and brightly coloured orchestration. In France we see DEBUSSY who in his one operatic

work, a setting of Maeterlinck's *Pelléas and Mélisande* (1902), cut right adrift from all tradition, providing a delicate score that to some who first heard it seemed, in its avoidance of set forms, to have become 'one long recitative'. In Italy there was now a determined effort, on the part of some younger men, to get away from the long-established It. traditions of flowing tune and melodramatic effect. In this connexion may be mentioned PIZZETTI (*Phaedra*, 1915; *Deborah and Jael*, 1922). The Viennese ALBAN BERG, a pupil and follower of Schönberg, produced a work (*Wozzeck*, 1925) of which the scenes followed set instrumental forms. The Spaniard FALLA achieved success with 2 works of modernistic-nationalistic character (*La Vida breve*, 1905; *El Retablo de Maese Pedro* = 'Master Peter's Puppet Show', 1923). Amongst Russian composers of opera in this period were PROKOFIEF (1891–1953) and SHOSTAKOVICH (b. 1906).

(5) It may have been noticed that the names of BRITISH COMPOSERS are conspicuously absent from the lists just given, and, indeed, it has to be admitted that, so far as the permanent world-repertory of opera is concerned they have made little or no contribution. Opera began in Britain during the mid-17th-c. Puritan régime with Davenant's London performances of specially commissioned works by leading Eng. composers (see *Siege of Rhodes*). PURCELL, later, though he composed much for the stage, left only one true opera (*Dido and Æneas*, written for private perf., abt. 1688). In the early 18th c. a new type of simple opera appeared, the *Ballad Opera* (*The Beggar's Opera*, q.v., 1728), and its many successors to 1753), in which existing popular tunes were used, interspersed with spoken dialogue; this led to the later composition of what is called 'English Opera', in which, whilst spoken dialogue is still employed, the music is not borrowed from existing sources but composed *ad hoc*. Of this latter type notable composers were ARNE (1710–78) and in the next century BISHOP, BALFE, WALLACE, and BENEDICT; some of the works of this last group of composers had considerable temporary success abroad. Opera

composers of a later period have been GORING THOMAS, COWEN, MACKENZIE, STANFORD, ETHEL SMYTH, HOLST, VAUGHAN WILLIAMS, and BRITTEN. A special type which has enjoyed (and still enjoys) enormous success in the English-speaking world is that of the light operas of Gilbert (as librettist, providing much witty spoken dialogue) and Sullivan (as composer): they were produced over a period of about 20 years (1875–96).

(6) The 1st opera performed in the AMERICAN colonies seems to have been *Flora, or Hob in the Well* (Charleston, S. Carolina, 1735), of unknown authorship, but performed and publ. in London 6 years earlier: it was on the general lines of *The Beggar's Opera*; Eng. works of this type had the field to themselves for over half a century, i.e. until 1790, when, in the French-speaking part of the South, Fr. opera was introduced. Performance of It. opera apparently dates from about the same time (1794—Paesiello's *Barber of Seville* in various cities). The earliest Amer. operas (on the lines of the 'English Opera' of the period—see 5) were Hewitt's *Tammany* (New York, 1794) and Carr's *The Archers of Switzerland* (New York, 1796), but these composers were not Amer. born, being immigrants from Britain. It was not until half a century later that the 1st work of the 'Grand Opera' type (see 7) was performed, its composer being W. H. Fry (*Leonora*, Philadelphia, 1845).

(7) Some CONVENTIONAL TERMS may now be explained. By *Grand Opera* is meant such as has its libretto entirely set to music (other definitions are given by some writers, but that is the traditional meaning of the term). In French, *Opéra-Comique* does not mean 'Comic Opera' but such opera as includes spoken dialogue, whatever the nature of its literary theme and treatment. *Opéra Bouffe* (Fr.) or *Opera Buffa* (It.), on the other hand, does mean 'Comic Opera'—but not necessarily opera that descends to farce (e.g. it covers such works as Rossini's *Barber of Seville* and even Mozart's *Don Giovanni*). *Opera Seria* (It.) is merely serious opera, as opposed to *Opera Buffa*.

Cf. *Bouffons, Guerre des*; *Singspiel*; *Festspiel*; *Light Opera*; *Loewenberg*.

Opera Buffa (It.), **Opéra Bouffe** (Fr.), **Opéra-Comique** (Fr.), **Opera Seria** (It.). See *Opera* 7.

Operetta. (1) A short opera. (2) A light opera—this being now the common sense of the word, and generally with the implication of spoken dialogue; the word is now, indeed, often almost a synonym for 'Musical Comedy' (q.v.).

Ophicleide. (1) See *Cornett and Key Bugle*. (2) Organ stop; sort of loud *Tuba* (q.v.).

Opp. Abbrev. for the plur. of *Opus* (q.v.).

Op. post. See *Opus*.

Opus (Lat. 'work'). In the early 17th c. some composers began the convenient custom of numbering their works as they appeared, and this custom still continues ('Op. 17', or whatever it may be). Unfortunately the figures attached to the works are not always reliable, many anomalies occurring owing to the carelessness or perversity of some composers and also of some publishers.

Op. Posth. means 'Posthumous Work'.

Opus Clavicembalisticum. See *Sorabji*.

Orageux, orageuse (Fr. masc., fem.). 'Stormy.'

Ora pro nobis (Lat.). 'Pray for us'—a litany response in the Roman Catholic Church.

Oratorio. Considering the term in its original and stricter sense this is an extended setting of a religious libretto, for solo vocalists, chorus, and orch., and for either concert or church perf., i.e. usually without scenery, dresses, or action. Such works took their rise in popular plays given in the oratory of the good priest Philip Neri (later canonized) in Rome in 1556, the oratorio in something near its present musical sense originating about 1600, after the death of that pioneer. This makes the beginnings of oratorio, in Rome, and those of opera, in Florence, coeval; see *Opera*. The 1st oratorio was one by Cavalieri—*La Rappresentazione dell' Anima e del Corpo* ('The Representation of Soul and Body'), which was really a Morality (see *Miracle Plays*) set to music. The composer was a member of the Florentine

group of experimenters in the new art of opera, and the score of the work (with its use of recitative, &c.) looks much like the score of any of the earliest operas. It was, indeed, very much a religious opera, having dresses and action and even a final (optional) dance.

Amongst the many later It. composers who followed up this innovation (with works more on the modern lines) were Carissimi (abt. 1604–74) and Alessandro Scarlatti (1660–1725). Amongst Germany's prominent oratorio composers have been Schütz (1585–1672), Handel (1685–1759; he wrote his oratorios in England), C.P.E. Bach (1714–88), Spohr (1784–1859), and Mendelssohn (1809–47). There have been many Fr. oratorio composers and, of course, the Brit. ones (especially in the 19th c.) have been innumerable—the examples by Elgar, produced during the decade 1896–1906, ranking especially high, both from their technical competence and complexity and their poetical and emotional appeal.

It is to be noted that the word 'oratorio' has, from the early 18th c., often been loosely applied, so as to include works in oratorio style but not treating of religious subjects (e.g. Handel's *Semele*, 1743). Moreover, in the later 18th c. and the early 19th c. the name was commonly given to miscellaneous concert programmes made up of extracts from various oratorios. Choral singers often speak of a Mass, a Passion, a setting of the Seven Last Words, &c., as an oratorio: such works as these are in the present book treated under their separate headings.

Orb and Sceptre. March by Walton, written for coronation of Queen Elizabeth II (1953).

Orchard, William Arundel (b. London 1867). Conductor Sydney Orch., Madrigal Soc., &c. Then Director State Conserv., N.S.W., 1923–34. Lecturer Univ. Tasmania 1935–8.

Orchestra. As long as instruments have existed, we may suppose, they have been combined in perf., but their effective organization into standard groups of (*a*) Strings, (*b*) Wood Wind, (*c*) Brass Wind, and (*d*) Percussion has come about gradually and late in the history of mankind, the following being the main stages of development.

(1) THE PERIOD OF THE EARLY OPERAS

(1600 onwards). The orch. was, apparently, much a chance combination of whatever instruments happened to be available—viols (big and little), violins, flutes, hautboys, cornetts (the old wooden instruments—see *Cornett and Key Bugle Families*), trumpets and trombones, drums, harp, harpsichord, organ, &c.

(3) THE MODERN ORCHESTRA (abt. 1800 onwards). By the year 1800 we find that the modern classical orch. is in being. There is no longer a background of harpsichord or organ tone, the Strings having taken their place as the orch.'s solid basis. The various Wind instruments (some of them much improved) have their well-defined types

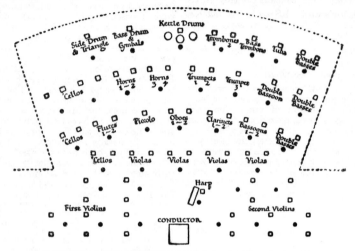

A COMMON 20TH-CENTURY PLACING OF THE ORCHESTRA

A frequent variant of this arrangement places the Second Violins adjacent to the Firsts (on the conductor's left) and the 'Cellos on the conductor's right, with the Double-basses behind them

(2) THE PERIOD OF BACH AND HANDEL (abt. 1700 onwards). Many instruments had now been improved and effective combinations of them discovered. As a background a keyboard instrument (harpsichord or organ) was used: its player had before him merely the bass part with an indication of the chords to be erected upon it (see *Figured Bass*). The viols were now little used, having been superseded by the violin family. The Wood Wind included various kinds of flutes, oboes, and bassoons; the Brass, horns, trumpets, and sometimes trombones. In Bach (especially) the instruments used in any movement of a work are a selection from the above, varying in the different movements. Their functions are as yet comparatively little differentiated, i.e. as to the kind of passage allotted to them.

of passage, corresponding to their individual capacities. Generally speaking all the instruments appear in all the movements throughout a score: delicacy of combination has been studied and by the momentary dropping out or reappearing of an instrument there is attained a kaleidoscopic play of orch. colour. Haydn and Mozart wrote for an orch. of this kind and in this way. The standard basic make-up of the orch. is that which we see in Beethoven's 1st symphony (performed 1800), i.e. violins (divided into 1st and 2nd), violas, 'cellos, and double-basses (these last two usually duplicating one another at the interval of an 8ve and so supplying a firm bass); a pair each of flutes, oboes, clarinets, bassoons; trumpets, and horns; 2 kettledrums. Such changes as took place during the succeeding century and more were merely amplifications of this, often considerable but observing the same principles.

(4) ORCHESTRATION AT THE BEGINNING OF THE 20TH CENTURY. Overleaping the developments due to the later Beethoven and then to Wagner and coming down to 1900 we may take any typical Strauss score, where we shall find something like this—strings as in Beethoven (but more of each instrument); 3 flutes and piccolo, 3 oboes and cor anglais, 2 clarinets plus a high clarinet, and a bass clarinet, 3 bassoons and a double bassoon; 8 horns, 5 trumpets, 3 trombones, a tenor tuba and a bass tuba; kettledrums, bass drum, side drum, military drum, cymbals; 2 harps. Here are both greatly increased dynamic power and high capacity for dramatic characterization.

(5) ORCHESTRATION FROM THE 1930's. Musical composition, including orchestration, had now passed into a highly experimental period, in which composers of different races and different temperaments were at work in their own individual ways. There was an occasional tendency to use instruments out of their proper ways (or what had long been considered as such), giving them passages to perform for which composers of the previous periods would have said they were never intended. Some composers produced on occasion works for smaller combinations (e.g. Stravinsky's *Soldier's Tale* is scored for 1 each of violin, doublebass, clarinet, bassoon, cornet, and trombone, with 8 percussion instruments in the hands of 1 player). And there was a ceaseless effort to discover new colours.

What the future of the orch. will be cannot be predicted. Just possibly it is doomed to disappear as electrical devices for producing varieties of musical tone are perfected (see *Electric Musical Instruments*).

(6) ORCHESTRAL SCORES. The conventional arrangement of instruments in a conductor's score is as follows, reading downwards: Wood Wind, Brass, Percussion, Strings. In general principle the instruments of each of these groups are placed in pitch order, the higher ones above, not however separating instruments of the same family, e.g. in the wood wind we may see piccolo, flutes, and bass flute; oboes and cor anglais; clarinets and bass clarinet; bassoon and double bassoon. If the harp appears it is placed under the percussion; if voices, they are to be seen interpolated between the lower and upper strings (i.e. above the 'cellos). In concertos the part for the solo instrument is placed above the string parts.

See also references under *History of Music*.

Orchestral oboe. Organ stop. See *Oboe* 2.

Orchestral score. See *Score*.

Orchestras in church. See *Anglican Parish Church Music*.

Orchestration. The art or act of scoring for an orch. (cf. *Instrumentation*).

Orchestre de genre. This term, which during the 1930's became common in French-speaking countries, appears to mean the same as *Tipica Orchestra* (q.v.).

Ord, Bernhard ('Boris'); (b. Bristol 1897; d. Cambridge 1961). Organist and choral trainer. Studied R.C.M. and Cambridge (Fellow King's College 1923–61; organist there 1929–57, conductor university choral soc., &c.). Hon. D.Mus. Durham 1955. C.B.E. 1958.

Ordinaire (Fr.). 'Ordinary', 'normal'; sometimes used to rescind some direction to play in an unusual way.

Ordinario (It.). 'Ordinary', 'normal', e.g. *tempo ordinario*.

Ordinary. See *Mass*.

Ordre. See *Suite*.

Orefice, Giacomo (b. Vicenza 1865; d. Milan 1922). Prof. of composition at Milan Conserv. and composer of many operas, orch., chamber, and piano works, &c.; also writer on music.

O'Reilly, Miles. See *Lochaber no more*.

Orfeo, La favola d' ('The Orpheus Fable'). Opera by Monteverdi. (Prod. Mantua 1607; after early 17th c. not performed until early 20th; then widely taken up.)

Very many other operas on same subject by composers of various periods (e.g. see *Rossi*).

Orfeo ed Euridice. It. opera by Gluck—the first in which he introduced his reforms. Libretto by Calzabigi. (Prod. Vienna 1762; London 1770; New York 1863; re-modelled with Fr. text, Paris 1774. Earliest full-length opera still in the international repertory.) See also *Orpheus*.

Orff, Carl (b. Munich 1895). Composer, teacher, and conductor. Best known for operas or stage cantatas in an individual neo-archaic style (*Carmina Burana*, q.v., *Catulli Carmina*, &c.).

Organ. The principles of the construction of the organ, in primary outline, are as follows:

(1) A row of PIPES, graduated as to size (and hence as to pitch), is placed in a corresponding row of holes in a WINDCHEST, which is fed by a BELLOWS.

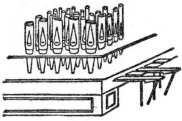

WINDCHEST

Showing position of Pipes and Sliders. (Two of the sliders are pulled out, showing that two of the stops are in operation)

Under each hole in the Windchest is a PALLET, i.e. a sort of hinged cover which can be opened and closed.

The Pallets are operated, in the older organs, by a series of rods, called STICKERS, and these are connected with the keyboard of the instrument by levers called BACKFALLS and rods called TRACKERS: thus on depressing a finger-key a current of air is admitted to its particular pipe, and on releasing it the current of air is again cut off. In the more modern organs, instead of the Sticker-Backfall-Tracker action there are the tubes of a PNEUMATIC ACTION or the wires of an ELECTRIC ACTION.

The above brief statement must now be somewhat amplified. What has been described is a theoretical organ of only 1 row of pipes. We will now imagine the Windchest to have several such rows, the pipes being some of wood and some of metal, some of normal pitch and some of a pitch an 8ve below or above that pitch, &c., some being mere simple ('flue') pipes and others supplied with a vibrating tongue of metal called a REED, and so on. The Pallets already spoken of extend, *from front to back*, under each of these rows, so admitting air to, or excluding it from, the pipes related to 1 finger-key of the organ, whilst *from side to side* of the Windchest, under each row of pipes, runs a board with holes in it, called a SLIDER: when slid into one position the holes in this board coincide with those under the pipes and so permit the pallets to operate as regards that row; when slid into another position they no longer coincide, and so cut off the operation of the pallets in admitting air. The sliding is accomplished (mechanically, pneumatically, or electrically) by connexion with handles or other devices; these are the DRAWSTOPS, STOP-KEYS, &c., respectively, each of which operates 1 row of pipes—called a REGISTER or STOP (we speak of an organ of '20 stops', of '100 stops', &c.).

A keyboard to be operated by the hands is called a MANUAL and one to be operated by the feet, a PEDAL-BOARD. All organs nowadays possess both sorts of keyboard. When an instrument contains any considerable number of stops, differentiation in their use is made easier by their being distributed over 2, 3, or 4 manuals (occasionally more). These are banked up stepwise before the player. The chief manual is that of the GREAT ORGAN, which contains a variety of stops, including especially many of robust tone. Above it is that of the SWELL ORGAN, the pipes belonging to which are enclosed in a *Swell Box*—with Venetian shutters which by means of a *Swell Pedal* can be opened or closed, so increasing or diminishing the volume of tone. Below the Great Organ manual, in a 3-manual organ, is that of the CHOIR ORGAN which contains softer stops, intended originally chiefly, in a church, for the accompaniment of the choral body. If there is a 4th manual (above the Swell manual) it is that of the SOLO ORGAN (with special stops of the character indicated by that

A MODERN ORGAN CONSOLE

name), and there may also be an ECHO ORGAN, with very soft stops.

(2) We now pass to some important details. We have already seen that there are two main varieties of stop, those which are mere whistles (as we may say) and those which possess 'reeds'; these two varieties are respectively called FLUE PIPES and REED PIPES. Both are graduated in size, the largest producing the lowest notes and the smallest the highest. The normal pitch of an organ (the same, properly, as that of a piano) is the product of any set of open-ended flue pipes of which the largest (representing C 2 lines below the bass staff) is 8 feet long, the length of the remaining pipes of the set diminishing

by half as each 8ve is ascended. The tone from the stops with these pipes of normal size can be reinforced by that from others of abnormal size, with their pipe for low C 4 feet, or 2 feet long (so that the whole stop concerned gives an effect 1 8ve or 2 8ves higher than the normal) or, on the other hand, 16 feet, or even 32 feet long (so that the stop concerned gives an effect 1 8ve or 2 8ves lower than the normal). There are also stops of other lengths which

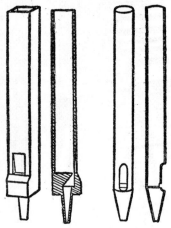

TWO FLUE PIPES
(Respectively wood and metal)

give intermediate pitches reinforcing some of the natural harmonics of the normally pitched stops (cf. *Acoustics* 7): these are called MUTATION STOPS or, if several rows ('Ranks') of them are operated in chorus as though they made one, MIXTURE STOPS (q.v.). The chief stops on the Pedal Organ are pitched an 8ve below those of the manuals (i.e. whereas the chief stops of the manuals are what we call 8-foot stops those of the Pedal are 16-foot stops).

The term 'open-ended flue pipes' was used above. There are also flue pipes which have a stopper at the top ('End-plugged' is a term used in various entries in the present book), which lowers their pitch by an 8ve. The chief manual stop of the organ is the 8-foot *Open Diapason*: but there is generally

also a *Stopped Diapason*, also, from its pitch, spoken of as an 8-foot stop although, in actual physical length, a 4-foot one. (These stops are also to be found in the pedal department.)

By a system of COUPLERS the Pedal organ can have 1 or more of the manuals

A REED PIPE

Diagrammatic representation of lower section of Clarinet. A is a solid lead block holding all the mechanism; B is the boot (corresponding to the mouth cavity of a wood-wind instrument player); C is the brass tube holding the reed; D is the reed (of thin brass); E (a piece of hard-wood) holds the reed in place; F is the moveable tuning wire; G is the lower portion of the pipe (which above this point becomes cylindrical). The arrows show the direction of the wind

connected with it, so that the effect of its stops is reinforced; further, 2 manuals can be connected with one another in the same way—e.g. the Swell may be joined up with the Great. There are also 'Super-octave' and 'Sub-octave' couplers, which duplicate the notes played—an 8ve higher or lower (on the same stop).

To facilitate rapid changing of tone-colour effects there are COMPOSITION PEDALS (or COMBINATION PEDALS), or Pistons having the same effect—that of throwing instantly into action certain selected groups of stops instead of their having to be operated individually by hand.

Some of the organ's stops are imitative of other instruments such as the FLUTE, the ORCHESTRAL OBOE, CLARINET, and TRUMPET (these 3 being Reed Stops), and the GAMBA (a STRING-TONED stop, supposed to reproduce the tone of the old viola da gamba; see *Viol Family* 2). Stops presumably intended to be imitative are the VOX HUMANA (a reed stop) and the VOX ANGELICA or VOIX CÉLESTE (with 2 flue pipes to each note slightly out of tune with each other, so producing a somewhat mysterious effect—or, if only one, by the drawstop bringing into action some normally tuned soft stop simultaneously). The TREMULANT is not a stop, though operated by the player by similar means: it causes a slight fluctuation of the tone and should be rarely used lest the effect pall.

(3) A few organ terms not yet explained are the following:

CONSOLE. The ensemble of manuals, pedal board, stop handles, pistons, or levers, swell pedals, composition pedals, &c., in fact all that part of the machinery of the instrument which stands in front of and on each side of the player and by which he operates. A DETACHED CONSOLE is one placed at a distance from the organ itself, so that the player has the advantage of hearing the full effect as his listeners hear it: in electric organs such a console may be movable.

UNIT ORGAN. One built on the principle of saving space and expense by making a comparatively small number of pipes yield something of the effect of a larger number. This is done by 'borrowing', e.g. the pipes of an 8-foot stop may be made to do duty also for a 4-foot one by a connexion for the latter purpose which draws on them an 8ve higher throughout. The term EX-TENSION ORGAN is also used. (Cinema organs are of this character.)

ELECTROPHONIC ORGANS (sometimes wrongly styled 'Electronic'). These produce their tone not from pipes but by means of radiophone lamps, &c. (cf. *Electric Musical Instruments* 4).

(4) A few facts as to the HISTORY OF THE ORGAN are as follows:

There are records of the existence of crude instruments of this class long before the opening of the Christian era (see *Hydraulus*). By the 10th c. development had got so far as (in very

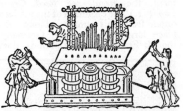

A 10TH-CENTURY ORGAN

(From a manuscript psalter in the library of Trinity College, Cambridge.) The blowers do not appear to be giving perfect satisfaction to the duet players

advanced specimens) 2 manuals each with a range of 20 notes and each note with as many as 10 different pipes, making 400 in all: the keyboard (if

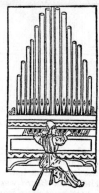

A 15TH-CENTURY ORGAN

(From the *Theorica Musica* of Gaffurius; Milan 1492)

there was one) had broad notes requiring the blow of the whole fist, but it is possible that the organist's function was accomplished by some other means than that of the keyboard, such as sliders moving from front to back, one for each note. (It must be remembered that nothing more would at this date be required from an ecclesiastical organ than a purely melodic accompaniment of the plainsong.) In the period which followed there were 2 types of organ, a PORTATIVE ORGAN which could be carried in processions, and one fixed in its position, a POSITIVE ORGAN. (For a particular kind of Portative instrument, the *Regal*, see *Reed Organ Family* 1.) The evolution of the modern organ from this simple infancy took place largely in northern Germany, though France, at some periods, does

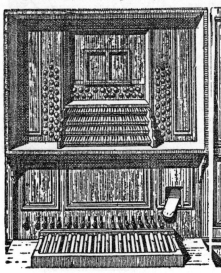

A MID-19TH-CENTURY ORGAN
(St. Eustache, Paris)

not seem to have been far behind. By the 17th c. something like the present form of the instrument had come into being. The *Pedal-Board* was of German introduction: it dates from at least as early as the mid-15th c., but, strangely, did not reach Britain until about 3 centuries later. The *Swell* device, on the other hand, is of Eng. invention, dating, in a crude form, from the early years of the 18th c. (cf. a similar device s.v. *Harpsichord Family*). *Pneumatic action* is also of Eng. origin (1832).

The 1st organ to be installed in any Amer. church was, apparently, one in Philadelphia abt. 1694. In recent times the Amer. development of the organ has been rapid, having profited by the attention of many ingenious inventors.

About 170 organ terms have their own entries in this book. Every effort has been made to attain complete accuracy, but, so far as names of stops are concerned, it cannot quite be guaranteed that no organ builder whatever has used any of these in some sense slightly varying from that here given, for any two firms in this business are apt to call the same stop by different names and to use the same name for somewhat different stops. (Where the Brit. and Amer. applications of a name are definitely known to differ this has been indicated.)

See also *Anglican Parish Church Music*; *Barocco* (for 'Barock Organ'); *Cathedral Music*; *Fingering*; *Hymns and Hymn Tunes* 6 (for Organ Accompaniment); *Puritans and Music*.

Organ Mass. Title (not very apt) of the sequence of chorale preludes forming part 3 of Bach's *Clavierübung* of 1739. They are for the most part a gathering together of earlier works.

Organ, Mechanical. See *Mechanical Reproduction of Music*.

Organistrum. The Hurdy-Gurdy (q.v.).

Organo (It.). 'Organ'.

Organo d'assolo (It.). *Solo Organ* (see *Organ* 1).

Organo d'eco (It.). *Echo Organ* (see *Organ* 1).

Organo d'espressione (It.). *Swell Organ* (see *Organ* 1).

Organo di coro (It.). *Choir Organ* (see *Organ* 1).

Organo di legno (It.). (1) Organ flue stops (see *Organ* 2). (2) Xylophone.

Organ Solo Mass. Mozart's in C, K. 259 (1776). The name has become attached on account of an important organ passage in the Benedictus.

Organum. See *History of Music* 2.

Orgatron. See *Electric Musical Instruments* 4.

Orgel (Ger.). 'Organ.' So *Orgelwalze*, 'organ cylinder', i.e. a clockwork organ, functioning by means of a barrel (see *Mechanical Reproduction* 4).

Orgelbüchlein ('Little Organ-book'). Unfinished collection of 46 short Chorale Preludes by Bach (164 having been intended), 'for the instruction of the tyro organist' in the extemporization of such works and 'to perfect himself in the study of the pedal'.

Orgia (It.). 'Orgy.'

Orgue (Fr.). 'Organ.'

Orgue de barbarie. See *Mechanical Reproduction of Music* 5.

Orgue expressif. A Fr. name for the Harmonium.

Orgue plein. 'Full Organ.'

Orgue positif. (1) 'Choir Organ'. (2) 'Positive Organ' (see *Organ* 4).

Ormandy, Eugene (b. Budapest 1899). Infant prodigy as violinist, entering Budapest Conserv. aged 5; pupil there of Hubay (q.v.); later on staff. After touring Hungary and Central Europe as violinist settled U.S.A.; naturalized 1927. Conductor Minneapolis Symphony Orch. 1931–6; then Philadelphia Orch. (at first with Stokowski). D.Mus., New York and Pensylvania, &c.

Ornaments or **Graces.** These terms are applied to melodic decorations such as are not given in full in the notation but either (*a*) In vocal music (especially), added by the performer according to his or her own taste and invention, partly guided, in some instances, by convention (this practice was universal in the 18th c.), or (*b*) In vocal or instrumental music, indicated by the composer by a series of signs conventionally adopted everywhere (see Tables 12–16) but in some degree changing their meaning in various periods.

The practice alluded to under (*a*) above often led to remarkably florid embellishment of the music. It occurred not only in solo perf. but also in choral and orch., and even in the congregational singing of metrical psalms and hymns (in such uses as these it must often have led to clashes through the lack of unanimity on the part of the participants).

Ornithoparcus (real name Andreas Vogelsang). Author of celebrated theoretical book *Musicae activae micrologus* (Leipzig 1517. Eng. transl. by John Dowland, 1609).

Ornstein, Leo (b. Krementchug, Russia, 1895). Of Jewish ancestry; resident in U.S.A. since childhood. Studied Imperial Conserv. Petrograd, 1905–7. Gifted pianist; as composer for some time considered very advanced; orch., chamber, and piano works, &c.

Orpharion or **Orphareon.** See *Cittern*.

Orphée aux enfers (Eng. title, 'Orpheus in the Underworld'). Offenbach's very popular comic opera. (Prod. Paris 1858; New York 1861; London 1865.)

Orphée et Euridice. See *Orfeo*.

Orphéon (Fr.). Male-voice choral soc. The Orphéoniste movement began abt. 1835 and in 1880 there were 1,500 societies. Cf. *Wilhem*.

Orpheus. Symphonic Poem by Liszt. Written 1854 as an introduction to the composer's production at Weimar of Gluck's *Orfeo ed Euridice* (q.v.).

Orpheus and Euridice. See *Orfeo*.

Orpheus Fable (Monteverdi). See *Orfeo, La favola d'*.

Orpheus in the Underworld (Offenbach). See *Orphée aux Enfers*.

Orr, (1) **Charles Wilfrid** (b. Cheltenham 1893). Song composer, setting fine Eng. poetry, with special leaning to Housman's verse; also writer of critical articles in musical periodicals.

(2) **Robin** (b. Brechin 1909). Studied Cambridge (M.A., D.Mus.) and R.C.M., and in Paris under Nadia Boulanger. Fellow of St. John's College, Cambridge (Organist 1938–51), and University Lecturer in Music. Professor at R.C.M. 1950; Glasgow Univ. 1956; Cambridge 1965. Compositions include orchestral, choral, and chamber music, songs, &c.

Orthodox Church. See *Greek Church*.

Ortiz, Diego (mid-16th c.). Composer of church music, lute music, &c.; author of famous book on art of playing divisions (q.v.) on bass viol (1553).

O Salutaris Hostia. A hymn sung in the Roman Catholic Church at the service of Benediction and sometimes at other services. It has a very elaborate traditional plainsong borrowed from the Ascensiontide hymn, *Æterne Rex altissime*, and has also been set by various composers. J. M. Neale's translation is now an official alternative to *Gloria in Excelsis* in the Communion office of the Protestant Episcopal Church of America.

Osanna. It. form of 'Hosanna'.

Osborne, George Alexander (b. Limerick 1806; d. London 1893). Studied in Paris under Kalkbrenner and became friend of Berlioz and Chopin; settled in London as piano teacher; composed chamber music, violin music (33 duets in collaboration with de Bériot), and piano salon music (see *Pluie de Perles*).

Oscillators. See *Electric Musical Instruments 1*.

Ospedali. See *Schools of Music*.

Osservanza (It.). 'Observation', hence 'care'.

Ossia (It., lit. 'or may be'). This expression is attached to passages added by the composer (or some editor) as alternatives to the original—sometimes on grounds of greater facility (hence the ingenious bad guess of some young musicians that 'Ossia' is It. for 'Easier').

Ostinato (It.). 'Obstinate', 'persistent'. So *basso ostinato*, ground bass (q.v.).

Ostrčil, Ottokar (b. nr. Prague 1879; d. Prague 1935). School teacher turned musician; conductor and composer of operas, symphonies, &c., generally of intellectual appeal.

O'Sullivan, (1) **Denis** (b. San Francisco 1868; d. Columbus, Ohio, 1908). Operatic and concert baritone. Trained London under Santley, &c., and in Paris. Concert début London and opera début Dublin both 1895. High reputation Britain and U.S.A.

(2) **Donal** (b. Liverpool 1893). Antiquarian and folk-music expert. Studied London Univ.; Irish Bar 1922. Ed. Irish Folk-song journal 1920–39; books on Irish music.

Oswald, (1) **James** (b. Scotland abt. 1710; d. Knebworth, Herts., 1769). Dancing-master, organist, violinist, &c., in Edinburgh; settled in London (1741) and developed music publishing business; chamber composer to George III (1761).

(2) **Arthur Lewis** (b. Brighton 1858; d. 1932). Pianist; then baritone vocalist (studying R.A.M. and Milan). Operatic appearances Italy. Prof. R.A.M. (1886) and G.S.M. (1896).

Otello (Verdi). See *Othello*.

Ôter (Fr.). 'To take off.' *Ôte*, *ôtent* are the indicative 3rd person sing. and plur. (He 'takes off', they 'take off'.) *Ôtez* is the imperative, 'take off'; so *Ôtez les sourdines*, 'take off the mutes'.

In organ music this verb means to throw out of use some stop up to that point in use.

Otger (late 9th and early 10th cs.). Shadowy personage now supposed to be composer of some works formerly credited to Hucbald.

O that we were maying! See *Hullah*.

Othello (Overture by Dvořák). See *Triple Overture*.

Othello (*Otello*). Opera by Verdi. Libretto by Boito, after Shakespeare. (Prod. Milan 1887; New York 1888; London 1889.) The composer had been 15 years silent when this work appeared. Also opera by Rossini (1816).

Ottava (It., sometimes abbrev. '8va'). 'Octave.'

Expressions meaning 'At the 8ve higher' are *all' ottava* ('at the 8ve'), *ottava alta* ('high 8ve'), and *ottava sopra* ('8ve above').

Expressions meaning 'At the 8ve below' are *ottava bassa* ('low 8ve') and *ottava sotto* ('8ve below').

An expression meaning 'play in 8ves' is *coll' ottava* ('with the 8ve').

Ottetto. See *Octet*.

Otto (It.). 'Eight.'

Ottone (It.). 'Brass.'

Ou (Fr.). 'Or.' **Où** (Fr.). 'Where.'

Ours, L' ('The Bear'). Nickname for Haydn's Symphony in C, the first of the 'Paris Symphonies' (q.v.) and no.

82 (1786) of Breitkopf edn. of the Symphonies. The bagpipe-like theme of the finale suggests the performance of a bear-leader (others have heard a 'growling' theme in the bass in the same movt.).

Ouseley, Frederick Arthur Gore (b. London 1825; d. Hereford 1889). Son of Sir Gore Ouseley, Brit. Ambassador to Persia; remarkable child prodigy in music; succeeded father in baronetcy 1844; educated Oxford (M.A. 1849; D.Mus. 1854); ordained clergyman (1849); Precentor Hereford Cathedral (1855); Prof. of Music, Oxford (1855 to death). Founded St. Michael's Coll., Tenbury (1854), boys' school for general education and cultivation of church music (daily choral service; fine library); became its resident warden. Good pianist and organist (clever fugue extemporizer); composer of much church music, 2 oratorios, organ works, &c., exercising much influence both on condition of church music and that of music in universities; several theoretical works, now out of date. (See *Degrees*.)

Ouvert, ouverte (Fr. masc., fem.). 'Open.'

Ouverture (Fr.). 'Overture.'

Ouvrir (Fr.). 'To open.' The imperative is *ouvrez*—often used in organ music in connexion with the swell-box or in the sense of to put into action some stop mentioned.

Overblowing. See *Clarinet Family*.

Overdamper. See *Pianoforte*.

Over-stringing. See *Pianoforte*.

Overtones. See *Acoustics* 6, 7.

Overture has come to have 2 meanings: (a) A piece of instrumental music intended as the introduction to an opera, oratorio, &c.; (b) A piece of instrumental music (generally keyboard or orch.) modelled on such a piece but intended for independent performance.

There were in the 17th and 18th cs. 2 types, the *Italian Overture* with 3 movements, quick-slower-quick (see reference under *Symphony*); and the *French Overture*, also with 3 move-

ments, but slow-quick-slow (or relatively slow; often a dance such as the minuet, or, in some cases, the 1st movement repeated as a whole or in part).

In the later 18th c. Gluck, in his later operas, sought a more intimate correspondence between the overture and what was to follow, designing, as he said, 'to prepare the audience for the plot of the play'. Mozart had a similar ideal: as regards form his operatic overtures resemble the 1st movement of a symphony (see *Form* 3); sometimes he anticipated, by allusion, some of the music of the opera to follow. Beethoven (4 overtures written for the opera *Fidelio*, or *Leonora*) and Weber were similarly allusive. Wagner's *Mastersingers* overture (called Prelude) is a fine example of the anticipatory and allusive type. Carrying the idea further, there are overtures that are no mere introduction but a part of the work itself, e.g. Haydn's 'Chaos' overture to the oratorio *Creation* and Wagner's river music preceding *Rhinegold*. Wagner often uses the word *Vorspiel* ('Fore-play') for the instrumental introductions to his music-dramas. Descending to a lower level we find a sort of Medley Overture in use by some 19th-c. Fr. composers, as also by Sullivan, who made overtures to his comic operas by stringing together tunes from the work to follow. Many fine overtures have been written for spoken plays, e.g. Beethoven's to Goethe's *Egmont*.

The word overture has sometimes been used as the equivalent of 'Suite' (e.g. by Bach and Handel) and of 'Symphony' (e.g. Haydn in his London programmes in 1791).

The practice of using as concert pieces overtures originally written for operas or dramas (e.g. Mozart's *Figaro* overture, Beethoven's *Egmont* overture, &c.) suggested to composers the composition of independent single-movement works in overture style but for concert perf. So came into existence the *Concert Overture* (Mendelssohn's *Hebrides*, &c.). Some such works are in the form of the 1st movement of a symphony and others are indistinguishable from the *Symphonic Poem* (q.v.).

Overture, Scherzo, and Finale. See *Schumann's Symphonies.*

Ovvero (It.). 'Or.'

O.W., in Ger. organ music = *Oberwerk*, i.e. 'swell organ'.

Owen, (1) **John**, called 'Owain Alaw' (b. Chester 1821; there d. 1883). Chester organist; composed oratorio *Jeremiah*, cantata *The Prince of Wales* (said to be earliest Welsh cantata), glees, anthems, &c.; publ. collections of Welsh national airs (see *Land of my Fathers*).

(2) **William Henry** (b. Chester 1854; killed in railway accident at Abergele 1868). Composed Welsh anthems, &c., publ. by his father, John (above).

(3) **David**. See *Dafydd y Garreg Wen*; *Rising of the Lark*.

(4) **Wilfred** (1893–1918). See *War Requiem.*

O who will o'er the downs. See *Pearsall.*

Oxenford, Edward (b. 1847; d. Haddenham, Bucks., 1929). Copious provider of 'lyrics' for song writers— 7,000 original and others translated from almost every European language. Also librettist—about 200 operas, operettas, and cantatas.

Oxford and Cambridge Musical Club. See *Clubs for Music Making.*

Oxford Movement. See *Anglican Chant*; *Anglican Parish Church Music*; *Cathedral Music*; *Hymns and Hymn Tunes* 4.

Oxford Symphony. Nickname for Haydn's Symphony in G, no. 92 in Breitkopf edn. of the Symphonies. Perf. when Haydn visited the Univ. to receive his honorary D.Mus.

Oxford Triple Bob. See *Bell.*

Oxford University. See *Degrees.* The Professors of Music have been—1626 Richard Nicholson; 1639 Arthur Philipps; 1656 John Wilson; 1661 Edward Lowe (s.v. *Cathedral Music*); 1682 Richard Goodson; 1718 Richard Goodson (jun.); 1741 Wm. Hayes; 1777 Philip Hayes; 1797 Wm. Crotch; 1848 H. R. Bishop; 1854 F. A. G. Ouseley; 1889 John Stainer; 1900 C. H. H. Parry; 1908 Walter Parratt; 1918 Hugh P. Allen; 1946 J. A. Westrup; 1971 Joseph Kerman.

Oxford University Musical Club and Union. See *Clubs for Music Making.*

Oxford University Press. Founded 1478; music publishing dept. 1924 (London address, 44 Conduit Street, W. 1; New York address, 200 Madison Avenue).

Ox Minuet. Attributed to Haydn but by a musician called Von Seyfried, who introduced it into an opera called *Die Ochsenmenuett* (prod. Vienna 1823). There have been 3 operas on the queer story that Haydn wrote a minuet for a butcher who rewarded him with the gift of an ox.

Oxon. Oxford—from 'Oxonia', latinized name of 'Ox(en)ford'.

P

P. Short for *piano* (It.). 'Soft.' (See *PP*.)

P. in Fr. organ music is sometimes used for *Pédales*, i.e. Pedals, and sometimes for *Positif*, i.e. Choir Organ.

Paar (Ger.). When this word is used as an ordinary noun (with capital—Paar) it means 'Pair', 'couple'; otherwise it means 'Few' (*Ein paar*, 'A few').

Pacato; pacatamente (It.). 'Placid'; 'placidly'.

Pachelbel, (1) Johann (b. Nuremberg 1653; there d. 1706). Held various positions as organist; keyboard compositions important for influence on Bach. For his son see below. (2) **Wilhelm Hieronymus** (b. Erfurt abt. 1685; d. Nuremberg 1764). Son of Johann above, whose life and work his much resembled.

Pachmann, Vladimir de (b. Odessa 1848; d. Rome 1933). Pianist. Trained at Vienna Conserv.; appeared in public in Russia at age 21 but retired for further study till 29; came before public again and again retired for 2 years. From age 32 won highest international fame, especially as Chopin interpreter. Odd gestures and remarks addressed to audiences an amusing feature of his appearances. (Cf. *Oakey*.)

Pacific 231. By Honegger. Realistic locomotive tone-poem (1924).

Pacini, Giovanni (b. Catania 1796; d. Pescia 1867). Famous teacher of composition and himself composer of about 90 operas, orch. works, chamber music, &c.

Pack up your troubles in your old kit bag and smile! smile! smile! This song, which must have been worth many thousand men to the Brit. Empire and Amer. troops during the Great War of 1914–18, was the work of two Welsh brothers, George and Felix Powell, as poet and composer (the former professionaly known as 'George Asaf').

Paderewski, Ignacy Jan (b. Kurilowka, Russian Poland, 1860; d. New York 1941). Studied piano at Warsaw Conserv., later under Leschetizky in Vienna; climbed into highest popularity throughout civilized world as pianist; composed an opera, *Manru*, a piano concerto, a symphony, &c., but only 2 or 3 piano trifles (e.g. Minuet in G) widely known. After war of 1914–18 elected Prime Minister of Poland; during early part of war of 1939–45 Speaker of Polish Parliament assembled at Angers, France.

Padiglione (It.). 'Pavilion', 'tent'; hence (from the shape) the 'bell' of a wind instrument. (But *Padiglione cinese* = Turkish Crescent, q.v.)

Padovana. See *Pavan and Galliard*.

Paean. A song of triumph or praise (originally one to Apollo).

Paër, Ferdinando (b. Parma 1771; d. Paris 1839). Active opera conductor; wrote over 40 operas as well as cantatas and some orch. music; musical director at court of Napoleon I (1807).

Paesiello (or **Paisiello**), **Giovanni** (b. Taranto 1740; d. Naples 1816). Famous dramatic composer at courts of Joseph Bonaparte and Murat at Naples, Catharine the Great at St. Petersburg, and Napoleon I at Paris; good taste and simplicity features of his 100 operas; composed also symphonies, chamber music, many masses, &c.

Paganini, Niccolò (b. Genoa 1782; d. Nice 1840). Poor boy with natural talent for violin and almost superhuman perseverance in mastering and developing its technique, of which later players and composers have been able to reap advantage; travelled everywhere in Europe (Brit. tour 1831–2; profits £16,000); died of consumption. Composed violin concertos, caprices for violin alone, and other pieces (e.g. *La Campanella*, q.v., *Carnival of Venice*, q.v.); also some music for guitar, on which he was for a time a performer.

See entries below.

Paganini Quartet. A leading string quartet of U.S.A. Founded 1946; appeared in London from 1947. Name derived from the fact that the four instruments (all by Stradivarius) were once owned by Paganini: the leader (Henri Temianka) plays the violin used at his recitals and the viola is that for which Berlioz wrote *Harold in Italy* (q.v.).

Paganini Studies. See below.

Paganini Transcriptions, &c. The following are either piano transcriptions (more or less close) of Paganini's violin compositions or are piano pieces based on his themes:

BRAHMS: *28 Variations on a Theme of Paganini* (op. 35, 1866). Two books of 14 each. LISZT: *Grande Fantaisie de Bravoure sur la Clochette* (1831–2; on theme from B minor violin concerto, op. 7: same theme as *Campanella*—see below). *Études d'exécution transcendante d'après Paganini* (1838; transcription of 6 of Paganini's caprices: no. 3 is the celebrated *La Campanella*—see above). Revised and reissued 1851 as *Grandes Études de Paganini*. SCHUMANN: *Six Études de Concert, composées d'après des Caprices de Paganini. First set* (op. 3, 1832). *Six Études de Concert, composées d'après des Caprices de Paganini. Second set* (op. 10, 1833). RACHMANINOF. *Rhapsodie pour Piano et Orchestre* (op. 43, 1934). Twenty-four variations on same theme as that used by Brahms.

Pagan Requiem (Delius). See *Requiem*.

Paget, Richard Arthur Surtees (1869–1955). Legal authority and physicist. Authority on acoustics; author valuable research work, *Human Speech* (1930). Some compositions. Succeeded father in baronetcy 1908.

Pagliacci, I ('The Buffoons'). Tragedy-opera by Leoncavallo. Libretto by composer. (Prod. Milan under Toscanini 1892; London and New York 1893.)

Paine, John Knowles (b. Portland, Maine, 1839; d. Cambridge, Mass., 1906). Had thorough training in Germany; later became Instructor, asst. Prof., and finally (1875) Prof. of Music at Harvard Univ., which created for him the 1st Chair of Music in any Amer. univ. He composed much but his lasting influence has been through his university work.

Pair (Fr.). 'Even' (numbers), as opposed to *impair*, 'odd'.

Pair of Virginals. See *Harpsichord Family.*

Paisiello. See *Paesiello.*

Palabra (Sp.). 'Word.'

Paladilhe, Émile (b. nr. Montpellier 1844; d. Paris 1926). At Paris Conserv. won chief piano prize at age of 13 and Rome Prize at 16: later a prof. there. Of high repute as composer of operas.

Palate. The roof of the mouth, the front being the *Hard Palate* and the back (movable and closing or opening the passage to the nose) the *Soft Palate*.

Palcoscenico (It.). 'Stage.'

Palestine. See *Crotch.*

Palestrina, Alla (It.). 'In the style of Palestrina', i.e. *a cappella* (see *Cappella*).

Palestrina, Giovanni Pierluigi da (b. Palestrina, nr. Rome, probably 1525; d. Rome 1594). At about 18 organist and choirmaster of cathedral of native town (from which he takes his name); his bishop being elected Pope invited him to Rome (1551) as choirmaster of the Julian chapel in St. Peter's; he later occupied other similar positions in Rome, including, for a time, that of director of the music to his friend St. Philip Neri, founder of the oratorio (q.v.). His first publication of church music was in 1554 (dedicated to the Pope, the first ever so dedicated by an Italian, Flanders having for long supplied the capital of Christendom with its chief singers and composers: see *Dufay*; *Josquin des Prés*; *Willaert*; *Arcadelt*; *de Rore*; *Lassus*). In later years appeared many publications of masses, motets, &c., and also of madrigals, in all a mountain of fine unaccompanied choral music, sacred and secular, all of which has, after 2 centuries of comparative neglect, been republished and so made available for the use of those who regard it as ranking high amongst the greatest music ever written.

See also under *Baini*; *History of Music* 5; *Litaniae Lauretanae*; *Missa Papae Marcelli*; *Stabat Mater*.

Palestrina (Opera). See *Pfitzner*.

Palindrome. Properly a word or verse that reads the same backwards as forwards; hence applied to a composition on same principle.

Pallet. See *Organ* 1.

Palmer, Samuel Ernest (b. London 1858; there d. 1948). Business man (biscuit firm, Huntley & Palmer) and railway magnate. Created baronet (1916) and then Baron Palmer of Reading (1933); 1st man to be raised to peerage for services to music (Council R.C.M.; scholarships there; Patron's Fund (q.v.), Palmer's Opera Study Fund, &c.).

Palmgren, Selim (b. Björneborg, Finland, 1878; d. Helsinki 1951). Studied at Conserv. of Helsinki (otherwise Helsingfors), and then in Germany, with Busoni and others, and in Italy; became choral conductor, &c., in native city, making tours as pianist. Prof. of piano and composition in Eastman School of Music, Rochester, N.Y., 1921–6, then returned to Helsinki, where Chairman of Sibelius Foundation, &c. Composed operas, orch. works, piano concertos, and smaller piano pieces.

Palotache (properly *Palotás*). A Hungarian type of instrumental piece in dance style (2-in-a-measure)—a derivative of the Verbunkos (q.v.).

Pammelia. See *Ravenscroft, Thomas*.

Pan and the Priest. Symphonic Poem with piano obbligato, by Hanson. (Op. 26; 1st perf. Rome 1926.)

Pandean Pipes. See *Panpipes*.

Pandore. See *Cittern*.

Pandurina. A very small instrument of the lute type, strung with wire—probably the ancestor of the mandoline.

Pange, lingua. There are 2 hymns so opening:

(1) *Pange, lingua, gloriosi praelium certaminis.* Passion hymn by Venantius Fortunatus (530–609). A modification of J. M. Neale's translation of this is

often sung—'Sing, my tongue, the glorious battle, Sing the last, the dread affray'.

(2) *Pange, lingua, gloriosi corporis mysterium.* By St. Thomas Aquinas, written 1263, and modelled on 1. A translation based on J. M. Neale and E. Caswall is often sung—'Now, my tongue, the mystery telling'. This hymn was written for the feast of Corpus Christi, as a part of the Office (q.v.) for that day. *Tantum ergo* (q.v.) is a part of the hymn.

Each of the above has its own plainsong tune.

Panharmonicon. See *Mechanical Reproduction of Music* 8.

THE ROMAN SYRINX

Panpipes, Pandean Pipes, or Syrinx. An instrument of high antiquity and widespread use, consisting of a series of small wooden whistles, graduated in size to give the pitches of the different notes. It is held in front of the mouth and the player blows across the open ends of the whistles.

Panseron, Auguste Mathieu (b. Paris 1795; there d. 1859). Noted singing teacher; trained Paris Conserv. and later on staff. Wrote books on singing. Also composer (Prix de Rome at age 18), producing operas, church music, songs, &c.

Pantaleon. An elaborate dulcimer (q.v.) invented by a German, Pantaleon Hebenstreit (1667–1750): he travelled Europe with it, giving performances. Others seem also to have performed on it and to have kept it in use for some time after his death. A Worcester (England) newspaper of 1767, announcing a perf., describes it as being 11 feet in length and having 276 strings. The name was later transferred to a type of horizontal piano in which the hammers struck downwards, and also to a certain stop found in some harpsichords.

Pantomime (from the Gr., meaning 'all imitating'). (1) A species of entertainment (Gr. or Roman) in which the actors performed in dumb show (cf. *Mimodrama*; also 'Ballet d'Action', s.v. *Ballet*), whilst a 'chorus' described the purport of the acting and commented thereon. In this sense Gluck, Berlioz, Wormser (*The Prodigal Son*, 1890), Bartók, and others have used the word. (2) In Britain the word has become loosely applied to a sort of gay Christmas entertainment, bearing the title of (and ostensibly based upon) some traditional fairy-tale, or the like. At one time this sort of entertainment had more coherence than it now has (Arne, Dibdin, Shield, and other 18th-c. composers): until well into the 19th c. it made a good deal of certain characters (Harlequin, Columbine, Pantaloon, &c.) borrowed from the It. 'Commedia dell' Arte' (or play with written plot and extemporized dialogue): the clown's importance in such pantomime is said to have been established by Grimaldi (1779–1837). Many of the popular street songs of the year used (in the 19th and earlier 20th cs.) to come from the Christmas pantomimes.

Pantoum (or *Pantum, Pantun*). Properly the name of a type of poem introduced by Victor Hugo—based on a Malay type. Ravel has used the word as the description of the scherzo in his Piano Trio.

Panufnik, Andrzej (b. Warsaw 1914). Trained Warsaw Conserv. and under Weingartner. Conductor of Warsaw Philharmonic 1946; in Britain from 1954; cond. Birmingham Orch. 1957–9. Compositions, of advanced school, include symphony and other orch. works, choral music, &c.

Papillons ('Butterflies'). Schumann's op. 2 for Piano (1829–31). Twelve short dance pieces inspired by the masked-ball scene that closes Jean Paul Richter's *Flegeljahre* ('Age of Indiscretion').

Papini, Guido (b. nr. Florence 1847; d. London 1912). Distinguished violinist; as such and as teacher lived latterly in Dublin and London; composed tuneful music (solo and concerted) still enjoyed by violin students.

Pâque, Désiré—in full Marie Joseph Léon Désiré (b. Liège 1867; d. Bessancourt 1939). Pupil of Liège Conserv.; periods as teacher in various cities of Bulgaria, Greece, Portugal, and Germany; then in Paris and naturalized as French. Compositions included 8 symphonies, much chamber music, a requiem, &c.

Paradies (or **Paradisi**), **Pietro Domenico** (b. Naples 1707; d. Venice 1791). Harpsichord player and composer who lived in London for some years beginning 1747. Composed sonatas, &c. (best remembered today by a certain sparkling Toccata).

Paradise and the Peri. Cantata by Schumann, a setting of his own trans. of words from Moore's *Lalla Rookh*. (Op. 50, 1843.)

Paradise Lost. See *Markevich*.

Paradisi. See *Paradies*.

Parallel Motion. See *Motion*.

Paraphrases. Collection of Piano duets—3 hands (24 variations and 14 other pieces) based on *Chopsticks* (q.v.). By Borodin, Rimsky-Korsakof, and some of their Russian contemporaries, with one by Liszt.

Paray, Paul (b. Le Tréport 1886). At Paris Conserv. won Rome Prize; later career as conductor (Lamoureux 1923; Colonne 1944; Detroit 1952–64). Compositions include choral and orch. works, chamber music, &c.

Pardessus de Viole. See *Viol Family* 3 h.

Pardon de Ploërmel, Le (Meyerbeer). See *Dinorah*.

Parergon to the Symphonia Domestica. See under *Domestic Symphony*.

Paris—A Night Piece. The Song of a Great City. Symphonic Poem by Delius. (1899; 1st perf. Elberfeld 1901; London 1908.) It has been used for a ballet—*Nocturne*.

Paris, Aimé and **Nanine.** See *Galin-Paris-Chevé*.

Paris Conservatory. See *Schools of Music*.

Parish Church Music. See *Anglican Parish Church Music*.

Parish Clerk. This official for centuries exercised a strong musical influence in England. He was an important functionary. He was lower than the vicar but higher than the sexton, and these three constituted the salaried officials of the parish church. Amongst the duties the parish clerk came in time to perform were those of making or leading the responses in the service, pronouncing a loud 'Amen' at the end of every prayer and of the sermon, and giving out the metrical psalm, and, when on great occasions there was an anthem, that also. He would act as precentor (q.v.), giving the note for the psalm tune (or the 4 notes for the 4 voices) on his adjustable pitch-pipe. Often he taught the choir: occasionally he played the 'barrel organ' (see *Mechanical Reproduction of Music* 10) or 'finger organ'. He was, indeed, in many cases the chief musical functionary.

The London Parish Clerks constitute one of the City Livery Companies; it has now been in existence for 700 years, for it was incorporated by Henry III in 1232. It had a fine hall in Bishopsgate that was taken from it, another in Broad Lane that was burnt in the fire of London in 1666, and since 1671 a hall in Silver Street which was destroyed by enemy action in 1941. When James I and then Charles II renewed its Charter it was laid down that 'Every person that is chosen Clerk of a Parish shall first give sufficient proof of his abilities to sing at least the tunes which are used in parish churches'. A century later William Riley, in *Parochial Music Corrected*, says this test is no longer applied, but he makes it clear that the London clerks were not forgetful of their musical duties, for he says they hold weekly meetings in their hall 'where they sing psalms, accompanied by an organ, for about an hour'. The name of Clerkenwell recalls the fact that this district of London got its name (when it was still open fields) from the parish clerks' coming there once a year to perform mystery plays and moralities (see *Miracle Plays*).

Parisian Tones or **Parisian Gregorians.** The Gregorian Tones (q.v.) supposedly according to the ancient Use of Paris (cf. *Use of Sarum, Hereford, &c.*) but actually more according to the Use of Rouen. In the latter half of the 19th c. they had considerable popularity in 'high' Anglican circles.

Paris Symphonies (Haydn). A set of 6 written (abt. 1786) for the famous 'Concert Spirituel'—nos. 82–87 in Breitkopf edn. of the Symphonies.

See *Ours*; *Poule*; *Reine*.

Paris Symphony (Mozart). Nickname of one written in Paris in 1778 (in D; K. 297).

Parker, (1) **Louis Napoleon** (b. Calvados, France 1852; d. Bishops Teignton, Devon, 1944). Trained R.A.M. Then Director of Music, Sherborne School (1873). A pioneer in developing musical education in boys' boarding-schools, as later in introducing and developing the 'Pageant' (sort of open-air masque, q.v., based on history of locality). Successful playwright.

(2) **William Frye** (b. Dunmow 1855; d. 1919). Violinist. Trained R.A.M. (afterwards on staff). Début London 1871. Chief violin of Philharmonic Soc. 1895–1909 and of many festivals. Conductor Civil Service Orchestra, &c.

(3) **Horatio William** (b. Auburndale, Mass., 1863; d. Cedarhurst, N.Y., 1919). Studied in Munich with Rheinberger and then took various positions as organist in the eastern U.S.A. Prof. of Music Yale Univ. 1894 to death. Composed 2 prize operas and especially a series of choral-orch. works highly popular for a time at various West of England festivals (e.g. *Hora Novissima*, produced New York 1893; Worcester Fest., England, 1899;

Chester 1900, &c.). Hon. D.Mus., Cambridge, 1902.

See *Legend of St. Christopher*.

Parlando, parlante (It.). 'Speaking'—either literally or in style of perf.; for the latter see *Aria*; *Recitative*.

Parlato (It.). 'Spoken.'

Parma, Ildebrando da. See *Pizzetti*.

Parody. In a musical sense this word has its more general meaning, i.e. *in the style of* some previous work or making use of thematic and harmonic material, &c., from such a work. Hence 'Parody Mass', &c.

Parramon, R. See *Viole-Ténor*.

Parratt, Walter (b. Huddersfield 1841; d. Windsor 1924). Son of organist of Huddersfield parish church; himself followed organist's career including Magdalen Coll., Oxford (1872), and St. George's Chapel, Windsor Castle (1882 to death); great influence on standard of Brit. organ playing exercised largely through teaching at R.C.M. (1883 to death). Prof. of Music, Oxford, 1908–18; Hon. D.Mus., Oxford and Cambridge. Knighted 1892.

Parrott, (Horace) Ian (b. London 1916). Composer, conductor, writer on music. Studied R.C.M.; music scholar New College, Oxford (M.A., D.Mus.). Lecturer, Birmingham Univ. 1947–50; Prof. Univ. Coll., Aberystwyth, 1950. Compositions for orch., piano, &c.

Parry, (1) John (d. 1782). Famous blind Welsh harper and collector-editor of Welsh airs.

(2) **John,** known as 'Bardd Alaw' (b. Denbigh 1776; d. London 1851). Composed theatre music; wrote book on the harp; publ. collections of Welsh airs; also London music critic.

(3) **John Orlando** (b. London 1810; d. East Molesey 1879). Son of John (2) above. Very popular humorous singer; also composer of songs (e.g. *Flow gently, Deva*).

(4) **Joseph** (b. Merthyr Tydfil 1841; d. Penarth 1903). Spent part of early life in U.S.A.; compositions made him popular there and in Wales; sent by fund raised on both sides of Atlantic to R.A.M. 1868; became D.Mus., Cambridge (1878); held positions in Welsh univ. colls.; composed operas (see *Blodwen*), oratorios, cantatas, songs, &c.; several hymn tunes still widely sung (e.g. *Aberystwyth* to 'Jesu, Lover of my soul').

(5) **(Charles) Hubert (Hastings)** (b. Bournemouth 1848; d. Rustington, Sussex, 1918). Son of artist and country gentleman, Gambier Parry; began to compose at 8 and whilst still a schoolboy at Eton took B.Mus., Oxford; active in music whilst Oxford undergraduate; then entered business but joined staff of R.C.M., of which succeeded Grove as Director 1894; Prof. of Music, Oxford, 1900. Knighted 1898; created baronet 1903; many honorary doctorates. As composer very prolific, producing choral-orch. works for Eng. festivals, all of very Eng. character (*Blest Pair of Sirens*, a setting of Milton's 'At a Solemn Music', Bach Choir, London, 1887, one of finest works); purely instrumental compositions not so successful; many songs; a choral setting of Blake's *Jerusalem* (q.v.); unaccompanied motets, towards end of life, particularly admired. Wrote several thoughtful works (*Evolution of the Art of Music*; *Bach*; *Style in Musical Art*).

A great open-air man, constantly endangering his life (and many times injuring himself) on land or sea; genial, generous, and of highest ideals, and thus an inspiring force in Brit. music.

See also *Job*; *Judith*; *King Saul*; *Prometheus Unbound*.

Parsifal. Religious Music-drama by Wagner. Libretto by composer based on medieval legends; see *Grail*. (Prod. Bayreuth 1882; New York 1903; London 1914. But there were earlier concert performances in Britain and U.S.A.—London 1884, New York 1886.)

Parsley (Parslie, Persley, &c.), **Osbert** (b. 1511; d. 1585). For over half a century singing man of Norwich Cathedral, his qualities being recorded in a highly eulogistic epitaph on one of the pillars; composer of church music, some of which also exists in arrangements for viols.

Parsons, (1) Robert (b. Exeter; drowned in Trent at Newark 1570). Gentleman of Chapel Royal and famous as composer of church music.

(2) **John** (d. 1623). Probably son of Robert above. Organist of St. Margaret's, Westminster (1616), master of choristers of Westminster Abbey (1621); composed a Burial Service.

(3) **Sir William** (b. 1746; d. London 1817). Choir-boy of Westminster Abbey; studied in Italy; became Master of the King's Music (1786); D.Mus., Oxford (1790); when in Ireland knighted by Viceroy (1795). London police magistrate.

(4) **Sir Chas. A.** See *Auxetophone*.

(5) **William** (b. Bristol 1907). Basso cantante. Trained R.C.M. Opera and concert appearances; radio, &c. European tours.

Part (Fr. *partie* or *voix*; It. *parte* or *voce*; Ger. *Part* or *Stimme*). In concerted music of any kind a single line of notes to be performed by any instrument or voice, or group of instruments or voices. *Part-writing* means that aspect of the process of composition which consists in the devising of the parts for the different participants. (See also *Part Song*.)

Partant pour la Syrie ('Departing for Syria'). This song passed as the composition of Queen Hortense (Hortense de Beauharnais, daughter of Josephine by her 1st marriage), and was appointed as the official march for fest. use during the reign of her son, Napoleon III, so superseding for a time the Marseillaise. It is now thought that the real author of the words was Count Alex. de Laborde (1774–1842), and that the music was largely the work of the Dutchman Philip Drouet (1792–1873), a solo flute player to the Court of Holland under Hortense's husband, Louis Napoleon, and then to the court of Napoleon Bonaparte in Paris, and afterwards a flute manufacturer in London, conductor of various orchs. and for a time resident in New York.

Parte, parti (It.). 'Part', 'parts'. So *colla parte*, 'with the (solo) part', i.e. much the same as *col canto*; *a tre parti*, 'in 3 parts' (i.e. 3 vocal or instrumental strands).

Parthenia (Gr. 'maidens' songs'). The 1st book of music publ. in England for the virginal (see *Harpsichord Family*). Its date is 1611, but it has been republ. in 1847 and 1908. The composers represented are Byrd, Bull, and O. Gibbons. A companion work, *Parthenia Inviolata*, was also publ.: of this only 1 copy exists (New York Public Library).

Partials. As explained under *Acoustics* 6, an individual note heard is not, as we are apt to imagine, a mere single sound, but a sound plus its *Overtones* (see *Acoustics* 7). All these sounds so heard in combination are 'Partials', the main note (or 'fundamental note') being called *First Partial* and the rest the *Upper Partials*. (Note that the term 'Upper Partial' and the term 'Harmonic' have not necessarily the same significance, since certain sound-producing agents, used in certain ways, can evoke Upper Partials that are inharmonic; cf. *Voice* 13.)

Partie. See *Part*; *Suite*.

Partita (It.). Usually this means 'Suite' (q.v.): occasionally, however, it means 'Air with Variations'. (For Bach's choral Partitas see under *Choral Prelude*.)

Partition (Fr.), **partitura** or **partizione** (It.), **Partitur** (Ger.). 'Score.'

Partito (It.). 'Divided.'

Partiturophone. See *Electric Musical Instruments* 1.

Part-song. Etymologically any song composed in parts, i.e. for several voices. In practice, however, restricted, excluding compositions of the types of madrigal (q.v.) and glee (q.v.). It may be defined as a composition for male, female, or mixed voices, not markedly contrapuntal in style (as the madrigal is) but rather of the nature of a melody in the highest voice with accompanying harmonies in the other voices, and not divided into little separate movements each closely representing the feeling of a section of the poem set (as the glee is), but either through-composed (see *Durchkomponiert*), or (more often) verse-repeating (strophic). The nearest historical resemblance is to the ayre (see *Madrigal*), but that, like the madrigal proper and the glee, was intended to be sung by 1 voice to a part whereas the part-song is intended for several or many voices to a part.

The normal part-song has no instrumental accompaniment. There exist, however, 'Accompanied Part Songs', employing the pianoforte or orch.

The part-song style dates from the early 19th c. and seems to have had its origin in the great extension of choral soc. activities which took place during that century. It is very much a Brit. style (Pearsall, Goss, Hatton, Smart, Barnby, Stanford, Elgar, &c.), but there are many part-song composers in the U.S.A., and in Germany there have been composers of much the same kind of thing (Schubert, Schumann, Abt, Mendelssohn, &c.).

Pas (Fr.). (1) 'Not', 'not any'. (2) 'Step' (see below).

Pas d'acier, Le ('The Step [or Tread] of Steel'; paraphrased as 'The Age of Steel'). Ballet by Prokofief (op. 41, 1924; prod. Paris and London 1927). Also as 'Symphonic Suite'.

Pas d'action. A ballet with a dramatic basis.

Pas de basque (Fr.). In ballet, an alternating step, with one foot on the floor all the time—a little step used as contrast with bigger ones and as a connecting link. (See also *Basques*.)

Pas d'echarpes (Fr.). 'Scarf dance.'

Pas de deux (Fr.). (1) Any stage dance for 2 performers. (2) A particular dance of the early 18th c., something like the gavotte.

Pasdeloup, Jules Étienne (b. Paris 1819; d. Fontainebleau 1887). Trained Paris Conserv.; later on staff. Became able orch. conductor and concert organizer, 'Concerts Pasdeloup' greatly extending Fr. orch. repertory.

Pas de quatre. Any stage dance for 4 performers.

Pas glissé (Fr.). In ballet, a single gliding step.

Pasodoble. A kind of lively one-step (q.v.), though the name means 'double-step'. It became popular in the early 20th c. The music is in compound duple time.

Pasquier Trio (brothers Jean, Étienne, Pierre). A leading French string trio, formed 1930, first visited London 1934.

Pasquini, Bernardo (b. nr. Lucca 1637; d. Rome 1710). Organist, &c., in Rome, and director there of the concerts of Queen Christiana of Sweden; famous as performer and teacher. Composed operas, oratorios, and (most important) work for harpsichord and organ.

Passacaglia. See *Chaconne and Passacaglia*.

Passage work. This term usually implies inferior quality in composition, being applied to some part of a piece serving as 'padding' and usually calling for rapid and brilliant execution, upon which its effect depends.

Passamezzo or **passemezzo** (It. 'pace-and-a-half'). An old dance in 2-beats-in-a-measure time.

Passecaille (Fr.). 'Passacaglia' (see *Chaconne and Passacaglia*).

Passemezzo. See *Passamezzo*.

Passend (Ger.). 'Fitting' (cf. *Commodo*).

Passepied (Fr. 'pass-foot') or **paspy** (Eng.). A gay, rapid dance, in 3-in-a-measure time. (Debussy incorrectly uses the term for a piece in 2-in-a-measure.)

Pas seul. A stage dance for 1 performer.

Passing by. Song. Words not by Herrick (as often stated) but from Ford's *Musick of Sundry Kinds* (1607): music not by Henry Purcell (as also stated) but by 'Edward C. Purcell'—really E. Purcell Cockram (d. 1932).

Passing note. See Harmony 2 g.

Passing of Beatrice. See *Wallace, William*.

Passionato; passionatamente (It.). 'Passionate'; 'passionately'. *Passionatissimo* is the superlative.

Passione (It.). 'Passion.'

Passione, La ('The Passion'). Nickname for Haydn's Symphony in F minor, no. 49 in Breitkopf edn. of the Symphonies.

Passion Music. The practice of setting to music the Passion of Christ, for perf. during Holy Week, has 2 connected origins—the old mysteries (see

Miracle Plays) and (a more direct and obvious source) a very ancient Holy Week practice of reading or reciting in church, in a more or less dramatic fashion, the story of the Passion of Christ. It is known to have existed in the 4th c.; by the 8th its character is determined as follows: a priest recited, in Latin, the story of the Passion from one of the Gospels, in a speaking voice except for the words of Christ, which he gave out to a traditional plainsong. By the 12th c. the general method had become a little more elaborate. Three of the clergy took part, a tenor as Narrator, a bass as Christ, and an alto as the Crowd (Turba). By the 15th c., the art of composition being now advanced to a sufficient point, Passions of a somewhat more elaborate character, musically, became common. The Reformation brought a further development. The Ger. (Lutheran) reformers, acting on their principle that the people should be able to follow the words of the service, adapted it to the Ger. language.

A parting of the ways had now come. The old Lat. form remained in use in Roman Catholic countries, the modern form in Germany and northern Europe generally. Amongst those who set the Passion in Latin during the 16th c. were Lassus, Victoria, and Byrd. Outstanding examples of the Ger. type of Passion are the settings of Schütz (1585–1672). He adopted a type of recitative that doubtless derived from the new It. style (see *Recitative, Opera* 1, and *Oratorio*), but that also had considerable affinity with the old plainsong. The whole works are without any instrumental parts, so presumably this recitative was to be sung unaccompanied, though some think that an organ was used. The various characters are allotted to different vocal soloists. The choruses are frequently dramatic in character, but are contrapuntal. The music is very austere in feeling.

The Passion reached its highest point with the work of Bach. He wrote 5 settings, including one according to each gospel, of which only those of St. Matthew and St. John and a part of that of St. Mark are now extant (there is a *St. Luke Passion*, partly in

his handwriting, which is not thought to be a work of his). The *St. Matthew Passion* (q.v.) is, by general consent, technically, emotionally, and devotionally the greatest work of its kind ever written. The forces employed are large—soloists, double chorus (with in one case an additional unison chorus of sopranos), double orch., and organ. Chorales are interspersed as reflection or personal application by the congregation of the lessons of the events of the story; it is uncertain whether these were intended to be sung by or merely to the congregation—most likely by them; they are, however, very subtly harmonized.

Pasta, Giuditta—*née* Negri (b. Saronno, nr. Como, 1798; d. in that district 1865). Operatic soprano of extended compass and high dramatic qualities. Before public 1815–50, but during last part of period with diminished powers. Husband was operatic tenor.

Pasticcio (It. 'pie' or 'pasty'). As applied to music—(1) A medley, especially one of operatic character in which favourite airs from previous operas (often by different composers) were worked into a new scheme with a new libretto: such entertainments were popular in the 18th c. The words *Cento* and *Centone* (It.) and *Centon* (Fr.) have also been applied to such works. (2) An opera in which each act is written by a different composer. (3) An instrumental composition of which different sections are the work of different composers.

Pastiche (Fr.). Same as It. *Pasticcio* (q.v.).

Pastoral. (1) From the 15th c. to the 18th a type of stage work embodying music, ballet, &c.—really a forerunner of the opera, but continuing after opera had come into being. (2) A type of instrumental composition generally in a compound time (e.g. 6/8 or 12/8) and with something of a musette (bagpipe) suggestion.

Pastoral ('Lie strewn the white flocks'). By Bliss. Choral-orch. Suite; a setting of poems by various authors (1st perf. London 1929).

Pastorale (Fr.). Pastoral (q.v.).

Pastoral Sonata (Beethoven). For Piano. In D major, op. 28. The name was added by the publisher.

Pastoral Symphony. (1) By HANDEL. Orch. movement in *Messiah*, depicting the calm of the 1st Christmas Eve. Its melody is said to be one heard by the composer in Italy, played by shepherds on their bagpipes, and there is a suggestion of the 'drone' effect of those instruments. (2) By BEETHOVEN. The 6th of his Symphonies (1826; op. 68, in F). A piece of Programme Music; the title is authentic and the movements also have titles, showing their inspiration in scenes of nature and country life. (1st perf. Vienna 1808; London 1811.) (3) By VAUGHAN WILLIAMS. (1st perf. London and Norfolk, Conn., 1922.) It has a touch of vocal tone at the end—wordless modal tune sung by a distant soprano.

Pastoso (It. 'soft' or 'sticky', from *Pasta*, 'Paste', 'dough'). The application of this adj. to musical perf. calls for an effort of the imagination: 'Soft', 'mellow' are suggestions given in some musical books of reference in English.

Patent Notes. See *Lancashire Sol-fa*.

Pater Dominicus Mass (Mozart). See *Dominicus Mass*.

Paterson & Sons. Scottish music publishers (27 George Street, Edinburgh; and elsewhere). Founded 1819.

Patetico (It.). 'Pathetic.' So *pateticamente*, 'pathetically'.

Patey, (1) **Janet Monach**—*née* Whytock (b. London 1842; d. Sheffield 1894). Contralto vocalist. Considered in Britain greatest concert and oratorio contralto of her day and popular also on continent and in U.S.A. Married J. G. Patey (see below). (2) **John George** (b. Stonehouse, Devon, 1835; d. Falmouth 1901). Baritone vocalist. Popular opera, oratorio, and concert artist (later music publisher). Husband of the above.

Pathetic Sonata (Beethoven). See *Grande Sonate Pathétique*.

Pathetic Symphony. See *Tchaikovsky's symphonies*.

Pathétique (Fr.), **pathetisch** (Ger.). 'Pathetic'. So *Pathétiquement* (Fr.), 'pathetically'.

Patience, or Bunthorne's Bride. Comic opera by Gilbert and Sullivan. (Prod. Opéra Comique, London, also St. Louis and New York 1881.)

Patimento (It.). 'Suffering.'

Patrem Omnipotentem. See *Mass*.

Patrick (or **Pattrick**), (1) **Nathaniel** (d. 1595). Organist of Worcester Cathedral and active as composer of church music (some still in use).
  (2) **Richard.** Lay-vicar of Westminster Abbey, abt. 1616–abt. 1625. Mentioned here merely to avoid the confusion that occurs between him and Nathaniel, above.
  (3) **Millar** (b. Ladybank, Fife, 1868; d. Edinburgh 1951). Ecclesiastic, hymnologist, and chief originator of the *Scottish Students' Songbook* (1891); author of monumental *Four Centuries of Scottish Psalmody* (1948). M.A., D.D., St. Andrews.

Patrie Overture. See *Bizet*.

Patron's Fund. R.C.M. fund, gift of Lord Palmer (see *Palmer, Ernest*) in order to enable young composers and performers to gain a hearing. Concerts and rehearsals are given at the R.C.M., participants not being confined to its students or former students.

Patterson, Banjo. See *Waltzing Matilda*.

Patter Song. A type of song having a rapid iteration of a string of words.

Patti, (1) **Adelina**—really Adela Juana Maria Patti (b. Madrid 1843; d. in her castle of Craig-y-Nos, Wales, 1919). Coloratura soprano vocalist of unrivalled fame. Of It. parents, both vocalists, who settled in New York when she was child. Appeared in public at 7; in England, in opera, at 18; henceforward welcomed, admired, and lavishly remunerated, in all civilized countries. Retired 1907 (appearing once for charity 1914). Three times married (see *Nicolini* 2). (2) **Carlotta** (b. Florence 1835; d. Paris 1889). Like sister, above, coloratura soprano.

Favourite concert singer (debarred from opera by lameness). Finally a singing teacher in Paris.

Pattrick. See *Patrick*.

Patzak, Julius (b. Vienna 1898). Tenor. Member State Opera, Munich, 1928–45. Since 1946 State Opera Vienna; on staff Conserv. there from 1948. Recitalist, concert artist, in many European centres.

Pauer, (1) **Ernst** (b. Vienna 1826; d. nr. Darmstadt 1905). Pianist, teacher (R.C.M., &c.), author of books on music, composer, &c. In London 1852–96. For son see below. (2) **Max** (b. London 1866; d. Jugenheim 1945). Pianist. Pupil of father (above). London début 1885. On staff of various conservs. (1924–32 head of that of Leipzig). Toured U.S.A., &c. Piano compositions and arrangements.

Pauken (Ger., plur. of 'Pauke'). 'Kettledrums' (see *Percussion Family* 1 a).

Paukenmesse ('Kettledrum Mass'). Popular name for Haydn's 10th Mass, in C. The composer called it *Missa in tempore belli* ('War-time Mass').

Paukenschlag ('Drumstroke'). Symphony by Haydn. See under *Surprise*.

Paukenwirbel (Haydn). See *Drum-Roll Symphony*.

Paul, Lady Dean. See *Poldowski*.

Paulus ('St. Paul'). See *Mendelssohn*.

Pausa (It.). 'Rest' (not 'pause', which is 'fermata').

Pause (Eng.). The sign ⌢, indicating that the note, chord, or rest over which it appears is to be prolonged at the performer's will.

It is occasionally placed over a bar line, indicating a short silence. Another use sometimes made of the sign is to intimate that the composition is finished; it is then placed over the final double bar and corresponds to 'finis' in a book.

Pause (Fr.). (1) 'Pause.' (2) 'Rest', especially (*a*) Semibreve (whole-note) rest (thus *demi-pause* means minim or half-note rest) and (*b*) Measure rest (whatever the length of the measure).

Pause (Ger.). (1) 'Pause.' (2) 'Rest.'

Pavana. See *Pavan and Galliard*.

Pavan and Galliard. The Pavan was of It. origin, and as the name sometimes appears as *Padovana* it is assumed that its original home was Padua, the once-accepted derivation of the word from Lat. *Pavo*, peacock, being now generally discredited. It was in simple duple time, and stately in character. Old forms of the word are *Pavin, Pavyn, Pavane, Pavana, Paven*, &c.

With the Pavan was often associated the Galliard (or Gagliarda), in simple triple time, rapid and, as the name implies, gay (cf. *Nachtanz*). A group of 5 steps was a feature and hence it was sometimes called *Cinque passi* (It.), *Cinque pas* (Fr.), and *Cinque pace* or *Sink-a-pace* (Eng.). The association of these 2 contrasted dances was the origin of the Suite (q.v.).

Pavane. See *Pavan and Galliard*.

Pavane pour une infante défunte ('Pavane for a Dead Infanta'). By Ravel. For piano (1899; 1st perf. Paris 1902); also existing in a version for small orch. (1910). It recalls the old Spanish court custom of a solemn ceremonial-dance on occasions of mourning.

Paven. See *Pavan and Galliard*.

Paventato, paventoso (It.). 'Timid.'

Pavillon (Fr.). 'Pavilion', 'tent'; hence (from the shape) the 'Bell' of a wind instrument. But *pavillon chinois* = Turkish Crescent (q.v.).

Pavin. See *Pavan and Galliard*.

Pavlova. See *Ballet*.

Pavyn. See *Pavan and Galliard*.

Paxton, (1) **Stephen** (b. London 1735; there d. 1787). 'Cellist and famous composer of part-songs and glees. For his brother see below. (2) **William** (b. 1737; d. 1781). Like his brother (above) 'cellist and composer of glees (e.g. *Breathe soft, ye winds*).

Payne, Albert (b. Leipzig 1842; there d. 1921). Son of an Eng. music publisher in Leipzig. Trained at Leipzig Conserv. and then entered family business, creating the series of miniature scores that bore his name (in 1892 taken over by Eulenburg).

Peabody Conservatory, Baltimore. See *Schools of Music*.

Peace, Albert Lister (b. Huddersfield 1844; d. Liverpool 1912). Organist from age 9; from 1897 to death at St. George's Hall, Liverpool. Composer of church and organ music. D.Mus., Oxford.

Peal. The sound made by a ring of bells. (See *Bell* 3.)

Pearl Fishers (Bizet). See *Pécheurs de perles*.

Pears, Peter (b. Farnham 1910). Operatic and concert tenor. Organ scholar Hertford Coll., Oxford; then schoolmaster. Scholarship R.C.M.; also lessons Elena Gerhardt. Joined New Eng. Singers. Glyndebourne Opera 1938; Sadler's Wells Co. 1943. Much associated with Britten; great success in *Peter Grimes*, &c.

Pearsall, Robert Lucas de (b. Clifton, Bristol, 1795; d. Wartensee, Lake Constance, 1856). Practised at the bar; then settled in Germany, studying works of Eng. madrigal school and composing (often finely) on their model; also composed church music (e.g. *In dulci jubilo*), choral ballads, &c. (popular part-song, *O who will o'er the downs so free?*). Was a poet and of romantic temperament (the 'de' of his name was his own addition).

Pearson, H. H. See *Pierson*.

Peasant Cantata (Ger. *Bauerncantate*). Humorous cantata by Bach (1742). The libretto, by Picander, turns on the rustic rejoicings on the appointment of a new local official.

Peasgood, Osborne Harold (b. London 1902; d. there 1962). Sub-organist Westminster Abbey. Trained R.C.M. (later on staff). Lecturer Reading Univ. D.Mus. Dublin. C.V.O. 1953.

Peau (Fr.). 'Skin' (e.g. of a drumhead).

Pêcheurs de Perles, Les ('The Pearl Fishers'). Tragedy-opera by Bizet. (Prod. Paris 1863; London 1887; Philadelphia 1893.)

Pedal. This word has a great variety of applications in music. See *Harmony* 2 i, *Harp*, *Organ*, *Pianoforte*, *Pianoforte Playing and Teaching*, and *Trombone Family*.

On the various members of the *Saxhorn Family* (q.v.) 'Pedal C' is the C below middle C (i.e. notationally, the actual pitch differing with different members of the family), and so for other notes in this range ('Pedal D', &c.).

Pedal Drums are such as have their pitch changed by means of pedals.

Pedal Board. See *Organ*; *Pianoforte*.

Pedal Clarinet. See *Clarinet Family*.

Pedalcoppel (Ger.). 'Pedal coupler.'

Pedale (It.). 'Pedal' or 'pedals'.

Pedalflügel (Ger.). 'Pedal piano' (grand).

Pedalgebrauch (Ger.). 'Pedal-use' (in piano playing).

Pedalier. (1) The pedal-board of an organ. (2) A similar pedal-board attached to a harpsichord (Bach composed for this) or piano (Schumann composed for this).

Pedaliera (It.). 'Pedal-board.'

Pedalpauken (Ger.). Mechanically tuned kettledrums (tuned by pedals). (See *Percussion Family* 1 a.)

Pedrell, Felipe (b. Tortosa, Catalonia, 1841; d. Barcelona 1922). Choirboy in cathedral of Tortosa; self-taught student of music; opera produced at Barcelona, 1874, first made him known; on staff of Madrid Conserv. (1894-1904), and then in Barcelona till death. Composed orch. music, cantatas, church music, chamber music, and songs; wrote books on Spanish music of past, and ed. complete works of Victoria and much other Spanish music. Importance lies in the inspiration he gave to Spanish composers to cultivate a national style.

Peel, Graham—in full Gerald Graham Peel (b. nr. Manchester 1877; d. Bournemouth 1937). Composer of a large number of popular and attractive songs.

Peerce, Jan (orig. Jacob Pincus Perelmuth) (b. New York 1904). Opera and concert tenor. Educ. Columbia Univ.; at first violinist and singer on lighter side; opera début Philadelphia 1938; Metropolitan 1941; then international career.

Peer Gynt. Incidental Music by Grieg to Ibsen's play. Composed 1875; later arranged for Piano 4 hands and then as 2 Orch. Suites. Also Opera by Werner Egk (q.v.).

Peerson, Martin (b. probably nr. Ely abt. 1572; d. London 1651). Organist of St. Paul's Cathedral, London; composer of ayres, instrumental music, &c.

Peeters, Flor (b. Thielen, Belgium, 1903). Organist; notable recitalist; on staff Ghent Conserv. from 1931; from 1952 dir. Antwerp Conserv.; active composer for his instrument and author of an exhaustive organ method.

Peine (Fr.). The expression *à peine* means 'scarcely', 'hardly at all'.

Peiris, H. C. J. See *Sena, Devar Surya.*

Pelléas et Mélisande. (1) Opera by DEBUSSY. (Prod. Paris 1902; New York 1908; London 1909.) A setting of Maeterlinck's play (prod. 1892). (2) Incidental Music by SIBELIUS (op. 46), for same play. (3) Incidental Music by FAURÉ (op. 80, 1898; written for London perf. same year). (4) Symphonic Poem by SCHÖNBERG (op. 5, 1903). (5) Early Overture by CYRIL SCOTT.

Pelletier, Wilfrid (b. Montreal 1896). Studied in Paris. Asst. conductor Metropolitan Opera, New York 1916; chief conductor 1932–50. Many other operatic activities—Ravinia Park (q.v.), San Francisco, &c.

Pendant (Fr.). 'During.'

Penderecki, Krzystof (b. Debica, Poland, 1933). Studied at Superior School of Mus. in Cracow; later on staff. Compositions, much performed at international festivals, are original both as to style and notation.

Pénélope. Opera by Fauré. Libretto by R. Fauchois. (Prod. Monte Carlo and Paris 1913.)

Pénétrant (Fr.). 'Penetrating.'

Penillion. An ancient yet still existing form of singing known only in Wales. It consists in singing extemporized verses or set poems in counterpoint to some well-known melody which is played in a harmonized version by a harper.

Pentatonic Scale. See *Scale.*

Penthesilea. Symphonic Poem by Hugo Wolf (1883). Based, via Kleist's tragedy, on the Gr. legend of the Amazon Queen.

Pepusch, John Christopher (b. Berlin 1667; d. London 1752). Settled in London abt. 1700, and was active as player in theatre orch., adapter of stage musical works (chose and arranged music for Gay's *Beggar's Opera*, q.v., 1728), and organist. Learned theorist and teacher of composition. D.Mus., Oxford, 1713; Fellow of Royal Soc. Wife was the great singer Margarita de l'Epine.

Pepys, Samuel (b. 1633; d. 1703). Admiralty official whose diary (1660–9) records many interesting facts and incidents in London musical life.

Per (It.). 'By', 'in order to', &c.

Percossa (It.). 'Percussion.'

Percussion Band. See *Rhythm Band.*

Percussion Family. This is probably the most ancient instrumental family in existence and is certainly the most primitive family represented in modern orch. and band combinations. Members of the family in such use are:

(1) INSTRUMENTS OF DEFINITE PITCH. (*a*) The KETTLEDRUM (It. *Timpano*; plur. *Timpani*). An inverted bowl of metal with, stretched over its open end, a membrane of which the tension can be increased or decreased by turning screws (in *Machine Drums*) or by some mechanical method. The playing is by means of 2 drumsticks, with heads of material which varies according to the tone-quality desired. Up to and including Beethoven the orch. player had 2 kettledrums normally tuned to the Tonic and Dominant (*Doh* and *Soh*) of the key in use: nowadays he has usually 3, and sometimes more. Both repeated notes and rolls are played. Forms of 'muffling' (= muting, see *Mute*) are possible. Most composers up to and including Mozart notated for the kettledrums as one of the 'transposing instruments' (q.v.), the part being written in Key C (i.e. the notes shown being C and G) and the actual pitch of the 2 notes being indicated at the outset by some such indication as *Timpani in D, A* (according to the key

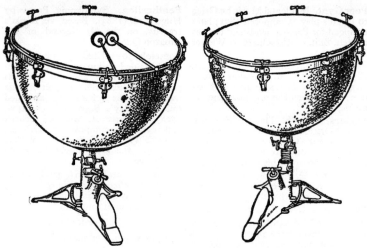

THE KETTLEDRUMS

of the piece). The current method is to show the actual notes to be played—except that sharps or flats are indicated merely in the preliminary notification and not otherwise. (*b*) BELLS. The normal orch. form is that of *Tubular Bells*, hung on a wooden frame and struck by drum-sticks. About an 8ve of notes can be played, generally a diatonic scale but sometimes a chromatic one. Thus simple actual tunes are possible. (*c*) GLOCKENSPIEL (Ger. 'Bell-play').

THE GLOCKENSPIEL

A set of steel plates, played, dulcimer-wise, with 2 little hammers. (See also *Bell Lyra*.) There is a form with tubes instead of plates and played from a key-

board—the TUBOPHONE. (*d*) CELESTA. Like the Glockenspiel but with wooden resonators under the steel plates, giving

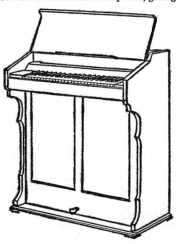

THE CELESTA

an ethereal quality of tone: it is operated from a keyboard. (*e*) DULCITONE (in Fr. 'Typophone'). Like the Celesta but with a series of tuning-forks as the sound-producing agent. It is rarely used orchestrally. (*f*) XYLOPHONE. A graduated series of hard wooden bars, played with 2 beaters held in the hands.

left clear for the use of 2 drumsticks. It can be muted by placing a handkerchief or a wooden wedge between the snares and the parchment. (*j*) TENOR DRUM.

THE SIDE DRUM

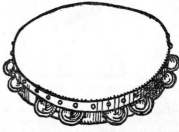

THE TAMBOURINE

Some examples now possess resonators and so fall, properly, into the class mentioned below. (*g*) MARIMBA. A sort of xylophone (see above) of which each wooden bar has under it a gourd (in the primitive instruments) or metal

Larger than the above and without snares. It is little used in the orch. (*k*) BASS DRUM. The biggest drum now in use. It has no snares. (*l*) TABOR or TABORET (see *Recorder Family* 2). It is in occasional orch. use. (*m*) TAMBOURINE. A shallow wooden hoop with a

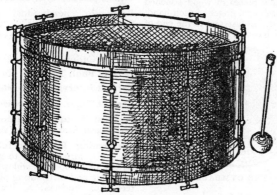

THE BASS DRUM

resonator (in the sophisticated ones). See *Marimba*. (*h*) MARIMBA GONGS. Like the Marimba but with metal plates instead of wooden bars.

(2) INSTRUMENTS OF INDEFINITE PITCH. (*i*) SIDE DRUM or SNARE DRUM. A small cylindrical drum with parchment at each end, one end having strings (*snares*) across it, to add a rattling effect and so increase the brilliance of the tone, the other end being

parchment head: the hoop has circular metal *jingles* inserted. It is played by striking with the knuckles, or (to produce a continuous sound from the jingles) shaking or rubbing the thumb over the parchment. (*n*) TRIANGLE. A small steel bar bent into 3-cornered shape and played by striking with a small metal rod. (*o*) CYMBALS. Plates of brass with leather handles. They are played by being held one in each hand

and clashed together—or fixed in a contrivance enabling the foot to promote the clashing; or one can be fixed to the side of the big drum and the

THE TRIANGLE

other clashed on to it; or they can be rattled at their edges; or a single cymbal can be struck with a drumstick or a roll performed on it with drumsticks. (See also *Chinese Crash Cymbal*; *Choke Cymbals*; *Sizzle Cymbal*; *Sting Cymbal*.) (*p*) GONG. A big, round sheet of metal turned up at the edge so as to form a sort of dish. It is beaten with a soft drumstick. (*q*) CASTANETS. A distinctively Spanish instrument. Two small hollow pieces of wood attached to the thumb or a finger of each hand, or (in the orch.) fastened to the end of a stick which can be shaken as required.

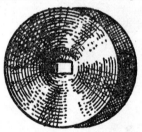

THE CYMBALS

(*r*) RATTLE. A small frame bearing strips of wood, revolved so that they catch in the cogs of a wheel. (*s*) ANVIL. An imitative instrument of steel bars and a striker: Wagner's *Rhinegold* calls for 18 such instruments in 3 different sizes. (*t*) JAZZ STICK. A 'slap-stick' of flapping wood. (*u*) RUSTLING TIN SHEET. (*v*) THUNDER STICK, BULL ROARER, or WHIZZER (see *Thunder Stick*). (*w*) WIRE BRUSHES. Used for producing a characteristic effect from the snare drum, cymbals, &c. (*x*) TYPEWRITER. Used in a few orch. compositions. (*y*) BIG IRON

CHAINS. Prescribed by Schönberg in the score of his *Gurrelieder*. When, however, this point is reached in the list 'anything is possible' and further

THE CASTANETS

particularization may be abandoned, leaving one letter of the alphabet still unused. (For a pretty detailed history of the gradual introduction of the various percussion effects see *OCM*.)

Perdendo, perdendosi (It., lit. 'losing', 'losing itself'). 'Gradually dying away'. *Se perdant* (Fr.) means the same.

Perfect Cadence. See *Cadence*.

Perfect Fool, The. See *Holst*.

Perfect Intervals. See *Interval*.

Perfect Time. See *Common Time*.

Perforated Roll Instruments. See *Mechanical Reproduction of Music* 13.

Performing Right Society. British body, formed 1914 to guard interests of composers and publishers, collecting and distributing performing fees, &c. Address: 29 Berners St., London, W. 1.

Pergolese (or **Pergolesi**), **Giovanni Battista** (b. Jesi, nr. Ancona, 1710; d. nr. Naples 1736). In his brief lifetime composed 15 operas (especially *La Serva Padrona*, q.v. = 'The Maid as Mistress', 1733), some church music (especially *Stabat Mater* 1736; still performed), and instrumental music (authenticity of some of this doubtful).

Peri, Jacopo (b. Rome 1561; d. Florence 1633). Great musician of the days of the Medicis and member of circle which originated Opera; composer of the 2 earliest operas, *Dafne* (now lost) and *Eurydice* (1600). (See also *Caccini* and *Gagliano*.)

Périgourdine. An old Fr. dance to music in compound duple time which was sung by the dancers. Its native home was Périgord.

Però (It.). 'However', 'therefore'.

Perosi, Lorenzo (b. Tortona, Piedmont, Italy, 1872; d. Rome 1956). It. priest-musician, who from 1897 to 1916 produced a series of New Testament oratorios that caused a sensation in Italy and Britain and are now already almost forgotten; also more than 30 masses, 120 motets, orch. works, &c. In charge of music at St. Mark's, Venice (1896), and then of Sistine Chapel, Rome (1915–17; resigned through recurring mental disturbance). Said to have influenced Pius X in issuing (1903) *Motu Proprio* (q.v.) on church music.

Pérotin-le-Grand—or **Perotinus Magnus** (c. 1160–1220). In charge of music of chapel on site of present Notre Dame, Paris. Developed polyphonic music and also its notation.

Perpetual Canon. See *Canon*.

Perpetuum Mobile (Lat. 'perpetually in motion'). Same as It. *moto perpetuo*. A title sometimes attached to a rapid instrumental composition proceeding throughout in notes of equal values—a sort of toccata (q.v.).

Perrin, Harry Crane (b. Wellingborough 1865; d. Exeter 1953). Organist Canterbury Cathedral 1898–1908. Prof. of Music and Director Conserv. McGill Univ., Montreal, 1908–30. D.Mus., Dublin.

Perséphone. Opera-ballet by Stravinsky. Libretto by André Gide. (Prod. Paris 1934; concert form London 1934, Boston 1935, New York 1936.)

Persian. A languorous, melancholy type of dance, e.g. in Delibes's *Lakmé*.

Persiani, Fanny—*née* Tacchinardi (b. Rome 1812; d. nr. Paris 1867). Famous opera soprano. Appeared frequently in London and Paris from 1837.

Persichetti, Vincent (b. Philadelphia 1915). Pianist, composer, and conductor (pupil of Olga Samaroff, Roy Harris, Fritz Reiner, &c.). On staff Philadelphia Conserv. 1942; Juilliard Sch. 1948. Numerous works include 7 symphonies and chamber and piano music. Notable book on modern harmony.

Persinger, Louis (b. Rochester, Ill., 1887; d. New York 1966). Violinist. Trained Leipzig Conserv. and in Brussels under Ysaÿe. Toured extensively, then holding orch. positions Berlin, San Francisco (Menuhin his pupil there), and Cleveland. Auer's successor at Juilliard School from 1930.

Persley. See *Parsley*.

Pertile, Aureliano (b. nr. Padua 1885; d. Milan 1952). Operatic tenor. Début Vicenza 1911. Of great reputation Milan, London, New York, &c. Settled in California. Composer of choral works, songs, piano music, &c.

Pes (Lat. 'Foot'). (1, 13th c.; cf. *Sumer is icumen in*) 'Ground bass' (q.v.). (2, in Plainsong) Synonym for *Podatus*, a particular melodic figure as indicated in the old neume notation.

Pesant (Fr.), **pesante** (It.). 'Weighing', i.e. heavy, heavily. So, too, *pesamment* (Fr.), *pesantemente* (It.), 'heavily'.

Pessl, Yella—properly Gabriella Elsa (b. Vienna 1906). Virtuoso woman pianist and harpsichordist and editor of and writer on the music for harpsichord. Resident New York 1931; on staff Columbia Univ. 1938.

Pestalozzi. See *Education and Music* 1.

Petenera. (1) Sort of traditional Spanish song (so called after a 19th-c. singer): it is in brisk triple time. (2) A guitar 'break' (see *Ragtime and Jazz*), often with alternating simple triple and compound duple time.

Peter and the Wolf. By Prokofief (op. 67). Children's piece for Orch. with Narrator. (Prod. Moscow 1936; London 1940.)

Peter Grimes. 3-act opera by Britten. Libretto by Montague Slater derived from poem by Crabbe. (Prod. London 1945; Stockholm, Zürich, Tanglewood, Rome, &c., 1946; New York 1948.)

Peter Ibbetson. Opera by Deems Taylor. Libretto based on Du Maurier's novel. (Prod. New York 1931.)

Peterkin, (1) **W. A.** Bass. Trained by Henry J. Wood (q.v.). Popular in Britain from about 1896 onwards.

(2) **Norman** (b. Liverpool 1886). Self-taught composer, who has produced sensitive songs, piano music, chamber music, &c. He was for some years manager of the music dept. of the Oxford Univ. Press (retiring 1947).

Peters. Great Leipzig music publishing firm, estd. 1814. Cheap edn. of classics, 'Peters Edition', very important. Large musical library, open to public. After 1900 in hands of Hinrichsen family.

Peters, Roberta (b. New York 1930). Coloratura soprano. Metropolitan début 1950 and regularly appearing there; Covent Garden 1951; international tours.

Peter Schmoll und seine Nachbarn ('Peter Schmoll and his Neighbours'). Opera by Weber. (Prod. Augsburg 1803.) The Overture is sometimes heard.

Peterson-Berger, (Olof) Wilhelm (b. Ullånger, Sweden, 1867; d. Oestersund 1942). Studied at Conserv. of Stockholm and in Germany and devoted himself to composition of music in definitely Swedish idiom; poet and music critic; translator of Wagner libretti into Swedish.

Petit, petite (Fr. masc., fem.). 'Small', 'little'.

Petit détaché (Fr.). See *Détaché*.

Petites Michu (Messager). See *P'tites Michu*.

Petite Suite (Bizet). See *Jeux d'enfants*.

Petrassi, Goffredo (b. nr. Rome 1904). Trained Rome Conserv., and under Casella (q.v.). Has composed choral, orch., and chamber works.

Petri, Egon (b. Hanover 1881; d. Berkeley, Calif., 1962). Pianist. As such pupil of Carreño, Busoni, &c. (in youth played also organ, violin, and horn). Recitalist from 1902, winning international acclaim. On staff Royal

Manchester Coll. of Music 1905–11 (Hon. D.Mus., Manchester Univ. 1938); various other posts including Berlin Hochschule 1921–5. Resident Poland from 1925; U.S.A. from 1939. Collaborated with Busoni in edn. of Bach.

Petrie, George (b. Dublin 1789; there d. 1866). Eminent painter, painstaking antiquary, amateur violinist, and collector of the standard collection of Irish folk tunes (1855; new edn. by Stanford 1902–5, including tunes Petrie left in MS. and containing nearly 1,600 airs).

Petrillo, James C. See *American Federation of Musicians*.

Petrouchka (or *Petrushka*). Ballet by Stravinsky on subject of a Russian Carnival. (Prod. Paris 1911.) Music also heard as Suite; new version of this, reorchestrated, 1946.

Petto (It.). 'Chest', e.g. *voce di petto*, 'chest voice'.

Peu (Fr.). 'Little.' So *peu à peu*, 'little by little'.

Pevernage, Andreas (b. Courtrai 1543; d. Antwerp 1591). Choirmaster of Antwerp Cathedral. Publ. masses, motets, and chansons (see *Chanson*), and edited important book of madrigals (*Harmonia Celeste*, 1583).

Pezzo (It., plur. *pezzi*). 'Piece.'

Pfeife (Ger.). 'Pipe.'

Pfiffig (Ger.). 'Artful.'

Pfitzner, Hans Erich (b. Moscow 1869; d. Salzburg 1949). Of German parentage and spent life in Germany; active as opera conductor and composer of operas of romantic type (e.g. *Palestrina*, Munich 1917); composed also orch., choral, and chamber works, &c.

Phaedra. See *Pizzetti*.

Phaëton. Symphonic Poem by Saint-Saëns (op. 39, 1873). It suggests the story of the son of Apollo allowed to guide the chariot of the sun and brought thereby to disaster. Also opera by Lully (prod. Paris 1683).

Phagotum. Elaborate early 16th-c. instrument, with wind-bag and bellows, invented by Canon Afranio—from its name mistakenly supposed to be the original of the fagotto (bassoon).

Phantasie (Ger., plur. *Phantasien*). 'Fancy', 'imagination', 'reverie'. *Phantasieren*, 'to imagine or improvise'. *Phantasiestück* (plur. *Phantasiestücke*) and *Phantasiebild* (plur. *Phantasiebilder*) are probably best translated lit. as 'fantasy piece' and 'fantasy picture', respectively.

Cf. *Phantasy* below.

Phantasy. A term introduced by W. W. Cobbett (1847–1937), wealthy chamber music enthusiast, who offered prizes for, and commissioned the composition of, single-movement pieces of chamber music, taking the idea from the Old Eng. 'Fancy' (q.v.).

Pharynx. The cavity which serves as the communicating chamber of nose, mouth, and larynx.

Philadelphia. See under *Schools of Music*.

Philadelphia Festival March. By Wagner. Commissioned for the Centennial of the Declaration of Independence in 1876 (fee $5,000).

Philadelphia Orchestra. Founded 1900. Stokowski conductor 1912–38; then Ormandy.

Phile, Philip. See *Hail, Columbia*.

Philémon et Baucis. Opera by Gounod. Libretto based on Ovid. (Prod. Paris 1860; Liverpool 1888; London 1891; New York 1893.)

Philharmonia Orchestra. Founded 1945, primarily as a recording unit, by the H.M.V. Gramophone Co. Cond. Karajan, Klemperer, &c.

Philharmonic Society. See *Royal Philharmonic Society*.

Philharmonic Society of Guitarists. See *Guitar*.

Philidor Family (real name 'Danican'). Like the Purcells, Couperins, and Bachs includes musicians of several generations—in their case abt. 1600–1800. Larger works of reference include 12–14 musician members of family—and even then omit some: only the most important one can be treated here—**François André** (b. Dreux 1726; d. London 1795). Famous chess-player, welcomed in London from 1749, where its Chess Club gave him a pension in return for annual visits (once played 3 simultaneous games without seeing boards). In music pupil of Campra (q.v.); heard Handel's music when first in London and composed choral music in same style; then (1756) turned to comic opera and produced long series of highly successful works in Paris (e.g. *Tom Jones* 1765). Also wrote church music, chamber music, &c.

Philipp, Isidor (b. Budapest 1863; d. Paris 1958). Pianist and teacher. In Paris at age 3 and naturalized French; trained at Paris Conserv.; later on its staff. High renown as performer and teacher (many famous pupils); also as author of works on piano technique, &c. In U.S.A. 1941–55.

Philips, Peter (b. England abt. 1560; d. probably Brussels abt. 1628–30). Held important musical positions in Spanish Netherlands, including that of Organist of Royal Chapel at Brussels; publ. in Antwerp madrigals, motets, &c.; composed also instrumental music. Of high importance in history of music in his period.

Phillips, (1) Henry (b. Bristol 1801; d. London 1876). Baritone and author. Studied under Sir George Smart. Appeared in opera in London. Also gave 'Table Entertainments'. Wrote books of reminiscences, angling, &c.; composed songs and edited those of Dibdin (q.v.).

(2) **Montague Fawcett** (b. London 1885; d. Esher, Sy., 1969). Org. & comp. of orch. and chamber music; songs; light opera, *The Rebel Maid* (1921).

(3) **Frank**—really Francis Hugh Addison Phillips (b. Sidmouth 1901). Baritone. Toured South Africa with Marie Hall 1926. Then in London and prominent in oratorio, &c. Later joined B.B.C. staff.

Philosoph, Der ('The Philosopher'). Nickname of Haydn's Symphony in E flat, no. 22 (1764) in Breitkopf edn. of the Symphonies.

Philosopher (Haydn). See *Philosoph*.

Phoebus and Pan (*Der Streit zwischen Phoebus und Pan*, 'The Contention between Phoebus and Pan'). Lively and satirical allegorical Cantata of Bach (1731). Libretto, by Picander, based on Ovid. (Occasionally staged as an opera.)

Phoneuma. Very soft organ stop of *Dulciana* (q.v.) tone and *Quintatön* (q.v.) effect.

Phonodeik. An ingenious apparatus invented by the late Prof. Dayton C. Miller, of Cleveland, Ohio, to cause sounds photographically to produce diagrams representing their so-called 'wave-forms'. (Cf. *Acoustics* 10.)

Phonogram, Phonograph. See *Gramophone*.

Photo-electric Cell. See *Electric Musical Instruments* 5.

Photona. See *Electric Musical Instruments* 5.

Phrase. No such thing as a continuous melody seems to be conceivable by the human mind. If any folk song, hymn tune, or other simple melody be hummed through it will be felt to fall into sections corresponding to the lines of the words, and if any instrumental composition be listened to with care it will, similarly, be felt to fall into sections, these sections being the music's 'phrases'.

The normal phrase-length is 4 measures but 3-measure and 5-measure phrases occur, and, indeed, there is no strict rule as to phrase-length, and the introduction of a change of length often contributes an acceptable effect of variety. The phrase, closely observed, will often be found to fall into half-phrases, and these into motifs (see *Motif*). Two or more phrases will be found to adhere together making up what is often called a 'Sentence'.

See *Phrase Marks* and *Phrasing* below.

Phrase Marks (see *Phrase* above), in musical notation, are the slurs placed over or under the notes as a hint of the proper punctuation of the perf. They are often very carelessly inserted, even by the greatest composers, a confusion occurring between (*a*) the slur which indicates the limits of a phrase and (*b*) that which suggests that a passage should be performed *legato*. Really 2 sets of marks are required and it has

been suggested that horizontal straight lines, square-ended or curve-ended, should be used as phrase marks, the present curved lines being reserved for the indication of legato (and in music for bowed instruments, the bowing). See Table 22.

Phrasing in perf. means the neat and artistic observance of what may be called the punctuation of a composition—its phrases and half-phrases, and motifs (see *Phrase* and *Phrase Marks* above). It has to be carried out clearly yet unobtrusively, as the result of genuine feeling and not of a mere intellectual analysis of the structure of the music: so achieved it constitutes one of the greatest refinements in the art of perf.—instrumental or vocal.

Phrygian Cadence. See *Cadence*.

Phrygian Mode. See *Modes*.

Phyle, Philip. See *Hail, Columbia*.

Piacere (It.). 'Pleasure.' So *A piacere*, 'at pleasure' (i.e. the same as *Ad libitum*, q.v.).

Piacevole (It.). 'Agreeable.'

Pianamente (It.). 'Softly.'

Piangendo, piangente (It., 'weeping'); **piangevole, piangevolmente** (It.). 'Plaintive'; 'plaintively'.

Piano (It.). 'Soft.' **Pianissimo** (It.). Superlative of *Piano*.

Piano-accordion. See *Reed-Organ Family* 3.

Piano à queue (Fr., lit. 'tailed-piano'). Grand Piano.

Pianoforte. This instrument is, as to its strings and hammers, a descendant of the dulcimer and, as to its keyboard, a descendant of the harpsichord (q.v.) and clavichord (q.v.). In the 18th c. the desire seems to have come about for a domestic instrument combining the gentle clavichord's power of accentuation, crescendo, diminuendo, and cantabile, with the force and brilliance of the harpsichord. In Florence, about 1709, Cristofori produced what he called a *gravicembalo col piano e forte*, i.e. a 'harpsichord with loudness and softness': for the harpsichord's plucking of the strings he had substituted the blows of a series of hammers, and it was this that gave the players of his instrument their new power of control of degrees of force. (For other claimants to the invention see *OCM*, s.v. *Pianoforte*.)

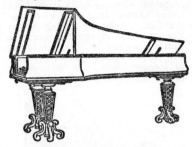

A CRISTOFORI PIANOFORTE, 1726
(In the Museum at Florence)

CRISTOFORI'S PRIMITIVE
ACTION, 1712

Cristofori's idea was taken up in Germany by the organ builder Silbermann, who in 1726 made 2 pianofortes which he submitted to J. S. Bach for his opinion, one that was not entirely

SILBERMANN GRAND
PIANOFORTE, 1746

favourable and perhaps led to the improvements which apparently were introduced. In 1747 Bach visiting the court of Frederick the Great, at Potsdam, played upon the Silbermann pianofortes there, of which the king possessed several. All pianofortes up to this point were of the harpsichord shape—much that of what we now call the grand piano, with the strings horizontal and in a line with the relevant finger-keys. One of Silbermann's apprentices, Zumpe, came to London and became famous as the inventor of the rectangular form of the instrument, called the SQUARE PIANOFORTE. This

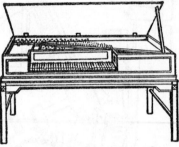

'SQUARE' PIANOFORTE, 1789
(By Albrecht of Philadelphia)

had great popularity and was largely exported to the Continent. John Broadwood (1732–1812; cf. *Shudi*) was an early maker of it who enjoyed high fame. Early Amer. makers were Brent (1774), Belmont (1775), Jarvis (1785), and Juhan (1786); all of these worked in Philadelphia.

Square pianofortes can still be seen occasionally in the shops of second-hand furniture dealers who mistakenly call them spinets. Their strings, like those of the earlier form, lie horizontally, but, unlike that form, from left to right, i.e. not at right angles to the keyboard.

The UPRIGHT PIANOFORTE, in which the strings run perpendicularly, we owe to Hawkins of Philadelphia (1800) and Robert Wornum, jun., of London (1811, perfected 1829): the existing model is largely founded on that of Wornum. From the middle of the 19th c. it drove the square form from the field, but from the 1930's it has looked as though it might itself in turn disappear before the small-size 'GRAND'. Constructionally the 'grand' has amongst other advantages that of not being capable of being placed against a brick or other unresonant wall and also that of the fall by gravity of the *dampers* (i.e. the deadeners to stop the sound as the player's finger releases the key).

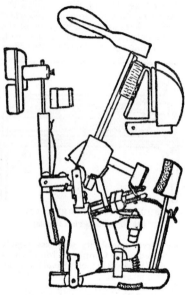

THE ACTION OF A MODERN UPRIGHT
(The Schwander action)

The IRON FRAME (for pianofortes of either shape) is another Amer. contribution: it was Hawkins of Philadelphia who introduced it—in his upright instrument already mentioned. One advantage of it has been the possibility of using strings at higher tension than the wooden frame allowed, so making possible the use of thicker wire, producing a fuller tone. The tension of a single string today may be 180–200 lb., the varying stress of the different sizes of strings being more or less equally distributed by OVER-STRINGING, i.e. by one group of strings passing more or less diagonally over another: this principle as applied to the pianoforte dates from about 1835, but there had previously been occasional overstrung clavichords.

The 18th-c. harpsichords had more than 1 string to each note and Cristofori's pianoforte had 2 throughout: the pianoforte of today has 1 string for a few of the very lowest notes, 2 for those that follow, and 3 for the highest (on account of the decrease of resonance with the shorter strings): the lowest strings are wrapped with a copper coil to increase their mass without too greatly decreasing their flexibility.

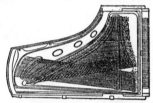

FRAME, SOUNDBOARD, AND STRINGS
of a Grand Pianoforte

The SOUND-BOARD of a pianoforte (lying behind the strings in an upright and below them in a grand) fulfils the same function as the body of a violin: without it the tone of the instrument would be very faint and thin. The SUSTAINING PEDAL, when depressed, removes the whole series of dampers from the strings: thus any note or chord played can be given some duration, even though the finger or fingers have been removed from the keys, and also the harmonics of the strings sounded are enriched by the sympathetic resonance of those derived from other strings, now left free to vibrate (cf. *Acoustics* 19), so resulting in a fuller tone. (It is a vulgar mistake to call this pedal the 'Loud Pedal' as it is as much used in soft passages as in loud.) This pedal must of course normally be lifted at a change of harmony, as otherwise confusion will result. There is in most instruments manufactured in the U.S.A. and Canada a SOSTENUTO PEDAL. It ingeniously enables the player to make (within limits) a selection as to the notes he wishes to be held over. Its introduction is due to the Steinway firm and it was perfected in 1874. The SOFT PEDAL may act in one of several ways: (*a*) In grands by moving the keyboard and set of hammers sideways, so as to leave unstruck 1 string of each note (cf. *Corda*); (*b*) In uprights by moving the whole set of hammers nearer to the strings, so that the force of their blows is diminished, or by interposing a piece of felt between hammer and strings (a crude method now little used).

The COMPASS of the Pianoforte has gradually been extended from Cristofori's 4 or 4½ 8ves to 7 or 7¼ (or even 8) 8ves.

Experiments in the construction of the pianoforte have been frequent; these have included PIANOFORTES WITH DOUBLE KEYBOARD; PIANOFORTES WITH INDEFINITELY PROLONGED SOUNDS (by means of a revolving wheel or other imitation of the violin bow, or of a current of air tending to keep the string in vibration, or by some electrical device); PIANOFORTES WITH TUNING-FORKS IN PLACE OF STRINGS (incapable of getting out of tune); COMBINATIONS OF THE PIANOFORTE PRINCIPLE WITH THAT OF SOME OTHER INSTRUMENT (e.g. flute, organ, harpsichord, clavichord); QUARTER-TONE PIANOFORTES (cf. *Microtones*); various applications of electricity, &c. As to experimental keyboards see *Keyboard*.

There have, of course, been many PIANOFORTES PROVIDED WITH A PEDAL-BOARD like that of the organ and such instruments are still used by organists for home practice.

SOME TERMS USED IN MAKERS' CATALOGUES, &c., are as follows (alphabetically arranged):

Aliquot Scaling (a speciality of the Blüthner firm): an arrangement by which the weak upper notes are provided with sympathetic strings (cf. 'Duplex Scaling' below, and also *Acoustics* 19), tuned an 8ve higher, so increasing the tone volume. *Baby Grand*: simply a small size grand. *Barless iron frame* (for the grand; a Broadwood speciality): made so as not to require the usual strengthening bars which are considered to be inimical to tone. *Cabinet Pianoforte*: a tall cupboard-like instrument now obsolete. *Concert Grand*: one of the largest size. *Console Piano*: a term used by Amer. manufacturers for a type of miniature upright piano. *Cottage Pianoforte*: a small upright. *Duplex Scaling*: a system by which those portions of the string which are normally dumb, lying beyond each end

of the vibrating portion, are left free and tuned so as to correspond with some of the harmonics of the main note of the string (cf. 'Aliquot Scaling' above). *Full Trichord*: 3 strings to each note (except the very lowest). *Giraffe*: an obsolete form of very tall upright. *Oblique*: in upright instruments the strings running at an angle, instead of perpendicularly, so securing increased length and fullness of tone. *Overdamper* and *Underdamper*: a term applied to uprights in which the dampers are respectively above or below the hammers. *Upright Grand*: a term of various meanings now usually applied to a large upright with overstringing and all improvements.

See also *Pianoforte Playing and Teaching*; *Electric Musical Instruments* 3.

Pianoforte Playing and Teaching.

The pianoforte in the 18th c., being a new instrument, called for a new technique as to touch and the various means by which expressive perf. could be achieved. The early pianists were, necessarily, all harpsichordists, and they would not readily discover all the ways in which the treatment of their new instrument should differ from that of their old one. By the end of the 18th c. there were 2 recognized 'schools' of piano playing, the 'Viennese' and the 'English'. To some extent the doctrines and practices of these schools were conditioned by the different action, touch, and tone of the instrument as manufactured in Vienna and London—the Viennese type being lighter and the tone less sonorous than the Eng. (or Fr.) type. The piano playing of Mozart was that of the Viennese school, and his piano compositions reflect this. Following him came a series of player-composers of the same school, Hummel (1778–1837), Czerny (1791–1857), and Moscheles (1794–1870) being outstanding examples. They sought in their playing equality and purity of tone, delicacy of nuance, lightness, and speed, and their style tended to the *bravura* of such younger men as Herz (1803–88), whose work has now been completely put aside.

The deeper fall of the keys of the Eng. instrument (which, it must be remembered, had a considerable sale in continental Europe) made it, with the Fr. models based on it, attractive to players and composers of more serious aims. Clementi (1752–1832), whose life was passed in England, being brought up on the Eng. instruments, wrote with them in mind, and himself became a maker of them. Beethoven's very dramatic piano sonatas are based, as to general style and methods, on those of Clementi. Beethoven's playing had 'tremendous power and character, and unheard-of brilliance and facility' (reported by Czerny); Hummel's supporters called it 'noisy' and Cherubini used the word 'rough'. Clementi's pupil, Field, who was employed for some time in his London warehouse, developed in a high degree the singing touch, and introduced the Nocturne style, so influencing Chopin.

The successors of the early Viennese School were exponents of the principle of the unmoving wrist, and of the fingers as the true producers of the tone. This idea was not so fully accepted by followers of the other school. Beethoven was the first fully to profit by the great extension in effect offered by the understanding use of the SUSTAINING PEDAL—which we are told he used much more than the markings on his compositions betray: his example in this matter was, of course, followed by the romantics, his younger contemporary, Schubert, and, later, Schumann, Chopin, and Mendelssohn, whose works would be unimaginable on a pedal-less instrument (Moscheles had actually taught that the pianist should use the pedals as little as possible). A little-known point bearing on the interpretation of Chopin's works concerns the significance of his pedal markings: examination of an instrument that belonged to him in his later years shows that the resonance of its pedal, as we ascend the keyboard, ceases to take effect about an 8ve lower than is usual in our modern instruments, so that when we see in his works markings indicating that the pedal should be held continuously through middle-keyboard passages we are not to take it that if the composer were now living he would insist on our observing his original instructions as reproduced in our printed copies.

The mid- and later 19th c. produced a crop of pianistic giants—virtuosi such as Liszt (1811–86), Thalberg (1812–71), Tausig (1841–71), Rubinstein (1829–94), and Von Bülow

1830–94). These were pianistic athletes with an immense command of the keyboard; moreover, they had studied minutely the powers of the instrument and had learnt how to exploit all of them to the full. We have nowadays no greater players than these but our *average standard* is probably far higher than that of their time, since keenly analytical minds have been at work and have discovered the principles which those giants, to some extent no doubt, applied merely empirically.

Famous teachers have been Plaidy (1810–74), Kullak (1818–82), and Leschetizky (1830–1915). Kullak was perhaps the first to realize the importance of arm and hand weight, a doctrine enforced and extended by Matthay in his *Act of Touch* (1903) and by Steinhausen in works publ. about the same time. Matthay's close analysis of the means by which good tone is produced and his insistence upon the need for the player to listen keenly to his tone have been of the highest value to many young Brit. and Amer. players. With the 20th c. new ideas as to piano tone have been promulgated by such composers as Bartók, who wrote music calling for a percussive touch. Such were not the ideas of the most accomplished artist of the piano in the recollection of living music critics of today—Busoni (1866–1924). It remains to be seen which line will be followed by piano composers and pianists of the next quarter or half century.

The earliest publ. music for 2 players at 1 keyboard is Burney's *Four Sonatas or Duets* (1777), but earlier music of this sort existed in manuscript (back to the 16th c. virginal composers). During the 20th c. the composition and arrangement of music for 2 players at 2 instruments has become common.

Music for left hand alone has been written by Kalkbrenner, Scriabin, Ravel, Korngold, Strauss, and others; and for right hand alone by Alkan and others.

See also the following entries: *Fingering*; *Expression*; *Interpretation*; *Memory*; *Accompaniment*; for a strange experiment dating from the 1940's, *Cage, John*.

Pianola. See *Mechanical Reproduction of Music 13*.

Piano Quartet, Quintet. See *Quartet*; *Quintet*.

Piano, Reproducing. See *Mechanical Reproduction of Music* 13.

Piano Score. See *Score*.

Piano, Street. See *Mechanical Reproduction of Music* 12.

Pianto (It.). 'Plaint', 'lamentation'.

Piatigorsky, Gregor (b. Ekaterinoslav, Russia, 1903). Violoncellist. Trained Moscow Conserv. Leading 'cellist Moscow opera and then Berlin Philharmonic. As soloist toured widely. U.S.A. citizen 1942; on staff Curtis Institute. Various compositions and transcriptions.

Piatti, Alfredo Carlo (b. Bergamo 1822; there d. 1901). Famous It. 'cellist, much associated with Joachim, with whom he made 1st appearance in London 1844. Composed sonatas and concertos for 'cello and edited music for it.

Piatti (It.). 'Cymbals' (see *Percussion Family* 2 o).

Pibcorn or **Pibgorn.** A Welsh instrument, much the same as the Scottish stockhorn (q.v.).

Pibroch. A type of Scottish Highland bagpipe music, a peculiar sort of air with variations (original word *Piobaireachd*).

Picardie, Tierce de ('Picardy Third'). See *Tierce de Picardie*.

Piccaver, Alfred (b. Long Sutton, Lincs., 1889; d. Vienna 1958). Tenor. Trained New York, Prague, Italy. Vienna State Opera, 1912–34.

Picchettato, picchiettato, picchiettando (It., 'knocked', 'knocking'). In the playing of bowed instruments, detaching the notes (cf. *Spiccato*).

Picchi, Giovanni (early 17th c.). Composer for harpsichord, whose work abounds in consecutive 5ths (see *Harmony* 2 j) and the tritone (q.v.) deliberately used.

Piccini (Picinni, &c.)**, Nicola** (b. Bari 1728; d. Passy, nr. Paris, 1800). Favourite pupil of Leo and Durante; in 1754 suddenly created furore with an opera at Naples; invited to Paris where a party ran him as rival to Gluck (q.v.)—who won. Composed 139 operas, also oratorios.

Piccolo, piccola (It. masc., fem.). 'Little.'

Piccolo. (1) See *Flute Family*. (2) Organ stop (metal or wood) of 2-foot length and pitch.

Piccolomini, Henry—real name Marie Henri Pontet (b. Dublin 1835; d. Hanwell 1902). Enormously popular composer of drawing-room ballads (*Whisper and I shall hear, Ora pro nobis*, &c.). Spent last years in extreme poverty and died in a lunatic asylum.

Picinni. See *Piccini*.

Pick-Mangiagalli, Riccardo (b. Strakonice, Bohemia, 1882; d. Milan 1949). Of half It., half Czech parentage; naturalized Italian. Head of Milan Conserv. Composer of operas and ballets, well-known piano pieces, &c.

Pickwick. See *Coates, Albert*.

Pictures at an Exhibition. Series of 10 piano pieces by Mussorgsky, inspired by paintings of Victor Hartmann seen in the Memorial Exhibition of his works in St. Petersburg in 1874. Various orch. arrangements are to be heard (Ravel, Henry Wood, Stokowski, and several others).

Pied (Fr.). 'Foot' (used in connexion with organ stops).

Pied en l'air (Fr. 'foot in the air'). A particular motion in the Galliard (see *Pavan and Galliard*).

Pieno, piena (It. masc., fem.). 'Full'; e.g. *organo pieno*, 'full organ'; *coro pieno*, 'full choir' (as contrasted with passages for quartet, &c.); *a voce piena*, 'with full voice'.

Pierné (Henri Constant) Gabriel (b. Metz 1863; d. Ploujean, Finistère, 1937). Student of Paris Conserv.; at 17 won Rome Prize; succeeded César Franck as organist of St. Clothilde (1890), and Colonne as conductor of his orch. concerts (1910). Composed operas, ballets, incidental music, chamber and piano music, songs, &c., and a musical legend, *The Children's Crusade* (q.v.), making much use of children's voices, as does *The Children of Bethlehem* (1907).

Pierrot Lunaire. Melodrama by Schönberg (op. 21, 1912); 21 poems by Giraud, recited in *Sprechgesang* (q.v.), with accompaniment of 5 instruments (rarely all employed).

Pierrot of the Minute, The. 'Comedy Overture' by Bantock. Based on a fantastic play by Ernest Dowson. (1st perf. Worcester Fest. 1908.)

Pierson (originally **Pearson**), **Henry Hugo** (b. Oxford 1815; d. Leipzig 1873). Son of Dean of Salisbury; educated Harrow and Cambridge; studied music in Germany; songs praised by Schumann in his musical magazine; became Prof. of Music at Edinburgh Univ. 1844 but resigned almost at once and returned to Germany. Had great success at Norwich Fest., 1852, with oratorio *Jerusalem*; composed music to 2nd part of Goethe's *Faust* (often performed in Germany). Part-song *Ye Mariners of England* very popular.

See *O Deutschland, hoch in Ehren!*

Pietà; pietoso; pietosamente (It.). 'Pity'; 'Piteous'; 'piteously'.

Pijper, Willem (b. Zeist, nr. Utrecht, 1894; d. Leidschendam 1947). Composer of orch. and chamber music, songs, &c.—latterly in an atonal idiom. Writer on musical subjects.

Pikieren (Ger.). To play *spiccato*.

Pilgrim's March (Mendelssohn). See *Italian Symphony*.

Pilgrim's Progress. (1) Work for solo vocalists, choir, and orch. by Bantock (1926). (2) Operatic 'Morality' by Vaughan Williams (Covent Garden 1951). See also *Austin, Ernest*.

Pilkington, Francis (b. abt. 1562; d. Chester 1638). In orders and a minor canon of Chester Cathedral; composed ayres and madrigals of high value.

Pinafore (Sullivan). See *H.M.S Pinafore*.

Pincé (Fr.). 'Pinched', i.e. *pizzicato*. (There was also an old mordent called by this name.)

Pincherle, Marc (b. Algiers 1888). Musicologist. Educ. Sorbonne; dir. Pleyel concerts from 1927; pres. French musicological society 1948–55;

Prof. of Mus. History, École Normale, Paris. Much research on history of violin; books on various aspects of his subject, including important work on Vivaldi.

Pines of Rome (*Pini di Roma*). Symphonic Poem by Respighi. Four movements devoted to the pines of (*a*) *The Villa Borghese*; (*b*) *A Catacomb*; (*c*) *The Janiculum*; (*d*) *The Appian Way*. (1st perf. Rome 1924. London 1925. New York 1926.)

Pini, Anthony (b. Buenos Aires 1902). Violoncellist. In Britain since age 12. Principal 'cellist in Beecham's original London Philharmonic Orch. 1932–9. As soloist has many times toured Europe and U.S.A. On staff G.S.M.

Pinsuti, Ciro (b. nr. Siena 1829; d. Florence 1888). Studied in London under Cipriani Potter (q.v.), and in Bologna under Rossini; fashionable London singing-master 1848 to retirement; on staff of R.A.M. Composed large number of songs, very popular part-songs; some operas, prod. in Italy.

Pinza, Ezio (b. Rome 1892; d. Stamford, Conn., 1957). Operatic bass. Studied Ravenna and Conserv. of Bologna. Début La Scala, Milan, afterwards appearing frequently in Rome, Vienna, Salzburg, Paris, &c. Mainly U.S.A. from 1926; also musical comedy, films, &c., from 1949.

Piobaireachd. See *Pibroch*.

Pioneers, The. See *Weinberg*.

Pipe. (1) In a general sense any gentle-sounding wooden or metal instrument. (2, in Scotland) Bagpipe. (3) For the 'Pipe and Tabor' see *Recorder Family* 2. (4) See *Organ*.

Piqué (Fr. 'pricked'). A bowed instrument term—same as *Spiccato* (q.v.).

Pique Dame (Tchaikovsky). See *Queen of Spades*.

Piquiren (Ger.). To play *Spiccato* (q.v.).

Pirani, Max (b. Melbourne, Australia, 1898). Pianist. Trained Melbourne Conserv., and London and New York. On staff R.A.M. 1925. Director Dept. of Music, Banff School of Fine Art (Univ. Alberta) 1941–7, and Prof. Univ. Western Ontario,

1944-8; founded and directed Music Teachers Coll. there (1945-8). Returned London 1948.

Pirates of Penzance, The, or The Slave of Duty. Comic opera by Gilbert and Sullivan. (Prod. Opéra Comique, London, 1880, after preliminary performances, to guard copyright, at Fifth Avenue Theatre, New York, and Paignton, Devon, previous year.)

Pirouette (Fr.). In ballet, a complete revolution of the body, made whilst balanced on the toe of one foot or whilst the whole body is in the air. The *Grande Pirouette* is the same thing with the spare leg held out at right angles.

Pirro, André (b. Saint-Dizier, Haute Marne, 1869; d. Paris 1943). After univ. study (Dr. ès Lettres) gave himself to musical and musicological labours, occupying various academic positions, finally that of Prof. of History of Mus. at the Sorbonne. Publ. many important works on Buxtehude, Schütz, Bach, &c.

Pisk, Paul Amadeus (b. Vienna 1893). Took doctorate at Vienna Univ. with musicological thesis; studied composition with Schreker and Schönberg; conducted theatre orchs.; composer of orch., chamber, piano, and organ music, songs, &c.; also music critic. In 1937 emigrated to U.S.A., becoming Prof. at Redlands Univ., California; 1951 Univ. Texas; 1963 Washington Univ., St. Louis.

Piston. (1, in brass instruments) A type of valve, bored with passages which, when it is depressed within its casing, deflect the air-stream passing through it into the valve tubing. (2, Fr. and Ger.) The Cornet (q.v.).

Piston, Walter (b. Rockland, Maine, 1894). Studied at Harvard Univ. and in Paris; became member of Harvard staff 1940 (Walter W. Naumberg Prof. 1948). Composer of orch. and chamber music, &c. (7th symph. 1961). Writer on musical subjects (e.g. *Harmony*, 1941; *Counterpoint*, 1947).

Pistone (It. 'piston', plur. *pistoni*). (1) Valve in brass instruments. (2) The high (E flat or F) cornet. (3) *Corno a pistoni*, the Valve Horn (see *Horn Family*).

Pitch. For the scientific explanation of the production of notes of differing pitches ('high' or 'low') see *Acoustics* 2 and 5.

The pitch allotted to the note C or A (and consequently the pitches of all the other notes) has varied greatly at different periods, e.g. in the Tudor period in England the usual domestic keyboard pitch was about 3 semitones lower than the usual pitch of today, the secular vocal pitch much the same as today, and the church music pitch more than 2 semitones higher than today. The pitch now internationally agreed upon (1960) is that in which the A (2nd space of treble staff) has 440 vibrations per second. This is, then, what is now meant by the old term 'Concert Pitch'.

Pitch-carrying instruments have been invented, for giving the pitch to singers, testing the pitch of instruments, &c.: of these the one now most in use is the Tuning-fork, usually sounding C or A. (Cf. *Resonoscope*.)

Pitfield, Thomas Baron (b. Lancashire 1903). Had some training at Royal Manchester Coll. of Music (later Hon. F.R.M.C.M.) and then became active as composer (also as poet, draughtsman, and craftsman in wood, &c.). Piano pieces, chamber music, orch. works, &c.

Pitt, Percy (b. London 1870; there d. 1932). Trained at Leipzig Conserv. Orch. and opera conductor, long attached to Covent Garden, Beecham Co., and Brit. National Opera Co.; Musical Director B.B.C. 1924–30. Many early compositions, largely orch. or vocal-orch.

Più (It.). 'More.'

Pius X. See *Motu Proprio*; *Plainsong* 3.

Pius XI. See *Motu Proprio* (end).

Piuttosto (It.). 'Rather' (cf. *Tosto*).

Pixis, Johann Peter (b. Mannheim 1788; d. Baden-Baden 1874). Pianist, famous teacher of his instrument, and lavish composer for it. (See *Hexameron*.)

Pizzetti, Ildebrando—also known as Ildebrando da Parma (b. Parma 1880; d. Rome 1968). Studied and taught at Conserv. of Parma; then prof. and director in that of Florence, and (1924) director of that of Milan; then prof. of composition in Conserv. of Santa Cecilia, Rome. Active as opera composer (*Phaedra*, Milan 1915; *Deborah and Jael*, Milan 1922, &c.—see *Opera* 4); composed also ballets, orch., choral, and chamber music, &c Wrote much on musical subjects.

See *Assassinio nella catedrale*.

Pizzicato (It., generally abbrev. to *Pizz.*, plur. *Pizzicati*). 'Plucked', i.e. pluck the strings (violin, &c.) with the fingers instead of bowing them.

P.K. (in Ger. organ music) = *Pedalkoppel*, i.e. 'pedal coupler' (followed by an indication of the particular manual to be coupled to the pedal).

Pk. Short for *Pauken*, i.e. 'kettledrums' (see *Percussion Family* 1 a).

Placabile; placabilmente (It.). 'Peaceful'; 'peacefully'.

Placido; placidezza (It.). 'Placid'; 'placidity'. *Placidamente*, 'peacefully'.

Placito (It.). 'Pleasure.' So *A bene placito*, 'at [one's] good pleasure' (same as *Ad libitum*, q.v.).

Plagal. See *Modes*; *Cadence*.

Plaidy, Louis (b. Hubertsburg, Saxony, 1810; d. Grimma 1874). Famous piano teacher and compiler of books of technical studies.

Plainchant. Same as *Plainsong* (q.v.).

Plainsong. (1) The large body of traditional ritual melody of the Western Christian Church. The word is a translation of *Cantus planus*—in contradistinction to *Cantus figuratus* (florid song, implying a counterpoint added to the traditional melody) or *Cantus mensuratus* (measured song, implying the regularity of rhythm associated with harmonic music). *Plainchant* and *Gregorian Chant* are common synonyms, the latter for a reason that will become evident later in this article. The Eastern (or 'Greek') branch of the Christian Church (see *Greek Church*) and the Jewish Church have similar bodies of melodic ritual song, but the term *Plainsong*, as ordinarily used, does not include them.

(2) Plainsong rhythm is the free rhythm of speech; it is a prose rhythm, which of course arises from the unmetrical character of the words to be recited—psalms, prayers, and the like.

In character, plainsong falls into two essentially distinct groups—the responsorial (developed from recitation of psalms round a 'dominant'), and antiphonal (developed as pure melody).

The character of the psalmodic plainsong is best seen in the familiar simple psalm tone. Usually there will be found an opening note or two (*Intonation*), leading to a monotone (*Reciting Note*), which is retained for some time and then merges into a cadence (here called *Mediation*); the monotone is then resumed and another cadence (called the *Ending*) closes the verse. The intonation is, in the Psalms, used for the 1st verse only. The reciting note is always the dominant of the mode (see *Modes*). Many pieces of psalmodic plainsong that are not marked by the comparative simplicity just described will be found on examination to circle around or touch frequently upon one special note (clearly the original reciting note), and then to drop to a cadence in some sort of a florid figure (a *Melisma*, q.v.). For the ancient scales represented by plainsong and for the influence of the reciting note in creating the idea of a scale 'dominant' see the article *Modes*. Each mode naturally developed its own type of cadence and melisma.

The repertory of plainsong is very large. The traditional notation of plainsong still in use (see *Notation*) employs a stave of only 4 lines, instead of 5.

(3) Plainsong grew up during the earliest centuries of Christianity, influenced possibly by the music of the Jewish synagogue and certainly by the Gr. modal system (see *Modes*). At the end of the 4th c. Ambrose, Bishop of Milan, finding a great disorder in the church music of Christendom, fixed upon 4 scales to be used (see *Modes*) and set the repertory in order. At the end of the 6th c. Pope Gregory is said to have taken the whole subject under review again, added 4 more scales, or modes, and again collected and recast the repertory.[1]

A reform was attempted at the end of the 16th c., but the results were disastrous. Palestrina was charged with the work of revising the plainsong of

[1] But cf. footnote on p. 375.

the Gradual, Antiphonal, and Psalter, but died almost immediately after accepting the commission. Felice Anerio and Soriano undertook the work, and their edn. was publ. by the Medicean Press in 2 vols. in 1614–15. This *Medicean Edition*, as it is called, with its addition and suppression of melismata, its altered melodies, and its new ones, became the basis for many cheaper performing edns. In the 18th c. there was a craze for introducing grace notes and passing notes into the plainsong (called in France *Machicotage*, q.v.). In the 19th c. there was another cry for reform and the famous Ratisbon (Regensburg) edns. appeared—unfortunately based on the Medicean Edition (see *Cecilian Movement*). Years of controversy followed, for the Benedictine monks of Solesmes, in France, had long been at work in the most scientific spirit, photographing and collating innumerable manuscripts, in all the libraries of Europe. They publ. their Gradual in 1883 and their Antiphonal in 1891. The Ratisbon edn. had had papal privileges conferred upon it, but in 1903 these expired and in the same year Pius X was chosen Pope and he at once issued his famous *Motu Proprio* (q.v.) on church music, laying down, amongst other things, the importance of plainsong and the necessity of taking it from early and pure sources.

Amongst the reforms of the Solesmes monks (who, temporarily driven from France by anti-clerical legislation in 1901, carried on their work for some years in England) was the introduction of a lighter and more rhythmic manner of performance.

Beyond the Versicles and Responses of the Prayer Book little plainsong was heard in the Anglican Church between the Reformation and the Oxford Movement of the 19th c., but since the beginning of that movement it has gradually gained large ground. In addition to its use for the Psalms and in the liturgy generally it has found its way, in the shape of the later metrical melodies, into many hymn books (see *Hymns and Hymn Tunes* 1), and this has accustomed the ears of congregations to its modal and rhythmic characteristics, and prepared the way for its larger adoption, which has been fairly widespread.

In America numerous Roman Catholic churches have made plainsong familiar to a large public; from about 1925 it has seemed that the interest in it was greatly widening.

(4) Plainsong is complete in itself; it is pure melody and needs no instrumental accompaniment, for it belongs to a pre-harmonic age. It is now customary, however, to support it with a background of organ harmonies. If simple concords are used (in root position and 1st inversion), the modal style of harmonization observed, and a chord-to-a-note method largely avoided in favour of a less laboured manner, in which chords are set only at the rhythmic points, and if only the lighter 8-foot stops are called upon (rarely 16 feet, even on the pedals), then the accompaniment is unobtrusive and is felt by most people to be in keeping. Nevertheless, it is, properly, an anachronism.

Cf. *Gregorian Tones*; *Parisian Tones*; *Gregorian Association*.

Plainsong and Mediaeval Music Society. Brit. soc. founded 1888. Publishes books on and edns. of old music, maintains a library and a choir, &c.

Plaisant (Fr.). 'Merry.'

Planchette ronflante. See *Thunder Stick*.

Plançon, Pol Henri (b. Fumay 1851; d. Paris 1914). Operatic and concert bass vocalist. Equally successful in Fr., It., and Eng. operas. Famous exponent of part of Mephistopheles in *Faust*.

Planets, The. Orch. Suite by Holst (op. 32, 1915). Seven movements based on astrological associations. (1) *Mars, the Bringer of War*; (2) *Venus, the Bringer of Peace*; (3) *Mercury, the Winged Messenger*; (4) *Jupiter, the Bringer of Jollity*; (5) *Saturn, the Bringer of Old Age*; (6) *Uranus, the Magician*; (7) *Neptune, the Mystic*, with female voice wordless chorus. (1st perf. London semi-privately 1918; with 5 movements publicly 1918. In full London and Chicago 1920.)

Planquette, Robert (b. Paris 1848; there d. 1903). Studied at Paris Conserv. and then made name as composer of gay songs and operettas (see *Cloches de Corneville*; *Rip van Winkle*).

Planté, Francis (b. Orthez, Basse Pyrenées, 1839; d. St. Avit 1934). Pianist. Trained Paris Conserv. Won success with Paris public; then took offence at something and disappeared to native place for 10 years. From 1872 again heard, touring many countries.

Plaqué (Fr.). A keyboard and stringed instrument term applied to chord-playing, meaning to play all the notes simultaneously, avoiding 'spreading'. (The reverse of this meaning is sometimes given; the above has, however, been carefully checked in reliable Fr. works and may be accepted as accurate.)

Plateau, plateaux (Fr.). 'Plate', 'plates' (of cymbals).

Plaudernd (Ger.). 'Chattering', 'babbling'.

Playera (Sp.). A Gipsy Seguidilla (q.v.), sung and danced. Another name is *Seguidillas gitanas*.

Playford Family. (1) **John I** (b. Norfolk 1623; d. London 1686). The great London music publisher of later 17th c. See reference under *Puritans and Music*. (2) **Henry** (b. 1657; d. 1706 or 1710, or later—according to various authorities). Son of John, above, and successor to his father in the important music publishing business. (3) **John II** (b. Stanmore Magna 1655; d. 1685). Nephew of John I; a printer employed by his cousin Henry in the production of all his musical publications.

Play of Robin and Marion. See *Adam de la Halle*.

Pleasure Dome of Kubla Khan, The. Symphonic Poem by Griffes, based on Coleridge's poem. (1st perf. Boston 1919.)

Plectrum. The small piece of wood, metal, ivory, or other material, used to actuate the strings of the mandoline, zither, and 1 or 2 other instruments. The quills of the harpsichord are, of course, also plectra.

Pleeth, William (b. London 1916). Violoncellist. Trained London Violoncello School and Leipzig Conserv. Soloist in concertos with Brit. orchs. Associated in recordings with wife Margaret Good. Member Philharmonia Quartet from 1948. On staff G.S.M.

Plein, pleine (Fr. masc., fem.). 'Full.'

Plein jeu. (*a*) Organ stop of Mixture type (see *Mixture Stop*), including only unison, 8ve, and 12th. (*b*) The term may in Fr. music indicate 'Full Organ' or this without reeds on the manuals (though with them on pedal).

Pleno. (It.). 'Full.'

Pleyel, (1) **Ignaz Joseph** (b. nr. Vienna 1757; d. Paris 1831). A favourite pupil of Haydn; also studied in Italy; became choirmaster of Strasbourg Cathedral; conducted concerts in London 1792; became music-seller in Paris; founded the still-existing piano-making business 1807. Composed immense quantities of instrumental music; some of 64 string quartets still played by amateurs and violin music by students; 29 symphonies, concertos, &c., now forgotten, for son and daughter-in-law see below. (2) **Camille** (b. Strasbourg 1788; d. Paris 1855). Son and pupil of Ignaz; pianist of high reputation; joined father's piano firm. Some time resident in London. Publ. some compositions. For wife see below. (3) **Marie Félicité Denise**—*née* Mocke or Mooke (b. Paris 1811; d. nr. Brussels 1875). Wife of Camille, above. Pianist, pupil of Herz, Moscheles, and Kalkbrenner; admired throughout Europe.

Pleyel, Wolff et Cie. Paris pianomaking firm, founded by Ignaz Pleyel (q.v.) 1807.

Pleyel Chromatic Harp. See *Harp*.

Plötzlich (Ger.). 'Suddenly.'

Plugging. A 20th-c. term, presumably derived from the 19th-c. slang expression, 'plugging away' for 'persisting perseveringly'. It is applied to the practice of so incessantly introducing an attractive melody (generally a song), by radio, cinema, &c., as to make it universally known, thus widely sold, and hence commercially profitable.

Pluie de perles. Piano composition by Osborne, once known to every Brit. drawing-room. About 1840 in the catalogues of 14 London music publishers.

Plus (Fr.). 'More.'

Pneuma (Gr., lit. 'breath' or a 'breathing'). The term is applied to the florid passages sung to a single vowel at the end of certain pieces of plainsong. Such final vocalizes were also known as *Jubili*, indicating their intention as expressions of pious joy.

Pneumatic Action. See *Organ* 1, 4.

Pochetto, pochettino (It.). 'Very little', 'very little indeed' (cf. *Poco*).

Pochissimo (It., diminutive of *poco*, 'little'). 'The least possible.'

Pochon, Alfred (b. nr. Lausanne 1878; d. there 1959). Violinist. Trained Liège Conserv. under César Thomson. Second Violin of Flonzaley Quartet (which he organized) throughout its existence (see *Coppet*). Principal Lausanne Conserv. Chevalier de la Légion d'Honneur, 1952.

Poco (It.). 'A little', i.e. 'rather', e.g. *poco lento*, 'rather slow'. *Poco a poco* means 'little by little', e.g. *poco a poco animando*, 'becoming lively by degrees' (cf. *Pochetto, Pochissimo*).

Podatus. See *Pes*.

Poème symphonique (Fr.), **poema sinfonico** (It.). Symphonic poem (q.v.).

Poem of Ecstasy. By Scriabin (op. 54, 1908); inspired by some of his theosophical ideas and mystical feelings, which he also expressed in an actual poem intended as an interpretation of the music. (1st perf. New York 1908; Moscow and St. Petersburg 1909; London 1910.)

Poet and Peasant. See *Suppé*.

Poet's Love (Schumann). See *Dichterliebe*.

Poggiato (It.). 'Dwelt upon', 'leant upon'.

Pohjola's Daughter. Symphonic Fantasia by Sibelius (op. 49, 1906). Based on the Finnish national epic, the *Kalevala*. (Pohjola is Lapland; the 'daughter' is Louhi, the whirr of whose spinning-wheel is one feature of the music.)

Pohl, Carl Ferdinand (b. Darmstadt 1819; d. Vienna 1887). Eminent musical author (standard biography of Haydn, completed by Botstiber, 1927).

Poi (It.). 'Then', e.g. (after some direction for the repetition of a passage) *poi la coda*, 'then the Coda'.

Poids (Fr.). 'Weight.'

Point (of bow of violin, &c.). The end opposite to that at which it is held (cf. *Heel*).

Point d'orgue. This Fr. term ('Organ Point') has 3 meanings: (*a*) The Pause sign ⌢; (*b*) The harmonic Pedal (see *Harmony* 2 i); (*c*) A Cadenza (q.v.) in a Concerto.

Pointe (Fr.). 'Point', as *pointe d'archet*, 'point of the bow'.

Pointing. See *Anglican Chant*.

Poisoned Kiss, The, or The Empress and the Necromancer. 'Romantic Extravaganza' by Vaughan Williams. (Prod. Cambridge 1935; London 1936; New York 1937.)

Poissons d'Or (Debussy). See under *Images*.

Polacca. See *Polonaise*.

Polacco, Giorgio (b. Venice 1875; d. New York 1960). Opera conductor. Trained Conserv. Milan; won high position Europe, S. America, and U.S.A. (Metropolitan, New York 1912–18; Chicago Civic Opera 1922–32). Retired 1932.

Poldini, Ede or **Eduard** (b. Budapest 1879; d. Vevey 1957). Composer of popular piano music, operas, ballets, &c.

'Poldowski'—really Lady Dean Paul (b. Brussels 1880; d. London 1932). Daughter of the famous violinist Wieniawski. Composed graceful songs, sometimes appearing as their singer and accompanist.

Pole, William (b. Birmingham 1814; d. London 1900). London organist (D.Mus., Oxford, 1876), Prof. of Civil Engineering in Univ. Coll., London (1859–76), and examiner for musical degrees in London Univ. (1878–90); authority on Pitch; author of several valuable books (especially *The Philo-sophy of Music*, 1879; 6th edn. 1924); publ. a few compositions. F.R.S.

Polish Symphony. Tchaikovsky's 3rd (in D, op. 29).

Polka. A Bohemian dance which originated in the early 19th c. and quickly overspread Europe. It was a round dance in a quick duple time, with steps on the 1st 3 half-beats of the measure and a sort of rest on the 4th. The music has some resemblance to that of the Schottische and a particular kind was, indeed, called *Schottische bohème* (another name for this was *Polka tremblante*).

For Polka-Mazurka see under *Mazurka* and for Ger. Polka see under *Schottische*.

Pollak, Anna (b. Manchester 1915). Contralto. Began as repertory actress, then studied opera. Appearances Sadler's Wells, Glyndebourne, Holland, &c.; frequent broadcasts. O.B.E. 1962.

Polly. See under *Beggar's Opera*.

Polnisch (Ger.). 'Polish.' *Polnischer Tanz*, 'Polonaise' (q.v.).

Polo. (1) Type of Spanish folk song, in simple triple time with syncopation. (2) Sort of Seguidilla (q.v.), also known as *Ole* or *Romalis*.

Polonaise (Fr.), **Polonäse** (Ger.), **Polacca** (It.). One of the national dances of Poland, in simple triple time and at moderate speed; it is, perhaps, more properly to be described as a stately ceremonial procession than as a dance. Certain rhythms are characteristic, such as the frequent division of the 1st beat of the measure, with accentuation of its 2nd half, the ending of the phrases on the 3rd beat of the measure, &c. Many of the great composers, from Bach and Handel onwards, have written polonaises; Chopin's 13 examples, in which he found an outlet for his patriotic feeling, are outstanding.

Polonäse. See *Polonaise*.

Polonia. (1) Early Concert-overture by WAGNER. Composed probably 1832. Expressive of sympathy with the Polish Revolution of 1831. (Score lost; found 1879; 1st perf. Palermo 1881; London 1905.) (2) Symphonic Prelude by

ELGAR (op. 76, 1915), a tribute to Poland early in the First World War, and dedicated to Paderewski. Three of the themes are Polish. (3) Symphony by Mlynarski.

Polovetz (or **Polovtsian**) **Dances.** By Borodin. Sequence of Choral and Orch. pieces forming a Ballet scene in the opera, *Prince Igor* (q.v.). The Polovtsy were a nomadic people who had invaded Russia.

Polska. A Scandinavian dance in simple triple time. Its name comes from its origin in Poland (it derives from the Mazurka), and dates from the union of the crowns of Sweden and Poland in 1587.

Polski. Same as *Polonaise* (q.v.).

Polstertanz (Ger. 'pillow dance'). Same as *Kissentanz* or *Cushion Dance* (q.v.).

Polyphony, Polyphonic. Terms applied to 'many-sound' (i.e. 'many-voice') music, in other words music of the contrapuntal type (see *Counterpoint*; *History* 2). The converse terms are 'Homophony' (q.v.), 'Homophonic' ('like-sounding').

Polyrhythmophone. See *Electric Musical Instruments* 5.

Polytonality. See *Harmony* 3.

Pommer. See *Oboe Family*.

Pomone. See *Cambert*.

Pomp and Circumstance. Set of 5 Military Marches by Elgar (op. 39, 1900–30). A melody in no. 1 was used for the section *Land of Hope and Glory* in the setting of A. C. Benson's Coronation Ode for Edward VII and has come into independent use as a patriotic community song.

Pompeux, pompeuse (Fr. masc., fem.). 'Pompous.'

Pomposo (It.). 'Pompous.'

Ponchielli, Amilcare (b. nr. Cremona 1834; d. Milan 1886). Popular composer of operas (especially *La Gioconda*, q.v.).

Ponderoso (It.). 'Ponderous.'

Poniatowski (Prince) Joseph Michael Xavier Francis John (b. Rome 1816; d. Chislehurst 1873).

Grand-nephew of last King of Poland and nephew of Napoleon's famous Marshal; attached to Napoleon III; after Sedan followed him into exile in England. Tenor vocalist and composer of many operas; remembered by his popular *The Yeoman's Wedding Song*.

Pons, Lily (b. Draguignan, Var, France, 1904). Operatic soprano. Trained Paris Conserv. Toured widely. Very popular U.S.A. and there settled.

Ponselle, Rosa—really Rose Melba Ponzillo (b. Meriden, Conn., 1897). Operatic and concert soprano—Metropolitan Opera House, Covent Garden, &c. Retired 1937.

Pontet, M. H. See *Piccolomini*.

Ponticello (It., 'little bridge'). Bridge of a stringed instrument. *Sul ponticello* ('on the bridge') means 'play with the bow as close to the bridge as possible'.

Pontifical. See *Liturgy*.

Poole, Elizabeth (b. London 1820; d. Langley, Bucks., 1906). Mezzo-soprano. Operatic début Drury Lane age 14. Thenceforward very popular until retirement 1870.

Poot, Marcel (b. nr. Brussels 1901). Pupil of Gilson and Dukas; member of group of 7 Belgian modernists, the 'Synthétistes'; music critic and ed. of *Revue musicale belge*; director Brussels Conserv. 1949; composer of operas, ballets, orch. and chamber works, &c.

Pope and Turk Tune. The tune of Luther (one of the few that can with confidence be assigned to him) to his own hymn for the young. This tune and a translation of the hymn appeared in a good many of the Eng. psalters of the 16th and 17th cs. and were very well known. The hymn began—'Preserve us, Lord, by Thy dear Word; From Turk and Pope defend us, Lord'. The tune is still in some Brit. (and possibly Amer.) hymn books, under the name of *Spires*.

Pope John XXII. See *Church Music*.

Pope Pius X. See *Motu Proprio*.

Popper, David (b. Prague 1843; d. nr. Vienna 1913). Famous virtuoso 'cellist, latterly a prof. at Conserv. of Budapest; composed much for his instrument.

The well-known pianist Sophie Menter (q.v.) was temporarily his wife.

Pordon Danza (Sp.). A men's dance with lances (in Ger. *Lanzentanz*).

Porgy and Bess. See *Gershwin*.

Porpora, Niccolo Antonio (b. Naples 1686; there d. 1767). Prolific opera composer and famous singing-master; as former produced several operas in rivalry with Handel in London in 1730's and as latter had the young Haydn as accompanist and valet in Vienna in 1740's. Composed not only 53 operas but also songs, chamber music, harpsichord music, &c., but remaining reputation is as the world's greatest voice-trainer.

Port á Beul. Scottish Highland type of vocal perf., used for dancing in the absence of any instrument.

Portamento (It. 'carrying'). (1, with voice or a bowed instrument) Carrying on the tone from note to note without gaps, hence very *legato* and momentarily sounding the pitches in between any two indicated by the notation (see Table 22); the same effect is possible on the trombone. (2, with the piano) A half-staccato (a curious use of the word).

For 'Aria di Portamento' see *Aria*.

Portando; portato (It.). 'Carrying'; 'carried'. The same (usually) as *Portamento* (q.v.).

Portative Organ. See *Organ* 4.

Port de voix (Fr. 'Carrying of the voice'). A vocal *portamento* (q.v.). One or two obsolete 'graces' also bore this name, either as it stands or with some added adjective.

Porté, portée (Fr.). 'Carried.' Same as *Portamento* (q.v.). As a noun, however, *portée* means 'stave', or 'staff'.

Porter, (1) Walter (b. abt. 1595; d. 1659). Gentleman of Chapel Royal; publ. 1632 'Madrigals and Ayres' (not the normal kind but with instrumental accompaniment and interpolations). Said to have been pupil of Monteverdi.

(2) **Quincy** (b. New Haven, Conn., 1897; d. Bethany, Conn., 1966). Educ. Yale and Paris (Schola Cantorum, q.v.). Held Guggenheim Fellowship (1929–31). Various academic positions.

Dean of New England Conserv., Boston (1938). Prof. of Mus., Yale Univ., 1947–65. Viola player in chamber music combinations. Many chamber music and orch. comps., &c.

Porter la voix (Fr. 'To carry the voice'). To use the *Portamento* (q.v.).

Portsmouth Point. Concert-overture by Walton 'after a print by Rowlandson'. (1st perf. Zürich International Fest. of Modern Music 1926.)

Portunal, Portunalflöte (Ger.). An organ stop of open wooden pipes wider at the top than the bottom. It has a smooth tone.

Pos. (1, in Fr. organ music) *Positif*, i.e. 'Choir Organ'. (2, in violin music, &c.) *Posizione* (It.), or *Position* (Fr.), i.e. 'Position' (q.v.).

Posaune (Ger.). (1) Trombone. (2) Organ Reed Stop of 8- or 16-foot pitch.

Posément (Fr.). 'Steadily', 'sedately'.

Positif (Fr.). Choir organ (see *Organ* 1).

Position (1, in stringed instrument playing). The shift, i.e. the moving of the left hand up or down the fingerboard so that the fingers may produce different sets of notes. So '1st Position', '2nd Position', &c. (But for 'Position naturelle' see *Pos. nat.* below.) (2, in trombone playing). The shifting of the slide (see *Trombone Family*).

Positive Organ. See *Organ* 4. (A modern type of organ, 1887, has also taken this name. It is, by ingenious methods, devised to economize expense, and is cleverly arranged to give much the effect of a 2-manual organ with pedals though normally consisting of only 1 manual without pedals. It has also an automatic transposing device. The inventor was Thomas Casson.)

Posizione (It.). 'Position' (q.v.).

Pos. nat = *Position naturelle* (Fr.). Used in string parts to countermand (say) *Sur la touche* (see *Touche*).

Possibile (It.). 'Possible.' Generally used in some such connexion as *il più forte possible*, 'as loud as possible'.

Post, Joseph (b. Sydney 1906; d. Queensland, 1972). Studied piano and

oboë at N.S.W. Conserv. (later on staff as teacher of both instruments). Took up opera conducting and toured Australia and New Zealand. Then joined Australian Broadcasting Co. in 1939, becoming resident conductor at Melbourne station. In 1950 three months in England as chief conductor B.B.C. Northern Orchestra.

Postans, Mary. See *Shaw, Mrs. Alfred.*

Posthorn. A straight, oblong-coiled or circular-coiled brass instrument, without valves or other means of producing any notes except those of the harmonic series (see *Acoustics* 6, 7) of its fundamental note. Its longer varieties have been given the name of *Coach-horn*.

Postlude. Converse of 'prelude'. Anything played as an after-piece to anything else can be so called.

Poston, Elizabeth (b. Highfield Stevenage 1905). Trained R.A.M. Composer of songs, chamber music, &c. On staff B.B.C. 1940–5.

Pothier, Joseph (b. nr. St. Die 1835; d. Solesmes 1924). Benedictine (Abbot of Solesmes 1898 to death). Great authority on plainsong and reformer whose efforts led to Papal *Motu Proprio* (q.v.) of 1903.

Pot-pourri (Fr., lit. 'rotten-pot'). Properly rose leaves and spices kept in a pot for their scent, but in music fancifully applied to a composition which consists of a string of popular tunes.

Potter, (Philip) Cipriani (Hambly) (b. London 1792; there d. 1871). Studied in Vienna, where Beethoven encouraged and advised him; became well known as pianist, piano teacher, and Principal of R.A.M. (1832–59), choral and orch. conductor, writer on music, &c. Composed 9 symphonies, piano concertos, and pieces for piano solo, &c.

Pouce (Fr.). 'Thumb.'

Pougnet, Jean (b. Mauritius 1907). Violinist. Trained R.A.M. 1918–25. Début London 1923. Leader London Philharmonic Orch. 1942–5; then devoted himself to solo playing.

Pouishnoff, Leff Nicolas (b. Odessa 1891; d. London 1959). Pianist. Appeared at age 5. Trained St. Petersburg

Conserv. Recitals in England 1912; in U.S.A. 1923. Composer of piano music, &c.

Poule, La ('The Hen'). Nickname for Haydn's Symphony in G minor (1786), no. 83 in Breitkopf edn. of the Symphonies, i.e. the 2nd of the 'Paris Symphonies' (q.v.). The reference is to the clucking character of the 1st movement's 2nd subject.

Poulenc, Francis (b. Paris 1899; there d. 1963). Disciple of Satie (q.v.) and member of 'Les Six' (see *Six*); neat and effective pianist; composer of ballet music, chamber and piano music, songs, &c. See *Bernac*; *Biches*; *Dialogues des carmélites*.

Pounds, (Charles) Courtice (b. London 1862; d. 1928). Operatic tenor and actor. Trained R.A.M. Joined D'Oyly Carte Co. and made name in Gilbert and Sullivan and other light operas, &c., also Shakespeare's comedies, &c.

Poupée, La ('The Doll'). Very popular operetta by Audran. (Prod. Paris 1896; London and New York 1897.)

Pour (Fr.). 'For.'

Poussé (Fr.). 'Pushed', i.e. 'up-bow' (as contrasted with *tiré*, 'pulled', i.e. 'down-bow').

Powell, (1) Maud (b. Peru, Ill., 1868; d. Uniontown, Pa., 1920). Violinist. Pupil of Joachim, &c. Played in London from age 15. Founded own String Quartet. Enjoyed high Amer. and world repute.

(2) **John** (b. Richmond, Va., 1882; d. Charlottesville, Va., 1963). Concert pianist (pupil of Leschetizky); in 1920 became widely known as composer by *Rhapsodie nègre*; also composed orch. works, concertos for piano and for violin, piano sonatas, chamber and choral music, songs, an opera, &c.

(3) **Ioan Lloyd** (b. Ironbridge, Salop, 1888). Pianist. Trained R.C.M. (later on staff) and under Busoni. Has travelled much as player and Examiner. 1951 res. Canada.

Power, (1) Lionel (d. Winchester 1445). Famous composer of church music; also writer of important theoretical work *Treatise upon the Gamme*.

(2) **Sir George**, Bt. (b. Dublin 1846; d. London 1928). Operatic tenor and singing teacher. Trained Italy under

Lamperti, &c., 1873–6. Début Malta 1875. Appeared in production Sullivan's *H.M.S. Pinafore* (1878) and *Pirates of Penzance* (1879).

Pp, Ppp, &c. Abbreviations for *pianissimo*, i.e. very soft.

P.R. (in Fr. organ music) = *Positif-Récit*, i.e. 'Choir-Swell' (Swell to Choir coupler).

Prächtig, prachtvoll (Ger.). 'Grand', 'grandly', 'with high dignity', 'pompously'.

Präcis (Ger.). 'Precise' (in rhythm).

Praeludium (Lat.). 'Prelude.' See *Järnefelt*.

Praetorius (latinized form of Schulz, Schultz, or Schultze); larger books of reference give particulars of many 16th- and 17th-c. Ger. musicians of this name: the one which the present work can include is **Michael** (b. Kreuzburg, Thuringia, 1571; d. Wolfenbüttel 1621). Author of *Syntagma musicum* (3 vols., 1615–19), a valuable synopsis of musical knowledge of the period; also composer of very many motets, hymns, madrigals, instrumental pieces, &c.

Prague Symphony. Nickname of Mozart's Symphony in D, K. 504, 1st perf. in Prague (1787).

Pralltriller (Ger.). 'Upper Mordent' (see Table 12).

Präludium (Ger.). 'Prelude.'

Pratella, Balilla—in full Francesco Balilla (b. in the Romagna 1880; d. Ravenna 1955). Composer of operas, orch. music, &c., and musical writer of futurist views.

Pratt, (1) Silas Gamaliel (b. Addison, Vermont, 1846; d. Pittsburgh 1916). Composer of operas (*Zenobia*, Chicago 1882), orch. works (*Centennial Overture* 1876; Berlin and London), piano pieces, songs, &c.

(2) **Waldo Selden** (b. Philadelphia 1857; d. Hartford, Conn., 1939). Archaeologist and Egyptologist, who turned to music and was from 1882 on staff of Hartford Theological Seminary and other institutions. Wrote scholarly books on Church Music, the History

of Music in general, &c., and also a valuable Encyclopaedia of Music (1924).

Prayer of Habakkuk, The. See *Lloyd, J. A.*

Préambule (Fr.). 'Prelude.'

Pré aux Clercs, Le. Opera by Hérold. (Prod. Paris 1832; London 1833; New York 1843. Still very popular with Fr. audiences.)

Précédemment (Fr.). 'Previously.'

Precentor. The term (as old as the 4th c.) means 'First Singer', and is attached to the official in charge of the song in a cathedral or monastic establishment or a church. In the Eng. cathedrals the dignity of the precentor varies (for this see *Cathedral Music*). The SUCCENTOR is his deputy (this official exists only in cathedrals of the Old Foundation). The organist nowadays tends to get more control, but is nevertheless officially subject to his clerical superior. The precentor sits opposite the dean, whence the name for the 2 sides of the choir, Decani (i.e. 'of the Dean') and Cantoris (i.e. 'of the Precentor').

In the Presbyterian Churches of Scotland, which until the latter part of the 19th c. had no organs, the precentor was formerly a very important official. He was supplied with a pitchpipe and gave out and led the metrical psalm. Sometimes he was called the 'Uptaker of the Psalms'. In the earlier-settled parts of America the precentor has also had a place in the life of the religious community. As late as 1902 Prof. Edward Dickinson, in his *Music in the History of the Western Church,* alludes to churches where the congregation 'led by a precentor with voice or cornet assumes the whole burden of song'.

Preces (plur. of *prex*, 'prayer'). In liturgical worship, short petitions uttered by the priest and responded to by the congregation (or by the choir representing it). In the Church of England the prayers of this character that precede the Creed are called *Preces* and those that follow it *Versicles*; the harmonized plainsong settings of the Preces differ somewhat in different churches.

Precipitato, precipitoso, precipitosamente, precipitando, precipitandosi, con precipitazione, &c. (It.), **précipité** (Fr.). 'With precipitation'). 'Impetuously.'

Preciso; precisione (It.). 'Precise'; 'precision' (in the rhythmic sense).

Preface. The Versicles and Responses preceding the *Sanctus* in the Roman Catholic Mass (q.v.). A traditional plainsong is used. In the Anglican Communion Service there are 'Proper Prefaces' sung by the celebrant only on special festivals.

Pregando (It.). 'Praying', i.e. in a devotional manner. **Preghiera** (It.). 'Prayer.'

Prelude. Any piece of music composed to be played before any other piece of music, or play, ceremony, &c., can be so called. Each fugue of Bach's '48' is preceded by a prelude, and some of his suites open with one. Chopin has left 24 piano compositions (one in each major and minor key) under the name of 'Preludes' and other composers of piano music have similarly used the term for short compositions; here the idea, apparently, is that the music is such as an able pianist might extemporize before a performance of a set programme or a particular piece (a sort of 'trying the piano') which perhaps seems rather far-fetched. Wagner in some of his music-dramas dispenses with a long, formal overture, and applies to the shorter introductory orch. piece which takes its place the term 'Prelude'.

For 'Chorale Prelude' see under that head.

Prélude à l'Après-midi d'un Faune (Debussy). See *Après-midi.*

Prelude in C Sharp Minor of Rachmaninof. For Piano, being 1 of the 5 *Morceaux de Fantaisie* (op. 3, 1893; introduced into Britain by Siloti in recitals the same year and by him into the U.S.A. 5 years later). Soon so popular as to become known by many simply as 'The Prelude'. A curse to its composer, from his early twenties compelled by audiences to play it on every occasion when he appeared, to the neglect of his 23 other Preludes. Many absurd and unauthorized stories attached to it treating it as 'Programme Music' (one relates it to Napoleon's Moscow débacle, another to the premature burial of a young woman, &c.). Orch. versions by Henry Wood, Lucien Caillet, and possibly others.

Préluder (Fr.). 'To prelude'; often also 'to tune up' or 'to play a few introductory chords in an extempory manner'. So the present participle, *préludant*.

Préludes. Two books on piano pieces by Debussy. BOOK I (1910): (1) *Danseuses de Delphes* ('Dancing Women of Delphi'), suggested by a pillar in the Louvre on which are sculptured 3 Bacchantes; (2) *Voiles* ('Sails'); (3) *Le vent dans la plaine* ('The wind in the plain'); (4) *Les sons et les parfums tournent dans l'air du soir* ('Sounds and perfumes in the evening air'); (5) *Les collines d'Anacapri* ('The hills of Anacapri'); (6) *Des pas sur la neige* ('Footsteps on the snow'); (7) *Ce qu'a vu le vent d'Ouest* ('What the west wind saw'); (8) *La fille aux cheveux de lin* ('The girl with the flaxen hair'), suggested by a poem of Leconte de Lisle; (9) *La sérénade interrompue* ('The interrupted serenade'), Spanish in its idioms; (10) *La cathédrale engloutie* ('The submerged cathedral'), based on the legend of the cathedral of Ys, with its bell-tolling and chanting under the sea; (11) *La danse de Puck* ('Puck's dance'); (12) *Minstrels*—Negro or music-hall type. BOOK II (1910–13): (1) *Brouillards* ('Mists'); (2) *Feuilles mortes* ('Dead leaves'); (3) *La Puerta del Vino*—name of famous gate of Alhambra; suggestions of Spanish street-life; (4) *Les fées sont d'exquises danseuses* ('Fairies are exquisite dancers'); (5) *Bruyères* ('Heaths'); (6) *General Lavine—eccentric*—wooden puppet who appeared in Paris music-hall performance; (7) *La terrasse des audiences du clair de lune* ('Terrace of Moonlight Audiences'), with a hint of the ceremonies connected with it; (8) *Ondine*—the water-spirit maiden of the early 19th-c. story of de la Motte Fouqué; (9) *Hommage à S. Pickwick Esq., P.P.M.P.C.*—with a touch of the Brit. national anthem; (10) *Canope* ('Canopic vase'), ancient Egyptian cinerary urn; (11) *Les tierces*

alternées ('Alternating 3rds'); (12) *Feux d'artifice* ('Fireworks').

Préludes, Les. One of the earliest Symphonic Poems of Liszt (1848; revised 1850). Professedly based on one of Lamartine's *Méditations poétiques* of the same name. According to Liszt's 'programme' rather than to Lamartine, Life is treated as but a prelude to the Unknown which is to follow. (This piece of Liszt really began its existence in a different form, as an Overture to a set of 4 male choruses with words by Joseph Autran.)

Preludio (It.). 'Prelude' (q.v.).

Premier, première (Fr. masc., fem.). 'First.' So *première fois*, 'first time'.

Prendre (Fr.). 'To take.' *Prenez* is the imperative.

'Prentice Sorcerer (Dukas). See *Apprentice Sorcier*.

Preparation. See *Harmony* 2 g.

Près (Fr.). 'Near', e.g. *près de la touche*, 'near the finger board'—of the violin, &c. (referring to manner of bowing).

Presanctified, Mass of the. See *Mass*.

Presbyterian Church. See *Precentor*.

President's March. See *Hail Columbia*.

Presque (Fr.). 'Almost.'

Pressando, pressante (It.), **pressant** (Fr.). 'Pressing on', i.e. *accelerando*. Sometimes the Fr. infinitive is used, *presser*.

Presser, Theo, & Co. Philadelphia music publishing firm. Est. on basis of journal *The Étude* (pubd. 1883–1957). Cf. *Ditson; Church Company; Presser Foundation*.

Presser Foundation. Estd. 1916 by Theodore Presser, founder of Presser, Theo., & Co. (q.v.). Owns above company and awards music scholarships in various univs., &c., maintains near Philadelphia a large Home for Retired Music Teachers (1906), &c. President from 1918, James Francis Cooke (q.v.).

Pressez (Fr.); **pressieren** (Ger.). 'Press on', i.e. *accelerando*.

Prestant. Organ stop, same as Principal (q.v.) in Brit. and Amer. instruments.

Presto (It.). 'Quick.' So *prestezza*, 'quickness'; *prestamente*, 'quickly'; *prestissimo*, 'very quick'; *prestissimamente*, 'very quickly'.

Prêtre, Georges (b. Waziers, France, 1924). Début Paris 1946; then career as opera and concert conductor.

Previtali, Fernando (b. Adria, Italy, 1907). Trained Conservs. Turin and Rome. 1936-53 conductor of Rome Radio Orch. From 1959 dir. Acad. St. Cecilia.

Prey, Hermann (b. Berlin 1929). Trained Berlin Hochschule; then career as opera and concert baritone.

Price, Leontyne (b. Laurel, Miss., 1927). Dramatic soprano. Trained Juilliard. New York début 1952; Vienna 1958; Covent Garden 1959; La Scala 1960; Metropolitan 1961.

Prick Song (in older Eng. to 'prick' is to 'mark'). Composed and written music, as distinct from (*a*) the traditional plainsong, and (*b*) mere extempore warbling.

Prière (Fr.). 'Prayer.'

Prigioniero, Il. ('The Prisoner'). 1-act opera, libretto and music by Dallapiccola. (Prod. Turin 1949.)

Prima (It., fem. form of 'primo'). 'First.' Thus *prima donna* (q.v.), 'first lady'; *prima volta*, 'first time' (see Table 20); *prima vista*, 'first sight'; *come prima*, 'as at first'.

Prima Donna (It. 'First Lady'; plur. 'Prime Donne'). Properly the chief female vocalist in an opera cast. The term dates from the 1st c. of opera, i.e. some time before 1700. At that period the term *Primo uomo* ('First Man') was also in use—for the leading castrato singer (see *Voice* 5). Nowadays the term 'Prima Donna' is often used with a less definite significance—merely that of a woman vocalist of high reputation and earning power.

Prima Donna Assoluta (It. 'Absolute First Lady'). See *Prima Donna* above. On account of too free a use of that term, which may sometimes be applied to more than one lady in an opera cast, this extension of the term has been adopted to secure the *very first* one in her cherished pre-eminence.

Primary Tones. See *American Terminology* 6.

Prime. (1) The 3rd of the 8 Canonical Hours (see *Divine Office*) of the Roman Catholic Church, properly sung at 6 a.m. (i.e. the 1st hour of the working day). (2) The lower of 2 notes forming an interval (q.v.). (3) The root of a chord (see *Harmony* 2e). (4) The generator of a series of harmonics (see *Acoustics* 7). (5) A unison. (6) The 1st note of a scale. (7) The interval formed by 2 notes which are written on the same line or space (e.g. F and F sharp).

Primo (It.). 'First', e.g. *primo uomo*, 'first man', or leading male singer in an opera cast; *tempo primo*, 'first tempo', i.e. same speed as at the beginning; *primo violino*, 'first violin'.

Primrose, William (b. Glasgow 1903). Viola player. Trained as violinist at G.S.M.; later with Ysaÿe. Toured extensively; transferred to viola and joined London String Quartet (1930-5). Settled U.S.A.

Prince Igor. Opera by Borodin. Libretto by composer; posthumous and completed and edited by Rimsky-Korsakof and Glazunof. (Prod. St. Petersburg 1890; London 1914; New York 1915.)

See *Polovetz Dances.*

Prince of Wales, The. See *Owen, John.*

Princess Ida, or Castle Adamant. Comic opera by Gilbert and Sullivan. (Prod. Savoy Theatre, London, also New York and Boston, 1884.)

Princess of Kensington, A. Light opera by Edward German. (Prod. London 1903.)

Princess Royal, The. See *Arethusa.*

Principal. Open Diapason organ stop (see *Organ* 2) of 4-foot length on manuals or 8-foot on pedal. (In Ger. organ music it means an Open Diapason of 8, 4, or 16-foot pitch.)

Principale (It.). Great Organ (see *Organ* 1).

Printemps. (1, 2) By DEBUSSY (1887). Early Symphonic Suite. Also an early chorus for female voices of the same name (1882). (3-5) By MILHAUD. Piece for Violin and Piano (1914). Also

Chamber Symphony (1917). Also 6 Piano Pieces (1920).

Prinz von Homburg. Opera by Henze. Libretto by I. Bachmann after Kleist's play. (Prod. Hamburg 1960.)

Pritchard, John (Michael) (b. London 1921). Conductor. On Glyndebourne staff 1947; cond. 1952; cond. and mus. dir. Liverpool Orch. 1957; London Philharmonic 1961–6; Mus. dir. Glyndebourne 1969. C.B.E. 1962.

Prix de Rome. (1) FRANCE. The Academy of Fine Arts has since 1803 awarded annually, after prolonged and severe competitive examination, what would in English be called 'bursaries' or 'exhibitions' or 'scholarships', entitling the winners to live in Rome for 4 years, engaged in study and creative work. The subjects in which the competition is held are painting, sculpture, engraving, architecture, and music. The winner of a 1st prize (who henceforth styles himself 'Grand Prix de Rome') resides in the Fr. Academy, the Villa Medici. The form of the competition in music is the composition of a cantata on a given subject, the competitors being locked up (*en loge*) for some days to carry out their task. A 2nd prize is given, but consists merely of a gold medal.

(2) BELGIUM has a similar prize, under the same name, but the winner is not necessarily tied to residence in Rome during the tenure of his prize.

(3) THE UNITED STATES in 1905 instituted a similar Rome Prize, the winner of which resides at the Amer. Academy in Rome.

Procesión del Rocío, La ('The Procession of Rocío'). Symphonic Poem by Turina (1912). The Rocío is a well-known place of pilgrimage near Seville. In 2 parts: (*a*) *Triana en Fête*—Triana being a suburb of Seville; passing without break into (*b*) *The Procession*.

Procter-Gregg, Humphrey (b. Kirkby, Lancs., 1895). B.A., B.Mus., Cambridge; then R.C.M. Opera producer, &c. On staff Manchester Univ. 1946; Prof. of Music 1954; Dir. London Opera Centre 1961.

Prodaná Nevěsta (Smetana). See *Bartered Bride*.

Prodigal Son, The. (1) Oratorio by Sullivan. (1st perf. Worcester Fest. 1869. Boston 1879.) (2–5) See *Enfant prodigue*.

Proemio. 'Preface'; so 'Prelude'.

Profession of Music. The 1st conception of music as a distinct vocation seems to have been that of minstrelsy, and in all countries this was early regulated more or less rigidly by bodies on the lines of the craft guilds (see *Minstrels*). For some centuries an important branch of musical activity in England and elsewhere was that of the official Waits (q.v.).

The earliest church musicians were priests and monks, but a separate class of laymen church musicians in time emerged. For a treatment of this part of the subject see *Cathedral Music*; *Vicar Choral*; *Parish Clerk*.

Opera-houses began to be erected (first in Italy) during the early part of the 17th c. and public concert-schemes developed towards the end of that century. With these, new opportunities for professional activity came into existence.

It is only with the development of music printing and publishing that composition, as such, can be said to have declared itself as a separate and potentially self-supporting branch of the musical profession—and then it did so only very slowly. Up to the beginning of the 19th c. most of the great composers held official positions, and composition was with them a part of the work done in return for a regular salary. At the present time the number of composers is enormous, but comparatively few of them (unless engaged in the production of 'popular' ephemeral music) are able to maintain themselves purely by composition.

Teaching has always constituted a financially important part of the work of the musician. For a little information on the history of music teaching see *Education and Music*. For the organization of schools of music (which, except in Italy, dates only from the 18th c.) see the article *Schools of Music*. For official qualifications of teachers see *Degrees and Diplomas in Music*.

The loss of the craft-guild system has been, to an extent, made good in every country by the bringing into existence of professional societies, such as, in Britain, the Royal Coll. of Organists (1864), the Incorporated Soc. of Musicians (founded in 1882, reconstituted 1928), and the Music Teachers' Assoc. (1908), and in America the Music Teachers' National Assoc. (1876), the Amer. National Assoc. of Organists (1908), and the Music Supervisors' Conference (first held 1907; later the Music Educators' National Conference). Benevolent organizations must also be considered as partly supplying the place of one side of activity of the crafts guilds. Of these the oldest in Britain is the Royal Soc. of Musicians, founded in 1738, Handel being one of the foundation members.

The Brit. movement towards the registration of teachers of all subjects has included those of music. For the Royal Soc. of Teachers see information under *Degrees and Diplomas* 2.

See also *Musicians' Union*; *Musicians' Benevolent Fund*; *Incorporated Association of Organists*; *Musicians' Company*.

Programme Music. A term introduced by Liszt, who prefixed passages of explanatory matter to his symphonic poems, and called these 'programmes'. It is now applied to any instrumental music which reproduces or suggests literary ideas or evokes mental pictures. Such music has been composed in all periods from the 16th c. onwards. The contrary term is *Absolute Music* or *Abstract Music*.

Progression. See *Harmony* 2c.

Progressivo; progressivamente (It.). 'Progressive', 'progressively'.

Prokofief (Prokofiev, &c.), Serge (b. govt. of Ekaterinoslav, Russia, 1891; d. Moscow 1953). Studied at Conserv. of St. Petersburg under Liadof, Rimsky-Korsakof, and others; became brilliant pianist; at 23 won Rubinstein Prize with his 1st piano concerto; later composed operas (see *Love of Three Oranges*; *War and Peace*), ballets (see *Chout*; *Enfant prodigue*; *Pas d'acier*; *Romeo and Juliet*), more piano concertos, orch. works (e.g. *Scythian Suite*, q.v.; several symphonies), choral, chamber, and piano works, &c. Expressed primitive emotion with unconventional harmonies

and directness of utterance. He returned permanently to Russia in 1934.

See also *Alexander Nevsky*; *Lieutenant Kije*; *Peter and the Wolf*.

Promenade Concerts. See *Concert.*

Prometheus. (1) Symphonic Poem by LISZT. (1st version 1850, scored by Raff; 2nd version 1855, scored by the composer.) Composed as an Overture to Herder's dramatic treatment of the subject. (2) By BEETHOVEN. In full *Die Geschöpfe des Prometheus* ('The Creatures of Prometheus'). Ballet (op. 43, 1801), of which the Overture is the portion now best known. See *Prometheus Variations.*

Prometheus—The Poem of Fire. Symphonic Poem by Scriabin (op. 60, 1911). For Orch. with Piano, Chorus (*ad lib.*), and (properly) 'Keyboard of Light', throwing colours on a screen (cf. *Colour and Music*). It expresses some of the composer's theosophical ideas. The harmony is largely based on a chord of 4ths. (1st perf., without 'Keyboard of Light', Moscow and Chicago 1911 and London 1913; with that Keyboard, New York 1915.)

Prometheus Unbound. By Parry. Solo vocal, choral, and orch. setting of Shelley's poem (Gloucester Fest. 1880).

Prometheus Variations. By Beethoven for Piano (in E flat, op. 35, 1802). On a theme from his *Prometheus* Ballet (see above). The same theme was used in no. 7 of the 12 Contredanses for Orch. (op. 141, 1802); also in the finale of the *Eroica* Symphony (1804), hence the alternative name *Eroica Variations.*

Promised Land, The. Oratorio by Saint-Saëns. (1st perf. Gloucester Fest. 1913.)

Promptement (Fr.). 'Promptly.'

Pronto (It.). 'Ready', 'prompt'. So *prontamente*, 'promptly'.

Pronunciation. See *Voice* 8, 9.

Proper. See *Mass*; *Common.*

Prophète, Le. Historical tragedy-opera by Meyerbeer. Libretto by Scribe. (Prod. Paris and London 1849; New Orleans 1850; New York 1853.)

Prophet in the Land, A. See *Milford.*

Proportion. A conception that pervades medieval musical theory. It concerns the relations between the vibration numbers of notes (see *Acoustics* 13) and also between their time-lengths.

Proportional Notation. See *Notation.*

Proporz, Proportz. Same as *Nachtanz* (q.v.).

Prosa or **Prose.** See *Sequence* 2.

Proses lyriques. Four songs by Debussy to his own texts (1892–3).

Proske, Karl (1794–1861). See *Cecilian Movement.*

Protagonist, The. See *Weill, Kurt.*

Protestant Boys. See *Lilliburlero.*

Prout, Ebenezer (b. Oundle 1835; d. London 1909). Had long and active career as organist, conductor, composer (many works for various media, now all forgotten), a prof. of composition at R.A.M., Prof. of Music, Dublin Univ. (1894 to death), and especially author of a long series of valuable theoretical textbooks, the most exact and complete of their period. (See *Day, A.*)

Provençale (Fr. masc., fem.). Apparently a vague name for any dance of Provence.

Prowo. Ger. composer of early 18th c., of whom practically nothing is known. A concerto of his for 2 flutes, 2 oboes, and 2 bassoons is tuneful and well laid out.

Prowse. See *Keith Prowse.*

Prussian Quartets. Three string quartets by Mozart, in D (K. 575), B flat (K. 589), and F (K. 590), comp. in 1789–90 and dedicated to the 'cellist King of Prussia (Frederick William III). The 'cello parts are suitably prominent.

Ps. Short for *Posaunen*, i.e. trombones.

Psalm. The word 'Psalm' means a hymn accompanied by stringed instruments. The Book of Psalms is the oldest book of songs still in use. Some of the various Psalms are definitely accredited to particular authors; their titles give 73 to David. Some are ascribed simply to 'the chief musician'.

The VERSE SYSTEM of the psalms is that peculiar to Hebrew poetry. It is not to a great extent metrical, even in the original, and there is no rhyme: its rhyme and rhythm are, so to speak, those of thought rather than of words, expressing themselves especially in parallelism of thought. This parallelism should be grasped by all who are concerned with the musical rendering of the poems. It consists either in 2 balanced clauses of a verse, expressing the same or a similar thought, or in an antithesis between 2 clauses, or by a 2nd clause stating the result of the 1st.

The Psalms form the backbone or essential part of the Offices (Matins, Vespers, &c.) of the Roman Breviary and to some extent (following this tradition of 1,000 years) of Morning and Evening Prayer in the Anglican Church. (See *Common Prayer.*)

The MUSIC ATTACHED TO THE PSALMS in services of the Christian Church is referred to under *Gregorian Tones* and *Anglican Chant.* They are sung antiphonally either (as often in the Roman Catholic Church) by priest and choir, or, as in the Anglican Church, by the 2 sides of the choir. This antiphonal treatment is traditional and dates from the time of Solomon's Temple, as a number of biblical references show.

The PENITENTIAL PSALMS are in the Eng. Authorized Version, 6, 32, 38, 51, 102, 130, and 143, and in the Lat. Version (Vulgate), 6, 31, 37, 50, 101, 129, and 142. The numeration of these 2 translations differs from no. 10 onwards, 10 and 11 of the Eng. version being put together as one Psalm in the Latin. The Eng. version agrees with the Jewish prayer book.

The METRICAL PSALM, or verse paraphrase, holds a very important place in the history of English-speaking Protestantism; it is treated in this volume under *Hymns and Hymn Tunes* 3.

Single Psalms, and groups of them, have repeatedly been set by composers, as, for instance, Schütz, Bach, Mendelssohn, Franck, Florent Schmitt, Kodály, and, indeed, perhaps one may say most composers in history.

Psalmody. By this term is generally meant the study of the tunes for metrical versions of the psalms and for hymns, but it can, obviously, have a wider range of meaning. See *Hymns and Hymn Tunes*; *Psalms*; *Plainsong*; *Gregorian Tones*; *Anglican Chant.*

Psalmus Hungaricus. See *Kodály*.

Psaltery. An early stringed instrument (very widespread in the 14th and 15th cs.), like a dulcimer (q.v.) but played by plucking with a plectrum or the fingers. It may be considered a simple form of zither (q.v.). Cf. *Bell Harp*.

Psaume (Fr.). Psalm.

Pskovitianka (Rimsky-Korsakof), alias *Ivan the Terrible* (q.v.).

p.s.m. See *Degrees and Diplomas* 2.

P'tites Michu, Les. Very popular operetta by Messager. (Prod. Paris 1897; London 1905; New York 1907.)

Puccini, Giacomo Antonio Domenico Michele Secondo Maria (b. Lucca 1858; d. Brussels 1924). Represents 5th generation of family of musicians holding official positions in Italy. Trained at Milan Conserv. under Ponchielli and others; from 26th year recognized as important opera composer. Chief works, *Manon Lescaut*, 1893; *La Bohème*, 1896; *Tosca*, 1900; *Madame Butterfly*, 1904; *Trittico*, 1918 (consisting of *Il Tabarro*, i.e. 'The Cloak', *Suor Angelica*, 'Sister Angelica', and *Gianni Schicchi*); *Turandot* (posthumous, finished by Alfano, 1926). Style was typically Italian—easy-flowing melody, highly coloured orchestration, strong dramatic effects.

See separate entries under the name of the operas given above and also under *Girl of the Golden West*; *Rondine*; *Villi*.

Pueyo, Eduardo del (b. Saragossa, Spain, 1905). Pianist. Trained Madrid Conserv.; later on staff of that of Brussels. International career as concert artist.

Pugnani, Gaetano (b. Turin 1731; there d. 1798). Great violinist and composer for strings, of best 18th-c. type. (Familiar *Praeludium and Allegro* in E minor admitted by Kreisler to be entirely his own work.) Also composed a few operas, ballets, and cantatas.

Pugno, Raoul—in full Stépane Raoul (b. Montrouge, N. France, 1852; d. Moscow 1914). Pianist and composer. Italian by race. Trained Paris Conserv. A Paris organist to age 40; then on staff of Conserv., meantime

winning international reputation as solo pianist and in joint recitals with Ysaÿe. Many successful compositions, especially for stage.

Pujol (a series of musicians of Catalonia, apparently unrelated), (1) **Juan** (b. Barcelona abt. 1573; there d. 1626). Choirmaster of cathedral of his native city; composed valuable church music.

(2) **Juan Bautista** (b. Barcelona 1835; there d. 1898). Pianist, composer of piano music, and author of book on piano playing.

(3) **Francisco** (b. Barcelona 1878; d. there 1945). Composer of many Sardanas (q.v.), orch. and choral music, &c.; writer on Catalan folk music.

(4) **Emilio** (b. Lérida 1886). World-touring guitarist.

Pulcinella. Ballet, with songs, by Stravinsky after Pergolesi. (Prod. Paris 1920; music also heard as Orch. Suite.)

Pulitzer Scholarships. Travelling scholarships for U.S.A. music students founded under will of Joseph Pulitzer. First award 1917.

Pult (Ger. 'desk', plur. *Pulte*). Orch. music stand (shared by 2 performers, playing the same part). *Pultweise*, 'deskwise', i.e. in order of the players' desks.

Punta (It.). 'Point', e.g. *a punta d'arco*, 'with the point of the bow'.

Punto coronato, Punto d'organo (It., lit. 'crowned point', 'organ point'). The sign ⌒.

Pupitre (Fr. 'desk'). Orch. music stand (shared by 2 performers, playing the same part).

Purcell (London musical family, active in 4 generations, of whom 3 members can be mentioned here), (1) **Henry** (b. London 1659; there d. 1695). Son of a Gentleman of Chapel Royal and himself became a boy in its choir; at 18 appointed a 'Composer in Ordinary with fee, for the Violins' (i.e. the orch. of the Chapel); at 21 organist of Westminster Abbey (at £10 per annum) and at 23 organist also of Chapel Royal. Composed much church music, stage music (one real opera, *Dido and Æneas*, q.v.), many complimentary Odes to royalty, harpsichord pieces, chamber music, &c. Reckoned Britain's 'greatest composer' and certainly so of his period and style. For his brother and son see below.

See also *Bell Anthem*; *Bonduca*; *Dioclesian*; *Don Quixote*; *Fairy Queen*; *Golden Sonata*; *Gordian Knot Untied*; *Indian Queen*; *King Arthur*; *Lillibullero*; *Macbeth*; *Te Deum*; *Tempest*; *Trumpet Voluntary*.

(2) **Daniel** (b. London abt. 1663; there d. 1717). Brother of Henry, above. Organist of Magdalen Coll., Oxford (1688–95), then in London, where extremely popular composer of incidental music for plays; organist of St. Andrew's, Holborn (1713 to death).

(3) **Edward** (b. London 1689; there d. 1740). Son of Henry, above. Organist St. Clement's, Eastcheap, and then (1726) St. Margaret's, Westminster.

Purcell Cockram, E. See *Passing by*.

Purcell Society. Brit. body dating from 1876, object being complete publication of Purcell's works.

Purday, Charles Henry (b. Folkestone 1799; d. London 1885). Vocalist, precentor of Presbyterian Church, Crown Court, London, music publisher; composer of songs, hymn tunes (*Sandon*), &c.

Puritani di Scozia, I ('The Scottish Puritans'). Last opera of Bellini. (Prod. Paris and London 1835; Dublin 1837; Philadelphia 1843; New York 1844.)

See *Hexameron*.

Puritans and Music. As the influence of Puritanism on music has often been discussed, and as false views have often been expressed, it seems desirable that any reference book of music should give the actual facts.

Puritanism has been antagonistic to music, as such, only in the case of certain quite exceptional individuals or sects. But it has always been somewhat strict in what concerns music as a part of, or aid to, worship. (It is an error to suppose that this kind of musical Puritanism has been confined to certain Protestant bodies or to the Anglo-Saxon peoples: throughout the whole history of the Christian Church it has reappeared at intervals, and certain Popes and Councils have been in this sense amongst the most rigid Puritans. Nevertheless, the churches whose doctrines and practices have most closely followed those of the church of Calvin at Geneva have the most steadily held to the stricter view.)

During the Eng. Puritan rule of the 17th c. secular music flourished as never before, but there was an objection to elaborate church music, with church organs and choirs. Simplicity and sincerity were aimed at, but no doubt we must consider that a misreading of scripture, and consequent prejudice, was a factor in excluding so much that was beautiful from the service of the church. To the organ, as such, there was no objection; domestic organs were common and so were, apparently, tavern organs.

A very large quantity of music was publ. during the Commonwealth and Protectorate, which (perhaps through the suppression of spoken stage plays and church music activities) released a great flood of secular musical publication. Playford's famous *Dancing Master* then first appeared and during this period it went into 3 edns., each time enlarged by the addition of extra tunes and dances: there was, in general, no objection to dancing, but a few of the stricter Puritans feared the results of 'mixed dancing' (i.e. of the sexes together). Rounds and catches, madrigals, string fantasias, collections of 'Lessons' for lute and for viol, tunes for the violin, books on the theory of music, and other musical works of every possible kind, were poured out in a profusion much greater than that of the periods immediately preceding or immediately following. The masque (q.v.) was one of the occasional diversions and opera first began in Britain then (see *Opera* 5).

It is often charged against the Puritan control of the country that *a cappella* compositions, and particularly the madrigals, ceased to be written about this time, but this is equally true of the same period in Italy, Germany, France, and other countries, and is to be put down to the general change of fashion. There is evidently not the very slightest ground for the often repeated statement that the Commonwealth and Protectorate (1649–60) 'killed' Eng. music, as the career of the great Purcell immediately followed this period.

The Pilgrim Fathers of 1620, and those who followed them across the Atlantic, had their attention taken up with work and the anxieties of winning a living and of self-defence, and they do not seem to have practised the arts to any high degree. It is often stated in books on Amer. music that they strongly objected to music and even legislated against it; but no supporting evidence can be found for this statement, which seems to be a mere reflection of that one which attributes such an objection to the Puritans in England. The Pilgrim Fathers themselves were Brownists, i.e. Independents (Congregationalists), and they could certainly have drawn no hatred of music from their founder, Robert Browne, who was 'a singular good lutenist' and taught his children to perform.

Whilst to some extent the misconception as to the feeling towards music of the Eng. and Colonial 17th-c. Puritans is due to a mistaken deduction from the fact that they disliked elaborate music in church, yet to some extent it is doubtless also due to a confusion with an objection to music that did

exist in some degree amongst the late 18th- and early 19th-c. Evangelicals, who sometimes felt music to be 'worldly' and 'a snare'.

See *Calvin*; *Anglican Parish Church Music*; *Cathedral Music*; *Deering* (for ref. to Cromwell); *Milton* 2.

Puy. See *Competitions in Music*.

Pyne. Musical family, members of which were before public for 125 years. The most important are: (1) **James Kendrick I** (b. 1785; d. 1857). Tenor. (2) **James Kendrick II** (b. Crayford, Kent, 1810; d. Bath 1893). Organist Bath Abbey; composed glees, &c. (3) **Louisa Fanny** (b. 1832; d. London 1904). Niece of (2). Operatic soprano. Very successful in Britain and U.S.A. Partner in Pyne-Harrison Opera Co. 1856–64. Married (1868) the baritone Frank Bodda (abt. 1823–1892) and retired from stage. (4) **James Kendrick III** (b. Bath 1852; d. 1938). Son of (2). Pupil of S. S. Wesley. Many organist positions, culminating Manchester Cathedral 1876–1908; also Town Hall same period. On staff of Royal Manchester Coll. of Music and Univ. Hon. D.Mus., Lambeth, 1901.

Q

Quadrat (Ger.). The sign of the Natural (see Table 7).

Quadrille. A square dance which first became popular at the court of Napoleon I and then in France generally, and was imported in 1816 into Britain, where it soon became the rage. The music fell in 5 sections in different kinds of time. Independently of dancing multitudes of quadrilles were composed, often based on airs from some opera, or the like. The LANCERS, introduced about 40 years later, was a variant of the Quadrille.

Quadruple Chants. See *Anglican Chant*.

Quadruple Counterpoint. See *Counterpoint*.

Quadruple-Croche. (Fr. 'quadruple-hook'). Hemidemisemiquaver or Sixty-fourth note (see Table 3).

Quadruplet. See Table 11.

Quadruple Time. See Table 10.

Quail. An instrument that imitates the cry of the bird of that name and is used in Toy Symphonies (q.v.), such as that of Haydn.

Qual (Ger.). 'Agony.' So *qualvoll*, 'agonized'.

Quanto (It.). 'As much', 'so much'.

Quantz, Johann Joachim (b. nr. Göttingen 1697; d. Potsdam 1773). Great flautist and flute composer (300 concertos, &c.) in service (1741 to death) of that other flautist Frederick the Great. Book on flute playing (many edns. 1752–1926), gives much general information on musical ideas of period.

Quartal. Term applied to harmony (medieval or modern) of which chords are constructed on basis not of superposed 3rds but 4ths.

Quarter-note. Crotchet (see Table 3).

Quarter-tone. See *Microtones*.

Quartet (Fr. *Quatuor*; Ger. *Quartett*; It. *Quartetto*). (1) Any body of 4 performers, vocal or instrumental. (2) Any piece of music composed for such.

The following are some specific instances of the use of the word: (*a*) *Mixed Voice Quartet* (or often simply 'Vocal Quartet'), Soprano, Alto or Contralto, Tenor, and Bass—often abbreviated 'S.A.T.B.'; (*b*) *Double Quartet*, the same with 2 voices to a part, or sometimes 8 voices each with its own part (properly this is an 'Octet'); (*c*) *Male Voice Quartet*, generally either alto, 1st and 2nd tenor, and bass, or 1st and 2nd tenor and 1st and 2nd bass (the terms 'With alto lead' and 'With tenor lead' express the distinction; (*d*) *String Quartet*, 2 violins, viola, and violoncello; (*e*) *Piano Quartet*, 3 bowed instruments and piano (and similarly with *Flute Quartet*, &c.).

Quartett (Ger.). 'Quartet' (q.v.).

Quartetto (It.). 'Quartet' (q.v.).

Quarto (It.). 'Fourth.'

Quasi (It.). 'As if.' Thus often 'almost'.

Quatre (Fr.). 'Four.' Hence *quatrième*, 'fourth'.

Quattro (It.). 'Four'; e.g. *quattro mani*, 'four hands'; *quattro voci*, 'four voices'.

Quattro pezzi sacri. A comprehensive title for 4 short choral works by Verdi: *Ave Maria, Stabat Mater, Laudi alla Vergine Maria, Te Deum* (1st perf. Paris 1898).

Quattro rusteghi. See *I quatro rusteghi*.

Quatuor (Fr.). 'Quartet' (q.v.).

Quaver (♪). The eighth-note, i.e. ⅛ the time-value of the whole-note or semibreve (see Table 1).

Que (Fr.). 'That', 'as'.

Queen, or Queen of France Symphony (Haydn). See *Reine*.

Queen Dido (Wilson). See *Brenhines Dido*.

Queen Elizabeth's Virginal Book. See *Fitzwilliam Virginal Book*.

Queen of Sheba (Goldmark). See *Königin*.

Queen of Spades (Also known as *Pique Dame*). Opera by Tchaikovsky. Libretto based on Pushkin's novel. (Prod. St. Petersburg 1890; New York 1910; London 1915.)

Queen's Hall (London). Built 1893 and the chief place of London music-making up to destruction by enemy aircraft 1941. See *Concert*; *Wood* (2); *Newman, Robert*.

Quelque, Quelques (Fr. sing., plur.). 'Some.'

Querflöte (Ger.). 'Transverse (i.e. modern) flute' (see *Flute Family*).

Querimonia di S. Maria Maddalena. See *Mazzocchi, Domenico*.

Questo, questa (It. masc., fem.; plur. *questi, queste*). 'This.'

Queue (Fr. 'tail'). *Piano à queue*, 'grand piano'.

Quid sum miser. See *Requiem*.

Quiet City. By Copland. For trumpet, cor anglais, and strings. Originally Incidental Music to play by Irwin Shaw. (Prod. New York 1939; as self-dependent music 1941.)

Quiet flows the Don. See *Dzerzhinsky*.

Quieto (It.). 'Quiet', 'calm'. *Quietissimo* is the superlative.

Quilter, Roger (b. Brighton 1877; d. London 1953). Studied in Germany. Composer of light, pleasant songs and music for plays, &c. Also *Children's Overture* (1920); light opera *Julia* (produced London 1936), &c.

Quint. Organ stop making use of the acoustical phenomenon of 'differential tones' (see *Acoustics* 14). When on the pedal it is a 10⅔-foot stop designed to be used in conjunction with a 16-foot stop, producing the effect of a 32-foot stop.

Quintadena. Much the same as *Quintatön* (q.v.) but with the additional harmonic sound more strongly heard.

Quintatön. Organ stop of type of *Bourdon* (q.v.) but so constructed that

the harmonic (see *Acoustics* 7) octave-5th (i.e. 12th) is faintly heard with the normal sound.

Quintenquartett ('Fifths Quartet'). Nickname of Haydn's String Quartet 'No. 69' or 'No. 76', in D minor, sometimes described as op. 76, no. 2. The name arises from the leaps of the interval of a 5th in the chief theme of the 1st movement. One movement is sometimes called *Hexenmenuett* ('Witch Minuet').

Quintet (Fr. *Quintette* or *Quintuor*; It. *Quintetto*; Ger. *Quintett*). (1) Any body of 5 performers. (2) Any music composed for such.

The following are some specific instances of uses of the word: (a) *String Quintet*, for 2 violins, 2 violas, and 'cello; or 2 violins, viola, and 2 'cellos—or (rarely) 1 'cello and double-bass. (b) *Piano Quintet*, string quartet plus piano. (c) *Clarinet Quintet*, string quartet plus clarinet. (d) *Vocal Quintet*, usually for 2 sopranos, contralto, tenor, and bass.

Quinto, quinta (It. masc., fem.). 'Fifth.'

Quintsaite (Ger.). E string of violin.

Quintuor (Fr.). 'Quintet' (q.v.).

Quintuple Counterpoint. See *Counterpoint*.

Quintuplet. See Table 11.

Quintuple Time. See Table 10 (notes at end).

Qui sedes. See *Mass*.

Qui tollis peccata mundi. See *Mass*.

Quitter (Fr.), 'To quit', 'To leave'.

Quodlibet (Lat. 'what you please' or 'what pleases'). Collection of tunes or fragments of compositions (vocal or instrumental) brought together as a joke, being arranged either (a) for perf. successively (cf. *Musical Switch*), or (b) for perf. simultaneously.

Quoniam tu solus sanctus. See *Mass*.

Quo Vadis. Oratorio by DYSON. Text from various poets. (1st complete perf. Three Choirs Fest. 1949.)

R

R. (in Fr. organ music) = *Récit*, i.e.
Swell Organ.

Rabaud, Henri (b. Paris 1873; d.
there 1949). Pupil of Massenet at Paris
Conservatory and won Rome Prize
1894; opera conductor at Paris Opéra
Comique and then Grand Opera; conductor of Boston Symphony Orch.,
U.S.A. (1918); director of Paris Conserv. 1920. Composed many operas
(see *Mârouf*), orch. and choral works,
&c.

Rabbia (It.). 'Rage.'

Rachmaninof   (**Rachmaninov,
Rakhmaninoff,** &c.), **Serge** (b. in
govt. of Novgorod 1873; d. California
1943). Studied under Arensky, Taneief,
and others at Conserv. of St. Petersburg; did much orch. and opera conducting (Imperial Opera, Moscow,
1905–6); left Russia 1917; made high
reputation in old and new worlds as
pianist of great artistry; composed
operas (*Aleko* 1892), 3 symphonies,
4 piano concertos, symphonic poem
(*Island of the Dead*, q.v.), works for
orch. and chorus (Poe's *The Bells*,
Birmingham 1921), chamber music,
songs, and piano solos (see *Prelude in
C sharp minor*; *Paganini Transcriptions*), &c.

Raddolcendo,   raddolcente (It.
'sweetening'). 'Becoming gentler',
'calming down'. So, too, *Raddolciato*,
'calmer'.

Raddoppiare (It.). 'To double.'
Hence *raddoppiamento*, 'doubling'.

Radford, Robert (b. Nottingham
1874; d. London 1933). Operatic,
oratorio, and concert bass vocalist.
Trained R.A.M. Of high Brit. reputation in all his 3 capacities. One of
founders and directors of Brit. National
Opera Co. (1922–9).

Radiant Morn, The. See *Woodward,
H. H.*

Radical Cadence. See *Cadence.*

Radio. See *Broadcasting of Music.*

Radiotone. See *Electric Musical Instruments 2.*

Raff, Joseph Joachim (b. Lachen, on
Lake Zürich, 1822; d. Frankfort-on-
Main 1882). School teacher; encouraged by Mendelssohn, Liszt, and von
Bülow, fought his way, poor and self-
taught, to great prominence in musical
world of Germany; attached to the
'Music of the Future' movement of
Liszt and Wagner. As composer very
prolific: operas, symphonies, concertos, chamber music, &c., brought high
fame in many countries, which quickly
faded with his death. (Now known to
general public by only a trifle, the ever-
popular 'Raff's Cavatina'.)

Raffrenando (It., from *freno*, 'brake').
'Putting on the brake', i.e. checking the
speed.

Rage over a lost penny (Beethoven,
op. 129). Youthful unfinished piano
piece publ. posthumously. Original
title *Alla ingharese* [sic], *quasi un
capriccio* ('In Hungarian style; a sort
of Capriccio'); composer later added
title *Leichter Kaprice* ('Easy Capriccio').
Present title added by unknown hand.
New edn. based on autograph discovered (abt. 1947) in U.S.A.

Rageur (Fr.). 'Ill-tempered.'

Ragtime. The Ragtime era began in
1897. As distinct from Jazz (q.v.),
which is an art of improvisation, Ragtime was essentially composed music,
usually played on the piano, with
many printed and published examples:
characteristically piano ragtime consisted of regular melodic lines, simply
syncopated over a four-square march-
style bass. Its popularity with an
enormous international audience lasted
until the early 1920's, by which time
it had been replaced by jazz (q.v.).

Raimondi, Pietro (b. Rome 1786;
there d. 1853). Composed 64 operas,
21 ballets, &c., but chiefly famous for
the ingenuity with which he contrived
4-voice fugues, each capable of being
performed separately or in combination

with 3, or 5 others, 3 oratorios similarly performable retail or wholesale, 2 operas on the same lines. These valuable time-saving devices await revival.

Raindrop Prelude for Piano. Chopin's op. 28, no. 15, in D flat. The nickname is based on the idea that it was composed whilst rain was falling, and was influenced thereby.

Rainier, Priaulx (b. Natal, S. Africa, 1903). Violinist and composer. Trained Cape Town and R.A.M., then under Nadia Boulanger in Paris; from 1942 on staff R.A.M. Her works include string quartet and other chamber music; also songs.

Rains, Leon (b. New York 1870; d. Los Angeles 1954). Operatic and concert bass. Training under Bouhy (q.v.), Paris, &c., followed by successes in old and new worlds.

Raisa, Rosa (b. Bialystok, Poland, 1893; d. Los Angeles 1963). Operatic soprano. Toured Poland as child singer, then trained Naples Conserv. Operatic début Parma 1913. Taken (in the same year) to U.S.A. by Cleofonte Campanini (q.v.), making début Chicago. In later days teaching in California.

Raisbeck, Rosina (b. Ballarat, Victoria, 1918). Operatic soprano singer. Trained N.S.W. State Conserv., Sydney, and with Bouhy (q.v.). Début Sydney (as contralto) 1944; Covent Garden (as mezzo) 1947; (as soprano) 1950.

Rake's Progress, The. 3-act opera by Stravinsky. Libretto by W. H. Auden and Chester Kallman, after Hogarth. (Prod. Venice 1951.)

See also *Gordon, Gavin*

Rákóczy March. Francis Rákóczy was the heroic leader in the Hungarian insurrection of 1703–11. The march named after him dates from 1809, but is based on old Hungarian airs. It was composed by János Bihari, a typical Hungarian gipsy violin virtuoso, specially for the use of a Pesth regiment about to march against Napoleon. It fell into forgetfulness until 1838, when Liszt included it in the programme of a recital tour in Hungary, and the arrangement of Berlioz (*Marche Hongroise*, 1846) estd. it in full favour. Berlioz then added it to his *Scenes from 'Faust'*, publ. 17 years earlier and now remodelled as *The Damnation of Faust*.

Ralentir (Fr.). 'To slow down.'

Ralf, (1) Torsten (b. Malmö, Sweden, 1901; d. Stockholm 1954). Tenor. Trained Stockholm Conserv. and in Berlin. Opera career in Ger. and other European cities. Metropolitan Opera, New York, 1945–8.

(2) **Eileen** (b. Perth, W. Australia, 1913). Pianist. Studied R.A.M. London; début 1936. Commonwealth and European tours, alone and with husband Thomas Matthews (see *Matthews* 2).

Rallentare; rallentando; rallentato (It.). 'To slow', 'slowing', 'slowed' (in each case gradually). So the noun *rallentamento*.

R.A.M. Royal Academy of Music, London. (See *Schools of Music*; *Degrees and Diplomas* 2.)

Rambert, Marie (Myriam Ramberg) (b. Warsaw 1888). Dancer and teacher. Paris 1906; own school in London 1920; 'Ballet Rambert' from 1926 important training ground for dancers and choreographers.

Rameau, Jean Philippe (b. Dijon 1683; d. Paris 1764). Son of organist of Dijon Cathedral; himself organist at many Fr. towns; when organist at Clermont-Ferrand wrote his famous *Treatise on Harmony* (Paris 1726), in which novel doctrines, such as that explaining some chords as 'inversions' of other chords (see *Harmony* 2 e), were first brought forward. Now became fashionable Paris harpsichord teacher, &c.; composed much fine music for harpsichord. At 50 (1733) produced opera *Hippolyte et Aricie*; henceforth many operas and ballets which are of very high importance in the history of Fr. music from their musical beauty and dramatic truth, the recitative being a strong feature, the orchestration another (*Castor and Pollux* 1737, his masterpiece). Was in the thick of the 'Guerre des Bouffons' (see *Bouffons*), writing many pamphlets. Public honours poured on him at the last; was allotted a pension by the director of the Opera, was exempted from payment of municipal taxes, was appointed chamber music composer to the King, was ennobled, and when he died was accorded a public funeral.

See *Opera* 2.

Rameaux, Les. See *Faure, J. B.*

Ramsbotham, Alexander (b. Leeds 1862; d. London 1932). Anglican clergyman (Preacher of Charterhouse, London) and distinguished musical scholar; edited 'Old Hall Manuscript' (q.v.), &c.

Ranalow, Frederick Baring (b. Dublin 1873; d. London 1953). Baritone. Trained R.A.M. Quickly won high position in concerts and festivals, &c.; then prominent exponent of varied leading parts in Beecham Opera Co. With London revival of *Beggar's Opera*, 1920, became its Macheath, playing the part 1,600 times; also in many light operas, films, &c. On Staff G.S.M.

Randegger, Alberto (b. Trieste 1832; d. London 1911). Settled London 1854. Active as theatre, opera, orch., and choral conductor. Attained great favour as singing teacher (R.A.M. and R.C.M.). Some compositions and a book on singing.

Ranelagh. See *Concert*.

Rangertone. See *Electric Musical Instruments* 4.

Rank (referring to 'mixture' stops). See *Organ* 2.

Rankl, Karl (b. Gaden, Austria, 1898; d. Austria 1968). Orch. and operatic conductor. Pupil of Schönberg, &c. Held many important positions in Germany, Czechoslovakia, &c. Came to Britain 1939; musical director Covent Garden 1946–51. Cond. Scottish Nat. Orch. 1952–4; Sydney Opera 1958. Various compositions.

Rant. Old Eng. dance of a character now not easily determined.

Ranz des Vaches; or Kuhreigen or Kuhreihen (Swiss-Fr. and Swiss-Ger. respectively, meaning 'cow-rank', i.e. 'cow procession'). A type of Swiss Alpine melody, sung or played on the Alphorn (q.v.) to call (for milking, &c.) the cows scattered over the mountain-side. Every district has its own version and some of the versions

(or modifications thereof) have been introduced into compositions, e.g. Rossini's *William Tell* overture, Beethoven's *Pastoral Symphony*, Berlioz's *Fantastic Symphony*, Schumann's *Manfred*, and Strauss's *Don Quixote*. Kienzl has an opera *Der Kuhreigen* (see *Kuhreigen*).

Rape of Lucretia, The. 2-act opera by Britten. Libretto by R. Duncan, derived from Livy and Shakespeare via A. Obey's play. Chamber orch. of about a dozen. (Prod. Glyndebourne 1946; Basle and elsewhere 1947; New York 1948.)

Rapido; rapidamente; rapidità (It.). 'Rapid'; rapidly'; 'rapidity'.

Rapper. See *Sword Dance*.

Rapports. See *Reports*.

Rappresentazione dell' Anima e del Corpo, La (Cavalieri). See *Oratorio*.

Rapprocher (Fr.). 'To bring closer together.' So the present and past participles *rapprochant, rapproché*.

Rapsodia (It.). 'Rhapsody' (q.v.).

Rapsodie norvègienne. By Lalo. (1st perf., by Sarasate, Paris, 1881.) An enlargement of his earlier *Fantaisie norvègienne* (1879).

Raptak. A whirlwind type of dance that appears in Delibes's opera *Lakmé*. Another name is *Rektah*.

Rasch; rascher (Ger.). 'Quick'; 'quicker'.

Rasiermesserquartett ('Razor Quartet'). Nickname of Haydn's String Quartet, 'No. 54' or 'No. 61', in F minor, sometimes described as op. 55, no. 2 (cf. *Tostquartette*). The story is of the composer, when shaving, crying, 'I'd give my best quartet for a new razor', and being taken at his word by a visitor, the London music-publisher, Bland.

Rasoumoffsky Quartets. See *Beethoven's String Quartets*.

Rathaus, Karol (b. Tarnopol, Poland, 1895; d. New York 1954. A naturalized Austrian). Studied composition under Schreker in Berlin. Composer of a number of operas, symphonies, &c.; chamber music; piano sonatas, &c. Style inclines to atonality.

Ratisbon Edition. See *Plainsong* 3.

Ratsche (Ger.). 'Rattle.'

Rattenere; rattenendo; rattenuto (It.). 'To hold back'; 'holding back'; 'held back' (in each case gradually).

Rattle. See *Percussion Family* 2 r.

Rauh (Ger.). 'Rough', 'coarse'.

Rauschend (Ger.). 'Rushing', 'dashing'. But perhaps more commonly 'rustling', 'murmuring'.

Rauzzini, Venanzio (b. Camerino 1746; d. Bath 1810). Famous tenor vocalist, singing teacher with many pupils, and concert organizer. Composer of operas, piano sonatas, chamber music, songs, &c. Last part of life spent in London and then Bath.

Ravel, Maurice Joseph (b. Ciboure, nr. St. Jean de Luz, 1875; d. Paris 1937). Trained in Paris Conserv. under Fauré and others; unsuccessfully competed 4 times for Rome Prize (1901-2-3-5); on last occasion eliminated in preliminary test as incompetent although some fine piano music and the string quartet already publ. (1903); this occasioned loud public protests against academic intolerance and the resignation of the director of the Conservatory, Dubois.

Works include fine piano music, orch. music, 2 operas (see *Enfant et les sortilèges; Heure espagnole*), ballets (see *Daphnis and Chloë*), many songs (largely settings of symbolist poets), and chamber music.

His music often classed with that of Debussy; both looked on as Impressionists but Ravel's music less fluid than Debussy's, making no use of whole-tone scale.

See also *Bolero; Gaspard de la nuit; Ma mère l'oye; Miroirs; Pavane pour une enfante défunte; Sheherazade; Tombeau de Couperin; Valse; Valses nobles et sentimentales.*

Ravenscroft, (1) Thomas (b. abt. 1590; d. abt. 1633). Chorister of St. Paul's Cathedral, London; then music master of Christ's Hospital. Publ. *Pammelia* and *Deuteromelia* (both 1609), being books of rounds and catches including round, *Three Blind Mice*, still well known); also *Melismata* (1611), being madrigals, rounds, and catches. Also a theoretical work, and famous book of metrical psalm tunes.

(2) **John** (d. abt. 1745). One of waits of a London district and theatre violinist; composed some hornpipes and a set of sonatas for 2 violins and bass viol (Rome 1695). Or it may be that these 2 series of compositions were the work of 2 composers of same name.

Ravinia Park. A Chicago suburb where during the summer months large-scale fest. performances are annually given. This dates from 1911 when the Ravinia Opera Co. was founded, which continued its operations for 20 years being then superseded by the present fest. organization.

Ravogli sisters, often appearing together in opera. (1) **Sofia** (b. Rome 1855; there d. 1910). Soprano. (2) **Giulia.** Contralto.

Ravvivando; ravvivato (It.). 'Quickening'; 'quickened'.

Rawsthorne, Alan (b. Haslingden, Lancs., 1905; d. Cambridge 1971). Began music study late 'owing to parental opposition'. Then trained Royal Manchester Coll. of Music. Composed many successful works, including 3 symphonies, 2 piano concertos, 2 violin concertos, chamber music and choral pieces. C.B.E. 1960.

See *Cortèges.*

Ray. See *Re.*

Raybould, Clarence (b. Birmingham 1886). Trained Birmingham Univ. (B.Mus.). First career as church organist (F.R.C.O.). On staff of Midland Inst. School of Music, Birmingham, and later on that of G.S.M. (opera class); 9 years associated with Covent Garden; a conductor, &c., of B.B.C. 1936-45. On staff R.A.M. 1944-61. Frequent conducting tours abroad. Composer of piano music, opera, &c. Hon. D.Mus. (Swansea).

Raymond. See *Thomas, C. L. A.*

Razor Quartet (Haydn). See *Rasier-messerquartett.*

R.C.M. Royal Coll. of Music, London (q.v.).

R.C.O. Royal Coll. of Organists. (See *Degrees and Diplomas* 2.)

Re. The 2nd degree of the major scale, according to the system of vocal syllables derived from Guido d'Arezzo (see *Hexachord*), and so used (spelt *Ray*) in Tonic Sol-fa (also in that system the 4th degree of the minor scale; see *Tonic Sol-fa*). In many countries, however, the name has become attached (on 'fixed-doh' principles; see *Sight-Singing*) to the note D, in whatever key this may occur (see Table 5).

Read, (1) **Gardner** (b. Evanston, Ill., 1913). Studied with Pizzetti. Composer of orch., chamber, organ, and piano works. First Symphony won prize of New York Philharmonic-Symphony Soc. 1937. On staff Boston University.

(2) **Ernest** (b. nr. Guildford, Surrey, 1879; d. London 1965). Conductor and educationist. Trained R.A.M.; on staff from 1914. Founder of London Junior Orch. (1926) and Ernest Read Orch. Concerts for children; very active in many phases of music education. Books on aural training, &c. C.B.E. 1956.

Reading, John (d. Winchester 1692). Vicar-choral of Lincoln Cathedral (1667), master of choristers there (1670); organist of Winchester Cathedral (1675), and of Winchester Coll. (1681); for latter composed well-known song, *Dulce domum*, q.v. (Note: larger books of reference list 3 or 4 other John Readings.)

Real Answer, Real Fugue. See *Form* 6.

Real Sequence. See *Sequence* 1.

Rebec or **Rebeck.** An early bowed instrument of which there existed a family, from treble to bass. Other names were *Ribible* or *Rubible*, and *Humstrum* (q.v.).

Rebel Maid, The. Light Opera by Montague Phillips. (1st perf. London 1921.)

Rebikof (Rebikow, Ryebikoff, &c.), Vladimir (b. Krasnoyarsk, Siberia, 1866; d. Yalta, Crimea, 1920). Studied, lived, and worked in various places in Russia and in Berlin and Vienna. As composer exploited whole-tone scale

(see *Scale*), new harmonies, &c. Composed 'Melomimics' (short piano or vocal pieces allied with pantomime), 'Rhythmodeclamations' and 'Musical Psychological Sketches' (i.e. dramas, e.g. *The Christmas Tree* 1903). Much piano music.

Rebute (Fr.). Jew's Harp (q.v.).

Recapitulation. See *Form* 3.

Recht, Rechte (Ger. masc., fem.). 'Right.'

Récit. Short for *Recitative* (q.v.).

Récit (Fr.). 'Swell Organ.' Note that this is not, as stated in some Eng. books, an abbrev. for 'Récitatif', but a complete word in itself.

Recital. According to Busby's *Dictionary of Music*, in 1811, this word was 'formerly the general name for any performance with a single voice' but had by then come to be 'applied only to recitative'. Apparently the earliest use of it in something like its present sense was in 1840, when the young Liszt, in London, was announced to give 'on Tuesday morning, June 9, Recitals on the Pianoforte' and 'on Wednesday evening a recital of one of his great fantasias'. The present sense of the word is that of a complete programme presented by 1 chief performer or 2 such performers, e.g. 'Organ Recital', 'Pianoforte Recital', 'Pianoforte and Violin Recital', 'Vocal Recital'.

Recitando, recitante (It.), **récitant** (Fr.). 'Reciting' (i.e. more like speech than song). So also *recitato*, 'recited'.

Recitative. A style of solo vocal composition in which ordered melody, rhythm, and metre are largely disregarded in favour of some imitation of the natural inflections of speech. Another name is *Musica parlante* (It. 'Speaking music'). In opera or oratorio it commonly serves for dialogue, or narrative, or dramatic expression, whilst the Aria (q.v.) serves for extended soliloquy and the more lyrical type of expression. For the purpose behind the original introduction of recitative see *Opera* 1.

There are various types of recitative, including the following: (1) RECITATIVO

SECCO (It. 'Dry Recitative') is a quick-moving type, with a mere background of simple chords as accompaniment; the 18th-c. practice was to confide the accompaniment to a mere harpsichord, the string basses thickening the lowest notes of the chords. (In the earlier part of the 19th c. it became usual, in Britain at any rate, to leave the whole duty of accompaniment to a 'cello, which played the chords in arpeggio). (2) RECITATIVO STROMENTATO (It. 'Instrumented Recitative') has orch. accompaniment: this type, which dates from about 1630, was carried to its point of greatest elaboration by Wagner.

Reciting Note. See *Plainsong 2*; *Anglican Chant.*

Recordare. See *Requiem.*

Recorder Family. Under this head are here included all flutes of the end-blown, whistle-mouthpiece type. These are, as a genus, described as FIPPLE FLUTES (fipple = the plug in the mouthpiece).

EARLY 16TH-CENTURY RECORDER

Right and left hands in two positions
(From Virdung's *Musica getutscht*, Basle, 1511)

(1) The Recorder proper has a mainly conical bore and 8 holes. It had, in the 16th and 17th cs. and the early 18th, much solo use, as also use in sets of different sizes (like the instruments of a string quartet). Handel and Bach wrote for it. After disuse during the later 18th c. and the 19th it has in the 20th had a very considerable revival.

(2) Other members of the family are (*a*) the FLAGEOLET, a small pipe with 6 holes, 2 of them being at the back and

THE 17TH-CENTURY RECORDER

(From Salter's *Exact Directions for the Recorder* 1683)

played with the thumbs. (*b*) The TIN WHISTLE, also with 6 holes but all at the front. (*c*) PIPE (and TABOR), WHITTLE (and DUB), or GALOUBET (and TAMBOURIN). This simple combination of a wind instrument and a percussion instrument, the 2 played by 1 performer, was for centuries in much rustic use. The pipe, having merely 3 holes,

PIPE AND TABOR

A French Fool in 1486

could be played with 1 hand, leaving the other free for the small drum.

See *Society of Recorder Players.*

Recte et retro (or **rectus et inversus**). See *Canon.*

Recueilli (Fr.). 'Meditative'.

Redemption, The. (1) Oratorio by GOUNOD. (1st perf. Birmingham Fest. 1882; New York 1882.) Enjoyed enormous popularity all over the civilized world. (2) 'Poem-Symphony' by FRANCK, for Soprano Solo, Chorus, and Orch. (1st perf. Paris 1873; new version 1st perf. 1890.)

Redend (Ger.). 'Speaking', hence same as *parlando* (It.).

Red Flag. The author of the words of this Socialist song was Jim Connell. The original tune used was that of *The White Cockade*. Later the Ger. tune of *Der Tannenbaum* (sometimes known as *Maryland*, q.v.) was adopted.

Redford, John (1st half of 16th c.). Organist of St. Paul's Cathedral and composer of church music.

Redlich, Hans Ferdinand (b. Vienna 1903; d. Manchester 1968). Conductor and musicologist. Studied univs. Vienna, Munich, and Frankfurt. Cond. municipal operas Berlin and Mainz. In England from 1939 (conductor, Extension Lecturer Cambridge Univ., &c.). Prof. Manchester Univ. 1962. Composer; author; authority on and ed. of Monteverdi, &c.

Redman, Reginald (b. London 1892.) Trained G.S.M. Composer of songs, piano music, chamber music, incidental music to plays, &c.; arrangements of Chinese songs. B.B.C. Director of Music, West Region (1936–52).

Redoubler; redoublement (Fr.). 'To double'; 'doubling'.

Redowa. A Bohemian dance in a pretty quick triple time. It resembles the Polish dance, the Mazurka. See also *Rejdováčka*.

Reduire (Fr.), **reduzieren** (Ger.). 'To reduce', 'arrange'.

Reed. The sound-producing agent (of thin cane or metal) of various instruments. A reed which vibrates *against* an air slot is a BEATING REED, whilst one which vibrates *through* such a slot (i.e. from one side to the other) is a *Free Reed*. Reeds may be either single (cf. *Clarinet Family*) or double (in the latter the 2 halves of the mouthpiece itself being pieces of reed vibrating against each other; cf. *Oboe Family*).

(In addition to the articles above-mentioned see *Bagpipe Family, Reed-Organ Family, Organ*.)

Reed, (1) **Thomas German** (b. Bristol 1817; d. East Sheen 1888). Conductor, singer, and founder of famous 'German Reed Entertainments'. These were dramatic performances designed to attract a public which normally objected to the theatre; the scene of the earlier operettas of Sullivan.

(2) **William Henry** (b. Frome 1876; d. Dumfries 1942). Violinist. Pupil of Sauret at R.A.M. Leader of London Symphony Orch. 1912–35; latterly on staff of R.C.M.; friend, helper, and biographer of Elgar. Composer of violin concerto, &c. D.Mus. Lambeth.

Reed-Organ Family. A large family, whose most important members are listed below, one of these being ancient and the others comparatively recent and enjoying present-day popularity.

(1) REGAL. This came into use in the 15th c. and remained popular into the 17th. In appearance it was a tiny, portable, 1-manual organ of small compass, but the pipes (all short) were at first all reed-pipes (cf. *Organ* 2), the reeds being of that type

A 15TH-CENTURY REGAL

Bas-relief by Luca della Robbia (1399–1482). Now in the Museum at Florence

A BIBLE REGAL

called 'Beating Reeds' (cf. *Reed*): later flue pipes were sometimes added. There was a kind called *Bible Regal*: it folded in two like a book.

(2) MOUTH ORGAN (in Germany, U.S.A., and elsewhere called *Harmonica*—but see under that word for other applications of it). It is one of the simplest applications of the Free Reed principle (see *Reed*). A number of small metal reeds of graduated size are enclosed in slots in a short narrow box, which is held against the lips and moved from side to side according to the note desired. It came into use in the 1830's. It is, to a point, easily played, but feats of virtuosity are possible to the gifted and persevering.

(3) ACCORDION (or ACCORDEON) and BANDONEON. The Accordion is in principle the same as the Mouth Organ (see above) but it is provided with bellows and studs for producing the notes required (or, in the *Piano-Accordion*, a small keyboard—up to 3½ octaves). It is so designed that it can be held in the 2 hands, the one approaching and separating from the other, so expanding and contracting the bellows part of the instrument: melody studs or keys are operated by the fingers of the right hand whilst the fingers of the left operate studs which provide certain simple chords. This instrument dates from about the same period as the Mouth Organ, or slightly earlier.

The Bandoneon is an Argentine type of Accordion, with no keyboard—merely buttons producing single notes, so that to produce chords several buttons must be depressed.

(4) CONCERTINA. This dates from the same period as the Mouth Organ and Accordion. It differs from the Accordion in having hexagonal (instead of rectangular) ends, and always studs (no keyboard). The *English Concertina* is a form of the instrument from which a very good effect can be obtained, and the *German Concertina* is cruder. At one time the Eng. form seemed to be establishing itself in serious musical circles in London and elsewhere, but this has not continued. There were then several sizes in use, roughly of the range of the instruments of the string quartet, and concerted music was performed.

(5) HARMONIUM. This dates from the early years of the 19th c. and has existed in many different forms and under many different names. Its perfecting is due to Debain, of Paris (abt. 1840; the instruments of the later Paris maker, Alexandre, have enjoyed high popularity throughout the civilized world). It is a free-reed keyboard instrument, blown by 2 pedals operated by left and right foot working in alternate strokes. When the *Expression Stop* is drawn the passage of the air is

made to short-circuit the reservoir through which it otherwise passes, and this gives the feet great control over degrees of force and accent: the effective operation of this stop, however, calls for a good deal of practice. (See reference under *Anglican Parish Church Music*.)

(6) AMERICAN ORGAN (in U.S.A. CABINET ORGAN). This resembles the Harmonium, but the air is sucked through the reeds instead of being forced through them and the tone is less pungent. There is no 'Expression' device and so where other means than the player's feet can be applied for operating the bellows a pedal-board like that of an organ can be built in as a part of the instrument. The invention of this instrument is due to one of the workmen in Alexandre's factory (see under *Harmonium*, above) but its development was carried out by Messrs. Mason & Hamlin, of Boston, U.S.A.

(7) MUSTEL ORGAN, ESTEY ORGAN, &c. These also are developments of the general 'Cabinet Organ' principle.

SOME GENERAL REMARKS ON THE LARGER REED INSTRUMENTS WITH KEYBOARDS. (*a*) A swell device (cf. *Organ*) has been applied to these instruments: it is operated by the player's knee. (*b*) The stops, each operating on a set of reeds, resemble those of an organ in that some are of normal pitch and some of a pitch an 8ve higher or lower. (*c*) A great disadvantage in nearly all such instruments is that the stops are divided, so that there are two for each set of reeds, one for the treble and the other for the bass. The object is said to be to allow an adroit performer to play a melody by the right hand and the accompaniment in the left an 8ve below the usual position—using for the latter a stop of 8ve pitch, so raising its pitch to normal. This is, however, difficult to achieve, owing to the necessity of keeping the melody strictly within the limited range of its portion of the keyboard and the accompaniment within its limited range also, and the real reason of the device may be suspected to be the impressing of the innocent purchaser by the display of a large number of stop knobs. (*d*) Another awkward detail is that if a stop of 8ve below pitch is provided (equivalent to a 16-foot stop in an organ) its range is usually only over a short bass portion of the keyboard, so that, in playing, awkward breaks occur. (*e*) A further troublesome detail sometimes found is that 1 set of reeds is made to do duty for 2 stops, by being acted upon in 2 different ways: thus when both stops are drawn there is not the expected increase of tone. (*f*) A defect of the Harmonium is that the carrying power of the sound diminishes as the square of the distance (or something like that), so that only the player and those near him hear the tone as he intends it to be heard: further the 'speech' of this instrument is slow, making rapid passages ineffective. However, when all these defects have been listed it has to be admitted that a number of important composers have taken such instruments seriously—Dvořák, Franck, Reger, and Karg-Elert being amongst those who have composed for them.

Reed Pipe and **Reed Stop.** See *Organ* 2.

Reel. Dance common in Scotland and Ireland, for 2 couples or more. The music is rapid and smoothly flowing and generally in simple quadruple time. The *Highland Fling* is a particularly vigorous form of the Scottish reel. What is called the *Virginia Reel* is said to be the same as the English *Sir Roger de Coverley* (q.v.). Scandinavian countries have similar dances. North Yorkshire people, who are largely Scandinavian in origin, possess the reel as a part of a sword dance.

Reese, Gustave (b. New York 1899). On staff of Univ. of New York (of which he is Mus.B. and LL.B.); for some time asst. ed. and then ed. of *Musical Quarterly* (q.v.); one of active spirits in Amer. Musicological Soc.; dir. of publications, G. Schirmer (1940); then Carl Fischer (1945). Author of scholarly work on *Music in the Middle Ages* (1940).

Reeves, Sims—in full John Sims (b. Shooter's Hill, Kent, 1818; d. Worthing 1900). Tenor vocalist (at first baritone). Began professional life at 14 as church organist; at 17 appeared as opera singer; studied in Paris and Milan and attained high position in opera, oratorio, and concert singing, being regarded as chief Eng. tenor of his day. Wrote book *Art of Singing*, &c.

Reflets dans l'eau (Debussy). See under *Images*.

Reformation. See *Anglican Parish Church Music*; *Education and Music* 1; *Hymns and Hymn Tunes* 2; *Passion Music*; *Roman Catholic Church Music in Britain*; *Service*.

Reformation Symphony. By Mendelssohn (op. 107, 1830). Composed for the Tercentenary of the Augsburg Confession of 1530. (1st perf., however, Berlin 1832. Crystal Palace 1867; Boston 1868.) A feature is the use of the tune *Ein' feste Burg* ('A safe stronghold').

Refrapper (Fr.). 'To strike again.'

Regal. See *Reed-Organ Family* 1.

Regale (It.), **régale, régale à vent** (Fr.). 'Regal' (see *Reed-Organ Family* 1).

Regensburg Edition. See *Plainsong* 3.

Reger, Max (b. Brand, Bavaria, 1873; d. Leipzig 1916). Began as school teacher who devoted himself to composition, studying under Riemann; then became pianist and toured as such; from 1905 took important academic positions including professorship of composition at Leipzig Conserv. (1907 to death); visited England (1909); conductor of famous Meiningen Orch. (1911–15). Composed organ music, orch. music, chamber music, piano music, choral music, &c.; list of works reveals an amazingly extensive output for a life of little over 40 years. May be described as a classical romanticist in sympathies and methods. (See *Italienisches Liederbuch*.)

Regina Coeli Laetare. See *Antiphons of the Blessed Virgin Mary*.

Register. (1) In connexion with the organ the word means the set of pipes belonging to a particular stop (see *Organ* 1), and 'to register' a piece of music means to choose the stops to be employed in its various passages. (2) See *Voice* 4.

Registrieren; Registrierung (Ger.). 'To register'; 'registration'.

Registro (It.). 'Register.'

Regnal, Frédéric. See *Erlanger.*

Regondi, Giulio (b. Geneva 1822; d. 1872). Great performer on the Concertina (the Eng. form; see *Reed-Organ Family* 4), also on the Guitar and Melophone (a sort of Harmonium). Eminent throughout Europe before the age of 9, from which age was resident in England.

Regular Singing. See *Hymns and Hymn Tunes* 7.

Reicha, Anton (Joseph) (b. Prague 1770; d. Paris 1836). Flautist; friend of Haydn and Beethoven; also teacher of piano and theory; author of many books on composition, &c.; a prof. of counter-point, &c., at Paris Conserv. (1818). Prolific composer: some operas and symphonies and piano sonatas, &c., and quantities of chamber works, especially for wood-wind.

Reichardt, Johann Friedrich (b. Königsberg 1752; d. Giebichenstein, nr. Halle, 1814). Pianist and violinist; wrote much on music and violently attacked Burney's book on his German Tour (see *Burney*); Kapellmeister to Frederick the Great and Frederick William II (1776–94). Composed many operas, songs, symphonies, sonatas, &c.

See *Annotated Programmes*; *Erl King*.

Reigen, Reihen (Ger.). Round dance or (more casually used) merely 'dance'. So such compounds as *Elfenreigen*, 'elf dance'; *Gnomenreigen*, 'gnome dance'.

Rein (Ger.). 'Pure.'

Reincken. See *Reinken*.

Reine, La ('The Queen's), or **La Reine de France**. Nickname for Haydn's Symphony in B flat, no. 85 in Breitkopf edn. of the Symphonies (no. 4 of the 'Paris Symphonies', q.v.)— much admired by Marie Antoinette; hence, possibly, the name.

Reinecke, Carl Heinrich Carsten (b. Altona 1824; d. Leipzig 1910). Younger member of Mendelssohn-Schumann circle; international reputation as pianist; conductor of Leipzig Gewandhaus Orch. (1860–95); a prof. of piano and composition at Leipzig Conserv. (from 1860) and then director (1892–1902). Composed operas, masses, songs, symphonies, chamber works,

and much piano music; also wrote much on music.

Reiner, Fritz (b. Budapest 1888; d. New York 1963). Conductor. Trained Budapest Conserv. Then conducted opera in that city and Dresden. Cincinnati Orch. 1922–31. Then head orch. and opera depts. of Curtis Institute: also conductor Pittsburgh Orch. 1938–48; Chicago Orch. 1953–62. Wide conducting tours North and South America and Europe (London début 1924).

Reinken (or **Reincken**), **Johann Adam**, or **Jan Adams** (b. Lower Alsace 1623; d. Hamburg 1722). Pupil of Sweelinck; organist in Holland; moved to Hamburg (1663) where playing so famous as to induce Bach several times to walk great distances to that city to hear him. Few of his compositions preserved.

Reissiger, Karl Gottlieb (b. nr. Wittenberg 1798; d. Dresden 1859). After varied life of study, teaching, and composition, settled in Dresden (1826), succeeding Weber as conductor of the German Opera. Composed operas, church music, &c. (see *Weber's Last Waltz*).

Reiterquartett (Haydn). See *Rittquartett*.

Reizenstein, Franz (b. Nuremberg 1911; d. London 1968). Pianist, composer, and conductor. Trained Berlin Conserv. under Hindemith, R.C.M. under Vaughan Williams, &c. Compositions include piano and chamber music, piano and 'cello concertos, &c.

Rejdováčka or **Rejdovák**. A Bohemian dance in duple time, somewhat like the Polka but considered to be a variant of the *Redowa* (q.v.).

Rejoice in the Lord alway (Purcell). See *Bell Anthem*.

Réjouissance (Fr. 'rejoicing', 'merry-making'). Term used by Handel and Bach as title of a movement in a suite.

Rektah. See *Raptak*.

Relâché (Fr.). 'Loosened' (e.g. snare of drum).

Related Keys. See *Modulation*.

Relative Major and Minor. See Table 8.

Relative Pitch, Sense of. See under *Absolute Pitch.*

Religieux, religieuse (Fr. masc., fem.), **religioso** (It.). 'Religious.' So *religieusement* (Fr.), 'religiously', *religiosamente* (It.), 'devotional in feeling'.

Remember, O thou man. See *God save the Queen.*

Reményi, Eduard (b. Hungary 1830; d. San Francisco 1898). Virtuoso violinist; as youth toured with Brahms; helped by Liszt; much applauded in Britain and appointed solo violinist to Queen Victoria (1854); died during a concert at San Francisco. Composer (for violin) of slight value.

Remettre (Fr.). 'To put back.' Hence the imperative *remettez* in Fr. organ music means to bring into use some stop that has been temporarily out of action.

Remick Music Corporation. See *Music Publishers Holding Corporation.*

Renard. 1-act 'Burlesque, to be sung and played', by Stravinsky. Russian text by composer; Fr. version by Ramuz. (Prod. Paris 1922; New York, concert form 1923; London, broadcast 1935.)

Renforcer (Fr.). 'To reinforce', 'increase'. The imperative is *renforcez.*

Rentrée (Fr.). 'Re-entry.'

Renvoi (Fr.). The 'sending back', i.e. the sign to repeat.

Repeat Marks. See Tables 20, 21.

Répétiteur (Fr.), **repetitore** (It.), **Repetitor** (Ger.). Choirmaster of an opera-house (in ordinary French it means 'assistant teacher', 'coach', &c.). The Fr. *répétition* and It. *repetizione* mean 'rehearsal'.

Répétition (Fr.). 'Rehearsal.' A *répétition générale* is a final rehearsal—often one to which the public are admitted.

Repiano. See *Ripieno.*

Replica (It.). 'Repeat.'

Replicato (It.). 'Doubled.'

Reports or **'Rapports'** (apparently from Fr. *rapporter*, 'to carry back'). 'Report', in 17th-c. musical parlance, was the equivalent of 'imitation' today.

It meant the bringing in again by one voice or 'part' of a melodic phrase just heard from another.

In the Scottish Psalter of 1635 appeared some tunes with the heading 'Heere are some Psalmes in Reports'. These are really little motets, or anthem-like treatments.

Repos (Fr.). 'Repose.'

Reprendre (Fr.). 'To take up again.' *Reprenez* is the imperative.

Reprise (Fr.). (1) A 'Repeat'. (2) 'Recapitulation section' (see *Form* 3). (3) 'Revival.'

Reproducing Piano. See *Mechanical Reproduction of Music* 13.

Requiem. The word is generally used as meaning the Mass for the Dead (*Missa pro defunctis*), which begins with the introit, 'Requiem aeternam'. The text is much the same as that of the normal Mass (q.v.), but with the more joyful parts (e.g. the *Gloria in excelsis* and the *Credo*) omitted, with certain small changes of wording, and with the *Dies irae* (q.v.) interpolated. The traditional plainsong of the Requiem is very beautiful, but the text has, of course, been repeatedly set by composers. Some notable settings are the following: (1) PALESTRINA. (2) MOZART (composed on his death-bed, 1791, and finished by Süssmayr, q.v.). (3) BERLIOZ (with Orch. and 4 Brass Bands; 1st perf. Paris 1837; Crystal Palace 1883). (4) VERDI (composed on the death of the novelist, Manzoni, 1873; 1st perf. Milan 1874; London, conducted by composer, 1875). (5) FAURÉ (op. 48, 1887). (6) DVOŘÁK (op. 89, 1st perf. Birmingham Fest. 1891).

As a typical disposition of the text in a large-scale setting, upon what we may call oratorio lines, we may take Verdi's—(*a*) *Requiem aeternam* and *Kyrie eleison* ('Rest eternal' and 'Have mercy'); (*b*) *Dies irae*—divided into movements as follows: *Dies irae* ('Day of wrath'), *Tuba mirum* ('Hark the trumpet'), *Liber scriptus* ('How the record'), *Quid sum miser* ('What affliction'), *Rex tremendae* ('King of Glories'), *Recordare* ('Ah! remember'), *Ingemisco* ('Sadly groaning'), *Confutatis* ('From the accursed'), *Lacrimosa* ('Ah! what weeping'); (*c*) *Domine Jesu Christe* ('Lord Jesus'); (*d*) *Sanctus* ('Holy'); (*e*) *Agnus Dei* ('Lamb of God'); (*f*) *Lux aeterna* ('Light eternal'); (*g*) *Libera me* ('Deliver me'). Liturgically the Requiem Mass has its place at funerals and memorial services and on All Souls' Day (2 November).

For BRAHMS's work see *German Requiem*. The Requiem of DELIUS (1916) is not such in the ordinary sense, but a setting of Nietzsche, and was originally announced as *A Pagan Requiem* (1st perf. London 1922).

Requiem Symphony. See *Kabalevsky*.

Résolument (Fr.). 'Resolutely.'

Resolution. See *Harmony* 2 f.

Resoluto, risoluto (It.). 'Resolute.'

Resoluzione, risoluzione (It. 'resolution'). Firmness and steady rhythm.

Resonance, Resonator. See *Acoustics* 19.

Resonoscope. An electrical pitch-carrying instrument (cf. *Pitch*) introduced in 1936 in U.S.A. and the following year in Britain. It sounds any note desired and shows it in visual terms as a wave form (see *Acoustics* 10) on a small screen.

Respighi, Ottorino (b. Bologna 1879; d. Rome 1936). Studied in Bologna; chief violin player in opera at St. Petersburg, studying composition under Rimsky-Korsakof; then in Berlin; prof. of composition at Liceo de S. Cecilia, Rome (1913); its director (1923–5). Composer of operas, ballets, chamber music, orch. music, songs, &c.; also edited works of Monteverdi, &c.

See also *Birds*; *Boutique fantasque*; *Church Windows*; *Fountains of Rome*; *Mary of Egypt*; *Old Dances and Airs for the Lute*; *Pines of Rome*; *Roman Festivals*.

Respond. Same as *Responses* (q.v.), but the word is specifically used as a name for the long and elaborate plainsong or choral settings sung by the choir, in answer to passages by the priest, as a part of the chanting of psalms. Such settings occur both in the Mass (between the Epistle and the Gospel) and in the other services of the Church; the description *Responsorium graduale* (or, briefly, 'Gradual') is applied to that sung in the Mass, whilst *Responsorium*, without the addition of 'Graduale', means one sung in the ordinary services. (Cf. *Responsorial*.)

Responses. The replies of the congregation (or the choir, representing them) to the Preces (q.v.) or Versicles (q.v.) of the priest, in the Roman and Anglican service.

The traditional Anglican settings are the ancient plainsong, adapted by Merbecke to the Eng. words at the time of the Reformation. Tallis a little later made two harmonized versions of these, one in 4 parts and one in 5. These are now usually known as the FESTAL RESPONSES: they have the plainsong in the tenor part and it is observed that congregations naturally mistake the treble for it, and sing in 8ves or unison with the choir-boys instead of in 8ves or unison with the tenors, as they should do. The FERIAL RESPONSES (see *Ferial*) have the plainsong in the treble, the harmonization being by any of the thousand-and-one organists who have undertaken to produce a version.

Responsorial. Old name for gradual—the *book* 'Gradual', that is (see *Gradual*). The name is also used for a collection of the solo passages of the Mass.

Responsorio. A sort of motet in which a soloist and the choir sing responsively—in English a sort of 'Solo Anthem'.

Responsorium. See *Respond*.

Ressortir (Fr.). 'To come out.' So used of making a melody stand out.

Restez (Fr.). 'Remain', e.g. remain on a note—not hurry off it; or (in string music) remain in the same 'position'.

Rests. See Table 2.

Resultant Bass. Organ stop; same as *Quint* (q.v.). See also *Acoustics* 16.

Resultant Tone. See *Acoustics* 16.

Resurrection Symphony. See *Mahler's Symphonies* (no. 2).

Reszke, (1) **Jean de**—really Jan Mieczyslaw de Reszke (b. Warsaw 1850; d. Nice 1925). Tenor vocalist (until age 34 a baritone). Of sensational reputation and world fame on opera stage. In his early 50's ceased public appearances and practised as highly successful teacher. (2) **Édouard de** (b. Warsaw 1853; d. Garneck, Poland, 1917). Bass vocalist; brother and pupil of above, and of equal fame. For a years taught in London. (3) **Josephine de** (b. Warsaw 1855; there d. 1891). Soprano vocalist; sister of the two above and, like them, of high reputation as operatic artist.

Retablo de Maese Pedro, El ('Master Peter's Puppet Show'). 1-act puppet-opera of Falla, based on incident in *Don Quixote*. (Prod. Seville 1923; Bristol 1924; New York 1925; London 1928.)

Retardando (It.). Same as *Ritardando* (q.v.).

Retardation. See *Harmony* 2 g.

Retenant; retenu (Fr.). 'Holding back'; 'held back' (immediately, like *ritenuto*, q.v.—not gradually, like *rallentando*).

Rethberg (really Sättler), **Elisabeth** (b. Schwarzenberg, Saxony, 1894). Trained Dresden Conserv. At first pianist; then soprano vocalist. High international reputation in concert and opera; New York 1922; Covent Garden 1925. Settled in U.S.A.

Retirer (Fr.). 'To withdraw.' The imperative *retirez*, in Fr. organ music, means 'withdraw from use' the stop in question.

Retour de basse danse. See *Basse Danse*.

Retrouvez (Fr.). 'Find again', 're-attain'.

Returning Tone. See under *Changing Note*.

Return of Lemminkäinen (Sibelius). See *Lemminkäinen*.

Reubke, Julius R. (b. Hausniendorf 1834; d. Pillnitz 1858). Son of a famous Ger. organ builder. Fine pianist and a favourite pupil of Liszt; his chief work is the great organ sonata (showing Lisztian influences)—*The Ninety-Fourth Psalm*, a detailed piece of 'programme music' of high technical difficulty.

Réunis (Fr.). 'United', 'reunited' (e.g. after *Divisés*, q.v.). In organ music it means 'coupled'.

Reutter, Hermann (b. Stuttgart 1900). Pianist and composer. Studied in Munich; dir. Frankfurt Music Sch. 1936–45; then unattached. Works

include numerous operas and choral works; concertos, piano pieces, and songs.

Rêve, Le. See *Bruneau*.

Reveille (from *réveil*, Fr., 'wakening'). The military signal beginning the day (in the Brit. army pronounced 'revelly' or 'revally').

Revenge, The. 'Choral-ballad' by Stanford; a setting of Tennyson's poem. (1st perf. Leeds Fest. 1886.)

Revenir (Fr.). 'To return.' *Revenez* is the imperative.

Rêveur (Fr.). 'Dreamy.' So the adverb *rêveusement*.

Revidiert (Ger.). 'Revised.'

Revolutionary Étude for Piano. Chopin's op. 10, no. 12, in C minor, the nickname arising from the tradition that in it the composer expressed his feelings on the taking of Warsaw by the Russians in 1831, and the consequent partition of his native country.

Revueltas, Silvestre (b. Santiago Papasquiaro, Mexico, 1899; d. Mexico City 1940). Début as violinist 1920; asst. cond. Mexico City Orch. 1929; in Spain 1937. Compositions are mostly shorter pieces for small orchestra of national flavour, though without actual folk-song borrowing.

Rex Tremendae. See *Requiem*.

Reyer, Ernest—originally Louis Étienne Ernest Rey (b. Marseilles 1823; d. nr. Hyères 1909). Fr. composer and critic of Wagnerian and general Ger. sympathies; operas (*Sigurd*, Brussels 1884; *Salammbô*, Brussels 1890); some church music, &c.

Reynolds, Alfred Charles (b. Liverpool 1884; d. Bognor 1969). Trained Paris and Berlin Hochschule. Became London theatre conductor and popular composer of theatre music.

Rezitativ (Ger.). 'Recitative.'

Rezniček, Emile Nikolaus von (b. Vienna 1860; d. Berlin 1945). Studied at Leipzig Conserv.; held various conductorships (orch., military band, theatrical); settled in Berlin (1901) as conductor, prof. of composition at

Hochschule, &c. Composition include operas, symphonies, &c., church, chamber, and organ music, &c.

Rf., Rfz. = *Rinforzando* (q.v.).

R.H. = Right Hand.

Rhapsodie Nègre. See *Powell, John.*

Rhapsody. A term imported into music by Tomaschek (about 1813; Rhapsodies for piano) and adopted by Liszt (15 *Hungarian Rhapsodies*, 1853-4), Dvořák (*Slavonic Rhapsodies*), and others. Compositions so called are often of the nature of fantasies on folk melodies, but Brahms and Dohnányi and many others have written Rhapsodies using entirely original material.

Rhapsody in Blue. Symphonic Poem, by Gershwin. Orchestration (by F. Grofé) includes Solo Pianist and Jazz Band. (1st perf. New York 1924.)

Rheinberger, Josef Gabriel (b. in Liechtenstein 1839; d. Munich 1901). Studied at Munich Conserv.; then earned living as organist and teacher; a prof. of composition at Conserv. 1859, pupils flocking to him from whole civilized world; received many honours, and raised to nobility (1894). Composed 20 organ sonatas and long list of solo vocal, choral, and instrumental music.

Rheingold (Wagner). See *Ring des Nibelungen.*

Rhené-Baton—really René Baton (b. Normandy 1879; d. Le Mans 1940). Trained at Paris Conserv.; took high position in Paris as orch. conductor. Composed orch. and chamber music, songs, &c.

Rhenish Symphony. See *Schumann's Symphonies.*

Rhine Gold (Wagner). See *Ring des Nibelungen.*

Rhythm (in the full sense of the word) covers everything pertaining to the *time* side of music as distinct from the side of pitch, i.e. it includes the effects of beats, accents, measures (or bars), grouping of notes into beats, grouping of beats into measures, grouping of measures into phrases, &c. When all these factors are judiciously treated by the performer (with due regularity yet with artistic purpose—an effect of

forward movement—and not mere machine-like accuracy) we feel and say that the performer possesses 'a sense of rhythm'.

The human ear seems to demand the perceptible presence of a unit of time (the BEAT); even in the 'Free Rhythm' of Plainsong (q.v.) or of Recitative (q.v.) this can be felt, though in such sort of music the grouping into measures is not present.

Apart from such music as that just mentioned it will be found that the beats fall into regular groups of twos or threes, or of combinations of these (as a group of 4 made up of 2+2, or a group of 6 made up of 3+3). Such groups or combinations of groups are indicated in our notation by the drawing of bar-lines at regular intervals, so dividing the music into MEASURES (or 'bars'; cf. Table 10). The measures, in their turn, can be felt to build up into larger groups, or PHRASES (4 measures to a phrase being a very common but not invariable combination; cf. *Phrase*).

It is chiefly ACCENT that defines these groupings, e.g. taking the larger groupings, a 4-bar phrase is normally accentuated something like this:

and if the beats are in any part of the music subdivided into what we may call shorter beat-units sub-accentuations are felt, as

Where the measures have 3 beats an accented note is followed by 2 unaccented:

and similarly in a 3-measure phrase the 1st measure will be more heavily accentuated than the 2 following measures

It will be seen, then, that what we may call the official beat-unit of a composition is a convention, there being often present smaller units and always present larger units, both of which may be considered beats.

It has been said above that Plainsong and Recitative are examples of Free Rhythm. Another example is to be seen in much of the choral music of the polyphonic period (madrigals, motets, &c.): borrowing from the terminology of literature we may say that all these types of music are frequently in 'prose rhythm', as distinguished from 'verse rhythm'.

'Verse rhythm' in music is, of course, found in its most pronounced form in tunes composed for marching and dancing. (During the 1930's an attempt was made by dance-music composers, performers, and publishers, to arrogate to themselves the proprietorship of the ancient term 'rhythm'. Thus they spoke of 'rhythm playing' and attached the word 'rhythm' to some not readily definable development of the earlier forms of 'Jazz', which development they, curiously, spoke of as 'Rhythm Music'—as though other music existed which lacked rhythm.)

Cf. *Melody*; *Ragtime*; *Jazz*.

Rhythm, Sprung. See *Sprung Rhythm*.

Rhythm Band or **Percussion Band.** A type of musical activity introduced into infant schools mainly during the 1920's and 1930's, though not unknown earlier. The children play various types of percussion instruments, the melody and harmony being supplied by a piano. The dulcimer was a later addition to the resources of such bands.

Rhythmé, rhythmique (Fr.). 'Rhythmic.'

Rhythmicon. See *Electric Musical Instruments* 5.

Rhythmisch (Ger.). 'Rhythmic.'

Rhythmus (Ger.). 'Rhythm.'

Ribible or **Rubible.** The rebec (q.v.).

Ributhe (Scottish). The Jew's harp (q.v.).

Ricci, (1) **Luigi** (b. Naples 1805; d. Prague 1859). Prolific and successful opera composer; became choirmaster of cathedral at Trieste (1836); collaborated with Federico (below) in comic opera *Crispino e la Comare* (1850);

went insane and died in asylum. For brother and son, see below.

(2) **Federico** (b. Naples 1809; d. Conegliano 1877). Like brother (above) opera composer (*Crispino e la Comare*, Venice 1850; an international success; see *Luigi*, above); for some years musical director of Imperial opera, St. Petersburg; composed masses, songs, &c.

(3) **Luigi** (b. Trieste 1852; d. Milan 1906). Like his father, Luigi above, opera composer.

(4) **Conrado** (b. Ravenna 1858; d. Rome 1934). Director of Fine Arts in Ministry of Education; writer of opera libretti and books and articles on music.

(5) **Ruggiero** (b. San Francisco 1918). Violinist; Pupil of Persinger. Appeared as prodigy briefly from age 10; then successful international career as mature artist.

Rice, Thomas. See *Negro Minstrels*.

Ricercare (It. 'to seek out'; cf. Eng. 'research' and Fr. 'recherché'). In music this word is used as a noun and applied (*a*; 16th to 18th cs.) to an elaborate contrapuntal composition in fugal or canonic style, and (*b*) more loosely to any sort of a prelude (usually, however, more or less contrapuntal in style).

Ricercata (It., past participle of verb *ricercare*, and used as a noun in same sense). See above.

Richard Coeur-de-Lion. Grétry's most successful opera. (Prod. Paris 1784; London 1786; Boston 1797; Philadelphia 1798; New York 1800.)

Richards, Henry Brinley (b. Carmarthen 1817; d. London 1885). Pianist, teacher, and popular composer of piano music and of national song, *God bless the Prince of Wales* (1863).

Richard the Third. Incidental Music to Shakespeare's play by German. (1st perf. London 1889.)

Richettato (It.). Same as *Spiccato* (q.v.).

Richter, (1) **Ernst Friedrich Eduard** (b. Gross-Schönau, Saxony, 1808; d. Leipzig 1879). Cantor of Thomas School, Leipzig, and notable and prolific author of theoretical works.

(2) **Hans** (b. Raab, Hungary, 1843;

d. Bayreuth 1916). Horn player; copyist for Wagner; became leading Wagnerian conductor. High popularity as orch. conductor in England. Conducted Hallé Orch., Manchester (1897–1911), 'Richter Concerts', London, &c.

(3) **Sviatoslav** (b. Zhitomir, Russia, 1914). Pianist; trained Odessa and Moscow. Foremost virtuoso of wide repertory; extensive foreign tours.

Richtig (Ger.). 'Right', 'precise'.

Ricordi (Milan). The leading It. music publishing firm, estd. 1808; publishers of Rossini, Verdi, Puccini, &c.

Riddick, (Clara) Kathleen (b. Epsom 1907). Cellist and conductor. Trained G.S.M. and Salzburg under Malko (q.v.). Formed Riddick String Orch. (1938) and Surrey Philharmonic Orch., performing many contemporary Brit. works. Has conducted B.B.C. and London Symphony Orch., &c.

Riddle, Frederick (Craig) (b. Liverpool 1912). Viola player. Trained R.C.M. (later on staff there, as also of T.C.M.). In London Symphony Orch. 1933–8, then London Philharmonic Orch., of which he is a Director. As soloist prominent exponent of Walton viola concerto.

Rideau (Fr.). 'Curtain.'

Riders to the Sea. Opera by Vaughan Williams. Text by J. M. Synge. (Prod. at R.C.M., London, 1937.)

Ridotto (It.). (1) 'Reduced', i.e. arranged for a smaller body of performers than that demanded by the original. (2) The same as Fr. 'redoute', i.e. an 18th-c. type of fashionable entertainment, generally a sort of masquerade with song and dance in which not only the paid performers but also the audience took part.

Riduzione (It.). 'Reduction', 'arrangement'.

Riegger, Wallingford (b. Albany, Georgia, 1885; d. New York 1961). Studied in New York and Berlin; conducted opera in Germany; held various academic positions in U.S.A. from 1917; published under pseudonyms many potboiling choral and other arrangements; at last after a struggle became recognized as able composer of atonal school.

Riego, Teresa Clotilde del—Mrs. Leadbitter (b. London 1876; d. there 1968). Composer of innumerable popular songs (e.g. *O dry those tears*), also of larger (unperformed) works of a more ambitious kind. Stated in *Who's Who*: 'Completed her 50 years of composition in 1944, having commenced song writing at a very early age.'

Riemann, Karl Wilhelm Julius Hugo (b. nr. Sondershausen 1849; d. Leipzig 1919). Prof. of Music at Univ. of Leipzig and highly productive author of theoretical works; famous *Musiklexikon* (1882 and later edns.).

Rienzi, der letzte der Tribunen ('Rienzi, the last of the Tribunes'). Historical opera by Wagner, founded on Bulwer Lytton's novel. (Prod. Dresden 1842; New York 1878; London 1879.)

Ries Family. Important family of active musicians, of whom most important have been (1) **Franz Anton** (b. Bonn 1755; d. Godesberg 1846). Good violinist in town of Beethoven's birth and boyhood and one of his best teachers and helpers. (2) **Ferdinand** (b. Godesberg 1784; d. Frankfort 1838). Son of above; befriended and taught by Beethoven. Settled in London where he had great success as pianist and composer. (3) **Hubert** (b. Bonn 1802; d. Berlin 1886). Also a son of Franz Anton. Specially remembered today for his violin 'School' and studies. (4) **Louis** (b. Berlin 1830; d. London 1913). Violinist. Son of (3) above. Settled in London 1853. Chamber music player of repute.

Rieti, Vittorio (b. Alexandria, Egypt, 1898). Italian composer, educated at Milan and Rome. Has composed ballets (see *Barabau*), operas, and orch. and other instrumental works of 'modernist' tendencies. In U.S.A. from 1940.

Rigaudon (Fr.), **Rigadoon** (Old Eng.). Ancient Provençal type of dance, in simple duple or quadruple time, somewhat resembling the bourrée.

Rigby, George Vernon (b. Birmingham 1840; d. Ramsgate 1928). Tenor. London début 1861. Then studied Milan and appeared in various continental opera houses. Returned England 1867 and took very high place in oratorio, &c. Retired early (abt. 1887).

Right-hand Pianoforte Music. See *Pianoforte Playing*.

Right Little, Tight Little Island. See *Rogue's March.*

Rignold, Hugo Henry (b. Kingston-on-Thames 1905). Conductor. Trained R.A.M. Cairo Symphony Orch., 1944; Covent Garden Ballet, 1947; Liverpool Philharmonic Orch. 1948–54; Cape Town 1956; Royal Ballet 1957; Birmingham 1960.

Rigoletto. 4-act tragedy-opera by Verdi. Libretto by Piave, based on Victor Hugo's play *Le Roi s'amuse*. (Prod. Venice 1851; London 1853; New York 1855.)

Rigore; rigoroso (It.). 'Rigour'; 'rigorous' (referring to exactitude in point of time).

Rig Veda (Holst). See *Hymns from the Rig Veda.*

Rilasciando, rilasciante (It.). 'Releasing' or 'relinquishing', i.e. getting gradually slower; the equivalent of 'rallentando'. *Rilassando, rilassato* mean the same thing.

Rimbault, Edward Francis (b. London 1816; there d. 1876). London organist and musical antiquary; usefully edited old music and wrote books (especially, with E. J. Hopkins, q.v., *The Organ, its History and Construction*). LL.D. of some univ. untraced (not Harvard or Oxford as variously stated); also stated to be Ph.D. of the univ. of Stockholm.

Rimettendo, rimettendosi (It.). 'Putting back' (in the sense of resuming the old tempo).

Rimonte. Same as *Ruimonte* (q.v.).

Rimsky-Korsakof (Korsakov, &c.), Nicholas (b. govt. of Novgorod 1844; d. Lyubensk, nr. St. Petersburg, 1908). Early life spent on a country estate where he heard the native folk music which influenced his life-work; whilst studying at Naval Academy met Balakiref and worked at music; became naval officer 1862; 1st symphony performed 1865; 1st opera (*The Maid of Pskov = Ivan the Terrible*, q.v.) 1873; had become prof. of composition at St. Petersburg Conserv. 1871; director of Free Music School founded by Balakiref 1874–81; notable orch. conductor; an important member of Russian national group (see *Five*). Compositions not above mentioned include operas (*The Snow Maiden; Sadko—* also subject of a symphonic poem; *Kitej; The Golden Cockerel*); 3 symphonies; symphonic suite, *Sheherazade*; choral music, songs, &c.

See entries under the names of the operas above-mentioned and under *Antar; Ballad of the Doom of Oleg; Capriccio espagnol; Christmas Eve; Czar's Bride; Dubinushka; Kaschey the Immortal; Legend of Tsar Saltan; Mlada; Mozart and Salieri; Night in May; Russian Easter; Sheherazade.*

Rinaldo. (1) HANDEL's 1st London opera (1711). Libretto based on Tasso. (2) Male-voice Cantata by BRAHMS. (Op. 50; 1st perf. Vienna 1869.) A setting of Goethe.

Rinck, Johann Christian Heinrich (b. in Thuringia 1770; d. Darmstadt 1846). Famous organist; composer of many organ works still played and author of a standard *Practical Organ School* (6 books of graded compositions).

Rincón, E. G. C. = *Astorga, Baron d'* (q.v.).

Rinforzando; rinforzato (It.). 'Reinforcing'; 'reinforced', i.e. stress is applied to individual notes or chords. So *rinforza, rinforzamente*; 'reinforcement'.

Ring des Nibelungen, Der ('The Ring of the Nibelung'). 'Festival Play for Three Days, with a Preliminary Evening', by Wagner. (Prod. as a whole at Bayreuth 1876; London 1882; New York 1889.) The 4 portions are: *Das Rheingold* ('The Rhine Gold'. Munich 1869; New York and London as above). *Die Walküre* ('The Valkyrie'. Munich 1870; New York, incomplete, 1877; London as above). *Siegfried* (Bayreuth as above; Vienna 1878; New York 1887; London as above). *Götterdämmerung*

('Dusk of the gods'. Bayreuth as above; New York 1888; London as above).

Ringing of Bells. See *Bell* 2.

Ring of Bells. See *Bell* 3, 4.

Rio Grande, The. By Constant Lambert. Choral-orch. setting, with solo piano, of poem by Sacheverell Sitwell (1st perf. Manchester 1929).

Ripetizione (It.). 'Repetition.'

Ripieno (It.). Lit. 'full'. (1) The term is used in older music to make a distinction between passages to be played by the full body and others to be played by some group of solo performers (these latter spoken of as *Concertante*; see *Concerto*). The term is in this sense still used in Eng. brass bands—generally misspelt RIPIANO or REPIANO. (2) In It. organ music the word means 'Mixture' (see *Mixture Stop* and *Organ* 2).

Ripieno Maggiore and **Ripieno Minore.** Types of organ mixture, respectively louder and softer.

Ripley, (Maud) Gladys (b. Essex 1908; d. Chichester 1955). Contralto vocalist. Largely self-taught. Popular in Britain, particularly in oratorio. Many appearances Covent Garden.

Riposo; riposato (It.). 'Repose'; 'reposeful'. So *riposatamente*, 'with a feeling of repose'.

Riprendere (It.). 'Take up again', i.e. resume (e.g. the original tempo).

Ripresa (It.). (1) 'Repeat' of a section of a composition. (2) 'Recapitulation Section' of a movement in Sonata form (see *Form* 3). (3) 'Revival'—of an opera, &c.

Rip van Winkle. (1) Opera by G. F. BRISTOW—New York 1855; revived New York and Philadelphia 1870. (2) Opera by PLANQUETTE—prod. London and New York 1882. (3) Opera by DE KOVEN—prod. Chicago and New York 1920.

Riscaldano (It., from *caldo*, 'warm'). Lit. 'They warm up', i.e. the players are to become more lively.

Rise and Fall of the City of Mahagonny. See *Weill, Kurt.*

Rise, Columbia; See *Rule, Britannia*

Rising of the Lark. This is the old Welsh song *Codiad yr Ehedydd* said to have been composed by the harper David Owen (see *Dafydd y Garreg Wen*) as, going home from a long-extended feast at 3 in the morning, he saw a lark mount and heard it herald the break of day.

Risoluto; risolutamente (It.). 'Resolute'; 'resolutely'. So the superlative *risolutissimo*. **Risoluzione,** 'resolution'.

Rispetto (plur. *Rispetti*). A type of It. folk song—with 8 lines to the stanza. Wolf-Ferrari, Malipiero, and others have written music under this title.

Ristringendo (It. 'drawing-together'). 'Quickening.'

Risvegliato (It.). 'Wakened up', i.e. 'Animated'.

Rit. Short for *ritardando*, &c. (see below).

Ritardare; ritardando; ritardato (It.). 'To hold back'; 'holding back'; 'held back' (gradually, i.e. the same as *rallentando*). The abbrev. 'Rit.' occurs (but cf. *Ritenuto* below). **Ritardo** (It.). The act of holding back (i.e. of gradually diminishing the speed).

Ritchie, Margaret (b. Grimsby 1903; d. London 1969). Soprano. Early education in Austria. Then trained R.C.M. Recitalist in Britain and on Continent. Covent Garden, Glyndebourne, Eng. Opera Group, &c.

Ritenendo, ritenente (It.). 'Holding back.' **Ritenuto** (It.). 'Held back', i.e. 'slower' (immediately, not gradually as with *ritardando* and *rallentando*; but it may be that some composers have not observed this distinction). Abbreviations sometimes seen are *Riten.* and *Rit.*

Rite of Spring, The ('Le Sacre du Printemps'). Ballet by Stravinsky. Usually heard in concert form. (Prod. Paris and London 1913.)

Ritmo (It.). 'Rhythm.' **Ritmico** (It.). 'Rhythmic.'

Ritornel (Fr. *ritournelle*; It. *ritornello*; Ger. *Ritornell*). Lit. anything 'returned to'. The following are examples: (1) The refrain in some of the older (14th- and 15th-c.) It. madrigal types. (2) Sort of It. folk song, 3 lines to stanza, the last line rhyming with the first. (3) The repetition of the instrumental introduction to a song (and hence, by loose use of the term, the instrumental introduction itself, even when never 'returned to'). (4) In the classical concerto the return of the full orch. after a solo passage—the same as 'tutti'. (5) A mere synonym for *da capo*.

Ritorno (It.). 'Return' (noun).

Ritournelle. See *Ritornel*.

Ritter, (1) **Alexander** (1833–96). See *Symphonic Poem.*
(2) **Hermann.** See *Viola Alta.*

Ritterlich (Ger.). 'Knightly.'

Rittquartett, or **Reiterquartett** (Rider Quartet, or in Eng. 'Horseman Quartet'). Nickname of Haydn's String Quartet 'No. 67' or 'No. 74', in G minor, sometimes described as op. 74, no. 3. The name arises from the rhythm of the 1st movement.

Rituale. See under *Liturgy.*

Rivarde, Serge Achille (b. New York 1865; d. London 1940). Violinist. Trained Paris Conserv. In U.S.A. again 1881–4; then leading violin Lamoureux Orch., Paris. London début 1894. On staff of R.C.M. 1899–1936. Book on violin playing.

Riverso, Al (It.), or **Al rovescio.** By contrasting motion, i.e. the upward intervals of a melody all turned into downward intervals of the same numerical value, and vice versa.

Rivière, Jules Prudence (b. Aix-en-Othe 1819; d. Colwyn Bay, Wales, 1901). Popular orch. conductor, resident in Britain 1857 to death. Cf. *Concert*; *Weldon*.

Rk. = 'Rank', referring to the 'mixture' stops of an organ (see *Organ* 2).

R.M.C.M. Royal Manchester Coll. of Music (q.v.).

Roast beef of Old England. See *Leveridge, Richard.*

Robert, Camille. See *Madelon, La.*

Robert le diable ('Robert the Devil'). Meyerbeer's 1st Fr. Opera, on libretto by Scribe. Enormously successful. (Prod. Paris 1831; at 3 London theatres and Dublin 1832; New York 1934.)

Roberton, Hugh S. (= Stevenson) (b. Glasgow 1874; d. there 1952). Choral trainer; founder and conductor of remarkable Glasgow Orpheus Choir (1906–51); annual tours in U.S.A., Canada, &c. Popular competition adjudicator. Many choral arrangements of Scottish folk songs, &c. Knighted 1931.

Roberts, (1) **John** = Ieuan Gwyllt (b. nr. Aberystwyth 1822; d. Carnarvon 1877). Active force in Welsh musical life, introducing works of Bach, Handel, and Mendelssohn, and bringing about reform in hymn singing by his collections of tunes (composed tune *Moab*, &c.), but also publ. a Welsh translation of Sankey and Moody.
(2) **John Varley** (b. Stanningley, nr. Leeds, 1841; d. Oxford 1920). Organist at Magdalen Coll., Oxford (1882 to death; an Oxford 'character'); able choir trainer and author of book on boy's voice; composed popular church music, &c.
(3) **William.** See *Newman* 2.

Robertson, (1) **Alec** (b. Southsea 1892). Studied at R.A.M.; became lecturer for Gramophone Co. on educational use of gramophone; some years in Rome. Authority on plainsong; considerable author on musical subjects and editor of talks on music to B.B.C. (to 1952).
(2) **Rae** (b. Ardersier, Scotland, 1893; d. Los Angeles 1956). Pianist. Studied Edinburgh Univ. (M.A.); then R.A.M. under Matthay. After short career as solo pianist married Ethel Bartlett and with her enjoyed international reputation in perf. of music for 2 pianos; latterly resident U.S.A.
(3) **James** (b. Liverpool 1902). Conductor and pianist. Educated Cambridge (M.A.), Leipzig Conserv., and R.C.M. On staff Glyndebourne and Carl Rosa Opera Co. 1937–9. Conductor in Winnipeg of Canadian Broadcasting Corpn., 1939–40. Direc-

tor of opera Sadler's Wells 1946; N.Z. Broadcasting Service 1954; Carl Rosa 1958; London Opera Centre 1964.

Robeson, Paul Le Roy (b. Princeton, N.J., 1898). Educated for law at Rutgers and Columbia Univs.; then bass vocalist and actor (plays and films). Of high reputation in U.S.A. and Britain as vocal recitalist, especially (being a Negro) as sympathetic interpreter of 'Spirituals'.

Robespierre. See *Litolff*.

Robin Adair. The tune of this song is the old Irish one of *Eileen Aroon* (q.v.). It appears to have been popularized in Scotland about 1715 by the famous blind Irish harper, Hempson, then touring there. The Scotch Snap which pervades the tune is no part of the original.

The 1st introduction of the name 'Robin Adair' seems to have been in a parody which in 1734 welcomed to Puckstown (County Dublin) an Irish M.P. of the name. The words now used date from about 1750 and are by Lady Caroline Keppel, being addressed to another Robin Adair, a young Irish surgeon, with whom she was in love, and whom (after a long fight with her relatives) she married in 1758; he became Surgeon-General to George III. Presumably the name 'Robin Adair' in the song as then circulated suggested to her a version with a personal application.

Robin and Marion. See *Adam de la Halle*.

Robin Hood. Popular operetta by de Koven. (Prod. Chicago, Boston, and London 1890; New York 1891.)

Other operas of the same name are those by Shield (1784) and Macfarren (1860).

Robin Hood Dell (Fairmount Park, nr. Philadelphia). Open air amphitheatre where nightly summer orch. concerts or opera performances are given. Inaugurated 1930.

Robinson, Douglas (b. Leeds 1912). Organist and choral conductor. Chorus master Covent Garden from 1946. B.Mus., Dunelm.

Robinson, Stanford (b. Leeds, 1904). Orch. and opera conductor. Trained R.C.M. Joined B.B.C. staff 1924, since occupying increasingly important positions on it—Opera Director (Sound), 1951.

Rob Roy Overture. Concert-overture by Berlioz (1832). Inspired by Scott's novel.

Robusto (It.). 'Robust' (e.g. *tenore robusto*—a powerful tenor voice). So *robustamente*, 'in a robust spirit'.

Rochberg, George (b. Paterson, N.J., 1918). Composer; pupil of Szell, Leopold Mannes, and at Curtis Institute (on staff 1948–54). Chmn. mus. dept., Univ. Pa., 1960. Works include 2 symphonies.

Rochester, N.Y. See under *Schools of Music*.

Rockstro (originally **Rackstraw**), **William Smyth** (b. North Cheam, Surrey, 1823; d. London 1895). Pupil of Sterndale Bennett, and, at Leipzig Conserv., of Mendelssohn and others. Active London pianist and piano teacher, ed. of piano arrangements of orch. music, &c.; then settled in Torquay, returning to London 1891 and teaching counterpoint and plainsong at R.C.M. Minor composer, but now remembered by his *Life of Handel* and other literary works covering a wide variety of subjects.

Roco (It.). 'Raucous.'

Rococo (Fr., from *rocaille*, fancy rockwork in architecture). In ordinary Eng. usage 'tawdry', 'tastelessly florid'; in music applied to the 'galant' or homophonic style (see *Style galant*) of e.g. Telemann, the sons of Bach, and the early Haydn and Mozart (roughly 1730–70).

Rode, Jacques Pierre Joseph (b. Bordeaux 1774; there d. 1830). Virtuoso violinist; became solo violinist to Napoleon I; toured in Russia; Beethoven composed for him sonata in G, op. 6; latterly skill and artistry declined and he abandoned public appearance. Composed 13 violin concertos, string quartets, famous violin caprices in all 24 keys, Variations in G (still performed), &c.

Rodeo. Ballet by Copland (prod. New York 1942). A 4-movt. concert suite from this.

Rodzinski, Artur (b. Split, Dalmatia, 1892; d. Boston, Mass., 1958). Conductor. Studied Vienna Conserv. and Univ. (law doctorate). Conducted Warsaw Opera 1920–4; then in Philadelphia; on staff Curtis Institute. Conducted orchs. Los Angeles 1929–33, Cleveland 1933–43; New York Philharmonic 1943–7; Chicago; then freelance. Naturalized in U.S.A.

Roeckel Family. (1) **Joseph August** (b. Neumberg vorm Wald 1783; d. Anhalt-Coethen 1870). Operatic vocalist; then director of opera at Aachen; settled in Paris (1823–32) and there introduced Ger. operas; visited London with his Paris company (1832); returned to Germany (1853). For 3 sons and daughter-in-law see below. (2) **August** (b. Graz 1814; d. Budapest 1876). Son of Joseph August, above; colleague of Wagner in Dresden Opera; like Wagner implicated in Revolution of 1848; in prison 1849–62. Wagner's letters to him published 1894. (3) **Edward** (b. Trier 1816; d. Bath 1899). Also son of Joseph August. Pupil of his uncle J. N. Hummel; settled in England 1848; estd. at Bath. Composer of much piano music. (4) **Joseph Leopold** (b. London 1838; d. Vittel, Vosges, 1923). Also son of Joseph August. Lived Clifton, Bristol; composed cantatas, glees, and popular tuneful Victorian songs (e.g. *Angus Macdonald*). For wife see below. (5) **Jane**, *née* Jackson (b. 1834; d. Clifton 1907). Wife of Joseph Leopold, above. Pianist, pupil of Hallé, Clara Schumann, and others; practised as teacher. Composed piano music ('Jules de Sivrai'); invented 'Pamphonia' for learning notation.

Rogan. See *Mackenzie-Rogan*.

Roger-Ducasse. Jean Jules Amable (b. Bordeaux 1873; d. there 1954). Trained Paris Conserv.; Inspector of Singing in Paris schools (1909); succeeded Dukas as a prof. of composition at the Conserv. (1935). Compositions include comic opera, ballets, orch. works, chamber and piano works, &c.

Rogers, (1) **Benjamin** (b. Windsor 1614; d. Oxford 1698). Lay-clerk at St. George's Chapel, Windsor; organist Christ Church Cathedral, Dublin, 1639–41; then in Windsor again; after Commonwealth (1660) organist of Eton Coll. and lay-clerk of St. George's Chapel again; organist Magdalen Coll., Oxford, 1664; D.Mus., Oxford, 1669. Composed much church music, &c. His *Hymnus eucharisticus* (1660) still sung from top of Magdalen Coll. tower at 5 a.m. on May Day.
(2) **Bernard** (b. New York 1893; d. Rochester, N.Y., 1968). Composer and teacher of composition (Eastman School).

Roger's Farewell. See *Auld Lang Syne*.

Roger the Cavalier. See *Sir Roger de Coverley*.

Rogue's March. This tune is almost identical with that of the well-known *Right little, tight little Island* of Dibdin (q.v.). In the Brit. Army it was used in the ceremony of expelling (or 'drumming out') a soldier from the army—hence its name.

Roh (Ger.). 'Rough', 'coarse'.

Rohrflöte, or **Rohr Flute** (Ger., lit. 'Reed flute', reed here meaning 'tube'). Organ stop; metal end-plugged pipes with narrow tube through plug; 4-foot length and 8-foot pitch (see *Organ* 2).

Rohrwerk, Rohrstimmen (Ger.). The reed dept. of the organ.

Roi David (Honegger). See *King David*.

Roi d'Ys, Le. Successful tragedy-opera by Lalo. Libretto based on Breton legend. (Prod. Paris 1888; New Orleans 1890; London 1901; New York 1922.)

Roi l'a dit, Le ('The King has said it'). Comedy-opera by Delibes. (Prod. Paris 1873; London 1894.)

Roi malgré lui, Le. See *Chabrier*.

Roland-Manuel. See *Manuel*.

Rolland, Romain (b. Clamecy 1866; d. Vezelay 1944). Man of high musical learning; author of very many important historical and biographical works (many vols. on Beethoven); also novels (e.g. *Jean-Christophe*, in 12 vols., 1904–12), on musical subjects, and plays. Dr. ès Lettres (1895) and lecturer at Sorbonne and elsewhere. In Switzerland 1913–38; then in France again.

Rollschweller (Ger.). The 'General Crescendo' pedal of an organ (the one which gradually brings out all the stops).

Rolltrommel (Ger.). Tenor drum (see *Percussion Family* 2 j).

Romalis (Sp.). A sort of Seguidilla (q.v.). Other names are *Ole* and *Polo*.

Roman Carnival, The (Berlioz). See *Carnaval Romain*.

Roman Catholic Church Music in Britain. The Reformation in Britain, which may be dated from 1534, entailed the destruction of a vast number of buildings in which church music was carried on at various degrees of efficiency (600 in England alone from 1536 to 1539). Henceforth the tradition of a high musical culture was confined entirely to those comparatively few buildings retained as cathedrals for the new national church. Except for the 5 years of Queen Mary's reign (1553–8) the Romanists, who had formerly sternly suppressed heresy, were now regarded as heretics themselves, and this and their real or supposed allegiance to a foreign power led to their worship being prohibited, so that for long the Mass could be celebrated only in secrecy or quasi-secrecy. Gradually, towards the very end of the 18th c., the disabilities of Roman Catholics were lessened. Complete freedom came only with the Catholic Emancipation Act of 1829. Except for the Embassy Chapels Roman Catholic service music may be said to have been virtually non-existent in Britain for about 300 years.

A series of able English-born musicians latterly directed the music at some of these embassies, as Samuel Webbe, sen., at the Sardinia Chapel, Lincoln's Inn Fields, and perhaps, too, at the Portuguese Chapel, Grosvenor Square; Samuel Webbe, jun., at the Spanish Chapel, Manchester Square; and Vincent Novello, who in turn had posts as chorister or as organist at all these 3 chapels. The Roman Church on the Continent was then passing through what we may consider a bad phase musically. The Masses most valued were not those of the high polyphonic period of Palestrina, Victoria, and their immediate predecessors and contemporaries, but the orchestrally accompanied Viennese Masses of Haydn, Mozart, Weber, Hummel, Beethoven, and their contemporaries, or those of Kalliwoda (1801–66) and others of his period, in which the spirit is rarely that of the Church and more often that of the concert-room or even, in some instances, of the opera-house, and in all of which the form is quite unliturgical (see *Mass*). One of the 3 musicians mentioned, Vincent Novello, founded the music-publishing house that still bears his name, and amongst his issues were many Masses of this type, which henceforth dominated Catholic music in Britain until well into the 20th c. (When Brit. Catholic musicians themselves wrote Masses these were their models.) Later came Gounod and other composers whose Masses, whatever their musical attractions or value, were in no real sense church music. The use of music of this sort was by no means the only or, indeed, the worst abuse. Both in Britain and on the Continent, until the 19th c. was far advanced, the organ music was often entirely unsuitable. The vernacular hymns sung in Roman Catholic churches until near the end of the 19th c. were usually not on a high level. The Webbe–Novello period left behind it a small supply of sound diatonic tunes, which, however, dropped almost out of use when, in the middle of the c., the hymns of Faber (1814–63) came into use and popularized a type of tune of much slighter worth.

In the middle of the 19th c. a change of taste, form, and spirit in continental Catholic music came about as the result of the movement in Germany promoted by the Cäcilienverein (or St. Cecilia Soc.), but the influence of this movement, partly good and partly bad, though it extended to Britain, left many churches untouched, and in any case the new music introduced, though not objectionable, as the old had been, showed few positive virtues (see *Cecilian Movement*). The change of ideal that has happily now largely come about dates from the issue of a *Motu Proprio* on the subject, by Pius X, in 1903 (see *Motu Proprio*) and the appointment in 1901 of Richard Terry (q.v.) to the newly erected Roman Catholic Cathedral at Westminster, where, during the following quarter-century, a remarkable revival took place not only of the works of Palestrina and his continental predecessors and contemporaries but also of Eng. music of the same periods. The authority given by Pius X to the plainsong publications of the monks of Solesmes (see *Plainsong*), in the same year as that of his *Motu Proprio*, naturally supported this movement for a higher standard of music and of perf. in the Catholic church in Britain—a movement that is not yet exhausted and, indeed, has still much to accomplish.

Romance. (1, in Fr.) 'Song'. (2, in Sp.) A type of ancient ballad. (3, in Eng.) Often a song-like instrumental piece.

Romancero (Sp.). A collection of novels; hence a series of instrumental compositions of romantic tendency.

Romance sans paroles (Fr.). 'Song without Words' (q.v.).

Romanesca (It.), **Romanesque** (Fr.). (1) Said to be the same as the Galliard (see *Pavan and Galliard*)—probably a kind of galliard danced in the Romagna. (2) A certain melody in the 17th c. much used as a ground bass (q.v.). (3) A type of song (e.g. by Monteverdi).

Roman Festivals. Orch. Suite by Respighi. (1st perf. New York 1929.) Four movements: (*a*) *Circus Maximus*; (*b*) *The Jubilee*; (*c*) *The October Festival*; (*d*) *The Epiphany*.

Romantic. This word is applied in music to the works of the period of Weber, Mendelssohn, Schumann, Chopin, Wagner, Berlioz, Liszt, and so on, in which the expression of emotion takes precedence over the element of beauty of form (though this is not necessarily or generally absent). There is so much in the work of Schubert and Beethoven that comes under the above description that the Romantic Movement in music can also logically be considered to include them. That movement was, of course, merely a part of a general Romantic Movement, affecting all the arts, especially literature and painting and including in Eng. literature the works of Wordsworth, Coleridge, and Scott, the novels of the last of whom exercised direct influence on the literature of the continent of Europe. It is very observable that the composers of the Romantic period were much influenced by literature, often (as in much 'Programme Music', q.v.) borrowing definite literary themes. They were also strongly influenced by the growing nationalistic feeling of the period (see *Nationalism in Music*). Romanticism in music began to decline in the early years of the 20th c.; nevertheless the music of Debussy represents a sensitive development of it (cf. *Impressionism*), and is often clearly related to the work of certain poets and painters.

A definite Anti-romantic or Neo-Classical School may be said to have begun with Stravinsky (b. 1882) and Bartók (1881–1945), who in many of their works have deliberately avoided the expression of strong emotion: meanwhile a Neo-Romantic School (though it has never candidly admitted itself to be such) flourished in Germany and Austria under the influence of Schönberg (1874–1951).

The above is a brief attempt at a fair generalized statement but it will be recognized that apart from the definite 'Romantic Movement' (the characteristic movement of the 19th c.) there has been more or less romantic feeling in much music of all ages. Romanticism is then a question of balance—greater or lesser stress laid upon what may be called respectively poetry and pattern (cf. *Classical*).

Romantic Symphony. (1) By HANSON. (For 50th anniversary of Boston Symphony Orch., 1930.) (2) By BRUCKNER. See *Bruckner's Symphonies*.

Romanza (It.). A song or a song-like instrumental composition.

Romanzero. See *Romancero*.

Rombando (It.). 'Humming.'

Romberg. Important family of musicians, of whom a dozen are to be found in larger books of reference; only the following can be accommodated here:

(1) **Andreas Jakob** (b. nr. Münster 1767; d. Gotha 1821). Eminent violinist, touring Europe; succeeded Spohr as Kapellmeister at Gotha (1815). Composed 8 operas, cantatas (e.g. *The Lay of the Bell*, very popular with Brit. choral societies); 10 symphonies, over 20 violin concertos, over 30 string quartets, &c. (Ironically, now remembered chiefly by his Toy Symphony, q.v.) For his cousin see below.

(2) **Bernhard** (b. Dinklage, Oldenburg, 1767; d. Hamburg 1841). Cousin of Andreas Jakob, above. 'Cellist of high repute; toured widely, sometimes with his cousin; prof. of Paris Conserv. (1801–3); improved 'cello technique and wrote 'Method' for the instrument. Composed 10 'cello concertos, string quartets, operas, &c.

Romberg, Sigmund (b. Hungary 1887; d. New York 1951). Popular composer of operettas, film music, &c. Settled in New York 1913: later Hollywood. Long list of works includes *Blossom Time* (1921; see *Dreimäderlhaus*), *Student Prince* (1924), and 70 similar.

Rome. See *Bizet*.

Romeo and Juliet. Opera by GOUNOD. (Prod. Paris, London, and New York 1867.)

There have been many other operatic treatments of Shakespeare's play including one by J. E. BARKWORTH (Middlesbrough 1916; London 1920). BERLIOZ's 3rd Symphony, with solos and chorus, is on the same subject and has the same title. And there are TCHAIKOVSKY's Fantasy Overture (Moscow 1870); also PROKOFIEF's Ballet (op. 64, 1935) and 2 Suites made from it, as also his set of 10 Piano pieces (op. 75, 1937).

Romeo und Julia auf dem Dorfe (Delius). See *Village Romeo and Juliet*.

Rome Prize (French, Belgian, American). See *Prix de Rome*.

Ronald, Landon—originally Landon Ronald Russell (b. London 1873; there d. 1938). Son of Henry Russell (q.v.); studied at R.C.M.; became conductor of opera and musical comedy, accompanist to Melba, &c.; Principal of G.S.M. (1910–37). In high repute as orch. conductor, especially of Elgar's works. Composed theatre music, songs, &c. Knighted 1922.

Ronconi Family—father (**Domenico**, tenor, 1772–1839) and 3 sons, **Giorgio** (baritone), **Felice** (1811–75), and **Sebastiano** (baritone, b. 1814). All highly popular singers and teachers of singing. Giorgio (b. Milan 1810; d. Madrid 1890) was of great reputation on both sides of Atlantic: Donizetti wrote parts specially for him: he lived latterly in Spain.

Ronda, Rondalla (Sp.). Young men making their evening rounds in the streets to play and sing before people's houses. (For Ronda, the place, see *Rondeña*.)

Rond de jambe. (Fr.). In ballet, the tracing of semicircles by one foot, the other being used as axis.

Ronde (Fr. 'Round'). The Whole-Note or Semibreve (see Table 3); also a round dance to which the music is supplied by the dancers' own singing.

Rondeau, rondel (Fr.). (1) 13th- and 14th-c. type of song, sometimes accompanied by dancing. In it a solo voice and choral refrain alternated. The music tended, as time went on, to become polyphonically complex. It was cultivated by the Troubadours and Trouvères (see *Minstrels* 2). (2) An instrumental form deriving from the above, i.e. the earlier, simpler type of Rondo.

Ronde des lutins, La. See *Bazzini, Antonio.*

Rondeña. A kind of fandango (q.v.) of southern Spain, with the same harmonic peculiarity as the malagueña (q.v.). It takes its name from Ronda in Andalusia.

Rondes de printemps (Debussy). See under *Images*.

Rondine, La ('The Swallow'). Comedy-opera by Puccini. (Prod. Monte Carlo, Bologna, and Milan 1917; New York 1928; broadcast perf. London 1929.)

Rondo à la clochette (Paganini). See *Campanella.*

Rondo Form. See *Form* 4.

Röntgen, Julius (b. Leipzig 1855; d. Utrecht 1932). Of Dutch parentage. Director of Amsterdam Conserv. (1918–24); friend of Liszt, Brahms, and Grieg. Composed operas, orch. and piano works, songs, &c.

Root, G. F. See *Battle Cry of Freedom.*

Rootham, Cyril Bradley (b. Bristol 1875; d. Cambridge 1938). Son of distinguished Bristol musician. Studied at Cambridge Univ. (M.A., D.Mus.) and R.C.M.; became organist St. John's Coll., Cambridge. Composed orch. and choral-orch. works, chamber music, &c.

Root of a Chord. See *Harmony* 2 e.

Ropartz, (Joseph) Guy (Marie) (b. Guingamp, Brittany, 1864; d. there 1955). Barrister who took to music and studied under Massenet; later with Franck. Compositions include opera, symphonies, chamber music, organ and piano music, &c.

Roper, Edgar Stanley (b. Croydon, nr. London, 1878; there d. 1953). Choir-boy of Westminster Abbey; then organ scholar at Corpus Christi Coll., Cambridge (M.A., B.Mus.); asst. organist Westminster Abbey 1917, organist Chapel Royal 1919; Principal T.C.M. 1929–44; Dean of Faculty of Music, London Univ. Composer and ed. of church music, &c. M.V.O. 1930, C.V.O. 1943. D.Mus. Lambeth.

Rore, Cipriano de—or Van Rore (b. Antwerp or Malines 1516; d. Parma 1565). Pupil of Willaert (q.v.) at Venice; held various positions in Italy. In high repute as composer of madrigals, motets, &c.

Rory O'More. The words and air of this popular Irish song are by the novelist-poet-painter, Samuel Lover (1797–1868): he wrote it as the result of a challenge to make something better than the Irish comic songs of which he complained. He based a novel on the song and a play on the novel.

Rosa, (1) Carl August Nicolas— really 'Karl Rose' (b. Hamburg 1842; d. Paris 1889). Appeared as violinist in Britain and other countries at age 12. Then studied Leipzig and Paris Conserv. Became chief violin of Hamburg Orch. Toured in U.S.A.; there married; got together opera company (wife as prima donna), touring U.S.A. Wife died 1874 and Rosa organized 'Carl Rosa Opera Co.' (for opera in English), which had London seasons and toured Britain, introducing many works hitherto unknown to Brit. stage and many new works by Brit. composers. Company continued after his death and was chief means of bringing opera to Brit. provincial centres. Ceased 1958.

(2) **Salvator** (b. nr. Naples 1615; d. Rome 1673). Painter; also satirist, poet, and musician. His satire *La Musica* (attacking the church music of his day and period) appeared posthumously, led to violent discussion, and was often reprinted. Most or all of the songs long attributed to Rosa are by other composers. (See Frank Walker in *Monthly Mus. Record*, Oct. 1949, &c.)

Rosalia. See *Sequence* 1.

Rosamunde Music. Schubert's Overture and Incidental Music to a play by Wilhelmine von Chezy (1823). But the piece which is publ. and now performed as the *Overture to 'Rosamunde'* (in C; op. 26) was composed in 1820 for a melodrama by Hoffmann called *Die Zauberharfe* ('The Magic Harp'), whilst the actual *Rosamunde* Overture (in D; op. 69) was later publ. as *Alfonso and Estrella* and is now so known.

Rosary, The. By Ethelbert Nevin (q.v.). Sentimental song (1898) with a sale of 6 million copies in the 1st 30 years.

Rosbaud, Hans (b. Graz 1895; d. Lugano 1962). Conductor and pianist. Trained Frankfurt-on-Main. Opera and concert conductor, holding positions in Ger. cities, Mainz, Münster, Strasbourg, Munich, &c. Chief conductor, Baden-Baden Radio 1948; also Zürich Tonhalle. Recognized as outstanding interpreter of advanced modern works.

Rose, (1) Billy (b. New York 1899; d. Jamaica 1966). Amateur shorthand champion of U.S.A. (at age 17, 350 words a minute, various languages); later successful saloon, restaurant, and night club proprietor; theatrical producer, &c.; popular newspaper columnist, author *Wine, Women, and Words.* Included here as composer of highly successful songs; scientifically studied hundreds of existing specimens of the species and discovered predominant importance of 1st line of chorus and of vowel combinations, found 'oo' to be most popular vowel and made hit with *Barney Google with the Goo-Goo-Googly Eyes*, &c.

(2) **Leonard** (b. Washington, D.C., 1918). 'Cellist. Pupil of Salmond at Curtis Institute; played for Cleveland and N.Y. Philharmonic Orchs.; solo career from 1951. On staff Juilliard Sch. and Curtis Institute.

Rosé, Arnold Josef (b. Jassy, Rumania, 1863; d. London 1946). Violinist. Trained Vienna Conserv. Leading violin Vienna Philharmonic Soc. for 57 years. Also Vienna State Opera. Bayreuth fest. about 20 years. Founded and led famous string quartet. Refugee in London from 1938.

Roseingrave (or **Rosingrave**), (1) **Daniel** (d. Dublin 1727). Pupil of Purcell; organist of cathedrals of Gloucester, Winchester, Salisbury, and Dublin (both St. Patrick's and Christ Church). Most of compositions lost. For his sons see below. (2) **Thomas** (b. Winchester 1690; d. Dunleary, Ireland, 1766). Son of Daniel, above. Studied in Italy (friend of the 2 Scarlattis); engaged in theatre music activities in London; organist St. George's, Hanover Square. Crossed in love and henceforth intermittently mad. Composed organ and harpsichord music, &c. (3) **Ralph** (b. Salisbury abt. 1695; d. Dublin 1747). Like Thomas a son of Daniel, above, and succeeded him in his Dublin organistships. Composed church music.

Rosenberg, Hilding C. (b. Bosjökloster, Sweden, 1892). Composer of modernist tendencies. Trained Stockholm Conserv. and Dresden. Symphonies (e.g. *Apocalyptic Symphony* for orch., chorus, and recitation, 1940), concertos, oratorios, chamber music, &c.

Rosenbloom, Sydney (b. Edinburgh 1889). Pianist, teacher, and composer. Trained R.A.M. and had successful recital career. Settled Bloemfontein, South Africa.

Rosenkavalier, Der ('The Cavalier of the Rose'). Opera ('Comedy for Music') by Richard Strauss. Libretto by Hofmannsthal. (Prod. Dresden 1911; London, Birmingham, and New York 1913.)

Rosenstock, Joseph (b. Cracow 1895). Conductor, trained Vienna. Piano prodigy from age 11; then at Stuttgart under F. Busch; mus. dir. Darmstadt 1922; Wiesbaden 1927; Metropolitan 1929; Mannheim 1930; Tokyo 1936–41 and 1945–6; N.Y. City Opera 1948–56; Cologne 1958. Some compositions.

Rosenthal, Moriz (b. Lwow 1862; d. New York 1946). Pianist. Pupil of Joseffy and Liszt. Of great international repute. Settled New York 1939.

Rose of Persia, The. Comic opera by Sullivan. Libretto by Basil Hood. (Prod. Savoy Theatre, London, 1899; New York 1901.)

Rose of Sharon, The. Oratorio by Mackenzie. (1st perf. Norwich Fest. 1884.)

Rosiera, La. See *Gnecchi*.

Rosing, Vladimir (b. St. Petersburg 1890; d. Santa Monica, Calif., 1963.) Operatic and concert tenor. Trained for bar; then in singing by Jean de Reszke (q.v.), &c. Petrograd opera 1912–13; début London 1913. Producing director Covent Garden Eng. Opera Co. 1936–9; then of South California Opera Co., Hollywood, 1939–41.

Rosingrave. See *Roseingrave*.

Roslavets (Roslavyets, Rosslavetz, &c.), **Nikolai Andreivich** (b. district of Chernigov, Russia, 1881; d. Moscow 1944). Studied violin and composition at Moscow Conserv. Composer of orch. and chamber music, songs, &c.

Rosseter, Philip (b. abt. 1575; d. London 1623). Lutenist and composer of songs, ayres, and chamber music; active in Queen Elizabeth's court theatricals, and friend of Campion.

Rossi (nearly 30 musicians of this name, living in 3 centuries, find a niche in various books of reference; here there is space for only the one of greatest historical importance), **Luigi** (b. Torremaggiore, S. Italy, 1597; d. Rome 1653). Singer, organist, and composer; popular in Paris, whither invited by Mazarin 1646; there produced his *Orfeo*, earliest It. opera there heard. Composed over 100 solo cantatas, &c.

Rossignol, Le (Stravinsky). See *Nightingale*.

Rossini, Gioacchino Antonio (b. Pesaro 1792; d. nr. Paris 1868). Trained at Conserv. of Bologna as 'cellist and composer; specially devoted to music of Mozart; soon became famous as composer, providing 36 operas in 19 years, 1810–29; then no more to end of life; most important are *The Barber of Seville* (see *Barbiere di Siviglia*), *William Tell* (see *Guillaume Tell*). Famous *Stabat Mater* (q.v.). Thoroughly understood human voice and orchestration; had gift of melody and sense of humour; hence his high success; in England for 5 months in 1823, earning the then immense sum of £7,000 by concerts, &c.

See also *Boutique fantasque*; *Cenerentola*; *Comte Ory*; *Gazza ladra*; *Italiana in Algeri*; *Mosè in Egitto*; *Scala di seta*; *Semiramide*; *Siege of Corinth*; *Tancredi*.

Rosslavetz. See *Roslavets*.

Rostal, Max (b. Teschen, Silesia, 1905). Violinist. Child prodigy: then studied under Arnold Rosé (q.v.) and Flesch (q.v.). On staff State Academy of Music, Berlin, 1930–3. In Britain since 1934 (naturalized). On staff G.S.M.

Rostropovich, Mstislav (b. Baku 1927). 'Cellist. Trained by father and at Moscow Conserv. (later on staff). Début aged 8; from 1950 distinguished international career. Wife is Galina Vishnevskaya.

Rota. (1) A round (q.v.); 'Sumer is icumen in' (q.v.) is often called the 'Reading Rota' (from its place of composition). (2) A Lat. name for the hurdy-gurdy (q.v.).

Rotary Valve. See *Cylinder or Rotary Valve*.

Rote or **Rotte.** Another name for Crwth (q.v.), though it may sometimes mean harp, perhaps. It occurs in Chaucer, &c.

Rothmüller, Marko (b. Trnjani, Jugoslavia, 1908). Operatic baritone. Studied Zagreb and Vienna (com-

position under Berg); since 1932 constant appearances in theatres of Europe, Britain, and U.S.A. Active as composer. On staff Indiana Univ.

Rothwell, (1) **Walter Henry** (b. London 1872; d. California 1927). Pianist, conductor, and composer. Trained Vienna Conserv. After successful career as pianist became asst. conductor to Mahler at Hamburg Opera (1895); then Amsterdam, New York, St. Paul (1908), Los Angeles (1919), and Hollywood Bowl.

(2) **Evelyn** (b. Wallingford, Berks., 1911). Oboist. Trained R.C.M. under Leon Goossens. Member of many chief London orchs. (1931–9); much solo oboe gramophone recording. Many oboe works dedicated to her. Edits series, *Music for Oboe*, so increasing repertory. Wife of Sir John Barbirolli (q.v.) 1939.

Rotondo (It.). 'Round', i.e. full in tone.

Rotte. See *Rote*.

Rouet d'Omphale, Le ('Omphale's Spinning-wheel'). The earliest Fr. Tone Poem; by Saint-Saëns (op. 31, 1871). It vividly reproduces in tone the idea of Hercules in servitude to the Lydian princess, 'the triumph of weakness over strength'.

Rouget de Lisle, Claude Joseph (b. in Franche-Comté 1760; d. nr. Paris 1836). Engineer officer in Fr. Army; stationed in Strasbourg 1792; composer at that time of the *Marseillaise*, 1st sung by the mayor of Strasbourg at a party, 25 April, hastily arranged for military band, and played at a review the following day; then 2 months later sung at a patriotic banquet at Marseilles. (For further particulars, differing in some respects from those usually given, see *OCM*.)

Rough Music. See *Charivari*.

Roulade (Fr.). Much the same as a vocal *Division*.

Roulant, roulante (Fr. masc., fem.). 'Rolling.' *Caisse roulante*, 'Tenor Drum' (see *Percussion Family* 2 j).

Round. A short vocal canon at the unison or 8ve (see *Canon*) for unaccompanied singing. It was a popular form in England in the 16th c. and is still current, though few fresh rounds are now composed. (Cf. *Catch*.)

Round, Catch, and Canon Club. London singing club, founded 1843.

Round Dance. (1) A dance in which the performers turn round. (2, a more common use of the term). A dance in which they move round in a circle, i.e. a ring dance. (Cf. *Square Dance*.)

Rousseau, Jean Jacques (b. Geneva 1712; d. nr. Paris 1778). (For his life, literary work, and philosophical and social influences see general books of reference.) Connexion with music began with activity as an ill-equipped music teacher at Lausanne; in Paris (1742) read a paper on a new (numeral) system of notation to Académie des Sciences, and next year publ. this as *Dissertation on Modern Music*; for extended periods of life earned living as music copyist; produced single opera *Le Devin du village* ('The Village Soothsayer') before King at Fontainebleau 1752; this had great success, being frequently performed for three-quarters of a century (in English, arranged by Burney, as 'The Cunning-Man', Drury Lane, London, 1766. Cf. *Bastien und Bastienne*).

Letter on French Music, decrying it on various grounds and lauding It. music (1753); similar attacks appear in some of the articles on music supplied to the famous Fr. *Encyclopedia* (1751–65), afterwards collected as a *Dictionary of Music* (1767; Eng. transl. 1770). Other (smaller) musical-literary works —invariably of a polemic nature. Dramatic piece (with Coignet as collaborator) *Pygmalion* (Lyons 1770; Paris 1775; declamation with interspersed orch. music). About 100 songs.

See reference under *Education* 1.

Rousseau's Dream. This tune comes from Rousseau's opera, *Le Devin du village* (1752; see *Rousseau*), where it appears, without words, to accompany action. The title *Rousseau's Dream* was given by J. B. Cramer (q.v.). The tune appears in many hymn collections.

Roussel, Albert (b. Tourcoing, N. of France, 1869; d. Royan 1937). Began life in navy; then studied under d'Indy at Schola Cantorum, of which later

(1902–14) a prof. Composed 4 symphonies and other orch. music, ballet music, choral and chamber music, songs, &c. Of the Impressionist School yet in later works influenced by Stravinsky.

See *Spider's Feast*.

Rovescio, Al (It.). The same as *Al riverso* (see *Riverso*).

Rowley, Alec (b. London 1892; d. there 1958). Composer of songs, chamber music, organ music, piano teaching music, &c. Vice-chairman T.C.L.

Roxolane, La. Nickname for Haydn's Symphony in C, no. 63 in Breitkopf edn. of the Symphonies. See remarks in *OCM*, s.v. *Nicknamed Compositions*.

Royal Academy of Music (London). (1) An operatic organization (1719–28) with which Handel was connected. (2) The present-day educational institution (opened 1822; see *Schools of Music*): the Principals have been Crotch (1823), Potter (1832), Lucas (1859), Sterndale Bennett (1866), G. A. Macfarren (1875), Mackenzie (1888), McEwen (1924), Marchant (1936), Thatcher (1949), Armstrong (1955); A. Lewis (1968). Cf. *Associated Board*.

Royal Albert Hall. See *Albert Hall, Royal*.

Royal Amateur Orchestral Society. London organization founded 1872 and still in existence. First President and leading violin was Duke of Edinburgh (son of Queen Victoria).

Royal Charlie. See *Will ye no come back again?*

Royal College of Music (London). Opened 1883 succeeding the National Training School of Music (q.v.). Directors, Grove (1883), Parry (1894), Allen (1918), Dyson (1937), Bullock (1953), Falkner (1960), Willcocks (1974).

Royal College of Organists. See *Profession of Music*; *Degrees and Diplomas* 2.

Royal Festival Hall, London. On south bank of Thames. Inauguration 1951 as first musical event of Festival of Britain. Seats 3000.

Royal Irish Academy of Music (Dublin). See *Schools of Music*.

Royal Manchester College of Music. Founded by Hallé in 1893. Later Principals, Brodsky (1895), Forbes (1929), Frederick R. Cox (1965). Cf. *Associated Board*.

Royal Military School of Music. See *Schools of Music*; *Degrees and Diplomas* 2; *Kneller Hall*.

Royal Musical Association. Founded (in London) 1874 'for the investigation and discussion of subjects connected with the art and science of music'. Incorporated 1904; 'Royal' since 1944.

Royal Palace. See *Weill, Kurt*.

Royal Philharmonic Orchestra. Formed 1946 by Beecham. Conductor 1960 Rudolf Kempe.

Royal Philharmonic Society. Famous concert-giving soc. founded in London, by members of the musical profession, 1813. Its 'membership' and 'associateship' are open only to members of that profession, but 'fellowship' is open to others, and the public can gain admission to concerts. (Cf. *Hanover Square Rooms*; *St. James's Hall*.)

Royal Philharmonic Society Prizes. See *Wood, Thomas*.

Royal School of Church Music. Founded 1927 as 'School of English Church Music' by Sydney Hugo Nicholson (q.v.) and members of Church Music Soc. (q.v.), Archbishop of Canterbury being President, and choirs all over country becoming affiliated. Royal Charter 1945. Coll. of St. Nicolas opened 1929 as chief training centre; successively at Chislehurst, Canterbury, and (1953) Croydon. Director, G. H. Knight (q.v.).

Royal Schools of Music. See *Associated Board*; *Degrees and Diplomas* 2.

Royal Scottish Academy of Music. A development (1929) of the Glasgow Athenaeum School of Music (founded 1890). Principals W. G. Whittaker (1929), Sir Ernest Bullock (1941), Henry Havergal (1953). Cf. *Associated Board*.

Royal Society of Musicians. See *Profession of Music*.

Royal Society of Teachers. See *Degrees and Diplomas* 2.

Royal Victoria Hall. See *Victoria Hall*.

Roze, Marie Hippolyte—*née* Pousin (b. Paris 1846; there d. 1926). Operatic and concert soprano. Trained Paris Conserv. Début Paris 1865; London 1872 (there long remained highly popular). For a time married to the impresario J. H. Mapleson.

Rózsa, Miklos (b. Budapest 1907). Composer; trained Leipzig. From 1940 in California. On staff Univ. S. Calif.; has composed in many forms; best known for his film scores.

Rubato or **Tempo rubato.** This word, though often used in various wide senses, is best reserved for a sort of rhythmic give-and-take in perf., within a limited unit of the time-scheme of a composition—that time unit being the Phrase (q.v.). A lingering or hurrying over some note or notes earlier in the phrase is compensated by a corresponding hurrying or lingering over others later in it, and if this be artistically carried out a keen-eared observer following the beat of a metronome would find that the departure from the beat earlier was later corrected by a return to it (always provided that the whole passage of which the phrase forms a part does not happen to be subjected to a general accelerando or rallentando, in which case the metronome would not offer a proper indication). A feeling of freedom, instead of mechanical regularity, is thus imparted to the perf. Time is kept—'bent but not broken', as Matthay puts it. For some of the melodic, harmonic, and other factors which suggest to the conscious or unconscious mind of the sensitive performer the employment of rubato cf. *Agogic*.

It is sometimes stated that whilst rubato occurs in the upper parts of a composition the bass should go on its way with undeviating regularity. This doctrine first appears in 18th-c. musical literature and continues to appear in the 19th c. in accounts of Chopin's playing of his own music and his teaching. It is obvious that such a doctrine is of limited application if grave harmonic clashes are to be avoided.

The employment of Tempo Rubato (lit. 'robbed time') must, if it is to sound natural, spring from genuine innate or cultivated musical feeling:

otherwise instead of adding to the beauty and emotional effect of a perf. it will produce an effect of discomfort in the mind of the listener.

Rubbra, Edmund (b. Northampton 1901). Studied with Cyril Scott and then at R.C.M. under Holst and others. Long list of compositions, symphonies, piano concerto, chamber music, vocal works, &c. Lecturer at Oxford Univ. (M.A.) 1947. Hon. D.Mus. Dunelm. 1949. C.B.E. 1960.

Rubens Cantata. See *Benoît*.

Rubens, Paul (b. 1876; d. nr. Falmouth 1917). Educated Oxford Univ. Became highly popular composer of songs for musical comedies (*Country Girl* 1902, *Miss Hook of Holland* 1907, &c.).

Rubible. The rebec (q.v.).

Rubini, Giovanni Battista (b. nr. Bergamo 1794; d. nr. there 1854). Famous tenor. Début Paris at 19. Toured Europe and gained immense wealth.

Rubinstein, (1) **Anton** (b. in govt. of Podolsk, Russia, 1829; d. nr. St. Petersburg 1894). Studied piano in Moscow, then at age 10–13 played in France, England, Holland, Germany, and Sweden, encouraged by Liszt; from 15 to 18 studied composition in Germany and Austria; henceforth accorded on both sides of Atlantic admiration as most remarkable pianist. Founded St. Petersburg Conserv. 1862 and was its principal for 5 years. As composer very prolific—20 operas, 6 symphonies (see *Ocean*), 5 piano concertos, piano solos, chamber music and over 100 songs, &c.—all now represented in the repertory by only a few trifles (see *Melody in F*). Not one of Russian nationalist school (cf. *Five*), but cosmopolitan or inclined to Teutonicism. For his brother see below.

(2) **Nicholas** (b. Moscow 1835; d. Paris 1881). Brother of Anton above, and like him a fine pianist; founded Moscow Conserv. 1859 (as his brother did that of St. Petersburg) and was its principal till his death; conductor of repute. Composed some piano music.

(3) **Artur** (b. Warsaw 1886). Pianist. Trained in Berlin and under Lesche-

tizky, &c. Since early age has been before the public of both sides of Atlantic. Composer of piano music, chamber music, &c. Resident in California.

(4) **Beryl** (b. Athens, Georgia, U.S.A., 1898; d. Cleveland 1952). Pianist. Had early career as boy prodigy; then pupil of Busoni. Recital career; director Cleveland Inst. of Music 1932. Composed piano concertos, &c.

Rubio, Augustin (b. Murcia, Spain, 1856; d. London 1940). Violoncellist. Trained Madrid Conserv. and Berlin. Settled London. Composed 'cello concerto, &c.

Rücksicht (Ger.). 'Consideration.'

Ruddigore, or The Witch's Curse. Comic opera by Gilbert and Sullivan. (Prod. Savoy Theatre, London, and New York, 1887.)

Rudement (Fr.). 'Roughly.'

Rudhyar, Dane—real name Daniel Chennevière (b. Paris 1895). Settled in U.S.A. 1917. Composer of orch., chamber, and piano works, usually of esoteric tendency; author of book on *The Rebirth of Hindu Music* (Madras 1928); also book on Debussy publ. at age 18, &c.

Rueda. A Spanish round dance popular in Castile: its music is in quintuple time, i.e. has 5 beats to the measure.

Ruffo, Vincenzo (b. Verona abt. 1520). Choirmaster, in turn, of cathedrals of Verona, Milan, Pistoia, and again Milan; publ. many books of church music and madrigals (a book of masses in 1592) and was looked upon as one of most accomplished composers of his day.

Rugby. 'Symphonic Movement' by Honegger (1928); suggestive of a football game.

Ruggles, Carl (b. Marion, Mass., 1876). Studied at Harvard; then influenced by Schönberg; attached to Univ. of Miami, Florida, 1937. Composed orch., piano, and vocal works of individual cast.

Ruhe (Ger.). 'Peace.' So *ruhig*, 'peaceful'; *ruhelos*, 'peace-less'.

Ruhepunkt; Ruhezeichen (Ger.). 'Rest-point'; 'rest-sign', i.e. the sign ⌒

Ruhig (Ger.). 'Peaceful.'

Ruhrtrommel (Ger.). 'Tenor drum' (see *Percussion Family* 2 j).

Rührung (Ger.). 'Feeling.'

Ruimonte (or **Rimonte**), **Pedro** (b. Saragossa towards end of 16th c.). Attached to Spanish vice-regal court at Brussels. Composed madrigals and unaccompanied sacred music.

Ruins of Athens Overture. From Beethoven's Incidental Music (op. 113) for an Epilogue by Kotzebue, written for the opening evening of the Ger. Theatre in Budapest, 1812 (cf. *King Stephen*). A Turkish March from the same Incidental Music is occasionally heard.

Rule, Britannia! The music of this is by Arne (q.v.) and the words by James Thomson. It was 1st performed in the masque *Alfred*, produced in the grounds of Frederick, Prince of Wales, (Cliefden House, Maidenhead), on 1 August 1740. In Handel's *Occasional Oratorio*, 6 years after *Alfred* was produced, he introduced the opening strain, evidently confident that the audience would recognize it.

Beethoven wrote piano variations on the tune (poor ones), and many composers who were no Beethovens have done the like. Beethoven also introduced it into his 'Battle' Symphony (see *Wellington's Victory*). It appears also in Attwood's anthem *O Lord, grant the King a long life*. Wagner wrote an overture based upon it (an early work; 1836: 1st perf. Königsberg 1837; 2nd perf. London 1905). Mackenzie (q.v.) has a brilliant *Britannia* Overture, partly based on the tune.

The chorus of 'Rule, Britannia!' is the only part of it the ordinary Brit. man, woman, or child can repeat when called upon, and then he, she, or it makes the confident but unauthorized statement 'Britannia *rules* the waves', instead of uttering the hopeful command, 'Britannia, rule the waves!'

In 1794 an Americanized version of the song appeared—'Rise, Columbia!' by Robert Treat Paine.

Rule of the Octave. A simple formula for the harmonization of the ascending and descending scale in the bass. It was taught to every harmony pupil in Europe during the 18th and early 19th cs.

Ruler of the Spirits, The (*Der Beherrscher der Geister*). Concert-overture by Weber, being revision (1804) of Overture to uncompleted Opera *Rubezahl*.

Rullante, Tamburo. 'Rolling drum', i.e. tenor drum (see *Percussion Family* 2 j).

Rumanian Rhapsody. See *Golestan.*

Rumba. A Cuban dance of somewhat complex rhythm which became popular in the U.S.A. and Europe from about 1930. It derives from a Negro dance of an erotic kind.

Rumba Bongos. Merely *Bongos* (q.v.); they are sometimes used in playing rumbas.

Rumford, Robert Kennerley (b. London 1870; d. North Stoke, Oxon., 1957). Baritone. Pupil of Henschel. Popular oratorio and concert singer. Clara Butt was his 1st wife (1900).

Rummel, (1) **Franz** (b. London 1853; d. Berlin 1901). Pianist. Came of a Bavarian family of musicians prominent in 4 generations. Trained Brussels Conserv. (later on staff). Début Antwerp 1872; London Albert Hall 1873. In U.S.A. 1878–81. Finally in Berlin. (2) **Walter Morse** (b. Berlin 1887; d. Bordeaux 1953). Pianist. Son of above: after his death some years in U.S.A. Pupil of Godowsky, &c. Début Paris 1913 (there friend of Debussy). Settled in Paris but toured widely. Some comps. (40 songs) and arrangements for piano of Bach organ works, &c.

Runciman, John F. (b. 1866; d. London 1916). London music critic (*Saturday Review*, &c.) and author of books on Purcell, Wagner, &c. Vigorous, outspoken and heedless, so that description of the R.A.M. (1896) as 'a cesspool of academic musical life', and as 'dominated by commercial men who, without shame, perpetrate feats of dishonesty', became the subject of a *cause célèbre.*

Running Set. Eng. folk dance still in use in the Appalachian mountain region of the U.S.A. The tunes to which it is danced are in simple quadruple time and its steps and movements are very active.

Rural Music Schools. These represent an Eng. movement for the encouragement of musical culture in the villages. They began in Hertfordshire, in 1929. Since then the movement has been widely extended. Violin classes, orchestras, choral societies, and lectures constitute a good deal of the activity. (Headquarters: Little Benslow Hills, Hitchin, Herts.)

Russalka (or Rusalka). (1) Opera by DARGOMÏJSKY; text based on Pushkin. (Prod. St. Petersburg 1856, New York 1922, London 1931). (2) DVOŘÁK's most popular opera. (Prod. Prague 1901.)

Russell, (1) **Henry** (b. Sheerness 1812; d. London 1900). Pupil of Rossini in Italy; singer on London stage; organist at Rochester, N.Y.; then celebrated provider (on both sides of Atlantic) of one-man musical entertainments, singing own songs (composed about 800—*Cheer, boys, cheer, There's a good time coming, boys!, A Life on the Ocean Wave,* &c.).

Cf. *Ronald, Landon.*

(2) (really Leonard), **Lillian** (b. Clinton, Iowa, 1861; d. Pittsburgh 1922). Operatic soprano. Became highly popular in light opera, her personal appearance contributing.

(3) **Ella—Countess di Righini** (b. Cleveland, Ohio, 1864; d. Florence 1935). Operatic and concert soprano. Trained Paris and Milan. Opera début Sicily 1882; Covent Garden 1885. Lived in London but toured widely. Died in poverty.

(4) **Thomas Alfred** (b. London 1902). Violinist and later viola player (pupil of Tertis). Member of London Philharmonic Orch. from 1935; head of its administration 1939–53. Ed. of *Philharmonic Post*; Hon. Sec., National Assoc. of Symphony Orchs. Author of many books and pamphlets relevant to his work. Chevalier of the Légion d'Honneur 1947.

Russia. Symphonic Poem by Balakiref. 'Composed for the inauguration at Novgorod in 1862 of a memorial of Russia's 1000th Anniversary.'

Russian Bassoon. See *Cornett and Key Bugle Families.*

Russian Church Music. See *Greek Church.*

Russian Concerto. For Violin. By Lalo (1883).

Russian Easter. Concert-overture by Rimsky-Korsakof, based on Russian church melodies (op. 36, 1888).

Russian Quartets (Haydn). See *Russischen Quartette.*

Russischen Quartette, Die ("The Russian Quartets'). Nickname of Haydn's String Quartets nos. 37–42 (reason for name unknown). They are also known as *Gli Scherzi* ('The Scherzos', or 'The Jokes'), from the character and marking of the minuets. Still another name is *Jungfernquartette* ('Maiden Quartets').

Russlan and Ludmilla. Opera by Glinka. Libretto based on poem of Pushkin. (Prod. St. Petersburg 1842; London 1931.)

Russo, Russa (It. masc., fem.). 'Russian.' So *Alla russa,* 'in the Russian style'.

Rust, (1) **Friedrich Wilhelm** (b. nr. Dessau 1739; d. Dessau 1796). Pupil of Friedemann and C. P. E. Bach, also, in Italy, of Benda, Tartini, and Pugnani; active in Dessau as director of music in theatre, &c. Composed extensively operas, songs, piano sonatas (considered as precursors of Beethoven's), sonatas for unaccompanied violin (one on E string), &c. For son and grandson see below. (2) **Wilhelm Karl** (b. Dessau 1787; there d. 1855). Fine pianist; in Vienna 1807–27 and there friend of Beethoven. (3) **Wilhelm** (b. Dessau 1822; d. Leipzig 1892). Grandson of Friedrich Wilhelm and nephew of Wilhelm Karl, above. Pianist and violinist; organist of St. Thomas's Church, Leipzig, from 1878 and cantor of St. Thomas's School from 1880; helped in preparation of Bachgesellschaft edn. A few compositions for piano and some songs.

Rustle of Spring (in Ger. *Frühlingsrauschen*). Early Piano piece of Sinding.

One of *Six Pieces*, op. 32. His most popular composition (50 edns. in U.S.A. alone).

Rustling Tin Sheet. See *Percussion Family* 2 u.

Rute, Ruthe (Ger. 'rod'). A sort of birch brush used to beat the bass drum for a particular effect.

Ruth. (1) Oratorio by COWEN. (1st perf. Worcester Fest. 1887). (2) Another by GAUL (Birmingham 1881). (3) A notorious (unintentionally comic) setting by GEORGE TOLHURST (1864).

Rutland, Harold (b. London 1900). Pianist, composer, and journalist. Trained G.S.M.; then Cambridge (B.A., Mus.B.) and R.C.M. On staff B.B.C. 1940–56; ed. *Mus. Times* 1957–60; Examiner T.C.L. 1959.

Ruy Blas Overture. By Mendelssohn. Hastily written for a Ger. perf. of Victor Hugo's play (op. 95, 1839).

Ruyneman, Daniel. See *Electrophone.*

Rysanek, Leonie (b. Vienna 1926). Dramatic soprano. Trained Vienna Conserv.; début 1948; Saarbrucken 1950; Bayreuth 1951; with Munich Opera from 1952; San Francisco 1957; New York 1959.

Rythme; rythmique (Fr.). 'Rhythm'; 'rhythmic'.

S

Sabaneef (Sabanyeff, &c.**), Leonid** (b. Moscow 1881). Dr. of Mathematics of Univ. of Moscow and trained in Conserv. there as pianist, organist, and composer. Settled in Paris 1926. Active as writer on Russian music; composer of symphonic and choral works, &c.

Sabata, Victor de (b. Trieste 1892; d. nr. Genoa 1967). Conductor and composer. Trained Milan Conserv. Monte Carlo Opera; concerts and opera in Italy, &c.; début U.S.A. 1927. Often in London. La Scala 1931–54. Composer of operas, symphonic poems, &c.

Sabatini, Renzo (b. Cagliari, Italy, 1905). Player of viola and viola d'amore; on staff, Conserv. San Pietro di Maiello, Naples. Tours of Europe, including Britain. Publ. arrangements of old music for viola, &c.

Sacbut, or Sackbut, or Sagbut. Old name for Trombone (see *Trombone Family*).

Saccadé (Fr. 'Jerked'). 'Sharply accented.'

Sacchini, Antonio Maria Gasparo (b. nr. Florence 1730; d. Paris 1786). One of most prolific, able, and famous opera composers of his period; lived 10 years in London composing for its stage; then in Paris. Also composed oratorios, masses, chamber music, &c.

Sacher, Paul (b. Basle 1906). Conductor. Studied Basle Univ. and, later, Conserv. Founded Basle Chamber Orch. (1926) and Chamber Choir (1928), specializing pre-classical and contemporary music. Also (1933) founded, and remains Director of, *Schola Cantorum Basiliensis*, for study of old music. Conductor *Collegium Musicum Zürich* (1941) and guest conductor to leading European orchs. President Assoc. Swiss Musicians.

Sachs, (1) **Hans.** See *Minstrels* 4.

(2) **Curt** (b. Berlin 1881; d. New York 1959). D.Phil. of Univ. of Berlin 1904; then musicological research; on staff of his univ. and in charge of state collection of musical instruments. Then lived and worked in Paris, organizing gramophone record issue, *L'Anthologie sonore*, and later (1937) became a prof. of Univ. of New York. Author of many works on instruments (including important lexicon), history of dance, &c.

Sackbut or **Sacbut,** or **Sagbut.** Old name for Trombone (see *Trombone Family*).

Sackville-West, Hon. Edward (Charles) (b. London 1901; d. Clogheen, Co. Tipperary, 1965). Educ. Oxford. Mus. critic and author. On staff *New Statesman* 1926–45. Well known as record reviewer and broadcaster. 5th Baron Sackville 1962.

Sacred Harmonic Society. London's outstanding large-scale choral body, 1832–89. At Exeter Hall (q.v.) 1834–80; then ejected by Y.M.C.A. which had bought Hall and objected to 'oratorios for amusement'; migrated to St. James's Hall (q.v.) and lasted another 7 years.

Sacre du Printemps, Le (Stravinsky). See *Rite of Spring*.

Sacre rappresentazioni (It. 'Sacred Representations', i.e. 'Sacred Dramas'). A kind of miracle play (see *Miracle Plays*, &c.) popular in Italy up to the middle of the 16th c. Latterly they were entirely sung, not spoken, and had the relief of interludes with dances. They thus rank as precursors of the opera.

Sadko. 'Symphonic Picture' by Rimsky-Korsakof (op. 5, 1867); later developed into a 'Musical Legend', or Ballet-Opera. (Prod. Moscow 1898; New York 1930; London 1931.)

Sadler's Wells. A place of entertainment on the north side of London, dating from the 1680's. It takes its name from a Mr. Sadler, who rediscovered an ancient well of reputedly medicinal waters, and exploited it by setting up a garden for the drinking of those waters combined with musical enjoyments: later he developed this into a

'Musick House' and it enjoyed varied fortunes up to 1915, when, after a brief period as a cinema, it became derelict. It was reopened by Lilian Baylis (see *Victoria Hall*) in 1931, as a theatre and opera house, then purely the latter. It was rebuilt and became famous as a centre for the perf. of both works in the existing operatic and ballet repertory and new works. Its ballet company (directed by the Irish-born Dame Ninette de Valois) has become famous and has made highly successful foreign tours (from 1956 'Royal Ballet' and moved to Covent Garden). Mus. dirs. Joan Cross, Norman Tucker 1948; A. Gibson 1957; Colin Davis 1961; Charles Mackerras 1967. Opera co. housed in London Coliseum from 1968 ('English Opera Co.' from 1974).

Sad Waltz (Schubert). See *Mourning Waltz*.

Saeta. A sort of Spanish folk song sung without the guitar or other instrument (cf. *Carcelera*).

Safe Stronghold (Luther). See *Ein' feste Burg*.

Safonof, Vassily Ilich (b. Itsyursk, Northern Caucasus, 1852; d. Kislovodsk, in same region, 1918). Pianist and conductor. Pupil of Leschetizky and at Conserv. of St. Petersburg. Toured as pianist; head of Moscow Conserv. 1889–1905. Became known as conductor in various parts of Europe and in U.S.A.; New York Philharmonic Orch. 1904–9, also directing National Conserv., New York.

Saga, A (Sibelius). See *En Saga*.

Sagbut, Sacbut, or **Sackbut.** Old name for Trombone (see *Trombone Family*).

Sainete (Sp.), **Saynète** (Fr.). A sort of Spanish musical farce.   [*song* 3.

Saint Ambrose. See *Modes*; *Plain-*

Saint Anne Fugue (Bach). For Organ. In E flat. Eng. nickname due to chance that main subject is same as opening line of Croft's hymn tune *St. Anne*. (The Prelude and Fugue—first connected by Mendelssohn—are respectively the first and last items of Bach's *Clavierübung*, Book 3.)

Saint Elizabeth (*Die Legende von der heiligen Elisabeth*, 'The Legend of the Holy Elizabeth'). Oratorio by Liszt. (1st perf. Budapest 1865. London 1870. Often performed as opera.)

Saint-Foix, Marie Olivier Georges du Parc Poullain, Comte de (b. Paris 1874; d. Aix en Provence 1954). Authority on 18th-c. music, especially Mozart (collaborator with Wyzewa, q.v., in standard book on Mozart, last 3 vols. being by him alone; 1912–46).

Saint Francis. Ballet by Hindemith composed for the 'Ballet Russe de Monte Carlo'. (Prod. London 1938 under title *Nobilissima visione*—this title being now attached to a Suite made from the Ballet.)

Saint Francis of Assisi. See *Gagnebin*.

Saint-George, (1) George (b. Dresden 1841; d. London 1924). Violinist who settled in London; studied old viol music and made viols and lutes. Composed favourite string suite, *L'Ancien Régime*, &c. (2) **Henry** (b. London 1866; d. there 1917). Violinist. Son of above and on staff T.C.M. Wrote book on the Bow (1896).

Saint Gregory (Pope). See *Modes*; *Plainsong* 3.

St. James's Hall. London's leading concert hall from 1858 to 1905. In Regent Street. Place of popular chamber concerts known as 'Monday Pops' (1859–98) and 'Saturday Pops' (1865–98). Also Ella's Musical Union (1845–80; see *Annotated Programmes*), Philharmonic Soc. (see *Royal Philharmonic Soc.*), Richter Concerts (see *Richter, Hans*), &c. The Queen's Hall eventually took its place.

Saint John Passion of Bach. (1st perf. Leipzig 1723 or 1724; 1st Brit. perf. London, under Barnby, 1872.)

St. John's Night on the Bare Mountain. See *Night on the Bare Mountain*.

Saint Ludmila. Oratorio by Dvořák. (1st perf. Leeds Fest. 1886.)

Saint Matthew Passion of Bach. Text compiled by Picander. (1st perf. Leipzig 1729; revived by Mendelssohn, Berlin 1829; London, nearly complete, under Sterndale Bennett 1854; complete under Barnby 1870.) See also under *Passion Music*.

St. Michael's College, Tenbury. See *Ouseley.*

Saint Patrick's Day. This air, which was played by the Irish bagpipes at the battle of Fontenoy (1745), was a popular Irish patriotic song earlier than that. Its 1st appearance in print seems to be in Rutherford's *Country Dances* (an Eng. publication) in 1749. The same air is traditionally known in the north of England as *Barbary Bell*, and in the south of England as a morris dance tune, *Bacon and Greens*. Moore (q.v.) wrote to the tune his song 'Though dark are our sorrows' (1811). Many different lyrics, Irish and English, had been previously sung to it.

Saint Paul (*Paulus*). See *Mendelssohn.*

Saint Paul's Suite. For String Orch., by Holst. Written 1913 for the girls of St. Paul's School, Hammersmith, London, where the composer was musical director.

Saint-Saëns, (Charles) Camille (b. Paris 1835; d. Algiers 1921). Studied at Paris Conserv. and privately under Gounod; then took up organist's career (at Madeleine 1858–77); from age 16 to death incessantly composing—symphonic poems (see *Rouet d'Omphale*; *Danse macabre*; *Jeunesse d'Hercule*; *Phaëton*); operas (see *Samson et Dalila*; *Henry the Eighth*); and works in almost every possible medium and form. Considerable author of books on music. Often in London as pianist, organist, or conductor; Hon. D.Mus., Cambridge, 1893.

See also *Carnival of Animals*; *Promised Land.*

Saints in Glory Fugue. Samuel Wesley's nickname for Fugue 9 (in E major) of the 2nd book of Bach's 'Forty-eight'.

Saite (Ger., plur. *Saiten*). 'String.' So *Saiteninstrumente*, 'stringed instruments'.

Salammbô. See *Reyer.*

Salazar, (1) **Juan Garcia** (d. 1710). Spanish priest and important composer for the church.

(2) **Adolfo** (b. Madrid 1890; d. Mexico City 1958). Pupil of Falla and others. Composer of orch. works, chamber and piano music, &c.; critic and author. Living in Mexico from 1939.

Salicet. Same as Salicional (q.v.) but of 4-foot length and pitch.

Salicional. Soft-toned organ stop, in Britain of slightly reedy quality and in U.S.A. of string quality; 8-foot length and pitch (sometimes 16 or 4).

Salieri, Antonio (b. Legnago, Italy, 1750; d. Vienna 1825). Highly popular conductor and composer of operas, &c.; resident in Vienna 1766 onwards, composing operas, &c., and teaching—amongst his pupils being Beethoven, Schubert, and Liszt; friend of Haydn, Gluck, and others.

Salinas, Francisco de (b. Burgos 1513; d. Salamanca 1590). Blind from birth yet a good organist and famous theorist. (*De Musica libri septem*, 1577.)

Sally in our Alley. Poem and original tune by Henry Carey (q.v.). Present tune the traditional old Eng. one of *What though I am a country lass.*

Salmo (It.). 'Psalm.'

Salmond, Felix (b. London 1888; d. New York 1952). Violoncellist. Trained R.C.M., &c. In Britain especially prominent in chamber music. Début New York 1922. Settled in U.S.A.; on staff of Curtis Inst. and Juilliard School.

Salome. (1) One-act Music-drama by RICHARD STRAUSS. Libretto based on Oscar Wilde. Produced Dresden 1905; New York 1907; London 1910. (2) Opera by MARIOTTE, composed somewhat before above; also based on Wilde. Prod. Lyons 1908; Paris 1910. (3) Symphonic poem by HENRY HADLEY. 1st perf. Boston 1905. (4) 'Drama without words' by FLORENT SCHMITT, *La Tragédie de Salomé*. Prod. Paris 1907; in final form 1910.

Salomé, Théodor César (b. Paris 1834; d. Saint-Germain-en-Laye 1896). Studied at Paris Conserv.; became successful organist and composer of organ music; also composed some orch. works.

Salomon, (1) **Johann Peter** (b. Bonn 1745; d. London 1815). Violinist and concert organizer, &c.; settled in London 1781; brought Haydn to England (1791 and 1794); hence Haydn's 'Salomon Symphonies' **and** *Creation* composed for perf. in England. Much respected by Beethoven. Buried in cloister of Westminster Abbey.

(2) **Karel** (b. Heidelberg 1897). Baritone vocalist and conductor. Studied Univs. Heidelberg and Berlin. Vocalist and conductor in Germany before 1933; then Palestine. Music Director Palestine Radio 1936–48; now in charge of 'Kol Israel' ('Voice of Israel') Broadcasting station, Tel-Aviv. Varied compositions include a marionette opera, piano concerto, oratorio, &c.

Salomon Symphonies (Haydn). See *London Symphonies*.

Salón México, El (Copland). See under *El*.

Saltando; saltato (It.). 'Leaping'; 'leapt'—generally in connexion with bowed instrument playing, meaning with a springing bow; i.e. same as *Spiccato*, q.v. (Cf. *Sautillé*.)

AN ITALIAN SALTARELLO

Saltarello. (1) The name of the after-dance (see *Nachtanz*) to the passamezzo (q.v.), usually based on the same theme, but turned from simple duple time to simple triple. (2) A Roman dance in simple triple or compound duple time, and resembling the tarantella. It is sometimes considered to be a variety of the galliard (see *Pavan and Galliard*).

Saltbox. A traditional handy instrument used when joyous music was to be extemporized, domestically or publicly. The lid was flapped up and down and the side battered with a rolling-pin. (For instruments of similar humble standing see *Marrow Bone and Cleaver*; *Bellows and Tongs*; *Tongs and Bones*; *Bladder and String*.)

Salvation Army. See *Hymns and Hymn Tunes* 7.

Salve Regina. See *Antiphons of the Blessed Virgin Mary*.

Salzédo, Carlos (b. Arcachon, S. France, 1885; d. Waterville, Me., 1961). Harpist, winning many distinctions at Paris Conserv., touring Europe, settling in New York (naturalized 1923), where he founded a soc. of harpists, publ. books on the harp, and also took a central position as propagandist of extreme modernist school of composition. Has written many orch. and chamber works employing his instrument.

Samaroff, Olga—known also as Samaroff-Stokowski; *née* Hickenlooper (b. San Antonio, Texas, 1882; d. New York 1948). Pianist. Trained Paris Conserv. Highly popular player until arm injury 1926. On staff Juilliard Sch. and Philadelphia Conserv. Author of musical-educational books, &c. From 1911 to 1923 wife of Leopold Stokowski (q.v.).

Samazeuilh, Gustave (b. Bordeaux 1877). Pupil of Chausson and d'Indy; music critic and composer of symphonic poems, chamber and piano music, songs, &c.

Saminsky, Lazare (b. Odessa 1882; d. New York 1959). Studied mathematics and philosophy at Univ. of St. Petersburg and composition at its Conserv. under Rimsky-Korsakof, &c.; emigrated to U.S.A. 1920; well known as conductor and composer (symphonies, &c.); authority on Jewish music and propagandist for contemporary composers.

Samisen. (1) A 3-stringed Japanese instrument of the banjo type played with a plectrum. (2) An instrument, wrongly called by this name, used in Puccini's *Madame Butterfly* and Mascagni's *Iris*; it consists of hollow bronze vessels of various sizes, struck with a drumstick.

Sammarco, Mario—in full Giuseppe Mario (b. Palermo 1873; d. Milan 1930). Operatic baritone. Highly popular in New York and London. Sang in many languages, including Russian.

Sammartini (or **San Martini**), (1) **Giuseppe** (b. Milan abt. 1693; d. abt. 1750). Finest hautboy player ever heard up to his period; active and reputable composer in London from 1727. For brother see below. (2) **Giovanni Battista** (b. Milan 1698; there d. 1775). Brother of Giuseppe, above. Organist of Milan Cathedral; teacher of Gluck. Composed 2,000 works; his 24 symphonies prefigure Haydn's.

Sammlung (Ger.). 'Collection.'

Sammons, Albert (Edward) (b. London 1886; d. nr. Bognor 1957). Violinist. Largely self-taught; discovered by Beecham playing in London restaurant orch. and engaged as leader of his orch.; quickly made name also as chamber music player and soloist (esp. in Elgar Concerto). Compositions; book on technique. C.B.E. 1944.

Samson. Oratorio by Handel. Text compiled from Milton's works. (1st perf. London 1743.)

Samson et Dalila. Biblical opera by Saint-Saëns. (Produced at Weimar in 1877; in Britain and U.S.A. at first as oratorio; as opera New York 1895; London 1909.)

Sämtlich (Ger.). 'Complete', 'collected'. So used of the works of a composer, the body of stops of an organ (*Sämtliche Stimmen*), &c.

Samuel Pepys. See *Coates, Albert.*

Samuel, Harold (b. London 1879; there d. 1937). Pianist. Played as a child in public houses, &c.; trained at R.C.M. of which later joined staff. Of highest fame as perfect interpreter of Bach, playing all his clavier music from memory in series of daily recitals in London and New York lasting a week or more.

San Carlo, Teatro di (Naples). Ital. opera house, second to La Scala, Milan. Built 1737; rebuilt 1816 (seats 3,500).

Sancta Civitas. Oratorio by Vaughan Williams. Setting of passages from *Book of Revelation*. (1st perf. Oxford and London 1926.)

Sanctus. 'Holy.' (See *Mass*; *Requiem*; *Common Prayer*; *Ter Sanctus*.)

Sands of Dee, The. See *Clay.*

Sanft (Ger.). 'Soft', 'gentle', 'gently'. So, too, *Sanftmütig.*

Sang Schoolis, Sang Scuils. See *Schola Cantorum.*

Sankey, Ira D. See *Hymns and Hymn Tunes* 7.

Sans (Fr.). 'Without.' So *sans les sourdines*, 'without the mutes'.

Santley, Charles (b. Liverpool 1834; d. London 1922). Baritone vocalist. Trained in Italy and there appeared in opera; then studied in London with Garcia (q.v.). Quickly made name both in opera and oratorio and great favourite at festivals. Knighted 1907 on completing half-century before the public. Last appearance 1915. Some compositions and books.

Santoliquido, Francesco (b. nr. Naples 1883). Trained at the Saint Cecilia Conserv. in Rome. When approaching 30 settled in Tunisia, returning to Rome for a part of each year; has made a study of Arab music, which has influenced the idiom of some of his compositions. Works include operas, orch. music, chamber music, piano music, &c., as also books on musical subjects.

Sanz, Gaspar (17th c.). Spanish guitar player and composer and author of important work on guitar playing (1694).

Sanzogno, Nino (b. Venice 1911). Pupil of Malipiero and Scherchen; as conductor appeared La Fenice and Scala; compositions include concertos for viola and cello; other orch. works.

Sapelnikof, Vassily (b. Odessa 1868; d. San Remo 1941). Pianist. Trained St. Petersburg Conserv. International virtuoso. Friend and interpreter of Tchaikovsky. Composed piano music, &c.

Sapho. Opera by Gounod. Libretto by Augier. (Prod. Paris and London 1851.)
Also operas of this name by Massenet (1897) and others.

Sappho Songs. By Bantock. Nine contralto songs with orch. accompaniment and prelude.

Sarabande or **Saraband.** An ancient dance type, probably Spanish in origin (possibly oriental but developed in Spain): it was once popular almost throughout Europe. It is dignified and steady in speed and rhythm, usually beginning on the first beat of the bar. It is usually in triple time. A sarabande movement generally forms an item in the classical suite.

Sarasate, Pablo de—in full **Pablo Martin Meliton Sarasate y Navascuez** (b. Pamplona 1844; d. Biarritz 1908). Trained as violinist at Paris Conserv. under Alard (q.v.) and quickly became world known. Composed attractively for his instrument.

Sardana. The national dance of Catalonia, performed to the accompaniment of the Spanish equivalent of the pipe and tabor (see *Recorder Family* 2). It is in sections, partly in compound duple and partly in simple duple time. There is motion with linked hands, as in the farandole (q.v.).

Sargent, Malcolm—in full Harold Malcolm Watts Sargent (b. Stamford 1895; d. London 1967). Conductor. Took A.R.C.O. (with Sawyer Prize) at 16 and became church organist; as pianist pupil of Moiseiwitch; came forward in his late 20's as orch. conductor (later opera, ballet, and choral conductor); many foreign and Empire tours. Director Courtauld-Sargent Concerts, London (1929–40): also Robert Mayer Children's Concerts, &c. Conductor, Royal Choral Soc. (Albert Hall), Hallé Orch. 1939; Liverpool Phil. 1942; B.B.C. Symphony Orch. 1950–7, thereafter continuing as chief conductor of the Promenade Concerts. On staff R.C.M. Some compositions. Many degrees. Knighted 1947.

Šàrka (Smetana). See *My Fatherland*.

Sarrusophone. See *Oboe Family*.

Sarti, Giuseppe (b. Faenza 1729; d. Berlin 1802). Organist of Cathedral of Faenza 1748; director of It. opera, &c., at Copenhagen 1753–75; then in Venice, Milan, and St. Petersburg 1784–1801. Composed over 50 operas, some church works, &c.; has importance as an acoustician.

Sartoris, Mrs. See *Kemble, Adelaide*.

Sarum Use. See *Use of Sarum*.

Sassofono (It.). 'Saxophone' (see *Saxophone Family*).

S.A.T.B. 'Soprano, Alto, Tenor, Bass' (see *Quartet*).

Satie, Erik—really Alfred Eric Leslie Satie (b. Honfleur 1866; d. Paris 1925). His father was French and his mother Scottish, both being composers. Studied for a year at Paris Conserv.; played in cabarets, &c. When nearly 40 entered Schola Cantorum (see *d'Indy*) and went through a 3 years' course of study. Adopted a defiantly modernistic technique and attached whimsical titles to his compositions. Debussy and Ravel encouraged him and a group of the young Fr. composers of the 2nd decade of the 20th c. adopted him as their standard-bearer.

'Saturday Pops.' See *St. James's Hall*.

Satyricon. Overture by John Ireland, based on the picaresque Lat. novel of Petronius (1st perf. 1946).

Satz (Ger.). 'Movement.' Also, confusingly, (1) Theme, subject. (2) Phrase. (3) Composition, piece. (4) Texture. (5) Style.
  Hauptsatz = 1st Subject. *Nebensatz*, or *Seitensatz* = 2nd Subject. *Schlusssatz* = either 'Finale' or 'Coda'.

Saudades (Portuguese). A term said to be expressive of the haunting sense of sadness and regret for days gone by. It has been used (e.g. by Milhaud) as a title for pieces of instrumental or vocal music.

Sauer, Emil von (b. Hamburg 1862; d. Vienna 1942). Pianist; pupil of Nicholas Rubinstein and Liszt; attained world fame. Composed music for piano and edited some of its classics—especially complete Brahms.

Sauguet, Henri (b. Bordeaux 1901). Composer. Pupil of Koechlin and Satie; works include over 20 ballets as well as orch. and chamber music, &c.

Saul. Oratorio by Handel. (1st perf. London 1739.)

Saul, King. Oratorio by C. H. H. Parry. (1st perf. Birmingham Fest. 1894.)

Saunders, Charles (b. Stratton, Cornwall, 1868; d. London 1917). Tenor. Trained G.S.M. Well-known oratorio singer.

Sauret, Émile (b. Dun-le-Roi, France, 1852; d. London 1920). Violinist. Pupil of de Bériot (q.v.) and Vieuxtemps (q.v.). London début age 10. In U.S.A. 1872 and often later. Various teaching positions Berlin, Chicago, London (R.A.M., &c.). Composed violin concertos, and a violin *Gradus ad Parnassum* (1894), &c. (Cf. *Carreño*.)

Sautillé. Sometimes used as synonymous with *spiccato* (q.v.); sometimes, more specifically, of a lighter form of *spiccato* used for very rapid passages (the term *sautillé modéré* being used for the heavier *spiccato*).

Savile, Jeremy (mid-17th c.). Known as composer of a few songs and part-songs, e.g. *Here's a health unto His Majesty.*

Savitri. 1-act chamber-opera by Holst. Libretto, on an Indian subject, by composer. (Prod. London 1916; Cincinnati 1939.)

Savonarola. Opera by Stanford. (Prod., in Ger., Hamburg, and London 1884.)

Savoy Operas. The operas of Gilbert and Sullivan (see *Sullivan*)—produced or revived at the Savoy Theatre, London, opened in 1881. The band of artists associated with these performances dubbed themselves (or were dubbed) 'Savoyards'.

Saw, Singing. See *Singing Saw.*

Sax, Adolphe—in full Antoine Joseph Adolphe (b. Dinant 1814; d. Paris 1894). See *Saxhorn* and *Saxophone*.

Saxhorn and Flügelhorn Families. Both are families of brass instruments with cup-shaped mouthpieces (like trumpets, trombones, and genuine tubas). Both are on the bugle model, with a conical bore (like the Fr. horn: but the bore of the Saxhorns is wider, and that of the Flügelhorns wider still).

The bell of the larger Saxhorns is held upwards and that of the Flügelhorns forward. The upper members of both families are almost exclusively wind-band instruments.

The nomenclature of the 2 families is in complete confusion. The following attempts to remove this, but as the names used in different countries vary greatly, and as no 2 books on instru-

mentation (even within the same country) agree, a complete and indisputably accurate clearing up of the muddle is impossible.

(1) The SAXHORNS (introduced by the Belgian Adolph Sax in 1845) are a set of 7 instruments, ranging from deep bass to high treble. The 3 lower ones are 'whole-tube' instruments and the 4 higher 'half-tube' instruments (see *Whole-tube and Half-tube*): the highest instrument of one group and the lowest of the other are identical in pitch, the difference lying in the rather fuller tone of the highest instrument of the lower group. The instruments of the lower pitched group are usually considered to be tubas and play tuba parts in the orch.: they are treated under *Tuba Group*. The higher-pitched ones are as follows: (*a*) SOPRANINO SAXHORN IN E FLAT (OR F), also called *Soprano Saxhorn*, or (mistakenly) *Soprano Flügelhorn* or *Flügelhorn piccolo*. This is little different from the E flat cornet (see *Cornet*). (*b*) SOPRANO SAXHORN IN B FLAT (OR C), also called *Alto Saxhorn*, or (mistakenly) *Alto Flügelhorn*. This is little different from the B flat cornet (see *Cornet*). (*c*) ALTO SAXHORN IN E FLAT (OR F). Also called simply *Saxhorn*, or *Tenor*, or *Tenor Saxhorn*, or *Tenor Horn*, or *Alto*, or *Althorn in E flat* (or F). There is a variety made in the form of a Fr. horn and called the *Tenor Cor.* (*d*) TENOR IN B FLAT (OR C), also called *Baritone*, or *Baritone Saxhorn*, or *Althorn in B flat.*

The various Saxhorns in E flat and B flat above mentioned are those in use in wind bands; those in F and C are occasionally used in orchs.

The Saxhorns are regarded as 'transposing instruments' (q.v.): the treble clef is used for all the higher 4 and sometimes also for the lower 3.

See a reference to Saxhorn terminology under *Pedal.*

(2) The FLÜGELHORNS are as follows: (*a*) SOPRANO FLÜGELHORN IN E FLAT (rare). (*b*) FLÜGELHORN IN B FLAT; also called *Alto Flügelhorn*, or simply *Alto*: it is used in wind bands amongst the cornets, than which its tone is somewhat mellower. (*c*) FLÜGELHORN IN E FLAT, or *Tenor Flügelhorn*, or *Altflügelhorn in E flat*, or *Alto Flügelhorn*

in E flat, or *Althorn in E flat* (sometimes it is in F and is used to play the upper tuba parts in Wagner).

(3) The FLICORNI. There is an It. series of instruments (alternately in E flat and B flat) of which those of higher pitch correspond to the Saxhorn family and those of lower pitch to the Flügelhorn family (cf. *Tuba Group* 4).

See also *Ballad Horn*.

Saxofonia, saxofono (It.). **Saxofon** (Ger.). 'Saxophone' (see *Saxophone Family*).

TENOR SAXOPHONE

Saxophone Family. This family had for father the Belgian instrument maker, Adolph Sax, and came into notice in the early 1840's. It was welcomed into Fr. military bands and gradually spread its activities until with the rise of Jazz (see *Ragtime*; *Jazz*) it became ubiquitous. Its constructional principles are hybrid, combining the conical tube of the oboe family and the single reed of the clarinet family; brass is its material. It numbers 12 members, little and big, but only 2 or 3 are in general use—written for as transposing instruments (q.v.) and

being usually in the regular wind-band keys of B flat and E flat (cf. *Brass Band*). The family has occasionally received recognition from serious orch. composers.

Saynète (Fr.), **Sainete** (Sp.). A sort of Spanish musical farce.

Sbalzo, sbalzato (It.). 'Jerk' or 'dash'; 'dashed' (generally with the sense of impetuosity).

Scacciapensieri (It., lit. 'chase-thoughts'). 'Jew's harp' (q.v.).

Scala, Teatro alla ('La Scala, Milan'). Chief Italian opera house. Built 1778; seats 3,600.

Scala di Seta, La ('The Silken Ladder'). 1-act opera by Rossini. (Prod. Venice 1812. Overture still popular.)

Scalchi, Sofia (b. Turin 1850; d. Rome 1922). Operatic contralto (also sang soprano roles). Début Mantua 1866; London 1868; Metropolitan Opera 1883. Of world reputation.

Scale. A scale is a stepwise arrangement (for a theoretical purpose, or for vocal or instrumental practice) of all the chief notes in a particular passage of music or in the musical system of some period or people. The number of scales in use throughout the world is incalculable and the varieties of effect represented enormous.

For the older European scales, as used in the Church's plainsong and in folk song, see under *Modes*. As is there stated, 2 of these ancient Modes remained in use by composers, when the other 10 were almost abandoned, and these are our Major and Minor Scales— the latter, however, subject to some variations in its 6th and 7th notes. Taking C as the keynote these scales (which have provided the chief material of music from about A.D. 1600 to 1900) run as follows:

Major Scale (Semitones 3–4 and 7–8—the two halves thus being alike).

Minor Scale—'Harmonic' Form (Semitones 2– 3, 5–6, 7–8; there is the interval of the Augmented Second, 6–7).

Minor Scale—'Melodic' Form (Semitones 2–3, 7–8 ascending; 6–5, 3–2 descending; this avoids the interval of the augmented second, whilst allowing the Leading Note to retain its function of 'leading' to the Tonic).

The Major and Minor scales are spoken of as DIATONIC SCALES, as distinct from a scale using nothing but semitones, which is the CHROMATIC SCALE, for which 2 different notations are employed:

Chromatic Scale (in 'melodic' notation—sharps upwards, flats downwards; this notation economizes accidentals).

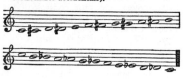

Chromatic Scale (in 'harmonic' notation).

This scale when begun on other notes is 'harmonically' notated according to the same principles; for instance, beginning on D it reads:

The scheme is as follows: the notes of the major scale, plus those of the harmonic minor scale, plus the minor second and augmented fourth.

A scale comprising the same notes as the Chromatic Scale is the DODECA-PHONIC SCALE, used by some contemporary composers (see *Note-row*), in which, however, the 12 notes are considered to be all of equal status and are so treated, whereas the Chromatic Scale beginning on any particular note is considered to comprise the Diatonic Scale of that note 'coloured' (this is the literal meaning of 'Chromatic') by the addition of the extra semitones.

Scales with smaller intervals than the semitone have been introduced—MICROTONAL SCALES (see *Microtones*).

A scale occasionally used by several composers (Glinka, Dargomijsky, Liszt, &c.), and much exploited by Debussy, is the WHOLE-TONE SCALE, which is free of semitones and thus allows of only 2 different series, each with 6 notes:

The Whole-tone Scale.

An extremely widespread scale is this 5-note or PENTATONIC SCALE (common in Scottish, Chinese, and other music):

The Pentatonic Scale (commonest order of the intervals).

The Scottish Highland Bagpipe is tuned to a scale that cannot be represented in our orthodox notation. It is roughly that of the white notes of the piano with the C and F about a quarter of a tone sharp.

Cf. *Key*.

Scalero, Rosario (b. nr. Turin 1870; d. nr. there 1954). Violinist. Pupil of Wilhelmj, &c. In U.S.A. from 1919; composition teacher at Curtis Institute. Composer of violin concerto, &c.

Scampanata. See *Charivari*.

Scapino. Comedy overture by Walton (1942), 'after an etching by Callot (1622)'. (Scapino was the comic valet in the old It. 'commedia dell' arte' and is also the hero of Molière's *Les Fourberies de Scapin*.)

Scarbo (Ravel). See *Gaspard de la Nuit*.

Scarlatti, (1) **Alessandro** (b. Sicily 1660; d. Naples 1725). Prolific and gifted opera composer and founder of Neapolitan school of opera; as to posts and residence oscillated between Naples and Rome; composed 115 operas, 500 chamber cantatas, 200 masses, 14 oratorios, &c. For his son see below. (2) **(Giuseppe) Domenico** (b. Naples 1685; d. Madrid 1757). Son of Alessandro, above. Held important court positions, and was for a time in charge of the music at St. Peter's; Rome (1714–19); in royal chapel Lisbon (1720–9), and then in court appointment at Madrid (1729 to death). Composed operas, but especially over 500 sonatas, &c., for harpsichord, on which instrument he was a most skilful and artistic performer. The standard edn. of the harpsichord works is that of Longo (q.v.); individual sonatas, &c., are identified in programmes as 'L 27' &c. The technique of keyboard composition and perf. owes much to him.

See also *Cat's Fugue*; *Good-humoured Ladies*; *Isola disabitata*.

Scat Song. A type of popular song with improvised nonsense words which, as an item in the 20th-c. outbreak of Americanized popular music, came into vogue in the early 1930's. It has been learnedly described as 'an unhampered musical figuration just barely held to the melodic line—the atonal exuberance of a racial melancholy' (for 'Atonality' see *Harmony* 3).

Scemando (It.). 'Diminishing', i.e. in volume of tone. Same as *diminuendo*.

Scena. An elaborate solo vocal composition in several sections, like the cantata in the old sense of the word (see *Cantata*).

Scenario. The skeleton libretto that precedes the writing of the full text of a play or libretto of an opera.

Scenes from Goethe's Faust (Schumann). See *Faust*.

Scenes from the Bavarian Highlands. Choral-orch. Suite by Elgar; text an adaptation by composer's wife of Bavarian folk songs. (1st perf. Worcester Choral Soc. 1896.)

Scènes historiques. Two suites each of 3 Orch. Pieces (with this Fr. title) by Sibelius (op. 25, 1899 and op. 66, 1912).

Scenes of Childhood (Schumann). See *Kinderscenen*.

Schafe können sicher weiden ('Sheep may safely graze'). By Bach. Recitative and air, with obbligato for 2 flutes (end-blown, i.e. Recorders), from the secular cantata *Was mir behagt* ('What I enjoy'). This came into enormous popularity in Britain about 1939, and has since been arranged for many instruments and combinations.

Schale; Schalen (Ger.). 'Cymbal'; 'cymbals' (see *Percussion Family* 2 o).

Schalk, Franz (b. Vienna 1863; d. Edlach, Lower Austria, 1931). Operatic and orch. conductor. Pupil of Bruckner. Various Ger. and Austrian opera houses with New York début, Metropolitan Opera 1898; Covent Garden same year. Main career in Vienna (State Opera, &c.).

Schalkhaft (Ger.). 'Roguish.'

Schallbecken (Ger.). 'Cymbals' (see *Percussion Family* 2 o).

Schalmey. See *Oboe Family*.

Scharf (Ger.). 'Sharply'—in various connexions, as *scharf betont*, 'given out with emphatic accent'. **Schärfe.** 'Sharpness', 'definiteness', 'precision'.

Scharrer, Irene (b. London 1888; d. there 1971). Pianist. Studied with Matthay at R.A.M.; high international reputation as accomplished and refined player.

Scharwenka, (1) **(Ludwig) Philipp** (b. nr. Posen 1847; d. Bad Nauheim 1917). Studied and taught in Berlin; latterly in charge of private conservatory founded by his brother (below). Composed symphonies, &c., chamber music; and much agreeable piano music. (2) **(Franz) Xaver** (b. nr. Posen 1850; d. Berlin 1924). Brother of Philipp, above. Had great success as piano virtuoso; popular as such and as piano composer in England; opened a conserv. in Berlin (1880) with later a branch in New York (1891). Composed an opera, piano concerto, small piano pieces, &c.; compiled books of graduated studies, &c., for pianists.

Schaurig, Schauerig, Schauerlich (Ger.). 'Ghastly', 'gruesome'.

Schauspieldirektor, Der ('The Impresario'). 1-act 'Comedy with Music' by Mozart. (Prod. Schönbrunn, Vienna, 1786; London 1857; New York 1870. Many performances have been with new libretti.)

Scheherazade. See *Sheherazade.*

Scheibler, Johann Heinrich (b. in the Aachen district 1777; d. Crefeld 1838). Silk manufacturer and acoustician especially useful by his acute experiments in the measurement of pitch and in the solution of problems of tuning.

Scheidemann, Heinrich (b. Hamburg abt. 1596; there d. 1663). Famous organist, pupil of Sweelinck at Amsterdam and predecessor of Reinken at St. Catherine's Church, Hamburg. Composed organ and harpsichord music and religious songs.

Scheidt, Samuel (b. Halle 1587; there d. 1654). Pupil of Sweelinck; very famous organist and important organ composer: his book of organ music *Tabulatura nova* (3 vols. 1624) and other books laid down a new standard in organ technique and artistry; in his own day his vocal works were highly valued.

Schein, Johann Hermann (b. Grünhain, Saxony, 1586; d. Leipzig 1630). Cantor of St. Thomas's School, Leipzig, a century before Bach (1616 to death). Prolific and valuable composer of church music, madrigals, and instrumental works, and compiler of important book of 200 chorales (*Cantional* 1627).

Schelle; Schellen (Ger.). 'Bell'; 'bells'.

Schellenbaum (Ger., lit. 'bell-tree'). The Turkish Crescent (q.v.).

Schellengeläute (Ger. 'bell-ringing'). 'Sleigh-bells.'

Schellentrommel (Ger., lit. 'bell-drum'). 'Tambourine' (see *Percussion Family* 2 m).

Schelling, Ernest (b. Belvedere, N.J., 1876; d. New York 1939). Virtuoso pianist, pupil of Paderewski, &c. Composer of orch. works, piano music, &c.; did valuable work in organizing orch. concerts for young people in various cities of U.S.A.

Schelmisch (Ger.). 'Roguish.'

Schelomo ('Solomon'). By Bloch. Rhapsody for 'Cello solo and Orch. (1st perf. New York 1916; London 1930).

Schemelli Hymn Book. Collection of 954 hymns and 69 tunes (*Musikalisches Gesangbuch*) issued in 1736, by a Ger. Cantor, G. C. Schemelli, who employed Bach as his musical ed.: some of the tunes are of Bach's composition.

Schenker, Heinrich (b. Galicia 1868; d. Vienna 1935). Pupil of Bruckner; composer; ed. of piano classics; voluminous author of theoretical works of Teutonic profundity and reasoned psychological basis.

Scherchen, Hermann (b. Berlin 1891; d. Florence 1966). Orch. conductor (at first viola player). Active in many countries, especially Germany (to 1932) and Switzerland; resident in Winterthur. Prominent in efforts to bring forward contemporary works. Author of *Handbook of Conducting* (Eng. edn. 1933; also It. and Spanish edns.). Some compositions. Hon. Dr. Univ. of Königsberg (1930).

Scherz (Ger.). 'Fun', 'joke'. So *Scherzend, Scherzhaft,* 'Jocular'. **Scherzando, scherzante, scherzevole, scherzevolmente** (It.). 'Jokingly', 'playfully'; so the superlative *scherzantissimo.* **Scherzare** (It.). 'To joke.'

Scherzetto, scherzino (It.). A short scherzo (q.v.).

Scherzi, Gli (Haydn). See *Russischen Quartette.*

Scherzo (It., plur. *scherzi*) means 'joke', and with this suggestion as to the style of the music to which it is applied the word has been in occasional use since Monteverdi publ. some choral Scherzi in 1628. Nowadays the application is solely to instrumental music, sometimes to independent 1-movement compositions but more commonly to that movement in the Sonata, Symphony, String Quartet, &c., where previously a Minuet and Trio had appeared (cf. *Minuet*). Beethoven is looked upon as the father of the modern Scherzo. Mendelssohn has left us a delightfully feathery type;

Chopin's 4 Scherzi are no jokes, but are works not only of high vigour but of great emotional intensity.

Scherzoso; scherzosamente (It.). 'Playful'; 'playfully'.

Schicksalslied (Brahms). See *Song of Destiny*.

Schietto (It.). 'Sincere', 'unadorned'. So the adverb *schiettamente* and the noun *schietezza*.

Schikaneder, Emanuel Johann—really Johannes Joseph (b. Straubing 1751; d. Vienna 1812). A Vienna theatre director and opera librettist; author of the text of Mozart's *The Magic Flute*.

Schillinger, Joseph (b. Kharkof 1895; d. New York 1943). Active in many official educational positions in Russia and collector of Georgian folk song; settled in New York 1929. Author of speculative treatises on *Electricity, a Liberator of Music*, &c., and composer of *First Airphonic Suite*, for the Thérémin (see *Electric Musical Instruments* 1), &c. Promulgator of the mechanistic or mathematical *Joseph Schillinger System of Musical Composition* (2 vols. posthumous).

Schillings, Max von (b. Düren 1868; d. Berlin 1933). Noted opera conductor (asst. conductor Bayreuth 1892 onwards; director of Berlin State Opera 1919–25). Composed operas, orch. and chamber music, &c.

Schindler, Kurt (b. Berlin 1882; d. New York 1935). Orch. and choral conductor, composer, and man of wide musical learning (especially interested in Russian and Spanish music—folk music and other). Settled New York; active as choral conductor, editor of collections of vocal music, &c. Founded Schola Cantorum.

Schiøler, Victor (b. Copenhagen 1899). Pianist and conductor. Pupil of Friedman and Schnabel. Leading Danish pianist; international tours. President Union of Danish Soloists and member Danish Musical Council. Director Royal Opera, Copenhagen, 1929–32.

Schiøtz, Aksel (b. Roskilde, Denmark, 1906). Tenor vocalist. Musical education in Copenhagen and Stockholm. Début at Royal Opera House, Copenhagen, 1939. Glyndebourne Opera 1946 in Britten's *Rape of Lucretia*. Toured U.S.A. 1948. Numerous recordings of Lieder and opera. Knighted by King Christian X of Denmark for behaviour during Nazi occupation of his country.

Schipa, Tito (b. Lecce 1889; d. Wickersham, N.Y., 1965). Lyric operatic tenor. Début Vercelli 1911; thenceforward popular all over Italy, in Spain, Britain, U.S.A., South America, &c. Various compositions and a comprehensive treatise on singing. Resident Hollywood to 1941; then Rome; later New York.

Schippers, Thomas (b. Kalamazoo, Mich., 1930). Conductor. Trained Curtis Institute. Début New York 1948; Cincinnati Orch. from 1970.

Schirmer, G., Inc. New York music publishers. Estd. 1861. Cf. *Musical Quarterly*.

Schlacht (Ger.). 'Battle.'

Schlag (Ger.). 'Stroke', 'blow'.

Schlägel (Ger.). 'Drumstick.'

Schlagen (Ger.). 'To strike.'

Schlaginstrumente (Ger.). Percussion instruments (see *Percussion Family*).

Schlagobers ('Whipped Cream'). Ballet by Richard Strauss. (Prod. Vienna 1924.)

Schlagzither (Ger.). 'Striking-zither'—one in which the strings are struck instead of plucked, i.e. a form of dulcimer (q.v.), 'zither' being a misnomer.

Schlangenrohr (Ger.). Serpent (see *Cornett and Key Bugle Families*).

Schleifer. (1) *Ländler* (q.v.). (2) Old ornament in instrumental music, the essential feature of which was the filling in of an interval between 2 melodic notes.

Schleppend (Ger.). 'Dragging' (generally used in the negative—*Nicht schleppend*).

Schlesinger, Kathleen (1862–1953). High authority on history of musical instruments—Ancient Greek, Roman, and Hebrew, Medieval and Modern. Gave series of 'peripatetic lectures' in Brit. Museum, &c., and publ. several standard works of original research.

Schlummerlied (Ger.). 'Slumber Song.'

Schluss (Ger.). 'Conclusion', 'end'.

Schluss-Satz. See under *Satz*.

Schlüssel (Ger.). Clef (see *Notation*).

Schlusszeichen (Ger., lit. 'close-sign'). The double-bar with pause indicating the end of a repeated portion which is to close a movement.

Schmachtend (Ger.). 'Languishing.'

Schmeichelnd (Ger.). 'Coaxingly.'

Schmelzend (Ger. 'melting'). 'Dying away.'

Schmerz (Ger.). 'Pain', 'sorrow'. So *schmerzlich, schmerzhaft, schmerzvoll*, 'painful', 'sorrowful'.

Schmetternd (Ger.).'Blared' in horn-playing—notes produced as 'stopped' (i.e. with the hand inserted in the bell), combined with hard blowing. The usual indication with Brit. composers is + together with an *ff*.

Schmidt, (1) **Bernhard.** See *Smith* 1.

(2) **Franz** (b. Pressburg, or Pozsony, now Bratislava, 1874; d. nr. Vienna 1939). Originally 'cellist; became director of Vienna Conserv. Composed operas, orch. and chamber music, organ music, &c.

Schmidt-Isserstedt, Hans (b. Berlin 1900; d. Hamburg 1973). Conductor. Studied with Schreker. Chief conductor Opera Hamburg, then Berlin. Founder and chief conductor, Nordwestdeutscher Rundfunk Orch.

Schmitt, (1) **Aloys** (b. Erlenbach-am-Main 1788; d. Frankfurt 1866). Fine pianist and composer especially for piano—including much instructive material.

(2) **Florent** (b. Blâmont, nr. Nancy, 1870; d. Neuilly 1958). Studied at Paris Conserv. under Massenet, Fauré, &c.; won Rome prize (1900). Varied compositions, of Impressionist stamp; skilful orchestrator. Writer on music.

See *Salome*.

Schmitz, Elie Robert (b. Paris 1889; d. San Francisco 1949). Pianist

of high reputation France, U.S.A., &c. Trained Paris Conserv. Espec. interested in contemporary music; founded Pro-Musica (1920; then called 'Franco-Amer. Mus. Soc.').

Schnabel, (1) **Artur** (b. Lipnik, Carinthia, 1882; d. Switzerland 1951). Pianist. Trained under Leschetizky. Then on staff of Berlin Hochschule; appeared frequently in Britain, U.S.A., &c.; famous as Beethoven player and edited and recorded all sonatas. Composer of orch. and chamber works; also author. (2) **Karl Ulrich** (b. Berlin 1909). Pianist. Son of above. Since 1933 resident U.S.A. Composer of piano music, &c.

Schnarre (Ger.). 'Rattle.' So *Schnarrtrommel*, 'Snare Drum' (see *Percussion Family* 2 i); *Schnarrsaite*, 'rattle-string', i.e. the snare. But the *Schnarrwerk* of an organ is the reed department.

Schneidend (Ger.). 'Cutting sharply', 'defining'.

Schneider, Johann Christian Friedrich (b. Alt-Waltersdorf, Saxony, 1786; d. Dessau 1853). Diligent composer of oratorios, masses, symphonies, male-voice choruses, songs, &c., and author of books on musical subjects.

Schneiderhan, Wolfgang (b. Vienna 1915). Violinist. Leader Vienna Symphony Orch. 1942; Vienna Philharmonic 1950; on staff Lucerne Conserv. 1949; active chamber-music player. Married Irmgard Seefried.

Schnell; schneller (Ger.). 'Quick'; 'Quicker'. So *Schnelligkeit*, 'Speed'.

Schobert, Johann (b. abt. 1720; d. Paris 1767). As harpsichordist and composer exercised influence on the music of Haydn–Mozart period. Spent last years in Paris and there d. (with whole household) from mistaking toadstools for mushrooms.

Schoeck, Othmar (b. Brunnen, Lake Lucerne, 1886; d. Zürich 1957). Choral and orch. conductor; lived in Zürich. Composer of operas, choral and orch. music, song cycles, &c.

Schoeffler, Paul (b. Dresden 1907). Bass-baritone vocalist. Studied Milan. Became leading baritone in opera at

Dresden and Vienna, appearing also Milan, Paris, London, Rome, &c. Also Lieder singer.

Schoenberg. See *Schönberg*.

Schofar. Same as *Shofar* or *Shophar*, the ancient synagogue horn of the Jews.

Schola Cantorum. Schools for church song are of very ancient origin. That of Rome is said to have been founded in the 4th c. St. Gregory (cf. *Plainsong* 3 and *Modes*) at the end of the 6th c. much developed the system. It soon became the custom for cathedrals and abbeys to maintain such schools (the existing choir school of York Minster dates from 627), and in Church Latin the term is still in use to signify the choral body of such a foundation. The Eng. song schools and the Scottish 'Sang Scuils' or 'Sang Schoolis' carried on the tradition up to the Reformation, and in some cases beyond (see *Education and Music* 1).

Modern institutions for the study or practice of sacred song have sometimes taken the name. See *d'Indy* (also *Bordes*; *Guilmant*) for that of Paris, which is, however, a full-scale conservatory.

See *Motu proprio*.

Scholes, Percy Alfred (b. Leeds 1877; d. Vevey 1958). Writer on music and lecturer. Privately educated; at first organist and schoolteacher; then active in 'Music Appreciation' movement; founded (1908) and ed. *Music Student* (later *Music Teacher*); much journalism; *Observer* (1920–7); *Radio Times* (1923–9). Author of valuable books on music appreciation, as well as more scholarly works, esp. *The Puritans and Music* (1934) and *The Great Dr. Burney* (1948), &c.; best known for 1-vol. *Oxford Companion to Music* (1938; many editions).

Schönberg, Arnold (b. Vienna 1874; d. Los Angeles 1951). Began professional life as an orchestrator of theatre music and conductor of theatre orchs. As composer developed an uncompromising style, expressing Ger. romantic mentality by means of original harmonic system, avowedly 'Expressionistic' (see *Expressionism*). Amongst many later works are a string quartet, a violin

concerto, a piano concerto, &c. In works of this period he employs the Dodecaphonic Scale (see *Scale*) and the device of the Note-Row (q.v.).

Prof. of Music Univ. California 1936–44. Author of textbooks of harmony; painter of Expressionist School.

See also *Buch der hängenden Gärten*; *Erwartung*; *Glückliche Hand*; *Gurrelieder*; *Hauer*; *Herzgewächse*; *History* 8; *Moses and Aaron*; *Ode to Napoleon*; *Pelléas et Mélisande*; *Pierrot lunaire*; *Verklärte Nacht*.

Schonberg, Harold C. (b. New York 1915). Educ. Brooklyn Coll. and N.Y. Univ.; music critic (*N.Y. Times* 1950; chief music critic 1960) and author; Pulitzer Prize 1970.

Schöne Melusine, Die (Mendelssohn). See *Melusina*.

Schöne Müllerin, Die ('The Beautiful Maid of the Mill'). Song Cycle by Schubert (op. 25, 1823), with piano accompaniment. Settings of 20 poems by Wilhelm Müller.

Schönning, Soffi (b. Lofoten, Norway, 1898). Soprano. Opera career Stockholm, Covent Garden, Glyndebourne, &c. Lieder singer.

School for Fathers. See *I Quattro rusteghi*.

Schoolmaster, The (*Der Schulmeister*). Nickname for Haydn's Symphony in E flat, no. 55 in Breitkopf edn. of the Symphonies.

School Music. See *Education*.

School of English Church Music. See under *Royal School*.

Schools of Music. The earliest schools of music were those organized by the church to secure the proper rendering of her plainsong (see *Education and Music*; *Schola Cantorum*). The introduction of schools of music of the modern kind, in which a wide range of musical subjects is taught and a professional training given, occurred first in Italy. The first such schools were orphanages and the name 'Conservatorio' (with its Fr. equivalent 'Conservatoire') records the fact. Naples was the great centre for conservatories for boys, the first being founded in 1537, and Venice for those for girls, though these latter were at first called Ospedali, i.e. Hospitals.

The first professional school of music

in England was not founded until 1822—the Royal Academy of Music (q.v.); it was not an orphanage, but pupils were at first admitted at an early age and all lived on the premises. It is, of course, still active, in a very much enlarged and modernized form. The Royal Coll. of Music (q.v.) followed half a century after this (1873 as the National Training School of Music; reorganized 1882 under its present title). Trinity Coll. of Music dates from 1875. These are national institutions situated in London, the first two of them operating on royal charters. The City of London maintains its own institution, the Guildhall School of Music (1880; see under *Guildhall*). Amongst schools of music outside London are the Royal Irish Academy of Music in Dublin (1848; reorganized 1856; 'Royal' since 1872), the Royal Manchester Coll. of Music (founded by Hallé in 1893), and the Royal Scottish Academy of Music, Glasgow (founded in 1929 on the basis of the Glasgow Athenaeum School of Music, dating from 1890). Specialist schools are the Royal Military School of Music, Kneller Hall, Twickenham (1857), and the Royal School of Church Music (formerly the School of Eng. Church Music, founded 1927, now at Croydon).

Apart from the It. conservatories the earliest founded school of music now existing in Europe is the Paris Conserv., or 'Conservatoire national de Musique et de Déclamation', founded, under another name, in 1784; it has had a very distinguished history. Many of the smaller cities of France also have conservatories. Central and northern Europe have many such institutions.

There is an immense number of institutions of the conservatory kind in the U.S.A., some of them independent and some attached to universities. It was in the 1860's that they began to appear. That of Oberlin, Ohio, was founded in 1865; those of Boston (New England Conserv), Cincinnati, and Chicago (Musical Coll.) in 1867; the Peabody Conserv., Baltimore, in 1868, and so on. Amongst specially endowed institutions of this kind are the New York Inst. of Musical Art

(1904; since 1926 connected with the Juilliard Foundation); the Eastman School of Music, Rochester, N.Y. (1919); the Curtis Inst., Philadelphia (1924); and the Juilliard School of Music, New York (1924). There is no other country in the world in which, at the present time, such generous provision is made for the training of talented young musicians of small financial resources as the U.S.A.

In Canada, notable institutions are the Conservs. of Montreal (McGill Univ.) and Toronto. Australia has several important conservatories. South Africa has a school of music at Cape Town, as well as smaller institutions.

Schöpfung, Die (Haydn). See *Creation*.

Schöpfungsmesse ('Creation Mass'). Popular name for Haydn's 13th Mass, in B flat. In the 'Qui Tollis' is a theme already familiar in *The Creation*.

Schott. One of largest firms of music publishers. At Mainz; estd. 1773.

Schottische (Eng.), **Schottisch** (Ger. 'Scottish'; a misnomer since there is no evidence of Scottish origin). The 'German Polka', a round dance of the mid-19th c. Some books of reference confuse it with the Écossaise (q.v.) which is a country dance, and thus very different. Both are, however, in simple duple time.

Schottische bohème. See under *Polka*.

Schötz. Spelling adopted in Brit. appearances by Aksel Schiøtz (q.v.).

Schrammel Quartet. A Viennese type of instrumental combination for the perf. of light music; it consists of 2 violins, accordion, and guitar—or some such instruments. The name comes from Joseph Schrammel (1850–93), leader of a quartet of this kind and composer of waltzes, &c., for it. There are also *Schrammel Orchestras* on similar lines.

Schreker, Franz (b. Monaco 1878; d. Berlin 1934). Studied violin at Vienna Conserv., of which later became a prof.; conductor of Vienna Popular Opera (Volksoper); founded Vienna Philharmonic Choir; director of Berlin State High School of Music

1920–32; died of a stroke due to Nazi threats based on his alleged Jewish descent. Composer of many successful operas of romantic, erotic, and Expressionist cast (see *Expressionism*), of which he wrote own libretti. See *Birthday of the Infanta*.

Schrittmässig, Schrittweise (Ger. 'step-style', 'step-wise', 'at a walking pace'). Same as *Andante* (q.v.).

Schröder-Devrient, Wilhelmine (b. Hamburg 1804; d. Coburg 1860). Operatic and Lieder soprano. Début Vienna 1821; Paris 1830; London 1832. Enormous reputation, largely due to dramatic powers.

Schröter, Corona. See *Erl King*.

Schtscherbatchew (and similar transliterations). See *Stcherbatchef*.

Schubert, Franz (b. Dresden 1808; there d. 1878). Violinist, &c., of Dresden; included here since sometimes confused with his greater namesake; e.g. his popular violin solo *L'Abeille* ("The Bee") has often been wrongly attributed.

Schubert, Franz Peter (b. Vienna 1797; there d. 1828). Son of a poor schoolmaster who, with his family, loved and practised music; at 11 admitted to choir of Royal Chapel, and there received good general and musical education; on voice breaking assisted in father's school but soon abandoned this for music; was admired and helped by a group of cultured middle-class people, including painters and poets of the place and time; never married.

As composer very fluent and prolific; known to have written 8 songs in 1 day and 144 in a year; wrote over 600 in all (generally settings of good poetry); operas (unsuccessful); masses, &c.; symphonies (see below), overtures, &c.; much chamber music (15 string quartets); many piano compositions (22 sonatas, see below, and large number of smaller pieces); choral works.

See also *Death and the Maiden*; *Erl King*; *Lilac Time*; *Mourning Waltz*; *Rosamunde music*; *Schöne Müllerin*; *Schwanengesang*; *Trout Quintet*; *Valse triste*; *Wanderer Fantasia*; *Winterreise*; also reference under *Loder*.

Schubert's Pianoforte Sonatas, as numbered in their various edns. and their mention in recital programmes, are in a very confused state. The following list rectifies this. It was supplied by Richard Capell in the *Daily Telegraph* of 12 Nov. 1938, being based by him on the researches of H. Költzsch (*Schubert in seinen Klaviersonaten*, 1927). No. 1, in E, 3 movements (1815). No. 2, in C, 3 movements; there may have been a finale now lost (1815). No. 3 in E, 5 movements (1816; publ. 1843 as *5 Klavierstücke*, '5 Piano Pieces'). No. 4 in A flat, with finale in E flat (1817). No. 5 in E minor, 2 movements (1817); an unpublished scherzo may belong to it, and the Rondo called op. 145 may be its finale. No. 6, in E flat (op. 122, 1817); 1st publ. in 1830. No. 7 in F sharp minor (1817); unfinished, but completions exist by Heinz Jolles and W. Rehberg. No. 8 in B (op. 147, 1817). No. 9 in A minor (op. 164, 1817). No. 10 in C (1818); unfinished. No. 11 in F minor (1818); unfinished; completion exists by W. Rehberg. No. 12 in C sharp minor (1819); fragmentary. No. 13 in A (op. 120, 1819—not later as sometimes stated). No. 14 in A minor (op. 143, 1823). No. 15 in C (1825); minuet and finale unfinished, completions by L. Stark, E. Křenek, and W. Rehberg. No. 16 in A minor (op. 42, 1825). No. 17 in D (op. 53, 1825). No. 18 in G (op. 78, 1826). No. 19 in C minor (1828). No. 20 in A (1828). No. 21 in B flat (1828).

Schubert's Symphonies are as follows (but a few are sometimes differently numbered): No. 1, in D (1813). No. 2, in B flat (1814–15). No. 3, in D (1815). No. 4, in C minor, nicknamed the *Tragic* (1816). No. 5, in B flat (1816). No. 6, in C (1817 or 1818). No. 7, in E (1821); sketched out in 4 movements; it has been completed and orchestrated by J. F. Barnett (1883) and Weingartner (1935). No. 8, in B minor, the *Unfinished* (2 movements only, 1822; 1st perf. 1865; publ. 1867); completions have been supplied by Frank Merrick and others. No. 9, in C (1829, sometimes called No. 7, sometimes No. 10—the latter counting the *Gastein* (see below) as No. 9). There is a mere sketch of one in E minor (1820). The *Grand Duo*, for Piano (op. 140) has been scored as a Symphony by Joachim, and also by Anthony Collins. There is supposed to be one lost symphony, called the *Gastein Symphony* from the place (in the Tyrol) of its composition; the date is thought to be 1825: some think the *Grand Duo* to be an arrangement of it.

Schüchtern (Ger.). 'Shy.'

Schulhoff, (1) **Julius** (b. Prague 1825; d. Berlin 1898). Pianist. Protégé of Chopin in Paris; lived there many years, but toured Europe widely. Then Dresden (1870) and Berlin (1897). Compositions for piano.

(2) **Erwin** (b. Prague 1894; died in Wüllsburg Concentration Camp 1942). Distant relative of Julius, above, and also fine pianist. Composer of 'advanced' tendencies and great productivity.

Schuller, Gunther (b. New York 1925). At first horn player from age 16; with Metropolitan 1945–59; as a composer largely self-taught and of great virtuosity, following paths opened by Webern; notable expounder of modern jazz developments; opera, *The Visitation* (Hamburg 1966). Head of New England Conserv. 1967.

Schulman, Jeremy (b. London 1896). Conductor and violinist. In S. Africa since 1924. Music director and chief conductor S. African Broadcasting Corporation from 1933.

Schulmeister, Der (Haydn). See *Schoolmaster*.

Schuman, William Howard (b. New York 1910). Studied at Columbia Univ. and joined staff of Sarah Lawrence Coll., Bronxville, N.Y. (1935–45). Pulitzer Prize for *A Free Song* 1945. Head of Juilliard School of Music (1945–61); President, Lincoln Center (1962–8). Has composed 7 symphonies and other orch. works, choral works, chamber music, &c.

See *Undertow*.

Schumann, (1) **Robert Alexander** (b. Zwickau, Saxony, 1810; d. in mental asylum nr. Bonn, 1856). Nominally educated for the law, but devoted his time largely to music; piano pupil of Wieck; engaged in journalism and editing musical journal by which he helped to bring into notice Chopin and other younger composers; married daughter of his teacher Wieck (see below); was of a dreamy and unpractical nature and his music reflects the romantic feeling of the Ger. literature of the period (e.g. Hoffmann and Jean Paul Richter) as also that of Eng. literature (especially Scott and Byron).

Composed 4 symphonies (see below) and other orch. works; chamber music; much piano music (often with novel and fanciful titles); many songs; choral works. His critical writings from his journal (*Die neue Zeitschrift*) have been publ. in collected form.

See also *Abegg Variations*; *Albumblätter*; *Bargiel*; *Carnaval*; *Davidsbündler-Tänze*; *Dichterliebe*; *Études symphoniques*; *Fantaisiestücke*; *Faschingsschwank aus Wien*; *Faust*; *Frauenliebe und Leben*; *Humoresque*; *Kinderscenen*; *Kreisleriana*; *Liederkreis*; *Manfred*; *Novelette*; *Paganini Transcriptions*; *Papillons*; *Paradise and the Peri*; *Träumerei*; *Waldscenen*.

Schumann's Symphonies are as follows: No. 1, in B flat, the *Spring Symphony* (op. 38, 1841). No. 2, in C (op. 61, 1846). No. 3, in E flat, the *Rhenish* (op. 97, 1850; inspired by Cologne Cathedral). No. 4, in D minor (withdrawn after 1st perf. in 1841; revised in 1851 and publ. as op. 120).

To these may be added the *Overture, Scherzo, and Finale* (op. 52, 1841; finale revised 1845).

Schumann, (2) **Clara Josephine** (b. Leipzig 1819; d. Frankfurt-on-Main 1896). Daughter of Wieck (see above) and (1840) wife of Robert Schumann. Gifted pianist, playing in public from age 9; frequently in England 1856–88 and a great favourite there; admirable teacher. Composed some music for piano, &c., and edited her husband's compositions. Cf. *Bargiel*.

(3) **Elisabeth** (b. Mersburg 1885; d. New York 1952). Soprano (operatic, oratorio, and Lieder). Internationally famous in Mozart, Strauss, &c. As result of Nazi régime settled U.S.A. 1937 (Curtis Inst.).

Schumann-Heink (*née* Rössler), **Ernestine** (b. Prague 1861; d. Hollywood 1936). Opera and concert contralto. Début Graz 1878; then

Hamburg, Bayreuth, Berlin, Paris, London, New York, &c. First appeared as 'Heink' (name of 1st husband, 1882); added 'Schumann' (name of 2nd husband, 1893); married (3rd—temporarily; 1905–14) an American, becoming U.S.A. citizen 1908.

Schusterfleck (Ger. 'cobbler-patch'). The Rosalia (see *Sequence* 1).

Schütt, Eduard (b. St. Petersburg 1856; d. Merano 1933). Fine pianist and good conductor, resident in Vienna, becoming naturalized Austrian. Composed piano concerto and smaller piano pieces, chamber music, songs, &c.

Schütteln (Ger.). 'To shake.'

Schütz, Heinrich (b. Köstritz, Saxony, 1585; d. Dresden 1672). Born exactly a century before Bach and ranks as one of his greatest precursors, bridging gap between earlier contrapuntal school (Palestrina period) and later contrapuntal school (Bach and Handel period).

Studied as young man in Venice under G. Gabrieli; then Kapellmeister to Elector of Saxony at Dresden (1615 to death, with interruptions); often revisited Italy and for 3 periods was court conductor at Copenhagen. Settings of Passion very important (see *Passion Music*); psalm settings, motets, madrigals, &c.; earliest Ger. opera (*Dafne* 1627, music lost); complete works publ. (1885–94, 16 vols. edited Spitta, and supplementary vol. 1927).

See *Gabrieli, G.*; *Seven Last Words*.

Schwab, Frederick. See *Criticism*.

Schwach; schwächer (Ger.). 'Weak' (soft); 'weaker'. So *schwächen*, 'to weaken'.

Schwanda, the Bagpiper. Opera by Weinberger. (Prod. Prague 1927; New York 1931; London 1934; translated into nearly 20 languages.)

Schwanendreher, Der ('The Swan-turner'—on a spit, that is). 3-movt. concerto by Hindemith for viola and orch. (1935), the musical material being old German songs.

Schwanengesang ('Swan Song'). Collection of 14 Songs by Schubert, so entitled by the publisher, as they were the composer's last songs (1828) and appeared posthumously. Poems by Rellstab and Heine, with one by Seidl.

Schwankend (Ger.). 'Swaying.'

Schwarz, Rudolf (b. Vienna 1905). Conductor. Trained Vienna and conducted in Ger. cities before 1933. After 1941 in various concentration camps until rescued from Belsen by Brit. troops 1945. Taken by Red Cross to Sweden for recovery. Then conducted Copenhagen. Musical Director Bournemouth Municipal Orch. 1947; Birmingham Orch. 1951; B.B.C. 1957–62; Northern Sinfonia 1964.

Schwarzendorf. See *Martini* 2.

Schwarzkopf, Elisabeth. (b. nr. Poznán 1915). Opera and concert soprano of very high reputation for voice and artistry, both opera and Lieder, Europe and America. Husband is Walter Legge (q.v.).

Schwebung (Ger. 'fluctuation'). (1) The 'beats' between 2 notes nearly but not quite in tune (see *Acoustics* 16). (2, Organ) The tremulant.

Schweigen (Ger.). 'Silence' or 'to be silent'. So *schweigt = tacet* (see *tacere*), and *Schweigezeichen* ('silence-sign') = 'rest'.

Schweigsame Frau, Die ('The Silent Woman'). 3-act opera by Richard Strauss. Libretto by Stefan Zweig after Ben Jonson's *Epicoene*. (Prod. Dresden 1935.)

Schweitzer, Albert (b. Kaysersberg, Upper Alsace, 1875; d. Lambaréné, Gabon, 1965). Philosopher, theologian, medical man (founder and director of a missionary hospital in Equatorial Africa), organist, and leading authority on Bach, editing his organ works (with Widor) and writing important biographical and critical study (1905). M.D., Hon. D.D., Zürich and Edinburgh, D.Phil., Prague, Hon. D.Mus., Oxford and Edinburgh.

Schwellen (Ger.). 'To swell', i.e. to increase in tone (*crescendo*). So *Schweller* is the swell of an organ, *Schwellwerk* being the Swell Organ and *Schwellkasten* the Swell Box.

Schwellwerk (Ger., lit. 'swell work'). Swell Organ (see *Organ* 1).

Schwer (Ger.). (1) 'Heavy' (in style). (2) 'Difficult.' **Schwermütig, Schwermutsvoll.** 'Heavy-hearted.'

Schwieger, Hans (b. Cologne 1910). Conductor, trained Cologne and Bonn. Assisted Kleiber, Berlin 1930; Mainz 1932. Career Asia and U.S.A. 1938; Kansas City 1948–70; many guest appearances elsewhere.

Schwindend (Ger.). 'Diminishing' (in tone, i.e. *diminuendo*).

Schwindl (or **Schwindel**), **Friedrich** (b. Amsterdam 1737; d. Karlsruhe 1786). Violinist, harpsichordist, flautist, and composer, living and working at different periods in Holland, Switzerland, and Germany. Composed symphonies, chamber music, &c., some of which was popular in England and publ. in London.

Schwirrholz. See *Thunder Stick*.

Schwung (Ger.). 'Swing.' Hence *Schwungvoll*, 'full of go' or 'vigour'.

Schytte, Ludwig Theodor (b. Denmark 1848; d. Berlin 1909). Pianist and composer, especially of piano concerto and many piano pieces.

Scintillante (It.). 'Sparkling.'

Sciolto, scioltamente (It. 'untied'). 'Loosely', i.e. in a free and easy manner. So the corresponding noun, *scioltezza*.

Scivolando (It.). 'Sliding', i.e. *glissando* (q.v.).

Scontrino, Antonio (b. Sicily 1850; d. Florence 1922). Eminent double-bass player, teacher of composition, and composer of operas, chamber music, &c.

Scordato (It.). 'Out of tune.' **Scordatura.** 'Out-of-tuning.' Abnormal tuning of a stringed instrument for the purpose of producing some unusual note, facilitating some type of passage, or changing the general tonal effect. The most common instance remaining today is the tuning of the lowest string a semitone or tone lower in order temporarily to increase the compass (e.g. in the Andante of Schumann's Piano Quartet the C string of the violoncello is tuned down to B flat).

Score. A music copy which shows the whole of the music, as distinct from 'parts' each of which shows that of 1 instrument or voice (or 1 group of instruments or voices performing in unison with one another). (1) A *Full Score* shows all the parts separately displayed. (2) An *Orchestral Score* is the full score of an orch. work (see *Orchestra* 6). (3) A *Vocal Score* shows all the voice parts of an oratorio, opera, &c., but with the orch. parts reduced to a piano part. (4) A *Piano Score* or *Short Score* is the reduction of an orch. score, &c., to a piano version.

Scoring has 2 meanings. (a) Deciding and writing down the orchestration of a work already conceived. (b) Taking the separate parts of a work and assembling them in a score (as has had to be done with, e.g. 16th-c. madrigals, &c., which had been preserved only as sets of parts).

Scorrendo, scorrevole (It.). 'Scouring' (a country), &c. Hence (1) Gliding from note to note = *glissando*; (2) In a flowing style.

Scotch Catch. Same as 'Scotch Snap.' See below.

Scotch Snap. A short note, on the beat, followed by a longer one occupying the remaining time-value before the next beat begins. It is a feature of the Strathspey (q.v.) and is found in some Scottish songs. It does not seem to be earlier than the 18th c. and the problem of its origin is unsolved.

Gin a bo-dy meet a bo-dy

com-ing thro' the rye.

Scotch Symphony. By Mendelssohn (op. 56). Inspired, in the first instance, by a visit to Holyrood in 1829 but not completed until 1842. Dedicated to Queen Victoria.

Scotland. See *Festival*.

Scots Snap. See *Scotch Snap*.

Scots Symphony (Mendelssohn). See *Scotch Symphony*.

Scots wha hae. The poem is by Burns; the air is the old traditional Scottish one of *Hey, tutti tatti*, also sung to Lady Nairne's *Land o' the Leal.*

Scott, (1) Charles Kennedy (b. Romsey 1876; d. 1965). Noted London choral trainer, authority on and ed. of Eng. madrigals; composer (*Everyman, a Mystery Play*, &c.). On staff T.C.M. Books on singing, &c.

(2) **Cyril Meir** (b. nr. Birkenhead 1879; d. Eastbourne 1970). Studied Frankfurt-on-Main; then Liverpool; at 21 heard his *Heroic Suite* performed there and in Manchester under Richter; 1st symphony at Darmstadt same year; thence onward became known to public as composer. A good pianist, he composed effectively for his instrument, also for orch., chamber combinations, choral bodies, &c.; also composed songs and 3 operas (*The Alchemist*, Essen 1925). Had a personal harmonic style inclining to Impressionism. In addition to compositions wrote books—autobiographical and philosophical, mystical, esoteric, and many medical (e.g. *Victory over Cancer*; and *Crude Black Molasses the Natural Wonder Food*).

(3) **Francis George** (b. Hawick 1880; d. Glasgow 1958). Composer of distinctively national mind and aims, setting Scottish poems and choosing Scottish subjects for orch. and other works. On staff of Jordanhill Teachers' Training College. B.Mus., Durham.

(4) **Marion Margaret** (b. London 1877; d. London 1953). Trained at R.C.M.; frequent contributor to musical press, especially on Haydn, on whose life and works she was leading authority.

(5) **Lady John Douglas.** See *Annie Laurie*; *Loch Lomond.*

Scotti, Antonio (b. Naples 1866; there d. 1936). Operatic baritone of great dramatic power. High reputation both sides of Atlantic, especially for interpretation of It. composers (Verdi, Puccini, &c.). For a time directed his own opera company in U.S.A. Made fortune but invested badly and spent last years in poverty.

Scottish National Academy. See *Royal Scottish.*

Scottish National Orchestra. Founded 1891; headquarters Glasgow. 1st condr. George Henschel; later ones include Barbirolli (1933–7); Szell (1937); Süsskind (1946); Rankl (1952); Alexander Gibson (1959).

Scottish Puritans (Bellini). See *Puritani di Scozia.*

Scottish Symphony (Mendelssohn). See *Scotch Symphony.*

Scozzese (It.). 'Scottish.'

Scriabin (Skryabin, &c.), Alexander (b. Moscow 1872; there d. 1915). Studied at Moscow Conserv. under Taneief and Arensky; was taken up by Belaief (q.v.), who published his compositions and planned recital tours; also owed much to conductor, Koussevitzky; toured in U.S.A. 1906–7; in London the year before early death from a tumour on the lip.

Early piano compositions, though original in content, resemble Chopin in style; later, as he developed very personal theosophical ideas, adopted own harmonic combinations and distinctive melodic shapes, with complexity of rhythm—highly emotional and working to points of powerful climax: for chief orch. works see *Divine Poem, Poem of Ecstasy*, and *Prometheus: the Poem of Fire.*

Scucito (It. 'unsewed'). 'Disconnected.'

Scythian Suite—Ala and Lolli. Orch. Suite by Prokofief. (Op. 20, 1914; 1st perf. St. Petersburg 1916. Chicago 1918; London 1920.)

Sdegno (It.). 'Disdain.' So *sdegnante*, 'disdaining'; *sdegnoso*, 'disdainful'; *sdegnosamente*, 'disdainfully'.

Sdrucciolando (It. 'sliding'). *Glissando* (q.v.).

Se (It.). 'If.'

Sea Drift. (1) Cantata by DELIUS; a setting of Whitman. (1st perf. Essen 1906, Sheffield and London 1908.) (2) Symphonic Poem by J. A. CARPENTER. (1st perf. Chicago 1933.) (3) Long discarded setting by COLERIDGE-TAYLOR (op. 69).

Sea Pictures. By Elgar (op. 37, 1899). Five songs for contralto with orch. (words by various poets).

Searle, Humphrey (b. Oxford 1915). Educ. Winchester, Oxford (B.A.), R.C.M., Vienna Conserv., and under Webern. On staff B.B.C. 1938–48. Many orch. and other compositions; much musical journalism (authority on Liszt). C.B.E. 1968.

Sea Shanty or **Sea Chanty**. See *Shanty*.

Seasons, The (*Die Jahreszeiten*). Secular oratorio by Haydn; libretto imitated from Thomson's *Seasons*. (1st perf. Vienna 1801.)

Sea Symphony. See *Vaughan Williams's Symphonies*.

Sec, sèche (Fr. masc., fem.). 'Dry', 'crisp'; so *sécheresse*, 'dryness'. **secco** (It. 'dry'), 'staccato' (but see also *Recitative*).

Sechs (Ger.). 'Six.'

Sechsviertelmesse ('Six-four-time Mass'). Popular name for Haydn's Mass No. 6, in G. The opening ('Kyrie') is in 6/4 time and of a pastoral character.

Sechzehntel or **Sechzehntelnote** (Ger.). 'Sixteenth' or 'sixteenth-note', i.e. Semiquaver (see Table 3).

Second. See *Interval*.

Second Inversion of a chord. See *Harmony* 2 e.

Second Violin. See *Violin Family*.

Secondando (It. 'seconding'). Same as *colla voce* and similar expressions.

Secondo, seconda (It. masc., fem.; the respective plurals are *secondi, seconde*). 'Second'. (For *Seconda volta* see Table 20.)

Secret Marriage, The (Cimarosa). See *Matrimonio segreto*.

Sedlák. The same as Furiant (q.v.).

Seefried, Irmgard (b. Bavaria 1919). Opera and concert soprano. Début Aachen 1939; Vienna 1943; world career after the war. Wife of W. Schneiderhan.

Seele (Ger. 'Soul'). (1) 'Feeling.' (2) The soundpost of a bowed instrument. *Seelenvoll* = 'soulful'.

See our oars, with feathered spray. See *Stevenson, J. A.*

Segno (It.). The 'sign' (see *Dal segno* and *Al segno*; also Table 20).

Segovia, Andrés (b. Linares, Spain, 1893). Guitarist, of high international fame for virtuosity and musicianship, whose performances brought back to public notice the capabilities of an instrument that had fallen into some neglect.

Segreto di Susanna, Il ('Susanna's Secret'). 1-act comedy-opera by Wolf-Ferrari. (Prod., as *Susannens Geheimnis*, Munich 1909; New York and London 1911.)

Segue (It.). 'Follows', e.g. *segue la coda*, 'the coda follows'. **Seguente, seguendo.** 'Following.'

Seguidilla. An ancient Spanish dance, in simple triple time, much like the bolero but quicker. There is a good deal of singing by the participants; the vocal passages, called *coplas*, are in short lines of alternately 7 and 5 syllables and have assonance (agreement of vowels) instead of rhyme. The castanets (see *Percussion Family* 2 q) are used. There are many regional varieties of this dance.

Seguidillas Gitanas. See *Playera*.

Sehnsucht (Ger.). 'Longing' (noun). So the adjs. *sehnsuchtsvoll* and *sehnsüchtig*.

Sehnsuchtswalzer (Schubert). See *Mourning Waltz*.

Sehr (Ger.). 'Very', 'much'. *Nicht zu sehr*, 'not too much'.

Sei (It.). 'Six.'

Seiber, Mátyás (b. Budapest 1905; d. in car crash nr. Johannesburg 1960). Trained Budapest Conserv. as 'cellist (with composition under Kodály). On staff Frankfurt-on-Main Conserv. 1928–33. Settled England 1935. Lecturer Morley Coll., London: conductor 'Dorian Singers'. Chamber, orch., and choral compositions, &c.; also booklets, articles, and lectures. Notable teacher.

Seidl, Anton (b. Budapest 1850; d. New York 1898). Internationally famous opera and orch. conductor, especially in Wagner works. Assisted Wagner at 1st Bayreuth performances. Held important posts Bremen, New York, &c.

Seises. Choir-boys who sing, dance, and clash their castanets on high festival days before the high altar in the Cathedral of Seville, at Jaca in Aragon, and in Majorca, as formerly also in the cathedrals of Toledo and Valencia. The name comes from *seis*, 'six', but at Seville the boys now number 10.

Seite (Ger.). 'Side', e.g. page of book or end of drum.

Seitensatz. See under *Satz*.

Selby, William (b. England 1738; d. Boston, Mass., 1798). Expert harpsichordist and organist; emigrated to America 1771 and sold groceries and liquor; performed and taught music, organized concerts, and composed some keyboard music, songs, anthems, &c.

Sellick, Phyllis. See under *Smith, Cyril*.

Sembrich (real name Kochanska), **Marcella** (b. Galicia 1858; d. New York 1935). Famous operatic soprano (also pianist and violinist). Pupil of Lamperti, &c. Latterly on staff of Curtis Inst., Philadelphia, and Juilliard School, New York.

Semel. See under *Gymel*.

Semele. Secular oratorio by Handel. Libretto taken from Congreve. (1st perf. London 1744.)

Semibiscroma (It.). Hemidemisemiquaver or Sixty-fourth note (see Table 3).

Semibreve (𝅜). The 'Whole-Note', half the time-value of the breve (q.v.) and double the value of the minim or Half-Note (see Table 1).

Semicroma (It.). Semiquaver or Sixteenth-note (see Table 3).

Semidemisemiquaver (𝅘𝅥𝅲) or **Hemidemisemiquaver.** The Sixty-fourth note, i.e. ¼ the time-value of the whole-note or semibreve (see Table 1).

Semi-luna. The Nail Fiddle (q.v.).

Semiminima (It.). Crotchet or Quarter-note (see Table 3).

Semi-perfect Cadence. See *Cadence*.

Semiquaver (𝅘𝅥𝅯). The Sixteenth-note, i.e. ¹⁄₁₆ the time-value of the whole-note or semibreve (see Table 1).

Semiramide ('Semiramis'—Empress of Nineveh). Tragedy-opera by Rossini. (Prod. Venice 1823; London 1824; New York 1845.)
Many other composers have written operas on the same subject.

Semitone. The smallest interval used in normal European music (as distinct from Asiatic, &c.), e.g. B–C, C–C sharp, E flat–E natural, and so forth.

Semplice; semplicità (It.). 'Simple' (in all the Eng. senses); 'Simplicity'. So *semplicemente*, 'simply'; *semplicissimo*, 'extremely simple'.

Sempre (It.). 'Always'; e.g. *sempre legato*, the whole passage or composition to be played smoothly.

Sena, Devar Surya. (Original name H. C. J. Peiris; b. Colombo 1899). Baritone vocalist, conductor, writer, &c. Educated Cambridge (M.A., LL.B.) and R.C.M. Collector and singer of folk-songs of Ceylon and India. Frequent broadcasts; tours of India, Europe, and U.S.A. Music director, Royal Coll., Colombo, &c. Books and articles on music of Ceylon.

Senaillé (or **Senallié**), **Jean Baptiste** (b. Paris 1687; there d. 1730). Violinist, pupil in Italy of Vitali; became member of orch. of Louis XV. Composed 50 violin sonatas.

Senior, Evan (b. Adelaide 1907). Music critic and journalist; in London from 1947; editor *Music and Musicians* 1952–63, *Music Magazine* 1963.

Sensibile; sensibilità (It.). 'Sensitive'; 'sensitiveness' (the *nota sensibile* is the leading note).

Sentence. See under *Phrase*.

Sentito (It.). 'Felt', i.e. 'with expression'.

Senza (It.). 'Without.'

Senza sordina or **senza sordino; senza sordini** (It.). (1, violin, &c.) 'Without mute'; 'without mutes'. (2, pianoforte) *Senza sordini* means 'without dampers', i.e. use the right pedal, which throws this part of the mechanism out of action, leaving the strings to vibrate freely.

Separé (Fr. 'Separated'). In Fr. organ music, 'uncoupled'.

Sept (Fr.). 'Seven'; hence *septième*, 'seventh'.

Septet (Fr. *septette*, or *septuor*; It. *settimino* or *septetto*; Ger. *Septett*). Any combination of 7 performers (usually instrumental), or any piece of music for such.

Septième (Fr. 'seventh'). Organ stop; same as *Flat Twenty-first* (q.v.).

Septimole or **Septolet**. See Table 11.

Septuor. See *Septet*.

Septuplet. See Table 11.

Sequence. The term has 2 applications:

(1) In musical construction it is applied to the more or less exact repetition of a passage at a higher or lower level of pitch. If the repetition be of only the melody we have a MELODIC SEQUENCE; if it be of a series of chords we have a HARMONIC SEQUENCE. If the quality of the intervals between the notes of the melody is to some extent

A 'REAL' SEQUENCE

(From the hymn tune, 'St. George')

altered (a major interval becoming a minor one and so forth, as is practically inevitable if the key is unchanged) we have a TONAL SEQUENCE; if there is no such variation in the intervals (usually achieved by altering not merely the pitch of the notes but also the key) we have a REAL SEQUENCE. If there are several repetitions, some of them Tonal and some Real, we have a MIXED SEQUENCE. A Harmonic Real Sequence is sometimes called ROSALIA

(some authorities, however, require as an additional qualification for this description a rise of one degree of the scale at each repetition).

(2) In ecclesiastical use the term Sequence is applied to a type of hymn which began as one of the many forms of interpolation in the original liturgy of the Western Christian Church. As the traditional plainsong did not provide for such interpolations special melodies were composed. In the Church's service Sequences follow (whence the name) the Gradual (q.v.) and Alleluia (q.v.). The earliest Sequences were in prose, not, as later, in rhymed verse, and the term 'Prose' is still sometimes used instead of 'Sequence'. The following are examples of the Sequence: *Dies Irae* (now a part of the Requiem, q.v.), *Veni Sancte Spiritus* (q.v.), *Victimae Paschali* (q.v.), *Lauda Sion* (q.v.), and *Stabat Mater dolorosa* (q.v.).

Sequential. Of the nature of sequence (q.v.), in melodic and possibly also harmonic construction.

Serafin, Tullio (b. Venice 1878; d. Rome 1968). Operatic conductor. Studied Milan. At first violinist in La Scala orch.; cond. there 1898; Metropolitan 1925–35, then returned to Italy.

Seraglio, The (Mozart). See *Entführung*.

Serenade (Fr. 'evening music'). Properly, music sung and played at night below a lady's window. The Ger. is *Nachtmusik* ('night music'—mostly applied to instrumental compositions) or *Ständchen* (implying performances by a performer standing below the window and usually applied to vocal music).

Serenade. By Britten. Song cycle for tenor with horn and strings (1943).

Serenata (It. 'serenade', but in ordinary musical use not the same thing). (1) A dramatic cantata, much like an opera but without the stage concomitants, e.g. Handel's *Acis and Galatea*. (2) A sort of orch. wind-band suite, opening with a march and including a minuet: much the same as *Divertimento* or *Cassation* (see *Suite*).

Serenatella (It.). Diminutive of *Serenata* (see above).

Sereno; serenità (It.). 'Serene'; 'serenity'.

Serf, The. See *Lloyd, George*.

Seria (It. fem. of *serio*). 'Serious'; e.g. *opera seria*, serious (or tragic) opera—as distinct from *opera buffa*, comic opera.

Seriamente. 'Seriously.'

Sérieux, sérieuse (Fr. masc., fem.). 'Serious.'

Serinette. See *Mechanical Reproduction of Music* 6.

Serio, seria; serioso, seriosa (It. masc., fem.). 'Serious.'

Seriosamente (It.). 'Seriously.'

Serkin, Rudolf (b. Eger, Bohemia, 1903; both parents Russian). Pianist. Début Vienna 1915, but full concert career began 1920. First appeared U.S.A. 1933. On staff Curtis Institute (Dir. 1968). Much associated in recitals with father-in-law Adolf Busch.

Sermisy, Claude de, known also simply as 'Claudin' (b. abt. 1490; d. 1562). Priest and musician of Sainte Chapelle, Paris, and royal private chapel; famous as composer of chansons (q.v.), masses, and motets.

Serof (Serov, Serow, &c.**), Alexander Nikolaievich** (b. St. Petersburg 1820; there d. 1871). Civil servant who turned to musical criticism and composition; became ardent Wagnerian and in tastes and propaganda rather eclectic than nationalist. Composed operas to own libretti, some of them very successful (see *Judith*).

Serpent. See *Cornett and Key Bugle Families*.

Serrando, serrato (It.); **serrant, serré** (Fr.). 'Pressing', 'pressed', i.e. 'getting quicker'.

Servais, (1) **Adrien François** (b. Hal, nr. Brussels, 1807; there d. 1866). Very high European reputation as 'cellist and composed music for his instrument. For sons see below. (2) **François Matthieu** (b. St. Petersburg 1846; d. nr. Paris 1901). Adopted son of A. F. Servais, above. Pianist and conductor

(earliest to perform some of Wagner's works in Belgium). Composed opera *Iôn* (Carlsruhe 1899). (3) **Joseph** (b. Hal, nr. Brussels, 1850; there d. 1885). Also son of A. F. Servais, above, and like him very fine solo 'cellist; prof. at Brussels Conservatory.

Serva Padrona, La ('The Maid as Mistress'). 2-act intermezzo by Pergolese. The oldest opera in the present-day international repertory. (Prod. Naples 1733; Paris 1748; London 1750; New York 1917. Performances in Paris by an It. troupe in 1752 led to great disputes and a pamphlet war between partisans of Fr. and It. schools— 'La Guerre des Bouffons'; see *Bouffons*.)

Service. A 'service', in the Anglican Church musical vocabulary, implies a more or less elaborate and continuous setting of the canticles for Morning Prayer or Evening Prayer, or of the Communion Service (see *Common Prayer* and *Canticle*). Strictly the use of such service settings (unless very simple) is proper only in cathedrals, college chapels, and the like, as in the parish church it is frequently, if not usually, desirable to give every member of the congregation the opportunity to participate audibly in the choral items.

The effect of the Reformation on the composition of service music was mainly twofold: (a) the canticles had now to be set in the vernacular, and (b) preferably without lengthening by repetition of phrases and as much as possible on the principle of a syllable to a note—this last point being apparently found unacceptable, or even impracticable, by the musicians, and, from the start of vernacular composition, generally disregarded. The terms *Short Service* and *Great Service* were often used by 16th- and early 17th-c. composers to distinguish between the settings which came within the normal scope of daily performance and those which, by their elaboration, and use of larger forces, were designed for special occasions. Byrd, Gibbons, Weelkes, and Tomkins wrote settings of both kinds. During the 18th c. almost all services were composed on the 'short' principle; this was, however, in all ways, a period of poverty in service composition.

An antiphonal treatment (by the Decani and Cantoris sides of the choir; see *Precentor*) is frequent in 'service' music. 'Verse' and 'Full' passages are also used (see *Verse*).

A rather curious feature of 'Service' music, as distinct from anthems, is the long observed tradition of writing it without independent organ part. Byrd, Morley, and Gibbons made experiments in the introduction of such a part, but after them such a thing is hardly found until the composition of 'Walmisley in D minor' 2 centuries later. Since Walmisley (q.v.) composers have made much effective use of the organ. S. S. Wesley (q.v.) exercised a great influence on the composition of service music. The publication of 'Stanford in B flat', in 1879 (see *Stanford*), marked the beginning of a more economical and consistent use of material in service composition, a whole movement (and indeed the whole service) being bound together by a repetition and development of thematic material, treated flexibly; the organ takes a large share in this treatment.

Sesquialtera. On organ a *Mixture stop* (q.v.), properly of 2 ranks (12th and 17th), but sometimes of 3–5 ranks.

Sessions, Roger (b. Brooklyn 1896). Graduate of Harvard; also studied at Yale under Horatio Parker; held various academic positions; in Europe 1925–33, successively with Guggenheim Fellowship, Rome Prize, and Carnegie Fellowship; then further academic work. Compositions include 8 symphonies, chamber music, organ music, songs, &c.

Sestetto. See *Sextet*.

Sette (It.). 'Seven.'

Settimino. See *Septet*.

Seufzend (Ger.). 'Sighing.'

Seul, seule; seuls, seules (Fr. masc., fem. sing.; masc., fem. plur.). 'Alone.'

Ševčik, Ottokar (Josef) (b. Horaž-dowitz, Bohemia, 1852; d. Pisek 1934). Violin teacher. Trained at Prague Conserv. and then appeared as solo violinist and as leader of orchs. Joined successively staffs of Kieff Conserv., that of Prague, and that of Vienna; Kubelik his 1st famous pupil (1892–8); many others followed. Method of study (publ.) most minutely detailed.

Seven Last Words. The last 7 utterances of Christ, drawn from the gospels. The texts of Passion Music (q.v.) have sometimes been based on these, as, especially, that of Haydn (1785). This was commissioned for the Cathedral of Cadiz, for use on Good Friday, and was publ. in Vienna as *7 sonate, con un' introduzione, ed al fine un terremoto* ('7 sonatas, with an introduction, and at the end an earthquake'), and had 3 opus numbers; op. 47 is its original form for orch.; op. 48 for strings; and op. 49 for harpsichord or piano (other opus nos. sometimes attached). After each of the Seven Words (given by Haydn to a bass in recitative) would come the bishop's commentary and exhortation, and then, whilst he prostrated himself at the altar, the appropriate 'Sonata' would be played: in fact the music was a series of 7 intermezzi in a sermon. Later the composer turned the whole into a cantata (publ. 1801).

Other settings of the Seven Words include those of Schütz (perf. about 1645; 1st printed 1873) and Gounod.

Seven Sonnets of Michelangelo. By Britten, for Tenor and Piano (1942).

Seventeenth. Organ mutation stop (see *Mutation*); length and pitch 1⅗ foot, sounding 2 octaves and a third (i.e. 17th) above normal.

Seventh. See *Interval*.

Sévérac, (Joseph Marie) Déodat de (b. in Haute-Garonne 1873; d. in Pyrenees 1921). Studied under d'Indy at Schola Cantorum and then composed symphonic poems, chamber music, songs, piano pieces, &c.—of fresh and original character.

Severn Suite. For Brass Band. By Elgar (op. 87), written for the Crystal Palace Brass Band Fest. of 1930. Orch. arrangement by the composer, Worcester Fest. 1932.

Severo; severamente (It.). 'Severe'; 'severely'. Hence *severità*, 'severity'.

Sevillana. The Seville type of the seguidilla (q.v.).

Sext. The 5th of the Canonical Hours (see *Divine Office*) of the Roman Catholic Church. Properly it takes place at midday (i.e. the 'sixth hour').

Sextet (Fr. *sextette* or *sextuor*; It. *sestetto*; Ger. *Sextett*). Any body of 6 performers, or any piece of music intended for such.

Sextolet. See Table 11.

Sextuor. See *Sextet*.

Sextuplet. See Table 11.

Seyfried, von. See *Ox Minuet*.

Sf. = *Sforzando, sforzato* (q.v.). So **Sff.** means *sforzatissimo.*

Sfogato (It. 'freely given out'). 'Light and easy in style' (*soprano sfogato* = light soprano voice).

Sfoggiando (It.). 'Flauntingly', 'ostentatiously'.

Sforzando; sforzato (It.). 'Forcing'; 'forced', i.e. strongly accenting a note or chord. The letters *Sf.* are sometimes used in abbreviation. The superlative is *sforzatissimo* (abbreviated, *Sff.*).

Sfp. *Sforzato* (see above) followed immediately by *piano*.

Sfz. = *Sforzando* (q.v.).

Sgambati, Giovanni (b. Rome 1841; there d. 1914). Son of It. father and Eng. mother. Piano pupil of Liszt in Rome; adherent to 'Music of the Future' group of Wagner and Liszt (see *Liszt*) and father of a modern musical movement in Italy; head of the piano section of Liceo Musicale in Rome. Composed much music that at once became highly valued—orch., chamber, church, and piano music, and songs.

Sgambato (It. 'walked off one's legs'). 'In weary style.'

Shacklock, Constance (b. Sherwood, Notts., 1913). Mezzo-contralto. Trained R.A.M. First reputation as concert singer; Covent Garden Opera 1946–56.

Shadwell, Charles Murray Winstanley (b. Dormans Park, Surrey, 1898). Conductor. At various times musical director of Portsmouth, Brighton, and Coventry Hippodromes. Musical director B.B.C. Variety Orch. 1936–46.

Shake or Trill. See Table 16. This is the most important of all the conventional 'Ornaments'. In the 18th c. the vocalist's ability to make a good shake (a 'natural shake') was valued very highly, and instrumental performers are still required to be equally accomplished.

See *Nachschlag*.

Shakespeare, William (b. Croydon 1849; d. London 1931). Tenor and singing teacher of high standing. Trained R.A.M. (later on staff), Leipzig Conserv. (Mendelssohn Scholar), and Milan under Lamperti. Conductor and composer. Author *Plain Words on Singing*.

Shaliapin. See *Chaliapine*.

Shamus O'Brien. Stanford's most successful opera. Libretto based on poem by J. Sheridan Le Fanu. (Prod. London 1896; New York 1897.)

Shanewis, or the Robin Woman. Opera by Cadman. (Prod. New York 1918.)

Shanks (and **Crooks**). See *Acoustics* 7; *Horn Family*; *Trumpet Family*.

Shanty or Chanty (both pronounced 'sh'). Working songs, rhythmically suitable for the accompaniment of various communal seafaring activities, such as pulling at ropes or pushing the capstan, and serving to secure unanimity of movement. They are sung by a 'shanty man', placed apart, the workers joining in the chorus. The tunes and words are traditional, but a certain amount of extemporization of the latter often occurs, an opportunity thus being afforded for topical allusions.

Shape-note Singing. Same as 'Buckwheat Notation' (q.v.).

Shaporin, Yuri (b. Glukhof, Ukraine, 1887; d. Moscow 1966). Studied at Conserv. of St. Petersburg and after the Revolution became known as composer of music in a traditional idiom, often inspired by Russia's past.

Sharp (♯). (1, Noun) The sign which, placed before a note, raises its pitch by a semitone. See Table 6. (There is a slight difference of usage in the language of Britain and the U.S.A.—in the former 'to sharpen' and 'sharpened'; in the latter 'to sharp' and 'sharped'.) (2, Adj.) Sharp singing or playing is such as departs from correct intonation, on the upward side.

Sharp, (1) **Cecil James** (b. London 1859; there d. 1924). Educated at Cambridge (B.Mus.) and then went to Australia; organist Adelaide Cathedral 1889–92; on return became principal of Hampstead Conserv., London (1896–1905). Then gave himself to collection, publication, and perf. of Eng. folk songs and folk dances, accomplishing more than any other person in salvage of this national heritage; travelled in eastern U.S.A., collecting tunes amongst descendants of Eng. settlers in Appalachians. Latterly enjoyed small govt. pension in recognition of work. Cecil Sharp House, London, built 1930 (Eng. Folk Dance and Song Soc., q.v.) as memorial and centre for carrying on his work.

(2) **Geoffrey.** See *Music Review.*

Sharpe, Cedric (b. London 1891). Violoncellist. Trained R.C.M. Later on staff of R.A.M. Principal 'cellist in London Symphony Orch., &c. Composer of songs, orch. music, &c.

Sharp Mixture. Organ *Mixture stop* (q.v.) of high-pitched pipes and bright tone.

Shaw, (1) **George Bernard** (b. Dublin 1856; d. Welwyn, Herts., 1950). Dramatist, socialist writer, &c. Music critic ('Corno di Bassetto') of London *Star* (1888–9), *World* (1890–4); contributions reprinted 1937 and 1932 respectively.

(2) **Martin (Edward Fallas)** (b. London 1875; d. Southwold, Suffolk, 1958). Trained R.C.M. and held London posts as organist (St. Martin-in-the-Fields 1920–4). One of leaders in movement for better type of church music. Compositions include ballad opera *Mr. Pepys* (Hampstead 1926), songs, chamber music, choral works, &c. Edited many books of Brit. songs; co-editor with Vaughan Williams of *Songs of Praise* and *Oxford Book of*

Carols. Autobiography 1929. D.Mus., Canterbury, 1932. For brother see below.

(3) **Geoffrey (Turton)** (b. London 1879; there d. 1943). Brother of Martin, above. Main career was as H.M. Inspector of Music in Schools and Training Colleges; also engaged in campaign for better church music, &c. Composed songs, part-songs, and with his brother edited collections of Brit. songs. D.Mus., Canterbury, at same time as brother.

(4) **Harold Watkins** (b. Bradford 1911). Educ. Wadham Coll., Oxford (M.A.), and R.C.M. Apart from educational work (with Hertfordshire County Council, &c.) has specialized in music of Eng. Restoration period; publications in both of these and other fields. Hon. Librarian St. Michael's Coll., Tenbury (cf. *Ouseley*), 1948.

(5) **Robert (Lawson)** (b. Red Bluff, Calif., 1916). Conductor. Educ. Pomona Coll.; founded Collegiate Chorale 1941; Robert Shaw Chorale 1948; assoc. cond. Cleveland Orch. from 1956; Atlanta 1967.

Shawe-Taylor, Desmond Christopher (b. Dublin 1907). Literary and music critic. Scholar Oriel Coll., Oxford. Occasional journalism (*The Times, Spectator,* &c.) before 1939. On staff *New Statesman* 1945–58; then *Sunday Times*; broadcasts, espec. on singing. Books, *Covent Garden* (1948), &c. C.B.E. 1965.

Shawm. See *Oboe Family.*

Shebalin, Vissarion (b. Omsk, 1902; d. Moscow 1963). Studied under Miaskovsky at the Moscow Conserv., of which he became director. Composed chamber music, a number of symphonies (including one choral), concertos, and operas.

Sheep may safely graze (Bach). See *Schafe können sicher weiden.*

Sheherazade. (1) Symphonic Suite by RIMSKY-KORSAKOF (op. 35, 1888). On *Arabian Nights* stories. The Ballet treatment of Diaghilef (1910) does not follow the programme outlined by the composer in his section-titles. (2) Overture by RAVEL (1898). (3) Cycle of 3 songs by RAVEL (1903), poems by 'Tristan Klingsor'.

Shepherd, (1) **John** (1st half of 16th c.). Orgst. Magdalen Coll., Oxford, 1542. Some church mus. compositions.

(2) **Arthur** (b. Paris, Idaho, 1880; d. Cleveland 1958). Pupil of Chadwick, &c., at New England Conserv.; then in Salt Lake City (1897–1908); at New England Conserv. as prof. of harmony, &c. (to 1920); Asst. Conductor Cleveland Symphony Orch. 1920–6; Prof. of Music Western Reserve Univ. Composer of orch. music, choral works, piano music, &c., also critic.

Shepherd Boy Étude, for Piano. Chopin's op. 25, no. 1, in A flat. Not so entitled by the composer, the nickname arising from his statement, however, that he had imagined a little shepherd taking refuge from a storm and playing a melody on his flute.

Shepherd Fennel's Dance. Orch. piece by Balfour Gardiner (1910), based on Thomas Hardy's story *The Three Strangers* (in *Wessex Tales*).

Shepherds of the Delectable Mountains, The. 1-act 'Pastoral Episode' or short opera (prod. London 1922), by Vaughan Williams. Incorporated in *Pilgrim's Progress* (q.v.).

Shera, Frank Henry (b. Sheffield 1882; there d. 1956). Studied R.C.M. and Cambridge (M.A., Mus.M.); classical master various schools; Director of Music Malvern Coll. 1916–28. Prof. of Music Sheffield Univ. (1928–48) (also Dean of Faculty of Arts 1933–6 and Public Orator 1934–6). Compositions include orch. and chamber music, songs, &c.; books on music.

Sheridan, Margaret (b. Castlebar, Co. Mayo, 1889; d. Dublin 1958). Operatic soprano. Trained R.A.M. and Italy, where appeared at La Scala, Milan—as often in later years. Covent Garden début 1919.

Sherman, Alec (b. London 1907). Conductor. First joined B.B.C. Orch. as violinist; began conducting 1938. Founded New London Orch. (1941), which (from 1945) gave weekly Sunday concerts at Cambridge Theatre. Co-conductor Sadler's Wells Ballet Co. 1943–5. Has also conducted abroad. Wife is Gina Bachauer.

Sherrington. See *Lemmens-Sherrington.*

She wandered down the mountain side. See *Clay.*

Shield, William (b. Whickham, Durham, 1748; d. London 1829). Boat builder's apprentice; studied music under Avison (q.v.); in orch. of It. Opera, London, as chief viola player (1773–91); Master of King's Musick 1817. Composed operas and much other theatre music, and songs (e.g. *The Thorn* and *The Wolf*), chamber music, &c., and wrote books on harmony.

See *Arethusa*; *Auld Lang Syne*; *Robin Hood.*

Shimmy. A dance of U.S. origin, popular about 1920. It was in a simple duple ragtime (see *Ragtime*).

Shingandi. Ballet Suite of primitive African flavour for 2 Pianos by Guion.

Shinn, Frederick George (b. London 1867; d. there 1950). Organist, &c. Trained R.C.M. On staff R.A.M. Long Hon. Sec. R.C.O. A pioneer in Ear-training and Memory-training, publishing useful books on these subjects.

Shinner, Emily—Mrs. Liddell (b. Cheltenham 1862; d. London 1901). Violinist. Pupil of Joachim. Prominent soloist and founder of Shinner Quartet of women players—the first such to appear in public in Britain.

Shivaree. This word is an Amer. corruption of 'Charivari' (q.v.).

Shock of the Glottis. See *Voice 4.*

Shofar (or **Shophar**). The ancient synagogue horn of the Jews.

Shop Ballad. See *Ballad.*

Shophar. See *Shofar.*

Shore, (1) **Samuel Royle** (b. Birmingham 1856; d. Hindhead 1946). Anglican organist. Authority on plainsong, Tudor church music, &c.

(2) **Bernard Alexander Royle** (b. 1896). Viola player. Trained R.C.M. and under Tertis. Quickly took high place as orch. and chamber music player, and soloist. Chief inspector of music to Brit. Board of Education; Director, Rural Music Schools Assn. (1948–59). Author of *The Orchestra*

Speaks (1938) and composer. C.B.E. 1955.

Short, Horace. See *Auxetophone.*

Short Metre. See *Hymns and Hymn Tunes* 8.

Short Octave and Broken Octave. These were devices for avoiding expenditure on the lowest and biggest (and consequently most costly) pipes of the organ, and as they were adopted also in the domestic keyboard instruments, virginals, spinet, and clavichord, the economic motive (though less weighty) probably operated in their case also.

(1) Where the SHORT OCTAVE device was adopted the lowest 8ve included only 9 notes instead of 13 (C, D, E, F, G, A, B flat, B, and C) and these were distributed over 6 long finger-keys and 3 short ones, the omitted notes being those which in the days previous to equal temperament (see *Temperament*) were not very likely to be needed in the bass.

(2) Where the BROKEN OCTAVE device was adopted the arrangement was generally the following or something like it. The lowest 8ve was complete from C to C, except that the lowest C sharp was replaced by a more useful note, the A from below. This device was still to be seen in some Eng. organs at the beginning of the 19th c.

For more detailed information see *OCM.*

Short Score. See *Score* 4.

Short Service. See under *Service.*

Shostakovich, Dmitri (b. St. Petersburg 1906). Studied under Glazunof and others at Conservatory of native city; then composed symphonies (7th, dedicated to 'ordinary Soviet heroes' of war, performed in Russia, Britain, and U.S.A., 1942), operas (see *Lady Macbeth of Mtsensk*), piano music, &c. Spoken of for a time as 'composer-laureate of Soviet state', but suffered temporary eclipse, as 'bourgeois in temperament' (1936).

See also *First of May*; *Leningrad Symphony*; *October Symphony*.

Shropshire Lad, A. Poems by Housman, many of which have been set by Brit. composers, e.g. G. Butterworth, who composed his orch. piece *A Shropshire Lad*, as epilogue to his setting of a group of them.

See *On Wenlock Edge.*

Showboat. See *Kern, Jerome.*

Shuard, Amy (b. London 1924). Dramatic soprano. Trained T.C.L. Sadler's Wells Opera Company.

Shudi, Burkat, or Tschudi, Burkhardt (b. Canton Glarus, Switzerland, 1702; d. London 1773). Came to England 1718 as joiner, estd. as harpsichord maker in London abt. 1728 and won highest fame for excellence of his instruments. The original Broadwood was his son-in-law and successor and the present-day Broadwood piano firm carries on the tradition.

Si (1) (It.). The mark of a reflexive verb, e.g. *si replica*, 'it repeats itself'; *si segue*, 'it follows on'; *si tace*, 'it keeps silence' (i.e. silence is to be kept), and so on.

(2) The 7th degree of the major scale, according to the system of vocal syllables derived from Guido d'Arezzo (see *Hexachord*). In Tonic Sol-fa (q.v.) it has for a certain convenience been changed to *Te*. In many countries, however, 'Si' has become attached (on 'fixed-doh' principles; see *Sight-Singing*) to the note B, in whatever key this may occur (see Table 5).

Sibelius, Jean (b. Tavastehus, Finland, 1865; d. Järvenpää 1957). Studied in Helsinki, Berlin, and Vienna; from 32 govt. life pension enabled him to devote himself to composition. Music expresses austerity and beauty of a land of long winter and short brilliant summer, also influenced by racial legend as found in national epic *Kalevala*. Works include 7 symphonies, tone-poems, violin concerto, over 100 songs, &c.; very individual style in themes and their treatment, and in orchestration.

See also *Bantock Society*; *En Saga*; *Everyman*; *Finlandia*; *Kajanus*; *Karelia*; *Kullervo*; *Lemminkäinen*; *Oceanides*; *Pelléas et Mélisande*; *Pohjola's Daughter*; *Scènes historiques*; *Tapiola*; *Tempest*; *Valse triste*; *Voces intimae.*

Sibyl. This 'Welsh air' is in reality a 'Cibel' (or 'Cebell', q.v.) in *Bremner's Harpsichord and Spinnet Miscellany* (Edinburgh, 1761). It appeared complete, treble and bass, in Jones's *Relicks of the Welsh Bards* (1784 and 1794), with the changed spelling of the title.

Sich (Ger.). 'Oneself', 'himself', 'herself', 'itself', 'themselves'.

Siciliano (It.), **Sicilienne** (Fr.). 'Sicilian'; hence an old dance type, presumably of Sicilian origin, in compound duple or quadruple time and with a swaying rhythm; often in the minor and generally in ternary form. So *alla siciliana*, 'in the Sicilian style', or 'in the style of the Siciliano'. (The *Pastorale* and *Gondoliera* are much the same.)

Side drum. See *Percussion Family* 2 i.

Sieben (Ger.). 'Seven.'

Sieg (Ger.). 'Victory.' So several compounds such as *Siegesmarsch*, a march celebrating victory.

Siege of Corinth, The. Opera by Rossini. (Prod. Naples 1820 as *Maometto II*; then with new libretto and title, Paris 1826, London 1834, New York 1835).

Siege of Rhodes. Earliest opera performed in England (1656), composed by Henry Lawes, Henry Cooke, Matthew Locke, Charles Coleman, and George Hudson. Libretto by Davenant. Music now lost.

Siegfried (Wagner). See *Ring des Nibelungen*.

Siegfried Idyll. Piece for Small Orch. by Wagner, composed 1870. 1st perf. in his Villa at Triebschen (Lake Lucerne) on the Christmas morning following the birth of his son Siegfried. All but one of the themes come from *Siegfried* and *The Valkyrie*. The original title was *Triebschen Idyll*.

Siegmeister, Élie (b. New York 1909). Studied at Columbia Univ., École Normale de Musique, Paris, and Juilliard School; then became known as collector and arranger of Amer. folk music and composer of orch. and stage music inspired by Amer. themes.

Siepi, Cesare (b. Milan 1923). Operatic bass. Début Venice 1941; La Scala 1946; international career from 1950; from 1951, principal bass, Metropolitan Opera.

Siesta. By Walton. For Orch. (1926).

Sifflöte (Ger.). 'Whistle-flute'—a high-pitched organ stop (2 ft. or 1 ft.).

Sight-singing. In early days there was no sight-singing, since there was no notation. The traditional plainsong of the churches was learnt by ear and so passed down from generation to generation. When notation began it was so rudimentary that, whilst enough to remind a singer which piece of memorized music was to be performed, it could do little more. Definite sight-singing study and practice began, apparently, in the early 11th c., with the monk, Guido d'Arezzo. His system was based on recurring groups of notes, with the tones and semitones falling in the same order every time (see *Hexachord*): this makes it the logical ancestor of the 'movable-doh' system of today (see *Tonic Sol-fa*). When in the 16th and 17th cs. this system broke down it was followed by one in which the alphabetical names of the notes were the guide to the singer. In this system if Guido's syllables were also used they were generally mere singable substitutes for the letters and were attached to fixed notes (C = ut; D = re; E = mi, &c.): such systems are the ancestors of the 'fixed-doh' systems of today, in which the singer depends on his sense of Absolute Pitch (q.v.), if he, happily, possesses such, or rapidly calculates his leaps and steps from note to note by identification of the intervals they represent. (For a curious system current in England throughout the 17th and 18th cs. and still current in the southern U.S.A., see *Lancashire Sol-fa*.) Roughly speaking, the English-speaking countries of the world now tend to use movable-doh systems and other civilized countries fixed-doh systems, but there are exceptions to the latter (e.g. see *Galin-Paris-Chevé*). A disadvantage of all fixed-doh systems is the progressive difficulty as the keys take on more sharps or flats: in movable-doh systems, on the other hand, all keys are equally easy.

So far we have considered sight-singing merely on the side of pitch, and the side of rhythm now demands a word. Roughly speaking movable-doh systems, as they regard the key and its degrees, i.e. the *relative* values in pitch, rather than the absolute values (A, B, C, &c.), so do they regard the measure (bar) and the pulse (beat), i.e. the *relative* values of time, rather than the absolute values, as semibreve, minim, &c.

The class teaching of sight-singing (which usually suffers from the neglect of a number of elementary considerations) is discussed in the *OCM*, to which the teacher-reader of the present book must be referred: the history of the remarkably enthusiastic Brit. movement for the teaching of sight-singing which began in the 1840's (Mainzer, Hullah, Curwen, &c.) is told in *The Mirror of Music 1844–1944*.

See *Hullah*; *Mainzer*; *Tonic Sol-fa*.

Signal Horn. Bugle (q.v.).

Signature. A 'sign' placed at the opening of a composition or of a section of a composition, indicating the key ('Key Signature') or the value of the beat and the number of beats in each measure ('Time Signature'). The 'Key Signature' consists of one or more sharps or flats (see Table 8), the 'Time Signature' usually of figures resembling a fraction (see Table 10).

Signature Tune. This is a term dating from the 1920's when dance bands enjoyed enormous favour. It became the custom (when broadcasting, at all events) for each band to pick a popular tune with which to 'sign' its work, this tune being played at the end of every perf. (sometimes at the beginning, too). 'Concert Parties', &c., use the same device. (Cf. *Wait* for an apparently similar practice in the 16th and 17th cs.)

Sigurd. See *Reyer*.

Sigurd Jorsalfar ('Sigurd the Crusader'). Three Orch. pieces by Grieg, written for a perf. of Björnson's play at Christiania, to celebrate the dramatist's 70th birthday.

Silas, Édouard (b. Amsterdam 1827; d. London 1909). Studied at Paris Conserv.; fine pianist and organist; settled in London 1850. Composed orch. and choral works (oratorio *Joash*, Norwich Fest. 1863), a mass, piano and organ music, &c.

Silbermann. See *Pianoforte*.

Silent Woman, The (R. Strauss). See *Schweigsame Frau, Die*.

Silenzio (It.). 'Silence.'

Silk, Dorothy (b. nr. Birmingham 1884; d. Alvechurch 1942). Soprano vocalist. Studied in Vienna. Publicly prominent only from her mid-thirties; very much valued for high artistic standards and choice repertory.

Silken Ladder (Rossini). See *Scala di seta*.

Siloti, Alexander (b. nr. Charkov 1863; d. New York 1945). Pianist. Studied Moscow Conserv. (afterwards on staff) and under Liszt. Won high international reputation. Conducted own orch. St. Petersburg. After Russian revolution settled New York, teaching at Juilliard School 1924–42.

Silver Band. A 'Brass Band' of which the instruments are (or are reputed to be) of silver.

Silvestri, Constantin (b. Bucharest 1913; d. London 1969). Appeared as piano prodigy; aged 11. Cond. Bucharest radio 1930; Opera 1935; Bournemouth Symphony Orchestra 1961.

Similar Motion. See *Motion*.

Simile, simili (It. sing., plur.). 'Similar.' Some direction having been given, the composer avoids the necessity for constant repetition of it by thus intimating that its effect is to continue.

Simionato, Giulietta (b. Forlì 1910). Mezzo-soprano. Début Florence 1933; small parts at Milan from 1940; then appeared Edinburgh 1947; Metropolitan 1949; Covent Garden 1952; in wide variety of mezzo roles. Retired 1966.

Simoneau, Leopold (b. Quebec 1918). Lyric operatic tenor. Trained Laval Univ. International career: Paris Opera 1949; La Scala 1953. Many recordings.

Simone Boccanegra. Opera by Verdi. Libretto by Piave, later revised by Boito; after Guttiérrez. (Prod. Venice 1857; revised version at Milan 1881; 1st perf. in England, Sadler's Wells, 1948.)

Simon the Cellarer. See *Hatton*.

Simple Aveu. See *Thomé*.

Simple Binary. See *Form 1*.

Simple Duple. See Table 10.

Simplement (Fr.). 'Simply', 'in a simple manner'.

Simple Quadruple, Simple Triple. See Table 10.

Simple Ternary. See *Form 2*.

Simpson (or **Sympson**), **Christopher** (b. Yorkshire abt. 1610; d. 1669). Famous player of viola da gamba, and author of important treatises (e.g. *The Division Violist*, 1659 and later edns.; *Principles of Practical Musick*, 1665 and 8 later edns.); composed string music (mostly unpublished).

Sin' (It.). Abbreviation of *sino*, 'until', e.g. *sin' al segno*, 'until the sign'.

Sinding, Christian (b. Kongsberg, Norway, 1856; d. Oslo 1941). Studied in Christiania (now Oslo); sent by govt. to Leipzig Conserv., Dresden, Munich, and Berlin; from 1890 granted pension by govt. so as to devote time to composition; taught composition at Eastman School of Music, Rochester, N.Y., 1921–2, then again in Oslo. Composed 2 violin concertos and piano concerto, 3 symphonies, chamber music, violin music, piano music, choral music, more than 200 songs, &c. A nationalist-romantic in feeling.

See *Rustle of Spring*.

Sinfonia da Requiem. By Britten. Three-movement symphony on an elegiac theme. (1st perf. New York 1941; London 1942.)

Sinfonia Eroica (Beethoven). See *Eroica*.

Sinfonico, sinfonica (It. masc., fem.). 'Symphonic.'

Sinfonietta (It.). A symphony on smaller scale—smaller as to length, or as to orch. forces employed, or as to both.

Singbar (Ger.). 'Singable' or 'in a singing style'.

Singend (Ger.). 'Singing' (cf. *Cantabile*).

Singet dem Herrn (Bach). See under *Motet*.

Singhiozzando (It.). 'Sobbingly.'

Singing. The development of the technique of the use of the voice in song is largely due to Italy, whose language (with its wealth of pure un-diphthongic vowels and absence of final consonants) makes it particularly suitable for song, and whose position from the 4th c. as the headquarters of the Western Church and from the early 17th as that of the cultivation of opera and oratorio have encouraged interest in the subject. From the latter period the art of song, both as a means of dramatic expression and as one of lyrical or florid expression in beautiful tone (*Bel Canto*), was greatly cultivated and It. singers were much in demand all over Europe. The 18th-c. It. singing masters enjoyed high fame. With the change in the requirements of the opera house that came in with the more definitely dramatic demands of 19th-c. composers such as Meyerbeer, Wagner, and Verdi, there occurred some decay in the Bel Canto school of song, and, of course, a high fidelity in poetical interpretation was one of the chief demands of the German 'Lieder' school (Schubert, Schumann, Wolf, &c.).

There is a consensus of opinion that during the 20th c. there has been some general decline in standard as regards both quality of tone and technical skill in the use of the voice.

See also *Voice*.

Singing by note. See *Hymns and Hymn Tunes* 7.

Singing Saw. An ordinary hand saw held between the player's knees and played on by a violin bow (or, more rarely, struck with a drumstick); its blade is meanwhile bent, under a lesser or greater tension, by the player's left hand, so producing the different pitches.

Single Chants. See *Anglican Chant*.

Single tonguing. See *Tonguing*.

Singspiel (Ger. 'sing-play') is practically the Ger. equivalent of 'English Opera' (see *Opera* 5), i.e. it has spoken dialogue with interpolated songs. It had a great vogue in Germany in the 2nd half of the 18th c. as the result of the successful perf. (Leipzig, 1764) of the Englishman Coffey's ballad opera, *The Devil to Pay* (q.v.). A very prolific composer of works of this class was J. A. Hiller (1728–1804).

Mozart on the title-page of his *The Seraglio* calls it a 'Singspiel', and this would entitle us to apply the term widely, e.g. to Beethoven's *Fidelio* and nearly all

Weber's operas; but it is better to restrict its application to works of a simpler type than these.

Sing ye to the Lord (Bach). See under *Motet*.

Sinigaglia, Leone (b. Turin 1868; there d. 1944). It. composer who ignored attractions of stage, composing orch., choral, and chamber music, piano pieces, songs, &c.

Sinistra (It.). 'Left' (hand).

Sink-a-pace. See *Pavan and Galliard*.

Sino, Sin' (It.). 'Until', e.g. *Sin' al segno* = '[Go on] until the sign'.

Sinus. An anatomical recess or cavity, such as those which are situated above the nose and communicate with it by small orifices (these are valuable as resonators for the voice, q.v.).

Sir Alexr. Don's Strathspey. See *Auld Lang Syne*.

Sir John in Love. 4-act opera by Vaughan Williams, based on *The Merry Wives of Windsor*. (Prod. London 1929.) See *In Windsor Forest*.

Sir Roger de Coverley. This is an old Eng. dance (see *Country Dance*), long used as the finale for a ball, and still in use. The tune is a variant of the Scottish one of *The Maltman*, sometimes also called *Roger the Cavalier*, but it is not proved that this is of actual Scottish origin. In Virginia the same tune used to be (perhaps still is) known as *My Aunt Margery* and the dance is said to be the same as the 'Virginia Reel'.

Sister Angelica (Puccini). See under *Trittico*.

Sistrum. A sort of tinkling instrument (rings on a metal frame with a handle by which to shake it) used by many ancient nations and occasionally revived by 19th-c. composers.

Sitt, Hans (b. Prague 1850; d. Leipzig 1922). Violinist and viola player. On staff Leipzig Conserv. Composer of violin, viola, and 'cello concertos, violin studies, &c.

Sivigliano, sivigliana (It. masc., fem.). 'In the style of Seville.'

Sivori, Ernesto Camillo (b. Genoa 1815; there d. 1894). Violinist. Pupil of Paganini. Début Turin and Paris 1827;

London 1828. Very popular with Brit. audiences and made world tours. Composed violin concertos, &c.

Sivrai, Jules de. See *Roeckel, Jane*.

Six (Fr.). 'Six'; hence *Sixième*, 'Sixth'.

Six, The. Name given to a temporarily associated group of Paris composers of the earlier 20th c.—Durey, Honegger, Milhaud, Tailleferre, Auric, Poulenc.

Six épigraphes antiques ('Six Ancient Inscriptions'). Set of Piano Duets by Debussy (1914). (1) *To invoke Pan*; *God of the Summer Wind*; (2) *For a Nameless Tomb*; (3) *That Night may be propitious*; (4) *For the Dancing Girl with the Castanets*; (5) *For the Egyptian Woman*; (6) *To thank the Morning Rain.*

Six-four-time Mass (Haydn). See *Sechsviertelmesse*.

Sixteenth-note. 'Semiquaver' (see Table 3).

Sixth. See *Interval*.

Sixty-fourth-note. Hemidemisemiquaver (see Table 3).

Sizzle Cymbal. Much like the normal cymbal (see *Percussion Family* 2 o) with 5 or 6 small jingles ('sizzlers') lying on its upper surface, to which they are loosely attached. It is played with a special kind of snare drumstick. The dance band is its home.

Sjögren, (Johann Gustav) Emil (b. Stockholm 1853; there d. 1918). Studied in Stockholm and Berlin, and became organist in former. Composed prolifically for solo voice, choirs, organ, piano, and violin. Romantic-nationalist in feeling.

Skalkottas, Nikos (b. Chalcis, Greece, 1904; d. Athens 1949). Composer. Studied under Weill and Schönberg, but on return to Greece had difficulty in making his way, his gifts being made known only after his early death. Works include orchestral pieces, concertos, chamber music, and songs, in a style influenced by his teachers but individual none the less.

Sketch (Fr. *Esquisse*; Ger. *Skizze*). (1) A brief, slight instrumental composition, usually for piano. (2) A composer's rough draft of a composition or of some part of it, e.g. we speak of

Beethoven's 'Sketch Books'—in which he stored up musical ideas of which he intended later to make use.

Skizze, Skizzen (Ger.). 'Sketch', 'sketches'.

Skrowaczewski, Stanislav (b. Lvov 1923). Conductor. Pupil of N. Boulanger, &c. Warsaw Philharmonic Orch. 1946; Cracow Philharmonic 1955; Minneapolis 1962.

Skye Boat Song. One half of the tune is a sea-shanty heard in 1879 by Miss Annie MacLeod (later Lady Wilson) when going by boat from Toran to Loch Coruisk; the other half is by Miss MacLeod herself. The words, by Sir Harold Boulton, Bt., date from 1884. Later some other words were written to the tune by Robert Louis Stevenson and a confusion has thus originated.

Skyscrapers. Ballet by J. A. Carpenter. (Prod. Monte Carlo 1925; New York 1926; Munich 1928.)

Sladen, Victoria (b. London 1910). Soprano. Trained Berlin, Vienna, London. With Sadler's Wells 1943–7; then Covent Garden. Recitalist, soloist with Brit. orchs. and choral societies, &c.

Slancio (It.). 'Impetus', 'outburst', i.e. impetuosity.

Slargando, slargandosi (It.). 'Slowing up', i.e. *rallentando*.

Slater, Edward. See *Barri*.

Slavonic Dances. By Dvořák. Sixteen in number; originally for Piano Duet (1–8, op. 46, 1878; 9–16, op. 72, 1886); orch. arr. by the composer.

Slavonic Rhapsodies. By Dvořák. Three in number (op. 45, 1879).

Sleeping Princess, The ('La Belle au bois dormant'). Ballet by Tchaikovsky. (Prod. St. Petersburg 1890; version retouched by Stravinsky, London 1921.) Last act often separately performed as *Aurora's Wedding*.

Slegato (It.). 'Un-legato' (see *Legato*).

Slentando (It., from *lento*, 'slow'). 'Slowing', i.e. the same as *rallentando*.

Slider. See *Organ* 1.

Slide Trumpet. See *Trumpet Family*.

Slobodskaya, Oda (b. Vilno 1895; d. London 1970). Operatic and concert soprano. Trained Petrograd Conserv. Extended tours both sides Atlantic, specializing in Russian opera and songs. Created role of Prasha in Stravinsky's *Mavra* (q.v.), Paris 1922.

Slonimsky, Nicolas (b. Petrograd 1894). Studied at the conserv. of his native city and in 1923 went to U.S.A. as member of staff of Eastman School of Music, Rochester, N.Y.; later in Boston and Calif.; active as conductor, journalist, editor, and author, and as composer. Authority on dates of birth and death of musicians. Ed. 5th edn. Baker's *Dictionary*, &c.; contributor to Grove, &c.

Sloper, Lindsay—in full Edward Hugh Lindsay Sloper (b. London 1826; d. 1887). Pianist and composer. Pupil of Moscheles, &c. London début 1846. Fecund and popular provider of music for 19th-c. drawing-room pianos.

Slug-horn (Browning), **Slughorne** (Chatterton). No musical instrument of this name exists, poets with a taste for the archaic having apparently been misled by the old Scottish Border word 'sloggorn' ('slogan' = battle cry).

Slur. The curved line in musical notation, of which the various applications are shown in Tables 22 and 23. (See also *Phrase Marks*.)

Small Cornett. See *Cornett and Key Bugle Families*.

Smallens, Alexander (b. St. Petersburg 1889). Taken to U.S.A. 1890; naturalized 1919. Trained New York Inst. Musical Art (1905–9), and Paris Conserv. (1909–11). Opera conductor Boston 1911, Chicago 1919–22, Berlin and Madrid 1923, Philadelphia 1923–30; from 1931 conductor Robin Hood Dell (q.v.). Musical director Philadelphia Civic Opera 1924–30; International Ballet 1944; also radio activities.

Smania (It.). 'Craze', 'frenzy'. So the adj. *smaniato* and *smanioso* and the adverb *smaniante*.

Smareglia, Antonio (b. Pola, Istria, 1854; d. Trieste 1929). Trained at Milan Conserv.; at 25 appeared as opera composer and brought out in all 9 operas (Wagnerian in style)—popular both in Italy and Germany.

Smart Family. In larger books of reference 6 members, in 6 generations, are mentioned; only the 2 chief members can be included here.

(1) **George Thomas** (b. London 1776; there d. 1867). Chorister at Chapel Royal, of which he was later one of the organists; became noted conductor, in charge of music at all chief festivals; when in Dublin knighted by Lord Lieutenant of Ireland (1811). Visited Beethoven in Vienna; Weber died at his house in London. For nephew see below. (2) **Henry Thomas** (b. London 1813; there d. 1879). Nephew of Sir George Smart, above. Organist at Blackburn, Lancs. (1831–6); then at important churches in London (St. Pancras 1864 to death); particularly noted for extemporization. Blind for last 15 years of life but fully continued activities. Composed festival choral-orchestral works, part-songs, and effective organ music.

Smetana, Bedřich or **Frederick** (b. Litomyšl, otherwise Leitomischl, Bohemia, 1824; d. Prague 1884). Played in a Haydn String Quartet at age 5 and early showed remarkable skill as pianist; estd. himself as teacher in Prague; encouraged by Liszt; conductor in Gothenburg, Sweden (1856–61), then again in Prague; connected with National Theatre founded 1862, and its chief conductor from 1866; suffered from a nervous disorder (constantly hearing a high note sounding) and resigned position 1874, then suddenly became totally deaf; died in a mental asylum.

Compositions include operas (see *Bartered Bride*; *Dalibor*), symphonic poems on national subjects (see *My Fatherland*), choral music, piano pieces, chamber music (including 2 string quartets, 1876 and 1882, *From my Life*—the second with high note representing malady above-mentioned), and songs. Strongly romantic and nationalist in feeling—'the Father of Bohemian Music'.

Smeterlin, Jan (b. Bielsko, Poland, 1892; d. London 1967). Pianist. Trained Vienna; pupil of Godowsky.

International repute as recitalist. Became British subject.

Sminuendo; sminuito (It.). 'Diminishing'; 'diminished' (in power), i.e. *diminuendo*.

Smith, (1) **'Father'**, really Bernhard Schmidt (b. Germany abt. 1630; d. London 1708). Came to England on Restoration of monarchy and of Anglican Church (with renewal of use of organ), 1660. Built important instruments (St. Paul's Cathedral, Temple Church, Sheldonian Theatre, Oxford, &c.).

(2) **John Stafford** (b. Gloucester 1750; d. London 1836). Son of organist of Gloucester Cathedral and choir-boy of Chapel Royal, London, of which later organist; had high reputation as tenor singer, organist, antiquary, and composer of glees, catches, anthems, &c. (The music of his song *Anacreon in Heaven* was taken as that for *The Star-spangled Banner*, q.v.)

(3) **Theodore** (date unknown). Eng. pianist and composer who seems to have lived in Germany as some works were publ. there. Dates of his publications range from abt. 1770 to abt. 1810.

(4) **Alfred Montem** (b. Windsor 1828; d. London 1891). Tenor. In choirs Westminster Abbey and Chapel Royal. Popular in oratorio and ballads. On staff R.A.M. and G.S.M. Composer of songs and glees.

(5) **(Edward) Sydney** (b. Dorchester 1839; d. London 1889). Noted pianist and piano teacher in London; composed light and lively drawing-room piano music, at one time enormously popular.

(6) **Alice Mary** (b. London 1839; there d. 1884). Well-known composer of orch., chamber, and large-scale choral works, now remembered by a few songs (married name Meadows White).

(7) **David Stanley** (b. Toledo, Ohio, 1877; d. New Haven, Conn., 1949). Studied under Horatio Parker at Yale (B.A., B.Mus.) and then at Munich and Paris; instructor in music theory, Yale; Prof. of Music 1916; Dean of School of Music 1920–40; known as orch. conductor. Hon. D.Mus., Northwestern Univ., &c. Composer of orch. and chamber works, songs, &c.

(8) **William Charles** (b. London 1881; d. Kent 1972). Brit. Museum Music Dept. 1901–44 (chief charge from 1920). Specializes in Handel research and possesses large Handelian collection. Books on Handel and on the 18th-c. music publisher, Walsh.

(9) **Joseph Dale** (b. Stockport 1893). Baritone vocalist. Trained Royal Manchester Coll. of Music and in Leipzig. Broadcaster, recitalist, &c., specially interested in interpretation of old Eng. music and folk songs. Also educational work, lecturer, competition adjudicator, &c.

(10) **Carleton Sprague** (b. New York 1905). Leading Amer. musicologist. Educ. Harvard (M.A.). Varied activities as critic, librarian, radio commentator, flautist, &c. Pres. Amer. Musicological Soc. (1938). 1931–59, in charge of important Music Dept. of New York Public Library. Dir. Nat. Art Foun., New York. D.Phil., Vienna.

(11) **Cyril** (b. Middlesbrough 1909). Pianist. Trained R.C.M. (later on staff). Appeared Queen's Hall Promenade concerts 1929. Married fellow pianist, Phyllis Sellick, and joined her in 2-piano recital tours.

Smoldon, William Lawrence (b. London 1892). Lecturer and writer; trained T.C.M. and London Univ. School-teacher; as author specialist in subjects connected with medieval music.

Smorfioso (It.). 'Mincing', 'affected'.

Smorzando (It.). 'Extinguishing', &c. (abbrev. *Smorz*). Gradually dying away. *Smorzato* is the past participle of the same verb.

Smyth, Ethel Mary (b. Foots Cray, Kent, 1858; d. Woking 1944). Studied at Leipzig Conserv. and then in Berlin; came into notice as composer with Mass (Albert Hall, London, 1893; sole perf. for over 30 years). Operas: *The Forest* ('Der Wald'), *The Wreckers* ('Strandrecht'), *The Boatswain's Mate*; *Fête Galante* (see separate entries under these titles). Also wrote orch. music (concerto for violin and horn, 1927) and a little choral music. A number of entertaining books, largely autobiographical.

In jail 1911 as militant suffragist;

created 'Dame' (feminine equivalent of knighthood) 1922.

Snare Drum. Side Drum (see *Percussion Family* 2 i).

Snegourotchka (Rimsky-Korsakof). See *Snow Maiden*.

Snello; snellamente (It.). 'Nimble'; 'nimbly'.

Snetzler, John. Ger. organ builder who settled London 1740 (cf. *Hill & Son, W.*).

Snow Maiden, The (*Snegourotchka*). Opera by Rimsky-Korsakof. Libretto based on Ostrovsky. (Prod. St. Petersburg 1882; Seattle and New York 1922; London 1933.)

So (Ger.). 'As', 'so'.

Soap Operas. An Amer. name for an Amer. type of radio entertainment— not musical, but merely a sentimental serial story strung out over years of daily development and designed to advertise some product (originally soap). In 1947 it was stated that some examples had already been running 10 years and that the estimated (female) audience for the type was 20,000,000.

Soave; soavità (It.). 'Suave'; 'suavity' (or 'gentle'; 'gentleness'). *Soavemente*, 'suavely'.

Sobald (Ger.). 'So soon as', and similar expressions. Sometimes 'should', in such phrases as 'should [a certain instrument] not be available then [do so-and-so]'.

Société Internationale de Musicologie. See *Musicology*.

Society for the Advancement of Musical Education. Founded in London about 1935 'to encourage the adequate recognition of the cultural and recreational value of music in all its forms'.

Society for the Promotion of New Music. See *Committee for the Promotion*, &c.

Society of British Composers. This Society, whose lifetime was from 1905 to 1918, publ. the works of its members and in other ways promoted their interest (see *Avison Edition*). Its chief founder and chairman was Frederick Corder (q.v.).

Society of College Youths. See *Bell* 3.

Society of Recorder Players. Brit. society, with large membership. Headquarters in London; branches in Manchester, Birmingham, Bristol, &c. Publishes a journal.

Society of St. Gregory. A Brit. Roman Catholic society, founded 1929, 'to help our parish congregations to sing the Ordinary and Responses of the Mass, according to the Pope's express wish and their own aspirations'.

Society of Women Musicians. Founded in London in 1911. It possesses a library, a chamber music section, &c., and carries on a 'Composers' Conference'.

Söderman, August Johann (b. Stockholm 1832; there d. 1876). Trained at Leipzig Conserv.; then attached to opera house of native place as subconductor. Composed operettas, choral music, a mass (of high repute in Sweden), songs, &c. On his death a national subscription for his widow and children; also Swedish govt. publ. many of his works.

Soeben (Ger.). 'Just', in the sense of (1) 'Barely', (2) 'A moment ago'.

Sofort (Ger.). 'Immediately.'

Soft Palate. See *Palate*.

Soggetto (It.). 'Subject', meaning, in a musical sense, the subject of a fugue (see *Form* 7; also *Attacco* and *Andamento*).

Sogleich (Ger.). 'Immediately.'

Soh. See *Sol*.

Soir, Le (Haydn). See under *Matin*.

Sol. The 5th degree of the major scale, according to the system of vocal syllables derived from Guido d'Arezzo (see *Hexachord*), and so used (spelt *Soh*) in Tonic Sol-fa (q.v.). In many countries, however, the name has become attached (on 'fixed-doh' principles; see *Sight-Singing*) to the note G, in whatever key this may occur. (See Table 5; also *Lancashire Sol-fa*.)

Sola (It., fem. of *Solo*). 'Alone.'

Soldat, Marie (b. Graz 1863; there d. 1955). Violinist. Trained Berlin Hochschule, &c., and by Joachim.

Undertook international tours (London début 1888). Formed and led quartets Berlin, then Vienna.

Soldatenzug (Ger.). 'Soldiers' procession.' *Soldatenmarsch*, 'Soldiers' March'.

Soldiers of the Queen. See *Stuart, Leslie*.

Soldier's Tale, The ('L'Histoire du Soldat'). Work by Stravinsky of a semi-operatic and ballet character, 'to be read, played, and danced'. Text by Ramuz. The score provides for 7 players of whom the drummer operates 8 instruments: sometimes heard as concert suite. (Lausanne 1918; London, concert form 1920; New York, concert form 1928; Cambridge, staged 1928.) One version of the Suite is for Clarinet, Violin, and Piano (1918).

Soleá (plur. *Soleares*). A type of folk song in Andalusia (Spain). Its poetry is in a 3-lined stanza, with assonance (agreement of vowels, instead of rhyme) between the 1st and 3rd lines.

Solemnis, Solennis (Lat.). 'Solemn.'

Solenne; solennemente; solennità (It.). 'Solemn'; 'solemnly'; 'solemnity'. **Solennel, solennelle** (Fr. masc., fem.). 'Solemn'; so *solennellement*, 'solemnly'. **Solennis.** See *Solemnis*.

Solesmes. See *Plainsong* 3; *Motu Proprio*.

Sol-fa. See *Tonic Sol-fa*, also *Conducting*.

Solfeggio (It.), **solfège** (Fr.). A type of vocal exercise in which the names of the notes are used throughout (on the continental *fixed-doh* system; see *Sight-Singing*). The object may be either voice exercise or sight-reading exercise.

The plural of *solfeggio* is *solfeggi*. (The Fr. word *solfège* is sometimes used as the equivalent of the Eng. 'rudiments', 'elements', or 'theory' of music, i.e. knowledge of notation, intervals, &c.)

Soli (It.). 'Alone' (plur. of *solo*, but in Eng. 'solos' is now more accepted).

Solito (It.). 'Usual.' So *al solito*, 'as usual'.

Sollecitando (It.). 'Hastening forward.' **Sollecito** (It.). 'Eager.'

Solmization. Singing a passage at sight to the sol-fa syllables in any of the various ways in which they have been used since Guido d'Arezzo introduced them in the 11th c. (Cf. *Hexachord, Tonic Sol-fa, Bocedization.*)

Solo (It.). 'Alone.' This word has now been adopted into most languages. (The plur. in It. is *soli*, in everyday Eng. *solos*.)

Solo Bells. A small Glockenspiel (see *Percussion Family* 1 c) of an easily portable type, used in dance bands, &c.

Solo Klavier (Ger.). Solo Organ (see *Organ* 1).

Solomon. Oratorio by Handel. (1st perf. London 1749.)

Solomon. (orig. Solomon Cutner) (b. London 1902). Pianist. First appearance (Queen's Hall) age 8; from 14 adopted and trained by Mathilde Verne (q.v.); also studied in Paris. Has toured the world. C.B.E. 1946.

Solomon, Izler (b. St. Paul, Minn., 1910). Conductor. Lansing Symphony 1932; Illinois Symphony 1936; Columbus Philharmonic 1941; Indianapolis Symphony 1956.

Solo Organ. See *Organ* 1.

Soltanto (It.). 'Solely.'

Solti, Georg (b. Budapest 1912). Conductor. Pupil of Kodály, Bartók, and Dohnányi. Budapest Opera 1933; in Switzerland 1939; Munich Op. 1947; Frankfurt 1951; Covent Garden 1961–71; Chicago 1969; also London Phil. 1971. Hon. K.B.E. 1971.

Sombre (Fr.). 'Dark', 'melancholy'.

Sombrero de tres picos, El (Falla). See *Three-cornered Hat.*

Somervell, Arthur (b. Windermere 1863; d. London 1937). Studied at Cambridge and at R.C.M.; also at Berlin Hochschule. Composed fest. choral-orch. works, a symphony, &c., chamber music, 5 song-cycles (Tennyson's *Maud*, &c.), and smaller pieces. Chief Inspector of Music to national Board of Education. Knighted 1929.

Sommesso (It.). 'Subdued.'

Sommo, somma (It. masc., fem.). 'Utmost.'

Son; sons (Fr.). 'Sound'; 'sounds'. (*Son* also means 'his', 'her', 'its'.)

Son and Stranger (Ger. title *Die Heimkehr aus der Fremde*, 'The Return from Abroad'). Operetta by Mendelssohn (op. 89, 1829) for family perf. in celebration of his parents' Silver Wedding.

Sonare (It.). 'To sound', i.e. play. So *sonante*, 'sounding', 'resonant'.

Sonata. The word (It.) means simply 'sounded', thus implying an instrumental composition, in distinction from Cantata ('sung').

In the 17th and early 18th cs. (the period when the Sonata was first developing) there were 2 varieties—the *Sonata da camera*, or 'Chamber Sonata', and *Sonata da chiesa*, or 'Church Sonata'. Both were for strings, with a keyboard background, the Chamber type being a chain of pieces in dance rhythms and the Church type a string of movements of a more abstract and serious character. The Chamber Sonata, then, is little distinguishable from the Suite (q.v.).

The earliest sonatas for keyboard instrument alone (i.e. for Harpsichord) are those of Kuhnau, Bach's Leipzig predecessor, dating from 1695 onwards. During the late 18th c. the term 'Sonata' became restricted to compositions for 1 instrument (usually Harpsichord), or for 2 (e.g. Harpsichord and Violin). Further, the dance implication was now lost. Normally such works were (like the *Sonata da Camera* from which they derived) in several movements, but there was a certain looseness in the use of the term, and Domenico Scarlatti's Sonatas (of which over 500 exist) are usually 1-movement works.

The modern Sonata is chiefly the creation of one of J. S. Bach's sons, Carl Philipp Emanuel Bach (1714–88), who wrote 70 such works for Harpsichord. One characteristic is the use in 1 movement or more of what we call 'Sonata Form' or 'Compound Binary Form' (see *Form* 3). In the early Sonatas, as in the Suites, all the movements were in the same key (or, at least, had the same key-signature, some being in the relative minor or major). Haydn, Mozart, and a great many other composers followed C. P. E. Bach, further developing the Sonata. It now became common, and even usual, to bring back the Suite's dance element as regards one of the movements of the Sonata: this was the *Minuet* (q.v.), which at that time was enjoying an immense ballroom vogue throughout Europe. It tended in time to increased brightness and speed and the losing of its true dance character, and was transformed into the *Scherzo* of Beethoven and other composers.

From Beethoven's day the normal movements of the Sonata were as follows: (*a*) A quick extended movement in 'Sonata Form'; (*b*) A slower and more lyrical movement; (*c*) A Minuet or Scherzo, gay in feeling; (*d*) An extended Rondo, or another movement in Sonata Form, rapid and lively. The greatest innovation of Beethoven, however, was the importation of a more dramatic element. Since Beethoven the Sonata form and style have been practised by most of the greater composers, some of them submerging the standard form in a flood of self-expression. Sometimes the whole work has been made continuous (being then spoken of as 'in one movement', which is hardly correct, as both time and tempo may be greatly changed in the various sections).

Throughout nearly 3 centuries the Sonata (like the Symphony, the String Quartet, &c., which are really Sonatas in other media) has been recognized as by far the most important type in instrumental music.

Cf. *Canzona.*

Sonata del diavolo. See *Devil's Trill.*

Sonata Form. See *Form* 3.

Sonata-rondo Form. See *Form* 4.

Sonata sopra Sancta Maria (Monteverdi). See *Vespers* 2.

Sonate (Fr., Ger.). 'Sonata.' The Fr. plur. is *Sonates,* the Ger. plur. *Sonaten.*

Sonate caractéristique, les Adieux, &c. (Beethoven). See *Adieux.*

Sonatina. A term not consistently used, but generally indicating either (1) A short and easy sonata, or (2) A less serious and less developed (but not necessarily easy) sonata.

Sonatine (Fr.). 'Sonatina' (q.v.).

Sonevole (It.). 'Sonorous', 'resonant'.

Song is a natural means of self-expression and although songless species of birds exist no songless people has ever been discovered. Different races tend to develop different song idioms—the use of particular scales, melodic intervals, rhythmic motifs, &c. To some extent these may be the result of chance and fashion but to a considerable degree they seem to express racial temperament.

The development of song amongst European races has been greatly influenced by certain institutions. Thus the CHRISTIAN CHURCH early made use of song, developed it, and from time to time sought to control it as to the scales used and the melodies recognized (see *Modes, Plainsong, Gregorian Tones*). The FEUDAL SYSTEM, with its few great families secure enough to attain a degree of culture, exercised influence through the patronage of minstrels and the movement of the 11th to 13th cs. associated with the names of the Troubadours, Trouvères, and Minnesingers (see *Minstrels*). In the 16th c. the LUTE COMPOSERS of various countries cultivated the art of singing to their instruments (the 1st book of accompanied songs ever publ. is that of the Spanish lutenist Don Luis Milán in 1536; similar books later appeared in other countries, as, for instance, those of the Englishman Dowland, whose 1st one appeared in 1597: a striking characteristic of the Eng. collections of lute songs is the fine poetry they contain). The introduction of OPERA at the opening of the 17th c. had an enormous effect upon the development of song, leading to the devising of new styles and forms (see *Recitative* and *Aria*), and also to a high cultivation of vocal skill, making possible greater elaboration in the style of composition for the voice.

All this while the peasantry had been singing their traditional songs (see *Folk Song*), and in the 18th c. the Eng. BALLAD OPERA (see *Opera* 5) carried their simple melodies on to the stage. The ROMANTIC MOVEMENT of the early 19th c. (see *Romantic*) brought with it the development of the Ger. 'Lied' by

Schubert, Schumann, Brahms, Wolf, and others (see *Lied*). A later 19th-c. development was the 1-artist perf. known as the 'SONG RECITAL'. The big dramatic demands of Wagner had, of course, their influence on the style of song composition.

It must be recognized that the art of song involves a compromise, since musical beauty and poetical or dramatic expressiveness have to be reconciled: in different periods and with different composers the balance between these 2 elements has necessarily greatly varied, but from the mid-19th c. onwards the tendency has been towards close interpretation of the meaning and emotion of the words rather than towards the production of 'tune', satisfying in itself.

Song before Sunrise. By Delius. For Small Orch. (1918).

Song-circle (Schumann). See *Liederkreis*.

Song-cycle. A string of songs of related thought and congruous musical style, thus constituting an entity and being capable of being sung as a series.

Song form. Another name for simple ternary form (see *Form* 2), generally as applied in the more lyrical type of instrumental piece.

Song of Destiny (*Schicksalslied*). Choral setting by Brahms (op. 54, 1871) of parts of a poem of Hölderlin.

Song of Summer, A. Symphonic Poem by Delius.

Song of the Earth (Mahler). See *Lied von der Erde*.

Song of the Fates (*Gesang der Parzen*). Choral Ballad (with Orch.) by Brahms (op. 89, 1882); a setting of Goethe.

Song of the Flea. By Mussorgsky (1879). Setting of Mephistopheles' song in Goethe's *Faust*.

Song of the Haulers of the Volga. Same as *Song of the Volga Boatmen*, q.v.

Song of the High Hills. By Delius. For wordless chorus and orch. (1st perf. London 1920.)

Song of the Volga Boatmen (or *Song of the Haulers of the Volga*, &c.). A

folk song originating amongst the class of men who, walking along the tow path, drag the Volga barges. During the earlier 20th c. it was made widely known by its inclusion in the programmes of the great Russian bass, Chaliapin.

Songs and Dances of Death. By Mussorgsky. Four Songs (1875–7), including his most famous song, *Field-Marshal Death*.

Song School. See *Schola Cantorum*; *Education and Music* 1.

Songs from the Greek Anthology. By Elgar. Set of 5 male-voice partsongs (op. 45, 1903).

Songs my Mother taught me. By Dvořák, being one of his 7 Gipsy songs for Tenor (op. 55, 1880).

Songs of a Wayfaring Man (Mahler). See *Lieder eines fahrenden Gesellen*.

Songs of Farewell. Last choral work of Delius; Double Choir and Orch. (1st perf. London 1932.)

Songs of Gurra (Schönberg). See *Gurrelieder*.

Song Without Words. A term introduced by Mendelssohn to cover a type of 1-movement Piano Solo piece in which a well-marked singing melody progresses against an accompaniment. The style was not new, though the term was. The 1st book of 6 pieces (op. 19), publ. in London by Novello, was composed in 1832 (original title, *Melodies for the Pianoforte*). Other books (op. 30, 38, 53, 65, 67, 85, 102), with 6 pieces in each, followed at intervals up to the composer's death. The Ger. term is *Lied ohne Worte*, with the plur. *Lieder ohne Worte* (not *Wörter*, as sometimes printed). The Fr. is *Chanson sans paroles* or *Romance sans paroles*. Mendelssohn composed also one 'Song without Words' for 'Cello and Piano (op. 109).

Sonnambula, La ("The Woman Sleep-walker'). Opera by Bellini. Libretto by Romani. (Prod. Milan and London 1831; New York 1835.)

Sonneck, Oscar George Theodore (b. Jersey City 1873; d. New York 1928). Author of many publications usually based on research into various aspects of Amer. musical history. Received general and musical education in Germany; became earliest chief music librarian of Library of Congress (1902–17), producing valuable catalogues, and earliest ed. of *Musical Quarterly*; later in charge of publication dept. of firm of G. Schirmer.

Sonnenquartette ('Sun Quartets'). Nickname of Haydn's String Quartets nos. 31–36, from a rising sun used as a trade-mark in an early edn. They are sometimes called the *Grosse Quartette* ('Great Quartets').

Sonnerie (Fr.). 'Sounding.'

Sonore (Fr.), **sonoro** (It.). 'Sonorous'; so *sonorité* (Fr.) and *sonorità* (It.), 'sonority'; *sonoramente* (It.), 'sonorously'.

Sons bouchés (Fr.). Stopped notes in horn playing (see *Horn Family*; also *Gestopft* and *Schmetternd*).

Sons, Maurice (b. Amsterdam 1857; d. London 1942). Violinist. Pupil of Wieniawski, &c. Leader of Scottish Orch. 1885; then Queen's Hall Orch. 1904–27. On staff of R.C.M. (retired 1937).

Sons of the Clergy. See *Festival*.

Sontag, Henriette Gertrude Walpurgis—Countess Rossi (b. Coblenz 1805; d. Mexico 1854). Operatic soprano of high international fame. First Brit. appearances 1828.

Sopra (It.). 'On', 'above'. So *sopra una corda*, 'on one string' (of violin, &c.; for piano see under *Corda*); *come sopra*, or *come di sopra*, 'as above'.

Sopran (Ger.). 'Soprano' (see *Voice* 14).

Soprana (It.). Fem. of *Soprano*; so *corda soprana*, the highest string (violin &c.).

Sopranino Saxhorn. See *Saxhorn and Flügelhorn Families* 1.

Sopranist. A Castrato Singer (see *Voice* 5) with a voice of soprano range.

Soprano. See *Voice* 14, 16. For 'Male Soprano' see *Voice* 5.

Soprano Clef. See Table 4.

Soprano Flügelhorn. See *Saxhorn and Flügelhorn Families* 1 a, 2.

Soprano Saxhorn. See *Saxhorn and Flügelhorn Families* 1.

Soprano Staff. See under *Great Staff*.

Sor (properly Sors), **Fernando** (b. Barcelona 1778; d. Paris 1839). Guitar virtuoso, touring Europe. Settled Paris 1828. Composer of works for his instrument; also operas, &c.

Sorabji, Kaikhosru Shapurji (originally Leon Dudley Sorabji; b. Chingford, Essex, 1892). Son of a Parsee father and a Spanish mother. Composer of piano music of such difficulty, complexity, and length as to reduce its potential performers and willing auditors to a small group of highly equipped and abnormally patient musical people; also of orch. music that demands a huge body of performers. Amongst his works are that for piano, *Opus Clavicembalisticum* (12 movements, occupying 250 pages, taking over 2 hours to perform), and an organ symphony which takes the time of a whole recital.

In the first eight editions of *The Oxford Companion to Music* this composer's birth date was given as 1895—as to which he publicly complained that 'a number of years had been clapped on to his age'. Research by Mr. Slonimsky has, however, brought to light the entry in the official Register of Births for the district of Epping. This gives the date not as 1895 but actually three years earlier and the baptismal first names not the two now used but 'Leon Dudley'.

In a communication to the present compiler, dated 22 February 1952, the composer lays down his attitude when 'dealing with stupid and impudent enquiries from lexecographical persons' and explains that his practice has been 'deliberately to mislead them as to dates and places'.

It is hoped that this frank admission will preclude further public complaints.

Sorcerer, The. Comic opera by Gilbert and Sullivan. (Prod. Opéra Comique, London, 1877; New York 1879.)

Sorcerer's Apprentice (Dukas). See *Apprenti sorcier*.

Sordina or **sordino**; **sordini** (It. sing. and plur.). 'Mute'; 'mutes'. So (violin, &c.) *sordini alzati* or *sordini levati*, 'mutes raised', i.e. taken off. (As to pianoforte see *senza sordino*.) **Sordo, sorda** (It., masc., fem.), **sordamente** (It.). 'Dull in tone', 'muffled'.

Sordun (Ger.). Organ stop of muffled tone (8 ft. and 16 ft.).

Sorgfalt (Ger.). 'Care.' So *sorgfältig*, 'carefully'.

Soriano (or **Suriano**), **Francesco** (b. Rome 1549; there d. 1620). Pupil of Palestrina; held important positions in churches of Rome and publ. motets, masses, madrigals, &c. (See reference under *Plainsong* 3.)

Soriano, Gonzalo (b. Alicante, Spain, 1916). Pianist. Trained Madrid Conserv. Continental and British tours.

Sortie (Fr.). 'Exit', 'departure', hence 'Closing Voluntary' and the like.

Sospirando, sospirante, sospirevole, sospiroso (It.). 'Sighing', i.e. plaintive in style.

Sostenendo, sostenente (It.). 'Sustaining.' **sostenuto**. 'Sustained.' (For Sostenuto Pedal see *Pianoforte*.)

Sotto voce (It. 'under the voice'). 'Under the breath', 'undertone', i.e. 'in a barely audible manner'. The term is, musically, applied to both vocal and instrumental performance.

Soubasse (Fr.). Contra-bourdon organ stop (32 ft.).

Soudainement (Fr.). 'Suddenly.'

Soul and Body (Cavalieri). See *Oratorio*.

Sound, Properties of. See *Acoustics*; *Broadcasting of Music*.

Sound-board. See *Pianoforte*.

Sound-holes. The '*f*' holes cut in the belly (i.e. the upper surface) of a violin, &c.

Sound-post. The piece of wood fixed within a violin, &c., to counter the downward pressure of the bridge (cf. *Âme, Anima*).

Soupirant (Fr.). 'Sighing.'

Souple (Fr.). 'Supple', 'flexible'.

Sourd, sourde (Fr. masc., fem). 'Muffled.' So *Pédale sourde*, 'soft pedal'.

Sourdine (Fr.). This word is used in the same senses as It. *sordino* (q.v.).

Sous (Fr.). 'Under.'

Sousa, John Philip (b. Washington, D.C., 1854; d. Reading, Pa., 1932). 'The March King'—composer of popular marches for military band, *The Washington Post, El Capitán, Stars and Stripes forever*, &c. Also composed light operas. Became conductor of Marine Band, Washington, 1880; after 12 years organized 'Sousa's Band', with which he toured not only his own country and Europe but, on one occasion (1910–11), the world. A man of remarkable personality and musical ability. (Cf. *Capitán, El*.)

Sousaphone. See *Tuba Group* 2.

Sousedska. A Bohemian peasant dance, slow, and in simple triple time. It was often danced as a change after the Furiant (q.v.), and at one time was given a devotional tinge by the singing of a certain traditional Chorale.

Soutenu (Fr.). 'Sustained.'

Souter Liedekens. See *Old Hundredth*.

Souzay, Gérard (b. Angers, France, 1918). Baritone. Trained Paris Conservatory. European and N. American career as concert artist.

Sower, D. See *Tonic Sol-fa*.

Sowerby, Leo (b. Grand Rapids, Mich., 1895; d. Port Clinton, Ohio, 1968). Trained in Chicago and won Rome Prize 1921; then again in Chicago as organist, pianist, and teacher of composition. 1962 dir. Coll. of Church Musicians, Washington, D.C. Composer of orch., chamber, organ, piano, and choral works.

Spagnoletti, P.—real name Paolo Diana (b. Cremona 1768; d. London 1834). Settled London in 1st years 19th c. and became leading violin all chief orchs.; admired by Paganini. Composed violin music, &c.

Spagnoletto, spagnoletta, spagniletta, spagnicoletta. An old round dance, probably related to the Pavan (q.v.).

Spain (España). See *Chabrier*.

Spalding, (1) **Walter Raymond** (b. Northampton, Mass., 1865; d. Cambridge, Mass., 1962). Studied Harvard (M.A.); then Paris and Munich. Asst. Prof. Harvard 1903; Prof. 1912. Publ. textbooks.

(2) **Albert** (b. Chicago 1888; d. New York 1953). Violinist. Début Paris age 17; New York 3 years later. Wide tours and many compositions.

Spandendo (It.). 'Expanding' (in power).

Spanisches Liederbuch ('Spanish Song-book'). Solo Song settings by Hugo Wolf (1890) of 44 poems translated by Goethe and Heyse. Piano accompaniment, but some later orchestrated by the composer.

Spanish Song-book (Wolf). See under *Spanisches*.

Spanish Symphony. See *Symphonie espagnole*.

Sparta, sparto; spartita, spartito (It.). 'Score.'

Spass; spasshaft (Ger.). 'Joke'; 'jocular'.

Spassapensieri (It.). Jew's harp (q.v.).

Spasshaft (Ger.). 'Jocular.'

Später (Ger.). 'Later.'

Speaker-key in wind instruments. A key opening a hole which divides the wind column, so making easier the production of harmonics required in the production of the higher notes (see *Acoustics* 7).

Speaks, Oley (b. Canal Winchester, Ohio, 1874; d. New York 1948). Baritone vocalist and composer. Began career as church soloist and teacher. Became prolific composer of songs, some enjoying enormous popularity (e.g. *On the Road to Mandalay*; *When the Boys come Home*); also some part-songs and anthems.

Species. See *Counterpoint*.

Spectre de la Rose. See *Aufforderung*.

Spectre's Bride, The. By Dvořák. Dramatic Cantata (1st perf. Pilsen 1885, Birmingham 1886).

Spediendo (It.). 'Speeding', 'hurrying'.

Spelman, Timothy Mather (b. Brooklyn 1891). Graduate of Harvard; studied music also at Munich and has lived for many years in Florence. Composer of orch., choral, and chamber works.

Spem in alium. See *Tallis*.

Spencer, Charles Child (b. London 1797; there d. 1869). London organist, composer of glees, &c., and writer of textbooks and the *Concise Explanation of the Church Modes* (1846)—for long the standard work on its subject.

Sperdendosi (It.). 'Fading out.'

Spherophone. See *Electric Musical Instruments* 1.

Spianato (It. fem., *spianata*). A 'spiana' is a carpenter's plane, and this adj. means 'planed', 'levelled', 'smoothed'.

Spiccato. Form of staccato bowing in which the bow is allowed to bounce upon the strings; produced by rapid movements with restricted (central) portion of the bow. Same as *Saltando*. (Cf. *Sautillé*.)

Spider's Feast, The ('Le Festin de l'araignée'). Ballet-pantomime by Roussel (1912). Score originally designed for Oriental ballet and then used for one based on a book of the entomologist Fabre. Often heard in concert performance.

Spiegando (It.). 'Unfolding', 'becoming louder'.

Spiel; Spielen (Ger.). 'Play'; 'To play'. So *Spielend*, 'playing', 'playful'; *Volles Spiel*, 'Full Organ'; *Spieler*, 'Player'.

Spinet. See *Harpsichord Family*.

Spinnen des Tons (Ger.). Same as *Filar la voce* (q.v.).

Spinnerlied (Ger.). 'Spinning Song', e.g. that of Mendelssohn (see below).

Spinning Song. By Mendelssohn. Unauthorized (but appropriate) name for *Song without Words* no. 34 in C: a more fanciful name is *The Bee's Wedding*. (See also *Litolff*.)

Spinnlied (Ger.). 'Spinning Song.'

Spirante (It.). 'Expiring', 'dying away'.

Spires (hymn tune). See *Pope and Turk tune*.

Spirito (It.). 'Spirit', 'vigour'. So *spiritoso*, 'spirited'; *spiritosamente*, 'spiritedly'.

Spirit of England. Three Poems by Laurence Binyon, set by Elgar for Soprano or Tenor Solo, Chorus, and Orch.; 1st perf. Leeds 1916–17. (1) *The Fourth of August*; (2) *To Women*; (3) *For the Fallen* (op. 80, 1916).

Spirit Trio or **Das Geistertrio** (Beethoven). Ger. nickname for Piano Trio in D, op. 70, no. 1, due to mysterious opening of 2nd movement.

Spirituals. Name given to Negro religious songs of Southern U.S.A. first generally heard through the post-Civil War tours of of Fisk Univ. choir.

Spitta, Philipp—in full Julius August Philipp (b. Wechold, Hanover, 1841; d. Berlin 1894). Author of standard life of Bach (1873–80; Eng. translation 1884–5); ed. of the works of Schütz, the organ works of Buxtehude, &c.

Spitze (Ger.). 'Point.' Hence, in string playing, *an der Spitze*, 'at the point' (of the bow).

Spitzflöte (Ger., lit. 'point-flute'). Metal organ stop of slightly conical shape; 8-, 4-, or 2-foot length and pitch.

Spitzig (Ger.). 'Pointed', 'cutting'.

Spivakovsky, Tossy (b. Odessa 1907). Violinist, trained Berlin; now resident New York. Has toured Europe, American Continent, Australia, and New Zealand.

Spofforth, Reginald (b. Southwell, Notts., 1770; d. London 1827). Well known as able composer of glees, of which one simple specimen, *Hail smiling morn*, is widely known.

Spohr, Louis (b. Brunswick 1784; d. Cassel 1859). Virtuoso violinist, opera conductor, and composer, in his day eminent in all 3 capacities.

At 14 in orch. of Duke of Brunswick; at 20 toured, arousing enthusiasm both as performer and composer; then held various positions in Vienna, Frankfurt, and elsewhere; first visited England in 1820, playing and conducting his own compositions at Philharmonic Soc.'s concerts; became court conductor at Cassel (1821) and there remained until within 2 years of death; early appreci-

ated Wagner, performing *The Flying Dutchman* (1843) and *Tannhäuser* (1853); as teacher turned out many eminent violinists; publ. important *Violin School* (1831). Wrote interesting autobiography.

Compositions include 11 operas, several oratorios, 10 symphonies, 15 violin concertos, 8 overtures, 34 string quartets, and other chamber music, &c. All these works very much admired in their day but later (partly from their over-chromaticism) neglected.

See also *Calvary*; *Fall of Babylon*; *Jessonda*; *Last Judgement*; *Weihe der Töne*.

Spontini, Gasparo Luigi Pacifico (b. Jesi, nr. Ancona, 1774; there d. 1851). Son of a peasant; studied in Naples and became prominent as opera composer; estd. himself in Paris (1803); there made great success with *La Vestale* (q.v.); court conductor at Berlin (1820), where he received an enormous salary and was long highly influential, at last, however, suffering from opposition, retired (1842) to Paris and finally returned to native place, devoting himself to good works and leaving his fortune to the poor.

Spöttisch (Ger.). 'Mocking.'

Sprechchor (Ger.). 'Speech-choir.' A choral body for the perf. of *Sprechgesang* ('speech-song'), i.e. music in *Sprechstimme* ('speech-voice')—a form of utterance half speech and half song.

Sprechend (Ger.). 'Speaking.'

Sprechstimme; Sprechgesang (Ger. 'speaking-voice'; 'speech-song'). (*a*) A type of vocal perf. in which Schönberg and a few others have experimented; in it the tone of the voice is that of speech (or nearly so) but modulated, as in song, according to the composer's notation. (*b*) *Sprechgesang* is also (and more properly) a synonym for *Rezitativ*, 'recitative'.

Springar. A popular dance of the Telemark district of southern Norway. It is danced by 2 people.

Springdans (or 'Leaping dance' to distinguish it from the *Gangar*, or 'Walking dance'). A Norwegian dance in simple triple time.

Springend (Ger.). 'Springing.' Hence *mit springendem Bogen*, 'with springing bow'.

Spring Sonata or Frühlingssonate. Nickname for Beethoven's Sonata for Piano and Violin, op. 24, in F.

Spring Song (Ger. *Frühlingslied*). Unauthorized name for Mendelssohn's *Song without Words* no. 30 in A. An earlier nickname was *Camberwell Green*, from the place of its composition in South London.

Spring Symphony. See *Schumann's Symphonies*. Benjamin Britten's symphony of the same name (1st perf. Amsterdam 1949) is for solo singers, chorus, and orchestra.

Sprung Rhythm. Term introduced by poet Gerard Manley Hopkins and quite unnecessary in application to music, since it covers merely the various devices already familiar as form of syncopation; hence better dropped.

Spugna, Bacchetta di (It.). Sponge-headed drumstick (see *Percussion Family* 1 a).

Square Dance. A dance of which the ground plan, so to speak, is rectangular, as contrasted with the 'Round Dance' (q.v.).

Square Pianoforte. See *Pianoforte*.

Squillante, squillanti (It. sing., plur.). 'Clanging.' (Applied to cymbals, it means that they shall be suspended and struck with drumsticks.)

Squire, (1) **William Barclay** (b. London 1855; there d. 1927). Studied Cambridge (M.A.); became solicitor; then on staff of Brit. Museum as music specialist (1885–1917); music critic various London journals; ed. of Purcell's keyboard works and (with brother-in-law, J. A. Fuller Maitland, q.v.) of Fitzwilliam Virginal Book, &c.

(2) **William Henry** (b. Ross, Herefordshire, 1871; d. London 1963). Trained R.C.M. (later on staff) and became well-known solo 'cellist; composed many popular songs, &c.

Staatskapelle (Ger.). State Orchestra.

Stabat Mater dolorosa. A sequence (q.v.) of the Roman Catholic liturgy, appointed for the Friday of Passion Week and 15 Sept. Its authorship is unknown, but it is often attributed to Jacopone da Todi (abt. 1228–1306), the It. Franciscan. Apart from its traditional plainsong, the *Stabat Mater dolorosa* has had many composed settings, e.g. by the following: (1) PALESTRINA, abt. 1590. (2) ASTORGA, abt. 1707. (3) PERGOLESE, 1736. (4) HAYDN, 1773. (5) ROSSINI, 1832–41; partial perf. Paris and London 1841; complete perf. Paris 1842. (6) VERDI; 1st perf. Paris 1898. (7) DVOŘÁK; 1st perf. Prague 1880; London 1883. (8) STANFORD; 1st perf. Leeds Fest. 1907.

Stäbchen (Ger. 'little staff'). The beater for a triangle.

Stabile (It.). 'Stable', i.e. firm.

Staccato (It.). 'Detached', i.e. the opposite of *legato*. The superlative is *staccatissimo*. (See Table 23 for the various signs used.)

Stadium Concerts (New York). Summer series of open-air concerts and opera performances in Lewisohn Stadium. Inaugurated 1918.

Stadlen, Peter (b. Vienna 1910). Pianist and critic. Trained Vienna; début 1934. From 1939 in England. Has specialized in music of Schönberg and his school, giving 1st performances of many atonal works. On staff *Daily Telegraph* 1960.

Stadler Quintet. Nickname of Mozart's Clarinet Quintet (K. 581), composed for the celebrated clarinet-tist, Anton Stadler.

Staff. See *Notation*; *Great Staff*.

Stainer, (1) Violin makers: see *Violin Family*.

(2) **John** (b. London 1840; d. Verona 1901). Choir-boy at St. Paul's Cathedral; at 16 1st organist appointed at St. Michael's Coll., Tenbury (cf. *Ouseley*); at 19 B.Mus., Oxford; at 20 organist Magdalen Coll., Oxford, taking B.A. 1863 and D.Mus. 1865; very active in all Oxford musical activities till left (1872) to become organist of St. Paul's Cathedral, where his example greatly raised standard of Eng. church music; also inspector to national Board of Education (1882). Knighted on resigning St. Paul's (1888); Prof. of Music, Oxford (1889).

Did valuable musicological work. Composed oratorios (especially *Daughter of Jairus*, q.v.; *Crucifixion* 1887), church music, &c.; also wrote useful textbooks.

Stainer & Bell, Ltd. London Music Publishers (69 Newman St., W. 1). Founded 1907.

Stamitz family. By their conducting and composing activities in mid- and late- 18th c. exercised immense influence on the standard of orch. playing and the form and style of the symphony. Chief members were: (1) **Johann Wenzel Anton** (b. Deutsch-Brod, Bohemia, 1717; d. Mannheim 1757). Remarkable violinist and famous violin teacher. Kapellmeister at court of Mannheim (from 1745), where estd. new standard of conducting; composed 50 symphonies (greatly influencing symphonic form and style), many violin concertos, sonatas, &c. (2) **Karl** (b. Mannheim 1745; d. Jena 1801). Son of J. W. A. Stamitz, above; also violinist (and viola player) of very high reputation; spent some time in Paris, London, Cassel, and St. Petersburg; conductor at Jena (from 1794). Composed 70 symphonies, violin concertos, chamber music, and 2 operas. (3) **(Johann) Anton** (b. Mannheim 1754; d. before 1809). Likewise son of J. W. A. Stamitz, above. Like his brother Karl spent some time in Paris. Composed 13 symphonies, 3 piano concertos, chamber music, &c.

Ständchen (Ger.). 'Serenade' (q.v.).

Standhaft; Standhaftigkeit (Ger.). 'Firm'; 'firmness'.

Stanford, Charles Villiers (b. Dublin 1852; d. London 1924). Organ Scholar at Queens' Coll., Cambridge, 1870; organist of Trinity Coll. 1873-92; graduated with classical honours 1874; in 1875-6 on leave in Germany studying composition at Leipzig and Berlin. Chief Prof. of Composition at R.C.M. 1883 to death and there responsible for training many Brit. composers; Prof. of Music, Cambridge, 1887 to death; conductor of Bach Choir (1885-92), of several Leeds Festivals, &c. Composed 7 operas (some 1st prod. in Germany), 7 symphonies, 5 Irish Rhapsodies, 3 piano concertos, chamber music,

church music (see *Service*), songs, &c., and edited collections of Irish songs, &c.; also wrote several valuable books. Knighted 1901.

See also *Canterbury Pilgrims*; *Critic*; *Eden*; *Much Ado about Nothing*; *Revenge*; *Savonarola*; *Shamus O'Brien*; *Stabat Mater*; *Te Deum*; *Travelling Companion*; *Veiled Prophet*.

Stanley, John (b. London 1713; there d. 1786). Blind from age 2, but became able organist of London churches, his voluntaries attracting other musicians to hear them—including Handel; at Temple Church from 1734; much occupied with management of oratorio series in London; for last 14 years of life Master of the Band to George III. Composed oratorios, orch. music, chamber music, and organ music (some still in use).

Stanton, Walter Kendall (b. Dauntsey, Wilts., 1891). Educ. Oxford (M.A., D.Mus.). School music master (St. Edward's, Oxford; Wellington), also in charge music dept. of Univ. of Reading; then Director of Music in Midland Region B.B.C.; in 1947 1st Prof. of Music at Bristol Univ. Composer of choral works, &c.

Stark (Ger.). 'Strong', 'loud'; so *stärker*, 'stronger', 'louder'. **Stark anblasen, stark blasend.** 'Strongly blown' (wind instruments).

Starker, Janos (b. Budapest 1924). Principal 'cellist, Budapest Opera 1945; Metropolitan Opera 1949; Chicago Symphony 1953; on staff Indiana Univ. from 1958. Eminent as soloist, particularly well-known via numerous recordings.

Starlight Express. Incidental Music by Elgar (op. 78, 1915) to a play by Violet Pearn based on Algernon Blackwood's *A Prisoner in Fairyland*.

Stars and Stripes forever. March for Military Band by Sousa—said to be most popular ever composed.

Star-spangled Banner, The. This is the official national anthem of the U.S.A., by a Bill which passed the Senate on 3 March 1931. The words of this song, beginning 'O say, can you see by the dawn's early light What so proudly we hailed at the twilight's last gleaming?' first appeared as a handbill, hastily struck off the day after they were written, i.e. 15 Sept. 1814 (during the war between the U.S.A. and Great Britain). They then appeared in *The Baltimore Patriot*, on 20 Sept. Their author was Francis Scott Key, of Baltimore. The peculiar metre adopted shows that the writer had in mind as the tune of his poem the one to which it was at once, and is still, sung, the 'Anacreontick Song' or 'Anacreon in Heaven', composed by John Stafford Smith (q.v.), of London, for the Anacreontic Soc. of London, and then popular in America as the official song of several Anacreontic Societies there.

Statt (Ger.). 'Instead of.'

Stave. Same as Staff. See *Notation*; *Great Staff*.

Stcherbatchef, (1) **Nicholas** (b. St. Petersburg 1853). Pianist and composer, in his youth attached to the 'young Russian' school, but somewhat influenced by Ger. romanticism.

(2) **Andrew** (b. nr. Poltava 1869; d. Kiev 1916). Trained at Conserv. of St. Petersburg. Composer of songs, piano music, orch. music, &c.

(3) **Vladimir** (b. Warsaw 1889; d. Leningrad 1952). Trained at Conserv. of Leningrad. Composer of symphonies, chamber music, &c., said to be somewhat in the Mahler vein.

Steber, Eleanor (b. Wheeling, W. Va., 1916). Operatic soprano. After early years with radio, church choirs, &c., won Metropolitan Opera auditions in 1940. Thereafter internationally successful in exceptionally wide range of parts.

Steffani, Agostino (b. Castelfranco 1654; d. Frankfurt-on-Main 1728). It. composer, organist, singer, mathematician, theologian (eventually a bishop), and man of general learning; occupied important positions in Germany both as musician and as diplomat; Kapellmeister at court of Hanover 1688 to 1711. Composed many It. operas, an immense quantity of duet cantatas, church music, and dance music; much influenced Handel (his immediate successor at Hanover) and other Ger. composers.

Steg (Ger.). 'Bridge'—of violin, &c. Thus *am Steg = sul ponticello* (It.), i.e. 'bow near the bridge'.

Steggall, Charles (b. London 1826; there d. 1905). London organist and composer of church music. D.Mus., Cambridge.

Steibelt, Daniel (b. Berlin 1765; d. St. Petersburg 1823). Famous pianist of showy type and fashionable piano teacher in Paris (1790–7); in London (1800–5). Composed many piano sonatas (a few still in use for teaching purposes), sonatas for piano and violin, piano fantasias, &c., and 5 piano concertos.

Stein, Richard Heinrich (b. Halle 1882; d. Sta. Brigida, Canary Is., 1942.) Law student, D.Phil. (with thesis on psychology of ethics); in Spain (1914–19), then in Berlin; settled in Canary Islands (1933). As composer a pioneer of quarter-tones (see *Microtones*), being earliest to publish music using these (1906); author of a book on the subject (1909). Also composed much music for the normal piano.

Steinbach, (1) **Emil** (b. in Duchy of Baden 1849; d. Mainz 1919). Conductor (Wagner exponent) and composer. (2) **Fritz** (b. in Duchy of Baden 1855; d. Munich 1916). Conductor (brother of above). For 16 years (1886–1902) in charge of famous Meiningen Orch. as successor to von Bülow; in last years visited Britain with it; then conductor of Gürzenich Concerts and director of Conservatory at Cologne. Some compositions.

Steinberg, (1) **Maximilian** (b. Vilna 1883; d. Leningrad 1946). Son-in-law and literary executor of Rimsky-Korsakof, of whom had been a pupil at Conserv. of St. Petersburg; later (1908) prof. of composition and then director of that Conservatory (1934). Composer of symphonies, ballet music, an opera, chamber music, &c.

(2) **William** (b. Cologne 1899). Conductor, pupil of Abendroth. Cologne Opera 1920; Prague 1925; Dir. Frankfurt Opera 1929–33; San Francisco 1944; Buffalo Orch. 1945; Pittsburgh 1952; also Boston 1969.

Steiner, Rudolf. See *Eurhythmy.*

Steinert, Alexander Lang (b. Boston, Mass., 1900). Graduate of Harvard; then studied composition with Loeffler; won Amer. Rome Prize 1927; conductor and pianist. Composer of orch., choral, and chamber works, &c.

Steinitz, Paul—in full Charles Paul Joseph (b. Chichester 1909). Organist and choral conductor. Trained R.A.M. (then on staff). Organist St. Bartholomew the Great, Smithfield. Conductor South London Bach Soc., &c., D.Mus., London.

Steinway & Sons. New York pianomaking firm, estd. 1853 by 4 members of Steinweg family (cf. *Grotrian-Steinweg*).

Steinweg. See *Grotrian-Steinweg.*

Stelle; Stellen (Ger.). 'Place'; 'places'.

Stendendo (It.). 'Extending', i.e. spacing the notes out = *rallentando*.

Stenhammar, Vilhelm Eugen (b. Stockholm 1871; there d. 1927). Studied at Conserv. of Stockholm and in Berlin; then held important positions as orch. and opera conductor in Sweden. Composer of music dramas, orch., choral, and piano works, &c.

Stenka Razin. Symphonic Poem by Glazunof (op. 13, 1885). Based on a lurid story of a 17th-c. pirate of the Volga. (1st perf. Berlin 1889; London 1914.)

Stentare (It. 'to work hard'). To play in a laborious way. So *stentando*, 'labouring', 'retarding'; *stentatamente*, 'laboriously', 'slowly'; *stentato*, 'laboured' (i.e. held back and every note stressed).

Step Dance. See under *Figure* 2.

Stéphan, Dom John. See *Adeste Fideles.*

Stéphanie Gavotte. See *Czibulka.*

Stephen, (1) **Edward**—known as 'Tanymarian' (b. nr. Festiniog 1822; d. nr. Bangor 1885). Welsh congregational minister; composer of earliest Welsh oratorio *Ystorm Tiberias* ('The Storm of Tiberias'), anthems, hymn tunes, &c.

(2) **David** (b. Dundee 1869; d. West Linton 1946). Organist, &c. Director

of Music to Carnegie Trust, Dunfermline, 1903–27 (see *Carnegie, Andrew*). Compositions of Scottish flavour. Hon. D.Mus., Edinburgh, 1945.

Stephens, Catherine—or 'Kitty' (b. London 1794; there d. 1882). Concert and operatic soprano of high repute. Married 82-year-old Earl of Essex 1838 and ceased public appearances.

Steppes of Central Asia (Borodin). See *In the Steppes.*

Sterbend (Ger.). 'Dying away.'

Sterling, Antoinette (b. Sterlingville, N.Y., 1850; d. London 1904). Contralto vocalist. Trained by Mathilde Marchesi, Viardot-Garcia, and Manuel Garcia, jun. Highly popular in Britain and U.S.A.; appeared in opera but soon devoted herself to oratorio and latterly completely to songs; settled in London; many popular Eng. songs (e.g. Sullivan's *The Lost Chord*) composed for her. Two of her children attained popularity—**Jean Sterling Mackinlay** (1882–1958), actress, diseuse, singer of folk songs, &c., and **Malcolm Sterling Mackinlay** (1870–1952), vocalist, author, &c.

Sterling Mackinlay. See *Sterling.*

Stern, Isaac (b. Kremenetz, Russia, 1920). Violinist; trained San Francisco Conserv.; début San Francisco 1931; then world-wide tours as foremost virtuoso.

Sternhold and Hopkins. See *Hymns and Hymn Tunes* 3.

Steso (It. 'Spread out'). 'Slow.

Stesso, stessa, stessi, stesse (It. masc. and fem., sing. and plur.). 'Same.'

Stets (Ger.). 'Steadily', 'always'.

Stevens, (1) **Richard John Samuel** (b. London 1757; there d. 1837). London organist—concurrently of Temple Church and Charterhouse; also Gresham Prof. of Music. Composer of fine and still-popular glees (e.g. *Ye spotted snakes, The cloud-capt Towers*).

(2) **Horace Ernest** (b. Melbourne, Australia, 1876; there d. 1950). Bassbaritone. In choir of St. Paul's Cathedral; then won public recognition in oratorio and opera (especially Wagner). Appeared frequently in U.S.A.

(3) **Bernard** (b. London 1916). **He**

studied at Cambridge Univ. (M.A., B.Mus.) and the R.C.M. (later on staff). He has composed a violin concerto (1943), a *Symphony of Liberation* (1946), and other works.

(4) **Denis (William)** (b. High Wycombe, Bucks, 1922). Violinist and viola player, musicologist, &c. Studied Oxford (M.A. 1948). Much musical journalism and lecturing (especially medieval music). On staff B.B.C. 1949–54. In U.S.A. from 1962.

(5) **Halsey** (b. Scott, N.Y., 1908). Composer and teacher. Educ. Syracuse Univ. and under Bloch. Taught at Syracuse Univ. 1935; Dakota Wesleyan Univ. 1937; Bradley Univ. 1941; Univ. S. Calif. 1946. Works include symphonies and other orch. and choral works, and chamber music. Important book on Bartók; other critical writings.

Stevenson, (1) **John Andrew** (b. Dublin 1761; d. Headfort House, co. Meath, 1833). Vicar-choral of the 2 Cathedrals of Dublin; organist to Viceroy of Ireland (1814); and composer of music for church and theatre; also glees (e.g. *See our oars, with feathered spray*); edited and arranged music for Moore's Irish Melodies (1807–34). Hon D.Mus., Dublin, 1791. Knighted by Viceroy of Ireland (1803).

(2) **Robert Louis** (b. Edinburgh 1850; d. Samoa 1894). Novelist, essayist, and poet. Amateur flautist. (See *Skye Boat Song*.)

Stewart, (1) **Robert Prescott** (b. Dublin 1825; there d. 1894). Organist Christ Church Cathedral, Dublin, at age 19; later also organist St. Patrick's Cathedral there; D.Mus., Dublin, 1851; Prof. of Music, Dublin Univ. (1861), where estd. 1st preliminary examination in general education for musical candidates in any Brit. univ. Composer of choral works, &c., including many glees. Knighted by Viceroy of Ireland 1872.

(2) **Charles Hylton** (b. Chester 1884; d. Windsor 1932). Organist Cathedrals of Rochester (1916), Chester (1930), and of St. George's Chapel, Windsor Castle, a few weeks before his death. Composer of church music.

(3) **Jean**—Mrs. Hadley (b. Tonbridge 1914). Viola player. Trained R.C.M. Soloist and chamber music

player; Menges Quartet since 1941 (see *Menges* 1). Specially interested in contemporary Brit. works, of which many dedicated to her (e.g. Vaughan Williams's A minor Quartet, *For Jean on her Birthday*).

Stickers. See *Organ* 1.

Stierhorn (Ger.). 'Cow-horn' (sounding only 1 note), e.g. the watchman's instrument in *The Mastersingers*.

Stignani, Ebe (b. Naples 1907). Operatic mezzo-soprano. Trained Naples. Début there 1925; Milan 1926–56, with guest appearances in many countries, esp. in such parts as Azucena.

Stile rappresentativo (It. 'representative style'). A term used by some of the early It. composers of opera and oratorio as describing their invention of recitative (see *Opera* 1; *Recitative*), which aimed at representing the natural inflections of the voice rather than at recording agreeable tune.

Stiles-Allen, Lilian (b. London 1896). Concert soprano. Trained G.S.M. and Vienna. Of repute in Britain and known also in U.S.A.

Still, William Grant (b. Woodville, Miss., 1895). Studied Oberlin Conserv. and under Chadwick in Boston; Guggenheim Fellowship (1934); 1st Negro to conduct important orch. and to compose a symphony (*Afro-American Symphony* 1931). Also composed ballets, opera, film music, &c. Hon. D.Litt., Bates Coll., Mass.

Still (Ger.). 'Quiet', 'calm'.

Stilt, The. This is the name given in Hart's Psalter of 1615 to the well-known common-metre tune now always called *York*. It moves by large steps, and doubtless this suggested the striding of a walker on stilts.

Stimmbogen. See *Krummbogen*.

Stimme (Ger. 'voice'; plur. *Stimmen*). (1) The human voice. (2) Organ register (stop). (3) Sound-post of violin, &c.

Stimmen (Ger.). 'To tune.'

Stimmflöte, Stimmhorn, Stimmpfeife (Ger.). 'Pitch pipe.' **Stimmgabel** (Ger.). 'Tuning-fork'.

Stimmung (Ger.). (1) 'Tuning.' (2) 'Mood'; so *Stimmungsbild*, 'mood picture' (not 'tone picture', as in some books of reference).

Sting Cymbal. The normal cymbal (see *Percussion Family* 2 o), but made of specially tempered metal so as to give a hard tone.

Stingo. See *Cold and Raw*.

Stinguendo (It.). 'Extinguishing', i.e. 'fading out'.

Stirando, stirato; stiracchiando, stiracchiato (It.). 'Stretching', 'stretched', i.e. making the music last out = *ritardando*.

Stirling, Elizabeth (b. Greenwich 1819; d. London 1895). Prominent London organist; one of first to include Bach in recital programmes. Composer of organ music, songs, and part-songs (e.g. *All among the Barley*). Fulfilled test for B.Mus., Oxford (1856), but no women then could take degrees in any British university.

Stirrup Bone. See *Ear and Hearing*.

St. John, Florence—really Maggie Greig (b. Kirkcaldy 1854; d. 1912). Operatic and concert soprano. London début 1875.

Stock, Frederick August (b. Jülich, Prussia, 1872; d. Chicago 1942). Succeeded Theodore Thomas as conductor of Chicago Symphony Orch. (1905). Composed orch., chamber, piano, violin, and vocal works.

Stockend (Ger.) 'coming to a standstill'). 'Slackening the time gradually.'

Stock Exchange Orchestral and Choral Society. A London organization founded 1883 and still active.

Stockhausen Family. (1) **Franz** (b. Cologne 1792; d. Colmar 1868). Harpist and composer for harp. Founder of an Academy of Singing in Paris. (2) **Margarete**—*née* Schmuck (b. Gebweiler, Alsace, 1803; d. 1877). Concert and oratorio singer. Wife of above. Very popular in Britain. (3) **Julius** (b. Paris 1826; d. Frankfurt 1906). Concert baritone. Son of two above. Trained Paris Conserv. and under Manuel Garcia. Won very high popularity by his artistic qualities (dedicatee of some of Brahms's Lieder)

and especially popular with Brit. audiences. Also able choral conductor and teacher of singing. (4) **Franz** (b. Gebweiler, Alsace, 1839; d. Strasbourg 1926). Brother of above. Studied Leipzig Conserv. Long musical director of Strasbourg Cathedral and head of Strasbourg Conserv., &c.

Stockhausen, Karlheinz (b. nr. Cologne 1928). Composer. Trained Cologne and Bonn and under Milhaud and Messiaen. Noted representative of most advanced Ger. Note-row school; much study of electrophonic music; some works partly improvised by performer, who selects 'running order' of the various sections, playing them in sequence or simultaneously. Active and successful lecturer, esp. in connexion with his own works.

Stockhorn or **Stock and Horn**, or **Stock in Horn.** An obsolete Scottish instrument consisting of a wooden tube (or the thigh bone of a sheep) bored

WELSH STOCKHORN
(or Pibcorn)

with finger-holes, and having a cow's horn at one end and a mouthpiece with a reed (a single beating reed; see *Reed*) at the other. The name *Hornpipe* was sometimes used for the same thing, as was the Welsh *Pibcorn*.

Stoessel, Albert (b. St. Louis 1894; d. New York 1943). Studied at Berlin Hochschule and had early career as concert violinist; became well-known conductor in eastern U.S.A.; head of music dept. New York Univ. (1923–30); head of orch. and opera depts. of Juilliard School (1930 to death). Composer of opera and orch., chamber, and choral works.

Stojowski, Sigismund (b. Strzelce, Poland, 1869; d. New York 1946). As pianist largely trained at Paris Conserv.; later under Paderewski; naturalized in U.S.A. (1938). Compositions include orch., choral, and piano works, &c.

Stokowski, Leopold Anton Stanislav (b. London 1882). Conductor.

Studied Oxford (B.Mus.) and R.C.M. Began career as organist St. James, Piccadilly (1900), then St. Bartholomew's, New York (1905); naturalized U.S.A. 1915. Conductor Cincinnati Orch. 1909–12, Philadelphia 1914–36, N.B.C. Symphony 1941–4, Hollywood Bowl 1945, then New York Philharmonic, &c. Has made orch. transcriptions of works of Bach and interested himself in film music.

See *Samaroff, Olga.*

Stone, (1) **Christopher Reynolds** (b. Eton 1882; d. Maidenhead 1965). Educ. Oxford. Novelist and miscellaneous writer. Long London ed. of *The Gramophone* (cf. *Mackenzie, Compton*—his brother-in-law). Popular broadcaster, especially on gramophone record issues.

(2) **Norman** (b. London 1890; d. 1967). Tenor. Choir-boy Chapel Royal and Temple Church, London. Trained G.S.M. Leader of 'English Singers Quartet'. Publ. folk song arrangements, &c.

Stone Guest, The (also known as *The Marble Guest*). Posthumous opera by Dargomijsky; a setting (intact) of Pushkin's poem. Orchestrated and revised by Rimsky-Korsakof; overture by Cui. (Prod. St. Petersburg 1872.) See also under *Dargomijsky.*

Stop and Stop-key. See *Organ* 1.

Stopped diapason. See *Organ* 2.

Stopped notes. See *Horn Family.*

Stopped pipes (Diapason, &c.). See *Organ* 2.

Stopping, on stringed instruments, is merely the placing of the tips of the fingers of the left hand so that they shorten the vibrating length of a string. (Cf. 'Double Stopping' under *Double.*)

Storace, Stephen (b. London 1763; there d. 1796). Son of It. double-bass player and brother of well-known vocalist Ann Storace; at 12 sent to one of Conservatories at Naples to study violin, composition, &c., became friend of the young Mozart; produced 2 operas in Vienna (1785–6); became prominent in London as theatrical arranger and prolific composer of operas (e.g. *The Haunted Tower* 1789, kept stage for half a century; *No Song,*

No Supper another popular work); had definite melodic gift; early death, due to 'gout on the stomach', a loss to Brit. music.

Storm, The. See *Hullah.*

Storm, The (Organ piece). See *Lemmens.*

Storm Symphony (Haydn). See under *Matin.*

Stornello (It., plur. *Stornelli*). A traditional type of Tuscan folk song often improvised by a *Stornellatore* (masc.) or *Stornellatrice* (fem.). The stanza has 3 lines.

Story of a Flemish Farm, The. Suite by Vaughan Williams (1945), using music written for a film.

Stracciacalando (It.). 'Prattling.'

Straccinato (It.). 'Stretched out', i.e. *ritardando.*

Strad, The. Journal for players of bowed instruments (2 Duncan Terrace, N. 1). Founded 1890. Also publishes books of interest to same constituency.

Stradella, Alessandro (b. Montefestino 1642; murdered Genoa 1682). Little known of life, and traditional romantic stories of details of assassination lack proof. Able composer of operas, oratorios, motets, cantatas, string concertos, &c.

Stradivari. See *Violin Family.*

Straeten, van der (1) **Edmond** (b. Oudenarde, Belgium, 1826; there d. 1896). Learned author of *La Musique aux Pays-Bas* (9 vols. 1867–88) and very many similar works of research. Also composer and music critic.

(2) **Edmund Sebastian Joseph** (b. Düsseldorf 1855; d. London 1934). Violoncellist and author of *History of the Violin* (2 vols. 1933) and many similar works.

Straff; straffer (Ger.). 'Strict'; 'stricter'. Also 'tight'; 'tighter' (drum head, &c.).

Straffando; straffato (It.). 'Throwing off'; 'thrown off'.

Strakosch, (1) **Moritz** (b. Moravia 1825; d. Paris 1887). Pianist and concert and opera impresario (New York and Chicago). Brother-in-law and manager of Adelina Patti; husband of Clara Kellogg. (2) **Max** (b. 1834; d. New York 1892). Brother and successor (as impresario) of above.

Strambotto (It.). An It. Renaissance poetical form, often set to music on the lines of the Frottola (q.v.). See *Rispetto*.

Strandrecht (Smyth). See *Wreckers*.

Stransky, Josef (b. nr. Deutschbrod, Bohemia, 1872; d. New York 1936). Conductor (originally medical man). Pupil of Bruckner, Dvořák, &c. After holding important positions in Germany followed Mahler at New York Philharmonic (1911–23). Then entered New York art-dealer business. Some compositions.

Strascicando; strascinando; strascinato (It.). 'Dragging'; 'dragged' (e.g. heavily slurring notes in bowing, singing *portamento*, &c.).

Strathspey. The slow dance of Scotland, as the reel is its quick dance. Its music is in simple quadruple time, with many dotted notes and some use of the 'Scotch Snap' (q.v.).

Stratton, George (Robert) (b. London 1897; d. London 1954). Violinist. Trained Guildhall School of Music. Leader of London Symphony Orch. 1933 and later associate conductor. Founded Stratton String Quartet; book on Chamber Music. O.B.E. 1954.

Straube, Karl (b. Berlin 1873; d. Leipzig 1950). Organist St. Thomas's Church, Leipzig, from 1902; cantor of St. Thomas's School from 1918. Choral conductor, ed. of organ music, &c.

Straus, Oscar (b. Vienna 1870; d. Bad Ischl 1954). Theatrical conductor and then very popular composer of light operas (e.g. *Der tapfere Soldat*, Vienna 1908; known in English-speaking countries as 'The Chocolate Soldier', q.v.) also composed a little orch. and chamber music. Fr. naturalization 1939.

Strauss Family of Viennese dance musicians.

(1) **Johann I** (b. Vienna 1804; there d. 1849). Known as 'The Father of the Waltz'. Graduated from dance orch. of Lanner (q.v.), organizing his own, with which he toured many countries; 1st visit to England and Scotland at time

of Queen Victoria's coronation 1838. Publ. over 150 waltzes and quantities of other dances. (2) **Johann II** (b. Vienna 1825; there d. 1899). Known as 'The Waltz King'. Son of Johann I, above, and had similar career. Composed many of world's best waltzes (see *Beautiful Blue Danube*; *Morgenblätter*); also operettas (see *Fledermaus*; *Zigeunerbaron*). (3) **Joseph** (b. Vienna 1827; there d. 1870). Also son of Johann I; graduated from his father's orch. and pursued similar career as conductor and composer of waltzes, &c. (4) **Eduard** (b. Vienna 1835; there d. 1916). Also son of Johann I. Had career as conductor and composer similar to that of his father and brothers; great success in London 1885 and 1895. (5) **Johann III** (b. Vienna 1866; d. Berlin? 1939). Son of Eduard, above, and had similar career.

Strauss, Richard—in full Richard Georg (b. Munich 1864; d. Garmisch-Partenkirchen, Bavaria, 1949). The most vital and successful of the successors of Wagner, with similar operatic methods and harmonies and orch. technique developed from his. Unlike Wagner he wrote much instrumental music, especially of the nature of the symphonic poem (q.v.). His songs are noteworthy, and he enjoyed a high reputation as an opera conductor. Amongst his operas are *Salome*, *Elektra*, and *Der Rosenkavalier*. Amongst his orch. works are the symphonic poems, *Macbeth*, *Don Juan*, *Tod und Verklärung* ('Death and Transfiguration'), *Till Eulenspiegels lustige Streiche* ('Till Eulenspiegel's Merry Pranks'), *Also sprach Zarathustra* ('Thus spake Zoroaster'), *Don Quixote*, and *Heldenleben* ('A Hero's Life'). All these, however, constitute but a portion of his copious output.

See also under *Aegyptische Helena*; *Aerophor*; *Alpine Symphony*; *Arabella*; *Ariadne auf Naxos*; *Capriccio*; *Death and Transfiguration*; *Domestic Symphony*; *Don Juan*; *Don Quixote*; *Elektra*; *Feuersnot*; *Frau ohne Schatten*; *Gnecchi*; *Guntram*; *Hero's Life*; *Intermezzo*; *Josephs Legende*; *Macbeth*; *Nietzsche*; *Rosenkavalier*; *Salome*; *Schlagobers*; *Schweigsame Frau*; *Till Eulenspiegel's Merry Pranks*.

Stravagante (It.). 'Extravagant', 'fantastic'.

Stravinsky, (1) Igor (b. Oranienbaum, nr. St. Petersburg, 1882; d. New York 1971). Son of an opera singer. He studied music under Rimsky-Korsakof and then, meeting in his middle twenties the ballet impresario, Diaghilef (see *Ballet*), made Paris his centre and devoted himself largely to the production of ballet scores, of which the most important are *The Firebird, Petrouchka, The Rite of Spring, The Nightingale, The Wedding,* and *Apollo Musagetes* (for these ballets see entries under their names). It was *The Rite of Spring* that first clearly revealed to a wide public the fact that new melodic, harmonic, rhythmic, and orch. idioms had to be grasped, and thence onwards the composer's innovations became daring and various. In the mid-1920's debate on these took a new turn, since in the Piano Concerto (1924) and Piano Sonata (1925) all Russian characteristics were abandoned and a neo-classical style adopted; he had now reached a point where he claimed to have discarded all 'extra-musical' influences and emotions.

Some major compositions in addition to those already mentioned are the stage works *Renard* and *The Soldier's Tale*, the so-called *Symphonies of Wind Instruments* (1920), the comic opera *Mavra* (1922), the secular oratorio, *Œdipus Rex* 1927), the choral-orch. *Symphony of Psalms* (1930), the *Violin Concerto* (1931), the opera-ballet *Perséphone* (1934), the ballet *Jeu de Cartes* (1936), the *Concerto for 16 Instruments* (1938), the Symphony in C (1940), the Mass (1948), and the opera *The Rake's Progress* (q.v.; 1951). There are also several books.

In 1934 Stravinsky became a Fr. citizen and later (1945) a citizen of the U.S.A.

See also *Agon*; *Baiser de la Fée*; *Dumbarton Oaks*; *Fireworks*; *Jeu de Cartes*; *Mavra*; *Oedipus Rex*; *Perséphone*; *Pulcinella*; *Renard*; *Soldier's Tale*; *Symphony of Psalms*.

(2) **(Sviatoslav) Soulima** (b. Lausanne 1910). Second son of (1). Pianist. U.S.A. début 1948. Some compositions.

Straziante (It.). 'Tearing.'

Street Piano. See *Mechanical Reproduction of Music* 12; *Hurdy-Gurdy*.

Streich (Ger.). 'Stroke' (of bow). Hence *Streichquartett*, 'string quartet', *Streichstimmen*, 'string-toned stops' (organ), and so on.

Streit zwischen Phoebus und Pan (Bach). See *Phoebus and Pan.*

Streng (Ger.). 'Strict.'

Strepito; strepitoso; strepitosamente (It.). 'Noise'; 'noisy'; 'noisily'.

Stretto (It. 'Drawn together'). (1) *Accelerando*. (2) For Stretto in Fugue see *Form* 6.

Strich or **Bogenstrich** or **Anstrich** (Ger.). A stroke (with a bow); hence *mit breitem Strich*, 'with the breadth of the whole bow', and so forth. So also *Strichart*, 'manner of bowing'; *Aufstrich*, 'up-bow'; *Niederstrich*, 'down-bow'.

Strict Canon. See *Canon.*

Strict Counterpoint. See *Counterpoint.*

Strict Faburden. See *Faburden.*

Strike Note. See *Bell* 1.

Strike the Lyre. See *Cooke* (3).

Striking Reed. Same as 'Beating Reed' (see *Reed*).

Strimpellata (It.). 'Strumming', 'scraping', &c. (a pejorative term).

String Band and **String Orchestra.** Properly both terms imply combinations of stringed instruments alone; in popular speech, however, they are sometimes used to cover dance bands, &c., provided such *include* strings, the intention apparently being to distinguish these from purely wind bands.

Stringendo (It. 'squeezing'). The notes following one another more and more quickly = *accelerando*.

Stringham, Edwin John (b. Kenosha, Wisconsin, 1890). After study in U.S.A., Rome (under Respighi), and Germany, he occupied various important academic positions at Denver, the Juilliard School, and elsewhere. He has written many orch. and choral works, &c. D.Mus. Northwestern Univ. 1914.

String Orchestra. See *String Band.*

String Quartet, Quintet. See *Quartet*; *Quintet.*

String-toned stops. Organ stops whose tone quality resembles that of stringed instruments, e.g. *Gamba* (q.v.).

Strisciando; strisciato (It., 'trailing'; 'trailed'). 'Smooth', 'slurred', &c., or, sometimes, *Glissando* (q.v.).

Strohfiedel (Ger.). 'Xylophone' (see *Percussion Family* 1 f). 'Stroh' = 'straw', on ropes of which the wooden blocks of the instrument formerly rested. (Avoid confusion with Stroh Violin below.)

Stroh Violin, Viola, 'Cello, Mandolin, Guitar, and Japanese Fiddle. In each of these the usual body of the instrument ('sound-box', &c.) is replaced by mechanism connected with an amplifying horn. Its inventor was Charles Stroh and the date of the introduction of his inventions 1901. (Avoid confusion with *Strohfiedel*: see above.)

Strolling Players' Amateur Orchestral Society. A London amateur body founded 1882 and still active.

Stromenti a corde, 'Stringed instruments'. **Stromenti d'arco,** 'Bowed instruments'. **Stromenti di legno,** 'Wood (wind) instruments'. **Stromenti d'ottone,** 'Brass instruments'. **Stromenti a percossa,** 'Percussion instruments'. **Stromenti a fiato,** 'Wind instruments'. **Stromenti da tasto,** 'Keyboard instruments'.

Stromento, stromenti (It.). 'Instrument', 'instruments'. So *stromentato*, 'instrumented' (cf. *Recitative*).

Strong, George Templeton (b. New York 1856; d. Geneva, Switzerland, 1948). Close friend of MacDowell and member of the circles of Liszt and Raff. During a long life spent almost entirely in Europe composed a symphonic poem *Undine*, a Symphony *Sintram*, and many other works and also showed himself to be a watercolour painter of distinction. His 8oth and 9oth birthdays were publicly celebrated in Geneva, where he had been long resident.

Strophic (Song). In stanzas each set to the same music, i.e. not 'through-composed'.

Strube, Gustav (b. Ballenstadt 1867; d. Baltimore 1953). Violinist, conductor, composer. Trained Leipzig Conserv.

Settled U.S.A. 1890; naturalized 1896. First violin Boston Symphony Orch. 1890–1912. On staff Peabody Conserv., Baltimore, 1913–46 and conductor Baltimore Symphony Orch. 1915–30. Composer of symphonies, concertos, chamber music, &c.

Strumento; strumenti (It.). 'Instrument'; 'instruments' (see *Stromento*).

Strunk, Oliver—in full William Oliver (b. Ithaca, N.Y., 1901). Educ. Cornell Univ., Ithaca, and Berlin Univ.; joined Library of Congress music staff 1928; later univ. professor (Catholic Univ. 1934; Princeton 1937). Various musicological writings. Hon. D.Litt., Univ. Rochester, N.Y.

Stuart, Leslie—real name Thomas A. Barrett (b. Southport 1866; d. Richmond, Surrey, 1928). Organist in Manchester; then in London as composer of very popular songs (e.g. *Soldiers of the Queen*) and musical plays (e.g. *Floradora*, 1899).

Stück (Ger.). 'Piece.'

Stucken, Frank Valentin van der (b. Fredericksburg, Texas, 1858; d. Hamburg 1929). Studied at Antwerp and Leipzig; returning to U.S.A. became well known as choral and orch. conductor in New York (men's choral soc., Arion) and then (1895–1907) Cincinnati (Symphony Orch.), after which lived chiefly in Germany. Composed an opera, orch. pieces, songs, &c.

Student's Festival Overture (Brahms). Same as *Academic Festival Overture* (q.v.).

Stürmend, Stürmisch (Ger.). 'Stormy', 'passionate'.

Style Galant (Fr.), **Galanter Stil** (Ger.). The light elegant style of the late 18th-c. harpsichord composers, e.g. C. P. E. Bach, Haydn, Mozart.

Su (It.). (1) 'On', 'near'. It commonly occurs with various forms of the definite article (masc. and fem., sing. and plur.), as *sul, sull', sulla, sui, sugli, sulle*, e.g. *sul G* (in violin playing), 'on the G string'. (2) 'Up', e.g. *arcata in su*, 'up-bowed'.

Suabe Flöte. Much the same as *Hohlflöte* (q.v.) but usually of 4-foot length and pitch.

Suave; suavità (It.). 'Suave'; 'suavity'.

Sub-Bass. Organ pedal stop, same as *Bourdon* (q.v.).

Sub-bourdon. Organ pedal end-plugged stop of 16-foot length and 32-foot pitch.

Subdominant. The 4th degree of the major or minor scale ('Sub' in the sense of less important, cf. *Submediant*; 'dominant' in the sense of exercising a degree of harmonic control in the key, as the dominant proper does).

Subito (It. 'suddenly'). 'Quickly', 'immediately', as in *volti subito*, 'turn over at once' (sometimes abbrev. to *V.S.*). *Subitamente* is another adverbial form.

Subject in Sonata, see *Form* 3; in Fugue, &c., see *Form* 6.

Submediant. The 6th degree of the major or minor scale ('Sub' in the sense of less important, cf. *Subdominant*; 'mediant' in the sense of midway between the subdominant and tonic, as the mediant proper is between the tonic and dominant).

Submerged Cathedral (Debussy). See *Préludes*.

Sub-octave Coupler. See *Organ* 2.

Subsidiary, or Subsidiary Theme. A term sometimes used to designate one of the less important pieces of subject-matter in a Sonata movement (see *Form* 3). What we speak of as the 'Subject' in such a movement may consist of several sections, the first being usually the most important and the others 'Subsidiary'.

Succentor. See *Precentor*.

Such, (1) **Henry** (b. London 1872; d. Philadelphia 1929). Violinist. Trained Berlin Hochschule 1885–92, and under Wilhelmj. Début Berlin (1893), London 1896. Joined staff G.S.M. For brother see below. (2) **Percy (Frederick)** (b. London 1878; d. New York 1959). Violoncellist. Trained Berlin Hochschule (1892–8). Début Berlin 1898; London 1901. Settled U.S.A. 1928. Brother of (1).

Suggia, Guilhermina (b. Oporto 1888; d. there 1950). Violoncellist. Pupil of Klengel at Leipzig. Before public as soloist age 17, soon enjoying highest international reputation. Wife of Casals 1906–12; married again 1927. Famous portrait of her by Augustus John.

Sugli, sui (It. plur.). 'On the.'

Suite (Fr. and Eng.), **Lesson** (old Eng.), **Ordre** (old Fr.), **Partie** or **Partita** (old Ger.), **Sonata da Camera** (old It.). Initially these things were sets of instrumental compositions, each piece in the set normally in the style of some particular dance, the whole sometimes preceded by an introductory piece or Prelude. The general convention in the 17th and 18th cs. (e.g. in Bach) was a framework as follows: Allemande, Courante, Sarabande, Gigue (see under these heads), Minuets and other dance types being often interpolated in the scheme (cf. *Galanterien*). In Couperin we find long Suites of as many as 17 or 18 pieces, some of them not in dance styles at all and bearing 'fancy' titles such as *Les Abeilles* ('The Bees'), or *Les Plaisirs de St.-Germain-en-Laye* ('The Pleasures' of that town of royal residence).

In that classic period of the Suite (e.g. Bach and Handel) it was usual (though not invariable) to adhere to one key for all the pieces forming the set, or, at least, to keys in the relation of tonic major and minor (occasionally relative major and minor).

Nearly all the movements of the Suite, from Purcell and Corelli in the late 17th c. to the deaths of Bach and Handel in the mid-18th, were in Simple Binary Form (see *Form* 1).

Some of Bach's orch. Suites he called by the name *Overture* (q.v.). In the second half of the 18th c. strings of orch. compositions of different styles were composed for recreative (sometimes open-air) use: these were, in effect, Suites, but were given such names as *Serenata* or *Serenade*, *Cassation* or *Cassazione*, and *Divertimento*.

The composition of Suites (our

oldest cyclic form) still to some extent continues, and, from the nature of things, is not likely entirely to cease. As a medium for the deepest expression it has, however, been mostly superseded by the Sonata and Symphony. The *Song-Cycle* (q.v.) has an obvious relation to the Suite.

Suivez (Fr.). 'Follow' (imperative).

Suk, Josef (b. Křečovice, Bohemia, 1874; d. Prague 1935). A fine violinist and at 17 one of the founders of the famous Bohemian Quartet. He studied under Dvořák and married his daughter. In his earlier compositions he shows the influence of Dvořák's style, in his later he becomes rhythmically and harmonically freer, sometimes approaching atonality.

Sul, sull', sulla, sui, sugli, sulle (It., termination according to gender and number). 'On the'.

Sul G or **Sul IV** (It.). 'On the G', 'on the fourth' (string)—a term used in violin music.

Sulla tastiera (It.). 'On the fingerboard', i.e. bow on or near it. *Sul tasto* means the same. (*Tastiera* also means keyboard.)

Sullivan, Arthur Seymour (b. London 1842; there d. 1900). Son of a military band clarinettist. He became a choir-boy of the Chapel Royal, and then won the Mendelssohn Scholarship, being thus enabled to study at the R.A.M. and the Leipzig Conserv. At 20 he made his name with his music to Shakespeare's *Tempest*, performed at the Crystal Palace. He composed orch. music, oratorios, songs, and part-songs, church music, &c., but especially that famous series of humorous, satirical operas of which the chief librettist was W. S. Gilbert. In these he showed decided gifts of melody, apt lighthanded orchestration, and dramatic characterization. The 'Gilbert and Sullivan Operas' are as follows: *Thespis* (1871); *Trial by Jury* (1875); *The Sorcerer* (1877); *H.M.S. Pinafore* (1878); *The Pirates of Penzance* (1880); *Patience* (1881); *Iolanthe* (1882); *Princess Ida* (1884); *The Mikado* (1885); *Ruddigore* (1887); *The Yeomen of the Guard* (1888); *The Gondoliers* (1889);

Utopia Limited (1893); *The Grand Duke* (1896).

For a time (1876–81) he directed the National Training School of Music (now the R.C.M.). He received honorary doctorates in music of Cambridge and Oxford and in 1883 was knighted.

See also *Beauty Stone*; *Contrabandista*; *Cox and Box*; *Di Ballo*; *Emerald Isle*; *Golden Legend*; *Haddon Hall*; *Henry the Eighth*; *In Memoriam*; *Ivanhoe*; *Kenilworth*; *Light of the World*; *Lost Chord*; *Martyr of Antioch*; *Prodigal Son*; *Rose of Persia*; *Te Deum*; *Tempest*; *Zoo*.

Sul ponticello (It.). 'On the bridge', i.e. bowing near it (violin, &c.).

Sul tasto (It.). 'On the touch' (meaning that the bow of the violin, &c., shall be kept over or near the fingerboard). *Sulla tastiera* means the same.

Sumer is icumen in. An early 13th-c. rota, or round—a spring song for 4 tenor voices in canon at the unison (see *Canon*) and 2 bass voices repeating a Pes, or short ground (see *Ground Bass*), which is also in canon at the unison. This elaborate construction and some other technical points make it a very remarkable production for its period. It is conjecturally attributed to John of Fornsete, monk of Reading Abbey. In 1945 Manfred Bukofzer put forward a theory that the earliest possible date, by internal evidence, is 1280, but this is not yet accepted by the best Brit. authorities. He admits that 'the rota can still claim to be the first composition for 6 voices and the first canon as a form in its own right'.

Summation Tone. See *Acoustics* 9.

Summend (Ger.). 'Humming.'

Summer Night on the River. Delicate piece for orch. by Delius. (1911; 1st Brit. perf. London 1914.)

Summer's Last Will and Testament. By Constant Lambert. Choral-orch. settings of lyrics (1st perf. London 1936) from a play of that name (1593) by Thomas Nashe.

Summy Co., Clayton F. (Inc.). Chicago music publishing firm. Estd. 1888.

Sumner, William Leslie (b. Airmyn, Yorks., 1904; d. 1973). Organist and writer on his instrument. Educ. London Univ. (Ph.D., B.Sc.).

Sumsion, Herbert (Whitton) (b. Gloucester 1899). Chorister Gloucester Cathedral. Studied R.C.M. On staff Curtis Institute, Philadelphia, 1926–8, then organist Gloucester Cathedral 1928–67 and conductor Choral and Orch. Societies and Fest. D.Mus., Lambeth.

Sung Mass. See *Mass*.

Sun Quartets (Haydn). See *Sonnenquartette*.

Sunrise Quartet. Eng. nickname of Haydn's String Quartet 'No. 71' or 'No. 78', in B flat, sometimes described as op. 76, no. 4.

Sun Worshippers, The. See *Thomas, A. Goring*.

Suo (It.). 'Its own' (e.g. *suo loco*, 'its own place'—after performing an 8ve higher or lower).

Suonare (same as *sonare*). To 'sound', i.e. to play; *suonante*, 'resonant'.

Suono; suoni (It.). 'Sound'; 'sounds'.

Suor Angelica (Puccini). See under *Trittico*.

Superbo, superba (It. masc., fem.). 'Proud.'

Super-octave coupler. See *Organ* 2.

Super-piano. See *Electric Musical Instruments* 5.

Supertonic. The 2nd degree of the major or minor scale.

Supervia, Conchita (b. Barcelona 1895; d. London 1936). Coloratura operatic and concert mezzo-soprano. Début age 14, Buenos Aires; age 15 Italy. Highly popular Great Britain and U.S.A.

Suppé, Franz von—really Francesco Ezecchiele Ermenegildo Cavaliere Suppé-Demelli (b. in Dalmatia 1819; d. Vienna 1895). A theatrical conductor who wrote over 150 operas and operettas which had a high popularity, especially in Vienna. His overture to *Poet and Peasant* is still everywhere performed and exists in nearly 60 arrangements for different instrumental combinations. (See *Boccaccio*.)

Suppliant (Fr.). 'Supplicating.' **Supplichevole; supplichevolmente** (It.). 'Supplicating'; 'supplicatingly'.

Supprimez (Fr.). 'Suppress.' In Fr. organ music it means to put out of use the stop in question.

Sur (Fr.). 'On', or 'over'.

Suriano. See *Soriano*.

Sur la touche (Fr.). 'On the fingerboard', i.e. (violin, &c.) bow over it.

Sur le chevalet (Fr.). 'On the bridge', i.e. (violin, &c.) bow near it.

Surprise Cadence. See *Cadence*.

Surprise Symphony. Nickname for Haydn's Symphony in G, no. 94 in Breitkopf edn. of the Symphonies (1791; no. 2 of the 'London Symphonies'). So called because of a loud stroke of drum in the slow movement. In Ger. the nickname is *Paukenschlag*, 'Drum Stroke' (not to be confused with *Paukenwirbel*; see *Drum-Roll*).

Sursum Corda. 'Lift up your hearts', included in all known Christian liturgies of all ages. The Eng. words occur in the Communion Service of the Anglican Church.

Surtout (Fr.). 'Above all', 'especially'.

Susanna. Oratorio by Handel. (1st perf. London 1749.)

Susannah. 2-act opera; libretto and music by Carlisle Floyd. (Prod. Florida 1955; New York 1956.)

Susanna's Secret (Wolf-Ferrari). See *Segreto di Susanna*.

Suspended Cadence. See *Cadence*.

Suspension. See *Harmony* 2 f.

Süss (Ger.). 'Sweet.'

Süsskind, Walter (b. Prague 1913). Trained Prague Conserv. Toured as pianist. Resident Britain from 1939, conducting Carl Rosa Opera Co. (q.v.), Sadler's Wells (q.v.), &c. Permanent condr. Scottish Orch. 1946–54, then Melbourne, Toronto, St. Louis Orchs. Some compositions.

Süssmayr, Franz Xaver (b. Steyer, Austria, 1766; d. Vienna 1803). Kapellmeister at Vienna opera and composer of stage works. Pupil and friend of Mozart and completed his *Requiem*.

Sustaining Pedal. See *Pianoforte; Pianoforte Playing*.

Susurrando, susurrante (It.). 'Whispering.'

Sutherland, Joan (b. Sydney 1926). Operatic soprano. Trained Sydney Conserv. Career at first Australia, then from 1952 at Covent Garden in supporting roles. Appeared there 1959 as Lucia, then rapidly gained first-rank position as dramatic coloratura of exceptional range, agility, and power. C.B.E. 1961.

Svanholm, Set (b. Vasteras 1904; d. nr. Stockholm 1964). Début as operatic baritone 1930; from 1936 tenor. Trained Stockholm Conserv. (later on staff) and in Germany, Austria, and France. With Royal Opera, Stockholm, from 1932. Guest appearances as opera and concert artist in Europe and North and South America. (Covent Garden 1948, &c.) Dir. Swedish Royal Opera 1956–63.

Svegliando; svegliato (It.). 'Awakening'; 'awakened', i.e. 'brisk', 'alert'.

Svelto (It.). 'Smart', 'quick'.

Svendsen, Johan Severin (b. Christiania, now Oslo, 1840; d. Copenhagen 1911). Norwegian conductor and composer, associate in Germany of Liszt and Wagner. His works include 2 symphonies, a violin concerto, and a 'cello concerto, songs, &c. He was a nationalist-romantic, but less pronouncedly nationalist than his countryman Grieg.

See *Carnival at Paris*.

Svolgimento (It. 'Unfolding'). 'Development' (q.v.).

Swain, Freda Mary (b. Portsmouth 1902). Composer and pianist. Trained under Stanford and Arthur Alexander at R.C.M. (later on staff), marrying latter. Publ. works include piano and chamber music, songs, &c.

Swainson, Willan (b. Harrogate 1886; d. Aberdeen 1970). Organist and choral conductor. Lecturer in Music, Univ. Aberdeen, 1925; Director of Music Dept. 1942.

Swallow, The (Puccini). See *Rondine*.

Swan, The (Saint-Saëns). See *Carnival of Animals*.

Swan and the Skylark, The. See *Thomas, A. Goring*.

Swan Lake ('Lac des Cygnes'). Tchaikovsky's 1st ballet (op. 20, 1876). Some of the music was afterwards made up as a 5-movt. Suite.

Swan of Tuonela (Sibelius). See *Lemminkäinen*.

Swan Song (Schubert). See *Schwanengesang*.

Swarthout, Gladys (b. Deepwater, Mo., 1904; d. nr. Florence 1969). Mezzo-soprano. Began career as church singer. Opera début Chicago 1924. Metropolitan Opera 1929. Novelist.

Sweelinck, Jan Pieterzoon (b. either Deventer or Amsterdam 1562; d. Amsterdam 1621). Famous organist, influencing the art of organ playing throughout northern Europe. His works for organ exhibit almost the earliest examples of independent pedal playing and include the earliest fully-worked-out fugues for the instrument. His choral works (sacred and secular) are important. (See *Gabrieli, A.; Hol.*)

Sweet Honey-sucking Bees. See *Wilbye*.

Swell Organ, Swell Box, Swell Pedal. See *Organ* 1.

Swert, Jules de (b. Louvain 1843; d. Ostend 1891). Well-known violoncellist. Composer for his instrument, &c.; author of *Primer of Violoncello*.

Swing. Variously interpreted, in common with most terms in Jazz: generally taken as meaning that subtle form of rubato which renders a skilled performer acceptable to initiates. In the 1930's 'Swing Bands' were widely popular.

Swinstead, Felix (Gerald) (b. London 1880; d. Southwold 1959). Pianist. Trained under Matthay, Corder, and others at R.A.M.; later a prof. of piano there and well-known public recitalist. Publ. chamber music, very many piano works, &c.

Swinyard, Laurence (b. London 1901). Music critic; ed. *Musical Opinion* and *The Organ*. Numerous articles, reviews, and translations.

Sword Dance. A type of folk dance for men. In Eng. sword dances each carries a wooden or blunt steel blade with, at each end, a handle ('rapper'), and with the other hand he grasps the handle of a neighbour's sword. The evolutions are those of an elaborate figure dance, in which the performers jump over or pass under the swords, and so on. Sometimes there is at the close a ceremony symbolical of cutting off a head, the whole dance having had its origin in some primitive religious exercise of nature worship and sacrifice.

Syllable Mark. See Table 22.

Sylphides, Les. Ballet by Fokine, set to various pieces of Chopin. (Prod. Paris 1909.)

Sylvia. See *Delibes.*

Symbolism. See *Debussy.*

Sympathetic Strings. Those on a bowed, plucked, or hammered instrument which are not played upon but vibrate merely by sympathetic resonance (cf. *Acoustics* 19; also *Viol Family* 3 g; and 'Aliquot Scaling', s.v. *Pianoforte*), so enriching the tone.

Symphonia domestica (Strauss). See *Domestic Symphony.*

Symphonic Dance. An orch. piece of serious value yet in dance rhythm and style.

Symphonic Poem, or Tone Poem. This term and the type of composition it represents are a legacy of Liszt. Influenced by the Romantic movement of his day (see *Romantic*), he brought into music literary, dramatic, and pictorial elements—in other words wrote *Programme Music* (q.v.): this tendency is seen in his two actual symphonies (*Dante* and *Faust*, each with 3 movements, expressive of the feelings connected with 3 phases of his subject). He realized, however, that in a 1-movement work of a free type he would be less constrained by formal considerations and could more readily let the form mould itself to the thought: to this new type of composition he gave the name Symphonic Poem. His Bohemian follower Smetana took up the idea, as have done A. Ritter and his disciple, Richard Strauss, and

Saint-Saëns, and others. The 1st Brit. composer of such a work was William Wallace, in his *The Passing of Beatrice* (1892). The fashion of composing Symphonic Poems died down in the 2nd decade of the 20th c., composers then favouring a more abstract application of their art.

Cf. the Concert Overture, s.v. *Overture.*

Symphonie Cévenole. See *Symphonie sur un chant montagnard.*

Symphonie de Psaumes (Stravinsky). See *Symphony of Psalms.*

Symphonie espagnole. By Lalo (op. 21). Really a violin concerto in 5 movements (one or two, however, often omitted). Dedicated to Sarasate and 1st perf. by him Paris 1875; Crystal Palace, London, 1878.

Symphonie fantastique (Berlioz). See *Fantastic Symphony.*

Symphonie funèbre et triomphale. For Orch. and Military Band. By Berlioz (op. 15), composed to celebrate the 10th anniversary of the Revolution of 1830 and performed in the Place de la Bastille, at the inauguration of the Bastille Column and the translation of the remains of the 'Combattants de Juillet'. The 3 movements are: (1) *Funeral March*; (2) *Funeral Oration*; leading into (3) *Apotheosis.*

Symphonie sur un chant montagnard français ('Symphony on a French Song from the Mountains'). By d'Indy. For Piano and Orch. (op. 25, 1886). Also known as *Symphonie Cévenole.*

Symphonique (Fr.). **symphonisch** (Ger.). 'Symphonic.'

Symphony, from the Greek, means a 'sounding together'. The word has had numerous applications at different periods in the history of music, nearly all of them explicable by its literal significance. It still has more than one meaning, being sometimes applied to an introducing, closing, or interpolated instrumental passage in a song, &c., to such a piece as the instrumental movement in Handel's *Messiah* called 'Pastoral Symphony', or, in U.S.A., to a full orch. (this last use, though strange to Brit. ears, justified by precedent, as in Milton's 'the whole symphony with artful and unimaginable touches adorn and grace the well-studied chords of some choice composer').

A Symphony, as the word is now used, is a Sonata for orch. and its history resembles, in a general way, that of the Sonata (q.v.). The It. operatic overture of the 18th c., consisting of 3 movements (quick-slow-quick), has an obvious resemblance to what we now call a Symphony. Overtures of that type, naturally, sometimes received separate perf., and from that fact came to be composed as independent works. The Concerto Grosso (see *Concerto*) had its influence, also, on the evolution of the Symphony.

Early composers of the Symphony, as we now normally use the word, with the 1st movement of its 4 in what we call 'Sonata Form' or 'Compound Binary Form' (see *Form* 3), were, in Italy, G. B. Sammartini (1704–74); in Germany, J. W. A. Stamitz (1717–57) and his sons; and, in France, Gossec (1734–1829). There was in their period no settled constitution for the symphonic orch., which might consist of strings, or of these with a pair of flutes, oboes, or horns, and, perhaps, bassoons, and (later) clarinets. The harpsichord (represented by a *Figured Bass*, q.v.) was usually a part of the force employed.

Carl Philipp Emanuel Bach (1714–88), the Father of the Sonata (as we understand the word), is also important in the history of its orch. counterpart, but Haydn is usually considered to be the Father of the Symphony; Mozart profited by Haydn's example and then developed the style further, so that, in turn, Haydn was able to learn a good deal from him. The 12 great symphonies composed by Haydn for England and the 3 greatest of Mozart (E flat, G minor, and the so-called 'Jupiter') are prominent landmarks in the history of the Symphony. Beethoven in his 9 Symphonies carried the serious development of the form and style still further. With these 3 composers we find a form that had begun as a means of cheerful entertainment turning into a means of deepest emotional expression.

The 1st movement of a Symphony (as already stated, normally in 'Sonata Form') is invariably its most important one. The 2nd movement is usually slower and more lyrical; the 3rd may be a Minuet and Trio (see *Minuet*) or a Scherzo (q.v.); the 4th is (like the 1st) of considerable length, but usually of lighter style: it is often in Rondo Form, but may be in Sonata Form, or any other form suitable for a longish piece of music.

During and following the Brahms period some development took place in all the various types of cyclic instrumental composition (sonatas, string quartets, symphonies, &c.). Sometimes the various movements were linked by the use of musical material common to all of them: at other times there was the intention of expressing some literary, dramatic, or pictorial idea—e.g. Berlioz's *Fantastic Symphony*, subtitled 'Episodes in the Life of an Artist', which is an example of the principle of Programme Music (q.v.), here applied in what had been considered an abstract form (Berlioz also employed the device of the 'Idée Fixe'; see *Berlioz*). The Symphonic Poem (q.v.) may be considered to be a child of the Symphony in this 'Programme Music' phase.

Symphony of a Thousand. Name that has become attached to Mahler's 8th in E flat (1907) which calls for Orch. of 130 players (including Piano, Harmonium, Organ, and Mandoline), 8 Vocal Soloists, 2 full Choirs and Choir of 400 children. Text of 1st part from *Veni Creator Spiritus* and 2nd part from conclusion of Goethe's Faust. (1st perf. Munich 1910. London 1930.)

Symphony of Liberation. See *Stevens, Bernard.*

Symphony of Psalms. Choral-orch. work by Stravinsky. (Dedicated to Boston Symphony Orch. and 1st perf. Boston 1930.)

Symphony to Dante's Divina Commedia. By Liszt (1856).

Sympson. See *Simpson.*

Syncopation is a displacement of either the beat or the normal accent of a piece of music.

It is, then, *rhythmic contradiction*

that constitutes syncopation. Sometimes (a) The effect of contradiction is brought about by the occurrence of rests on the normally accented parts of the measure, with notes on the unaccented; sometimes (b) By notes being first sounded on the normally unaccented parts of the measure and then merely held on over the normally accented parts; sometimes (c) By the introduction of a stress mark over notes that would normally be unstressed. In any case, the rhythmic effect is the same: there is a shifting of accent.

All composers of all periods have used syncopation, and, being a very simple and natural device, it often occurs in the folk song music of certain races. The Scotch Snap (q.v.) is an instance of syncopation, though here the normal divisions of the beat, rather than those of the measure, are contradicted. (But this is little more than a matter of notation, for a beat is really a sub-measure.)

The prevalence of syncopation in African music, and hence in that of the Amer. Negroes, is an important influence in the history of jazz, and thus of jazz-influenced ballroom dancing and 20th-c. popular music generally.

Improvement introduced into a theme from Schubert's 'Unfinished' Symphony. (The London Revue *Joy Bells*, during the early 1920's.)

Synthétistes. See *Poot.*

Syrinx. See *Panpipes.*

Syvspring ('Seven jumps'). A popular dance of Jutland.

Székely, Zoltán (b. Hungary 1903). Violinist. Pupil of Hubay. Leader of Hungarian String Quartet. Composed chamber music, &c. Resident U.S.A. (1950).

Szell, George (b. Budapest 1897; d. Cleveland 1970). Operatic and orch. conductor. Child prodigy pianist. Then conductor at various Ger. opera houses. Scottish Orch. 1937. Australia 1938 and 1939; U.S.A. 1942, &c. (Cleveland Orch. from 1946).

Szenkar, Eugen (b. Budapest 1891). Operatic and orch. conductor. Positions in Prague, Budapest, Salzburg (Mozarteum 1915–16), Altenburg, Frankfurt, Berlin, Cologne, &c. Composer of orch., chamber, and piano music, songs, &c.

Szigeti, Joseph (b. Budapest 1892; d. Lucerne 1973). Violinist. Pupil of Hubay. Appeared in public from age 9. Lived in London 1906–13. On staff of Geneva Conserv. 1917–24; later in Paris and Berlin, with world tours. Publ. transcriptions, &c. Book, '*With Strings Attached* (1948). Long resident U.S.A.; Switzerland from 1959.

Szymanowski, Karol (b. Tymoszowka, Ukraine, 1882; d. Lausanne 1937). Of Polish race and studied at Warsaw Conserv., becoming its Principal in 1927. Composed at first in Chopin manner, later in polytonal or even atonal style. Works include 3 symphonies, symphonic poems, 2 violin concertos, 2 operas, chamber music, piano music, choral music, and songs.

T

Tabarro, Il (Puccini). See under *Trittico.*

Tabatière à musique. See *Mechanical Reproduction of Music* 7.

Tablature. A system of indicating the music to be performed other than by notation (i.e. other than by the use of 'notes'). Such a system might use figures, letters, and similar signs. The older instrumental music was often represented in Tablature (e.g. the lute accompaniment to a song—see *Lute Family*) and there are still some instances of Tablature today in music supplied for such instruments as ukeleles, zithers, ocarinas, and mandolines, and even for simple piano accompaniment as taught in some 'Vamping Tutors'.

Tabor. See *Recorder Family* 2.

Tabor (Smetana). See *My Fatherland.*

Tacere (It.). 'To be silent.' So *tace,* 'is silent'; *tacciono,* 'are silent'. Often the Lat. sing. and plur. forms are used, *tacet, tacent.*

Tafelklavier (Ger. 'table-keyboard'). The virginals or the spinet (either); for these see *Harpsichord Family.*

Tafelmusik (Ger.) 'Table Music', i.e. (1) music to be performed whilst a meal is proceeding. Telemann has left a fine example in 3 sections for various combinations of instruments, each with 6 movements. (2) Choral music at table after a meal. (The term is a vague one and has possibly other applications.)

Tagliavini, Ferruccio (b. Reggio Emilia 1913). Lyric tenor. Début Florence 1939, then international career.

Taglioni, Marie. See *Ballet.*

Tailleferre, Germaine. See *Six.*

Takt (Ger.). (a) 'Time', (b) 'Beat', (c) 'Measure' (i.e. bar). So *im Takt,* 'in time' (= 'A tempo'); *ein Takt wie vorher zwei,* 'one beat as previously two' (one beat allowed as much time as two beats previously).

A good many compounds and derivatives of *Takt* are met with; e.g. *Taktart,* 'time-species'—duple, triple, &c.; *taktfest* ('time-firm'), 'in steady time'; *Takt halten,* 'to hold [keep] time'; *taktieren,* 'to beat time'; *Taktschlag* ('time-stroke'), 'beat'; *Taktzeichen* ('time-sign'), 'signature'; *Taktwechsel,* 'time-change'; *taktmässig* ('time moderated'), generally meaning the same as 'Tempo commodo', q.v.; *Taktnote* ('bar-note'), 'semibreve'; *Taktpause,* 'measure-rest' (i.e. bar-rest); *Taktstock* ('time-stick'), 'baton'; *Taktstrich* ('bar-stroke'), 'bar-line'; *taktig,* 'bar-ish', in such connexion as 3-*taktig,* 'three-bar-ish', i.e. having 3-bar (3-measure) phrases.

Tale of Czar Saltan (Rimsky-Korsakof). See under *Legend.*

Tale of the Invisible City (Rimsky-Korsakof). See *Kitej.*

Tale of Tsar Saltan. See under *Legend.*

Tales of Hoffman. Fantastic opera by Offenbach, based on 3 stories by Ger. romantic writer, E. T. A. Hoffmann. Posthumous and orchestrated by Guiraud. (Prod. Paris 1881; New York 1882; London 1907.)

See also *Barcarolle.*

Talich, Václav (b. Moravia 1883; d. nr. Prague 1961). Violinist (pupil of Ševčik), conductor (pupil of Nikisch), and composer (pupil of Reger). Conductor Czech National Orch. (1919–41), Prague National Opera (1933–48), &c. Many tours, including Britain (Scottish Orch. season of 1926–7).

Tallis, Thomas (b. abt. 1505; d. Greenwich 1585). Seems to have been organist of Waltham Abbey, nr. London, until the dissolution of the monasteries in 1540; Gentleman of the Chapel Royal under both Henry VIII and Elizabeth; latterly joint organist with Byrd; these two granted a monopoly of music printing in England (1575); arranged in harmony the plainsong responses (see *Responses*) of the Eng. church service as adapted by Merbecke; these still in use, as also famous setting of canticles in Dorian Mode. Wrote some English anthems; greater part of output Latin masses, motets, lamentations, &c.; motet, *Spem in alium*, in 40 voice-parts, a remarkable work.

Tallis Fantasia. By Vaughan Williams, based on a metrical psalm tune by Tallis. For String Quartet and 2 String Orchs. (1st perf. Gloucester Fest. 1910.)

Tallis's Canon. This well-known tune dates from about 1567. It is one of the 9 tunes (1 in each of the 8 modes, with an additional 1) which Tallis (q.v.) composed for Archbishop Parker's metrical *Whole Psalter*, where it is attached to the 67th Psalm. The tenor and treble are in canon in the 8ve throughout. Nowadays the treble leads and the tenor follows at a measure's distance; in the original the tenor (then looked upon as the chief part in vocal harmony) led and the treble followed. The tune was then, by repetition of each line, twice as long as it is now.

The words traditionally associated with the tune are those of Bishop Ken's evening hymn for the Winchester Coll. boys, 'Glory to Thee, my God, this night' (1692). The earliest connexion of this hymn with the tune, in print, is 1732.

Talon (Fr. 'Heel'). The nut end of the bow of the violin, &c.

Tamagno, Francesco (b. Turin 1851; d. Varese 1905). Operatic tenor of the heroic type. Trained Turin Conserv. Great success from début in 1873. Verdi's 1st Othello (Milan 1887; London 1889; New York 1891).

Tamara. Symphonic Poem by Balakiref (1882). Based on a poem of Lermontof concerning an angeldemon-queen who lured men to destruction. Dedicated to Liszt. (1st London perf. 1896; New York 1908.) Fokine arranged a ballet to the music.

Tambour (Fr.). 'Drum' (see *Percussion Family*).

Tambour de Basque (Fr.). Tambourine (see *Percussion Family* 2 m).

Tambourin (Fr.). (1) The tabor: elaborations of the name are *Tambourin de Provence* and *Tambourin genre Watteau* (but *Tambourin de Béarn* is a sort

of small dulcimer). (2) In Ger. and It. either tabor or tambourine. (3) An old Provençal dance, in which are used the tambourin (tabor) and galoubet (see *Recorder Family* 2). (4) A keyboard piece in the style of the music for 3 above, and with much use of the device of repeated notes in a harmonic 'pedal' (see *Harmony* 2 i), in imitation of the tabor.

Tambourine. See *Percussion Family* 2 m.

Tambour militaire (Fr.). Side drum (see *Percussion Family* 2 i).

Tamburin (Ger.), **tamburino** (It.). Tabor or tambourine (either). (See *Percussion Family* 2 l, m.)

Tamburini, Antonio (b. Faenza 1800; d. Nice 1876). Operatic baritone. Made early reputation all over Italy; London and Paris 1832. Extreme flexibility of voice and high versatility features of his performances. Retired about 1859.

Tamburo basco (It. 'Basque drum'). The tambourine (see *Percussion Family* 2 m).

Tamburo grande or **tamburo grosso**, or **gran tamburo** (It.). Bass Drum (see *Percussion Family* 2 k).

Tamburo militare (It.). Snare Drum, Side Drum (see *Percussion Family* 2 i).

Tamburone (It.). Bass Drum (see *Percussion Family* 2 k).

Tamburo piccolo (It. 'little drum'). The Side Drum (see *Percussion Family* 2 i).

Tamburo rullante (It. 'rolling drum'). Tenor Drum (see *Percussion Family* 2 j).

Taming of the Shrew (Goetz). See *Widerspenstigen Zähmung*.

Tammany, or The Indian Chief; also known as *America Rediscovered*. Early Amer. Ballad-opera; by James Hewitt. Music lost. (Prod. New York and Philadelphia 1794; Boston 1796.)

Tam O'Shanter. (1) MACKENZIE'S Scottish Rhapsody No. 3, for Orch. (1st perf. London 1911.) (2) Symphonic Ballad by CHADWICK. (1st perf. Norfolk, Conn., Fest. 1915.) (3)

Scherzo by E. Goossens (1916). (4) Overture by Malcolm Arnold.

Tampon (Fr.). Drumstick. The *Tampon double* is a double-headed stick used occasionally with the Bass Drum for thunder effects.

Tam-tam. Gong (see *Percussion Family* 2 p).

Tancredi. Opera by Rossini. Libretto based on Tasso and on Voltaire. (Prod. Venice 1813; London 1820; New York 1825.)

Tändelei (Ger.). Same as *Badinage*, i.e. 'Playfulness'. *Tändelnd*, 'Playfully'.

Taneief, (1) **Alexander Sergeivich** (b. St. Petersburg 1850; there d. 1918). Important civil servant who studied music under Rimsky-Korsakof and others and composed operas, symphonies, chamber music, &c.

(2) **Serge Ivanovich** (b. govt. of Vladimir 1856; d. Moscow 1915). Studied at Moscow Conserv. under Nicholas Rubinstein and Tchaikovsky, later becoming prof. of both composition and piano and finally director; toured as pianist. Composed 6 symphonies, 6 string quartets, 2 string trios, songs, an operatic trilogy, &c. Wrote treatises on counterpoint and canon.

Tangent. See *Clavichord.*

Tango. Argentine dance, performed by couples moving at a slow walking pace. The music is in simple duple time and shares with the Habanera (q.v.) a characteristic dotted rhythm (♩♩ ♫).

Tannenbaum. See *Maryland, my Maryland; Red Flag.*

Tannhäuser und der Sängerkrieg auf Wartburg ('Tannhäuser and the Contest of Song on the Wartburg'). Dramatic opera by Wagner. (Prod. Dresden 1845; New York 1859; London 1876.)

Tansman, Alexandre (b. Łódź 1897). Polish composer, pianist, and conductor, who has made Paris his centre since 1920. Works include symphonies, piano concertos, string quartets, operas, ballets, songs, film music, &c.

Tans'ur, William—really 'Tanzer' (b. Dunchurch, War., probably 1706; d. St. Neots, Hunts., 1783). Bookseller and teacher of psalmody, composer and ed. of metrical psalm tunes, author of quaint but highly popular theoretical treatises which appeared in many edns. from 1724 to 1829.

Tant (Fr.). 'As much' (or sometimes simply 'much').

Tantivy Towers. See *Dunhill.*

Tanto (It.). 'So much', 'as much', 'too much'. *Non tanto*, after an adj. or adv., is a frequent expression, meaning 'But don't overdo it!' (e.g. 'Allegro non tanto'). *Tantino* is the diminutive— 'A very little'.

Tantum ergo ('Therefore we before Him bending, this great sacrament revere', in a familiar Eng. version). These are the opening words of the last section of St. Thomas Aquinas's Corpus Christi hymn, *Pange lingua* (q.v.). It is used in other services than that of Corpus Christi and especially in that of Benediction (q.v.). It has its own plainsong, but has often been set by composers.

Tanymarian. See *Stephen* 1.

Tanz, Tänze (Ger.). 'Dance', 'dances'. *Tänzchen* is a diminutive.

Tap Box. See *Chinese Wood Block.*

Tap-dancing. What was formerly called 'step-dancing' (though this term has also a wider sense). Repeated taps on the floor with toes and heels are its distinguishing feature.

Tapfere Soldat, Der (Straus). See *Chocolate Soldier.*

Tapiola. The most important of the Symphonic Poems of Sibelius. (Op. 112, 1925. Dedicated to Walter Damrosch.) The name signifies the sombre domains of the Forest God, Tapio.

Tarantella (It.), **Tarantelle** (Fr.). A dance which takes its name from Taranto, in the heel of Italy, or from a spider common there, called the Tarantula, whose bite is alleged to be poisonous and to cause the disease known as Tarantism, of which disease the dance is supposed to be a cure. The music is in compound duple time and of great rapidity with an approach to the *perpetuum mobile* (q.v.). The saltarello is a similar type.

THE TARANTULA SPIDER

(From *Observations Rares de Médecine*, 1758. This work credulously asserts that the insects will dance rhythmically if a Tarantella tune is played to them)

Tarbouka. A flower-pot-shaped drum from North Africa, used by Berlioz in the Slave Dance in his *The Trojans*.

Tardo, tarda (It. masc., fem.). 'Slow.' So *tardamente*, 'slowly'; *tardando*, *tardantemente*, 'slowing' (gradually); *tardato*, 'slowed' (gradually).

Tartini, Giuseppe (b. Pirano 1692; d. Padua 1770). Son of nobleman, educated in turn for church, law, and army, but became famous violinist and also composer and acoustical theorist (discovered resultant tones, 1714: see *Acoustics*); attached as violinist and orch. director to church of St. Anthony, Padua; in that city visited by violin students of many nations seeking instruction. Composed 150 sonatas for violin and harpsichord (including 'Devil's Trill' sonata, q.v.), 140

concertos for violin and strings, 50 string trios; many of these works never printed. Also wrote important treatises on harmony, violin playing, &c.

Tasso. Symphonic Poem by Liszt (1849). Partly inspired by Byron's *Lament of Tasso*.

Taste, Tasten (Ger.). 'Key', 'keys' (in the sense of the finger-keys of a keyboard instrument).

Tasti. See *Tasto*.

Tastiera (It.). This has the same 2 meanings as *Tasto*, below. Thus *sulla tastiera* = *sul tasto*.

Tastiera per luce ('Keyboard for Light'). See *Prometheus* (Scriabin).

Tasto, tasti (It. sing. and plur.). (1) Key, keys (i.e. of a keyboard). Hence in old music with figured bass (q.v.) *Tasto solo* means 'play the key alone', i.e. the mere bass line as shown, without adding chords. (2) The fingerboard of a bowed instrument. Thus *sul tasto*, 'on the finger-board', means that one is to bow well up the strings. (Cf. *Tastiera*, above.)

Tate, (1) Nahum (b. Dublin 1652; d. London 1715). Minor poet; Poet Laureate (1690 to death); associate of Purcell and collaborator with Brady (q.v.) in long-famous metrical version of Psalms (see *Hymns and Hymn Tunes* 3).

(2) **Phyllis (Margaret Duncan)** (b. Gerrards Cross, Bucks., 1911). Trained R.A.M. Composer of chamber and vocal works; concerto for saxophone and strings, an opera and other vocal works, &c. Wife of Alan Frank.

Tattoo. The music of bugles and drums, recalling soldiers to their barracks at night. In the Brit. Army it begins with the *First Post*, lasts about 20 minutes, and ends with the *Last Post* (q.v.).

Tauber, Richard (b. Linz 1892; d. London 1948). Operatic tenor of the *bel canto* type. Special reputation in Mozart. Composed light operas, &c., and composed for and appeared in films. Naturalized British 1940.

Taubert, (Karl Gottfried) Wilhelm (b. Berlin 1811; there d. 1891). Pianist and conductor; voluminous and refined composer of operas, symphonies, chamber music, piano sonatas, and (especially) about 300 songs.

Taubmann. See *Electric Musical Instruments* 1.

Tausig, Karl (b. Warsaw 1841; d. Leipzig 1871). Member of Liszt circle and as pianist ranked with Liszt and von Bülow; able to play from memory the complete classical repertory. Composed piano music (including studies still used) and produced many piano transcriptions.

Tavan, Émile (b. Aix-en-Provence 1849; d. Gassicourt-près-Menthes 1930). Incessantly active and very resourceful 'arranger' for small orchs. of music composed for larger ones or for some other medium; wrote a book on orchestration and was for nearly 20 years mayor of Menthes.

Taverner, John (b. abt. 1495; d. Boston, Lincs., 1545). Master of the Choristers and organist (1526–30) at St. Frideswide's, Oxford (now Christ Church Cathedral); imprisoned in a cellar for premature Protestantism; then lived in Boston; one of chief agents for suppression of the monasteries. One of greatest of 16th-c. Eng. church composers. (See *In Nomine.*)

Taylor, (1) **Franklin** (b. Birmingham 1843; d. London 1919). Pianist. Trained Leipzig Conserv. Settled in London as performer and teacher (holding church organ positions also). On staff (1876 to death) of National Training School and its successor the R.C.M.; partner with Beringer (q.v.) in founding Academy for the Higher Development of Pianoforte-playing (1873–97).

(2) See *Coleridge-Taylor.*

(3) **(Joseph) Deems** (b. New York 1885; d. New York 1966). General journalist and then music critic; also popular broadcaster. Composer of operas (see *King's Henchman*; *Peter Ibbetson*), orch. works, &c., and author of some books on music.

Tchaikovsky (Chaykovski, &c.), **Peter Ilich** (b. Kamsko-Votinsk, govt. of Viatka, 1840; d. St. Petersburg 1893). Began life as civil servant, then

turned to music and studied at Conserv. of St. Petersburg under Anton Rubinstein; later influenced by Balakiref and Rimsky-Korsakof, but never in full sympathy with their nationalist group of 'The Five' (q.v.); was the 1st Russian composer to capture the attention of Brit. and Amer. audiences, his melodic vein, brilliant orch. colour, and strong emotional expression making strong appeal. Composed 10 operas, 6 symphonies (see below), 3 piano concertos, violin concerto, 3 ballets, chamber and piano music, and songs.

See also *Baiser de la fée*; *Capriccio italien*; *Eighteen-Twelve Overture*; *Eugen Onegin*; *Iolanthe*; *Nutcracker*; *Queen of Spades*; *Romeo and Juliet*; *Sleeping Princess*; *Swan Lake*.

Tchaikovsky's Symphonies are as follows: No. 1, in G minor (op. 13, 1867); known as *Winter Dreams.* No. 2, in C minor (op. 17, 1873); known as the *Little Russian* one. No. 3, in D (op. 29, 1875); known as the *Polish.* No. 4, in F minor (op. 36, 1878). No. 5, in E minor (op. 64, 1888). No. 6, in B minor (op. 74, 1893); known as the *Pathetic.* There is also the *Manfred Symphony* (op. 58, 1885); which can be considered rather as a Tone-poem, and is not numbered amongst the Symphonies proper.

Tchaikovsky's Concertos, &c., are as follows:

PIANOFORTE. No. 1, B flat minor (op. 23, 1875). No. 2, G (op. 44, 1880, revised 1893). No. 3, E flat (op. 75, left incomplete; the *Andante and Finale*, op. 79, belong to this work). There is also the Concert Fantasia (op. 56, composed 1884).

VIOLIN. D (op. 35, composed 1878). Sérénade Mélancolique (op. 26, composed 1875). Valse Scherzo (op. 34, composed 1877).

VIOLONCELLO. Variations on a Rococo Theme (op. 33, composed 1876). Pezzo capriccioso (op. 62, composed 1887).

Tchardache. See *Czardas.*

Tcherepnin (Cheryepnin, &c.), (1) **Nicholas** (b. St. Petersburg 1873; d. Issy-les-Moulineaux 1945). Pupil of Rimsky-Korsakof at Conserv. of St. Petersburg; toured as conductor of Diaghilef's Russian Ballet (see *Ballet*)

1909–14; settled in Paris. Composer of operas, ballets, piano concerto, &c.

(2) **Alexander** (b. St. Petersburg 1899). Son of Nicholas, above. Studied at Conservs. of St. Petersburg and Paris; able pianist, playing own works, &c.; European tours; lived in Far East 1934–7 and edited collection of modern Chinese and Japanese compositions; then Chicago. Composer of operas, piano concertos, chamber music, &c.

T.C.L., T.C.M. Trinity College of Music, London (q.v.).

Te. See *Si*. It may be added that in Tonic Sol-fa (q.v.) Te is also the 2nd degree of the minor scale.

Teachers' Registration Council. See *Degrees and Diplomas* 2.

Teatro alla moda, Il. See *Marcello*.

Tebaldi, Renata (b. Pesaro 1922). Dramatic soprano. After thorough private general musical training made début Trieste and La Scala 1946; Covent Garden 1950; Metropolitan 1955; then acclaimed as a leading international guest artist.

Tedesca. It. for 'German' (i.e. in the fem. sing., with plur. *tedesche*, and masc. sing. and plur. *tedesco* and *tedeschi*). The term has been used with different meanings at different periods, e.g. *alla tedesca* at one time meant 'in the style of the Allemande' (q.v.), but later came to mean 'in the style of the German waltz'.

Te Deum Laudamus ('We praise Thee, O God'). The long hymn which constitutes the supreme expression of rejoicing in the Roman Catholic, Anglican, and other Christian Churches. In the liturgy of the Roman Catholic Church it finds a place as the outpouring of praise at the moment of climax of the service of Matins on the occasion of festivals; in the Anglican Church its Eng. version is a part of the service of Morning Prayer, except when replaced by the *Benedicite* (q.v.).

The ancient traditional plainsong to the Lat. hymn is of a very magnificent character; it has a great popularity amongst the peasantry of Italy. In the Anglican cathedrals and larger churches elaborate 'service' settings are used

(see *Service*); in the smaller churches series of Anglican chants, or, nowadays frequently, simple 'service' settings. The hymn has inspired innumerable composers of all periods and many of their settings, from the late 17th c. onwards, have been on extended lines, with solos, choruses, and orch. accompaniment, in the style of the oratorio.

Some notable settings are the following: (1) PURCELL. (Composed, with the Jubilate, for St. Cecilia's Day 1694.) (2) HANDEL. See *Utrecht* and *Dettingen*. (3) BERLIOZ. (Composed 1854; 1st perf. Paris 1855; Crystal Palace 1885.) (4) DVOŘÁK. (Op. 103, 1892.) (5) SULLIVAN. (Composed for Queen Victoria's Diamond Jubilee and perf. London 1897.) (6) VERDI. (1st perf. Paris 1898.) (7) STANFORD. (1st perf. Leeds Fest. 1898.) (8) VAUGHAN WILLIAMS.

Teichmüller, Robert (1863–1939). Eminent German pianist and teacher; 42 years on staff of Leipzig Conserv.

Teil or **Theil** (Ger.). 'Part', in the sense of 'portion' or 'section'. So *Teilen* or *Theilen*, 'to divide'.

Telemann, Georg Philipp (b. Magdeburg 1681; d. Hamburg 1767). Held many posts as Kapellmeister and director of church music and in his day ranked high as composer; very prolific (40 settings of Passion; 40 operas; 600 overtures, and very many other works).

Telephone. See *Broadcasting of Music*.

Telephone, The. 1-act chamber opera by Menotti. (Prod. New York 1947; London 1948.)

Teller (Ger.). 'Plate' (e.g. of cymbal).

Telmányi, Emil (b. Arad, then Hungary, now Rumania, 1892). Violinist; pupil of Hubay, &c. At 19 gave 1st Ger. perf. Elgar Concerto at Berlin. Frequently heard in Britain. In Copenhagen since 1919. Wife is daughter of Carl Nielsen.

Telyn. See *Harp*.

Tema (It.). 'Theme', i.e. a main subject of a composition. *Tema con Variazioni*, 'Air and Variations' (see *Form* 5).

Temperament is adjustment in tuning whereby (e.g. to avoid in keyboard instruments an unmanageable number of finger-keys) such pairs of notes as B sharp and C, or C sharp and D flat are combined instead of being treated as individuals, a compromise being effected which leaves neither note of the pair accurate but both sufficiently near accuracy for the ear tolerantly to accept them.

Equal Temperament treats every note in this fashion, so that any particular interval in any key is exactly of the same 'size' as the same interval in any other key. Modulation from key to key can thus be freely made, Bach's 48 Preludes and Fugues (*Das wohltemperirte Klavier*—'The Well-tempered Keyboard') constituting a manifesto for this system, which is now universally adopted: Bach was not, however, as frequently stated, its originator. Before the adoption of Equal Temperament a system frequently employed was that of *Mean-tone Temperament*, which left certain keys quite tolerable, others less so, and some so intolerable that they could not be used. This system was still to be found in some organs until after the middle of the 19th c.

It is a common delusion that voices singing unaccompanied, or string instrumentalists so playing, being free of 'the tyranny of the keyboard', use *Just Intonation*, i.e. the untempered scale: a moment's reflection will show that (*a*) They could not (either unconsciously or consciously) momentarily throw off habits acquired when performing with accompaniment, and (*b*) In any case this would almost necessitate their confining themselves to compositions remaining entirely in one of the 12 major and 12 minor scales, i.e. compositions free of all modulation. In fact such departures from equal temperament as are commonly made, such as very sharp major thirds and leading-notes, are really in the *opposite* direction from the corresponding notes in the theoretical 'just intonation' scale. *Expressive Intonation* is the most descriptive term for this, and has been used by Casals and others.

Tempest, The. Incidental Music to Shakespeare's play has been provided by many composers, including (1) PURCELL (1695—a perversion of the play by Shadwell and others). (2) SULLIVAN

(op. 1, 1861). (3) CHAUSSON (1st perf. Paris 1888). (4) SIBELIUS (1st perf. Helsingfors 1929).

There is also a symphonic poem of the name by Paine (op. 31).

Tempesta, La (Haydn). See under *Matin*.

Tempestoso; tempestosamente (It.). 'Tempestuous'; 'tempestuously'.

Temple, Hope—really Dotie Davies (b. Dublin 1859; d. 1938). Composer of popular songs (e.g. *An Old Garden*). Cf. *Messager*.

Temple Block. See *Korean Temple Block*.

Templeton, (1) **Alec Andrew** (b. Cardiff 1909; d. Greenwich, Conn., 1963). Pianist (blind). Trained R.C.M. and R.A.M. After London career settled U.S.A. 1936. Popular concert and radio pianist (including improvisation) and entertainer. Composed piano, vocal, and orch. works.

(2) **John** (b. nr. Kilmarnock 1802; d. New Hampton 1886). Famous tenor; frequent stage companion of Malibran (known as 'Malibran's Tenor').

Tempo, tempi (It. sing., plur.). (1) 'Speed', 'speeds'. So *a tempo*, 'at proper speed' (after a *rallentando* or *accelerando* has taken place). (2) In the It. language the word is used also in a derived sense—'Movement' (of a sonata and the like).

Tempo comodo or **tempo commodo** (It.). 'Convenient speed', i.e. a speed convenient to the player.

Tempo di ballo (It.). (1) 'Dance speed.' (2) A movement in dance style.

Tempo di minuetto (It.). 'Minuet speed' (and so for other dances).

Tempo giusto (It.). (1) 'Just', i.e. exact, rhythm. (2) The speed that the style of the music demands (usually *Moderato*).

Tempo maggiore (It.). The same as 'Alla breve' (see *Breve*).

Tempo minore (It.). The same as *Tempo ordinario* (3), below.

Tempo ordinario (It.). 'Ordinary time.' (1) Neither fast nor slow, in fact 'Moderato' or perhaps 'Andante'. (2) The same speed as before, i.e. equivalent to 'Tempo primo'. (3) A time in which the beats have their normal value, as opposed to 'Alla breve' (see *Breve*), i.e. the quarter-note, or crotchet, as the unit, instead of the half-note, or minim.

Tempo primo (It.). Lit. 'first time', i.e. resume the original speed. (This is sometimes abbreviated to *Tempo 1mo*.)

Tempo rubato. See *Rubato*.

Tempo wie vorher (Ger.). 'Time as before', i.e. resume (or continue) the original speed.

Temps (Fr.). 'Time', often in the sense of 'beat' (see, for instance, *Deux Temps*).

Ten. Short for *tenuto* (q.v.).

Tender Land, The. 2-act opera by Copland. Libretto by H. Everett. (Prod. New York 1954.)

Tendre; tendrement (Fr.). 'Tender'; 'tenderly'.

Tenebrae (Lat. 'darkness'). In the Roman Catholic Church the name applied to Matins and Lauds of the following day sung during the afternoon or evening from Wednesday to Friday of Holy Week. The candles are extinguished one by one as each psalm is sung. (See reference under *Lamentations*.)

Tenebroso (It. 'dark'). 'Gloomy.'

Tenendo (It.). 'Sustaining', e.g. *tenendo il canto*, 'sustaining the melody'.

Tenero (It.). 'Tender.' So *teneroso*, *teneramente*, 'tenderly'; *tenerezza*, 'tenderness'.

Tenete (It.). 'Hold', i.e. 'sustain'.

Tenor. See *Voice* 14, 16.

Ténor (Fr.), **Tenor** (Ger.). (1) The tenor voice (see *Voice* 14). (2) The Viola (see *Violin Family*).

Tenor-bass Trombone. See *Trombone Family*.

Tenor Clef. See Table 4.

Tenor Cor. A high-pitched instrument of horn-like character intended to take horn parts when proper horns are not available (see *Saxhorn and Flügelhorn Families* 1).

Tenor Drum. See *Percussion Family* 2 j.

Tenore (It.). 'Tenor.'

Tenore leggiero (It.). 'Light tenor.'

Tenore robusto (It.). 'Robust tenor' (see *Voice* 16).

Tenor Flügelhorn. See *Saxhorn and Flügelhorn Families* 2.

Tenorgeige (Ger. 'tenor fiddle'). The Viola.

Tenor Horn. See *Saxhorn and Flügelhorn Families* 1.

Tenoroon. See *Oboe Family* h.

Tenorposaune (Ger.). 'Tenor trombone' (see *Trombone Family*).

Tenor Saxhorn. See *Saxhorn and Flügelhorn Families* 1.

Tenor Staff. See under *Great Staff*.

Tenorstimme (Ger.). 'Tenor voice.'

Tenor Trombone. See *Trombone Family*.

Tenor Tuba. See *Tuba Group* 1 a, 2 a.

Tenor Viol. See *Viol Family* 2 b.

Tenu, tenue (Fr. masc., fem.). 'Held.'

Tenuta (It. fem. 'held'). The Pause $\frown$ (probably short for *nota tenuta*, i.e. 'held note').

Tenuto (It. masc.). 'Held', i.e. sustained to the end of its value (and perhaps sometimes a little more).

Tepido (It. 'tepid', 'lukewarm'). 'Unimpassioned.' So *tepidità*, 'lukewarmness'; *tepidamente*, 'in a lukewarm manner'.

Terana. An original type of dance, 6 beats in a measure occasionally changing to 3 beats (the measure remaining equal in duration).

Terce. The 4th of the Canonical Hours (see *Divine Office*) of the Roman Catholic Church. Properly it takes place at 9 a.m.

Ternary Form. See *Form* 2.

Ternina, Milka (b. Croatia 1863; d. Zagreb 1941). Operatic and Lieder soprano. Great Wagner exponent (especially at Munich 1890–9). Successful Bayreuth, London, New York.

Terpodion. (1) A keyboard instrument introduced in 1816 and now obsolete. In principle it somewhat resembled the clavicylinder (q.v.). (2) A kind of Harmonium. (3) An organ stop whose tone presumably resembles that of one of the above.

Terry, (1) **Richard Runciman** (b. Ellington, Northumb., 1865; d. London 1938). Organist Antigua Cathedral, West Indies (1892–6), Downside Abbey, nr. Bath (1896–1901), Westminster Roman Catholic Cathedral (1901–24); at this last did remarkable work in revival of 16th-c. church music, especially English; also authority on Calvinistic metrical psalm-tunes, on carols, and on sea-shanties. Hon. D.Mus., Durham. Knighted 1922. Cf. *Andrews, Hilda*; *Roman Catholic Church Music*.

(2) **Charles Sanford** (b. Newport Pagnell, Bucks., 1864; d. Aberdeen 1936). Choir-boy St. Paul's Cathedral; at Cambridge Univ., graduating 1886. Lecturer and then Prof. of History, Aberdeen Univ. (1898–1930). Many historical works (particularly Scottish history); latterly devoted himself to study of career and works of Bach, becoming chief European authority and publishing series of books of very thorough research on all aspects of subject.

Ter Sanctus. Properly the same as 'Trisagion' (q.v.), but sometimes improperly applied to the Sanctus as found in the Roman Catholic Mass or the Anglican Communion service.

Tertis, Lionel (b. West Hartlepool 1876). Viola player. Trained as violinist at Leipzig Conserv. and R.A.M. Became viola virtuoso of international reputation and carried on propaganda for his instrument, arranging music for it, inducing composers to write for it, and introducing a new model ('Tertis Model').

Tessitura. See *Voice* 15.

Testa (It.). 'Head.' So *voce di testa*, 'head voice' (see *Voice* 4).

Testo (It.). 'Text', i.e. Libretto.

Tests and Measurements of musical capacity have gradually become common during the present century, especially in U.S.A. Much ingenuity has been expended in the effort to devise such as will enable teachers to direct students away from courses of study for which they are not by nature fitted and, on the other hand, to encourage students to take up and persevere in courses for which it is clear that they possess genuine aptitude. In this way the musical profession may gain by the exclusion of less gifted people. On the other hand there exist mental and moral qualities which if absent may bring the gifted musician to failure and which if present may help the less gifted to achieve a happy and relatively successful career, and it is doubtful if any test can be devised which will reveal the presence or absence of these qualities, or any system of psychological accounting which will permit of the drawing up of a reliable balance sheet, i.e. one allotting the due value to each factor. Probably it is best to say that there is usefulness in such tests and measurements, but that caution should be adopted in accepting too absolutely their results and that experimentation and recording of such results may meantime continue with some prospect of ultimate profit to the art.

Tetrachords. The 2 halves of the 8ve of the major or minor scale (e.g. in key C, the notes C–F and G–C), or of any mode. In all the modes, as in the major scale, the 2 tetrachords are exactly similar in order of tones and semitones. (See *Modes* and *Scale*.)

Tetrazzini, (1) **Eva** (b. Milan 1862; d. Salsomaggiore 1938). Operatic soprano. Début Florence 1882; took part in 1st U.S.A. perf. Verdi's *Othello* 1888; married its conductor (see *Campanini, Cleofonte*). For sister see below. (2) **Luisa** (b. Florence 1871; d. Milan 1940). Coloratura soprano. Sister of above. Trained at Florence Conserv. Début Florence 1890. Quickly won international repute in opera by brilliance of voice and execution. Before public to 1933.

Teyte, Maggie (b. Wolverhampton 1888). Soprano vocalist. Studied R.C.M. and Paris under Jean de Reszke. From age 18 appeared on Fr. opera stage (name originally 'Tate' changed to secure correct pronunciation in France); then popular in

Britain (Covent Garden, &c.) and U.S.A. Delicate interpreter of Fr. song (Debussy, &c.). D.B.E. 1958.

Thaïs. Romantic opera by Massenet. Libretto based on Anatole France's novel. (Prod. Paris 1894; New York 1907; London 1911.)

Thalben-Ball, George Thomas (b. Sydney, N.S.W., 1896). Organist. Trained R.C.M. (later on staff). Succeeded Walford Davies at Temple Church, London, 1923. Curator-organist Royal Albert Hall. Has toured extensively Europe, Dominions, and U.S.A. D.Mus., Lambeth. C.B.E. 1967.

Thalberg, Sigismond (b. Geneva 1812; d. nr. Naples 1871). Astonishing virtuoso of piano; composed for it works exploiting its technical possibilities. (See *Hexameron*.)

Thamar, Thamara (Balakiref). See *Tamara*.

Thatcher, Reginald Sparshatt (b. Midsomer Norton 1888; d. Cranleigh, Surrey, 1957). Trained R.C.M. and Oxford (M.A., D.Mus.). Taught various public schools (Harrow 1928–36). Deputy Director of Music B.B.C. 1928; Vice-Principal of R.A.M. 1945; Principal 1949–55. O.B.E.; Kt. 1952.

Thayer, Alexander Wheelock (b. South Natick, Mass., 1817; d. Trieste 1897). Enthusiast for works of Beethoven who contrived to spend many years in Germany and Austria, pursuing researches in the composer's life. Publ. (in German) the standard and definitive biography 1866–79 and final volume, posthumous, 1908; Eng. edn. in New York 1921; revised 1963.

Theater (Ger.). 'Theatre', but often used in the sense of 'stage', as distinct from 'auditorium'.

Thebom, Blanche (b. Monessen, Pa., 1918). Mezzo-soprano, of Swedish parentage. After private study appeared New York 1944; then for 10 years leading singer at Metropolitan, with many international guest appearances.

Theil or Teil (Ger.). 'Part', in the sense of 'portion' or 'section'. So *theilen* or *teilen*, 'to divide'.

Theile, Johann (b. Naumburg 1646; there d. 1724). Pupil of Schütz; became a noted contrapuntist; one of the earliest Ger. opera composers; publ. a Passion (1675), a book of 20 masses, and another book of instrumental pieces.

Thematic Material. The whole body of musical subject-matter out of which a composition is constructed, including definite 'Themes' or 'Subjects' and less definite scraps of material used in the course of the construction.

Theme. The same as 'Subject' (q.v.). *Theme and Variations* is the same as 'Air and Variations' (see *Form* 5).

Theme and Six Diversions. Orch. variations by German. (1st perf. London 1919.)

Theme Song. The term originates in cinema practice. In 1928, in a film called *The Singing Fool*, there was introduced something like a sort of recurring Leitmotiv (see *Leading Motive*), a song called 'Sonny Boy', which contributed greatly to the success of the film, and apparently the term 'Theme Song' was introduced in connexion with this film or others which imitated it. We may almost say that there is a theme song in the Prize Song of *The Mastersingers*, which crops up from time to time during the course of the action and, indeed, tends to dominate it. An earlier example is 'Home, Sweet Home' (q.v.), which pervaded Bishop's opera of *Clari, or the Maid of Milan* (1829).

Thème sur le nom Abegg (Schumann). See *Abegg*.

Theodora. Oratorio by Handel. (1st perf. London 1750.)

Theorbo. See *Lute Family*.

Thérémin or Théréminovox. See *Electric Musical Instruments* 1.

There's a good time coming. See *Russell, H.*

Theresa Mass (Haydn). See *Theresienmesse*.

Theresienmesse ('Theresa Mass'). Popular name for Haydn's 12th Mass, in B flat (1799). Probably named after consort of Emperor Francis II (*not* Empress Maria Theresa, d. 1780).

There's nae luck aboot the hoose. The poem has been variously attributed to William Julius Mickle (1734–88) and to a schoolmistress, Jean Adams (1710–65). The air is the old Scottish one of *Up and waur at them a'*, *Willie!*

There was an old woman. See *Lilliburlero*.

Thespis, or The Gods Grown Old. 'Grotesque Opera' by Gilbert and Sullivan—their first association. (Prod. Gaiety Theatre, London, 1871.)

Thibaud, Jacques (b. Bordeaux 1880; killed in air crash over French Alps 1953). Violinist. Trained Paris Conserv. under Marsick. Début Paris 1898; rapidly gained world fame. Much trio perf. with Casals and Cortot.

Thieving Magpie, The (Rossini). See *Gazza ladra*.

Thiman, Eric Harding (b. Ashford, Kent, 1900). London organist (City Temple, London, from 1957); dean of London Univ. music faculty; on staff of R.A.M. Composer of widely used church music.

Third. See *Interval*.

Third Inversion of a chord. See *Harmony* 2 e.

Thirty-second Note. 'Demisemiquaver' (see Table 3).

Thomas, (1) **(Charles Louis) Ambroise** (b. Metz 1811; d. Paris 1896). Won high honours at Paris Conserv. culminating in Rome Prize (1832); on return to Paris prod. many highly successful operas, both light and serious (e.g. *Mignon*, q.v.; *A Midsummer Night's Dream* 1850; *Raymond* 1851; *Hamlet* 1868); also composed popular male voice choruses, &c. Became director of Conservatory 1871 and then practically dropped composition.

(2) **Theodore** (b. Esens, Hanover, 1835; d. Chicago 1905). In U.S.A. from age 10 began musical life as violinist; at 27 first organized an orch.; henceforward the leading conductor of the country; from 1891 in Chicago, founding its (still existent) Symphony Orch. and conducting it until his death, which occurred 3 weeks after opening of the hall specially built for its activities. Exercised great influence on development of musical taste in U.S.A.

(3) **Arthur Goring** (b. nr. Eastbourne 1850; d. London 1892). Studied in Paris and then at R.A.M.; made name with cantata *The Sun Worshippers* (Norwich Fest. 1881), confirmed by operas *Esmeralda* (London and Cologne 1883; Hamburg 1884; Breslau 1890) and *Nadeshda* (London and Dublin 1885); also composed many songs. Mental derangement ended career 1891; cantata *The Swan and the Skylark* orchestrated by Stanford after his death (Birmingham Fest. 1894).

(4) **Thomas**—known as 'Ap Thomas' (b. Bridgend, Glam., 1829; d. Ottawa 1913). Famous Welsh harpist; played in many parts of Europe and when approaching age 70 settled in U.S.A. (1895); composed a cantata, &c., and wrote history of harp. For elder brother see 6 *b* below.

(5) **John Charles** (b. nr. Carlisle, Pa., 1891; d. Apple Valley, Calif., 1960). Operatic and concert baritone. Trained Baltimore Conserv. First successes in light opera and in musical comedy; then grand opera débuts Washington, D.C., 1924; Brussels 1925; Metropolitan Opera, New York, 1934.

(6 *a*–*d*) **John.** As there have been a number of public musicians of this name there are listed below those (more or less important) concerning whom confusion is liable to occur:

(*a*) (b. nr. Carmarthen 1795; d. Treforest, Glam., 1871.) Bardic name, 'Ieuan Ddu'. Schoolmaster, poet, promoter of choral singing, collector of old Welsh minstrelsy, and composer of various airs to be found in collections of Welsh music.

(*b*) (b. Bridgend 1826; d. London 1913.) Like his brother Thomas (4 above) known as 'Ap Thomas'. Studied at R.A.M. and later became prof. of harp there; toured Europe and U.S.A. and was harpist to Queen Victoria; great adjudicator at Eisteddfodau; at a National Eisteddfod (Chester 1866) presented with purse of 500 guineas in recognition of services to Welsh music. Composed symphonies, operas, cantatas, &c., also much harp music. When 'John Thomas' is mentioned it is generally he who is meant. Bardic name, 'Pencerdd Gwalia'.

(c) (b. Blaenanerch, Cardiganshire, 1839; d. Llanwrtyd Wells, Brecon, 1922.) Composed glees, part-songs, anthems, &c.

(d) **John Rogers** (b. Newport, Mon., 1829; d. New York 1896). Lived some time in U.S.A. Publ. collections of sacred music; composed cantata, &c., and once-popular songs (e.g. *'Tis but a little faded flower*).

(7) **Marjorie** (b. Sunderland 1923). Contralto. Trained Royal Manchester Coll. of Music. Frequent recitalist and broadcaster in Britain.

(8) **Mansel Treharne** (b. Rhondda 1909). Conductor and composer. Scholar R.A.M. B.Mus. (Dunelm). Career in B.B.C.: Welsh Region asst. music director, 1936; conductor Revue Orch. 1941; conductor Welsh Orch. 1946; head of Welsh Music, 1950–65. Orch., chamber, and vocal compositions. F.R.A.M. 1951.

Thomé, Francis—really François Lucien Joseph Thomé (b. Mauritius 1850; d. Paris 1909). Pianist and composer. Trained Paris Conserv. Composed operas, &c. Best known by little piece, *Simple aveu* ('Simple Avowal').

Thompson, (1) **Arthur John** (b. London 1856; there d. 1926). Concert tenor. Trained R.A.M. (later on staff, as also on that of G.S.M.).

(2) **Oscar** (b. Crawfordsville, Ind., 1887; d. New York 1945). On staff *Musical America* 1919–43. Also various New York daily journals. On staff Curtis Institute, &c. Many books on music; 1st ed. *International Cyclopedia of Music*.

(3) **Randall** (b. New York 1899). After his course at Harvard held Amer. Rome Fellowship (1922–5); also studied under Ernest Bloch in New York. Guggenheim Fellowship (1929 and 1930). Then in various univ. positions and (1939–41) Director of Curtis Inst., Philadelphia. Prof. Univ. Virginia 1941, Princeton 1945, Harvard 1948. Composer of symphonies and various other orch. and choral works. Hon. D.Mus., Rochester Univ.

Thompson, Lady. See *Loder, Kate.*

Thomson, (1) **George** (b. Limekilns, Fife, 1757; d. Leith 1851). For half a century (1780–1830) Secretary to the Board for the Encouragement of Arts and Manufactures in Scotland. Great collector of Scottish, Irish, and Welsh airs; publ. volumes of these, also sets of variations and some sonatas using them as subjects; new poems often supplied by Burns, Sir Walter Scott, &c.; on the writing of accompaniments employed Pleyel, Haydn, Beethoven, Hummel, Weber, &c. Publication covered period 1793–1841. (Cf. *Hogarth, George.*)

(2) **John** (b. Ednam, Kelso, 1805; d. Edinburgh 1841). Friend of Mendelssohn; studied at Leipzig; first Prof. of Music at Edinburgh Univ. (1839).

See *Annotated Programmes.*

(3) **César** (b. Liège 1857; d. Lugano 1931). Studied violin at Liège Conserv., of which became a prof., as later of Conservs. of Brussels, Paris, and (1924–7) Ithaca, N.Y. (teaching, too, at Juilliard School, New York). Famous virtuoso, touring civilized world. Edited early violin music.

(4) **Virgil** (b. Kansas City 1896). Graduate of Harvard who studied under Nadia Boulanger in Paris; won Juilliard Fellowship (1923). Set to music some of Gertrude Stein's literary productions (especially opera *Four Saints in Three Acts*, q.v.); has also composed symphonies, chamber music, film music, &c. Music critic *New York Herald Tribune* 1940–54.

Thorax. The upper part of the body, shut off from the abdomen by the flexible partition called the *Diaphragm* (see *Voice* 3).

Thorn, The. See *Shield, William.*

Thorough Bass. See *Figured Bass.*

Though dark are our sorrows. See *Saint Patrick's Day.*

Three Blind Mice. A round (q.v.) familiar to all children in Britain and most in the U.S.A. It is found in the *Deuteromelia* (1609) of Ravenscroft (q.v.), but in the minor, in a shorter form, and with somewhat different words.

The tune has in certain quarters an

absurd reputation of being very 'un-lucky'. Were it played in a circus no performer would dare to do his 'turn'.

Three Choirs Festival. See *Festival*.

Three-cornered Hat, The (*El Sombrero de tres picos*). Ballet by Falla, based on the novel by Alarcón. (Prod. London 1919.) (Cf. *Corregidor*.)

Three Fishers, The. See *Hullah*.

Threepenny Opera, The ('Die Dreigroschenoper'). See *Weill, Kurt*.

Threnody. Dirge.

Thring, Edward. See *Education* 2.

Through-composed. See *Durchcomponiert*.

Thuille, Ludwig Wilhelm Andreas Mario (b. Bozen or Bolzano, Trentino, 1861; d. Munich 1907). Pupil at Munich of Rheinberger and others; became a prof. at Munich Conserv. Composed 3 operas, some chamber and choral music, songs, and piano pieces.

Thunder Machine. This is called for by the score of Strauss's 'Alpine' Symphony and perhaps some scores by other composers; it is also in use in theatres. It usually consists of a big drum with balls of some material inside it; it is so fixed on pivots as to be capable of rotation, and the balls then strike the parchment.

Thunder Stick, Bull Roarer, or **Whizzer.** An instrument in use among the Amer. Indians, the Australian aborigines, the natives of Central Africa, &c.—a thin, flat piece of wood, swung to produce a whirring noise, and rising or falling in pitch with the changing speed of the motion. The Ger. name of this instrument is *Schwirrholz* ('whirling-wood') and the Fr. *planchette ronflante* ('roaring board').

Thuner-Sonata. Nickname given to Brahms's Sonata for Pianoforte and Violin in D minor, op. 108, composed at Thun, in Switzerland, 1888. (1st perf. by Brahms and Joachim, Vienna, 1889.)

Thurston, Frederick (b. Lichfield 1901; d. 1953). Clarinettist. Trained R.A.M. On staff R.C.M. Principal clarinet B.B.C. orch., &c. C.B.E. 1952.

Thus spake Zoroaster (Strauss). See under *Nietzsche*.

Thyroid Cartilage. See *Larynx*.

Thy Voice, O Harmony. See *Webbe, Samuel* 1.

Tibbett, Lawrence Mervil (b. California 1896; d. New York 1960). Operatic and concert baritone. At first actor (Shakespeare, &c.); then light opera; lastly grand opera. Operatic début, Hollywood Bowl, 1923; Metropolitan Opera, New York, 1923; European tour, with Covent Garden début, 1937. Hon. D.Mus., New York.

Tibia. Organ stop, not brilliant but full-toned. Varieties are: *Tibia Major* (8- or 16-foot length and pitch); *Tibia Minor* (4- or 8-foot); *Tibia Plena* (8-foot, loud); *Tibia Profunda* (16-foot); *Tibia Dura* (4-foot, hard in tone); *Tibia Clausa* (4-foot).

Tie or Bind. The curved line placed over a note and its repetition to show that the two shall be performed as one unbroken note of their total time-value. The object is (*a*) To get over the obstacle of an intervening bar-line, or (*b*) To make up a value such as no single note could give. The word *ligature* is sometimes used, but better avoided, as it has other applications.

See also Table 22. For an attempt to introduce a slur sign not liable to be confused with phrasing marks, &c., see *Phrase Marks*.

Tief (Ger.). 'Deep', 'low'.

Tiefgespannt. 'Deep-stretched', i.e. [of a drum] loosely braced, so as to give a low sound.

Tiefland ('Lowlands'). Opera by d'Albert. (Prod. Prague 1903; New York 1908; London 1910.)

Tiepido and derivatives. Same as *Tepido* (q.v.) and derivatives.

Tierce (Fr.) (1). 'Third'—the interval. (2) Organ stop; same as *Seventeenth* (q.v.).

Tierce de Picardie. For some obscure reason the name given to a major Tonic chord ending a composition in a minor key (e.g. in Key C minor, the chord C–E natural–G instead of the expected

C–E flat–G). This ending is found in many compositions as late as Bach and even at the present day.

Tietjens. See *Titiens*.

Tilkin. See *Caryll*.

Till Eulenspiegel's Merry Pranks (*Till Eulenspiegels lustige Streiche*). Symphonic Poem by Richard Strauss (op. 28, 1895). It recalls the exploits of the rascally vagabond hero of a 15th-c. Ger. chap-book—familiar also in Eng. literature under a translated form of his second name, 'Owlglass'.

Tillyard, Henry Wetenhall (b. Cambridge 1881; d. 1968). Prof. of Greek, Univ. Coll., Cardiff (1926–46); prev. posts included Professorship of Latin at Johannesburg, and of Russian at Birmingham, &c. High authority on Byzantine music.

Timbales (Fr.). Kettledrums (see *Percussion Family* 1 a).

Timbre means that 'tone-quality' or 'tone-colour' which distinguishes the effect of a flute from that of an oboe, a note sung by a soprano choir-boy from that of the same note sung by a contralto, and so on.

For the scientific explanation of the varying timbres of different instruments and voices see *Acoustics* 6.

Timbrel. An ancient Tambourine (see *Percussion Family* 2 m).

Timbrer (Fr.). 'To stamp' (as, for instance, with a rubber stamp). So Debussy's *Doucement timbré*, 'Softly accented'.

Time Signature. See *Signature*; also Table 10.

Timido; timidezza (It.). 'Timid'; 'timidity'.

Timore (It.). 'Fear.' So *timoroso*, 'fearful'; *timorosamente*, 'fearfully'.

Timothy, Miriam (later Mrs. Deane; d. Mauritius 1950). Harpist. Trained R.A.M. and R.C.M. (later on staff). Long member of Queen's Hall Orch., &c.

Timpani (*not* Tympani): It. for 'kettledrums' (plur. of *timpano*). See *Percussion Family* 1 a.

Tinayre, Yves Jean (b. Paris 1891). Tenor. Pupil of Beigel (q.v.), &c. Of high international repute for wide repertory (largely result of own research) and artistic interpretation.

Tinctoris, Johannes de (b. prob. Nivelles, *c.* 1435; d. 1511). Celebrated musical theorist and author earliest dictionary of musical terms (Treviso abt. 1498).

Tinel, (1) **Edgar** (b. Sinay, Flanders, 1854; d. Brussels 1912). At Brussels Conserv. won Rome Prize (1877); became head of Malines School for Church Music (cf. Lemmens); later head of Brussels Conserv. (1909). Composed 2 music-dramas, oratorio *Franciscus*, much church music, &c., and wrote treatise on plainsong. For son see below. (2) **Paul** (b. Malines 1892). Son of (1). Composer and organist, music critic.

Tin sheet (Rustling). See *Percussion Family* 2 u.

Tintagel. Symphonic Poem by Bax (1917), inspired by the castle-crowned cliff and the wide spaces of the Atlantic as seen from the Cornish coast.

Tinter; tintement (Fr.). 'To tinkle'; 'tinkling' (noun).

Tintinnare (It.). 'To tinkle'; so *tintinnando*, 'tinkling' (present participle).

Tinto (It.). 'Colour.' So *con tinto*, 'colourfully', i.e. with expression.

Tin Whistle. See *Recorder Family* 2.

Tipica Orchestra. This term became common in many European countries during the 1930's. 'Tipica' is Italian and Spanish for 'typical', and orchs. bearing this name specialize in mixed programmes of music of markedly national and racial traits (Spanish, South American, Gipsy, &c.), claiming to play each type in its true native style. *Orchestre de genre* appears to be the same thing.

Tipperary. This song, beginning 'It's a long way to Tipperary' (composed in 1912), had an immense popularity in the Brit. Army during the Great War of 1914–18, and also with the civil population of Britain. The song was the joint production of Harry J. Williams, of Temple Balsall, Warwickshire (the 1st line of the words is inscribed on his tombstone), and Jack Judge, a music-hall performer, of Oldbury, near Birmingham.

Tippett, Michael (Kemp) (b. London 1905). Trained R.C.M. In charge of the musical organization of Morley Coll., London, 1940–52. His compositions include chamber music, piano music, orchestral music, an oratorio, *A Child of Our Time* (q.v.), and the operas *Midsummer Marriage* (1955) and *King Priam* (q.v.). C.B.E. 1959. Hon. D.Mus., Cambridge, 1964.

Tirana. A Spanish song-dance popular in Andalusia.

Tirare; tirando; tirato (It.). 'To draw'; 'drawing'; 'drawn'. Used in connexion with the violin, &c., and implying the down-bow. *Tira tutto* ('draws all') is the Full Organ composition-pedal or piston.

Tirasse (Fr.). Coupler of organ—generally a pedal coupler. So *Tirasse du Positif, du Récit, du Grande Orgue,* mean respectively 'Choir to Pedal', 'Swell to Pedal', 'Great to Pedal'. These may be abbreviated to *Tir. P., Tir. R.,* and *Tir. G.O.,* whilst *Tirasse G.P.R.* means that all 3 couplers are to be used.

Tirer, tiré (Fr.). 'To draw'; 'drawn'. Used in connexion with the violin, &c., and implying down-bow (cf. *Poussé*). Sometimes the imperative, *Tirez,* is used.

Tir. G.O. See *Tirasse.*

Tir. P., Tir. R. See *Tirasse.*

'Tis but a little faded flower. See *Thomas* 6 d.

Titelouze, Jean (b. St. Omer 1563; d. Rouen 1633). Organist and canon of Rouen Cathedral; famous as performer on, and composer for, his instrument and an authority on its construction. Looked on as the founder of the Fr. school of organ composition.

Titiens (also spelt Tietjens), **Thérèse Cathline Johanna Alexandra** (b. Hamburg 1831; d. London 1877). Operatic and oratorio soprano of great fame. Before public from age 18. Lived in London 1858 to death.

Titof (or Titov), **Nikolai Alexandrovich** (b. St. Petersburg 1800; there d.

1875). General in Russian Army; composer of highly popular songs.

Titterton, Frank (b. Birmingham 1896; d. Roehampton 1956). Well-known operatic, oratorio, and concert tenor.

To Anthea. See *Hatton, J. L.*

Tobend (Ger.). 'Blustering.'

Tobin, (1) **Joseph Raymond** (b. Liverpool 1886; d. Mansfield 1967). Ed. *The Music Teacher* from 1934. Chairman Music Teachers' Assoc. from 1947. Author of educational books.

(2) **John** (b. Liverpool 1891). Director of Music Toynbee Hall, London. Founder and Director Liverpool Repertory Opera, Conductor Liverpool Philharmonic Choir, London Choral Soc., &c. Various compositions. (Became L.R.A.M. at age 14½; F.R.C.O., and Choir Training Diploma of R.C.O. by age 19.)

Toccata (It. past participle of *toccare,* 'to touch'). A rapid type of keyboard piece in which the notes are just 'touched' and left (not dwelt on). But there are earlier uses of the word in all of which it seems to mean little more than 'played', i.e. not sung (cf. Fr. 'toucher du piano', 'to play the piano').

Toccatina, toccatino. A miniature toccata (see above).

Toch, Ernst (b. Vienna 1887; d. Los Angeles 1964). Self-taught composer who won many prizes and taught in several cities, settling in U.S.A. 1935 (Prof. of Composition, Univ. of California). Composed film music for Hollywood, operas, chamber music, and (from 1950) symphonies.

Todi, Jacopone da. See *Stabat Mater Dolorosa.*

Tod Jesu, Der ('The Death of Jesus'). Passion Cantata by Graun. Text by Ramler. (1st perf. Berlin 1755; London 1877.) Of great fame in Germany.

Todt (Ger.). 'Dead.' So such compounds as *Todtenmesse,* 'Mass for the Dead', i.e. Requiem (q.v.); and *Todtenmarsch,* 'Dead March'.

Todtentanz (*Danse macabre*). A 'Paraphrase on the Dies Irae', for

Piano and Orch., by Liszt (1850). Inspired by Orcagna's fresco, *The Triumph of Death*, at Florence. (Cf. *Danse macabre*.)

Tod und Verklärung (Strauss). See *Death and Transfiguration*.

Toe-dancing. See *Ballet*.

Toeschi, Carlo Giuseppe (b. in the Romagna, abt. 1723; d. Munich 1788). Violinist in the famous Mannheim Orch., and composer of chamber music, symphonies, &c.

Togli (It.). 'Take away' (imperative)— used in organ music for the shutting off of any stop, &c.

Toile (Fr.). 'Curtain' (theatre).

Tolhurst, George (1827–77). See *Ruth*.

Tomaschek, Johann Wenzel (b. Skuch, Bohemia, 1774; d. Prague 1850). Great pianist and piano teacher in Prague with many famous pupils; also organist. Composed orch. and chamber music, operas, vocal works, and especially piano works. (See *Rhapsody*.)

Tomasi, Henri (b. Marseilles 1901; d. Avignon 1971). Of Corsican parentage. Studied at Paris Conserv. Composed operas and other works and conducted orch. of Radio-Paris.

Tombeau (Fr.). 'Tomb' (the term is fancifully used a good deal in compositions written in memory of some person).

Tombeau de Couperin, Le. ('Couperin's Tomb'). Suite of 6 Piano Pieces by Ravel (1917) of which 4 were also scored for Orch. (1919). A tribute to the great Fr. composer of the late 17th and early 18th c. The music has been adapted to a Ballet (*The Enchanted Grove*; Sadler's Wells, 1932).

Tomb of Askold, The. See *Verstovsky*.

Tom Bowling. See *Dibdin*.

Tome (Fr.). 'Volume' (of a series).

Tom Jones. Light Opera by Edward German. Libretto based on Fielding's novel. (Prod. London 1907.)

Another of same name and subject by Philidor, 1765.

Tomkins. For 12 members of this highly musical family see Fellowes's article in Grove's Dictionary: here only the most important member can be included:

Thomas (b. St. David's, Pembrokeshire, 1573; d. Martin Hussingtree, Worcs., 1656). One of Organists of Chapel Royal, London, and then of Worcester Cathedral (abt. 1596–1646). Composed very fine madrigals, services, anthems, and music for virginals and for viols. B.Mus., Oxford, 1607.

Tommasini, Vincenzo (b. Rome 1878; d. there 1950). Studied at the Univ. and Conserv. of Rome and then in Berlin, Paris, London, and New York; then settled in Rome. Composed operas, orch. music, chamber music, &c., and arranged music of Scarlatti for the ballet (Diaghilef company) *The Good-humoured Ladies*. An adherent of the movement which seeks to detach It. music from the inevitability of operatic association.

Tommy Talker. See *Mirliton*.

Tom-Tom. (1) Native Indian or Chinese drum—used in dance bands, &c., in both a tunable and non-tunable form. (2, less correctly) Gong (i.e. the same as 'Tam-tam'; see *Percussion Family* 2 p).

Ton (Fr., Ger.). (1) In Fr. the word means:

(*a*) PITCH, as *Donner le ton*, 'to give the pitch'. (*b*) 'KEY', 'MODE', as *Ton d'ut*, 'key C'; *Ton majeur*, 'major key'; *Ton d'église*, 'church mode'. (*c*) 'TONE', in the sense of 'Gregorian tone' (see *Gregorian Tones*). Somewhat akin to this are such expressions as *Ton de chasse*, 'hunting signal'—on the horn. (*d*) 'CROOK', as *Ton de trompette*, 'trumpet crook'; *Ton de cor*, 'horn crook'; *Ton de rechange*, 'spare crook'. (*e*) The INTERVAL THE 'TONE', as distinct from *Demiton*, 'semitone'. (*f*) 'SOUND', 'NOTE', &c., so *Ton aigre*, 'shrill sound'; *Ton bouché*, 'stopped note of horn'; *Ton doux*, 'Sweet tone-quality'.

(2) In Ger. (plur. *Töne*) the word means:

(*a*) PITCH, as *Den Ton angeben*, 'to give the pitch'. (*b*) 'KEY', 'MODE', in compounds such as *Tongeschlecht* ('tone-gender', or some such idea), Major or Minor. (*c*) 'NOTE', &c., as in such expressions and compounds as *Den Ton halten*, 'to hold the note'; *Tonabstand* ('note-stand-off') 'interval'; *Tonfarbe* ('tone-colour'), 'timbre'; *Tonfolge* ('note following'), 'melody'; *Tonfülle* ('tone-fulness'), 'volume of tone'; *Tonhöhe* ('note-height'), 'pitch'; *Tonlage* ('note-lie'), 'pitch', 'compass', 'register', &c.; *Tonleiter* ('note-ladder'), 'scale'; *Tonreihe* ('tone-row', see s.v. *Schönberg*); *Tonmass* ('tone-measure'), 'time'; *Tonschlüssel* ('note-key'), 'key-note'; *Tonsetzer* ('note setter'), 'composer'. (*d*) 'SOUND', 'MUSIC', in such compounds as *Tonkunst* ('tone art'), knowledge, &c.,' of music; *Tonkünstler* ('tone-artist'), 'musician'; *Tonlehre* ('tone knowledge'), 'acoustics'; *Tonbühne* ('music stage'), 'orchestra platform'; *Tonbild*, 'tone picture'; *Tonmalerei*, 'music-painting', e.g. programme music (q.v.); *Tondichter* ('tone-poet'), 'composer'; *Tondichtung*, 'tone-poem' (see 'Symphonic Poem', and note that *Tondichter* and *Tondichtung* are not quite corresponding terms).

Tonabstand. See *Ton* 2 c.

Tonada (Sp.). The tune set to any poem or for any dance.

Tonadilla (Sp.). (1) The diminutive of *Tonada*, above. (2) the use now customary). A cantata with vocal solos, and usually also choral and instrumental movements. Such works were used as comic intermezzi in the theatre; their popularity was established by Luís Misón, a Spanish flute virtuoso and conductor (who wrote over 100, beginning about 1757), and others.

Tonal Answer, Tonal Fugue. See *Form* 6.

Tonality is the observance of what may be called 'loyalty to a tonic', i.e. to the key-scheme of a composition. (Cf. 'Atonality' and 'Polytonality', s.v. *Harmony* 3.)

Tonal Sequence. See *Sequence* 1.

Tonante (It.). 'Thunderous.'

Tonart (Ger.). Lit. 'tone-kind' or 'tone-type'; applied both to the modes (as Dorian, Lydian, &c.) and to the scales (as major and minor). (See *Modes* and *Scale*.)

Tonbild, Tonbühne, Tondichter. See *Ton* 2 d.

Tondichtung (Ger.). Symphonic poem (q.v.).

Tondo (It. 'round'). 'Full-toned.'

Tone. (1) Musical sound. (2) Interval of major 2nd (e.g. C–D, E–F sharp).

(3) Resultant tone (see *Acoustics* 14).
(4) For Amer. use of the word see *American Terminology* 1.

Töne (Ger.). Plur. of 'Ton' (see *Ton* 2), generally in the sense of 'sounds' or 'notes'.

Tone Poem. See *Symphonic Poem*.

Tone-rows. See *Note-row*.

Tonfarbe, Tonfolge, Tonfülle. See *Ton* 2 c.

Tongeschlecht. See *Ton* 2 b.

Tongs and Bones. A ready-to-hand means of domestic musical merriment (cf. Shakespeare's *A Midsummer Night's Dream*).

Tonguing in the playing of wind instruments. The interruption of the flow of wind by a motion of the tongue. *Single Tonguing* is effected by a motion equivalent to that required for the enunciation of the letter T; *Double Tonguing* by one equivalent to that of TK; and *Triple Tonguing* by one equivalent to that of TTK or some such group. Double and Triple Tonguing allow of more rapid performance of passages or of repeated notes. (See references under *Flute Family, Clarinet Family, Cornet, Trumpet Family, Horn Family*.)

Flutter Tonguing is a special variety introduced by Richard Strauss (chiefly on the flute but possible also on the clarinet and some brass): it consists of a trilling of the letter R whilst playing a chromatic scale. (Ger. *Flatterzunge*.)

Tonhöhe. See *Ton* 2 c.

Toni (It.). See *Tono*.

Tonic. The 1st degree of the major or minor key. The 'key-note' from which the key takes its name, as Key of A, &c. (See *Key*.)

Tonic Sol-fa. (Read first the article *Sight-Singing*.) A system of singing at sight introduced in the early 1840's by a Congregational minister, John Curwen (1816–80), but acknowledging indebtedness to the *Norwich Sol-fa System* of Sarah Ann Glover (1785–1867) and in some ways anticipated (unknown to Miss Glover and Curwen) by the system of D. Sower (*Norristown New and Much Improved Music Reader*, 1832). It possesses a letter notation of its own but its principles can be (and are constantly) applied when singing from the staff notation.

On the side of pitch, the root principle is the treatment of all major keys (since they are identical in interval) as one, with the note-names (slightly adapted from those of Guido d'Arezzo in the 11th c.; see *Hexachord*), *Doh-ray-me-fah-soh-lah-te*. The minor is treated as a mode of the major, its 1st note being *lah*, its 2nd *te*, its 3rd *doh*, &c. In the special notation the notes are reduced to their initial letters, *d*, *r*, *m*, *f*, *s*, *l*, *t*. Passing sharps and flats are named by changing the vowel, as regards the sharps to 'e' and as regards the flats to 'a' (pronounced 'aw'). Thus *doh* sharpened becomes *de*; *me* flattened becomes *ma*; and so on.

As concerns the side of time and rhythm, the older time-names semibreve, minim, &c. (or whole-note, half-note, &c.), are abandoned: in the Tonic Sol-fa notation the beat is the unit and occupies the same amount of linear space throughout a score, the half-beats occupying half that space, and so on. Double dots (like a colon) separate beat from beat; single dots are used, when necessary, to divide a beat into half-beats, and commas to divide half-beats into quarter-beats. Horizontal lines show that notes are held and blanks indicate rests. And so forth, the rhythmic layout being graphic and avoiding the large amount of calculation of relative time-values inseparable (in any complicated composition) from reading in the staff notation. A valuable series of time-names has been incorporated into the Tonic Sol-fa teaching system from the Fr. system of Galin-Paris-Chevé (q.v.). These are based on the practical idea that the mind measures time in music not by duration but by accents, greater and smaller, which mark off the duration. Thus a beat is always called *taa*; a beat extended into another beat, *taa-aa*; a beat divided into half-beats, *taa-tai*; and so on. These names, when first introduced to the learner, are pronounced rhythmically and thereafter remain in the mind not as mere names but as rhythm expressed in words.

Early practice in the pitch side of the system is, in class instruction, carried out by means of a *Modulator* in which the note-names are ranged in order perpendicularly, the teacher pointing to them and the class singing the notes to which he points. Converse to this is the practice of ear-tests, in which the teacher sings several notes and the pupils name them.

For a fuller account of the Tonic Sol-fa system see *OCM* and for a complete account the textbooks of John Curwen himself and some of his followers.

See *English Schools Music Association*.

Tonic Sol-fa College. See *Degrees and Diplomas* 2.

Tonitruone (It.). Sheet of iron, loosely hanging and shaken to produce a thunder effect.

Tonkunst, Tonkünstler (Ger.). See *Ton* 2 d. **Tonlage.** See *Ton* 2 c. **Tonlehre.** See *Ton* 2 d. **Tonleiter.** See *Ton* 2 c. **Tonlos** (Ger.). 'Toneless.'

Tonmalerei. See *Ton* 2 d. **Tonmass.** See *Ton* 2 c.

Tonnerre (Fr.). 'Thunder.'

Tono (Sp.). Sort of part-song or madrigal, of 2 or 3 stanzas, sung before a play in 17th c.

Tono (It., pl. *toni*). 'Tone'—in all the various senses of the English word (see *Tone*). Also 'mode', 'key'.

Tonreihe. See *Note-row*. **Tonschlüssel, Tonsetzer.** *Ton* 2 c.

Tonsils. The 2 almond-shaped projecting glands, one on each side of the top of the throat.

Tonus (Lat.). (1) Mode. (2) Gregorian tone—see *Gregorian Tones*.

Tonus peregrinus ('Foreign Mode'). A piece of plainsong used for the psalm *In Exitu Israel* ('When Israel went out of Egypt'; Ps. 114 in the Eng. Authorized Version). It exists also formalized into an Anglican Chant and has been harmonized by Bach as a chorale.

Torch Dance. The name carries its own meaning (see also *Fackeltanz*).

Torch Song. One of the many Amer. manifestations of exuberant emotionalism that found a place in the popular music of the 1930's. The term is probably Negro in origin, 'to carry the torch' meaning to suffer the pangs of unrequited love. 'Torch singers' are those ladies who have the right emotional flavour, voice, and personality to put over the sensations of unrequited love at full force.

Tordion (or 'Tourdion'). See *Basse danse.*

Torelli, Giuseppe (b. Verona 1658; d. Bologna 1709). Violinist and composer of violin music of high reputation (wrongly regarded as originator of *concerto grosso*). Was attached to court of Margrave of Brandenburg (1698 to death).

Tornada (Sp.). A type of refrain in many of the folk songs of Catalonia.

Tornare; tornando (It.). 'To return'; 'returning'.

Tortelier, Paul (b. Paris 1914). 'Cellist. Orchestral experience with Paris Conserv. Concert Soc. and Boston Symphony Orch.; then solo tours U.S.A., Britain, &c. Composer for his instrument.

Torvo (It.). 'Grim.'

Tosca. 3-act tragedy-opera by Puccini. Libretto by Giacosa and Illica, based on the play *La Tosca* by Sardou. (Prod. Rome and London 1900; New York 1901.)

Toscanini, Arturo (b. Parma 1867; d. New York 1957). Orch. and operatic conductor of world renown, with activities especially centred on Milan and New York. Began professional career as orch. violoncellist. Severely near-sighted but gifted with phenomenal musical memory conducted entirely without score. From 1937 until his retirement in 1954 he had a particular connexion with the orch. of the National Broadcasting Co., New York. During Fascist régime in Italy and Nazi régime in Germany and Austria refused to appear further in those countries.

Toselli, Enrico (b. Florence 1883; there d. 1926). Composer of instrumental music, some of it of high popularity (especially a Serenata).

Tosti, Francesco Paolo (b. in Abruzzi 1846; d. Rome 1916). Singing-master to Queen of Italy and later to Brit. royal family. Settled in London and

was knighted (1908). Composed graceful and highly popular drawing-room songs (e.g. *Goodbye*, q.v.).

Tostissimo (adj.), **tostissimamente** (adv.). Superlative of *Tosto* (below).

Tosto (It.). (1) 'Rapid'; so *più tosto*, 'more rapid'. But *più tosto*, or *piùttosto*, as ordinary It. expressions mean 'rather', in either sense of this word. (2) 'Immediately.'

Tostquartette ('Tost Quartets'). Nickname of 2 series of Haydn's String Quartets, 6 in each series—nos. 57–68 (sometimes described as op. 54, nos. 1–3; op. 55, nos. 1–3; and op. 64, nos. 1–6). They were dedicated to a Vienna amateur violinist of the name of Tost. (Cf. *Lerchenquartett*.)

Totentanz. See *Todtentanz.*

To the Distant Beloved (Beethoven). See *An die ferne Geliebte.*

Touche (Fr.). Finger-board—of violin, &c., e.g. *sur la touche*, 'bow over the finger-board'.

Toujours (Fr.). 'Always.'

Tourel, Jennie (b. Montreal 1910; d. New York 1973). Operatic mezzo-soprano. Educated France and Switzerland. Opera début (as Carmen) Paris 1932. From 1941 in U.S.A., making 1st appearance there with Toscanini and N.Y. Philharmonic Orch. Has also toured South America (1945).

Tournemire, Charles Arnould (b. Bordeaux 1870; d. Arcachon 1939). Pupil of Franck and d'Indy and a notable Paris organist and composer of organ music, and also operas, &c.

Tours, Berthold (b. Rotterdam 1838; d. London 1897). For latter half of life musical adviser to Messrs. Novello; composer of Eng. church music, songs, violin pieces, &c.

Tourte, François (b. Paris 1747; there d. 1835). Violin bow maker; introduced the present bow (with concave curve of stick, &c.).

Tout, toute; tous, toutes (Fr. masc., fem. sing.; masc., fem. plur.). 'All.'

Tout à coup (Fr.). 'Suddenly.'

Tout à fait (Fr.). 'Completely.'

Tout ensemble (Fr.). The whole, the general effect.

Tovey, Donald Francis (b. Eton 1875; d. Edinburgh 1940). Took classical degree at Oxford and then appeared very successfully in London and on Continent as solo pianist. Prof. of Music Edinburgh Univ. 1914 to death. Composer of chamber music, a piano concerto, a 'cello concerto, a symphony, and an opera (*The Bride of Dionysus*, Edinburgh 1929). Wrote much on music. D.Mus., Oxford. Knighted 1935.

See *Annotated Programmes*.

Toward the Unknown Region. Choral-orch. setting by Vaughan Williams of poem by Whitman. (1st perf. Leeds Fest. 1907.)

To Women (Elgar). See *Spirit of England*.

Toy-box (Debussy). See *Boîte à joujoux*.

Toye. Occasional 16th- and early 17th-c. title for any light virginal composition.

Toye, (1) **Francis**—in full John Francis (b. Winchester 1883; d. Florence 1964). Well-known critic of London newspapers and general writer on musical subjects (books on Rossini, Verdi, &c.). Director of Brit. Inst. in Florence 1936–9; Brazil 1941; Florence 1945. C.B.E. 1954.
(2) **Geoffrey** (b. London 1889; there d. 1942). Held scholarship at R.C.M. and then, whilst pursuing his profession as marine underwriter, was active as orch., choral, and opera conductor and also as composer. Manager of Covent Garden 1934–6.

Toy Symphony (Ger. *Kindersymphonie*, i.e. 'Children's Symphony'; Fr. *La Foire des enfants*, i.e. 'The Children's Fair', or *Symphonie burlesque*). A simple symphony in which toy instruments are employed (in addition to strings and usually piano). Haydn (or possibly Leopold Mozart) is said to have been its 1st composer. His example is often played today, as also one by A. Romberg. At least 20 or 30 other composers have also contributed to the repertory.

Tr. Short for *Trumpet*.

Tracey, Hugh (Travers) (b. Willand, Devon, 1903). Director, Durban Broadcasting Studios, 1935–46. Student of native music of S. Africa, and founder and director African Music Society, q.v. Books on his subject.

Trachea. The 'windpipe', the air passage leading from the bronchial tubes to the larynx.

Trackers. See *Organ* 1.

Tract. One of the psalmodic interludes in the Roman Catholic liturgy, occurring between the Epistle and the Gospel, replaced since the time of St. Gregory by the Alleluia (q.v.) and now only surviving in use from Septuagesima to Easter. It has, of course, its traditional plainsong.

Tradotto (It.), **traduit** (Fr.). (1) 'Translated.' (2) 'Arranged' (see *Arrangement*). (3) 'Transposed.' **Traduzione** (It.), **traduction** (Fr.). (1) 'Translation.' (2) 'Arrangement', q.v. (3) 'Transposition.'

Traetta, Tommaso (b. Naples 1727; d. Venice 1779). Pupil of Durante who early won fame as opera composer. For 7 years at Russian court and then a short time in London. Composed church music, &c.

Tragédie de Salomé, La (Schmitt). See *Salome*.

Tragic Overture (*Tragische Ouvertüre*). By Brahms, being his op. 81, 1st perf. 1881 on the same occasion as the *Academic Festival Overture* (q.v.). The composer stated that it was inspired by no particular tragedy.

Tragic Symphony. See *Schubert's Symphonies*.

Tragische Ouvertüre (Brahms). See *Tragic Overture*.

Traîné (Fr.). 'Dragged.'

Tranquillo (It.). 'Tranquil.' So *tranquillamente*, 'tranquilly'; *tranquillità*, *tranquillezza*, 'tranquillity'.

Transatlantic. First opera by Antheil; libretto by himself. (First opera by an American to be presented in a Ger. opera house—Frankfurt 1930.)

Transcription. See *Arrangement*.

Transfigured Night (Schönberg). See *Verklärte Nacht.*

Transient Shake. Another name for *Upper Mordent* (see Table 12).

Transition. (1) A very brief and passing modulation. (2) A change of key effected with abruptness rather than by the regular process of modulation (see *Modulation*).

Transposing Instruments. These are such instruments as are not notated at their true pitch but (mechanically and without any effort on the player's part) produce the effect of that pitch. Take the clarinet as an example. It is found best to make it in 2 sizes, of which the normal keys are respectively B flat and A (the object of this is to reduce the difficulty of playing in the flat and sharp keys, respectively, by reducing the number of flats or sharps with which the player has to cope). Taking the B flat instrument as our example, that key is to its player the 'natural key' (as C is to the pianist): the player faced with music in (say) the key of E flat finds his music written in the key of F, i.e. he has 2 flats less to consider. Similarly with the A instrument a piece written in the key of B is notated in the key of D, i.e. he has 3 sharps less to consider. Thus music for the B flat clarinet is notated a tone higher than it is to sound and music for the A clarinet a minor 3rd higher than it is to sound. It may here be pointed out that many players of today, with improved mechanism and developed technique, use the B flat instrument for all keys, making the necessary transposition mentally. The abolition of the out-of-date method of notation would save unnecessary mental effort in conductors and other readers of scores, in which there may be as many as 10 transposing instruments in use at any moment, and these requiring transposition by a number of different intervals; this effort, however, becomes, with practice, subconscious and does not seem unduly to worry practised musicians.

The transposing instruments are as follows: (*a*) Bass Flute; (*b*) Cor Anglais, Oboe d'Amore, Oboe in E flat, Heckelphone, Sarrusophone (for all

these see *Oboe Family*); (*c*) Clarinet in B flat and A, Bass Clarinet, High Clarinet in E flat and D, Alto Clarinet in E flat and F, Basset Horn, Pedal Clarinet (for all these see *Clarinet Family*); (*d*) Saxophones (see *Saxophone Family*); (*e*) Cornets (see *Cornet*); (*f*) French Horns (see *Horn Family*); (*g*) Trumpets (see *Trumpet Family*); (*h*) Saxhorns (see *Saxhorn and Flügelhorn Family*); (*i*) Kettledrums (up to Mozart's period, but excluding Handel —see *Percussion Family* 1 a).

The brass band is a law to itself in the matter of transposition (see *Brass Band*).

The following instruments, which are notated an 8ve higher or lower than their actual sounds, are not looked upon as 'transposing instruments': Piccolo, Double Bassoon, String Double-Bass.

Transposition is the changing of the pitch of a composition without other change, e.g. the raising of the pitch of a piece in the key of C to that of key D, or its lowering to the key of B or A (cf. *Key*).

Transverse Flute. See *Flute Family.*

Traps. The nondescript collection of noise and rhythm producers in a jazz band, &c.

Trascinando (It. 'dragging'). Holding back (= *rallentando*).

Trascrizione (It.). 'Arrangement' (q.v.).

Trattenuto (It.). (1) 'Held back.' (2) 'Sustained.'

Tratto (It.). 'Dragged' (used in the negative, *non tratto*, 'not dragged').

Traubel, Helen (b. St. Louis, Mo., 1899). Soprano. Début with Metropolitan Opera 1939, becoming its principal Wagnerian soprano. Also frequent concert appearances with Amer. orchs.

Trauer. Ger. for 'sorrow', and so used in various musical titles, as *Trauermarsch* (Funeral March), &c.

Trauersymphonie (Haydn). See *Mourning Symphony.*

Trauerwalzer (Schubert). See *Mourning Waltz.*

Traum \(Ger.). 'Dream.' So *Traumbild*, 'dreaming-picture'; *träumend*, 'dreaming'; *Träumerei*, 'reverie'; *träumerisch*, 'dreamy', &c. And *Liebestraum*, 'love-dream'.

Träumerei ('Dreaming'). By Schumann. One of his *Kinderscenen* ('Scenes of Childhood') for Piano (op. 15, 1839).

Traurig (Ger.). 'Sad.'

Trautmann, Marie. See *Jaell* 2.

Trautonium. See *Electric Musical Instruments* 1.

Trautwein. See *Electric Musical Instruments* 1.

Travelling Companion, The. Opera by Stanford. Libretto by H. Newbolt, based on Hans Andersen. (Posthumously prod., Liverpool, 1925.)

Travers, John (b. abt. 1703; d. 1758). Choir-boy of St. George's Chapel, Windsor Castle, who became organist of the Chapel Royal, London. Composed church music, organ voluntaries, &c.

Traviata, La ('The Woman led astray'). 4-act tragedy-opera by Verdi. Libretto by Piave, based on Dumas's novel *La Dame aux Camélias*. (Prod. Venice 1853; London and New York 1856.)

Tre (It.). 'Three.' So *A tre* means (*a*) In 3 parts, or (*b*) What have been 3 instrumental groups (e.g. 3 violins) now join together to play the same line of music (cf. *Due*; *Trois*).

Trebelli (original name Gilbert), **Zelia** (b. Paris 1838; d. Étretat 1892). Mezzo-soprano vocalist. Before the public 1859–89. Of very high reputation in opera in Europe and U.S.A. The vocalist **Antonia Dolores** (Antoinette Trebelli) was her daughter.

Treble. The highest voice in choral singing; same as 'Soprano'. But note that the Treble Clef and the Soprano Clef are not the same (see Table 4).

Treble Clef. See *Great Staff*; Table 4.

Treble Trombone. See *Trombone Family*.

Treble Viol. See *Viol Family* 2 a.

Tregian, Francis (*c.* 1574–1619). Cornish musical amateur. After living in France and Italy came to England, where he died in prison as Catholic recusant. Diligent collector and transcriber of music, including important *Fitzwilliam Virginal Book* (q.v.).

Treibend (Ger. 'driving'). 'Hurrying'.

Tremando, tremante, tremolando (It.). 'With tremolo' (q.v.).

Tremblant (Fr.). Tremulant of organ.

Tremendo (It.). 'Tremendous.' So the superlative *tremendissimo*.

Tremolando (It.). 'With tremolo.'

Tremolante (It.). (1) 'With tremolo.' (2) Name for organ tremulant.

Tremolo and **Vibrato**. Both these terms concern the playing of bowed instruments and singing. They are the names for two effects which are frequently carried to great excess by vocalists, so becoming detestable vices.

The one effect (*a*) is that of rapid iteration of a note (instead of steady holding of it) and the other (*b*) is that of a slight waving of the pitch of the note. The application of the terms to those effects varies as regards the voice, some applying (*a*) where others apply (*b*) and vice versa. As regards string playing, *Tremolo* is the rapid iteration of a note, or alternation of 2 notes (see Table 21). *Vibrato* is the undulation of the pitch of a note, caused by a controlled vibration of the finger stopping the string.

A third term, 'Judder', has been introduced into the vocal vocabulary by Field-Hyde (q.v.): it is a variant of (*a*) and is described as 'marked rapid changes of intensity during the emission of a tone, due to involuntary variations, small or great, in the vocal tension'.

Tremulant. See *Organ* 2.

Trend, John Brande (b. Southampton 1887; d. Cambridge 1958). Prof. of Spanish, Cambridge Univ. Author of many books on Spanish history, literature, and (especially) music (*Luis Milán* 1925; *Manuel de Falla*, 1929, &c.).

Trenodia (It.). 'Threnody', 'dirge'.

Trent, Council of. See *Church Music*; *Lauda Sion*; *Veni Sancte*; *Victimae Paschali*.

Trepak. A Russian popular dance, with music in simple duple time.

Très (Fr.). 'Very.'

Trescone. A highly popular Florentine dance, something like the Cushion Dance (q.v.) but with the dropping of a handkerchief instead of a cushion. The music is in simple duple time and rapid and lively.

Trevor, C. H. (Caleb Henry) (b. Shropshire 1895). Organist. Educ. Oxford (M.A.). Successive posts at Oxford, Calcutta, London (St. Peter's, Eaton Square, then Lincoln's Inn). On staff R.A.M. Sometime music director Sherborne School.

Trg. or Trge. Short for *Triangle*.

Triad. See *Harmony* 2 d.

Trial by Jury. Musical 'Extravaganza' by Gilbert and Sullivan. (Prod. Royalty Theatre, London, and New York 1875.)

Triangel (Ger.). 'Triangle' (see *Percussion Family* 2 n).

Triangle. (1) The tinkling orch. instrument—see *Percussion Family* 2 n. (2) A spinet was, from its shape, sometimes called a triangle—e.g. in Pepys and the later 17th and early 18th c. literature.

Triangolo (It.). 'Triangle' (see *Percussion Family* 2 n).

Trichord. See *Pianoforte*.

Trihory. A sort of branle (q.v.) formerly danced in Brittany.

Trill. See *Shake*; also Table 16.

Trillo del Diavolo. See *Devil's Trill*.

Trilogy (Eng.), **Trilogie** (Fr., Ger.), **trilogia** (It.). A series of 3 works of art (e.g. operas, oratorios) on a common theme.

Trimble, (1) **Joan** (b. Enniskillen 1915). Pianist and composer. Studied Dublin Univ. (B.A., B.Mus.) and R.C.M. (Sullivan and Cobbett compn. prizes, &c.) Associated with sister Valerie in perf. of 2 piano works. Compositions for orch., chamber combinations, voice, 2 pianos, &c. (2) **Valerie** (b. Enniskillen 1917). See (1) above.

Trinity College of Music (London). Founded 1875 on the basis of a somewhat earlier body. It is both a teaching and an examining institution, with an extensive system of overseas examinations.

Trinklied (Ger.). 'Drinking song.'

Trio. Any body of 3 performers together, or any piece of music for such. (a) A *Vocal Trio* may or may not have *accompaniment*. (b) The normal *String Trio* consists of Violin, Viola, and 'Cello. (c) *Pianoforte Trio* is the illogical name for the combination of Violin, 'Cello, and Piano.

Triolet. (1) A type of poem—see English Dictionary. (2) A triplet, see Table 11. (3) A short trio—this last use being regrettable since, as the title of a piece, the word suggests some relationship with the poetical form mentioned under (1).

Trionfale, trionfante (It.). 'Triumphant.'

Tripelkonzert, or **Tripelconcert** (Ger.). 'Triple concerto', i.e. a concerto with 3 solo instruments.

Triple Appoggiatura. See Table 12.

Triple Chants. See *Anglican Chant*.

Triple Concerto. A concerto with 3 solo instruments.

Triple Counterpoint. See *Counterpoint*.

Triple-croche (Fr. 'Triple-hook'). The demisemiquaver or Thirty-second note (see Table 3).

Triple Overture. By Dvořák. A cycle of 3 Overtures, constituting a sort of Symphony. (1st perf. Prague 1892, on the composer's departure for America, and then in New York, on his arrival.) They represent Nature, Life, and Love, and are entitled *In der Natur* (op. 91), *Carnival* (originally 'Bohemian Carnival'; op. 92), and *Othello* (op. 93). They are now performed as separate concert pieces.

Triplet. See Table 11.

Triple Time. See Table 10.

Triple Tonguing. See *Tonguing*.

Triptych (Puccini). See *Trittico*.

Trisagion or **Trishagion** ('O holy God, Holy and mighty, Holy and immortal, Have mercy on us'). This is a part of the liturgy of the Greek Church, and occurs also in that of the Roman Catholic Church in the service of the adoration of the cross on Good Friday, and in the ferial prayer at Prime for days of penitence; in the Roman Catholic use it appears in both Greek and Latin, sung antiphonally by 2 choirs, phrase by phrase, one uttering a phrase in Greek and the other repeating it in Latin to the same music. The name comes from the Gr. *Tris*, 'Thrice', and *Hagios*, 'Holy'. There are a number of well-known settings by Russian composers.

Tristan und Isolde. Tragic music-drama by Wagner. Libretto by composer, based on the medieval epic of Gottfried von Strassburg. (Prod. Munich 1865; London 1882; New York 1886.)

Triste (Fr.), **tristo** (It.). 'Sad.' **Tristesse** (Fr.), **tristezza** (It.). 'Sadness.'

Tritone. The interval of the augmented 4th (i.e. the sum of 3 full tones). In the major scale it occurs between the 4th and 7th notes (subdominant and leading note), and so too in the minor, except in the descending form of the melodic minor (see *Scale*). It is a difficult interval to sing and hence usually avoided in composing vocal music.

Trittico, Il ('The Triptych'). Set of 3 one-act operas for perf. on one evening, by Puccini. (Prod. New York 1918; Rome and Chicago 1919; London 1920.)—(1) *Il Tabarro* ('The Cloak', a tragedy); (2) *Suor Angelica* ('Sister Angelica', mystical opera); (3) *Gianni Schicchi* (a comedy).

Triumphal March (Grieg). See *Huldigungsmarsch*.

Triumphlied (*Hymn of Triumph*). Composed by Brahms in 1871 (his op. 55); dedicated to the Kaiser William I, and 1st performed in Vienna in 1872. It drew on Holy Writ to celebrate the Ger. victory in the Franco-Prussian War of 1870.

Triumph of Neptune, The. Ballet by Lord Berners; scenario by Sacheverell Sitwell. (Prod. London 1926.)

Triumphs of Oriana, The. An important book of madrigals (see *Madrigal*) in praise of Queen Elizabeth I, consisting of 29 examples by 26 composers, and edited by Thomas Morley (q.v.). It is dated 1601, but actually appeared in 1603, when the Queen was dead.

Troilus and Cressida. Opera in 3 acts by Walton. Libretto by Christopher Hassall, after Chaucer. (Prod. London 1954; New York and San Francisco 1955; Milan 1956.)

Trois (Fr.). 'Three.' So *À trois* means either (1) in 3 parts, or (2) what have been 3 instrumental groups (e.g. 3 violins) now join together to play the same line of music (cf. *Deux*; *Tre*).

Troisième (Fr.). 'Third'; so *troisième position*, 'third position' (see *Position*).

Tromba (It.). (1) 'Trumpet' (see *Trumpet Family*). (2) Organ stop; sort of loud *Tuba* (q.v.).

Tromba a macchina (It. 'machine trumpet'). 'Valve trumpet' (see *Trumpet Family*).

Tromba cromatica (It.). 'Valve trumpet' (see *Trumpet Family*).

Tromba da tirarsi (It. 'drawing-out trumpet'). 'Slide trumpet' (see *Trumpet Family*).

Tromba marina (It. 'marine trumpet'). A performing variety of the scientific monochord (q.v.). It consisted of a long, tapering box, with a

A 12TH-CENTURY TROMBA
MARINA

single string passing over a bridge and played by a bow. The notes obtained were all harmonics (see *Acoustics* 7) produced by touching the string lightly with the thumb of the left hand. Late specimens had sympathetic strings (q.v.) inside the box. The bridge was adjusted so that it was supported by one foot only, the other vibrating freely against the belly of the instrument, producing a clear and brassy tone, so possibly suggesting the name 'trumpet' (no plausible suggestion as to the sea-going element in the name has yet been made, though it may be worth mentioning that the term is used in Italian for a waterspout).

Tromba spezzata (It. 'broken trumpet'). 'Trombone' (see *Trombone Family*).

Tromba ventile (It.). 'Valve trumpet' (see *Trumpet Family*).

Trombone. (1) Organ stop, type of *Tromba* (q.v.) or *Tuba* (q.v.); 16-foot pitch; generally on pedal. (2) See *Trombone Family*.

Trombone a cilindri (It.). 'Valve trombone.'

Trombone Family. The trombone (anciently *Sackbut*) is like the trumpet in consisting of a tube of cylindrical bore, with a moderate-sized bell, and a cup-shaped mouthpiece. It differs from the trumpet as to its means of extending the tube, which is effected, normally, not by valves but by a sliding arrangement, one part of the tube inside another. Like all brass instruments its notes are obtained from the harmonic series (see *Acoustics* 7), the slides enabling it to change its fundamental note (and thus its harmonic series), so making available all the notes of the chromatic scale. The fundamental notes (7 in number, from 7 positions of the slides) can be obtained, but are not so easy to obtain as the harmonics: they

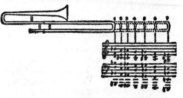

HARMONICS OF THE TROMBONE
Showing them as obtained by the 7 positions
of the slide

are called *Pedal Notes*. (For the means by which sound is brought into existence see *Acoustics* 4; *Brass*.) The tone is, in general, noble in character. A true legato is unobtainable, on account of the momentary breaks induced by the moving of the slides. Valve trombones exist but their tone is somewhat inferior.

The trombone is not a transposing instrument: its notes are written as they are to sound.

The members of the family are as follows: (*a*) TREBLE TROMBONE: found in a few scores of Purcell, Bach, &c. (*b*) ALTO TROMBONE: found in many older scores but now replaced by the tenor instrument. (*c*) TENOR TROMBONE: the most important member of the family. It is notated in either the tenor or bass clef, according to convenience. (*d*) BASS TROMBONE (peculiar to the Commonwealth). (*e*) TENOR-BASS

TROMBONE: with the pitch of the tenor instrument but the bore of the bass one: it is in general use in some continental countries and U.S.A. (*f*) CONTRABASS TROMBONE, or DOUBLE-BASS TROMBONE —in pitch an 8ve below the tenor trombone: it is very tiring to play.

Trombonino (It.). 'Alto trombone' (see *Trombone Family*).

Trommel (Ger.). 'Side drum' (generally called *kleine Trommel*, i.e. 'Little Drum'), or 'Bass Drum' (generally called *grosse Trommel*, i.e. 'Big Drum'). For these 2 instruments see *Percussion Family* 2 i, 2 k.

Trommelflöte (Ger.). Fife (q.v.).

Tromp, Trompe, Trompe de Béarn, Trompe de Berne, Trompe de Laquais. 'Jew's Harp' (q.v.).

Trompete (Ger.). 'Trumpet' (see *Trumpet Family*).

Trompette (Fr.). 'Trumpet'. **Trompette à Coulisse** (Fr.). Slide trumpet.

Trompette à Pistons (Fr.). The normal trumpet. **Trompette Basse** (Fr.). 'Bass trumpet.' **Trompette Chromatique** (Fr.). 'Valve trumpet' (see *Trumpet Family* for all these).

Trop (Fr.). 'Too much.'

Tropary or **Troper.** The collection of tropes (see below).

Trope. In the liturgy of the Roman Catholic Church, an intercalation of music or words or both. The practice began about the 9th c. and was abolished in the 15th c. Such tropes as survive in use now lead a separate existence as a form of hymn. (Cf. *Farcing*.)

Troper or **Tropary.** The collection of tropes (see above).

Troppo (It.). 'Too much.' Generally used with a negative and as part of a warning, e.g. *allegro ma non troppo*, 'quick, but not too much so'.

Trotère, Henry—really Trotter (b. London 1855; d. 1912). Composer of once highly popular drawing-room ballads (*The Toreador, My Old Shako, Asthore*, &c.).

Troubadours. See *Minstrels* 2.

Troutbeck, John (b. Cumberland 1832; d. Westminster 1899). Anglican clergyman, Precentor of Westminster Abbey; writer on choir-training, ed. of psalters and hymn-books, translator of texts of innumerable oratorios, &c. (Cf. *Hadow*.)

Trout Quintet. Nickname of Schubert's Piano Quintet in A, op. 114, of which the 4th movement (of 5) consists of variations on the composer's song *The Trout*.

Trouvères. See *Minstrels* 2.

Trovatore, Il ('The Troubadour'). 4-act tragedy-opera by Verdi. Libretto by Cammarano after a play by Guttiérez. (Prod. Rome 1853; London and New York 1855.)

Trowell, Arnold (b. Wellington, New Zealand, 1887; d. London 1966). Violoncellist. Studied under Gérardy, Becker, &c. Appeared Brussels 1906. Settled in England 1907. Composer— especially for own instrument.

Troyens, Les ('The Trojans'). Opera by Berlioz, libretto by himself. In 2 parts. (*a*) *La Prise de Troie* ('The Taking of Troy') and (*b*) *Les Troyens à Carthage* ('The Trojans at Carthage'). The 2nd part prod. Paris 1863; the opera as a whole at Carlsruhe 1890; the 1st part at Paris 1899.

Trüb, Trübe (Ger.). 'Sad.'

Trumpet. Organ Reed Stop of 8-foot pitch.

Trumpet Family. The trumpet is a cylindrical tube of narrow bore, which in the last quarter of its length widens out into a merely moderate-sized bell: it has a cup-shaped mouthpiece. In all these particulars it differs from the horn, but like that it is a 'half-tube' instrument (see *Whole-tube and Half-tube*). The principle on which the notes are obtained is that of all brass instruments (see *Brass*).

The horn's hand-stopped notes are impossible on the trumpet, as the bell is too far from the player. Like the horn it can be muted by the insertion in the bell of a pear-shaped stopper, or mute (q.v.), which may be used to subdue the tone or, with severer wind-pressure, to produce a peculiarly strident tone. Double and triple tonguing are possible on the trumpet and are more effective than on any other instrument.

The members of the family are as follows: (a) NATURAL TRUMPET WITHOUT CROOKS. The most ancient and simplest form: it can produce only notes of the harmonic series of its fundamental note (see *Acoustics* 7). (b) NATURAL TRUMPET WITH CROOKS. This was in use from the 17th c. until well on in the 19th. The crooks were additional lengths of tubing, lowering the pitch of the fundamental note and thus of the whole harmonic series. But a crook could not be very quickly removed, inserted, or changed, and so the limitations of the natural trumpet without crooks to some extent still existed, the main advantage being that the instrument could now at least be 'crooked' in the main key of the piece to be performed or a nearly related one. For the system of notation involved see *Transposing Instruments* (observe that trumpet parts are generally written without key signature, accidentals being inserted as required). (c) VALVE TRUMPET. This is a trumpet in a specified key, provided with 3 pistons or

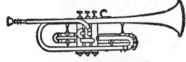

THE VALVE TRUMPET

rotary valves which admit air to additional lengths of tubing, so making available the harmonic series at 6 other pitches. The methods of notating music for this instrument (the one now in general use) are various: the best is that of writing the actual notes as they are to sound. (d) SLIDE TRUMPET. On the principle of the trombone (see *Trombone Family*). It is not commonly in use, some types of passage being found difficult or even impossible on it. (e) BACH TRUMPET. In the late 17th and 18th cs. high-lying florid trumpet parts were written, such as composers after that period avoided (rather surprisingly) as impossible of perf. In the 1880's instruments were prod. on which such passages could be played (cf. *Morrow, Walter*), and in the 1930's

an instrument which it was claimed closely reproduced that of Bach's day. The virtuosity of players now seems to remove the need for such special instruments. (f) BASS TRUMPET. This is really a valve trombone. Being pitched in Key C it is not a transposing instrument.

Trumpet Overture. By Mendelssohn (op. 101; but composed 1825, when the composer was 16; 1st perf. Berlin 1825; London 1833. Publ. 1867.) The brass has unusual prominence, hence the name.

Trumpet Voluntary. See *Voluntary* 5 for 'Cornet Voluntary'; the 17th c. 'Trumpet Voluntary', if the term was ever in use, was supposedly something of this sort, with the right hand playing on a manual in which the trumpet stop was in use and the left hand accompanying on another manual.

In the 20th c. the title became familiar to the Brit. public as that of a piece arranged (for orch. and also for piano) by Sir Henry Wood, working from a 19th-c. piano score whose title-page attributed it to Purcell, and marked by Wood on his own publ. score, 'On programmes this arrangement to be described as *Trumpet Voluntary*; *Purcell-Wood*'. Later it was pointed out that the attribution of origin should be to Purcell's contemporary, Jeremiah Clarke (q.v.), in whose *Choice Lessons for the Harpsichord or Spinett* (posthumous, 1711) it appears as 'The Prince of Denmark's March' (Prince George of Denmark = consort of Queen Anne; came to England 1683).

Try, Charles de. See *Tryphone*.

Tryangle. Same as *Triangle* 2, q.v. (Pepys spells it this way in his diary).

Tryphone. A Fr. form of xylophone. Ch. de Try introduced it about 1870 (see *Percussion Family* 1 f).

T.S. = *Tasto Solo* (see *Tasto*).

Tsar Saltan. See under *Legend*.

Tsar's Bride. See under *Czar's Bride*.

Tschaikowsky. See *Tchaikovsky*.

Tschudi. See *Shudi*.

Tsigane, Tzigane (Fr.). 'Gipsy.

Tuba. (1) Organ stop like *Trumpet* (q.v.) but on high wind pressure and very sonorous 8-, 16-, or 4-foot pitch. *Tuba Major, Tuba Minor, Tuba Mirabilis,* and *Tuba Sonora* are varieties. (2) See *Tuba Group.*

Tuba Group. It is impossible to define 'Tuba', the word apparently being indifferently applied to any sort of bass brass instrument other than the trombone. Moreover, the names of the different individual instruments coming under this very general description vary in different countries and even within the limits of any one country.

In the following attempt at a classification note that the indications (*a*), (*b*), and (*c*) are applied systematically, an instrument marked (*a*) in one section being replaceable by one marked (*a*) in another section, and so with (*b*) and (*c*).

(1) THE WAGNER TUBAS. These were introduced by Wagner in order to combine with his 4 horns when he wanted 8-part harmony. They are as follows: (*a*) TENOR TUBA. Of this he used 2: their bore was narrow, approaching that of horns, and their mouthpiece was much like the horn's funnel-shaped one. Thus their tone resembled that of the horn. Their fundamental key (see *Brass*) was B flat and they had 3 valves plus an extra one for correcting the intonation of the lowest octave. (*b*) BASS TUBA. Of this he used 2. They resembled (*a*) but their fundamental key was F. (*c*) DOUBLE-BASS TUBA, or CONTRA-BASS TUBA. Of this he used 1, to strengthen the bass of his 8-part harmony by doubling it an 8ve lower (as the string double-bass does the 'cello part). Unlike its companions it had a wide conical bore and a cup-shaped mouthpiece. Its fundamental key was C.

What are heard today as 'Wagner Tubas' represent a modification of the above, so far as the tenor and bass instruments are concerned. They retain the funnel-shaped mouthpiece but otherwise resemble the Saxhorn (see *Saxhorn and Flügelhorn Families*). Wagner's notation for his Tubas is not consistent and cannot be explained here.

(2) THE BRITISH TUBAS. What are usually played as 'tubas' in Britain are modelled on Wagner's one true tuba, i.e. (*c*) above. (The term 'British Tubas' is not an accepted one but is used here for convenience.) They are as follows: (*a*) EUPHONIUM or TENOR TUBA IN B FLAT. (*b*, i) E FLAT BASS TUBA or E FLAT BOMBARDON, or EE FLAT BASS TUBA.[1] (*b*, ii) F BASS TUBA. This is a reproduction of the preceding two semitones

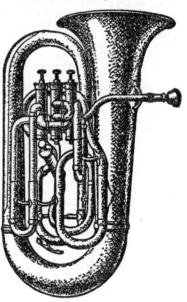

THE BASS TUBA

higher and is sometimes preferred for orchestral use. (*c*) B FLAT BASS TUBA, or B FLAT BOMBARDON, or BB FLAT BASS TUBA.[1] This is (but for the detail of a slightly shortened compass downwards) a reproduction of (*a*) an 8ve lower. When made in a circular form it is called the HELICON. The SOUSAPHONE, an Amer. innovation, is a helical form of (*b*, i) and (*c*) above; its bell is turned up through 2 right angles and terminates in an enormous flange, 2 feet wide; it lacks the lowest 7 notes of the range we should expect to find. It is a dance-band and wind-band instrument.

[1] Double letters indicate merely specimens with a wider bore.

The notation used for these instruments does not treat them as 'transposing instruments' (q.v.).

(3) THE LOWER SAXHORNS (cf. *Saxhorn and Flügelhorn Families*). These are: (*a*) BASS SAXHORN IN B FLAT (OR c); practically identical with the Euphonium. (*b*) BASS SAXHORN IN E FLAT (OR F); practically identical with the Brit. E flat Bass Tuba, otherwise *E flat Bombardon*. (*c*) DOUBLE-BASS SAXHORN IN B FLAT (OR C); practically identical with the B flat Bass Tuba (2 *c*) but with its range complete at the bottom.

Sometimes these instruments are treated as 'transposing instruments' and sometimes not; sometimes the bass clef is used and sometimes the treble clef showing the notes an 8ve higher than they would have been if the bass clef had been used and adopting the convention of representing by middle C, in each case, the 8ve of the fundamental note.

(4) THE LOWER FLÜGELHORNS.

For the FLÜGELHORN IN E FLAT see *Saxhorn and Flügelhorn Families* 2.

There is an It. variety of Saxhorn and Flügelhorn called *Flicorno* and of this there are tuba sizes as follows: *Flicorno basso* or *Bassflicorno*, *Flicorno basso grave*, and *Flicorno contrabasso*.

Tuba mirum. See *Requiem*.

Tubo di ricambio (It. 'changing-tube'). Crook or shank of a brass instrument (see *Acoustics* 7; *Trumpet Family*; *Horn Family*).

Tubophone or **Tubuphone.** See *Percussion Family* 1 c.

Tubular Bells. See *Percussion Family* 1 b; *Bell* 5.

Tucker, Richard (b. New York 1914). Dramatic tenor. At first synagogue cantor, then appeared Metropolitan 1945, and thenceforward with constant success.

Tucket. A flourish of trumpets and beating of drums—the word used by Shakespeare and his contemporaries.

Tudor, Antony (b. London 1909). Dancer and choreographer. Sadler's Wells 1933; Ballet Theater 1939; inventive and original deviser of numerous ballets.

Tudway, Thomas (d. 1726). Choirboy; later tenor in St. George's Chapel, Windsor Castle; organist, King's Coll. Cambridge (1670), Prof. of Music in the Univ. (1704) and D.Mus., 1705. Composed church music and compiled 6 MS. vols. of Eng. church compositions (now in Brit. Museum).

Tune. (1, noun) A melodic succession of notes that 'makes sense' or 'has meaning'. (2) The uppermost part in any simple composition. (3, verb) To establish correct intonation, e.g. 'To tune a piano'.

Tuning. See *Temperament*.

Tuning-fork. See *Pitch*.

Tunsted, Simon (b. Norwich; d. probably Bruisyard, Suffolk, 1369). Franciscan friar of Oxford, of reputation as writer on astronomy and music (though authorship on latter subject not certain).

Turandot. Opera on Chinese subject by PUCCINI—posthumous and completed by Alfano (q.v.). Libretto by Adami and Simoni, based on the 18th-cent. play by Gozzi. (Prod. Milan, New York, Philadelphia, &c., 1926. London 1927.)

BUSONI has an opera (prod. Zürich 1917) on the subject, also a suite.

WEBER wrote music for Schiller's play (1809).

Turca, Alla (It.). 'In the Turkish style.'

Turchaninof, Peter (1779–1856). Priest and choirmaster of cathedral of St. Petersburg; composer of music for the Russian church.

Tureck, Rosalyn (b. Chicago 1914, of Russo-Turkish parents). Pianist; trained Juilliard. Début 1935; became noted as Bach player. Res. England from 1956.

Turina, Joaquin (b. Seville 1882; d. Madrid 1949). Studied in Madrid and then in Paris under d'Indy. Pianist, conductor, and composer of music of distinctively Spanish cast (see *Procesión del Rocio*).

Turkey in the straw. American folk song transcribed for piano by Guion (q.v.) and other composers.

Turkish Crescent or **Turkish Jingle** or **Jingling Johnny.** A noise-maker once used in army bands. It consists of a long stick surmounted by a tent-shaped construction, with an inverted crescent a little lower down the stick, small bells and the like being suspended from both of these.

Turkish March (Beethoven). See *Ruins of Athens.*

Turle, James (b. Taunton, Somerset, 1802; d. London 1882). Holder of many London organ posts; assistant organist Westminster Abbey 1819; organist 1831, titular organist to death, with J. Frederick Bridge as deputy and then successor. Composed much church music.

Turmmusik (Ger. 'Tower Music'). Wind music played by the town band, at stated times, from the church tower.

Turn. See Tables 14, 15.

Turner, (1) **William** (b. Oxford 1651; d. London 1740). Choir-boy of Chapel Royal, London, under Cooke (q.v.), and associated with fellow choristers Blow (q.v.) and Humfrey (q.v.) in composition of 'Club Anthem'; in same choir as a man, and also in those of Westminster Abbey and St. Paul's Cathedral. Composed church music, &c.

(2) **James William** (b. Sutton-in-Ashfield, Notts., 1847; d. Birmingham 1913). Operatic tenor; début as such Crystal Palace 1872; then Carl Rosa Co. Formed own travelling company 1885 and in this had very successful career.

(3) **Laurence** (b. Huddersfield 1899). Violinist. Pupil of Ysaÿe, &c. In Hallé Orch. (see *Hallé*) 1920–4; again 1940, as its leading violin. Much solo and chamber music playing. On staff Royal Manchester Coll. of Music.

(4) **Eva** (b. Oldham 1892). Operatic soprano. Trained R.A.M. In Carl Rosa Co. 1916–24. Then La Scala, Milan; Covent Garden and other European, U.S.A., and South American opera houses. D.B.E. 1962.

Turn of the Screw, The. Opera by Britten. Libretto by Myfanwy Piper, after Henry James. (Prod. Venice 1954.)

Tusch (Ger.). (1) A fanfare (q.v.). (2) A Ger. orch.'s flourish of wind instruments and drums, as an expression of applause, sometimes called for by the audience.

Tutta, Tutte. See *Tutto.*

Tutte le corde (It.). 'All the strings', i.e. (in pianoforte music) cease to play *Una corda* (see *Corda*).

Tutti (It. 'all', plur. of *tutto*). Used of a full passage after one in which some of the performers have not been employed (e.g. in a concerto when after a passage for the solo instrument the orch. takes over).

Tutto il cembalo (It.). Same as *Tutte le corde* (q.v.).

Tutto, tutta, tutti, tutte (It. masc., fem. sing.; masc., fem. plur.). 'All.'

Twelfth. Organ stop of the Mutation kind (see *Mutation Stop*). Length and pitch 2⅔ foot, sounding an 8ve and a 5th (i.e. a 12th) above normal.

'Twelfth Mass' ('Mozart'). This once-popular work may contain some material by Mozart, but is otherwise spurious.

Twelve-note Technique (also ambiguously called 'Twelve-tone' Technique; and sometimes known as 'Twelve-tone Set Technique' and 'Dodecaphonist Technique'). See *Note-row.*

Twilight of the Gods, The; or The Dusk of the Gods (Wagner). See *Ring des Nibelungen.*

Tye, Christopher (b. probably 1497; d. 1572 or 1573). Master of the choristers at Ely Cathedral (abt. 1541–61) and Gentleman of the Chapel Royal. B.Mus., Cambridge, 1536; D.Mus., 1545; later also D.Mus., Oxford. Ordained 1560, becoming rector of Doddington, Isle of Ely. Publ. for domestic edification rhymed metrical version of Acts of the Apostles, with tunes (two of them still in use; see any hymn-tune book) and lute accompaniment; also choral music.

Tympani. A common misspelling of *timpani*, 'kettledrums' (see *Percussion Family* 1 a).

Typewriter. See *Percussion Family* 2 x.

Typophone. A sort of dulcitone (see *Percussion Family* 1 e).

Tyrer, Anderson (b. Accrington, Lancs., 1893; d. at sea between S. Africa and England 1963). Pianist and conductor. Trained Royal Manchester Coll. of Music. Début Hallé Concerts 1914. London 1919. Formed and conducted New Zealand National Symphony Orch. 1946–50. Orch., choral, and piano compositions.

Tyrwhitt, Gerald. See *Berners*.

Tzigane, Tsigane (Fr.). 'Gipsy.'

U

U. Frequent abbreviation of the German *und*, i.e. 'and'.

Über (Ger.). 'Over', 'above', 'too'.

Übung or **Uebung** (Ger., plur. *Übungen* or *Uebungen*). 'Exercise.'

Uccelli, Gli (Respighi). See *Birds*.

U.G.M. Union of Graduates in Music (see under *Union*, below).

Uguale, uguali (It. sing., plur.). 'Equal.' So *ugualmente*, 'equally'; *ugualità, uguaglianza*, 'equality'.

Uhr, Die (Haydn). See *Clock Symphony*.

Ukelele or **Ukulele**. An instrument of the guitar family, patented in Hawaii in 1917 and soon popular in the U.S.A. and elsewhere. A similar instrument, though larger and often electrically amplified, is the *Hawaiian Guitar*; in this the strings are stopped by a steel bar, giving the opportunity for a characteristically exaggerated portamento.

Ullogaun. A sort of Irish lament.

Ultimo, ultima (It. masc., fem.). 'Last.'

Umano, umana (It. masc., fem.). 'Human.'

Umkehrung (Ger.). 'Turning round', 'reversal'. Thus *Kanon in der Umkehrung*, 'Canon by Inversion' (see *Canon*).

Umore (It.). 'Humour.'

Umstimmen (Ger.). To tune in some special way (see *Scordatura*). So the noun *Umstimmung*.

Un', una, uno (It.); **un, une** (Fr.). 'A' or 'an', 'one'.

Una Corda. See *Corda*.

Unaufhörliche, Das ('The Unceasing'). Oratorio by Hindemith. (1st perf. Berlin 1931. London 1933.)

Unceasing, The (Hindemith). See under *Unaufhörliche*.

Und (Ger.). 'And.'

Unda Maris ('Wave of the sea'). Organ stop much like *Voix Céleste* (see *Organ* 2).

Underdamper. See *Pianoforte*.

Under the spreading chestnut tree. This song, with its gestures, was popularized in Britain in the late 1930's by the Boys' School Camp movement. The tune is the old Eng. one of *Go no more a-rushing* (i.e. gathering rushes).

Undertow. Ballet by William Schuman. (Prod. New York 1945.) Concert Suite from the same.

Unesco = Short name used for United Nations Educational, Scientific, and Cultural Organization (q.v.).

Unessential Notes. See *Essential Note*.

Unfinished Symphony. See *Schubert's Symphonies*.

Unfretted. See *Clavichord*.

Ungar, Ungarisch (Ger.). 'Hungarian.'

Ungebunden (Ger. 'unbound'). 'Free', 'unconstrained'.

Ungeduld (Ger.). 'Impatience.' So *ungeduldig*, 'impatient'.

Ungefähr (Ger.). 'About'—in the sense of approximately.

Unger, Heinz (b. Berlin 1895; d. Toronto 1965). Conductor Berlin Philharmonic Orch. 1919–33. Leningrad radio orch. 1934–6, then Britain. Toronto from 1948.

Ungestüm (Ger.). 'Impetuous.'

Ungezwungen (Ger. 'unforced'). 'Easy-going', 'natural'.

Ungherese (It.). 'Hungarian.'

Unheimlich (Ger.). 'Uncanny.'

Uni (Fr.; fem. *unie*, plur. *unis, unies*). (1) 'United.' (2) 'Smooth.'

Union of Graduates in Music (British). Founded 1893 to protect genuine degree holders; has been successful in suppressing spurious degrees. First president was Stainer.

Unisono, Aria all'. See *Aria*.

United Nations Educational, Scientific, and Cultural Organization ('Unesco'). Founded 1945. In 1949 it formed an International Music Council, which undertook the formulation and carrying out of very large projects (World Catalogue of Recorded Music, &c.).

Uniti (It.). 'United'; e.g. after *Divisi* (q.v.), to revoke this direction.

Unit Organ. See *Organ* 3.

Universal Edition. Vienna music publishing house (founded 1901 by combination of older houses).

Universities. See *Degrees and Diplomas*; *Education and Music*; *Choragus*; *Stirling, Elizabeth*.

Unmerklich (Ger.). 'Imperceptible.'

Uno, una, un' (It.). 'A' or 'an', 'one'.

Un peu (Fr.). 'A little' (often in the sense of 'rather').

Un poco (It., sometimes shortened to *un po'*). 'A little' (often in the sense of 'rather').

Unprepared suspension. See *Harmony* 2 g.

Unruhe (Ger.). 'Disquiet', 'lack of peace'. **Unruhig.** 'Unpeaceful.' 'Restless.'

Unschuldig (Ger.). 'Innocent.'

Unten (Ger.). 'Under', 'below'.

Unter (Ger.). '(1) 'Under', 'lower', 'beneath'. (2) 'Amidst.'

Unterwerk (Ger., lit. 'under work'). *Choir Organ* (see *Organ* 1).

Up and waur at them a', Willie! See *There's nae luck aboot the hoose*.

Upper Mordent. See Table 12.

Upper Partials. See *Acoustics* 6, 7; *Partials*.

Upright Grand. See *Pianoforte*.

Upright Pianoforte. See *Pianoforte*.

Uptaker of the Psalms. See *Precentor*.

Uranian Concert, Philadelphia. See *Annotated Programmes*.

Ursprünglich (Ger.). 'Original', 'originally'.

Urtext (Ger.). 'Original Text'; i.e. an edition purporting to give the composer's intentions without later editorial additions.

Use of Sarum, Hereford, &c. The liturgy, ritual, and manner of performing the plainsong in the diocese of Sarum (with its cathedral at Old Sarum, now destroyed and replaced by Salisbury), Hereford, York, Bangor, &c. The Eng. Prayer Book, as its preface states, had as one of its objects the abolition of these local 'uses' and the introduction of uniformity.

(The Scottish 'Use of Colmonell' is a 20th-c. order of Presbyterian worship, originating at Colmonell in Ayrshire, and adopted in some other parishes.)

U.S.F. = *Und so fort* (Ger.). 'And so forth'. Same as *U.S.W.* (q.v.) and *Simile* (q.v.).

U.S.W. = *Und so weiter* (Ger.). 'And so further' (same meaning as *U.S.F.*).

Ut. The keynote of the major scale, according to the system of vocal syllables derived from Guido d'Arezzo (see *Hexachord*), now replaced in most countries by the more singable syllable *Do* (*Doh*, q.v.). In many countries, however, the names *Ut* and *Doh* have become attached (on 'fixed-doh' principles; see *Sight-Singing*) to the note C, in whatever key this may occur (see Table 5).

Utopia Limited, or The Flowers of Progress. Comic Opera by Gilbert and Sullivan. (Prod. Savoy Theatre, London, 1893; New York 1894.)

Utrecht Te Deum and Jubilate. By Handel, to celebrate Peace of Utrecht 1713. (1st perf. St. Paul's Cathedral that year.)

Uvula. The fleshy part of the soft palate (see *Palate*) at the back of the mouth.

U.W. = *Unterwerk* (Ger.), i.e. 'Choir Organ'.

V

Va (It.). 'Go on', '[it] goes on'; i.e. 'Continue', 'it continues' (e.g. *Va diminuendo*, 'It continues to get softer').

Vacillant (Fr.); **vacillando** (It.). 'Wavering'—referring to the stringed instrument vibrato.

Vaghezza (It.). (1) 'Longing.' (2) 'Grace', 'charm'.

Vago (It.). 'Vague.'

Valeur (Fr.). 'Value.' So such expressions as Debussy's *La m.g. un peu en valeur sur la m.d.*, 'The left hand to have a little more value (importance, weight) than the right hand.' The same word also means 'valour'.

Valkyrie (Wagner). See *Ring des Nibelungen*.

Vallas, Léon (b. Roanne 1879; d. Lyons 1956). Distinguished man of musical learning, especially known for works on history of music in Lyons, on Migot, and on Debussy.

Valois, Dame Ninette de (Edris Stannus) (b. Ireland 1898). Dancer and noted choreographer. Director of Sadler's Wells Ballet from 1931.

Valore (It.). Same two meanings as Fr. *Valeur*: see above.

Valse. See *Waltz*.

Valse, La. 'Choreographic Poem' by Ravel. Written as a concert piece (1st perf. Paris 1920; London 1921), but later used also as a ballet.

Valses nobles et sentimentales. By Ravel (1911), for piano, but also arranged by him for orch. (1912); used, too, for ballet *Adelaïde*.

Valse triste ('Sad Waltz'). (1) SCHUBERT's op. 9, no. 2, for Piano. (2) Orch. waltz, by SIBELIUS, from the incidental music to a drama, *Kuolema*.

Valve Instruments. See *Brass*; *Horn Family*; *Trumpet Family*; *Tuba Group*; *Cornet*; *Trombone Family*.

Vamp Horn. A sort of megaphone that seems to have been used in some Eng. churches. It consisted of a long tube terminating in a bell, and an old parish clerk has reported that he sang through it 'to make more sound for the singing'. In some old Ger. cities such an instrument was in use by a watchman stationed on a church tower to give warning of fires.

Vamping. The extemporizing of a simple accompaniment to a singer—who has perhaps previously hummed the tune of his song into the ear of the obliging pianist. Many vampers know nothing of the notation of music, operating solely 'by ear'.

van Beinum. See *Beinum*.

van Biene. See *Biene*.

van den Borren. See *Borren*.

van der Gucht. See *Gucht*.

van der Straeten. See *Straeten*.

van der Stucken. See *Stucken*.

van Dieren. See *Dieren*.

Vanessa. 4-act opera by Barber. Libretto by Menotti. (Prod. New York 1958.)

Vanhall (or **Wanhall**, &c.), **Johann Baptist** (b. Neu-Nechanič, Bohemia, 1739; d. Vienna 1813). Pupil of Dittersdorf (q.v.) and like him a prolific composer (over 100 each symphonies and string quartets, many sonatas, 25 masses, &c.). Lived chiefly in Vienna.

van Hoogstraten. See *Hoogstraten*.

van Wyk. See *Wyk*.

Vaporeux, vaporeuse (Fr. masc., fem.). 'Vaporous.'

Varèse, Edgard—orig. Edgar (b. Paris 1885; d. New York 1965). Pupil at Schola Cantorum of d'Indy and Roussel and at the Conserv. of Widor; conducted choirs in Paris and Berlin and then settled in New York (1915). Active as supporter of daring modernist composers and himself one of these (chiefly for orch.—large or small).

Varga, Tibor (b. Györ, Hungary, 1921). Violinist. Studied Budapest Conserv. and Univ. International soloist (modern and classical works). Resident Britain.

Variante (Fr., It.). 'Variant.'

Variations. See *Form* 5.

Variato, variata (It. masc., fem.). 'Varied.' **Variazione; variazioni** (It.). 'Variation'; 'variations'.

Varié (Fr.). 'Varied.'

Varnay, Astrid (b. Stockholm 1918). Dramatic soprano. Début New York Metropolitan 1941; numerous appearances U.S.A., Canada, and S. America; also London.

Varsovienne. Originally a dance of Warsaw, a sort of mazurka (q.v.) which was popular in the ballrooms about 1850–70.

Vaterländisch (Ger.). Having to do with the Fatherland, i.e. 'Patriotic'.

Vaucanson. See *Mechanical Reproduction of Music* 9.

Vaudeville. Originally a type of satirical Parisian street song. Towards the end of the reign of Louis XIV the tunes of such songs, with topical words set to them, were intercalated into the comedies played at the Paris fairs, which from being styled 'Comedies with Vaudevilles' came to be called merely 'Vaudevilles'. Hence nowadays the name is sometimes used as a synonym for 'variety show'.

The word is also applied to a type of finale to a play or an opera, in which the individual soloists sing successive stanzas (e.g. the finale of Mozart's *The Abduction from the Seraglio*).

Vaughan Williams, Ralph (b. Down Ampney, Glos., 1872; d. London 1958). Educ. at Cambridge (M.A., D.Mus.) and the R.C.M., also studied in Berlin with Max Bruch and worked under the advice of Ravel in Paris. Became active as collector and student of Eng. folk song and of Tudor church music, both of which influenced his idiom.

Compositions include 9 symphonies; concertos for piano, for violin, and for tuba; choral works (e.g. Mass in G minor; *Sancta Civitas*; *Benedicite*; *In Windsor Forest*; *Magnificat*; *Dona nobis pacem*); operas (*Hugh the Drover*; *Sir John in Love*; *The Poisoned Kiss*; *Riders to the Sea*; *The Pilgrim's Progress*); ballets (*Old King Cole*; *Job*); chamber music; many songs.

Showed consistent interest in popular movements in music (e.g. Competition Fest. movement, Folk Dance movement). Musical ed. of *The English Hymnal*.

Hon. D.Mus., Oxford (1919), Bristol (1952). Order of Merit (1935).

See entries under the names of the works above-mentioned and under *Committee for the Promotion of New Music*; *Concerto Accademico*; *Five Tudor Portraits*; *Flos Campi*; *Greensleeves*; *Lark Ascending*; *Norfolk Rhapsodies*; *On Wenlock Edge*; *Shepherds of the Delectable Mountains*; *Story of a Flemish Farm*; *Tallis Fantasia*; *Toward the Unknown Region*; *Wasps*.

Vaughan Williams's Symphonies are as follows: No. 1, *A Sea Symphony* (1st perf. Leeds Fest. 1910; revised 1918; orch. and voices, text from Walt Whitman). No. 2, *A London Symphony* (1913; revised 1920). No. 3, *A Pastoral Symphony* (1922; see *Pastoral Symphony*). No. 4, in F minor (1935). No. 5, in D major (1943). No. 6, in E minor (1948). No. 7, *Sinfonia Antartica* (1952). No. 8, in D minor (1956). No. 9, in E minor (1958).

Vautor, Thomas. An Eng. madrigal writer of the early 17th c.

Vauxhall Gardens. See *Concert*.

Vc. Short for Violoncello.

Vecchi, Orazio (b. Modena 1550; there d. 1605). An ecclesiastic and chief musician at court of Modena; wrote important madrigals (see *Amfiparnaso*); also church music.

Vecsey, Franz von (b. Budapest 1893; d. Rome 1935). Violinist. Pupil of Hubay and Joachim. Child prodigy; then high international reputation. Composer of violin music.

Veemente (It.). 'Vehement.

Veiled Prophet, The. Opera by Stanford. Libretto based on Moore's *Lalla Rookh*. (Prod., in Ger., Hanover 1881; In It., London 1893.)

Velato, velata (It. masc., fem.). 'Veiled.'

Veloce, velocemente (It.). 'With velocity.' *Velocissimo, velocissima-mente*, are the superlatives; *velocità* means 'velocity'.

Velouté (Fr.). 'Velvety.'

Vendredis, Les ('Fridays'). Two sets of pieces for String Quartet, created in collaboration by the Russian composers who used to gather every Friday at the house of their inspirer and organizer, Belaief (q.v.). The pieces are 16 in all and their composers include Borodin, Rimsky-Korsakof, Glazunof, and Liadof.

Veni Creator Spiritus. An 8th-c. Whitsuntide hymn, of which transla-tions exist in all languages (Luther, Dryden, &c.). The Eng. translation generally used is the 17th-c. one of Bishop Cosin ('Come, Holy Ghost, our souls inspire'). This is one of the only two metrical hymns included in the Eng. Common Prayer, and thus offi-cially authorized; the other belongs to an alternative translation given in the same book (The Ordering of Priests): the tune usually sung is a harmonized adaptation of the proper plainsong.

The *Veni Creator Spiritus* is sung at the creation of a pope, the consecration of a bishop, the elevation or translation of a saint, and the coronation of a king (e.g. recent Brit. kings), and on many other occasions.

Veni Sancte Spiritus. A sequence (q.v.) of the Roman Catholic liturgy, appointed for Whitsunday. In medieval times it was called the Golden Se-quence. It is one of the sequences al-lowed to remain when the rest were abolished by the Council of Trent (1545–63). Its traditional plainsong is very beautiful. A version of Caswall's transl. ('Come, thou Holy Spirit, come') appears in some hymn-books, and Neale's ('Come, thou holy Paraclete') in others.

Venite. The 95th Psalm (in the Vul-gate the 94th; see *Psalm* for the differ-ing numeration), the Invitatorium or Invitatory Psalm—*O come, let us sing unto the Lord*. In the Common Prayer (q.v.) of the Anglican Church it is sung as a prelude to the morning Psalms, and is, even where there is a good choir, chanted, not (except by some of the Elizabethan composers and a few others) 'set' with the rest of the 'Ser-vice' (see *Service*). Some elaborate settings of this psalm exist, not in-tended for liturgical use, e.g. Mendels-sohn's.

The prayer book of the Amer. Epi-scopal Church joins part of the Venite with part of the *Cantate Domino*.

Vent (Fr.). 'Wind.' So *instruments à vent*, 'wind instruments'.

Ventil (Ger.). 'Valve.'

Ventilator. A word which occurs in at least one of Richard Strauss's scores as the supposed English of 'Wind Machine' (q.v.).

Ventile (It.). 'Valve.'

Ventile, Corno (It.). 'Valve horn' (see *Horn Family*).

Ventile, Trombone (It.). 'Valve trom-bone' (see *Trombone Family*).

Ventilhorn (Ger.). 'Valve horn' (see *Horn Family*).

Ventilposaune (Ger.). 'Valve trom-bone' (see *Trombone Family*).

Ventiltrompete (Ger.). 'Valve trum-pet' (see *Trumpet Family*).

Venus and Adonis. Masque by Blow 'for the Entertainment of the King', abt. 1684. Revived at Glastonbury 1920 and then performed in other places.

Venusto (It.). 'Pretty.'

Veracini, (1) **Antonio** (latter half of 17th c.). Florentine violinist and com-poser of instrumental music. For his nephew see below. (2) **Francesco (Maria)** (b. Florence 1690; d. possibly at Pisa 1750). Nephew of Antonio, above, and like him violinist and in-strumental composer (24 violin sonatas, &c.). Some contemporaries con-sidered him the world's greatest violinist. Spent some time in Dresden and London, in which latter he pro-duced several operas.

Veränderungen (Ger. 'changes'). A word sometimes used by Beethoven as a synonym for 'Variations'.

Verbrugghen, Henri (b. Brussels 1873; d. Northfield, Minn., 1934). Violinist and conductor. Trained Brussels Conserv. Became chief violinist Scottish Orch., &c.; conductor Glasgow Choral Union; founded String Quartet. Settled (with his quartet) Sydney, N.S.W., 1915, directing Conserv., &c.; conductor Minneapolis Orch. 1922–32.

Verbunko or **Verbounkoche.** A Hungarian dance of the late 18th c., originally danced by hussars in uniform, to the music of gipsy bands.

Verdelot, Philippe (d. abt. 1550). One of famous group of Flemish and Northern French musicians who practised their art in Italy (singer in St. Mark's, Venice, abt. 1525; then choirmaster at San Giovanni, Florence). Composer of masses, motets, and many madrigals— these last especially important.

Verdi, Giuseppe (b. nr. Busseto, district of Parma, 1813; d. Milan 1901). Being refused a scholarship at Conserv. of Milan, as being over-age and lacking in talent, studied in that city privately. At 25 had an opera performed at La Scala opera house there; many others followed and made his name world-famous; still important are *Rigoletto*, *La Traviata*, *Aida*, *Othello*, *Falstaff*: the last two here mentioned, written respectively at 73 and 79, showing a surprising development of style and method—reflecting the influence of Wagner. There exist also the remarkable *Requiem* (q.v.), and some other sacred music.

In him is found the It. gift of melody and understanding of vocal capabilities, with enriched harmony and orchestration, and enhanced sense of poetry and dramatic fitness.

See also *Aida*; *Ballo in maschera*; *Don Carlos*; *Ernani*; *Falstaff*; *Forza del destino*; *Macbeth*; *Nabucodonosor*; *Othello*; *Quattro pezzi sacri*; *Rigoletto*; *Simone Boccanegra*; *Stabat Mater*; *Te Deum*; *Traviata*; *Trovatore*.

Verdoppeln (Ger.). 'To double.' So *Verdoppelt*, 'doubled'; *Verdoppelung*, 'doubling'.

Verein (Ger.). 'Society.'

Vergnügt (Ger.). 'Contented.'

Verhallend (Ger.). 'Dying away.'

Verismo. Tendency in (chiefly Italian) opera of the late 19th c. to take subjects filled with naturalism (in the sense of strong realism) on the models of writers such as Zola and Verga. Early powerful examples of the trend are *I Pagliacci* and *Cavalleria Rusticana*; Puccini's works have a good share of the influence.

Verkaufte Braut, Die (Smetana). See *Bartered Bride*.

Verklärt (Ger.). 'Transfigured', 'glorified'.

Verklärte Nacht ("Transfigured Night'). String Sextet by Schönberg (op. 4, 1899). Based upon poem of Richard Dehmel. (1st perf. Berlin 1902. London 1914; Chicago 1915; arranged for String Orch. and perf. New York 1921.)

Verlauf (Ger.). 'Course', 'continuance'.

Verliebt (Ger.). 'Loved', i.e. performed in a tender manner.

Verlierend (Ger. 'losing itself'). 'Dying away.'

Verlöschend (Ger. 'extinguished'). 'Dying away.'

Verne—originally Wurm, q.v., (1) **Mathilde** (b. Southampton 1868; d. London 1936). Pianist. Studied with Mme Schumann. Long known as capable pianist and London teacher. (Cf. *Solomon*.) (2) **Adela** (b. Southampton 1886; d. London 1952). Pianist. Sister of above and of like reputation.

Vernehmbar (Ger.). 'Perceptible.'

Véronique. Popular opera by Messager. (Prod. Paris 1898; London 1903; New York 1905.)

Verschiebung (Ger.). 'Soft pedal (lit. 'shoving away'—from the character of the mechanism).

Verschieden (Ger.). 'Various.'

Verschwindend (Ger. 'disappearing'). 'Dying away.'

Verse, as contrasted with 'Full', is a term used in church music to mean a passage for solo voice, or for 2 or more voices (e.g. quartet), as constrasted with passages to be sung by the whole choir. A 'Service' (q.v.) or Anthem is called a 'Verse Service', 'Verse Anthem',

'Full Service', or 'Full Anthem', according as it has or has not some portion for solo voices. The words 'Verse' and 'Full' frequently occur in the scores of the 18th-c. and other anthems, as an indication to the singers of the alternation of quartet and full chorus.

Verse-repeating. Term applied to a song in which the same tune is used for every stanza.

Verset. The word simply means 'verse', but has also a special application in the Roman Catholic Church to a verse of a psalm, during which the singers are silent, the organist plays, and the clergy, choir, and congregation repeat the words of the verse to themselves.

A similar practice is sometimes used in connexion with the perf. of the Kyrie, Gloria, and Agnus Dei, the organ *supplying* (this is the technical term) alternate phrases. Similarly the Tract, Sequence, Offertory, and Communion may be 'supplied' by the organ and so may the repetition of the Introit. In some churches the verse of the Gradual is 'supplied'. The Antiphons at Vespers may be supplied on their repetition after the Psalm. The object may be either to relieve the choir or to add to the exultation of a festival by brilliant outbursts of extemporization. The practice is much in use in the Fr. cathedrals and large churches where there are fine organists. Organ versets were publ. as early as 1531, in which year Pierre Attaignant, the celebrated Paris publisher, issued 2 books of them.

Versetzung (Ger.). 'Transposition.'

Versicle. In the Roman or Anglican service a short verse spoken or chanted by the priest and responded to by the congregation (or the choir representing it). But see *Preces*.

Verstärken (Ger.). 'To strengthen.'
Verstärkt. 'Strengthened', i.e. the same as *rinforzandl* (q.v.).

Verstovsky (**Werstowsky**, &c.), **Alexis** (b. Tambov, Central Russia, 1799; d. Moscow 1862). Composer of operas in the It. style, with some mixture of the Ger. (Weber) style, and some Russian elements; of importance as the chief predecessor of the more definitely national Glinka (q.v.); *The Tomb of Askold* (1835) was long highly popular. Also composed songs, &c.

Verteilt, Vertheilt (Ger.). 'Divided.'

Verweilend (Ger.). 'Delaying', i.e. *rallentando*.

Verzierungen (Ger.). 'Embellishments' (see *Ornaments or Graces*; also Tables 12–16).

Vesperal. A Roman Catholic service book containing the liturgy and plainsong for Vespers (q.v.) and often for some of the other 'Hours' of the Church (see *Divine Office*). It is merely an extract from the Antiphonal (q.v.).

Vespéral, Vespérale (Fr. masc., fem.). As the title of a piece of music the word probably usually means 'Evening Mood' or something of that kind (see also entry above).

Vespers. (1) The 7th of the Canonical Hours (see *Divine Office*) of the Roman Catholic Church. Properly it is held at sunset. It is also known as Evensong.

(2) By Monteverdi. His first large-scale liturgical composition (1610) combining the contrapuntal style of the 16th c. with the revolutionary early 17th c. recitative, figured-bass and orch. accompaniment. (Revived in London 1946. The movement *Sonata sopra Sancta Maria* is sometimes performed with orch. only.)

Vestale, La. Chief opera of Spontini. (Prod. Paris 1807; London 1826; Philadelphia 1828.)

Vestris, Gaetano. See *Ballet*.

Vetrate di Chiesa (Respighi). See *Church Windows*.

Vetter Michel (Ger.). Another name for Rosalia (see *Sequence* 1).

Via (It.). 'Away!' So *via sordini*, 'remove mutes'.

Viadana (real name Grossi), **Ludovico** (b. Viadana, nr. Mantua, 1564; d. Gualtieri 1645). Franciscan who held at different times various positions in control of cathedral music, &c.; publ. many madrigals, motets (with organ accompaniment, *Concerti ecclesiastica*), &c. Has been credited with introduction of system of figured bass, but this is inexact.

Viardot-Garcia. See *García 4.*

Vibes. See below.

Vibraphone, Vibra-harp. A sort of marimba (q.v.) of which the resonators (tuned ones) of the (metal) bars are fitted with lids kept in motion (i.e. opening and closing) by an electric motor. This gives a pulsation to the sound coming from any bar of the instrument struck by the player. In the 1920's and 1930's dance bands (especially) largely adopted this instrument. In the U.S.A. it is familiarly called the 'Vibes'.

Vibrations. See *Acoustics*; *Broadcasting of Music*; *Gramophone.*

Vibrato. See *Tremolo.*

Vibrer (Fr.). 'To vibrate.'

Vicar Choral. The term is peculiar to the Anglican Church and designates a cathedral singing man (see *Cathedral Music*). The position varies in the details of its conditions in different cathedrals, and at some the term 'Lay Clerk' or 'Lay Vicar' is used. The word vicar indicates that the duties are really those of the canons, done vicariously: at one time every canon had either a vicar choral or a minor canon (the latter being in orders) attached to him. The office, as it now exists, is one which sprang up at the time of the Reformation (1533–6). Formerly all these various 'Clerks' and 'Vicars' were in holy orders.

Vicar of Bray, The. The hero of this song was a real personage who managed to keep his position through the reigns of Henry VIII (Roman Catholic and then Protestant), Edward VI (Protestant), Mary (Roman Catholic), and Elizabeth (Protestant). The Bray in question is in Berkshire and the poem expands a popular Berkshire proverb—'The Vicar of Bray will be Vicar still'.

The poem as we have it today is said to date from the early 18th c. and treats events of the 17th (not those with which the actual Vicar of Bray was concerned).

It was long sung to a Scottish tune, *Bessy Bell and Mary Gray*, but since about 1770 has been wedded to its present tune of *The Country Garden*, which still survives (or did recently)

amongst Eng. morris dancers, and apparently first appeared in print in *The Quaker's Opera* (1728).

Vicentino, Nicolà (b. Vicenza 1511; d. Rome 1572). Pupil of Willaert at Venice; then joined household of Cardinal Ippolito d'Este. Infatuated with idea of reviving ancient Gr. modes; invented multiple-keyboard instrument, capable of enharmonic distinctions, also publ. madrigals exemplifying his theories and a treatise on *The Ancient Music reduced to Modern Practice* (1555).

Vicino (It.). 'Near.'

Vickers, Jon(athan Stewart) (b. Prince Albert, Saskatchewan, 1926). Heroic tenor. Studied Toronto Conserv.; appeared New York 1956; with Covent Garden from 1957; also Bayreuth 1958, Vienna 1959, &c.

Victimae Paschali. A sequence (q.v.) of the Roman Catholic liturgy, appointed for Easter Day. It dates from the 11th c., and is one of the few allowed to remain when the rest were abolished by the Council of Trent (1545–63). It has, of course, its traditional plainsong.

Victor, Charles (b. London). Operatic and concert baritone. Trained G.S.M. Opera début London 1885. Then career on Continent and with Carl Rosa Co., &c., in Britain.

Victoria, Tomás Luis de (b. Avila, Old Castile, abt. 1548; d. Madrid 1611). One of greatest of contemporaries of Palestrina and, like him, a great composer of unaccompanied church music in the contrapuntal style; wrote no secular music whatever.

The common Italianization of his name (Vittoria) comes from his spending in Rome about 30 years of earlier part of life; there he became a priest. (See *Pedrell.*)

Victoria Hall, Royal (or 'Old Vic'). A London theatre south of the Thames, dating from 1818, later a low music hall, then (1880) taken over by Emma Cons and converted into a place of cheap clean entertainment, and still later (1898) by her niece, Lilian Baylis (afterwards Hon. M.A., Oxon., Hon. LL.D., Birmingham, and C.H.; d. 1937), into a notable home of Shakespearian drama and of opera (the latter later transferred to Sadler's Wells, q.v.).

Victory Symphony. Beethoven's 5th, as nicknamed during Second World War, when it was realized that its opening 4-note theme was, in rhythm, almost the same as the Morse signal 'V', so that this theme came to be used incessantly in broadcasting as a promise of 'Victory'.

Vida Breve, La ('Brief Life'). Opera by Falla. (Composed 1905. Prod. Paris and Madrid 1914; New York 1926.)

Vide (Fr.). 'Empty.' Thus *corde à vide* means 'open string'.

Viel (Ger., *viele*, *vielem*, &c., are all other grammatical forms of the same word). 'Much', 'many'.

Vielle (Fr.). (1) A medieval precursor of the viol. (2) Short for 'vielle à roue' (lit. 'wheel vielle'), i.e. Hurdy-gurdy (q.v.).

Vienna Philharmonic Orchestra. Founded 1842. Conductors include Nicolai (1842); Richter (1875); Mahler (1898); Furtwängler (1938); Karajan (1956); Abbado (1964).

Viennese Carnival Pranks (Schumann). See *Faschingsschwank*.

Vier (Ger.). 'Four.'

Vierfach (Ger.). 'Fourfold' (see *Fach*).

Vierhändig. 'Four-handed', i.e. 'piano duet'.

Vierling. See *Electric Musical Instruments* 2 and 3.

Vierne, (1) **Louis Victor Jules** (b. Poitiers 1870; d. Paris 1937). Pupil at Paris Conserv. of Franck and Widor; in 1900, though blind, appointed organist of Notre Dame; died whilst playing at a service there. Fine performer, touring Europe and▸U.S.A.; and composer for his instrument (especially 5 'symphonies'); also composed an orch. symphony, a mass, songs, &c. Many of the leading Fr. organists were his pupils. For his brother see below. (2) **René** (b. Lille 1878; killed at Verdun 1918). Brother of Louis, above, and like him a Paris organist and composer of organ music.

Vierte (Ger., *viertes*, *viertem*, *vierten* are other grammatical forms of the word). 'Fourth.'

Viertel or **Viertelnote** (Ger.). 'Quarter' or 'Quarter-note', i.e. Crotchet (see Table 3).

Vierundsechzigstel or **Vierundsechzigstelnote** (Ger.). 'Sixty-fourth' or 'sixty-fourth note', i.e. Hemidemisemiquaver (see Table 3).

Vieuxtemps, (1) **Henri** (b. Verviers, Belgium, 1820; d. Algeria 1881). At 7 played violin in public (a concerto of Rode), at 8 toured as virtuoso, at 9 appeared in Paris under auspices of his teacher, de Bériot; continued life of touring (in Europe and America), everywhere hailed as a marvel, until in 1871 settled in Brussels as violin prof. at Conserv.; in 1873 suffered partial paralysis. Composed 6 violin concertos, &c., all magnificently laid out for the instrument but sometimes merely showy. For his brothers see below. (2) **Jean Joseph Lucien** (b. 1828; d. Brussels 1901). Brother of Henri, above, and Jules, below. Pianist, piano teacher in Brussels, and composer of piano music. (3) **Jules Joseph Ernest** (b. Brussels 1832; d. Belfast 1896). Brother of Henri and Jean, above. 'Cellist, and as such engaged in Covent Garden opera, London; at time of death leading 'cellist in Hallé Orch., Manchester.

Vif, vive (Fr. masc., fem.). 'Lively.' *Vivement* is the adverb.

Vigueur, vigoureux, vigoureusement (Fr.); **vigore, vigoroso, vigorosamente** (It.). 'Vigour', 'vigorous', 'vigorously'.

Vihtol, Joseph (b. Wolmar, Latvia, 1863; d. Lübeck 1948). Pupil of Rimsky-Korsakof at Conserv. of St. Petersburg; after First World War founded Latvian Conserv. at Riga. Composer of orch. and chamber music, songs, &c.; also arranger of Latvian folk songs.

Vihuela. Sp. instrument, a sort of guitar (q.v.) strung and played like the lute (q.v.).

Village Blacksmith, The. See *Weiss, W. H.*

Village Romeo and Juliet, A (*Romeo und Julia auf dem Dorfe*). Chief opera of Delius. Libretto (in Ger.) by the composer, based on story by Gottfried Keller. (Prod. Berlin 1907; in Eng., London 1910.)

Village Soothsayer, The. See *Rousseau*.

Villa-Lobos, Heitor (b. Rio de Janeiro 1887; d. there 1959). Leading Brazilian composer (over 2,000 works) of operas, symphonies, chamber music, piano music, &c., all strongly influenced by Brazilian folk music idioms, and sometimes employing polytonality. Some of his technical devices appear to be arbitrary and even eccentric. Headed own conservatory.

Villancico (Sp., from *villano*, 'rustic'). A 16th-c. type of choral song, which later developed into a sort of big anthem or cantata for Christmas or other festivals; this began and ended with a choral movement, or *Estrabillo*, and had middle movements for solo voices, &c., called *Coplas*.

Villanella (It.). A sort of simple-minded, light-hearted Neapolitan madrigal, popular in the 16th c. It repeated the same music for each stanza of the poem. A feature was the prevalence of consecutive 5ths. The Villotta is ractically the same thing. (Cf. *Napolitana*.)

Villanesca (It. and Sp., much the same as *Villanella*, q.v., 'rustic'). Granados has a dance of this name.

Villi, Le ('The Wilis', i.e. ghosts of girls deserted by their lovers). Tragedy-opera by Puccini. (Prod. Milan 1884; Manchester 1897; New York 1908.)

Villon. See *Wallace, William*.

Villota or **Villotta** (It., plur. *Villote* or *Villotte*). Practically the Villanella (q.v.).

Vinay, Ramon (b. Chile 1912). At first sang baritone parts in Mexico, &c. Then from 1944 noted heroic tenor (esp. as Otello), leading active international career until 1962. Then baritone again.

Vinci, Leonardo (b. Strongoli, Calabria, 1690; d. Naples 1730). Attached to court of Naples and notable composer of opera in the style of Alessandro Scarlatti, as also of church music and some instrumental music.

Viñes, Ricardo (b. Lérida 1875; d. Barcelona 1943). Pianist. Trained Paris Conserv. Wide tours (both sides Atlantic), notable for introduction of many contemporary compositions.

Viol. See *Viol Family*.

Viola. (1) See *Violin Family*. (2) Organ stop; string-toned; 8-foot length and pitch.

Viola alta or **Altgeige.** A large-sized Viola, in which the size is in just proportion to its pitch, as compared with the violin (cf. *Violin Family*). It has 5 strings. It was introduced by Hermann Ritter in 1876 and used by Wagner in his Bayreuth orch., but the larger stretch of the hand for which it calls has hampered its acceptance.

Viola da gamba. (1) See *Viol Family* 2 c, 4. (2) Organ stop (see *Gamba*).

Viola d'amore. See *Viol Family* 3 i.

Viola pomposa. See *Viol Family* 3 i.

Viole (Fr.). (1) 'Viol.' (2) 'Viola.'

Viole (It.). Plur. of *Viola*.

Viole d'amour. (1) See *Viol Family* 3 i. (2) Organ stop, much like *Violin Diapason* (q.v.).

Viole d'orchestre. Organ stop; a small-scaled *Gamba* (q.v.), of rather biting quality.

Violen (Ger.). Plur. of *Viola*.

Violento; violentamente (It.). 'Violent'; 'violently'.

Violenza (It.). 'Violence.'

Viole-Ténor or **Alto moderne.** A large viola played like the 'cello. Introduced in the 1930's by R. Parramon of Barcelona; it avoids the weakness of the normal viola, which is made too small for its pitch (as compared with the Violin).

Viol Family. This preceded (and then for some time remained contemporary with) the violin family (q.v.) which finally superseded it. Latterly it has been revived and it has now again makers and players.

(1) The DIFFERENTIATION FROM THE VIOLIN FAMILY may be set out as follows: (*a*) Flat back, instead of convex; (*b*) Shoulders usually sloping to the neck, instead of meeting it at right angles; (*c*) Thinner wood and deeper

ribs; (*d*) Normal number of strings 6, not 4; (*e*) Finger-board not smooth but 'fretted' (see *Frets*); (*f*) Sound holes in shape of *c*, not of *f*; (*g*) Bridge less arched; (*h*) Strings lighter, longer, and under less tension; (*i*) Bow-stick curved outward from the hair (as those of the violin family once were), the hairs being tightened or loosened by finger pressure whilst playing (the hand held *under* the bow).

THE VIOL FAMILY

As depicted in Praetorius, *Syntagma musicum* (1615–19)

All viols were (normally) held downwards, the smaller resting on the knees and the larger between the legs.

(2) The SIZES of the chief members of the family are much like those of the Violin Family. A complete '*Chest*' *of Viols* (i.e. a domestic set, often kept in an actual chest) might comprise (*a*) 2 trebles (the treble viol being also called *Descant Viol*), (*b*) 2 tenors (or 1 alto and 1 tenor), and (*c*) 2 basses (the bass viol being often called *Viola da Gamba* = 'leg viol'; held as the violoncello is: when in later parlance we read of the 'bass viol' in church use it is this that is intended). A set like the above would be used in compositions written for a *Consort of Viols* (q.v.).

Cf. *Braccio and Gamba*.

(3) OTHER MEMBERS OF THE FAMILY were: (*d*) the *Double-Bass Viol* (or *Violone*, or *Consort Viol*), playing an 8ve below the bass viol; (*e*) the *Division Viol*, a small-sized bass viol, suitable for the playing of the popular sets of variations (often extemporized); (*f*) the *Lyra Viol*, another small bass viol; (*g*) the *Baryton*, another bass viol, but with sympathetic strings (q.v.); (*h*) the *Pardessus de Viole*, smaller than the treble viol; (*i*) the *Viola d'amore*, or *Viole d'amour*; with no frets and with sympathetic strings. There was also the *Viola pomposa*, really a small violoncello or large viola and so not a true member of the viol family.

(4) The latest survivor of the family in actual use was the Viola da Gamba, which could be heard in public until near the end of the 18th c. At an earlier period than that the Eng. players of this instrument were famous (cf. *Simpson, Christopher*, and *Brade, William*; also *Abel*).

Violin. See *Violin Family*.

Violinda. A violin with various practical helps for the young learner, introduced in Britain in the 1930's, especially for class instruction. It is the invention of J. Hullah Brown.

Violin Diapason. Organ stop; small-scaled diapason (see *Organ* 2) of 8-foot length and pitch.

Violin Family. This dates from the early 16th c. It does not, as often stated, derive from the Viol Family (except as to one member; see below), the resemblances between the two being mainly superficial; however, the two families may perhaps have derived from a common ancestor (see *Viol Family* 1 for differentiation).

The members of the violin family are (*a*) The VIOLIN itself ('First' or 'Second' Violin are mere distinctions of function, like First and Second Soprano in a choir). (*b*) The VIOLA (also called *Tenor* or *Alto*): it is larger than the Violin but not so large in proportion to its lower pitch, and consequently its tone is less bright. (*c*) The VIOLONCELLO or, for short, ''Cello', in perf. placed between the player's knees. (*d*) The DOUBLE-BASS (also called *Contra Bass*). Originally larger and more cumbrous than at present, but that form seems to have been early abandoned in favour of the Violone (see *Viol Family* 3 d) from which our modern double-bass derives: the player stands or sits on a high stool.

Each of these instruments has 4 strings except the Double-bass, which

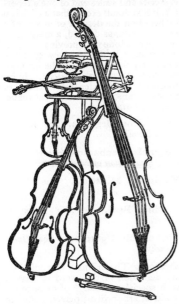

THE VIOLIN FAMILY

formerly had 3 and now has 4 or sometimes 5. Each has its strings tuned at the interval of a 5th from one another except the Double-bass which has them tuned at the interval of a 4th (however, tunings occasionally vary from this).

The normal orch. employment of the family is in 4 parts, as 1st Violins, 2nd Violins, Violas, and 'Cellos with Double-Basses playing an 8ve below. The String Quartet consists of 1st Violin, 2nd Violin, Viola, and 'Cello. As the strings constitute the very basis of the orch., and as the String Quartet is the most homogeneous and versatile combination of solo instruments that exists, the family can fairly claim to stand at the head of all the instrumental families. Its tone is very pleasant and extremely sensitive, and

can be easily varied in intensity: its compass, from the lowest note of the Double-bass to the highest of the Violin, is nearly 7 octaves; almost infinite variations of effect can be obtained by different groupings within one bow-motion and by different methods of applying the bow (see *Spiccato, Martelé, Sul ponticello, Col legno, Tremolo*): further, instead of the strings being bowed they can be plucked by the fingers (*Pizzicato*); double notes and chords can be played —with some limitations (see *Double Stopping*); flute-like Harmonic notes are possible (see *Acoustics* 7): and the Mute (a small clamp on the bridge) can be applied, so producing a curious silvery tone. All this justifies the claim made above as to the versatility of the family.

Whereas every other instrument has undergone steady and continual improvement the Violin remains essentially what it was in the period from the late 16th c. to the 18th, when the great makers were at work, the Amati, Guarneri, and Stradivari families of Cremona in north Italy, and the Stainer family in the Tyrol. The pitch in use today is higher and the strain on the strings therefore more severe (96 lb., as against 63), which has led to the necessity for some strengthening of parts of the old instruments still in use and equivalent alterations of detail in the modern ones; the compass of music having been extended, the finger-board has had to be lengthened in order to make the obtaining of higher notes possible; the bridge has been raised and its curve increased, so that the bow may press harder without catching a string other than the one that is being played upon; and so on. These are details: the bow, however, has undergone a radical change—the curve of its stick, which was convex (considered in its relation to the straight line of the hairs), has, since the late 18th c., become concave and had its tension increased. (The Double-bass players retained the convex bow to the end of the 19th c.)

The development of the performer's technique has gone forward unceasingly and the teaching of the instrument has, by thorough analysis of its elements, been methodized to the last degree.

The Viola was for long a somewhat neglected instrument to which mid-18th c. composers, in their orch. works, gave the simple duty of doubling the 'Cello part: moreover very few original solo compositions were then provided for it. Its orch. role has long been given importance and latterly composers have provided players with a more abundant repertory (cf. *Tertis*).

The Violoncello has long been a favourite solo instrument and the Double-bass has at times had its virtuosi (Dragonetti, q.v., 1763–1846; Bottesini, q.v., 1822–89; Koussevitzky, q.v., 1874–1951: all these, however, used a rather smaller size of the instrument, one easier to manipulate in rapid passages and quicker in the response of its strings).

Violino. Organ stop; string-toned; 4-foot length and pitch (sometimes 8 foot).

Violino; violini (It.). 'Violin'; 'violins'.

Violino Piccolo. Small violin, with strings tuned 8ve above those of Viola.

Violon (Fr.). 'Violin.'

Violoncelle (Fr.). 'Violoncello.'

Violoncello. See *Violin Family*.

Violone. (1) See *Viol Family* 3 d. (2) Organ stop; string-toned; of 16-foot length and pitch.

Viotti, Giovanni Battista (b. Piedmont 1755; d. London 1824). Son of a blacksmith; early showed remarkable ability as violinist and developed into the foremost player of his day and became the founder of modern violin technique; lived a very chequered life, largely at the Fr. court and in London (in latter a wine merchant, and one of founders of Philharmonic Soc.); died in poverty. His violin compositions (including 29 concertos) and chamber music rank amongst the classics of their kind.

Virdung, Sebastian (b. Amberg, Upper Palatinate). Priest and member of court musical staff at Heidelberg (1500); author of oldest book we possess on musical instruments (*Musica getutscht*, Basle 1511; includes valuable pictorial representations; modern facsimile reprints 1882 and 1931).

Virelai. A medieval French song-form (from Vire, in Normandy), with a refrain before and after each stanza.

Virgil Practice Clavier. A keyboard instrument purely for practice (both of exercises and scales and of one's repertory): it is dumb except that a click can be heard on the descent or ascent of a key—or both, as desired, a merging of two clicks in one then proving an absolute legato. The degree of key resistance can be regulated at will. The inventor was A. K. Virgil, an American. He introduced his Clavier into Britain in 1895 and for a time it had a great vogue. (Cf. *Digitorium*.)

Virginal or **Virginals.** See *Harpsichord Family*.

Virginals, Mechanical. See *Mechanical Reproduction of Music* 2.

Virginian Minstrels. See *Negro Minstrels*.

Virginia Reel. See *Sir Roger de Coverley.*

Virgin Soil Upturned. See *Dzerzhinsky.*

Virtuoso. The ordinary Eng. dictionary definition of this word is 'Person with special knowledge of or taste for works of art or virtu; person skilled in the mechanical part of a fine art'. In the 18th c. it was the former part of this definition which represented the more general usage: at present it is the latter part, and this is the sense in which it is applied in connexion with music, which art now tends towards monopoly of the term. The word is especially used to designate an instrumental performer who possesses the highest technical skill, so that he can render difficult music with the greatest ease and at any velocity required.

Properly virtuosity is a means to an end—that is Interpretation (q.v.). There has always been an inclination on the part of the public, however, to treat it as an end in itself, disregarding the distinction between mere virtuosity and artistry.

The term VIRTUOSO MUSIC implies the requirement of exceptional technical skill for its perf.

Visetti, Albert (b. Dalmatia 1848; d. London 1928). After youthful career in Italy and France as opera conductor came to England 1870. Won high position as singing teacher (R.C.M., G.S.M., T.C.M.).

Vishnevskaya, Galina (b. Leningrad 1926). Lyric-dramatic soprano. Eminent in Russia; appeared also Italy (1957); England (1959); U.S.A., &c. (1960). Wife of M. Rostropovitch, q.v.

Vision of Isaiah, The. See *Burkhard, Willy*.

Vitali, (1) **Filippo** (b. Florence abt. 1600; d. 1653). Priest and member of Vatican choir; composer of sacred music, madrigals, and opera *Aretusa* (said to be earliest heard in Rome; 1620). Important figure in history of new monodic style.

(2) **Giovanni Battista** (b. Cremona abt. 1644; d. Modena 1692). Director of music at court of Modena (1684); famous violinist and composer of string music; his sonatas (of the early type) had influence on the development of form. For his son see below.

(3) **Tommaso Antonio** (b. Bologna abt. 1665; d. after 1717). Son of Giovanni, above, and like him famous violinist and composer of string music, best known today by a much-played chaconne for violin and figured bass.

Vital Spark. See *Harwood, Edward*.

Vita nuova, La. See *Wolf-Ferrari*.

Vite; vitement (Fr.). 'Quick'; 'quickly'.

Vito (Sp.). A type of Baile (q.v.) danced in Andalusia.

Vittoria. See *Victoria*.

Vivace, vivacemente (It.). 'Vivacious.' So *vivacetto*, 'rather vivacious'; *vivacissimo*, *vivacissimamente*, 'very vivacious'. *Vivacità*, *vivacezza*, 'vivacity'.

Vivaldi, Antonio (b. probably Venice abt. 1676; d. Vienna 1741). Venetian priest, for most of life in charge of music at orphanage-conservatory for girls in Venice; noted violinist and instrumental composer—in some respects taken as a model by his contemporary, Bach. His string concertos (concertos only in older sense), which number

nearly 70, are important (Bach arranged 20 of these for keyboard and 1 for 4 harpsichords and strings); also composed about 40 operas.

Vivamente (It.). In 'lively' fashion.

Vive (Fr.). 'Lively' (*vif* is the masculine form of the word; *vivement* is the adv.).

Vivente (It.). In 'lively' fashion.

Vivezza. 'Liveliness.' **Vivido.** 'Lively' (same as *Vivace*).

Vivier, Eugène Léon (b. Corsica 1821; d. Nice 1900). Internationally famous horn player (by some secret device could produce up to 4 notes at once).

Vivo (It.). 'Lively'; *vivissimo* is the superlative.

Vl. Short for 'violin'.

Vltava (Smetana). See *My Fatherland*.

Vocal Compass. See *Voice* 14.

Vocal cords ('True' and 'False'). See *Voice* 4.

Vocalize. To sing to a vowel, as in the Fr. exercises called *vocalises* (cf. *Solfeggio*) or in the extended 'divisions' (q.v.) of a Handel vocal solo or chorus, &c. (cf. *Coloratura*).

Vocalizzo (It., plur. *vocalizzi*). Same as Fr. *Vocalise* (see above).

Vocal Quartet, Quintet. See *Quartet; Quintet*.

Vocal Registers. See *Voice* 4.

Vocal Score. See *Score*.

Voce; voci (It.). 'Voice'; 'voices'. So *colla voce*, 'with the voice', i.e. the accompanist carefully taking his time, &c., from the singer.

Voce di petto; Voce di testa (It.). 'Chest voice'; 'head voice'; see *Voice* 4.

Voces aequales (Lat.), **voci eguali** (It.). 'Equal voices' (q.v.).

Voces intimae. Name given by Sibelius to his only String Quartet (op. 56; 1909).

Voci eguali (It.). 'Equal voices' (q.v.).

Vogel, Vladimir (b. Moscow 1896). Son of Ger. father and Russian mother. In youth associated with Scriabin; then pupil and assistant to Busoni in Berlin;

since 1940 living in Switzerland. Has composed (largely under influence of Schönberg's 'expressionism', q.v.) chamber music, orch. music, piano pieces, &c.

Vogelquartett ('Bird Quartet'). Nickname of Haydn's String Quartet No. 39, one of the so-called *Russischen Quartette* (q.v.). It is in C and sometimes known as op. 33, no. 3. Some of the thematic material seems to be taken from bird-calls.

Vogl, Heinrich (b. nr. Munich 1845; d. Munich 1900). Operatic tenor; famous in Wagner roles. Took part in 1st Bayreuth performances (*Ring*, 1876), &c.

Vogler, Georg Joseph, known as Abbé (or Abt) Vogler (b. Würzburg 1749; d. Darmstadt 1814). Priest, organist (touring Europe as recitalist), theorist, teacher of composition, and composer, tireless experimenter in acoustics, and inventor of a new system of organ building. Amongst his many pupils were Weber and Meyerbeer. Has been idealized and immortalized in a poem by Browning.

Voglia (It.). 'Longing.'

Vogrich, Max Wilhelm Karl (b. Hermannstadt 1852; d. New York 1916). Pianist and composer. Trained Leipzig Conserv. Toured widely as pianist. Resided New York, Australia, London, &c., and again New York. Composed operas, symphonies, chamber music, piano music, &c. Edited Schumann's works, &c.

Vogt, Augustus Stephen (b. Washington, Ontario, 1861; d. Toronto 1926). Trained New England Conserv., Boston, and Leipzig Conserv. Organist in Toronto; founded famous Mendelssohn Choir (1894) of Toronto and directed Toronto Conserv. (1913–26). Hon. D.Mus., Univ. of Toronto.

Voice. (1) The voice-producing mechanism is a musical instrument like any other, but with the additional power of framing the particular kind of sounds called 'words' and producing these simultaneously with its musical tones.

(2) As an instrument the MECHANISM consists of a bellows (the lungs), a

sound-producing agent (the vocal cords), and a resonating cavity (the mouth, nose, upper throat, &c.).

(3) The WIND SUPPLY in singing is required to be much greater than in ordinary breathing. As air is taken in, the diaphragm (the partition between the upper and lower parts of the body) descends and the ribs expand, so leaving space for the inflation of the lungs. Capacity and control have to be developed because, in singing, the emission of breath has often to be maintained over a long period for a sustained note or a group of notes, and also because breath must often be taken abnormally rapidly in order to avoid interruption of the flow of the music.

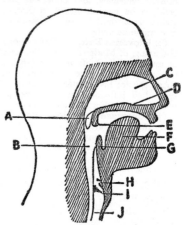

THE VOCAL CORDS AND ASSOCIATED CAVITIES

A, Soft Palate; B, Pharynx; C, Nasal Cavity; D, Hard Palate; E, Uvula; F, Tongue; G, Epiglottis; H, False Vocal Chords; I, Vocal Cords; J, Windpipe.

(4) The SOUND PRODUCTION, as already stated, is the work of the Vocal Cords. These are tiny (about half an inch long in a man and less in a woman or child). During the intake of breath they are wide apart, but when the sound is to be produced they come close together: the opening between them is called the *Glottis*, and when it is thus constricted the friction of the air is considerable enough to provoke vibration—resulting in a series of very

rapid puffs. Any particular note required is obtained by a subconscious varying of the tension of the vocal cords to the required degree.

There is a method of breath emission that has in the past been much insisted upon but is now generally held to be harmful. Above the true vocal cords are 2 membranes called the *False Vocal Cords*; they can be closed and quickly released, which constitutes the action of coughing: this action can be employed as a method of admitting air to the true vocal cords. The name given to this action is *Shock of the Glottis* or *Coup de Glotte* (Fr.).

There are differences of quality of tone in different ranges of the voice, which ranges are called *Registers*. (The causes of this are debated by both singing teachers and physiologists.) The terms 'Head Register' and 'Chest Register', frequently used, merely indicate a difference in the location of sensation when the upper and lower notes, respectively, are produced.

(5) There is a peculiar type of tone called FALSETTO: it is possible only in the upper part of the voice, generally beginning where the more natural tones leave off. It is usually said to be produced by the vibration of the mere edges of the vocal cords and with a high position of the larynx (of which the 'Adam's Apple' is the front portion). The adult male alto's voice is an example of falsetto (see *Alto Voice*).

Normally at puberty the boy's voice becomes for a time more or less uncontrollable owing to sudden and unequal growth of the various parts of the vocal cords and other parts of the sound-producing apparatus: then it gradually settles definitely to the pitch of a man's voice. During the 17th and 18th cs. adult male vocalists with soprano or contralto voices were highly popular; these had been subjected before puberty to a surgical operation on the sexual organs, such as left them, physiologically, in a certain sense, permanently boys. Names applied to such singers have been *Sopranists* or *Contraltists* (as the case may be), *Castrati* (sing. 'Castrato'), *Evirati* (sing. 'Evirato'), and *Musici* (sing. 'Musico').

(6) As RESONATING AGENTS (cf. *Acoustics* 19) the voice possesses that portion of the neck which lies between the vocal cords and the mouth, the mouth itself, the nose, the frontal sinuses (open spaces above the nose), and the chest. All of these are in direct communication with the air which has passed through the vocal cords, so receiving the vibrations originating in these, as well as any vibrations passed on in other ways.

(7) The mouth constitutes 2 resonators by the use of the tongue, which in speech assumes a more or less arched position, so dividing the space into 2 distinct yet connected cavities. By unconscious adjustment of the size of these cavities there are obtained the

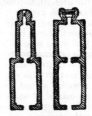

AN ARTIFICIAL LARYNX

Sir Richard Paget 'analysed his own vowel-sounds by ear, and then arranged an artificial larynx in which the part of the vocal cords is played by a reed and the air is blown past this reed into a double resonator. The two chambers of the resonator are tuned to give the required formants and thus the vowel-sound is synthesized' (Wood, *Physics of Music*, 1944)

varieties of VOWEL SOUNDS, every vowel being the result of a combination of 2 resonances at more or less fixed pitches; these resonances are evoked at any given moment by the corresponding upper partials (see *Acoustics* 6 and 7) amongst those of the note then uttered in song or speech.

(8) These 2 resonators to which the production of vowel sounds is assigned must be brought into action by vibrations emanating from the original impulse of the vocal cords. This creates a DIFFICULTY IN VOCAL PRONUNCIATION. One or both of the resonances required may, if a high note is being sung (say by a soprano voice), lie too low for any of the upper partials arising from that note to be able to evoke them. The vowel E is a familiar example: it is useless for composers to

set to a high note a syllable with that vowel, since to sing it on such a note is physically impossible.

(9) The large use of DIPHTHONGS in the Eng. language constitutes another difficulty for singers. As one small example, the 'i' in 'night' when sung to a long note has, perforce, to be given out as 'ah-ee', the 'ah' occupying most of the time occupied by the note and leaving the listener's ear in doubt as to what is to follow. This factor in the 'putting over' of speech in song is, like the one mentioned under 8 above, often overlooked in the criticism of a singer's 'diction'.

(10) For the purposes of a brief treatment like the present, CONSONANTS may be looked upon as merely ways of beginning and ending vowels. Most of them are momentary, but the nasals (*m*, *n*, &c.) offer the possibility of a sort of humming continuation, and the rolled *r* is also continuous.

(11) The ASPIRATE, as the word implies, is a *breathed* sound, i.e. one preceded by an escape of air between the vocal cords before these close in order to produce their notes.

(12) INTENSITY OF TONE, i.e. the degree of loudness with which a note is sung, is largely due to the greater or less force with which the stream of air is directed to the vocal cords, so affecting the amplitude of their vibrations (cf. *Acoustics* 3); lung-capacity is, then, a considerable factor in size of voice, but there are other factors, such as the freedom of passage from the larynx onwards, the size of the resonating chambers, and so on.

(13) The principles affecting QUALITY OF TONE (both as meaning tone-colour and the agreeableness or otherwise of the tone) can be seen by consulting *Acoustics* 6. Pronounced inharmonic upper partials (see *Partials*) in the original tone given out by the vocal cords, or 'parasite resonances' from the various resonating chambers, mean an ugly voice. Both of these elements allow of improvement under judicious training.

(14) Differences in the length of the vocal cords and the size of the resonating chambers bring about differences in the COMPASS OF VOICES, as between children and adults, men and women,

and also individuals. The usual classification of voices according to compass takes account of 6 ranges, with their distinctive qualities, the average voices in these ranges extending an 8ve to a 10th below and above the following notes:

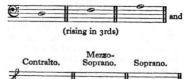

(male alto a note or two less)

(15) Distinct from the range of a song (i.e. its highest and lowest notes), which is necessarily conditioned by the definite compass of the voice for which it is written, is the general (or average) position of its vocal lines. This is called TESSITURA. It will be realized that a song may have a high range but a low tessitura and vice versa.

(16) There are recognized SUB-VARIETIES OF VOICE such as (*a*) *Dramatic Soprano* (powerful voice and high declamatory powers); *Lyric Soprano* (lighter quality and good cantabile style); *Coloratura Soprano* (with marked acrobatic ability and high range). (*b*) *Tenore robusto* (with full voice and much vigour); *Lyric Tenor* (also *Tenore leggiero*, i.e. 'light tenor', corresponding to the Lyric Soprano above). (*c*) *Basso profondo* ('deep bass', capable of the expression of solemnity and similar emotions); *Basso cantante* (with qualities similar to those of the Lyric Tenor and Soprano).

Voices in Fugue. See *Form* 6.

Voile (Fr.). 'Veil.' In music the cloth used for muffling a drum. Hence *voilé*, 'veiled' or 'muffled' (also used of a voice that lacks clarity, either temporarily, through a cold, or permanently).

Voix (Fr. sing., plur.). 'Voice' or 'voices'.

Voix céleste. See *Organ* 2.

Voix humaine (Fr.). 'Vox Humana' (see *Organ* 2).

Volante (It.). 'Flying', i.e. swift and light. Applied to violin playing it means a certain difficult sort of slurred staccato in which the bow has to bounce from the string.

Volga Boat Song. See *Song of the Volga Boatmen.*

Volkmann, (Friedrich) Robert (b. Lommatzsch, Saxony, 1815; d. Budapest 1883). One of the young composers encouraged by Schumann; spent most of life in Budapest as teacher of composition. Works include symphonies, overtures, string quartets, 2 masses, piano pieces (solo and duet), songs, &c.—some of them once highly popular, few of them now to be heard.

Volkslied (Ger.). Lit. 'Folk Song' (q.v.) and properly restricted to this sense, but often carelessly used for 'national song' or 'popular song' (cf. *Volkstümliches Lied*).

Volkston (Ger.). 'Folk style.'

Volkstümliches Lied (Ger.). 'Popular' or 'national' song, as distinct from folk song.

Voll (Ger., *volles, vollem,* &c., are grammatical forms of the word). 'Full.'

Volles Werk (Ger.). 'Full Organ.'

Völlig (Ger.). 'Complete.'

Volltönig, Volltönend (Ger.). 'Full-sounding', i.e. sonorous.

Volochaevko Days. See *Dzerzhinsky.*

Volonté (Fr.). 'Will.' So *A volonté* means 'at one's own pleasure' (= *Ad libitum*, q.v.).

Volta or Volte or Lavolta. (1) A quick dance in simple triple time, probably derived from the galliard. The name suggests the turning round which is one of the motions of the dance. (2) The same 2 words 'Volta' and 'Volte' are It. for 'time' and 'times', e.g. *prima volta,* 'first time'.

Volti (It.). 'Turn', in the sense of 'turn over', e.g. *volti subito* (sometimes abbrev. 'V.S.') 'Turn over quickly'.

Volubile; volubilmente (It.). 'Voluble' (flowing easily); 'volubly'.

Voluntary. (1) The word is found in a musical application as early as the mid-16th c., at first, apparently,

meaning an instrumental composition in which, instead of the composer adding parts to a plainsong theme, as was still common, he left himself free to fashion all his parts as he liked.

(2) But the idea of freedom implicit in the word allowed it to be applied in another way. Thus from the same date or a little later we find voluntary used as meaning what we now call 'Extemporization' or 'Improvisation', and this use of the word persists well into the 19th c., and for any extemporary perf. on any instrument.

(3) Because of the habit of 'voluntarizing' (as we may call it) before a song or the set perf. of a piece, the word early came to have as one of its senses (perhaps a less common one) that of 'prelude'. So we find a warrant of Charles I which lays down the rhythm to be used by army drummers including one as a 'Voluntary before the March'.

(4) Almost from the beginning of the introduction of the word 'voluntary' into musical parlance it had still another application. Composers from at least Purcell onwards (see his Voluntary on the 100th Psalm Tune) have loosely used this word 'voluntary' for written and printed music. It was thus applied even to string music.

(5) Organists have always been active extemporizers and the service in the cathedrals and such churches as possessed organs allowed them scope for the exercise of their skill in voluntary playing. Thus 'voluntary' has come in time to collect round it a special flavour of the ecclesiastical and to signify organ playing before, during, or after a service, whether extempore or not. In the 18th c. 3 voluntaries, at least, were commonly played—at the beginning and end of the Anglican service (as now) and also after the 1st lesson (or before the sermon, whilst the clergyman was changing from his surplice to his preaching gown).

There were several distinct types of voluntary in use in the Eng. Church during the 18th c., of which the principal were, perhaps, the solid *Diapason Voluntary* and the showy *Cornet Voluntary.* The Cornet was a powerful sort of mixture stop, and these voluntaries provided for it (in the right-hand part) a very florid runabout line of single notes, with (in the left-hand part) an accompaniment to be played on another manual. (Often the left-hand part was a line of mere single notes also.) If in addition to its loud cornet the organ had an 'Echo Cornet' (a soft stop), passages for the 2 alternated in the right-hand part (cf. *Cornet Stop*).

Vom (Ger.). 'From the.' So *vom Anfang*, 'from the beginning'.

Von (Ger.). 'From', 'of'.

Von hier (Ger.). 'From here.'

Von Seyfried. See *Ox Minuet*.

Vor (Ger.). 'For'; as a prefix, in many words, it carries the sense of 'before', 'forward', &c.

Voraus (Ger.). 'Beforehand'; *im Voraus*, in organ music, means that the stops in question are to be 'prepared'.

Vorbereiten (Ger.). 'To prepare' (applied to the registration of organ music, often in the form of *bereite vor*, mentioning a stop). So *Vorbereitung*, 'preparation'.

Vorhalt (Ger.). (1) Suspension, (2) Retardation, (3) Long appoggiatura, (4) Syncopation.

Vorhanden (Ger.). 'Available.'

Vorher; vorherig (Ger.). 'Formerly'; 'foregoing' (in various phrases indicating that something is to be performed like or unlike something preceding).

Vorig (Ger.). Same as *vorher*.

Vornehm (Ger.). 'Noble.'

Vorschlag (Ger.). Lit. 'forestroke'; the *Kurzer Vorschlag* (i.e. the 'short' one) is the Acciaccatura; the *Langer Vorschlag* (i.e. the 'long' one) is the Appoggiatura (see Tables 12, 13).

Vorspiel (Ger. 'fore-play'). 'Overture' (see *Overture* and *Prelude*, and for 'Choral Vorspiel' see *Chorale Prelude*).

Vortrag (Ger. 'forth-bringing'). 'Performance', 'execution'; so *Vortragsstück*, a piece designed to show off execution.

Vortragen, Vorzutragen (Ger.). 'To perform' or (more usually) 'to bring forward prominently'.

Vorwärts (Ger.). 'Forwards'; so *Vorwärts gehend*, 'Forwards going', i.e. 'faster'.

Votive Mass. See *Mass*.

Vowels (Production of). See *Voice* 7.

Vox Angelica. See *Organ* 2. (Sometimes, however, a single-rank stop of type of soft *Dulciana*, q.v.).

Vox Humana ('Human voice'). Organ Reed Stop; sort of Clarinet Stop with pipes of bigger bore and very short: 8-foot pitch. The resemblance of its tone to that of the human voice is not often close.

Vreuls, Victor (b. Verviers, Belgium, 1876; d. Brussels 1944). Studied at Liège Conserv.; pupil of d'Indy in Paris and then a prof. in his Schola Cantorum; later director of Conserv. of Luxembourg (1906–26). Compositions include an opera, symphonic poems, chamber music, piano music, songs, &c.

V.S. = *Volti subito*, 'turn over quickly'.

Vuillaume. Family of bowed instrument makers of 17th to 19th cs., first at Mirecourt and then at Paris. The most important member was J. B. Vuillaume (1798–1875).

See *Octo-bass*.

Vuillermoz, Emile (b. Lyons 1878; d. Paris 1960). Student of Fauré at Paris Conserv. and then, almost abandoning composition, a leading writer on music in the Paris press and author of many books.

Vulpius, Melchior (b. Wasungen 1560; d. Weimar 1615). Valuable composer of sacred music of all Protestant types of his period; ed. and translator of a Compendium of Music (1610; originally in Latin by Heinrich Faber, 1552).

Vuoto, vuota (It. masc., fem.). 'Empty'. So *corda vuota*, 'open string'.

Vycpálek, Ladislav (b. Vršavice, nr. Prague, 1882). Graduated as Doctor of Philosophy and became secretary of Prague Univ. Library. Pupil in composition of Novak. Works include choral music, song-cycles, &c.

Vyšehrad (Smetana). See *My Fatherland*.

W

Wachet auf ('Sleepers Awake'). Bach's Cantata 140; the choral movements being based on a chorale of this title.

Wachsend (Ger.). 'Growing', i.e. (generally) *crescendo*.

Wacht am Rhein, Die. See *Watch on the Rhine*.

Wachtel; Wachtelpfeife (Ger. 'Quail'; 'Quail-pipe'). An instrument imitating a bird-cry in Haydn's Toy Symphony, &c. Beethoven in the oboe part of his Pastoral Symphony uses this term where he makes the oboe attempt a similar imitation.

Wade, John Francis. See *Adeste Fideles*.

Waelrant, Hubert (b. Tongerloo, Brabant, abt. 1518; d. Antwerp 1595). Tenor singer in the cathedral of Antwerp, in which city he founded a school of music (1547); taught new system of solmization (see *Bocedization*); engaged also in music publishing business. Fine composer of madrigals, unaccompanied church music, chansons, &c.

Wagenaar, (1) **Johan** (b. Utrecht 1862; d. 1941). Organist of cathedral of Utrecht; then at Arnhem, Leyden, and elsewhere; from 1919 to 1937 director of Conserv. of The Hague. Composed operas, orch. works, organ music, &c., and enjoyed high esteem as teacher of composers.

(2) **Bernard** (b. Arnhem, Holland, 1894; d. nr. Kennebunkport, Me., 1971.) Settled in U.S.A. 1920; violinist in New York Philharmonic Orch. (1921–3); teacher of composition at Inst. of Musical Art, New York (1926–37), and at Juilliard Graduate School (from 1927). Composed symphonies, concertos, chamber and piano music, &c.

Wagenseil, (1) **Johann Christoph** (b. Nuremberg 1633; d. Altdorf 1708). Historian; author of book (1697) which includes treatise on the mastersingers.

(2) **Georg Christoph** (b. Vienna 1715; there d. 1777). Austrian organist, harpsichordist, composer of high reputation, and music-master to the Empress Maria Theresa. Works include harpsichord and organ music, symphonies, operas, &c.

Wagner, (1) **(Wilhelm) Richard** (b. Leipzig 1813; d. Venice 1883). Educ. in Dresden and Leipzig (finally at Thomas School, of whose staff Bach, 80 years earlier, had been a member) and for a short time at the Univ. of Leipzig.

From early years dabbled in composition; then took lessons and at 19 had a symphony performed in Prague and at the famous Gewandhaus concerts in Leipzig. Then wrote operas, with small success; held conductorships in opera houses at Würzburg, Magdeburg, Königsberg, and Riga; visited Paris (1839) hoping to get his opera *Rienzi* performed, but was unsuccessful; it was prod. at Dresden in 1842, as was his *The Flying Dutchman* in 1843. Success in Dresden led to his appointment as court music director, and to his perf. under favourable conditions, during 6 years' tenure of the post, of works of Gluck, Mozart, Beethoven, Weber, &c.; in 1845 he prod. his *Tannhäuser* there. Participation in the rebellion of 1848–9 caused his flight to Weimar and to Jena; at Weimar (but after he had left) Liszt prod. his *Lohengrin* (1850), thereafter remaining for life one of his warmest supporters.

He now went to Zürich (1849), remaining in Switzerland 8 years, writing essays explanatory of his views on music and drama, and working at his *The Ring of the Nibelung* (*Rhinegold, The Valkyrie, Siegfried, The Dusk of the Gods*; this 4-evening work not completed until a quarter of a century later) and *Tristan and Isolde*. In 1855 he spent a season in London as conductor of the Philharmonic Soc.'s concerts. *Tristan* was accepted by the Vienna opera but after nearly 80 rehearsals abandoned as not performable.

Always careless in money matters, he was deeply in debt when in 1864 the 'mad king', Ludwig of Bavaria, invited him to settle in Munich; here *Tristan* was prod. (1865, under von Bülow) and he worked at *Parsifal*; soon the opposition of enemies led to his being asked to leave the city and he settled at Triebschen, near Lucerne. He finished *The Mastersingers of Nuremberg*, which was prod. at Munich (1868, under von Bülow), as were *Rhinegold* (1869) and *The Valkyrie* (1870). In 1872 the little Bavarian city of Bayreuth offered him a site for a theatre of his own and the way to the fulfilment of a long-cherished dream was thus opened: here he settled and it was henceforth his home. Funds were raised by subscriptions from various parts of the world and in 1876 the theatre was opened with the 1st complete perf. of *The Ring* (under Richter). Next year he visited London for a series of concerts of his works at the Albert Hall. In 1882 *Parsifal* was completed and performed at Bayreuth (under Levi). The following year, whilst wintering in Venice on account of ill health, he died. He was buried in the garden of his villa, 'Wahnfried', at Bayreuth.

In these works of Wagner the Ger. Romantic movement of the 19th c. found its completest expression; the emotional intensity of Beethoven is in them further intensified. As the series grew, earlier operatic methods of set recitatives and arias, &c., were gradually abandoned in favour of a less formal and more speech-like mode of vocal utterance, accompanied by a flexible treatment of short pregnant orch. phrases (*Leitmotiven*—'Leading Motives') characterizing the personalities of the drama or particular situations, or ideas, and recurring again and again to underline the thought or emotion behind the dramatic position at the moment: the whole score of a scene thus became fluid. The composer, who was his own librettist, aimed to unite upon equal terms the literary, musical, and scenic arts and thus to achieve the fulfilment of the ideals of Gluck, making every element in the perf. subservient to dramatic effect; he aimed, indeed, at such a fusion of the arts as would amount to the creation of a new art; he desired not 'Opera' but 'Music Drama'.

In addition to dramatic works Wagner composed a few piano pieces (of small importance); a number of overtures (including a *Faust* overture and one on *Rule, Britannia*); the beautiful orch. *Siegfried Idyll*; a *Kaiser March*; a 'biblical scene', *The Love Feast of the Apostles*; and a few other things. His collected literary works occupy 10 volumes.

For his son see below.

See also under *Annotated Programmes*; *Chamberlain*; *Christopher Columbus*; *Dannreuther*; *Faust Overture*; *Feen*; *Festpiel*; *Fliegende Holländer*; *Funeral Marches*; *History* 7; *Huldigungsmarsch*; *Humperdinck*; *Kaisermarsch*; *King Enzio*; *Logier*; *Lohengrin*; *Love Feast of the Apostles*; *Meistersinger*; *Motif*; *Nietzsche*; *Opera* 3; *Parsifal*; *Philadelphia Festival March*; *Polonia*; *Rienzi*; *Ring des Nibelungen*; *Rule, Britannia*; *Siegfried Idyll*; *Tristan und Isolde*; *Tuba Group* 1.

(2) **(Helferich) Siegfried** (b. Triebschen, nr. Lucerne, 1869; d. Bayreuth 1930). Only son of Richard Wagner, by his wife Cosima (daughter of Liszt and formerly wife of von Bülow). After his father's death, when he was 14, continued to live, with his mother, at Villa Wahnfried, and, in time, took over the management of the Bayreuth festivals, conducting some of the performances; married, at age 46, an Englishwoman (Winifred Williams, adopted daughter of Klindworth). Composed many operas (e.g. *Der Bärenhäuter*, 'The Lazybones', Munich 1899) and other things. Conducted in the U.S.A. and in London. After his death his wife continued the festivals (with the support of Hitler) up to the outbreak of the Second World War.

(3) **Johanna**—married name Jachmann (b. nr. Hanover 1826; d. Würzburg 1894). Operatic soprano; also appearing (during 11-year period of loss of singing voice) in spoken drama. Pupil of Garcia. Niece of Richard Wagner and at 19 created part of Elisabeth in *Tannhäuser*. Appeared in London 1856.

(4) **Peter Josef** (b. nr. Trèves 1865; d. Fribourg, Switzerland, 1931). High authority on plainsong and early polyphonic music. Very many publications on Gregorian and Mozarabic chant, Palestrina's madrigals, &c. Prof. of

History of Music, &c., Univ. Fribourg. D.Phil., Strasbourg.

(5) **Georg Gottfried.** See *Lob und Ehre.*

Wagner Tubas. See *Tuba Group* 1.

Während (Ger.). 'During.'

Wainwright Family. Active Lancashire musical family of whom the following are the most important. (1) **John** (b. Stockport abt. 1723; d. 1768). Composer of the well-known tune *Yorkshire* (at first called 'Stockport' and then various other names), to Byrom's hymn 'Christians, Awake!'; in the year before his death appointed organist of what is now Manchester Cathedral. (2) **Robert** (b. 1748; d. 1782). Son of John, above, whom he succeeded in the Manchester appointment; then in Liverpool. D.Mus., Oxford. Composed an oratorio, hymn tunes, &c. (3) **Richard** (b. 1758; d. 1825). Also son of John, above, and also held same and other appointments in Manchester; later in Liverpool. Composed glees, hymn tunes, &c.

Wait or **Wayte.** The waits, in old Brit. life, were the watchmen of a city. They patrolled the streets during the night and used a musical instrument to show that they were at their duty and to mark the hours. The musical side of their work developed and they became good musicians, playing on a variety of instruments, forming a uniformed city band, and appearing with dignity on ceremonial occasions. Each body of waits had its own special tune: thus there have been preserved tunes called *London Waits, Chester Waits,* &c. (cf. *Signature Tune*).

The normal instrument of the waits was the hautboy, long a much-used instrument, and (being loud and coarse in its earlier form) very suitable for outdoor playing; thus the name 'Wayte' was often applied to that instrument, but the waits often played stringed instruments also and sometimes (as at Norwich) were renowned for their singing. Because the waits serenaded the public at Christmas time, any body of people so serenading has come to be called 'the Waits', and the term is still often so used in popular parlance in England today.

Wakefield, Mary—in full Augusta Mary (b. nr. Kendal 1853; d. Grange-over-Sands 1910). Contralto. Pupil of Randegger, Henschel, &c. Became popular with Brit. audiences: then engaged (1885) in development of competition festivals in Westmorland (see *Competitions*). Lectured on music and wrote book *Ruskin on Music* (1894).

Wald, Der (Smyth). See *Forest.*

Waldflöte (Ger. 'Woodland Flute'). Organ stop like *Clarabella* (q.v.), but often of 4-foot length and pitch and with inverted mouth.

Waldscenen. ('Woodland Scenes'). By Schumann. Nine Piano Pieces (op. 82, 1849).

Waldstein Sonata (Beethoven). For Piano. In C major, op. 53 (1804). Dedicated to Count Waldstein; hence the nickname.

Waldteufel, Emil (b. Strasbourg 1837; d. Paris 1915). Very popular waltz composer; pianist, chamber musician to Empress Eugénie and director of court balls.

Walenn, (1) **Arthur** (b. London). Baritone. Trained R.A.M. and under Santley and Henschel. Queen's Hall début 1905; then active career as singer and teacher.

(2) **Herbert** (b. London 1870; d. there 1953). Violoncellist. Trained R.C.M., R.A.M. (later on staff), and at Frankfurt. London début abt. 1902. Became member of Kruse Quartet. Founded London Violoncello School.

(3) **Gerald** (b. London 1871; d. Sydney 1942). Violinist. Trained R.A.M. and under Sauret (q.v.). After London career settled Adelaide 1918 and then Sydney—in each place on staff of State Conserv.

Wales. See *Festival.*

Walker, (1) **Edyth** (b. Hopewell, N.Y., 1870; d. New York 1950). Operatic mezzo-soprano. Trained Dresden. Début Berlin 1894. Appeared many Ger. opera houses (Bayreuth 1908), Covent Garden, Metropolitan Opera, &c.

(2) **Ernest** (b. Bombay 1870; d. Oxford 1949). Took classical honours

at Oxford at age 20 and then served his college (Balliol) in a musical capacity, succeeding John Farmer in direction of its series of Sunday evening chamber music concerts to 1925. Lecturer in the Univ. Faculty of Music. Pianist; composer of many orch. and choral works, songs, &c., and author of a standard *History of Music in England* (1907, 1924, 1952) and other works. D.Mus. 1898.

(3) **Norman** (b. Shaw, Lancs., 1907; d. 1963). Operatic and concert bass. Trained Royal Manchester Coll. of Music and G.S.M. Covent Garden 1935, &c., Glyndebourne, &c.

Walküre, Die (Wagner). See *Ring des Nibelungen.*

Wallace, (1) **William Vincent** (b. Waterford, Ireland, 1812; d. Château de Bages, in the Pyrenees, 1865). Dublin violinist who in his twenties led a highly adventurous life in Australia, New Zealand, North and South America, India, and elsewhere; then in London prod. opera *Maritana* which at once enjoyed (and long retained, and to some extent still retains) great popularity; travelled in North and South America again; settled in Germany for a time and on return prod. *Lurline* (1860), at first even more successful than *Maritana*; other operas and piano music also in high repute in their day; retired to south of France for health and there died.

(2) **William** (b. Greenock 1860; d. Malmesbury 1940). Graduated in medicine at Glasgow, and specialized in ophthalmology, studying in Vienna and Paris; then studied at R.A.M., of which later became a member of the staff. Compositions include the earliest Brit. symphonic poem (*The Passing of Beatrice,* based on Dante, Crystal Palace, 1892; later works of this type include *Wallace, A.D. 1305-1905,* and *Villon,* 1909); the *Freebooter Songs,* popular with a large public. Author of *The Threshold of Music* (1908), *The Musical Faculty* (1914), *A Study of Wagner* (1925). During 1914-18 war an inspector of army ophthalmic hospitals; presented to Army Medical War Museum 100 water-colour sketches by himself.

(3) **Lucille** (b. Chicago 1898).

Pianist and harpsichordist. Studied Bush Conserv., Chicago (B.Mus.), Vassar Coll., and Vienna Univ., Paris Sorbonne, &c. Also with Schnabel, Landowska, and Nadia Boulanger. Married Clifford Curzon (q.v.).

Walmisley, (1) **Thomas Forbes** (b. London 1783; there d. 1866). For 40 years organist of St. Martin-in-the-Fields, London; of reputation as a composer of glees. For his son see below. (2) **Thomas Attwood** (b. London 1814; d. Hastings 1856). Son of Thomas Forbes, above, and godson of Attwood. At 19 appointed organist of Trinity and St. John's Colls., Cambridge; had a distinguished academical career, showing strong mathematical and literary ability; took his B.A. 1838 and M.A. 1841, but before this had been elected Univ. Prof. of Music (1836, aged 22); held organ posts at 3 colls. and the Univ. Church, involving 8 Sunday services. Composer of fine church music still in use (especially the service 'Walmisley in D minor'). Friend of Mendelssohn and a pioneer in the Brit. appreciation of Bach.

Walpurgis Night (Mendelssohn). See *First Walpurgis Night.*

Walsh, John (d. 1736) and his son, also John (d. 1766). Important London music publishers (Handel's publishers).

Walter, Bruno—real surname Schlesinger (b. Berlin 1876; d. Beverly Hills, Calif., 1962). Conductor and pianist. Trained Stern Conserv., Berlin. Became conductor, in turn, of several Ger. opera houses and then Vienna (1901-12) and Munich (1913-22). Friend of Mahler and exponent of his music; devoted also to Bruckner's music. Frequently appeared in Britain (1909 onwards); Fr. nationality 1938; settled in U.S.A. 1939. Publ. autobiography 1946.

Walther, (1) **Johann** (b. Kahla, Thuringia, 1496; d. Torgau 1570). Friend and musical collaborator of Luther, helping him in the musical arrangements of the reformed church, for which he publ. much music.

(2) **Johann Gottfried** (b. Erfurt 1684; d. Weimar 1748). Relative and friend of Bach, a good organist, a composer of organ music, **and the 1st**

compiler of dictionaries of music (1728 and a much larger one 1732).

Walthew, Richard Henry (b. London 1872; d. East Preston, Sussex, 1951). Trained G.S.M. and R.C.M. Held various academic posts. Composer of orch. and choral music and (especially) chamber music. Writer on musical subjects.

Walton, William (Turner) (b. Oldham 1902). Chorister at Christ Church Cathedral, Oxford; then much associated with the literary Sitwell family (Sacheverell, Osbert, and Edith). As composer of serious aims and an obviously high standard of self-criticism has taken high rank. Amongst his compositions are *Façade* (q.v.); Overture *Portsmouth Point* (q.v.); *Sinfonia Concertante* for piano and orch. (1927); *Belshazzar's Feast* (q.v.); 2 symphonies (1934–5 and 1960); concertos for viola (1929), violin (1939), and 'cello (1956); String Quartet in A minor (1947); opera *Troilus and Cressida* (q.v.; 1954); important film music.

Hon. D.Mus. Oxford, Durham, Manchester, Dublin, and Cambridge. Knighted 1951. O.M. 1968. Res. Italy.

See also *Crown Imperial*; *Doctor Syntax*; *In Honour of the City*; *Orb and Sceptre*; *Scapino*; *Siesta*; *Wise Virgins*.

Waltz (Eng.), **Walzer** (Ger.), **valse** (Fr.). A dance in simple triple time derived from the old Ger. *Ländler* (q.v.) and first becoming prominent at the end of the 18th c. In the following century the light graceful productions of the Viennese composers Lanner and the 2 Strausses gave it enormous popularity. In general there are 7 or 8 different melodies with an introduction and a coda. An harmonic feature is the 1-chord-in-a-measure basis, with the bass of the chord on the 1st beat and 'lumps' of the chord on the 2nd and 3rd.

For *Valse à deux temps* see *Deux temps*.

Waltzing Matilda. The term is Australian slang for a man on the tramp. The song, highly popular in Australia, was the work of one Banjo Patterson (the words) and his sister (the music). Made widely known in Britain in ed. by Dr. Thomas Wood.

Walzer. See *Waltz*.

Walzertempo (a Ger.-It. compound). 'Waltz-time.'

Wanderer Fantasia. By Schubert. For Piano (op. 15, 1822). Based on material from his song, *The Wanderer*.

Wand of Youth. Music by Elgar written when a boy of 12 for a children's play and later rewritten by him and arranged as 2 Orch. Suites. (Op. 1 a and b; 1907.)

Wanhall. See *Vanhall*.

Wankend (Ger.). 'Wavering', 'shaking'.

War and Peace. Opera by Prokofief. Libretto by Mira Mendelssohn, based on Tolstoy's novel. (Prod. Moscow 1945.)

Ward, (1) **John** (reigns of Elizabeth and James I). Domestic musician to Sir Henry Fanshaw, of Ware Park, Herts. Composed church music, very fine madrigals, and viol music.

(2) **S. A.** See *America the Beautiful*.

(3) **Robert** (b. Cleveland 1917). Trained Eastman and Juilliard Schools (on staff of latter). Composer of three symphonies, numerous shorter works, and two operas. Pulitzer Prize 1962.

See *Crucible*.

Warlich, Reinhold von (b. St. Petersburg 1879; d. New York 1939). Bass-baritone. Studied Florence; also Cologne Conserv. Début Florence 1899. Toured both sides Atlantic. Especially famous in *Lieder*.

Warlock, Peter. See *Heseltine, Philip*.

War March of the Priests (Mendelssohn). See under *Athalie*.

Wärme (Ger.). 'Warmth.'

Warner, (1) **H. Waldo** (b. Northampton 1874; d. London 1945). Fine violist, member (1907–28) of the much-travelled London String Quartet. As composer known by his chamber music.

(2) **Sylvia Townsend** (b. 1893). Distinguished novelist and general writer; also high authority on Tudor Church Music and one of editors of great Carnegie Trust collection of such publ. by Oxford Univ. Press.

Warr, Eric (b. Nottingham 1905). Chorister Manchester Cathedral 1914–20; Cambridge Univ. 1923–6 (M.A., B.Mus.); R.C.M. 1926–9. Carl Rosa

Co. and Covent Garden 1930–6. Conductor, B.B.C., 1936; Home Service music supervisor 1947; Asst. Head of Music 1950.

Warrack, (1) Guy Douglas Hamilton (b. Edinburgh 1900). Educ. Oxford (B.A.), and R.C.M. (on staff 1925–35). Conducted B.B.C. Scottish Orch. (1936–45); then Sadler's Wells Ballet (from 1948). Composed orch. and other music; much film music.

(2) **John (Hamilton)** (b. London 1928). Educ. Winchester Coll. and R.C.M. Son of (1). Oboist; then music critic with *Daily Telegraph* (1954); *Sunday Telegraph* (1961). Broadcasts, reviews, &c.

Warren (really Warenoff), **Leonard** (b. New York 1911; d. there 1960). Baritone. Won Metropolitan Opera audition 1938; then, after study in Milan, from 1939 until he died on-stage, a leading Metropolitan baritone of great musical and dramatic power.

War Requiem. By Britten; the Latin text, interspersed with nine war poems of Wilfred Owen. (Perf. Coventry Cathedral 1962; Tanglewood 1963.)

Warsaw Concerto. For piano; by Richard Addinsell. Composed for the film *Dangerous Moonlight* (1942). One movement.

'War-time Mass' (Haydn). See *Paukenmesse.*

Washboard. A kitchen utensil of corrugated metal, now promoted to the dance band. The drumstick moved over it produces a rhythmic humming sound.

Washington, Henry (b. Birmingham 1904). Organist and choral conductor. Trained Birmingham School of Music. Music director various Birmingham churches; then Brompton Oratory, London. Specialist early Latin church music; conductor choir 'Schola Polyphonica'.

Washington Post. Very popular march for Military Band by Sousa.

Wasielewski, Josef Wilhelm von (b. nr. Danzig 1822; d. Sondershausen 1896). Pupil of Mendelssohn at Leipzig Conserv. and (as violinist) of Ferdinand David. Composed a few small pieces, especially a popular

Nocturne for violin and piano. Did much musical journalism and wrote many books on musical subjects.

Was mir behagt (Bach). See *Schafe können.*

Wasps, The. Incidental Music by Vaughan Williams for Cambridge perf. (1909) of Aristophanes' comedy. The Overture is often heard.

Wassail. A festive occasion with drinking. The word often occurs in Christmas carols.

Watch on the Rhine, The (*Die Wacht am Rhein*). A Ger. national song of great popularity. The words were written in 1840, at a moment of special fear of France, by Max Schneckenburger (1819–49), a wealthy ironmaster. They were more than once set to music. The tune that has lived is that of Carl Wilhelm (1815–73), who composed it in 1854: the war of 1870 brought his setting into popularity. During the Great War of 1914–18 there was an ingenious Eng. rejoinder-song, 'When we've wound up the Watch on the Rhine'.

Water Carrier (Cherubini). See *Deux Journées.*

Waterhouse, John Fitzwalter (b. Southport 1904). Educ. Oxford (M.A.). Lecturer, Birmingham Univ. 1927–46; music critic, *Birmingham Post* 1946.

Water Music. Instrumental Suite by Handel, pub. 1740 and thought to include pieces composed for a royal progress on the Thames abt. 1715 (the circumstances a matter of dispute).

Water Organ. See *Hydraulus.*

Waters, Thorold Dalrymple (b. London 1876). Music critic and adjudicator. Journalist in Sydney and Melbourne; then career as tenor soloist (from 1904). After First World War music critic Melbourne *Sun*; competition adjudicator.

Watson, (1) Henry (b. Burnley 1846; d. Salford 1911). Organist and active choral conductor (for long period directing 8 societies). On staff Royal Manchester Coll. of Music. Gave it his fine collection of instruments and to Manchester Corporation collection of

30,000 vols. musical books and scores ('Henry Watson Music Library').

(2) **Sydney** (b. Denton, Lancs., 1903). Studied R.C.M. and Oxford (M.A., D.Mus.). Organist New Coll., Oxford, 1933–8, and conductor orch. and choral societies there. In charge music Winchester Coll. 1938–45; then Eton. Christ Church, Oxford, 1955.

Watts, Isaac. See *Hymns and Hymn Tunes* 4.

Waverley. Early Concert-overture by Berlioz (his 'Op. 1 bis'; 1828). It bears as motto a quotation from Scott.

Wayte. 'Wait' (q.v.). Also an old name for the hautboy (see *Oboe Family*; *Chapel Royal*).

Wearing of the green, The. The words of this song date from 1797. The author is unknown. The tune is earlier. The song has had great vogue at times of patriotic excitement in Ireland.

Webb, Dorothea (b. London 1886; d. London 1949). Soprano. Trained R.A.M. 8 years under Lierhammer (q.v.), &c.; prizes singing, elocution, piano. On staff R.A.M., R.C.M. (1921), also Royal Academy Dramatic Art (1947).

Webbe, the two **Samuels** (father and son).

(1) (b. London 1740; there d. 1816). Organist at the Sardinian Embassy Chapel, London, providing ecclesiastical music still in use in Roman Catholic Church. Prolific composer of catches, canons, and glees, winning 26 of the annual medals of the Catch Club; some glees still widely sung (e.g. *When winds breathe soft, Glorious Apollo*, and *Thy voice, O Harmony!*).

(2) (b. London abt. 1770; d. there 1843). Organist of the Spanish Embassy, London, and at various Liverpool churches; continued the composing activities of his father; wrote 2 textbooks of harmony.

Weber, Carl Maria Friedrich Ernst von (b. nr. Lübeck 1786; d. London 1826). Chorister in the cathedral of Salzburg and there pupil of Michael Haydn (afterwards of the Abbé Vogler at Vienna); at 13 composed his 1st opera (never performed); many other operas followed of which chief are *Der*

Freischütz, Euryanthe, and *Oberon:* these works estd. his position as the effective founder of the Ger. national opera school and of romantic opera in general. His death in London (from consumption) occurred during his visit there for the production of *Oberon.*

In addition to his operas he left independent orch. compositions, and chamber music, which has now practically faded out of public knowledge, but some of his piano music (he was an able pianist) is still to be heard.

See also under *Abu Hassan; Annotated Programmes; Aufforderung zum Tanz; Euryanthe; Freischütz; Oberon; Peter Schmoll und seine Nachbarn; Ruler of the Spirits.*

Webern, Anton von (b. Vienna 1883; d. Mittersill, nr. Salzburg, 1945). Musicologist (D.Phil., Vienna 1906) and composer; in latter capacity pupil of Schönberg (his collaborator also in various musical enterprises); adopted the 12-note system of his master (see 'Dodecuple Scale', s.v. *Scale*); most of his works are of delicate texture, small dimensions, and great concentration; they are largely for chamber combinations or for voice.

See also *Note-row.*

Weber's last Waltz or **Weber's last Thought.** Not by Weber but by K. G. Reissiger (1798–1859), being no. 5 of his *Danses brillantes,* op. 26.

Webster, David (Lumsden) (b. Dundee 1903; d. London 1970). Educ. Oxford. Business career; Chairman, Liverpool Orch. 1940; Gen. Administrator, Covent Garden Opera 1946–70. Knighted 1960.

Wechseln (Ger.). 'To change.' **Wechselnote,** Changing Note (q.v.).

Weckerlin, Jean Baptiste Théodore (b. Alsace 1821; there d. 1910). Librarian of the Paris Conserv., notable bibliographer, and re-discoverer and ed. of much old Fr. vocal music. Also composer of songs, a mass and other choral works, and several operas.

Wedding, The ('Les Noces'). Cantata-Ballet by Stravinsky, with Vocal Soloists, Chorus, 4 pianos, and 17 percussion instruments. (Prod. Paris 1923.)

Wedding Marches. Music of this nature has been composed for special occasions at many periods. The pieces especially used by Brit. organists are Wagner's Bridal Chorus from *Lohengrin* and Mendelssohn's Wedding March from the incidental music to Shakespeare's *Midsummer Night's Dream* (first so used 1847; popularized by use at the wedding of the Princess Royal to the future Ger. Emperor, Frederick III, at Windsor, 1858).

Wedding of the Camacho, The (*Die Hochzeit des Camacho*). Comic opera by the boy Mendelssohn (op. 10; 1825; prod. Berlin 1827). Libretto based on an episode in *Don Quixote*.

Wedge Fugue (Bach). For Organ. In E minor. Nickname arises from melodic shape of subject.

&c.

Weekes & Co. London music publishing firm now part of Galliard (q.v.).

Weelkes, Thomas (b. abt. 1575; d. London 1623). Organist of Winchester Coll. and then of Chichester Cathedral; notable composer of madrigals (e.g. *As Vesta was from Latmos Hill descending*); also wrote much church music and some music for viols.

Weg (Ger.). 'Away', 'off'.

Wehmut, Wehmuth (Ger., lit. 'woemood') 'sorrow'. So *wehmütig* or *wehmüthig*, 'sorrowful'.

Weich (Ger.). 'Soft', 'tender', 'light' (sometimes also 'minor').

Weidig, Adolf (b. Hamburg 1867; d. Chicago 1931). Became a naturalized citizen of the U.S.A. and a valued teacher of composition; composed orch. and chamber music, unaccompanied choruses, &c.

Weihe der Töne, Die ('The Consecration of Sound'), by Spohr. His 4th Symphony, in F (op. 86, 1832), in 8 movements, programmatically based on a poem by Carl Pfeiffer.

Weihe des Hauses (Beethoven). See *Consecration of the House*.

Weihnachtslieder. See *Carol*.

Weihnachts Oratorium (Bach). See *Christmas Oratorio*.

Weihnachtssymphonie ('Christmas Symphony'). Nickname for Haydn's Symphony in D minor, no. 26 in Breitkopf edn. of the Symphonies. Also called *Lamentations*.

Weill, Kurt (b. Dessau 1900; d. New York 1950). Studied under Busoni at Berlin; became opera composer with as chief literary colleague, in later period, Bert Brecht (see *Gebrauchsmusik*), the two sharing the view that in stage works 'music should not cooperate in the action but only interrupt it at suitable spots'; among his many operas are *The Protagonist* (Dresden 1926), *Royal Palace* (Berlin 1927), *Rise and Fall of the City of Mahagonny* (Baden-Baden 1927; new version Leipzig 1929), and a Ger. version (or rather perversion—with altered plot and new music) of *The Beggar's Opera*, *Die Dreigroschenoper* ('The threepenny opera'; Berlin 1928; 2,000 performances in Germany; London in concert form 1935). His non-dramatic works include some chamber music, orch. music, and choral music. The coming to power of the Nazis led to his emigration to the U.S.A. (1935).

See *Down in the Valley*.

Weinberg, Jacob (b. Odessa 1879; d. New York 1956). Studied at Moscow Conserv.; then piano pupil of Leschetizky at Vienna; on staff of Odessa Conserv. (1915–21); lived in Palestine; emigrated to U.S.A. (1926), occupying various posts in New York. Opera *The Pioneers* (prod. New York 1934) uses musical material (partly Arab) found in Palestine; composed choral music, piano concerto, &c., and wrote books on musical theory.

Weinberger, Jaromir (b. Prague 1896; d. St. Petersburg, Fla., 1967). Studied at Prague Conserv. and with Reger in Berlin; in U.S.A. 1922–6, then active in various European countries and returned to U.S.A. in 1939. Composer of operas (see *Schwanda the Bagpiper*), orch. works, &c.

Weinend (Ger.). 'Wailing.'

Weingartner, (Paul) Felix (b. Zara, Dalmatia, 1863; d. Winterthur, Switzerland, 1942). Born into poverty, struggled upwards; secured training at Leipzig Conserv. became protégé of Liszt, and gradually estd. himself as one of foremost orch. conductors, worthily holding many of chief positions in Ger. centres, in Vienna (where he succeeded Mahler in 1907), and in Basle. Often conducted in U.S.A. and Britain. Composed a number of operas, symphonies, and other orch. works, chamber music, &c., and wrote valuable books on conducting and other musical subjects, including an autobiographical work. Frequently married.

Weinlied (Ger. 'Wine Song'). 'Drinking Song.'

Weinrich, Carl (b. Paterson, N.J., 1904). Organist. Trained Curtis Institute. On staff Princeton Univ. 1934–40 and from 1943; Columbia Univ. 1942–52; many recordings of Bach, &c.

Weinzweig, John Jacob (b. Toronto 1913). Composer, teacher, and conductor. Trained Eastman School and Toronto Univ. (M.Mus.) Prominent Canadian exponent of Note-row (q.v.) technique; numerous vocal, orchestral, and chamber music compositions.

Weiss, (1) Willoughby Hunter (b. Liverpool 1820; d. London 1867). Well-known opera and oratorio bass vocalist. Composed about 1854 a song that long enjoyed overwhelming popularity, a setting of Longfellow's *The Village Blacksmith*.

(2) **Adolph** (b. Baltimore 1891; d. Van Nuys, Calif., 1971). Pupil of Schönberg in Berlin; played bassoon in Amer. orchs.; won Guggenheim Fellowship in composition (1932). Works include orch. and chamber music, &c. Helped to organize a conductorless orch. in New York.

(3) **Amelia**. See *Joachim*.

Weissenburg, Heinz. See *Albicastro*.

Weldon, (1) John (b. Chichester 1676; d. London 1736). At school at Eton; then took lessons from Purcell. Organist of New Coll., Oxford (1694). Gentleman of Chapel Royal (1701) and later one of its organists and composers;

held other organistships in London churches. Composed good church music, also operas, &c.

(2) **Mrs. Georgina**—maiden name Thomas, changed to Treherne (b. nr. London 1837; d. Brighton 1914). Soprano vocalist of high standing; before public as such 1870–84. Became friend and supporter of Gounod when he was in England (1870–5); then quarrelled with him, winning lawsuit against him with £12,000 damages (he issued in Paris, privately, *Mémoires de Georgina Weldon*, with sub-title *Justice? Anglaise*). Habitual and able litigant, bringing action against medical man who signed lunacy certificate, and 20 slander and libel actions, total favourable verdicts amounting to £20,000; herself spent 6 months in jail for libel on Rivière; founded and conducted orphanage for musical children. Publ. many books and pamphlets.

(3) **George** (b. Chichester 1908; d. Cape Town 1963). Orch. and operatic conductor. Trained R.C.M. Conductor of City of Birmingham Orch. (1943); second condr. Hallé Orch. (1952); free-lance from 1956.

Welitsch, Ljuba (b. Bulgaria 1913). Soprano. Trained Vienna Conserv. Opera career Graz, Hamburg, Dresden, Munich, Vienna, &c.; also Metropolitan Opera, New York, Covent Garden, &c.

Wellesley. See *Mornington*.

Wellesz, Egon (b. Vienna 1885). Learned musicologist (D.Phil., Vienna 1908) and active composer of operas, ballets, orch., choral, and chamber music, songs, &c. On staff Univ. of Vienna, but settled in England on Nazi invasion of Austria, being elected Fellow of Lincoln Coll., Oxford, and appointed lecturer on the music faculty of the Univ. and (1948) Reader in Byzantine Music. Hon. D.Mus., Oxford, 1932; M.A. 1939. Many books and articles. C.B.E. 1957.

See also *Note-row*.

Wellington's Victory, or the Battle of Victoria (sometimes called 'Battle Symphony'). A naïve and noisy piece of 'Programme Music' composed by Beethoven for perf. by the mechanical orch. of his friend Maelzel but actually performed by a real orch. at a Vienna concert (1813) for the benefit of Austrian soldiers wounded in the Battle. It brings in the tunes *Rule, Britannia, Malbrouck* (= 'For he's a jolly good fellow'), and *God save the King*, and imitates cannon fire, &c. It was dedicated to the Prince Regent.

Well-tempered. See *Wohltemperirte Clavier, Das.*

Welsh Harp. See *Harp.*

Welsh Rhapsody. Orch. piece by German. (1st perf. Cardiff 1904.)

Welte Photophone. See *Electric Musical Instruments* 5.

Wenig (Ger.). 'Little', in the expression *ein wenig,*, 'a little' (i.e. a small amount, rather). *Weniger,* 'less'.

Wenlock Edge. See *On Wenlock Edge.*

Weprik, Alexander (b. Lodz 1899). Russian musician trained at Conservs. of Leipzig, St. Petersburg, and Moscow; then on staff of last. Compositions combine Slavonic and Jewish elements.

Werden (Ger.). 'To become.' So *werdend,* 'becoming'; *es wird,* 'it becomes'.

Werstowsky. See *Verstovsky.*

Wert, Giaches, or **Jacques de Wert,** or **Jakob von Wert,** &c. (b. possibly at Antwerp 1525; d. Mantua 1596). Sent to Italy as boy chorister and there remained, chiefly at Mantua, where at some periods he was attached to the court. Publ. many books of madrigals, &c., which brought him high fame.

Werther. Tragedy-opera by Massenet. Libretto based on Goethe's novel, *The Sorrows of Werther.* (Prod. Vienna 1892; New York and London 1894.)

Wesley, (1) **Charles** (b. Bristol 1757; d. London 1834). Son of Charles Wesley, the Methodist divine and hymn writer. Astonishing child prodigy in music; trained by Kelway and Boyce; became organist of London churches, composing organ and other music. For his brother see below. (2) **Samuel** (b. Bristol 1766; d. London 1837). Like his brother (above)

child prodigy. Became fine organist and valuable composer (see *In exitu Israel*). Friend of Mendelssohn and, like him, enthusiastic champion of Bach in days when his music was little known. For his son see below. (3) **Samuel Sebastian** (b. London 1810; d. Gloucester 1876). Natural son of Samuel, above. Choir-boy of Chapel Royal, organist of London churches and then of cathedrals of Hereford (1832) and Exeter (1835), Leeds Parish Church (1842), and cathedrals of Winchester (1849) and Gloucester (1865 to death); considered finest organist of the country and enjoyed special fame as extemporizer. Cherished high ideals in church music in days when the general standard was low and engaged in constant warfare on behalf of his views (see *Cathedral Music*). Many of his church compositions are in regular use and are highly admired.

Wessely, Hans (b. Vienna 1862; d. Innsbruck 1926). Violinist. Trained Vienna Conserv. London début 1888; on staff R.A.M. from following year, with many distinguished pupils. Founded Wessely String Quartet and publ. *Practical Guide to Violin Playing,* &c.

West, John Ebenezer William (b. London 1863; there d. 1929). Organist, &c. Trained R.A.M.; held various London church posts; on editorial staff of Novello's 1884 onwards; composed cantatas, church music, &c.; edited large collection of Eng. organ music, and publ. useful book on Eng. Cathedral Organists (edns. 1899 and 1921).

Westrup, Jack Allan (b. London 1904). Educ. Oxford (M.A., B.Mus., Hon. D.Mus.). Schoolmaster (classics); then London music critic and ed. of *Monthly Musical Record* (1933–45); Lecturer in Music, King's College, Newcastle, in Durham Univ. (1941); Prof. of Music, Birmingham Univ. (1944) and then Oxford Univ. (1946–71). Active musicologist, authority on Purcell (standard life 1937), conductor of operas of Monteverdi and others; ed. of *New Oxford History of Music.* Knighted 1960.

West Side Story. See *Bernstein, L.*

We won't go home till morning.
See *Malbrouck's s'en va-t-en guerre*.

What I enjoy (Bach). See *Schafe können*.

What though I am a Country Lass.
See *Sally in our Alley*.

When a little farm we keep. See *Mazzinghi*.

When Johnny comes marching home. See *Gilmore*.

When the King enjoys his own again. This is a ballad of the time of the beginning of the Civil War in England (1643), and served to keep up the spirits of the Cavalier party at that time, and after the revolution of 1689 those of the adherents of the Pretender. It is by the celebrated ballad-monger Martin Parker, who probably wrote it to an existing tune. The original refrain was 'When the king comes home in peace again'.

When the stormy winds do blow.
See *You Gentlemen of England*.

When we've wound up the Watch on the Rhine. See *Watch on the Rhine*.

When winds breathe soft. See *Webbe, Samuel* 1.

Whiffle. A Fife (q.v.). A whiffler was a fifer who preceded a great personage in ceremonial. The instrument was used in the old Eng. morris dance.

Whinyates, Seymour (b. Fretherne, Glos., 1892). She studied violin, Dresden, Berlin, R.C.M., and Paris; then tours of Europe. Own quartet 1929–39. Brit. Council music dept. 1943; head of this 1946–62. Officier d'Académie de France, 1948.

Whipped Cream (R. Strauss). See *Schlagobers*.

Whistle. See *Recorder Family* 2.

Whistling. The human whistle is acoustically a very peculiar instrument, since the lips produce a sound the pitch of which is not controlled by their tension (as might be supposed) but by the shaping of the mouth as a resonating chamber behind them. There have been world-famous virtuosi of this instrument. Occasionally individuals can whistle 2 notes at a time, presumably by means of 2 resonances,

respectively in the back and front of the mouth (cf. vowel production, s.v. *Voice* 7). Others, whilst humming one part, can whistle another simultaneously.

White, (1) **Robert** (b. abt. 1535; d. Westminster 1574). Probably son-in-law to Tye (q.v.) whom he succeeded as organist of Ely Cathedral; seems from there to have moved to Chester Cathedral; and later to have been Master of the Choristers at Westminster Abbey; died of plague, with his wife and 3 of his children. As composer enjoyed high reputation in lifetime, then almost forgotten; now recognized as one of the very greatest of his great period.

(2) **William** (earlier part of 17th c.). Singing man of Westminster Abbey; wrote some church music and music for viols; has sometimes been confused with Robert, above.

(3) **Matthew** (end of 16th c. and beginning of 17th). Gentleman of the Chapel Royal; in 1611 is found to be in orders and a Vicar Choral of Wells Cathedral; in 1629 D.Mus., Oxford. Is taken to be the composer of various catches and anthems, but there may be confusion here with the Whites above.

(4) **Maude Valérie** (b. Dieppe 1855; d. London 1937). Held Mendelssohn Scholarship at R.A.M. Composed chiefly songs.

(5) **Felix Harold** (b. London 1884; there d. 1945). Self-taught musician who became successful composer of orch. and chamber music, songs, &c., all showing refinement.

(6) **Mrs. Meadows.** See *Smith* 6.

(7) **Eric Walter** (b. Bristol 1905). Educated Clifton and Oxford (B.A.). Has held positions in League of Nations (1929), National Council of Social Service (1935), C.E.M.A., and Arts Council, q.v. (1942). Author of books on Stravinsky, Britten, &c.

White Cockade. See *Red Flag*.

Whitehill, Clarence Eugene (b. Marengo, Iowa, 1871; d. New York 1932). Operatic bass. Trained Paris and under Stockhausen. Début Brussels 1899. Won great favour as powerful exponent of Wagner roles U.S.A., Britain, and Germany.

Whitehouse, William Edward (b. London 1859; there d. 1935). Violoncellist. Pupil of Piatti at R.A.M. (later on staff). Prominent in chamber music.

White Lady (Boïeldieu). See *Dame Blanche*.

Whiteman, Paul (b. Denver 1890; d. Doylestown, Pa., 1967). Highly popular bandleader; brought jazz into the concert hall in 1920's.

Whithorne, (1) **Thomas.** See *Whythorne*.

(2) **Emerson** (originally 'Whittern'; b. Cleveland, Ohio, 1884; d. Lyme, Conn., 1958). Studied piano and composition in Europe; composed orchestral and chamber music, songs, &c.; lived in England 1907–14.

Whiting, Arthur Battelle (b. Cambridge, Mass., 1861; d. Beverly, Mass., 1936). Studied composition with Chadwick and Rheinberger; composed orchestral and chamber music, piano music, songs, &c., and was active in giving chamber concerts and reviving old instruments and music.

Whitlock, Percy William (b. Chatham 1903; d. Bournemouth 1946). Studied at R.C.M. and became organist of various provincial churches and then borough organist of Bournemouth. Compositions chiefly organ and church music—including long and highly praised organ sonata in C minor (1938).

Whittaker, William Gillies (b. Newcastle-on-Tyne 1876; d. Orkney 1944). Active for many years as general musical practitioner in Newcastle-on-Tyne and lecturer on music in Armstrong Coll. there (Univ. of Durham); founded Newcastle-on-Tyne Bach Choir, which gave performances in London and also on continent of Europe and revived neglected music of Byrd, &c. In Glasgow, 1930–41, as head of Scottish National Academy of Music and Prof. of Music in the Univ.; throughout career showed great interest in educational treatment of music and became president of Tonic Sol-fa Coll. (now Curwen Memorial Coll.). Composed choral and other music; edited northcountry folk songs, music of Bach, &c.; wrote valuable books on various musical subjects. M.A., Glasgow; D.Mus., Edinburgh and Durham; LL.D., Edinburgh.

Whittle and Dub. See *Recorder Family* 2.

Whizzer. See *Thunder Stick.*

Whole Consort. See *Consort.*

Whole-note. 'Semibreve' (see Table 3).

Whole-tone Scale. See *Scale.*

Whole-tube and **Half-tube Instruments.** This distinction is applied to brass instruments. Those of wide bore, able to produce their fundamental note (see *Acoustics* 7), are 'Whole-tube', that note being prod. by the vibration of the tube's column of air as a whole, whereas those of narrow bore, whose lowest note is the 2nd harmonic (i.e. the 8ve of the fundamental note) are called 'Half-tube', that note being prod. by the vibration of the air column in a halves. Thus the tubas belong to the 'Whole-tube' class and the trumpets, horns, and Saxhorns are considered to be 'Half-tube' class. However, the distinction has lost a good deal of its validity today, owing to the virtuosity of modern players which enables the best of them to get a whole-tube vibration out of any instrument except the Fr. horn.

Whyte, Ian (b. Dunfermline 1901; d. Glasgow 1960). Studied at R.C.M. and on Continent. Director of Music of Scottish Regional Station of B.B.C. 1931–46; then chief conductor B.B.C. Scottish Orch. Composer of operas, cantatas, symphonies, chamber music, songs, &c.; and ed. of old Scottish music.

Whythorne (or **Whithorne**), **Thomas** (b. 1528; d. after 1590). Publ. (1571) an important secular book of songs in 3 to 5 parts (in effect, early Ayres, see *Madrigal*), also (1590) one of vocal duets, sacred and secular. Autobiography published 1961.

Widdop, Walter (b. nr. Halifax, Yorks., 1892; d. London 1949). Operatic and concert tenor. Début in *Aida*, Leeds 1923. Brit. National Opera Co., Covent Garden, &c.; also Holland, Germany, Spain.

Widerspenstigen Zähmung, Der ('The Taming of the Shrew'). Comedy-opera by Goetz. Libretto based on Shakespeare. (Prod. Mannheim 1874; London 1878; New York 1886.)

Widor, Charles Marie Jean Albert (b. Lyons 1844; d. Paris 1937). Studied at Brussels under Lemmens; became organist of St. Sulpice, Paris (1869-1933), and prof. of organ at the Conserv. (1890, succeeding Franck) and of composition (1896, succeeding Dubois); from boyhood a notable improviser. Composed organ symphonies, &c., wrote music criticism in a Paris journal, publ. valuable books on the organ, orchestration, &c., and (with Schweitzer) ed. the organ works of Bach. Permanent Sec. of the Academy of Fine Arts.

Wie (Ger.). 'As', 'like', 'as if'. *Wie anfänglich*, 'as at the beginning'.

Wieder (Ger.). 'Again.' So *Wiederholung*, 'repetition'.

Wiegenlied. 'Lullaby' or 'Berceuse'. (Ger. *Wiege* = 'cradle'; *wiegen* = 'to rock'; so *wiegend*, 'rocking', 'swaying'.)

Wiele, Aimée van de (b. Brussels 1907). Harpsichordist. Trained Brussels Conserv., gaining first prizes composition, piano, musical history. After study with Landowska made numerous appearances Britain and Continent: broadcasts and recordings.

Wienerisch (Ger.). 'Viennese.'

Wieniawski, (1) Henri (b. Lublin, Poland, 1835; d. Moscow 1880). Trained as violinist at Paris Conserv. and quickly attained international fame; lived in St. Petersburg (1860-72); toured the U.S.A. with Rubinstein (1872); succeeded Vieuxtemps as prof. of violin at Brussels Conserv. (1874-7). Composed violin concertos, fantasias, &c. For his brother see below. (2) **Joseph** (b. Lublin, Poland, 1837; d. Brussels 1912). Brother of the above. A distinguished pianist and a composer of piano and chamber music.

Wife of Martin Guerre. See *Bergsma*.

Wilbye, John (b. Diss, Norfolk, 1574; d. Colchester 1638). On attaining manhood took service with Sir Thomas Kytson, at Hengrave Hall, near Bury St. Edmunds, remaining there and in the house of a younger member of the family to the end of his life. Composer of some of the very best madrigals, English or foreign (e.g. *Adieu, sweet Amaryllis, Flora gave me fairest flowers, Sweet honey-sucking bees*).

Wilderness, The. See *Goss*.

Wilhelm, Carl. See *Watch on the Rhine*.

Wilhemj, August Emil Daniel Ferdinand (b. Usingen, Nassau, 1845; d. London 1908). Famous from childhood as violin virtuoso and as such toured the old and new worlds; for the last 14 years of his life prof. at G.S.M., London. Wrote (with James Brown) a *Modern School for the Violin*. (See *G String*.)

Wilhem (real name Bocquillon), **Guillaume Louis** (b. Paris 1781; there d. 1842). Organized teaching of sight-singing, &c., in Paris schools (cf. *Hullah*); instituted 'Orphéons' (popular male-voice choral societies) throughout France. Publ. many textbooks of sight-singing ('fixed-doh'), &c., and composed songs.

Wilis (Puccini). See *Villi*.

Willaert, Adrian (b. in Flanders abt. 1480; d. Venice 1562). Studied law and music in Paris and then travelled widely in Europe; from 1527 to death was in charge of the music at St. Mark's, Venice. Composed and publ. motets, masses, madrigals, &c., of the highest importance; excelled in works for double choir.

Willan, Healey (b. Balham, Surrey, 1880; d. Toronto 1968). Organist in London; in Toronto from 1913; on staff of Conserv. and Univ. till 1950 (D.Mus. 1921); also held positions as organist. Composed symphonies, cantatas, church music, organ music, chamber music, &c., and operas.

Willcocks, David (Valentine) (b. Newquay 1919). Trained R.C.M., Cambridge Univ. Organist, Worcester Cathedral 1950; King's Coll., Camb., 1957, also cond. Bach Choir 1960. Skilful choral arranger, &c. C.B.E. 1971.

Will Forster's Virginal Book. A MS. collection of music compiled 1624. It is in the Brit. Museum and has never been publ. (Forster's identity seems to be untraced.)

Williams, (1) **Ralph Vaughan.** See *Vaughan Williams.*

(2) **Charles Lee** (b. Winchester 1853; d. Gloucester 1935). Organist of Gloucester Cathedral (1882–97), and so one of conductors of the Three Choirs Festival, for which he composed short oratorios, &c. (see *Last Night at Bethany*). Also composed anthems, service music, &c.

(3) **Alberto** (b. Buenos Aires 1862; d. there 1952). Studied at Paris Conserv.; then returned to Argentina; founded Conserv. of Buenos Aires (1903) of which he remained director. Composed symphonies, chamber and piano music, songs, &c.

(4) **John Gerrard** (b. London 1888; d. Caterham 1947). Trained as an architect, and as a composer almost entirely self-taught. Composer of chamber and piano music, songs, a ballad opera (*Kate, the Cabin Boy*, London 1924), &c.

(5) **Christopher à Becket** (b. Dorchester 1890; d. London 1956). Composer of chamber and piano music, &c.

(6) **Harold** (b. Sydney 1893). Operatic and concert baritone (Covent Garden, Brit. National Opera Co., &c.). Toured Australia and New Zealand. One of earliest Brit. broadcasters.

(7) **William Sidney Gwynn** (b. Llangollen, N. Wales, 1896). Ed. of Welsh musical journals, publisher of Welsh music, Sec. Welsh Folk Song Soc., Mus. Director Internat. Eisteddfod (Llangollen), composer, author of *Welsh National Music and Dances* (1932), &c. O.B.E. 1953.

(8) **Tom** (b. Burry Port, Llanelly, S. Wales, 1902; d. nr. Ilfracombe 1957). Baritone. Trained R.A.M. Soloist with Brit. orchs. and choral societies. With Sadler's Wells Opera Co. 1937–45, then Covent Garden.

(9) **Thomas E.** See *Britannia, the Pride of the Ocean.*

(10) **Joseph, Ltd.** London Music Publishers. Founded 1808; oldest existing Brit. firm in the trade, now part of Galliard (q.v.).

(11) **Grace** (b. Barry, Wales, 1906). Trained R.C.M. and Vienna. Schoolteacher and composer of numerous choral and orch. works.

Williamson, (1) **John Finley** (b. Canton, Ohio, 1887). Choral conductor. Founder (1921) and dean of famous Westminster Choir which has toured principal cities of U.S.A. and Europe. Also founder (1926) and president (to 1958) Westminster Choir Coll., Princeton.

(2) **Malcolm** (b. Sydney 1931). Studied under Eugene Goossens, then under Elizabeth Lutyens in London. His compositions include concertos for piano and for violin and an opera.

William Tell (Rossini). See *Guillaume Tell.*

Willis, Henry (b. 1821; d. London 1901). Famous London organ builder, grandfather of the present head of the firm, also Henry Willis (b. 1889).

Will ye no come back again? The tune is the old one of *Royal Charlie*; the lyric is by Lady Nairne.

Wilson, (1) **John** (b. probably at Faversham, Kent, 1595; d. London 1674). Singer, lutanist, and violist, and possibly at one time, or on one occasion, a player in Shakespeare's company; composed music for some of Shakespeare's songs and this is sometimes still sung. Musician to Charles I (1635); then during the Commonwealth Prof. of Music in Oxford Univ. (1656); at the Restoration Musician to Charles II and Gentleman of the Chapel Royal (1662). Composer of songs, catches, &c.; also a little church music. (See *Brenhines Dido.*)

(2) **Lady.** See *Skye Boat Song.*

(3) **James Steuart** (b. Clifton, Bristol, 1889; d. Petersfield 1966). Tenor vocalist. Studied Cambridge; then as singer with Jean de Reszke and Henschel. On staff Curtis Inst., Philadelphia, 1939–42; then Music Director (Overseas) B.B.C. 1942; Arts Council 1945; Head of Music, B.B.C., 1948; Deputy General Administrator, Covent Garden, 1950–5. Knighted 1948.

(4) **Marie** (b. London 1903). Violinist. Studied R.C.M. (later on staff). Early career as soloist and leader of

string quartet. In 1929 became sub-leader (and frequently leader) of B.B.C. Symphony Orch., but returned to solo playing in 1944; high reputation in both capacities.

Wind-band Mass (Haydn). See *Harmoniemesse*.

Windchest See *Organ* 1.

Windingstad, Ole (b. Sandefjord, Norway, 1886; d. Kingston, N.Y., 1959). Conductor. Studied Leipzig Conserv. In U.S.A. since 1913. Composer of orch. works, &c.

Wind Machine. A barrel framework covered with silk and revolved by a handle, and working in friction with wood or cardboard. Used by Richard Strauss (cf. *Ventilator*).

Windpipe. See *Trachea*.

Winter Dreams. See *Tchaikovsky's Symphonies*.

Winter Journey (Schubert). See *Winterreise*.

Winterreise, Die ('The Winter Journey'). Song Cycle by Schubert (op. 89; 1827), with Piano accompaniment. Settings of 24 poems by Wilhelm Müller.

Winter-Spring. By Bloch. Two connected symphonic poems (1904–5).

Winter Wind Étude for Piano. Chopin's op. 25, no. 11, in A minor. The title has no authority.

Wirbel (Ger. 'whirl'). 'Drum roll.'

Wirbeltrommel (Ger.). Tenor drum (see *Percussion Family* 2 j).

Wire Brushes. See *Percussion Family* 2 w.

Wirén, Dag (b. Sweden 1905). Composer and musical writer. Trained Conserv. Stockholm. Has composed orch. and chamber music, &c.

Wir fahren gegen Engelland ('We are marching against England'). The official Ger. song of the Second World War. Composer, Hermes Niel (1888–1954).

Wirth, Emanuel (b. Luditz, Bohemia, 1842; d. Berlin 1923). Violinist and viola player. At Rotterdam (on Conserv. staff, &c.) 1864; then (1877) Berlin; viola player of Joachim Quartet.

Founded Trio (with Barth and Hausmann).

Wise, Michael (b. probably at Salisbury abt. 1648; there d. 1687). One of 1st choir-boys in the Chapel Royal at the Restoration (cf. *Cooke, Humfrey, Blow, Purcell*); lay clerk of St. George's Chapel, Windsor Castle (1663); organist Salisbury Cathedral (1668); Gentleman of the Chapel Royal (1676); master of the choristers of St. Paul's Cathedral (1687). Being in Salisbury quarrelled with his wife, rushed into the street, ran into a watchman who hit him on the head with his bill-hook and broke his skull. Composed church music, some of it still in use.

Wiseman, Herbert (b. Bucksburn, Aberdeen, 1886; d. Edinburgh 1966). Trained Aberdeen Univ. and R.C.M. Various organ positions and then Director of Music Edinburgh Education Committee and Head of Music, B.B.C., Scotland (1946–52). Active adjudicator, editor of school music, &c.

Wise Virgins, The. Ballet with music arranged by Walton from various Bach sources. (Prod. London 1940.) Music also as Orch. Suite.

Witch Minuet (Haydn). See *Quintenquartett*.

Witch of Salem. Opera by Cadman. Libretto by N. R. Eberhardt. (Prod. Chicago 1926.)

Withers, Herbert (b. London 1880). Violoncellist. Studied R.A.M. (later on its staff) and under Becker at Frankfurt. London début 1897. Became leading 'cellist Beecham Orch., &c.; member in turn of several important String Quartets.

Within a Mile of Edinburgh Town. The words are an altered version of some by Tom D'Urfey (1653–1723), and the tune (composed 1780) is not Scottish but by James Hook (q.v.).

With the Horn Call (Haydn). See *Auf dem Anstand*.

Witkowski, Georges Martin (b. Mostaganem, Algeria, 1867; d. Lyons 1943). Of mixed Fr. and Polish descent; brought up in France, a pupil of d'Indy; director of Conserv. of Lyons

(1924). Many and varied compositions —an opera, an oratorio, symphonies, &c.

Witmark & Sons, Inc., M. See *Music Publishers Holding Corporation.*

Witt, Franz Xaver. See *Cecilian Movement.*

Wittgenstein, Paul (b. Vienna 1887; d. nr. Manhasset, N.Y., 1961). Pianist; pupil of Leschetizky, &c. Début Vienna 1913. Lost right arm in 1914–18 war and developed astonishing left-hand technique; many compositions specially written for him (Strauss, Ravel, &c.). Cf. *Domestic Symphony*; *Zichy*. From 1938 in U.S.A.

Wohin (Schubert). See reference under *Loder* 1.

Wohlgefällig (Ger.). 'Pleasant', 'pleasantly'.

Wohl mir, dass ich Jesum habe. Chorale setting in Bach's Cantata 147. Arranged for piano solo by Myra Hess as *Jesu, Joy of Man's desiring* (poem by Robert Bridges made for a choral arrangement by H. P. Allen many years earlier). Later very popular in arrangements for other media.

Wohltemperirte Klavier, Das ('The Well-tempered Keyboard-instrument'; known also as 'Bach's 48'). Made up of 2 collections, each of 24 pairs of pieces (Prelude and Fugue), each collection including 1 pair in each major and minor key, in ascending order from C major to B minor. An object served was the demonstration of the advantage of Equal Temperament (see *Temperament*). The 2 collections date from 1722 and 1744 but were not publ. until 1800. (See reference under *Klavier*.)

Wöldike, Mogens (b. Copenhagen 1895). Conductor. Studied Univ. Copenhagen. Orch. and choral conductor in Scandinavian cities and elsewhere (e.g. Danish State Radio Madrigal Choir).

Wolf, (1) Hugo (b. 1860, Windisch-graz, Southern Styria, Austria, now Slovenski Grades, Jugoslavia; d. Vienna 1903). As student at Vienna Conserv. dismissed on a false charge; made a poor living by music lessons and criticism; settled in a village near Vienna and poured out songs in as-

tonishing quantity; at 37 was in a mental asylum where after 7 years he died. Works include an opera (*The Corregidor*, q.v.), a string quartet, a little orch. music, and the many songs that have caused him to be hailed by some as one of the greatest song writers of the world.

See also *Goethe Songs*; *Italian Serenade*; *Italienisches Liederbuch*; *Mörike Songs*; *Penthesilea*; *Spanisches Liederbuch*.

(2) **Johannes** (b. Berlin 1869; d. Munich 1947). Musicologist, long a Prof. in the Univ. of Berlin and Music Librarian of the Prussian State Library.

Wolf. (1) A jarring sound sometimes heard from some note in bowed instruments, due to the body of the instrument as a whole resonating to that particular note (see *Acoustics* 19). (2) An out-of-tune effect on the organ when the playing passed into extreme keys. It disappeared when Equal Temperament was introduced (cf. *Temperament*).

Wolf, The. See *Shield.*

Wolff, (1) Werner (b. Berlin 1883; d. Ruschlikon, Switzerland, 1961). Opera conductor in various Ger. cities. In U.S.A. 1938–59. Composer of orch. music, &c.

(2) **Albert Louis** (b. Paris 1884; d. 1970). Conductor. Studied at Paris Conserv. Cond. Opéra Comique (1911–34), also of Fr. works at Metropolitan Opera House, New York (1919–21); and of Paris 'Concerts Lamoureux' (1928) and then 'Concerts Pasdeloup'. Composer of operas.

Wolf-Ferrari, Ermanno (b. Venice 1876; there d. 1948). Son of Ger. father and It. mother; pupil of Rheinberger. Composer of many successful lyrical and realistic operas (e.g. *The Jewels of the Madonna*), of the oratorio *La Vita nuova* (1903), &c.

See *Donne curiose*; *Gioielli della Madonna*; *I Quattro rusteghi*; *Segreto di Susanna.*

Wölfl, Joseph (b. Salzburg 1773; d. London 1812). Pupil of Mozart's father and Haydn's brother Michael; famous pianist and rival of Beethoven in art of piano improvisation. Composed symphonies, sonatas, chamber music, operas, &c.

Wolle, John Frederick (b. Bethlehem, Pa., 1863; there d. 1933). See *Bach Choir*.

Wolstenholme, William (b. Blackburn, Lancs., 1865; d. London 1931). Born blind and born musical; trained at Coll. for Blind, Worcester; taught violin by Elgar. B.Mus., Oxford; organist many years in Blackburn and then in London; toured U.S.A. as organist; also a brilliant pianist. Compositions are chiefly for organ.

Woman of Samaria, The. Oratorio by Sterndale Bennett. (1st perf. Birmingham Fest. 1867.) The quartet *God is a Spirit* has had much separate performance.

Woman without a Shadow (Strauss). See *Frau ohne Schatten*.

Women of Troy. See *Gray, Cecil*.

Women's Love and Life (Schumann). See *Frauenliebe und Leben*.

Wonderful Mandarin (Bartók). See *Amazing Mandarin*.

Wood (or À Wood), Anthony (1632–95). Oxford antiquary; historian of the university and keen amateur musician who has left us much information on Oxford music during his period.

Wood, (1) Charles (b. Armagh, Ireland, 1866; d. Cambridge 1926). Studied at R.C.M. (of which he later became a prof.), and at Cambridge (M.A., D.Mus.). Prof. of Music, Cambridge, 1924. Composed choral and orch. works, music to Gr. plays, church music, chamber music, songs, &c.

(2) **Henry Joseph** (b. London 1869; d. Hitchin, Herts., 1944). At 10 was an organist; studied at R.A.M.; at 19 was conducting operas and at 25 was engaged as conductor of the newly founded Queen's Hall Promenade Concerts (see *Concert*), in which capacity, over a period of half a century, he did a great work in training the musical taste of Londoners and introducing new composers; also a great singing teacher and choral trainer. Hon. D.Mus., Oxford, 1926. Knighted 1911.

See also *Klenovsky* 2.

(3) **Haydn** (b. nr. Huddersfield 1882; d. London 1959). Violinist and

composer, trained R.C.M. Of his compositions it is the lighter ones that are chiefly heard and some of these have great popularity (200 songs).

(4) **Thomas** (b. Chorley, Lancs., 1892; d. Bures Hamlet, Halstead, Essex, 1950). Spent much of early life at sea. B.Mus., M.A., D.Mus., Oxford; then R.C.M. (1918). Musical Director of Tonbridge School (1919–24); Lecturer Oxford (1924–9); travelled extensively in Australasia, Canada, &c., as musical examiner and on various government service, writing lively and popular travel books. Composer of many choral and orch. works, &c. With his wife founded annual Royal Philharmonic Society Prizes for best student compositions.

(5) **Anne** (b. Crawley, Sussex, 1908). Contralto. Trained under Gerhardt, &c. Oratorio and Lieder singer. General Manager Eng. Opera Group 1946–8; then one of its artistic directors.

(6) **Arthur** (b. Heckmondwike, Yorks., 1875; d. 1953). Conductor and composer. Mus. director, Apollo Theatre, London (*Véronique* 1904, &c.), then other theatres during runs of musical comedies of the period to 1932. Composed and arranged much light music.

Wood Block. See *Chinese Wood Block.*

Wooden Prince, The. Ballet by Bartók (op. 13; 1916).

Woodforde-Finden (*née* Ward,) **Amy** (b. Valparaiso; d. 1919). Composer of very popular songs (e.g. *Indian Love Lyrics*).

Woodgate, Leslie (b. London 1902; d. 1961). Trained R.C.M. Held London organ positions. From 1928 on staff B.B.C.; chorus master from 1934; some compositions, also textbooks. O.B.E. 1959.

Woodhouse, (1) Frederick Erwin (b. London 1892; d. 1966). Baritone. Trained T.C.M. Sang at many festivals. Founded and sang in Intimate Opera Co. (1931).

(2) **(Mrs.) Violet Gordon**—*née* Gwynne (b. London 1872; there d. 1948). Highly accomplished harpsichordist and clavichordist with enormous repertory.

Woodland Scenes (Schumann). See *Waldscenen*.

Wood Nymphs, The. See *Bennett, William Sterndale*.

Woodward, (1) **Richard** (b. Dublin 1744; there d. 1777). Organist Christ Church Cathedral, Dublin, 1765 and Vicar Choral St. Patrick's Cathedral there 1772. Publ. volume of his anthems, chants, &c. D.Mus., Dublin (1771).

(2) **Herbert Hall** (b. nr. Liverpool 1847; d. London 1909). Anglican clergyman and very popular composer of church music (e.g. Communion Service in E flat and anthem *The Radiant Morn* (1881)). Precentor of Worcester Cathedral 1890. B.Mus., Oxford, 1866.

(3) **George Ratcliffe** (b. Birkenhead 1848; d. London 1934). Anglican clergyman who became great authority on hymnology; several publications based on research on carols (e.g. *Cowley Carol Book*, 2 series: 1901 and 1919).

Wooing of Joan and John, The. See *Nicholson, Richard*.

Wooldridge, Harry Ellis (b. Winchester 1845; d. London 1917). Slade Prof. of Fine Arts, Oxford. Author of vols. on Polyphonic Period in 1st edn. of *Oxford History of Music*. See also s.v. *Chappell, William*.

Worcester, Mass. See *Festival*.

Wordsworth, William (Brocklesby) (b. London 1908). Studied under Tovey (q.v.) at Edinburgh; composer of symphonies, chamber music, &c.

Work, H. C. See *Marching through Georgia*.

Working-out. Same as 'Development' in Compound Binary Form, &c. (see under *Development* and also *Form* 3).

World Requiem. See *Foulds, John Herbert*.

Wormser. See *Enfant Prodigue*.

Wornum, Robert. See *Pianoforte*.

Worshipful Company of Musicians. See *Musicians' Company*.

Would I were Erin's Apple Blossom o'er You. See *Londonderry Air*.

Wozzeck. Opera by Alban Berg. Libretto based on Büchner's drama *Woyzeck*. (Prod. Berlin 1925; Philadelphia and New York 1931; London, concert form 1934, staged Covent Garden 1952.)

Wranitsky, (1) **Paul** (b. Neureisch, Moravia, 1756; d. Vienna 1808). One of Haydn's violinists in the Esterházy orch., and then director of the court opera at Vienna. Composer of operas, ballets, 27 symphonies, 45 string quartets and much other chamber music, &c. For his brother see below. (2) **Anton** (b. Neureisch, Moravia, 1761; d. Vienna 1820). Brother of Paul, above. Pupil of Haydn and Mozart; well-known violin teacher. Composer of masses, a violin concerto, chamber music, &c.

Wreath, The. See *Mazzinghi*.

Wreckers, The. Opera by Ethel Smyth. (Prod. in Ger. as *Strandrecht*, Leipzig and Prague 1906; London concert form 1908, staged 1909.)

Wright, (1) **Kenneth Anthony** (b. Norfolk 1899). Head of Music, Television, B.B.C. At first engineer (M.Eng., Sheffield Univ.). Then B.B.C. career 1922–59. Composed orch., military band, &c., music. Chev. Lég. Honneur; O.B.E. 1953.

(2) **Denis** (b. London 1895; d. 1967). Brass band composer, conductor, &c., and competition adjudicator. Trained R.C.M. In charge of B.B.C. brass band broadcasts 1936; Transcription Service 1945. Books on brass-band scoring, &c. O.B.E. 1959.

Wuchtig (Ger.). 'Weighty.'

Wüllner, (1) **Franz** (b. Munster 1832; d. Braunsels-on-the-Lahn 1902). Pianist and conductor; succeeded von Bülow at Munich 1869. (For son see below.)

(2) **Ludwig** (b. Münster, Westphalia, 1858; d. Berlin 1938). Lieder baritone; previously prof. of philology (Ph.D.) and then actor; appeared also as violinist. Début as vocal recitalist Berlin 1895; then world tours.

Wunsch (Ger.). 'Wish.' So *Nach Wunsch*, 'according to one's wish' (= *Ad Libitum*, q.v.).

Würde (Ger. 'worth'). 'Dignity.' So *Würdig*, 'dignified'.

Wurlitzer Electronic Piano. See *Electric Musical Instruments* 1.

Wurm, Marie (b. Southampton 1860; d. Munich 1938). Pianist. Studied with Raff and Mme Schumann; then won Mendelssohn Scholarship (q.v.) at R.A.M.; in high repute as recitalist; retained original name when sisters changed theirs to 'Verne' (q.v.); retired to Germany and taught in Hanover, Berlin, and Munich.

Wut, Wuth (Ger.). 'Rage.' So *wütend* or *wüthend, wütig* or *wüthig*, 'raging', 'furious'.

Wyk, Arnold van (b. Calvinia, Cape Province, S.A., 1916). Composer and pianist. Trained Stellenbosch Univ. and R.A.M. Composer of orch., chamber, and piano music, &c.

Wylde, (1) **Henry** (b. Bushey, Herts., 1822; d. London 1890). Orch. conductor, &c. Founded New Philharmonic Soc. (1852) and London Academy of Music (1861). Composer and author of books on music. Gresham Prof. 1863 to death.

(2) **Harold Eustace** (b. Glenelg, S. Australia, 1888). Organist. Trained R.C.M. Eng. church positions. City organist, Adelaide, 1933. On staff Adelaide Conserv.

Wyss, Sophie (b. Neuveville, Switzerland, 1897). Soprano. Settled in Britain 1925. Wide repertory including much Fr. and contemporary Brit. song. Tours in Australia, &c.

Wyton, Alec (b. London 1921). Organist; trained R.A.M. and Oxford. In U.S.A. from 1950; St. John the Divine, New York 1954. Various compositions.

Wyzewa, Théodore de (b. Kalusik 1862; d. Paris 1917). Of Polish origin. Writer on music; authority on Mozart (cf. *Saint-Foix*).

X

Xabo. See *Jabo*.

Xácara. See *Jácara*.

Xaleo. See *Jaleo*.

Xylophone. See *Percussion Family* 1 f.

Xylorimba. An Amer. form of light-weight marimba (q.v.).

Y

Yaddo. Estate of Saratoga Springs, N.Y., left by Mrs. Spencer Trask for artistic purposes. Festivals are held (1st in 1932) at which Amer. composers have an opportunity of bringing forward their works. Also quarters are provided in which composers can settle for periods of work and discussion.

Yaniewicz. See *Janiewicz*.

Yankee Doodle. This is a burlesque song, to a very gay tune, used by the Brit. troops in derision of the revolutionary colonial troops of North America and then adopted by the revolutionists for their own purposes. Its history is confused, both as to words and music. A version of the tune first appears in print about 1778 in Aird's *Selection of Scottish, English, Irish, and Foreign Airs*, publ. at Glasgow (this publication contains several Amer. airs, which suggest that *Yankee Doodle* may be actually American in origin). Other versions appeared shortly afterwards. The 1st Amer. publication to include it is believed to be the *Federal Overture* of Benjamin Carr, 1795.

Years of Pilgrimage (Liszt). See *Années de Pèlerinage*.

Ye Banks and Braes. The poem is by Burns (1st publ. 1792). The tune was called *The Caledonian Hunt's Delight*. Niel Gow, sen. (q.v.), in whose *Second Collection of Strathspey Reels* (1788) it appears, was probably the first to give it this name; his book is dedicated to the Hunt and opens with this tune. Gow adds the sub-title 'A favourite Air', which suggests that the tune was already well known.

Ye Mariners of England. The words (written 1800) are by the poet Thomas Campbell, who was fond of the traditional tune to *You Gentlemen of England* (q.v.) and expressed his patriotism by supplying it with a new lyric. (See also *Pierson*.)

Yeomen of the Guard, The, or The Merryman and his Maid. Romantic Opera by Gilbert and Sullivan. (Prod. Lyceum Theatre, London, and New York, 1888.)

Yeoman's Wedding Song, The. See *Poniatowski*.

Ye Spotted Snakes. See *Stevens, Richard*.

Yodel. An Eng. spelling of *Jodel* (see *Jodelling*).

Yolande. See *Magnard*.

Yon, Pietro Alessandro (b. Settimo Vittone, Italy, 1886; d. nr. New York 1943). Organist. At 18 asst. organist St. Peter's, Rome. Settled New York 1907 (from 1926 organist St. Patrick's Cathedral). Composer of organ music, &c.

Yonge, Nicholas (b. Lewes, Sussex, date unknown; d. London 1619). Thought to have been a singer in choir of St. Paul's Cathedral. Notable as having introduced into England the It. madrigal (q.v.).

York (hymn tune). See *Stilt.*

Yorkshire (hymn tune). See *Wainwright, J.*

Yorkshire Symphony Orchestra. Founded 1947, Leeds being headquarters. Conductor Maurice Miles (1947), Nicolai Malko (1952). Ceased 1955.

You Gentlemen of England. This is an altered version of a ballad of the celebrated ballad-monger Martin Parker (cf. *When the King enjoys his own again*). The tune is the older one of *When the stormy winds do blow*, which words appear in the refrain of the song. *Ye Mariners of England* (q.v.) is an early 19th-c. imitation.

Youll, Henry (end of 16th c. and beginning of 17th). Circumstances of life unknown but famous for his canzonets and balletts (see *Madrigal*).

Young, (1) **William** (d. 1672). Flute player and then violinist in band of Charles II; appears to have previously held position at court of Archduke of Austria; at Innsbruck (1653) publ. collection of sonatas and dance pieces for 2, 3, and 4 violins, viola da gamba, and keyboard (modern edn. by W. G. Whittaker 1931)—these anticipating Purcell's style.

(2) **Gibson.** See *Community Singing.*

(3) **Percy M.** (= Marshall) (b. Northwich, Ches., 1912). Educ. Cambridge Univ. (M.A., Mus.B.). From 1934 adviser and mus. director various teacher training colls., &c.; organist; some compositions; many books, on Handel, Elgar, &c. Mus.D., Dublin.

(4) **Alexander** (b. London 1920). Lyric tenor. Trained G.S.M., R.C.M., and briefly in Naples. Small parts at Glyndebourne from 1949. international career from 1953.

Youth of Abraham, The. See *Gniessin.*

Youth of Hercules (Saint-Saëns). See *Jeunesse d'Hercule.*

Ysaÿe, (1) **Eugène** (b. Liège 1858; d. Brussels 1931). One of remarkable Liège group of violinists and as a virtuoso world-famous; founded Ysaÿe Orch. Concerts, Brussels (1894); conducted Cincinnati Orch. (1918–22). Composed an opera in Walloon dialect (1929), 6 violin concertos, &c. For his brother see below. (2) **Théophile** (b. Verviers, Belgium, 1865; d. Nice 1918). Pianist, sometimes heard in sonata programmes with his brother Eugène, above. Composed orch. music, &c.

Ystorm Tiberias. See *Stephen, E.*

Z

Zacconi, Ludovico (b. Pesaro 1555; d. nr. there 1627). Augustinian Canon of Venice, whose *Prattica di Musica* (2 parts 1592, 1619) is valuable for information on musical thought of his day.

Zählzeit (Ger.). 'Beat.'

Zambra. A Spanish dance showing Moorish influence.

Zampa, ou La Fiancée de Marbre ('Zampa, or The Marble Bride'). Romantic Opera of the supernatural by Hérold. (Prod. Paris 1831; London and New York 1833.)

Zandonai, Riccardo (b. Sacco, Trentino, 1883; d. Pesaro 1944). Composer of many operas (see *Conchita*; *Francesca da Rimini*), a Requiem, orch. music, &c.

Zapateado. A Spanish clog-dance, 3-in-a-measure, with a savage rhythm, marked by stamping instead of by the usual Spanish castanets.

Zarlino, Gioseffo (b. Chioggia 1517; d. Venice 1590). Pupil of Willaert with de Rore; Franciscan friar, choirmaster of St. Mark's, Venice, composer, and theoretical writer of high importance (chief work *Istitutioni harmoniche*, Venice 1558 and later edns., also translations into several languages).

Zart (Ger.). 'Tender.' So *Zartheit*, 'tenderness'; *zärtlich*, 'tenderly'.

Zarzuela. The traditional Spanish comic opera (generally in 1 act); it has spoken dialogue with songs and choruses (cf. *Albéniz* 3).

Zauberflöte (Ger.). 'Magic Flute.' Organ stop, a sort of *Harmonic Flute* (q.v.) of 8-foot pitch; end-plugged with the hole pierced in such a place that the harmonic heard is no. 3 of the harmonic series (see *Acoustics* 7), the length of the pipes being adjusted to bring the pitch to normal.

Zauberflöte, Die (Mozart). See *Magic Flute*.

Zauberharfe, Die (Schubert). See *Rosamunde*.

Zaza. Opera by Leoncavallo; libretto by himself, based on French play by C. Simon and P. Berton. (Prod. Milan 1900; many translations.)

Zehn (Ger.). 'Ten.'

Zeichen (Ger.). 'Sign.'

Zeisler, Fanny Bloomfield. See *Bloomfield-Zeisler*.

Zeitmass (Ger. 'time-measure'). 'Tempo.'

Zelo; zeloso; zelosamente (It.). 'Zeal'; 'zealous'; 'zealously'.

Zelter, Carl Friedrich (b. nr. Berlin 1758; d. Berlin 1832). Learned musician, friend of Goethe, teacher of Mendelssohn, and champion of Bach at a time when his music was largely forgotten. One of earliest composers of the Ger. Lied (q.v.).

Zemlinsky, Alexander (b. Vienna 1872; d. New York 1942). Notable conductor in Vienna, Prague, and Berlin; early supporter (later brother-in-law) of Schönberg. Composed 6 operas, symphonies, chamber music, &c.

Zenatello, Giovanni (b. Verona 1876; d. New York 1949). Operatic tenor. High It. reputation; appeared Covent Garden 1905 onwards; New York 1907. Retired from stage 1930, becoming vocal teacher. For wife see *Gay, Maria*.

Zenobia. (1) See *Coerne*. (2) See *Pratt, Silas G.*

Zich, Ottokar (b. Kralove Mestec, now in Czechoslovakia, 1879; d. Prague 1934). Prof. of philosophy and aesthetics at Univ. of Brno; student of Czech folk music; author of books on musical subjects. Composed operas, choral music, songs, &c.

Zichy, (Count) Géza (b. Sztára, Hungary, 1849; d. Budapest 1924). Lawyer by profession. Lost right arm as boy but studied piano with Liszt and others and became notable left-hand player. Composed left-hand concerto, &c. (Cf. *Wittgenstein*.)

Ziehen (Ger.). 'To draw out.'

Ziehharmonika (Ger.). 'Accordion.'

Ziehn, Bernard (b. Erfurt, Germany, 1845; d. Chicago 1912). Noted theorist and teacher of counterpoint, &c. Author of textbooks of high repute.

Ziemlich (Ger.). 'Rather.'

Zierlich (Ger.). 'Elegant.'

Zigeuner (Ger.). 'Gipsy.' So *Zigeunerlied*, 'gipsy song'.

Zigeunerbaron, Der ('The Gipsy Baron'). Very popular operetta by Johann Strauss junior. (Prod. Vienna 1885; New York 1886; London 1935.)

Zilafone (It.). Xylophone (see *Percussion Family* 1 f).

Zilcher, Hermann (b. Frankfurt-on-Main 1881; d. Würzburg 1948). Director of Conserv. of Würzburg; well-known pianist: composer of symphonies, concertos for piano and for violin, &c., an oratorio, chamber and piano music, many songs, &c.

Zimbalist, Efrem (b. Rostov on Don, Russia, 1889). Violinist. Pupil of Auer. Appeared in public Berlin and London 1907; Boston 1911. Settled in U.S.A.; joined staff Curtis Institute, Philadelphia; its director 1941; married 1943 Mrs. M. L. Curtis-Bok, daughter of its founder (1st wife was vocalist Alma Gluck, q.v., d. 1938). Composed Violin Concerto (1947), &c.

Zimbalon. A developed Dulcimer (q.v.) found in Hungarian and Rumanian popular orchs. and capable of virtuoso treatment.

Zimmermann, Agnes (b. Cologne 1847; d. London 1925). Pianist. Trained from age 9 at R.A.M. Won high position as able interpreter of classics, publicly appearing (in Britain and on Continent) from age 16 to nearly 80. Some compositions. Edited piano works of Mozart, Beethoven, and Schumann: in last introduced into Britain 'Continental Fingering' (thumb not as + but as 1). See *Fingering*.

Zingarelli, Nicola Antonio (b. Naples 1752; d. nr. there 1837). Once-famous composer of over 30 operas, sacred music; choirmaster of Milan Cathedral 1792, Loreto 1794, and St.

Peter's, Rome, 1804. Teacher of Bellini, Mercadante, Costa, &c.

Zingaro, zingara (It. masc., fem.). 'Gipsy.' Hence *alla zingarese*, 'in gipsy style'; *zingaresca*, 'gipsy song', &c.

Zither. The favourite instrument of the Tyrol and adjacent mountain regions. It consists of a closed wooden box with 30–45 strings stretched over its surface. A few melody strings lie over frets (q.v.); these are 'stopped' by the thumb of the left hand whilst that of the right hand, equipped with a plectrum, plucks them. Meanwhile the 3 larger fingers of the left hand pluck accompaniment strings (unfretted and used as 'open' strings).

Cf. information given under *Psaltery*, *Dulcimer*, *Cittern*, and *Tablature*, and for Zither-banjo see *Banjo*.

Zither Banjo. See *Banjo*.

Zitternd (Ger.). 'Trembling' (= *tremolando*).

Zögernd (Ger.). 'Delaying', i.e. *rallentando*.

Zoo, The. Comic Opera by Sullivan. Libretto by B. C. Stephenson. (Prod. St. James's Theatre, London, 1875.)

Zopf (Ger. 'pigtail'). Nickname for the conventional style in music and the other arts during much of the 18th c.

Zoppa, Alla. *Zoppo* (fem. *zoppa*) in It. is 'lame', 'limping', and so it has been applied to music in the sense of 'syncopated'.

Zortziko, or Zortzico. A sort of Basque folk dance in 5-in-a-measure time (cf. *Aurresku*), like the Rueda except that the 2nd and 4th beats are almost constantly dotted notes.

Zu (Ger.). 'To', or 'too'. Also 'for' and other translations which the context may suggest.

Zu 2. (1) Two instruments to play the same part. (2) All the instruments in question (e.g. 1st violins) to divide into 2 parts.

Zuerst (Ger.). 'First', 'at first'.

Zug (Ger.). (1) 'Procession'; thus *Brautzug*, 'bridal procession', and so on. (2) The action of pulling; thus organ-stop knob; piano pedal (which pulls down some mechanism). So the compounds *Zugposaune*, 'slide trombone' (see *Trombone Family*), and *Zugtrompete*, 'slide trumpet' (see *Trumpet Family*).

Zugeeignet (Ger.). 'Dedicated.'

Zugehen (Ger.). 'To go.' So *zugehend*, 'going'.

Zum, Zur (Ger.). 'To the', 'at the', &c.

Zumpe. See *Pianoforte*.

Zumsteeg, Johann Rudolf (b. Baden 1760; d. Stuttgart 1802). Remarkable composer of songs and a pioneer of the narrative and dramatic ballad (as such Schubert's early model); composed also operas, &c.

Zunge (Ger., plur. *Zungen*). 'Tongue', 'reed'.

Zur Mühlen, Raimund von (b. Livonia 1854; d. Steyning, Sussex, 1931). Tenor. Celebrated Lieder singer; apparently the first to give one-singer all-song recitals in London (1882).

Zurück (Ger.). 'Back again.' So *zurückgehend*, 'going back' (i.e. to original tempo); *zurückhaltend*, 'holding back (i.e. *rallentando*).

Zusammen (Ger.). 'Together'; used sometimes of instruments.

Zutraulich (Ger.). 'Confidingly', 'intimately'.

Zuvor (Ger.). 'Before.'

Zwei (Ger.). 'Two.' So *zweihändig*, 'Two-handed'; *zweistimmig*, 'Two-voiced', &c.

Zweifach. 'Twofold' (see *Fach*).

Zweimal (Ger.). 'Twice.'

Zweite, zweites (Ger., various terminations according to case, gender, &c.). 'Second.'

Zweiunddreissigstel or **Zweiunddreissigstelnote** (Ger.). 'Thirty-second' or 'Thirty-second note', i.e. Demisemiquaver (see Table 3).

Zwischen (Ger.). 'Between', 'amongst'. There are many compounds, such as *Zwischenspiel* (see below).

Zwischenspiel (Ger. 'between-play'). Anything of an interlude or intermezzo character, e.g. (1) Organ-playing between the stanzas of a hymn. (2) Episodes of a fugue. (3) Solo portions between the *tuttis* of a concerto.

Zwo (Ger.). To some extent now adopted instead of *zwei* ('two'), the original object having been, apparently, to avoid mis-hearing for *drei* ('three') in telephoning and in radio announcements. (*Zwote* is, in conformity, used for *zweite*, 'second'.)

Zwölf (Ger.). 'Twelve.'

Zwote (Ger.). Same as *zweite* (q.v.).

Zymbalum. See *Zimbalon*.